6TH EDITION

ECONOMICS
for Today

IRVIN B. TUCKER
UNIVERSITY OF NORTH CAROLINA CHARLOTTE

SOUTH-WESTERN
CENGAGE Learning™

Australia • Brazil • Canada • Mexico • Singapore • Spain • United Kingdom • United States

SOUTH-WESTERN
CENGAGE Learning

Economics for Today, Sixth Edition
Irvin B. Tucker

Editorial Director: Jack W. Calhoun

Editor-in-Chief: Alex von Rosenberg

Senior Acquisitions Editor: Steven Scoble

Developmental Editor:
Michael Guendelsberger

Editorial Assistant: Lena Mortis

Marketing Communications Manager:
Sarah Greber

Senior Marketing Manager: John Carey

Marketing Coordinator: Suellen Ruttkay

Content Project Manager:
Jacquelyn K Featherly

Technology Project Manager:
Deepak Kumar

Technology Production Analyst:
Adam Grafa

Senior Manufacturing Coordinator:
Sandee Milewski

Production House/Compositor:
Pre-Press PMG

Senior Art Director: Michelle Kunkler

Cover and Internal Designer:
Beckmeyer Design

Cover Image:
©David Muir/Digital Vision

For product information and technology assistance, contact us at
Cengage Learning Customer & Sales Support, 1-800-354-9706

For permission to use material from this text or product,
submit all requests online at **www.cengage.com/permissions**
Further permissions questions can be emailed to
permissionrequest@cengage.com

ExamView® and ExamView Pro® are registered trademarks of FSCreations, Inc. Windows is a registered trademark of the Microsoft Corporation used herein under license. Macintosh and Power Macintosh are registered trademarks of Apple Computer, Inc. used herein under license.

Library of Congress Control Number: 2008939441
Student Edition ISBN 13: 978-0-324-59136-1
Student Edition ISBN 10: 0-324-59136-5
Instructor's Edition ISBN 13: 978-0-324-78381-0
Instructor's Edition ISBN 10: 0-324-78381-7

South-Western Cengage Learning
5191 Natorp Boulevard
Mason, OH 45040
USA

Cengage Learning products are represented in Canada by
Nelson Education, Ltd.

For your course and learning solutions, visit **www.cengage.com**
Purchase any of our products at your local college store or at our
preferred online store **www.ichapters.com**

Printed in Canada
1 2 3 4 5 6 7 12 11 10 09 08

Irvin B. Tucker

Irvin B. Tucker has more than 30 years of experience teaching introductory economics at the University of North Carolina Charlotte and the University of South Carolina. He earned his B.S. in economics at N.C. State University and his M.A. and Ph.D. in economics from the University of South Carolina. Dr. Tucker is former director of the Center for Economic Education at the University of North Carolina Charlotte and is a longtime member of the National Council on Economic Education. He is recognized for his ability to relate basic principles to economic issues and public policy. His work has received national recognition by being awarded the Meritorious Levy Award for Excellence in Private Enterprise Education, the Federation of Independent Business Award for Postsecondary Educator of the Year in Entrepreneurship and Economic Education, and the Freedom Foundations George Washington Medal for Excellence in Economic Education. In addition, his research has been published in numerous professional journal articles on a wide range of topics, including industrial organization, entrepreneurship, and economics of education. Dr. Tucker is also the author of the highly successful *Survey of Economics*, sixth edition, a text for the one-semester principles of economics courses, published by South-Western Publishing. Also, Dr. Tucker has coauthored, with professors Allan Layton and Tim Robins of Queensland University of Technology, a one-semester edition of *Economics for Today* for Australia, New Zealand, and Southeast Asia, published by Nelson/Cengage Learning.

BRIEF CONTENTS

CONTENTS

PART 3
MARKET STRUCTURES   197

Chapter 8

Chapter 9

PART 4
MICROECONOMIC POLICY ISSUES

301

Chapter 23

PART 7
MONEY, BANKING, AND MONETARY POLICY

Chapter 24

The Four Versions of This Book

Economics for Today	Economics for Today	Microeconomics for Today	Macroeconomics for Today	Survey of Economics for Today
1 Introducing the Economic Way of Thinking	X	X	X	X
2 Production Possibilities, Opportunity Cost, and Economic Growth	X	X	X	X
3 Market Demand and Supply	X	X	X	X
4 Markets in Action	X	X	X	X
5 Price Elasticity of Demand and Supply	X	X		X
6 Consumer Choice Theory	X	X		
7 Production Costs	X	X		X
8 Perfect Competition	X	X		X
9 Monopoly	X	X		X
10 Monopolistic Competition and Oligopoly	X	X		X
11 Labor Markets	X	X		
12 Income Distribution, Poverty, and Discrimination	X	X		X
13 Antitrust and Regulation	X	X		
14 Environmental Economics	X	X		
15 Gross Domestic Product	X		X	X
16 Business Cycles and Unemployment	X		X	X
17 Inflation	X		X	X
18 The Keynesian Model	X		X	
19 The Keynesian Model in Action	X		X	
20 Aggregate Demand and Supply	X		X	X
21 Fiscal Policy	X		X	X
22 The Public Sector	X		X	X
23 Federal Deficits, Surpluses, and the National Debt	X		X	X
24 Money and the Federal Reserve System	X		X	X
25 Money Creation	X		X	X
26 Monetary Policy	X		X	X
27 The Phillips Curve and Expectations Theory	X		X	
28 International Trade and Finance	X	X	X	X
29 Economies in Transition	X	X	X	X
30 Growth and the Less-Developed Countries	X	X	X	X

Note: Chapter numbers refer to the complete book, *Economics for Today*

PREFACE

Text with a Mission

The purpose of *Economics for Today,* Sixth Edition, is to teach, in an engaging style, the basic operations of the U.S. economy to students who will take a two-term economics course. Rather than taking an encyclopedic approach to economic concepts, *Economics for Today* focuses on the most important tool in economics—supply and demand analysis—and applies it to clearly explain real-world economic issues.

Every effort has been made to make *Economics for Today* the most "student friendly" text on the market. This text was written because so many others expose students to a confusing array of economic analyses that force students to simply memorize in order to pass the course. Instead, *Economics for Today* presents a straightforward and unbiased approach that effectively teaches the application of basic economic principles. After reading this text, the student should be able to say "now that economics stuff in the news makes sense."

How It Fits Together

The text presents the core principles of microeconomics, macroeconomics, and international economics. The first 14 chapters introduce the logic of economic analysis and develop the core of microeconomic analysis. Here students learn the role of demand and supply in determining prices in competitive versus monopolistic markets. This part of the book explores such issues as minimum wage laws, rent control, and pollution. The next 13 chapters develop the macroeconomics part of the text. Using the modern, yet simple, aggregate demand and aggregate supply model, the text explains measurement of and changes in the price level, national output, and employment in the economy. The study of macroeconomics also includes how the supply of money and the demand for money influence the economy. Finally, the text concludes with three chapters devoted entirely to global issues. For example, students will learn how the supply of and demand for currencies determine exchange rates and what the complications of a strong or a weak dollar are.

Text Flexibility

The full version of *Economics for Today* is easily adapted to an instructor's preference for the sequencing of microeconomics and macroeconomics topics. The text can be used in a macroeconomic-microeconomic sequence by teaching the first four chapters and then Parts 5 through 7. Next, microeconomics is covered in Parts 2 through 4. Finally, the course can be completed with Part 8, consisting of three chapters devoted to international economics.

An important design of this text is that it accommodates the two camps for teaching principles of macroeconomics: (1) those who cover both the Keynesian Cross and *AD/AS* models and (2) those who skip the Keynesian model and cover only the *AD/AS* model. For instructors who prefer the former model sequence, *Economics for Today* moves smoothly in Chapters 18–19 (8–9) from the Keynesian model (based on the Great Depression) to the AD/AS model in Chapter 20 (10). For instructors using the latter approach, this text is written so that instructors can skip the Keynesian model in Chapters 18–19 (8–9) and proceed from Chapter 17 (7) to

Chapter 20 (10) without losing anything. For example, the spending multiplier is completely covered both in the Keynesian and AD/AS model chapters.

For instructors who wish to teach the self-correcting AD/AS model, emphasis can be placed on the appendixes to Chapters 20 (10) and 26 (16). Instructors who choose not to cover this model can simply skip these appendixes. In short, *Economics for Today* provides more comprehensive and flexible coverage of macroeconomics models than is available in other texts. Also, a customized text might meet your needs. If so, contact your South-Western/Cengage sales representative for information.@

How Not to Study Economics

To some students, studying economics is a little frightening because many chapters are full of graphs. Students often make the mistake of preparing for tests by trying to memorize the lines of graphs. When their graded tests are returned, the students using this strategy will probably exclaim, "What happened?" The answer to this query is that the students should have learned the economic concepts *first*; then they would understand the graphs as *illustrations* of these underlying concepts. Stated simply, superficial cramming for economics quizzes does not work.

For students who are anxious about using graphs, the appendix to Chapter 1 provides a brief review of graphical analysis. In addition, *The Graphing Workshop* and the *Study Guide* contain step-by-step features on how to interpret graphs.

New to the Sixth Edition

The basic layout of the sixth edition remains the same. The following are changes:

- New feature titled "Road Map" at the end of each part provides review questions linked to an interactive causation chain game.
- New Global Economics feature, titled "How Does Public Capital Affect a Nation's Curve?"
- New Checkpoint feature titled "Why the Higher Price for Ethanol?"
- New You're the Economist feature titled "Why is That Web Site You're Using Free?"
- New You're the Economist feature titled "Social-Networking Sites: The New Advertising Game."
- New box insert feature titled "Social Security: Past, Present, and Future."
- New Global Economics feature titled "How Should Carbon Emissions be Reduced: Cap-and-Trade or Carbon Taxes?"
- New Checkpoint feature titled "What is the Real Price of Gasoline?"
- New Checkpoint feature titled "What is the MPC for Uncle Sam's Stimulus Package?"
- New You're the Economist feature titled "America's Housing Market Bubble Bursts."
- Added story of Wizard of Oz in the Global Economics feature on the gold standard.
- Over 600 new questions added to the test bank.
- Over 700 new question added to the online quizzes.
- A new feature on classroom games added to the Instructor's Manual.
- Revised Lecture PowerPoint Slides

Alternate Versions of the Book

For instructors who wish to spend various amounts of time for their courses and offer different topics of this text:

- *Economics for Today.* This complete version of the book contains all 30 chapters. It is designed for two-semester introductory courses that cover both microeconomics and macroecnomics.
- *Microeconomics for Today.* This version contains 17 chapters and is designed for one-semester courses in introductory microeconomics.
- *Macroeconomics for Today.* This version contains 20 chapters and designed for one-semester courses in introductory macroeconomics.
- *Survey of Economics.* This version of the book contains 23 chapters. It is designed for one-semester courses that cover the basics of both microeconomics and macroeconomics.

The accompanying table shows precisely which chapters are included in each book. Instructors who wish more information about these alternative version should contact their local Cengage South-Western representative.

Motivational Pedagogical Features

Economics for Today strives to motivate and advance the boundaries of pedagogy with the following features:

Part Openers

Each part begins with a statement of the overall mission of the chapters in the part. In addition, there is a nutshell introduction of each chapter in relation to the part's learning objective.

Chapter Previews

Each chapter begins with a preview designed to pique the student's interest and reinforce how the chapter fits into the overall scheme of the book. Each preview appeals to the student's "Sherlock Holmes" impulses by posing several economics puzzles that can be solved by understanding the material presented in the chapter.

Margin Definitions

Key concepts introduced in the chapter are highlighted in bold type and then defined in the text and again in the margins. This feature therefore serves as a quick reference.

Conclusion Statements

Throughout the chapters, highlighted conclusion statements of key concepts appear at the ends of sections and tie together the material just presented. Students will be able to see quickly if they have understood the main points of the section. A summary of these conclusion statements is provided at the end of each chapter.

You're the Economist

Each chapter includes boxed inserts that provide the acid test of "relevance to everyday life." This feature gives the student an opportunity to encounter timely, real-world extensions of economic theory. For example, students read about Fred Smith as he writes an economics term paper explaining his plan to create FedEx. To ensure that the student wastes no time figuring out which concepts apply to the article, applicable concepts are listed after each title. Many of these boxed features include quotes from newspaper articles over a period of years demonstrating that economics concepts remain relevant over time.

Global Economics

Today's economic environment is global. *Economics for Today* carefully integrates international topics throughout the text and presents the material using a highly readable and accessible approach designed for students with no training in international economics. All sections of the text that present global economics are identified by a special global icon in the text margin and in the International Economics boxes. In addition, the final three chapters of the book are devoted entirely to international economics.

Analyze the Issue

This feature follows each *You're the Economist* and *Global Economics* feature and asks specific questions that require students to test their knowledge of how the material in the boxed insert is relevant to the applicable concept. To allow these questions to be used in classroom discussions or homework assignments, answers are provided in the Instructor's Manual rather than the text.

Checkpoint

Watch for these! Who said learning economics can't be fun? This feature is a unique approach to generating interest and critical thinking. These questions spark students to check their progress by asking challenging economics puzzles in game-like style. Students enjoy thinking through and answering the questions, and then checking the answers at the end of the chapter. Students who answer correctly earn the satisfaction of knowing they have mastered the concepts.

Illustrations

Attractive large graphical presentations with grid lines and real-world numbers are essential for any successful economics textbook. Each exhibit has been carefully analyzed to ensure that the key concepts being represented stand out clearly. Brief descriptions are included with graphs to provide guidance for students as they study the graph. When actual data are used, the Web site reference is provided so that students can easily locate the data source.

Causation Chains Game

This will be one of your favorites. The highly successful causation chains are included under many graphs throughout the text. This pedagogical device helps students visualize complex economic relationships in terms of simple box diagrams that illustrate how one change causes another change. Each exhibit having a causation chain in the text is included in the animaed Causation Chains game on the text website (www.cengage.com/economics/tucker). This game makes it fun to learn. Arrange the blocks correctly and hear the cheers.

Key Concepts

Key concepts introduced in the chapter are listed at the end of each chapter and on the Tucker Web site (www.cengage.com/economics/tucker). As a study aid, you can use the key concepts as flashcards to test your knowledge. First state the definition and then click on the term to check for correctness.

Visual Summaries

Each chapter ends with a brief point-by-point summary of the key concepts. Many of these summarized points include miniaturized versions of the important graphs and causation chains that illustrate many of the key concepts. These are intended to serve as visual reminders for students as they finish the chapters and are also useful in reviewing and studying for quizzes and exams.

Study Questions and Problems

The end-of-chapter questions and problems offer a variety of levels ranging from straightforward recall to deeply thought-provoking applications. The answers to odd questions and problems are in the back of the text. This feature gives students immediate feedback without requiring the instructor to check their work.

End-of-Chapter Practice Quizzes

A great help before quizzes. Many instructors test students using multiple-choice questions. For this reason, the final section of each chapter provides the type of multiple-choice questions given in the instructor's Test Bank. The answers to all of these questions are given in the back of the text. In addition, students may visit the Tucker Web site (www.cengage.com/economics/tucker) and then click the tutorial to obtain a visual explanation of each correct answer and a reference to page numbers in the text that explain the answer. Here students can actually see the graphs shift as arrows point to key changes in prices, output, and other key variables.

Online Quizzes

In addition to the end-of-chapter practice quizzes, there are multiple-choice questions on the Tucker Web site (cengage.com/economics/tucker). Each question explains why an answer is incorrect or correct. Between this feature and the end-of-chapter practice quizzes, students are well prepared for tests.

Part Road Map

This feature concludes each part with review questions listed by chapter from the previous part. To reinforce the concepts, each set of questions relates to the interactive causation chain game. Click on the Tucker Web site and make learning fun listening to the cheers when correct and jeers for a wrong answer. Answers to the questions are in the back of the text.

Online Exercises

These exercises are designed to spark students' excitement about researching on the Internet by asking them to access economic data and then answer questions related to the content of the chapter. All Internet exercises are on the Tucker Web site (www.cengage.com/economics/tucker) with direct links to the addresses so that students will not have the tedious and error-prone task of entering long Web site addresses.

Internet Links

Visit the Tucker Web site, www.cengage.com/economics/tucker, and find up-to-date links pertaining to relevant topics in the subject matter. These addresses provide students with access to specific content and real-world application. There's no need to type in the links; they're a mere click away!

A Supplements Package Designed for Success

To learn more about the supplements for *Economics Today,* visit the Tucker Web site, www.cengage.com/economics/tucker. For additional information, contact your Cengage South-Western sales representative.

Instructor Resources

Instructor's Manual

This manual, prepared by Douglas Copeland of Johnson County Community College, provides valuable course assistance to instructors. It includes chapter outlines, instructional objectives, critical thinking/group discussion questions, hints for effective teaching, answers to the Analyze the Issue questions, answers to even-numbered questions and problems, summary quizzes with answers, and classroom games. Instructor's Manual ISBN: 0324781997.

Test Bank

Prepared by the text author to match the text, the Test Bank includes over 7,000 multiple-choice, true-false, and short essay questions. The questions are arranged by the order presented in the chapter and are grouped with concept headings that make it easy to select questions. Most questions have been thoroughly tested in the classroom by the author and are classified by topic and degree of difficulty. Text page references help locate pages where material related to the questions is explained.

Macro Test Bank ISBN: 032478208X.
Micro Test Bank ISBN: 0324782098.

ExamView

ExamView Computerized Testing Software contains all of the questions in the printed *Test Bank.* ExamView is an easy-to-use test creation software compatible with both Microsoft Windows and Apple Macintosh. Instructors can add or edit questions, instructions, and answers; select questions by previewing them on the screen; or select them randomly or by number. Instructors can also create and administer quizzes online, whether over the Internet, a local area network (LAN), or a wide area network (WAN). Available on the Instructor's Resource CD: ISBN: 0324782071

PowerPoint Lecture Slides

This state-of-the-art slide presentation provides instructors with visual support in the classroom for each chapter. Lecture Slides contain vivid highlights of important concepts. Instructors can edit the PowerPoint presentations or create their own exciting in-class presentations. These slides are available on the Instructor's Resource CD as well as for downloading from the Tucker Web site www.cengage.com/economics/tucker.

PowerPoint Exhibit Slides

These slides contain figures, charts, and tables from the text. Instructors can easily incorporate them into their own PowerPoint presentations from the Tucker Web site.

Instructor's Resource CD-ROM

Get quick access to all instructor ancillaries from your desktop. This easy-to-use CD lets you review, edit, and copy exactly what you need in the format you want. This supplement contains the Instructor's Manual, Test Bank, ExamView Testing software, and the PowerPoint presentation slides. IRCD ISBN: 0324782071.

Student Resources
Study Guide

The Study Guide is recommended for each student using the text. It is perhaps the best way to prepare for quizzes. Too often, study guides are not written by the author, and the material does not really fit the text. Not so here. The Study Guide was prepared by the text author to prepare students before they take tests in class. The Study Guide contains student-friendly features such as the chapter in a nutshell, key concepts review, learning objectives, fill-in-the-blank questions, step-by-step interpretation of the graph boxes, multiple-choice questions, true-false questions, and crossword puzzles.
ISBN: 0324782004

The Tucker EconCentral Web site

The EconCentral Web site: (www.cengage.com/economics/tucker6e/econcentral) features a content-rich, robust set of multimedia learning tools. These Web features have been specifically developed with the student in mind:

- **The Graphing Workshop.** The Graphing Workshop is a one-stop learning resource for help in mastering the language of graphs, one of the more difficult aspects of an economics course for many students. It enables students to explore important economic concepts through a unique learning system made up of tutorials, interactive drawing tools, and exercises that teach how to interpret, reproduce, and explain graphs.
- **ABC News Video Segments.** ABC video segments bring the "real world" right to students' desktops. The ABC News videos illustrate how economics is an important part of students' daily lives and help them learn the material by applying it to current events.
- **Ask the Instructor Video Clips.** Via streaming video, difficult concepts are explained and illustrated. These video clips are extremely helpful review and clarification tools if a student has trouble understanding an in-class lecture or is a visual learner.
- **Economic Applications** *(EconApps)*. EconNews Online, EconDebate Online, and EconData Online features help to deepen students' understanding of the theoretical concepts through hands-on exploration and analysis of the latest economic news stories, policy debates, and data.

For Students and Instructors
The Wall Street Journal

The Wall Street Journal is synonymous with the latest word on business, economics, and public policy. *Economics for Today* makes it easy for students to apply economic concepts to this authoritative publication, and for you to bring the most up-to-date, real-world events into your classroom. For a nominal additional cost, *Economics for Today* can be packaged with a card entitling students to a 15-week subscription to both the print and online versions of *The Wall Street Journal*. Instructors with at least seven students who activate their subscriptions will automatically receive their own free subscription. Contact your Cengage South-Western sales representative for package pricing and ordering information.

TextChoice: Economic Issues and Activities

TextChoice is the home of Cengage Learning's online digital content. TextChoice provides the fastest, easiest way for you to create your own learning materials. South-Western's Economic Issues and Activities content database includes a wide variety of high-interest, current event/policy applications as well as classroom activities that are designed specifically to enhance introductory economics courses. Choose just one reading, or many—even add your own material—to create an accompaniment to the textbook that is perfectly customized to your course. Contact your Cengage South-Western sales representative for more information.

Tucker Web Site

The Tucker Web site (www.cengage.com/economics/tucker) provides open access to: PowerPoint chapter review slides, tutorials for the text's end-of-chapter Practice Quizzes, online quizzing, direct links to the Internet activities mentioned in the text, updates to the text, the opportunity to communicate with the author, and other downloadable teaching and learning resources.

Acknowledgments

A deep debt of gratitude is owed to the reviewers for their expert assistance. All comments and suggestions were carefully evaluated and served to improve the final product. To each of the reviewers of all six editions, I give my sincerest thanks.

Jack E. Adams
University of Arkansas-Little Rock

John W. Alderson, III
East Arkansas Community College

Irma Alonso
Florida International University

Hasaan Aly
The Ohio State University

James Q. Aylsworth
Lakeland Community College

Randy Barnes
Mirimar College

Atin Basu
Virginia Military Institute

Klaus G. Becker
Texas Tech University

Randall W. Bennett
Gonazaga University

John P. Blair
Wright State University

Orn B. Bodvarsson
St. Cloud State University

Tantatape Brahmasrene
Purdue University, North Central

Joyce Bremer
Oakton Community College

Anne Bresnock
California State University, Pomona

Stacey Brook
University of Sioux Falls

Stephanie Campbell
Mineral Area College

Juan Castro
ETX Baptist University

Dell Champlin
Eastern Illinois University

Doug Copeland
Johnson County Community College

John P. Dahlquist
College of Alameda

James P. D'Angelo
University of Cincinnati

Jan L. Dauve
University of Missouri

Gregory J. Delemeester
Marietta College

Robert C. Dolan
University of Richmond

William Dougherty
*Carroll County Community
College*

James W. Eden
Portland Community College

Ronald Elkins
Central Washington University

Tommy Eshleman
University of Nebraska, Kearney

John L. Ewing-Smith
Burlington County College

Chris Fawson
Utah State University

Arthur A. Fleisher, III
*Metropolitan State College of
Denver*

Kaya Ford
*Northern Virginia Community
College*

Arthur Friedberg
*Mohawk Valley Community
College*

Scott Gabeheart
Mesa Community College

Linda Ghent
Eastern Illinois Univeristy

Cindy Gibson
Keuka College

J.P. Gilbert
Mira Costa College

Deborah Goldsmith
City College of San Francisco

Sanford D. Gordon
University of South Florida

Gary Green
Manatee Community College

Serge S. Grushchin
*ASA College of Advanced
Technology*

Steven Hackett
Humbolt State University

Gail A. Hawks
*Miami Dade Community
College*

Michael G. Heslop
*Northern Virginia Community
College*

Yu-Mong Hsiao
Campbell University

R. Jack Inch
Oakland Community College

Hans R. Isakson
University of Northern Iowa

Barbara H. John
University of Dayton

Petur O. Jonsson
Fayetteville State University

Paul Jorgensen
Linn-Benton Community College

Louise Keely
University of Wisconsin

Randall G. Kesselring
Arkansas State University

Harry T. Kolendrianos
Danville Community College

William F. Kordsmeier
University of Central Arkansas

Margaret Landman
Bridgewater State College

David Latzko
*Pennsylvania State University,
York*

Ralph F. Lewis
Orange Coast College

Stephen E. Lile
Western Kentucky University

Dandan Liu
Bowling Green State University

Melody Lo
*University of Southern
Mississippi*

Thomas Maloy
Muskegon Community College

Dayle Mandelson
University of Wisconsin-Stout

Robert A. Margo
Vanderbilt University

Melanie Marks
Longwood College

Michael Marlow
*Cal Polytechnic State
University-SLO*

Fred May
Trident Technical College

James C. McBrearty
University of Arizona

Diana L. McCoy
*Truckee Meadows Community
College*

Donald P. McDowell
Florida Community College

Fazlul Miah
Fayetteville State University

David S. Moewes
Concordia College

Margaret Moore
Franklin University

Marie Mora
New Mexico State University

Kevin J. Murphy
Oakland University

Jack Muryn
*University of Wisconsin-
Washington County*

Lee Nordgren
Indiana University

Peter K. Olson
Indiana University

Patrick B. O'Neill
University of North Dakota

Jan Palmer
Ohio University

Michael L. Palmer
Maple Woods Community College

Elliott Parker
University of Nevada in Reno

Kathy Parkison
Indiana University-Kokomo

Donald W. Pearson
Eastern Michigan University

Martin Perline
Wichita State University

Maurice Pfannestiel
Wichita State University

L. Wayne Plumly, Jr.
Valdosta State University

Ray Polchow
Muskingum Area Technical College

Elaine Peterson
California State University, Stanislaus

Michael J. Pisani
Texas A&M University

Renee Prim
Central Piedmont Community College

Fernando Quijano
Dickinson State University

R. Larry Reynolds
Boise State University

Kathryn Roberts
Chipola Junior College

Steve Robinson
University of North Carolina at Wilmington

Craig Rogers
Canisius College

Lawrence P. Schrenk
University of Baltimore

Kurt A. Schwabe
Ohio University

Lisa Simon
California Polytechnic State University

Larry Singell
University of Oregon

Alden W. Smith
Anne Arundel Community College

Tricia Snyder
William Patterson University

Angela M. Sparkman
Itawamba Community College

Larry Spizman
SUNY-Oswego

Rebecca Summary
Southeast Missouri State University

Daniel A. Talley
Dakota State University

Daryl Thorne
Valencia Community College

Larry Towle
Eastern Nazarene College

Greg Trandel
University of Georgia

Richard Trieff
Des Moines Area Community College

Tracy M. Turner
Kansas State University

Roy van Til
University of Maine-Farmington

Lee Van Scyok
University of Wisconsin-Oshkosh

Darlene Voeltz
Rochester Community and Technical College

Rosemary Walker
Washburn University

Harold Warren
East Tennessee State University

Robert G. Welch
Midwestern State University

Herbert D. Werner
University of Missouri

Michael D. White
St. Cloud State University

Leo M. Weeks
Northwestern University

Gwen Williams
Alvernia College

Virginia S. York
Gulf Coast Community College

Paul Young
Dodge City Community College

Michael J. Youngblood
Rock Valley College

Special Thanks

I especially wish to express my deepest appreciation to Peter Schwarz, my colleague at UNC Charlotte. Many of the ideas in the Checkpoint sections are the result of brainstorming sessions with him. Special thanks also go to Douglas Copeland of Johnson County Community College for preparing the Instructor's Manual and Bob Sandman of the University of Cincinnati, who provided PowerPoint slides and new ideas for the You're the Economist and Global Economics.

My appreciation goes to Steve Scoble, Senior Acquisitions Editor for Cengage Learning/South-Western. My thanks also to Mike Guendelsberger, Developmental Editor; Jaci Featherly, Content Project Manager; Lena Mortis, Editorial Assistant; and Suellen Ruttkay, Marketing Coordinator, who put all the pieces of the puzzle together and brought their creative talent to this text. Kelly Birch was superb in her copyediting of the manuscript. I am also grateful to John Carey for his skillful marketing. Finally, I give my sincere thanks for a job well done to the entire team at Cengage Learning/South-Western.

Introduction to Economics

The first two chapters introduce you to a foundation of economic knowledge vital to understanding the other chapters in the text. In these introductory chapters, you will begin to learn a valuable reasoning approach to solving economics puzzles that economists call "the economic way of thinking." Part 1 develops the cornerstone of this type of logical analysis by presenting basic economic models that explain such important topics as scarcity, opportunity cost, production possibilities, and economic growth.

CHAPTER

1

Introducing the Economic Way of Thinking

© David Muir/Digital Vision/Getty Images.

W elcome to an exciting and useful subject economists call "the economic way of thinking." As you learn this reasoning technique, it will become infectious. You will discover that the world is full of economics problems requiring more powerful tools than just common sense. As you master the methods explained in this book, you will appreciate economics as a valuable reasoning approach to solving economics puzzles. Stated differently, the economic way of thinking is important because it provides a logical framework for organizing your thoughts and understanding an economic issue or event. Just to give a sneak preview, in later chapters you will study the perils of government price fixing for gasoline and health care. You will also find out why colleges and universities charge students different tuitions for the same education. You will investigate whether you should worry if the federal government fails to balance its budget. You will learn that the island of Yap

uses large stones with holes in the center as money. In the final chapter, you will study why some countries grow rich while others remain poor and less developed. And the list of fascinating and relevant topics continues throughout each chapter. As you read these pages, your efforts will be rewarded by an understanding of just how economic theories and policies affect our daily lives—past, present, and future.

Chapter 1 acquaints you with the foundation of the economic way of thinking. The first building blocks joined are the concepts of scarcity and choice. The next building blocks are the steps in the model-building process that economists use to study the choices people make. Then we look at some pitfalls of economic reasoning and explain why economists might disagree with one another. The chapter concludes with a discussion of why you may wish to be an economics major.

In this chapter, you will learn
to solve these economic puzzles:

- Can you prove there is no person worth a trillion dollars?

- Why would you purchase more Coca-Cola when the price increases?

- How can we explain the relationship between the Super Bowl winner and changes in the stock market?

- What famous people majored in economics?

The Problem of Scarcity

Our world is a finite place where people, both individually and collectively, face the problem of scarcity. Scarcity is the condition in which human wants are forever greater than the available supply of time, goods, and resources. Because of scarcity, it is impossible to satisfy every desire. Pause for a moment to list some of your unsatisfied wants. Perhaps you would like a big home, gourmet meals, designer clothes, clean air, better health care, shelter for the homeless, more leisure time, and so on. Unfortunately, nature does not offer the Garden of Eden, where every desire is fulfilled. Instead, there are always limits on the economy's ability to satisfy unlimited wants. Alas, scarcity is pervasive, so "You can't have it all."

You may think your scarcity problem would disappear if you were rich, but wealth does not solve the problem. No matter how affluent an individual is, the wish list continues to grow. We are familiar with the "rich and famous" who never seem to have enough. Although they live well, they still desire finer homes, faster planes, and larger yachts. In short, the condition of scarcity means all individuals, whether rich or poor, are dissatisfied with their material well-being and would like more. What is true for individuals also applies to society. Even Uncle Sam can't escape the problem of scarcity because the federal government never has enough money to spend for the poor, education, highways, police, national defense, Social Security, and all the other programs it wishes to fund.

Scarcity is a fact of life throughout the world. In much of South America, Africa, and Asia, the problem of scarcity is often life threatening. On the other hand, North America, Western Europe, and some parts of Asia have achieved substantial economic growth and development. Although life is much less grueling in the more advanced countries, the problem of scarcity still exists because individuals and countries never have as much of all the goods and services as they would like to have.

Scarce Resources and Production

Because of the economic problem of scarcity, no society has enough resources to produce all the goods and services necessary to satisfy all human wants. Resources are the basic categories of inputs used to produce goods and services. Resources are

Scarcity
The condition in which human wants are forever greater than the available supply of time, goods, and resources.

Resources
The basic categories of inputs used to produce goods and services. Resources are also called *factors of production*. Economists divide resources into three categories: land, labor, and capital.

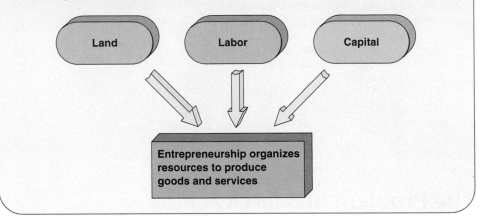

EXHIBIT 1   Three Categories of Resources

Resources are the basic categories of inputs organized by entrepreneurship (a special type of labor) to produce goods and services. Economists divide resources into the three categories of land, labor, and capital.

Land   Labor   Capital

Entrepreneurship organizes resources to produce goods and services

also called *factors of production*. Economists divide resources into three categories: *land, labor,* and *capital* (see Exhibit 1).

Land

Land is a shorthand expression for any natural resource provided by nature. *Land* includes those resources that are gifts of nature available for use in the production process. Farming, building factories, and constructing oil refineries would be impossible without land. Land includes anything natural above or below the ground, such as forests, gold, diamonds, oil, wildlife, and fish. Other examples are rivers, lakes, seas, wind and the sun. Two broad categories of natural resources are *renewable resources* and *nonrenewable resources*. Renewable resources are basic inputs that nature can automatically replace. Examples include lakes, crops, and clean air. Nonrenewable resources are basic inputs that nature cannot automatically replace. There is only so much coal, oil, and natural gas in the world. If these fossil fuels disappear, we must use substitutes.

Labor

Labor is the mental and physical capacity of workers to produce goods and services. The services of farmers, assembly-line workers, lawyers, professional football players, and economists are all *labor*. The labor resource is measured both by the number of people available for work and by the skills or quality of workers. One reason nations differ in their ability to produce is that human characteristics, such as the education, experience, health, and motivation of workers, differ among nations.

Entrepreneurship is a special type of labor. Entrepreneurship is the creative ability of individuals to seek profits by taking risks and combining resources to produce innovative products. An *entrepreneur* is a motivated person who seeks profits by undertaking such risky activities as starting new businesses, creating new products, or inventing new ways of accomplishing tasks. Entrepreneurship is a scarce human resource because relatively few people are willing or able to innovate and make decisions involving greater-than-normal chances for failure.

Land
A shorthand expression for any natural resource provided by nature.

Labor
The mental and physical capacity of workers to produce goods and services.

Entrepreneurship
The creative ability of individuals to seek profits by taking risks and combining resources to produce innovative products.

Entrepreneurs are the agents of change who bring material progress to society. The birth of the Levi Strauss Company is a classic entrepreneurial success story. In 1853, at the age of 24, Levi Strauss, who was born in Bavaria, sailed from New York to join the California Gold Rush. His intent was not to dig for gold, but to sell cloth. By the time he arrived in San Francisco, he had sold most of his cloth to other people on the ship. The only cloth he had left was a roll of canvas for tents and covered wagons. On the dock, he met a miner who wanted sturdy pants that would last while digging for gold, so Levi made a pair from the canvas. Later a customer gave Levi the idea of using little copper rivets to strengthen the seams. Presto! Strauss knew a good thing when he saw it, so he hired workers, built factories, and became one of the largest pants makers in the world. As a reward for taking business risks, organizing production, and introducing a product, the Levi Strauss Company earned profits, and Strauss became rich and famous.

Capital

Capital is the physical plants, machinery, and equipment used to produce other goods. Capital goods are human-made goods that do not directly satisfy human wants. Before the Industrial Revolution, *capital* meant a tool, such as a hoe, an axe, or a bow and arrow. In those days, these items served as capital to build a house or provide food for the dinner table. Today, capital also consists of factories, office buildings, warehouses, robots, trucks, and distribution facilities. College buildings, the printing presses used to produce this textbook, and pencils are also examples of capital.

The term *capital* as it is used in the study of economics can be confusing. Economists know that capital in everyday conversations means money or the money value of paper assets, such as stocks, bonds, or a deed to a house. This is actually *financial* capital. In the study of economics, capital does not refer to money assets. Instead, capital in economics means a factor of production, such as a factory or machinery. Stated simply, you must pay special attention to this point: Money is not capital and is therefore not a resource.

> **Conclusion** *Financial capital by itself is not productive; instead, it is only a paper claim on economic capital.*

Capital
The physical plants, machinery, and equipment used to produce other goods. Capital goods are human-made goods that do not directly satisfy human wants.

Economics: The Study of Scarcity and Choice

The perpetual problem of scarcity forcing people to make choices is the basis for the definition of economics. Economics is the study of how society chooses to allocate its scarce resources to the production of goods and services in order to satisfy unlimited wants. You may be surprised by this definition. People often think economics means studying supply and demand, the stock market, money, and banking. In fact, there are many ways one could define *economics,* but economists accept the definition given here because it includes the link between *scarcity* and *choices.*

Society makes two kinds of choices: economywide, or macro choices, and individual, or micro, choices. The prefixes *macro* and *micro* come from the Greek words meaning "large" and "small," respectively. Reflecting the macro and micro perspectives, economics consists of two main branches: *macroeconomics* and *microeconomics.*

Economics
The study of how society chooses to allocate its scarce resources to the production of goods and services in order to satisfy unlimited wants.

Macroeconomics

The old saying "Looking at the forest rather than the trees" describes macroeconomics. Macroeconomics is the branch of economics that studies decision making for the economy as a whole. Macroeconomics applies an overview perspective to an economy by examining economywide variables, such as inflation, unemployment, growth of the economy, the money supply, and the national incomes of developing countries. Macroeconomic decision making considers such "big picture" policies as the effect that federal tax cuts will have on unemployment and the effect that changing the money supply will have on prices.

Microeconomics

Examining individual trees, leaves, and pieces of bark, rather than surveying the forest, illustrates microeconomics. Microeconomics is the branch of economics that studies decision making by a single individual, household, firm, industry, or level of government. Microeconomics applies a microscope to study specific parts of an economy, as one would examine cells in the body. The focus is on small economic units, such as economic decisions of particular groups of consumers and businesses. An example of microeconomic analysis would be to study economic units involved in the market for ostrich eggs. Will suppliers decide to supply more, less, or the same quantity of ostrich eggs to the market in response to price changes? Will individual consumers of these eggs decide to buy more, less, or the same quantity at a new price?

We have described macroeconomics and microeconomics as two separate branches, but they are related. Because the overall economy is the sum, or aggregation, of its parts, micro changes affect the macro economy, and macro changes produce micro changes.

The Methodology of Economics

As used by other disciplines, such as criminology, biology, chemistry, and physics, economists employ a step-by-step procedure for solving problems by developing a theory, gathering data, and testing whether the data are consistent with the theory. Based on this analysis, economists formulate a conclusion. Exhibit 2 summarizes the model-building process.

Problem Identification

The first step in applying the economic method is to define the issue. Suppose an economist wishes to investigate the microeconomic problem of why U.S. motorists cut back on gasoline consumption in a given year from, for example, 400 million gallons per day in May to 300 million gallons per day in December.

Model Development

The second step in our hypothetical example toward finding an explanation is for the economist to build a model. A model is a simplified description of reality used to understand and predict the relationship between variables. The terms *model* and *theory* are interchangeable. A model emphasizes only those variables that are most important to explaining an event. As Albert Einstein said, "Theories should be as simple as possible, but not more so." The purpose of a model is to construct an abstraction from real-world complexities and make events understandable. Consider a model airplane that is placed in a wind tunnel to test the aerodynamics of a new design. For this purpose, the model must represent only the shapes of the wings and fuselage, but it does not need to include tiny seats, electrical wiring, or other

---

EXHIBIT 2   The Steps in the Model-Building Process

The first step in developing a model is to identify the problem. The second step is to select the critical variables necessary to formulate a model that explains the problem under study. Eliminating other variables that complicate the analysis requires simplifying assumptions. In the third step, the researcher collects data and tests the model. If the evidence supports the model, the conclusion is to accept the model. If not, the model is rejected.

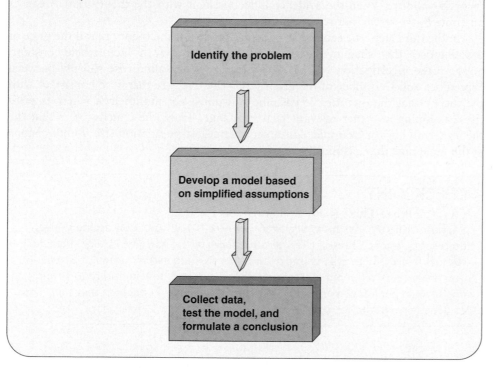

---

interior design details. A highway map is another example. To find the best route to drive between two distant cities, you do not want extraneous information on the location of all roads, streets, potholes, telephone lines, trees, stoplights, schools, hospitals, and firehouses. This would be too much detail, and the complexity would make it difficult to choose the best route.

To be useful, a model requires simplified assumptions. Someone must decide, for example, whether a map will include only symbols for the major highways or the details of hiking trails through mountains. In our gasoline consumption example, several variables might be related to the quantity of gasoline consumed, including consumer incomes, the prices of substitutes for gasoline, the price of gasoline, the fuel economy of cars, and weather conditions. Because a theory focuses only on the main or critical variables, the economist must be a Sherlock Holmes and use a keen sense of observation to form a model. Using his or her expertise, the economist must select the variables that are related to gasoline consumption and reject variables that have only slight or no relationship to gasoline consumption. In this simple case, the economist removes the cloud of complexity by formulating the theory that increases in the price of gasoline *cause* the quantity of gasoline consumed to decrease during the time period.

Testing a Theory

An economic model can be stated as a verbal argument, numerical table, graph, or mathematical equation. You will soon discover that a major part of this book is devoted to building and using economic models. The purpose of an economic model is to *forecast* or *predict* the results of various changes in variables. An economic theory can be expressed in the form "If *A*, then *B*, other things held constant." An economic model is useful only if it yields accurate predictions. When the evidence is consistent with the theory that *A* causes outcome *B*, there is confidence in the theory's validity. When the evidence is inconsistent with the theory that *A* causes outcome *B*, the researcher rejects this theory.

In the third step, the economist gathers data to test the theory that if the price of gasoline rises, then gasoline purchases fall—all other relevant factors held constant. Suppose the investigation reveals that the price of gasoline rose sharply between September and December of the given year. The data are therefore consistent with the theory that the quantity of gasoline consumed per month falls when its price rises, assuming no other relevant factors change. Thus, the conclusion is that the theory is valid if, for example, consumer incomes or population size do not change at the same time that gasoline prices rise.

CHECKPOINT

Can You Prove There Is No Trillion-Dollar Person?

Suppose a theory says no U.S. citizen is worth $1 trillion. You decide to test this theory and send researchers to all corners of the nation to check financial records to see whether someone qualifies by owning assets valued at $1 trillion or more. After years of checking, the researchers return and report that not a single person is worth at least $1 trillion. Do you conclude that the evidence proves the theory?

Hazards of the Economic Way of Thinking

Models help us understand and predict the impact of changes in economic variables. A model is an important tool in the economist's toolkit, but it must be handled with care. The economic way of thinking seeks to avoid reasoning mistakes. Two of the most common pitfalls to clear thinking are (1) failing to understand the *ceteris paribus assumption* and (2) confusing *association* and *causation*.

The Ceteris Paribus Assumption

As you work through a model, try to think of a host of relevant variables assumed to be "standing still," or "held constant." Ceteris paribus is a Latin phrase that means while certain variables change, "all other things remain unchanged." In short, the ceteris paribus assumption allows us to isolate or focus attention on selected variables. In the gasoline example discussed earlier, a key simplifying assumption of the model is that changes in consumer incomes and certain other variables do not occur and complicate the analysis. The ceteris paribus assumption holds everything else constant and therefore allows us to concentrate on the relationship between two key variables: changes in the price of gasoline and the quantity of gasoline purchased per month.

Now suppose an economist examines a model explaining the relationship between the price and quantity purchased of Coca-Cola. The theory is "If the price

Ceteris paribus

A Latin phrase that means while certain variables change, "all other things remain unchanged."

increases, then the quantity of Coca-Cola purchased decreases, ceteris paribus."
Now assume you observe that the price of Coca-Cola increased one summer and
some people actually bought more, not less. Based on this real-world observation,
you declare the theory is incorrect. Think again! The economist responds that this is
a reasoning pitfall because the model is valid based on the assumption of ceteris
paribus, and your observation gives us no reason to reject the model. The reason
the model appeared flawed is because another factor, a sharp rise in the temperature, *caused* people to buy more Coca-Cola in spite of its higher price. If the temperature and all other factors are held constant as the price of Coca-Cola rises, then
people will indeed buy less Coca-Cola, as the model predicts.

> **Conclusion** *A theory cannot be tested legitimately unless its ceteris paribus*
> *assumption is satisfied.*

Association versus Causation

Another common error in reasoning is confusing *association* (or correlation) and
causation between variables. Stated differently, you err when you read more into a
relationship between variables than is actually there. A model is valid only when a
cause-and-effect relationship is stable over time, rather than being an association
that occurs by chance and eventually disappears. Suppose a witch doctor performs
a voodoo dance during three different months and stock market prices skyrocket
during each of these months. The voodoo dance is *associated* with the increase in
stock prices, but this does not mean the dance *caused* the event. Even though there
is a statistical relationship between these two variables in a number of observations,
eventually the voodoo dance will be performed and stock prices will fall or remain
unchanged. The reason is that there is no true economic relationship between voodoo dances and stock prices.

Further investigation may reveal that stock prices actually responded to
changes in interest rates during the months that the voodoo dances were performed.
Changes in interest rates affect borrowing and, in turn, profits and stock prices. In
contrast, there is no real economic relationship between voodoo dances and stock
prices, and, therefore, the voodoo model is not valid.

> **Conclusion** *The fact that one event follows another does not necessarily*
> *mean that the first event caused the second event.*

CHECKPOINT

Should Nebraska State Join a Big-Time Athletic Conference?
Nebraska State (a mythical university) stood by while Penn State, Florida State,
the University of Miami, and the University of South Carolina joined big-time
athletic conferences. Now Nebraska State officials are pondering whether to
remain independent or to pursue membership in a conference noted for high-
quality football and basketball programs. An editorial in the newspaper advocates joining and cites a study showing that universities belonging to major
athletic conferences have higher graduation rates than nonmembers. Because
educating its students is the number one goal of Nebraska State, will this
evidence persuade Nebraska State officials to join a big-time conference?

YOU'RE THE ECONOMIST   Mops and Brooms, the Boston
Snow Index, the Super Bowl, and Other Economic Indicators
Applicable Concepts: association versus causation

© Laurin Rinder, 2008/Used under license from Shutterstock.com.

Although the Commerce Department, the Wharton School, the Federal Reserve Board, and other organizations publish economic forecasts and data on key economic indicators, they are not without armchair competition. For example, the chief executive of Standex International Corporation, Daniel E. Hogan, reported that his company can predict economic downturns and recoveries from sales reports of its National Metal Industries subsidiary in Springfield, Massachusetts. National makes metal parts for about 300 U.S. manufacturers of mops and brooms. A drop in National's sales always precedes a proportional fall in consumer spending. The company's sales always pick up slightly before consumer spending does.[1]

The Boston Snow Index (BSI) is the brainchild of a vice president of a New York securities firm. It predicts a rising economy for the next year if there is snow on the ground in Boston on Christmas Day. The BSI predicted correctly about 73 percent of the time over a 30-year period. However, its creator, David L. Upshaw, did not take it too seriously and views it as a spoof of other forecasters' methods.

Greeting card sales are another tried and true indicator, according to a vice president of American Greetings. Before a recession sets in, sales of higher-priced greeting cards rise. It seems that people substitute the cards for gifts, and since there is no gift, the card must be fancier.

A Super Bowl win by an NFC team predicts that in the following December the stock market will be higher than the year before. A win by an old AFL team predicts a dip in the stock market.

Several other less well-known indicators have also been proposed. For example, one economist suggested that the surliness of waiters is a countercyclical indicator. If they are nice, expect that bad times are coming, but if they are rude, expect an upturn. Waiters, on the other hand, counter that a fall in the average tip usually precedes a downturn in the economy.

Finally, Anthony Chan, chief economist for Bank One Investment Advisers, studied marriage trends over a 34-year period. He discovered that when the number of marriages increases, the economy rises significantly, and a slowdown in marriages is followed by a decline in the economy. Chan explains that there is usually about a 1-year lag between a change in the marriage rate and the economy.[2]

ANALYZE THE ISSUE

Which of the above indicators are examples of causation? Explain.

---

1. "Economic Indicators, Turtles, Butterflies, Monks, and Waiters," *The Wall Street Journal*, Aug. 27, 1979, pp. 1, 16.
2. Sandra Block, "Worried? Look at Wedding Bell Indicator," *The Charlotte Observer*, Apr. 15, 1995, p. 8A.

Throughout this book, you will study economic models or theories that include variables linked by stable cause-and-effect relationships. For example, the theory that a change in the price of a good *causes* a change in the quantity purchased is a valid microeconomic model. The theory that a change in the money supply *causes* a change in interest rates is an example of a valid macroeconomic model. The You're the Economist gives some amusing examples of the "association means causation" reasoning pitfall.

Why Do Economists Disagree?

Why might one economist say a clean environment should be our most important priority and another economist say economic growth should be our most important goal? If economists share the economic way of thinking and carefully avoid reasoning pitfalls, then why do they disagree? Why are economists known for giving advice by saying, "On the one hand, if you do this, then *A* results, and, on the other hand, doing this causes result *B*?" In fact, President Harry Truman once jokingly exclaimed, "Find me an economist with only one hand." George Bernard Shaw offered another famous line in the same vein: "If you took all the economists in the world and laid them end to end, they would never reach a conclusion." These famous quotes imply that economists should agree, but they ignore the fact that physicists, doctors, business executives, lawyers, and other professionals often disagree.

Economists may appear to disagree more than other professionals partly because it is more interesting to report disagreements than agreements. Actually, economists agree on a wide range of issues. Many economists, for example, agree on free trade among nations, the elimination of farm subsidies and rent ceilings, government deficit spending to recover from a recession, and many other issues. When disagreements do exist, the reason can often be explained by the difference between *positive economics* and *normative economics*.

Positive Economics

Positive economics deals with facts and therefore addresses "what is" or "verifiable" questions. Positive economics is an analysis limited to statements that are verifiable. Positive statements can be proven either true or false. Often a positive statement is expressed: "If *A*, then *B*." For example, if the national unemployment rate rises to 7 percent, then teenage unemployment exceeds 80 percent. This is a positive "if-then" prediction, which may or may not be correct. Accuracy is not the criterion for being a positive statement. The key consideration is whether the statement is *testable* and not whether it is true or false. Suppose the data show that when the nation's overall unemployment rate is close to 7 percent, the unemployment rate for teenagers never reaches 80 percent. For example, the overall unemployment rate was 6.9 percent in 1993, and the rate for teenagers was 19 percent—far short of 80 percent. Based on the facts, we would conclude that this positive statement is false.

Now we can explain one reason why economists' forecasts can diverge. The statement "If event *A* occurs, then event *B* follows" can be thought of as a *conditional* positive statement. For example, two economists may agree that if the federal government cuts spending by 10 percent this year, prices will fall about 2 percent next year. However, their predictions about the fall in prices may differ because one economist assumes Congress will not cut spending, while the other economist assumes Congress will cut spending by 10 percent.

> **Conclusion** *Economists' forecasts can differ because, using the same methodology, economists can agree that event* A *causes event* B, *but disagree over the assumption that event* A *will occur.*

Normative Economics

Instead of using objective statements, an argument can be phrased subjectively. Normative economics attempts to determine "what should be." Normative

Positive economics
An analysis limited to statements that are verifiable.

Normative economics
An analysis based on value judgment.

economics is an analysis based on value judgments. Normative statements express an individual or collective opinion on a subject and cannot be proven by facts to be true or false. Certain words or phrases, such as *good, bad, need, should,* and *ought to,* tell us clearly that we have entered the realm of normative economics.

The point here is that people wearing different-colored glasses see the same facts differently. Each of us has individual subjective preferences that we apply to a particular subject. An animal rights activist says that no one *should* purchase a fur coat. Or one senator argues, "We *ought to* see that every teenager who wants a job has one." Another senator counters by saying, "Maintaining the purchasing power of the dollar is *more important* than teenage unemployment."

> **Conclusion** *When opinions or points of view are not based on facts, they are scientifically untestable.*

When considering a debate, make sure to separate the arguments into their positive and normative components. This distinction allows you to determine if you are choosing a course of action based on factual evidence or on opinion. The material presented in this textbook, like most of economics, takes pains to stay within the boundaries of positive economic analysis. In our everyday lives, however, politicians, business executives, relatives, and friends use mostly normative statements to discuss economic issues. Economists also may associate themselves with a political position and use normative arguments for or against some economic policy. When using value judgments, an economist's normative arguments may have no greater validity than those of others. Biases or preconceptions can cloud an economist's thinking about deficit spending or whether to increase taxes on gasoline. Like beginning economics students, economists are human.

Careers in Economics

The author of this text entered college more years ago than I would like to admit. In those days, economics was not taught in high school, so I knew nothing of the subject. Like many students taking this course, I was uncertain about which major to pursue, but selected electrical engineering because I was an amateur radio operator and enjoyed building radio receivers and transmitters. My engineering curriculum required a course in economics. I signed up thinking that "econ is boring." Instead, it was an eye-opening experience that inspired me to change my major to economics and pursue an economics teaching career.

The study of economics has attracted a number of well-known people. For example, the Rolling Stones' Mick Jagger attended the London School of Economics, and Tiger Woods studied economics at Stanford. Other famous people who majored in economics include former Supreme Court Justice Sandra Day O'Connor, California Governor Arnold Schwarzenegger, and three former presidents—George H. W. Bush, Ronald Reagan, and Gerald Ford.

An economics major can choose many career paths. Most economics majors work for business firms. Because economists are trained in analyzing financial matters, they find good jobs in management, sales, or as a market analyst interpreting economic conditions relevant to a firm's markets. For those with an undergraduate degree, private-sector job opportunities exist in banking, securities brokering, management

YOU'RE THE ECONOMIST   Does Raising the Minimum Wage
Help the Working Poor?   *Applicable Concepts: positive and normative analyses*

In 1938, Congress enacted the federal Fair Labor Standards Act, commonly known as the "minimum-wage law." Today, a minimum-wage worker who works full-time still earns a deplorably low annual income. One approach to help the working poor earn a living wage might be to raise the minimum wage.

The dilemma for Congress is that a higher minimum wage for the employed is enacted at the expense of jobs for unskilled workers. Opponents forecast that the increased labor cost from a large minimum-wage hike would jeopardize hundreds of thousands of unskilled jobs. For example, employers may opt to purchase more capital and less expensive labor. The fear of such sizable job losses forces Congress to perform a difficult balancing act to ensure that a minimum-wage increase is large enough to help the working poor, but not so large as to threaten their jobs.

Some politicians claim that raising the minimum wage is a way to help the working poor without cost to taxpayers. Others believe the cost is hidden in inflation and lost employment opportunities for marginal workers, such as teenagers, the elderly, and minorities. One study by economists, for example, examined a national data set and reported evidence that

minimum wage increases resulted in reduced employment and hours of work for low-wage workers.[1]

Another problem with raising the minimum wage to aid the working poor is that minimum wage is a blunt weapon for redistributing wealth. Studies show that only a small percentage of minimum-wage earners are full-time workers whose family income falls below the poverty line. This means that most increases in the minimum wage go to workers who are not poor. For example, many minimum-wage workers are students living at home or workers whose spouse earns a much higher income. To help only the working poor, some economists argue that the government should target only those who need assistance, rather than using the "shotgun" approach of raising the minimum wage.

Supporters of raising the minimum wage are not convinced by these arguments. They say it is outrageous that a worker can work full-time and still live in poverty. Moreover, people on this side of the debate believe that opponents exaggerate the dangers to the economy from a higher minimum wage. For example, one could argue that a higher minimum wage will force employers to upgrade the skills and productivity of their workers. Increasing the minimum wage may therefore be a win-win proposition,

rather than a win-lose proposition. Finally, across the United States, numerous localities have implemented living-wage laws, while dozens more are considering them. Note that we will return to this issue in Chapter 4 as an application of supply and demand analysis.

ANALYZE THE ISSUE

1. Identify two positive and two normative statements given above concerning raising the minimum wage. List other minimum-wage arguments not discussed in this You're the Economist, and classify them as either positive or normative economics.

2. Give a positive and a normative argument why a business leader would oppose raising the minimum wage. Give a positive and a normative argument why a labor leader would favor raising the minimum wage.

3. Explain your position on this issue. Identify positive and normative reasons for your decision. Are there alternative ways to aid the working poor?

---

1. David Neumark, Mark Schweitzer, and William Wascher, "Minimum Wage Effects throughout the Wage Distribution," *The Journal of Human Resources,* Vol. 39, No. 2 (Spring, 2004), pp. 425–450.

consulting, computer and data processing firms, the power industry, statistical and market research and analysis, finance, health care, and many other industries. Other economics majors work for government agencies and in colleges and universities.

Government economists work for federal, state, and local governments. For example, a government economist might compile and report national statistics for economic growth or work on projects such as how to improve indexes to measure trends in consumer prices. Economists in academe not only enjoy the challenge of teaching economics, but have great freedom in selecting research projects.

Studying economics is also an essential preparation for other careers. Those preparing for law school, for example, find economics an excellent major because of its emphasis on a logical approach to problem solving. Economics is also great preparation for an MBA. In fact, students majoring in any field will benefit throughout their lives from learning how to apply the economic way of thinking to analyze real-world economic issues.

Finally, economics majors shine in salary offers upon graduation. Exhibit 3 shows average yearly salary offers for bachelor's degree candidates for January 2007.

EXHIBIT 3	Average Yearly Salary Offers for Selected Majors
Undergraduate Major	**Average Offer, January 2007**
Computer engineering	$55,936
Electrical engineering	54,599
Economics	**51,631**
Computer science	51,070
Mathematics	47,417
Management information systems	46,568
Accounting	46,500
Nursing	44,633
Business administration	43,523
Marketing	41,323
Environmental science	37,133
Animal science	36,250
Liberal arts and sciences	36,154
Journalism	35,100
Foreign language	32,103
Visual and performing arts	31,157
Criminal justice	30,570
Political science	29,900
Sociology	29,808
Social work	28,846
Psychology	28,820

SOURCE   National Association of Colleges and Employers, *Salary Survey,* Winter 2007, pp. 4–5.

KEY CONCEPTS

Scarcity	Capital	Ceteris paribus
Resources	Economics	Positive economics
Land	Macroeconomics	Normative economics
Labor	Microeconomics	
Entrepreneurship	Model	

SUMMARY

- **Scarcity** is the fundamental economic problem that human wants exceed the availability of time, goods, and resources. Individuals and society therefore can never have everything they desire.
- **Resources** are factors of production classified as land, labor, and capital. Entrepreneurship is a special type of labor. An entrepreneur seeks profits by taking risks and combining resources to produce innovative products.
- **Economics** is the study of how individuals and society choose to allocate scarce resources in order to satisfy unlimited wants. Faced with unlimited wants and scarce resources, we must make choices among alternatives.

- **Macroeconomics** applies an economywide perspective that focuses on such issues as inflation, unemployment, and the growth rate of the economy.
- **Microeconomics** examines individual decision-making units within an economy, such as a consumer's response to changes in the price of coffee

and the reasons for changes in the market price of personal computers.
- **Models** are simplified descriptions of reality used to understand and predict economic events. An economic model can be stated verbally or in a table, a graph, or an equation. If the evidence is not consistent with the model, the model is rejected.

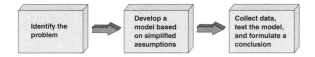

- **Ceteris paribus** holds "all other factors unchanged" that might affect a particular relationship. If this assumption is violated, a model cannot be tested. Another reasoning pitfall is to think that *association* means *causation*.
- Use of **positive versus normative economic analysis** is a major reason for disagreements among economists. **Positive economics** uses testable statements. Often a positive argument is expressed as an *if-then* statement. **Normative economics** is based on value judgments or opinions and uses words such as *good, bad, ought to,* and *should.*

SUMMARY OF CONCLUSION STATEMENTS

- Financial capital by itself is not productive; instead, it is only a paper claim on economic capital.
- A theory cannot be tested legitimately unless its ceteris paribus assumption is satisfied.
- The fact that one event follows another does not necessarily mean that the first event caused the second event.

- Economists' forecasts can differ because, using the same methodology, economists can agree that event *A* causes event *B*, but disagree over the assumption that event *A* will occur.
- When opinions or points of view are not based on facts, they are scientifically untestable.

STUDY QUESTIONS AND PROBLEMS

1. Explain why both nations with high living standards and nations with low living standards face the problem of scarcity. If you won $1 million in a lottery, would you escape the scarcity problem?

2. Why isn't money considered capital in economics?

3. Computer software programs are an example of
   a. capital.
   b. labor.
   c. a natural resource.
   d. none of the above.

4. Explain the difference between macroeconomics and microeconomics. Give examples of the areas of concern to each branch of economics.

5. Which of the following are microeconomic issues? Which are macroeconomic issues?
   a. How will an increase in the price of Coca-Cola affect the quantity of Pepsi-Cola sold?
   b. What will cause the nation's inflation rate to fall?
   c. How does a quota on textile imports affect the textile industry?
   d. Does a large federal budget deficit reduce the rate of unemployment in the economy?

6. A model is defined as a
   a. value judgment of the relationship between variables.
   b. presentation of all relevant aspects of real-world events.
   c. simplified description of reality used to understand the way variables are related.
   d. data set adjusted for irrational actions of people.

7. Explain why it is important for an economic model to be an abstraction from the real world.

8. Explain the importance of the ceteris paribus assumption for an economic model.

9. Suppose Congress cuts spending for the military, and then unemployment rises in the U.S. defense industry. Is there causation in this situation, or are we observing an association between events?

10. Which of the following is an example of a proposition from positive economics?
    a. If John Kerry had been elected president, taxpayers would have been treated more fairly than under George W. Bush.
    b. The average rate of inflation was higher during George W. Bush's presidency than during Bill Clinton's presidency.
    c. In economic terms, George W. Bush is a better president than Bill Clinton.
    d. Bill Clinton's policies were more just toward poor people than George W. Bush's.

11. "The government should collect higher taxes from the rich and use the additional revenues to provide greater benefits to the poor." This statement is an illustration of a
    a. testable statement.
    b. basic principle of economics.
    c. statement of positive economics.
    d. statement of normative economics.

12. Analyze the positive versus normative arguments in the following case. What statements of positive economics are used to support requiring air bags? What normative reasoning is used?

Should the Government Require Air Bags?

Air bag advocates say air bags will save lives and the government should require them in all cars. Air bags add an estimated $600 to the cost of a car, compared to about $100 for a set of regular seat belts. Opponents argue that air bags are electronic devices subject to failure and have produced injuries and death. For example, air bags have killed both adults and children whose heads were within the inflation zone at the time of deployment. Opponents therefore believe the government should leave the decision of whether to spend an extra $600 or so for an air bag to the consumer. The role of the government should be limited to providing information on the risks of having versus not having air bags.

For Online Exercises, go the text Web site at www.cengage.com/economics/tucker.

CHECKPOINT ANSWERS ✓

Can You Prove There Is No Trillion-Dollar Person?

How can researchers ever be certain they have seen all the rich people in the United States? There is always the possibility that somewhere there is a person who qualifies. If the researchers had found one, you could have rejected the theory. Because they did not, you cannot reject the theory. If you said that the evidence can support, but never prove, the theory, **YOU ARE CORRECT.**

Should Nebraska State Join a Big-Time Athletic Conference?

Suppose universities that belong to big-time athletic conferences do indeed have higher graduation rates than nonmembers. This is not the only possible explanation for the statistical correlation (or association) between the graduation rate and membership in a big-time athletic conference. A more plausible explanation is that improving academic variables, such as tuition, quality of faculty, and student-faculty ratios, and not athletic conference membership, increases the graduation rate. If you said correlation does not mean causation, and therefore Nebraska State officials will not necessarily accept the graduation rate evidence, **YOU ARE CORRECT.**

PRACTICE QUIZ

For visual explanation of the correct answers, please visit the tutorial at www.cengage.com/economics/tucker.

1. Scarcity exists
   a. when people consume beyond their needs.
   b. only in rich nations.
   c. in all countries of the world.
   d. only in poor nations.

2. Which of the following would eliminate scarcity as an economic problem?
   a. Moderation of people's competitive instincts
   b. Discovery of sufficiently large new energy reserves
   c. Resumption of steady productivity growth
   d. None of the above because scarcity cannot be eliminated

3. Which of the following is *not* a resource?
   a. Land
   b. Labor
   c. Money
   d. Capital

4. Economics is the study of
   a. how to make money.
   b. how to operate a business.
   c. people making choices because of the problem of scarcity.
   d. the government decision-making process.

5. Microeconomics approaches the study of economics from the viewpoint of
   a. individual or specific markets.
   b. the operation of the Federal Reserve.
   c. economywide effects.
   d. the national economy.

6. A review of the performance of the U.S. economy during the 1990s is primarily the concern of
   a. macroeconomics.
   b. microeconomics.
   c. both macroeconomics and microeconomics.
   d. neither macroeconomics nor microeconomics.

PRACTICE QUIZ CONTINUED

7. An economic theory claims that a rise in gasoline prices will cause gasoline purchases to fall, ceteris paribus. The phrase *ceteris paribus* means that
   a. other relevant factors like consumer incomes must be held constant.
   b. gasoline prices must first be adjusted for inflation.
   c. the theory is widely accepted but cannot be accurately tested.
   d. consumers' need for gasoline remains the same regardless of price.

8. An economist notices that sunspot activity is high just prior to recessions and concludes that sunspots cause recessions. The economist has
   a. confused association and causation.
   b. misunderstood the ceteris paribus assumption.
   c. used normative economics to answer a positive question.
   d. built an untestable model.

9. Which of the following is a statement of positive economics?
   a. The income tax system collects a lower percentage of the incomes of the poor
   b. A reduction in tax rates of the rich makes the tax system more fair
   c. Tax rates ought to be raised to finance health care
   d. All of the above are primarily statements of positive economics

10. Which of the following is a statement of positive economics?
    a. An unemployment rate greater than 8 percent is good because prices will fall.
    b. An unemployment rate of 7 percent is a serious problem.
    c. If the overall unemployment rate is 7 percent, unemployment rates among African-Americans will average 15 percent.
    d. Unemployment is a more severe problem than inflation.

11. Which of the following is a statement of normative economics?
    a. The minimum wage is good because it raises wages for the working poor.
    b. The minimum wage is supported by unions.
    c. The minimum wage reduces the number of jobs for less-skilled workers.
    d. The minimum wage encourages firms to substitute capital for labor.

12. Select the normative statement that completes the following sentence: If the minimum wage is raised rapidly, then
    a. inflation will increase.
    b. workers will gain their rightful share of total income.
    c. profits will fall.
    d. unemployment will rise.

13. Computer programs, or software, are an example of
    a. land.
    b. labor.
    c. capital.
    d. none of the above.

14. Which of the following would *not* be classified as a capital resource?
    a. The Empire State Building.
    b. A Caterpillar bulldozer.
    c. A Macintosh computer.
    d. 100 shares of stock in General Motors.

15. A model (or theory)
    a. is a general statement about the causal relationship between variables based on facts.
    b. helps explain and predict the relationship between variables.
    c. when expressed as a downward (negatively) sloping graph implies an inverse relationship between the variables.
    d. all of the above.

Applying Graphs to Economics

Economists are famous for their use of graphs. The reason is "a picture is worth a thousand words." Graphs are used throughout this text to present economics models. By drawing a line, you can use a two-dimensional illustration to analyze the effects of a change in one variable on another. You could describe the same information using other model forms, such as verbal statements, tables, or equations, but a graph is the simplest way to present and understand the relationship between economic variables.

Don't be worried that graphs will "throw you for a loop." Relax! This appendix explains all the basic graphical language you will need. The following illustrates the simplest use of graphs for economic analysis.

A Direct Relationship

Basic economic analysis typically concerns the relationship between two variables, both having positive values. Hence, we can confine our graphs to the upper-right (northeast) quadrant of the coordinate number system. In Exhibit A-1, notice that the scales on the horizontal axis (*x*-axis) and the vertical axis (*y*-axis) do not necessarily measure the same numerical values.

The horizontal axis in Exhibit A-1 measures annual income, and the vertical axis shows the amount spent per year for a personal computer (PC). In the absence of any established traditions, we could decide to measure income on the vertical axis and expenditure on the horizontal axis. The intersection of the horizontal and vertical axes is the *origin,* and the point at which both income and expenditure are zero. In Exhibit A-1, each point is a coordinate that matches the dollar value of income and the corresponding expenditure for a PC. For example, point *A* on the graph shows that people with an annual income of $10,000 spent $1,000 per year for a PC. Other incomes are associated with different expenditure levels. For example, at $30,000 per year (point *C*), $3,000 will be spent annually for a PC.

The straight line in Exhibit A-1 allows us to determine the direction of change in PC expenditure as annual income changes. This relationship is *positive* because PC expenditure, measured along the vertical axis, and annual income, measured along the horizontal axis, move in the same direction. PC expenditure increases as annual income increases. As income declines, so does the amount spent on a PC. Thus, the straight line representing the relationship between income and PC expenditure is a direct relationship. A direct relationship is a positive association between two variables. When one variable increases, the other variable increases, and when one variable decreases, the other variable decreases. In short, both variables change in the *same* direction.

Finally, an important point to remember: A two-variable graph, like any model, isolates the relationship between two variables and holds all other variables constant under the ceteris paribus assumption. In Exhibit A-1, for example, such fac-

---

Direct relationship

A positive association between two variables. When one variable increases, the other variable increases, and when one variable decreases, the other variable decreases.

EXHIBIT A-1   A Direct Relationship between Variables

The line with a positive slope shows that the expenditure per year for a personal computer has a direct relationship to annual income, ceteris paribus. As annual income increases along the horizontal axis, the amount spent on a PC also increases, as measured by the vertical axis. Along the line, each 10-unit increase in annual income results in a 1-unit increase in expenditure for a PC. Because the slope is constant along a straight line, we can measure the same slope between any two points. Between points B and C or between points A and D, the slope = $\Delta Y/\Delta X = +3/+30 = +1/+10 = 1/10$.

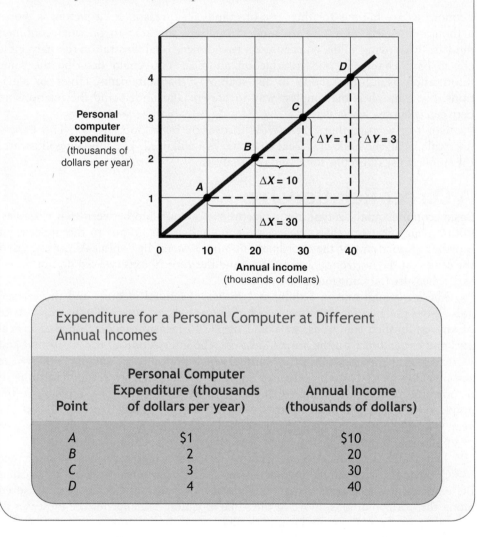

Expenditure for a Personal Computer at Different Annual Incomes

Point	Personal Computer Expenditure (thousands of dollars per year)	Annual Income (thousands of dollars)
A	$1	$10
B	2	20
C	3	30
D	4	40

tors as the prices of PCs and education are held constant by assumption. In Chapter 3, you will learn that allowing variables not shown in the graph to change can shift the position of the curve.

An Inverse Relationship

Now consider the relationship between the price of compact discs (CDs) and the quantity consumers will buy per year, shown in Exhibit A-2. These data indicate

EXHIBIT A-2   An Inverse Relationship between Variables

The line with a negative slope shows an inverse relationship between the price per compact disc and the quantity of CDs consumers purchase, ceteris paribus. As the price of a CD rises, the quantity of CDs purchased falls. A lower price for CDs is associated with more CDs purchased by consumers. Along the line, with each $5 decrease in the price of CDs, consumers increase the quantity purchased by 25 units. The slope = $\Delta Y/\Delta X = -5/+25 = -1/5$.

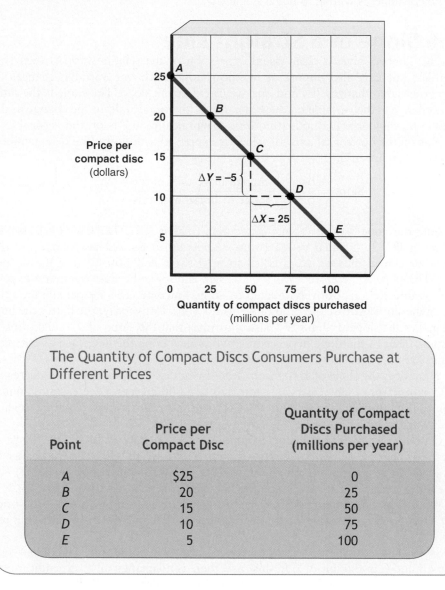

The Quantity of Compact Discs Consumers Purchase at Different Prices

Point	Price per Compact Disc	Quantity of Compact Discs Purchased (millions per year)
A	$25	0
B	20	25
C	15	50
D	10	75
E	5	100

a *negative* relationship between the price and quantity variables. When the price is low, consumers purchase a greater quantity of CDs than when the price is high.

In Exhibit A-2, there is an inverse relationship between the price per CD and the quantity consumers buy. An inverse relationship is a negative association between two variables. When one variable increases, the other variable decreases, and

Inverse relationship
A negative association between two variables. When one variable increases, the other decreases, and when one variable decreases, the other variable increases.

when one variable decreases, the other variable increases. Stated simply, the variables move in *opposite* directions.

The line drawn in Exhibit A-2 is an inverse relationship. By long-established tradition, economists put price on the vertical axis and quantity on the horizontal axis. In Chapter 3, we will study in more detail the relationship between price and quantity called the *law of demand*.

In addition to observing the inverse relationship (slope), you must interpret the *intercept* at point *A* in the exhibit. The intercept in this case means that at a price of $25 no consumer is willing to buy a single CD.

The Slope of a Straight Line

Plotting numbers gives a clear visual expression of the relationship between two variables, but it is also important to know how much one variable changes as another variable changes. To find out, we calculate the slope. The slope is the ratio of the change in the variable on the vertical axis (the rise or fall) to the change in the variable on the horizontal axis (the run). Algebraically, if *Y* is on the vertical axis and *X* is on the horizontal axis, the slope is expressed as follows (the delta symbol, Δ, means "change in"):

Slope The ratio of the change in the variable on the vertical axis (the rise or fall) to the change in the variable on the horizontal axis (the run).

$$\text{Slope} = \frac{\text{rise}}{\text{run}} = \frac{\text{change in vertical axis}}{\text{change in horizontal axis}} = \frac{\Delta Y}{\Delta X}$$

Consider the slope between points *B* and *C* in Exhibit A-1. The change in expenditure for a PC, *Y*, is equal to +1 (from $2,000 up to $3,000 per year), and the change in annual income, *X*, is equal to +10 (from $20,000 up to $30,000 per year). The slope is therefore +1/+10. The sign is positive because computer expenditure is directly, or positively, related to annual income. The steeper the line, the greater the slope because the ratio of Δ*Y* to Δ*X* rises. Conversely, the flatter the line, the smaller the slope. Exhibit A-1 also illustrates that the slope of a straight line is constant. That is, the slope between any two points along the line, such as between points *A* and *D*, is equal to +3/+30 = 1/10.

What does the slope of 1/10 mean? It tells you that a $1,000 increase (decrease) in PC expenditure each year occurs for each $10,000 increase (decrease) in annual income. The line plotted in Exhibit A-1 has a *positive slope*, and we describe the line as "upward sloping."

On the other hand, the line in Exhibit A-2 has a *negative slope*. The change in *Y* between points *C* and *D* is equal to –5 (from $15 down to $10), and the change in *X* is equal to +25 (from 50 million up to 75 million CDs purchased per year). The slope is therefore –5/+25 = –1/5, and this line is described as "downward sloping."

What does this slope of –1/5 mean? It means that raising (lowering) the price per CD by $1 decreases (increases) the quantity of CDs purchased by 5 million per year.

Suppose we calculate the slope between any two points on a flat line—say, points *B* and *C* in Exhibit A-3. In this case, there is no change in *Y* (expenditure for toothpaste) as *X* (annual income) increases. Consumers spend $20 per year on toothpaste regardless of annual income. It follows that Δ*Y* = 0 for any Δ*X*, so the slope is equal to 0. The two variables along a flat line (horizontal or vertical) have an independent relationship. An independent relationship is a zero association between two variables. When one variable changes, the other variable remains unchanged.

Independent relationship A zero association between two variables. When one variable changes, the other variable remains unchanged.

EXHIBIT A-3	An Independent Relationship between Variables

The flat line with a zero slope shows that the expenditure per year for toothpaste is unrelated to annual income. As annual income increases along the horizontal axis, the amount spent each year for toothpaste remains unchanged at 20 units. If annual income increases 10 units, the corresponding change in expenditure is zero. The slope = $\Delta Y/\Delta X = 0/+10 = 0$.

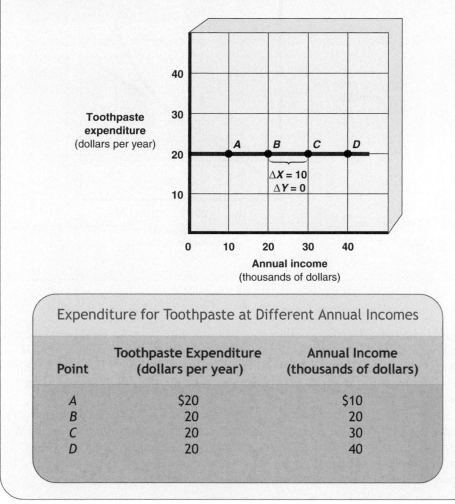

Expenditure for Toothpaste at Different Annual Incomes

Point	Toothpaste Expenditure (dollars per year)	Annual Income (thousands of dollars)
A	$20	$10
B	20	20
C	20	30
D	20	40

The Slope of a Curve

The slope of a curve changes from one point to another. Suppose the relationship between the expenditure for a PC per year and annual income is not a straight line, but an upward-sloping curve, as drawn in Exhibit A-4. This means the slope of the curve is *positive* as we move along the curve. To calculate the slope of a given point on the curve requires two steps. For example, at point *A*, the first step is to draw a tangent line that just touches the curve at this point without crossing it. The second

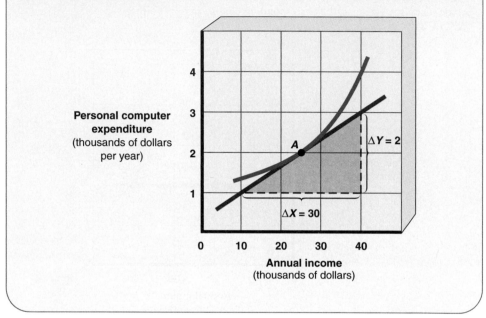

EXHIBIT A-4   The Slope of an Upward-Sloping Curve

The slope of a curve at any given point, such as point A, is equal to the slope of the straight line drawn tangent to the curve at that point. The tangent line just touches the curve at point A without crossing it. The slope of the upward-sloping curve at point A is +2/+30 = +1/+15 = 1/15.

step is to determine the slope of the tangent line. In Exhibit A-4, the slope of the tangent line, and therefore the slope of the curve at point A, is +2/+30 = 1/15. What does this slope of 1/15 mean? It means that at point A there will be a $1,000 increase (decrease) in PC expenditure each year for each $15,000 increase (decrease) in annual income.

Now consider that the relationship between the price per CD and the quantity demanded by consumers per year is the downward-sloping curve shown in Exhibit A-5. In this case, the slope of the curve is *negative* as we move along the curve. To calculate the slope at point A, draw a line tangent to the curve at point A. Thus, the slope of the curve at point A is −10/+50 = −1/+5 = −1/5.

A Three-Variable Relationship in One Graph

The two-variable relationships drawn so far conform to a two-dimensional flat piece of paper. For example, the vertical axis measures the price per CD variable, and the horizontal axis measures the quantity of CDs purchased variable. All other factors, such as consumer income, that may affect the relationship between the price and quantity variables are held constant by the ceteris paribus assumption. But reality is frequently not so accommodating. Often a model must take into account

EXHIBIT A-5   The Slope of a Downward-Sloping Curve

In this exhibit, the negative slope changes as one moves from point to point along the curve. The slope at any given point, such as point *A*, can be determined by the slope of the straight line tangent to that point. The slope of the downward-sloping curve at point *A* is −10/+50 = −1/+5 = −1/5.

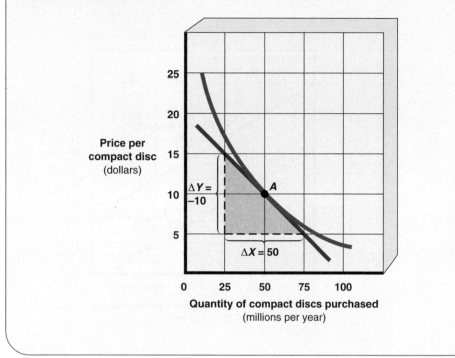

the impact of changes in a third variable (consumer income) drawn on a two-dimensional piece of graph paper.

Economists' favorite method of depicting a three-variable relationship is shown in Exhibit A-6. As explained earlier, the cause-and-effect relationship between price and quantity of CDs determines the downward-sloping curve. A change in the price per CD causes a movement downward along either of the two separate curves. As the price falls, consumers increase the quantity of CDs demanded. The location of each curve on the graph, however, depends on the annual income of consumers. As the annual income variable increases from $30,000 to $60,000 and consumers can afford to pay more, the price-quantity demanded curve shifts rightward. Conversely, as the annual income variable decreases and consumers have less to spend, the price-quantity demanded curve shifts leftward.

This is an extremely important concept that you must understand: Throughout this book, you must distinguish between *movements along* and *shifts in* a curve. Here's how to tell the difference. A change in one of the variables shown on either of the coordinate axes of the graph causes *movement along* a curve. On the other hand, a change in a variable not shown on one of the coordinate axes of the graph causes a *shift in* a curve's position on the graph.

EXHIBIT A-6 — Changes in Price, Quantity, and Income in Two Dimensions

Economists use a multicurve graph to represent a three-variable relationship in a two-dimensional graph. A decrease in the price per CD causes a movement downward along each curve. As the annual income of consumers rises, there is a shift rightward in the position of the demand curve.

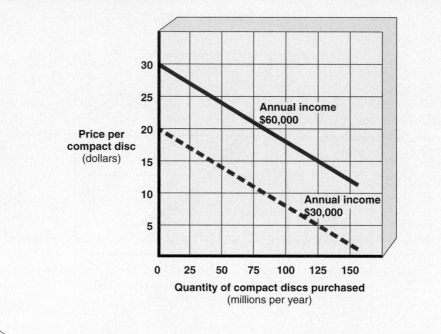

Conclusion *A shift in a curve occurs only when the ceteris paribus assumption is relaxed and a third variable not shown on either axis of the graph is allowed to change.*

A Helpful Study Hint for Using Graphs

To some students, studying economics is a little frightening because many chapters are full of graphs. An often-repeated mistake is to prepare for tests by trying to memorize the lines of graphs. When their graded tests are returned, the students using this strategy will probably exclaim, "What happened?" The answer is that if you learn the economic concepts first, then you will understand the graphs as illustrations of these underlying concepts. Stated simply, superficial cramming for economics quizzes does not work. For students who are anxious about using graphs, in addition to the brief review of graphical analysis in this appendix, the Graphing Workshop on the EconCentral Web site and the Study Guide contains step-by-step features on how to interpret graphs.

KEY CONCEPTS

Direct relationship   Slope
Inverse relationship   Independent relationship

SUMMARY

- **Graphs** provide a means to clearly show economic relationships in two-dimensional space. Economic analysis is often concerned with two variables confined to the upper-right (northeast) quadrant of the coordinate number system.
- A **direct relationship** occurs when two variables change in the *same* direction.

Direct Relationship

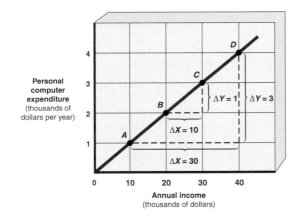

- An **inverse relationship** occurs when two variables change in *opposite* directions.

Inverse Relationship

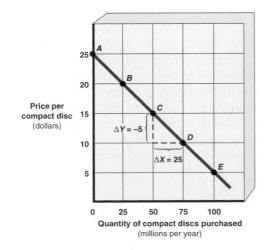

- An **independent relationship** occurs when two variables are unrelated.

Independent Relationship

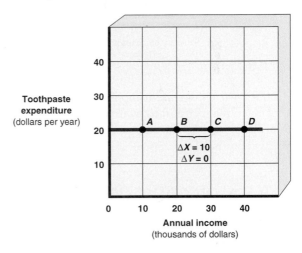

- **Slope** is the ratio of the vertical change (the rise or fall) to the horizontal change (the run). The slope of an *upward-sloping* line is *positive*, and the slope of a *downward-sloping* line is *negative*.

Positive Slope of an Upward-Sloping Curve

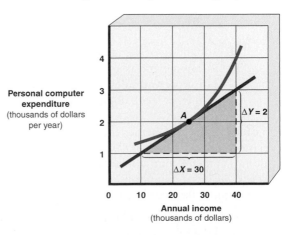

Negative Slope of a Downward-Sloping Curve

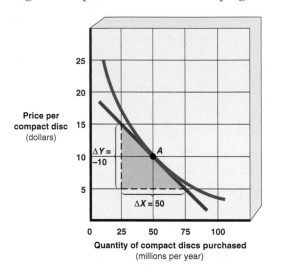

assumption is relaxed and a third variable (such as annual income) not on either axis of the graph is allowed to change.

Three-Variable Relationship

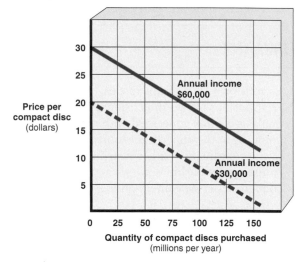

- A **three-variable relationship** is depicted by a graph showing a shift in a curve when the ceteris paribus

SUMMARY OF CONCLUSION STATEMENT

- A shift in a curve occurs only when the ceteris paribus assumption is relaxed and a third vari- able not shown on either axis of the graph is al- lowed to change.

STUDY QUESTIONS AND PROBLEMS

1. Draw a graph without specific data for the expected relationship between the following variables
   a. The probability of living and age
   b. Annual income and years of education
   c. Inches of snow and sales of bathing suits
   d. The number of football games won and the athletic budget

   In each case, state whether the expected relationship is *direct* or *inverse*. Explain an additional factor that would be included in the *ceteris paribus* assumption because it might change and influence your theory.

2. Assume a research firm collects survey sales data that reveal the relationship between the possible selling prices of hamburgers and the quantity of hamburgers consumers would purchase per year at alternative prices. The report states that if the price of a hamburger is $4, 20,000 will be bought. However, at a price of $3, 40,000 hamburgers will be bought. At $2, 60,000 ham- burgers will be bought, and at $1, 80,000 hamburgers will be purchased.

   Based on these data, describe the relevant relationship between the price of a hamburger and the quantity consumers are willing to purchase, using a verbal statement, a numerical table, and a graph. Which model do you prefer and why?

PRACTICE QUIZ

For an explanation of the correct answers, please visit the tutorial at www.cengage.com/economics/tucker.

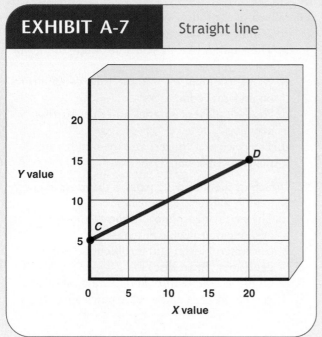

EXHIBIT A-7 | Straight line

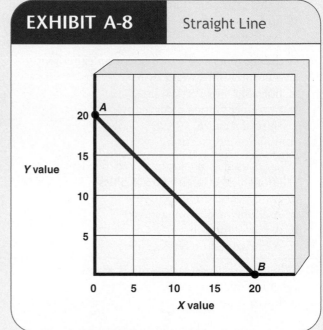

EXHIBIT A-8 | Straight Line

1. Straight line *CD* in Exhibit A-7 shows that
   a. increasing the value of *X* will increase the value of *Y*.
   b. decreasing the value of *X* will decrease the value of *Y*.
   c. there is a direct relationship between *X* and *Y*.
   d. all of the above are true.

2. In Exhibit A-7, the slope of straight line *CD* is
   a. 3.
   b. 1.
   c. −1.
   d. 1/2.

3. In Exhibit A-7, the slope of straight line *CD* is
   a. positive.
   b. zero.
   c. negative.
   d. variable.

4. Straight line AB in Exhibit A-8 shows that
   a. increasing the value of *X* reduces the value of *Y*.
   b. decreasing the value of *X* increases the value of *Y*.
   c. there is an inverse relationship between *X* and *Y*.
   d. all of the above are true.

5. As shown in Exhibit A-8, the slope of straight line *AB*
   a. decreases with increases in *X*.
   b. increases with increases in *X*.
   c. increases with decreases in *X*.
   d. remains constant with changes in *X*.

6. In Exhibit A-8, the slope of straight line *AB* is
   a. 3.
   b. 1.
   c. −1.
   d. −5.

PRACTICE QUIZ CONTINUED

7. A shift in a curve represents a change in
   a. the variable on the horizontal axis.
   b. the variable on the vertical axis.
   c. a third variable that is not on either axis.
   d. any variable that is relevant to the relationship being graphed.

8. A change in a third variable *not* on either axis of a graph is illustrated by a
   a. horizontal or vertical line.
   b. movement along a curve.
   c. shift of a curve.
   d. point of intersection.

9. What is used to illustrate an independent relationship between two variables?
   a. An upward-sloping curve
   b. A downward-sloping curve
   c. A hill-shaped curve
   d. A horizontal or vertical line

10. When an inverse relationship is graphed, the resulting line or curve is
   a. horizontal.
   b. vertical.
   c. upward sloping.
   d. downward sloping.

11. Which of the following pairs is the *most* likely to exhibit an inverse relationship?
   a. The amount of time you study and your grade point average
   b. People's annual income and their expenditure on personal computers
   c. Baseball players' salaries and their batting averages
   d. The price of a concert and the number of tickets people purchase

12. Which of the following pairs is the *most* likely to exhibit a direct relationship?
   a. The price of gasoline and the amount of gasoline that people purchase
   b. Cholesterol levels and the likelihood of developing heart disease
   c. Outdoor temperature and heating oil sales
   d. Annual income and weekly pawn shop visits

Production Possibilities, Opportunity Cost, and Economic Growth

T his chapter continues building on the foundation laid in the preceding chapter. Having learned that *scarcity* forces *choices,* here you will study the choices people make in more detail. This chapter begins by examining the three basic choices: *What, How,* and *For Whom* to produce. The process of answering these basic questions introduces two other key building blocks in the economic way of thinking: *opportunity cost* and *marginal analysis.* Once you understand these important concepts stated in words, it will be easier to interpret our first formal economic model, the *production possibilities curve.* This model illustrates how economists use graphs as a powerful tool to supplement words and develop an understanding of basic economic principles. You will discover that the production possibilities model teaches many of the most important concepts in economics, including scarcity, the law of increasing opportunity costs, efficiency, investment, and economic growth. For example, the chapter concludes by using the production possibilities curve to explain why underdeveloped countries do not achieve economic growth and thereby improve their standard of living.

In this chapter, you will learn to solve these economic puzzles:

- Why do so few rock stars and movie stars go to college?

- Why would you spend an extra hour reading this text rather than going to a movie or sleeping?

- Why are investment and economic growth so important?

Three Fundamental Economic Questions

Whether rich or poor, every nation must answer the same three fundamental economic questions: (1) *What* products will be produced? (2) *How* will they be produced? (3) *For Whom* will they be produced? Later, the chapter on economies in transition introduces various types of economic systems and describes how each deals with these three economic choices.

What to Produce?

Should society devote its limited resources to producing more health care and fewer military goods? Should more capital goods be produced instead of consumer goods, or should small hybrid cars and fewer SUVs be produced? The problem of scarcity restricts our ability to produce everything we want during a given period, so the choice to produce "more" of one good requires producing "less" of another good.

How to Produce?

After deciding which products to make, the second question for society to decide is how to mix technology and scarce resources in order to produce these goods. For instance, a towel can be sewn primarily by hand (labor), partially by hand and partially by machine (labor and capital), or primarily by machine (capital). In short, the *How* question asks whether a production technique will be more or less capital-intensive.

Education plays an important role in answering the *How* question. Education improves the ability of workers to perform their work. Variation in the quality and quantity of education among nations is one reason economies differ in their capacities to apply resources and technology to answer the *How* question. For example, the United States is striving to catch up with Japan in the use of robotics. Answering the question *How do we improve our robotics?* requires engineers and employees with the proper training in the installation and operation of robots.

For Whom to Produce?

Once the *What* and *How* questions are resolved, the third question is *For Whom*. Among all those desiring the produced goods, who actually receives them? Who is fed well? Who drives a Mercedes? Who receives organ transplants? Should economics professors earn a salary of $1 million a year and others pay higher taxes to support economists? The *For Whom* question means that society must have a method to decide who will be "rich and famous" and who will be "poor and unknown."

Opportunity Cost

Because of scarcity, the three basic questions cannot be answered without sacrifice or cost. But what does the term *cost* really mean? The common response would be to say that the purchase price is the cost. A movie ticket *costs* $8, or a shirt *costs* $50. Applying the economic way of thinking, however, *cost* is defined differently. A well-known phrase from Nobel Prize-winning economist Milton Friedman says, "There is no such thing as a free lunch." This expression captures the links among the concepts of scarcity, choice, and cost. Because of scarcity, people must make choices, and each choice incurs a cost (sacrifice). Once one option is chosen, another option is given up. The money you spend on a movie ticket cannot also buy a DVD. A business may purchase a new textile machine to manufacture towels, but this same money cannot be used to buy a new recreation facility for employees.

The DVD and recreation facility examples illustrate that the true cost of these decisions is the opportunity cost of a choice, not the purchase price. Opportunity cost is the best alternative sacrificed for a chosen alternative. Stated differently, it is the cost of not choosing the next best alternative. This principle states that some highly valued opportunity must be forgone in all economic decisions. The actual good or use of time given up for the chosen good or use of time measures the opportunity cost. We may omit the word *opportunity* before the word *cost*, but the concept remains the same. Exhibit 1 illustrates the causation chain linking scarcity, choice, and opportunity cost.

Examples are endless, but let's consider a few. Suppose your economics professor decides to become a rock star in the Rolling in Dough band. Now all his or her working hours are devoted to creating hit music, and the opportunity cost is the educational services no longer provided. Now a personal example: The opportunity cost of dating a famous model or movie star (name your favorite) might be the loss of your current girlfriend or boyfriend. Opportunity cost also applies to national economic decisions. Suppose the federal government decides to spend tax revenues on a space station. The opportunity cost depends on the next best program *not* funded. Assume roads and bridges are the highest-valued projects not built as a result of the decision to construct the space station. Then the opportunity cost of the decision to devote resources to the space station is the forgone roads and bridges and not the money actually spent to build the space station.

To personalize the relationship between time and opportunity cost, ask yourself what you would be doing if you were not reading this book. Your answer might be watching television or sleeping. If sleeping is your choice, the opportunity cost of studying this text is the sleep you sacrifice. Rock stars and movie stars, on the other hand, must forfeit a large amount of income to attend college. Now you know why you see so few of these stars in class.

Decisions often involve sacrifice of *both* goods and time. Suppose you decide to see a movie at a theater located 15 minutes from campus. If you had not spent the money at the movie theater, you could have purchased a DVD and watched a movie at home. And the time spent traveling to and from the movie and sitting through it

Opportunity cost
The best alternative sacrificed for a chosen alternative.

EXHIBIT 1   The Links between Scarcity, Choice, and Opportunity Cost

Scarcity means no society has enough resources to produce all the goods and services necessary to satisfy all human wants. As a result, society is always confronted with the problem of making choices. This concept is captured in the famous phrase, "There is no such thing as a free lunch." This means that each decision has a sacrifice in terms of an alternative not chosen.

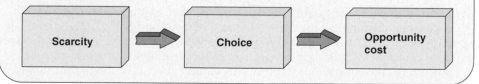

could have been devoted to studying for your economics exam. The opportunity cost of the movie consists of giving up (1) a DVD and (2) study time needed to score higher on the economics exam.

Marginal Analysis

At the heart of many important decision-making techniques used throughout this text is marginal analysis. Marginal analysis examines the effects of additions to or subtractions from a current situation. This is a very valuable tool in the economic-way-of-thinking toolkit because it considers the "marginal" effects of change. The rational decisionmaker decides on an option only if the marginal benefit exceeds the marginal cost. For example, you must decide how to use your scarce time. Should you devote an extra hour to reading this book, going to a movie, watching television, talking on the phone, or sleeping? Which of your many options do you choose? The answer depends on marginal analysis. If you decide the benefit of a higher grade in economics exceeds the opportunity cost of, say, sleep, then you allocate the extra hour to studying economics. Excellent choice!

Businesses use marginal analysis. Hotels, for example, rent space to student groups for dances and other events. Assume you are the hotel manager and a student group offers to pay $400 to use the ballroom for a party. To decide whether to accept the offer requires marginal analysis. The marginal benefit of renting otherwise vacant space is $400, and the marginal cost is $300 for extra electricity and janitorial service. Since the marginal benefit exceeds the marginal cost, the manager sensibly accepts the offer.

Similarly, farmers use marginal analysis. For example, a farmer must decide whether to add fertilizer when planting corn. Using marginal analysis, the farmer estimates that the corn revenue yield will be about $75 per acre without fertilizer and about $100 per acre using fertilizer. If the cost of fertilizer is $20 per acre, marginal analysis tells the farmer to fertilize. The addition of fertilizer will increase profit by $5 per acre because fertilizing adds $25 to the value of each acre at a cost of $20 per acre.

Marginal analysis is an important concept when the government considers changes in various programs. For example, as demonstrated in the next section, it is useful to know that an increase in the production of military goods will result in an opportunity cost of fewer consumer goods produced.

The Production Possibilities Curve

The economic problem of scarcity means that society's capacity to produce combinations of goods is constrained by its limited resources. This condition can be represented in a model called the production possibilities curve. The production possibilities curve shows the maximum combinations of two outputs that an economy can produce in a given period of time with its available resources and technology. Three basic assumptions underlie the production possibilities curve model:

1. **Fixed Resources.** The quantities and qualities of all resource inputs remain unchanged during the time period. But the "rules of the game" do allow an economy to shift any resource from the production of one output to the production of another output. For example, an economy might shift workers from producing consumer goods to producing capital goods. Although the number of

---

Marginal analysis

An examination of the effects of additions to or subtractions from a current situation.

Production possibilities curve

A curve that shows the maximum combinations of two outputs an economy can produce in a given period of time with its available resources and technology.

workers remains unchanged, this transfer of labor will produce fewer consumer goods and more capital goods.

2. **Fully Employed Resources.** The economy operates with all its factors of production fully employed and producing the greatest output possible without waste or mismanagement.

3. **Technology Unchanged.** Holding existing technology fixed creates limits, or constraints, on the amounts and types of goods any economy can produce. Technology is the body of knowledge applied to how goods are produced.

Technology
The body of knowledge applied to how goods are produced.

Exhibit 2 shows a hypothetical economy that has the capacity to manufacture any combination of military goods ("guns") and consumer goods ("butter") per year along its production possibilities curve (*PPC*), including points *A*, *B*, *C*, and *D*. For example, if this economy uses all its resources to make military goods, it can produce a *maximum* of 160 billion units of military goods and zero units of consumer goods (combination *A*). Another possibility is for the economy to use all its resources to produce a *maximum* of 100 billion units of consumer goods and zero units of military goods (point *D*). Between the extremes of points *A* and *D* lie other production possibilities for combinations of military and consumer goods. If combination *B* is chosen, the economy will produce 140 billion units of military goods and 40 billion units of consumer goods. Another possibility (point *C*) is to produce 80 billion units of military goods and 80 billion units of consumer goods.

What happens if the economy does not use all its resources to their capacity? For example, some workers may not find work, or plants and equipment may be idle for any number of reasons. The result is that our hypothetical economy fails to reach any of the combinations along the *PPC*. In Exhibit 2, point *U* illustrates an *inefficient* output level for any economy operating without all its resources fully employed. At point *U*, our model economy is producing 80 billion units of military goods and 40 billion units of consumer goods per year. Such an economy is underproducing because it could satisfy more of society's wants if it were producing at some point along *PPC*.

Even if an economy fully employs all its resources, it is impossible to produce certain output quantities. Any point outside the production possibilities curve is *unattainable* because it is beyond the economy's present production capabilities. Point *Z*, for example, represents an unattainable output of 140 billion units of military goods and 80 billion units of consumer goods. Society would prefer this combination to any combination along, or inside, the *PPC*, but the economy cannot reach this point with its existing resources and technology.

> **Conclusion** *Scarcity limits an economy to points on or below its production possibilities curve.*

Because all the points along the curve are *maximum* output levels with the given resources and technology, they are all called *efficient* points. A movement between any two efficient points on the curve means that *more* of one product is produced only by producing *less* of the other product. In Exhibit 2, moving from point *A* to point *B* produces 40 billion additional units of consumer goods per year, but only at a cost of sacrificing 20 billion units of military goods. Thus, a movement between any two efficient points graphically illustrates that "There is no such thing as a free lunch."

EXHIBIT 2	The Production Possibilities Curve for Military Goods and Consumer Goods

All points along the production possibilities curve (*PPC*) are maximum possible combinations of military goods and consumer goods. One possibility, point *A*, would be to produce 160 billion units of military goods and zero units of consumer goods each year. At the other extreme, point *D*, the economy uses all its resources to produce 100 billion units of consumer goods and zero units of military goods each year. Points *B* and *C* are obtained by using some resources to produce each of the two outputs. If the economy fails to utilize its resources fully, the result is the inefficient point *U*. Point *Z* lies beyond the economy's present production capabilities and is unattainable.

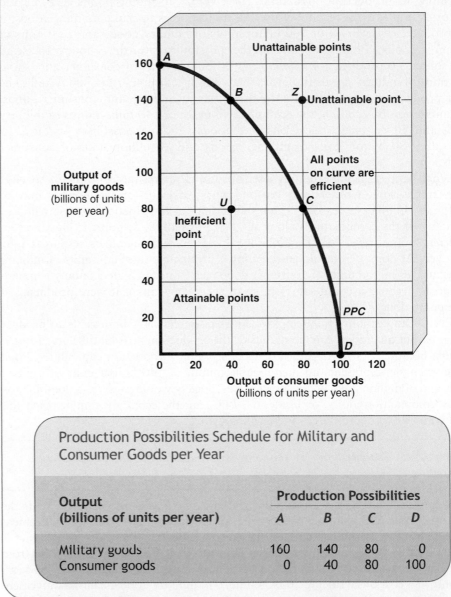

Production Possibilities Schedule for Military and Consumer Goods per Year

Output (billions of units per year)	Production Possibilities			
	A	B	C	D
Military goods	160	140	80	0
Consumer goods	0	40	80	100

> **Conclusion** *The production possibilities curve consists of all efficient output combinations at which an economy can produce more of one good only by producing less of the other good.*

The Law of Increasing Opportunity Costs

Why is the production possibilities curve shaped the way it is? Exhibit 3 will help us answer this question. It presents a production possibilities curve for a hypothetical economy that must choose between producing tanks and producing sailboats. Consider expanding the production of sailboats in 20,000-unit increments. Moving from point *A* to point *B*, the *opportunity cost* is 10,000 tanks; between point *B* and point *C*, the *opportunity cost* is 20,000 tanks; and the *opportunity cost* of producing at point *D*, rather than point *C*, is 50,000 tanks.

Exhibit 3 illustrates the law of increasing opportunity costs, which states that the opportunity cost increases as production of one output expands. Holding the stock of resources and technology constant (ceteris paribus), the law of increasing opportunity costs causes the production possibilities curve to display a *bowed-out* shape.

Why must our hypothetical economy sacrifice larger and larger amounts of tank output in order to produce each additional 20,000-sailboats? The reason is that all workers are not equally suited to producing one good, compared to another good. Expanding the output of sailboats requires the use of workers who are less suited to producing sailboats than producing tanks. Suppose our hypothetical economy produces no sailboats (point *A*) and then decides to produce them. At first, the least-skilled tank workers are transferred to making sailboats, and 10,000 tanks are sacrificed at point *B*. As the economy moves from point *B* to point *C*, more highly skilled tank makers become sailboat makers, and the opportunity cost rises to 20,000 tanks. Finally, the economy can decide to move from point *C* to point *D*, and the opportunity cost increases even more to 50,000 tanks. Now the remaining tank workers, who are superb tank makers, but poor sailboat makers, must adapt to the techniques of sailboat production.

Finally, it should be noted that the production possibilities curve model could assume that resources can be substituted and the opportunity cost remains constant. In this case, the production possibilities curve would be a straight line, which is the model employed in the chapter on international trade and finance.

Sources of Economic Growth

The economy's production capacity is not permanently fixed. If either the resource base increases or technology advances, the economy experiences economic growth, and the production possibilities curve shifts outward. Economic growth is the ability of an economy to produce greater levels of output, represented by an outward shift of its production possibilities curve. Exhibit 4 illustrates the importance of an outward shift. (Note the causation chain, which is often used in this text to focus on a model's cause-and-effect relationship.) At point *A* on PPC_1, a hypothetical full-employment economy produces 40,000 computers and 200 million pizzas per year. If the curve shifts outward to the new curve PPC_2, the economy can expand its full-employment output options. One option is to produce at point *B* and increase computer output to 70,000 per year. Another possibility is to increase

Law of increasing opportunity costs
The principle that the opportunity cost increases as production of one output expands.

Economic growth
The ability of an economy to produce greater levels of output, represented by an outward shift of its production possibilities curve.

EXHIBIT 3   The Law of Increasing Opportunity Costs

A hypothetical economy produces equal increments of 20,000 sailboats per year as we move from point *A* through point *D* on the production possibilities curve (*PPC*). If the economy moves from point *A* to point *B*, the opportunity cost of 20,000 sailboats is a reduction in tank output of 10,000 per year. This opportunity cost rises to 20,000 tanks if the economy moves from point *B* to point *C*. Finally, production at point *D*, rather than point *C*, results in an opportunity cost of 50,000 tanks per year. The opportunity cost rises because workers are not equally suited to making tanks and sailboats.

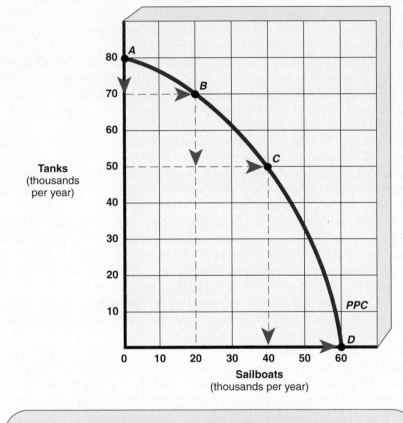

Production Possibilities Schedule for Tanks and Sailboats per Year

Output	Production Possibilities			
(thousands per year)	A	B	C	D
Tanks	80	70	50	0
Sailboats	0	20	40	60

pizza output to 400 million per year. Yet another choice is to produce more of both at some point between points B and C.

Changes in Resources

One way to accelerate economic growth is to gain additional resources. Any increase in resources—for example, more natural resources, a "baby boom," or more factories—will shift the production possibilities curve outward. In Exhibit 4, assume curve PPC_1 represents Japan's production possibilities for clothing and food in a given year. Suddenly, Japan discovers within its borders new sources of labor and other resources. As a result of the new resources, Japan will have an expanded capacity to produce any combination along an expanded curve, such as curve PPC_2.

Reductions in resources will cause the production possibilities curve to shift inward. Assume curve PPC_2 describes Japan's economy before World War II and the destruction of its factors of production during the war caused Japan's curve to shift leftward to curve PPC_1. Over the years, Japan trained its workforce, built new factories and equipment, and used new technology to shift its curve outward and surpass its original production capacity at curve PPC_2.

Technological Change

Another way to achieve economic growth is through research and development of new technologies. The knowledge of how to transform a stone into a wheel vastly improved the prehistoric standard of living. Technological change also makes it possible to shift the production possibilities curve outward by producing more from the same resources base. One source of technological change is *invention*. Computer chips, satellites, and the Internet are all examples of technological advances resulting from the use of science and engineering knowledge.

Technological change also results from the innovations of entrepreneurship, introduced in the previous chapter. Innovation involves creating and developing new products or productive processes. Seeking profits, entrepreneurs create new, better, or less expensive products. This requires organizing an improved mix of resources, which expands the production possibilities curve.

One entrepreneur, Henry Ford, changed auto industry technology by pioneering the use of the assembly line for making cars. Another entrepreneur, Chester Carlson, a law student, became so frustrated copying documents that he worked on his own to develop photocopying. After years of disappointment, a small firm named Xerox Corporation accepted Carlson's invention and transformed a good idea into a revolutionary product. These, and a myriad of other business success stories, illustrate that entrepreneurs are important because they transform their new ideas into production and practical use.

The phrase "new economy" refers to economic growth resulting from technological advances that make businesses and workers more productive. Success stories in the new economy are endless. The dizzying array of technological changes marches on cutting costs, boosting productivity and profits. Oil companies, for example, use new computer technology to generate three-dimensional maps, and they now hit oil with half as many "dry holes" as they previously drilled. New technology is even saving tropical fish at pet stores. Computer-controlled monitors that track water temperatures, acidity, and chlorine levels are resulting in fewer fish deaths per store. Such widespread technological gains mean real progress in the way we work and live.

EXHIBIT 4

An Outward Shift of the Production Possibilities Curve for Computers and Pizzas

The economy begins with the capacity to produce combinations along the first production possibilities curve PPC_1. Growth in the resource base or technological advances can shift the production possibilities curve outward from PPC_1 to PPC_2. Points along PPC_2 represent new production possibilities that were previously impossible. This outward shift permits the economy to produce greater quantities of output. Instead of producing combination A, the economy can produce, for example, more computers at point B or more pizzas at point C. If the economy produces at a point between B and C, more of both pizzas and computers can be produced, compared to point A.

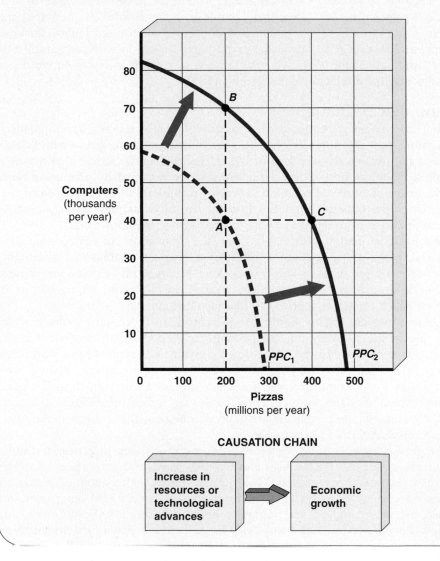

CAUSATION CHAIN

Increase in resources or technological advances → Economic growth

It can be argued that there is nothing really "new" in the new economy concept. Throughout history, technological advances have fostered economic growth by increasing our nation's productive power. Today, the Internet and computers are "new" technologies, but railroads, electricity, and automobiles, for example, were also "new" technologies in their time.

FedEx Wasn't an Overnight Success
Applicable Concept: entrepreneurship

Frederick W. Smith is a classic entrepreneurial success story. Young Fred went to Yale University, had a good new idea, secured venture capital, worked like crazy, made a fortune, and the Smithsonian Institution rendered its ultimate accolade. It snapped up an early Federal Express jet for its collection, displaying it for a time in the Air and Space Museum in Washington, D.C., not far from the Wright brothers' first airplane.

Smith's saga began with a college economics term paper that spelled out a nationwide overnight parcel delivery system that would be guaranteed to "absolutely, positively" beat the pants off the U.S. Postal Service. People, he said, would pay much more if their packages would arrive at their destination the next morning. To accomplish his plan, planes would converge nightly on Memphis, Tennessee, carrying packages accepted at any location throughout the nation. Smith chose this city for its central U.S. location and because its airport has little bad weather to cause landing delays. In the morning hours, all items would be unloaded, sorted, and rerouted to other airports, where vans would battle rush-hour traffic to make deliveries before the noon deadline.

Smith's college term paper got a C grade. Perhaps the professor thought the idea was too risky, and lots of others certainly agreed. In 1969, after college and a tour as a Marine pilot in Vietnam, the 24-year-old Smith began pitching his parcel delivery plan to mostly skeptical financiers. Nevertheless, with $4 million of his family's money, he persuaded a few venture capitalists to put up $80 million. At this time, this was the largest venture capital package ever assembled. In 1973, delivery service began with 33 jets connecting 25 cities, but on the first night only 86 packages showed up.

It was years before Smith looked like a genius. The company posted a $27 million loss the first year, turned the corner in 1976, and then took off, helped by a 1981 decision to add letters to its basic package delivery service. Today, Smith's basic strategy hasn't changed, but the scale of the operation has exploded. FedEx is the world's largest express transportation company, serving over 200 countries.

ANALYZE THE ISSUE

Draw a production possibilities curve for an economy producing only pizzas and computers. Explain how Fred Smith and other entrepreneurs affect the curve.

CHECKPOINT

What Does a War on Terrorism Really Mean?

With the disappearance of the former Soviet Union and the end of the Cold War, the United States became the world's only superpower and no longer engaged in an intense competition to build up its military. As a result, in the 1990s Congress and the White House had the opportunity to reduce the military's share of the budget and spend more funds for nondefense goods. This situation was referred to as the "peace dividend." Now consider that the need to combat terrorism diverts resources back to military and security output. Does the peace dividend or a reversal to more military spending represent a possible shift of the production possibilities curve or a movement along it?

EXHIBIT 5 — Alpha's and Beta's Present and Future Production Possibilities Curves

In part (a), each year Alpha produces only enough capital (K_a) to replace existing capital being worn out. Without greater capital and assuming other resources remain fixed, Alpha is unable to shift its production possibilities curve outward. In part (b), each year Beta produces K_b capital, which is more than the amount required to replenish its depreciated capital. In the year 2010, this expanded capital provides Beta with the extra production capacity to shift its production possibilities curve to the right (outward). If Beta chooses point B on its curve, it has the production capacity to increase the amount of consumer goods from C_b to C_c without producing fewer capital goods.

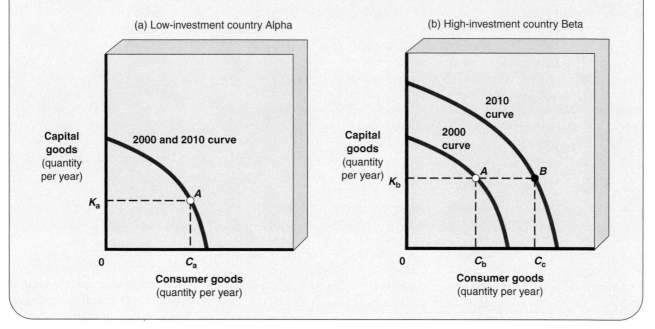

Present Investment and the Future Production Possibilities Curve

GLOBAL ECONOMICS

When the decision for an economy involves choosing between capital goods and consumer goods, the output combination for the present period can determine future production capacity.

Exhibit 5 compares two countries producing different combinations of capital and consumer goods. Part (a) shows the production possibilities curve for the low-investment economy of Alpha. This economy was producing combination A in 2000, which is an output of C_a of consumer goods and an output of K_a of capital goods per year. Let's assume K_a is just enough capital output to replace the capital being worn out each year (depreciation). As a result, Alpha fails to accumulate the net gain of factories and equipment required to expand its production possibilities curve outward in future years.[1] Why wouldn't Alpha simply move up along its production curve by shifting more resources to capital goods production? The problem

---

1. *Recall from the Appendix to Chapter 1 that a third variable can affect the variables measured on the vertical and horizontal axes. In this case, the third variable is the quantity of capital worn out per year.*

Alex Melnick, 2008/Used under license from Shutterstock.com.

The discussion of low-investment country Alpha versus high-investment country Beta explained that sacrificing production of consumer goods for an increase in capital goods output can result in economic growth and a higher standard of living. Stated differently, there was a long-run benefit from the accumulation of capital that offset the short-run opportunity cost in terms of consumer goods. Here the analysis was in terms of investment in private capital such as factories, machines, and inventories. However, public or government capital can also influence the production of both capital goods and consumption goods. For example, the government provides infrastructure such as roads, schools, bridges, ports, dams, and sanitation that makes the accumulation process for private capital more efficient, and in turn an economy grows at a greater rate.

Using data from 21 high-investment countries, a recent study by economists investigated how government investment policy affected the productivity of new private capital goods.[1] Countries included in the research were, for example, Canada, Japan, New Zealand, Spain, and the United States. A key finding was that a 1 percent increase in public investment increased the productivity of private investment by 27 percent. As a result, public capital caused the stock of private capital to rise more quickly over time.

Finally, economic growth and development is a major goal of countries throughout the world, and there are numerous factors that cause some countries to experience greater economic growth compared to other countries. Note that this topic is discussed in more depth in the last chapter of the text.

ANALYZE THE ISSUE

Construct a production possibilities curve for a hypothetical country. Put public capital goods per year on the vertical axis and consumer goods per year on the horizontal axis. Not shown directly in your graph, assume that this country produces just enough private capital per year to replace its depreciated capital. Assume further that this country is without public capital and is operating at point A where consumer goods are at a maximum. Based on the above research and using a production possibilities curve show and explain what happens to this country's private capital, production possibilities curve, and standard of living if it increases its output of public capital.

1. Stuart Fowler and Bichaka Fayissa, "Public Capital Spending Shocks and the Price of Investment: Evidence from a Panel of Countries," The 2007 Missouri Economics Conference, http://www.mtsu.edu/~sfowler/research/fs1.pdf.

is that sacrificing consumer goods for capital formation causes the standard of living to fall.

Comparing Alpha to Beta illustrates the importance of being able to do more than just replace worn-out capital. Beta operated in 2000 at point *A* in part (b), which is an output of C_b of consumer goods and K_b of capital goods. Assuming K_b is more than enough to replenish worn-out capital, Beta is a high-investment economy, adding to its capital stock and creating extra production capacity. This process of accumulating capital (*capital formation*) is investment. Investment is the accumulation of capital, such as factories, machines, and inventories, used to produce goods and services. Newly built factories and machines in the present provide an economy with the capacity to expand its production options in the future. For

> **Investment**
>
> The accumulation of capital, such as factories, machines, and inventories, that is used to produce goods and services.

example, the outward shift of its curve allows Beta to produce C_c consumer goods at point B in the year 2010. This means Beta will be able to improve its standard of living by producing C_c–C_b extra consumer goods, while Alpha's standard of living remains unchanged because the production of consumer goods remains unchanged.

> **Conclusion** *A nation can accelerate economic growth by increasing its production of capital goods in excess of the capital being worn out in the production process.*

KEY CONCEPTS

What, How, and *For Whom*
  questions
Opportunity cost
Marginal analysis

Production possibilities curve
Technology
Law of increasing
  opportunity costs

Economic growth
Investment

SUMMARY

- **Three fundamental economic questions** facing any economy are *What, How,* and *For Whom* to produce goods. The *What* question asks exactly which goods are to be produced and in what quantities. The *How* question requires society to decide the resource mix used to produce goods. The *For Whom* problem concerns the division of output among society's citizens.

- **Opportunity cost** is the best alternative forgone for a chosen option. This means no decision can be made without cost.

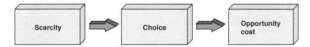

- **Marginal analysis** examines the impact of changes from a current situation and is a technique used extensively in economics. The basic approach is to compare the additional benefits of a change with the additional costs of the change.

- A **production possibilities curve** illustrates an economy's capacity to produce goods, subject to the constraint of scarcity. The production possibilities curve is a graph of the maximum possible combinations of two outputs that can be produced in a given period of time, subject to three conditions: (1) All resources are fully employed. (2) The resource base is not allowed to vary during the time period. (3) **Technology,** which is the body of knowledge applied to the production of goods, remains constant. **Inefficient** production occurs at any point inside the production possibilities curve. All points along the curve are **efficient** points because each point represents a maximum output possibility.

Production Possibilities Curve

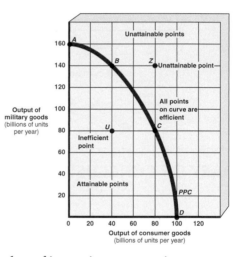

- The **law of increasing opportunity costs** states that the opportunity cost increases as the production of an output expands. The explanation for this law is that the suitability of resources declines sharply as greater amounts are transferred from producing one output to producing another output.

- **Economic growth** is represented by the production possibilities curve shifting outward as the result of an increase in resources or an advance in technology.

Economic Growth

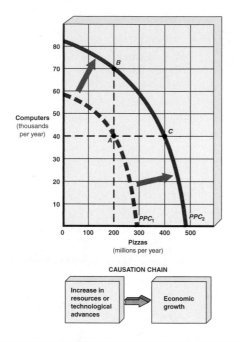

CAUSATION CHAIN

| Increase in resources or technological advances | → | Economic growth |

- **Investment** means that an economy is producing and accumulating capital. Investment consists of factories, machines, and inventories (capital) produced in the present that are used to shift the production possibilities curve outward in the future.

SUMMARY OF CONCLUSION STATEMENTS

- Scarcity limits an economy to points on or below its production possibilities curve.
- The production possibilities curve consists of all efficient output combinations at which an economy can produce more of one good only by producing less of the other good.

- A nation can accelerate economic growth by increasing its production of capital goods in excess of the capital being worn out in the production process.

STUDY QUESTIONS AND PROBLEMS

1. Explain why scarcity forces individuals and society to incur opportunity costs. Give specific examples.

2. Suppose a retailer promotes its store by advertising a drawing for a "free car." Is this car *free* because the winner pays *zero* for it?

3. Explain verbally the statement "There is no such thing as a free lunch" in relation to scarce resources.

4. Which of the following decisions has the greater opportunity cost? Why?
   a. A decision to use an undeveloped lot in Tokyo's financial district for an apartment building.
   b. A decision to use a square mile in the desert for a gas station.

5. Attending college is expensive, time-consuming, and it requires effort. So why do people decide to attend college?

6. The following is a set of hypothetical production possibilities for a nation.

Combination	Automobiles (thousands)	Beef (thousands of tons)
A	0	10
B	2	9
C	4	7
D	6	4
E	8	0

a. Plot these production possibilities data. What is the opportunity cost of the first 2,000 automobiles produced? Between which points is the opportunity cost per thousand automobiles highest? Between which points is the opportunity cost per thousand tons of beef highest?

b. Label a point *F* inside the curve. Why is this an inefficient point? Label a point *G* outside the curve. Why is this point unattainable? Why are points *A* through *E* all efficient points?

c. Does this production possibilities curve reflect the law of increasing opportunity costs? Explain.

d. What assumptions could be changed to shift the production possibilities curve?

7. The following table shows the production possibilities for pies and flower boxes. Fill in the opportunity cost (pies forgone) of producing the first through the fifth flower box.

Combination	Pies	Flower Boxes	Opportunity Cost
A	30	0	_____
B	26	1	_____
C	21	2	_____
D	15	3	_____
E	8	4	_____
F	0	5	_____

8. Why does a production possibilities curve have a bowed-out shape?

9. Interpret the phrases "There is no such thing as a free lunch" and "A free lunch is possible" in terms of the production possibilities curve.

10. Suppose, unfortunately, your mathematics and economics professors have decided to give tests 2 days from now and you can spend a total of only 12 hours studying for both exams. After some thought, you conclude that dividing your study time equally between each subject will give you an expected grade of C in each course. For each additional 3 hours of study time for one of the subjects, your grade will increase one letter for that subject, and your grade will fall one letter for the other subject.

a. Construct a table for the production possibilities and corresponding number of hours of study in this case.

b. Plot these production possibilities data in a graph.

c. Does this production possibilities curve reflect the law of increasing opportunity costs? Explain.

11. Draw a production possibilities curve for a hypothetical economy producing capital goods and consumer goods. Suppose a major technological breakthrough occurs in the capital goods industry and the new technology is widely adopted only in this industry. Draw the new production possibilities curve. Now assume that a technological advance occurs in consumer goods production, but not in capital goods production. Draw the new production possibilities curve.

12. The present choice between investing in capital goods and producing consumer goods now affects the ability of an economy to produce in the future. Explain.

For Online Exercises, go to the text Web site at www.cengage.com/economics/tucker.

CHECKPOINT ANSWER ✓

What Does a War on Terrorism Really Mean?

A "peace dividend" suggests resources are allocated away from military production and used for greater nonmilitary production. The war on terrorism arguably shifts resources in the opposite direction. If you said that this phrase represents a movement along the production possibilities curve, **YOU ARE CORRECT.**

PRACTICE QUIZ

For visual explanation of the correct answers, please visit the tutorial at www.cengage.com/economics/tucker.

1. Which of the following decisions must be made by all economies?
    a. How much to produce? When to produce? How much does it cost?
    b. What is the price? Who will produce it? Who will consume it?
    c. What to produce? How to produce it? For whom to produce?
    d. None of the above.

2. A student who has one evening to prepare for two exams on the following day has the following two alternatives:

Possibility	Score in Economics	Score in Accounting
A	95	80
B	80	90

    The opportunity cost of receiving a 90, rather than an 80, on the accounting exam is represented by how many points on the economics exam?
    a. 15 points
    b. 80 points
    c. 90 points
    d. 10 points

3. Opportunity cost is the
    a. purchase price of a good or service.
    b. value of leisure time plus out-of-pocket costs.
    c. best option given up as a result of choosing an alternative.

    d. undesirable sacrifice required to purchase a good.

4. On a production possibilities curve, the opportunity cost of good X in terms of good Y is represented by
    a. the distance to the curve from the vertical axis.
    b. the distance to the curve from the horizontal axis.
    c. the movement along the curve.
    d. all of the above.

5. If a farmer adds 1 pound of fertilizer per acre, the value of the resulting crops rises from $80 to $100 per acre. According to marginal analysis, the farmer should add fertilizer if it costs less than
    a. $12.50 per pound.
    b. $20 per pound.
    c. $80 per pound.
    d. $100 per pound.

6. On a production possibilities curve, a change from economic inefficiency to economic efficiency is obtained by
    a. movement along the curve.
    b. movement from a point outside the curve to a point on the curve.
    c. movement from a point inside the curve to a point on the curve.
    d. a change in the slope of the curve.

7. Any point inside the production possibilities curve is a(an)
   a. efficient point.
   b. unfeasible point.
   c. inefficient point.
   d. maximum output combination.

8. Using a production possibilities curve, unemployment is represented by a point located
   a. near the middle of the curve.
   b. at the top corner of the curve.
   c. at the bottom corner of the curve.
   d. outside the curve.
   e. inside the curve.

9. Along a production possibilities curve, an increase in the production of one good can be accomplished only by
   a. decreasing the production of another good.
   b. increasing the production of another good.
   c. holding constant the production of another good.
   d. producing at a point on a corner of the curve.

10. Education and training that improve the skill of the labor force are represented on the production possibilities curve by a(an)
    a. movement along the curve.
    b. inward shift of the curve.
    c. outward shift of the curve.
    d. movement toward the curve from an exterior point.

11. A nation can accelerate its economic growth by
    a. reducing the number of immigrants allowed into the country.
    b. adding to its stock of capital.
    c. printing more money.
    d. imposing tariffs and quotas on imported goods.

12. From the information in Exhibit 6, which of the following points on the production possibilities curve are attainable with the resources and technology currently available?
    a. A, B, C, E, U
    b. A, B, C, D, W
    c. E, U, W
    d. B, C, D, U
    e. A, B, C, E

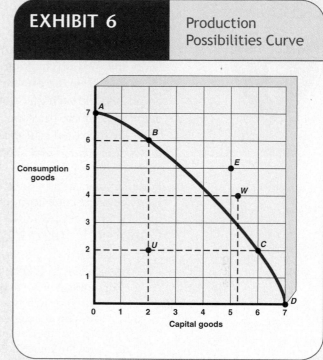

EXHIBIT 6   Production Possibilities Curve

13. In Exhibit 6, which of the following points on the production possibilities curve are efficient production points?
    a. A, B, C, U
    b. A, B, C, D, U
    c. E, U, W
    d. B, C, D, U
    e. A, B, C, D

14. In Exhibit 6, to move from U to B, the opportunity cost
    a. would be 4 units of consumption goods.
    b. would be 2 units of capital goods.
    c. would be zero.
    d. would be 5 units of capital goods.
    e. cannot be estimated.

15. In Exhibit 6, which of the following points on the production possibilities curve are full-employment production points?
    a. A, B, C, D
    b. A, B, C, D, U
    c. E, U, W
    d. B, C, D, U
    e. A, B, C, U

Road Map

INTRODUCTION TO ECONOMICS

This road map feature helps you tie material in the part together as you travel the Economic Way of Thinking Highway. The following are review questions listed by chapter from the previous part. The key concept in each question is given for emphasis, and each question or set of questions concludes with an interactive game to reinforce the concepts. Click on the Tucker Web site, select the chapter, and play the visual causation chain game designed to make learning fun. Enjoy the cheers when correct and suffer the jeers if you miss.

For an explanation of the correct answers, please visit the tutorial at www.cengage.com/economics/tucker.

Chapter 1. Introducing the Economic Way of Thinking

1. **Key Concept: Scarcity**
   Economists believe that scarcity forces everyone to
   a. satisfy all their wants.
   b. abandon consumer sovereignty.
   c. lie about their wants.
   d. create unlimited resources.
   e. make choices.

2. **Key Concept: Economics**
   The subject of economics is primarily the study of
   a. the government decision-making process.
   b. how to operate a business successfully.
   c. decision making because of the problem of scarcity.
   d. how to make money in the stock market.

 Causation Chain Game
   The Relationship Between Scarcity and Decision Making

3. **Key Concept: Model**
   When building a model, an economist must
   a. adjust for exceptional situations.
   b. provide a complete description of reality.
   c. make simplifying assumptions.
   d. develop a set of behavioral equations.

4. **Key Concept: Ceteris Paribus**
   If the price of a textbook rises and then students purchase fewer textbooks, an economic model can show a cause-and-effect relationship only if which of the following conditions hold:
   a. students' incomes fall.
   b. tuition decreases.
   c. the number of students increases.
   d. everything else is constant.
   e. the bookstore no longer accepts used book trade-ins.

5. **Key Concept: Association vs. Causation**
   Someone notices that sunspot activity is high just prior to recessions and
   concludes that sunspots cause recessions. This person has
   a. confused association and causation.
   b. misunderstood the ceteris paribus assumption.
   c. used normative economics to answer a positive question.
   d. built an untestable model.

Causation Chain Game
The Steps in the Model-Building Process-Exhibit 2

Chapter 2. Production Possibilities, Opportunity Cost, and Economic Growth

6. **Key Concept: Production Possibilities Curve**
   Which of the following is *not true* about a production possibilities curve? The
   curve
   a. indicates the combinations of goods and services that can be produced with
      a given technology.
   b. indicates the efficient production points.
   c. indicates the non-efficient production points.
   d. indicates the feasible (attainable) and non-feasible production points.
   e. indicates which production point will be chosen.

7. **Key Concept: Production Possibilities Curve**
   Which of the following is *true* about the production possibilities curve when a
   technological progress occurs? The curve
   a. Shifts inward to the left.
   b. Becomes flatter at one end and steeper at the other end.
   c. Becomes steeper.
   d. Shifts outward to the right.
   e. Does not change.

8. **Key Concept: Shifting the Production Possibilities Curve**
   An outward shift of an economy's production possibilities curve is caused by
   a. entrepreneurship.
   b. an increase in labor.
   c. an advance in technology.
   d. all of the above.

9. **Key Concept: Shifting the Production Possibilities Curve**
   Which would be *least likely* to cause the production possibilities curve to shift
   to the right?
   a. An increase in the labor force
   b. Improved methods of production
   c. An increase in the education and training of the labor force
   d. A decrease in unemployment

10. **Key Concept: Investment**
    A nation can accelerate its economic growth by
    a. reducing the number of immigrants allowed into the counry.
    b. adding to its stock of capital.
    c. printing more money.
    d. imposing tariffs and quotas on imported goods.

Causation Chain Game
Economic Growth and Technology-Exhibit 4

Microeconomic Fundamentals

I n order to study the microeconomy, the chapters in Part 2 build on the basic concepts learned in Part 1. Chapters 3 and 4 explain the market demand and supply model, which has a wide range of real-world applications. Chapter 5 takes a closer look at movements along the demand curve introduced in Chapter 3. Chapter 6 returns to the law of demand and explores in more detail exactly why consumers make their choices among goods and services. Part 2 concludes in Chapter 7 with an extension of the concept of supply that explains how various costs of production change as output varies.

Market Demand and Supply

© David Muir/Digital Vision/Getty Images.

A cornerstone of the U.S. economy is the use of markets to answer the basic economic questions discussed in the previous chapter. Consider baseball cards, DVDs, physical fitness, gasoline, soft drinks, alligators, and sneakers. In a *market economy*, each is bought and sold by individuals coming together as buyers and sellers in markets. This chapter is extremely important because it introduces basic supply and demand analysis. This technique will prove to be valuable because it is applicable to a multitude of real-world choices of buyers and sellers facing the problem of scarcity. For example, the Global Economics feature asks you to consider the highly controversial issue of international trade in human organs.

Demand represents the choice-making behavior of consumers, while supply represents the choices of producers. The chapter begins by looking closely at demand and then supply. Finally, it combines these forces to see how prices and quantities are determined in the marketplace. Market demand and supply analysis is the basic tool of microeconomic analysis.

In this chapter, you will learn to solve these economic puzzles:

- What is the difference between a "change in quantity demanded" and a "change in demand"?

- Can Congress repeal the law of supply to control oil prices?

- Does the price system eliminate scarcity?

The Law of Demand

Economics might be referred to as "graphs and laughs" because economists are so fond of using graphs to illustrate demand, supply, and many other economic concepts. Unfortunately, some students taking economics courses say they miss the laughs.

Exhibit 1 reveals an important "law" in economics called the law of demand. The law of demand states there is an inverse relationship between the price of a good and the quantity buyers are willing to purchase in a defined time period, ceteris paribus. The law of demand makes good sense. At a "sale," consumers buy more when the price of merchandise is cut.

In Exhibit 1, the *demand curve* is formed by the line connecting the possible price and quantity purchased responses of an individual consumer. The demand curve therefore allows you to find the quantity demanded by a buyer at any possible selling price by moving along the curve. For example, Bob, a sophomore at Marketplace College, loves watching movies on DVDs. Bob's demand curve shows that at a price of $15 per DVD his quantity demanded is six DVDs purchased annually (point *B*). At the lower price of $10, Bob's quantity demanded increases to 10 DVDs per year (point *C*). Following this procedure, other price and quantity possibilities for Bob are read along the demand curve.

Note that until we know the actual price, we do not know how many DVDs Bob will actually purchase annually. The demand curve is simply a summary of Bob's buying intentions. Once we know the market price, a quick look at the demand curve tells us how many DVDs Bob will buy.

> **Conclusion** *Demand is a curve or schedule showing the various quantities of a product consumers are willing to purchase at possible prices during a specified period of time, ceteris paribus.*

Market Demand

To make the transition from an *individual* demand curve to a *market* demand curve, we total, or sum, the individual demand schedules. Suppose the owner of Zap Mart, a small retail chain of stores serving a few states, tries to decide what to charge for DVDs and hires a consumer research firm. For simplicity, we assume Fred and Mary are the only two buyers in Zap Mart's market, and they are sent a questionnaire that asks how many DVDs each would be willing to purchase at several possible prices. Exhibit 2 reports their price-quantity demanded responses in tabular and graphical form.

The market demand curve, D_{total}, in Exhibit 2 is derived by summing *horizontally* the two individual demand curves, D_1 and D_2, for each possible price. At a price of $20, for example, we sum Fred's two DVDs demanded per year and Mary's one DVD demanded per year to find that the total quantity demanded at $20 is three DVDs per year. Repeating the same process for other prices generates the market demand curve, D_{total}. For example, at a price of $5, the total quantity demanded is 12 DVDs.

Law of demand

The principle that there is an inverse relationship between the price of a good and the quantity buyers are willing to purchase in a defined time period, ceteris paribus.

Demand

A curve or schedule showing the various quantities of a product consumers are willing to purchase at possible prices during a specified period of time, ceteris paribus.

EXHIBIT 1   An Individual Buyer's Demand Curve for DVDs

Bob's demand curve shows how many DVDs he is willing to purchase at different possible prices. As the price of DVDs declines, the quantity demanded increases, and Bob purchases more DVDs. The inverse relationship between price and quantity demanded conforms to the law of demand.

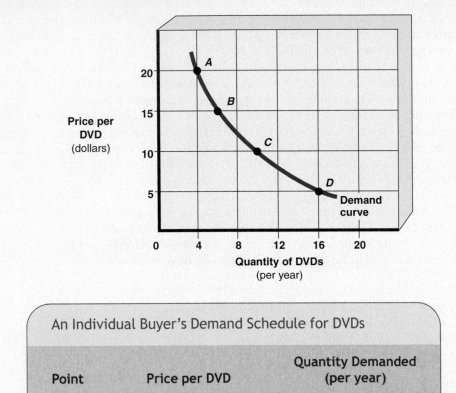

An Individual Buyer's Demand Schedule for DVDs

Point	Price per DVD	Quantity Demanded (per year)
A	$20	4
B	15	6
C	10	10
D	5	16

The Distinction between Changes in Quantity Demanded and Changes in Demand

Price is not the only variable that determines how much of a good or service consumers will buy. Recall from Exhibit A-6 of Appendix 1 that the price and quantity variables in our model are subject to the ceteris paribus assumption. If we relax this assumption and allow other variables held constant to change, a variety of factors can influence the position of the demand curve. Because these factors

| EXHIBIT 2 | The Market Demand Curve for DVDs |

Individual demand curves differ for consumers Fred and Mary. Assuming they are the only buyers in the market, the market demand curve, D_{total}, is derived by summing horizontally the individual demand curves, D_1 and D_2.

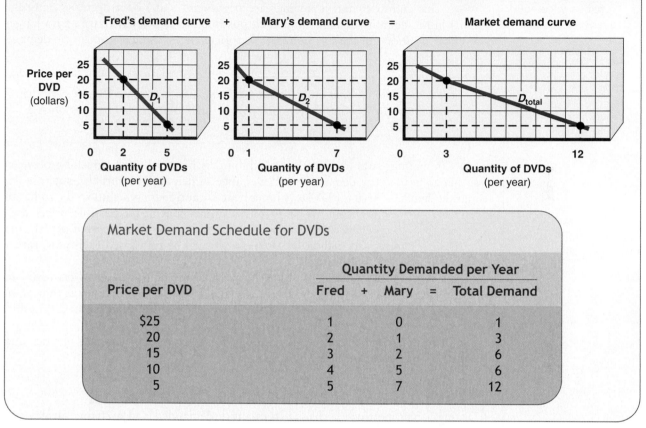

Market Demand Schedule for DVDs

Price per DVD	Quantity Demanded per Year		
	Fred +	Mary =	Total Demand
$25	1	0	1
20	2	1	3
15	3	2	6
10	4	5	6
5	5	7	12

are not the price of the good itself, these variables are called *nonprice determinants,* or simply, *demand shifters.* The major nonprice determinants include (1) the number of buyers; (2) tastes and preferences; (3) income; (4) expectations of future changes in prices, income, and availability of goods; and (5) prices of related goods.

Before discussing these nonprice determinants of demand, we must pause to explain an important and possibly confusing distinction in terminology. We have been referring to a change in quantity demanded, which results solely from a change in the price. A change in quantity demanded is a movement between points along a stationary demand curve, ceteris paribus. In Exhibit 3(a), at the price of $15, the quantity demanded is 20 million DVDs per year. This is shown as point A on the demand curve, D. At a lower price of, say, $10, the quantity demanded increases to 30 million DVDs per year, shown as point B. Verbally, we describe the impact of the price decrease as an increase in the quantity demanded of 10 million DVDs per year. We show this relationship on the demand curve as a movement down along the curve from point A to point B.

> **Change in quantity demanded**
>
> A movement between points along a stationary demand curve, ceteris paribus.

> **Conclusion** *Under the law of demand, any decrease in price along the vertical axis will cause an increase in quantity demanded, measured along the horizontal axis.*

Change in demand

An increase or a decrease in the quantity demanded at each possible price. An increase in demand is a rightward shift in the entire demand curve. A decrease in demand is a leftward shift in the entire demand curve.

A change in demand is an increase (rightward shift) or a decrease (leftward shift) in the quantity demanded at each possible price. If ceteris paribus no longer applies and if one of the five nonprice factors changes, the location of the demand curve shifts.

> **Conclusion** *Changes in nonprice determinants can produce only a shift in the demand curve and not a movement along the demand curve, which is caused by a change in the price.*

Comparing Parts (a) and (b) of Exhibit 3 is helpful in distinguishing between a change in quantity demanded and a change in demand. In Part (b), suppose the market demand curve for DVDs is initially at D_1 and there is a shift to the right (an increase in demand) from D_1 to D_2. This means that at *all* possible prices consumers wish to purchase a larger quantity than before the shift occurred. At $15 per DVD, for example, 30 million DVDs (point *B*) will be purchased each year, rather than 20 million DVDs (point *A*).

Now suppose a change in some nonprice factor causes demand curve D_1 to shift leftward (a decrease in demand). The interpretation in this case is that at *all* possible prices consumers will buy a smaller quantity than before the shift occurred.

Exhibit 4 summarizes the terminology for the effects of changes in price and nonprice determinants on the demand curve.

Nonprice Determinants of Demand

Distinguishing between a change in quantity demanded and a change in demand requires some patience and practice. The following discussion of specific changes in nonprice factors will clarify how each nonprice variable affects demand.

Number of Buyers

Look back at Exhibit 2, and imagine the impact of adding more individual demand curves to the individual demand curves of Fred and Mary. At all possible prices, there is extra quantity demanded by the new customers, and the market demand curve for DVDs shifts rightward (an increase in demand). Population growth therefore tends to increase the number of buyers, which shifts the market demand curve for a good or service rightward. Conversely, a population decline shifts most market demand curves leftward (a decrease in demand).

The number of buyers can be specified to include both foreign and domestic buyers. Suppose the market demand curve D_1 in Exhibit 3(b) is for DVDs purchased in the United States by customers at home and abroad. Also assume Japan restricts the import of DVDs into Japan. What would be the effect of Japan removing this trade restriction? The answer is that the demand curve shifts rightward from D_1 to D_2 when Japanese consumers add their individual demand curves to the U.S. market demand for DVDs.

EXHIBIT 3 | Movement along a Demand Curve versus a Shift in Demand

Part (a) shows the demand curve, D, for DVDs per year. If the price is $15 at point A, the quantity demanded by consumers is 20 million DVDs. If the price decreases to $10 at point B, the quantity demanded increases from 20 million to 30 million DVDs.

Part (b) illustrates an increase in demand. A change in some nonprice determinant can cause an increase in demand from D_1 to D_2. At a price of $15 on D_1 (point A), 20 million DVDs is the quantity demanded per year. At this same price on D_2 (point B), the quantity demanded increases to 30 million.

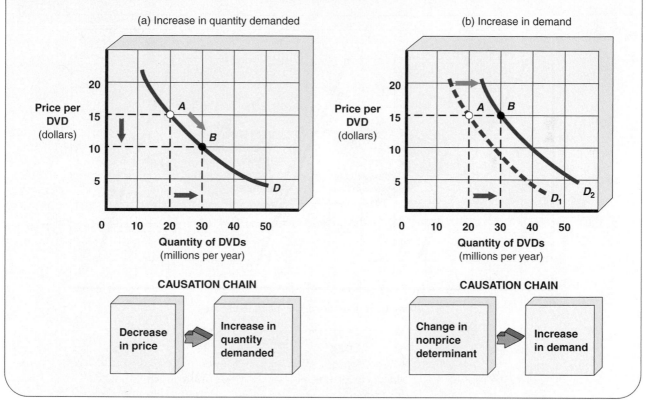

(a) Increase in quantity demanded

(b) Increase in demand

CAUSATION CHAIN

Decrease in price ⇨ Increase in quantity demanded

CAUSATION CHAIN

Change in nonprice determinant ⇨ Increase in demand

Tastes and Preferences

Fads, fashions, advertising, and new products can influence consumer preferences to buy a particular good or service. Beanie Babies became the rage in the 1990s, and the demand curve for these products shifted to the right. When people tire of a product, the demand curve will shift leftward. The physical fitness trend has increased the demand for health clubs and exercise equipment. On the other hand, have you noticed many stores selling hula hoops? Advertising can also influence consumers' taste for a product. As a result, consumers are more likely to buy more at every price, and the demand curve for the product will shift to the right.

Income

Most students are all too familiar with how changes in income affect demand. There are two possible categories for the relationship between changes in income and changes in demand: (1) normal goods and (2) inferior goods.

Normal good
Any good for which there is a direct relationship between changes in income and its demand curve.

Inferior good
Any good for which there is an inverse relationship between changes in income and its demand curve.

EXHIBIT 4 — Terminology for Changes in Price and Nonprice Determinants of Demand

Caution! It is important to distinguish between a change in quantity demanded, which is a movement along a demand curve (D_1) caused by a change in price, and a change in demand, which is a shift in the demand curve. An increase in demand (shift to D_2) or decrease in demand (shift to D_3) is not caused by a change in price. Instead, a shift is caused by a change in one of the nonprice determinants.

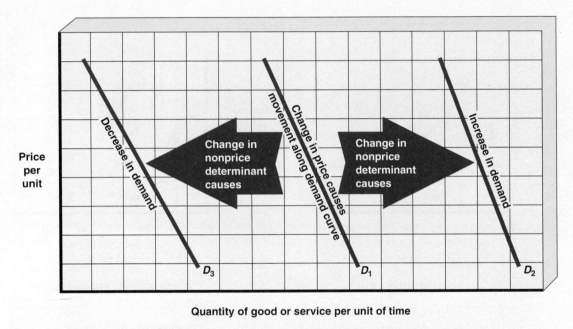

Quantity of good or service per unit of time

Change	Effect	Terminology
Price increases	Upward movement along the demand curve	Decrease in the quantity demanded
Price decrease	Downward movement along the demand curve	Increase in the quantity demanded
Nonprice determinant	Leftward or rightward shift in the demand curve	Decrease or increase in demand

A **normal good** is any good for which there is a direct relationship between changes in income and its demand curve. For many goods and services, an increase in income causes buyers to purchase more at any possible price. As buyers receive higher incomes, the demand curve shifts rightward for such *normal goods* as cars, steaks, vintage wine, cleaning services, and DVDs. A decline in income has the opposite effect, and the demand curve shifts leftward.

An **inferior good** is any good for which there is an inverse relationship between changes in income and its demand curve. A rise in income can result in reduced purchases of a good or service at any possible price. This might happen with such *inferior* goods as generic brands, Spam, discount clothes, and used cars. Instead of buying these inferior goods, higher incomes allow consumers to buy brand-name products, steaks, designer clothes, or new cars. Conversely, a fall in income causes the demand curve for inferior goods to shift rightward.

Expectations of Buyers

What is the effect on demand in the present when consumers anticipate future changes in prices, incomes, or availability? What happens when a war breaks out in the Middle East? Expectations that there will be a shortage of gasoline induce consumers to say "fill-er-up" at every opportunity, and demand increases. Suppose students learn that the prices of the textbooks for several courses they plan to take next semester will double soon. Their likely response is to buy now, which causes an increase in the demand curve for these textbooks. Another example is a change in the weather, which can indirectly cause expectations to shift demand for some products. Suppose a hailstorm destroys a substantial portion of the peach crop. Consumers reason that the reduction in available supply will soon drive up prices, and they dash to stock up before it is too late. This change in expectations causes the demand curve for peaches to increase.

Prices of Related Goods

Possibly the most confusing nonprice factor is the influence of other prices on the demand for a particular good or service. The term *nonprice* seems to forbid any shift in demand resulting from a change in the price of *any* product. This confusion exists when one fails to distinguish between changes in quantity demanded and changes in demand. Remember that ceteris paribus holds all prices of other goods constant. Therefore, movement along a demand curve occurs solely in response to changes in the price of a product, that is, its "own" price. When we draw the demand curve for Coca-Cola, for example, we assume the prices of Pepsi-Cola and other colas remain unchanged. What happens if we relax the ceteris paribus assumption and the price of Pepsi rises? Many Pepsi buyers switch to Coca-Cola, and the demand curve for Coca-Cola shifts rightward (an increase in demand). Coca-Cola and Pepsi-Cola are one type of related goods called substitute goods. A substitute good competes with another good for consumer purchases. As a result, there is a direct relationship between a price change for one good and the demand for its "competitor" good. Other examples of substitutes include margarine and butter, domestic cars and foreign cars, email and the U.S. Postal Service, and Internet movie downloads and DVDs.

DVDs and DVD players illustrate a second type of related goods called complementary goods. A complementary good is jointly consumed with another good. As a result, there is an inverse relationship between a price change for one good and the demand for its "go together" good. Although buying a DVD and buying a DVD player can be separate decisions, these two purchases are related. The more DVD players consumers buy, the greater the demand for DVDs. What happens when the price of DVD players falls sharply? The market demand curve for DVDs shifts rightward (an increase in demand) because new owners of players add their individual demand curves to those of persons already owning players and buying DVDs. Conversely, a sharp rise in college tuition that reduces the number of students would decrease the demand for textbooks.

Substitute good
A good that competes with another good for consumer purchases. As a result, there is a direct relationship between a price change for one good and the demand for its "competitor" good.

Complementary good
A good that is jointly consumed with another good. As a result, there is an inverse relationship between a price change for one good and the demand for its "go together" good.

EXHIBIT 5	Summary of the Impact of Changes in Nonprice Determinants of Demand on the Demand Curve		
Nonprice Determinant of Demand	**Relationship to Changes in Demand Curve**	**Shift in the Demand Curve**	**Examples**
1. Number of buyers	Direct	*[graph: Price vs Quantity, shift from D₁ to D₂]*	○ Immigration from Mexico increases the demand for Mexican food products in grocery stores.
		[graph: Price vs Quantity, shift from D₁ to D₂]	○ A decline in the birthrate reduces the demand for baby clothes.
2. Tastes and preferences	Direct	*[graph: Price vs Quantity, shift from D₁ to D₂]*	○ For no apparent reason, consumers want Beanie Babies and demand increases
		[graph: Price vs Quantity, shift from D₂ to D₁]	○ After a while, the fad dies and demand declines.
3. Income a. Normal goods	Direct	*[graph: Price vs Quantity, shift from D₁ to D₂]*	○ Consumers' incomes increase, and the demand for steaks increases.
		[graph: Price vs Quantity, shift from D₂ to D₁]	○ A decline in income decreases the demand for air travel.
b. Inferior goods	Inverse	*[graph: Price vs Quantity, shift from D₂ to D₁]*	○ Consumers' incomes increase, and the demand for hamburger decreases.
		[graph: Price vs Quantity, shift from D₁ to D₂]	○ A decline in income increases the demand for bus service.
4. Expectations of buyers	Direct	*[graph: Price vs Quantity, shift from D₁ to D₂]*	○ Consumers expect that gasoline will be in short supply next month and that prices will rise sharply. Consequently, consumers fill the tanks in their cars this month, and there is an increase in demand for gasoline.

Continued

Continued from previous page

Nonprice Determinant of Demand	Relationship to Changes in Demand Curve	Shift in the Demand Curve	Examples
		Price / Quantity (D_2 D_1)	○ Months later consumers expect the price of gasoline to fall soon, and the demand for gasoline decreases.
5. Prices of related goods a. Substitute goods	Direct	Price / Quantity (D_2 D_1)	○ A reduction in the price of tea decreases the demand for coffee.
		Price / Quantity (D_1 D_2)	○ An increase in the price of airfares causes higher demand for bus transportation.
b. Complementary goods	Inverse	Price / Quantity (D_1 D_2)	○ A decline in the price of cellular service increases the demand for cell phones.
		Price / Quantity (D_2 D_1)	○ A higher price for peanut butter decreases the demand for jelly.

Exhibit 5 summarizes the relationship between changes in the nonprice determinants of demand and the demand curve, accompanied by examples for each type of nonprice factor change.

CHECKPOINT

Can Gasoline Become an Exception to the Law of Demand?
Suppose war in the Middle East threatened oil supplies and gasoline prices began rising. Consumers feared future oil shortages, and so they rushed to fill up their gas tanks. In this case, as the price of gas increased, consumers bought more, not less. Is this an exception to the law of demand?

The Law of Supply

In everyday conversations, the term *supply* refers to a specific quantity. A "limited supply" of golf clubs at a sporting goods store means there are only so many for sale

Law of supply

The principle that there is a direct relationship between the price of a good and the quantity sellers are willing to offer for sale in a defined time period, ceteris paribus.

and that's all. This interpretation of supply is *not* the economist's definition. To economists, supply is the relationship between ranges of possible prices and quantities supplied, which is stated as the law of supply. The law of supply states there is a direct relationship between the price of a good and the quantity sellers are willing to offer for sale in a defined time period, ceteris paribus. Interpreting the individual *supply curve* for Entertain City shown in Exhibit 6 is basically the same as interpreting Bob's demand curve shown in Exhibit 1. Each point on the curve represents a quantity supplied (measured along the horizontal axis) at a particular price (measured

EXHIBIT 6 An Individual Seller's Supply Curve for DVDs

The supply curve for an individual seller, such as Entertain City, shows the quantity of DVDs offered for sale at different possible prices. As the price of DVDs rises, a retail store has an incentive to increase the quantity of DVDs supplied per year. The direct relationship between price and quantity supplied conforms to the law of supply.

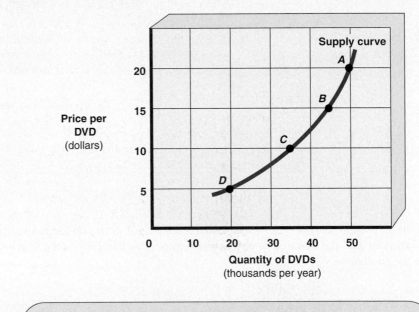

An Individual Seller's Supply Schedule for DVDs

Point	Price per DVD	Quantity Supplied (thousands per year)
A	$20	50
B	15	45
C	10	35
D	5	20

along the vertical axis). For example, at a price of $10 per disc (point C), the quantity supplied by the seller, Entertain City, is 35,000 DVDs per year. At the higher price of $15, the quantity supplied increases to 45,000 DVDs per year (point B).

> **Conclusion** *Supply is a curve or schedule showing the various quantities of a product sellers are willing to produce and offer for sale at possible prices during a specified period of time, ceteris paribus.*

Why are sellers willing to sell more at a higher price? Suppose Farmer Brown is trying to decide whether to devote more of his land, labor, and barn space to the production of soybeans. Recall from Chapter 2 the production possibilities curve and the concept of increasing opportunity cost developed in Exhibit 3. If Farmer Brown devotes few of his resources to producing soybeans, the opportunity cost of, say, producing milk is small. But increasing soybean production means a higher opportunity cost, measured by the quantity of milk not produced. The logical question is: What would induce Farmer Brown to produce more soybeans for sale and overcome the higher opportunity cost of producing less milk? You guessed it! There must be the *incentive* of a higher price for soybeans.

> **Conclusion** *Only at a higher price will it be profitable for sellers to incur the higher opportunity cost associated with producing and supplying a larger quantity.*

Supply
A curve or schedule showing the various quantities of a product sellers are willing to produce and offer for sale at possible prices during a specified period of time, ceteris paribus.

CHECKPOINT

Can the Law of Supply Be Repealed for the Oil Market?
The United States experienced two oil shocks during the 1970s in the aftermath of Middle East tensions. Congress said no to high oil prices by passing a law prohibiting prices above a legal limit. Supporters of such price controls said this was a way to ensure adequate supply without allowing oil producers to earn excess profits. Did price controls increase, decrease, or have no effect on U.S. oil production during the 1970s?

Market Supply

To construct a *market* supply curve, we follow the same procedure used to derive a market demand curve. That is, we *horizontally* sum all the quantities supplied at various prices that might prevail in the market.

Let's assume Entertain City and High Vibes Company are the only two firms selling DVDs in a given market. As you can see in Exhibit 7, the market supply curve, S_{total}, slopes upward to the right. At a price of $25, Entertain City will supply 25,000 DVDs per year, and High Vibes will supply 35,000 DVDs per year. Thus, summing the two individual supply curves, S_1 and S_2, *horizontally*, the total of 60,000 DVDs is plotted at this price on the market supply curve, S_{total}. Similar calculations at other prices along the price axis generate a market supply curve, telling us the total amount of DVDs these businesses offer for sale at different selling prices.

EXHIBIT 7   The Market Supply Curve for DVDs

Entertain City and High Vibes are two individual businesses selling DVDs. If these are the only two firms in the DVD market, the market supply curve, S_{total}, can be derived by summing horizontally the individual supply curves, S_1 and S_2.

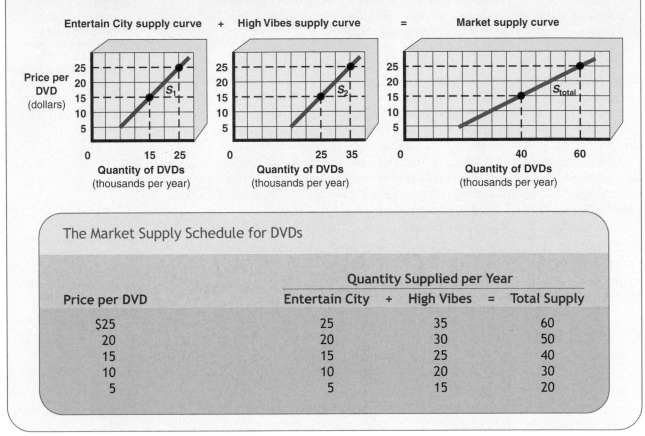

The Market Supply Schedule for DVDs

Price per DVD	Quantity Supplied per Year		
	Entertain City +	High Vibes =	Total Supply
$25	25	35	60
20	20	30	50
15	15	25	40
10	10	20	30
5	5	15	20

Change in quantity supplied

A movement between points along a stationary supply curve, ceteris paribus.

Change in supply

An increase or a decrease in the quantity supplied at each possible price. An increase in supply is a rightward shift in the entire supply curve. A decrease in supply is a leftward shift in the entire supply curve.

The Distinction between Changes in Quantity Supplied and Changes in Supply

As in demand theory, the price of a product is not the only factor that influences how much sellers offer for sale. Once we relax the ceteris paribus assumption, there are six principal *nonprice determinants* (or simply, *supply shifters*) that can shift the supply curve's position: (1) the number of sellers, (2) technology, (3) resource prices, (4) taxes and subsidies, (5) expectations, and (6) prices of other goods. We will discuss these nonprice determinants in more detail momentarily, but first we must distinguish between a change in quantity supplied and a change in supply.

A change in quantity supplied is a movement between points along a stationary supply curve, ceteris paribus. In Exhibit 8(a), at the price of $10, the quantity supplied is 30 million DVDs per year (point *A*). At the higher price of $15, sellers offer a larger "quantity supplied" of 40 million DVDs per year (point *B*). Economists describe the effect of the rise in price as an increase in the quantity supplied of 10 million DVDs per year.

EXHIBIT 8   Movement along a Supply Curve versus a Shift in Supply

Part (a) presents the market supply curve, *S*, for DVDs per year. If the price is $10 at point *A*, the quantity supplied by firms will be 30 million DVDs. If the price increases to $15 at point *B*, the quantity supplied will increase from 30 million to 40 million DVDs.

Part (b) illustrates an increase in supply. A change in some nonprice determinant can cause an increase in supply from S_1 to S_2. At a price of $15 on S_1 (point *A*), the quantity supplied per year is 30 million DVDs. At this price on S_2 (point *B*), the quantity supplied increases to 40 million.

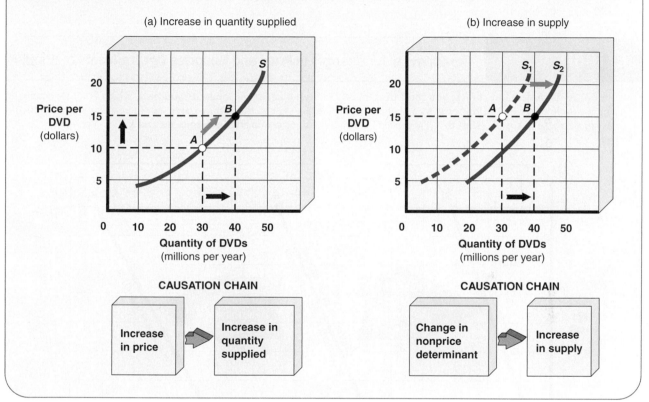

Conclusion *Under the law of supply, any increase in price along the vertical axis will cause an increase in the quantity supplied, measured along the horizontal axis.*

A change in supply is an increase (rightward shift) or a decrease (leftward shift) in the quantity supplied at each possible price. If ceteris paribus no longer applies and if one of the six nonprice factors changes, the impact is to alter the supply curve's location.

Conclusion *Changes in nonprice determinants can produce only a shift in the supply curve and not a movement along the supply curve.*

In Exhibit 8(b), the rightward shift (an increase in supply) from S_1 to S_2 means that at all possible prices sellers offer a greater quantity for sale. At $15 per DVD, for instance, sellers provide 40 million for sale annually (point B), rather than 30 million (point A).

Another case is that some nonprice factor changes and causes a leftward shift (a decrease in supply) from supply curve S_1. As a result, a smaller quantity will be offered for sale at any price.

Exhibit 9 summarizes the terminology for the effects of changes in price and nonprice determinants on the supply curve.

EXHIBIT 9   Terminology for Changes in Price and Nonprice Determinants of Supply

Caution! As with demand curves, you must distinguish between a change in quantity supplied, which is a movement along a supply curve (S_1) in response to a change in price, and a shift in the supply curve. An increase in supply (shift to S_2) or decrease in supply (shift to S_3) is caused by a change in some nonprice determinant and not by a change in the price.

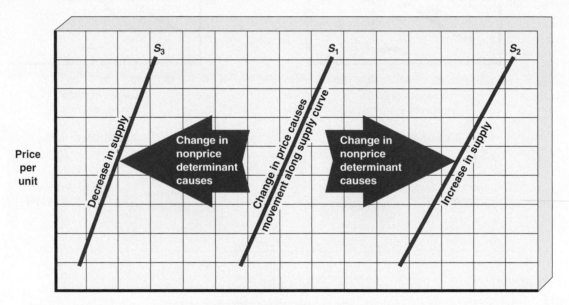

Quantity of good or service per unit of time

Change	Effect	Terminology
Price increases	Upward movement along the supply curve	Increase in the quantity supplied
Price decreases	Downward movement along the supply curve	Decrease in the quantity supplied
Nonprice determinant	Leftward or rightward shift in the supply curve	Decrease or increase in supply

Nonprice Determinants of Supply

Now we turn to how each of the six basic nonprice factors affects supply.

Number of Sellers

What happens when a severe drought destroys wheat or a frost ruins the orange crop? The damaging effect of the weather may force orange growers out of business, and supply decreases. When the government eases restrictions on hunting alligators, the number of alligator hunters increases, and the supply curve for alligator meat and skins increases. Internationally, the United States may decide to lower trade barriers on textile imports, and this action increases supply by allowing new foreign firms to add their individual supply curves to the U.S. market supply curve for textiles. Conversely, higher U.S. trade barriers on textile imports shift the U.S. market supply curve for textiles leftward.

Technology

Never have we experienced such an explosion of new production techniques. Throughout the world, new and more efficient technology is making it possible to manufacture more products at any possible selling price. New, more powerful computers reduce production costs and increase the supply of all sorts of goods and services. For example, computers are now milking cows. Computers admit the cows into the milking area and then activate lasers to guide milking cups into place. Dairy farmers no longer must wake up at 5:30 a.m., and cows get milked whenever they fancy, day or night. As this technology spreads across the United States, it will be possible to offer more milk for sale at each possible price, and the entire supply curve for milk shifts to the right.

Resource Prices

Natural resources, labor, capital, and entrepreneurship are all required to produce products, and the prices of these resources affect supply. Suppose many firms are competing for computer programmers to design their software, and the salaries of these highly skilled workers increase. This increase in the price of labor adds to the cost of production. As a result, the supply of computer software decreases because sellers must charge more than before for any quantity supplied. Any reduction in production cost caused by a decline in the price of resources will have an opposite effect and increase supply.

Taxes and Subsidies

Certain taxes, such as sales taxes, have the same effect on supply as an increase in the price of a resource. The impact of an increase in the sales tax is similar to a rise in the salaries of computer programmers. The higher sales tax imposes an additional production cost on, for example, DVDs, and the supply curve shifts leftward. Conversely, a payment from the government for each DVD produced (an unlikely subsidy) would have the same effect as lower prices for resources or a technological advance. That is, the supply curve for DVDs shifts rightward.

Expectations of Producers

Expectations affect both current demand and current supply. Suppose a war in the Middle East causes oil producers to believe that oil prices will rise dramatically. Their initial response could be to hold back a portion of the oil in their storage tanks so they

Applicable Concepts: nonprice determinants of demand and supply

Radio was in existence for 38 years before 50 million people tuned in. Television took 13 years to reach that benchmark. Sixteen years after the first PC kit came out, 50 million people were using one. Once opened to the public, the Internet crossed that line in 4 years.[1]

An Associated Press article reported in 1998:

Personal computers, which tumbled below the $1,000-price barrier just 18 months ago, now are breaking through the $400-price-mark—putting them within reach of the average U.S. family. The plunge in PC prices reflects declining wholesale prices for computer parts, such as microprocessors, memory chips, and hard drives. "We've seen a massive transformation in the PC business," said Andrew Peck, an analyst with Cowen & Co., based in Boston. Today's computers costing below $1,000 are equal or greater in power than PCs costing $1,500 and more just a few years ago—working well for word processing, spreadsheet applications, and Internet access, the most popular computer uses.[2]

In 1999, a *Wall Street Journal* article reported that PC makers and distributors were bypassing their industry's time-honored sales channels. PC makers such as Hewlett-Packard are now using the Internet to sell directly to consumers. In doing so, they are following the successful strategy of Dell, which for years has bypassed storefront retailers and the PC distributors who traditionally keep them stocked, going instead straight to the consumer with catalogs, an 800 number, and Web sites.[3]

In 2001, a *New York Times* article described a computer price war:

We reached a situation where the market was saturated in 2000. People who needed computers had them. Vendors are living on sales of replacements, at least in the United States. But that doesn't give you the kind of growth these companies were used to. In the past, most price cuts came from falling prices for processors and other components. In addition, manufacturers have been narrowing profit margins for the last couple years. But when demand dried up last fall, the more aggressive manufacturers decided to try to gain market share by cutting prices to the bone. This is an all-out battle for market share.[4]

In 2006, an analyst in *USA Today* observed that users could pick up good deals on desktop and notebook PCs following computer chip price cuts. Chipmakers Intel and AMD reduced the cost of computer chips in a price war. This article concluded that prices were falling at the right time and users will get good specification for their investment.[5] And in 2008, Dell, Gateway, and CompUSA sold computers for less that $400 that outperformed most middle-of-the-road PCs from only a few years previously. Also, ASUS sells a small laptop called the Eee for only $299.

ANALYZE THE ISSUE

Identify changes in quantity demanded, changes in demand, changes in quantity supplied, and changes in supply described in the article. For any change in demand or supply, also identify the nonprice determinant causing the change.

1. The Emerging Digital Economy (U.S. Department of Commerce, 1998), Chap. 1, p. 1 (http://www.ecommerce.gov/chapter1.htm).
2. David E. Kalish, "PC Prices Fall Below $400 Luring Bargain-Hunters," Associated Press/*Charlotte Observer*, Aug. 25, 1998, p. 3D.
3. George Anders, "Online Web Seller Asks: How Low Can PC Prices Go?" *The Wall Street Journal*, Jan. 19, 1999, p. B1.
4. Barnaby J. Feder, "Five Questions for Martin Reynolds: A Computer Price War Leaves Buyers Smiling," *New York Times*, May 13, 2001.
5. Michelle Kessler, "School Shoppers See PC Prices Fall," *USA Today*, Aug. 14, 2006, p. B1.

can sell more and make greater profits later when oil prices rise. One approach used by the major oil companies might be to limit the amount of gasoline delivered to independent distributors. This response by the oil industry shifts the current supply curve to the left. Now suppose farmers anticipate the price of wheat will soon fall sharply. The reaction is to sell their inventories stored in silos today before the price declines tomorrow. Such a response shifts the supply curve for wheat to the right.

Prices of Other Goods the Firm Could Produce

Businesses are always considering shifting resources from producing one good to producing another good. A rise in the price of one product relative to the prices of other products signals to suppliers that switching production to the product with the higher relative price yields higher profit. Suppose the price of corn rises because of government incentives to grow corn for ethanol, while the price of wheat remains the same, then many farmers will divert more of their land to corn and less to wheat. The result is an increase in the supply of corn and a decrease in the supply of wheat. This happens because the opportunity cost of growing corn, measured in forgone corn profits, increases.

Exhibit 10 summarizes the relationship between changes in the nonprice determinants of supply and the supply curve, accompanied by examples for each type of nonprice factor change.

A Market Supply and Demand Analysis

A drumroll please! Buyer and seller actors are on center stage to perform a balancing act in a market. A market is any arrangement in which buyers and sellers interact to determine the price and quantity of goods and services exchanged. Let's consider the retail market for sneakers. Exhibit 11 displays hypothetical market demand and supply data for this product. Notice in column 1 of the exhibit that price serves as a common variable for both supply and demand relationships. Columns 2 and 3 list the quantity demanded and the quantity supplied for pairs of sneakers per year.

The important question for market supply and demand analysis is: Which selling price and quantity will prevail in the market? Let's start by asking what will happen if retail stores supply 75,000 pairs of sneakers and charge $105 a pair. At this relatively high price for sneakers, consumers are willing and able to purchase only 25,000 pairs. As a result, 50,000 pairs of sneakers remain as unsold inventory on the shelves of sellers (column 4), and the market condition is a surplus (column 5). A surplus is a market condition existing at any price where the quantity supplied is greater than the quantity demanded.

How will retailers react to a surplus? Competition forces sellers to bid down their selling price to attract more sales (column 6). If they cut the selling price to $90, there will still be a surplus of 40,000 pairs of sneakers, and pressure on sellers to cut their selling price will continue. If the price falls to $75, there will still be an unwanted surplus of 20,000 pairs of sneakers remaining as inventory, and pressure to charge a lower price will persist.

Now let's assume sellers slash the price of sneakers to $15 per pair. This price is very attractive to consumers, and the quantity demanded is 100,000 pairs of sneakers each year. However, sellers are willing and able to provide only 5,000 pairs at this price. The good news is that some consumers buy these 5,000 pairs of sneakers at $15. The bad news is that potential buyers are willing to purchase 95,000 more pairs at that price, but cannot because the shoes are not on the shelves for sale. This out-of-stock condition signals the existence of a shortage. A shortage is a market condition existing at any price where the quantity supplied is less than the quantity demanded.

Market
Any arrangement in which buyers and sellers interact to determine the price and quantity of goods and services exchanged.

Surplus
A market condition existing at any price where the quantity supplied is greater than the quantity demanded.

Shortage
A market condition existing at any price where the quantity supplied is less than the quantity demanded.

EXHIBIT 10 — Summary of the Impact of Changes in Nonprice Determinants of Supply on the Supply Curve

Nonprice Determinant of Supply	Relationship to Changes in Supply Curve	Shift in the Supply Curve	Example
1. Number of sellers	Direct	$S_1 \to S_2$ (rightward)	○ The United States lowers trade restrictions on foreign textiles and the supply of textiles in the United States increases.
		$S_2 \leftarrow S_1$ (leftward)	○ A severe drought destroys the orange crop, and the supply of oranges decreases.
2. Technology	Direct	$S_1 \to S_2$ (rightward)	○ New methods of producing automobiles reduce production costs, and the supply of automobiles inceases.
		$S_2 \leftarrow S_1$ (leftward)	○ Technology is destroyed in war, and production costs increase; the result is a decrease in the supply of good X.
3. Resource prices	Inverse	$S_1 \to S_2$ (rightward)	○ A decline in the price of computer chips increases the supply of computers.
		$S_2 \leftarrow S_1$ (leftward)	○ An increase in the cost of farm equipment decreases the supply of soybeans.
4. Taxes and subsidies	Inverse and direct	$S_2 \leftarrow S_1$ (leftward)	○ An increase in the per-pack tax on cigarettes reduces the supply of cigarettes.
		$S_1 \to S_2$ (rightward)	○ Government payments to ethanol refiners based on the number of gallons produced increases the supply of ethanol.
5. Expectations	Inverse	$S_2 \leftarrow S_1$ (leftward)	○ Oil companies anticipate a substantial rise in future oil prices, and this expectation causes these companies to decrease their current supply of oil.
		$S_1 \to S_2$ (rightward)	○ Farmers expect the future price of wheat to decline, so they increase the present supply of wheat.

Continued

Continued from previous page

Nonprice Determinant of Supply	Relationship to Changes in Supply Curve	Shift in the Supply Curve	Example
6. Prices of other goods and services	Inverse		○ A rise in the price of brand-name drugs causes drug companies to decrease the supply of generic drugs. ○ A decline in the price of tomatoes causes farmers to increase the supply of cucumbers.

In the case of a shortage, unsatisfied consumers compete to obtain the product by bidding to pay a higher price. Because sellers are seeking the higher profits that higher prices make possible, they gladly respond by setting a higher price of, say, $30 and increasing the quantity supplied to 20,000 pairs annually. At the price of $30, the shortage persists because the quantity demanded still exceeds the quantity supplied. Thus, a price of $30 will also be temporary because the unfulfilled quantity demanded provides an incentive for sellers to raise their selling price further and offer more sneakers for sale. Suppose the price of sneakers rises to $45 a pair. At this price, the shortage falls to 25,000 pairs, and the market still gives sellers the message to move upward along their market supply curve and sell for a higher price.

Equilibrium Price and Quantity

Assuming sellers are free to sell their products at any price, trial and error will make all possible price-quantity combinations unstable except at equilibrium. Equilibrium

Equilibrium

A market condition that occurs at any price and quantity where the quantity demanded and the quantity supplied are equal.

EXHIBIT 11		Demand, Supply, and Equilibrium for Sneakers (Pairs per Year)			
(1) Price per Pair	(2) Quantity Demanded	(3) Quantity Supplied	(4) Difference (3) − (2)	(5) Market Condition	(6) Pressure on Price
$105	25,000	75,000	+50,000	Surplus	Downward
90	30,000	70,000	+40,000	Surplus	Downward
75	40,000	60,000	+20,000	Surplus	Downward
60	50,000	50,000	0	Equilibrium	Stationary
45	60,000	35,000	−25,000	Shortage	Upward
30	80,000	20,000	−60,000	Shortage	Upward
15	100,000	5,000	−95,000	Shortage	Upward

There is a global market in human organs, in spite of attempts to prevent these transactions. For example, China banned organ sales in 2006, and India did the same in 1994.

The National Transplant Organ Act of 1984 made sale of organs illegal in the United States. Economist James R. Rinehart wrote the following on this subject:

If you were in charge of a kidney transplant program with more potential recipients than donors, how would you allocate the organs under your control? Life and death decisions cannot be avoided. Some individuals are not going to get kidneys regardless of how the organs are distributed because there simply are not enough to go around. Persons who run such programs are influenced in a variety of ways. It would be difficult not to favor friends, relatives, influential people, and those who are championed by the press. Dr. John la Puma, at the Center for

Clinical Medical Ethics, University of Chicago, suggested that we use a lottery system for selecting transplant patients. He feels that the present rationing system is unfair.

The selection process frequently takes the form of having the patient wait at home until a suitable donor is found. What this means is that, at any given point in time, many potential recipients are just waiting for an organ to be made available. In essence, the organs are rationed to those who are able to survive the wait. In many situations, patients are simply screened out because they are not considered to be suitable candidates for a transplant. For instance, patients with heart disease and overt psychosis often are excluded. Others with end-stage liver disorders are denied new organs on the grounds that the habits that produced the disease may remain to jeopardize recovery . . . .

Under the present arrangements, owners receive no monetary compensation; therefore,

occurs at any price and quantity where the quantity demanded and the quantity supplied are equal. Economists also refer to *equilibrium* as *market clearing*.

In Exhibit 11, $60 is the *equilibrium* price, and 50,000 pairs of sneakers is the *equilibrium* quantity per year. Equilibrium means that the forces of supply and demand are "in balance" or "at rest" and there is no reason for price or quantity to change, ceteris paribus. In short, all prices and quantities except a unique equilibrium price and quantity are temporary. Once the price of sneakers is $60, this price will not change unless a nonprice factor changes demand or supply.

English economist Alfred Marshall (1842–1924) compared supply and demand to a pair of scissor blades. He wrote, "We might as reasonably dispute whether it is the upper or the under blade of a pair of scissors that cuts a piece of paper, as whether value is governed by utility [demand] or cost of production [supply]."[1] Joining market supply and market demand in Exhibit 12 allows us to clearly see the "two blades," that is, the demand curve, *D*, and the supply curve, *S*. We can measure the amount of any surplus or shortage by the horizontal distance between the demand and supply curves. At any price *above* equilibrium—say, $90—there is an

---

1. Alfred Marshall, *Principles of Economics*, 8th ed. (New York, 1982), p. 348.

suppliers are willing to supply fewer organs than potential recipients want. Compensating a supplier monetarily would encourage more people to offer their organs for sale. It also would be an excellent incentive for us to take better care of our organs. After all, who would want an enlarged liver or a weak heart…?[1]

The following excerpt from a newspaper article illustrates the controversy:

Mickey Mantle's temporary deliverance from death, thanks to a liver transplant, illustrated how the organ-donations system is heavily weighted against poor potential recipients who cannot pass what University of Pennsylvania medical ethicist Arthur Caplan calls the "wallet biopsy." … Thus, affluent patients like Mickey Mantle may get evaluated and listed simultaneously in different regions to increase their odds of finding a donor. The New Yorker found his organ donor in Texas' Region 4. Such a system is not only highly unfair, but it leads to other kinds of abuses.[2]

Based on altruism, the organ donor distribution system continues to result in shortages. In 2007, the United Network for Organ Sharing (UNOS) reported that there were over 90,000 patients waiting on the list for organs. To address the shortage of organ donation, some European countries such as Spain, Belgium, and Austria have implemented an "opt-out" organ donation system. In the "opt-out" system, people are automatically considered to be organ donors unless they officially declare that they do not wish to be donors.

ANALYZE THE ISSUE

1. Draw supply and demand curves for the U.S. organ market and compare the U.S. market to the market in a country where selling organs is legal.
2. What are some arguments against using the price system to allocate organs?
3. Should foreigners have the right to buy U.S. organs and U.S. citizens have the right to buy foreign organs?

---

1. James R. Rinehart, "The Market Approach to Organ Shortages," *Journal of Health Care Marketing* 8, no. 1 (March 1988): 72–75.
2. Carl Senna, "The Wallet Biopsy," *Providence Journal*, June 13, 1995, p. B-7.

---

excess quantity supplied (surplus) of 40,000 pairs of sneakers. For any price *below* equilibrium—$30, for example—the horizontal distance between the curves tells us there is an *excess quantity demanded* (shortage) of 60,000 pairs. When the price per pair is $60, the market supply curve and the market demand curve intersect at point *E*, and the quantity demanded equals the quantity supplied at 50,000 pairs per year.

> **Conclusion** *Graphically, the intersection of the supply curve and the demand curve is the market equilibrium price-quantity point. When all other nonprice factors are held constant, this is the only stable coordinate on the graph.*

Rationing Function of Prices

Our analysis leads to an important conclusion. The predictable or stable outcome in the sneakers example is that the price will eventually come to rest at $60 per pair. All other factors held constant, the price may be above or below $60, but the forces of surplus or shortage guarantee that any price other than the equilibrium price is

EXHIBIT 12   The Supply and Demand for Sneakers

The supply and demand curves represent a market for sneakers. The intersection of the demand curve, *D*, and the supply curve, *S*, at point *E* indicates the equilibrium price of $60 and the equilibrium quantity of 50,000 pairs bought and sold per year. At any price above $60, a surplus prevails, and pressure exists to push the price downward. At $90, for example, the excess quantity supplied of 40,000 pairs remains unsold. At any price below $60, a shortage provides pressure to push the price upward. At $30, for example, the excess quantity demanded of 60,000 pairs encourages consumers to bid up the price.

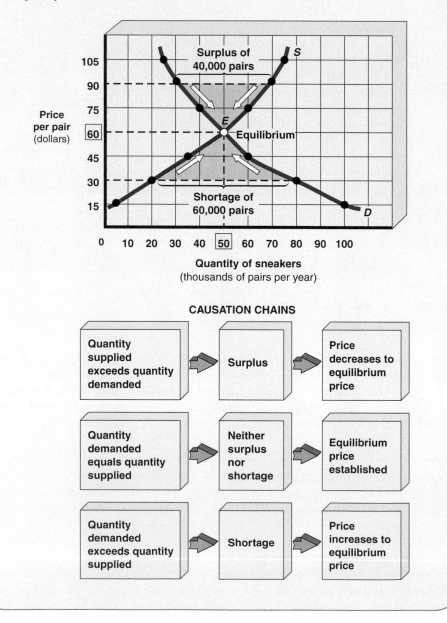

temporary. This is the theory of how the price system operates, and it is the corner-stone of microeconomic analysis. The price system is a mechanism that uses the forces of supply and demand to create an equilibrium through rising and falling prices. Stated simply, price plays a *rationing* role. The price system is important because it is a mechanism for distributing scarce goods and services. At the equilib-rium price of $60, only those consumers willing to pay $60 per pair get sneakers, and there are no shoes for buyers unwilling to pay that price.

Price system

A mechanism that uses the forces of supply and demand to create an equilibrium through rising and falling prices.

CHECKPOINT

Can the Price System Eliminate Scarcity?

You visit Cuba and observe that at "official" prices there is a constant short-age of consumer goods in government stores. People explain that in Cuba scarcity is caused by low prices combined with low production quotas set by the government. Many Cuban citizens say that the condition of scarcity would be eliminated if the government would allow markets to respond to supply and demand. Can the price system eliminate scarcity?

KEY CONCEPTS

Law of demand	Inferior good	Change in supply
Demand	Substitute good	Market
Change in quantity demanded	Complementary good	Surplus
	Law of supply	Shortage
Change in demand	Supply	Equilibrium
Normal good	Change in quantity supplied	Price system

SUMMARY

- The **law of demand** states there is an inverse relationship between the price and the quantity demanded, ceteris paribus. A market demand curve is the horizontal summation of individual demand curves.
- A **change in quantity demanded** is a movement along a stationary demand curve caused by a change in price. When any of the nonprice determinants of demand changes, the demand curve responds by shifting. An *increase in demand* (rightward shift) or a *decrease in demand* (leftward shift) is caused by a change in one of the nonprice determinants.

Change in Quantity Demanded

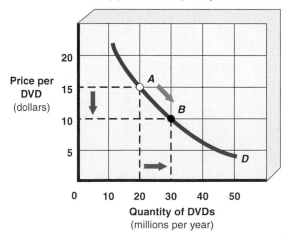

(a) Increase in quantity demanded

Change in Demand

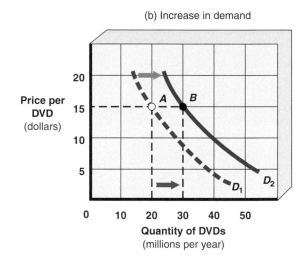

(b) Increase in demand

- **Nonprice determinants of demand** are as follows:
  a. Number of buyers
  b. Tastes and preferences
  c. Income (normal and inferior goods)
  d. Expectations of future price and income changes
  e. Prices of related goods (substitutes and complements)
- The **law of supply** states there is a direct relationship between the price and the quantity supplied, ceteris paribus. The market supply curve is the horizontal summation of individual supply curves.

- A **change in quantity supplied** is a movement along a stationary supply curve caused by a change in price. When any of the nonprice determinants of supply changes, the supply curve responds by shifting. An increase in supply (rightward shift) or a *decrease in supply* (leftward shift) is caused by a change in one of the nonprice determinants.

Change in Quantity Supplied

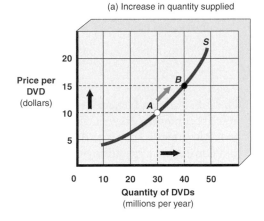

(a) Increase in quantity supplied

Change in Supply

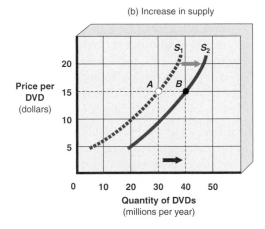

(b) Increase in supply

- **Nonprice determinants of supply** are as follows:
  a. Number of sellers
  b. Technology
  c. Resource prices
  d. Taxes and subsidies
  e. Expectations of future price changes
  f. Prices of other goods and services
- A **surplus or shortage** exists at any price where the quantity demanded and the quantity supplied are not equal. When the price of a good is higher than the equilibrium price, there is an excess quantity supplied, or a *surplus*. When the price is less than the equilibrium price, there is an excess quantity demanded, or a *shortage*.
- **Equilibrium** is the unique price and quantity established at the intersection of the supply and demand curves. Only at equilibrium does quantity demanded equal quantity supplied.

Equilibrium

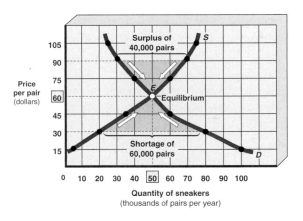

- The **price system** is the supply and demand mechanism that establishes equilibrium through the ability of prices to rise and fall.

SUMMARY OF CONCLUSION STATEMENTS

- Demand is a curve or schedule showing the various quantities of a product consumers are willing to purchase at possible prices during a specified period of time, ceteris paribus.

- Under the law of demand, any decrease in price along the vertical axis will cause an increase in quantity demanded, measured along the horizontal axis.

- Changes in nonprice determinants can produce only a shift in the demand curve and not a movement along the demand curve, which is caused by a change in price.
- Supply is a curve or schedule showing the various quantities of a product sellers are willing to produce and offer for sale at possible prices during a specified period of time, ceteris paribus.
- Only at a higher price will it be profitable for sellers to incur the higher opportunity cost associated with producing and supplying a larger quantity.

- Under the law of supply, any increase in price along the vertical axis will cause an increase in quantity supplied, measured along the horizontal axis.
- Changes in nonprice determinants can only produce a shift in the supply curve and not a movement along the supply curve.
- Graphically, the intersection of the supply curve and the demand curve is the market equilibrium price-quantity point. When all other nonprice factors are held constant, this is the only stable coordinate on the graph.

STUDY QUESTIONS AND PROBLEMS

1. Some people will pay a higher price for brand-name goods. For example, some people buy Rolls Royces and Rolex watches to impress others. Does knowingly paying higher prices for certain items just to be a "snob" violate the law of demand?

2. Draw graphs to illustrate the difference between a decrease in the quantity demanded and a decrease in demand for Mickey Mantle baseball cards. Give a possible reason for change in each graph.

3. Suppose oil prices rise sharply for years as a result of a war in the Persian Gulf region. What happens and why to the demand for
   a. cars.
   b. home insulation.
   c. coal.
   d. tires.

4. Draw graphs to illustrate the difference between a decrease in quantity supplied and a decrease in supply for condominiums. Give a possible reason for change in each graph.

5. Use supply and demand analysis to explain why the quantity of word processing software exchanged increases from one year to the next.

6. Predict the direction of change for either supply or demand in the following situations:
   a. Several new companies enter the home computer industry.
   b. Consumers suddenly decide SUVs are unfashionable.

   c. The U.S. Surgeon General issues a report stating that tomatoes prevent colds.
   d. Frost threatens to damage the coffee crop, and consumers expect the price to rise sharply in the future.
   e. The price of tea falls. What is the effect on the coffee market?
   f. The price of sugar rises. What is the effect on the coffee market?
   g. Tobacco lobbyists convince Congress to remove the tax paid by sellers on each carton of cigarettes sold.
   h. A new type of robot is invented that will pick peaches.
   i. A computer game company anticipates that the future price of its games will fall much lower than the current price.

7. Explain the effect of the following situations:
   a. Population growth surges rapidly.
   b. The prices of resources used in the production of good X increase.
   c. The government is paying a $1-per-unit subsidy for each unit of a good produced.
   d. The incomes of consumers of normal good X increase.
   e. The incomes of consumers of inferior good Y decrease.
   f. Farmers are deciding what crop to plant and learn that the price of corn has fallen relative to the price of cotton.

8. Explain why the market price may not be the same as the equilibrium price.

9. If a new breakthrough in manufacturing technology reduces the cost of producing DVD players by half, what will happen to the
   a. supply of DVD players?
   b. demand for DVD players?
   c. equilibrium price and quantity of DVD players?
   d. demand for DVDs?

10. The U.S. Postal Service is facing increased competition from firms providing overnight delivery of packages and letters. Additional competition has emerged because communications can be sent by emails, fax machines, and text messaging. What will be the effect of this competition on the market demand for mail delivered by the post office?

11. There is a shortage of college basketball and football tickets for some games, and a surplus occurs for other games. Why do shortages and surpluses exist for different games?

12. Explain the statement "People respond to incentives and disincentives" in relation to the demand curve and supply curve for good X.

For Online Exercises, go the text Web site at www.cengage.com/economics/tucker.

CHECKPOINT ANSWERS

Can Gasoline Become an Exception to the Law of Demand?

As the price of gasoline began to rise, the expectation of still higher prices caused buyers to buy more now, and, therefore, demand increased. As shown in Exhibit 13 below, suppose the price per gallon of gasoline was initially at P_1 and the quantity demanded was Q_1 on demand curve D_1 (point A). Then the war in the Middle East caused the demand curve to shift rightward to D_2. Along the new demand curve, D_2, consumers increased their quantity demanded to Q_2 at the higher price of P_2 per gallon of gasoline (point B).

The expectation of rising gasoline prices in the future caused "an increase in demand," rather than "an increase in quantity demanded" in response to a higher price. If you said there are no exceptions to the law of demand, **YOU ARE CORRECT.**

Can the Law of Supply Be Repealed for the Oil Market?

There is not a single quantity of oil—say, 3 million barrels—for sale in the world on a given day. The supply curve for oil is not vertical. As the law of supply states, higher oil prices will cause greater quantities of oil to be offered for sale. At lower prices, oil producers have less incentive to drill deeper for oil that is more expensive to discover.

EXHIBIT 13

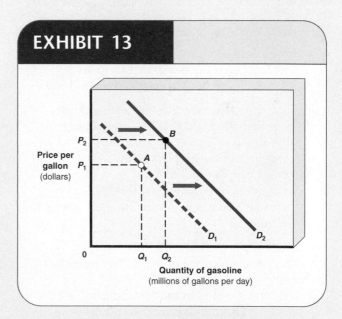

The government cannot repeal the law of supply. Price controls discourage producers from oil exploration and production, which causes a reduction in the quantity supplied. If you said U.S. oil production decreased in the 1970s when the government put a lid on oil prices, **YOU ARE CORRECT.**

Can the Price System Eliminate Scarcity?

Recall from Chapter 1 that scarcity is the condition in which human wants are forever greater than the resources available to satisfy those wants. Using markets free from government interference will not solve the scarcity problem. Scarcity exists at any price for a good or service. This means scarcity occurs at any disequilibrium price at which a shortage or surplus exists, and scarcity remains at any equilibrium price at which no shortage or surplus exists.

Although the price system can eliminate shortages (or surpluses), if you said it cannot eliminate scarcity, **YOU ARE CORRECT.**

PRACTICE QUIZ

For visual explanation of the correct answers, please visit the tutorial at www.cengage.com/economics/tucker.

1. If the demand curve for good X is downward sloping, an increase in the price will result in
   a. an increase in the demand for good X.
   b. a decrease in the demand for good X.
   c. no change in the quantity demanded for good X.
   d. a larger quantity demanded for good X.
   e. a smaller quantity demanded for good X.

2. The law of demand states that the quantity demanded of a good changes, other things being equal, when
   a. the price of the good changes.
   b. consumer income changes.
   c. the prices of other goods change.
   d. a change occurs in the quantities of other goods purchased.

3. Which of the following is the result of a decrease in the price of tea, other things being equal?
   a. A leftward shift in the demand curve for tea
   b. A downward movement along the demand curve for tea
   c. A rightward shift in the demand curve for tea
   d. An upward movement along the demand curve for tea

4. Which of the following will cause a movement along the demand curve for good X?
   a. A change in the price of a close substitute
   b. A change in the price of good X
   c. A change in consumer tastes and preferences for good X
   d. A change in consumer income

5. Assuming beef and pork are substitutes, a decrease in the price of pork will cause the demand curve for beef to
   a. shift to the left as consumers switch from beef to pork.
   b. shift to the right as consumers switch from beef to pork.
   c. remain unchanged, because beef and pork are sold in separate markets.
   d. none of the above.

6. Assuming coffee and tea are substitutes, a decrease in the price of coffee, other things being equal, results in a (an)
   a. downward movement along the demand curve for tea.
   b. leftward shift in the demand curve for tea.
   c. upward movement along the demand curve for tea.
   d. rightward shift in the demand curve for tea.

7. Assuming steak and potatoes are complements, a decrease in the price of steak will
   a. decrease the demand for steak.
   b. increase the demand for steak.
   c. increase the demand for potatoes.
   d. decrease the demand for potatoes.

8. Assuming steak is a normal good, a decrease in consumer income, other things being equal, will
   a. cause a downward movement along the demand curve for steak.
   b. shift the demand curve for steak to the left.
   c. cause an upward movement along the demand curve for steak.
   d. shift the demand curve for steak to the right.

9. An increase in consumer income, other things being equal, will
   a. shift the supply curve for a normal good to the right.
   b. cause an upward movement along the demand curve for an inferior good.
   c. shift the demand curve for an inferior good to the left.
   d. cause a downward movement along the supply curve for a normal good.

10. Yesterday, seller A supplied 400 units of good X at $10 per unit. Today, seller A supplies the same quantity of units at $5 per unit. Based on this evidence, seller A has experienced a (an)
    a. decrease in supply.
    b. increase in supply.
    c. increase in the quantity supplied.
    d. decrease in the quantity supplied.
    e. increase in demand.

11. An improvement in technology causes a (an)
    a. leftward shift of the supply curve.
    b. upward movement along the supply curve.
    c. firm to supply a larger quantity at any given price.
    d. downward movement along the supply curve.

12. Suppose autoworkers receive a substantial wage increase. Other things being equal, the price of autos will rise because of a (an)
    a. increase in the demand for autos.
    b. rightward shift of the supply curve for autos.
    c. leftward shift of the supply curve for autos.
    d. reduction in the demand for autos.

13. Assuming soybeans and tobacco can be grown on the same land, an increase in the price of tobacco, other things being equal, causes a (an)
    a. upward movement along the supply curve for soybeans.
    b. downward movement along the supply curve for soybeans.
    c. rightward shift in the supply curve for soybeans.
    d. leftward shift in the supply curve for soybeans.

14. If Q_d = quantity demanded and Q_s = quantity supplied at a given price, a shortage in the market results when
    a. Q_s is greater than Q_d.
    b. Q_s equals Q_d.
    c. Q_d is less than or equal to Q_s.
    d. Q_d is greater than Q_s.

15. Assume that the equilibrium price for a good is $10. If the market price is $5, a
    a. shortage will cause the price to remain at $5.
    b. surplus will cause the price to remain at $5.
    c. shortage will cause the price to rise toward $10.
    d. surplus will cause the price to rise toward $10.

16. In the market shown in Exhibit 14 the equilibrium price and quantity of good X are
    a. $0.50, 200.
    b. $1.50, 300.
    c. $2.00, 100.
    d. $1.00, 200.

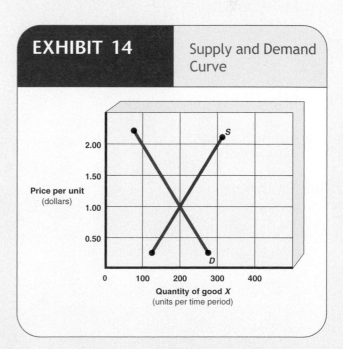

EXHIBIT 14   Supply and Demand Curve

PRACTICE QUIZ CONTINUED

17. In Exhibit 14, at a price of $2.00, the market for good X will experience a
    a. shortage of 150 units.
    b. surplus of 100 units.
    c. shortage of 100 units.
    d. surplus of 200 units.

18. In Exhibit 14, if the price of good X moves from $1.00 to $2.00, the new market condition will put
    a. upward pressure on price.
    b. no pressure on price to change.
    c. downward pressure on price.
    d. no pressure on quantity to change.

19. In Exhibit 14, if the market price of good X is initially $0.50, a movement toward equilibrium requires
    a. no change, because an equilibrium already exists.
    b. the price to fall below $0.50 and both the quantity supplied and the quantity demanded to rise.
    c. the price to remain the same, but the supply curve to shift to the left.

    d. the price to rise above $0.50, the quantity supplied to rise, and the quantity demanded to fall.

20. In Exhibit 14, if the market price of good X is initially $1.50, a movement toward equilibrium requires
    a. no change, because an equilibrium already exists.
    b. the price to fall below $1.50 and both the quantity supplied and the quantity demanded to fall.
    c. the price to remain the same, but the supply curve to shift to the left.
    d. the price to fall below $1.50, the quantity supplied to fall, and the quantity demanded to rise.

Consumer Surplus, Producer Surplus, and Market Efficiency

This chapter explained how the market forces of demand and supply establish the equilibrium price and output. Here it will be demonstrated that the equilibrium price and quantity determined in a competitive market are desirable because the result is *market efficiency.* To understand this concept, we use the area between the market price and the demand and supply curves to measure gains or losses from market transactions for consumers and producers.

Consumer Surplus

Consider the market demand curve shown in Exhibit A-1(a). The height of this demand curve shows the maximum willingness of consumers to purchase ground beef at various prices per pound. At a price of $4.00 (point X) no one will purchase ground beef. But if the price drops to $3.50 at point A, consumers will purchase one million pounds of ground beef per year. Moving downward along the demand curve to point B, consumers will purchase an additional million pounds of ground beef per year at a lower price of $3.00 per pound. If the price continues to drop to $2.50 per pound at point C and lower, consumers are willing to purchase more pounds of ground beef consistent with the law of demand.

Assuming the market equilibrium price for ground beef is $2.00 per pound, we can use the demand curve to measure the net benefit, or *consumer surplus,* in this market. Consumer surplus is the value of the difference between the price consumers are willing to pay for a product on the demand curve and the price actually paid for it. At point A, consumers are willing to pay $3.50 per pound, but they actually pay the equilibrium price of $2.00. Thus, consumers earn a surplus of $1.50 ($3.50 − $2.00) per pound multiplied by one million pounds purchased, which is a $15 million consumer surplus. This value is represented by the shaded vertical rectangle formed at point A on the demand curve. At point B, consumers who purchase an additional million pounds of ground beef at $3.00 per pound receive a lower extra consumer surplus than at point A, represented by a rectangle of lower height. At point C, the marginal consumer surplus continues to fall until at equilibrium point E, where there is no consumer surplus.

The total value of consumer surplus can be interpreted from the explanation given above. As shown in Exhibit A-1(b), begin at point X and instead of selected prices, now imagine offering ground beef to consumers at each possible price downward along the demand curve until the equilibrium price of $2.00 is reached at point E. The result is that the entire green triangular area between the demand curve and the horizontal line at the equilibrium price represents total consumer surplus. Note that a rise in the equilibrium price decreases total consumer surplus and a fall in the equilibrium price increases total consumer surplus.

Consumer surplus
The value of the difference between the price consumers are willing to pay for a product on the demand curve and the price actually paid for it.

EXHIBIT A-1 Market Demand Curve and Consumer Surplus

As illustrated in Part (a), consumers are willing at point *A* on the market demand curve to pay $3.50 per pound to purchase one million pounds of ground beef per year. Since the equilibrium price is $2.00, this means they receive a consumer surplus of $1.50 for each pound of ground beef and the vertical shaded rectangular area is the consumer surplus earned only at point *A*. Others who pay less at points *B*, *C*, and *E* receive less consumer surplus and the height of the corresponding rectangles falls at each of these prices. In Part (b), moving downward along all possible prices on the demand curve yields the green shaded triangle, which is equal to total consumer surplus (net benefit).

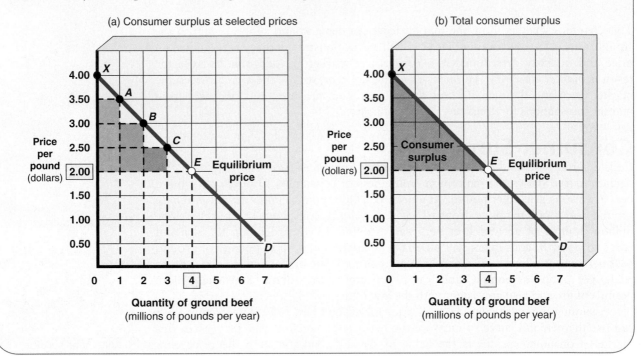

Conclusion *Total consumer surplus measured in dollars is represented by the total area under the market demand curve and above the equilibrium price.*

Producer Surplus

Similar to the concept of consumer surplus, the height of the market supply curve in Exhibit A-2(a) shows the producers' minimum willingness to accept payment for ground beef offered for sale at various prices per pound. At point *X*, firms offer no ground beef for sale at a price of zero and they divert their resources to an alternate use. At a price of $0.50 (50 cents) per pound (point *A*), the supply curve tells us that one million pounds will be offered for sale. Moving upward along the supply curve to point *B*, firms will offer an additional million pounds of ground beef for sale at the higher price of $1.00 per pound. If the price rises to $1.50 at point *C* and higher, firms allocate more resources to ground beef production and another million pounds will be supplied along the supply curve.

Again we will assume the equilibrium price is $2.00 per pound, and the supply curve can be used to measure the net benefit, or *producer surplus*. Producer surplus

Producer surplus

The value of the difference between the actual selling price of a product and the price producers are willing to sell it for on the supply curve.

EXHIBIT A-2 | Market Supply Curve and Producer Surplus

In Part (a), firms are willing at $0.50 (point *A*) to supply one million pounds of ground beef per year. Because $2.00 is the equilibrium price, the sellers earn a producer surplus of $1.50 per pound of ground beef sold. The first vertical shaded rectangle is the producer surplus earned only at point *A*. At points *B*, *C*, and *E*, sellers receive less producer surplus at each of these higher prices and the sizes of the rectangles fall. In Part (b), moving upward along all possible selling prices on the supply curve yields the red-shaded triangle that is equal to total producer surplus (net benefit).

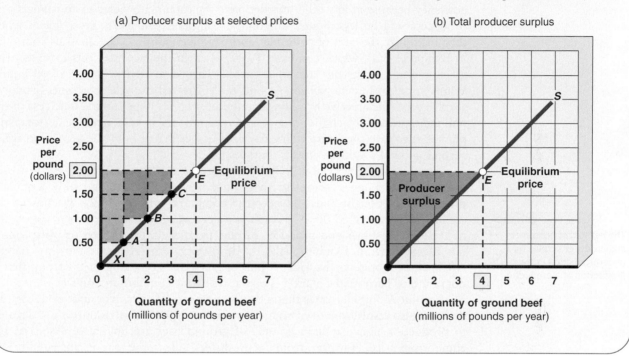

(a) Producer surplus at selected prices

(b) Total producer surplus

is the value of the difference between the actual selling price of a product and the price producers are willing to sell it for on the supply curve. Now assume the first million pounds of ground beef is sold at point *A* on the supply curve. In this case, producer surplus is the difference between the equilibrium selling price of $2.00 and the $0.50 price that is the minimum price that producers will accept to supply this quantity of ground beef. Thus producer surplus is equal to $1.50 ($2.00 − $0.50) per pound multiplied by one million pounds sold, which is $1.5 million producer surplus. This value is represented by the vertical shaded rectangle formed at point *A* on the supply curve. The second million pounds of ground beef offered for sale at point *B* also generates a producer surplus because the selling price of $2.00 exceeds the $1.00 price at which firms are willing to supply this additional quantity of ground beef. Note that producer surplus is lower at point *B* compared to point *A*, and marginal producer surplus continues to fall at point *C* until it reaches zero at the equilibrium point *E*.

The total value of producer surplus is represented in Exhibit A-2(b). Start at point *X* where none of the product will be supplied at the price of zero. Now consider the quantities of ground beef producers are willing to offer for sale at each possible price upward along the supply curve until the equilibrium price of $2.00 is reached at point *E*. The result is that the entire red triangular area between the horizontal line at the equilibrium price and the supply curve represents total producer surplus.

> **Conclusion** *Total producer surplus measured in dollars is represented by the total area under the equilibrium price and above the supply curve.*

Market Efficiency

In this section, the equilibrium price and quantity will be shown to achieve market efficiency because at any other market price the total net benefits to consumers and producers will be less. Stated differently, competitive markets are efficient when they maximize the sum of consumer and producer surplus. The analysis continues in Exhibit A-3(a), which combines Parts (b) from the two previous exhibits. The green triangle represents consumer surplus earned in excess of the $2.00 equilibrium price consumers pay for ground beef. The red triangle represents producer surplus producers receive by selling ground beef at $2.00 per pound in excess of the minimum price at which they are willing to supply it. The total net benefit (total surplus) is therefore the entire triangular area consisting of both the green consumer surplus and red producer surplus triangles.

Now consider in Exhibit A-3(b) the consequences to market efficiency of producers devoting fewer resources to ground beef production and only 2 million pounds being bought and sold per year compared with 4 million pounds at the equilibrium price of $2.00. The result is a deadweight loss. Deadweight loss is the net loss of consumer and producer surplus from underproduction or overproduction of a product. In Exhibit A-3(b), the deadweight loss is equal to the gray triangle *ABE*, which represents the total surplus of green and red triangles in Part (a) that is not obtained because the market is operating below equilibrium point *E*.

Exhibit A-3(c) illustrates that a deadweight loss of consumer and producer surplus can also result from overproduction. Now suppose more resources are devoted to production and 6 million pounds of ground beef are bought and sold at the equilibrium price. However, from the producers' side of the market, the equilibrium selling price is only $2.00 and below any possible selling price on the supply curve between points *E* and *C*. Therefore, firms have a net loss for each pound sold, represented by the area under the supply curve and bounded below by the horizontal equilibrium price line. Similarly, consumers pay the equilibrium price of $2.00, but this price exceeds any price consumers are willing to pay between points *E* and *D* on the demand curve. This means consumers experience a total net benefit loss for each pound purchased, represented by the rectangular area between the horizontal equilibrium price line above and the demand curve below. The total net loss of consumer and producer surplus (deadweight loss) is equal to the gray-shaded area *EDC*.

> **Deadweight loss**
>
> The net loss of consumer and producer surplus for underproduction or overproduction of a product.

> **Conclusion** *The total dollar value of potential benefits not achieved is the deadweight loss resulting from too few or too many resources used in a given market.*

Looking ahead, the conclusion drawn from this appendix is that market equilibrium is efficient, but this conclusion is not always the case. In the next chapter, the topic of *market failure* will be discussed in which market equilibrium under certain conditions can result in too few or too many resources being used to produce goods and services. For example, the absence of a competitive market, existence of pollution, or vaccinations to prevent a disease can establish equilibrium conditions with

EXHIBIT A-3   Comparison of Market Efficiency and Deadweight Loss

In Part (a), the green triangle represents consumer surplus and the red triangle represents producer surplus. The total net benefit, or total surplus, is the entire triangle consisting of the consumer and producer surplus triangles.

In Part (b), too few resources are used to produce 2 million pounds of ground beef compared to 4 million pounds at equilibrium point *E*. The market is inefficient because the deadweight loss gray triangle *ABE* is no longer earned by either consumers or producers. As shown in Part (c), overproduction at the equilibrium price of $2.00 can also be inefficient. If 6 million pounds of ground beef are offered for sale, too many resources are devoted to this product and a deadweight loss of area *EDC* occurs.

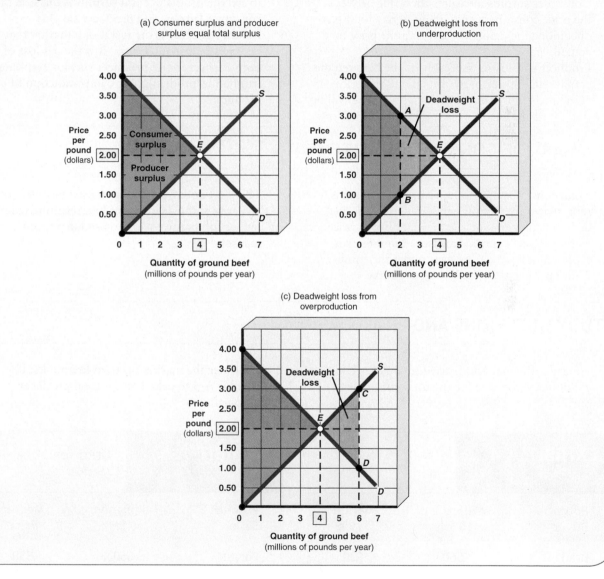

misallocations of resources. In these cases, government intervention may be preferable in order to achieve optimal allocation of resources. In other cases, such as the government imposing price ceilings and price floors, the result of government intervention is a market that is no longer efficient.

KEY CONCEPTS

Consumer surplus   Producer surplus   Deadweight loss

SUMMARY

- **Consumer surplus** measures the value between the price consumers are willing to pay for a product along the demand curve and the price they actually pay.
- **Producer surplus** measures the value between the actual selling price of a product and the price along the supply curve at which sellers are willing to sell the product. Total surplus is the sum of consumer surplus and producer surplus.
- **Deadweight loss** is the result of a market that operates in disequilibrium. It is the net loss of both consumer and producer surplus resulting from underproduction or overproduction of a product.

SUMMARY OF CONCLUSION STATEMENTS

- Total consumer surplus measured in dollars is represented by the total area under the market demand curve and above the equilibrium price.
- Total producer surplus measured in dollars is represented by the total area under the equilibrium price and above the supply curve.
- The total dollar value of potential benefits not achieved is the deadweight loss resulting from too few or too many resources used in a given market.

STUDY QUESTIONS AND PROBLEMS

1. Consider the market for used textbooks. Use Exhibit A-4 to calculate the total consumer surplus.

2. Consider the market for used textbooks. Use Exhibit A-5 to calculate the total producer surplus.

EXHIBIT A-4	Used Textbook Market	
Potential Buyer	**Willingness to Pay**	**Market Price**
Brad	$60	$30
Juan	45	30
Sue	35	30
Jamie	25	30
Frank	10	30

EXHIBIT A-5	Used Textbook Market	
Potential Seller	**Willingness to Sell**	**Market Price**
Forest	$60	$30
Betty	45	30
Allen	35	30
Paul	25	30
Alice	10	30

EXHIBIT A-6	Used Textbook Market

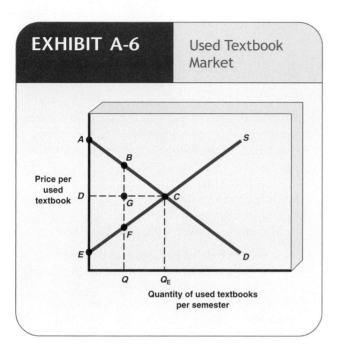

Quantity of used textbooks per semester

3. Using Exhibits A-4 and Exhibit A-5 above, calculate the total surplus. Now calculate the effect on consumer surplus, producer surplus, and total surplus of a fall in the equilibrium price of textbooks from $30 to $15 each. Explain the meaning of your calculations.

4. Using Exhibit A-6, and assuming the market is in equilibrium at Q_E, identify areas *ACD*, *DCE*, and *ACE*. Now explain the result of underproduction at Q in terms of areas *BCG*, *GCF*, and *BCF*.

PRACTICE QUIZ

For an explanation of the correct answers, please visit the tutorial at www.cengage. com/economics/tucker.

1. If Bill is willing to pay $10 for one good X, $8 for a second, and $6 for a third, and the market price is $5, then Max's consumer surplus is
   a. $24.
   b. $18.
   c. $9.
   d. $6.

2. Suppose Gizmo Inc. is willing to sell one gizmo for $10, a second gizmo for $12, a third for $14, and a fourth for $20, and the market price is $20. What is Gizmo Inc.'s producer surplus?
   a. $56
   b. $24
   c. $20
   d. $10

3. In an efficient market, deadweight loss is
   a. maximum.
   b. minimum.
   c. constant.
   d. zero.

4. Deadweight loss results from
   a. equilibrium.
   b. underproduction.
   c. overproduction.
   d. none of the above are correct.
   e. Either b. or c.

5. Total surplus equals
   a. consumer surplus + producer surplus − deadweight loss.
   b. consumer surplus − producer surplus − deadweight loss.
   c. consumer surplus − producer surplus + deadweight loss.
   d. consumer surplus + producer surplus.

6. Which of the following statements is *correct*?
   a. Total surplus is the sum of consumer and producer surplus.
   b. Deadweight loss is the net loss of both consumer and producer surplus.

PRACTICE QUIZ CONTINUED

EXHIBIT A-7   Demand and Supply Curves for Good *X*

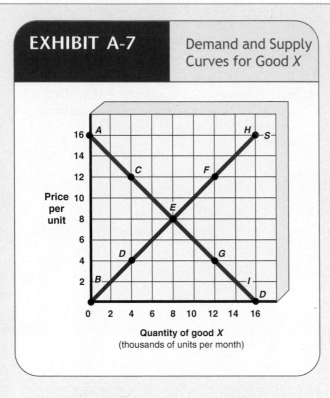

Quantity of good *X*
(thousands of units per month)

c. Deadweight loss is a measure of market inefficiency.
d. All of the above.

7. In Exhibit A-7, suppose firms devote resources sufficient to produce 4,000 units of good *X* per month. The result is a deadweight loss of triangle
a. *ABE*.
b. *CDE*.

c. *EGE*.
d. *EDE*.

8. Suppose in Exhibit A-7 that exchange in the market for good *X* yields triangle *ABE*, this means that which of the following conditions exists in the market?
a. Only consumer surplus
b. Only producer surplus
c. Deadweight loss
d. Maximum consumer plus producer surplus

9. As shown in Exhibit A-7, assume that the quantity of good *X* exchanged results in triangle *EIH*. This would be caused by _____ resources being used by producers to produce good *X*.
a. too many
b. too few
c. an optimal amount of
d. asymmetric

10. As shown in Exhibit A-7, assume that the quantity of good *X* exchanged results in triangle *CDE*. This would be caused by _____ resources being used by producers to produce good *X*.
A. too many
b. too few
c. an optimal amount of
d. asymmetric

Markets in Action

O nce you understand how buyers and sellers respond to changes in equilibrium prices, you are progressing well in your quest to understand the economic way of thinking. This chapter begins by showing that changes in supply and demand influence the equilibrium price and quantity of goods and services exchanged around you every day. For example, you will study the impact of changes in supply and demand curves on the markets for Caribbean cruises, new homes, and AIDS vaccinations. Then you will see why the laws of supply and demand cannot be repealed. Using market supply and demand analysis, you will learn that government policies to control markets have predictable consequences. For example, you will understand what happens when the government limits the maximum rent landlords can charge and who benefits and who loses from the federal minimum-wage law.

In this chapter, you will also study situations in which the market mechanism fails. Have you visited a city and lamented the smog that blankets the beautiful surroundings? Or have you ever wanted to swim or fish in a stream, but could not because of industrial waste? These are obvious cases in which market-system magic failed and the government must consider cures to reach socially desirable results.

In this chapter, you will learn to solve these economic puzzles:

- How can a spotted owl affect the price of homes?

- How do demand and supply affect the price of ethanol fuel?

- Why might government warehouses overflow with cheese and milk?

- What do ticket scalping and rent controls have in common?

Changes in Market Equilibrium

Using market supply and demand analysis is like putting on glasses if you are near-sighted. Suddenly, the fuzzy world around you comes into clear focus. In the following examples, you will open your eyes and see that economic theory has something important to say about so many things in the real world.

Changes in Demand

The Caribbean cruise market shown in Exhibit 1(a) assumes market supply, S, is constant and market demand increases from D_1 to D_2. Why has the demand curve shifted rightward in the figure? We will assume the popularity of cruises to these vacation islands has suddenly risen sharply due to extensive advertising that influenced tastes and preferences. Given supply curve S and demand curve D_1, the initial equilibrium price is $600 per cruise, and the initial equilibrium quantity is 8,000 cruises per year, shown as point E_1. After the impact of advertising, the new equilibrium point, E_2, becomes 12,000 cruises per year at a price of $900 each. Thus, the increase in demand causes both the equilibrium price and the equilibrium quantity to increase.

It is important to understand the force that caused the equilibrium to shift from E_1 to E_2. When demand initially increased from D_1 to D_2, there was a temporary shortage of 8,000 cruises at $600 per cruise. Firms in the cruise business responded to the excess demand by hiring more workers, offering more cruises to the Caribbean, and raising the price. The cruise lines therefore move upward along the supply curve (increasing quantity supplied, but not changing supply). During some period of trial and error, Caribbean cruise sellers increase their price and quantity supplied until a shortage no longer exists at point E_2. Therefore, the increase in demand causes both the equilibrium price and the equilibrium quantity to increase.

What will happen to the demand for gas-guzzling automobiles (for example, SUVs) if the price of gasoline triples? Because gasoline and automobiles are complements, a rise in the price of gasoline decreases the demand for gas guzzlers from D_1 to D_2 in Exhibit 1(b). At the initial equilibrium price of $30,000 per gas guzzler ($E_1$), the quantity supplied now exceeds the quantity demanded by 20,000 automobiles per month. This unwanted inventory forces automakers to reduce the price and quantity supplied. As a result of this movement downward on the supply curve, market equilibrium changes from E_1 to E_2. The equilibrium price falls from $30,000 to $20,000, and the equilibrium quantity falls from 30,000 to 20,000 gas guzzlers per month.

Changes in Supply

Now reverse the analysis by assuming demand remains constant and allow some nonprice determinant to shift the supply curve. In Exhibit 2(a), begin at point E_1 in a market for babysitting services at an equilibrium price of $9 per hour and 4,000 babysitters hired per month. Then assume there is a population shift and the number of people available to babysit rises. This increase in the number of sellers shifts the market supply curve rightward from S_1 to S_2 and creates a temporary surplus of 4,000 babysitters at point E_1 who offer their services but are not hired. The unemployed babysitters respond by reducing the price and the number of babysitters available for hire, which is a movement downward along S_2. As the price falls, buyers move down along their demand curve and hire more babysitters per month. When the price falls to $6 per hour, the market is in equilibrium again at point E_2, instead of E_1, and consumers hire 6,000 babysitters per month.

EXHIBIT 1   The Effects of Shifts in Demand on Market Equilibrium

In Part (a), demand for Caribbean cruises increases because of extensive advertising, and the demand curve shifts rightward from D_1 to D_2. This shift in demand causes a temporary shortage of 8,000 cruises per year at the initial equilibrium of E_1. This disequilibrium condition encourages firms in the cruise business to move upward along the supply curve to a new equilibrium at E_2.

Part (b) illustrates a decrease in the demand for gas-guzzling automobiles (SUVs) caused by a sharp rise in the price of gasoline (a complement). This leftward shift in demand from D_1 to D_2 results in a temporary surplus of 20,000 gas guzzlers per month at the initial equilibrium of E_1. This disequilibrium condition forces sellers of these cars to move downward along the supply curve to a new equilibrium at E_2.

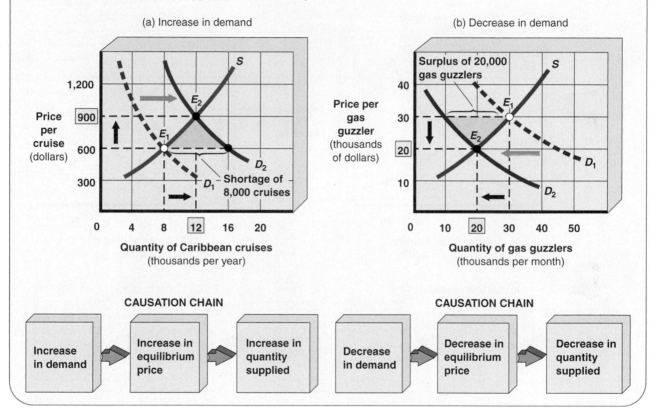

Exhibit 2(b) illustrates the market for lumber. Suppose this market is at equilibrium at point E_1, where the going price is $400 per thousand board feet, and 8 billion board feet are bought and sold per year. Now suppose a new Endangered Species Act is passed, and the federal government sets aside huge forest resources to protect the spotted owl and other wildlife. This means the market supply curve shifts leftward from S_1 to S_2, and a temporary shortage of 4 billion board feet of lumber exists at point E_1. Suppliers respond by hiking their price from $400 to $600 per thousand board feet, and a new equilibrium is established at E_2, where the quantity is 6 billion board feet per year. This higher cost of lumber, in turn, raises the price of a new 1,800-square-foot home by $4,000, compared to the price of an identical home the previous year.

Exhibit 3 gives a concise summary of the impact of changes in demand or supply on market equilibrium.

EXHIBIT 2   The Effects of Shifts in Supply on Market Equilibrium

In Part (a), begin at equilibrium E_1 in the market for babysitters, and assume an increase in the number of babysitters shifts the supply curve rightward from S_1 to S_2. This shift in supply causes a temporary surplus of 4,000 unemployed babysitters per month. This disequilibrium condition causes a movement downward along the demand curve to a new equilibrium at E_2. At E_2, the equilibrium price declines, and the equilibrium quantity rises.

In Part (b), steps to protect the environment cause the supply curve for lumber to shift leftward from S_1 to S_2. This shift in supply results in a temporary shortage of 4 billion board feet per year. Customer bidding for the available lumber raises the price. As a result, the market moves upward along the demand curve to a new equilibrium at E_2, and the quantity demanded falls.

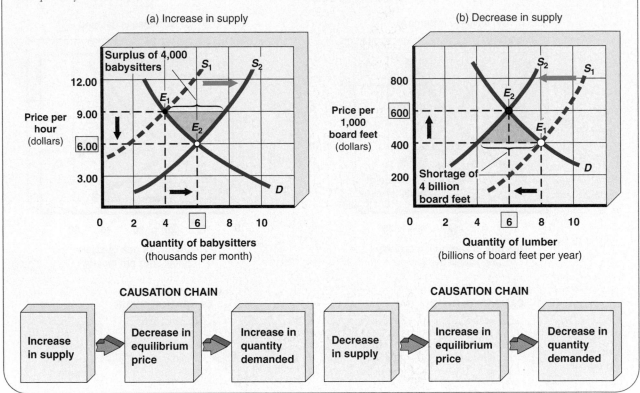

CHECKPOINT

Why the Higher Price for Ethanol Fuel?
Suppose more consumers purchased ethanol fuel for their cars, and at the same time, producers switched over to ethanol fuel production. Within a year, the price of ethanol fuel shot up $2 per gallon. During this year period, which increased more—demand, supply, or neither?

Trend of Equilibrium Prices over Time

Basic demand and supply analysis allows us to explain a trend in prices over a number of years. Exhibit 4 shows the effect of changes in nonprice determinants that increase both the demand and supply curves for good X between 2000, 2005, and 2010. A line connects the equilibrium prices for each year in order to summarize the

EXHIBIT 3	Effect of Shifts in Demand or Supply on Market Equilibrium	
Change	**Effect on Equilibrium Price**	**Effect on Equilibrium Quantity**
Demand increases	Increases	Increases
Demand decreases	Decreases	Decreases
Supply increases	Decreases	Increases
Supply decreases	Increases	Decreases

trend of equilibrium price and quantity changes over this time period. In this case, the observed prices trace an upward-sloping trend line.

Can the Laws of Supply and Demand Be Repealed?

The government intervenes in some markets with the objective of preventing prices from rising to the equilibrium price. In other markets, the government's goal is to intervene and maintain a price higher than the equilibrium price. Market supply and demand analysis is a valuable tool for understanding what happens when the government fixes prices. There are two types of price controls: *price ceilings* and *price floors*.

Price Ceilings

Case 1: Rent Controls   What happens if the government prevents the price system from setting a market price "too high" by mandating a price ceiling? A price ceiling is a legally established maximum price a seller can charge. Rent controls are an example of the imposition of a price ceiling in the market for rental units. New York City, Washington, D.C., Los Angeles, San Francisco, and other communities in the United States have some form of rent control. Since World War I, rent controls have been widely used in Europe. The rationale for rent controls is to provide an "essential service" that would otherwise be unaffordable by many people at the equilibrium rental price. Let's see why most economists believe that rent controls are counterproductive.

Exhibit 5 is a supply and demand diagram for the quantity of rental units demanded and supplied per month in a hypothetical city. We begin the analysis by assuming no rent controls exist and equilibrium is at point *E*, with a monthly rent of $1200 per month and 6 million units occupied. Next, assume the city council imposes a rent control (ceiling price) that by law forbids any landlord from renting a unit for more than $800 per month. What does market supply and demand theory predict will happen? At the low rent ceiling of $800, the quantity demanded of rental units will be 8 million, but the quantity supplied will be only 4 million. Consequently, the price ceiling creates a persistent market shortage of 4 million rental units because suppliers cannot raise the rental price without being subjected to legal penalties.

Price ceiling
A legally established maximum price a seller can charge.

EXHIBIT 4 — Trend of Equilibrium Prices over Time

Nonprice determinants of demand and supply for good *X* have caused both the demand and supply curves to shift rightward between 2000 and 2010. As a result, the equilibrium price and quantity in this example rise along the upward-sloping trend line connecting each observed equilbrium price.

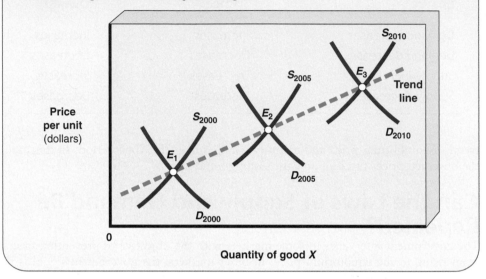

Note that a rent ceiling at or above $1200 per month would have no effect. If the ceiling is set at the equilibrium rent of $1200, the quantity of rental units demanded and the quantity of rental units supplied are equal regardless of the rent control. If the rent ceiling is set above the equilibrium rent, the quantity of rental units supplied exceeds the quantity of rental units demanded, and this surplus will cause the market to adjust to the equilibrium rent of $1200.

What is the impact of rent controls on consumers? First, as a substitute for paying higher prices, consumers must spend more time on waiting lists and searching for housing. This means consumers incur an *opportunity cost* added to the $800 rent set by the government. Second, an illegal market, or *black market,* can arise because of the excess quantity demanded. Because the price of rental units is artificially low, the profit motive encourages tenants to risk breaking the law by subletting their unit to the highest bidder over $800 per month.

From the seller's perspective, rent control encourages two undesirable effects. First, faced with a mandated low rent, landlords may cut maintenance expenses, and housing deterioration will reduce the stock of rental units in the long run. Second, landlords may use discriminatory practices to replace the price system. Once owners realize there is an excess quantity demanded for rentals at the controlled price, they may resort to preferences based on pet ownership, family size, or race to determine how to allocate scarce rental space.

Case 2: Gasoline Price Ceiling   The government placed ceilings on most nonfarm prices during World War II and, to a lesser extent, during the Korean War. In 1971, President Nixon "froze" virtually all wages, prices, and rents for 90 days in

EXHIBIT 5 — Rent Control Results in a Shortage of Rental Units

If no rent controls exist, the equilibrium rent for a hypothetical apartment is $1200 per month at point *E*. However, if the government imposes a rent ceiling of $800 per month, a shortage of 4 million rental units occurs. Because rent cannot rise by law, one outcome is that consumers must search for available units instead of paying a higher rent. Other outcomes include a black market, bribes, discrimination, and other illegal methods of dealing with a shortage of 4 million rental units per month.

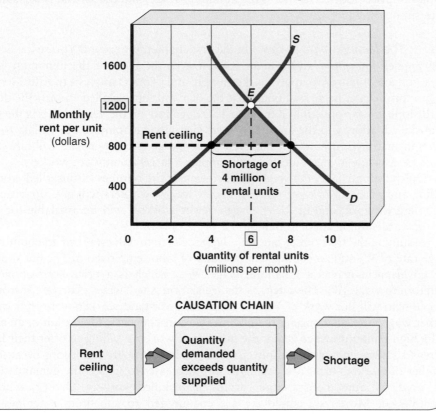

CAUSATION CHAIN

Rent ceiling ⇒ Quantity demanded exceeds quantity supplied ⇒ Shortage

an attempt to control inflation. As a result of an oil embargo in late 1973, the government imposed a price ceiling of 55 cents per gallon of gasoline. To deal with the shortage, nonprice rationing schemes were introduced in 1974. Some states used a first-come, first-served system, while other states allowed consumers with even-numbered license plates to buy gas on even-numbered days and those with odd-numbered license plates to buy on odd-numbered days. Gas stations were required to close on Friday night and not open until Monday morning. Regardless of the scheme, long waiting lines for gasoline formed, just as the supply and demand model predicts. Finally, in the past, legally imposed price ceilings have been placed on such items as natural gas shipped in interstate commerce and on interest rates for loans. Maximum interest rate laws are called *usury laws,* and state governments have adopted these ceilings in the past to regulate home mortgages and other types of loans. Internationally, as discussed later in the chapter on economies in transition, price ceilings on food and rent were common in the former Soviet Union. Soviet sociologists estimated that members of a typical urban household spent a combined total of 40 hours per week standing in lines to obtain various goods and services.

Price Floors

The other side of the price-control coin is a price floor set by government because it fears that the price system might establish a price viewed as "too low." A price floor is a legally established minimum price a seller can be paid. We now turn to two examples of price floors. The first is the minimum wage, and the second is agricultural price supports.

Price floor

A legally established minimum price a seller can be paid.

Case 1: The Minimum-Wage Law   In the first chapter, the second You're the Economist applied *normative* and *positive* reasoning to the issue of the minimum wage. Now you are prepared to apply market supply and demand analysis (positive reasoning) to this debate. Begin by noting that the demand for unskilled labor is the downward-sloping curve shown in Exhibit 6. The wage rate on the vertical axis is the price of unskilled labor, and the amount of unskilled labor employers are willing to hire varies inversely with the wage rate. At a higher wage rate, businesses will hire fewer workers. At a lower wage rate, they will employ a larger quantity of workers.

On the supply side, the wage rate determines the number of unskilled workers willing and able to work per year. At higher wages, workers will give up leisure or schooling to work, and at lower wages, fewer workers will be available for hire. The upward-sloping curve in Exhibit 6 is the supply of labor.

Assuming the freedom to bargain, the price system will establish an equilibrium wage rate of W_e and an equilibrium quantity of labor employed of Q_e. But suppose the government enacts a minimum wage, W_m, which is a price floor above the equilibrium wage, W_e. The intent of the legislation is to "wave a carrot" in front of people who will not work at W_e and to make lower-paid workers better off with a higher wage rate. But consider the undesirable consequences. One result of an artificially high minimum wage is that the number of workers willing to offer their labor increases upward along the supply curve to Q_s, but there are fewer jobs because the number of workers firms are willing to hire decreases to Q_d on the demand curve. The predicted outcome is a labor surplus of unskilled workers, $Q_s - Q_d$, who are unemployed. Moreover, employers are encouraged to substitute machines and skilled labor for the unskilled labor previously employed at equilibrium wage W_e. The minimum wage is therefore considered counterproductive because employers lay off the lowest-skilled workers, who ironically are the type of workers minimum-wage legislation intends to help. Also, loss of minimum wage jobs represents a loss of entry-level jobs to those who seek to enter the workforce.

Supporters of the minimum wage are quick to point out that those employed (Q_d) are better off. Even though the minimum wage causes a reduction in employment, some economists argue that a more equal or fairer income distribution is worth the loss of some jobs. Moreover, the shape of the labor demand curve may be much more vertical than shown in Exhibit 6. If this is the case, the unemployment effect of a rise in the minimum wage would be small. In addition, they claim opponents ignore the possibility that unskilled workers lack bargaining power versus employers.

Finally, a minimum wage set at or below the equilibrium wage rate is ineffective. If the minimum wage is set at the equilibrium wage rate of W_e, the quantity of labor demanded and the quantity of labor supplied are equal regardless of the

EXHIBIT 6 · A Minimum Wage Results in a Surplus of Labor

When the federal or state government sets a wage-rate floor above the equilibrium wage, a surplus of unskilled labor develops. The supply curve is the number of workers offering their labor services per year at possible wage rates. The demand curve is the number of workers employers are willing and able to hire at various wage rates. Equilibrium wage, W_e, will result if the price system is allowed to operate without government interference. At the minimum wage of W_m, there is a surplus of unemployed workers, $Q_s - Q_d$.

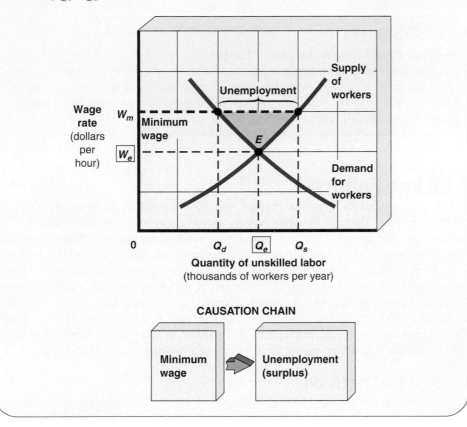

CAUSATION CHAIN

Minimum wage → Unemployment (surplus)

minimum wage. If the minimum wage is set below the equilibrium wage, the forces of supply of and demand for labor establish the equilibrium wage regardless of the minimum wage rate.

Case 2: Agricultural Price Supports   A farm price support is a well-known example of a price floor, which results in government purchases of surplus food and in higher food prices. Agricultural price support programs began in the 1930s as a means of raising the income of farmers, who were suffering from low market prices during the Great Depression. Under these programs, the government guarantees a minimum price above the equilibrium price and agrees to purchase any quantity the farmer is unable to sell at the legal price.

A few of the crops that have received price supports are corn, peanuts, soybeans, wheat, cotton, rice, tobacco, and dairy products. As predicted by market supply and demand analysis, a price support above the equilibrium price causes surpluses.

Government warehouses therefore often overflow with such perishable products as butter, cheese, and dry milk purchased with taxpayers' money. The following You're the Economist on the dairy industry examines one of the best-known examples of U.S. government interference with agricultural market prices.

> **Conclusion** *A price ceiling or price floor prevents market adjustment in which competition among buyers and sellers bids the price upward or downward to the equilibrium price.*

CHECKPOINT

Is There Price-Fixing at the Ticket Window?

At sold-out concerts, sports contests, and other events, some ticket holders try to resell their tickets for more than they paid—a practice known as scalping. For scalping to occur, must the original ticket price be legally set by a price floor, at the equilibrium price, or by a price ceiling?

Market Failure

In this chapter and the previous chapter, you have gained an understanding of how markets operate. Through the price system, society coordinates economic activity, but markets are not always "Prince Charmings" that achieve *market efficiency* without a misallocation of resources. It is now time to step back with a critical eye and consider markets that become "ugly frogs" by allocating resources inefficiently. Market failure occurs when market equilibrium results in too few or too many resources being used in the production of a good or service. In this section, you will study four important cases of market failure: lack of competition, externalities, public goods, and income inequality. Market failure is discussed in more detail in the chapter on environmental economics, except for the macroeconomics version of the text.

> **Market failure**
>
> A situation in which market equilibrium results in too few or too many resources used in the production of a good or service. This inefficiency may justify government intervention.

Lack of Competition

There must be competition among both producers and consumers for markets to function properly. But what happens if the producers fail to compete? In *The Wealth of Nations,* Adam Smith stated, "People of the same trade seldom meet together, even for merriment and diversion, but the conversation ends in a conspiracy against the public, or in some diversion to raise prices."[1] This famous quotation clearly underscores the fact that in the real world businesses seek ways to replace consumer sovereignty with "big business sovereignty." What happens when a few firms rig the market and they become the market's boss? By restricting supply through artificial limits on the output of a good, firms can enjoy higher prices and profits. As a result, firms may waste resources and retard technology and innovation.

Exhibit 7 illustrates how IBM, Apple, Gateway, Dell, and other suppliers of personal computers (PCs) could benefit from rigging the market. Without collusive action, the competitive price for PCs is $1,500, the quantity of 200,000 per month is sold, and efficient equilibrium prevails at point E_1. It is in the best interest of

Adam Smith (1723-1790). The father of modern economics, who wrote *The Wealth of Nations* published in 1776.

---

1. Adam Smith, *An Inquiry into the Nature and Causes of the Wealth of Nations* (1776; reprint, New York: Random House, The Modern Library, 1937), p. 128.

© Marc Dietrich, 2008/Used under license from Shutterstock.com

Each year the milk industry faces an important question: What does the federal government plan to do about its dairy price support program, which has helped boost farmers' income since 1949? Under the price support program, the federal government agrees to buy storable milk products, such as cheese, butter, and dry milk. If the farmers cannot sell all their products to consumers at a price exceeding the price support level, the federal government will purchase any unsold grade A milk production. Although state-run dairy commissions set their own minimum prices for milk, state price supports closely follow federal levels and are kept within 3 percent of levels in bordering states to reduce interstate milk price competition.

Members of Congress who advocate changes in the price support programs worry that milk surpluses are costing taxpayers too much. Each year the federal government pays billions of dollars to dairy farmers for milk products held in storage at a huge cost. Moreover, the problem is getting worse because the federal government encourages dairy farmers to use ultramodern farming techniques to increase the production per cow. Another concern is that the biggest government price support checks go to the largest farmers, while the number of dairy farmers continues to decline.

Congress is constantly seeking a solution to the milk price support problem. The following are some of the ideas that have been considered:

1. Freeze the current price support level. This prospect dismays farmers, who are subject to increasing expenses for feed, electricity, and other resources.

2. Eliminate the price supports gradually in yearly increments over the next 5 years. This would subject the milk market to the price fluctuations of the free market, and farmers would suffer some bad years from low milk prices.

3. Have the Department of Agriculture charge dairy farmers a tax of 50 cents for every 100 pounds of milk they produce. The farmers oppose this approach because it would discourage production and run small farmers out of business.

4. Have the federal government implement a "whole herd buyout" program. The problem is that using taxpayers' money to get farmers out of the dairy business pushes up milk product prices and rewards dairy farmers who own a lot of cows. Besides, what does the government do with the cows after it purchases them?

Finally, opponents of the dairy price support program argue that the market for milk is inherently a competitive industry and that consumers and taxpayers would be better served without government price supports for milk.

ANALYZE THE ISSUE

1. Draw a supply and demand graph to illustrate the problem described in the case study, and prescribe your own solution.

2. Which proposal do you think best serves the interests of small dairy farmers? Why?

3. Which proposal do you think best serves the interests of consumers? Why?

4. Which proposal do you think best serves the interest of a member of Congress? Why?

sellers, however, to take steps that would make PCs artificially scarce and raise the price. Graphically, the sellers wish to shift the competitive supply curve, S_1, leftward to the restricted supply curve, S_2. This could happen for a number of reasons, including an agreement among sellers to restrict supply (collusion) and government action. For example, the sellers could lobby the government to pass a law allowing an association of PC suppliers to set production quotas. The proponents might argue this action raises prices and, in turn, profits. Higher profits enable the industry to invest in new capital and become more competitive in world markets.

Opponents of artificially restricted supply argue that, although the producers benefit, the lack of competition means the economy loses. The result of restricting supply is that the efficient equilibrium point, E_1, changes to the inefficient equilibrium point, E_2. At point E_2, the higher price of $2,000 is charged, and the lower equilibrium quantity means that firms devote too few resources to producing PCs and charge an artificially high price. Note that under U.S. antitrust laws, the Justice Department is responsible for prosecuting firms that collude to restrict supply to force higher prices.

EXHIBIT 7   Rigging the PC Market

At efficient equilibrium point E_1, sellers compete. As a result, the price charged per PC is $1,500, and the quantity of PCs exchanged is 200,000. Suppose suppliers use collusion, government intervention, or other means to restrict the supply of this product. The decrease in supply from S_1 to S_2 establishes inefficient market equilibrium E_2. At E_2, firms charge the higher price of $2,000, and the equilibrium quantity of PCs falls to 150,000. Thus, the outcome of restricted supply is that the market fails because firms use too few resources to produce PCs at an artificially higher price.

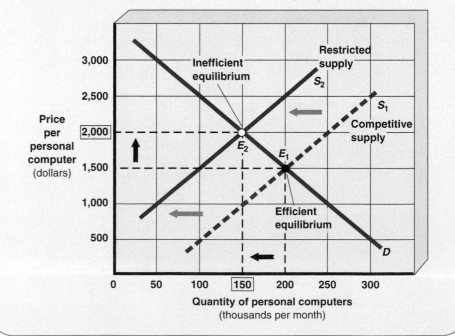

Externalities

Even when markets are competitive, some markets may still fail because they suffer from the presence of side effects economists call externalities. An externality is a cost or benefit imposed on people other than the consumers and producers of a good or service. Externalities are also called *spillover effects* or *neighborhood effects*. People other than consumers and producers who are affected by these side effects of market exchanges are called *third parties*. Externalities may be either negative or positive; that is, they may be detrimental or beneficial. Suppose you are trying to study and your roommate is listening to Steel Porcupines at full blast on the stereo. The action of your roommate is imposing an unwanted *external cost* or *negative externality* on you and other third parties who are trying to study or sleep. Externalities can also result in an *external benefit* or *positive externality* to nonparticipating parties. When a community proudly displays its neat lawns, gorgeous flowers, and freshly painted homes, visitors are third parties who did none of the work, but enjoy the benefit of the pleasant scenery.

Externality
A cost or benefit imposed on people other than the consumers and producers of a good or service.

A Graphical Analysis of Pollution   Exhibit 8 provides a graphical analysis of two markets that fail to include externalities in their market prices unless the government takes corrective action. Exhibit 8(a) shows a market for steel in which steel firms burn high-sulfur coal and pollute the environment. Demand curve, D, and supply curve, S_1, establish the inefficient equilibrium, E_1, in the steel market. Not included in S_1 are the *external costs* to the public because the steel firms are not paying for the damage from smoke emissions. If steel firms discharge smoke and ash into the atmosphere, foul air reduces property values, raises health care costs, and, in general, erodes the quality of life. Because supply curve, S_1, does not include these external costs, they are also not included in the price of steel, P_1. In short, the absence of the cost of pollution in the price of steel means the firms produce more steel and pollution than is socially desirable.

S_2 is the supply curve that would exist if the external costs of respiratory illnesses, dirty homes, and other undesirable side effects were included. Once S_2 includes the charges for environmental damage, the equilibrium price rises to P_2, and the equilibrium quantity becomes Q_2. At the efficient equilibrium point, E_2, the steel market achieves allocative efficiency. At E_2, steel firms are paying the full cost and using fewer resources to produce the lower quantity of steel at Q_2.

> **Conclusion** *When the supply curve fails to include external costs, the equilibrium price is artificially low, and the equilibrium quantity is artificially high.*

Regulation and pollution taxes are two ways society can correct the market failure of pollution:

1. **Regulation.** Legislation can set standards that force firms to clean up their emissions as a condition of remaining in business. This means firms must buy, install, and maintain pollution-control equipment. When the extra cost of the pollution equipment is added to the production cost per ton of steel, the initial supply curve, S_1, shifts leftward to supply curve S_2. This means regulation has forced the market equilibrium to change from E_1 to E_2. At point E_2, the firms use fewer resources to produce Q_2 compared to Q_1 output of steel per year, and, therefore, the firms operate efficiently.

EXHIBIT 8 — Externalities in the Steel and AIDS Vaccination Markets

In Part (a), resources are overallocated at inefficient market equilibrium E_1 because steel firms do not include the cost per ton of pollution in the cost per ton of steel. Supply curve S_2 includes the external costs of pollution. If firms are required to purchase equipment to remove the pollution or to pay a tax on pollution, the economy achieves the efficient equilibrium of E_2.

Part (b) demonstrates that external benefits cause an underallocation of resources. The efficient output at equilibrium point E_2 is obtained if people are required to purchase AIDS shots or if the government pays a subsidy equal to the external benefit per shot.

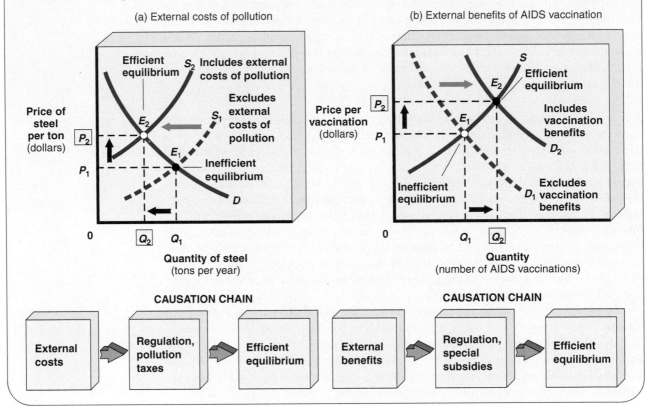

(a) External costs of pollution

(b) External benefits of AIDS vaccination

CAUSATION CHAIN

External costs → Regulation, pollution taxes → Efficient equilibrium

CAUSATION CHAIN

External benefits → Regulation, special subsidies → Efficient equilibrium

2. **Pollution Taxes.** Another approach would be for the government to levy a tax per ton of steel equal to the external cost imposed on society when the firm emits pollution into the air. This action inhibits production by imposing an additional production cost per ton of steel from the pollution taxes and shifts the supply curve leftward from S_1 to S_2. Again, the objective is to change the equilibrium from E_1 to E_2 and eliminate the overuse of resources devoted to steel production and its pollution. The tax revenue could be used to compensate those damaged by the pollution.

A Graphical Analysis of AIDS Vaccinations   As explained above, the supply curve can understate the *external costs* of a product. Now you will see that the demand curve can understate the *external benefits* of a product. Suppose a vaccination is discovered that prevents AIDS. Exhibit 8(b) illustrates the market for immunization against AIDS. Demand curve D_1 reflects the price consumers would pay for shots to receive the benefit of a reduced probability of infection by AIDS. Supply curve S shows the quantities of shots suppliers offer for sale at different prices. At equilibrium point E_1, the market fails to achieve an efficient allocation of resources. The reason is that when buyers are vaccinated, other people who do not purchase AIDS shots (called *free riders*) also benefit because this disease is less likely to spread. Once demand curve, D_2, includes external benefits to nonconsumers of AIDS vaccinations (increase in the number of buyers), the efficient equilibrium of E_2 is established. At Q_2, sellers devote greater resources to AIDS vaccinations, and the underallocation of resources is eliminated.

How can society prevent the market failure of AIDS vaccinations? Two approaches follow:

1. **Regulation.** The government can boost consumption and shift the demand curve rightward by requiring all citizens to purchase AIDS shots each year. This approach to capturing external benefits in market demand explains why all school-age children must have polio and other shots before entering school.

2. **Special Subsidies.** Another possible solution would be for the government to increase consumer income by paying consumers for each AIDS vaccination. This would mean the government pays each citizen a dollar payment equal to the amount of external benefits per shot purchased. Because the subsidy amount is payable at any price along the demand curve, the demand curve shifts rightward until the efficient equilibrium price and quantity are reached.

> **Conclusion** *When externalities are present, market failure gives incorrect price and quantity signals, and, as a result, resources are misallocated. External costs cause the market to overallocate resources, and external benefits cause the market to underallocate resources.*

Public Goods

Private goods are produced through the price system. In contrast, national defense is an example of a public good provided by the government because of its special characteristics. A public good is a good or service that, once produced, has two properties: (1) users collectively consume benefits, and (2) there is no way to bar people who do not pay (free riders) from consuming the good or service.

To see why the marketplace fails, imagine that Patriot Missiles Inc. offers to sell missile defense systems to people who want private protection against attacks from incoming missiles. First, once the system is operational, everyone in the defense area benefits from increased safety. Second, the *nonexclusive* nature of a public good means it is impossible or very costly for any owner of a Patriot missile defense system to prevent nonowners, the free riders, from reaping the benefits of its protection.

Given the two properties of a public good, why would any private individual purchase a Patriot missile defense system? Why not take a free ride and wait until someone else buys a missile system? Thus, each person wants a Patriot system, but does not want to bear the cost of the system when everyone shares in the benefits. As a result, the market fails to provide Patriot missile defense systems, and everyone hopes no missile attacks occur before someone finally decides to purchase one. Government can solve this public goods problem by producing Patriot missiles and

Public good

A good or service with two properties: (1) users collectively consume benefits, and (2) there is no way to bar people who do not pay (free riders) from consuming the good or service.

Applicable Concepts: public goods versus private goods

In their book, *Free to Choose*, published in 1980, economists Milton Friedman and his wife Rose Friedman proposed a voucher plan for schools.[1] The objective of their proposal was to retain government financing, but give parents greater freedom to choose the schools their children attend. The Friedmans pointed out that under the current system parents face a strong incentive not to remove their children from the public schools. This is because, if parents decide to withdraw their children from a public school and send them to a private school, they must pay private tuition in addition to the taxes that finance children enrolled in the public schools.

To remove the financial penalty that limits the freedom of parents to choose schools, the government could give parents a voucher, which is a piece of paper redeemable for a sum of money payable to any approved school. For example, if the government spends $8,000 per year to educate a student, then the voucher could be for this amount. The voucher plan embodies exactly the same principle as the GI Bill that provides educational benefits to military veterans. The veteran receives a voucher good only for educational expenses and is completely free to choose the school where it is used, provided the school satisfies certain standards.

The Friedmans argue that parents could, and should, be permitted to use the vouchers not only at private schools but also at other public schools—and not only at schools in their own district, city, or state, but at any school that is willing to accept their child. That would give every parent a greater opportunity to choose and at the same time would require public schools to charge tuition. The tuition would be competitive because public schools must compete for students both with other public schools and with private schools. It is important to note that this plan relieves no one of the burden of taxation to pay for schooling. It simply gives parents a wider choice as to which competing schools their children attend, given the amount of funding per student that the community has obligated itself to provide. The plan also does not affect the present standards imposed on private schools to ensure that students

1. Milton Friedman and Rose Friedman, *Free to Choose: A Personal Statement* (New York: Harcourt Brace Jovanovich, 1980), pp. 160–161.

taxing the public to pay. Unlike a private citizen, the government can use force to collect payments and prevent the free-rider problem. Other examples of public goods include the judicial system, the national emergency warning system, air traffic control, prisons, and traffic lights.

> **Conclusion** *If public goods are available only in the marketplace, people wait for someone else to pay, and the result is an underproduction or zero production of public goods.*

Income Inequality
In the cases of insufficient competition, externalities, and public goods, the marketplace allocates too few or too many resources to producing output. The market may

attending them satisfy the compulsory attendance laws.

In 1990, Milwaukee began an experiment with school vouchers. The program gave selected children from low-income families taxpayer-funded vouchers to allow them to attend private schools. There has been a continuing heated debate among parents, politicians, and educators over the results. In 1998, Wisconsin's highest court ruled in a 4–2 decision that Milwaukee could use public money for vouchers for students who attend religious schools without violating the constitutional separation of church and state.

A 2002 article in *USA Today* reported:

> *Opponents of vouchers have repeatedly argued that they would damage the public schools, draining them of resources and better students. A recent study of the Milwaukee voucher program by Caroline Hoxby, a Harvard economist,* suggests just the opposite. She wrote that "schools that faced the most potential competition from vouchers had the best productivity response." No doubt, the nation's experience with vouchers is limited, yet the evidence cited in a recent Brookings Institution report shows that they do seem to benefit African-American youngsters.[2]

The controversy continues: For example, in a 2002 landmark case, the U.S. Supreme Court ruled that government vouchers for private or parochial schools are constitutional. In 2003, however, a Denver judge struck down Colorado's new school voucher law, ruling that it violated the state's constitution by stripping local school boards of their control over education. And in 2006, the Florida Supreme Court ruled that Florida's voucher program for students in the lowest-rated public schools was unconstitutional.

Finally, in the 2007–2008 school year, over 20 percent of Milwaukee students received publicly funded vouchers to attend private schools.[3]

ANALYZE THE ISSUE

1. In recent years, school choice has been a hotly debated issue. Explain whether education is a public good. If education is not a public good, why should the government provide it?

2. The Friedmans present a very one-sided view of the benefits of a voucher system. Other economists disagree about the potential effectiveness of vouchers. Do you support a voucher system for education? Explain your reasoning.

---

2. Robert J. Bresler, "Vouchers and the Constitution," *USA Today*, May 2002, p. 15.
3. Data available at http://dpi.state.wi.us/sms/geninfo.html.

---

also result in a very unequal distribution of income, thereby raising a very controversial issue. Under the impersonal price system, movie stars earn huge incomes for acting in movies, while homeless people roam the streets penniless. The controversy is therefore over how equal the distribution of income should be and how much government intervention is required to achieve this goal. Some people wish to remove most inequality of income. Others argue for the government to provide a "safety net" minimum income level for all citizens. Still others see high income as an incentive and a "fair" reward for productive resources.

To create a more equal distribution of income, the government uses various programs to transfer money from people with high incomes to those with low incomes. Unemployment compensation and food stamps are examples of such programs. The federal minimum wage is another example of a government attempt to raise the earnings of low-income workers.

CHECKPOINT

Should There Be a War on Drugs?

The U.S. government fights the use of drugs, such as marijuana and cocaine, in a variety of ways, including spraying crops with poisonous chemicals; imposing jail sentences for dealers and users; and confiscating drug-transporting cars, boats, and planes. Which market failure motivates the government to interfere with the market for drugs: lack of competition, externalities, public goods, or income inequality?

KEY CONCEPTS

Price ceiling
Price floor

Market failure
Externality

Public good

SUMMARY

- **Price ceilings** and **price floors** are maximum and minimum prices enacted by law, rather than allowing the forces of supply and demand to determine prices. A *price ceiling* is a maximum price mandated by government, and a *price floor,* or *support price* for agricultural products, is a minimum legal price. If a price ceiling is set below the equilibrium price, a shortage will persist. If a price floor is set above the equilibrium price, a surplus will persist.

Price ceiling

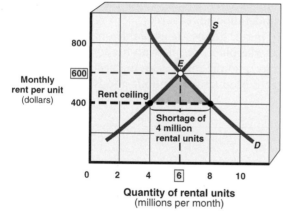

- **Market failure** occurs when the market mechanism does not achieve an efficient allocation of resources. Sources of market failure include lack of competition, externalities, public goods, and income inequality. Although controversial, government intervention is a possible way to correct market failure.
- An **externality** is a cost or benefit of a good imposed on people who are not buyers or sellers of that good. Pollution is an example of an *external cost,* which means too many resources are used to produce the product responsible for the pollution. Two basic approaches to solve this market failure are regulation and pollution taxes. Vaccinations provide *external benefits,* which means sellers devote too few resources to produce this product. Two basic solutions to this type of market failure are laws to require consumption of shots and special subsidies.

Externalities

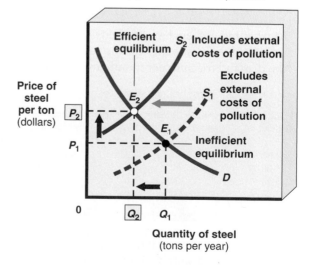

(a) External costs of pollution

Price floor

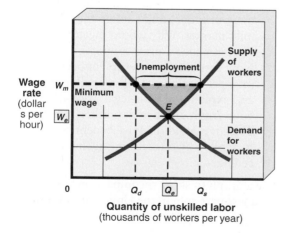

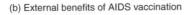

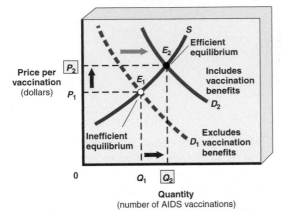

(b) External benefits of AIDS vaccination

- **Public goods** are goods that are consumed by all people in a society regardless of whether they pay or not. National defense, air traffic control, and other public goods can benefit many individuals simultaneously and are provided by the government.

SUMMARY OF CONCLUSION STATEMENTS

- A price ceiling or price floor prevents market adjustment in which competition among buyers and sellers bids the price upward or downward to the equilibrium price.
- When the supply curve fails to include external costs, the equilibrium price is artificially low, and the equilibrium quantity is artificially high.
- When externalities are present, market failure gives incorrect price and quantity signals, and as

a result, resources are misallocated. External costs cause the market to overallocate resources, and external benefits cause the market to underallocate resources.
- If public goods are available only in the marketplace, people wait for someone else to pay, and the result is an underproduction or zero production of public goods.

STUDY QUESTIONS AND PROBLEMS

1. Market researchers have studied the market for milk, and their estimates for the supply of and the demand for milk per month are as follows:

Price per Gallon	Quantity Demanded (millions of gallons)	Quantity Supplied (millions of gallons)
$10.50	100	500
8.00	200	400
6.50	300	300
4.00	400	200
2.50	500	100

a. Using the above data, graph the demand for and the supply of milk. Identify the equilibrium point as E, and use dotted lines to connect E to the equilibrium price on the

price axis and the equilibrium quantity on the quantity axis.

b. Suppose the government enacts a milk price support of $8 per gallon. Indicate this action on your graph, and explain the effect on the milk market. Why would the government establish such a price support?

c. Now assume the government decides to set a price ceiling of $4 per gallon. Show and explain how this legal price affects your graph of the milk market. What objective could the government be trying to achieve by establishing such a price ceiling?

2. Use a graph to show the impact on the price of Japanese cars sold in the United States if the

United States imposes import quotas on Japanese cars. Now draw another graph to show how the change in the price of Japanese cars affects the price of American-made cars in the United States. Explain the market outcome in each graph and the link between the two graphs.

3. Using market supply and demand analysis, explain why labor union leaders are strong advocates of raising the minimum wage above the equilibrium wage.

4. What are the advantages and disadvantages of the price system?

5. Suppose a market is in equilibrium and both demand and supply curves increase. What happens to the equilibrium price if demand increases more than supply?

6. Consider this statement: "Government involvement in markets is inherently inefficient." Do you agree or disagree? Explain.

7. Suppose coal-burning firms are emitting excessive pollution into the air. Suggest two ways the government can deal with this market failure.

8. Explain the impact of external costs and external benefits on resource allocation.

9. Why are public goods not produced in sufficient quantities by private markets?

10. Which of the following are public goods?
    a. Air bags
    b. Pencils
    c. Cycle helmets
    d. City street lights
    e. Contact lenses

For Online Exercises, go the text Web site at www.cengage.com/economics/tucker.

CHECKPOINT ANSWERS ✓

Why the Higher Price for Ethanol Fuel?

As shown in Exhibit 9, an increase in demand leads to higher prices, while an increase in supply leads to lower prices. Because the overall direction of price in the ethanol market was up, the demand increase must have been larger than the supply increase. If you said demand increased by more than supply because consumers reacted more quickly than producers, **YOU ARE CORRECT.**

Is There Price-Fixing at the Ticket Window?

Scalpers are evidence of a shortage whereby buyers are unable to find tickets at the official price. As shown in Exhibit 10, scalpers (often illegally) profit from the shortage by selling tickets above the official price. Shortages result when prices are restricted below equilibrium, as is the case when there is a price ceiling. If you said scalping occurs when there is a price ceiling because scalpers charge more than the official maximum price, **YOU ARE CORRECT.**

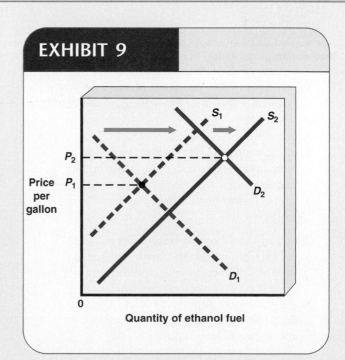

EXHIBIT 9

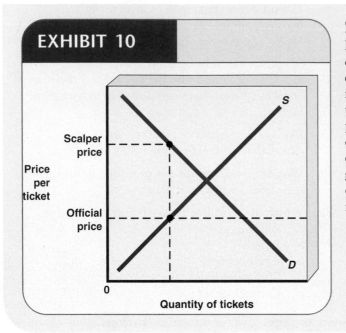

EXHIBIT 10

Should There Be a War on Drugs?

Drug use often affects not only the person using the drugs, but other members of society as well. For example, higher crime rates are largely attributable to increased drug usage, and AIDS is often spread when users inject drugs with nonsterile needles. When one person's actions affect others not involved in the decision to buy or sell, the market fails to operate efficiently. If you said the market failure motivating government intervention in the drug market is externalities because drug users impose costs on nonusers, **YOU ARE CORRECT.**

PRACTICE QUIZ

For visual explanation of the correct answers, please visit the tutorial at www.cengage.com/economics/tucker.

1. Suppose prices for new homes have risen, yet the number of homes sold has also risen. We can conclude that
   a. the demand for new homes has risen.
   b. the law of demand has been violated.
   c. new firms have entered the construction industry.
   d. construction firms must be facing higher costs.

2. Which of the following statements is *true*?
   a. An increase in demand, with no change in supply, will increase the equilibrium price and quantity.
   b. An increase in supply, with no change in demand, will decrease the equilibrium price and the equilibrium quantity.
   c. A decrease in supply, with no change in demand, will decrease the equilibrium

price and increase the equilibrium quantity.
   d. All of the above are true.

3. Consider the market for chicken. An increase in the price of beef will
   a. decrease the demand for chicken, resulting in a lower price and a smaller amount of chicken purchased in the market.
   b. decrease the supply of chicken, resulting in a higher price and a smaller amount of chicken purchased in the market.
   c. increase the demand for chicken, resulting in a higher price and a greater amount of chicken purchased in the market.
   d. increase the supply of chicken, resulting in a lower price and a greater amount of chicken purchased in the market.

4. An increase in consumers' incomes increases the demand for oranges. As a result of the adjustment to a new equilibrium, there is a (an)
   a. leftward shift of the supply curve.
   b. downward movement along the supply curve.
   c. rightward shift of the supply curve.
   d. upward movement along the supply curve.

5. An increase in the wage paid to grape pickers will cause the
   a. demand curve for grapes to shift to the right, resulting in higher prices for grapes.
   b. demand curve for grapes to shift to the left, resulting in lower prices for grapes.
   c. supply curve for grapes to shift to the left, resulting in lower prices for grapes.
   d. supply curve for grapes to shift to the left, resulting in higher prices for grapes.

6. If the federal government wants to raise the price of cheese, it will
   a. take cheese from government storage and sell it.
   b. encourage farmers to research ways to produce more cheese.
   c. subsidize purchases of farm equipment.
   d. encourage farmers to produce less cheese.

7. Which of the following is *least* likely to result from rent controls set below the equilibrium price for rental housing?
   a. Shortages and black markets will result.
   b. The existing rental housing will deteriorate.
   c. The supply of rental housing will increase rapidly.
   d. People will demand more apartments than are available.

8. Suppose the equilibrium price set by supply and demand is lower than the price ceiling set by the government. The eventual result will be
   a. a shortage.
   b. that quantity demanded is equal to quantity supplied.
   c. a surplus.
   d. a black market.

9. A good that provides external benefits to society has
   a. too few resources devoted to its production.
   b. too many resources devoted to its production.

   c. the optimal resources devoted to its production.
   d. not provided profits to producers of the good.

10. Pollution from cars is an example of
    a. a harmful opportunity cost.
    b. a negative externality.
    c. a production dislocation.
    d. none of the above.

11. Which of the following is the *best* example of a public good?
    a. Pencils
    b. Education
    c. Defense
    d. Trucks

12. A public good may be defined as any good or service that
    a. allows users to collectively consume benefits.
    b. must be distributed to all citizens in equal shares.
    c. is never produced by government.
    d. is described by answers (a) and (c) above.

13. In Exhibit 11, which of the following might cause a shift from S_1 to S_2?
    a. A decrease in input prices
    b. An improvement in technology
    c. An increase in input prices
    d. An increase in consumer income

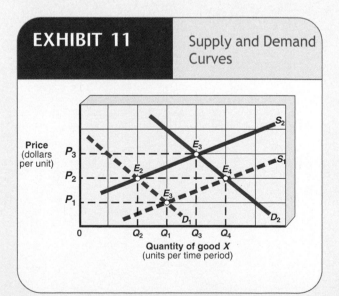

EXHIBIT 11 Supply and Demand Curves

PRACTICE QUIZ CONTINUED

14. In Exhibit 11, an increase in supply would cause a move from which equilibrium point to another, other things being equal?
    a. E_1 to E_2
    b. E_1 to E_3
    c. E_4 to E_1
    d. E_3 to E_4

15. Beginning from an equilibrium at point E_1 in Exhibit 11, an increase in demand for good X, other things being equal, would move the equilibrium point to
    a. E_1 (no change).
    b. E_2.
    c. E_3.
    d. E_4.

Applying Supply and Demand Analysis to Health Care

One out of every seven dollars spent in the United States is spent for health care services. This is a greater percentage than in any other industrialized country.[1] The topic of health care arouses deep emotions and generates intense media coverage. How can we understand many of the important health care issues? One approach is to listen to the normative statements made by politicians and other concerned citizens. Another approach is to use supply and demand theory to analyze the issue. Here again the objective is to bring textbook theory to life and use it to provide you with a deeper understanding of health service markets.

The Impact of Health Insurance

There is a downward-sloping demand curve for health care services just as there is for other goods and services. Following the same law of demand that applies to cars, clothing, entertainment, and other goods and services, movements along the demand curve for health care occur because consumers respond to changes in the price of health care. As shown in Exhibit A-1, we assume that health care, including doctor visits, medicine, hospital bills, and other medical services, can be measured in units of health care. Without health insurance, consumers buy Q_1 units of health care services per year at a price of P_1 per unit. Assuming supply curve S represents the quantity supplied, the market is in equilibrium at point A. At this point, the total cost of health care can be computed by the price of health care (P_1) times the quantity demanded (Q_1) or represented geometrically by the rectangle $0P_1AQ_1$.

Analysis of the demand curve for health care is complicated by the way health care is financed. About 80 percent of all health care is paid for by *third parties*, including private insurance companies and government programs, such as Medicare and Medicaid. The price of health care services therefore depends on the *copayment rate*, which is the percentage of the cost of services consumers pay out-of-pocket. To understand the impact, it is more realistic to assume consumers are insured and extend the analysis represented in Exhibit A-1. Because patients pay only 20 percent of the bill, the quantity of health care demanded in the figure increases to Q_2 at a lower price of P_2. At point B on the demand curve, insured consumers pay an amount equal to rectangle $0P_2BQ_2$, and insurers pay an amount represented by rectangle P_2P_3CB. Health care providers respond by increasing the quantity supplied from point A to point C on the supply curve S, where the quantity supplied equals the quantity demanded of Q_2. The reason that there is no shortage in the health care market is that the combined payments from the insured consumers and insurers equal the total payment required for the movement upward along the

---

1. U.S. Census Bureau, *Statistical Abstract of the United States*, 2007, http://www.census.gov/compendia/statab/, Table 1318.

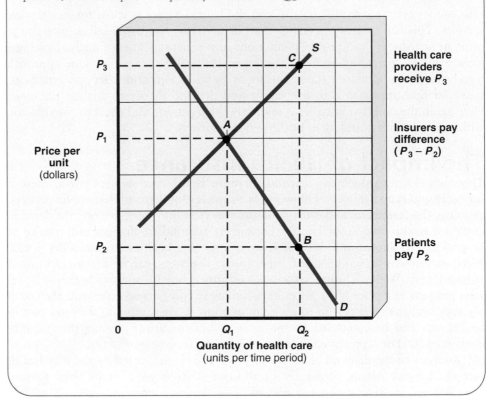

EXHIBIT A-1   The Impact of Insurance on the Health Care Market

Without health insurance, the market is in equilibrium at point A, with a price of P_1 and a quantity demanded of Q_1. Total spending is $0P_1AQ_1$. With copayment health insurance, consumers pay the lower price of P_2, and the quantity demanded increases to Q_2. Total health care costs rise to $0P_3CQ_2$, with $0P_2BQ_2$ paid by consumers and P_2P_3CB paid by insurers. As a result, the quantity supplied increases from point A to point C, where it equals the quantity demanded of Q_2.

supply curve. Stated in terms of rectangles, the total health care payment of $0P_3CQ_2$ equals $0P_2BQ_2$ paid by consumers plus P_2P_3CB paid by insurers.

> **Conclusion** *Compared to a health care market without insurance, the quantity demanded, the quantity supplied, and the total cost of health care are increased by copayment health care insurance.*

Finally, note that Exhibit A-1 represents an overall or general model of the health care market. Individual health care markets are subject to *market failure.* For example, there would be a lack of competition if hospitals, doctors, health maintenance organizations (HMOs), or drug companies conspired to fix prices. Externalities provide another source of market failure, as illustrated previously for vaccinations in Exhibit 8(b). We are also concerned that health care be distributed in a fair way. This concern explains why the government Medicare and Medicaid programs help the elderly and poor afford health care.

Shifts in the Demand for Health Care

While changes in the price of health care cause movements along the demand curve, other factors can cause the demand curve to shift. The following are some of the nonprice determinants that can change the demand for health care.

Number of Buyers

As the population increases, the demand for health care increases. In addition to the total number of people, the distribution of older people in the population is important. As more people move into the 65-and-older age group, the demand for health care services becomes greater because older people have more frequent and prolonged spells of illness. An increase in substance abuse involving alcohol, tobacco, or drugs also increases the demand for health care. For example, if the percentage of babies born into drug-prone families increases, the demand for health care will shift rightward. As this text is written in 2008, each of the candidates for president has a plan to expand health care insurance, including tax incentives and a government mandate. The impact of these programs would be to increase the demand curve for health care.

Tastes and Preferences

Changes in consumer attitudes toward health care can also change demand. For example, television, movies, magazines, and advertising may be responsible for changes in people's preferences for cosmetic surgery. Moreover, medical science has improved so much that we believe there must be a cure for most ailments. As a result, consumers are willing to buy larger quantities of medical services at each possible price.

Doctors also influence consumer preferences by prescribing treatment. It is often argued that some doctors guard against malpractice suits or boost their incomes by ordering more tests or office visits than are really needed. Some estimates suggest that fraud and abuse account for about 10 percent of total health care spending. These studies reveal that as many as one-third of some procedures are inappropriate.

Income

Health care is a normal good. Rising inflation-adjusted incomes of consumers in the United States cause the demand curve for health care services to shift to the right. On the other hand, if real median family income remains unchanged, there is no influence on the demand curve.

Prices of Substitutes

The prices of medical goods and services that are substitutes can change and, in turn, influence the demand for other medical services. For example, treatment of a back problem by a chiropractor is an alternative for many of the treatments provided by orthopedic doctors. If the price of orthopedic therapy rises, then some people will switch to treatment by a chiropractor. As a result, the demand curve for chiropractic therapy shifts rightward.

Shifts in the Supply of Health Care

Changes in the following nonprice factors change the supply of health care.

Number of Sellers

Sellers of health care include hospitals, nursing homes, physicians in private practice, HMOs, drug companies, chiropractors, psychologists, and a host of other suppliers. To ensure the quality and safety of health care, virtually every facet of the industry is regulated and licensed by the government or controlled by the American Medical Association (AMA). The AMA limits the number of persons practicing medicine primarily through medical school accreditation and licensing requirements. The federal Food and Drug Administration (FDA) requires testing that delays the introduction of new drugs. Tighter restrictions on the number of sellers shift the health care supply curve leftward, and reduced restrictions shift the supply curve rightward.

Resource Prices

An increase in the costs of resources underlying the supply of health care shifts the supply curve leftward. By far the single most important factor behind increasing health care spending has been technological change. New diagnostic, surgical, and therapeutic equipment is used extensively in the health care industry, and the result is higher costs. Wages, salaries, and other costs, such as the costs of malpractice suits, also influence the supply curve. If hospitals, for example, are paying higher prices for inputs used to produce health care, the supply curve shifts to the left because the same quantities may be supplied only at higher prices.

Price Elasticity of Demand and Supply

S uppose you are the manager of the Steel Porcu- pines rock group. You are considering raising your ticket price, and you wonder how the fans will react. You have studied economics and know the law of demand. When the price of a ticket rises, the quantity demanded goes down, ceteris paribus. So you really need to know how many tickets fans will purchase if the band boosts the ticket price. If the ticket price for a Steel Porcupines concert is $25, you will sell 20,000 tick- ets. At $30 per ticket, only 10,000 tickets will be sold. Thus, a $5 increase per ticket cuts the number of tickets sold in half.

Which ticket price should you choose? Is it better to charge a higher ticket price and sell fewer tickets or to charge a lower ticket price and sell more tickets? The answer depends on changes in *total revenue,* or sales, as we move upward along points on the Steel Porcupines' demand curve. At $30 per ticket, sales will be $300,000. If you charge $25, the group will take in $500,000 for a concert. Okay, you say, what happens at $20 per ticket?

This chapter teaches you to calculate the percentage change in the quantity demanded when the price changes by a given percentage. Then you will see how this relates to total revenue. This knowledge of the sensitivity of demand is vital for pricing and targeting markets for goods and services. Next, you will see how changes in consumer income and the prices of related goods affect percentage changes in the quantity de- manded. The chapter concludes by relating the concept of price elasticity to supply and the impact of taxation.

In this chapter, you will learn
to solve these economic puzzles:

- Can total revenue from a Steel Porcupines' concert remain unchanged regardless of changes in the ticket price?

- How sensitive is the quantity of cigarettes demanded to changes in the price of cigarettes?

- What would happen to the sales of Mercedes, BMWs, and Jaguars in the United States if Congress prohibited sales of luxury Japanese cars in this country?

Price Elasticity of Demand

In Chapter 3, when you studied the demand curve, the focus was on the law of demand. This law states there is an inverse relationship between the price and the quantity demanded of a good or service. In this chapter, the emphasis is on measuring the *relative size* of changes in the price and the quantity demanded. Now we ask: By *what percentage* does the quantity demanded rise when the price falls by, say, 10 percent?

The Price Elasticity of Demand Midpoints Formula

Price elasticity of demand

The ratio of the percentage change in the quantity demanded of a product to a percentage change in its price.

Economists use a price elasticity of demand formula to measure the degree of consumer responsiveness, or sensitivity, to a change in price. Price elasticity of demand is the ratio of the percentage change in the quantity demanded of a product to a percentage change in its price. Suppose a university's enrollment drops by 20 percent because tuition rises by 10 percent. Therefore, the price elasticity of demand is 2 (−20 percent/+10 percent). The number 2 means that the quantity demanded (enrollment) changes 2 percent for each 1 percent change in price (tuition). Note there should be a minus sign in front of the 2 because, under the law of demand, price and quantity move in *opposite* directions. However, economists drop the minus sign because we know from the law of demand that quantity demanded and price are inversely related.

The number 2 is an *elasticity coefficient*, which economists use to measure the degree of elasticity. The elasticity formula is

$$E_d = \frac{\text{percentage change in quantity demanded}}{\text{percentage change in price}}$$

where E_d is the elasticity of demand coefficient. Here you must take care. *There is a problem using this formula.* Let's return to our rock group example from the chapter preview. Suppose Steel Porcupines raises its ticket price from \$25 to \$30 and the number of seats sold falls from 20,000 to 10,000. We can compute the elasticity coefficient as

$$E_d = \frac{\%\Delta Q}{\%\Delta P} = \frac{\dfrac{10{,}000 - 20{,}000}{20{,}000}}{\dfrac{30 - 25}{25}} = \frac{50\%}{20\%} = 2.5$$

Now consider the elasticity coefficient computed between these same points on Steel Porcupines' demand curve when the price is lowered. Starting at $30 per ticket and lowering the ticket price to $25 causes the number of seats sold to rise from 10,000 to 20,000. In this case, the rock group computes a much different elasticity coefficient, as

$$E_d = \frac{\%\Delta Q}{\%\Delta P} = \frac{\dfrac{20{,}000 - 10{,}000}{10{,}000}}{\dfrac{25 - 30}{30}} = \frac{100\%}{17\%} = 5.9$$

There is a reason for the different elasticity coefficients between the same two points on a demand curve (2.5 if price is raised, 5.9 if price is cut). The natural approach is to select the initial point as the base and then compute a percentage change. But price elasticity of demand involves changes between two possible initial base points (P_1, Q_1 or P_2, Q_2). Economists solve this problem of different base points by using the *midpoints* as the base points of changes in prices and quantities demanded. The *midpoints formula* for price elasticity of demand is

$$E_d = \frac{\text{change in quantity}}{\text{sum of quantities/2}} \div \frac{\text{change in price}}{\text{sum of prices/2}}$$

which can be expressed as

$$E_d = \frac{\%\Delta Q}{\%\Delta P} = \frac{\dfrac{Q_2 - Q_1}{Q_1 + Q_2}}{\dfrac{P_2 - P_1}{P_1 + P_2}}$$

where Q_1 represents the first quantity demanded, Q_2 represents the second quantity demanded, and P_1 and P_2 are the first and second prices. Expressed this way, we divide the change in quantity demanded by the *average* quantity demanded. Then this value is divided by the change in the price divided by the *average* price.[1]

It does not matter if Q_1 or P_1 is the first or second number in each term because we are finding averages. Also note that you can drop the 2 as a divisor of both the $(Q_1 + Q_2)$ and $(P_1 + P_2)$ terms because the 2s in the numerator and the denominator cancel out. Now we can use the midpoints formula to calculate the price elasticity of demand of 3.7 regardless of whether Steel Porcupines raises the ticket price from $25 to $30 or lowers it from $30 to $25.

$$E_d = \frac{\dfrac{Q_2 - Q_1}{Q_1 + Q_2}}{\dfrac{P_2 - P_1}{P_1 + P_2}} = \frac{\dfrac{10{,}000 - 20{,}000}{20{,}000 + 10{,}000}}{\dfrac{30 - 25}{25 + 30}} = \frac{33\%}{9\%} = 3.7$$

---

1. The midpoints formula is also commonly called the *arc elasticity formula.*

and

$$E_d = \frac{\dfrac{Q_2 - Q_1}{Q_1 + Q_2}}{\dfrac{P_2 - P_1}{P_1 + P_2}} = \frac{\dfrac{20,000 - 10,000}{10,000 + 20,000}}{\dfrac{25 - 30}{30 + 25}} = \frac{33\%}{9\%} = 3.7$$

The Total Revenue Test of Price Elasticity of Demand

As reflected in the midpoints formula, the *responsiveness* of the quantity demanded to a change in price determines the value of the elasticity coefficient. There are three possibilities: (1) the numerator is greater than the denominator, (2) the numerator is less than the denominator, and (3) the numerator equals the denominator. Exhibit 1 presents three cases that the Steel Porcupines rock band may confront.

Elastic Demand ($E_d > 1$)

Suppose the Steel Porcupines' demand curve is as depicted in Exhibit 1(a). Using the above midpoints formula, which drops the 2 as a divisor, if the group lowers its ticket price from $30 to $20, the quantity demanded increases from 10,000 to 30,000. Using the midpoints formula, this means that a 20 percent reduction in ticket price brings a 50 percent increase in quantity demanded. Thus, $E_d = 2.5$, and demand is elastic. Elastic demand is a condition in which the percentage change in quantity demanded is greater than the percentage change in price. Demand is elastic when the elasticity coefficient is greater than 1. Because the percentage change in quantity demanded is greater than the percentage change in price, the drop in price causes total revenue (TR) to rise. Total revenue is the total number of dollars a firm earns from the sale of a good or service, which is equal to its price multiplied by the quantity demanded. Perhaps the simplest way to tell whether demand is elastic, unitary elastic, or inelastic is to observe the response of total revenue as the price of a product changes. For example, in Exhibit 1(a), the total revenue at $30 is $300,000. The total revenue at $20 is $600,000. Compare the shaded rectangles under the demand curve, representing total revenue at each price. The gray area is an amount of total revenue unaffected by the price change. Note that the green shaded area gained at $20 per ticket ($400,000) is greater than the red shaded area lost at $30 per ticket ($100,000). This net gain of $300,000 causes the total revenue to increase by this amount when Steel Porcupines lowers the ticket price from $30 to $20.

Inelastic Demand ($E_d < 1$)

The demand curve in Exhibit 1(b) is inelastic. The quantity demanded is less responsive to a change in price. Here a fall in Steel Porcupines' ticket price from $30 to $20 causes the quantity demanded to increase by just 5,000 tickets (20,000 to 25,000 tickets). Using the midpoints formula, a 20 percent fall in the ticket price causes an 11 percent rise in the quantity demanded. This means $E_d = 0.55$ and demand is inelastic. Inelastic demand is a condition in which the percentage change in quantity demanded is less than the percentage change in price. Demand is inelastic when the elasticity coefficient is less than 1. When demand is inelastic, the drop in price causes total revenue to fall from $600,000 to $500,000. Note the net change in the shaded rectangles.

Elastic demand

A condition in which the percentage change in quantity demanded is greater than the percentage change in price.

Total revenue

The total number of dollars a firm earns from the sale of a good or service, which is equal to its price multiplied by the quantity demanded.

Inelastic demand

A condition in which the percentage change in quantity demanded is less than the percentage change in price.

EXHIBIT 1 — The Impact of a Decrease in Price on Total Revenue

These three different demand curve graphs show the relationship between a decrease in concert ticket price and a change in total revenue.

In Part (a), the demand curve is elastic between points *A* and *B*. The percentage change in quantity demanded is greater than the percentage change in price, $E_d > 1$. As the ticket price falls from \$30 to \$20, total revenue increases from \$300,000 to \$600,000.

Part (b) shows a case in which the demand curve is inelastic between points *C* and *D*. The percentage change in quantity demanded is less than the percentage change in price, $E_d < 1$. As the ticket price decreases over the same range, total revenue falls from \$600,000 to \$500,000.

Part (c) shows a unitary elastic demand curve. The percentage change in quantity demanded equals the percentage change in price between points *E* and *F*, $E_d = 1$. As the concert ticket price decreases, total revenue remains unchanged at \$600,000.

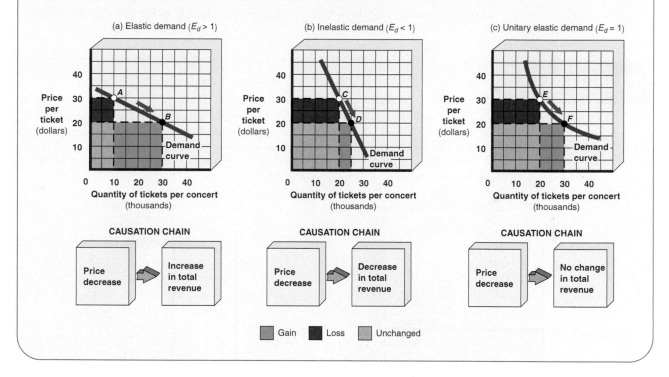

Unitary Elastic Demand ($E_d = 1$)

An interesting case exists when a demand curve is neither elastic nor inelastic. Exhibit 1(c) shows a demand curve for which any percentage change in price along the curve causes an exact proportional change in quantity demanded. When this situation occurs, the total amount of money spent on a good or service does not vary with changes in price. If Steel Porcupines drops the ticket price from \$30 to \$20, the quantity demanded rises from 20,000 to 30,000. Therefore, using the midpoints formula, a 20 percent decrease in price brings about a 20 percent increase in quantity demanded. If this is the case, demand is unitary elastic ($E_d = 1$), and the total revenue remains unchanged at \$600,000. Unitary elastic demand is defined as a condition in which the percentage change in quantity demanded is equal to the percentage change in price. Because the percentage change in price equals the percentage change in quantity, total revenue does not change regardless of changes in price.

Unitary elastic demand
A condition in which the percentage change in quantity demanded is equal to the percentage change in price.

Perfectly Elastic Demand ($E_d = \infty$)

Two extreme cases are shown in Exhibit 2. These represent the limits between which the three demand curves explained above fall. Suppose for the sake of argument that a demand curve is perfectly horizontal, as shown in Exhibit 2(a). At a price of $20, buyers are willing to buy as many tickets as the Steel Porcupines band is willing to offer for sale. At higher prices, buyers buy nothing. For example, at $20.01 per ticket or higher buyers will buy zero tickets. If so, $E_d = \infty$, and demand is perfectly elastic. Perfectly elastic demand is a condition in which a small percentage change in price brings about an infinite percentage change in quantity demanded.

> **Perfectly elastic demand**
>
> A condition in which a small percentage change in price brings about an infinite percentage change in quantity demanded.

Perfectly Inelastic Demand ($E_d = 0$)

Exhibit 2(b) shows the other extreme case, which is a perfectly vertical demand curve. No matter how high or low the Steel Porcupines' ticket price is, the quantity

---

EXHIBIT 2	Perfectly Elastic and Perfectly Inelastic Demand

Here two extreme demand curves for Steel Porcupines concert tickets are presented. Part (a) shows a demand curve that is a horizontal line. Such a demand curve is perfectly elastic. At $20 per ticket, the Steel Porcupines can sell as many concert tickets as it wishes. At any price above $20, the quantity demanded falls from an infinite number to zero.

Part (b) shows a demand curve that is a vertical line. This demand curve is perfectly inelastic. No matter what the ticket price, the quantity demanded remains unchanged at 20,000 tickets.

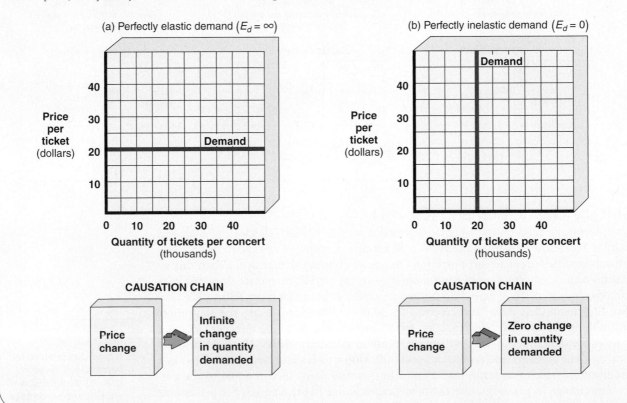

EXHIBIT 3	Price Elasticity of Demand Terminology		
Elasticity Coefficient	**Definition**	**Demand**	**Graph**
$E_d > 1$	Percentage change in quantity demanded is greater than the percentage change in price	Elastic	
$E_d < 1$	Percentage change in quantity demanded is less than the percentage change in price	Inelastic	
$E_d = 1$	Percentage change in quantity demanded is equal to the percentage change in price	Unitary elastic	
$E_d = \infty$	Percentage change in quantity demanded is infinite in relation to the percentage change in price	Perfectly elastic	
$E_d = 0$	Quantity demanded does not change as the price changes	Perfectly inelastic	

demanded is 20,000 tickets. Such a demand curve is perfectly inelastic, and $E_d = 0$. Perfectly inelastic demand is a condition in which the quantity demanded does not change as the price changes.

Exhibit 3 summarizes the ranges for price elasticity of demand.

Perfectly inelastic demand

A condition in which the quantity demanded does not change as the price changes.

Price Elasticity of Demand Variations along a Demand Curve

The price elasticity of demand for a downward-sloping straight-line demand curve varies as we move along the curve. Look at Exhibit 4, which shows a linear demand curve in Part (a) and the corresponding total revenue curve in Part (b). Begin at $40 on the demand curve and move down to $35, to $30, to $25, and so on. The table in Exhibit 4 lists variations in the total revenue and the elasticity coefficient (E_d) at different ticket prices. As we move down the upper segment of the demand curve, price elasticity of demand falls, and total revenue rises. For example, measured over the price range of $35 to $30, the price elasticity of demand is 4.33, so this segment of demand is elastic ($E_d > 1$). Between these two prices, total revenue increases from $175,000 to $300,000. At $20, price elasticity is unitary elastic ($E_d = 1$),

EXHIBIT 4 — The Variation in Elasticity and Total Revenue along a Hypothetical Demand Curve

Part (a) shows a straight-line demand curve and its three elasticity ranges. In the $40–$20 price range, demand is elastic. As price decreases in this range, total revenue increases. At $20, demand is unitary elastic, and total revenue is at its maximum. In the $20–$5 price range, demand is inelastic. As price decreases in this range, total revenue decreases. The total revenue (TR) curve is plotted in Part (b) to trace its relationship to price elasticity.

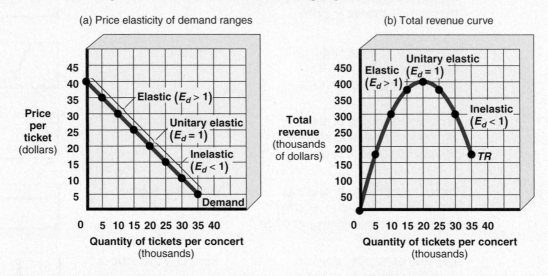

Calculation of Total Revenue and Elasticity along a Hypothetical Demand Curve

Price	Quantity	Total Revenue (thousands of dollars)	Elasticity Coefficient (E_d)	Price Elasticity of Demand
$40	0	$ 0		
			15.00	Elastic
35	5	175		
			4.33	Elastic
30	10	300		
			2.20	Elastic
25	15	375		
			1.29	Elastic
20	20	400	1.00	Unitary elastic
			0.78	Inelastic
15	25	375		
			0.45	Inelastic
10	30	300		
			0.23	Inelastic
5	35	175		

and total revenue is maximized at $400,000. As we move down the lower segment of the demand curve, price elasticity of demand falls below a value of 1.0, and total revenue falls. Over the price range of $15 to $10, for example, the price elasticity of demand is 0.45, and, therefore, this segment of demand is inelastic ($E_d < 1$). Between these two prices, total revenue decreases from $375,000 to $300,000.

Conclusion *The price elasticity coefficient of demand applies only to a specific range of prices.*

It is no coincidence that the demand curve in Exhibit 4(a) has elastic, unitary elastic, and inelastic segments. In fact, *any downward-sloping straight-line demand curve has ranges of all three of these types of price elasticity of demand.* As we move downward, first, there is an elastic range; second, a unitary elastic range; and, third, an inelastic range. Why? Recall that price elasticity of demand is a ratio of percentage changes. At the upper end of the demand curve, quantities demanded are lower, and prices are higher. A change of 1 unit in quantity demanded is a large percentage change. On the other hand, a $1 price change is a relatively small percentage change. At the lower end of the curve, the situation reverses. A 1-unit change in quantity demanded is a small percentage change. A $1 price change is a relatively larger percentage change. Now pause and refer back to Parts (a) and (b) of Exhibit 1. If we examine changes in price along the entire length of these demand curves, we will find elastic, unitary elastic, and inelastic segments.

Exhibit 5 summarizes the relationships between elasticity, price change, and total revenue.

EXHIBIT 5	Relationships among Elasticity, Price Change, and Total Revenue		
Price Elasticity of Demand	**Elasticity Coefficient**	**Price**	**Total Revenue**
Elastic	$E_d > 1$	↑	↓
Elastic	$E_d > 1$	↓	↑
Unitary elastic	$E_d = 1$	↑ ↓	No change
Inelastic	$E_d < 1$	↑	↑
Inelastic	$E_d < 1$	↓	↓

CHECKPOINT

Will Fliers Flock to Low Summer Fares?

US Airways is concerned over low sales and announces special cuts in its fares this summer. The New York to Los Angeles fare, for example, is reduced from $500 to $420. Does US Airways think demand is elastic, unitary elastic, or inelastic?

Determinants of Price Elasticity of Demand

Economists have estimated price elasticity of demand for various goods and services. Exhibit 6 presents some of these estimates, and as you can see, the elasticity coefficients vary a great deal. For example, the demand for automobiles and for chinaware is elastic. On the other hand, the demand for jewelry and watches and for theater and opera tickets is inelastic. The demand for tires and tubes is approximately unitary elastic. Why do the price elasticities of demand for these products vary so much? The following factors cause these differences.

Availability of Substitutes

By far the most important influence on price elasticity of demand is the availability of substitutes. Demand is more elastic for a good or service with close substitutes. If the

EXHIBIT 6	Estimated Price Elasticities of Demand	
	Elasticity Coefficient	
Item	**Short Run**	**Long Run**
Automobiles	1.87	2.24
Chinaware	1.54	2.55
Movies	0.87	3.67
Tires and tubes	0.86	1.19
Commuter rail fares	0.62	1.59
Jewelry and watches	0.41	0.67
Medical care	0.31	0.92
Housing	0.30	1.88
Gasoline	0.20	0.70
Theater and opera tickets	0.18	0.31
Foreign travel	0.14	1.77
Air travel	0.10	2.40

SOURCES: Robert Archibald and Robert Gillingham, "An Analysis of the Short-Run Consumer Demand for Gasoline Using Household Survey Data," *Review of Economics and Statistics 62* (November 1980): 622–628; Hendrik S. Houthakker and Lester D. Taylor, *Consumer Demand in the United States: Analyses and Projections* (Cambridge, MA: Harvard University Press, 1970: pp. 56–149); Richard Voith, "The Long-Run Elasticity of Demand for Commuter Rail Transportation," *Journal of Urban Economics 30* (November 1991): 360–372.

price of cars rises, consumers can switch to buses, trains, bicycles, and walking. The more public transportation is available, the more responsive quantity demanded is to a change in the price of cars. When consumers have limited alternatives, the demand for a good or service is more price inelastic. If the price of tobacco rises, people addicted to it have few substitutes because not smoking is unappealing to most users.

> **Conclusion** *The price elasticity coefficient of demand is directly related to the availability of good substitutes for a product.*

Price elasticity also depends on the market used to measure demand. For example, studies show the price elasticity of Chevrolets is greater than that of automobiles in general. Chevrolets compete with other cars sold by GM, Ford, Chrysler, Toyota, and other automakers and with buses and trains—all of which are substitutes for Chevrolets. But using the broad class of cars eliminates these specific types of cars as competitors. Instead, substitutes for automobiles include buses and trains, which are also substitutes for Chevrolets. In short, there are more close substitutes for Chevrolets than there are for all cars.

> ## CHECKPOINT
> **Can Trade Sanctions Affect Elasticity of Demand for Cars?**
> Assume Congress prohibits the sale of Japanese luxury cars, such as Lexus, Acura, and Infiniti, in the United States. How would this affect the price elasticity of demand for Mercedes, BMWs, and Jaguars in the United States?

Share of Budget Spent on the Product

When the price of salt changes, consumers pay little attention. Why should they notice? The price of salt or matches can double, and this purchase will remain a small percentage of one's budget. If, however, college tuition, the price of dinners at restaurants, or housing prices double, people will look for alternatives. These goods and services account for a large part of people's budgets.

> **Conclusion** *The price elasticity coefficient of demand is directly related to the percentage of one's budget spent for a good or service.*

Adjustment to a Price Change over Time

Exhibit 6 separates the elasticity coefficients into short-run and long-run categories. As time passes, buyers can respond fully to a change in the price of a product by finding more substitutes. Consider the demand for gasoline. In the short run, people find it hard to cut back the amount they buy when the price rises sharply. They are accustomed to driving back and forth to work alone in their cars. The typical short-run response is to cut luxury travel and reduce speed on trips. If high prices persist over time, car buyers will find ways to cut back. They can buy cars with better fuel economy (more miles per gallon), form car pools, and ride buses or commuter trains. This explains why the short-run elasticity coefficient of gasoline in the exhibit is more inelastic at 0.2 than the long-run elasticity coefficient of 0.7.

© Obak, 2008/Used under license from Shutterstock.com

Tobacco use is one of the chief preventable causes of death in the world. Since 1964, health warnings have been mandated in the United States on tobacco advertising, including billboards and printed advertising. In 1971, television advertising was prohibited. Most states have banned smoking in state buildings, and the federal government has restricted smoking in federal offices and military facilities. In 1998, the Senate engaged in heated debate over proposed legislation to curb smoking by teenagers. This bill would have raised the price of cigarettes by $1.10 a pack over 5 years, and the tobacco industry would have paid $369 billion over the next 25 years. Opponents argued that this price increase would be a massive tax on low-income Americans that would generate huge revenues to finance additional government programs and spending. Proponents countered that the bill was not about taxes. Instead, the bill was an attack on the death march of Americans who die early from tobacco-related diseases. Ultimately, the Senate was so divided on the issue that it was impossible, at least for that year, to pass a tobacco bill.

Estimates of the price elasticity of demand for cigarettes in the United States and other high-income countries fall in the inelastic range of 0.62. This means that if prices rise by 10 percent, cigarette consumption will fall by about 6 percent.[1] Moreover, estimates of the price elasticity of demand range significantly across states from 2.00 (Kentucky) to 0.09 (Mississippi).[2] The price elasticity of demand for cigarettes also appears to vary by education. Less-educated adults are more responsive to price changes than better-educated adults. This finding supports the theory that less-educated people are more present-oriented, or "myopic," than people with more education. Thus, less-educated individuals tend to be more influenced by current changes in the price of a pack of cigarettes.[3]

Another study in 2000 confirmed that education has strong negative effects on the quantity of cigarettes smoked, especially for high-income individuals. The presence of young children reduces smoking, with the effect most pronounced for women.[4]

A study published in *Health Economics* estimated the relationship between cigarette smoking and price for 34,145 respondents, aged 15–29 years. The price elasticity of smoking was inelastic and varied inversely with age: 0.83 for ages 15–17, 0.52 for ages 18–20, 0.37 for ages 21–23, 0.20 for ages 24–26, and 0.09 for ages 27–29. Thus, younger people were more likely to reduce the number of cigarettes smoked in response to increased prices.[5]

ANALYZE THE ISSUE

According to the above discussion, what factors influence the price elasticity of demand for cigarettes? What other factors not mentioned in the article might also influence the price elasticity of demand for cigarettes?

1. Jon P. Nelson, "Cigarette Demand, Structural Change, and Advertising Bans: International Evidence, 1970–1995," *Contribution to Economic Analysis and Policy* 2, no. 1 (2003): article 10.1.
2. Craig A. Gallet, "Health Information and Cigarette Consumption: Supply and Spatial Consideration," *Empirica* 33, no. 1 (March 2006): 35–47.
3. Frank Chaloupka et al., "Tax, Price and Cigarette Smoking," *Tobacco Control* 11, no. 1 (March 2002): 62–73.
4. Joni Hersch, "Gender, Income Levels, and the Demand for Cigarettes," *Journal of Risk and Uncertainty* 21, no. 2–3 (November 2000): 263–282.
5. Jeffrey E. Harris and Sandra W. Chan, "The Continuum of Addiction: Cigarette Smoking in Relation to Price among Americans Aged 15–29," *Health Economics* 8, no. 1 (February 1999): 81–86.

> **Conclusion** *In general, the price elasticity coefficient of demand is higher the longer a price change persists.*

Other Elasticity Measures

The elasticity concept has other applications beyond calculating the price elasticity of demand. Broadly defined, it is a technique for measuring the response of one variable to changes in some other variable.

Income Elasticity of Demand

Recall from Chapter 3 that an increase in income can increase demand (shift the demand curve rightward) for a normal good or service and decrease demand (shift the demand curve leftward) for an inferior good or service. To measure exactly how consumption responds to changes in income, economists calculate the income elasticity of demand. Income elasticity of demand is the ratio of the percentage change in the quantity demanded of a good or service to a given percentage change in income. We use a midpoints formula similar to the one we used for calculating price elasticity of demand:

$$E_I = \frac{\text{percentage change in quantity demanded}}{\text{percentage change in income}}$$

$$E_I = \frac{\% \, \Delta Q}{\% \Delta I} = \frac{\dfrac{Q_2 - Q_1}{Q_1 + Q_2}}{\dfrac{I_2 - I_1}{I_1 + I_2}}$$

Where E_I is the income elasticity of demand coefficient, Q_1 and Q_2 represent quantities demanded before and after the income change, and I_1 and I_2 represent income before and after the income change.

For a *normal* good or service, the income elasticity of demand is *positive*, $E_I > 0$. Recall that for this type of good demand and income move in the same direction. Thus, the variables in the numerator and denominator change in the same direction. For an *inferior* good or service, the reverse is true, and the income elasticity of demand is *negative*, $E_I < 0$.

Why is the income elasticity coefficient important? Returning to our rock group example, the Steel Porcupines band needs to know the impact of a recession on ticket sales. During a downturn when consumers' incomes fall, if a rock concert is a *normal good*, the quantity of ticket sales falls. Conversely, if a rock concert is an *inferior good*, the quantity of ticket sales rises. To illustrate, suppose consumers' incomes increase from $1,000 to $1,250 per month. As a result, the quantity of tickets demanded increases from 10,000 to 15,000. Based on these data, is a rock concert a normal or an inferior good? We compute as follows:

$$E_I = \frac{\dfrac{Q_2 - Q_1}{Q_1 + Q_2}}{\dfrac{I_2 - I_1}{I_1 + I_2}} = \frac{\dfrac{15,000 - 10,000}{10,000 + 15,000}}{\dfrac{1,250 - 1,000}{1,250 + 1,000}} = \frac{0.20}{0.11} = 1.8$$

Income elasticity of demand
The ratio of the percentage change in the quantity demanded of a good or service to a given percentage change in income.

EXHIBIT 7	Estimated Income Elasticities of Demand	
	Elasticity Coefficient	
Item	**Short Run**	**Long Run**
Potatoes	N.A.	0.81
Furniture	2.60	0.53
Dental services	0.38	1.00
Automobiles	5.50	1.07
Physician services	0.28	1.15
Clothing	0.95	1.17
Shoes	0.90	1.50
Gasoline and oil	0.55	1.36
Jewelry and watches	1.00	1.60
Toilet articles	0.25	3.74

SOURCES: Hendrik S. Houthakker and Lester D. Taylor, *Consumer Demand in the United States: Analyses and Projections* (Cambridge, MA: Harvard University Press, 1970); Dale M. Helen, "The Structure of Food Demand: Interrelatedness and Duality," *American Journal of Agricultural Economics* 64, no. 2 (May 1982): 213–221.

The computed income elasticity of demand coefficient of 1.8 summarizes the relationship between changes in rock concert ticket purchases and changes in income. First, E_I is a positive number; therefore, a rock concert is a normal good because people buy more when their incomes rise. Second, ticket purchases are very responsive to changes in income. When income rises by 11 percent, ticket sales increase by more (20 percent).

Exhibit 7 lists estimated income elasticity of demand for selected products.

Cross-Elasticity of Demand

In Chapter 3, we learned that a change in the price of one good, say, Y, can cause the consumption of another good, say, X, to change (see prices of related goods in Exhibit 5 in Chapter 3). In Exhibit 1(b) in Chapter 4, for example, a sharp rise in the price of gasoline (a complement) causes the number of gas guzzlers purchased to decline. This responsiveness of the quantity demanded to changes in the price of some other good is estimated by the cross-elasticity of demand. Cross-elasticity of demand is the ratio of the percentage change in the quantity demanded of a good or service to a given percentage change in the price of another good or service. Again, we use the midpoints formula as follows to compute the cross-elasticity coefficient of demand:

Cross-elasticity of demand

The ratio of the percentage change in the quantity demanded of a good or service to a given percentage change in the price of another good or service.

$$E_c = \frac{\text{percentage change in quantity demanded of one good}}{\text{percentage change in price of another good}}$$

$$E_c = \frac{\%\Delta Q_X}{\%\Delta P_Y} = \frac{\dfrac{Q_{X_2} - Q_{X_1}}{Q_{X_1} + Q_{X_2}}}{\dfrac{P_{Y_2} - P_{Y_1}}{P_{Y_1} + P_{Y_2}}}$$

where E_c is the cross-elasticity coefficient, Q_1 and Q_2 represent quantities before and after the price of another good or service changes, and P_1 and P_2 represent the price of another good or service before and after the price change.

The cross-elasticity coefficient reveals whether a good or service is a *substitute* or a *complement*. For example, suppose Coke increases its price 10 percent, which causes consumers to buy 5 percent more Pepsi. The cross-elasticity of demand for Pepsi is a *positive* 0.50 (+5 percent/+10 percent). Since $E_c > 0$, Coke and Pepsi are *substitutes* because the numerator and denominator variables change in the same direction. The larger the positive coefficient, the greater the substitutability between the two goods.

Now suppose there is a 50 percent increase in the price of motor oil and the quantity demanded of gasoline decreases by 10 percent. The cross-elasticity of demand for gasoline is a *negative* 0.20 (−10 percent/+50 percent). Since $E_c < 0$, these two goods are complements. The larger the negative coefficient, the greater the complementary relationship between the two goods. The variables in the numerator and denominator change in opposite directions.

Price Elasticity of Supply

The price elasticity of supply closely follows the price elasticity of demand concept. Price elasticity of supply is the ratio of the percentage change in the quantity supplied of a product to the percentage change in its price. This elasticity coefficient is calculated using the following formula:

$$E_s = \frac{\text{percentage change in quantity supplied}}{\text{percentage change in price}}$$

where E_s is the price elasticity of supply coefficient. Since price and quantity supplied change in the same direction, the elasticity coefficient is a positive value. Economists use terminology corresponding to that for the elasticity of demand. Supply is *elastic* when $E_s > 1$, *unit elastic* when $E_s = 1$, *inelastic* when $E_s < 1$, *perfectly elastic* when $E_s = \infty$, and *perfectly inelastic* when $E_s = 0$. Exhibit 8 shows three of these cases.

In Chapter 8, we will explain why the time period of analysis is a primary determinant of the shape of the supply curve. More specifically, it will be shown that

> **Price elasticity of supply**
> The ratio of the percentage change in the quantity supplied of a product to the percentage change in its price.

EXHIBIT 8	Price Elasticity of Supply

This figure shows three supply curves. As shown in Part (a), a small change in price changes the quantity supplied by an infinite amount: $E_s = \infty$. Part (b) shows the quantity supplied is unaffected by a change in price: $E_s = 0$, and supply is perfectly inelastic. In Part (c), the percentage change in quantity supplied is equal to the percentage change in price: $E_s = 1$.

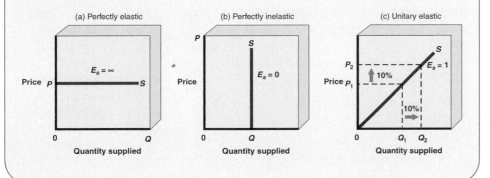

price elasticity of supply is greater in the long run than in the short run. Thus, the long-run supply curve will be flatter.

Exhibit 9 gives a summary of the three elasticity concepts presented in this section.

Price Elasticity and the Impact of Taxation

Who pays a tax levied on sellers of goods such as gasoline, cigarettes, and alcoholic beverages? One way to answer this question is to say that if the government places a tax on, say, gasoline, the gasoline companies pay the tax. They collect the tax when they sell gas and write the checks to the government for the tax. But this is not the whole story. Instead of looking simply at who writes the checks, economists use the elasticity concept to analyze who "really" pays a tax. Tax incidence is the share of a tax ultimately paid by consumers and sellers. In this section, we show that even though taxes are collected from sellers, buyers do not escape a share of the tax burden. The tax incidence depends on the price elasticities of demand and supply. Let's look at two examples.

Suppose the federal government decides to raise the gasoline tax $0.50 per gallon. Exhibit 10 shows the impact of the tax on different demand curves. At E_1 in Part (a), the equilibrium price before the tax is $3.00 per gallon and the equilibrium quantity is 30 million gallons per day. The effect of the tax is to shift the supply curve leftward from S_1 to S_2. From the sellers' viewpoint, the cost of each gallon of gasoline increases $0.50 per gallon at any possible selling price. The effect is exactly the same as if the price of crude oil or any resource used to produce gasoline increased.

Tax incidence

The share of a tax ultimately paid by consumers and sellers.

EXHIBIT 9	Summary of Other Elasticity Concepts		
Type	**Definition**	**Elasticity Coefficient Possibilities**	**Terminology**
Income elasticity of demand	$$\frac{\text{percentage change in quantity demanded}}{\text{percentage change in income}}$$	$E_I > 0$ $E_I < 0$ $E_I > 1$ $E_I < 1$ $E_I = 1$	Normal good Inferior good Income elastic Income inelastic Income unitary elastic
Cross-elasticity of demand	$$\frac{\text{percentage change in quantity demanded of one good}}{\text{percentage change in price of another good}}$$	$E_c < 0$ $E_c > 0$	Complements Substitutes
Price elasticity of supply	$$\frac{\text{percentage change in quantity supplied}}{\text{percentage change in price}}$$	$E_s > 1$ $E_s = 1$ $E_s < 1$ $E_s = \infty$ $E_s = 0$	Elastic Unitary elastic Inelastic Perfectly elastic Perfectly inelastic

EXHIBIT 10 | The Tax Incidence of a Tax on Gasoline

In Parts (a) and (b), S_1 is the supply curve before the imposition of a tax of $0.50 per gallon on gasoline. The demand curve is not affected by this tax collected from the sellers. The initial equilibrium is E_1. Before the tax, the price is $3.00 per gallon, and 30 million gallons are bought and sold.

In Part (a), the equilibrium price rises to $3.25 per gallon at E_2 as a result of the tax. After the tax is paid, sellers receive only $2.75 per gallon (point T) instead of the $3.00 they received before the tax. Thus, buyers pay $0.25 of the tax per gallon, and sellers bear the remaining $0.25. The shaded area is the total tax collected.

As shown in Part (b), a tax collected from sellers can be fully shifted to buyers in the unlikely case that demand is perfectly inelastic. Since the quantity of gasoline purchased is unresponsive to a change in price, sellers receive $3.00 per gallon before and after they pay the tax.

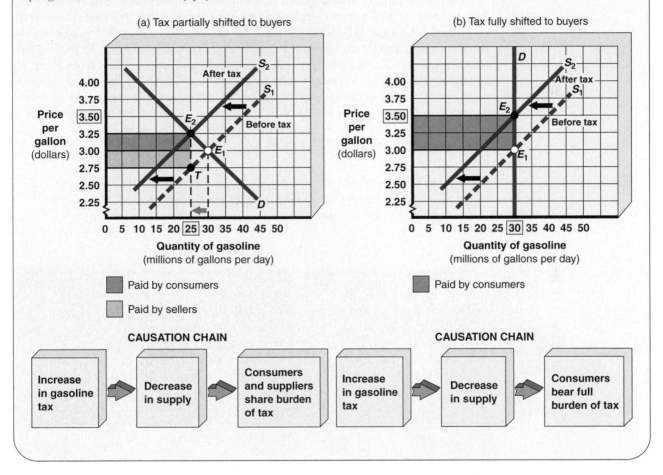

Sellers would like consumers to pay the entire amount of the tax. This would occur if consumers would pay $3.50 per gallon for the same 30 million gallons per day they purchased before the tax. But the leftward shift in supply establishes a new equilibrium at E_2. The new equilibrium price is $3.25 per gallon, and the equilibrium quantity falls to 25 million gallons per day. At E_2, the entire shaded area represents the tax revenue. The government collects $12.5 million per day, which equals the $0.50 per gallon tax times the 25 million gallons sold each day. The vertical line between points E_2 and T represents the $0.50 tax per gallon.

Since consumers now pay $3.25 instead of $3.00 per gallon, they pay one-half of the tax. The sellers pay the remaining half of the tax. Now the sellers send $0.50 to Uncle Sam and keep $2.75 compared to the $3.00 per gallon they kept before the tax.

> **Conclusion** *If the demand curve slopes downward and the supply curve slopes upward, sellers cannot raise the price by the full amount of the tax.*

Part (b) of Exhibit 10 is a special case in which the market price increases by the full amount of the tax per gallon. Here the demand for gasoline is perfectly inelastic. In this case, buyers do not decrease the quantity demanded in response to the decrease in supply caused by the tax. The quantity demanded is 30 million gallons per day before and after the tax. The price, however, increases from E_1 to E_2 by exactly the amount of tax per unit from $3.00 to $3.50 per gallon, and therefore consumers pay the entire burden of the tax. After paying the tax, sellers receive a net price of $3.00 per gallon. The total tax revenue collected by the government is the shaded area. Each day $15 million is collected, which equals the $0.50 per gallon tax multiplied by 30 million gallons sold each day.

> **Conclusion** *In the case where demand is perfectly inelastic, sellers can raise the price by the full amount of a tax.*

CHECKPOINT

Can Honda Compete with Itself?
When Honda introduced the Acura to compete with European luxury cars, there was a danger that the new line would take sales away from Honda's Accord. To make Acura more competitive with other luxury cars, suppose Honda cuts the price of Acura while keeping the price of Accord unchanged. If Honda's fear comes true, will it find a negative cross-elasticity of demand, a negative income elasticity of demand, or a positive cross-elasticity of demand?

KEY CONCEPTS

Price elasticity of demand
Elastic demand
Total revenue
Inelastic demand

Unitary elastic demand
Perfectly elastic demand
Perfectly inelastic demand
Income elasticity of demand

Cross-elasticity of demand
Price elasticity of supply
Tax incidence

SUMMARY

- *Price elasticity of demand* is a measure of the responsiveness of the quantity demanded to a change in price. Specifically, price elasticity of demand is the ratio of the percentage change in quantity demanded to the percentage change in price.

$$E_d = \frac{\%\Delta Q}{\%\Delta P} = \frac{\dfrac{Q_2 - Q_1}{Q_1 + Q_2}}{\dfrac{P_2 - P_1}{P_1 + P_2}}$$

- *Elastic demand* occurs where there is a change of more than 1 percent in quantity demanded in response to a 1 percent change in price. Demand is elastic when the elasticity coefficient is greater than 1 and *total revenue* (price times quantity) varies inversely with the direction of the price change.

- *Inelastic demand* occurs where there is a change of less than 1 percent in quantity demanded in response to a 1 percent change in price. Demand is inelastic when the elasticity coefficient is less than 1 and total revenue varies directly with the direction of the price change.

- *Unitary elastic demand* occurs where there is a 1 percent change in quantity demanded in response to a 1 percent change in price. Demand is unitary elastic when the elasticity coefficient equals 1 and total revenue remains constant as the price changes.

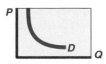

- *Perfectly elastic demand* occurs when the quantity demanded declines to zero for even the slightest rise or fall in price. This is an extreme case in which the demand curve is horizontal and the elasticity coefficient equals infinity.

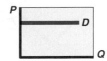

- *Perfectly inelastic demand* occurs when the quantity demanded does not change in response to price changes. This is an extreme case in which the demand curve is vertical and the elasticity coefficient equals zero.

- *Determinants of price elasticity of demand* include (a) the availability of substitutes, (b) the percentage of one's budget spent on the product, and (c) the length of time allowed for adjustment. Each of these factors is directly related to the elasticity coefficient.
- *Income elasticity of demand* is the percentage change in quantity demanded divided by the percentage change in income. For a *normal* good or service, income elasticity of demand is positive. For an *inferior* good or service, income elasticity of demand is negative.
- *Cross-elasticity of demand* is the percentage change in the quantity demanded of one product caused by a change in the price of another product. When the cross-elasticity of demand is negative, the two products are complements.
- *Price elasticity of supply* is a measure of the responsiveness of the quantity supplied to a change in price. Price elasticity of supply is the ratio of the percentage change in quantity supplied to the percentage change in price.
- *Tax incidence* is the share of a tax ultimately paid by buyers and sellers. Facing a downward-sloping demand curve and an upward-sloping supply curve, sellers cannot raise the price by the full amount of the tax. If the demand curve is vertical, sellers will raise the price by the full amount of the tax.

Tax Incidence of Gasoline Tax

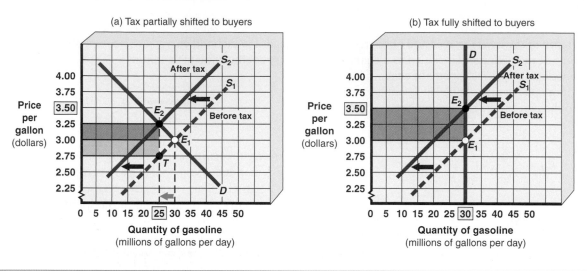

SUMMARY OF CONCLUSION STATEMENTS

- The price elasticity coefficient of demand applies only to a specific range of prices.
- The price elasticity coefficient of demand is directly related to the availability of good substitutes for a product.
- The price elasticity coefficient of demand is directly related to the percentage of one's budget spent for a good or service.

- In general, the price elasticity coefficient of demand is higher the longer a price change persists.
- If the demand curve slopes downward and the supply curve slopes upward, sellers cannot raise the price by the full amount of the tax.
- In the case where demand is perfectly inelastic, sellers can raise the price by the full amount of a tax.

STUDY QUESTIONS AND PROBLEMS

1. If the price of a good or service increases and the total revenue received by the seller declines, is the demand for this good over this segment of the demand curve elastic or inelastic? Explain.

2. Suppose the price elasticity of demand for farm products is inelastic. If the federal government wants to follow a policy of increasing income for farmers, what type of programs will the government enact?

3. Suppose the price elasticity of demand for used cars is estimated to be 3. What does this mean? What will be the effect on the quantity demanded for used cars if the price rises by 10 percent?

4. Consider the following demand schedule:

Price	Quantity Demanded	Elasticity Coefficient
$25	20	
20	40	_____
15	60	_____
10	80	_____
5	100	_____

What is the price elasticity of demand between
a. $P = \$25$ and $P = \$20$?
b. $P = \$20$ and $P = \$15$?
c. $P = \$15$ and $P = \$10$?
d. $P = \$10$ and $P = \$5$?

5. Suppose a university raises its tuition from $3,000 to $3,500. As a result, student enrollment falls from 5,000 to 4,500. Calculate the price elasticity of demand. Is demand elastic, unitary elastic, or inelastic?

6. Will each of the following changes in price cause total revenue to increase, decrease, or remain unchanged?
   a. Price falls, and demand is elastic.
   b. Price rises, and demand is elastic.
   c. Price falls, and demand is unitary elastic.
   d. Price rises, and demand is unitary elastic.
   e. Price falls, and demand is inelastic.
   f. Price rises, and demand is inelastic.

7. Suppose a movie theater raises the price of popcorn 10 percent, but customers do not buy any less popcorn. What does this tell you about the price elasticity of demand? What will happen to total revenue as a result of the price increase?

8. Charles loves Mello Yello and will spend $10 per week on the product no matter what the price. What is his price elasticity of demand for Mello Yello?

9. Which of the following pairs of goods has the higher price elasticity of demand?
   a. Oranges or Sunkist oranges
   b. Cars or salt
   c. Foreign travel in the short run or foreign travel in the long run

10. The Energizer Bunny that "keeps going and going" has been a very successful ad campaign for batteries. Explain the relationship between this slogan and the firm's price elasticity of demand and total revenue.

11. Suppose the income elasticity of demand for furniture is 3.0 and the income elasticity of demand for physician services is 0.3. Compare the impact on furniture and physician services of a recession that reduces consumers' incomes by 10 percent.

12. How might you determine whether Nikes and Reeboks are in competition with each other?

13. Assume the cross-elasticity of demand for car tires with respect to the price of cars is −2. What does this tell you about the relationship between car tires and cars when the price of cars rises by 10 percent?

14. Consider the following supply schedule:

Price	Quantity Supplied	Elasticity Coefficient
$10	50	
8	40	_____
6	30	_____
4	20	_____
2	10	_____
0	0	_____

What is the price elasticity of supply between
   a. $P = \$10$ and $P = \$8$?
   b. $P = \$8$ and $P = \$6$?
   c. $P = \$6$ and $P = \$4$?
   d. $P = \$4$ and $P = \$2$?
   e. $P = \$2$ and $P = \$0$?

15. Why would consumers prefer that the government tax products with elastic, rather than inelastic, demand?

16. Opponents of increasing the tax on gasoline argue that the big oil companies just pass the tax along to the consumers. Do you agree or disagree? Explain your answer.

For Online Exercises, go to the text Web site at www.cengage.com/economics/tucker.

CHECKPOINT ANSWERS

Will Fliers Flock to Low Summer Fares?

US Airways must believe the quantity of airline tickets demanded during the summer is quite responsive to a price cut. For total revenue to rise with a price cut, the quantity demanded must increase by a larger percentage than the percentage decrease in the price. For this to occur, the price elasticity of demand must exceed 1. If you said US Airways believes demand is elastic, **YOU ARE CORRECT.**

Can Trade Sanctions Affect Elasticity of Demand for Cars?

Because substitutes (Japanese luxury cars) are no longer available to U.S. consumers, the quantity demanded of Mercedes, BMWs, and Jaguars in the United States would be less responsive to changes in the prices for these cars. If you said the price elasticity of demand for Mercedes, BMWs, and Jaguars would become less elastic, **YOU ARE CORRECT.**

Can Honda Compete with Itself?

Determining the effect of cutting the Acura's price on sales of Accords calls for cross-elasticity. Once the price of Acura is cut, Honda would calculate the change in the quantity of Accords demanded. If Acura's decrease in price causes people to buy fewer Accords, Honda is indeed competing with itself. If you said a positive cross-elasticity of demand indicates the two goods are substitutes, **YOU ARE CORRECT.**

PRACTICE QUIZ

For an explanation of the correct answers, please visit the tutorial at www.cengage.com/economics/tucker.

1. If an increase in bus fares in Charlotte, North Carolina, reduces the total revenue of the public transit system, this is evidence that demand is
   a. price elastic.
   b. price inelastic.
   c. unitary elastic.
   d. perfectly elastic.

2. Which of the following will result in an increase in total revenue?
   a. Price increases when demand is elastic.
   b. Price decreases when demand is elastic.
   c. Price increases when demand is unitary elastic.
   d. Price decreases when demand is inelastic.

3. You are on a committee that is considering ways to raise money for your city's symphony program. You would recommend increasing the price of symphony tickets only if you thought the demand curve for these tickets was
   a. inelastic.
   b. elastic.
   c. unitary elastic.
   d. perfectly elastic.

4. The price elasticity of demand for a horizontal demand curve is
   a. perfectly elastic.
   b. perfectly inelastic.
   c. unitary elastic.
   d. inelastic.
   e. elastic.

5. Suppose the quantity of steak purchased by the Jones family is 110 pounds per year when the price is $2.10 per pound and 90 pounds per year when the price is $3.90 per pound. The price elasticity of demand coefficient for this family is
   a. 0.33.
   b. 0.50.
   c. 1.00.
   d. 2.00.

6. If a 5 percent reduction in the price of a good produces a 3 percent increase in the quantity demanded, the price elasticity of demand over this range of the demand curve is
   a. elastic.
   b. perfectly elastic.
   c. unitary elastic.
   d. inelastic.
   e. perfectly inelastic.

7. A manufacturer of Beanie Babies hires an economist to study the price elasticity of demand for this product. The economist estimates that the price elasticity of demand coefficient for a range of prices close to the selling price is greater than 1. The relationship between changes in price and quantity demanded for this segment of the demand curve is
   a. elastic.
   b. inelastic.
   c. perfectly elastic.
   d. perfectly inelastic.
   e. unitary elastic.

8. A downward-sloping straight-line demand curve will have a
   a. higher price elasticity of demand coefficient along the top of the demand curve.
   b. lower price elasticity coefficient along the top of the demand curve.
   c. constant price elasticity of demand coefficient throughout the length of the demand curve.
   d. positive slope.

9. The price elasticity of demand coefficient for a good will be lower
   a. if there are few or no substitutes available.
   b. if a small portion of the budget will be spent on the good.
   c. in the short run than in the long run.
   d. if all of the above are true.

10. The income elasticity of demand for shoes is estimated to be 1.50. We can conclude that shoes
    a. have a relatively steep demand curve.
    b. have a relatively flat demand curve.
    c. are a normal good.
    d. are an inferior good.

11. To determine whether two goods are substitutes or complements, an economist would estimate the
    a. price elasticity of demand.
    b. income elasticity of demand.
    c. cross-elasticity of demand.
    d. price elasticity of supply.

12. If the government wanted to raise tax revenue and shift most of the tax burden to the sellers, it would impose a tax on a good with a
    a. steep (inelastic) demand curve and a steep (inelastic) supply curve.
    b. steep (inelastic) demand curve and a flat (elastic) supply curve.

c. flat (perfectly elastic) demand curve and a steep (inelastic) supply curve.
d. flat (perfectly elastic) demand curve and a flat (elastic) supply curve.

13. As shown in Exhibit 11, assume the government places a $1 per pack sales tax on cigarettes. The percentage of the burden of taxation paid by consumers of a pack of cigarettes is
    a. zero.
    b. 25 percent.
    c. 50 percent.
    d. 100 percent.

14. As shown in Exhibit 11, assume the government places a $1 per pack sales tax on cigarettes. The percentage of the burden of taxation paid by tobacco sellers is:
    a. zero.
    b. 50 percent.
    c. 75 percent.
    d. 100 percent.

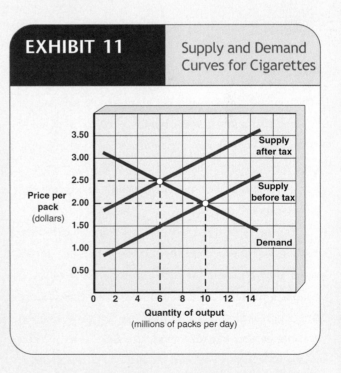

EXHIBIT 11   Supply and Demand Curves for Cigarettes

15. As shown in Exhibit 11, the $1 per pack sales tax on cigarettes raises tax revenue per day totaling:
    a. $5 million.
    b. $6 million.
    c. $10 million.
    d. $15 million.

Consumer Choice Theory

© David Muir/Digital Vision/Getty Images.

This chapter expands our understanding of demand by investigating more deeply *why* people buy goods and services. In Chapter 3, the law of demand rested on a foundation of common sense and everyday observation. When the price of a Big Mac falls, people *do* buy more, and a price rise causes people to buy less. But there is more to the story.

The focus of this chapter is the logic of consumer choice. Why does a consumer buy one bundle of goods, rather than another? Suppose someone asked why you bought a milkshake and french fries rather than a Coke and a hot dog. You would probably answer that given the money you had to spend, the Coke and hot dog would have given you less satisfaction. In this chapter, you will transform this simple explanation into consumer choice theory and then connect this theory to the law of

demand. The chapter ends with another way to explain the demand curve, which involves effects related to income and the prices of other goods.

In this chapter, you will learn to solve these economic puzzles:

- Under what conditions might you be willing to pay $10,000 for a gallon of water and 1 cent for a one-carat diamond?

- When ordering Big Macs, milkshakes, pizza, and other goods, how can you obtain the highest possible satisfaction?

- Do white rats obey the law of demand?

From Utility to the Law of Demand

The basis of the law of demand is self-interested behavior. Consumers spend their limited budget to satisfy some want, such as listening to a compact disc or driving a new car. The motivation to consume goods and services is to gain utility. Utility is the satisfaction, or pleasure, that people receive from consuming a good or service. Utility is want-satisfying power "in the eye of the beholder." Just as wants differ among people, utility received from consumption varies from person to person. Fred's utility from consuming a BMW will probably differ from Maria's utility. In spite of the subjective nature of utility, this section develops in steps the derivation of a demand curve based on the utility concept.

Total Utility and Marginal Utility

Actual measurement of utility is impossible because only you know the satisfaction from consuming, say, four Big Macs in one day. But suppose we could gauge your total utility of consuming four Big Macs in a day. Total utility is the amount of satisfaction received from all the units of a good or service consumed. That is, the utility of the first unit consumed added to that of the second unit, and so on. What units can be used to measure total utility? Economists use a mythical unit called a *util*, which allows us to quantify our thinking about consumer behavior.

No one has invented a "utility meter," but assume we could connect such a meter to your brain. Like taking your temperature, we could read the marginal utility each time you eat a Big Mac. Marginal utility is the change in total utility from one additional unit of a good or service. Instead of the total pleasure from eating X number of Big Macs, the question is how much *extra* satisfaction the first, second, or third Big Mac gives you. For example, Exhibit 1(a) shows your marginal utility data for eating four Big Macs in a day. You munch down the first Big Mac. Ah, the util meter hits an 8. You grab another Big Mac and eat it a little more slowly. The util meter hits 4 this time. You're starting to feel full, but you eat a third Big Mac. This one gets a 2. Even though you are pretty full, there is room for one more. You eat the fourth Big Mac very slowly, and it gives you less satisfaction than any of the previous burgers. Your utility meter reads 1. This trend conforms to the law of diminishing marginal utility. The law of diminishing marginal utility is the principle that the extra satisfaction provided by a good or service declines as people consume more in a given period. Economists have found that this is a universal principle of human consumption behavior.

Exhibit 1(a) is a marginal utility, *MU*, graph. Consistent with the law of diminishing marginal utility, the *MU* curve slopes downward as you consume more Big Macs. This reflects a steady decline in the utility of each additional Big Mac consumed. If you continued to eat Big Macs, a quantity of Big Macs is eventually reached at which the marginal utility is zero. Here you say to yourself, "If I eat another bite, I'll be sick." Then if you did eat another bite after all, marginal utility would be negative. A rational person never consumes goods when the marginal utility is negative (disutility) unless he or she is paid enough to do so. In our example, we assume you are rational and will not eat a Big Mac that gives you a negative marginal utility and a stomachache. Also keep in mind that the *MU* curve for a good is different for different circumstances and individuals. Your *MU* curve would be much higher if you had not eaten in days. On the other hand, a vegetarian would receive no positive marginal utility from consuming a Big Mac.

Utility
The satisfaction, or pleasure, that people receive from consuming a good or service.

Total utility
The amount of satisfaction received from all the units of a good or service consumed.

Marginal utility
The change in total utility from one additional unit of a good or service.

Law of diminishing marginal utility
The principle that the extra satisfaction of a good or service declines as people consume more in a given period.

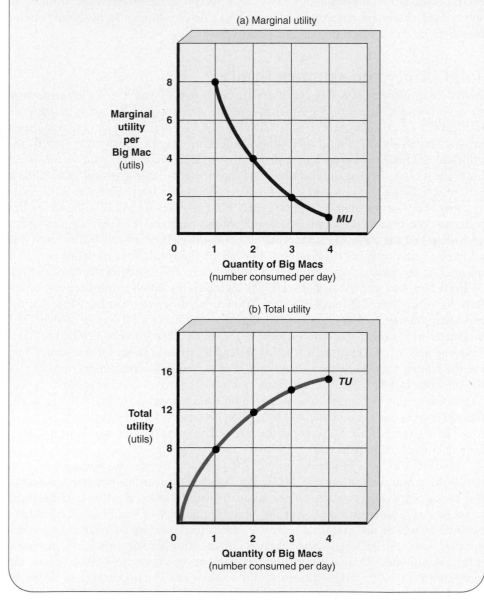

EXHIBIT 1   Diminishing Marginal Utility and Total Utility Curves for Consuming Big Macs

Part (a) shows that, as more Big Macs are consumed per day, the utility from each additional Big Mac declines. The utils are only imaginary because utility cannot be measured. When the marginal utility of each Big Mac consumed is summed, we obtain the total utility curve shown in Part (b).

(a) Marginal utility

Marginal utility per Big Mac (utils)

MU

Quantity of Big Macs
(number consumed per day)

(b) Total utility

Total utility (utils)

TU

Quantity of Big Macs
(number consumed per day)

Exhibit 1(b) shows how the shape of the total utility, *TU*, curve varies with marginal utility as you consume more Big Macs each day. The total utility of Big Macs increases steadily because each hamburger provides *additional* satisfaction to the sum of all the Big Macs already consumed. However, the *TU* curve becomes flatter as the

YOU'RE THE ECONOMIST   Why Is Water Less Expensive Than Diamonds?   *Applicable Concepts: total utility and marginal utility*

© Dragan Trifunovic/Used under license from Shutterstock.com.

Adam Smith posed a paradox in *The Wealth of Nations*. Water is essential to life and therefore should be of great value. On the other hand, diamonds are not essential to life, so people should value them less than water. Yet, even though water provides more utility, it is cheaper than diamonds. Smith's puzzle came to be known as the diamond-water paradox. Now you can use marginal utility analysis to explain something that baffled the father of economics.

Early economists failed to find the key to the diamond-water puzzle because they did not distinguish between marginal and total utility. Marginal utility theory was not developed until the late nineteenth century. Water is life-giving and does indeed yield much higher total utility than diamonds. However, marginal utility, and not total utility, determines the price. Water is plentiful in most of the world, so its marginal utility is low. This follows the law of diminishing marginal utility.

Jewelry-quality diamonds, on the other hand, are scarce. Because we have relatively few diamonds, the quantity of diamonds consumed is not large. As a result, the marginal utility of diamonds and the price buyers are willing to pay for them are quite high. Thus, scarcity raises marginal utility and price regardless of the size of total utility.

Exhibit 2 presents a graphical analysis that you can use to unravel the alleged paradox. Part (a) shows the marginal utility per carat you receive from each diamond consumed, and Part (b) represents marginal utility per gallon of water consumed. The vertical line, *S*, in each graph is the supply of water or diamonds available per year. Since water is much more plentiful than diamonds, the supply curve for water intersects the marginal utility curve at MU_w, which is close to zero. Conversely, the supply curve for diamonds intersects the marginal utility curve at a much higher marginal utility, MU_d. Because of the relative marginal utilities of water and diamonds, you are willing to pay much more for one more carat of a diamond than for one more gallon of water.

EXHIBIT 2   The Diamond-Water Paradox

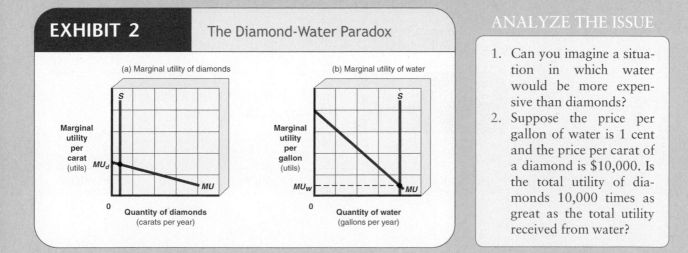

(a) Marginal utility of diamonds

Marginal utility per carat (utils) MU_d MU

0   Quantity of diamonds (carats per year)

(b) Marginal utility of water

Marginal utility per gallon (utils) MU_w MU

0   Quantity of water (gallons per year)

ANALYZE THE ISSUE

1. Can you imagine a situation in which water would be more expensive than diamonds?
2. Suppose the price per gallon of water is 1 cent and the price per carat of a diamond is $10,000. Is the total utility of diamonds 10,000 times as great as the total utility received from water?

marginal utility diminishes. This is because, as you consume more, the positive pleasure per Big Mac declines, and, in turn, each Big Mac adds less to total utility.

Consumer Equilibrium

We will now make our example of consumer choice more realistic. Let's examine how Bob Moore, a sophomore at Seaview College, might behave, given a limited budget and the choice between two goods. Suppose Bob goes to McDonald's for lunch with $8 in his pocket to spend for Big Macs and milkshakes. The price of a Big Mac is $2, and the price of a milkshake is also $2. How can Bob enjoy the maximum total utility with his limited money?

Recall from Chapter 2 the concept of *marginal analysis*. This is the method Bob uses to decide how many Big Macs and milkshakes to order. Exhibit 3 shows Bob's marginal utility for each Big Mac and milkshake consumed. The *marginal utility per dollar (MU/P)* is the ratio of the marginal utility of each good to its price. In making purchases, the key consideration is how additional satisfaction relates to price. Using marginal decision making before giving an order, Bob compares the marginal utility of one Big Mac to the marginal utility of one milkshake. Being a rational consumer, Bob sees that spending his first $2 on a Big Mac gives more "bang for the buck." The first Big Mac gives him 4 utils per dollar, but the same $2 spent on a milkshake gives him 3 utils per dollar. Next, Bob ponders how to spend his next $2. The best buy now is a milkshake because it gives 3 utils per dollar compared to 2 utils per dollar for a second Big Mac.

Spending Bob's last $4 is a tossup. Both the second Big Mac and the second milkshake give the same 2 utils per dollar. So Bob can spend $2 for a second Big Mac and his last $2 for a second milkshake. Or he can spend $2 for a second milkshake and his last $2 for a second Big Mac. The order does not matter. Now that Bob has spent all his income, the marginal utility per dollar of the last Big Mac is equal to the marginal utility per dollar of the last milkshake.

> **Conclusion** *If the marginal utility per last dollar spent on each good is equal and the entire budget is spent, total utility is maximized.*

To convince yourself that two Big Macs and two milkshakes do indeed maximize total utility, consider any other combination Bob could buy with $8. All others

EXHIBIT 3	Marginal Utility for Big Macs and Milkshakes (Utils per Day)				
	Big Macs			**Milkshakes**	
Quantity	MU	MU/P		MU	MU/P
1	8	4		6	3
2	4	2		4	2
3	2	1		1	1/2
4	1	1/2		0	0

Note: The price per Big Mac and per milkshake is $2.

yield lower total utility. Suppose Bob were to buy three Big Macs and one milk-shake. The third Big Mac adds 2 utils, but giving up the second milkshake subtracts 4 utils. As a result, total utility falls by 2 utils. Or can Bob maximize utility if he were to eat only one Big Mac and drink three milkshakes? The extra utility of the third milkshake is 1 util, but this is less than the 4 utils he would lose by saying no to the second Big Mac. In this case, total utility would fall by 3 utils.

The above example demonstrates the utility-maximizing concept of consumer equilibrium. Consumer equilibrium is a condition in which total utility cannot increase by spending more of a given budget on one good and spending less on another good. Suppose Bob knows not only the exact marginal utility of consuming Big Macs and milkshakes, but also the marginal utility of french fries, pizza, and other goods. To obtain the highest possible satisfaction, Bob allocates his budget so the last dollar spent on good *A*, the last on good *B*, and so on yield equal *MU/P* ratios. Consumer equilibrium can be restated algebraically as

$$\frac{MU \text{ of good } A}{\text{Price of good } A} = \frac{MU \text{ of good } B}{\text{Price of good } B} = \frac{MU \text{ of good } Z}{\text{Price of good } Z}$$

> **Consumer equilibrium**
> A condition in which total utility cannot increase by spending more of a given budget on one good and spending less on another good.

The letters *A, B, ... Z* indicate all the goods and services purchased by the consumer with a given budget.

From Consumer Equilibrium to the Law of Demand

Understanding the law of diminishing marginal utility and consumer equilibrium provides you with a new set of tools to explore the law of demand. Let's begin with a straightforward link between the law of diminishing marginal utility and the demand curve. Declining marginal utility from consuming more Big Macs and milkshakes means each extra quantity consumed is less important or valuable to the consumer. Therefore, as the quantity consumed increases and the marginal utility falls, Bob is willing to pay less per Big Mac and milkshake. Thus, Bob's individual demand curve conforms to the law of demand and is downward sloping.

A more complete explanation of the law of demand combines diminishing marginal utility and consumer equilibrium. Suppose Bob reaches consumer equilibrium as follows:

$$\frac{MU \text{ of Big Mac}}{\text{Price of Big Mac}} = \frac{MU \text{ of milkshake}}{\text{Price of milkshake}}$$

$$\frac{4 \text{ utils}}{\$2} = \frac{4 \text{ utils}}{\$2}$$

Now suppose the price of a Big Mac falls to $1 and upsets the above equality. This changes the formula to the following:

$$\frac{MU \text{ of Big Mac}}{\text{Price of Big Mac}} > \frac{MU \text{ of milkshake}}{\text{Price of milkshake}}$$

$$\frac{4 \text{ utils}}{\$1} > \frac{4 \text{ utils}}{\$2}$$

Now Bob gains more utility per dollar by buying a Big Mac rather than a milkshake. To restore maximum total utility, he spends more on Big Macs. The marginal utility of a Big Mac must fall as he buys more. At the same time, the marginal utility of a milkshake must rise as Bob buys fewer. A fall in the price of Big Macs therefore causes Bob to buy more Big Macs. Voilà! The law of demand.

CHECKPOINT

When Dining Out, Do You Eat Smart?

Welcome to José's Hacienda! Beside each dish, the menu lists the total utility from each item. If you have $15 to spend, which meal will you order to achieve consumer equilibrium?

José's Hacienda Menu

Tacos – $3 each	Flan* – $2 each	Coke – $1 each
1 taco (99 utils)	1 flan (40 utils)	1 Coke (25 utils)
2 tacos (162 utils)	2 flans (48 utils)	2 Cokes (29 utils)
3 tacos (174 utils)	3 flans (50 utils)	3 Cokes (32 utils)

* Mexican dessert.

Income and Substitution Effects and the Law of Demand

Since utility is not measurable, it is desirable to have an alternative explanation of demand. Economists offer the following two complementary explanations for the law of demand, which do not rely on utility.

Income Effect

One reason people buy more of a good when the price falls is the effect of a price change on real income. The *nominal,* or *money,* amount of your paycheck is simply the number of dollars you earn. On the other hand, price changes alter your *real* income. A rise in prices decreases purchasing power, and a fall in prices increases purchasing power, ceteris paribus.

Suppose your weekly nominal income is $100 and you decide to stock up on Pepsi-Cola (a normal good). If the price per quart is $1, you can afford to buy 100 quarts this week. If the price is instead $0.50 per quart and the prices of other goods remain constant, you are richer because of the rise in purchasing power. As a result, you can buy 200 quarts of Pepsi-Cola without giving up any other goods, or less than 200 quarts and more of other goods. As predicted by the law of demand, the lower price for Pepsi-Cola causes real income to rise and, in turn, causes the quantity demanded to rise. This relationship between changes in real income and your ability to buy goods and services is the income effect. The income effect is the change in quantity demanded of a good or service caused by a change in real income (purchasing power).

Income effect

The change in quantity demanded of a good or service caused by a change in real income (purchasing power).

YOU'RE THE ECONOMIST   Testing the Law of Demand
with White Rats   *Applicable Concepts: substitution effect*

Economists often envy the controlled laboratory experiments of biologists and other scientists. In the real world, the economist is unable to observe consumer behavior without prices of other goods, expectations, and other factors changing. So it is no wonder that the idea of studying the behavior of white rats to test the law of demand was intriguing. The question was whether the consumer choice of a white rat supports the downward-sloping demand curve.

Standard laboratory rats were placed in experimental cages with two levers. If a rat pressed one lever, nonalcoholic Collins mix was the reward. Pressing the second lever rewarded the rat with root beer. It seems rats are fond of these two beverages. Each rat was given a limited "income" of lever presses per day. After, say, 300 presses, a light above the lever went out, signaling the daily budget was gone. The next day the light was turned on, and the rat was given a new income of lever presses. The "price" of each good corresponded to the number of lever pushes required to obtain one

milliliter of liquid. For example, if the number of pushes per milliliter for Collins mix released increased by 10 percent, this equaled a 10 percent increase in the price of Collins mix.

The crucial test was to measure the substitution effect resulting from a change in price. As explained in the text, a change in price sets in motion both an income effect and a substitution effect. In the experiment, the price of Collins mix was lowered by decreasing the number of pushes required per milliliter. At the same time, the price of root beer was raised by increasing the number of pushes required per milliliter. To eliminate the income effect, the number of lever presses was raised to compensate for loss of purchasing power. For example, if a rat purchased 4 milliliters of Collins mix per day and 11 milliliters of root beer before the price change, it would be given enough extra pushes after the price change to still purchase these quantities.

In one experiment, a male albino rat was given 300 pushes per day for 2 weeks, and both liquids

were priced at 20 pushes per milliliter. The rat soon settled into a consistent consumption pattern of 4 milliliters of Collins mix and 11 milliliters of root beer per day. Then the experimenters made changes in prices and income. The price (pushes per milliliter) of Collins mix was cut in half, and the price of root beer was doubled. At the same time, the total income of pushes was increased just enough to allow the rat to afford its initial consumption pattern. Stated differently, the income effect was eliminated in order to focus on the substitution effect. After 2 weeks of decisions under the new conditions, the rat changed its consumption pattern to 17 milliliters of Collins mix and 8 milliliters of root beer per day.

ANALYZE THE ISSUE

Based on the behavior of the rat described above, what do you conclude about the substitution effect and the slope of the demand curve?

Source: From John H. Kagel, Raymond C. Battalio, Howard Rachlin, and Leonard Green, "Demand Curves for Animal Consumers," *The Quarterly Journal of Economics*, 96:1 (February 1981), pp. 1–16. © 1981 by the President and Fellows of Harvard College and the Massachusetts Institute of Technology.

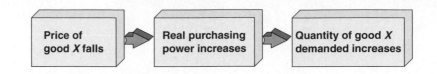

Substitution Effect

There is another reason why the change in a good's price causes a change in the quantity demanded. This reason has to do with changing *relative prices,* that is, the price of one good compared to that of another. If the price of Pepsi falls and the price of Coke remains unchanged, Pepsi becomes a better buy. As a result, many consumers will switch from Coke and other beverages and buy Pepsi. Just as the law of demand predicts, this is an increase in quantity demanded. With the price of Pepsi lower than before, the substitution effect causes people to substitute Pepsi for the now relatively more expensive Coke. The substitution effect is the change in quantity demanded of a good or service caused by a change in its price relative to substitutes.

Substitution effect

The change in quantity demanded of a good or service caused by a change in its price relative to substitutes.

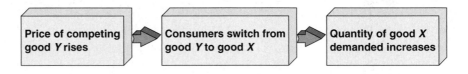

Above we discussed the income and the substitution effects separately, but they are complementary explanations for the downward-sloping demand curve.

> **Conclusion** *When the price of a normal good falls, the income effect and the substitution effect combine to cause the quantity demanded to increase.*

Some students express relief that this conclusion has no reference to the untidy word *utility.*

CHECKPOINT

Does the Substitution Effect Apply to Buying a Car?

Jenny Tanaka wants to buy a new car, and the annual gasoline expense is a major consideration. Her present car gets 25 miles per gallon (mpg), and she is looking at a new car that gets 40 mpg. Jenny now drives about 12,000 miles per year and pays $3.25 per gallon of gasoline. She therefore calculates an annual gasoline consumption of 480 gallons for her 25 mpg car (12,000 miles/25 mpg) compared to 300 gallons consumed per year for the 40 mpg car (12,000 miles/40 mpg). Since driving the higher mileage car would use 180 gallons less per year, Jenny estimates the new car will save her $585 in gasoline expense per year (180 gallons × $3.25 per gallon). Suppose Jenny buys the 40 mpg car. Do you predict Jenny will have an annual gasoline savings equal to $585, less than $585, or more than $585?

KEY CONCEPTS

Utility
Total utility
Marginal utility

Law of diminishing marginal
    utility
Consumer equilibrium

Income effect
Substitution effect

SUMMARY

- *Utility* is the satisfaction or pleasure derived from consumption of a good or service. Actual measurement of utility is impossible, but economists assume it can be measured by a fictitious unit called the *util*.
- *Total utility* is the total level of satisfaction derived from all units of a good or service consumed. *Marginal utility* is the change in total utility from a 1-unit change in the quantity of a good or service consumed.

Relationship between marginal and total utility

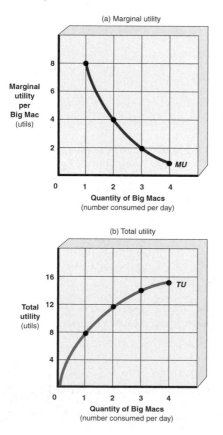

- The *law of diminishing marginal utility* states that the marginal utility of a good or service eventually declines as consumption increases.
- *Consumer equilibrium* is the condition of reaching the maximum level of satisfaction, given a budget, when the marginal utility per dollar spent on each good purchased is equal. Consumer equilibrium and the law of diminishing marginal utility can be used to derive a downward-sloping demand curve. When the price of a good falls, consumer equilibrium no longer holds because the marginal utility per dollar for the good rises. To restore equilibrium, the consumer must increase consumption. As the quantity demanded increases, the marginal utility falls until equilibrium is again achieved. Thus, the price falls, and the quantity demanded rises, as predicted by the law of demand.

$$\frac{MU \text{ of good } A}{\text{price of good } A} = \frac{MU \text{ of good } B}{\text{price of good } B} = \frac{MU \text{ of good } Z}{\text{price of good } Z}$$

- The *income effect* and the *substitution effect* are complementary explanations for the law of demand. When the price changes, these effects work in combination to change the quantity demanded in the opposite direction. As the price falls, real purchasing power increases, causing an increase in the consumer's willingness and ability to purchase a good or service. This is the *income effect*. Also, as the price falls, the consumer substitutes the cheaper good for other goods that are now relatively more expensive. This is the *substitution effect*.

SUMMARY OF CONCLUSION STATEMENTS

- If the marginal utility per last dollar spent on each good is equal and the entire budget is spent, total utility is maximized.

- When the price of a normal good falls, the income effect and the substitution effect combine to cause the quantity demanded to increase.

STUDY QUESTIONS AND PROBLEMS

1. Does a dollar given to a rich person raise the rich person's total utility more than a dollar given to a poor person raises the poor person's total utility?

2. Do you agree with the following statement? "If you like tacos, you should consume as many as you can."

3. This week you have gone to two parties. Assume the total utility you gained from these parties is 100 utils. Then you go to a third party, and your total utility rises to 110 utils. What is the marginal utility of the third party attended per week? Given the law of diminishing marginal utility, what will happen to total utility and marginal utility when you go to a fourth party this week?

4. Suppose your marginal utility for meals at the campus cafeteria this week has fallen to zero. Explain what has happened to your total utility curve derived from consuming these meals. Now explain what will happen to total utility if you eat more meals at the cafeteria this week.

5. Suppose you consume 3 pounds of beef and 5 pounds of pork per month. The price of beef is $1.50 per pound, and pork is $2.00 per pound. Assuming you have studied economics and achieved consumer equilibrium, what is the ratio of the marginal utility of beef to the marginal utility of pork?

6. Suppose the marginal utility of a Coke is 15 utils and its price is $1. The marginal utility of a pizza is 20 utils, and its price is $2. If you buy 1 unit of each good, will you achieve consumer

equilibrium? If not, how can greater total utility be obtained?

7. Explain the relationship between the law of diminishing marginal utility and the law of demand.

8. Consider the table below, which lists James's marginal utility schedule for steak and hamburger meals:

Steak meals per month	Marginal utility of steak meals	Price per steak meal	Hamburger meals per month	Marginal utility of hamburger meals	Price per hamburger meal
1	20	$10	1	15	$5
2	15	10	2	8	5
3	12	10	3	6	5
4	10	10	4	4	5
5	8	10	5	2	5

Given a budget of $45, how many steak and hamburger meals will James buy per month to maximize his total utility? What is the total utility realized?

9. Using the marginal utility schedule in question 8, begin in consumer equilibrium, and assume the price per hamburger meal falls from $5 to $2, all other factors held constant. What is the total utility realized?

10. Suppose the price of a BMW falls. Explain the law of demand based on the income and substitution effects.

For Online Exercises, go the text Web site at www.cengage.com/economics/tucker.

CHECKPOINT ANSWERS ✓

When Dining Out, Do You Eat Smart?
Start with one taco (99 marginal utils/$3, or 33 marginal utils/$1). Then order a Coke (25 marginal utils/$1). Next, order another taco (63 marginal utils/$3, or 21 marginal utils/$1). Now treat yourself to a flan (40 marginal utils/$2, or 20 marginal utils/$1). Finish it all with a second flan (4 marginal utils/$1), another Coke (4 marginal utils/$1), and a third taco (4 marginal utils/$1). You have now spent your entire $15 budget. If you said, following the principle of consumer equilibrium, you would order two Cokes, two flans, and three tacos, although not a very nutritious choice, **YOU ARE CORRECT.**

Does the Substitution Effect Apply to Buying a Car?
Buying a higher mpg car will reduce the cost per mile of driving relative to substitutes, such as riding a bus, train, or airplane. As the cost of driving falls, the substitution effect predicts Jenny will drive more in the 40 mpg car than the 12,000 miles she now drives per year in the 25 mpg car. The extra cost of gasoline for driving over 12,000 miles per year in the 40 mpg car must be subtracted from the $585 savings that was based on the assumption that Jenny's miles driven per year would remain unchanged when she bought the 40 mpg car. If you said Jenny will save less than $585, **YOU ARE CORRECT.**

PRACTICE QUIZ

For an explanation of the correct answers, please visit the tutorial at www.cengage.com/economics/tucker.

1. As an individual consumes more of a given good, the marginal utility of that good to the consumer
   a. rises at an increasing rate.
   b. rises at a decreasing rate.
   c. falls.
   d. rises.

2. The amount of added utility that a consumer gains from the consumption of one more unit of a good is called
   a. incremental utility.
   b. total utility.
   c. diminishing utility.
   d. marginal utility.

3. A certain consumer buys only food and compact discs. If the quantity of food bought increases, while that of compact discs remains the same, the marginal utility of food will
   a. fall relative to the marginal utility of compact discs.
   b. rise relative to the marginal utility of compact discs.
   c. rise, but not as fast as the marginal utility of compact discs rises.
   d. fall, but not as fast as the marginal utility of compact discs falls.

4. Rational consumers will continue to consume two goods until the
   a. marginal utility per dollar's worth of the two goods is the same for the last dollar spent on each good.
   b. marginal utility is the same for each good for the last dollar spent on each good.
   c. prices of the two goods are equal for the last dollar spent on each good.
   d. prices of the two goods are unequal.

5. Assume that a person's consumption of just the right amounts of pork and chicken is in equilibrium. We can conclude that the
   a. marginal utility of pork must equal the marginal utility of chicken.
   b. price of pork must equal the price of chicken.

PRACTICE QUIZ CONTINUED

c. ratio of marginal cost to price must be the same in both the pork and the chicken markets.

d. ratio of marginal utility to price must be the same for pork and chicken.

6. Assume an individual consumes only milk and doughnuts and has arranged consumption so that the last glass of milk yields 12 utils and the last doughnut 6 utils. If the price of milk is $1 per glass and the price of a doughnut is $0.50, we can conclude that the

a. consumer should consume less milk and more doughnuts.

b. price of milk is too high relative to doughnuts.

c. consumer should consume more milk and fewer doughnuts.

d. consumer is in equilibrium.

7. Suppose an individual consumes pizza and cola. To reach consumer equilibrium, the individual must consume pizza and cola so that the

a. price paid for the two goods is the same.

b. marginal utility of the two goods is equal.

c. ratio of marginal utility to price is the same for both goods.

d. ratio of the marginal utility of cola to the marginal utility of pizza is 1.

8. A state of consumer equilibrium for goods consumed prevails when the

a. marginal utility of all goods is the same for the last dollar spent for each good.

b. marginal utility per dollar's worth of two goods is the same for the last dollar spent for each good.

c. price of two goods is the same for the last dollar spent for each good.

d. marginal cost per dollar spent on two goods is the same for the last dollar spent for each good.

9. The change in quantity demanded resulting from a change in purchasing power is known as the

a. income effect.

b. substitution effect.

EXHIBIT 4

Total Utility for Multiplex Tickets, Video Rentals, and Popcorn

Total Utility from Multiplex Tickets	Total Utility from Video Rentals	Total Utility from Popcorn
1 movie (30 utils)	1 video (14 utils)	1 bag (8 utils)
2 movies (54 utils)	2 videos (24 utils)	2 bags (13 utils)
3 movies (72 utils)	3 videos (30 utils)	3 bags (15 utils)
4 movies (84 utils)	4 videos (32 utils)	4 bags (16 utils)

c. law of demand.

d. consumer equilibrium effect.

10. In Exhibit 4, assume Multiplex tickets cost $6 each, video rentals cost $2 each, and bags of popcorn cost $1 each. What is the marginal utility of renting a third video?

a. 6 utils

b. 8 utils

c. 10 utils

d. 30 utils

11. In Exhibit 4, assume Multiplex tickets cost $6 each, video rentals cost $2 each, and bags of popcorn cost $1 each. Suppose the consumer has $12 per week to spend on Multiplex tickets, video rentals, and popcorn. What combination of goods will give the consumer the most utility?

a. 1 movie, 3 videos, and no popcorn

b. 1 movie, 2 videos, and 2 bags of popcorn

c. 1 movie, 1 video, and 4 bags of popcorn

d. 2 movies, no videos, and no bags of popcorn

12. In Exhibit 4, assume the Multiplex tickets cost $6 each, video rentals cost $2 each, and bags of popcorn cost $1 each. Suppose the consumer has $12 per week to spend on multiplex tickets, video rentals, and popcorn. In consumer equilibrium, what is the marginal utility per dollar for each of the three goods?

a. 5 utils per dollar

b. 9 utils per dollar

c. 13 utils per dollar
d. 22 utils per dollar

13. The law of diminishing marginal utility exists for the first 4 units of a good if they have marginal utilities of
a. 1, 2, 4, 8.
b. 8, 4, 1, 2.
c. 4, 8, 2, 1.
d. 8, 4, 2, 1.

14. The demand curve is downward sloping because of the law of
a. diminishing marginal utility.
b. diminishing consumer equilibrium.
c. consumer equilibrium.
d. diminishing utility maximization.

15. The total utilities associated with the first 5 units of consumption of good X are 15, 30, 40, 47, and 50, respectively. What is the marginal utility associated with the third unit?
a. 15
b. 70
c. 85
d. 10
e. 45

Indifference Curve Analysis

This appendix explains another version of consumer choice theory based on indifference curves and budget lines.

Constructing an Indifference Curve

Let's begin with an experiment to find out a consumer's consumption preferences for quantities of two goods. The consumer samples a number of pairs of servings with various ounces of lobster tail and steak (surf and turf). Each time the same question is asked, "Would you prefer serving A or serving B?" After numerous trials, suppose the consumer states indifference between eating choices A-D shown in Exhibit A-1. This means the consumer is just as satisfied having either 7 ounces of steak and 4 ounces of lobster (A), or 3 ounces of steak and 8 ounces of lobster (D), or either of the other two combinations of B or C. Interpretation of the curve connecting these points is that each of these choices yields the same total utility because no choice is preferred to any other choice. Since, as explained in the chapter, there is no such thing as a utility meter, this approach is actually a method for determining equal levels of satisfaction or total utility for different bundles of goods without an exact measure of utils. The curve derived from this experimental data is called an indifference curve. Note that not only points A, B, C, and D but all other points on the smooth curve connecting them are equally satisfactory combinations to the consumer.

Why Indifference Curves Are Downward Sloping and Convex

If total utility is the same at all points along the indifference curve, then consuming more of one good must mean less of the other is consumed. Given this condition, movement along the indifference curve generates a curve with a negative slope. Suppose a consumer moves in marginal increments between any two combination points in Exhibit A-1. For instance, say the consumer decides to move from point A to point B and consume an extra ounce of lobster. To do so, the consumer increases total utility ($+MU$) by consuming an extra quantity of lobster.

However, since by definition total utility is constant everywhere along the curve, the consumer must give up a quantity of steak (2 ounces) in order to reduce total utility ($-MU$) by precisely enough to offset the gain in total utility from the extra lobster.

The inverse relationship between goods along the downward-sloping indifference curve means that the absolute value of the slope of an indifference curve equals what is called the marginal rate of substitution (MRS). The MRS is the rate at which a consumer is willing to substitute one good for another with no change in total utility. Begin at A and move to B along the curve. The slope and MRS of the curve is $-2/1$, or simply 2, when the minus sign is removed to give the absolute value. This is the

Indifference curve

A curve showing the different combinations of two products that yield the same satisfaction or total utility to a consumer.

Marginal rate of substitution (MRS)

The rate at which a consumer is willing to substitute one good for another without a change in total utility. The MRS equals the slope of the indifference curve at any point on the curve.

EXHIBIT A-1   A Consumer's Indifference Curve

Points *A, B, C, D* and each point along the curve represent a combination of steak and lobster that yields equal total utility for a given consumer. Stated differently, the consumer is indifferent between consuming servings having quantities represented by all points composing the indifference curve.

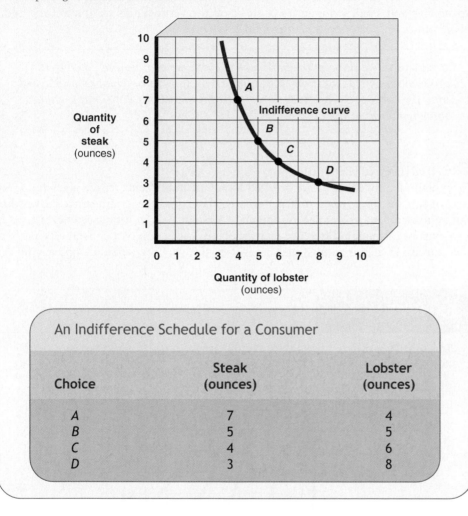

An Indifference Schedule for a Consumer

Choice	Steak (ounces)	Lobster (ounces)
A	7	4
B	5	5
C	4	6
D	3	8

consumer's subjective willingness to substitute *A* for *B*. At point *A*, the consumer has a substantial amount of steak and relatively little lobster. Therefore, the consumer is willing to forgo or "substitute" 2 ounces of steak to get 1 more ounce of lobster. In other words, the marginal utility of losing each ounce of steak between *A* and *B* is low compared to the marginal utility of gaining each ounce of lobster.

Now suppose the consumer moves from *B* to *C*, and the slope changes to 1/1 (*MRS* = 1). Between these two points, the consumer is willing to substitute 1 ounce of steak for an equal quantity of lobster. This means that between *B* and *C* the marginal utility lost per ounce of steak equals the marginal utility gained from each ounce of lobster, while total utility remains constant. Finally, assume the consumer moves from *C* to *D*. Here the slope equals 1/2 (MRS = 1/2) because the consumer at point C has a substantial amount of lobster and relatively little steak. Consequently, the marginal utility lost from giving up 1 ounce of steak equals twice the marginal utility gained from an additional ounce of lobster.

As we see in this example, as the quantity of lobster increases along the horizontal axis, the marginal utility of additional ounces of lobster decreases. Correspondingly, as the quantity of steak decreases along the vertical axis, its marginal utility increases. So moving down the curve means the consumer is willing to give up smaller and smaller quantities of steak on the vertical axis to obtain each additional ounce of lobster on the horizontal axis.

> **Conclusion** *The slope of the indifference curve is negative and equal to the marginal rate of substitution (MRS), which declines as one moves downward along the curve. The result is a curve with a diminishing slope that is convex (bowed inward) to the origin.*

The Indifference Map

Indifference map
A selection of indifference curves with each curve representing a different level of satisfaction or total utility.

As explained above, any point selected along an indifference curve gives the same level of satisfaction or total utility. Actually, there are other indifference curves that can be drawn for a consumer. As shown in Exhibit A-2, indifference curves I_1 to I_6 also exist to form an indifference map, which is a selection of a consumer's indifference curves. In fact, if all possible curves were drawn, they would completely fill the

---

EXHIBIT A-2   A Consumer's Indifference Map

An indifference map is a selected set of indifference curves. Along curves farther from the origin, it is possible to select more of both goods compared to indifference curves closer to the origin. Therefore, curves farther from the origin are preferred because they yield higher levels of total utility.

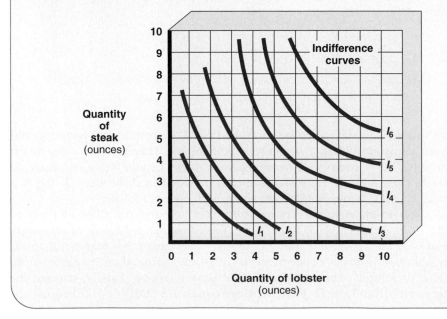

space between the axes because there would be so many. And it is important to note that each curve reflects a different level of total utility. Also, each curve moving from the origin in the northeasterly direction from I_1 to I_6 and beyond yields higher total utility. This is reasonable because at each higher indifference curve the consumer is able to select more of both goods and therefore be better off. To verify this concept, select a combination on one indifference curve in Exhibit A-2 and then select a combination of more of both goods on a higher indifference curve.

> **Conclusion** *Each consumer has a set of indifference curves that form a map. Since consumers wish to achieve the highest possible total utility, they always prefer curves farther from the origin where they can select more quantities of two goods.*

The Budget Line

Having considered the consumer's preferences for steak and lobster in the indifference map, the next step is to see what the consumer can afford. The consumer's ability to purchase steak and lobster is limited or constrained by the amount of money (income) that the consumer has to spend and the prices of the two goods. Suppose the consumer likes to go to a fine restaurant and budgets $10 per week to dine on surf and turf. The price of steak is $1 per ounce, and the price of lobster is $2 an ounce. If the consumer spends the entire budget on steak, 10 ounces of steak can be purchased. At the other extreme, the whole budget could be spent for lobster, and 5 ounces would be purchased. As shown in Exhibit A-3, and given the consumption possibilities of buying fractions of ounces of steak and lobster, a range of choices can be purchased along the budget line ranging from 10 ounces on the steak axis to 5 ounces on the lobster axis. The table in this exhibit computes selected whole-unit combinations that each equal a $10 total expenditure.

> **Budget line**
> A line that shows the different combinations of two goods a consumer can purchase with a given amount of money and prices for the goods.

> **Conclusion** *The budget line represents various combinations of goods that a consumer can purchase at given prices with a given budget.*

Computing the slope of the budget line requires some shorthand mathematical notation. Let B represent the amount of money the consumer has to spend on steak and lobster. Also, let P_l and P_s represent the prices of lobster and steak, respectively, and L and S represent the ounces of lobster and steak, respectively. Given this notation, the budget line may be expressed as

$$P_l L + P_s S = B$$

In order to express the equation in slope-intercept form, divide both sides by P_s and get

$$\frac{P_l}{P_s} L + S = \frac{B}{P_s}$$

Solving for S yields

$$S = \frac{B}{P_s} - \frac{P_l}{P_s} L$$

EXHIBIT A-3 A Consumer's Budget Line

A budget line shows all the possible combinations of goods that can be purchased with a given budget and given prices for these goods.

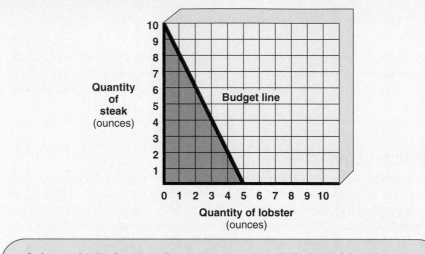

Selected Whole-Unit Consumption Possibilities of Steak and Lobster Affordable with a $10 Budget

Choice	Ounces of steak (price = $1/ounce)	Ounces of lobster (price = $2/ounce)	Total expenditure
A	10	0	$10 ($10 + $0)
B	8	1	$10 ($8 + $2)
C	4	3	$10 ($4 + $6)
D	2	4	$10 ($2 + $8)
E	0	5	$10 ($0 + $10)

Note that S is a linear function of L with a vertical intercept of B/P_s and a slope of $-P_l/P_s$. Since the price of lobster is $2 an ounce and the price of steak is $1 per ounce, the slope of the budget line is -2 or 2 as an absolute value.

Conclusion *The slope of the budget line equals the ratio of the price of good X on the horizontal axis divided by the price of good Y on the vertical axis. Expressed as a formula:*

$$\text{slope of budget line} = P_x/P_y$$

A Consumer Equilibrium Graph

Exhibit A-4 shows the budget line from Exhibit A-3 superimposed on an indifference map. This allows us to easily compare consumer preferences and affordability. The utility-maximizing combination is the equilibrium point X where the budget

EXHIBIT A-4 | Consumer Equilibrium

Consumer equilibrium is at point X, where the budget line is tangent to the highest attainable indifference curve, I_2. Only at this point does the marginal rate of substitution (MRS) along I_2 equal the slope of the budget line, which equals the price ratio P_l/P_s. Although point Y is on a higher curve, I_3, and would yield a greater total utility than X, point Y is beyond the budget line and therefore is unattainable by the consumer. Point Z is on a lower indifference curve, but it will not be chosen. The consumer can move upward along the budget line by shifting dollars from purchases of lobster to purchases of steak and reach point X on the higher indifference curve I_2.

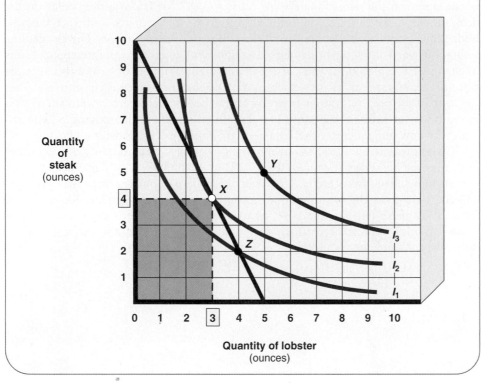

line is just tangent to the highest attainable indifference curve, I_2, and the quantity of steak purchased is tangent to the highest attainable indifference curve, I_2, and the quantity of steak purchased is 4 ounces and the quantity of lobster is 3 ounces.

As explained in Exhibit A-5 of the appendix to Chapter 1, the slope of a straight line tangent to a curve is equal to the slope of the curve at that point. This mathematical relationship translates into the economic interpretation of the tangency condition in this appendix. At the point of tangency, the MRS equals the slope of the budget line. At point X, the slope is the price ratio $P_l/P_s = 2$ from Exhibit A-3, and, therefore, it follows that $MRS = 2$ at point X on curve I_2 in Exhibit A-4. At any other combination, the MRS will not be equal to the price ratio, and the consumer will reallocate the budget until equilibrium is achieved at point X.

Conclusion *Consumer equilibrium occurs where the budget line is tangent to the highest attainable indifference curve. At this unique point, MRS = slope (price ratio of P_x/P_y).*

Derivation of the Demand Curve

This appendix concludes with Exhibit A-5, which shows how the demand curve for lobster can be derived from a map of two indifference curves. The table in this exhibit reproduces the table from Exhibit A-3 and adds column (4) with the price of lobster equal to $1 per ounce, rather than $2 per ounce. Now compare columns (3) and (4) in the table. Holding the price of steak constant at $1 per ounce and the budget equal to $10, the consumer can afford to purchase more lobster at each choice except A, where the entire budget is spent on steak. The top graph is drawn from Exhibit A-4 where at point X the price of lobster is $2 per ounce and the quantity demanded of lobster is 3 ounces. In the bottom graph of Exhibit A-5, this is one point on the demand curve for lobster at X'. To find another point on the demand curve, we decrease the price of lobster to $1 per ounce and trace the new budget line points from column (4) of the table onto the top graph. The budget line swings outward along the horizontal axis, but the original vertical intercept remains unchanged. The reason the vertical axis remains at 10 ounces of steak is because the price of steak is still at $1 per ounce, and if the consumer spends the entire $10 on steak, then the price of lobster is irrelevant to the vertical intercept. However, at a lower price for lobster, the consumer can afford more lobster moving downward along the new budget line with the same $10 budget because lobster is cheaper.

Given the new budget line shown in the top graph in Exhibit A-5, the consumer finds that the higher indifference curve, I_3, is now attainable. As a result, consumer equilibrium moves from point X to point Y', where 7 ounces of lobster are purchased. This gives the corresponding second point Y shown in the lower graph. Connecting these two points allows us to draw the consumer's demand curve for lobster. Voila! Consistent with the law of demand, the demand curve is indeed downward sloping.

EXHIBIT A-5 | Deriving the Demand Curve

In the top part of this exhibit, the initial budget line intersects the highest attainable indifference curve, I_2, at point X with the price of steak equal to $1 per ounce and the price of lobster equal to $2 per ounce. Holding the budget and the price of steak constant at $10 and $1, respectively, the price of lobster drops to $1 per ounce. As a result, the budget line shifts to intersect the higher indifference curve, I_3, at point Y.

The bottom part of the exhibit corresponds points X and Y to points X' and Y'. At $2 per ounce for lobster, the consumer buys 3 ounces. At $1 per ounce for lobster, the consumer buys 7 ounces. Connecting these two points results in a downward-sloping demand curve.

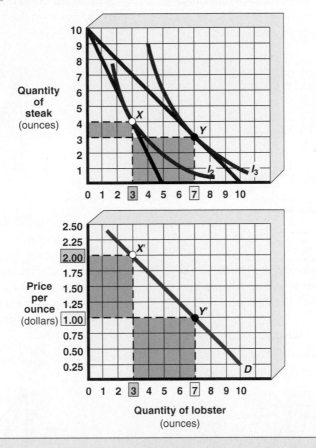

Selected Whole-Unit Combinations of Steak and Lobster Affordable with a $10 Budget

(1) Choice	(2) Ounces of steak (price = $1/ounce)	(3) Ounces of lobster (price = $2/ounce)	(4) Ounces of lobster (price = $1/ounce)	(5) Total expenditure
A	10	0	$0	$10 ($10 + $0)
B	8	1	2	$10 ($8 + $2)
C	4	3	6	$10 ($4 + $6)
D	2	4	8	$10 ($2 + $8)
E	0	5	10	$10 ($0 + $10)

KEY CONCEPTS

Indifference curve   Marginal rate of substitution (*MRS*)   Indifference map   Budget line

SUMMARY

- An *indifference curve* shows the different quantity combinations of two goods that give the same satisfaction or total utility to a consumer.

  Indifference curve

  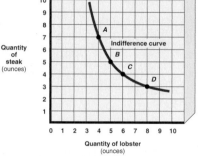

- The *marginal rate of substitution (MRS)* is the rate at which a consumer is willing to substitute one good for another with no change in total utility.
- An *indifference map* is a selection of a consumer's indifference curves.

  Indifference map

  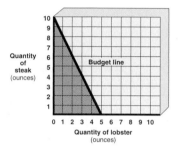

- The *budget line* gives the different combinations of two goods that a consumer can purchase with a given amount of money and relative prices for the goods. The slope of the budget line equals the

price of the good on the horizontal axis divided by the price on the vertical axis.

  Budget line

  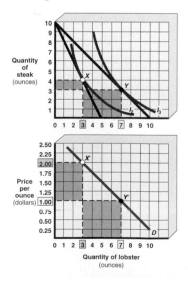

- *Consumer equilibrium* occurs where the budget line is tangent to the highest possible indifference curve, as shown originally at point *X*. If the price of one good falls, then the consumer equilibrium changes to point *Y* on a higher indifference curve. Connecting the two corresponding price-quantity points *X'* and *Y'* generates a downward-sloping demand curve.

  Consumer equilibrium

SUMMARY OF CONCLUSION STATEMENTS

- The slope of the indifference curve is negative and equal to the marginal rate of substitution (MRS), which declines as one moves downward along the curve. The result is a curve with a diminishing slope that is convex (bowed inward) to the origin.
- Each consumer has a set of indifference curves that form a map. Since consumers wish to achieve the highest possible total utility, they always prefer curves farther from the origin, where they can select more quantities of two goods.

- The budget line represents various combinations of goods that a consumer can purchase at given prices with a given budget.
- The slope of the budget line equals the ratio of the price of good X on the horizontal axis divided by the price of good Y on the vertical axis. Expressed as a formula: slope $= P_x/P_y$.
- Consumer equilibrium occurs where the budget line is tangent to the highest attainable indifference curve. At this unique point, $MRS =$ slope (price ratio of P_x/P_y).

STUDY QUESTIONS AND PROBLEMS

1. Suppose a consumer's marginal rate of substitution is three slices of pizza for one coke. If the price of a coke is $1 and the price of three slices of pizza is $2, would the consumer change his or her consumption combination?

2. Let M represent the quantity of medical services, such as the number of doctor visits, and let O represent the quantity of other goods purchased by a consumer in a given year. Let the budget (B) be in thousands of dollars and the price of medical services and other goods be in terms of dollars per unit, with $B = 60$, $P_m = 6$, and $P_o = 10$.
   a. Graph the budget line and determine the slope.
   b. Show the result if the price of medical services (P_o) decreases to $5.
   c. Add two indifference curves to the graph that are tangent to the budget line and explain the result.

3. Assume that the data in the following table are an indifference curve for a consumer:
   a. Graph this indifference curve and label "Quantity of Y" on the vertical axis and

   "Quantity of X" on the horizontal axis. Label the points A–D.
   b. Assume the consumer's budget is $12 and the prices of X and Y are $1.00 and $1.50, respectively. Draw the budget line in the above graph.
   c. What combination of X and Y will the consumer purchase?
   d. What is the value of the MRS and the slope (P_x/P_y) at consumer equilibrium?
   e. Beginning with the graph drawn in (a) above, explain and draw graphs to derive a demand curve for X.

Choice	Units of Y	Units of X
A	10	2
B	6	4
C	4	6
D	2	12

PRACTICE QUIZ

For an explanation of the correct answers, please visit the tutorial at www.cengage. com/economics/tucker.

1. An indifference curve consists of quantity combinations of two goods that yield
   a. equal marginal utilities.
   b. negative marginal utilities.
   c. the same price ratios.

   d. the same total satisfaction.

2. The absolute value of the slope of an indifference curve is called the
   a. marginal rate of transformation.

b. transitivity slope.
c. indifference rate of preference.
d. marginal rate of substitution.

3. The slope of the indifference curve for goods X and Y is called the marginal
   a. product rate.
   b. rate of transformation.
   c. rate of substitution.
   d. rate of utility.

4. Given the prices of two goods, all quantity combinations inside the budget line are
   a. indifferent.
   b. efficient.
   c. unattainable.
   e. attainable.

5. Assume the price of good X is P_x, price of good Y is P_y, and B is the budget. The formula for the budget line for these two goods is
   a. $P_y Q_y / P_x O_x$.
   b. $P_x B + P_y B = B$.
   c. $P_x X + P_y Y = B$.
   d. $(1 - P_y / B)\, P_x$.

6. The ratio of the price of good X on the horizontal axis to the price of good Y on the vertical axis is the _____ of the budget line.
   a. marginal rate
   b. slope
   c. marginal utility
   d. equalization rate

7. Assume P_x is the price of good X on the horizontal axis and P_y is the price of good Y on the vertical axis. The slope of the budget line equals
   a. $P_y / P_x Y$.
   b. $P_y Q_y / P_x Q_x$.
   c. $(1 - P_y / P_x)$.
   d. P_x / P_y.

8. Consumer equilibrium occurs where the budget line is tangent to the
   a. lowest possible indifference curve.
   b. highest possible indifference curve.
   c. utility-maximizing indifference curve.
   d. utility-equalization indifference curve.

9. Only at the point of consumer equilibrium does the marginal rate of substitution (MRS) equal the
   a. slope of the budget line.

b. slope of the indifference curve.
c. price ratio.
d. all of the above.

10. At point A in Exhibit A-6, consumers would be
    a. spending all of their income but not maximizing total utility.
    b. spending all of their income and maximizing total utility.
    c. maximizing total utility without spending all of their income.
    d. none of the above.

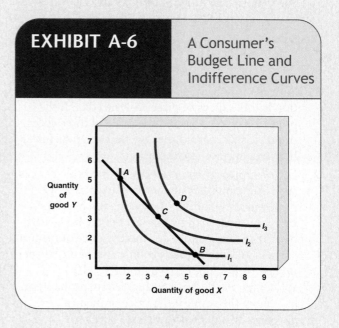

EXHIBIT A-6   A Consumer's Budget Line and Indifference Curves

11. The consumer equilibrium shown in Exhibit A-6 is located at point
    a. A.
    b. B.
    c. C.
    d. D.

12. In Exhibit A-6, point D is
    a. a consumer equilibrium.
    b. unattainable, given the consumer's current budget constraint.
    c. a point that does not exhaust all of the consumer's income.
    d. none of the above.

Production Costs

S uppose you dream of owning your own company. That's right! You want to be an entrepreneur. You crave the excitement of starting your own firm and making it successful. Instead of working for someone else, you want to be your own boss. You are under no illusions; it is going to take hard work and sacrifice.

You are an electrical engineer who is an expert at designing electronic components for cell phones and similar applications. So you quit your job and invest your nest egg in starting Computech (a mythical company). You lease factory space, hire employees, and purchase raw materials, and soon your company's products begin rolling off the assembly line. And then you find production cost considerations influence each decision you make in this new business venture.

The purpose of this chapter is to study production and its relationship to various types of costs. Whether your company is new and small or an international giant, understanding costs is essential for success. In this chapter and the next two chapters, you will follow Computech and learn the basic principles of production and the way various types of costs vary with output.

In this chapter, you will learn to solve these economic puzzles:

- Why would an accountant say a firm is making a profit and an economist say it is losing money?

- What is the difference between the short run and the long run?

- How can a company make a profit with a free Web site?

Costs and Profit

A basic assumption in economics is that the motivation for business decisions is profit maximization. Economists realize that managers of firms sometimes pursue other goals, such as contributing to the United Way or building an empire for the purpose of ego satisfaction. Nevertheless, the profit maximization goal has proved to be the best theory to explain why managers of firms choose a particular level of output or price. To understand profit as a driving force for business firms, we must distinguish between the way economists measure costs and the way accountants measure costs.

Explicit and Implicit Costs

Explicit costs

Payments to nonowners of a firm for their resources.

Economists define the total opportunity cost of a business as the sum of *explicit costs* and *implicit costs*. Explicit costs are payments to nonowners of a firm for their resources. In our Computech example, explicit costs include the wages paid to labor, the rental charges for a plant, the cost of electricity, the cost of materials, and the cost of medical insurance. These resources are owned outside the firm and must be purchased with actual payments to these "outsiders."

Implicit costs

The opportunity costs of using resources owned by the firm.

Implicit costs are the opportunity costs of using resources owned by the firm. These are opportunity costs of resources because the firm makes no actual payments to outsiders. When you started Computech, you gave up the opportunity to earn a salary as an electrical engineer for someone else's firm. When you invested your nest egg in your own enterprise, you gave up the opportunity to earn interest. You also used a building you own to warehouse Computech products. Although you made no payment to anyone, you gave up the opportunity to earn rental payments.

Economic and Accounting Profit

In everyday use, the word *profit* is defined as follows:

$$\text{Profit} = \text{total revenue} - \text{total cost}$$

Economists call this concept *accounting profit*. This popular formula is expressed in economics as

$$\text{Accounting profit} = \text{total revenue} - \text{total explicit cost}$$

Economic profit

Total revenue minus explicit and implicit costs.

Because economic decisions include implicit as well as explicit costs, economists use the concept economic profit instead of accounting profit. Economic profit is total revenue minus explicit and implicit costs. Economic profit can be positive, zero, or negative (an economic loss). Expressed as an equation:

$$\text{Economic profit} = \text{total revenue} - \text{total opportunity costs}$$

or

$$\text{Economic profit} = \text{total revenue} - (\text{explicit costs} + \text{implicit costs})$$

Exhibit 1 illustrates the importance of the difference between accounting profit and economic profit. Computech must know how well it is doing, so you hire an accounting firm to prepare a financial report. The exhibit shows that Computech

EXHIBIT 1	Computech's Accounting Profit versus Economic Profit	
Item	Accounting Profit	Economic Profit
Total revenue	$500,000	$500,000
Less explicit costs:		
Wages and salaries	400,000	400,000
Materials	50,000	50,000
Interest paid	10,000	10,000
Other payments	10,000	10,000
Less implicit costs:		
Forgone salary	0	50,000
Forgone rent	0	10,000
Forgone interest	0	5,000
Equals profit	$30,000	–$35,000

earned total revenue of $500,000 in its first year of operation. Explicit costs for wages, materials, interest, and other payments totaled $470,000. Based on standard accounting procedures, this left an accounting profit of $30,000.

If the analysis ends with accounting profit, Computech is profitable. But accounting practice overstates profit. Because implicit costs are subjective and therefore difficult to measure, accounting profit ignores implicit costs. A few examples will illustrate the importance of implicit costs. Your $50,000-a-year salary as an electrical engineer was forgone in order to spend all your time as owner of Computech. Also forgone were $10,000 in rental income and $5,000 in interest that you would have earned during the year by renting your building and putting your savings in the bank. Subtracting both explicit and implicit costs from total revenue, Computech had an economic loss of $35,000. The firm is failing to cover the opportunity costs of using its resources in the electronics industry. Thus, the firm's resources would earn a higher return if used for other alternatives.

How would you interpret a zero economic profit? It's not as bad as it sounds. Economists call this condition normal profit. Normal profit is the minimum profit necessary to keep a firm in operation. Zero economic profit signifies there is just enough total revenue to pay the owners for all explicit and implicit costs. Stated differently, there is no benefit from reallocating resources to another use. For example, assume an owner earns zero economic profit, including an implicit (forfeited) cost of $50,000 per year that could have been earned working for someone else. This means the owner earned as much as would have been earned in the next best employment opportunity.

Normal profit
The minimum profit necessary to keep a firm in operation. A firm that earns normal profits earns total revenue equal to its total opportunity cost.

Conclusion *Since business decision making is based on economic profit, rather than accounting profit, the word profit in this text always means economic profit.*

CHECKPOINT

Should the Professor Go or Stay?

Professor Martin is considering leaving the university and opening a consulting business. For her services as a consultant, she would be paid $75,000 a year. To open this business, Professor Martin must convert a house from which she collects rent of $10,000 per year into an office and hire a secretary at a salary of $15,000 per year. Also, she must withdraw $10,000 from savings for miscellaneous expenses and forgo earning 10 percent interest per year. The university pays Professor Martin $50,000 a year. Based only on economic decision making, do you predict the professor will leave the university to start a new business?

Short-Run Production Costs

Having presented the basic definitions of total cost, the next step is to study cost theory. In this section, we explore the relationship between output and cost in the short run. In the next section, the time horizon shifts to the long run.

Short Run versus Long Run

Suppose I asked you, "What is the difference between the short run and the long run?" Your answer might be that the short run is less than a year and the long run is over a year. Good guess, but wrong! Economists do not partition production decisions based on any specific number of days, months, or years. Instead, the distinction depends on the ability to vary the quantity of inputs or resources used in production. There are two types of inputs—*fixed inputs* and *variable inputs*. A fixed input is any resource for which the quantity cannot change during the period of time under consideration. For example, the physical size of a firm's plant and the production capacity of heavy machines cannot easily change within a short period of time. They must remain as fixed amounts while managers decide to vary output. In addition to fixed inputs, the firm uses *variable inputs* in the production process. A variable input is any resource for which the quantity can change during the period of time under consideration. For example, managers can hire fewer or more workers during a given year. They can also change the amount of materials and electricity used in production.

Now we can link the concepts of fixed and variable inputs to the *short run* and the *long run*. The short run is a period of time so short that there is at least one fixed input. For example, the short run is a period of time during which a firm can increase output by hiring more workers (variable input), while the size of the firm's plant (fixed input) remains unchanged. The firm's plant is the most difficult input to change quickly. The long run is a period of time so long that all inputs are variable. In the long run, the firm can build new factories or purchase new machinery. New firms can enter the industry, and existing firms may leave the industry.

The Production Function

Having defined inputs, we can now describe how these inputs are transferred into outputs using a concept called a production function. A production function is the relationship between the maximum amounts of output a firm can produce and

Fixed input

Any resource for which the quantity cannot change during the period of time under consideration.

Variable input

Any resource for which the quantity can change during the period of time under consideration.

Short run

A period of time so short that there is at least one fixed input.

Long run

A period of time so long that all inputs are variable.

Production function

The relationship between the maximum amounts of output that a firm can produce and various quantities of inputs.

various quantities of inputs. An assumption of the production function model we are about to develop is that the level of technology is fixed. Technological advances would mean more output is possible from a given quantity of inputs.

Exhibit 2(a) presents a short-run production function for Eaglecrest Vineyard. The variable input is the number of workers employed per day, and each worker is presumed to have equal job skills. The acreage, amount of fertilizer, and all other inputs are assumed to be fixed; therefore, our production model is operating in the short run. Employing zero workers produces no bushels of grapes. A single worker

---

EXHIBIT 2 — A Production Function and the Law of Diminishing Returns

Part (a) shows how the total output of bushels of grapes per day increases as the number of workers increases while all other inputs remain constant. This figure is a short-run production function, which relates outputs to a one-variable input while all other inputs are fixed.

Part (b) illustrates the law of diminishing returns. The first worker adds 10 bushels of grapes per day, and marginal product is 10 bushels per day. Adding a second worker adds another 12 bushels of grapes per day to total output. This is the range of increasing marginal returns. After two workers, diminishing marginal returns set in, and marginal product declines continuously.

Short-Run Production Function of Eaglecrest Vineyard

(1) Labor Input (number of workers per day)	(2) Total Output (bushels of grapes per day)	(3) Marginal Product (bushels of grapes per day) [Δ(2)/Δ(1)]
0	0	
		10
1	10	
		12
2	22	
		11
3	33	
		9
4	42	
		6
5	48	
		2
6	50	

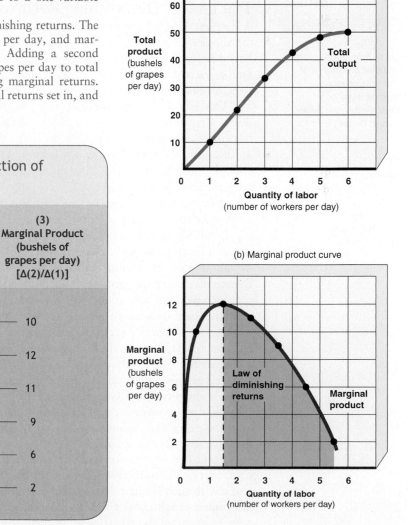

(a) Total output curve

(b) Marginal product curve

can produce 10 bushels per day, but a lot of time is wasted when one worker picks, loads containers, and transports the grapes to the winery. Adding a second worker raises output to 22 bushels per day because the workers divide the tasks and specialize. Adding four more workers raises total product to 50 bushels per day.

Marginal Product

The relationship between changes in total output and changes in labor is called the marginal product of labor. Marginal product is the change in total output produced by adding one unit of a variable input, with all other inputs used being held constant. When Eaglecrest increases labor from zero to one worker, output rises from zero to 10 bushels produced per day. This increase is the result of the addition of one more worker. Therefore, the marginal product so far is 10 bushels per worker. Similar marginal product calculations generate the marginal product curve shown in Exhibit 2(b). Note that marginal product is plotted at the midpoints shown in the table because the change in total output occurs between each additional unit of labor used.

The Law of Diminishing Returns

A long-established economic law called the law of diminishing returns determines the shape of the marginal product curve. The law of diminishing returns states that beyond some point the marginal product decreases as additional units of a variable factor are added to a fixed factor. Because the law of diminishing returns assumes fixed inputs, this principle is a short-run, rather than a long-run, concept.

This law applies to production of both agricultural and nonagricultural products. Returning to Exhibit 2, we can identify and explain the law of diminishing returns in our Eaglecrest example. Initially, the total output curve rises quite rapidly as this firm hires the first two workers. The marginal product curve reflects the change in the total output curve because marginal product is the slope of the total output curve. As shown in Exhibit 2(b), the range from zero to two workers hired is called *increasing marginal returns*. In this range of output, the last worker hired adds more to total output than the previous worker.

Diminishing returns begin after the second worker is hired and the marginal product reaches its peak. Beyond two workers, diminishing returns occur, and the marginal product declines. The short-run assumption guarantees this condition. Eventually, marginal product falls because the amount of land per worker falls as more workers are added to fixed quantities of land and other inputs used to produce wine. Similar reasoning applies to the Computech example introduced in the chapter preview. Assume Computech operates with a fixed plant size and a fixed number of machines and all other inputs except the number of workers are fixed. Those in the first group of workers hired divide the most important tasks among themselves, specialize, and achieve increasing returns. Then diminishing returns begin and continue as Computech employs each additional worker. The reason is that as more workers are added, they must share fixed inputs, such as machinery. Some workers are underemployed because they are standing around waiting for a machine to become available. Also, as more workers are hired, there are fewer important tasks to perform. As a result, marginal product declines. In the extreme case, marginal product would be negative. At some number of workers, they must work with such limited floor space, machines, and other fixed inputs that they start stepping on each other's toes. No profit-seeking firm would ever hire workers with zero or negative marginal product. Chapter 11 explains the labor market in more detail and shows how Computech decides exactly how many workers to hire.

Marginal product

The change in total output produced by adding one unit of a variable input, with all other inputs used being held constant.

Law of diminishing returns

The principle that beyond some point the marginal product decreases as additional units of a variable factor are added to a fixed factor.

Short-Run Cost Formulas

To make production decisions in either the short run or the long run, a business must determine the costs associated with producing various levels of output. Using Computech, you will study the relationship between two "families" of short-run costs and output: first, the total cost curves, and next, the average cost curves.

Total Cost Curves

Total Fixed Cost   As production expands in the short run, costs are divided into two basic categories—*total fixed cost* and *total variable cost*. Total fixed cost (*TFC*) consists of costs that do not vary as output varies and that must be paid even if output is zero. These are payments that the firm must make in the short run regardless of the level of output. Even if a firm, such as Computech, produces nothing, it must still pay rent, interest on loans, property taxes, and fire insurance. Fixed costs are therefore beyond management's control in the short run. The total fixed cost for Computech is $100, as shown in column 2 of Exhibit 3.

Total Variable Cost   As the firm expands from zero output, total variable cost is added to total fixed cost. Total variable cost (*TVC*) consists of costs that are zero when output is zero and vary as output varies. These costs relate to the costs of variable inputs. Examples include wages for hourly workers, electricity, fuel, and raw materials. As a firm uses more input to produce output, its variable costs will increase. Management can control variable costs in the short run by changing the level of output. Exhibit 3 lists the total variable cost for Computech in column 3.

Total Cost   Given total fixed cost and total variable cost, the firm can calculate total cost (*TC*). Total cost is the sum of total fixed cost and total variable cost at each level of output. As a formula:

$$TC = TFC + TVC$$

Total cost for Computech is shown in column 4 of Exhibit 3. Exhibit 4(a) uses the data in Exhibit 3 to construct graphically the relationships between total cost, total fixed cost, and total variable cost. Note that the *TVC* curve varies with the level of output and the *TFC* curve does not. The *TC* curve is simply the *TVC* curve plus the vertical distance between the *TC* and *TVC* curves, which represents *TFC*.

Average Cost Curves

In addition to total cost, firms are interested in the *per-unit cost,* or *average cost.* Average cost, like product price, is stated on a per-unit basis. The last three columns in Exhibit 3 are *average fixed cost (AFC), average variable cost (AVC),* and *average total cost (ATC).* These average, or per-unit, curves are also shown in Exhibit 4(b). These three concepts are defined as follows:

Average Fixed Cost   As output increases, average fixed cost (*AFC*) falls continuously. Average fixed cost is total fixed cost divided by the quantity of output produced. Written as a formula:

$$AFC = \frac{TFC}{Q}$$

Total fixed cost (*TFC*)
Costs that do not vary as output varies and that must be paid even if output is zero. These are payments that the firm must make in the short run, regardless of the level of output.

Total variable cost (*TVC*)
Costs that are zero when output is zero and vary as output varies.

Total cost (*TC*)
The sum of total fixed cost and total variable cost at each level of output.

Average fixed cost (*AFC*)
Total fixed cost divided by the quantity of output produced.

EXHIBIT 3   Short-Run Cost Schedule for Computech

(1) Total Product (Q)	(2) Total Fixed Cost (TFC)	(3) Total Variable Cost (TVC)	(4) Total Cost (TC)	(5) Marginal Cost (MC)	(6) Average Fixed Cost (AFC)	(7) Average Variable Cost (AVC)	(8) Average Total Cost (ATC)
0	$100	$ 0	$100		—	—	—
				$ 50			
1	100	50	150		$100	$50	$150
				34			
2	100	84	184		50	42	92
				24			
3	100	108	208		33	36	69
				19			
4	100	127	227		25	32	57
				23			
5	100	150	250		20	30	50
				30			
6	100	180	280		17	30	47
				38			
7	100	218	318		14	31	45
				48			
8	100	266	366		13	33	46
				59			
9	100	325	425		11	36	47
				75			
10	100	400	500		10	40	50
				95			
11	100	495	595		9	45	54
				117			
12	100	612	712		8	51	59

As shown in Exhibit 4(b), the *AFC* curve approaches the horizontal axis as output expands. This is because larger output numbers divide into *TFC* and cause *AFC* to become smaller and smaller.

Average variable cost (AVC)

Total variable cost divided by the quantity of output produced.

Average Variable Cost   The average variable cost (*AVC*) in our example forms a U-shaped curve. Average variable cost is total variable cost divided by the quantity of output produced. Written as a formula:

$$AVC = \frac{TVC}{Q}$$

EXHIBIT 4 Short-Run Cost Curves

The curves in this exhibit are derived by plotting data from Exhibit 3. Part (a) shows that the total cost (*TC*) at each level of output is the sum of total variable cost (*TVC*) and total fixed cost (*TFC*). Because the *TFC* curve does not vary with output, the shape of the *TC* curve is determined by the shape of the *TVC* curve. The vertical distance between the *TC* and the *TVC* curves is *TFC*.

In Part (b), the marginal cost (*MC*) curve decreases at first, then reaches a minimum, and then increases as output increases. The *MC* curve intersects both the average variable cost (*AVC*) curve and the average total cost (*ATC*) curve at the minimum point on each of these cost curves. The average fixed cost (*AFC*) curve declines continuously as output expands. *AFC* is also the difference between the *ATC* and the *AVC* curves at any quantity of output.

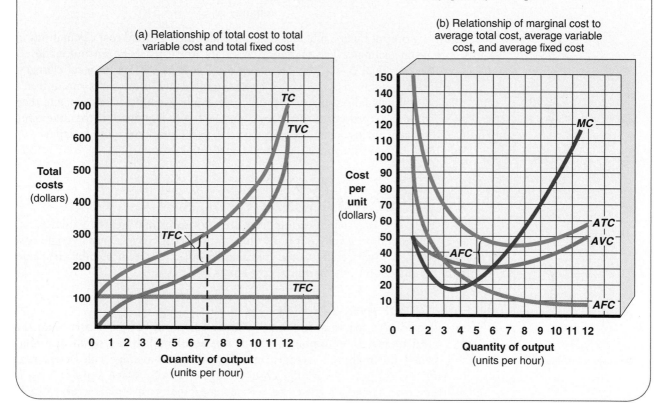

The *AVC* curve is also drawn in Exhibit 4(b). At first, the *AVC* curve falls, and then after an output of 6 units per hour, the *AVC* curve rises. Thus, the *AVC* curve is U-shaped. The explanation for the shape of the *AVC* curve is given in the next section.

Average Total Cost Average total cost (*ATC*) is sometimes referred to as *per-unit cost*. The average total cost is total cost divided by the quantity of output produced. Written as a formula:

> **Average total cost (ATC)**
> Total cost divided by the quantity of output produced.

$$AVC = AFC + AVC = \frac{TC}{Q}$$

Like the *AVC* curve, the *ATC* curve is U-shaped, as shown in Exhibit 4(b). At first, the *ATC* curve falls because its component parts—*AVC* and *AFC*—are falling. As output continues to rise, the *AVC* curve begins to rise, while the *AFC* curve falls continuously. Beyond the output of 7 units per hour, the rise in the AVC curve is greater than the fall in the AFC curve, which causes the ATC curve to rise in a U-shaped pattern.

Marginal Cost   Marginal analysis asks how much it costs to produce an *additional* unit of output. Column 5 in Exhibit 3 is marginal cost (MC). Marginal cost is the change in total cost when one additional unit of output is produced. Stated differently, marginal cost is the ratio of the change in total cost to a one-unit change in output. Written as a formula:

$$MC = \frac{\text{change in } TC}{\text{change in } Q}$$

Changing output by one unit at a time simplifies the marginal cost calculations in our Computech example. The marginal cost data are listed between output levels to show that marginal cost is the change in total cost as the output level changes. Exhibit 4(b) shows this marginal cost schedule graphically. In the short run, a firm's marginal cost initially falls as output expands, eventually reaches a minimum, and then rises, forming a J-shaped curve. Note that marginal cost is plotted at the midpoints because the change in cost actually occurs between each additional unit of output.

Exhibit 5 summarizes a firm's short-run cost relationships.

Marginal Cost Relationships

Part (b) of Exhibit 4 presents two important relationships that require explanation. First, we will explain the rule that links the marginal cost curve to the average cost curve. Second, we will return to the marginal product curve in Exhibit 2(b) and explain its connection to the marginal cost curve.

The Marginal-Average Rule

Observe that the MC curve in Exhibit 4(b) intersects both the AVC curve and the ATC curve at their minimum points. This is not accidental. It is a result of a relationship called the marginal-average rule. The marginal-average rule states that when marginal cost is below average cost, average cost falls. When marginal cost is above average cost, average cost rises. When marginal cost equals average cost, average cost is at its minimum point. The marginal-average rule applies to grades, weights, and any average figure.

Perhaps the best way to understand this rule is to apply it to a noneconomic example. Suppose there are 20 students in your class and each student has a grade point average (GPA) of 4.0. The average GPA of the class is therefore 4.0. Now assume another student who has a GPA of 2.0 joins the class. The new average GPA of 21 students in the class falls to 3.9. The average GPA was pulled down because the *marginal* GPA of the additional student was lower than the *average* GPA of the other students. Now suppose we start with a class of 20 students with a 2.0 GPA and add a student who has a 4.0 GPA. In this case, the new average GPA of the 21 students rises from 2.0 to 2.1. Thus, the *marginal* GPA of the last student was higher than the *average* GPA of all students in class before the addition of the new student.

Now consider the MC curve in Part (b) of Exhibit 4. In the range of output from zero to 6 units per hour, the MC curve is below the AVC curve, and AVC is falling. Beyond 6 units per hour, the MC curve is above AVC, and AVC is rising.

Marginal cost (MC)

The change in total cost when one additional unit of output is produced.

Marginal-average rule

The rule that states when marginal cost is below average cost, average cost falls. When marginal cost is above average cost, average cost rises. When marginal cost equals average cost, average cost is at its minimum point.

EXHIBIT 5	Short-Run Cost Formulas	
Cost Concept	**Formula**	**Graph**
Total Cost (TC)	$TC = TFC + TVC$	
Marginal cost (MC)	$MC = \dfrac{\text{change in } TC}{\text{change in } Q}$	
Average fixed cost (AFC)	$AFC = \dfrac{TFC}{Q}$	
Average variable cost (AVC)	$AVC = \dfrac{TVC}{Q}$	
Average total cost (ATC)	$ATC = \dfrac{TC}{Q}$	

Hence, the relationship between *AVC* and *MC* conforms to the marginal-average rule. It follows that the *MC* curve intersects the *AVC* curve at its lowest point. This analysis also applies to the relationship between the *MC* and *ATC* curves. Initially, the *MC* curve is lower than the *ATC* curve until it reaches its minimum, causing the *ATC* curve to fall. Beginning with 8 units of output, the *MC* curve exceeds the *ATC* curve, causing the ATC curve to rise.

CHECKPOINT

Did Michael Jordan Beat the Marginal-Average Rule?
`Michael Jordan, formerly of the Chicago Bulls, is one of the finest players in the history of basketball. Suppose he had an average of 33 points per game over the first 10 games of the season and then scored 20, 25, 40, 50, and 20 points in the next five games. Did Michael Jordan beat the marginal-average rule?

Marginal Cost's Mirror Image

Since the MC curve determines the U-shape of the AVC and ATC curves, we must explain the J-shape of the MC curve. Exhibit 6 illustrates that the shape of the MC curve is the mirror reflection of the shape of the marginal product (MP) curve. Comparing Parts (a) and (b) of Exhibit 6 gives the following:

> **Conclusion** *The marginal cost declines as the marginal product of a variable input rises if the wage rate is constant. Beginning at the point of diminishing returns, the marginal cost rises as the marginal product of a variable input declines.*

As explained earlier in this chapter, the law of diminishing returns is the declining portion of the MP curve that corresponds to the rising portion of the MC curve. To understand why this relationship exists, we return to the case of Eaglecrest Vineyard presented earlier in Exhibit 2. Now we again assume that labor is the only variable input and add the new important assumption that the wage rate is constant at $100 per day. When Eaglecrest moves from zero labor to hire one worker, its total output rises from zero to 10 bushels of grapes per day. As explained earlier, the marginal product is also 10 bushels, and the marginal cost is $100/10 = $10 ($\Delta TC/\Delta Q = \Delta TC/MP$). When Eaglecrest hires the second worker, total output rises by 12 bushels per day. Hiring this worker increases the firm's total cost by $100, while the marginal product rises to 12 bushels. The marginal cost of the second worker therefore falls to a minimum at $100/12 = $8.33. At this point, it is noteworthy that the minimum point on the MC curve corresponds to the maximum point on the MP curve. The third worker hired yields only 11 additional bushels of grapes per day, so marginal cost rises to $9.09. Thus, diminishing returns begin with the third worker, and the marginal cost continues to rise as more workers are hired.

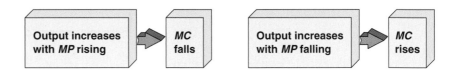

Long-Run Production Costs

As explained earlier in this chapter, the long run is a time period long enough to change the quantity of all fixed inputs. A firm can, for example, build a larger or smaller factory or vary the capacity of its machinery. In this section, we will discuss how varying factory size and *all* other inputs in the long run affects the relationship between production and costs.

Long-Run Average Cost Curves

Suppose Computech is making its production plans for the future. Taking a long-run view of production means the firm is not locked into a small, medium, or large factory. However, once a factory of any particular size is built, the firm operates in the short run because the plant becomes a fixed input.

EXHIBIT 6 — The Inverse Relationship between Marginal Product and Marginal Cost

Part (a) represents the marginal product of labor (*MP*) curve. At first, each additional worker hired adds more to output than does the previously hired worker, and the *MP* curve rises until a maximum is reached at two workers hired. At three workers, the law of diminishing returns sets in, and each additional worker hired adds less output than previously hired workers.

Part (b) shows the marginal cost (*MC*) curve is a J-shaped curve that is inversely related to the *MP* curve. Assuming the wage rate remains constant, as the *MP* curve rises, the *MC* curve falls. When the *MP* curve reaches a maximum at two workers, the *MC* curve is at a minimum. As diminishing returns set in and the *MP* curve falls, the *MC* curve rises.

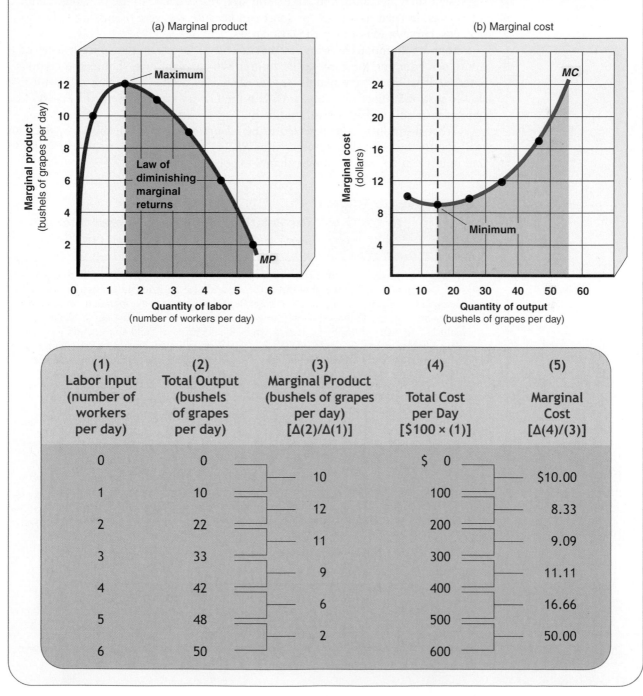

(1) Labor Input (number of workers per day)	(2) Total Output (bushels of grapes per day)	(3) Marginal Product (bushels of grapes per day) [Δ(2)/Δ(1)]	(4) Total Cost per Day [$100 × (1)]	(5) Marginal Cost [Δ(4)/(3)]
0	0		$ 0	
		10		$10.00
1	10		100	
		12		8.33
2	22		200	
		11		9.09
3	33		300	
		9		11.11
4	42		400	
		6		16.66
5	48		500	
		2		50.00
6	50		600	

> **Conclusion** *A firm operates in the short run when there is insufficient time to alter some fixed input. The firm plans in the long run when all inputs are variable.*

Exhibit 7 illustrates a situation in which there are only three possible factory sizes Computech might select. Short-run cost curves representing these three possible plant sizes are labeled $SRATC_s$, $SRATC_m$, and $SRATC_l$. SR is the abbreviation for short run, and ATC stands for average total cost. The subscripts s, m, and l represent small, medium, and large plant size, respectively. In the previous sections, there was no need to use SR for short run because we were discussing only short-run cost curves and not long-run cost curves.

Suppose Computech estimates that it will be producing an output level of 6 units per hour for the foreseeable future. Which plant size should the company choose? It will build the plant size represented by $SRATC_s$ because this affords a lower cost of $30 per unit (point A) than the factory size represented by $SRATC_m$, which has a cost of $40 per unit (point B).

What if production is expected to be 12 units per hour? In this case, the firm will choose the plant size represented by $SRATC_l$. At this plant size, the cost is $30 per unit (point C), which is lower than $40 per unit (point D).

EXHIBIT 7 — The Relationship between Three Factory Sizes and the Long-Run Average Cost Curve

Each of the three short-run ATC curves in the exhibit corresponds to a different plant size. Assuming these are the only three plant-size choices, a firm can choose any one of these plant sizes in the long run. For example, a young firm may operate a small plant represented by the U-shaped short-run average total cost ($SRATC_s$) curve. As a firm matures and demand for its product expands, it can decide to build a larger factory, corresponding to either $SRATC_m$ or $SRATC_l$. The long-run average cost ($LRAC$) curve is the green shaded scalloped curve joining the short-run curves below their intersections.

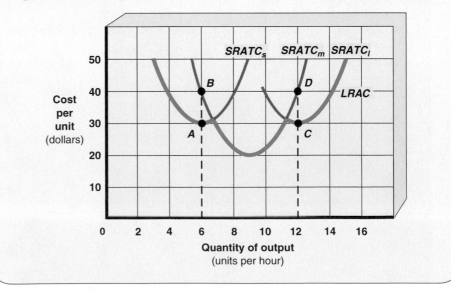

Conclusion *The plant size selected by a firm in the long run depends on the expected level of production.*

Using the three short-run average cost curves shown in Exhibit 7, we can construct the firm's long-run average cost curve (*LRAC*). The long-run average cost curve traces the lowest cost per unit at which a firm can produce any level of output after the firm can build any desired plant size. The *LRAC* curve is often called the firm's planning curve. In Exhibit 7, the green shaded curve represents the *LRAC* curve.

Exhibit 8 shows there are actually an infinite number of possible plant sizes from which managers can choose in the long run. As the intersection points of the short-run *ATC* curves move closer and closer together, the lumps in the *LRAC* curve in Exhibit 7 disappear. With a great variety of plant sizes, the corresponding short-run *ATC* curves trace a smooth *LRAC* curve in Exhibit 8. When the *LRAC* curve falls, the tangency points are to the left of the minimum points on the short-run *ATC* curves. As the *LRAC* curve rises, the tangency points are to the right of the minimum points on the short-run *ATC* curves.

Different Scales of Production

Exhibit 8 depicts long-run average cost as a U-shaped curve. In this section, we will discuss the reasons why the *LRAC* curve first falls and then rises when output

> **Long-run average cost curve (*LRAC*)**
>
> The curve that traces the lowest cost per unit at which a firm can produce any level of output when the firm can build any desired plant size.

EXHIBIT 8   The Long-Run Average Cost Curve When the Number of Factory Sizes Is Unlimited

There are an infinite number of possible short-run *ATC* curves that correspond to different plant sizes. The long-run average cost (*LRAC*) curve is the green curve tangent to each of the possible red short-run *ATC* curves.

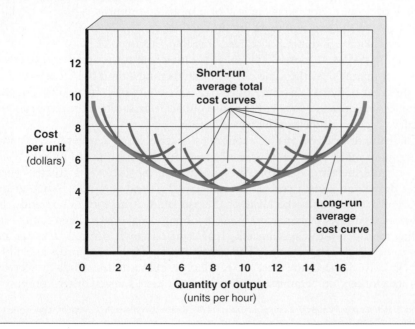

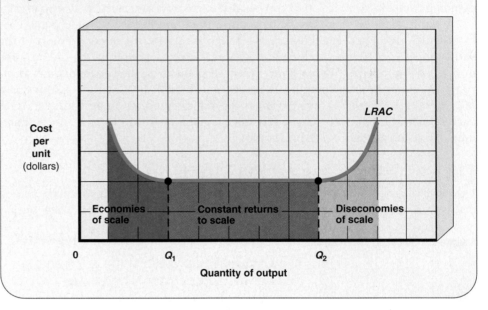

EXHIBIT 9   A Long-Run Average Cost Curve with Constant Returns to Scale

The long-run average cost ($LRAC$) curve illustrates a firm that experiences economies of scale until output level Q_1 is reached. Between output levels Q_1 and Q_2, the $LRAC$ curve is flat, and there are constant returns to scale. Beyond output level Q_2, the firm experiences diseconomies of scale, and the $LRAC$ curve rises.

expands in the long run. In addition, we will learn that the $LRAC$ curve can have a variety of shapes. Note that the law of diminishing returns is not an explanation here because in the long run there are no fixed inputs.

For simplicity, Exhibit 9 excludes possible short-run ATC curves that touch points along the $LRAC$ curve. Typically, a young firm starts small and builds larger plants as it matures. As the scale of operation expands, the $LRAC$ curve can follow three different patterns. Over the lowest range of output from zero to Q_1, the firm experiences economies of scale. Economies of scale exist when the long-run average cost curve declines as the firm increases output.

There are several reasons for economies of scale. First, a larger firm can increase its *division of labor* and *use of specialization*. Adam Smith noted in *The Wealth of Nations,* published in 1776, that the output of a pin factory is greater when one worker draws the wire, a second straightens it, a third cuts it, a fourth grinds the point, and a fifth makes the head of the pin. As a firm initially expands, having more workers allows managers to break a job into small tasks. Then each worker—ncluding managers—can specialize by mastering narrowly defined tasks rather than trying to be a jack-of-all-trades.[1] The classic example is Henry Ford's assembly line, which greatly reduced the cost of producing automobiles. Today, McDonald's trains its workers at "Hamburger University"; then some workers prepare food,

> **Economies of scale**
>
> A situation in which the long-run average cost curve declines as the firm increases output.

---

1. Adam Smith, *An Inquiry into the Nature and Causes of the Wealth of Nations* (1776; reprint, New York: Random House, 1937), pp. 4–6.

YOU'RE THE ECONOMIST

Why Is That Web Site You're Using Free?

Applicable Concepts: economies and diseconomies of scale

Pick the best price that you wish to pay for a product. Is zero reserved only for those who believe in Santa Claus? Recall the famous saying by economist Milton Friedman that "there's no such thing as a free lunch." Well, today more and more Web companies are using digital technology and the principles of *freeconomics* to make profits by giving something away free of charge. And the key to understanding this radical business model is the concept of economies of scale.

How is it possible for companies to cover their production costs with a price of zero? Don't Web businesses have huge fixed costs to buy computer servers and design Web pages? This is true, but once the servers are powered up and the sites are online, the cost of logging in each additional customer is very small. Then, as the companies scale expands over time, the cost of servers, bandwidth, and software are spread out over millions of users, and the long-run cost curve declines to almost zero, which is economies of scale.[1]

In the Web land of free payments called *freemiums,* the basic idea is to shift from the view of a market price matching buyers and sellers of a product to a free system with many participants and only a few who exchange cash. After customers get used to the free services, the companies hope that people will pay for more advanced services. Examples of freemiums are Adobe Reader, search engines, blogging platforms, and Skype-to-Skype phone calls. The revenue from the premiums for more powerful services covers the cost of both the premium and free activities. This is the cross-subsidy approach. A legendary example of this marketing strategy is King Gillette, who in the early 1900s was having no success selling men on the idea of shaving with disposable thin blades rather than with a straight razor. The solution was to bundle free razors with gum, coffee, marshmallows, and even new bank deposits with the slogan "Shave and Save" attached. The freebie razor without blades was useless so customers bought the blades—and the rest of this success story is history.

Another approach is to use free services to deliver advertising, just like traditional broadcast TV or radio. One company that has very successfully applied the advertising approach to freemiums is Google. There is no cost to use their search engine, but the results pages feature "Sponsored Links," which are advertisements paid for by Web sites related to your search terms. Google used this model to achieve impressive financial results.

ANALYZE THE ISSUE

Suppose a hugely successful Web company has used freeconomics, expanded its scale of operations, and spread its long-run costs over larger and larger audiences. After years of profits, the company's profits fell continuously. Using production costs theory, explain why this situation might be occurring.

---

1. Chris Anderson, "Why $0.00 is the Future of Business," March 2008, http://www.wired.com/images/press/pdf/free.pdf.

some specialize in taking orders, and a few workers specialize in the drive-through window operation.

Second, economies of scale result from greater *efficiency of capital*. Suppose machine A costs $1,000 and produces 1,000 units per day. Machine B costs $4,000, but it is technologically more efficient and has a capacity of 8,000 units per day. The low-output firm will find it too costly to purchase machine B, so it uses machine A, and its average cost is $1. The large-scale firm can afford to purchase machine B and produce more efficiently at a per-unit cost of only $0.50.

The *LRAC* curve may not turn upward and form the U-shaped cost curve in Exhibit 8. Between some levels of output, such as Q_1 and Q_2 in Exhibit 9, the *LRAC* curve no longer declines. In this range of output, the firm increases its plant size, but the *LRAC* curve remains flat. Economists call this situation constant returns to scale. Constant returns to scale exist when the long-run average cost curve does not change as the firm increases output. Economists believe this is the shape of the *LRAC* curve in many real-world industries. The scale of operation is important for competitive reasons. Consider a young firm producing less than output Q_1 and competing against a more established firm producing in the constant-returns-to-scale range of output. The *LRAC* curve shows that the older firm has an average cost advantage.

As a firm becomes large and expands output beyond some level, such as Q_2 in Exhibit 9, it encounters diseconomies of scale. Diseconomies of scale exist when the long-run average cost curve rises as the firm increases output. A very large-scale firm becomes harder to manage. As the firm grows, the chain of command lengthens, and communication becomes more complex. People communicate through forms instead of direct conversation. The firm becomes too bureaucratic, and operations bog down in red tape. Layer upon layer of managers are paid big salaries to shuffle papers that have little or nothing to do with beating the competition by producing output at a lower cost. Consequently, it is no surprise that a firm can become too big, and these management problems can cause the average cost of production to rise.

Steven Jobs, founder of Apple Computer Company, stated:

> When you are growing [too big], you start adding middle management like crazy... People in the middle have no understanding of the business, and because of that, they screw up communications. To them, it's just a job. The corporation ends up with mediocre people that form a layer of concrete.[2]

Constant returns to scale
A situation in which the long-run average cost curve does not change as the firm increases output.

Diseconomies of scale
A situation in which the long-run average cost curve rises as the firm increases output.

---

2. Deborah Wise and Catherine Harris, "Apple's New Crusade," *Business Week*, Nov. 26, 1984, p. 156.

KEY CONCEPTS

Explicit costs	Production function	Average variable cost (AVC)
Implicit costs	Marginal product	Average total cost (ATC)
Economic profit	Law of diminishing	Marginal cost (MC)
Normal profit	returns	Marginal-average rule
Fixed input	Total fixed cost (TFC)	Long-run average cost curve ($LRAC$)
Variable input	Total variable cost (TVC)	Economies of scale
Short run	Total cost (TC)	Constant returns to scale
Long run	Average fixed cost (AFC)	Diseconomies of scale

SUMMARY

- *Economic profit* is equal to total revenue minus both *explicit* and *implicit* costs. *Implicit costs* are the opportunity costs of forgone returns to resources owned by the firm. Economic profit is important for decision-making purposes because it includes implicit costs and accounting profit does not. Accounting profit equals total revenue minus explicit costs.

- The *short run* is a time period during which a firm has at least one fixed input, such as its factory size. The *long run* for a firm is defined as a period during which all inputs are variable.

- A *production function* is the relationship between output and inputs. Holding all other factors of production constant, the production function shows the total output as the amount of one input, such as labor, varies.

- *Marginal product* is the change in total output caused by a one-unit change in a variable input, such as the number of workers hired. The *law of diminishing returns* states that after some level of output in the short run, each additional unit of the variable input yields smaller and smaller marginal product. This range of declining marginal product is the region of diminishing returns.

- *Total fixed cost* (TFC) consists of costs that do not vary with the level of output, such as rent for office space. Total fixed cost is the cost of inputs that do not change as the firm changes output in the short run. *Total variable cost* (TVC) consists of costs that vary with the level of output, such as wages. Total variable cost is the cost of variable inputs used in production. *Total cost* (TC) is the

sum of total fixed cost (TFC) and total variable cost (TVC).

Total Cost Curves

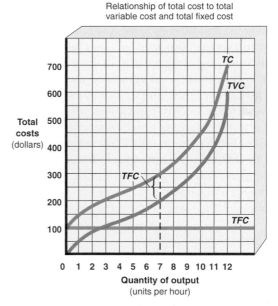

Relationship of total cost to total variable cost and total fixed cost

- *Marginal cost* (**MC**) is the change in total cost associated with one additional unit of output. *Average fixed cost* (**AFC**) is the total fixed cost divided by total output. *Average variable cost* (**AVC**) is the total variable cost divided by total output. *Average total cost* (**ATC**) is the total cost, or the sum of average fixed cost and average variable cost, divided by output.

Average and Marginal Cost Curves

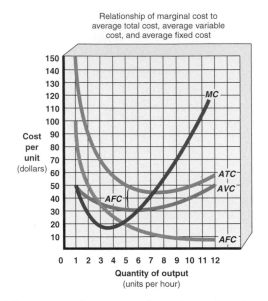

Relationship of marginal cost to average total cost, average variable cost, and average fixed cost

Marginal Cost

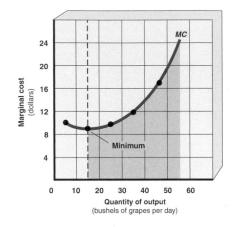

- The *marginal-average rule* explains the relationship between marginal cost and average cost. When marginal cost is less than average cost, average cost falls. When marginal cost is greater than average cost, average cost rises. Following this rule, the marginal cost curve intersects the average variable cost curve and the average total cost curve at their minimum points.
- *Marginal cost* (**MC**) and *marginal product* (**MP**) are mirror images of each other. Assuming a constant wage rate, marginal cost equals the wage rate divided by the marginal product. Increasing returns cause marginal cost to fall, and diminishing returns cause marginal cost to rise. This explains the J-shaped marginal cost curve.

Marginal Product

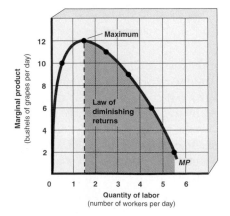

- The *long-run average cost curve* (**LRAC**) is a curve drawn tangent to all possible short-run average total cost curves. When the *LRAC* curve decreases as output increases, the firm experiences *economies of scale*. If the *LRAC* curve remains unchanged as output increases, the firm experiences *constant returns to scale*. If the *LRAC* curve increases as output increases, the firm experiences *diseconomies of scale*.

Long-run Average Cost Curve

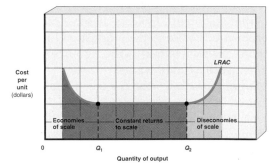

SUMMARY OF CONCLUSION STATEMENTS

- Since business decision making is based on economic profit, rather than accounting profit, the word *profit* in this text always means economic profit.
- The marginal cost declines as the marginal product of a variable input rises if the wage rate is constant. Beginning at the point of diminishing returns, the marginal cost rises as the marginal product of a variable input declines.

- A firm operates in the short run when there is insufficient time to alter some fixed input. The firm plans in the long run when all inputs are variable.
- The plant size selected by a firm in the long run depends on the expected level of production.

STUDY QUESTIONS AND PROBLEMS

1. Indicate whether each of the following is an explicit cost or an implicit cost:
   a. A manager's salary
   b. Payments to IBM for computers
   c. A salary forgone by the owner of a firm by operating his or her own company
   d. Interest forgone on a loan an owner makes to his or her own company
   e. Medical insurance payments a company makes for its employees
   f. Income forgone while going to college

2. Suppose you own a video game store. List some of the fixed inputs and variable inputs you would use in operating the store.

3. a. Construct the marginal product schedule for the production function data in the following table:

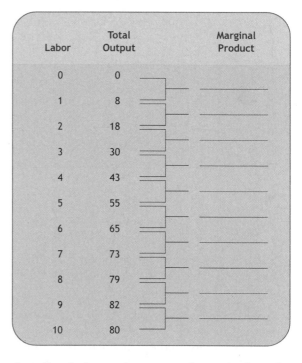

Labor	Total Output	Marginal Product
0	0	
1	8	
2	18	
3	30	
4	43	
5	55	
6	65	
7	73	
8	79	
9	82	
10	80	

   b. Graph the total output and marginal product curves, and identify increasing and diminishing marginal returns.

4. Consider this statement: "Total output starts falling when diminishing returns occur." Do you agree or disagree? Explain.

5. What effect might a decrease in the demand for high definition televisions have on the short-run average total cost curve for this product?

6. a. Construct the cost schedule using the data below for a firm operating in the short run:

Total Output (Q)	Total Fixed Cost (TFC)	Total Variable Cost (TVC)	Total Cost (TC)	Marginal Cost (MC)	Average Fixed Cost (AFC)	Average Variable Cost (AVC)	Average Total Cost (ATC)
0	$ 50	$ ———	$ 50		$ ———	$ ———	$ ———
				$ ———			
1	———	———	$ 70		———	———	———
				———			
2	———	———	$ 85		———	———	———
				———			
3	———	———	$ 95		———	———	———
				———			
4	———	———	$100		———	———	———
				———			
5	———	———	$110		———	———	———
				———			
6	———	———	$130		———	———	———
				———			
7	———	———	$165		———	———	———
				———			
8	———	———	$215		———	———	———
				———			
9	———	———	$275				

b. Graph the average variable cost, average total cost, and marginal cost curves.

7. Explain why the average total cost curve and the average variable cost curve move closer together as output expands.

8. Ace Manufacturing produces 1,000 hammers per day. The total fixed cost for the plant is $5,000 per day, and the total variable cost is $15,000 per day. Calculate the average fixed cost, average variable cost, average total cost, and total cost at the current output level.

9. An owner of a firm estimates that the average total cost is $6.71 and the marginal cost is $6.71 at the current level of output. Explain the relationship between these marginal cost and average total cost figures.

10. What short-run effect might a decline in the demand for electronic components for automatic teller machines have on Computech's average total cost curve?

11. For mathematically minded students, what is the algebraic relationship between the equation for output and the equation for marginal product in Exhibit 2? Explain the circumstances under which the long-run supply curve for an industry is a horizontal line. Next, explain the circumstances under which the long-run supply curve for an industry is an upward-sloping line.

For Online Exercises, go to the text Web site at www.cengage.com/economics/tucker.

CHECKPOINT ANSWERS ✓

Should the Professor Go or Stay?

In the consulting business, the accounting profit is $60,000. An accountant would calculate profit as the annual revenue of $75,000 less the explicit cost of $15,000 per year for the secretary's salary. However, the accountant would neglect implicit costs. Professor Martin's business venture would have implicit costs of $10,000 in forgone rent, $50,000 in forgone earnings, and $1,000 in forgone annual interest on the $10,000 taken out of savings. Her economic profit is –$1,000, calculated as the accounting profit of $60,000 less the total implicit costs of $61,000. If you said the professor will pass up the potential accounting profit and stay with the university to avoid an economic loss, **YOU ARE CORRECT.**

Did Michael Jordan Beat the Marginal-Average Rule?

Since Jordan's marginal points in games 11 and 12 were below his average points per game, his average points per game fell from 33 to 31. Games 13 and 14 lifted his average from 31 to 33 points per game because his marginal points in both of these games exceeded his average points per game. Finally, the 20 points in game 15 again reduced his average back to 32 points per game. Thus, when Jordan's marginal points scored in a game were below his season's average points per game, his average fell. When Jordan's marginal points scored in a game were above his season's average points per game, his average rose. If you said even Michael Jordan cannot beat the marginal-average rule, **YOU ARE CORRECT.**

Game	Marginal Points	Average Points
10		33 over 10 games
11	20	$32 = (33 \times 10 + 20)/11$ games
12	25	$31 = (32 \times 11 + 25)/12$ games
13	40	$32 = (31 \times 12 + 40)/13$ games
14	50	$33 = (32 \times 13 + 50)/14$ games
15	20	$32 = (33 \times 14 + 20)/15$ games

PRACTICE QUIZ

For an explanation of the correct answers, please visit the tutorial at www.cengage.com/economics/tucker.

1. Explicit costs are payments to
   a. hourly employees.
   b. insurance companies.
   c. utility companies.
   d. all of the above.

2. Implicit costs are the opportunity costs of using the resources of
   a. outsiders.
   b. owners.
   c. banks.
   d. retained earnings.

3. Which of the following equalities is *true*?
   a. Economic profit = total revenue − accounting profit

   b. Economic profit = total revenue − explicit costs − accounting profit
   c. Economic profit = total revenue − implicit costs − explicit costs
   d. Economic profit = opportunity cost + accounting cost

4. Fixed inputs are factors of production that
   a. are determined by a firm's plant size.
   b. can be increased or decreased quickly as output changes.
   c. cannot be increased or decreased as output changes.
   d. are none of the above.

PRACTICE QUIZ CONTINUED

5. An example of a variable input is
    a. raw materials.
    b. energy.
    c. hourly labor.
    d. all of the above.

6. Suppose a car wash has two washing stations and five workers and is able to wash 100 cars per day. When it adds a third station, but no more workers, it is able to wash 150 cars per day. The marginal product of the third washing station is
    a. 100 cars per day.
    b. 150 cars per day.
    c. five cars per day.
    d. 50 cars per day.

7. If the units of variable input in a production process are 1, 2, 3, 4, and 5 and the corresponding total outputs are 10, 22, 33, 42, and 48, respectively, the marginal product of the fourth unit is
    a. 2.
    b. 6.
    c. 9.
    d. 42.

8. The total fixed cost curve is
    a. upward sloping.
    b. downward sloping.
    c. upward sloping, then downward sloping.
    d. unchanged with the level of output.

9. Assuming the marginal cost curve is a smooth J-shaped curve, the corresponding total cost curve has a (an)
    a. linear shape.
    b. S-shape.
    c. U-shape.
    d. reverse S-shape.

10. If both the marginal cost and the average variable cost curves are J-shaped, at the point of minimum average variable cost, the marginal cost must be
    a. greater than the average variable cost.
    b. less than the average variable cost.
    c. equal to the average variable cost.
    d. at its minimum.

11. Which of the following is *true* at the point where diminishing returns set in?
    a. Both marginal product and marginal cost are at a maximum.
    b. Both marginal product and marginal cost are at a minimum.
    c. Marginal product is at a maximum, and marginal cost is at a minimum.
    d. Marginal product is at a minimum, and marginal cost is at a maximum.

12. As shown in Exhibit 10, total fixed cost for the firm is
    a. zero.
    b. $250.
    c. $500.
    d. $750.
    e. $1,000.

13. As shown in Exhibit 10, the total cost of producing 100 units of output per day is
    a. zero.
    b. $250.
    c. $500.
    d. $750.
    e. $1,000.

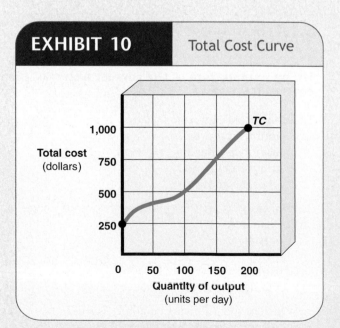

EXHIBIT 10   Total Cost Curve

14. In Exhibit 10, if the total cost of producing 99 units of output per day is $475, the marginal cost of producing the 100th unit of output per day is approximately
    a. zero.
    b. $25.
    c. $475.
    d. $500.

15. Each potential short-run average total cost curve is tangent to the long-run average cost curve at
    a. the level of output that minimizes short-run average total cost.
    b. the minimum point of the average total cost curve.
    c. the minimum point of the long-run average cost curve.
    d. a single point on the short-run average total cost curve.

16. Suppose a typical firm is producing x units of output per day. Using any other plant size, the long-run average cost would increase. The firm is operating at a point at which
    a. its long-run average cost curve is at a minimum.
    b. its short-run average total cost curve is at a minimum.
    c. both (a) and (b) are true.
    d. neither (a) nor (b) is true.

17. The downward-sloping segment of the long-run average cost curve corresponds to
    a. diseconomies of scale.
    b. both economies and diseconomies of scale.
    c. the decrease in average variable costs.
    d. economies of scale.

18. long-run diseconomies of scale exist when the
    a. short-run average total cost curve falls.
    b. long-run marginal cost curve rises.
    c. long-run average total cost curve falls.
    d. short-run average variable cost curve rises.
    e. long-run average cost curve rises.

19. long-run constant returns to scale exist when the
    a. short-run average total cost curve is constant.
    b. long-run average cost curve rises.
    c. long-run average cost curve is flat.
    d. long-run average cost curve falls.

20. Which of the following is *not* a source of economies of scale?
    a. Division and specialization of labor
    b. Increase in output
    c. More efficient use of capital
    d. All of the above
    e. Centralized marketing

Road Map

MICROECONOMIC FUNDAMENTALS

PART 2

This road map feature helps you tie material in the Part together as you travel the Economic Way of Thinking Highway. The following are review questions listed by chapter from the previous part. The key concept in each question is given for emphasis, and each question or set of questions concludes with an interactive game to reinforce the concepts. Click on the Tucker Web site, select the chapter, and play the visual causation chain game designed to make learning fun. Enjoy the cheers when correct and suffer the jeers if you miss.

For an explanation of the correct answers, please visit the tutorial at www.cengage.com/economics/tucker.

Chapter 3. Market Demand and Supply

1. **Key Concept: Movement along versus shift in demand**
   Which of the following would shift the demand curve for autos to the right?
   a. A fall in the price of autos
   b. A fall in the price of auto insurance
   c. A fall in consumers' incomes
   d. A fall in the price of steel

    Causation Chain Game
   Movement along a Demand Curve versus a Shift in Demand—Exhibit 3

2. **Key Concept: Movement along versus shift in supply**
   Assuming that soybeans and tobacco can both be grown on the same land, a decrease in the price of tobacco, other things being equal, causes a (an)
   a. rightward shift of the supply curve for tobacco.
   b. upward movement along the supply curve for soybeans.
   c. rightward shift in the supply curve for soybeans.
   d. leftward shift in the supply curve for soybeans.

    Causation Chain Game
   Movement along a Supply Curve versus a Shift in Supply—Exhibit 8

3. **Key Concept: Surplus**
   Assume Q_s represents the quantity supplied at a given price and Q_d represents the quantity demanded at the same given price. Which of the following market conditions produce a downward movement of the price?
   a. $Q_s = 1,000$, $Q_d = 750$
   b. $Q_s = 750$, $Q_d = 750$
   c. $Q_s = 750$, $Q_d = 1,000$
   d. $Q_s = 1,000$, $Q_d = 1,000$

4. **Key Concept: Shortage**
   Which of the following situations results from a ticket price to a concert set below the equilibrium price?
   a. A long line of people wanting to purchase tickets to the concert
   b. No line of people wanting to buy tickets to the concert

c.   Tickets available at the box office, but no line of people wanting
     to buy them
d.   None of the above

Causation Chain Game
The Effects of Shifts in Demand on Market Equilibrium—Exhibit 12

Chapter 4. Markets in Action

5. Key Concept: Change in demand
A decrease in consumer income decreases the demand for compact discs. As a
result of the change to a new equilibrium, there is a (an)
a.   leftward shift of the supply curve.
b.   rightward shift of the supply curve.
c.   upward movement along the supply curve.
d.   downward movement along the supply curve.

Causation Chain Game
The Effects of Shifts in Demand on Market Equilibrium—Exhibit 1

6. Key Concept: Change in supply
Consider the market for grapes. An increase in the wage paid to grape pickers
will cause the
a.   demand curve for grapes to shift to the right, resulting in a higher equili-
     brium price for grapes and a reduction in the quantity consumed.
b.   demand curve for grapes to shift to the left, resulting in a lower equilibrium
     price for grapes and an increase in the quantity consumed.
c.   supply curve for grapes to shift to the left, resulting in a lower equilibrium
     price for grapes and a decrease in the quantity consumed.
d.   supply curve for grapes to shift to the left, resulting in a higher equilibrium
     price for grapes and a decrease in the quantity consumed.

Causation Chain Game
The Effects of Shifts in Supply on Market Equilibrium—Exhibit 2

7. Key Concept: Rent control
Rent controls create distortions in the housing market by
a.   increasing rents received by landlords.
b.   raising property values.
c.   encouraging landlords to overspend for maintenance.
d.   discouraging new housing construction.
e.   increasing the supply of housing in the long run.

Causation Chain Game
Rent Control—Exhibit 5

8. Key Concept: Minimum wage
A good example of a price floor is
a.   rent controls on apartments in major cities.
b.   general admission tickets to concerts.

c.   the minimum-wage law.
d.   food stamp regulations.
e.   rock concert tickets.

 Causation Chain Game
Minimum Wage—Exhibit 6

Chapter 5. Price Elasticity of Demand

9. Key Concept: Tax incidence

Assuming the demand curve is more elastic (flatter) than the supply curve, which of the following is *true*?

a.   The full tax is always passed on to the consumer no matter how flat (elastic) the demand curve is.
b.   The full tax is always passed on to the seller no matter how flat (elastic) the demand curve is.
c.   The smaller the portion of a sales tax that is passed on to the consumer.
d.   It does not make any difference how flat (elastic) the demand curve is; the tax is always split evenly between buyer and seller.

 Causation Chain Game
The Incidence of a Tax on Gasoline—Exhibit 10

Chapter 6. Consumer Choice Theory

10. Key Concept: Income effect

The income effect refers to a change in

a.   income because of changes in the CPI.
b.   the quantity demanded of a good because of a change in the buyer's real income.
c.   the quantity demanded of a good because of a change in the buyer's money income.
d.   none of the above.

 Causation Chain Game
Income Effect

Chapter 7. Production Costs

11. Key Concept: Marginal product and marginal cost

Which of the following is *true* at the point where diminishing returns set in?

a.   Both marginal product and marginal cost are at a maximum.
b.   Both marginal product and marginal cost are at a minimum.
c.   Marginal product is at a maximum and marginal cost is at a minimum.
d.   Marginal product is at a minimum and marginal cost is at a maximum.

 Causation Chain Game
Marginal Products Effects on Marginal Cost

Market Structures

This part focuses on different types of markets, each defined by a set of characteristics that determine corresponding demand and supply conditions. Chapter 8 describes a highly competitive market consisting of an extremely large number of competing firms, and Chapter 9 explains the theory for a market with only a single seller. Between these extremes, Chapter 10 discusses two markets that have some characteristics of both competition and monopoly. The part concludes by developing labor market theory in Chapter 11.

Perfect Competition

© David Muir/Digital Vision/Getty Images.

O strich farmers in Iowa, Texas, Oklahoma, and other states in the Midwest "stuck their necks out." Many invested millions of dollars converting a portion of their farms into breeding grounds for ostriches. The reason was that mating pairs of ostriches were selling for $75,000 during the late 1990s. Ostrich breeders claimed that ostrich meat would become the low-cholesterol, low-fat health treat, and ostrich prices rose. The high prices for ostriches fueled profit expectations, and many cattle ranchers deserted their cattle and went into the ostrich business.

Adam Smith concluded that competitive forces are like an "invisible hand" that leads people who simply pursue their own interests and, in the process, serve the interests of society. In a competitive market, when the profit potential in the ostrich business looked good, firms entered this market and started raising ostriches. Over time more and more ostrich farmers flocked to this market, and the ostrich population exploded. As a result, the price of a breeding pair plummeted to only a few thousand dollars, profits tumbled, and the number of ostrich farms declined. A decade later demand increased unexpectedly because mad cow disease plagued Europe, and people bought alternatives to beef. Suppliers could not meet the demand for ostrich burgers and profits rose again, causing farmers to increase supply by investing in more ostriches.

This chapter combines the demand, cost of production, and marginal analysis concepts from previous chapters to explain how competitive markets determine prices, output, and profits. Here firms are small, like an ostrich ranch or an alligator farm, rather than huge, like Sears, Exxon-Mobil, or IBM. Other types of markets in which large and powerful firms operate are discussed in the next two chapters.

In this chapter, you will learn
to solve these economic puzzles:

- Why is the demand curve horizontal for a firm in a perfectly competitive market?

- Why would a firm stay in business while losing money?

- In the long run, can alligator farms earn an economic profit?

Perfect Competition

Firms sell goods and services under different market conditions, which economists call market structures. A market structure describes the key traits of a market, including the number of firms, the similarity of the products they sell, and the ease of entry into and exit from the market. Examination of the business sector of our economy reveals firms operating in different market structures. In this chapter and the two chapters that follow, we will study four market structures. The first is perfect competition, to which this entire chapter is devoted. Perfect, or pure, competition is a market structure characterized by (1) a large number of small firms, (2) a homogeneous product, and (3) very easy entry into or exit from the market. Let's discuss each of these characteristics.

Characteristics of Perfect Competition

Large Number of Small Firms How many sellers comprise a large number? And how small is a small firm? Certainly, one, two, or three firms in a market would not be a large number. In fact, the exact number cannot be stated. This condition is fulfilled when each firm in a market has no significant share of total output and, therefore, no ability to affect the product's price. Each firm acts independently, rather than coordinating decisions collectively. For example, there are thousands of independent egg farmers in the United States. If any single egg farmer raises the price, the going market price for eggs is unaffected.

> **Conclusion** *The large-number-of-sellers condition is met when each firm is so small relative to the total market that no single firm can influence the market price.*

Homogeneous Product In a perfectly competitive market, all firms produce a standardized or homogeneous product. This means the good or service of each firm is identical. Farmer Brown's wheat is identical to Farmer Jones's wheat. Buyers may believe the transportation services of one independent trucker are about the same as another's services. This assumption rules out rivalry among firms in advertising and quality differences.

Market structure

A classification system for the key traits of a market, including the number of firms, the similarity of the products they sell, and the ease of entry into and exit from the market.

Perfect competition

A market structure characterized by (1) a large number of small firms, (2) a homogeneous product, and (3) very easy entry into or exit from the market. Perfect competition is also referred to as *pure competition*.

> **Conclusion** *If a product is homogeneous, buyers are indifferent as to which seller's product they buy.*

Very Easy Entry and Exit   Very easy entry into a market means that a new firm faces no barriers to entry. Barriers can be financial, technical, or government-imposed barriers, such as licenses, permits, and patents. Anyone who wants to try his or her hand at raising ostriches needs only a plot of land and feed.

> **Conclusion** *Perfect competition requires that resources be completely mobile to freely enter or exit a market.*

No real-world market exactly fits the three assumptions of perfect competition. The perfectly competitive market structure is a theoretical or ideal model, but some actual markets do approximate the model fairly closely. Examples include farm products markets, the stock market, and the foreign exchange market.

The Perfectly Competitive Firm as a Price Taker

For model-building purposes, suppose a firm operates in a market that conforms to all three of the requirements for perfect competition. This means that the perfectly competitive firm is a price taker. A price taker is a seller that has no control over the price of the product it sells. From the individual firm's perspective, the price of its products is determined by market supply and demand conditions over which the firm has no influence. Look again at the characteristics of a perfectly competitive firm: A small firm that is one among many firms, sells a homogeneous product, and is exposed to competition from new firms entering the market. These conditions make it impossible for the perfectly competitive firm to have the market power to affect the market price. Instead, the firm must adjust to, or "take," the market price.

Exhibit 1 is a graphical presentation of the relationship between the market supply and demand for electronic components and the demand curve facing a firm in a perfectly competitive market. Here we will assume that the electronic components industry is perfectly competitive, keeping in mind that the real-world market does not exactly fit the model. Exhibit 1(a) shows market supply and demand curves for the quantity of output per hour. The theoretical framework for this model was explained in Chapter 4. The equilibrium price is $70 per unit, and the equilibrium quantity is 60,000 units per hour.

Because the perfectly competitive firm "takes" the equilibrium price, the individual firm's demand curve in Exhibit 1(b) is *perfectly elastic* (horizontal) at the $70 market equilibrium price. (Note the difference between the firm's units per hour and the industry's thousands of units per hour.) Recall from Chapter 5 that when a firm facing a perfectly elastic demand curve tries to raise its price one penny higher than $70, no buyer will purchase its product [Exhibit 5(a) in Chapter 5.] The reason is that many other firms are selling the same product at $70 per unit. Hence, the perfectly competitive firm will not set the price above the prevailing market price and risk selling zero output. Nor will the firm set the price below the market price because a lower price would reduce the firm's revenue, and the firm can sell all it wants to at the going price.

Price taker

A seller that has no control over the price of the product it sells.

EXHIBIT 1 — The Market Price and Demand for the Perfectly Competitive Firm

In Part (a), the market equilibrium price is $70 per unit. The perfectly competitive firm in Part (b) is a price taker because it is so small relative to the market. At $70, the individual firm faces a horizontal demand curve, D. This means that the firm's demand curve is perfectly elastic. If the firm raises its price even one penny, it will sell zero output.

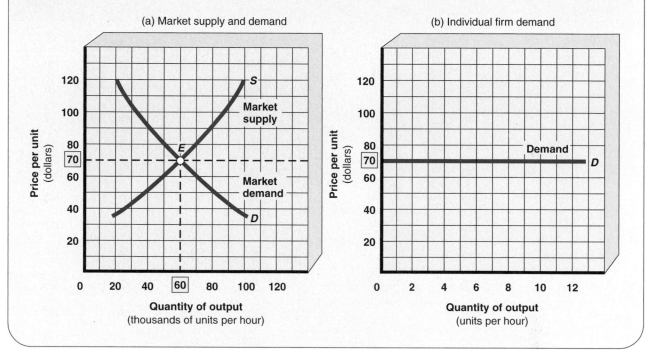

Short-Run Profit Maximization for a Perfectly Competitive Firm

Since the perfectly competitive firm has no control over price, what does the firm control? The firm makes only one decision—what quantity of output to produce that maximizes profit. In this section, we develop two profit maximization methods that determine the output level for a competitive firm. We begin by examining the total revenue-total cost approach for finding the profit-maximizing level of output. Next, we use marginal analysis to show another method for determining the profit-maximizing level of output. The framework for our analysis is the short run with some fixed input, such as factory size.

The Total Revenue-Total Cost Method

Exhibit 2 provides hypothetical data on output, total revenue, total cost, and profit for our typical electronic components producer—Computech. Using Computech as our example allows us to extend the data and analysis presented in previous chapters. The cost figures are taken from Exhibit 3 in Chapter 7. Total fixed cost at zero output is $100. Total revenue is reported in column 3 of Exhibit 2 and is computed as the product price times the quantity. In this case, we assume the market equilibrium price is $70 per unit, as determined in Exhibit 1. Because Computech is a

EXHIBIT 2 — Short-Run Profit Maximization Schedule for Computech as a Perfectly Competitive Firm

(1) Output (units per hour) (Q)	(2) Price per Unit (P)	(3) Total Revenue (TR)	(4) Marginal Revenue (MR)	(5) Marginal Cost (MC)	(6) Total Cost (TC)	(7) Average Variable Cost (AVC)	(8) Average Total Cost (ATC)	(9) Profit (+) or Loss (−) [(3) − (6)]
0	$70	$ 0			$100	—	—	−$100
			$70	$ 50				
1	70	70			150	$50	$150	−80
			70	34				
2	70	140			184	42	92	−44
			70	24				
3	70	210			208	36	69	2
			70	19				
4	70	280			227	32	57	53
			70	23				
5	70	350			250	30	50	100
			70	30				
6	70	420			280	30	47	140
			70	38				
7	70	490			318	31	45	172
			70	48				
8	70	560			366	33	46	194
			70	59				
9	70	630	70	70	425	36	47	205
			70	75				
10	70	700			500	40	50	200
			70	95				
11	70	770			595	45	54	175
			70	117				
12	70	840			712	51	59	128

price taker, the total revenue from selling 1 unit is $70, from selling 2 units is $140, and so on. Subtracting total cost in column 6 from total revenue in column 3 gives the total profit or loss (column 9) that the firm earns at each level of output. From zero to 2 units, the firm incurs losses, and then a *break-even point* (zero economic profit) occurs at about 3 units per hour. If the firm produces 9 units per hour, it earns the maximum profit of $205 per hour. As output expands between 9 and 12 units of output, the firm's profit diminishes. Exhibit 3 illustrates graphically that the maximum profit occurs where the vertical distance between the total revenue and the total cost curves is at a maximum.

The Marginal Revenue Equals Marginal Cost Method

A second approach uses *marginal analysis* to determine the profit-maximizing level of output by comparing marginal revenue (marginal benefit) and marginal cost. Recall from the previous chapter that marginal cost is the change in total cost as the output level changes one unit. Also recall that these marginal cost data are listed between the quantity of output line entries because the change in total cost occurs

EXHIBIT 3	Short-Run Profit Maximization Using the Total Revenue-Total Cost Method for a Perfectly Competitive Firm

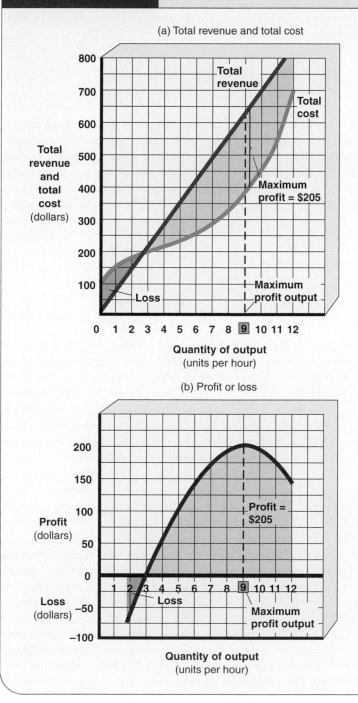

(a) Total revenue and total cost

(b) Profit or loss

This exhibit shows the profit-maximizing level of output chosen by a perfectly competitive firm, Computech. Part (a) shows the relationships between total revenue, total cost, and output, given a market price of $70 per unit. The maximum profit is earned by producing 9 units per hour. At this level of output, the vertical distance between the total revenue and the total cost curves is the greatest. At an output level below 3 units per hour, the firm incurs losses.

Profit maximization is also shown in Part (b). The maximum profit of $205 per hour corresponds to the profit-maximizing output of 9 units per hour, represented in Part (a).

between each additional whole unit of output rather than exactly at each listed output level.

Now we introduce marginal revenue (*MR*), a concept similar to marginal cost. Marginal revenue is the change in total revenue from the sale of one additional unit of output. Stated another way, marginal revenue is the ratio of the change in total revenue to a change in output.

Mathematically,

$$MR = \frac{\text{change in total revenue}}{\text{one-unit change in output}}$$

As shown in Exhibit 1(b), the perfectly competitive firm faces a perfectly elastic demand curve. Because the competitive firm is a price taker, the sale of each additional unit adds to total revenue an amount equal to the price (average revenue, *TR/Q*). In our example, Computech adds $70 to its total revenue each time it sells one unit. Therefore, $70 is the marginal revenue for each additional unit of output in column 4 of Exhibit 2. As with *MC*, *MR* is also listed between the quantity of output line entries because the change in total revenue occurs between each additional unit of output.

> **Conclusion** *In perfect competition, the firm's marginal revenue equals the price that the firm views as a horizontal demand curve.*

Columns 3 and 6 in Exhibit 2 show that both total revenue and total cost rise as the level of output increases. Now compare marginal revenue and marginal cost in columns 4 and 5. As explained, marginal revenue remains equal to the price, but marginal cost follows the J-shaped pattern introduced in Exhibit 4 of Chapter 7. At first, marginal cost is below marginal revenue, and this means that producing each additional unit adds less to total cost than to total revenue. Economic profit therefore increases as output expands from zero until the output level reaches 9 units per hour. Over this output range, Computech moves from a $100 loss to a $205 profit per hour. Beyond an output level of 9 units per hour, marginal cost exceeds marginal revenue, and profit falls. This is because each additional unit of output raises total cost by more than it raises total revenue. In this case, profit falls from $205 to only $128 per hour as output increases from 9 to 12 units per hour.

Our example leads to this question: How does the firm use its marginal revenue and marginal cost curves to determine the profit-maximizing level of output? The answer is that the firm follows a guideline called the *MR* = *MC* rule: *The firm maximizes profit by producing the output where marginal revenue equals marginal cost.* Exhibit 4 relates the marginal revenue curve equals marginal cost curve condition to profit maximization. In Exhibit 4(a), the perfectly elastic demand curve is drawn at the industry-determined price of $70. The average total cost (*ATC*) and average variable cost (*AVC*) curves are traced from Exhibit 2. Using marginal analysis, we can relate the *MR* = *MC* rule to the same profit data given in Exhibit 2. Between 8 and 9 units of output, the *MC* curve is below the *MR* curve ($59 < $70), and the profit curve rises to its peak at $205. Beyond 9 units of output, the *MC* curve is above the *MR* curve, and the profit curve falls. For example, between 9 and 10 units of output, marginal cost is $75, and marginal revenue is $70. Therefore, if

Marginal revenue (*MR*)

The change in total revenue from the sale of one additional unit of output.

EXHIBIT 4

Short-Run Profit Maximization Using the Marginal Revenue Equals Marginal Cost Method for a Perfectly Competitive Firm

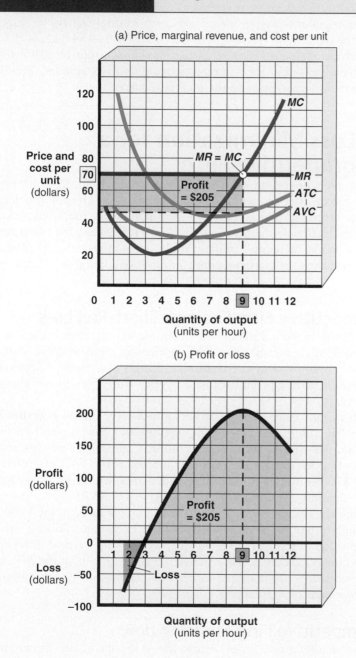

(a) Price, marginal revenue, and cost per unit

Quantity of output
(units per hour)

(b) Profit or loss

Quantity of output
(units per hour)

In addition to comparing total revenue and total cost, a firm can find the profit-maximizing level of output by comparing marginal revenue (*MR*) and marginal cost (*MC*). As shown in Part (a), profit is at a maximum where marginal revenue equals marginal cost at $70 per unit. The intersection of the marginal revenue and the marginal cost curves establishes the profit-maximizing output at 9 units per hour.

A profit curve is depicted separately in Part (b) to show that the maximum profit occurs when the firm produces at the level of output corresponding to the *MR* = *MC* point. Below 3 units per hour output, the firm incurs losses.

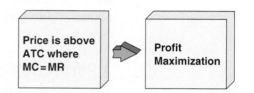

Price is above ATC where MC=MR ⟹ Profit Maximization

the firm produces at 9 units of output rather than, say, 8 or 10 units of output, the *MR* curve equals the *MC* curve, and profit is maximized.

You can also calculate profit directly from Exhibit 4(a). At the profit-maximizing level of output of 9 units, the vertical distance between the demand curve and the *ATC* curve is the *average profit per unit*. Multiplying the average profit per unit times the quantity of output gives the profit ($70 − $47.22) × 9 = $205.02.[1] The shaded rectangle also represents the maximum profit of $205 per hour. Note that we have arrived at the same profit maximization amount ($205) derived by comparing the total revenue and the total cost curves.

Short-Run Loss Minimization for a Perfectly Competitive Firm

Because the perfectly competitive firm must take the price determined by market supply and demand forces, market conditions can change the prevailing price. When the market price drops, the firm can do nothing but adjust its output to make the best of the situation. Here only the marginal approach is used to predict output decisions of firms. Our model therefore assumes that business managers make their output decisions by comparing the *marginal* effect on profit of a *marginal* change in output.

A Perfectly Competitive Firm Facing a Short-Run Loss

Suppose a decrease in the market demand for electronic components causes the market price to fall to $35. As a result, the firm's horizontal demand curve shifts downward to the new position shown in Exhibit 5(a). In this case, there is no level of output at which the firm earns a profit because any price along the demand curve is below the *ATC* curve.

Since Computech cannot make a profit, what output level should it choose? The logic of the *MR = MC* rule given in the profit maximization case applies here as well. At a price of $35, *MR = MC* at 6 units per hour. Comparing Parts (a) and (b) of Exhibit 5 shows that the firm's loss will be minimized at this level of output. The minimum loss of $70 per hour is equal to the shaded area, which is the *average loss per unit* times the quantity of output ($35 − $46.66) × 6 = −$70.

Note that although the price is not high enough to pay the average total cost, the price is high enough to pay the average variable cost. Each unit sold also contributes to paying a portion of the average fixed cost, which is the vertical distance between the *ATC* and the *AVC* curves. This analysis leads us to extend the *MR = MC* rule: *The firm maximizes profit or minimizes loss by producing the output where marginal revenue equals marginal cost.*

A Perfectly Competitive Firm Shutting Down

What happens if the market price drops below the *AVC* curve, as shown in Exhibit 6? For example, if the price is $25 per unit, should Computech produce some level of output? The answer is no. The best course of action is for the firm to shut down. *If the price is below the minimum point on the AVC curve, each unit*

---

1. In Exhibit 3 in Chapter 7, the average total cost figure at 9 units of output was rounded to $47. It also should be noted that there is often no level of output for which marginal revenue exactly equals marginal cost when dealing with whole units of output.

EXHIBIT 5

Short-Run Loss Minimization Using the Marginal Revenue Equals Marginal Cost Method for a Perfectly Competitive Firm

If the market price is less than the average total cost, the firm will produce a level of output that keeps its loss to a minimum. In Part (a), the given price is $35 per unit, and marginal revenue (*MR*) equals marginal cost (*MC*) at an output of 6 units per hour.

Part (b) shows that the firm's loss will be greater at any output other than where the marginal revenue and the marginal cost curves intersect. Because the price is above the average variable cost, each unit of output sold pays for the average variable cost and a portion of the average fixed cost.

Price is below ATC where MC = MR ⟹ Loss Minimization

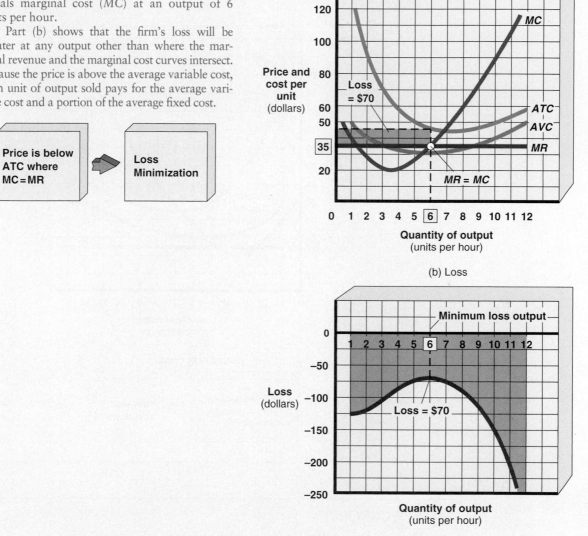

(a) Price, marginal revenue, and cost per unit

(b) Loss

produced would not cover the variable cost per unit; therefore, operating would increase losses. The firm is better off shutting down and producing zero output. While shut down, the firm might keep its factory, pay fixed costs, and hope for higher prices soon. If the firm does not believe market conditions will improve, it will avoid fixed costs by going out of business.

EXHIBIT 6 — The Short-Run Shutdown Point for a Perfectly Competitive Firm

The shutdown point of $30 per unit is the minimum point on the average variable cost curve (*AVC*). If the price falls below this price, the firm shuts down. The reason is that operating losses are now greater than total fixed cost. In this exhibit, the price of $25 per unit (*MR*) is below the *AVC* curve at any level of output, and the firm would shut down at this price.

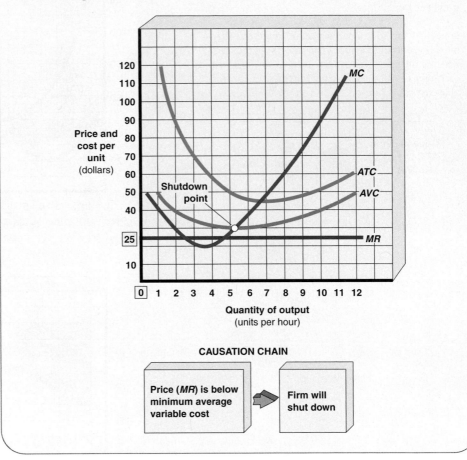

CAUSATION CHAIN

Price (*MR*) is below minimum average variable cost → Firm will shut down

---

CHECKPOINT

Should Motels Offer Rooms at the Beach for Only $50 a Night?
Myrtle Beach, South Carolina, with its famous Grand Strand and Calabash seafood, is lined with virtually identical motels. Summertime rates run about $200 a night. During the winter, one can find rooms for as little as $50 a night. Assume the average fixed cost of a room per night, including insurance, taxes, and depreciation, is $50. The average guest-related cost for a room each night, including cleaning service and linens, is $45. Would these motels be better off renting rooms for $50 in the off-season or shutting down until summer?

Short-Run Supply Curves under Perfect Competition

The preceding examples provide a framework for a more complete explanation of the supply curve than was given earlier in Chapter 3. We now develop the short-run supply curve for an individual firm and then derive it for an industry.

The Perfectly Competitive Firm's Short-Run Supply Curve

Exhibit 7 reproduces the cost curves from our Computech example. Also represented in the exhibit are three possible demand curves the firm might face—MR_1, MR_2, and MR_3. As the marginal revenue curve moves upward along the marginal cost curve, the $MR = MC$ point changes.

Suppose demand for electronic components begins at a market price close to $30. Point A therefore corresponds to a price equal to MR_1, which equals MC at the lowest point on the AVC curve. At any lower price, the firm cuts its loss by shutting

---

EXHIBIT 7	The Perfectly Competitive Firm's Short-Run Supply Curve

This exhibit shows how the short-run supply curve for Computech is derived. When the price is $30, the firm will produce 5.5 units per hour at point A. If the price rises to $45, the firm will move upward along its marginal cost curve (MC) to point B and produce 7 units per hour. At $90, the firm continues to set price equal to marginal cost, and it produces 10 units per hour. Thus, the firm's short-run supply curve is the MC curve above its AVC curve.

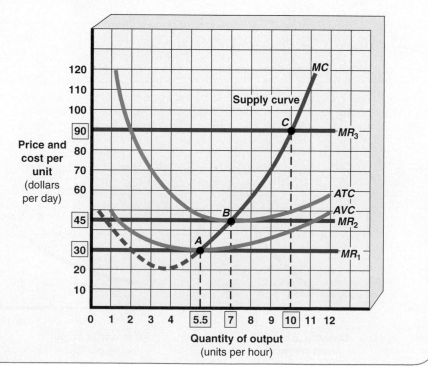

down. At a price of about $30, however, the firm produces 5.5 units per hour. Point A is therefore the lowest point on the individual firm's short-run supply curve.

If the price rises to $45, represented in the exhibit by MR_2, the firm breaks even and earns a normal profit at point B with an output of 7 units per hour. As the marginal revenue curve rises, the firm's supply curve is traced by moving upward along its MC curve. At a price of $90, point C is reached. Now MR_3 intersects the MC curve at an output of 10 units per hour, and the firm earns an economic profit. If the price rises higher than $90, the firm will continue to increase the quantity supplied and increase its maximum profit.

We can now define a perfectly competitive firm's short-run supply curve. The perfectly competitive firm's short-run supply curve is its marginal cost curve above the minimum point on its average variable cost curve.

The Perfectly Competitive Industry's Short-Run Supply Curve

Understanding that the firm's short-run supply curve is the segment of its MC curve above its AVC curve sets the stage for derivation of the perfectly competitive industry's short-run supply curve. The perfectly competitive industry's short-run supply curve is the horizontal summation of the marginal cost curves of all firms in the industry above the minimum point of each firm's average variable cost curve.

In Exhibit 7 in Chapter 3, we drew a market supply curve. Now we will reconstruct this market, or industry, supply curve using more precision. Although in perfect competition there are many firms, we suppose for simplicity that the industry has only two firms, Computech and Western Computer Co. Exhibit 8 illustrates the MC curves for these two firms. Each firm's MC curve is drawn for prices above the minimum point on the AVC curve. At a price of $40, the quantity

Perfectly competitive firm's short-run supply curve

The firm's marginal cost curve above the minimum point on its average variable cost curve.

Perfectly competitive industry's short-run supply curve

The supply curve derived from horizontal summation of the marginal cost curves of all firms in the industry above the minimum point of each firm's average variable cost curve.

EXHIBIT 8   Deriving the Industry Short-Run Supply Curve

Assuming input prices remain constant as output expands, the short-run supply curve for an industry is derived by horizontally summing the quantities supplied at each price by all firms in the industry. In this exhibit, we assume there are only two firms in an industry. At $40, Computech supplies 7 units of output, and Western Computer Co. supplies 11 units. The quantity supplied by the industry is therefore 18 units. Other points forming the industry short-run supply curve are obtained similarly.

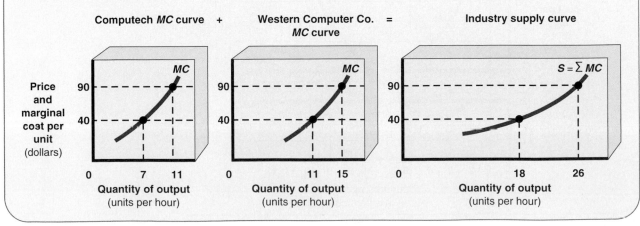

supplied by Computech is 7 units, and the quantity supplied by Western Computer Co. is 11 units. Now we horizontally add these two quantities and obtain one point on the industry supply curve corresponding to a price of $40 and 18 units. Following this procedure for all prices, we generate the short-run industry supply curve.

Note that the industry supply curve derived above is based on the assumption that input prices remain unchanged as output expands. In the next section, we will learn how changes in input prices affect derivation of the supply curve.

Short-Run Equilibrium for a Perfectly Competitive Firm

Exhibit 9 illustrates a condition of short-run equilibrium under perfect competition. Exhibit 9(a) represents the equilibrium price and cost situation for one of the many firms in an industry. As shown in the exhibit, the firm earns an economic profit in the short run by producing 9 units. Exhibit 9(b) depicts short-run equilibrium for the industry. As explained earlier, the industry supply curve is the aggregate of each firm's *MC* curve above the minimum point on the *AVC* curve. Including industry demand establishes the equilibrium price of $60 that all firms in the industry must take. The industry's equilibrium quantity supplied is 60,000 units. This state of

---

EXHIBIT 9   Short-Run Perfectly Competitive Equilibrium

Short-run equilibrium occurs at point *E*. The intersection of the industry supply and demand curves shown in Part (b) determines the price of $60 facing the firm shown in Part (a). Given this equilibrium price, the firm represented in Part (a) establishes its profit-maximizing output at 9 units per hour and earns an economic profit shown by the shaded area. Note in Part (b) that the short-run industry supply curve is the horizontal summation of the marginal cost (*MC*) curves of all individual firms above their minimum average variable cost points.

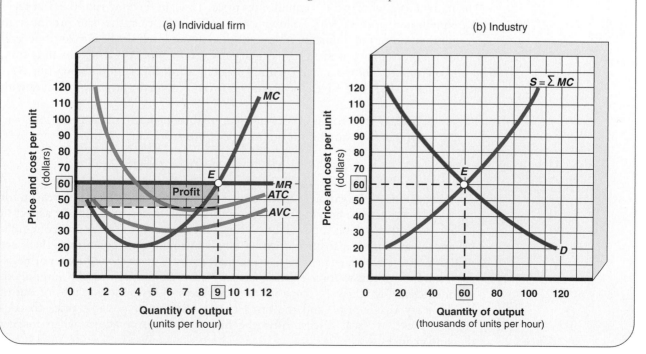

short-run equilibrium will remain until some factor changes and causes a new equilibrium condition in the industry.

Long-Run Supply Curves under Perfect Competition

Recall from Chapter 7 that *all* inputs are variable in the long run. Existing firms in an industry can react to profit opportunities by building larger or smaller plants, buying or selling land and equipment, or varying other inputs that are fixed in the short run. Profits also attract new firms to an industry, while losses cause some existing firms to leave the industry. As you will now see, the free entry and exit characteristic of perfect competition is a crucial determinant of the shape of the long-run supply curve.

Long-Run Equilibrium for a Perfectly Competitive Firm

As discussed in Chapter 7, in the long run a firm can change its plant size or any input used to produce a product. This means that an established firm can decide to *leave* an industry if it earns below normal profits (negative economic profits) and that new firms may enter an industry in which earnings of established firms exceed normal profits (positive economic profits). This process of entry and exit of firms is the key to long-run equilibrium. If there are economic profits, new firms enter the industry and shift the short-run industry supply curve to the right. This increase in short-run supply causes the price to fall until economic profits reach zero in the long run. On the other hand, if there are economic losses in an industry, existing firms leave, causing the short-run supply curve to shift to the left, and the price rises. This adjustment continues until economic losses are eliminated and economic profits equal zero in the long run.

Exhibit 10 shows a typical firm in long-run equilibrium. Supply and demand for the market as a whole set the equilibrium price. Thus, in the long run, the firm faces an equilibrium price of $60. Following the $MR = MC$ rule, the firm produces an equilibrium output of 6 units per hour. At this output level, the firm earns a normal profit (zero economic profit) because marginal revenue (price) equals the minimum point on both the short-run average total cost curve ($SRATC$) and the long-run average cost curve ($LRAC$). Given the U-shaped $LRAC$ curve, the firm is producing with the optimal factory size.

With $SRMC$ representing short-run marginal cost, the conditions for long-run perfectly competitive equilibrium can also be expressed as an equality:

$$P = MR = SRMC = SRATC = LRAC$$

As long as none of the variables in the above formula changes, there is no reason for a perfectly competitive firm to change its output level, factory size, or any aspect of its operation. Everything is just right! Because the typical firm is in a state of equilibrium, the industry is also at rest. Under long-run equilibrium conditions, there are neither positive economic profits to attract new firms to enter the industry nor negative economic profits to force existing firms to leave. In long-run equilibrium, maximum efficiency is achieved. The adjustment process of firms moving into or out of the industry is complete, and the firms charge the lowest possible price to consumers. Next, we will discuss how the firm and industry adjust when market demand changes.

EXHIBIT 10 — Long-Run Perfectly Competitive Equilibrium

Long-run equilibrium occurs at point *E*. In the long run, the firm earns a normal profit. The firm operates where the price equals the minimum point on its long-run average cost curve (*LRAC*). At this point, the short-run marginal cost curve (*SRMC*) intersects both the short-run average total cost curve (*SRATC*) and the long-run average cost curve (*LRAC*) at their minimum points.

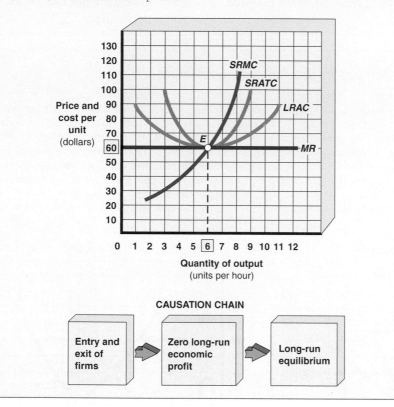

CAUSATION CHAIN

Entry and exit of firms ⇒ Zero long-run economic profit ⇒ Long-run equilibrium

CHECKPOINT

Are You in Business for the Long Run?

You are considering building a Rent Your Own Storage Center. You are trying to decide whether to build 50 storage units at a total economic cost of $200,000, 100 storage units at a total economic cost of $300,000, or 200 storage units at a total economic cost of $700,000. If you wish to survive in the long run, which size will you choose?

Three Types of Long-Run Supply Curves

There are three possibilities for a perfectly competitive industry's long-run supply curve. The perfectly competitive industry's long-run supply curve shows the quantities supplied by the industry at different equilibrium prices after firms complete their entry and exit. The shape of each of these long-run supply curves depends on the

Perfectly competitive industry's long-run supply curve
The curve that shows the quantities supplied by the industry at different equilibrium prices after firms complete their entry and exit.

Constant-cost industry

An industry in which the expansion of industry output by the entry of new firms has no effect on the individual firm's average total cost curve.

response of input prices as new firms enter the industry. The following sections discuss each of these three cases.

Constant-Cost Industry

In a constant-cost industry, input prices remain constant as new firms enter or exit the industry. A constant-cost industry is an industry in which the expansion of industry output by the entry of new firms has no effect on the firm's cost curves. Exhibit 11(a) reproduces the long-run equilibrium situation from Exhibit 10.

EXHIBIT 11   Long-Run Supply in a Constant-Cost Industry

Part (b) shows an industry in equilibrium at point E_1, producing 50,000 units per hour and selling them for $60 per unit. In Part (a), the firm is in equilibrium, producing 6 units per hour and earning a normal profit. Then industry demand increases from D_1 to D_2, and the equilibrium price rises to $80. Industry output rises temporarily to 70,000 units per hour and the individual firm increases output to 7 units per hour. Firms are now earning an economic profit, which attracts new firms into the industry. In the long run, the entry of these firms causes the short-run supply curve to shift rightward from S_1 to S_2, the price is reestablished at $60, and a new industry equilibrium point, E_3, is established. At E_3, industry output rises to 90,000 units per hour, and the firm's output returns to 6 units per hour. Now the typical firm earns a normal profit, and new firms stop entering the industry. Connecting point E_1 to point E_3 generates the long-run supply curve.

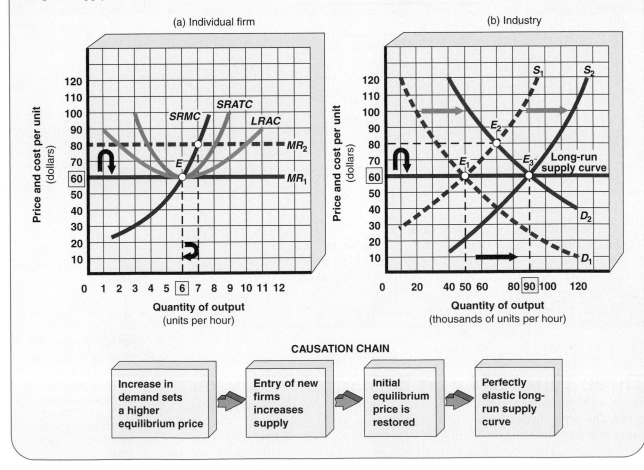

(a) Individual firm

(b) Industry

CAUSATION CHAIN

| Increase in demand sets a higher equilibrium price | Entry of new firms increases supply | Initial equilibrium price is restored | Perfectly elastic long-run supply curve |

Begin in Part (b) of Exhibit 11 at the initial industry equilibrium point E_1 with short-run industry supply curve S_1 and industry demand curve D_1. Now assume the industry demand curve increases from D_1 to D_2. As a result, the industry equilibrium moves temporarily to E_2. Correspondingly, the equilibrium price rises from $60 to $80, and industry output increases from 50,000 to 70,000 units.

The short-run result for the individual firm in the industry happens this way. As shown in Part (a) of Exhibit 11, the firm takes the increase in price and adjusts its output from 6 to 7 units per hour. At the higher price and output, the firm changes from earning a normal profit to making an economic profit because the new price is above its *SRATC* curve. All the other firms in the industry make the same adjustment by moving upward along their *SRMC* curves.

In perfect competition, new firms are free to enter the industry in response to a profit opportunity, and they will do so. The addition of new firms shifts the short-run supply curve rightward from S_1 to S_2. Firms will continue to enter the industry until profit is eliminated. This occurs at equilibrium point E_3, where short-run industry demand curve D_2 intersects short-run supply curve S_2. Thus, the entry of new firms has restored the initial equilibrium price of $60. The firm responds by moving downward along its *SRMC* curve until it once again produces 6 units and earns a normal profit.

As shown in the exhibit, the path of these changes in industry short-run equilibrium points traces a horizontal line, which is the industry's long-run supply curve.

> **Conclusion** *The long-run supply curve in a perfectly competitive constant-cost industry is perfectly elastic.*

Now we reconsider Exhibit 11 and ask what happens when the demand curve shifts leftward from D_2 to D_1. Beginning in Part (b) at point E_3, the decrease in demand causes the price to fall temporarily below $60. As a result, firms incur short-run losses, and some firms leave the industry. The exodus of firms shifts the short-run supply curve leftward from S_2 to S_1, establishing a new equilibrium at point E_1. This decrease in supply restores the equilibrium price to the initial price of $60 per unit. Once equilibrium is reestablished at E_1, there is a smaller number of firms, each earning a normal profit.

Decreasing-Cost Industry

Input prices fall as new firms enter a decreasing-cost industry, and output expands. A decreasing-cost industry is an industry in which the expansion of industry output by the entry of new firms decreases each individual firm's cost curve (cost curve shifts downward). For example, as production of electronic components expands, the price of computer chips may decline. The reason is that greater sales volume allows the suppliers to achieve *economies of scale* and lower their input prices to firms in the electronic components industry. Exhibit 12 illustrates the adjustment process of an increase in demand based on the assumption that our example is a decreasing-cost industry.

> **Conclusion** *The long-run supply curve in a perfectly competitive decreasing-cost industry is downward sloping.*

Decreasing-cost industry
An industry in which the expansion of industry output by the entry of new firms decreases the individual firm's average total cost curve (cost curve shifts downward).

EXHIBIT 12   Long-Run Supply in a Decreasing-Cost Industry

The long-run supply curve for a decreasing-cost industry is downward sloping. The increase in industry demand shown in Part (b) causes the price to rise to $80 in the short run. Temporarily, the individual firm illustrated in Part (a) earns an economic profit. Higher profits attract new firms, and supply increases. As the industry expands, the average total cost curve for the firm shifts lower, and the firm reestablishes long-run equilibrium at the lower price of $50.

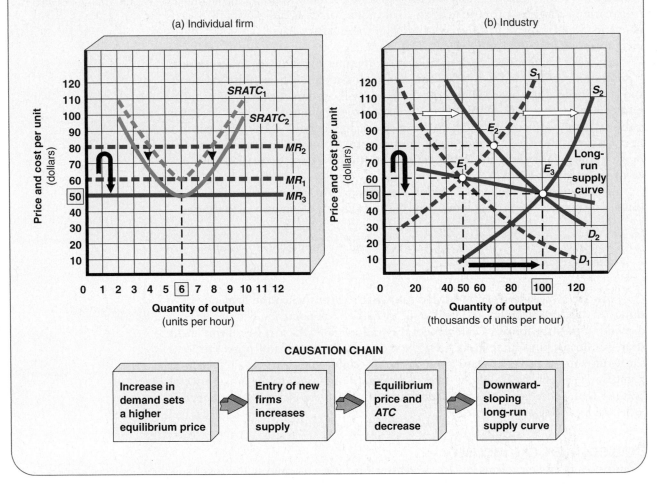

Increasing-Cost Industry

In an increasing-cost industry, input prices rise as new firms enter the industry, and output expands. As this type of industry uses more labor and machines, the demand for greater quantities of these inputs drives up input prices. An increasing-cost industry is an industry in which the expansion of industry output by the entry of new firms increases the individual firm's cost curve (cost curve shifts upward). Suppose the electronic component disc business uses a significant proportion of all electrical engineers in the country. In this case, electrical engineering salaries will rise as firms hire more electrical engineers to expand industry output. In practice, most industries are increasing-cost industries, and, therefore, the long-run supply curve is upward sloping.

EXHIBIT 13   Long-Run Supply in an Increasing-Cost Industry

This pair of graphs derives the long-run supply curve based on the assumption that input prices rise as industry output expands. Part (b) shows that an increase in demand from D_1 to D_2 causes the price to increase in the short run from $60 to $80. The individual firm represented in Part (a) earns an economic profit, and new firms enter the industry, causing an increase in industry supply from S_1 to S_2. As output expands, input prices rise and push up the firm's short-run average total cost curve from $SRATC_1$, to $SRATC_2$. As a result, a new long-run equilibrium price is established at $70, which is above the initial equilibrium price. The long-run supply curve for an increasing-cost industry is upward sloping.

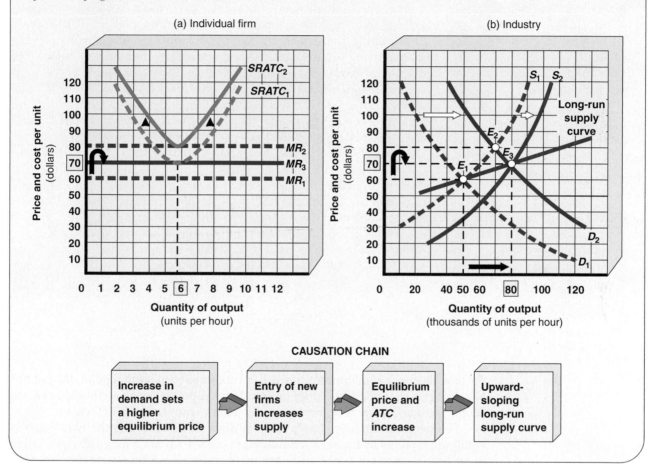

(a) Individual firm

(b) Industry

CAUSATION CHAIN

| Increase in demand sets a higher equilibrium price | ⇨ | Entry of new firms increases supply | ⇨ | Equilibrium price and *ATC* increase | ⇨ | Upward-sloping long-run supply curve |

Exhibit 13 shows what happens in an increasing-cost industry when an increase in demand causes output to expand. In Part (b), the industry is initially in equilibrium at point E_1. As in the previous case, the demand curve shifts rightward from D_1 to D_2, establishing a new short-run equilibrium at E_2. This movement upward along short-run industry supply curve S_1 raises the price in the short run from $60 to $80, resulting in profit for the typical firm. Once again, new firms enter the industry, and the short-run supply curve shifts rightward from S_1 to S_2. Part (a) of Exhibit 13 shows that the response of the firm's *SRATC* curve to the industry's expansion differs from the constant-cost industry case. In an increasing-cost industry, the firm's *SRATC* curve shifts upward from $SRATC_1$ to $SRATC_2$, corresponding to

YOU'RE THE ECONOMIST   Gators Snapping up Profits

Applicable Concepts: short-run and long-run competitive equilibrium

© David Huntley, 2008/Used under license from Shutterstock.com.

In the late 1980s, many farmers who were tired of milking cows, roping steers, and slopping hogs decided to try their hands at a new animal. Anyone feeding this animal, however, could require a gun for protection.

Prior to the late 1970s, alligators were on the endangered species list. Under this protection, their numbers grew so large that wandering alligators became pests in Florida neighborhoods and police were exhausted from chasing them around. Consequently, the ban on hunting was removed, and shrewd entrepreneurs began seeking big profits by turning gators into farm animals. In fact, gator farming became one of Florida's fastest-growing businesses.

The gators spawned several hot industries. The lizard "look" came back into vogue, and the fashionable sported gator-skin purses, shoes, and belts. Chic didn't come cheap. In New York, gator cowboy boots sold for $1,800, and attaché cases retailed for $4,000. And you could order gator meat at trendy restaurants all along the East Coast. "Why not gator?" asked Red Lobster spokesman Dick Monroe.

"Today's two-income households are looking for more variety. And they think it's neat to eat an animal that can eat them."

To meet the demand, Florida doubled the number of its licensed alligator farms compared to the previous four years, when they functioned almost entirely as tourist attractions. In 1985, Florida farmers raised 37,000 gators; in 1986, that figure increased by 50 percent. Revenues soared as well. Frank Godwin, owner of Gatorland in Orlando, netted an estimated $270,000 from the 1,000 animals he harvested annually. Improved technology was applied to gator farming in order to boost profits even higher. Lawler Wells, for example, owner of Hilltop

the new short-run equilibrium at point E_3. At this final equilibrium point, the price of $70 is higher than the initial price of $60. Normal profits are re-established because profits are squeezed from both the price fall and the rise in the *SRATC* curve.

The long-run industry supply curve is drawn by connecting the two long-run equilibrium points of E_1 and E_3. Equilibrium point E_2 is not a long-run equilibrium point because it is not established after the entry of new firms has restored normal profits.

> **Conclusion** *The long-run supply curve in a perfectly competitive increasing-cost industry is upward sloping.*

Finally, given the three models presented, you may ask which is the best choice. The answer is that all three versions are possible for any given industry. Only direct observation of the industry can tell which type of industry it is.

Farms in Avon Park, raised 7,000 gators in darkened hothouses that accelerated their growth.[1]

Seven years later, a 1993 article in the *Washington Post* continued the gator tale: "During the late 1980s, gator ranching was booming, and the industry was being compared to a living gold mine. People rushed into the industry. Some farmers became temporarily rich."[2]

In 1995, a *USA Today* interview with a gator hunter provided evidence of long-run equilibrium: "Armed with a pistol barrel attached to the end of an 8-foot wooden pole, alligator hunter Bill Chaplin fires his 'bankstick' and dispatches a six-footer with a single round of .44 magnum ammunition. What's in it for him? Financially, very little. At $3.50 a pound for the meat and $45 a foot for the hide, an alligator is worth perhaps $100 a foot. After paying for skinning and processing, neither hunter nor landowner gets rich."[3]

A 2000 article in *The Dallas Morning News* provided further evidence: Mark Glass, who began raising gators in 1995 south of Atlanta stated, "I can honestly say I haven't made any money yet, but I hope that's about to change."[4] And a 2003 article from *Knight Ridder/Tribune Business News* gave a pessimistic report for Florida: "Revenue from alligator harvesting has flattened in recent years, despite Florida's efforts to promote the alligator as part of a viable 'aquaculture' industry. It's a tough business."[5] And in 2007, in response to numerous complaints of nuisance alligators, the Florida Fish and Wildlife Conservation Commission considered eliminating some rules that have protected this species for years.

ANALYZE THE ISSUE

1. Draw short-run firm and industry competitive equilibriums for a perfectly competitive gator-farming industry before the number of alligator farms in Florida doubled. For simplicity, assume the gator farm is earning zero economic profit. Now show the short-run effect of an increase in demand for alligators.

2. Assuming gator farming is perfectly competitive, explain the long-run competitive equilibrium condition for the typical gator farmer and the industry as a whole.

1. Ron Moreau and Penelope Wang, "Gators: Snapping Up Profits," *Newsweek*, Dec. 8, 1986, p. 68.
2. William Booth, "Bag a Gator and Save the Species," *The Washington Post*, Aug. 25, 1993, p. A1.
3. J. Taylor Buckley, "S. Carolina Lets Hunters Go for Gators Again," *USA Today*, Sept. 21, 1995, News Section, p. A1.
4. "More Bite for the Buck," *Dallas Morning News*, Dec. 6, 2000, p. 2A.
5. Jerry W. Jackson, "Alligators Are Growing Part of Florida's Agricultural Landscape," *Knight Ridder/Tribune Business News*, Jan. 26, 2003.

KEY CONCEPTS

Market structure
Perfect competition
Price taker
Marginal revenue (*MR*)

Perfectly competitive firm's short-
   run supply curve
Perfectly competitive industry's
   short-run supply curve

Perfectly competitive industry's
   long-run supply curve
Constant-cost industry
Decreasing-cost industry
Increasing-cost industry

SUMMARY

- *Market structure* consists of three market charac-teristics: (1) the number of sellers, (2) the nature of the product, and (3) the ease of entry into or exit from the market.

- *Perfect competition* is a market structure in which an individual firm cannot affect the price of the product it produces. Each firm in the industry is very small relative to the market as a whole, all the firms sell a homogeneous product, and firms are free to enter and exit the industry.

- A *price-taker firm in perfect competition faces a perfectly elastic demand curve. It can sell all it wishes at the market-determined price, but it will sell nothing above the given market price. This is because so many competitive firms are willing to sell the same product at the going market price.*

- The *total revenue-total cost method* is one way a firm determines the level of output that maxi-mizes profit. Profit reaches a maximum when the vertical difference between the total revenue and the total cost curves is at a maximum.

Total revenue-total cost method

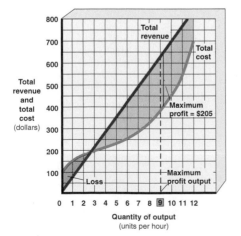

- The *marginal revenue equals marginal cost method* is a second approach to finding where a firm maximizes profits. *Marginal revenue (MR)* is the change in total revenue from a one-unit change in output. Marginal revenue for a per-fectly competitive firm equals the market price. The *MR = MC* rule states that the firm maxi-mizes profit or minimizes loss by producing the output where marginal revenue equals marginal cost. If the price (average revenue) is below the minimum point on the average variable cost curve, the *MR = MC* rule does not apply, and the firm shuts down to minimize its losses.

Marginal revenue-marginal cost method

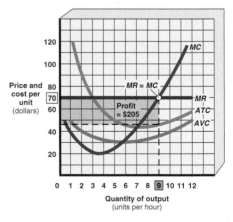

- The *perfectly competitive firm's short-run supply curve* is a curve showing the relationship between the price of a product and the quantity supplied in the short run. The individual firm always produces along its marginal cost curve above its intersection with the average variable cost curve. The *perfectly competitive industry's short-run supply curve* is the horizontal summation of the short-run supply curves of all firms in the industry.

Short-run supply curve

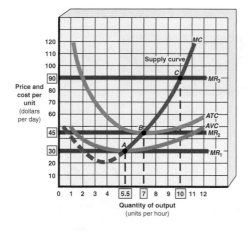

Long-run perfectly competitive equilibrium

- *Long-run perfectly competitive equilibrium* occurs when a firm earns a normal profit by producing where price equals minimum long-run average cost equals minimum short-run average total cost equals short-run marginal cost.
- In a *constant-cost industry*, total output can be expanded without an increase in the individual firm's average total cost. Because input prices remain constant, the long-run supply curve in a constant-cost industry is perfectly elastic.

- In a *decreasing-cost industry*, lower input prices result in a downward-sloping industry long-run supply curve. As industry output expands, an individual firm's average total cost curve declines (shifts downward), and the long-run equilibrium market price falls.
- In an *increasing-cost industry,* input prices rise as industry output increases. As a result, an individual firm's average total cost curve rises (shifts upward), and the industry long-run supply curve for an increasing-cost industry is upward sloping.

SUMMARY OF CONCLUSION STATEMENTS

- The large-number-of-sellers condition is met when each firm is so small relative to the total market that no single firm can influence the market price.
- If a product is homogeneous, buyers are indifferent as to which seller's product they buy.
- Perfect competition requires that resources be completely mobile to freely enter or exit a market.
- In perfect competition, the firm's marginal revenue equals the price that the firm views as a horizontal demand curve.
- In perfect competition, the firm maximizes profit or minimizes loss by producing the output where marginal revenue equals marginal cost.

- In perfect competition, if the price is below the minimum point on the *AVC* curve, each unit produced would not cover the variable cost per unit. Therefore, the firm shuts down.
- The long-run supply curve in a perfectly competitive constant-cost industry is perfectly elastic.
- The long-run supply curve in a perfectly competitive decreasing-cost industry is downward sloping.
- The long-run supply curve in a perfectly competitive increasing-cost industry is upward sloping.

STUDY QUESTIONS AND PROBLEMS

1. Explain why a perfectly competitive firm would or would not advertise.

2. Does a Kansas wheat farmer fit the perfectly competitive market structure? Explain.

3. Suppose the market equilibrium price of wheat is $2 per bushel in a perfectly competitive industry. Draw the industry supply and demand curves and the demand curve for a single wheat farmer. Explain why the wheat farmer is a price taker.

4. Assuming the market equilibrium price for wheat is $5 per bushel, draw the total revenue and the marginal revenue curves for the typical wheat farmer in the same graph. Explain how marginal revenue and price are related to the total revenue curve.

5. Consider the following cost data for a perfectly competitive firm in the short run:

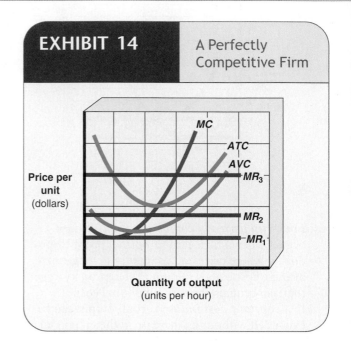

EXHIBIT 14   A Perfectly Competitive Firm

Output (Q)	Total Fixed Cost (TFC)	Total Variable Cost (TVC)	Total Cost (TC)	Total Revenue (TR)	Profit
1	$100	$120	$_____	$_____	$_____
2	100	200	_____	_____	_____
3	100	290	_____	_____	_____
4	100	430	_____	_____	_____
5	100	590	_____	_____	_____

If the market price is $150, how many units of output will the firm produce in order to maximize profit in the short run? Specify the amount of economic profit or loss. At what level of output does the firm break even?

6. Consider this statement: "A firm should increase output when it makes a profit." Do you agree or disagree? Explain.

7. Consider this statement: "When marginal revenue equals marginal cost, total cost equals total revenue, and the firm makes zero profit." Do you agree or disagree? Explain.

8. Consider Exhibit 14, which shows the graph of a perfectly competitive firm in the short run.
   a. If the firm's demand curve is MR_3, does the firm earn an economic profit or loss?
   b. Which demand curve(s) indicate(s) the firm incurs a loss?
   c. Which demand curve(s) indicate(s) the firm would shut down?
   d. Identify the firm's short-run supply curve.

9. Consider this statement: "The perfectly competitive firm will sell all the quantity of output consumers will buy at the prevailing market price." Do you agree or disagree? Explain your answer.

10. Suppose a perfectly competitive firm's demand curve is below its average total cost curve. Explain the conditions under which a firm continues to produce in the short run.

11. Suppose the industry equilibrium price of residential housing construction is $100 per square foot and the minimum average variable cost for a residential construction contractor is $110 per square foot. What would you advise the owner of this firm to do? Explain.

12. Suppose independent truckers operate in a perfectly competitive industry. If these firms are earning positive economic profits, what happens in the long run to the following: the price of trucking services, the industry quantity of output, the profits of trucking firms? Given these conditions, is the independent trucking industry a constant-cost, an increasing-cost, or a decreasing-cost industry?

For Online Exercises, go to the text Web site at www.cengage.com/economics/tucker.

CHECKPOINT ANSWERS ✓

Should Motels Offer Rooms at the Beach for Only $50 a Night?

As long as price exceeds average variable cost, the motel is better off operating than shutting down. Since $50 is more than enough to cover the guest-related variable costs of $45 per room, the firm will operate. The $5 remaining after covering variable costs can be put toward the $50 of fixed costs. Were the motel to shut down, it could make no contribution to these overhead costs. If you said the Myrtle Beach motels should operate during the winter because they can get a price that exceeds their average variable cost, **YOU ARE CORRECT.**

Are You in Business for the Long Run?

In the long run, surviving firms will operate at the minimum of the long-run average cost curve. The average cost of 50 storage units is $4,000 ($200,000/50), the average cost of 100 storage units is $3,000 ($300,000/100), and the average cost of 200 storage units is $3,500 ($700,000/200). Of the three storage-unit quantities given, the one with the lowest average cost is closest to the minimum point on the *LRAC* curve. If you chose 100 storage units, **YOU ARE CORRECT.**

PRACTICE QUIZ

For an explanation of the correct answers, please visit the tutorial at www.cengage.com/economics/tucker.

1. A perfectly competitive market is *not* characterized by
   a. many small firms.
   b. a great variety of different products.
   c. free entry into and exit from the market.
   d. any of the above.

2. Which of the following is a characteristic of perfect competition?
   a. Entry barriers
   b. Homogeneous products
   c. Expenditures on advertising
   d. Quality of service

PRACTICE QUIZ CONTINUED

3. Which of the following are the same at all levels of output under perfect competition?
   a. Marginal cost and marginal revenue
   b. Price and marginal revenue
   c. Price and marginal cost
   d. All of the above

4. If a perfectly competitive firm sells 100 units of output at a market price of $100 per unit, its marginal revenue per unit is
   a. $1.
   b. $100.
   c. more than $1, but less than $100.
   d. less than $100.

5. Short-run profit maximization for a perfectly competitive firm occurs where the firm's marginal cost equals
   a. average total cost.
   b. average variable cost.
   c. marginal revenue.
   d. all of the above.

6. A perfectly competitive firm sells its output for $100 per unit, and the minimum average variable cost is $150 per unit. The firm should
   a. increase output.
   b. decrease output, but not shut down.
   c. maintain its current rate of output.
   d. shut down.

7. A perfectly competitive firm's supply curve follows the upward-sloping segment of its marginal cost curve above the
   a. average total cost curve.
   b. average variable cost curve.
   c. average fixed cost curve.
   d. average price curve.

8. Assume the price of the firm's product in Exhibit 15 is $15 per unit. The firm will produce
   a. 500 units per week.
   b. 1,000 units per week.
   c. 1,500 units per week.
   d. 2,000 units per week.
   e. 2,500 units per week.

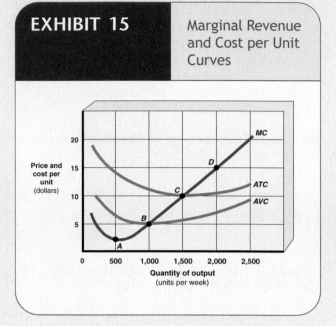

EXHIBIT 15 — Marginal Revenue and Cost per Unit Curves

9. In Exhibit 15, the lowest price at which the firm earns zero economic profit in the short run is
   a. $5 per unit.
   b. $10 per unit.
   c. $20 per unit.
   d. $30 per unit.

10. Assume the price of the firm's product in Exhibit 15 is $6 per unit. The firm should
    a. continue to operate because it is earning an economic profit.
    b. stay in operation for the time being even though it is incurring an economic loss.
    c. shut down temporarily.
    d. shut down permanently.

11. Assume the price of the firm's product in Exhibit 15 is $10 per unit. The maximum profit the firm earns is
    a. zero.
    b. $5,000 per week.
    c. $1,500 per week.
    d. $10,500 per week.

12. In Exhibit 15, the firm's total revenue at a price of $10 per unit pays for
   a. a portion of total variable costs.
   b. a portion of total fixed costs.
   c. none of the total fixed costs.
   d. all of the total fixed costs and total variable costs.

13. As shown in Exhibit 15, the short-run supply curve for this firm corresponds to which segment of its marginal cost curve?
   a. *A* to *D* and all points above
   b. *B* to *D* and all points above
   c. *C* to *D* and all points above
   d. *B* to *C* only

14. In long-run equilibrium, the perfectly competitive firm's price is equal to which of the following?
   a. Short-run marginal cost
   b. Minimum short-run average total cost
   c. Marginal revenue
   d. All of the above

15. In a constant-cost industry, input prices remain constant as
   a. the supply of inputs fluctuates.
   b. firms encounter diseconomies of scale.
   c. workers become more experienced.
   d. firms enter and exit the industry.

16. Suppose that, in the long run, the price of feature films rises as the movie production industry expands. We can conclude that movie production is a (an)
   a. increasing-cost industry.
   b. constant-cost industry.
   c. decreasing-cost industry.
   d. marginal-cost industry.

17. Which of the following is *true* of a perfectly competitive market?
   a. If economic profits are earned, then the price will fall over time.
   b. In long-run equilibrium, $P = MR = SRMC = SRATC = LRAC$.
   c. A constant-cost industry exists when the entry of new firms has no effect on their cost curves.
   d. All of the above are true.

18. Suppose that in a perfectly competitive market, firms are making economic profits. In the long run, we can expect to see
   a. some firms leave.
   b. the market price rise.
   c. market supply shift to the left.
   d. economic profits become zero.
   e. production levels remaining the same as in the short-run.

19. Assume the short-run average total cost for a perfectly competitive industry decreases as the output of the industry expands. In the long run, the industry supply curve will
   a. have a positive slope.
   b. have a negative slope.
   c. be perfectly horizontal.
   d. be perfectly vertical.

20. The long-run supply curve for a competitive constant-cost industry is
   a. horizontal.
   b. vertical.
   c. upward sloping.
   d. downward sloping.

Monopoly

© David Muir/Digital Vision/Getty Images.

P laying the popular board game of Monopoly teaches some of the characteristics of monopoly theory presented in this chapter. In the game version, players win by gaining as much economic power as possible. They strive to own railroads, utilities, Boardwalk, Park Place, and other valuable real estate. Then each player tries to bankrupt opponents by having hotels that charge high prices. A player who rolls the dice and lands on another player's property has no choice—either pay the price or lose the game.

In the last chapter, we studied perfect competition, which may be viewed as the paragon of economic virtue. Why? Under perfect competition, there are many sellers, each lacking any power to influence price. Perfect competition and monopoly are polar extremes. The word

monopoly is derived from two Greek words meaning "single seller." A monopoly has the market power to set its price and not worry about competitors. Perhaps your college or university has only one bookstore where you can buy textbooks. If so, students are likely to pay higher prices for textbooks than they would if many sellers competed in the campus textbook market.

This chapter explains why firms do not or cannot enter a particular market and compete with a monopolist. Then we explore some of the interesting actual monopolies around the world. We study how a monopolist determines what price to charge and how much to produce. The chapter ends with a discussion of the pros and cons of monopoly. Most of the analytical tools required here have been introduced in previous chapters.

The Monopoly Market Structure

The model at the opposite extreme from perfect competition is monopoly. Under monopoly, the consumer has a simple choice—either buy the monopolist's product or do without it. Monopoly is a market structure characterized by (1) a single seller, (2) a unique product, and (3) impossible entry into the market. Unlike perfect competition, there are no close substitutes for the monopolist's product. Monopoly, like perfect competition, corresponds only approximately to real-world industries, but it serves as a useful benchmark model. Following are brief descriptions of each monopoly characteristic.

Monopoly
A market structure characterized by (1) a single seller, (2) a unique product, and (3) impossible entry into the market.

Single Seller

In perfect competition, many firms make up the industry. In contrast, a monopoly means that a single firm *is* the industry. One firm provides the total supply of a product in a given market. Local monopolies are more common real-world approximations of the model than national or world market monopolies. For example, the campus bookstore, local telephone service, cable television company, and electric power company may be local monopolies. The only gas station, drug store, and grocery store in Nowhere County, Utah, and a hotdog stand at a football game are also examples of monopolies. Nationally, the U.S. Postal Service monopolizes first-class mail.

Unique Product

A unique product means there are *no close substitutes* for the monopolist's product. Thus, the monopolist faces little or no competition. In reality, however, there are few, if any, products that have no close substitutes. For example, students can buy used textbooks from sources other than the campus bookstore, and textbooks can be purchased over the Internet. Natural gas and oil furnaces are good substitutes for electric heat. Similarly, the fax machine and email are substitutes for mail service, and a satellite dish can replace your local cable television service.

Impossible Entry

In perfect competition, there are no constraints to prevent new firms from entering an industry. In the case of monopoly, extremely high barriers make it very difficult or impossible for new firms to enter an industry. Following are the three major barriers that prevent new firms from entering a market and competing with a monopolist.

Ownership of a Vital Resource

Sole control of the entire supply of a strategic input is one way a monopolist can prevent a newcomer from entering an industry. A famous historical example is Alcoa's monopoly of the U.S. aluminum market from the late nineteenth century until the end of World War II. The source of Alcoa's monopoly was its control of bauxite ore, which is necessary to produce aluminum. Today, it is very difficult for a new professional sports league to compete with the National Football League (NFL) and the National Basketball Association (NBA). Why? NFL and NBA teams have contracts with the best players and leases for the best stadiums and arenas.

Legal Barriers

The oldest and most effective barriers protecting a firm from potential competitors are the result of government franchises and licenses. The government permits a single firm to provide a certain product and excludes competing firms by law. For example, water and sewer service, natural gas, and cable television operate under monopoly franchises established by state and local governments. In many states, the state government runs monopoly liquor stores and lotteries. The U.S. Postal Service has a government franchise to deliver first-class mail.

Government-granted licenses restrict entry into some industries and occupations. For example, the Federal Communications Commission (FCC) must license radio and television stations. In most states, physicians, lawyers, dentists, nurses, teachers, real estate agents, hairstylists, taxicabs, liquor stores, funeral homes, and other professions and businesses are required to have a license.

Patents and copyrights are another form of government barrier to entry. The government grants patents to inventors, thereby legally prohibiting other firms from selling the patented product for 20 years. Copyrights give creators of literature, art, music, and movies exclusive rights to sell or license their works. The purpose behind granting patents and copyrights is to encourage innovation and new products by guaranteeing exclusive rights to profit from new ideas for a limited period.

Economies of Scale

Why might competition among firms be unsustainable so that one firm becomes a monopolist? Recall the concept of *economies of scale* from the chapter on production costs. As a result of large-scale production, the long-run average cost ($LRAC$) of production falls. This means a monopoly can emerge in time *naturally* because of the relationship between average cost and the scale of an operation. As a firm becomes larger, its cost per unit of output is lower compared to a smaller competitor. In the long run, this "survival of the fittest" cost advantage forces smaller firms to leave the industry. Because new firms cannot hope to produce and sell output equal or close to that of the monopolist, thereby achieving the monopolist's low costs, they will not enter the industry. Thus, a monopoly can arise over time and remain dominant in an industry even though the monopolist does not own an essential resource or obtain legal barriers.

Economists call the situation in which one seller emerges in an industry because of economies of scale a natural monopoly. A natural monopoly is an industry in which the long-run average cost of production declines throughout the entire

Natural monopoly

An industry in which the long-run average cost of production declines throughout the entire market. As a result, a single firm can supply the entire market demand at a lower cost than two or more smaller firms.

market. As a result, a single firm can supply the entire market demand at a lower cost than two or more smaller firms. Public utilities, such as the natural gas, water, and local telephone companies, are examples of natural monopolies. The government grants these industries an exclusive franchise in a geographic area so consumers can benefit from the cost savings that occur when one firm in an industry with significant economies of scale sells a large output. The government then regulates these monopolies through a board of commissioners to prevent exploitation.

Exhibit 1 depicts the *LRAC* curve for a natural monopoly. A single firm can produce 100 units at an average cost of $15 and a total cost of $1,500. If two firms each produce 50 units, the total cost rises to $2,500. With five firms producing 20 units each, the total cost rises to $3,500. In the chapter on antitrust and regulation, regulation of a natural monopoly will be explored in greater detail.

> **Conclusion** *Because of economies of scale, a single firm in an industry will produce output at a lower per-unit cost than two or more firms.*

Price and Output Decisions for a Monopolist

A major difference between perfect competition and monopoly is the shape of the demand curve, not the shapes of the cost curves. As explained in the previous

---

EXHIBIT 1 | Minimizing Costs in a Natural Monopoly

In a natural monopoly, a single firm in an industry can produce at a lower cost than two or more firms. This condition occurs because the *LRAC* curve for any firm decreases over the relevant range. For example, one firm can produce 100 units at an average cost of $15 and a total cost of $1,500. Two firms in the industry can produce 100 units of output (50 units each) for a total cost of $2,500, and five firms can produce the same output for a total cost of $3,500.

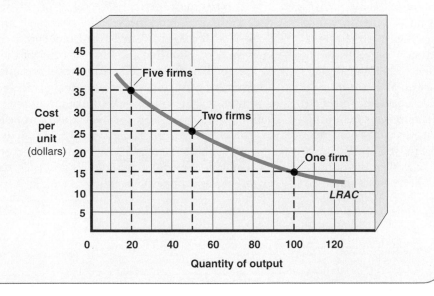

© North Wind Picture Archives.

Interesting examples of monopolies can be found in other countries. Let's begin with a historical example. In the sixteenth through eighteenth centuries, monarchs granted monopoly rights for a variety of businesses. For example, in 1600 Queen Elizabeth I chartered the British East India Company and gave it a monopoly over England's trade with India. This company was even given the right to coin money and to make peace or war with non-Christian powers. As a result of its monopoly, the company made substantial profits from the trade in Indian cotton goods, silks, and spices. In the late 1700s, the growing power of the company and huge personal fortunes of its officers provoked more and more government control. Finally, in 1858, the company was abolished, ending its trade monopoly, great power, and patronage.

"Diamonds are forever," and perhaps so is the diamond monopoly. DeBeers, a South African corporation, was close to a world monopoly. Through its Central Selling Organization (CSO) headquartered in London, DeBeers controlled 80 percent of all the diamonds sold in the world. DeBeers controlled the price of jewelry-quality diamonds by requiring suppliers in Russia, Australia, Congo, Botswana, Namibia, and other countries to sell their rough diamonds through DeBeers's CSO. Why did suppliers of rough diamonds allow DeBeers to set the price and quantity of diamonds sold throughout the world? The answer was that the CSO could put any uncooperative seller out of business. All the CSO had to do was to reach into its huge stockpile of diamonds and flood the market with the type of diamonds being sold by an independent seller. As a result, the price of diamonds would plummet in the competitor's market, and it ceased to sell diamonds.

In recent years, DeBeers lost some of its control of the market. Mines in Australia became more independent, diamonds were found in Canada, and Russian mines began selling to independents. To deal with the new conditions, DeBeers changed its policy in 2001 by closing the CSO and promoting DeBeers' own brand of diamonds rather than trying to control the world diamond supply. DeBeers proclaimed its strategy to be "the diamond supplier of choice." Will this monopoly continue? It is an interesting question.

Genuine caviar, the salty black delicacy, is naturally scarce because it comes from the eggs of sturgeon harvested by fisheries from the Caspian Sea near the mouth of the Volga River. After the Bolshevik revolution in Russia in 1917, a caviar monopoly was established under the control of the Soviet Ministry of Fisheries and the Paris-based Petrosian Company. The Petrosian brothers limited exports of caviar and pushed prices up as high as $1,000 a pound for some varieties. As a result of this worldwide monopoly, both the Soviet government and the Petrosian Company earned handsome profits. It is interesting to note that the vast majority of the tons of caviar harvested each year was consumed at government banquets or sold at bargain prices to top Communist Party officials. With the fall of the Soviet Union, it was impossible for the Ministry of Fisheries to control all exports of caviar. Various former Soviet republics claimed jurisdiction and negotiated independent export contracts. As a result, caviar export prices dropped sharply.

chapter, a perfectly competitive firm is a *price taker*. In contrast, the next sections explain that a monopolist is a price maker. A price maker is a firm that faces a downward-sloping demand curve. This means a monopolist has the ability to select the product's price. In short, a monopolist can set the price with its corresponding level of output, rather than being a helpless pawn at the mercy of the going industry price. To understand the monopolist, we again apply the marginal approach to our hypothetical electronics company—Computech.

Marginal Revenue, Total Revenue, and Price Elasticity of Demand

Suppose engineers at Computech discover an inexpensive miracle electronic device called SAV-U-GAS that anyone can easily attach to a car's engine. Once installed, the device raises gasoline mileage to over 100 miles per gallon. The government grants Computech a patent, and the company becomes a monopolist selling this gas-saver gizmo. Because of this barrier to entry, Computech is the only seller in the industry. Although other firms try to compete with this invention, they create poor substitutes. This means the downward-sloping demand curve for the industry and for the monopolist are identical.

Exhibit 2(a) illustrates the demand and the marginal revenue (*MR*) curves for a monopolist such as Computech. As the monopolist lowers its price to increase the quantity demanded, changes in both price and quantity affect the firm's total revenue (price times quantity), as shown graphically in Exhibit 2(b). If Computech charges $150, consumers purchase zero units, and, therefore, total revenue is zero. To sell 1 unit, Computech must lower the price to $138, and total revenue rises from zero to $138. Because the marginal revenue is the increase in total revenue that results from a 1-unit change in output, the *MR* curve at the first unit of output is $138 ($138 − 0). Thus, the price and the marginal revenue from selling 1 unit are equal at $138. To sell 2 units, the monopolist must lower the price to $125, and total revenue rises to $250. The marginal revenue from selling the second unit is $112 ($250 − $138), which is $13 less than the price received.

As shown in Exhibit 2(a), as the monopolist lowers its price, price is greater than marginal revenue after the first unit of output. Like all marginal measurements, marginal revenue is plotted midway between the quantities.

> **Conclusion** *The demand and marginal revenue curves of the monopolist are downward sloping, in contrast to the horizontal demand and corresponding marginal revenue curves facing the perfectly competitive firm* [compare Exhibit 2(a) with Exhibit 1(b) of the previous chapter].

Starting from zero output, as the price falls, total revenue rises until it reaches a maximum at 6 units, and then it falls, tracing the "revenue hill" drawn in Part (b). The explanation was presented earlier in the discussion of price elasticity of demand in Chapter 5. Recall that a straight-line demand curve has an elastic ($E_d > 1$) segment along the upper half, a unit elastic ($E_d = 1$) at the midpoint, and an inelastic ($E_d < 1$) segment along the lower half (see Exhibit 4 in Chapter 5). Recall from Chapter 5 that when $E_d > 1$, total revenue rises as the price drops, and total revenue reaches a maximum where $E_d = 1$. When $E_d < 1$, total revenue falls as the price falls.

As shown in Exhibit 2(b), total revenue for a monopolist is related to marginal revenue. When the *MR* curve is above the quantity axis (elastic demand), total revenue

EXHIBIT 2   Demand, Marginal Revenue, and Total Revenue for a Monopolist

Part (a) shows the relationship between the demand and the marginal revenue curves. The *MR* curve is below the demand curve. Between zero and 6 units of output, *MR* > 0; at 6 units of output, *MR* = 0; beyond 6 units of output, *MR* < 0.

The relationship between demand and total revenue is shown in Part (b). When the price is $150, total revenue is zero. When the price is set at zero, total revenue is also zero. In between these two extreme prices, the price of $75 maximizes total revenue. This price corresponds to 6 units of output, which is where the *MR* curve intersects the quantity axis, halfway between the origin and the intercept of the demand curve.

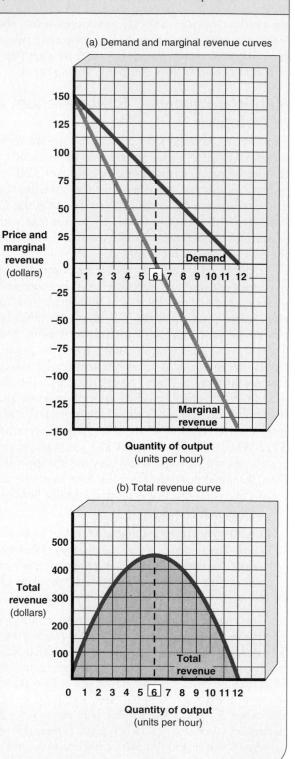

(a) Demand and marginal revenue curves

(b) Total revenue curve

Output per Hour	Price	Total Revenue	Marginal Revenue
0	$150	$ 0	
			$138
1	138	138	
			112
2	125	250	
			89
3	113	339	
			61
4	100	400	
			40
5	88	440	
			10
6	75	450	
			0
			−9
7	63	441	
			−41
8	50	400	
			−58
9	38	342	
			−92
10	25	250	
			−107
11	13	143	
			−143
12	0	0	

is increasing. At the intersection of the *MR* curve and the quantity axis (unit elastic demand), total revenue is at its maximum. When the *MR* curve is below the quantity axis, total revenue is decreasing (inelastic demand). The monopolist will never operate on the inelastic range of its demand curve that corresponds to a negative marginal revenue. The reason is that, in this inelastic range, the monopolist can increase total revenue by cutting output and raising price. In our example, Computech would not charge a price lower than $75 or produce an output greater than 6 units per hour. Now we turn to the question of what price the monopolist will charge to maximize profit.

In Exhibit 2(a), observe that the *MR* curve cuts the quantity axis at 6 units, which is half of 12 units. Following an easy rule helps locate the point along the quantity axis where marginal revenue equals zero: *The marginal revenue curve for a straight-line demand curve intersects the quantity axis halfway between the origin and the quantity axis intercept of the demand curve.*

Short-Run Profit Maximization for a Monopolist Using the Total Revenue-Total Cost Method

Exhibit 3 reproduces the demand, total revenue, and marginal revenue data from Exhibit 2 and adds cost data from the previous two chapters. These data illustrate a situation in which Computech can earn monopoly economic profit in the short run. Subtracting total cost in column 6 from total revenue in column 3 gives the total profit or loss in column 8 that the firm earns at each level of output. From zero to 1 unit, the monopolist incurs losses, and then a break-even point occurs before 2 units per hour. If the monopolist produces 5 units per hour, it earns the maximum profit of $190 per hour. As output expands between 5 and 8 units of output, the monopolist's profit diminishes. After 8 units of output, there is a second break-even point, and losses increase as output expands. Exhibit 4 illustrates graphically that where the vertical distance between the total revenue and total cost curves is maximum corresponds to the profit-maximizing output. Note that the total revenue-maximizing output level of 6 units is greater than the profit-maximizing output at 5 units.

Short-Run Profit Maximization for a Monopolist Using the Marginal Revenue Equals Marginal Cost Method

Exhibit 5 reproduces the demand and cost curves from the table in Exhibit 3. Like the perfectly competitive firm, a monopolist maximizes profit by producing the quantity of output where *MR* = *MC* and charging the corresponding price on its demand curve. In this case, 5 units is the quantity at which *MR* = *MC*. As represented by point *A* on the demand curve, the price at 5 units is $88. Point *B* represents an average total cost (*ATC*) of $50 at 5 units. Because the price of $88 is above the *ATC* curve at the *MR* = *MC* output, the monopolist earns a profit of $38 per unit. At the hourly output of 5 units, total profit is $190 per hour, as shown by the shaded area ($38 per unit × 5 units).

Observe that a monopolist charges neither the highest possible price nor the total revenue-maximizing price. In Exhibit 5(a), $88 is not the highest possible price. Because Computech is a *price maker*, it could have set a price above $88 and sold less output than 5 units. However, the monopolist does not maximize profit by charging the highest possible price. Any price above $88 does not correspond to the intersection of the *MR* and *MC* curves. Now note that 5 units is below the output level where *MR* intersects the quantity axis and total revenue reaches its peak. Since *MR* = 0 and

EXHIBIT 3		Short-Run Profit-Maximization Schedule for Computech as a Monopolist					
(1) Output per Hour (Q)	(2) Price per Unit (P)	(3) Total Revenue (TR)	(4) Marginal Revenue (MR)	(5) Marginal Cost (MC)	(6) Total Cost (TC)	(7) Average Total Cost (ATC)	(8) Profit (+) or Loss (−)
0	$150	$ 0			$100	—	−$100
			$138	$50			
1	138	138			150	$150	−12
			112	34			
2	125	250			184	92	66
			89	24			
3	113	339			208	69	131
			61	19			
4	100	400			227	57	173
			40	23			
5	88	440	25	25	250	50	190
			10	30			
6	75	450			280	47	170
			−9	38			
7	63	441			318	45	123
			−41	48			
8	50	400			366	46	34
			−58	59			
9	38	342			425	47	−83
			−92	75			
10	25	250			500	50	−250
			−107	95			
11	13	143			595	54	−452
			−143	117			
12	0	0			712	59	−712

$E_d = 1$ when total revenue is maximum at 6 units of output, $MC = 0$ must also hold to maximize revenue and profit at the same time. A monopolist producing with zero marginal cost is an unlikely case. Hence, the price charged to maximize profit is higher on the demand curve than the price that maximizes total revenue.

> **Conclusion** *The monopolist always maximizes profit by producing at a price on the elastic segment of its demand curve.*

A Monopolist Facing a Short-Run Loss

Having a monopoly does not guarantee profits. A monopolist has no protection against changes in demand or cost conditions. Exhibit 6 shows a situation in which the demand curve is lower at any point than the *ATC* curve, and total cost

EXHIBIT 4

Short-Run Profit Maximization for a Monopolist Using the Total Revenue-Total Cost Method

The profit-maximizing level of output for Computech as a monopolist is shown in this exhibit. Part (a) shows that maximum profit is earned by producing 5 units per hour and charging a price of $88 per unit where the vertical distance between the total revenue and total cost curves is the greatest. In Part (b), the maximum profit of $190 per hour corresponds to the profit-maximizing output of 5 units per hour illustrated in Part (a). At output levels below 2 or above 8, the monopolist incurs losses.

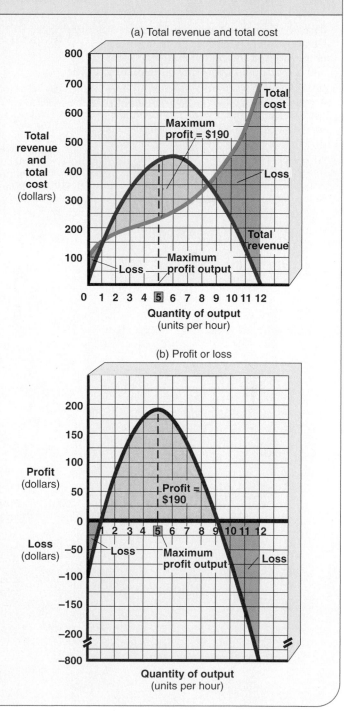

(a) Total revenue and total cost

(b) Profit or loss

EXHIBIT 5

Short-Run Profit Maximization for a Monopolist Using the Marginal Revenue Equals Marginal Cost Method

Part (a) illustrates a monopolist electronics firm, Computech, maximizing profit by producing 5 units of output where the marginal revenue (*MR*) and the marginal cost (*MC*) curves intersect. The profit-maximizing price the monopolist charges at 5 units of output is $88, which is point *A* on the demand curve. Because $88 is above the average total cost (*ATC*) of $50 at point *B*, the monopolist earns a short-run profit of $190 per hour, represented by the shaded area ($38 profit per unit × 5 units).

At a price of $88 and output of 5 units per hour in Part (a), the shaded area in Part (b) shows that the profit curve is maximized at $190 per hour. At output levels below 2 or above 8, the monopolist incurs losses.

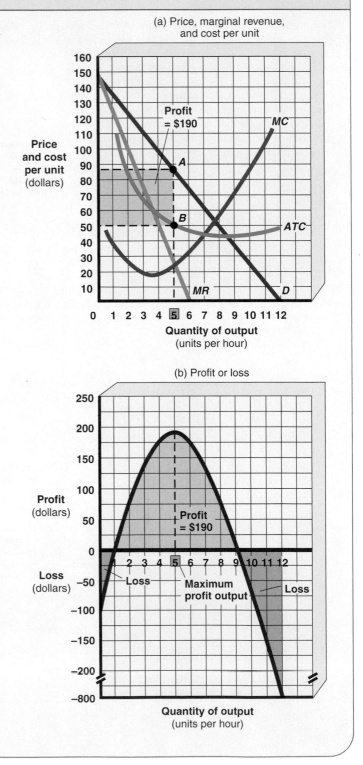

(a) Price, marginal revenue, and cost per unit

(b) Profit or loss

EXHIBIT 6	Short-Run Loss Minimization for a Monopolist Using the Marginal Revenue Equals Marginal Cost Method

In Part (a), all points along the demand curve lie below the *ATC* curve. If the market price charged corresponds to the output where the marginal revenue (*MR*) and marginal cost (*MC*) curves intersect, the firm will keep its loss to a minimum. At point *A*, the loss-minimizing price is $50 per unit, and marginal revenue equals marginal cost at an output of 5 units per hour with *ATC* equal to $70 per unit (point *B*). The short-run loss represented by the shaded area is $100 ($20 loss per unit × 5 units).

Part (b) shows that the firm's short-run loss will be greater at any output other than where the marginal revenue and the marginal cost curves intersect at an output of 5 units per hour. Because the price of $50 is above the average variable cost, each unit of output sold pays for the average variable cost and a portion of the average fixed cost.

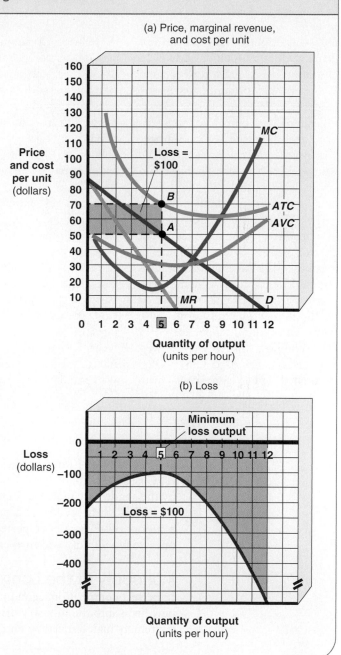

(a) Price, marginal revenue, and cost per unit

(b) Loss

therefore exceeds total revenue at any price charged. Because the point where *MR* = *MC* at a price of $50 (point *A*) on the demand curve is above the *AVC* curve, but below the *ATC* curve, the best Computech can do is to minimize its loss. This means the monopolist, like the perfectly competitive firm, produces in the short run

Oil was discovered in western Pennsylvania by Colonel Edwin L. Drake in 1859, and after the Civil War, oil wells sprang up across the landscape. Because oil was plentiful, there was cutthroat competition, and the result was low prices and profits. At this time, John D. Rockefeller, who had grown up selling eggs, was a young Cleveland produce wholesaler in his early twenties. He was doing well in produce, but realized that greater profits could be made in refining oil, where there was less competition than in drilling for oil. So, in 1869, Rockefeller borrowed all the money he could and began with two small oil refineries.

To boost his market power, Rockefeller's Standard Oil of Ohio negotiated secret agreements with the railroads. In addition to information on his competitors' shipments, Rockefeller negotiated contracts with the railroads to pay rebates not only on Standard Oil's oil shipments, but also on its competitors' shipments. Soon Standard Oil was able to buy 21 of its 26 refining competitors in the Cleveland area. As its profits grew, Standard Oil expanded its refining empire by acquiring its own oil fields, railroads, pipelines, and ships. The objective was to control oil from the oil well to the consumer. Over time, Rockefeller came to own a major part of the petroleum industry. Competitors found railroads and pipelines closed to their oil shipments. Rivals that could not be forced out of business were merged with Standard Oil.

In 1870, Standard Oil controlled only 10 percent of the oil industry in the United States. By 1880, Standard Oil controlled over 90 percent of the industry, and its oil was being shipped throughout the world. The more Standard Oil monopolized the petroleum industry, the higher its profits rose, and the greater its power to eliminate competition became. As competitors dropped out of the industry, Rockefeller became a price maker. He raised prices, and Standard Oil's profits soared. Finally, in 1911, Standard Oil was broken up under the Sherman Antitrust Act of 1890 into competing companies, including companies that eventually became Exxon and Mobil.

at a quantity of 5 units per hour where $MR = MC$. At a price of $50 (point A), the ATC is $70 (point B), and Computech incurs a loss of $100 per hour, represented by the shaded area ($20 × 5 units).

What if $MR = MC$ at a price on the demand curve that is below the AVC for a monopolist? As under perfect competition, the monopolist will shut down. To operate would only add further to its losses.

Monopoly in the Long Run

In perfect competition, economic profits are impossible in the long run. The entry of new firms into the industry drives the product's price down until profits reach zero. Extremely high barriers to entry, however, protect a monopolist.

> **Conclusion** *If the positions of a monopolist's demand and cost curves give it a profit and nothing disturbs these curves, the monopolist will earn profit in the long run.*

In the long run, the monopolist has great flexibility. The monopolist can alter its plant size to lower cost just as a perfectly competitive firm does. But firms such as

Computech will not remain in business in the long run when losses persist—regardless of their monopoly status. Facing long-run losses, the monopolist will transfer its resources to a more profitable industry.

In reality, no monopolist can depend on barriers to protect it fully from competition in the long run. One threat is that entrepreneurs will find innovative ways to compete with a monopoly. For example, Computech must fear that firms will use their ingenuity and new electronic discoveries to develop a better and cheaper gasoline-saving device. To dampen the enthusiasm of potential rivals, one alternative for the monopolist is to sacrifice short-run profits to earn greater profits in the long run. Returning to Part (a) of Exhibit 5, the monopolist might wish to charge a price below $88 and produce an output greater than 5 units per hour.

Price Discrimination

Our discussion so far has assumed the monopolist charges each customer the same price. What if Computech decides to sell identical SAV-U-GAS units for, say, $50 to truckers and $100 to everyone else? Under certain conditions, a monopolist may practice price discrimination to maximize profit. Price discrimination occurs when a seller charges different prices for the same product that are not justified by cost differences.

Conditions for Price Discrimination

All monopolists cannot engage in price discrimination. The following three conditions must exist before a seller can price discriminate:

1. The seller must be a price maker and therefore face a downward-sloping demand curve. This means that monopoly is not the only market structure in which price discrimination may occur.
2. The seller must be able to segment the market by distinguishing between consumers willing to pay different prices. Momentarily, this separation of buyers will be shown to be based on different price elasticities of demand.
3. It must be impossible or too costly for customers to engage in arbitrage. Arbitrage is the practice of earning a profit by buying a good at a low price and reselling the good at a higher price. For example, suppose your campus bookstore tried to boost profits by selling textbooks at a 50 percent discount to seniors. It would not take seniors long to cut the bookstore's profits by buying textbooks at the low price, selling these texts under the list price to all students who are not seniors, and pocketing the difference. In so doing, even without knowing the word *arbitrage,* the seniors would destroy the bookstore's price discrimination scheme.

Although not monopolies, college and university tuition policies meet the conditions for price discrimination. First, lower tuition increases the quantity of openings demanded. Second, applicants' high school grades and SAT scores allow the admissions office to classify "consumers" with different price elasticities of demand. Students with lower grades and SAT scores have fewer substitutes, and their demand curve is less elastic than that of students with higher grades and SAT scores. If the tuition rises at University *X,* few students with lower grades will be lost because they have few offers of admission from other universities. On the other hand, the loss of students with higher grades and SAT scores is greater because they have more admissions opportunities. Third, the nature of the product prevents arbitrage. A student cannot buy University *X* admission at one price and sell it to another student for a higher price.

> **Price discrimination**
> The practice of a seller charging different prices for the same product that are not justified by cost differences.

> **Arbitrage**
> The practice of earning a profit by buying a good at a low price and reselling the good at a higher price.

EXHIBIT 7   Price Discrimination

To maximize profit, University X separates students applying for admission into two markets. The demand curve for admission of average students in Part (a) is less elastic than the demand curve for admission of superior students in Part (b). Profit maximization occurs when $MR = MC$ in each market. Therefore, University X sets a tuition of T_1 for average students and gives scholarships to superior students, which lowers their tuition to T_2. Using price discrimination, University X earns a greater profit than it would by charging a single tuition to all students.

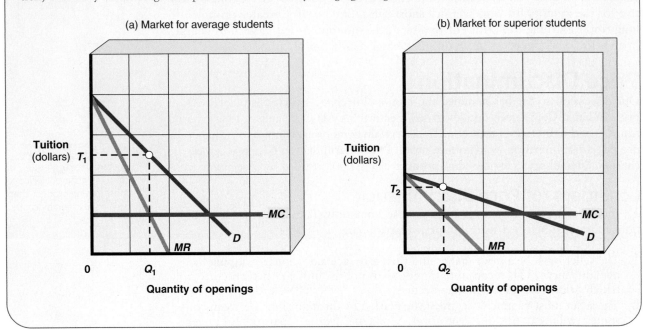

(a) Market for average students

(b) Market for superior students

Exhibit 7 illustrates how University X price discriminates. For simplicity, assume the marginal cost of providing education to students is constant and therefore is represented by a horizontal MC curve. To maximize profit, University X follows the $MR = MC$ rule in each market. Given the different price elasticities of demand, the price at which $MR = MC$ differs for average and superior students. As a result, University X sets a higher tuition, T_1, in the average-student market, where demand is less responsive to the higher price. In the superior-student market, where demand is more responsive, these students receive scholarships, and their tuition is lower at T_2.

Is Price Discrimination Unfair?

Examples of price discrimination abound. Movie theaters offer lower prices for children than for adults. Electric utilities, which are monopolies, charge industrial users of electricity lower rates than residential users. Hotels and restaurants often give discounts to senior citizens. Airlines offer lower fares to groups of vacationers.

The typical reaction to price discrimination is that it is unfair. From the viewpoint of buyers who pay the higher prices, it is. But look at the other side of price discrimination. First, the seller is pleased because price discrimination increases profits. Second, many buyers benefit from price discrimination by not being excluded from purchasing the product. In Exhibit 7, price discrimination makes it possible for superior students who could not afford to pay a higher tuition to attend University X. Price discrimination also allows retired persons to enjoy hotels and restaurants they could not otherwise afford and enables more children to attend movies.

CHECKPOINT

Why Don't Adults Pay More for Popcorn at the Movies?
At the movies, adults pay a higher ticket price than children, and each group gets a different-colored ticket. However, when adults and children go to the concession stand, both groups pay the same amount for popcorn and other snacks. Which of the following statements best explains why price discrimination stops at the ticket window? (1) The demand curve for popcorn is perfectly elastic. (2) The theater has no way to divide the buyers of popcorn based on different price elasticities of demand. (3) The theater cannot prevent resale.

Comparing Monopoly and Perfect Competition

Now that the basics of the two extremes of perfect competition and monopoly have been presented, we can compare and evaluate these market structures. This is an important assessment because the contrast between the disadvantages of monopoly and the advantages of perfect competition is the basis for many government policies, such as antitrust laws. To keep the analysis simple, we assume the monopolist charges a single price, rather than engaging in price discrimination.

The Monopolist as a Resource Misallocator

Recall the discussion of market efficiency in Chapter 4. This condition exists when a firm charging the equilibrium price uses neither too many nor too few resources to produce a product, so there is no *market failure*. Now you can state this definition of market efficiency in terms of price and marginal cost, as follows: *A perfectly competitive firm that produces the quantity of output at which* $P = MC$ *achieves an efficient allocation of resources.* This means production reaches the level of output when the price of the last unit produced matches the cost of producing it.

Exhibit 8(a) shows that a perfectly competitive firm produces the quantity of output at which $P = MC$. The price, P_c (marginal benefit), of the last unit produced equals the marginal cost of the resources used to produce it. In contrast, the monopolist shown in Exhibit 8(b) charges a price, P_m, greater than marginal cost, $P > MC$. Therefore, consumers are shortchanged because the marginal benefit of the last unit produced exceeds the marginal cost of producing it. Consumers want the monopolist to use more resources and produce additional units, but the monopolist restricts output to maximize profit.

Conclusion *A monopolist is characterized by inefficiency because resources are underallocated to the production of its product.*

EXHIBIT 8   Comparing a Perfectly Competitive Firm and a Monopolist

The perfectly competitive firm in Part (a) sets $P = MC$ and produces Q_c output. Therefore, at the last unit of output, the marginal benefit is equal to the marginal cost of resources used to produce it. This condition means perfect competition achieves efficiency.

Part (b) shows that the monopolist produces output Q_m where $P > MC$. By so doing, consumers are short-changed because the marginal benefit of the last unit produced exceeds the marginal cost of producing it. Under monopoly, inefficiency occurs because the monopolist underallocates resources to the production of its product. As a result, Q_m is less than Q_c.

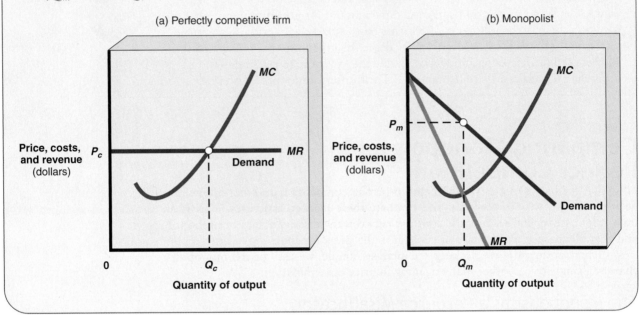

(a) Perfectly competitive firm

(b) Monopolist

Perfect Competition Means More Output for Less

Exhibit 9 presents a comparison of perfect competition and monopoly in the same graph. Suppose the industry begins as perfectly competitive. The market demand curve, D (equal to MR), and the market supply curve, S, establish a perfectly competitive price, P_c, and output, Q_c. Recall from Exhibit 8 in the previous chapter that the competitive industry's supply curve, S, is the horizontal sum of the marginal cost (MC) curves of all the firms in the industry.

Now let's suppose the market structure changes when one firm buys out all the competing firms and the industry becomes a monopoly. Assume further that the demand and cost curves are unaffected by this dramatic change. In a monopoly, the industry demand curve *is* the monopolist's demand curve. Because the single firm is a price maker, the MR curve lies below the demand curve. The industry supply curve now becomes the MC curve for the monopolist. To maximize profit, the monopolist sets $MR = MC$ by restricting the output to Q_m and raising the price to P_m.

> **Conclusion** *Monopoly harms consumers on two fronts. The monopolist charges a higher price and produces a lower output than would result under a perfectly competitive market structure.*

EXHIBIT 9 — The Impact of Monopolizing an Industry

Assume an industry is perfectly competitive, with market demand curve D and market supply curve S. The market supply curve is the horizontal summation of all the individual firms' marginal cost curves above their minimum average variable costs. The intersection of market supply and market demand establishes the equilibrium price of P_c and the equilibrium quantity of Q_c. Now assume the industry suddenly changes to a monopoly. The monopolist produces the $MR = MC$ output of Q_m, which is less than Q_c. By restricting output to Q_m, the monopolist is able to charge the higher price of P_m.

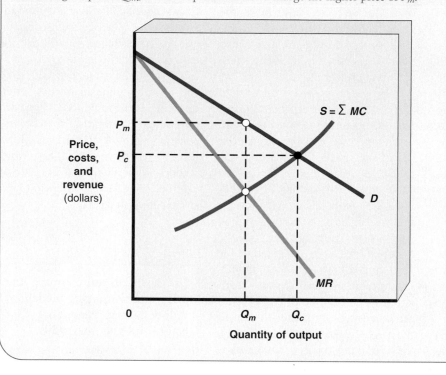

The Case against and for Monopoly

So far, a strong case has been made against monopoly and in favor of perfect competition. Now it is time to pause and summarize the economist's case against monopoly:

- A monopolist "gouges" consumers by charging a higher price than would be charged under perfect competition.
- Because a monopolist restricts output in order to maximize profit, too few resources are used to produce the product. Stated differently, the monopolist misallocates resources by charging a price greater than marginal cost. In perfectly competitive industries, price is set equal to marginal cost, and the result is an optimal allocation of resources.
- Long-run economic profit for a monopolist exceeds the zero economic profit earned in the long run by a perfectly competitive firm.
- To the extent that the monopolist is a rich John D. Rockefeller, for example, and consumers of oil are poor, monopoly alters the distribution of income in favor of the monopolist.

Not all economists agree that monopoly is bad. Joseph Schumpeter and John Kenneth Galbraith praised monopoly power. They argued that the rate of technological

YOU'RE THE ECONOMIST

New York Taxicabs: Where Have All the Fare Flags Gone?

Applicable Concepts: Perfect competition versus monopoly

Yellow taxi cabs in New York City, which are today one of the most famous icons of the city, are a love and hate relationship. Just pretend you're the Statue of Liberty, and stick your arm straight up in the sky to hail a cab that will take you to your destination. The downside of an abundance of cabs is the traffic jams speckled with yellow cabs that service the city. Flashback to the 1920s when New York taxicabs were competitive. There was no limit on the number of taxis, and hack licenses were only $10. With this low barrier to entry taxis engaged in price competition. Cabbies could choose among three different flags to attach to their cars. A red flag cab charged a surcharge for extra passengers. A white flag signaled no surcharge for extra passengers. A green flag meant the cabbie was offering a discount fare. Price wars often erupted, and the vast major-ity of cabbies flew green flags and charged bargain fares. One strategy was to fly the red flag (high rate) during rush hour and the green flag to offer discounts at off-peak times. Taxi companies also offered a variety of cabs—old, new, big, and small.[1]

As years passed, the system changed because of the concern that competition was causing an overabundance of taxies that congested city streets. The solution was to create a monopoly by law in 1937 designed to limit the number of cabs by requiring all cabs accepting street hails to be painted yellow and possess a medallion on the hood of the taxi. Currently, the Taxi and Limousine Commission (TLC) sets rates and imposes regulations. There are no price wars and the barrier to entry is high due to the high price of medallions. Today, the aluminum badges that give the rights to pick up passengers on the street cost more than $400,000, as determined at infrequent auctions. Because of their high prices, most cabs are owned by investment companies and are leased to the drivers. On the other hand, it is illegal for cabs without medallions to cruise and pick up passengers who hail them, although the law is often ignored. Nonmedallion cabs are authorized to respond only to customers who have ordered the cab in advance by phone or other means. There's no limit on the number of nonmedallion cabs or what the drivers may charge.

ANALYZE THE ISSUE

Use a graph to compare the price and output of medallion yellow cabs in New York City before and after the 1920s.

---

1. John Tierney, "You'll Wonder Where the Yellow Went," *The New York Times*, July 12, 1998, Section 6, p. 18.

---

change is likely to be greater under monopoly than under perfect competition. In their view, monopoly profits afford giant monopolies the financial strength to invest in the well-equipped laboratories and skilled labor necessary to create technological change.

The counterargument is that monopolists are slow to innovate. Freedom from direct competition means the monopolist is not motivated and therefore tends to stick to the "conventional wisdom." As Nobel laureate Sir John Hicks put it, "The best of all monopoly profit is a quiet life." In short, monopoly offers the opportunity to relax a bit and not worry about the "rat race" of technological change.

What does research on this issue suggest? Not surprisingly, many attempts have been made to verify or refute the effect of market structure on technological change. Unfortunately, the results to date have been inconclusive. For all we know, a mix of large and small firms in an industry may be the optimal mix to create technological change.

KEY CONCEPTS

Monopoly   Price maker   Arbitrage
Natural monopoly   Price discrimination

SUMMARY

- *Monopoly* is a single seller facing the entire industry demand curve because it is the industry. The monopolist sells a unique product, and extremely high barriers to entry protect it from competition.
- *Barriers to entry* that prevent new firms from entering an industry are (1) ownership of an essential resource, (2) legal barriers, and (3) economies of scale. Government franchises, licenses, patents, and copyrights are the most obvious legal barriers to entry.
- A *natural monopoly* arises because of the existence of economies of scale in which the long-run average cost ($LRAC$) curve falls as production increases. Without government restrictions, economies of scale allow a single firm to produce at a lower cost than any firm producing a smaller output. Thus, smaller firms leave the industry, new firms fear competing with the monopolist, and the result is that a monopoly emerges *naturally*.

Natural monopoly

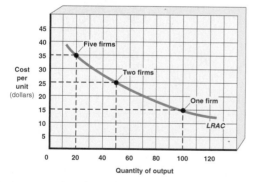

- A *price-maker* firm faces a downward-sloping demand curve. It therefore searches its demand curve to find the price-output combination that maximizes its profit and minimizes its loss.
- The *marginal revenue* and demand curves are downward sloping for a monopolist. The marginal revenue curve for a monopolist is below the demand curve, and the total revenue curve reaches its maximum where marginal revenue equals zero.
- *Price elasticity of demand* corresponds to sections of the marginal revenue curve. When MR is positive,

price elasticity of demand is elastic, $E_d > 1$. When MR is equal to zero, price elasticity of demand is unit elastic, $E_d = 1$. When MR is negative, price elasticity of demand is inelastic, $E_d < 1$.

- The *short-run profit-maximizing monopolist,* like the perfectly competitive firm, locates the profit-maximizing price by producing the output where the MR and MC curves intersect. If this price is less than the average variable cost (AVC) curve, the monopolist shuts down to minimize losses.

Short-run profit-maximizing monopolist

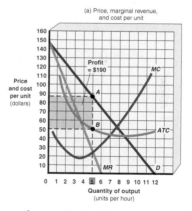

Short-run loss-minimizing monopolist

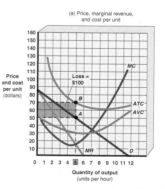

- The *long-run profit-maximizing monopolist* earns a profit because of barriers to entry. If demand and cost conditions prevent the monopolist from earning a profit, the monopolist will leave the industry.

- *Price discrimination* allows the monopolist to increase profits by charging buyers different prices rather than a single price. Three conditions are necessary for price discrimination: (1) the demand curve must be downward sloping, (2) buyers in different markets must have different price elasticities of demand, and (3) buyers must be prevented from reselling the product at a higher price than the purchase price.

- *Monopoly disadvantages* include the following: (1) a monopolist charges a higher price and produces less output than a perfectly competitive firm, (2) resource allocation is inefficient because the monopolist produces less than if competition existed, (3) monopoly produces higher long-run profits than if competition existed, and (4) monopoly transfers income from consumers to producers to a greater degree than under perfect competition.

Price discrimination

Monopoly disadvantages

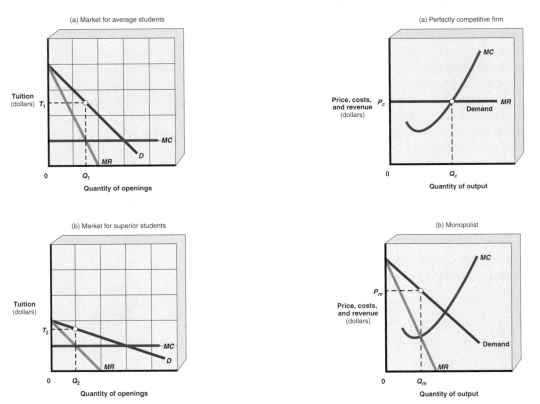

SUMMARY OF CONCLUSION STATEMENTS

- Because of economies of scale, a single firm in an industry will produce output at a lower per-unit cost than two or more firms.
- The demand and marginal revenue curves of the monopolist are downward sloping in contrast to the horizontal demand and corresponding marginal revenue curves facing the perfectly competitive firm.

- The marginal revenue curve for a straight-line demand curve intersects the quantity axis halfway between the origin and the quantity axis intercepts of the demand curve.
- The monopolist always maximizes profit by producing at a price on the elastic segment of its demand curve.
- If the positions of a monopolist's demand and cost curves give it a profit and nothing disturbs

these curves, the monopolist will earn profit in the long run.

- A monopolist is characterized by inefficiency because resources are underallocated to the production of its product.

- Monopoly harms consumers on two fronts. The monopolist charges a higher price and produces a lower output than would result under a perfectly competitive market structure.

STUDY QUESTIONS AND PROBLEMS

1. Using the three characteristics of monopoly, explain why each of the following is a monopolist:
   a. Local telephone company
   b. San Francisco 49ers football team
   c. U.S. Postal Service

2. Why is the demand curve facing a monopolist downward sloping while the demand curve facing a perfectly competitive firm is horizontal?

3. Suppose an investigator finds that the prices charged for drugs at a hospital are higher than the prices charged for the same products at drugstores in the area served by the hospital. What might explain this situation?

4. Explain why you agree or disagree with the following statements:
   a. "All monopolies are created by the government."

   b. "The monopolist charges the highest possible price."
   c. "The monopolist never takes a loss."

5. Suppose the average cost of producing a kilowatt-hour of electricity is lower for one firm than for another firm serving the same market. Without the government granting a franchise to one of these competing power companies, explain why a single seller is likely to emerge in the long run.

6. Use the following demand schedule for a monopolist to calculate total revenue and marginal revenue. For each price, indicate whether demand is elastic, unit elastic, or inelastic. Using the data from the demand schedule, graph the demand curve, the marginal revenue curve, and the total revenue curve. Identify the elastic, unit elastic, and inelastic segments along the demand curve.

Price	Quantity Demanded (Q)	Total Revenue (TR)	Marginal Revenue (MR)	Price Elasticity of Demand (E_d)
$5.00	0	$____		____
4.50	1	____	$____	____
4.00	2	____	____	____
3.50	3	____	____	____
3.00	4	____	____	____
2.50	5	____	____	____
2.00	6	____	____	____
1.50	7	____	____	____
1.00	8	____	____	____
.50	9	____	____	____
0	10	____	____	

7. Make the unrealistic assumption that production is costless for the monopolist in question 6. Given the data from the above demand schedule, what price will the monopolist charge, and how much output should the firm produce? How much profit will the firm earn? When marginal cost is above zero, what will be the effect on the price and output of the monopolist?

8. Explain why a monopolist would never produce in the inelastic range of the demand curve.

9. In each of the following cases, state whether the monopolist would increase or decrease output:
   a. Marginal revenue exceeds marginal cost at the output produced.
   b. Marginal cost exceeds marginal revenue at the output produced.

10. Suppose the demand and cost curves for a monopolist are as shown in Exhibit 10. Explain what price the monopolist should charge and how much output it should produce.

11. Which of the following constitute price discrimination?
   a. A department store has a 25 percent off sale.
   b. A publisher sells economics textbooks at a lower price in North Carolina than in New York.
   c. The Japanese sell cars at higher prices in the United States than in Japan.
   d. The phone company charges higher long-distance rates during the day.

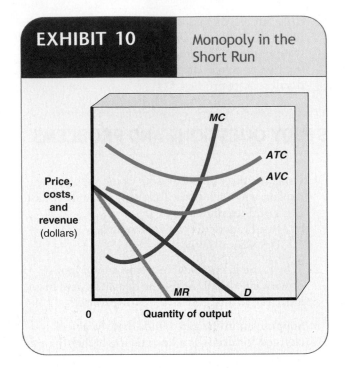

EXHIBIT 10   Monopoly in the Short Run

12. Suppose the candy bar industry approximates a perfectly competitive industry. Suppose also that a single firm buys all the assets of the candy bar firms and establishes a monopoly. Contrast these two market structures with respect to price, output, and allocation of resources. Draw a graph of the market demand and market supply for candy bars before and after the takeover.

For Online Exercises, go to the text Web site at www.cengage.com/economics/tucker.

CHECKPOINT ANSWERS ✔

Why Don't Adults Pay More for Popcorn at the Movies?

First, there are no other popcorn sellers in the lobby, so the theater is a price maker for popcorn and the demand curve slopes downward. Second, the theater could easily set up different lines for adults and children and charge different prices for popcorn.

Third, is there a practical way to prevent resale? Does the theater want to try to stop children who resell popcorn to their parents, friends, and other adults? If you said theaters do not practice price discrimination at the concession counter because resale cannot be prevented, **YOU ARE CORRECT.**

PRACTICE QUIZ

For an explanation of the correct answers, please visit the tutorial at www.cengage.com/economics/tucker.

1. A monopolist always faces a demand curve that is
   a. perfectly inelastic.
   b. perfectly elastic.
   c. unit elastic.
   d. the same as the market demand curve.

2. A monopolist sets the
   a. price at which marginal revenue equals zero.
   b. price that maximizes total revenue.
   c. highest possible price on its demand curve.
   d. price at which marginal revenue equals marginal cost.

3. A monopolist sets
   a. the highest possible price.
   b. a price corresponding to minimum average total cost.
   c. a price equal to marginal revenue.
   d. a price determined by the point on the demand curve corresponding to the level of output at which marginal revenue equals marginal cost.
   e. none of the above.

4. Which of the following is *true* for the monopolist?
   a. Economic profit is possible in the long run.
   b. Marginal revenue is less than the price charged.
   c. Profit maximizing or loss minimizing occurs when marginal revenue equals marginal cost.
   d. All of the above are true.

5. As shown in Exhibit 11, the profit-maximizing or loss-minimizing output for this monopolist is
   a. 100 units per day.
   b. 200 units per day.
   c. 300 units per day.
   d. 400 units per day.

6. As shown in Exhibit 11, this monopolist
   a. should shut down in the short run.
   b. should shut down in the long run.
   c. earns zero economic profit.
   d. earns positive economic profit.

7. To maximize profit or minimize loss, the monopolist in Exhibit 11 should set its price at
   a. $30 per unit.
   b. $25 per unit.

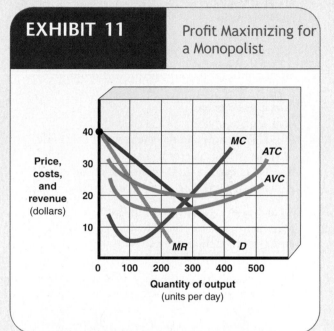

EXHIBIT 11   Profit Maximizing for a Monopolist

   c. $20 per unit.
   d. $10 per unit.
   e. $40 per unit.

8. If the monopolist in Exhibit 11 operates at the profit-maximizing output, it will earn total revenue to pay about what portion of its total fixed cost?
   a. None
   b. One-half
   c. Two-thirds
   d. All total fixed costs

9. For a monopolist to practice effective price discrimination, one necessary condition is
   a. identical demand curves among groups of buyers.
   b. differences in the price elasticity of demand among groups of buyers.
   c. a homogeneous product.
   d. none of the above.

PRACTICE QUIZ CONTINUED

10. What is the act of buying a commodity at a lower price and selling it at a higher price?
    a. Buying short
    b. Discounting
    c. Tariffing
    d. Arbitrage

11. Under both perfect competition and monopoly, a firm
    a. is a price taker.
    b. is a price maker.
    c. will shut down in the short run if price falls short of average total cost.
    d. always earns a pure economic profit.
    e. sets marginal cost equal to marginal revenue.

12. At any point where a monopolist's marginal revenue is positive, the downward-sloping straight-line demand curve is
    a. perfectly elastic.
    b. elastic, but not perfectly elastic.
    c. unit elastic.
    d. inelastic.

13. Suppose a monopolist charges a price corresponding to the intersection of the marginal cost and marginal revenue curves. If this price is between its average variable cost and average total cost curves, the firm will
    a. earn an economic profit.
    b. stay in operation in the short run, but shut down in the long run if demand remains the same.
    c. shut down.
    d. none of the above.

14. In contrast to a perfectly competitive firm, a monopolist operates in the long run at a quantity of output at which
    a. $P = MC$.
    b. $MR = MC$.
    c. $P = ATC$.
    d. $P > MR$.

15. The monopolist, unlike the perfectly competitive firm, can continue to earn an economic profit in the long run because of
    a. collusive agreements with competitors.
    b. price leadership.
    c. cartels.
    d. a dominant firm.
    e. extremely high barriers to entry.

Monopolistic Competition and Oligopoly

© David Muir/Digital Vision/Getty Images.

S uppose your favorite restaurant is Ivan's Oyster Bar. Ivan's does not fit either of the two extreme models studied in the previous two chapters. Instead, Ivan's characteristics are a blend of monopoly and perfect competition. For starters, like a monopolist, Ivan's demand curve is downward sloping. This means Ivan's is a *price maker* because it can charge a higher price for seafood and lose some customers, but many loyal customers will keep coming. The reason is that Ivan's distinguishes its product from the competition by advertising, first-rate service, a great salad bar, and other attributes. In short, like a monopolist, Ivan's has a degree of *market power*, which allows it to restrict output and maximize profit. But like a perfectly competitive firm and unlike a monopolist,

Ivan's is not the only place to buy a seafood dinner in town. It must share the market with many other restaurants within an hour's drive.

The small Ivan's Oyster Bar and the gigantic General Motors of the world represent most of the firms with which you deal. These firms compete in two different market structures: *monopolistic competition* or *oligopoly*. Ivan's operates in the former, and General Motors belongs to the latter. The theories of perfect competition and monopoly from the previous two chapters will help you understand the impact of monopolistic competition and oligopoly market structures on the price and output decisions of real-world firms.

In this chapter, you will learn
to solve these economic puzzles:

- Why will Ivan's Oyster Bar make zero
  economic profit in the long run?

- Why do OPEC and other cartels tend to
  break down?

- Are Cheerios, Rice Krispies, and other
  brands sold by firms in the breakfast cereal
  industry produced under monopolistic
  competition or oligopoly?

- How does the NCAA Final Four basketball
  tournament involve imperfect competition?

The Monopolistic Competition Market Structure

Monopolistic competition

A market structure characterized by (1) many small sellers, (2) a differentiated product, and (3) easy market entry and exit.

Economists define monopolistic competition as a market structure characterized by (1) many small sellers, (2) a differentiated product, and (3) easy market entry and exit. Monopolistic competition fits numerous real-world industries. The following is a brief explanation of each characteristic.

Many Small Sellers

Under monopolistic competition, as under perfect competition, the exact number of firms cannot be stated. Ivan's Oyster Bar, described in the chapter preview, is an example of a monopolistic competitor. Ivan assumes that his restaurant can set prices slightly higher or improve service *independently* without fear that competitors will react by changing their prices or giving better service. Thus, if any single seafood restaurant raises its price, the going market price for seafood dinners increases by a very small amount.

> **Conclusion** *The many-sellers condition is met when each firm is so small relative to the total market that its pricing decisions have a negligible effect on the market price.*

Differentiated Product

Product differentiation

The process of creating real or apparent differences between goods and services.

The key feature of monopolistic competition is product differentiation. Product differentiation is the process of creating real or apparent differences between goods and services. A differentiated product has close, but not perfect, substitutes. Although the products of each firm are highly similar, the consumer views them as somewhat different or distinct. There may be 25 seafood restaurants in a given city, but they are not all the same. They differ in location, atmosphere, quality of food, quality of service, and so on.

Product differentiation can be real or imagined. It does not matter which is correct so long as consumers believe such differences exist. For example, many customers think Ivan's has the best seafood in town even though other restaurants actually offer a similar product. The importance of this viewpoint is that consumers are willing to pay a slightly higher price for Ivan's seafood. This gives Ivan the incentive to appear on local TV cooking shows and to buy ads showing him personally catching the seafood he serves.

> **Conclusion** *When a product is differentiated, buyers are not indifferent as to which seller's product they buy.*

The example of Ivan's restaurant makes it clear that under monopolistic competition rivalry centers on nonprice competition in addition to price competition. With nonprice competition, a firm competes using advertising, packaging, product development, better quality, and better service, rather than lower prices. Nonprice competition is an important characteristic of monopolistic competition that distinguishes it from perfect competition and monopoly. Under perfect competition, there is no nonprice competition because the product is identical for all firms. Likewise, the monopolist has little incentive to engage in nonprice competition because it sells a unique product.

Nonprice competition
The situation in which a firm competes using advertising, packaging, product development, better quality, and better service, rather than lower prices.

Easy Entry and Exit

Unlike a monopoly, firms in a monopolistically competitive market face low barriers to entry. But entry into a monopolistically competitive market is not quite as easy as entry into a perfectly competitive market. Because monopolistically competitive firms sell differentiated products, it is somewhat difficult for new firms to become established. Many persons who want to enter the seafood restaurant business can get loans, lease space, and start serving seafood without too much trouble. However, these new seafood restaurants may at first have difficulty attracting consumers because of Ivan's established reputation as the best seafood restaurant in town.

Monopolistic competition is by far the most common market structure in the United States. Examples include retail firms, such as grocery stores, hair salons, gas stations, DVD rental stores, diet centers, and restaurants.

The Monopolistically Competitive Firm as a Price Maker

Given the characteristics of monopolistic competition, you might think the monopolistic competitor is a *price taker,* but it is not. The primary reason is that its product is differentiated. This gives the monopolistically competitive firm, like the monopolist, limited control over its price. When the price is raised, brand loyalty ensures some customers will remain steadfast. As for a monopolist, the demand curve and the corresponding marginal revenue curve for a monopolistically competitive firm are downward sloping. But the existence of close substitutes causes the demand curve for the monopolistically competitive firm to be more elastic than the demand curve for a monopolist. When Ivan's raises its prices 10 percent, the quantity of seafood dinners demanded declines, say, 30 percent. Instead, if Ivan's had a monopoly, no close substitutes would exist, and consumers would be less sensitive to price changes. As a monopolist, the same 10 percent price hike might lose Ivan's only, say, 15 percent of its quantity of seafood dinners demanded.

> **Conclusion** *The demand curve for a monopolistically competitive firm is less elastic (steeper) than for a perfectly competitive firm and more elastic (flatter) than for a monopolist.*

Advertising Pros and Cons

Before presenting the complete graphical models for monopolistic competition, let's pause to examine the topic of advertising further. As explained at the beginning of this chapter, a distinguishing feature of a monopolistically competitive firm is that it engages in nonprice competition by using expensive ads to differentiate its product. Instead of lowering the price, the firm's goal is to convince customers that its product is really different from its rivals' products. Monopolistically competitive firms are frequently running ads that feature lower prices, a higher quality of service, or new products to win customers. Ads proclaim that products make you smarter, better looking, or nicer to be around. Graphically, the firm hopes advertising will make the demand curve less elastic and shift it rightward by changing consumers' tastes in favor of its product. Profit rises when advertising increases the firm's revenue more than the cost of the advertising.

Exhibit 1 illustrates the effect of advertising on the long-run average cost ($LRAC$) curve for Yummy Frozen Yogurt. Yummy competes with It Can't Be Yogurt and five other stores in the northeastern part of town. Without advertising, the $LRAC_1$ curve represents Yummy's average cost. At the given price charged, the quantity demanded is 6,000 frozen yogurt dishes per month, and the average cost is $2.00 per dish (point A).

To increase profits in the short run, Yummy decides to advertise. Yummy knows, however, that in the long run new entrants and rising costs will shrink all yogurt stores' economic profits to zero. Then Yummy must come up with some new product to boost sales. But for now, suppose Yummy's advertising campaign is successful and demand increases. Then two short-run effects occur. One is an upward shift in the average cost curve at any level of output from $LRAC_1$ to $LRAC_2$. The vertical distance between these two curves measures the additional average fixed cost of advertising. Another effect is that the quantity demanded increases to 12,000 frozen yogurt dishes per month. Now the average cost is $1.50 at point B on $LRAC_2$.

So far, our story illustrates a social benefit of advertising. Look again at Exhibit 1. The increased volume of sales caused by advertising leads to *economies of scale*, explained in Chapter 7. Without advertising, Yummy operated with a lower output and a higher average cost. With advertising, the benefit to consumers from the reduction in average total cost from A to B outweighs the boost in cost per unit from advertising.

On the other hand, suppose Yummy's advertising campaign is not successful and demand remains unchanged. In this case, the quantity demanded remains at the original 6,000 frozen yogurt dishes per month, but the average total cost rises to $3.00 (point C). Critics of advertising argue this is the typical case and not the reduction from A to B. Instead of economies of scale, advertising is self-canceling. Yummy, It Can't Be Yogurt, and other firms spend large outlays on advertising just to keep their present market share. And in the process, the cost, and therefore the

EXHIBIT 1   The Effect of Advertising on Average Cost

When Yummy Frozen Yogurt increases its advertising costs to sell more yogurt, the firm's average cost curve shifts upward from $LRAC_1$ to $LRAC_2$. If advertising increases the quantity demanded from 6,000 to 12,000 dishes per month, average total cost falls from $2.00 (point A) to $1.50 (point B). However, if the extra cost of advertising fails to increase the quantity demanded, average total cost rises from $2.00 (point A) to $3.00 (point C).

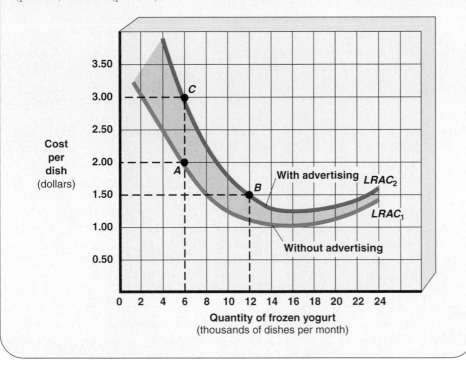

Quantity of frozen yogurt
(thousands of dishes per month)

price, of yogurt is increased. Moreover, the additional cost of advertising does not improve the yogurt at all. The only purpose is to persuade or mislead consumers into buying something they do not need. From society's viewpoint, the resources used in advertising could be used for schools, hospitals, bridges, or other more useful purposes.

Proponents of advertising counter the argument that advertising is valueless. They argue that ads provide information. Advertising informs consumers of sales, the availability of products, and the advantages of products. Although the product costs a little more, this information saves consumers money and time. Ads also increase price competition among sellers. When Yummy offers discount coupons, other yogurt stores see these ads and respond with lower prices. Finally, consumers are rational and cannot be fooled by advertising. If a product is undesirable, customers will not buy it.

Does monopolistic competition lead to lower prices, greater output, and better-informed consumers? Or does this market structure simply raise prices and annoy customers with useless and often misleading information? This fascinating and ongoing debate is perhaps best analyzed on a case-by-case basis. In a later section, you will learn that advertising to differentiate a product is also a key characteristic of oligopoly.

A key characteristic of the market structures discussed in this chapter is that they use advertising to promote product differentiation, which is a form of nonprice competition. The television commercial is considered the most effective method of mass-market advertising. This explains why TV networks charge such high prices for commercial airtime during prominent events, such as the Super Bowl football game. However, the days when television commercials dominate the advertising world could be fading away. Don't want to be bothered by those advertisements? It's easy: Just press the fast forward button on the remote of a digital video recorder (DVR). Advertisers are therefore struggling to figure out how to get the attention of consumers by tapping into the popularity of such social-networking sites as Facebook, MySpace, and YouTube. These sites connect individuals with others who interact through personal profiles, games, video clips, and more. There are also niche sites focused on very specific activities for a hyper-targeted audience. For example, Dogster.com is a site for dog lovers and Greenthumbs.com is a site for gardeners.

The challenge for Web economy entrepreneurs is to earn profits by differentiating their product and creating innovative ways to include advertising. The search engine is a highly successful business model. If someone Googles for golf clubs, sponsored links for golf clubs appear on the screen. Social networks provide the prospect of tailoring ads to people's specific interests. Now suppose a golf club company pays Facebook, the crown jewel of social networking, for a page where you and your friends can register and play a game of golf. What does the company get out of it—A database of tens of thousands of names, all potential customers.

However, some ideas are not winners. Facebook implemented a new approach that informed friends whenever a member purchased something from online retailers. Consumers protested this was an invasion of privacy, and the program was abandoned. Now consider this idea: Imagine being at a concert and text messaging a shout-out to your friends. Your message appears during the concert next to the stage on a big screen with a large ad from a company. Is this imposing a negative externality that distracts others in the audience from the performance?

ANALYZE THE ISSUE

Advertising is tasteless, offensive, and a nuisance that wastes resources. Give three arguments against this idea.

Price and Output Decisions for a Monopolistically Competitive Firm

Now we are prepared to develop the short-run and long-run graphical models for monopolistic competition. In the short run, you will see that monopolistic competition resembles monopoly. In the long run, however, entry by new firms leads to a more competitive market structure. This section presents a graphical analysis that shows why a monopolistically competitive firm is part perfectly competitive and part monopolistic.

Monopolistic Competition in the Short Run

Exhibit 2 shows the short-run equilibrium position for Ivan's Oyster Bar—a typical firm under monopolistic competition. As explained earlier, the demand curve slopes downward because customers believe, rightly or wrongly, that Ivan's product is a

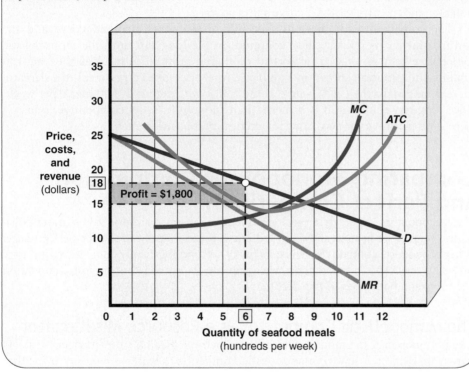

EXHIBIT 2   A Monopolistically Competitive Firm in the Short Run

Ivan's Oyster Bar is a monopolistically competitive firm that maximizes short-run profit by producing the output where marginal revenue equals marginal cost. At an output of 600 seafood dinners per week, the price of $18 per dinner is dictated by the firm's demand curve. Given the firm's costs, output, and prices, Ivan's will earn a short-run profit of $1,800 per week.

little better than its competitors' products. Customers like Ivan's family atmosphere, location, and quality of service. These nonprice factors differentiate Ivan's product and allow the restaurant to raise the price of sautéed alligator, shrimp, and oysters at least slightly without losing many sales.

Like the monopolist, the monopolistically competitive firm maximizes short-run profit by following the $MR = MC$ rule. In this case, the marginal cost (MC) and marginal revenue (MR) curves intersect at an output of 600 seafood meals per week. The price per meal of $18 is the point on the demand curve corresponding to this level of output. Because the price exceeds the average total cost (ATC) of $15 per meal, Ivan's earns a short-run economic profit of $1,800 per week. As under monopoly, if the price equals the ATC curve, the firm earns a short-run normal profit. If the price is below the ATC curve, the firm suffers a short-run loss, and if the price is below the average variable cost (AVC) curve, the firm shuts down.

Monopolistic Competition in the Long Run

The monopolistically competitive firm, unlike a monopolist, will not earn an economic profit in the long run. Rather, like a perfect competitor, the monopolistically competitive firm earns only a normal profit (that is, zero economic profit) in the long run. Recall from the chapter on production costs that *normal profit* is the minimum profit necessary to keep a firm in operation. The reason is that short-run profits and easy entry attract new firms into the industry. When Ivan's Oyster Bar earns a short-run profit, as shown in Exhibit 2, two things happen. First, Ivan's demand curve shifts downward as some of each seafood restaurant's market share is taken away by new firms seeking profit. Second, Ivan's, and other seafood restaurants as well, tries to recapture market share by advertising, improving its decor, and utilizing other forms of nonprice competition. As a result, long-run average costs increase, and the firm's *LRAC* curve shifts upward.

The combination of the leftward shift in the firm's demand curve and the upward shift in its *LRAC* curve continues in the long run until the monopolistic competitive firm earns zero or normal economic profit. The result is the long-run equilibrium condition shown in Exhibit 3. At a price of $17 per meal, the demand curve is tangent to the *LRAC* curve at the $MR = MC$ output of 500 meals per week. Once long-run equilibrium is achieved in a monopolistically competitive industry, there is no incentive for new firms to enter or established firms to leave.

Comparing Monopolistic Competition and Perfect Competition

Some economists argue that the long-run equilibrium condition for a monopolistically competitive firm, as shown in Exhibit 3, results in poor economic performance. Other economists contend that the benefits of a monopolistically competitive industry outweigh the costs. In this section, we again use the standard of perfect competition to understand both sides of this debate.

The Monopolistic Competitor as a Resource Misallocator

Like a monopolist, the monopolistically competitive firm fails the efficiency test. As shown in Exhibit 3, under monopolistic competition, Ivan's charges a price that exceeds the marginal cost. Thus, the value to consumers of the last meal produced is greater than the cost of producing it. Ivan's could devote more resources and produce more seafood dinners. To sell this additional output, Ivan's must move downward along its demand curve by reducing the $17 price per meal. As a result, customers would purchase the additional benefits of consuming more seafood meals. However, Ivan's uses less resources and restricts output to 500 seafood meals per week in order to maximize profits where $MR = MC$.

Monopolistic Competition Means Less Output for More

Exhibit 4(a) reproduces the long-run condition from Exhibit 3. Exhibit 4(b) assumes that the seafood restaurant market is perfectly competitive. Recall from Chapter 8 that the characteristics of perfect competition include the condition that customers perceive seafood meals as *homogeneous* and, as a result, no firms engage in advertising. Because we now assume for the sake of argument that Ivan's product is identical to all other seafood restaurants, Ivan's becomes a *price taker*. In this case, the industry's long-run supply and demand curves set an equilibrium price of $16 per meal. Consequently, Ivan's faces a horizontal demand curve with the price equal to marginal revenue. Also recall from Chapter 8 that long-run equilibrium for

---

EXHIBIT 3   A Monopolistically Competitive Firm in the Long Run

In the long run, the entry of new seafood restaurants decreases the demand for Ivan's seafood. In addition, Ivan's shifts its average cost curve upward by increasing advertising and other expenses in order to compete against new entrants. In the long run, the firm earns zero economic profit at a price of $17 per seafood meal and produces an $MR = MC$ output of 500 meals per week.

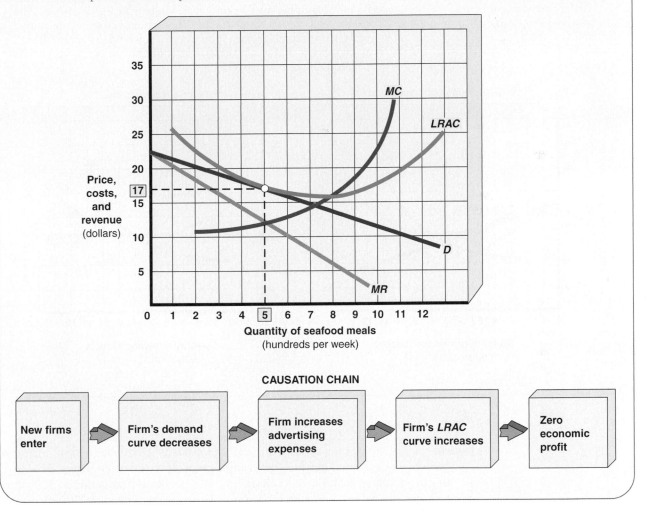

CAUSATION CHAIN

New firms enter ⇨ Firm's demand curve decreases ⇨ Firm increases advertising expenses ⇨ Firm's *LRAC* curve increases ⇨ Zero economic profit

---

a perfectly competitive firm is established by the entry of new firms until the minimum point of $16 per meal on the firm's *LRAC* curve equals the price, *MR* and *MC*. Stated as a formula:

$$P = MR = MC = LRAC$$

A comparison of Parts (a) and (b) of Exhibit 4 reveals two important points. First, both the monopolistic competitor and the perfect competitor earn zero economic profit in the long run. Second, the long-run equilibrium output of the monopolistically competitive firm is to the left of the minimum point on the *LRAC* curve and the price

EXHIBIT 4

A Comparison of Monopolistic Competition and Perfect Competition in the Long Run

In Part (a), Ivan's Oyster Bar is a monopolistically competitive firm that sets its price at $17 per seafood meal and produces 500 meals per week. As a monopolistic competitor, Ivan's earns zero economic profit in the long run and does not produce at the lowest point on its *LRAC* curve.

Under conditions of perfect competition in Part (b), Ivan's becomes a price taker, rather than a price maker. Here the firm faces a flat demand curve at a price of $16 per seafood meal, which is the equilibrium price set by the market demand and supply curves. The output is 800 meals per week, which corresponds to the lowest point on the *LRAC* curve. Therefore, the price is lower, and the excess capacity of 300 meals per week is utilized when Ivan's operates as a perfectly competitive firm, rather than as a monopolistically competitive firm.

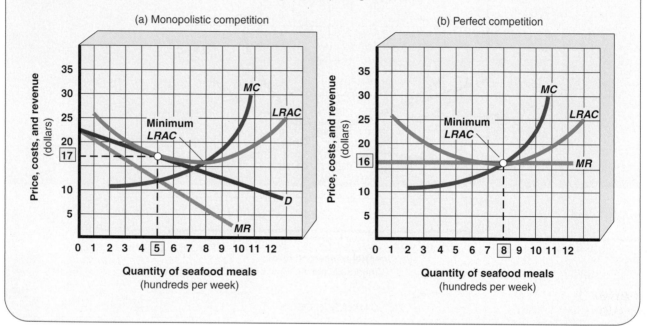

exceeds *MC*. Like a monopolist, the monopolistically competitive firm therefore charges a higher price and produces less output than a perfectly competitive firm.

In our example, Ivan's would charge $1 less per meal and produce 300 more seafood meals per week in a perfectly competitive market. The extra 300 meals not produced are *excess capacity*, which represents underutilized resources. The criticism of monopolistic competition, then, is that there are too many firms producing too little output at inflated prices and wasting society's resources in the process. For example, on many nights, there are not enough customers for all the restaurants in town. Servers, cooks, tables, and other resources are therefore underutilized. With fewer firms, each would produce a greater output at a lower price and with a lower average cost.

Opinions vary concerning whether the benefits of monopolistic competition exceed the costs. Having many seafood restaurants offers consumers more choice and variety of output. Having Ivan's Oyster Bar and many similar competitors gives consumers extra quality and service options. If you do not like Ivan's sautéed alligator, you may be able to find another restaurant that serves this dish. Also, having many restaurants in a market saves consumers valuable time. Chances are that you will not shed crocodile tears because the travel time required to enjoy an alligator meal is lower.

The Oligopoly Market Structure

Now we turn to oligopoly, an imperfectly competitive market structure in which a few large firms dominate the market. Many manufacturing industries, such as steel, aluminum, automobiles, aircraft, drugs, and tobacco, are best described as oligopolistic. This is the "big business" market structure, in which firms aggressively compete by bombarding us with advertising on television and filling our mailboxes with junk mail.

Economists define an oligopoly as a market structure characterized by (1) few sellers, (2) either a homogeneous or a differentiated product, and (3) difficult market entry. Like monopolistic competition, oligopoly is found in real-world industries. Let's examine each characteristic.

Few Sellers

Oligopoly is competition "among the few." Here we refer to the "Big Three" or "Big Four" to mean that three or four firms dominate an industry. But what does "a few" firms really mean? Does this mean at least two, but less than ten? As with other market structures, the answer is there is no specific number of firms that must dominate an industry before it is an oligopoly. Basically, an oligopoly is a consequence of mutual interdependence. Mutual interdependence is a condition in which an action by one firm may cause a reaction from other firms. Stated another way, a market structure with a few powerful firms makes it easier for oligopolists to collude. The large number of firms under perfect competition or monopolistic competition and the absence of other firms in monopoly rule out mutual interdependence and collusion in these market structures.

When General Motors (GM) considers a price hike or a style change, it must predict how Ford, Chrysler, and Toyota will change their prices and styling in response. Therefore, the decisions under oligopoly are more complex than under perfect competition, monopoly, and monopolistic competition.

> **Conclusion** *The few-sellers condition is met when these few firms are so large relative to the total market that they can affect the market price.*

Homogeneous or Differentiated Product

Under oligopoly, firms can produce either a homogeneous (identical) or a differentiated product. The steel produced by USX is identical to the steel from Republic Steel. The oil sold by Saudi Arabia is identical to the oil from Iran. Similarly, zinc, copper, and aluminum are standardized or homogeneous products. But cars produced by the major automakers are differentiated products. Tires, detergents, and breakfast cereals are also differentiated products sold in oligopolies.

> **Conclusion** *Buyers in an oligopoly may or may not be indifferent as to which seller's product they buy.*

Oligopoly
A market structure characterized by (1) few sellers, (2) either a homogeneous or a differentiated product, and (3) difficult market entry.

Mutual interdependence
A condition in which an action by one firm may cause a reaction from other firms.

Difficult Entry

Similar to monopoly, formidable barriers to entry in an oligopoly protect firms from new entrants. These barriers include exclusive financial requirements, control over an essential resource, patent rights, and other legal barriers. But the most significant barrier to entry in an oligopoly is *economies of scale*. For example, larger automakers achieve lower average total costs than those incurred by smaller automakers. Consequently, the U.S. auto industry has moved over time from more than 60 firms to only two major U.S. owned firms.

Price and Output Decisions for an Oligopolist

Mutual interdependence among firms in an oligopoly makes this market structure more difficult to analyze than perfect competition, monopoly, or monopolistic competition. The price-output decision of an oligopolist is not simply a matter of charging the price where $MR = MC$. Making price and output decisions in an oligopoly is like playing a game of chess. One player's move depends on the anticipated reactions of the opposing player. One player thinks, "If I move my rook here, my opponent might move her knight there." Likewise, a firm in an oligopoly can have many different possible reactions to the price, nonprice, and output changes of another firm. Consequently, there are different oligopoly models because no single model can cover all cases. The following is a discussion of five well-known oligopoly models: (1) nonprice competition, (2) the kinked demand curve, (3) price leadership, (4) the cartel, and (5) game theory.

Nonprice Competition

Major oligopolists often compete using advertising and product differentiation. Instead of "slugging it out" with price cuts, oligopolists may try to capture business away from their rivals through better advertising campaigns and improved products. This model of behavior explains why advertising expenditures often are large in the cigarette, soft drink, athletic shoe, and automobile industries. It also explains why the research and development (R&D) function is so important to oligopolists. For example, much engineering effort is aimed largely at developing new products and improving existing products.

Why might oligopolists compete through nonprice competition, rather than price competition? The answer is that each oligopolist perceives that its rival will easily and quickly match any price reduction. In contrast, it is much more difficult to combat a clever and/or important product improvement.

The Kinked Demand Curve

Unlike other market structures, different assumptions define different models for any given oligopolistic industry. Over time, the "rules of the game" change, and a new model becomes the best predictor of the behavior of oligopolists. We begin with the kinked demand curve. The strange shape of this curve explains why prices in an oligopolistic market selling cars change far less often than prices in a perfectly competitive market selling wheat.

The kinked demand curve is a demand curve facing an oligopolist that assumes rivals will match a price decrease, but ignore a price increase. Without collusion, the kinked demand curve exists because management tacitly believes that the

Kinked demand curve

A demand curve facing an oligopolist that assumes rivals will match a price decrease, but ignore a price increase.

EXHIBIT 5 | The Kinked Demand Curve

An oligopolist's demand curve may be kinked. In this graph, an automobile producer believes it faces two demand curves. A price hike from $25,000 to $27,250 per auto causes a sizable reduction in the quantity demanded from 3 million to 1.5 million autos (point X). Demand above the kink is elastic because rivals ignore the firm when it raises the price. Below the kink, the demand curve is less elastic. A price reduction from $25,000 to $22,250 per auto attracts very few new customers, and the quantity demanded increases from 3 million to only 3.2 million autos per year (point Y). Under the kinked demand curve theory, prices will be rigid.

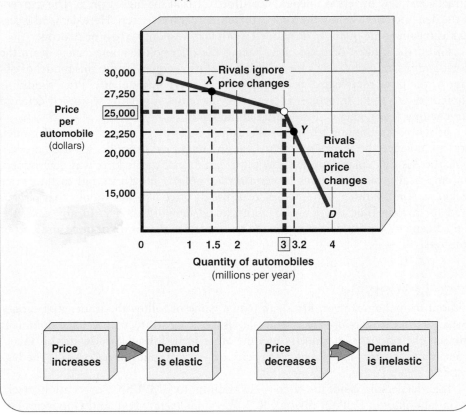

competition will not be "undersold." On the other hand, a price hike by one firm allows competitors to capture its share of the market. Oligopolistic firms must make pricing decisions, so they are *price makers*, rather than price takers. But as we will soon see in the kinked demand model, the high degree of interdependence among oligopolists restricts their pricing discretion.

In Exhibit 5, a kinked demand curve is drawn for Tucker Motor Company, which we assume competes with GM, Ford, Toyota, and Chrysler in the automobile market. (I suggest you check out the movie titled *Tucker* at your video rental store.) The current price per Tucker car is $25,000, and the quantity demanded at this price is 3 million cars per year. Tucker's management assumes that if it raises its price even slightly above $25,000, the other automakers *will not follow* with higher prices. This price gap between the Tucker and other cars would drive many of

Tucker's customers over to its rivals. The segment of the demand curve above $25,000 is therefore relatively flat. Stated differently, above the "kink" in the demand curve, demand is relatively elastic. If Tucker raises the price to, say, $27,250 at point *X,* this price hike cuts Tucker's quantity demanded to 1.5 million cars per year. Since raising its price is ill-advised, management can consider a price-reduction strategy. Suppose Tucker cuts the price of its cars from $25,000 to $22,250 at point *Y.* The model shows that Tucker gains few customers and the quantity demanded rises only slightly from 3 million to 3.2 million cars per year. The reason for such a small sales boost is that other automakers also cut their prices so that each firm can keep its initial market share. However, the lower price does attract some new buyers who could not afford a car at the higher price. The segment of the demand curve below the kink is therefore relatively steep. Here demand is less elastic, meaning the quantity demanded is not very responsive to a price drop.

Given the kinked demand curve facing the oligopolist, management fears the worst and is afraid to raise or lower the price of its product. Under this model of oligopoly, the price established at the kink changes very infrequently. Price rigidity is eliminated only after large cost increases or decreases force a new kinked demand curve with a new higher or lower price at the kink.

Economists continue to debate the importance of the kinked demand model. Critics challenge the theory on theoretical and empirical grounds. On a theoretical level, there is no explanation for how the original price at the kink was determined. On empirical grounds, studies of certain oligopolistic industries fail to find price stickiness. On the other hand, widespread use of price lists in catalogs that remain fixed for a long time is consistent with kinked demand theory. In any case, the kinked demand theory does not provide a complete explanation of price and output decisions.

Price Leadership

Without formal agreement, firms can play a game of follow-the-leader that economists call price leadership. Price leadership is a pricing strategy in which a dominant firm sets the price for an industry and the other firms follow. Following this tactic, firms in an industry simply match the price of perhaps, but not necessarily, the biggest firm.

Price leadership

A pricing strategy in which a dominant firm sets the price for an industry and the other firms follow.

Price leadership is not uncommon. In addition to GM, USX Corporation (steel), Alcoa (aluminum), DuPont (nylon), R. J. Reynolds (cigarettes), and Goodyear Tire and Rubber (tires) are examples of price leaders in U.S. industries.

The Cartel

The price leadership model assumes that firms do not collude to avoid price competition. Instead, firms avoid price wars by informally playing by the established pricing rules. Another way to avoid price wars is for oligopolists to agree to a peace treaty. Instead of allowing mutual interdependence to lead to rivalry, firms openly or secretly conspire to form a monopoly called a cartel. A cartel is a group of firms that formally agree to control the price and the output of a product. The goal of a cartel is to reap monopoly profits by replacing competition with cooperation. Cartels are illegal in the United States, but not in other nations. The best-known cartel is the Organization of Petroleum Exporting Countries (OPEC). The members of OPEC divide crude oil output among themselves according to quotas openly agreed

GLOBAL ECONOMICS

Cartel

A group of firms that formally agree to control the price and the output of a product.

Cartels flourished in Germany and other European countries in the first half of the twentieth century. Many had international memberships. After World War II, European countries passed laws against such restrictive trade practices. The following are some of the most important cartels today:

- **Organization of Petroleum Exporting Countries (OPEC).** OPEC was created by Iran, Iraq, Kuwait, Saudi Arabia, and Venezuela in Baghdad in 1960. Today, the Vienna-based OPEC's membership consists of 12 countries that control about 70 percent of the world's oil reserves. Cartels are anticonsumer. OPEC's objective is to set oil production quotas for its members and, in turn, influence global prices of oil and gasoline.

- **International Telecommunications Union (ITU).** Perhaps the world's least-known and most effective cartel is based in Geneva, Switzerland. The ITU was founded in 1865 and became an agency of the United Nations in 1947. It is responsible for international regulations and standards governing telecommunications. The ITU sets the minimum price you pay for an international telephone call.

- **International Air Transport Association (IATA).** Originally founded in 1919, most of the world's international airlines belong to the IATA. This cartel headquartered in Montreal sets international airline ticket prices and safety and security standards for passenger and cargo shipping. It controls access to airports, and challenges rules and regulations considered to be unreasonable. The IATA also is concerned with minimizing the impact of air transport on the environment.

upon at meetings of the OPEC oil ministries. Saudi Arabia is the largest producer and has the largest quota. The Global Economics feature provides a brief summary of some of today's major global cartels.

Using Exhibit 6, we can demonstrate how a cartel works and why keeping members from cheating is a problem. Our analysis begins before oil-producing firms have formed a cartel. Assume each firm has the same cost curve shown in the exhibit. Price wars have driven each firm to charge $75 a barrel, which is equal to the minimum point on its *LRAC* curve. Because oil is a standardized product, as under perfect competition, each firm fears raising its price because it will lose all its customers. Thus, the typical firm is in long-run competitive equilibrium at a price of $75 per barrel ($MR_1$), producing 6 million barrels per day. In this condition, economic profits are zero, and the firms decide to organize a meeting of all oil producers to establish a cartel.

Now assume the cartel is formed and each firm agrees to reduce its output to 4 million barrels per day and charge $120 per barrel. If no firms cheat, each firm faces a higher horizontal demand curve, represented by MR_2. At the cartel price, each firm earns an economic profit of $120 million, rather than a normal profit. But what if one firm decides to cheat on the cartel agreement by stepping up its output while other firms stick to their quotas? Output corresponding to the point at which $MR_2 = MC$ is 8 million barrels per day. If a cheating firm expands its output to this level, it can double its profit by earning an extra $120 million. Of course, if all firms cheat and the cartel breaks up, the price and output of each firm return to the initial levels, and economic profit again falls to zero.

EXHIBIT 6   Why a Cartel Member Has an Incentive to Cheat

A representative oil producer operating in a perfectly competitive industry would be in long-run equilibrium at a price of $75 per barrel, producing 6 million barrels per day and making zero economic profit. A cartel can agree to raise the price of oil from $75 to $120 per barrel by restricting the firm to 4 million barrels per day. As a result of this quota, the cartel price is above $90 on the *LRAC* curve, and the firm earns a daily profit of $120 million. However, if the firm cheats on the cartel agreement, it will set the cartel price equal to the *MC* curve and earn a total profit of $240 million by adding an additional $120 million. If all firms cheat, the original long-run equilibrium will be reestablished.

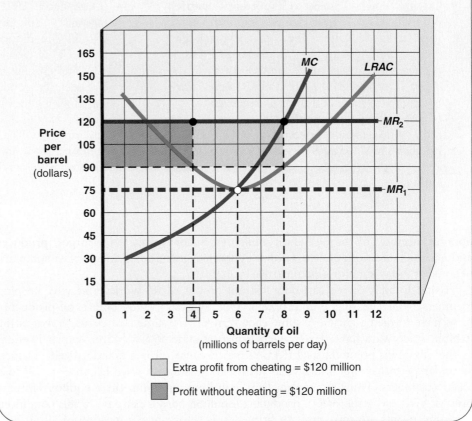

☐ Extra profit from cheating = $120 million

☐ Profit without cheating = $120 million

Game Theory

Game Theory

A model of the strategic moves and countermoves of rivals.

Game theory is a model of the strategic moves and countermoves of rivals. To illustrate, let's use a noncollusive example of USAirways competing with American Airlines. Each airline independently sets its fare, and Exhibit 7 is a *payoff matrix* that shows profit outcomes for the two airlines resulting from charging either a high fare or a low fare. If both charge the high fare in cell *A*, they split the market, and each makes a profit of $8 billion. If both decide to charge the low fare in cell *D*, they also split the market, and the profit for each falls to $5 billion. If one charges the high fare and the other the low fare in cell *B* or cell *C*, then the low-fare airline attracts

EXHIBIT 7 — A Two-Firm Payoff Matrix

Game theory is a method of analyzing the oligopoly puzzle. Two fare options of charging either a high fare or a low fare are given for USAirways and American Airlines. The profit or loss that each earns in cells *A–D* depends on the pricing decisions of these two rivals. Their collective interest is best served in cell *A* where each charges the high fare and each makes the maximum profit of $8 billion. But once either airline independently seeks the higher profit of $10 billion by using a low-fare strategy in cell *B* or *C*, the other airline counters with a low fare, and both end up charging the low fare in cell *D*. As a result, mutual profits are $5 billion, rather than $8 billion in cell *A*. Cell *D* is the equilibrium outcome because both fear changing the price and causing the other to counter.

	USAirways' options	
	High fare	**Low fare**
American Airlines' options **High fare**	*A* USAirways' profit = $8 billion / American Airlines' profit = $8 billion	*B* USAirways' profit = $10 billion / American Airlines' loss = −$2 billion
Low fare	*C* USAirways' loss = −$2 billion / American Airlines' profit = $10 billion	*D* USAirways' profit = $5 billion / American Airlines' profit = $5 billion

most of the customers and earns the maximum possible profit of $10 billion, while the high-fare airline loses $2 billion.

Both rivals in our example are clearly *mutually interdependent* because an action by one firm may cause a reaction from the other firm. Suppose both airlines initially select the most mutually profitable solution and both charge high fares in cell *A*. This outcome creates an incentive for either airline to charge a lower fare in cell *B* or cell *C* and earn the highest possible profit by pulling customers away from its rival. Consequently, assume the next day one airline cuts its fare to gain higher profits. In order to avoid losing customers, this action causes the other airline to counter with an equally low fare. Price competition has therefore forced both airlines to charge the low fare in cell *D* and earn less than maximum joint profits. Once cell *D* is reached, neither airline has an incentive to alter the fare either higher or lower because both fear their rival's countermoves. Note that when both firms charge the low fare in equilibrium at cell *D*, consumers benefit from not paying high fares in the other cells.

> **Conclusion** *The payoff matrix demonstrates why a competitive oligopoly tends to result in both rivals using a low-price strategy that does not maximize mutual profits.*

How can these oligopolists avoid the low-fare outcome in cell *D* and instead stabilize the more jointly profitable high-fare payoffs in cell *A*? One possible strategy is called *tit-for-tat*. Under this approach, a player will do whatever the other player did the last time. If one airline defects from cell *A* by cutting its fare to gain a

Suppose March Madness included your basketball team making it all the way to the Final Four and you were there. Before leaving, you checked the official Web site and noticed a Coke ad giving a prize to the person who submitted the best video commercial for a new Coke product. But this was only the beginning of the Great Cola Wars. Shortly after leaving the plane at the airport you encountered a group of students who were giving away huge inflatable plastic hands with index fingers sticking up in the air signaling that your team is number one. The plastic hands were imprinted with the Pepsi-Cola logo and your choice of a Final Four team. And the group was also giving away free ice-cold cans of Pepsi. As you walked along the streets to your hotel, giant inflatable "cans" of Pepsi appeared all over the downtown area on the sidewalks and on top of gas stations. And not to be outdone, the entire side of a prominent three-story building was painted Coca-Cola red and white with the 64 NCAA basketball finalists and all the winners listed, bracket by bracket. Following the first-round games, painters were three stories up on scaffolding, filling in the Coke sign's brackets for the final two teams, in school colors no less. Inside the arena the colas continued their battle by scrolling cola ads with other ads under the press rows along either side of the basketball court. This was indeed competition between showboating industry giants worthy of the Final Four competition among the basketball teams.

Many fascinating markets function during the Final Four basketball tournament, including competitive markets that determine prices for parking lots, restaurants, and tickets. (Recall the Checkpoint in Chapter 4 on ticket scalping.) Then there were the hotels surrounding the arena, which joined a centralized booking service. Each hotel had raised its normal price by 75 percent for the weekend.

ANALYZE THE ISSUE

In this feature, two forms of oligopoly were observed. Identify each of these forms and explain why it is being used by the oligopolists.

profit advantage, the other competitor will also cut its fare. After repeated trials, these price cutting responses serve as a signal that says, "You are not going to get the best of me so move your fare up!" Once the defector responds by moving back to the high fare, the other airline cooperates and also moves to the high fare. The result is that both players return to cell A without a formal agreement.

Another informal approach is for rivals to coordinate their pricing decisions based on price leadership, as discussed earlier in this chapter. For example, one airline may be much more established or dominant, and the other airline follows whatever price the leader sets. Another approach would be to informally rotate the leadership. Thus, without a formal agreement, the leader sets the profit-maximizing high price in cell A and the other competitor follows. However, this system does not eliminate the threat that the price follower will cheat.

Finally, if cartels were legal in the United States, the airlines could collude and make a formal agreement that each will charge the high fare. However, as explained in the previous section, there is always the incentive for one firm to cheat by moving from cell A to either cell B or cell C, and therefore cartels tend to break down. A remedy might be for the rivals to agree on a penalty for any party that reneges by lowering its fare.

> **Conclusion** *As long as the benefits exceed the costs, cheating can threaten formal or informal agreements among oligopolists to maximize joint profits.*

An Evaluation of Oligopoly

Oligopoly is much more difficult to evaluate than other market structures. None of the models just presented gives a definite answer to the question of efficiency under oligopoly. Depending on the assumptions made, an oligopolist can behave much like a perfectly competitive firm or more like a monopoly. Nevertheless, let's assume some likely changes that occur if a perfectly competitive industry is suddenly turned into an oligopoly selling a differentiated product.

First, the price charged for the product will be higher than under perfect competition. The smaller the number of firms in an oligopoly and the more difficult it is to enter the industry, the higher the oligopoly price will be in comparison to the perfectly competitive price.

Second, an oligopoly is likely to spend money on advertising, product differentiation, and other forms of nonprice competition. These expenditures can shift the demand curve to the right. As a result, both price and output may be higher under oligopoly than under perfect competition.

Third, in the long run, a perfectly competitive firm earns zero economic profit. The oligopolist, however, can earn a higher profit because it is more difficult for competitors to enter the industry.

CHECKPOINT

Which Model Fits the Cereal Aisle?

As you walk along the cereal aisle, notice the many different cereals on the shelf. For example, you will probably see General Mills' Wheaties, Total, and Cheerios; Kellogg's Corn Flakes, Cracklin' Oat Bran, Frosted Flakes, and Rice Krispies; Quaker Oats' Cap'n Crunch and 100% Natural; and Post's Super Golden Crisp, to name only a few. There are many different brands of the same-product cereal on the shelves. Each brand is slightly different from the others. Is the breakfast cereal industry's market structure monopolistic competition or oligopoly?

Review of the Four Market Structures

Now that we have completed the discussion of perfect competition, monopoly, monopolistic competition, and oligopoly, you are prepared to compare these four market structures. Exhibit 8 summarizes the characteristics and gives examples of each market structure.

EXHIBIT 8	Comparison of Market Structures			
Market Structure	Number of Sellers	Type of Product	Entry Condition	Examples
Perfect competition	Large	Homogeneous	Very easy	Agriculture*
Monopoly	One	Unique	Impossible	Public utilities
Monopolistic competition	Many	Differentiated	Easy	Retail trade
Oligopoly	Few	Homogeneous or differentiated	Difficult	Auto, steel, oil

*In the absence of government intervention.

KEY CONCEPTS

Monopolistic competition
Product differentiation
Nonprice competition

Oligopoly
Mutual interdependence
Kinked demand curve

Price leadership
Cartel
Game theory

SUMMARY

• *Monopolistic competition* is a market structure characterized by (1) many small sellers, (2) a differentiated product, and (3) easy market entry and exit. Given these characteristics, firms in monopolistic competition have a negligible effect on the market price.

• *Product differentiation* is a key characteristic of monopolistic competition. It is the process of creating real or apparent differences between products.

• *Nonprice competition* includes advertising, packaging, product development, better quality, and better service. Under monopolistic competition and oligopoly, firms may compete using nonprice competition, rather than price competition.

• *Short-run equilibrium for a monopolistic competitor* can yield economic losses, zero economic profits, or economic profits. In the long run, monopolistic competitors make zero economic profits.

Short-run equilibrium for a monopolistic competitor

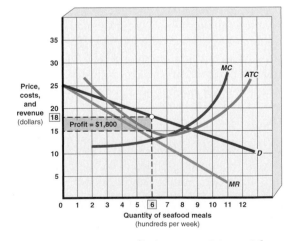

• *Comparing monopolistic competition with perfect competition,* we find that in the long run the monopolistically competitive firm does not achieve allocative efficiency, charges a higher price, restricts output, and does not produce where average costs are at a minimum.

Comparison of monopolistic and perfect competition

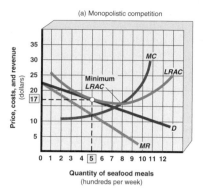

(a) Monopolistic competition

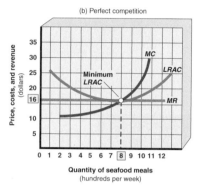

(b) Perfect competition

Kinked demand curve

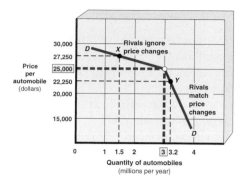

- *Oligopoly* is a market structure characterized by (1) few sellers, (2) either a homogeneous or a differentiated product, and (3) difficult market entry. Oligopolies are *mutually interdependent* because an action by one firm may cause a reaction from other firms.
- The *nonprice competition model* is a theory that might explain oligopolistic behavior. Under this theory, firms use advertising and product differentiation, rather than price reductions, to compete.
- The *kinked demand curve* model explains why prices may be rigid in an oligopoly. The kink occurs because an oligopolist assumes that rivals will match a price decrease, but ignore a price increase.

- *Price leadership* is another theory of pricing behavior under oligopoly. When a dominant firm in an industry raises or lowers its price, other firms follow suit.
- A *cartel* is a formal agreement among firms to set prices and output quotas. The goal is to maximize profits, but firms have an incentive to cheat, which is a constant threat to a cartel.

Cartel

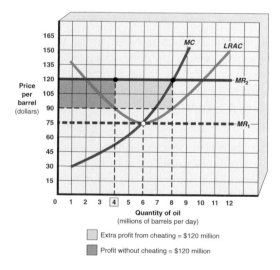

Extra profit from cheating = $120 million

Profit without cheating = $120 million

- *Game theory* reveals that (1) oligopolies are mutually interdependent in their pricing policies; (2) without collusion, oligopoly prices and mutual profits are lower; and (3) oligopolists have a temptation to cheat on any collusive agreement.
- *Comparing oligopoly with perfect competition,* we find that the oligopolist allocates resources inefficiently, charges a higher price, and restricts output so that price may exceed average cost.

SUMMARY OF CONCLUSION STATEMENTS

- The many-sellers condition is met when each firm is so small relative to the total market that its pricing decisions have a negligible effect on the market price.
- When a product is differentiated, buyers are not indifferent as to which seller's product they buy.
- The demand curve for a monopolistically competitive firm is less elastic (steeper) than for a perfectly competitive firm and more elastic (flatter) than for a monopolist.
- The few-sellers condition is met when these few firms are so large relative to the total market that they can affect the market price.

- Buyers in an oligopoly may or may not be indifferent as to which seller's product they buy.
- The payoff matrix demonstrates why a competitive oligopoly tends to result in both rivals using a low-price strategy that does not maximize mutual profits.
- As long as the benefits exceed the costs, cheating can threaten formal or informal agreements among oligopolists to maximize joint profits.

STUDY QUESTIONS AND PROBLEMS

1. Compare the monopolistically competitive firm's demand curve to those of a perfect competitor and a monopolist.

2. Suppose the minimum point on the $LRAC$ curve of a soft-drink firm's cola is $1 per liter. Under conditions of monopolistic competition, will the price of a liter bottle of cola in the long run be above $1, equal to $1, less than $1, or impossible to determine?

3. Exhibit 9 represents a monopolistically competitive firm in long-run equilibrium.
   a. Which price represents the long-run equilibrium price?
   b. Which quantity represents the long-run equilibrium output?
   c. At which quantity is the $LRAC$ curve at its minimum?
   d. Is the long-run equilibrium price greater than, less than, or equal to the marginal cost of producing the equilibrium output?

4. Consider this statement: "Because price equals long-run average cost and profits are zero, a monopolistically competitive firm is efficient." Do you agree or disagree? Explain.

5. Assuming identical long-run cost curves, draw two graphs, and indicate the price and output that result in the long run under monopolistic

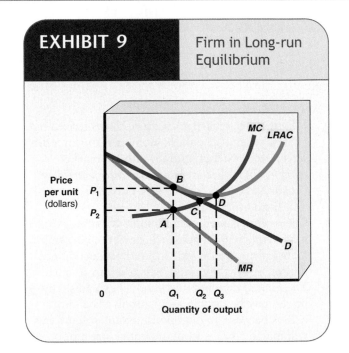

EXHIBIT 9   Firm in Long-run Equilibrium

competition and perfect competition. Evaluate the differences between these two market structures.

6. Draw a graph that shows how advertising affects a firm's ATC curve. Explain how advertising can lead to lower prices in a monopolistically competitive industry.

7. List four goods or services that you have purchased that were produced by an oligopolist. Why are these industries oligopolistic, rather than monopolistically competitive?

8. Why is mutual interdependence important under oligopoly, but not so important under perfect competition, monopoly, or monopolistic competition?

9. Suppose the jeans industry is an oligopoly in which each firm sells its own distinctive brand of jeans. Each firm believes its rivals will not follow its price increases, but will follow its price cuts. Explain the demand curve facing each firm. Does this demand curve mean that firms in the jeans industry do or do not compete against one another?

10. What might be a general distinction between oligopolists that advertise and those that do not?

11. Suppose IBM raised the price of its printers, but Hewlett-Packard (the largest seller) refused to follow. Two years later IBM cut its price, and Hewlett-Packard retaliated with an even deeper price cut, which IBM was forced to match. For the next 5 years, Hewlett-Packard raised its prices five times, and each time IBM followed suit within 24 hours. Does the pricing behavior of these computer industry firms follow the cartel model or the price leadership model? Why?

12. Evaluate the following statement: "A cartel will put an end to price war, which is a barbaric form of competition that benefits no one."

13. Assume the payoff matrix in Exhibit 7 applies to spending for advertising rather than airline fares. Substitute "Don't advertise" for "High fare" and "Advertise" for "Low fare." Assume the same profit and loss figures in each cell, but substitute "Marlboro" for "USAirways" and "Camel" for "American Airlines." Explain the dynamics of the model and why cigarette companies might be pleased with a government ban on all cigarette advertising.

For Online Exercises, go to the text Web site at www.cengage.com/economics/tucker.

CHECKPOINT ANSWER

Which Model Fits the Cereal Aisle?
The fact that there is a differentiated product does not necessarily mean that many firms are competing along the cereal aisle. The different cereals listed in this example are produced by only four companies: General Mills, Kellogg's, Quaker Oats, and Post. In fact, there are relatively few firms in the cereal industry, so even though they sell a differentiated product, the market structure cannot be monopolistic competition. If you said the cereal industry is an oligopoly, **YOU ARE CORRECT.**

PRACTICE QUIZ

For an explanation of the correct answers, please visit the tutorial at www.cengage.com/economics/tucker.

1. An industry with many small sellers, a differentiated product, and easy entry would *best* be described as which of the following?
   a. Oligopoly
   b. Monopolistic competition
   c. Perfect competition
   d. Monopoly

2. Which of the following industries is the *best* example of monopolistic competition?
   a. Wheat

PRACTICE QUIZ CONTINUED

b. Restaurant

c. Automobile

d. Water service

3. Which of the following is *not* a characteristic of monopolistic competition?

a. A large number of small firms

b. A differentiated product

c. Easy market entry

d. A homogeneous product

4. A monopolistically competitive firm will

a. maximize profits by producing where $MR = MC$.

b. not earn an economic profit in the long run.

c. shut down if price is less than average variable cost.

d. do all of the above.

5. The theory of monopolistic competition predicts that in long-run equilibrium a monopolistically competitive firm will

a. produce the output level at which price equals long-run marginal cost.

b. operate at minimum long-run average cost.

c. overutilize its insufficient capacity.

d. produce the output level at which price equals long-run average cost.

6. A monopolistically competitive firm is inefficient because the firm

a. earns positive economic profit in the long run.

b. is producing at an output where marginal cost equals price.

c. is not maximizing its profit.

d. produces an output where average total cost is not minimum.

7. A monopolistically competitive firm in the long run earns the same economic profit as a

a. perfectly competitive firm.

b. monopolist.

c. cartel.

d. none of the above.

8. One possible effect of advertising on a firm's long-run average cost curve is to

a. raise the curve.

b. lower the curve.

c. shift the curve rightward.

d. shift the curve leftward.

9. Monopolistic competition is an inefficient market structure because

a. firms earn zero profit in the long run.

b. marginal cost is less than price in the long run.

c. a wider variety of products is available compared to perfect competition.

d. all of the above.

10. The "Big Three" U.S. automobile industry is described as

a. a monopoly.

b. perfect competition.

c. monopolistic competition.

d. an oligopoly.

11. The cigarette industry in the United States is described as

a. a monopoly.

b. perfect competition.

c. monopolistic competition.

d. an oligopoly.

12. A characteristic of an oligopoly is

a. mutual interdependence in pricing decisions.

b. easy market entry.

c. both (a) and (b).

d. neither (a) nor (b).

13. The kinked demand curve theory attempts to explain why an oligopolistic firm

a. has relatively large advertising expenditures.

b. fails to invest in research and development (R&D).

c. infrequently changes its price.

d. engages in excessive brand proliferation.

14. According to the kinked demand curve theory, when one firm raises its price, other firms will

a. also raise their prices.

b. refuse to follow.

c. increase their advertising expenditures.

d. exit the industry.

15. Which of the following is evidence that OPEC is a cartel?

a. Agreement on price and output quotas by oil ministries

b. Ability to raise prices regardless of demand

c. Mutual interdependence in pricing and output decisions

d. Ability to completely control entry

16. Assume costs are identical for the two firms in Exhibit 10. If both firms were allowed to form a cartel and agree on their prices, equilibrium would be established by
a. Zeba Oil charging $100 and Tucker Oil charging $100.
b. Zeba Oil charging $100 and Tucker Oil charging $50.
c. Zeba Oil charging $50 and Tucker Oil charging $50.
d. Zeba Oil charging $50 and Tucker Oil charging $100.

17. Suppose costs are identical for the two firms in Exhibit 10. If both firms assume the other will compete and charge a lower price, equilibrium will be established by
a. Zeba Oil charging $100 and Tucker Oil charging $100.
b. Zeba Oil charging $100 and Tucker Oil charging $50.
c. Zeba Oil charging $50 and Tucker Oil charging $100.
d. Zeba Oil charging $50 and Tucker Oil charging $50.

18. Suppose costs are identical for the two firms in Exhibit 10. Each firm assumes without formal agreement that if it sets the high price, its rival will not charge a lower price. Under these "tit-for-tat" conditions, equilibrium will be established by
a. Zeba Oil charging $100 and Tucker Oil charging $100.
b. Zeba Oil charging $100 and Tucker Oil charging $50.
c. Zeba Oil charging $50 and Tucker Oil charging $50.
d. Zeba Oil charging $50 and Tucker Oil charging $100.

19. Which of the following is a game theory strategy for oligopolists to avoid a low-price outcome?
a. Tit-for-tat
b. Win-win
c. Last-in first-out
d. Second best

20. Which of the following is a game theory strategy for oligopolists to avoid a low-price outcome?
a. Tit-for-tat
b. Price leadership
c. Cartel
d. All of the above

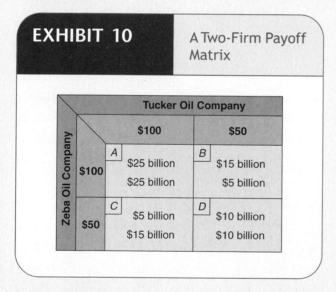

EXHIBIT 10   A Two-Firm Payoff Matrix

Labor Markets

© David Muir/Digital Vision/Getty Images.

I n 2007, champion golfer Tiger Woods earned the impressive figure of $100 million, but talk show host Oprah Winfrey did even better. She earned $260 million. While one headline reports a sports team signed their star player to a contract paying $10 million annually, another cites a recent survey showing chief executive officers (CEOs) of America's biggest corporations are paid millions of dollars in compensation. The president of the United States is paid $400,000 per year. The worker with only a bachelor's degree earns an average of about $55,000. The average high school graduate earns less than $30,000, while many others, including college students, toil for the minimum wage.

How are earnings determined? What accounts for the wide differences in earnings? This chapter provides answers by explaining different types of labor markets that determine workers' compensation and the quantity of workers firms hire. Understanding hiring decisions is indeed a key to understanding why some become rich and famous by playing baseball—a kid's game—while other workers might be exploited by firms with labor market power.

The chapter begins with the development of a competitive labor market in which no single buyer or seller can influence the price (wage rate) of labor. The chapter concludes with a discussion of power. As in the product markets, labor market determinations are affected by market power. Power on the side of either unions or employers can alter wage and employment outcomes. For example, the chapter explains how unions affect wages and examines trends in union membership around the world.

The Labor Market under Perfect Competition

In Chapters 8–10, you studied the price and quantity determinations of goods and services produced by firms operating under different market structures—perfect competition, monopoly, oligopoly, and monopolistic competition. As you have learned, market structure affects the price and the quantity of a good or service sold by firms to consumers. Similarly, as this chapter will demonstrate, the price (wage rate) paid to labor and the quantity of labor hired by firms are influenced by whether or not the labor market is competitive.

Recall from Chapter 8 that we assumed the hypothetical firm called Computech produces and sells electronic units for automated teller machines in a perfectly competitive market. Here we also assume Computech hires workers in a perfectly competitive labor market. In a perfectly competitive labor market, there are many sellers and buyers of labor services. Consequently, wages and salaries are determined by the intersection of the demand for labor and the supply of labor.

The Demand for Labor

How many workers should Computech hire? To answer this question, Computech must know how much workers contribute to its output. Column 1 of Exhibit 1 lists possible numbers of workers Computech might hire per day, and as discussed earlier in Chapter 7 on production costs, column 2 shows the total output per day. One worker would produce 5 units per day, two workers together would produce 9 units per day, and so on. Note that columns 1 and 2 constitute a *production function,* as represented earlier in Exhibit 2(a) in Chapter 7. Column 3 lists the additional output from hiring each worker. The first worker hired would add 5 units of output per day, the second would produce an additional 4 units (total product of 9—5 units produced), and so on. Recall from Chapter 7 that the additional output from hiring another unit of labor is defined as the *marginal product of labor* [see Exhibit 2(b) in Chapter 7]. Consistent with the *law of diminishing returns,* the marginal product falls as the firm hires more workers.[1]

The next step in Computech's hiring decision is to convert marginal product into dollars by calculating the marginal revenue product (MRP), which is the increase in

> **Marginal revenue product (*MRP*)**
> The increase in a firm's total revenue resulting from hiring an additional unit of labor or other variable resource.

---

1. Recall from Chapter 7 that at low rates of output marginal product may increase with the addition of more labor due to specialization and division of labor. Then, as output expands in the short run, the law of diminishing returns will cause marginal product to decrease.

EXHIBIT 1 — Computech's Demand for Labor

Points	(1) Labor Input (workers per day)	(2) Total Output (units per day)	(3) Marginal Product (units per day)	(4) Product Price	(5) Marginal Revenue Product [(3) × (4)]
	0	0		$70	
			5		$350
A	1	5		70	
			4		280
B	2	9		70	
			3		210
C	3	12		70	
			2		140
D	4	14		70	
			1		70
E	5	15		70	

a firm's total revenue resulting from hiring an additional unit of labor or other variable resource. Stated simply, MRP is the dollar value of worker productivity. It is the extra revenue a firm earns from selling the output of an extra worker. Returning to Exhibit 1 in Chapter 8 on perfect competition, suppose the market equilibrium price per unit is $70. Because Computech operates in a perfectly competitive market, the firm can sell any quantity of its product at the $70 market-determined price. Given this situation, the first unit of labor contributes an MRP of $350 per day to revenue ($70 per unit times the 5 units of output). Column 5 of Exhibit 1 lists the MRP of each additional worker hired.

Conclusion *A perfectly competitive firm's marginal revenue product is equal to the marginal product of its labor times the price of its product. Expressed as a formula:* **MRP = P × MP.**

Demand curve for labor

A curve showing the different quantities of labor employers are willing to hire at different wage rates in a given time period, ceteris paribus. It is equal to the marginal revenue product of labor.

Now assuming all other inputs are fixed, Computech can derive its demand curve for labor, which conforms to the law of demand explained in Chapter 3. The demand curve for labor is a curve showing the different quantities of labor employers are willing to hire at different wage rates. It is equal to the MRP of labor. The MRP numbers from Exhibit 1 are duplicated in Exhibit 2. As shown in Exhibit 2 the price of labor in terms of daily wages is measured on the vertical axis. The quantity of workers Computech will hire per day at each wage rate is measured on the horizontal axis. The demand curve for labor is downward sloping: As the wage rate falls, Computech will hire more workers per day. If the wage rate is above $350 (point A), Computech will hire no workers because the cost of a worker is more than the dollar value of any worker's contribution to total revenue (MRP). But what happens if Computech pays each worker $280 per day? At point B, Computech finds it profitable to hire two workers because the MRP of the first worker is greater than the wage rate (extra cost) and the second worker's MRP equals the

EXHIBIT 2   Computech's Demand Curve for Labor

Computech's downward-sloping demand curve for labor is derived from the marginal revenue product (*MRP*) of labor, which declines as additional workers are hired. The *MRP* is the change in total revenue that results from hiring one more worker (see Exhibit 1). At point *B*, Computech pays $280 per day and finds it profitable to pay this wage to two workers because each worker's *MRP* equals or exceeds the wage rate. If Computech pays a lower wage rate of $140 per day at point *D*, it is not profitable for the firm to hire the fifth worker because this worker's *MRP* of $70 is below the wage rate of $140 per day. At a wage rate of $70, the fifth worker would be hired.

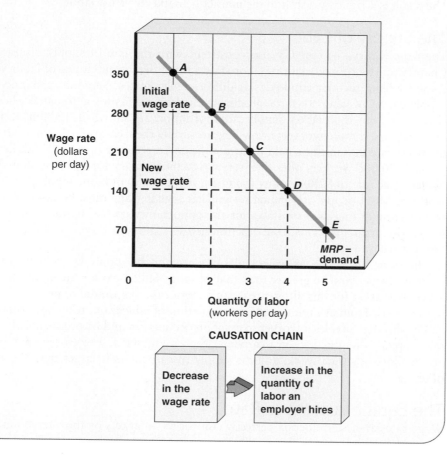

wage rate. If the wage rate is $140 per day at point *D*, Computech will find it profitable to hire four workers. In this case, Computech will not hire the fifth worker. Why? The fifth worker contributes an *MRP* of $70 to total revenue (point *E*), but this amount is below the wage rate paid of $140. Consequently, Computech cannot maximize profits by hiring the fifth worker because it would be adding more to costs than to revenue. Specifically, Computech would lose $70 per day by hiring the fifth worker. At a wage rate of $70, however, the fifth worker would be hired.

Conclusion *A firm hires additional workers up to the point where the MRP equals the wage rate.*

Each firm in the market has a demand for labor based on its *MRP* data. Summing these individual demand curves for labor provides the market demand curve for labor in the electronic components industry. Another important point must be made. The demand for labor is called derived demand. The derived demand for labor and other factors of production depends on the consumer demand for the final goods and services the factors produce. If consumers are not willing to purchase products requiring electronic components, such as bank teller machines, there is no *MRP*, and firms will hire no workers to make electronic components for them. On the other hand, if customer demand for bank teller machines soars, the price of units rises, and the *MRP* of firms in the electronic components industry also rises. The result is a rightward shift in the market demand curve for labor.

Derived demand

The demand for labor and other factors of production that depends on the consumer demand for the final goods and services the factors produce.

The Supply of Labor

The supply curve of labor is also consistent with the law of supply discussed in Chapter 3. The supply curve of labor shows the different quantities of labor workers are willing to offer employers at different wage rates. Summing the individual supply curves of labor for firms producing electronic units for automated teller machines provides the market supply curve of labor. As shown in Exhibit 3, as the wage rate rises, more workers are willing to supply their labor. Each point indicates the wage rate that must be paid to attract the corresponding number of workers. At point *A*, 20,000 workers offer their services to the industry for $140 per day. At the higher wage rate of $280 per day (point *B*), the quantity of labor supplied is 40,000 workers. More people are willing to work at higher wage rates because the incentive of earning more compensates for the opportunity cost of leisure time. Higher wages also attract workers from other industries that require similar skills, but have lower wage rates.

Supply curve of labor

A curve showing the different quantities of labor workers are willing to offer employers at different wage rates in a given time period, ceteris paribus.

Ignoring differences in wage scales, why might the supply of less-skilled workers (e.g., carpenters) be greater than that of more-skilled workers (e.g., physicians)? The explanation for this difference is the human capital required to perform various occupations. Human capital is the accumulation of education, training, experience, and health that enables a worker to enter an occupation and be productive. Less human capital is required to be a carpenter than a physician. Therefore, many people are qualified for such work, and the supply of carpenters is larger than the supply of physicians.

Human capital

The accumulation of education, training, experience, and health that enables a worker to enter an occupation and be productive.

The Equilibrium Wage Rate

Wage rates are determined in perfectly competitive markets by the interaction of labor supply and demand. The equilibrium wage rate for the entire electronic components market, shown in Exhibit 4(a), is $210 per day. This wage rate clears the market because the quantity of 30,000 workers demanded equals the quantity of 30,000 workers who are willing to supply their labor services at that wage rate. In a competitive labor market, no single worker can set his or her wage above the equilibrium wage. Such a worker fears not being hired because there are so many workers who will work for $210 per day. Similarly, so many firms are hiring labor that a single firm cannot influence the wage by paying workers more or less than the prevailing wage. Hence, a wage rate above $210 per day would create a surplus of workers seeking employment (unemployment) in the electronic components market, and a wage rate below $210 per day would cause a shortage.

Why does a cardiologist make a much higher hourly wage than a server in a restaurant? As demonstrated in Exhibit 4(a), wage differentials are determined by

EXHIBIT 3 — The Market Supply Curve of Labor

The upward-sloping supply curve of labor for the electronic components industry indicates that a direct relationship exists between the wage rate and the quantity of labor supplied. At point *A*, 20,000 workers are willing to work for $140 per day in this market. If the wage rate rises to $280 per day, 40,000 workers will supply their services to the electronic components labor market.

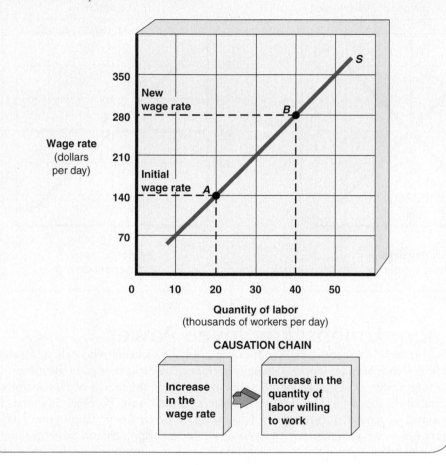

Wage rate
(dollars per day)

CAUSATION CHAIN

Increase in the wage rate → Increase in the quantity of labor willing to work

the demand and supply curves in labor markets for these two occupations. In this case, the equilibrium wage rate for cardiologists greatly exceeds the equilibrium wage rate for servers. In the next chapter, this labor market model is used to explain differences in wages resulting from racial discrimination.

Although the supply curve of labor is upward sloping for the electronic components market, this is not the case for an individual firm, such as Computech, shown in Exhibit 4(b). Because a competitive labor market assumes that each firm is too small to influence the wage rate, Computech is a "wage taker" and therefore pays the market-determined wage rate of $210 per day regardless of the quantity of labor it employs. For this reason, the labor supply to Computech is represented by a horizontal line at the equilibrium wage rate. Given this wage rate of $210 per day, Computech then hires labor up to the equilibrium point, *E*, where the wage rate equals the third worker's marginal revenue product.

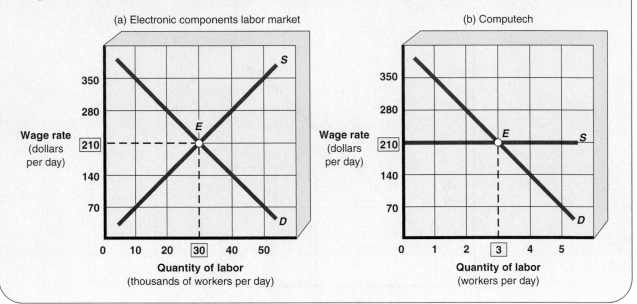

EXHIBIT 4   A Competitive Labor Market Determines the Firm's Equilibrium Wage

In Part (a), the intersection of the supply of labor and the demand for labor curves determines the equilibrium wage rate of $210 per day in the electronic components industry. Part (b) illustrates that a single firm, such as Computech, is a "wage taker." The firm can hire all the workers it wants at this equilibrium wage, so its supply curve, *S*, is a horizontal line. Computech chooses to hire three workers, where the firm's demand curve for labor intersects its supply curve of labor.

(a) Electronic components labor market

Wage rate (dollars per day)

350
280
210
140
70

E
S
D

Quantity of labor
(thousands of workers per day)
0   10   20   30   40   50

(b) Computech

Wage rate (dollars per day)

350
280
210
140
70

E
S
D

Quantity of labor
(workers per day)
0   1   2   3   4   5

Labor Unions: Employee Power

The perfectly competitive model does not apply to workers who belong to unions. Unions arose because workers recognized that acting together gave them more bargaining power than acting individually and being at the mercy of their employers. Some of the biggest unions are the Teamsters, United Auto Workers, National Education Association, and American Federation of Government Employees. Two primary objectives of unions are to improve working conditions and raise the wages of union members above the level that would exist in a competitive labor market. To raise wages, unions use three basic strategies: (1) increase the demand for labor, (2) decrease the supply of labor, and (3) exert power to force employers to pay a wage rate above the equilibrium wage rate.

Unions Increase the Demand for Labor

Now suppose the workers form a union. One way to increase wages is to use a method called *featherbedding*. This means the union forces firms to hire more workers than are required or to impose work rules that reduce output per worker. For example, contract provisions may prohibit any workers but carpenters from doing even the simplest carpentry work. Another approach is to boost domestic demand for labor by decreasing competition from other nations. For example, the union might lobby Congress to protect the U.S. electronic parts industry against competition from China. Another approach might be to advertise and try to convince the public to "Look for the Union Label." Effective advertising would boost the demand for electronic products with union-made components and, in turn, the demand for union labor because it is *derived demand*.

Exhibit 5 shows how union power can be used to increase the demand curve for labor. This exhibit reproduces the labor market for electronic components workers from Exhibit 4(a). Begin at equilibrium point E_1, with the wage rate of $210 per day paid to each of 30,000 workers. Then the union causes the demand curve for labor to increase from D_1 to D_2. At the new equilibrium point, E_2, firms hire an additional 10,000 workers and pay each worker an extra $70 per day.

Unions Decrease the Supply of Labor

Exhibit 6 shows another way unions can use their power to increase the wage rate of their members by restricting the supply of labor. Now suppose the labor market

EXHIBIT 5   A Union Causes an Increase in the Demand Curve for Labor

A union shifts the demand curve for labor rightward from D_1 to D_2 by featherbedding or other devices. As a result, the equilibrium wage rate increases from $210 per day at point E_1 to $280 per day at point E_2, and employment rises from 30,000 to 40,000 workers.

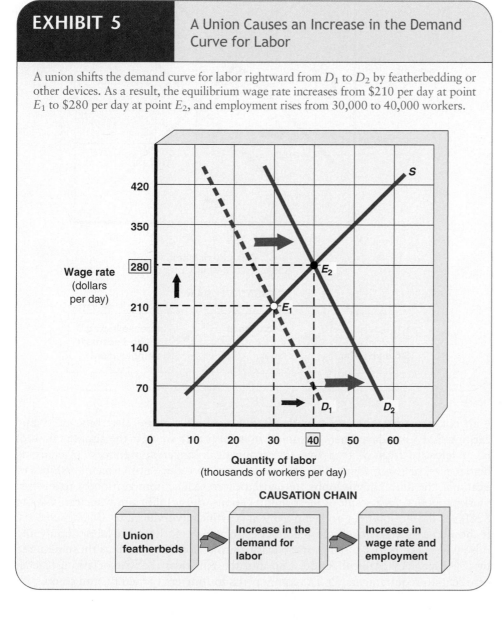

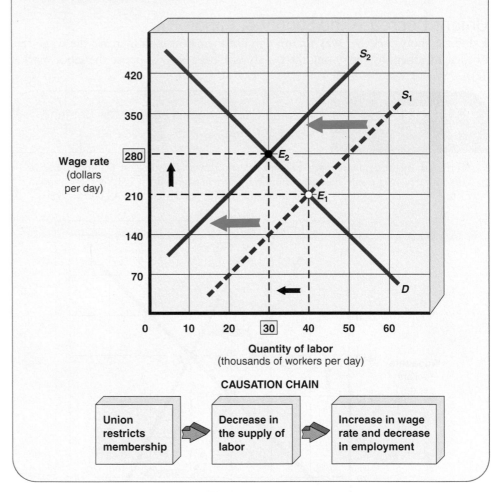

EXHIBIT 6   A Union Causes a Decrease in the Supply Curve of Labor

A union shifts the supply curve of labor leftward from S_1 to S_2 by restricting union membership or by using other techniques. As a result, the equilibrium wage rate rises from $210 per day at point E_1 to $280 per day at point E_2, and the number of workers hired falls from 40,000 to 30,000.

CAUSATION CHAIN

| Union restricts membership | → | Decrease in the supply of labor | → | Increase in wage rate and decrease in employment |

is in equilibrium at point E_1, with 40,000 workers making electronic units and earning $210 per day. Then the union uses its power to shift the supply curve of labor leftward from S_1 to S_2 by, say, requiring a longer apprenticeship, charging higher fees, or using some other device designed to reduce union membership. For example, the union might lobby for legislation to reduce immigration or to shorten working hours. As a result of these union actions, the equilibrium wage rate rises to $280 per day at point E_2, and employment is artificially reduced to 30,000 workers. It should be noted that self-serving practices of unions to limit the labor supply and raise wages can be disguised as standards of professionalism, such as those required by the American Medical Association and the American Bar Association, teacher certification requirements, Ph.D. requirements for university faculty, and so on.

Unions Use Collective Bargaining to Boost Wages

A third way to raise the wage rate above the equilibrium level is to use collective bargaining. Collective bargaining is the process of negotiating labor contracts between the union and management concerning wages and working conditions. By law, once a union has been certified as the representative of a majority of the workers, employers must deal with the union. If employers deny union demands, the union can strike and reduce profits until the firms agree to a higher wage rate.

The result of collective bargaining is shown in Exhibit 7. Again, we return to the situation depicted for the electronic components market in Exhibit 4(a). At the equilibrium wage rate of $210 per day (point E), there is no surplus or shortage of workers. Then the industry is unionized, and a collective bargaining agreement takes effect in which firms agree to pay the union wage rate of $280 per day. At the higher wage rate, employment falls from 30,000 to 20,000 workers. However, 40,000 workers wish to work for $280 per day, so there is a surplus of 20,000 unemployed workers in the industry. How might firms react to a situation in which they hire fewer workers and pay higher wages? Employers might respond by substituting capital for labor or by transferring operations overseas, where labor costs are lower than in the United States.

> **Collective bargaining**
> The process of negotiating labor contracts between the union and management concerning wages and working conditions.

EXHIBIT 7 — Union Collective Bargaining Causes a Wage Rate Increase

A union exerts its power through collective bargaining. Instead of the competitive wage rate of $210 at point E, firms in the industry avoid a strike by agreeing in a labor contract to $280 per day. The effect is to artificially create a labor surplus (unemployment) of 20,000 workers at the negotiated wage.

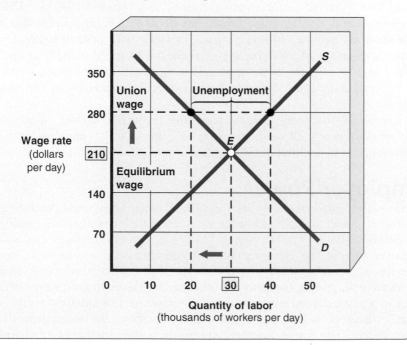

EXHIBIT 8	Factors Causing Changes in Labor Demand and Labor Supply

Changes in Labor Demand	Changes in Labor Supply
1. Unions	1. Unions
2. Prices of substitute inputs	2. Demographic trends
3. Technology	3. Expectations of future income
4. Demand for final products	4. Changes in immigration laws
5. Marginal product of labor	5. Education and training

GLOBAL ECONOMICS

Finally, several factors can cause either the demand curve for labor or the supply curve of labor to shift. Exhibit 8 provides a list of these factors.

Union Membership around the World

How important are unions as measured by the percentage of the labor force that belongs to a union? Let's start during the Great Depression, when millions of people were out of work and union membership was relatively low (see Exhibit 9). To boost employment and earnings, President Franklin D. Roosevelt's National Industrial Recovery Act (NIRA) of 1933 established the right of employees to bargain collectively with their employers, but the act was declared unconstitutional by the Supreme Court in 1935. However, the 1935 National Labor Relations Act (NLRA), known as the Wagner Act, incorporated the labor provisions of the NIRA. The Wagner Act guaranteed workers the right to form unions and to engage in collective bargaining. The combined impact of this legislation and the production demands of World War II created a surge in union membership between 1935 and 1945.

Since World War II, union power has declined. Union membership has fallen from about 35 percent of the labor force in 1945 to 12 percent today. Since 1983, union membership of public sector workers has changed little from 36.7 percent to 36.2 in 2006. On the other hand, union membership for private sector workers has declined significantly from 16.5 percent to 7.4 percent over the same period of time.

Exhibit 10 shows the unionization rates in other countries. While in Sweden and Denmark nearly all workers belong to a union, union membership in the United States is far below that of other industrialized countries.

Employer Power

So far, labor markets have been explained with employees possessing varying degrees of power to influence wage rates and employment while employers were competitive with no market power. However, significant power can exist on the employer side of the labor market. The extreme case occurs in a monopsony. Monopsony is a labor market in which a single firm hires labor. For example, a single textile mill, mining company, or housing contractor might be the only buyer of labor in a particular market. The classical phrase for this situation is the "company town," where for miles around a small town everyone's livelihood depends on a single employer. The reason for the monopsony is the absence of other firms in the

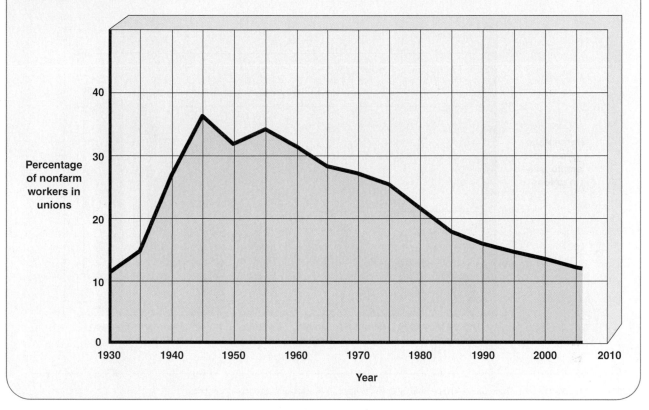

EXHIBIT 9   U.S. Union Membership, 1930-2006

As a percentage of nonfarm workers, union membership in the United States grew most rapidly during the decade 1935–1945. Since its peak in 1945, union membership as a percentage of the labor force has fallen to about the level in 1935.

Percentage of nonfarm workers in unions

SOURCE: *Statistical Abstract of the United States*, 2008, http://www.census.gov/compendia/statab/, Table 644.

area competing for relatively immobile labor because workers must acquire new skills to find work outside the company town market. Even if a firm doesn't dominate a local labor market, it may have monopsony power over certain types of labor. A hospital, for example, may be the only large employer of nurses in a local market; therefore, it has monopsony power.

Marginal Factor Cost

This chapter began by assuming Computech operated in a competitive labor market in which no single employer in the electronic components market had any direct influence on the market wage rate. Recall from Exhibit 4 that Computech is a wage taker. More precisely, Computech hires the quantity of labor at the prevailing labor market equilibrium wage rate, which is determined by the point where the firm's downward-sloping *MRP* curve (demand curve for labor) intersects the horizontal supply curve of labor. The equilibrium wage rate is established by a competitive labor market beyond Computech's power to control.

Now we visit the isolated small town of Plainsville and find General Griffin's, which is a monopsonist producing turkeys. As shown in Exhibit 11, the supply of

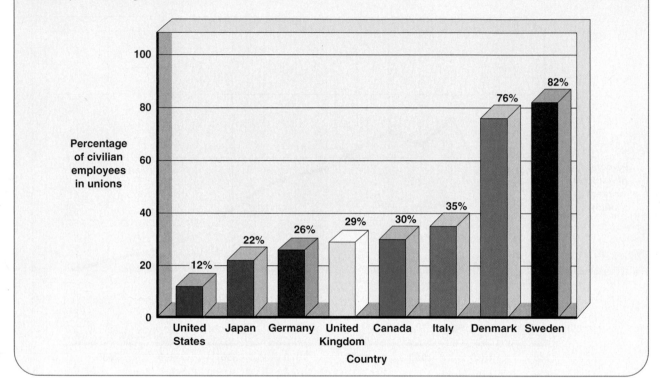

EXHIBIT 10   Union Membership for Selected Countries, 2006

Union membership as a percentage of the civilian labor force in Denmark and Sweden is far above that of the United States. The unionization rates of other industrialized countries, such as Japan, Canada, Germany, the United Kingdom, and Italy, are also higher than the rate in the United States.

SOURCE: NationMaster.com, *Trade Union Membership by Country,* http://www.nationmaster.com/statistics.

---

labor curve facing the monopsonist is upward sloping rather than horizontal. The reason is that General Griffin's is the only firm hiring workers in Plainsville, so it faces the industry, or entire, supply curve of labor in the Plainsville labor market. This situation compares to that of the monopolist, which faces the industry demand curve for a particular product. As a result, the monopolist in a product market cannot sell an additional unit of a good without lowering the price, and the marginal revenue curve falls below the demand curve. For the monopsonist, a distinction exists between the supply curve of labor and the marginal factor cost (*MFC*) curve. Marginal factor cost is the additional total cost resulting from a one-unit increase in the quantity of a factor. Note that the *MFC* curve starts above the bottom of the supply curve of labor and then rises above it. The *MFC* points are plotted at the midpoints because the change in total wage cost occurs between each additional unit of labor. Having made this observation, relax and take a deep breath; then we will proceed to the nuts and bolts of monopsonist theory.

If General Griffin's pays $3 per hour at point *A* on the upward-sloping supply curve of labor in Plainsville, only one worker will be willing to be hired. If the monopsonist wants to hire more labor, it must offer higher wages. If the firm raises its wage offer to $6 per hour for each worker (point *B*), the quantity of labor supplied

Marginal factor cost (*MFC*)

The additional total cost resulting from a one-unit increase in the quantity of a factor.

EXHIBIT 11   A Monopsonist Determines Its Wage Rate

The monopsonist, General Griffin's, faces the industry upward-sloping supply curve of labor in the small town of Plainsville. As the wage rate rises, all workers must be paid the same higher wage. As a result, the change in total wage cost (marginal factor cost in column 4) exceeds the wage paid to the last worker (column 1). The *MFC* curve therefore lies above the supply curve of labor.

The demand curve for labor is the marginal revenue product (*MRP*), or the worth to the monopsonist of each worker it hires. The intersection of the *MFC* and *MRP* curves at point *E* determines that General Griffin's hires two workers per hour. Because this firm has a monopsony in the Plainsville labor market, it can pay $6 per hour at point *B* on the supply curve of labor, which is enough to attract two workers. However, the worker is exploited because the *MRP* at point *E* for the second worker is $12 per hour and the wage rate is only $6. In a competitive labor market, the equilibrium would be at point *C*, and General Griffin's would pay a higher wage and employ more workers.

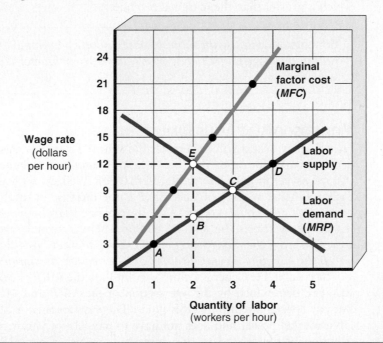

Points	(1) Wage Rate (per hour)	(2) Labor Input (workers per hour)	(3) Total Wage Cost (per hour) [(1) × (2)]	(4) Marginal Factor Cost (*MFC*) [Δ(3)/Δ(2)]
	$0	0	$0	
				$3
A	3	1	3	
				9
B	6	2	12	
				15
C	9	3	27	
				21
D	12	4	48	

increases to two workers per hour. In the exhibit, the total wage cost per hour in column 3 is computed by multiplying the wage rate per hour in column 1 times the number of workers per hour in column 2. At point *A*, the total wage cost per hour is $3, which equals the wage rate. At point *B*, the total wage cost per hour rises to $12, and *MFC* is greater than the wage rate of $6 per hour. The explanation is that all workers are assumed to perform the same job. Consequently, the first worker will demand to be paid the same wage rate as the second worker hired at the higher wage rate. Stated differently, General Griffin's must pay a higher wage not only to each additional worker but also to all previously hired workers. If General Griffin's attempts to pay different wage rates for the same job, worker morale will deteriorate, causing labor unrest. Comparing points *A* through *D* confirms that *MFC* is greater than the wage rate for a monopsonist, much like the monopolist's price, which is greater than the marginal revenue.

> **Conclusion** *Because the monopsonist can hire additional workers only by raising the wage rate for all workers, the marginal factor cost exceeds the wage rate.*

Monopsonistic Equilibrium

How many workers will General Griffin's hire? To answer this question requires the demand curve for labor that traces labor's marginal revenue product (*MRP*), explained earlier in this chapter. Recall that *MRP* reflects the value or contribution of each additional worker because *MRP* is the increase in total revenue produced by hiring each additional worker. Also, as explained in Chapter 8, the profit-maximizing producer selects the level of output where marginal revenue equals marginal cost. Similarly, *the monopsonist in the labor market hires the quantity of labor at which the marginal revenue product of labor equals its marginal factor cost.*

In Exhibit 11, General Griffin's will follow the *MRP* = *MFC* rule by hiring two workers, determined by the intersection of the *MRP* and *MFC* curves at point *E*. But pay special attention to this point: The monopsonist is a "wage maker." It has labor market power and does not have to pay $12 per hour, which equals the contribution of the second worker measured by his or her *MRP*. Instead of paying workers what their services are worth, the monopsonist follows the supply curve of labor, selects point *B*, and pays $6 per hour rather than $12 per hour. Since $6 per hour is all the firm must pay to attract and hire two workers, the monopsonist can exploit labor by paying less than its marginal revenue product.

One alternative for labor facing a powerful employer is to organize a powerful union and engage in collective bargaining. Totally successful collective bargaining by a labor union could raise the wage rate from $6 per hour at point *B* to $12 per hour at point *E*. General Griffin's will resist the union's demands and offer a lower wage closer to point *B*. Thus, points *B* and *E* represent the boundaries of a potential final settlement. What the negotiated final equilibrium wage rate will be depends on the tactics and resources of the negotiating parties.

Finally, suppose the monopsony is broken up into a large number of small firms. Recall from earlier in this chapter that in competitive labor markets additional workers are hired to the point where the wage rate is equal to the *MRP*. In this case, the supply curve of labor intersects the *MRP* (demand) curve at point *C*, and more workers would be hired with $9 per hour paid to each worker.

Image Source/Jupiterimages.

It was perfect football weather on a beautiful autumn Saturday at Nebraska State's stadium. There was a hush in the crowd of 80,000 as the clock showed 5 seconds left in the game and the scoreboard read Home 26, Visitor 30. The Screaming Eagles were playing the Fighting Irish, and the season was on the line. With time running out, the Eagles' All-American quarterback, Joe Wyoming, launched a desperation pass from his 45-yard line. The pass hit the extended fingers of a wide receiver who leaped over three defenders at the Irish 25-yard line and then ran into the end zone all alone. The home crowd roared with joy after staring defeat in the face.

So the season had been in the hands of Joe Wyoming, who received a full scholarship, which cost the university more than $40,000 over four years. Because Joe led the Eagles to victory over Notre Dame, the team played in the Sugar Bowl, which paid Nebraska State $5 million for the appearance. In addition, the next year's ticket sales, alumni contributions, and trademark licensing boosted revenues $10 million, while applications for admission to the university increased sharply.

Economist John Leonard argues that college athletes are clearly underpaid because players cannot be paid salaries under National Collegiate Athletic Association (NCAA) rules. His study estimated that a star college football player who is named to an All-American team generates a marginal revenue product of $100,000 per year for the university. Yet that athlete is paid only $10,000 scholarship per year.

In Chapter 10, a cartel was explained as a group of firms that use a collusive agreement to act as a monopoly. NCAA regulations serve as a collusive agreement among colleges and universities to act as a monopsony and hire the services of college-bound athletes. Just like an output or sellers' cartel, such as the Organization of Petroleum Exporting Countries (OPEC), the NCAA must enforce the rules against cheaters.

Because this agreement holds players' wages far below their marginal revenue product, the gap creates an incentive for schools to offer "illegal" inducements of cars, money, clothes, and trips to attract good players. Such cheating benefits the college athletes whose wages are raised closer to their marginal revenue products. A school that is not caught benefits by recruiting better players, achieving athletic success, and receiving greater sports revenue. Schools that follow the rules must depend on the NCAA to punish cheaters by taking away TV appearances, tournament play, bowl invitations, and scholarships.

ANALYZE THE ISSUE

Do you favor paying college athletes salaries determined by a competitive labor market rather than by an NCAA agreement? Explain.

Conclusion *A monopsonist hires fewer workers and pays a lower wage than a firm in a competitive labor market.*

CHECKPOINTS

Can the Minimum Wage Create Jobs?
In Chapter 4, Exhibit 5 explained that the effect of the minimum wage in a competitive labor market is to decrease the number of unskilled workers employed. Assume the minimum wage is $9, and consider the effect on the monopsonist represented in Exhibit 11. This means by law the monopsonist cannot hire a worker for a lower wage. In the case of monopsony, contrary to the case of perfect competition, can the minimum wage increase the number of persons working? Explain your answer using Exhibit 11.

If You Don't Like It, Mickey, Take Your Bat and Go Home
Mickey Mantle described his salary negotiations with the Yankees in his autobiography *The Mick*. After winning baseball's Triple Crown in 1955, his salary increased from about $85,000 to $100,000. The next season, he raised his batting average even higher, and the Yankee team owner offered him a pay cut. What is the most likely explanation for the owner's behavior—an increase in the supply of star baseball players, owner monopsony power, or the owner's desire that Mantle find another team?

KEY CONCEPTS

Marginal revenue product (*MRP*)
Demand curve for labor
Derived demand

Supply curve of labor
Human capital
Collective bargaining

Monopsony
Marginal factor cost (*MFC*)

SUMMARY

- *Marginal revenue product (MRP)* is determined by a worker's contribution to a firm's total revenue. Algebraically, the marginal revenue product equals the price of the product times the worker's marginal product: $MRP = P \times MP$.

- The *demand curve for labor* shows the quantities of labor a firm is willing to hire at different prices of labor. The marginal revenue product (*MRP*) of labor curve is the firm's demand curve for labor. Summing individual demand for labor curves gives the market demand curve for labor.

Demand curve for labor

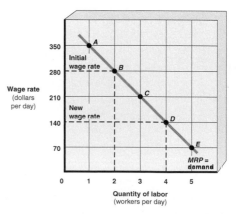

- *Derived demand* means that a firm demands labor because labor is productive. Changes in consumer demand for a product cause changes in the demand for labor and for other resources used to make the product.
- The *supply curve of labor* shows the quantities of workers willing to work at different prices of labor. The market supply curve of labor is derived by adding the individual supply curves of labor.

Supply curve of labor

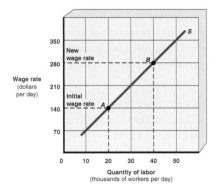

- *Human capital* is the accumulated investment people make in education, training, experience, and health in order to make themselves more productive. One explanation for earnings differences is differences in human capital.

- *Collective bargaining* is the process through which a union and management negotiate a labor contract.
- *Monopsony* is a labor market in which a single firm hires labor. Because the monopsonist faces the industry supply curve of labor and each worker is paid the same wage, changes in total wage cost exceed the wage rate necessary to hire each additional worker. As a result, the *marginal factor cost* (**MFC**) of labor curve, which measures changes in total wage cost per worker, lies above the supply curve of labor. The monopsonist's wage rate and quantity of labor are determined where the *MFC* equals *MRP*. Since at this point the worker's *MRP* is greater than the wage paid, the monopsonist exploits workers.

Monopsony

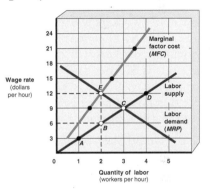

SUMMARY OF CONCLUSION STATEMENTS

- A perfectly competitive firm's marginal revenue product is equal to the marginal product of its labor times the price of its product. Expressed as a formula: $MRP = P \times MP$.
- A firm hires additional workers up to the point where the *MRP* equals the wage rate.

- Because the monopsonist can hire additional workers only by raising the wage rate for all workers, the marginal factor cost exceeds the wage rate.
- A monopsonist hires fewer workers and pays a lower wage than a firm in a competitive labor market.

STUDY QUESTIONS AND PROBLEMS

1. Consider this statement: "Workers demand jobs, and employers supply jobs." Do you agree or disagree? Explain.

2. The Zippy Paper Company has no control over either the price of paper or the wage it pays its workers. The following table shows the

relationship between the number of workers Zippy hires and total output:

Labor Input (workers per day)	Total Output (boxes of paper per day)
0	0
1	15
2	27
3	36
4	43
5	48
6	51

If the selling price is $10 per box, answer the following questions:

a. What is the marginal revenue product (MRP) of each worker?

b. How many workers will Zippy hire if the wage rate is $100 per day?

c. How many workers will Zippy hire if the wage rate is $75 per day?

d. Assume the wage rate is $75 per day and the price of a box of paper is $20. How many workers will Zippy hire?

3. Assume the Grand Slam Baseball Store sells $100 worth of baseball cards each day, with one employee operating the store. The owner decides to hire a second worker, and the two workers together sell $150 worth of baseball cards. What is the second worker's marginal revenue product (MRP)? If the price per card sold is $5, what is the second worker's marginal product (MP)?

4. What is the relationship between the marginal revenue product (MRP) and the demand curve for labor?

5. The market supply curve of labor is upward sloping, but the supply curve of labor for a single firm is horizontal. Explain why.

6. Assume the labor market for loggers is perfectly competitive. How would each of the following events influence the wage rate loggers are paid?

a. Consumers boycott products made with wood.

b. Loggers form a union that requires longer apprenticeships, charges high fees, and uses other devices designed to reduce union membership.

7. How does a human capital investment in education increase your lifetime earnings?

8. Suppose states pass laws requiring public school teachers to have a master's degree in order to retain their teaching certificates. What effect would this legislation have on the labor market for teachers?

9. Use the data in Question 2, and assume the equilibrium wage rate is $90 per day, determined in a perfectly competitive labor market. Now explain the impact of a union-negotiated collective bargaining agreement that changes the wage rate to $100 per day.

10. Some economists argue that the American Medical Association and the American Bar Association create an effect on labor markets similar to that of a labor union. Do you agree?

11. The Jacksonville Jaguars was an expansion professional football team in the National Football League (NFL). NFL draft and employment rules create monopsony power for each member club. In 1995, the Jaguars were in the process of hiring players. Using the following hypothetical table of data, construct a graph to determine the number of quarterbacks the Jaguars hired and the salary paid to each quarterback. Assuming the labor market was competitive, what would be the number of quarterbacks hired and the salary paid to each?

(1) Salary (thousands of dollars)	(2) Number of Quarterbacks	(3) Total Cost of Quarterbacks (thousands of dollars)	(4) Marginal Factor Cost (MFC) (thousands of dollars)	(5) Marginal Revenue Product (MRP) (thousands of dollars)
$ 0	0	$ 0	—	—
100	1	100	$100	$700
200	2	400	300	600
300	3	900	500	500
400	4	1,600	700	400
500	5	2,500	900	300

For Online Exercises, go to the text Web site at www.cengage.com/economics/tucker.

CHECKPOINT ANSWERS ✓

Can the Minimum Wage Create Jobs?

The minimum wage of $9 corresponds to point C in Exhibit 11. At this point, the labor supply and labor demand (MRP) curves intersect. Thus, the effect of the minimum wage is to force the monopsonist to operate at the equilibrium that would be established in a competitive labor market. If you said that under monopsony the minimum wage could raise the wage rate and create additional employment, **YOU ARE CORRECT.**

If You Don't Like It, Mickey, Take Your Bat and Go Home

Baseball players had no free-agent rights in the 1950s. If Mantle did not like the salary offer, his only choice was to go back to his home in Oklahoma. Faced with that alternative, he accepted the salary cut. If you said each team owner achieved monopsony power by prohibiting players from going to another team, **YOU ARE CORRECT.**

PRACTICE QUIZ

For an explanation of the correct answers, please visit the tutorial at www.cengage.com/ economics/tucker.

1. Marginal revenue product measures the increase in
    a. output resulting from one more unit of labor.
    b. total revenue resulting from one more unit of output.
    c. revenue per unit from one more unit of output.
    d. total revenue resulting from one more unit of labor.

2. Troll Corporation sells dolls for $10 each in a market that is perfectly competitive. Increasing the number of workers from 100 to 101 would cause output to rise from 500 to 510 dolls per day. Troll should hire the 101st worker only when the wage is
    a. $100 or less per day.
    b. more than $100 per day.
    c. $5.10 or less per day.
    d. none of the above.

3. Derived demand for labor depends on the
    a. cost of factors of production used in the product.
    b. market supply curve of labor.
    c. consumer demand for the final goods produced by labor.
    d. firm's total revenue less economic profit.

4. If demand for a product falls, the demand curve for labor used to produce the product will shift
    a. leftward.
    b. rightward.
    c. upward.
    d. remain unchanged.

5. The owner of a restaurant will hire waiters if the
    a. additional labor's pay is close to the minimum wage.
    b. marginal product is at the maximum.
    c. additional work of the employees adds more to total revenue than to costs.
    d. waiters do not belong to a union.

6. In a perfectly competitive market, the demand curve for labor
    a. slopes upward.
    b. slopes downward because of diminishing marginal productivity.
    c. is perfectly elastic at the equilibrium wage rate.
    d. is described by all of the above.

7. A union can influence the equilibrium wage rate by
    a. featherbedding.
    b. requiring longer apprenticeships.
    c. favoring trade restrictions on foreign products.

d. all of the above.

e. none of the above.

8. In which of the following market structures is the firm *not* a price taker in the factor market?
   a. Oligopoly
   b. Monopsony
   c. Monopoly
   d. Perfect competition

9. The extra cost of obtaining each additional unit of a factor of production is called the marginal
   a. physical product.
   b. revenue product.
   c. factor cost.
   d. implicit cost.

10. A monopsonist's marginal factor cost (*MFC*) curve lies above its supply curve because the firm must
    a. increase the price of its product to sell more.
    b. lower the price of its product to sell more.
    c. increase the wage rate to hire more labor.
    d. lower the wage rate to hire more labor.

11. To maximize profits, a monopsonist will hire the quantity of labor to the point where the marginal factor cost is equal to
    a. marginal physical product.
    b. marginal revenue product.
    c. total revenue product.
    d. any of the above.

12. BigBiz, a local monopsonist, currently hires 50 workers and pays them $6 per hour. To attract an additional worker to its labor force, BigBiz would have to raise the wage rate to $6.25 per hour. What is BigBiz's marginal factor cost?
    a. $6.25 per hour
    b. $12.50 per hour
    c. $18.75 per hour
    d. $20.00 per hour

13. Suppose a firm can hire 100 workers at $8.00 per hour, but must pay $8.05 per hour to hire 101 workers. Marginal factor cost (*MFC*) for the 101st worker is approximately equal to
    a. $8.00.
    b. $8.05.

c. $13.05.

d. $13.00.

14. A monopsonist in equilibrium has a marginal revenue product of $10 per worker hour. Its equilibrium wage rate must be
    a. less than $10.
    b. equal to $10.
    c. greater than $10.
    d. equal to $5.

15. If the labor market shown in Exhibit 12 is a monopsony, the wage rate and number of workers employed will be determined at point.
    a. *A*.
    b. *W*.
    c. *C*.
    d. *Y*.
    e. *Z*.

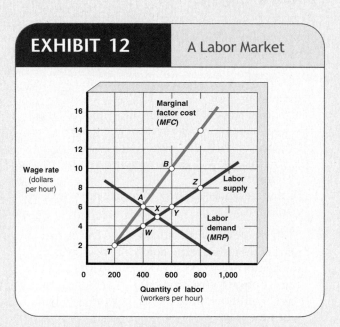

EXHIBIT 12   A Labor Market

MARKET STRUCTURES

This road map feature helps you tie material in the Part together as you travel the Economic Way of Thinking Highway. The following are review questions listed by chapter from the previous part. The key concept in each question is given for emphasis, and each question or set of questions concludes with an interactive game to reinforce the concepts. Click on the Tucker Web site, select the chapter, and play the visual causation chain game designed to make learning fun. Enjoy the cheers when correct and suffer the jeers if you miss.

For an explanation of the correct answers, please visit the tutorial at www .cengage.com/economics/tucker.

Chapter 8. Perfect Competition

1. **Key Concept: Short-Run Shut Down Point**
    Suppose product price is fixed at $24, $MR = MC$ at $Q = 200$, $AFC = \$6$, $AVC = \$25$. What do you advise this firm to do?
    a. Increase output.
    b. Decrease output.
    c. Shut down operations.
    d. Stay at the current output; the firm is earning a profit of $1,400.
    e. Stay at the current output; the firm is losing $1,400.

    Causation Chain Game
    The Short-Run Shutdown Point—Exhibit 6

2. **Key Concept: Long-Run Equilibrium**
    Consider a firm operating with the following: price = 10, $MR = 10$, $MC = 10$, $ATC = 10$. This firm is
    a. making an economic profit of 10.
    b. an example of monopolistic competition.
    c. going to go out of business in the long run.
    d. a monopolist for a product with a relatively inelastic demand.
    e. perfectly competitive in long-run equilibrium.

    Causation Chain Game
    Long-Run Perfectly Competitive Equilibrium—Exhibit 10

3. **Key Concept: Constant-cost Industry**
    Assume the short-run average total cost for a perfectly competitive industry remains constant as the output of the industry expands. In the long run, the industry supply curve will
    a. have a positive slope.
    b. have a negative slope.
    c. be perfectly horizontal.
    d. be perfectly vertical.

Causation Chain Game

Long-Run Supply in a Constant-Cost Industry—Exhibit 11

4. **Key Concept: Decreasing-cost Industry**

Assume the short-run average total cost for a perfectly competitive industry decreases as the output of the industry expands. In the long run, the industry supply curve will

a. have a positive slope.
b. have a negative slope.
c. be perfectly horizontal.
d. be perfectly vertical.

Causation Chain Game

Long-Run Supply in Decreasing-Cost Industry—Exhibit 12

5. **Key Concept: Increasing-Cost Industry**

Suppose that, in the long run, the price of feature films rises as the movie production industry expands. We can conclude that movie production is a (an)

a. increasing-cost industry.
b. constant-cost industry.
c. decreasing-cost industry.
d. marginal-cost industry.

Causation Chain Game

Long-Run Supply in an Increasing-Cost Industry—Exhibit 13

Chapter 9. Monopoly

6. **Key Concept: Profit Maximization**

Assume a monopolist's marginal cost and marginal revenue curves intersect and the demand curve passes above its average total cost curve. The firm will

a. make an economic profit.
b. stay in operation in the short run, but shut down in the long run.
c. shut down in the short run.
d. lower the price.

7. **Key Concept: Loss Minimization**

Assume a monopolist's marginal cost and marginal revenue curves intersect and the demand curve passes above its average total cost curve. The firm will

a. make an economic profit.
b. stay in operation in the short run, but shut down in the long run.
c. shut down in the short run.
d. lower the price.

Causation Chain Game

Profit Maximization and Loss Minimization

Chapter 10. Monopolistic Competition and Oligopoly

8. **Key Concept: Long-Run Monopolistic Competition**
    In the long run, the economic profits of Hoot's Chicken'n' Ribs, a monopolistic competitor are
    a. not eliminated, because competition is not perfect.
    b. not eliminated, because the demand curve slopes downward.
    c. eliminated due to firms entering the industry.
    d. eliminated due to firms leaving the industry.
    e. not eliminated, because firms cannot enter the industry.

 Causation Chain Game
    New Firms, Advertising, and Demand—Exhibit 3

Chapter 11. Labor Markets

9. **Key Concept: Market Supply Curve of Labor**
    Which of the following statements concerning the supply of labor is *true*?
    a. The supply of labor is determined by the prevailing wage rate.
    b. The labor supply curve is downward sloping.
    c. The wage rate has no effect on the supply of labor.
    d. None of the above.

Causation Chain Game
    The Market Supply Curve of Labor—Exhibit 3

10. **Key Concept: Increase in Demand for Labor**
    Featherbedding allows unions to increase wages by
    a. limiting the supply of labor.
    b. increasing firms' demand for labor.
    c. forcing firms to accept higher-than-equilibrium wages.
    d. reducing labor share of payroll taxes.

Causation Chain Game
    A Union Causes an Increase in the Demand Curve for Labor—Exhibit 5

11. **Key Concept: Decrease in Supply of Labor**
    Which of the following statements is *true*?
    a. Derived demand for labor depends on the demand for the product labor produces.
    b. Unions can either increase demand or decrease the supply of labor.
    c. Investment in human capital is expected to increase the demand for those workers.
    d. All of the above.

Causation Chain Game
    A Union Causes a Decrease in the Supply Curve of Labor—Exhibit 6

Microeconomic Policy Issues

These three chapters apply micro principles learned in previous chapters to explore policy issues concerning some important economic topics. The first chapter in this part extends the theory of labor markets into an examination of actual data on income and poverty. The second chapter mixes politics and economic theory to discuss such interesting topics as the Microsoft case and the deregulation of energy. The third chapter takes a closer look at ways to deal with externalities, such as pollution permits, which are actually traded on the Chicago Board of Trade.

Income Distribution, Poverty, and Discrimination

© David Muir/Digital Vision/Getty Images.

The previous chapter examined how variations in wages are determined in competitive and mono-psonistic labor markets. These labor supply and demand models do not give the complete picture of labor markets. In this chapter, we turn our attention to the distribution of income, poverty, and discrimination, which are important topics related to labor market wage decisions. The chapter begins by exploring the controversial issue of how the total family income "pie" is cut into various size "slices" or shares for different groups of families. You will examine government data that indicate the trend over the years in the share of income for the richest fifth of the population and the poorest fifth. Here the hotly contested issue of whether the "rich got richer" at the expense of the poor is addressed. In addition, the inequality of income in the United States is compared to that of other countries.

Poverty is an unhappy consequence of an unequal income distribution. Eighteenth-century English poet and essayist Samuel Johnson stated, "A decent provision for the poor is the true test of civilization." One purpose of this chapter is to define poverty and who are the poor. Another objective is to discuss government programs that aid the poor and provide criticisms of these programs. A special feature concerns the important issue of Social Security—past, present, and future.

The chapter concludes with the subject of discrimination, which is one possible explanation for unequal income distribution and poverty. Here you will apply the supply and demand model to explain why women earn less on average than men and African-Americans earn less than whites.

In this chapter, you will learn to solve these economic puzzles:

- Could the rich become richer and other income groups also become better off?

- How can a negative income tax solve the welfare controversy?

- Is pay for females fair?

The Distribution of Income

One function of labor markets is to determine the *distribution of income*—that is, how wages and salaries are divided among members of society. Recall from Chapter 2 that the For Whom question is one of the three basic questions that any economic system must answer. Here we study the For Whom question in more detail.

Trends in Income Distribution

One way to analyze the distribution of income in the United States is illustrated in Exhibit 1. In column 1 of this exhibit, families are divided into six groups according to the percentage of the total annual money income they received. The remaining columns of the table give the percentages of the total money income for each of the six groups in selected years since 1929. These data reveal changes in the distribution of income among families over time. For example, families with income in the top 5 percent in 1929 earned 10 percent more of the total income pie than they did in 2007. Otherwise, the distribution of income has not fluctuated greatly since 1947. Nonetheless, there is concern that since 1970 the percentage of income received by families in the lowest 20 percent group has fallen, while the income percentages received by the families in the highest fifth and the highest 5 percent have risen.

As shown in Exhibit 1, there is an unequal distribution of income among families. Why didn't each fifth of the families receive 20 percent of the total income? There are many reasons. For example, Exhibit 2 reveals that families headed by a college graduate fare better than those headed by an individual with less education. Recall from the previous chapter that human capital refers to education and skills that increase a worker's productivity. Workers with a greater investment in human capital are likely to be worth more to an employer. Data in this exhibit also indicate that families headed by a male generally earn more than those headed by a female.

Equality versus Efficiency

Because the data presented in Exhibits 1 and 2 show that an unequal distribution of income exists in the United States, the normative question to be debated concerns the pros and cons of a more equal income distribution. Those who favor greater equality fear the link between the rich and political power. The wealthy may well use their money to influence national policies that benefit the rich. It is also argued that income inequality results in unequal opportunities for various groups. For

EXHIBIT 1	The Division of Total Annual Money Income among Families, 1929–2007					
Percentage of Families	**1929**	**1947**	**1970**	**1980**	**1990**	**2007**
Highest 5%	30%	17%	16%	15%	17%	20%
Highest fifth	54	43	41	41	44	47
Second-highest fifth	19	23	24	24	24	23
Middle fifth	14	17	18	18	16	16
Second-lowest fifth	9	12	12	12	11	10
Lowest fifth	4	5	5	5	5	4

SOURCE: U.S. Bureau of the Census, Historical Income Tables, http://www.census.gov/hhes/income/income.html, Table F-2.

example, children of the poor have difficulty obtaining a college education. Consequently, their underutilized productive capacity is a waste of human capital. The poor are also unable to afford health care, and this is a national concern.

Advocates of income inequality pose this question. Suppose you had your choice of living in egalitarian society *A*, where every person earns $40,000 a year, or society *B*, where 20 percent earn $100,000 and 80 percent earn $30,000. You would likely choose society *B* because the incentive to earn more and live better is worth the risk of earning less and living worse. After all, why is the average income higher in society *B*? The answer is that income inequality gives people an incentive to be productive. In contrast, people in society *A* lack such motivation because everyone earns the same income. Those who favor equality of income believe that critics ignore the nonmonetary incentives, such as pride in one's work and nation, that can motivate people.

EXHIBIT 2	Median Money Income of Families, 2007
Characteristic	**Median Income***
All families	$61,355
Families headed by a male	44,358
Families headed by a female	30,296
Families with head aged 25–34 years	52,291
Families with head aged 65 years and over	41,851
Families headed by person with less than 9th grade education	26,973
Families headed by a high school graduate	49,739
Families headed by a person with at least a bachelor's degree	100,000

*Fifty percent of families earn less than the median income and 50 percent earn more.

SOURCE: U.S. Bureau of the Census, Historical Income Tables, http://www.census.gov/hhes/www/income/income.html, Tables F-7, F-11, and F-18.

A frequently debated topic concerning income inequality is whether the "rich are getting richer." As we observed earlier, the data in Exhibit 1 reveal that the percentages of total income received by the highest 5 percent and the highest fifth have increased in recent decades, while the percentages received by each of the fifths below the highest decreased slightly.

> **Conclusion** *Measured by distribution of family money income, the richest families have become a little richer and the rest of the family groups a little poorer in recent decades.*

It is important to note that simply observing changes in income distribution over time does not tell the whole story. Exhibit 3 traces real median family income, adjusted for rising prices, for the period 1980–2007. This measure indicates the trend of the average level of income received by all groups. Generally, the trend for real median income since the 1980s has been upward. This means the size of the income "pie" grew, and, therefore, all of the slices grew larger. However, consistent with the distribution data in Exhibit 1, the relative share of the pie for those with the biggest slice grew slightly larger. In 2000, real median income reached a new high before falling during the recession of 2001 and through 2004. In 2007, median family income rose to about the amount in 2000.

| EXHIBIT 3 | Real Median Family Income, 1980–2007 |

Real median income measures the income adjusted for inflation received by all families in the United States. Fifty percent of families earn less and 50 percent earn more than the median income. The trend of this measure was generally upward until 2000. In 2000, real median income reached a new high before falling during the recession of 2001 and through 2004. In 2007, median family income rose to about the amount in 2000.

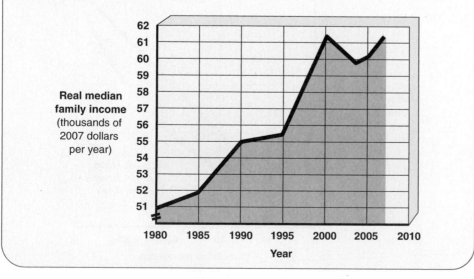

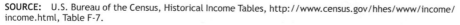

SOURCE: U.S. Bureau of the Census, Historical Income Tables, http://www.census.gov/hhes/www/income/income.html, Table F-7.

The Lorenz Curve

The distribution of income data presented in Exhibit 1 can be represented by the Lorenz curve. The Lorenz curve is a graph of the actual cumulative distribution of income compared to a perfectly equal cumulative distribution of income. This curve is a primary tool for measuring income distribution developed in 1905 by statistician M. O. Lorenz. Look at the hypothetical Lorenz curve in Exhibit 4. The vertical axis measures the *cumulative* percentage of family income, and the horizontal axis measures the *cumulative* percentage of families from poorest to richest. Starting at the lower left-hand corner on the graph, 0 percent of the families earned 0 percent of the cumulative percentage of money income. At the upper right-hand corner on the graph, 100 percent of the families earned 100 percent of the cumulative percentage of money income. The combination of other total family-total money income points between 0 and 100 percent forms the Lorenz curve.

Reading along the horizontal axis, each fifth (20 percent) of the cumulative percentage of families corresponds to its cumulative share of income earned

Lorenz curve
A graph of the actual cumulative distribution of income compared to a perfectly equal cumulative distribution of income.

EXHIBIT 4   A Hypothetical Lorenz Curve

The Lorenz curve shows the cumulative percentage of money income earned from 0 to 100 percent by the cumulative percentage of families, also from 0 to 100 percent. If the income distribution followed the 45-degree perfect equality line, 20 percent of the families earn 20 percent of total money income, 40 percent receive 40 percent of total money income, and so on. The shaded area between the perfect equality line and the Lorenz curve measures the degree of inequality in the distribution of income. The more the Lorenz curve is bowed outward, the more unequal the distribution of income is.

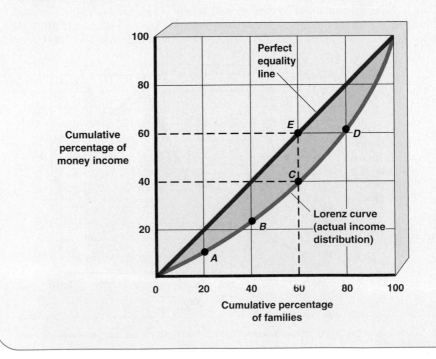

measured along the curve. At point *A*, the lowest 20 percent of families receive 10 percent of total or cumulative income. To read this, go from the 20 percent point on the horizontal axis up to point *A* on the Lorenz curve. Then draw a horizontal line to the vertical axis, and read that it intersects this axis at 10 percent. Point *B* is interpreted as the lowest 40 percent of families earn 10 percent plus 15 percent, which equals a cumulative share of 25 percent. Similarly, point *C* is the cumulative share earned by the lowest 60 percent of families, which equals 40 percent. Finally, point *D* is a bit tricky to interpret. At this point, the lowest 80 percent of families receive about 62 percent of total income. And here is the twist. You must interpret that the richest 20 percent of families earn 38 percent of income (100 percent –62 percent).

We now turn to the 45-degree line above the Lorenz curve that cuts the box in half. This line represents perfect equality: 20 percent of the families receive 20 percent of total income, 40 percent of the families receive 40 percent of total income, and so on. The distance of the Lorenz curve from the perfect equality line is therefore a measure of unequal income distribution. The gap between points *C* and *E*, for example, indicates that 60 percent of families earn 20 percent less of total income than required for perfect equality. Similar measurements generate the shaded area between the Lorenz curve and the perfect equality line. Thus, the shaded area is a measure of the degree of income inequality for our hypothetical data. A larger shaded area would mean greater income inequality, and the shape of the Lorenz curve would become more bowed outward. A smaller shaded area would represent a more equal income distribution, and the Lorenz curve would be a flatter curve.

It is very important to note that there are limitations associated with using money income statistics. Such data are not adjusted for government-provided food stamps, medical care, housing, or other goods and services. Money income also reflects income before taxes and does not measure unreported income or wealth. Still, used carefully, the Lorenz curve is a convenient tool for visualizing the degree of income inequality.

Income Distribution Trend in the United States

In Exhibit 1, we looked at income distributions for selected years between 1929 and 2007. What can we conclude from these data using the Lorenz curve? Has the overall income distribution become more or less equal? The table in Exhibit 5 restates the income share data for 1929 and 2007 from Exhibit 1, and the cumulative percentage shares of families of quintiles are calculated from the percentage shares.

Exhibit 5 suggests that overall money income distribution has changed little over the period. In the exhibit, there is only a small shaded area between the 1929 and 2007 Lorenz curves. However, the share of income received by the highest fifth of families fell from 54 percent in 1929 to 47 percent in 2007. Note that comparing other years can lead to different conclusions. For example, as shown in Exhibit 1, the distribution of income is less equal since 1970.

> **Conclusion** *The Lorenz curve has shifted only slightly inward, and therefore closer to the perfect equality line between 1929 and 2007.*

EXHIBIT 5	Lorenz Curves for Family Income Distribution in the United States, 1929 and 2007

Since 1929, the Lorenz curve has shifted somewhat inward toward the perfect equality line. Thus, there has been a reduction in the inequality of distribution of family money income since 1929.

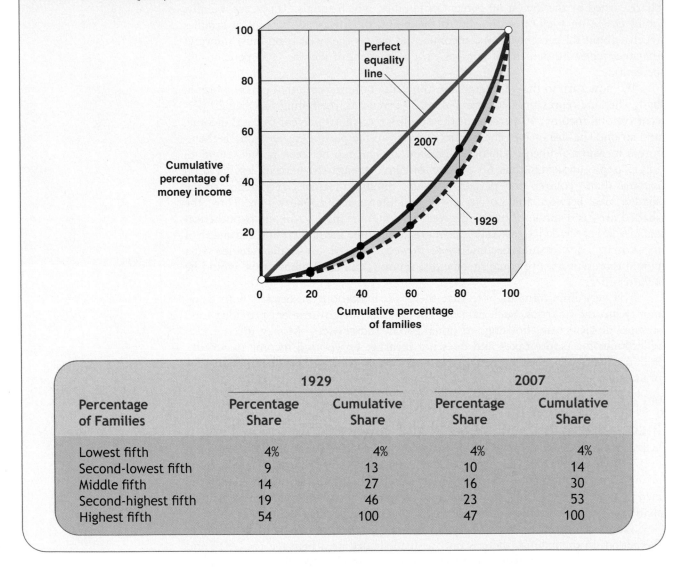

	1929		2007	
Percentage of Families	Percentage Share	Cumulative Share	Percentage Share	Cumulative Share
Lowest fifth	4%	4%	4%	4%
Second-lowest fifth	9	13	10	14
Middle fifth	14	27	16	30
Second-highest fifth	19	46	23	53
Highest fifth	54	100	47	100

GLOBAL ECONOMICS

Global Comparisons of Income Distribution

How does the distribution of income in the United States compare with that of other countries? Exhibit 6 presents separate Lorenz curves for the United States, the Czech Republic, and Brazil. This exhibit indicates that the degree of income inequality in the United States exceeds that of the Czech Republic. On the other hand, income distribution is more equal in the United States than in Brazil. In

EXHIBIT 6 | Lorenz Curves for Selected Countries

Comparing Lorenz curves for the United States, the Czech Republic, and Brazil reveals that income is distributed more equally in the Czech Republic than in the United States and Brazil. As illustrated by the Lorenz curve for Brazil, income inequality is usually greater in less-developed countries.

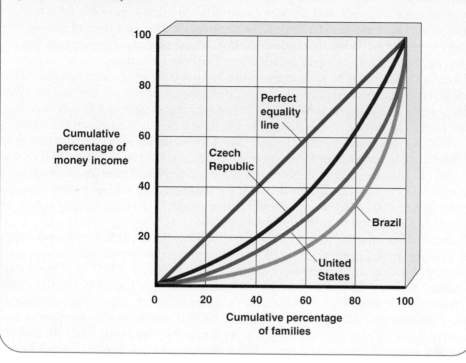

SOURCE: From 'The World Bank Group', http://devdata.worldbank.org/wd2005/Section2.htm, Table 2.8.

general, the distribution of income in developed nations, such as the United States, Germany, Italy, and Sweden, is more equal than in developing nations, such as Brazil, Mexico, and Zimbabwe.

Poverty

Having discussed the broader question of how the degree of income distribution inequality is measured, we now turn the spotlight on the fiercely debated issue of poverty. We are all disturbed by homelessness and hungry children. How can poverty exist in a nation of abundance such as the United States? Can economists offer useful ideas to reform and improve our current welfare system? Most of the nation agrees that the welfare system must undergo reforms to reduce poverty, cut welfare dependency, and save taxpayers money. The first step to understanding the problem is to ask this question: Who is poor?

Defining Poverty

What is poverty? Is it eating Spam when others are eating steak? Or is poverty a family having one car when others have two or more? Is the poverty standard only a matter of normative arguments? Indeed, the term *poverty* is difficult to define. A person whose income is comparatively low in the United States may be viewed as well-off in a less-developed country. Or what we in the United States regard as poverty today might have seemed a life of luxury 200 years ago.

There are two views of poverty. One defines poverty in *absolute* terms, and the other defines poverty in *relative* terms. Absolute poverty can be defined as a dollar figure that represents some level of income per year required to purchase some minimum amount of goods and services essential to meeting a person's or a family's basic needs. In contrast, relative poverty might be defined as a level of income that places a person or family in the lowest, say, 20 percent of all persons or families receiving incomes. An unequal distribution of income guarantees that some persons or families will occupy in relative terms the bottom rung of the income ladder. The U.S. government first established an official definition of the poverty line in 1964. The poverty line is the level of income below which a person or a family is considered poor. The poverty line is defined in absolute terms: It is based on the cost of a minimal diet multiplied by three because low-income families spend about one-third of their income on food. In 1964, the poverty income level for a family of four was $3,000 ($1,000 for food × 3). Since 1969, the poverty line figure has been adjusted upward each year for inflation. In 1988, for example, the official poverty income level was $12,092 or below for a family of four. In 2007, a family of four needed an income of $21,386 to clear the poverty threshold.

Exhibit 7(a) shows the percentage of all persons in the U.S. population below the poverty level, beginning with 1959. The poverty rate for all persons was on a downward trend until the early 1980s. From 1980 to 1995, the percentage remained between 13 and 14 percent until the rate dropped to 11 percent in 2000. This was the lowest level in more than a quarter-century. After the recession in 2001, the poverty rate rose to 13 percent in 2007. The exhibit also gives an idea of poverty levels by race for selected years. As shown by comparing Parts (b) and (c), the percentage of African-Americans below the poverty line remained almost three times the percentage of whites between 1970 and 1995. In 2007, the ratio was over twice as great.

The poverty rate shown in Exhibit 7 has two major problems. First, this percentage gives no indication of how poor the people included are. A person with an income $1 below the poverty line counts, and so does a person whose income is $5,000 below the threshold. Second, the poverty rate is computed by comparing a family's census cash income from all sources to the poverty line. Cash income includes cash payments from Social Security, unemployment compensation, and Temporary Assistance to Needy Families (TANF). Cash income for the poor does not include noncash transfers, called in-kind transfers. In-kind transfers are government payments in the form of goods and services, rather than cash, including such government programs as food stamps, Medicaid, and housing. These antipoverty programs will be discussed in more detail in the next section.

Who Are the Poor?

Exhibit 8 lists selected characteristics of families below the poverty level in 2007. Geographically, poor families are most likely to live in the South. An important characteristic of families living below the poverty line in the United States is family structure. The poverty rate was 28 percent for families headed by a female with no husband present and 14 percent for families headed by a male with no female present, compared to only 5 percent for married couples. Finally, poverty is greatly

---

Poverty line

The level of income below which a person or a family is considered to be poor.

In-kind transfers

Government payments in the form of goods and services, rather than cash, including such government programs as food stamps, Medicaid, and housing.

EXHIBIT 7

Persons below the Poverty Level as a Percentage of the
U.S. Population, 1959–2007

In Part (a), the official poverty rate for all persons declined sharply between 1959 and the 1970s. After the recession in
2001, the poverty rate rose. Comparison of Parts (b) and (c) reveals that the poverty rate for African-Americans fell
sharply between 1959 and 1970, but since then it remained almost three times the poverty rate of whites until 1995. In
2007, the ratio was 2.3 times as great.

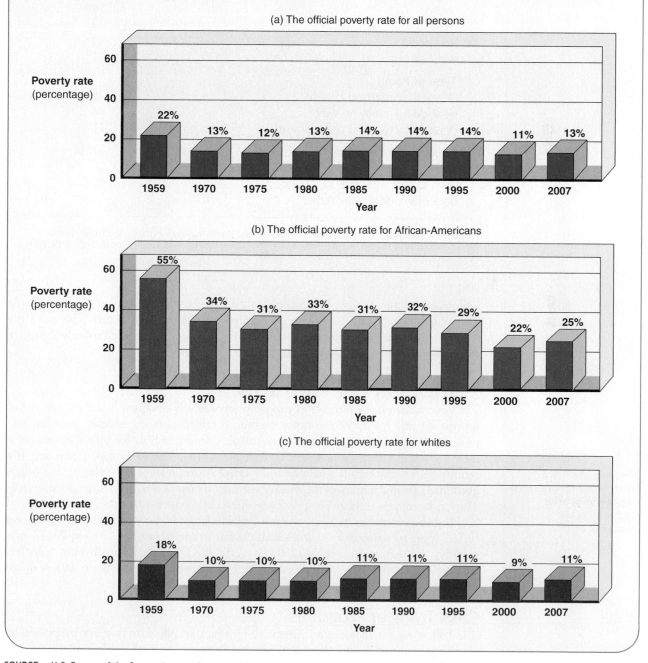

(a) The official poverty rate for all persons

(b) The official poverty rate for African-Americans

(c) The official poverty rate for whites

SOURCE: U.S. Bureau of the Census, *Income, Poverty, and Health Insurance in the United States: 2007*, http://www.census.gov/index.html, Table B-1.

| EXHIBIT 8 | Characteristics of U.S. Persons and Families below the 2007 Poverty Level |

Characteristic	Percentage below the Poverty Line
Region	
South	14%
West	12
Northeast	11
Midwest	11
Type of Family	
Headed by married couple	5
Headed by male, no wife	14
Headed by female, no husband	28
Education of Household Head	
No high school diploma	20
High school diploma, no college	10
Bachelor's degree or more	2

SOURCE: U.S. Bureau of the Census, *Income, Poverty, and Health Insurance in the United States: 2006,* http://www.census.gov/hhes/www/poverty.html, Table 3; and *Statistical Abstract of the United States,* 2008, http://www.census.gov/compendia/statab/, Table 691.

influenced by the lack of educational achievement of the head of household. As shown in the exhibit, 20 percent of families with household heads who have not received a high school diploma are below the poverty line compared to only 2 percent of families whose heads have at least a bachelor's degree.

Antipoverty Programs

The government has a number of programs specifically designed to aid the poor. The groups eligible for such assistance include disabled persons, elderly persons, and poor families with dependent children. People become eligible for public assistance if their income is below certain levels as measured by a *means test*. A means test is a requirement that a family's income not exceed a certain level to be eligible for public assistance. People who pass the means test may be *entitled* to government assistance. Thus, government welfare programs are often called *entitlement programs*.

Means test

A requirement that a family's income not exceed a certain level to be eligible for public assistance.

Federal programs to assist the poor in the United States are classified into two broad types of programs: *cash* assistance and *in-kind transfers*. As explained previously, the current definition of the poverty threshold excludes in-kind transfers because these programs did not exist when the poverty rate measure was adopted decades ago.

Cash Transfer Programs

The following are major government programs that alleviate poverty by providing eligible persons with cash payments needed to purchase food, shelter, clothing, and other basic needs.

Social Security (OASDHI)   The technical name for our gigantic social insurance program is Old Age, Survivors, and Disability Health Insurance, or OASDHI. Under the Social Security Act passed in 1935, each worker must pay a payroll tax matched in equal amount by his or her employer. Look at your paycheck, and you will find this deduction under FICA, which stands for Federal Insurance Contribution Act. Most of this money is used on a "pay-as-you-go" basis to pay current benefit recipients, and the remainder goes into the Social Security Trust Fund. Workers may retire between the ages 65 and 67, depending on year of birth, with full benefits, or at age 62, with reduced benefits. If a wage earner dies, Social Security provides payments to survivors, including spouse and children, until about 18 years of age (age 21 if they are in school). In addition, payments are made to disabled workers.

Earned-Income Tax Credit (EITC)   This is a refundable federal tax credit based on earned income below a maximum amount provided to low-income wage earners with the purpose of offsetting Social Security payroll taxes paid by the workers. In short, EITC is designed to avoid taxing the working poor further into poverty. Under this program, the tax credit reduces federal income taxes or provides a cash payment if the credit exceeds the tax liability.

Unemployment Compensation   Unemployment compensation is a government insurance program that pays income for a short time period to unemployed workers. This unemployment insurance is financed by a payroll tax on employers, which varies by state and according to the size of the firm's payroll. This means nothing is deducted from employees' paychecks for unemployment compensation. Although the federal government largely collects the taxes and funds this program, it is administered by the states. Any insured worker who becomes unemployed, and did not just quit his or her job, can become eligible for benefit payments after a short waiting period of usually one week.

Unemployment compensation
The government insurance program that pays income for a short time period to unemployed workers.

Temporary Assistance to Needy Families (TANF)   TANF gives states broad discretion to determine eligibility and benefit levels. However, families may not receive benefits for longer than 60 months. Unwed teenage parents must stay in school and live at home, and people convicted of drug-related felonies are banned from receiving TANF or food stamp benefits. In addition, nonworking adults must participate in community service within two months of receiving benefits, and must find work within two years. Parents with children under age one are exempt from the work requirements (under age six if child care is not available).

In-Kind Transfers

The following are important government in-kind transfer programs that raise the standard of living for the poor.

Medicare   This federal health care program is available to Social Security beneficiaries and persons with certain disabilities. Coverage is provided for hospital care and post-hospital nursing services. It also makes available supplementary low-cost insurance programs that help pay for doctor services and prescription drug expenses. Medicare is financed by payroll taxes on employers and employees.

Medicaid   This is the largest in-kind transfer program. Medicaid provides medical services to eligible poor under age 65 who pass a means test. TANF families qualify for Medicaid in all states. It is financed by general tax revenues.

SOCIAL SECURITY: PAST, PRESENT, AND FUTURE

Social Security Trust Fund Projections

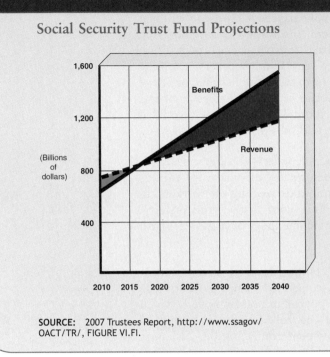

SOURCE: 2007 Trustees Report, http://www.ssagov/
OACT/TR/, FIGURE VI.FI.

President Franklin D. Roosevelt signed the Social Security Act as a bedrock of the New Deal program to help Americans besieged by the Great Depression. On December 1, 1936, the first official Social Security card was drawn arbitrarily from a stack of applications. The recipient was John D. Sweeney, Jr., who was the son of a wealthy factory owner and had grown up in a 15-room home staffed with servants. Unfortunately, Mr. Sweeney died at the age of 61 without ever receiving any benefits from the Social Security program.

Currently, the Social Security Trust Fund takes in more money in taxes and interest than it pays out in benefits, and the balance is invested exclusively in interest-bearing U.S. Treasury securities. However, as shown in the graph, revenue will fall

Food Stamps   The food stamp program began in 1964 as a federally financed program that is administered by state governments. The government issues coupons to the poor, who use them like money at the grocery store. The grocer cashes the stamps at a local bank, which redeems them at face value from the government. The cash value of stamps issued varies with the eligible recipient's income and family size. The food stamp program has become a major part of the welfare system in the United States.

Housing Assistance   Federal and state governments have a number of different programs to provide affordable housing for poor people. The federal agency overseeing most of these programs is the Department of Housing and Urban Development (HUD). These programs include housing projects owned and operated by the government and subsidies to assist people who rent private housing. In both cases, recipients pay less than the market value for apartments and therefore receive an in-kind transfer.

Welfare Criticisms

The majority of objections to welfare can be classified into the following major criticisms:

- **Work Disincentives.** Critics have argued that because welfare provides income that is easier to obtain than by working, the poor are often induced to reduce their work effort. In fact, the more a recipient earns from a job, the fewer the benefits he or she receives. Moreover, the taxes to finance welfare payments have some disincentive effects on the work effort of taxpayers. Taxes reduce take-home pay and thus reduce the reward for work.

below benefits in 2017, and the system will begin dipping into the trust fund to make up the difference. In 2040, it is estimated that the trust fund will be depleted. Excluding increasing the retirement age, the solution to financing a secure retirement program for future generations is to reduce benefits and/or increase revenues.

One idea to restore the trust fund is to allow people to obtain a higher return on their investment by channeling all or some of the money into their own private stock market account because stocks generally outperform U.S. Treasury securities by a significant margin. Unanswered questions of this partial privatization system include: (1) How much money could workers divert from Social Security into their private investment account? (2) What are the transition costs for new government debt required to pay benefits to current retirees not financed by payroll taxes because of money diverted to private accounts? and (3) How should workers be protected if their investments lose money?

Another reform idea is to increase tax revenue by lifting the cap on income subject to Social Security taxes. Currently, employers and employees each pay a fixed percentage of 12.4 percent (6.2 percent from employees and 6.2 percent from employers) payroll tax on their earnings up to a maximum amount of each employee's salary. However, no tax is paid on the income above that maximum amount, which is currently $102,000. The effect would be to raise revenue by expanding the tax base to include highest-paid employees.

- **Inefficiencies**. Critics have charged that the huge welfare bureaucracy in Washington, D.C., and throughout the nation results in more money in the pockets of bureaucrats than in the pockets of the poor. This major criticism was expressed by economics professor Thomas Sowell as follows:

> *The amount necessary to lift every man, woman, and child in America above the poverty line has been calculated, and it is one-third of what is in fact spent on poverty programs. Clearly, much of the transfer ends up in the pockets of highly paid administrators, consultants, and staff as well as higher income recipients of benefits from programs advertised as anti-poverty efforts.*[1]

- **Inequities**. Today, many critics argue that poor persons with equal needs receive different benefits. For example, a needy family in California might receive welfare benefits twice as great as those received by a needy family of the same size in South Carolina. The reason is that benefits under TANF and Medicaid are essentially controlled by the states.

Reform Proposals

Although there have been numerous proposals for reforming welfare, the various ideas can be classified into two broad approaches. First, the negative income tax offers a major transformation of the entire patchwork of federal, state, and local welfare programs. Second, workfare, which is the cornerstone of TANF, is a

---

1. Thomas Sowell, *Markets and Minorities* (New York, 1981), p. 122.

departure from the previous welfare system because it is based on work rather than entitlement. However, workfare is not without considerable debate and controversy.

Negative Income Tax

Negative income tax (NIT)

A plan under which families below a certain break-even level of income would receive cash payments that decrease as their incomes increase.

The idea of negative income tax (NIT) was first advanced by the prominent economist Milton Friedman in the early 1960s to reduce work disincentives and welfare bureaucracy while providing for the poor. NIT is a plan under which families below a certain break-even level of income would receive cash payments that decrease as their incomes increase. An NIT system would combine all cash and in-kind transfer welfare programs into a single program administered by a single agency.

Exhibit 9 illustrates how a negative income tax might work. A low-income family of four receives a cash payment until it reaches a *break-even income* at $20,000 per year, where the family neither receives a payment nor pays income taxes. Above $20,000, the family pays income taxes. For example, a family with an income of $30,000 pays $5,000 in taxes, while a family with an income of $10,000 is paid an NIT subsidy of $5,000. A family with zero income receives an NIT payment of $10,000. Thus, the government pays families an amount that varies inversely (negatively) with income.

> **Conclusion** *The negative income tax is the reverse of a positive income tax system, in which people pay the government an amount that varies directly with their income.*

The basic idea behind the NIT system is simple: Families with incomes above the break-even income finance payments to families with incomes below the break-even income. Begin at zero income in the exhibit, and assume the income guarantee is set at the poverty income threshold of $10,000. Beyond the guaranteed minimum

---

EXHIBIT 9   A Negative Income Tax Plan

In this example, a family with no earned income receives a $10,000 payment from the government. From $0 to $20,000, payments are reduced by a phase-out rate of $0.50 for each $1.00 of additional income. When income exceeds $20,000, payments fall to zero, and the family pays income taxes. Thus, a family with an income of $30,000 pays $5,000 in taxes.

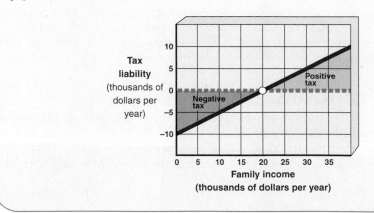

income of $10,000, government payments are reduced by, say, $0.50 for each $1.00 earned. This rate, called the *phase-out rate,* determines the cash transfers to low-income families until the break-even income is reached.

The NIT system offers several potential advantages. First, bureaucratic costs would be cut because an NIT program could be administered by a single agency. Second, poor people would not suffer the stigma of repeatedly standing in lines at the welfare office or using food stamps in the grocery store. The needy would simply file annual, or perhaps quarterly, income returns with the IRS. Third, many economists argue that individuals are rational and know best how to spend their money. Thus, a cash subsidy is preferable to an in-kind transfer.

After years of discussion and study, the NIT has not gained wide support. The NIT system is perceived as a political liability because voters perceive it as a "give-away" of taxpayers' money. These critics believe in-kind welfare is preferable to cash assistance. When a recipient is given food stamps or a housing subsidy, he or she acquires food and housing, rather than, say, buying drugs and gambling. NIT proponents point out, however, it is known that some food stamps are sold illegally for cash, which is used to buy drugs, alcohol, or whatever. Finally, some critics argue that a generous guaranteed minimum income paid in cash might create a disincentive to work rather than an incentive to work.

CHECKPOINT

Does a Negative Income Tax Discourage Work?

Under a negative income system, people who work receive reduced payments from the government. Even worse, beyond the break-even income, workers must pay taxes. This means there is no basis in an NIT system to argue that the poor will have an incentive to work. Explain why you agree or disagree. (Hint: Construct a table using Exhibit 9, and consider after-tax income.)

Workfare

The 1996 welfare reform bill titled the Personal Responsibility and Work Opportunity Act created TANF, and gave the states block grants to run welfare programs. To overcome the disincentive to work characteristic of earlier welfare programs based on entitlement, the current approach is to increase the work performed by welfare recipients and encourage their participation in job-training programs. To keep their benefits, welfare recipients must perform some work activities within two years of receiving welfare or risk losing benefits. This idea is called *workfare.* Workfare programs require able-bodied adults to work for the local government or any available private-sector employer in order to be eligible for welfare benefits. The paramount question thus becomes how to create jobs for welfare recipients who often lack basic literacy skills. A large public job plan would be costly and politically unpopular, especially among public employees who fear losing their jobs. Another option is for the government to pay employers to hire welfare recipients. A variation on this idea is for the government to hire personnel firms that would earn a fee for each person placed in a job.

There are potential problems with providing subsidies for companies that hire welfare recipients. One problem is that subsidies can stigmatize welfare recipients and reduce their long-term employment prospects. Another potential problem is that subsidies could be a windfall payment to employers for hiring people who

Welfare reform appears to be a success: The number of families on welfare has fallen sharply from 4.4 million in 1996 to 1.9 million in 2005.[1] The following is a sampling of articles describing the evolution of welfare under the Personal Responsibility and Work Opportunity Act of 1996.

As reported in *The Washington Post*, Los Angeles County provides a striking contrast of welfare prior to and after reform in 1996. Prior to 1996, Los Angeles County had a traditional welfare program that provided education and job training without work requirements. After the welfare reform act of 1996, inde-pendent researchers found that 43 percent of poor families who were required to participate in the city's new welfare reform pro-gram with work requirements got jobs, while only 32 percent of families randomly selected to remain in the traditional welfare program did. This represented an increase of one-third over the old welfare program. The typical wel-fare family subject to the new reform initiatives earned $1,286 in the first six months of the pro-gram, while "control group" families earned $879, a difference of 46 percent.[2]

A 2002 article in the *Los Angeles Times* concerned the new approach of the federal govern-ment providing block grants to states and mandating that the needy find jobs rather than just handing them welfare checks:

Before 1996, when the nation's welfare laws were radically altered, welfare families might have gotten a monthly welfare check for the rest of their lives. Martha Soria's job would have been mostly to shuffle their paperwork. But with welfare reform came time limits on such benefits and strict new work requirements. And while Soria still shuffles a lot of paperwork, her job as well as

would have been hired without the subsidies. Finally, there is a displacement problem because a subsidized welfare-recipient worker can take the job of an unsubsidized worker who has never received welfare benefits.

Discrimination

Poverty and discrimination in the workplace are related. Nonwhites and females earn less income when employer prejudice prevents them from receiving job opportunities. Discrimination also occurs when nonwhites and females earn less, but do basically the same work as whites and males. Exhibit 10 uses labor market theory to explain how discrimination can cause the equilibrium wage to be lower for nonwhites than for whites.

Exhibit 10(a) assumes that employers do not discriminate. This means employers hire workers regardless of race—that is, on the basis of their con-tribution to revenue (their marginal revenue products, *MRPs*). Hence, the intersec-tion of the market demand curve, *D*, and the market supply curve, *S*, determines the equilibrium wage rate of $245 per day paid by nondiscriminating employers.

the jobs of welfare caseworkers across the state and nation have changed. They have had to master hundreds of new rules and regulations under welfare reform and take on new responsibilities as guidance counselor, job finder, cheerleader, and taskmaster.[3]

The following article argues that the states must do more to avoid racial bias:

Under the 1996 law, states have the option to enforce time limits of their choosing. Because of this flexibility, states are left open to discriminate freely. Across the board, race was the determining factor affecting time limit lengths and their application. Observation of the enforcement of time limits shows that states with a higher proportion of African Americans or Latinos possess shorter time limits than the five-year guideline of the law. Over 20 states have opted to not allow exemptions to these time limits. Over 50 percent of African American families under welfare are subject to time limits shorter than the federal cutoff, as opposed to 30 percent of whites under welfare.[4]

A 2008 article in the Chronicle of Higher Education reported that a new federal rule would make it easier for some welfare recipients to attend college by counting a year's worth of study, including homework time, as work. The amount of time welfare recipients can spend in basic education and language courses was also expanded. The rule requires colleges to track recipients' class attendance, which some argue stigmatizes these students.[5]

ANALYZE THE ISSUE

The current approach to welfare reform is to cut the growth of welfare by shifting control from the federal government to the states. The idea is that because state and local officials are closer to the people, welfare programs will improve. Analyze the results presented above based on work disincentives, inefficiencies, and inequities.

1. U.S. Census Bureau, *Statistical Abstract of the United States*, 2008, http://www.census.gov/compendia/statab/, Table 546.
2. Judith Havemann, "Welfare Reform Success Cited in L.A.," *The Washington Post*, Aug. 20, 1998, p. A1.
3. Carla Rivera, "Welfare Reform's Enforcers," *Los Angeles Times*, May 28, 2002, p. A1.
4. Gordon Hurd, "Safety Net Sinking," *Colorline Magazine*, Summer 2002, p. 17.
5. Elyse Ashburn "New Federal Rule Could Help Welfare Recipients Stay Longer in College," *Chronicle of Higher Education*, Feb. 9, 2008, p. A26.

The total number of African-American and white workers hired is 14,000 workers.

Now assume for the sake of argument that employers do practice job discrimination against African-American workers. The result, shown in Exhibit 10(b), is two different labor markets—one for whites and one for African-Americans. Because discrimination exists, the demand curve for labor for African-Americans is to the left of the demand curve for labor for whites, reflecting unjustified restricted employment practices. The supply curve of labor for African-Americans is also to the left of the supply curve of labor for whites because there are fewer African-Americans seeking employment than whites.

Given the differences in the labor market demand and supply curves, the equilibrium wage rate for whites of $280 is higher than the $210 paid to African-Americans. Comparison of these wage rates with the labor market equilibrium wage rate of $245 reveals that the effect of discrimination is to change the relative wages of white and African-American workers. Whites earn a higher wage rate than they would earn in a labor market that did not favor hiring them. Conversely, the African-American wage rate is lower as a result of discrimination.

EXHIBIT 10 — Labor Markets without and with Racial Discrimination

In Part (a), there is no labor market discrimination against African-Americans. In this case, the equilibrium wage for all labor is $245 per day. Under discrimination in Part (b), the labor demand and labor supply curves for white and African-American workers differ. As a result, the equilibrium wage rate for whites, $280, is higher than that for African-Americans, $210.

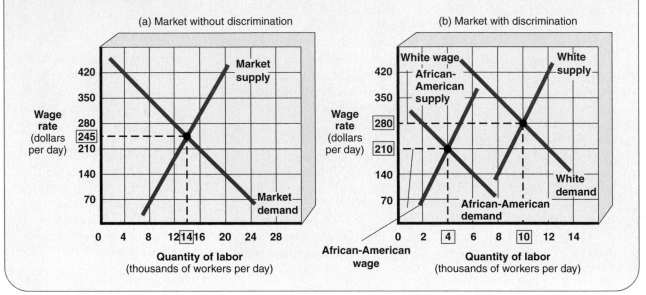

Comparable Worth

Comparable worth

The principle that employees who work for the same employer must be paid the same wage when their jobs, even if different, require similar levels of education, training, experience, and responsibility. A nonmarket wage-setting process is used to evaluate and compensate jobs according to point scores assigned to different jobs.

A controversial public policy aimed at eliminating labor market pay inequities is a concept called comparable worth. Comparable worth is the principle that employees who work for the same employer must be paid the same wages when their jobs, even if different, require similar levels of education, training, experience, and responsibility. Comparable worth is a nonmarket wage-setting remedy to the situation where jobs dominated by women pay less than jobs dominated by men. Because women's work is alleged to be undervalued, the solution is equal pay for jobs evaluated as having "comparable worth" according to point scores assigned to different jobs. In essence, comparable worth replaces labor-market–determined wages with bureaucratic judgments about the valuation of different jobs. For example, compensation paid to an elevator inspector and a nurse can be computed based on quantitative scores in a job-rating scheme. If the jobs' point totals are equal, the average elevator inspector and nurse must be paid equally by law.

CHECKPOINT

Should the Law Protect Women?

Do you want women, mining coal and building skyscrapers? Suppose laws are enacted that protect women by keeping them out of jobs deemed "too strenuous" or "too dangerous." Would the likely effect of such laws be to decrease wages in male-dominated occupations, increase wages in female-intensive occupations, or decrease wages in female-intensive occupations?

YOU'RE THE ECONOMIST   Is Pay for Females Fair?

Applicable Concepts: comparable worth

Women working full time earn on average about 20 percent less than men. Discrimination in wages and employment on the basis of sex was made illegal in 1963 by the Equal Pay Act (EPA), which outlawed pay discrimination between men and women doing substantially the same job. This does not mean that unequal pay for the same work cannot exist, but if it does, the differential must be due to factors other than gender.

Proponents of comparable worth argue that the equal-pay-for-equal-work idea has failed. They maintain that women crowd into such female-dominated occupations as secretarial work, nursing, school teaching, and social work because of discrimination against women in male-dominated occupations such as engineering. The increased supply of female labor in female-crowded professions lowers the prevailing wage. If the courts follow the comparable worth principle, they will not consider whether employers intentionally pay less for "women's jobs," but only whether the employers are in compliance with a quantitative rating scheme. The best-known case occurred in the 1980s, when the American Federation of State, County, and Municipal Employees won the first federal court case against the state of Washington. The state was found guilty of wage discrimination against women because it had not followed a comparable worth point system. According to the point system, male-dominated jobs often paid more than female-dominated jobs even though the female jobs had greater "worth," and, therefore, "underpaid" female job classes should be raised rather than lowering the "overpaid" male job classes. The court ordered Washington to upgrade nearly 15,000 female employees and award back-pay estimated at $377 million. The decision was appealed to higher courts, and the union ultimately lost the case.

Critics of comparable worth argue that it is nearly impossible to measure all of the factors that determine compensation for jobs, and the fact that female occupations earn less than male occupations is not necessarily evidence of discrimination. For example, women often seek occupations more compatible with childrearing.

Over the years it appeared that comparable worth had faded into a golden oldie until the Fair Pay Act of 2007 was introduced by Senator Tom Harkin (D-Iowa) and included Senator Barack Obama (D-Illinois) as one of the co-sponsors. The premise is that the government has the duty to decide a job's worth. Under its provisions, employers must send the Equal Employment Commission (EEOC) annual reports of how pay is determined in any jobs dominated by one gender. The goal is for the EEOC to decide pay for workers in dissimilar, but "equivalent" jobs based on criteria established by the EEOC. Such calculations would serve as a basis for workers to sue their employers based on not being paid the same for "equivalent" work. As this text is written in 2008, this act has not been enacted into law.

ANALYZE THE ISSUE

Suppose the EEOC uses a job-scoring system and determines that the wage rate for a secretary is $50 per hour, while the competitive labor market wage rate is $10 per hour. What would be the effect of such a comparable worth law?

KEY CONCEPTS

Lorenz curve	Means test	Comparable worth
Poverty line	Unemployment compensation	
In-kind transfers	Negative income tax (NIT)	

SUMMARY

- The *Lorenz curve* is a measure of inequality of income. Since 1947, the share of money income for each fifth of families ranked according to their income has been quite stable. Also, the degree of income inequality among families in the United States has changed little since 1929. In recent decades, the richest families have become richer; however, the median income of all groups has increased.

Lorenz curve

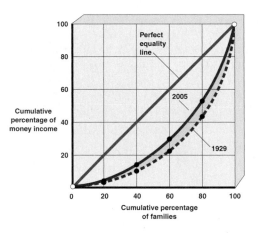

- The *poverty line* is a level of cash income below which a family is classified as poor. The poverty income threshold is three times the cost of a minimal diet for a family. Today, about 13 percent of the U.S. population is officially classified as poor.
- *In-kind transfers* are payments to the poor in the form of goods and services, rather than cash. Calculation of the poverty line counts only cash income. In-kind transfers, such as food stamps, Medicaid, and housing, do not count as income for families classified as officially poor. Government cash transfers counted in calculating the poverty line include payments from Social

Security, unemployment compensation, and Temporary Assistance to Needy Families.
- *Welfare criticisms* include three major arguments: (1) Welfare reduces the incentive to work for the poor and taxpayers. (2) Welfare is inefficient because much of the money covers administrative costs, rather than providing benefits for the poor. (3) Because many antipoverty programs are controlled by the state, welfare benefits vary widely.
- The *negative income tax* is a plan to guarantee a certain amount of income for all families. As a low-income family earns income, government payments (negative income tax) are phased out. After reaching a break-even income, families become taxpayers instead of being on the welfare rolls.

Negative income tax

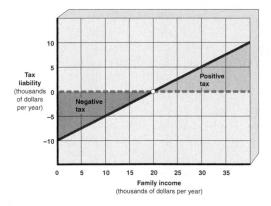

- *Comparable worth* is the theory that workers in jobs determined to be of equal value by means of point totals should be paid equally. Instead of allowing labor markets to set wages, independent consultants award points to different jobs on the basis of such criteria as knowledge, experience, and working conditions.

SUMMARY OF CONCLUSION STATEMENTS

- Measured by distribution of family money income, the richest families have become a little richer and the rest of the family groups a little poorer in recent decades.
- The Lorenz curve has shifted only slightly inward, and therefore closer to the perfect equality line between 1929 and 2007.

- The negative income tax is the reverse of a positive income tax system, in which people pay the government an amount that varies directly with their income.

STUDY QUESTIONS AND PROBLEMS

1. The following table contains data on the distribution of income in the countries of Alpha and Beta:

Percentage of Families	Alpha		Beta	
	Percentage Share	Cumulative Share	Percentage Share	Cumulative Share
Lowest fifth	17.7%	—	9.0%	—
Second-lowest fifth	19.9	—	14.2	—
Middle fifth	20.4	—	17.5	—
Second-highest fifth	20.7	—	21.9	—
Highest fifth	21.3	—	37.4	—

a. Compute the cumulative distribution of income for each country.
b. Construct the Lorenz curve for each country.
c. For which country is the distribution of income more equal?

2. Suppose each family in the United States earned an equal money income. What would be the effect?

3. Explain the difference between poverty defined absolutely and poverty defined relatively. Which definition is the basis of the poverty line?

4. Calculate the official poverty threshold annual income for a family of four. Assume the minimally acceptable diet is estimated to be $5 per person per day and the minimum wage is $5 per hour. Will a head of a family of four earn the poverty threshold you have calculated?

5. What are in-kind transfers? Give examples. How are in-kind transfers considered in determining whether a family is below the poverty income threshold?

6. Would free health care reduce poverty, as measured by the government? Would free public housing, day care, and job training for the poor reduce the poverty rate? Explain.

7. What percentage of families in the United States was classified as poor? Which demographic groups have higher poverty rates?

8. List the major government cash assistance and in-kind transfer programs to assist the poor. Which of the programs are not exclusively for the poor?

9. What are three major criticisms of welfare?

10. Assume the government implements a negative income tax plan with a guaranteed minimum income of $5,000 and a phase-out rate for payments of 50 percent. Provide the missing data in the following table:

Family Income	Negative Tax	Total After-Tax Income
$ 0	—	—
2,000	—	—
4,000	—	—
6,000	—	—
8,000	—	—
10,000	—	—

11. Critics of welfare argue that the role of government should be to break down legal barriers to employment rather than using programs that directly provide cash or goods and services. For example, advocates of this approach would remove laws mandating minimum wages, comparable worth, union power, professional licensing, and other restrictive practices. Do you agree or disagree? Why?

For Online Exercises, go the text Web site at www.cengage.com/economics/tucker.

CHECKPOINT ANSWERS

Does a Negative Income Tax Discourage Work?

The following table is interpreted from Exhibit 9. Even though payments from the government decrease, total after-tax income increases from the combination of the income earned and the negative tax. After the break-even income of $20,000, total after-tax income continues to rise. If you said the NIT system assumes the poor are rational people who are motivated to earn more total after-tax income by working, **YOU ARE CORRECT.**

Family Income	Negative Tax	Positive Tax	Total After-Tax Income
$ 0	$10,000	$ 0	$10,000
5,000	7,000	0	12,000
10,000	5,000	0	15,000
15,000	2,500	0	17,500
20,000	0	0	20,000
25,000	0	−2,500	22,500
30,000	0	−5,000	25,000
35,000	0	−7,500	27,500

Should the Law Protect Women?

A law that limits women's access to certain occupations results in their crowding into the remaining occupations. The obstacles facing women in male-dominated occupations artificially restrict competition with men. If you said the increased labor supply in female-intensive occupations decreases their wages, while the decreased labor supply in male-intensive occupations increases wages for males, **YOU ARE CORRECT.**

PRACTICE QUIZ

For an explanation of the correct answers, please visit the tutorial at www.cengage.com/economics/tucker.

1. Currently, the wealthiest 5 percent of all U.S. families earned what percentage of total annual money income among families?
   a. More than 20 percent
   b. Less than 10 percent
   c. More than 25 percent
   d. More than 50 percent

2. A figure that measures the relationship between the cumulative percentage of money income on the vertical axis and the cumulative percentage of families on the horizontal axis is called the
   a. family-income curve.
   b. Washington curve.
   c. Lorenz curve.
   d. Gini curve.

3. As shown in Exhibit 11, the perfect equality line is drawn between points
   a. W and Y along the curve.
   b. X and Z.
   c. W and Y along the straight line.
   d. W and X.

4. As shown in Exhibit 11, 20 percent of families earned a cumulative share of about _____ percent of income.
   a. 5
   b. 10
   c. 30
   d. 50

5. As shown in Exhibit 11, 40 percent of families earned a cumulative share of about _____ percent of income.
   a. 5
   b. 15
   c. 30
   d. 50

6. Since 1929, the overall family income distribution in the United States has become
   a. much more unequal.
   b. much less unequal.
   c. slightly more unequal.
   d. slightly more equal.

7. Comparing the family income distributions of the United States, the Czech Republic, and Brazil, the conclusion is that income is distributed
   a. most equally in Brazil.
   b. most equally in the United States.
   c. about the same in all three countries.
   d. most equally in the Czech Republic.

8. To establish the poverty line that divides poor and nonpoor families, the government
   a. multiplies the cost of a minimal diet by three.
   b. multiplies the cost of a minimal diet by five.

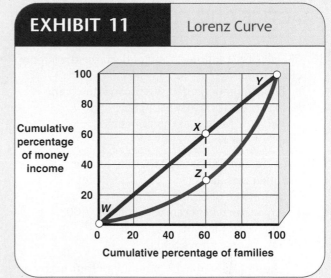

EXHIBIT 11   Lorenz Curve

Cumulative percentage of money income (vertical axis)
Cumulative percentage of families (horizontal axis)

   c. adds 50 percent to the cost of a minimal diet.
   d. adds 100 percent to the cost of a minimal diet.

9. The poverty line
   a. is defined as one-half average family income.
   b. includes in-kind transfers.
   c. includes Medicaid benefits.
   d. has been attacked for overstating poverty.

10. Which of the following is an in-kind transfer?
   a. Social Security payments
   b. Unemployment compensation
   c. Food stamps
   d. Welfare payments

11. Which of the following is a cash assistance (not an in-kind transfer) program?
   a. Temporary Assistance to Needy Families (TANF)
   b. Medicare
   c. Medicaid
   d. Food stamps

12. The negative income tax (NIT) is a plan under which families
   a. above a level of income pay no tax.
   b. pay the same tax rate except for the poor.
   c. below a level of income receive pay no tax.
   d. below a level of income receive a cash payment.

PRACTICE QUIZ CONTINUED

13. Which of the following might decrease the supply curve of labor?
    a. Discrimination against African-Americans
    b. Discrimination against women
    c. Difficult licensing requirements
    d. All of the above

14. As shown in Exhibit 12, a family of four pays income taxes at
    a. an income of $5,000.
    b. any income between zero and $40,000.
    c. all levels of income.
    d. any income above $40,000.

15. As shown in Exhibit 12, a family of four with no earned income receives _____ from the government.
    a. zero payment
    b. the break-even income of $40,000
    c. a $20,000 payment
    d. a $20,000 tax deferment

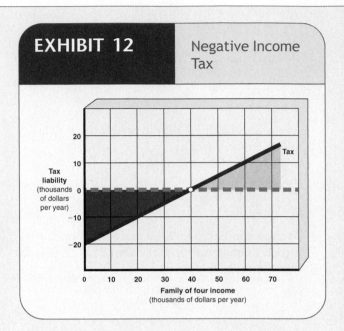

EXHIBIT 12   Negative Income Tax

Antitrust and Regulation

People of the same trade seldom meet together, even for merriment and diversion, but the conversation ends in a conspiracy against the public, or in some contrivance to raise prices.[1]

— **Adam Smith**

W hen Microsoft dominated the personal computer software industry, the U.S. government charged the firm and Bill Gates, its founder, with anticompetitive business practices. The media compared the case to John D. Rockefeller's Standard Oil monopoly and the robber barons of the 1890s. In the past, antitrust laws have been successfully used against the nation's largest corporations. This threat of the high legal costs of defending against an antitrust suit serves as a powerful deterrent, discouraging monopolies from engaging in

unfair actions intended to eliminate rivals. Here you will explore and form opinions on the Microsoft case, the Standard Oil case, and other major antitrust cases.

When antitrust policy is successful, consumers benefit from lower prices and more output. As you study antitrust policy in this chapter, you will learn that antitrust is somewhat of an art form that blends economic theory and politics—perhaps more politics than economic theory. Interestingly, certain industries and organizations are exempt from antitrust legislation: labor unions, professional baseball teams, public utilities, public transit companies, schools, hospitals, and suppliers of military equipment.

The second half of this chapter turns to government regulation, which affects virtually every business and consumer. Our food is regulated, our environment is regulated, airline safety is regulated, and most industries must deal with some form of regulation. What are the reasons for regulation, and what are its consequences?

---

1. Adam Smith, *An Inquiry into the Nature and Causes of the Wealth of Nations* (1776, reprint, New York, 1937), p. 128.

The explanation begins with a brief survey of regulation in the United States. In the last section, we discuss the rationale for three different types of regulation justified on the basis of market failure.

Antitrust

Before the Civil War, industries were populated by small firms, and few economic problems were caused by monopoly. After the Civil War, during the rapid industrialization of the 1870s and 1880s, the railroads and telegraph linked diverse regions of the country and enabled firms to expand into national markets. To gain more control of expanding industries, many competing companies merged or formed a trust. A trust is a combination or cartel consisting of firms that place their assets in the custody of a board of trustees. The trust allows firms that have not actually merged to form a cartel, or a cohesive group of firms that controls an industry in order to charge monopoly prices and earn higher profits. The long list of trusts formed during this period included the iron trust, sugar trust, copper trust, steel trust, coal trust, oil trust, tobacco trust, and even the paper-bag trust. The organizers of many of these trusts became widely known as *robber barons* because they exploited and bullied anyone in their way.

During the last decades of the nineteenth century, many trusts used various tactics to avoid competition. Recall from Chapter 9 on monopoly that Standard Oil acquired oil fields, railroads, pipelines, and ships and then denied access to rivals. Thus, competing firms had to merge with Standard Oil or go out of business. With the competition eliminated, John D. Rockefeller, the best-known so-called robber baron, raised Standard Oil's prices and limited production, and consumers suffered along with Standard Oil's competitors.

Another anticompetitive strategy used by the industrial giants was predatory pricing. Predatory pricing is the practice of one or more firms temporarily reducing prices in order to eliminate competition and then raising prices. Often trusts would sell a product below cost until their weaker competitors were unable to withstand mounting losses and were forced from the industry. Perhaps even more alarming, some trusts resorted to political corruption. For example, the railroad and petroleum trusts employed corrupt legislators and judges to gain a competitive edge.

By the end of the nineteenth century, the threat of continuing economic and political abuses created a public opinion quite hostile to big business. Newspapers regularly printed news of the trusts' questionable business practices. The numerous and politically influential farmers blamed the trusts for the high railroad charges that were making farming unprofitable. Consumers and labor unions also raised their voices against monopoly power. The influence of the trusts was discussed

Trust

A combination or cartel consisting of firms that place their assets in the custody of a board of trustees.

Predatory pricing

The practice of one or more firms temporarily reducing prices in order to eliminate competition and then raising prices.

constantly in the halls of Congress. In 1888, both major political parties added antimonopoly planks to their campaign platforms. Hatred and distrust of the centralization of economic and political power originated in the Jeffersonian tradition of the United States. Against this background of populist (pro-people) fear of big business and its political power, Congress passed laws aimed at preventing firms from engaging in anticompetitive activities.

The following is a brief description of the major antitrust legislation that constitutes basic antitrust law.

The Sherman Act

The first antitrust law was the Sherman Act. The Sherman Act of 1890 is the federal antitrust law that prohibits monopolization and conspiracies to restrain trade. Today, this act remains the cornerstone of antitrust policy in the United States. It has two main provisions:

> **Section 1:** Every contract, combination in the form of trust or otherwise, or conspiracy in restraint of trade or commerce among the several States, or with foreign nations, is hereby declared to be illegal....

> **Section 2:** Every person who shall monopolize, or attempt to monopolize, or combine or conspire with any other person or persons, to monopolize any part of the trade or commerce among the several States, or with foreign nations, shall be deemed guilty of a misdemeanor, and, on conviction thereof, shall be punished by a fine not exceeding five thousand dollars, or by imprisonment not exceeding one year, or by both said punishments, in the discretion of the court.[2]

In response to the public outcry, Congress intended to craft this law with sweeping language against the trusts. But what does the Sherman Act really say? It is unclear exactly which business practices constitute a "restraint of trade" and therefore a violation of the law. As a result of the extremely vague language, there were numerous court battles, and the act was ineffective for years. For example, the federal government did not win its first notable cases against Standard Oil and American Tobacco until 1911.

The serious consequences of violating the Sherman Act are reflected in the more recent case of Archer Daniels Midland Company (ADM). In 1995, this agribusiness giant pleaded guilty to price-fixing involving lysine and citric acid. It paid a $100 million fine. In 1998, a federal jury convicted three past and present executives of conspiring with competitors to fix the prices of these products. They were sentenced to serve two years in prison and to pay fines of $350,000 each.

The Clayton Act

As explained above, the Sherman Act initially proved to be little more than a legislative mandate for the courts to spell out the meaning of antitrust laws. To define anticompetitive acts more precisely, Congress passed the Clayton Act. The Clayton Act of 1914 is an amendment that strengthened the Sherman Act by making it illegal for firms to engage in certain anticompetitive business practices. Under this act, the following business practices are illegal with the important controversial

Sherman Act
The federal antitrust law enacted in 1890 that prohibits monopolization and conspiracies to restrain trade.

Clayton Act
A 1914 amendment that strengthens the Sherman Act by making it illegal for firms to engage in certain anticompetitive business practices.

---

2. In 1974, the act was amended so that violations would be treated as felonies.

condition that the effect must be to "substantially lessen competition or tend to create a monopoly":

1. **Price Discrimination.** A firm charges different customers different prices for the same product with the price differences not related to cost differences. (Recall the discussion of this topic in the chapter on monopoly.)
2. **Exclusive Dealing.** A manufacturer requires a retailer to sign an agreement stipulating the condition that the retailer will not carry any rival products of the manufacturer.
3. **Tying Contracts.** The seller of one product requires the buyer to purchase some other product(s). For example, movie distributors cannot force theaters to purchase projection rights to a blockbuster movie only on the condition that they pay for a bundle of films with much less box office potential.
4. **Stock Acquisition of Competing Companies.** One firm buys the stock of a competing firm.
5. **Interlocking Directorates.** The directors of one company serve on the board of directors of another company in the same industry. Interlocking directorates are illegal, whether or not the effect may be to "substantially lessen competition."

Although more specific than the Sherman Act, the Clayton Act is also vague and leaves a key question unanswered: Exactly when does a situation or action "substantially lessen competition"? To this day, the task of interpreting this ambiguous phrase remains with the courts, and the interpretation changes over time.

The Federal Trade Commission Act

Since the federal government faced a growing antitrust responsibility in the early 1900s, an agency was needed to investigate alleged anticompetitive practices and reach judgments. The Federal Trade Commission Act was enacted for this purpose. The Federal Trade Commission Act of 1914 established the Federal Trade Commission (FTC) to investigate unfair competitive practices of firms. This act contains perhaps the most general language of any antitrust act. It declares illegal "unfair methods of competition in commerce." The act established a five-member commission appointed by the president to determine the exact meaning of "unfair methods." Today, the FTC is concerned primarily with (1) enforcing consumer protection legislation, (2) prohibiting deceptive advertising, and (3) preventing collusion. When a complaint is filed with the FTC, the commission investigates. If there is a violation, the FTC can negotiate a settlement, issue a cease-and-desist order, or initiate a lawsuit.

Federal Trade Commission Act

The federal act that in 1914 established the Federal Trade Commission (FTC) to investigate unfair competitive practices of firms.

The Robinson-Patman Act

The Clayton Act has been amended twice. Although price discrimination became illegal under the Clayton Act, that section was not widely enforced at first. This situation changed with the passage of the Robinson-Patman Act. The Robinson-Patman Act of 1936 is an amendment to the Clayton Act that strengthens the Clayton Act's provisions against price discrimination. The Robinson-Patman Act is complex and controversial. Its basic purpose is to prevent large sellers from offering different prices to different buyers where the effect is to harm even a single small firm. In fact, the Robinson-Patman Act is often called the "Chain Store Act" because it was an outgrowth of the competition between small independent sellers and chain stores that developed after World War I.

Robinson-Patman Act

A 1936 amendment to the Clayton Act that strengthens the Clayton Act against price discrimination.

The Robinson-Patman Act encourages lawsuits by small independent firms because it broadens the list of illegal price discrimination practices. This act, for example, makes it illegal for a firm to offer quantity discounts, free advertising, or promotional allowances to one buyer if the firm does not offer the same concessions to all buyers. Be careful to note that the prohibition on price discrimination in the Robinson-Patman Act is limited to situations where the effect is to "substantially lessen competition or tend to create a monopoly." The first You're the Economist offers the opportunity to debate issues concerning this act.

The Celler-Kefauver Act

Prior to 1950, the U.S. Supreme Court interpreted the Sherman Act as prohibiting mergers between competing firms by stock acquisition, but not prohibiting mergers by the sale of physical assets (plant, equipment, and so on). The Celler-Kefauver Act was the second amendment to the Clayton Act, and it was enacted to address this problem. The Celler-Kefauver Act of 1950 is an amendment to the Clayton Act that prohibits one firm from merging with a competitor by purchasing its physical assets if the effect is to substantially lessen competition. Consequently, this act is sometimes called the "Antimerger Act" because it closed the loophole in the Clayton Act and thereby prohibited anticompetitive mergers, which were the target of the original Clayton Act.

The five major antitrust laws are summarized in Exhibit 1.

> **Celler-Kefauver Act**
> A 1950 amendment to the Clayton Act that prohibits one firm from merging with a competitor by purchasing its physical assets if the effect is to substantially lessen competition.

Key Antitrust Cases

Antitrust policy can be compared to the rules of baseball or other sports. The House and Senate of the U.S. Congress set the "rules of the game" for antitrust cases, just as the American and National Leagues set the rules of baseball. For example, the

EXHIBIT 1	Summary of Major Antitrust Laws
Law (date enacted)	**Key Provisions**
Sherman Act (1890)	○ Prohibits interstate price-fixing and other conspiracies and combinations that restrain trade and attempt to monopolize.
Clayton Act (1914)	○ Bolsters and clarifies the Sherman Act by prohibiting specific business practices, including exclusive dealing, tying contracts, stock acquisition of competitors, and interlocking directorates.
Federal Trade Commission Act (1914)	○ Established an agency (the FTC) to help enforce antitrust laws by investigating unfair and deceptive business practices.
Robinson-Patman Act (1936)	○ Amends the Clayton Act by broadening the list of illegal price discrimination practices to include quantity discounts, free advertising, and promotional allowances offered to large buyers and not to small buyers. The Robinson-Patman Act is often called the "Chain Store Act."
Celler-Kefauver Act (1950)	○ Amends the Clayton Act by closing the loophole that permitted a firm to merge by buying assets of a rival, rather than by acquisition of stocks, as outlawed in the original Clayton Act. The Celler-Kefauver Act is often called the "Antimerger Act."

YOU'RE THE ECONOMIST
Is Utah Pie's Slice of the Pie Too Small?
Applicable Concepts: Robinson-Patman Act

The following is a classic and controversial case: In the 1950s, the market for frozen dessert pies was small, but growing. The Salt Lake City market was supplied by distant plants in California that were owned by Carnation, Continental Baking, and Pet Milk. Until 1957, these three firms accounted for almost all the frozen fruit pies sold in the Salt Lake City market.

The Utah Pie Company had been baking dessert pies in Salt Lake City and selling them fresh for 30 years. This family-owned-and-operated business entered the frozen pie market in 1957. It was immediately successful and grabbed a huge share of the Salt Lake City market. During the relevant years, the market shares of the various competitors were as follows:

prices below those of its competitors. Due to its immediate success, it built a new plant in 1958. Its local plants gave Utah Pie a locational advantage over its competitors. For most of the time in question, Utah Pie's prices were the lowest in the Salt Lake City market. The incumbent firms, of course, responded to Utah Pie's entry and lower prices by reducing their own prices. As a result, all the larger firms sold frozen pies in Salt Lake City at prices lower than those charged for pies of like grade and quality in other geographic markets considerably closer to their California plants.

Utah Pie sued these three firms, claiming price discrimination. Ultimately, the case was reviewed by the Supreme Court [in 1967], which took a dim view

purchasers at different prices if the result may be to injure competition in either the sellers' or the buyers' market unless such discriminations are justified as permitted by the Act." Consequently, the Supreme Court found the defendants guilty of price discrimination. Inasmuch as no competitors had been forced from the market, it appears that price discrimination does not have to have an obviously predatory impact to be ruled illegal. All the Court saw in this case was a pattern of falling prices. It feared that such a pattern could result in a lessening of competition if one or more competitors dropped out of the market.

ANALYZE THE ISSUE

Utah Pie sued its three outside competitors under the Robinson-Patman Act. Some have criticized this case because it is an example of the type of bizarre result that can be produced by antitrust policy. Do you agree? Explain.

	1958	1959	1960	1961
Utah Pie	67%	34%	46%	45%
Pet	16	36	28	29
Carnation	10	9	12	9
Continental	1	3	2	8
All others	6	18	12	9

Utah Pie's strategy for penetrating the market was to set its of such pricing behavior: "Sellers may not sell like goods to different

Source: David L. Kaserman and John W. Mayo, *Government and Business: The Economics of Antitrust and Regulation* (Fort Worth, 1995), p. 282.

rules of baseball say that a player hitting a homer must run from first base to home plate, rather than from third base to home plate. Similarly, the Sherman Act forbids monopolization through predatory pricing by businesses. This brings us to the role of the umpire. After a game, a Little League player asked the first base umpire, "What do you call when the runner and the ball reach first base at exactly the same time?" The umpire replied, "There's no such thing as a tie. It's always the way I call it." That's how it is with court decisions on antitrust laws, and, just like many of the umpire's calls, all the courts' decisions are not "crowd pleasers." With this point in mind, let's look at some important "calls" of courts on antitrust cases.

The Standard Oil Case (1911)

President Theodore Roosevelt's administration took action to break up Standard Oil under the Sherman Act. After 10 years of litigation, the Supreme Court ruled in 1911 that Standard Oil had achieved its monopoly position in the oil refining industry through illegal business practices. John D. Rockefeller's trust had used railroad rebates, discounts, espionage, control of supplies to rivals, and predatory pricing to gain a monopoly. The remedy was for the Standard Oil Trust to be broken into competing companies: Standard Oil of New York became Mobil, Standard Oil of California became Chevron, Standard Oil of Indiana became Amoco, and Standard Oil of New Jersey became Exxon.

The Standard Oil Trust case established a standard for antitrust rulings. The Supreme Court ruled that (1) Standard Oil was a monopoly with a 90 percent share of the refined-oil market and (2) Standard Oil achieved its monopoly through illegal business behavior intended to exclude rivals. The Court stated that point (2) was critical to its decision and not point (1). This doctrine became known as the rule of reason. The rule of reason is the antitrust doctrine that the existence of monopoly alone is not illegal unless the monopoly engages in illegal business practices. Stated differently, monopoly *per se* is not illegal. Thus, "big is not necessarily bad." Standard Oil and other dominant firms would be broken up not merely because of their dominance, but also because of their abusive behavior.

Between 1911 and 1920, the courts applied the rule of reason in breaking up the American Tobacco Trust and other trusts. In 1920, the Supreme Court also applied the rule of reason when it decided that U.S. Steel was not guilty under the Sherman Act. Although U.S. Steel controlled almost 75 percent of the domestic iron and steel industry, the Supreme Court ruled that it is not *size* that violates the law. Since there was no evidence of unfair pricing practices, U.S. Steel was a "good citizen" not in violation of the Sherman Act.

The Alcoa Case (1945)

Thirty-four years after the Standard Oil case, the courts did a "flip flop" on the rule of reason. In 1940, the Aluminum Company of America (Alcoa) was the only producer of aluminum in the United States. Alcoa's monopoly was primarily the result of its patents and its ownership of a unique resource, bauxite. Moreover, Alcoa kept its prices low to avoid competition and prosecution, behaving as a "good citizen" despite its size. A federal appeals court ruled that Alcoa had violated the Sherman Act and declared:

> *Having proved that Alcoa had a monopoly of the domestic ingot market the government had gone far enough.... Congress did not condone "good trusts" and condemn "bad" ones; it forbade all.*[3]

With the Alcoa decision, the courts turned from "big is not necessarily bad" to "big is bad." The rule of reason was transformed into the per se rule. The per se

---

Rule of reason
The antitrust doctrine that the existence of monopoly alone is not illegal unless the monopoly engages in illegal business practices.

Per se rule
The antitrust doctrine that the existence of monopoly alone is illegal, regardless of whether or not the monopoly engages in illegal business practices.

---

3. U.S. v. Aluminum Co. of America, 148 F.2d 416 (2d Cir. 1945).

rule is the antitrust doctrine that the existence of monopoly alone is illegal, regardless of whether or not the monopoly engages in illegal business practices. Instead of judgments based on the performance of a monopoly, antitrust policy in the United States was switched by the court's interpretation to judgments based solely on the market structure. Interestingly, the court's solution was not to break up Alcoa. Instead, the federal government subsidized its competitors. War plants were sold at bargain prices to Reynolds Aluminum and Kaiser Aluminum, and later more rivals entered the aluminum industry.

The IBM Case (1982)

In 1969, the U.S. Department of Justice brought antitrust action against IBM because of its dominance in the mainframe computer market. The government argued that IBM had a 72 percent share of the electronic digital computing industry. IBM argued that the relevant market was broader and included programmable calculators and other information-processing products. After 13 years of litigation, IBM had spent over $100 million on its defense and had constructed an entire building to store case documents. Finally, in 1982, the government dropped the case. One reason was that Digital Equipment, Apple Computer, and Japanese companies were competing with IBM. Another reason illustrates the mix of politics and antitrust policy. In 1982, Ronald Reagan was president, and he believed in a much less restrictive interpretation of antitrust laws. In any event, the IBM case represented a shift in the general sentiment among those enforcing the antitrust laws from the per se rule back to the rule of reason.

The AT&T Case (1982)

In 1978, the U.S. Department of Justice brought an antitrust suit against AT&T and the Bell System. The issue was complicated. At this time, AT&T was a *natural monopoly* regulated by the government. (Regulation of a natural monopoly will be explained later in this chapter; see Exhibit 5.) The government allowed AT&T to have a monopoly in long-distance and local telephone service and in the production of telephones. The Federal Communications Commission (FCC) regulated long-distance rates, and state utility commissioners regulated local rates. What was the objective of giving one company the exclusive right to provide telephone services in the United States? In order to provide everyone with low-cost local services, the regulatory commissions set AT&T's local charges low and its long-distance rates high to cover the lower local rates.

In the 1970s, advances in technology changed the nature of the long-distance telephone industry. Telephone service was no longer a natural monopoly because fiber optics and satellites made cable connections obsolete. Competitors developed, and the government alleged that these rivals were being charged unfairly high fees for access to AT&T's local telephone lines.

On the same day the IBM case ended in 1982, AT&T and the Department of Justice announced this case was settled. AT&T ("Ma Bell") divested itself of 22 local companies ("Baby Bells"), but retained its long-distance telephone service, its research facilities (Bell Laboratories), and its manufacturing facilities (Western Electric Company). As a result, local companies became regulated monopolies in their areas, and local phone rates rose sharply. In nationwide long-distance telephone service, AT&T's competition with MCI and Sprint lowered the price of long-distance telephone service. Moreover, individual customers became responsible for buying their own phones, rather than using only AT&T phones. The result has been a highly competitive market, offering a wide range of phone prices and a wide variety of phones.

The MIT Case (1992)

For years, the presidents of many of the nation's top universities—Cornell, Harvard, Yale, Columbia, Brown, Princeton, The University of Pennsylvania, Dartmouth, and MIT—attended annual meetings to discuss tuition, faculty salaries, and financial aid packages. After such meetings, these schools often adjusted tuition charges, salary increases, and even fees for room and board. For example, one year Dartmouth planned to raise faculty salaries by 8.5 percent. The other schools wanted to hold the line at 6.5 percent, so Dartmouth was persuaded to cave in. At other meetings, the group's goal was to make sure each student who applied to more than one of the schools would be offered the same financial aid. At another meeting, Harvard and Yale accused Princeton of offering excessively generous scholarships to top students.

The U.S. Justice Department investigated and charged the eight Ivy League universities and MIT with an illegal conspiracy to fix prices. The Ivy League schools settled the case with a consent decree. This agreement required these schools to cease colluding on tuition, salaries, and financial aid in the future, and, in return, none of the schools admitted guilt for a price conspiracy. MIT refused to sign the consent order, and in 1992, a federal district judge ruled that MIT had violated antitrust laws and concluded that students and parents have the right to compare prices when choosing a university. In 1993, an appeals court ordered a new trial and the Justice Department dropped charges with the agreement that MIT would cease comparing financial packages.

CHECKPOINT

Does Price-Fixing Improve Your Education?

Price-fixing agreements are among the monopolistic restraint-of-trade practices prohibited by Section 1 of the Sherman Act. The Supreme Court has concluded that a formal agreement is not necessary to prove conspiracy. Instead, conspiracy may be inferred from the acts of the accused even if the consequences might be considered socially desirable. The presidents of the universities charged with price-fixing in the MIT case defended their business practices with the argument that they openly met to fix prices in order to improve education. With tuition and the amount of financial aid fixed, students and parents will choose their university on the basis of academic quality alone. Consider the discussion of pricing strategies for an oligopoly discussed in Chapter 10. Can you give the presidents a better argument for their defense?

The Microsoft Case (2001)

Microsoft Corporation dominated the personal computer (PC) software industry with about a 90 percent share of the PC operating system software and Internet browser markets. And Microsoft had tied its Windows operating systems at zero price (predatory pricing) to its Internet Explorer browser in order to eliminate competition and establish a monopoly in the browser market. The remedies discussed included both conduct and structural remedies. A conduct remedy was a judicial instruction against engaging in specific behavior. For example, Microsoft could be required to include major rival browsers with its browser. Bill Gates likened this proposal to "requiring Coca-Cola to include three cans of Pepsi in every six-pack it sells." Moreover, Microsoft claimed that by integrating Internet Explorer with Windows it was creating one product and not tying two products. In short, no one using the Windows operating system needed a separate browser.

A structural remedy is a "surgical fix" aimed at permanently altering a company so substantially that further violations are not possible. For example, Microsoft could be split into three companies. One company would have operating systems, such as Windows. A second company could have applications, such as Word, Excel, and PowerPoint. The third company would get Internet Explorer and related Internet business. A major concern with this remedy was that a three-headed monopoly monster might destroy innovation and a seamless transition between Windows and other software applications. Another fear was that prices might rise and software would become much more complicated.

In 2001, a federal appeals court ruled that Microsoft did violate antitrust law to protect a monopoly for its Windows operating system. However, the court ruled the government had failed to prove Microsoft illegally attempted to monopolize the Internet browser market. In response, Microsoft announced that it would allow PC manufacturers to continue adding icons of other technology companies to Microsoft's operating system. In 2002, a federal judge approved most of the provisions of the antitrust settlement reached the previous year with Microsoft.

The major antitrust cases are summarized in Exhibit 2.

EXHIBIT 2	Summary of Major Antitrust Cases
Case (date)	**Key Provision**
Standard Oil (1911)	○ This case established the rule of reason, allowing a monopoly unless it engages in illegal practices.
Alcoa (1945)	○ This case overturned the rule of reason and established the per se rule, under which all monopolies are illegal.
IBM (1982)	○ The government dropped its case after 13 years and shifted antitrust policy back to the rule of reason.
AT&T (1982)	○ Technology made this government-regulated natural monopoly obsolete, and AT&T was found guilty of anticompetitive pricing.
MIT (1992)	○ Eight Ivy League schools agreed to stop colluding to fix prices, and MIT was found guilty of price-fixing while attending open meetings. MIT and the Justice Department reached an agreement after an appeals court ordered a new trial.
Microsoft (2001)	○ Microsoft and the government reached a settlement after an appeals court held that the firm illegally protected its Windows monopoly.

Mergers and Global Antitrust Policy

The decades of the 1980s and 1990s were characterized by a wave of mergers. Mergers are a concern to antitrust regulators because firms can avoid charges of price-fixing by merging into one firm. The antitrust policy toward mergers depends on the type of merger and its likely effect on the relevant market.

Types of Mergers

A horizontal merger is a merger of firms that compete in the same market. The mergers of Coca-Cola and PepsiCo, Ford Motor Company and General Motors, and Anheuser Bush and Coors would be hypothetical examples of horizontal mergers. Horizontal mergers raise a "red flag" because they decrease competition in a market. For example, in 1986, the government blocked the proposed merger between Coca-Cola and Seven-Up.

A vertical merger is a merger of a firm with its suppliers. This type of merger occurs between companies at different stages of a production process. Hypothetical examples of vertical mergers would be General Motors merging with a major tire company and Ford Motor Company merging with a large number of car dealerships. Although the government often challenges vertical mergers, global competition has reduced antitrust scrutiny of vertical mergers. If this type of merger lowers costs by eliminating unnecessary supplier charges, U.S. firms will be more competitive in world markets.

A conglomerate merger is a merger between firms in unrelated markets. Suppose an insurance company buys a computer software company or a cigarette company merges with a hotel chain. Actual examples are Phillip Morris merging with Miller Brewing Company and General Motors merging with Electronic Data Systems Corporation. No antitrust action was taken to prevent these mergers because the products of the two firms were considered to be unrelated. Conglomerate mergers are generally allowed because they do not significantly decrease competition.

> **Horizontal merger**
> A merger of firms that compete in the same market.

> **Vertical merger**
> A vertical merger is a merger of a firm with its suppliers.

> **Conglomerate merger**
> A merger between firms in unrelated markets.

Antitrust Policies in Other Countries

Early antitrust laws were aimed at the domestic economy with little concern for global competitiveness. Because of the internationalization of competition in recent decades, some economists call for a relaxation of antitrust laws to allow firms to merge and compete more effectively in the world economy. Other economists disagree and argue that strong antitrust laws are necessary because small firms create most jobs and innovations.

One reason firms in other countries are so competitive with U.S. firms is that other countries' antitrust laws are weak in comparison to U.S. antitrust laws. For example, no other country breaks up companies for antitrust violations. There are two basic explanations. First, most other countries have smaller populations than the United States. Because other countries have fewer potential customers, they view the global market as the target and design weak antitrust laws accordingly. Stated differently, other countries must sell their products globally in order to achieve economies of scale and be competitive.

Second, other countries have weak antitrust laws based on their culture and history. In the United States, there is a strong belief in Adam Smith's individualistic competition among small firms. This "big is bad" ideology is the foundation of U.S. antitrust laws, but this belief is not prevalent in other countries. In other countries, "big is better," and in countries such as Japan and Germany, government and business work together to compete globally. In contrast, there is a general mistrust of government working directly with big businesses in the United States.

Regulation

The same distrust of big business that is the basis of antitrust laws also led to the evolution of regulation and federal regulatory agencies in the United States. The regulatory process in the United States has gone through several phases. In the first phase, from 1887 to the Great Depression, the railroads were the primary target. During the 1930s, the Great Depression created a favorable environment in which regulation spread to the communications, financial, and other industries. After 1970, regulation increased steadily in the areas of health, safety, and the environment until the 1980s, when a deregulation movement began and it continued to have momentum in the early 2000s.

Historical Origins of Regulation

The Early Years   The railroads came under regulation in the late nineteenth century as a result of their unfair pricing practices. At that time in history, railroads faced little competition from other carriers, so there was little to prevent railroads from overcharging. Railroads also practiced price discrimination against isolated rural customers by charging them higher rates for short hauls than they charged city customers for long hauls. In 1887, the Interstate Commerce Commission (ICC) was established to regulate rail prices and to cut the costs of rail transportation by reducing duplicate trains, depots, and tracks.

The Great Depression Era   During the 1930s, regulation was extended to other industries. The Food and Drug Administration (FDA) was established in 1931 to oversee the safety of food and drugs. All surface transportation, including trucks, barges, and oil pipelines, came to be regulated by the ICC. The Civil Aeronautics Board (CAB) was created in 1938 to regulate air travel, and the Federal Communications Commission (FCC) was established in 1934 to regulate telephones, telegraphs, and broadcasting industries. In 1934, as a result of the stock market crash of 1929, the Securities and Exchange Commission (SEC) was created to combat fraud and malpractice in the securities industry.

The Health, Safety, and Environment Era   The Occupational Safety and Health Administration (OSHA) was created in 1970 to reduce the incidence of injury and death in the workplace. This agency cites and fines employers who violate safety and health rules. In the same year, the Environmental Protection Agency (EPA) was established to set and enforce pollution standards. In 1972, the Consumer Product Safety Commission (CPSC) was established to protect the public against injury from unsafe products. The CPSC has the power to ban the sale of hazardous products.

The Deregulation Trend

In the 1970s, the higher production costs resulting from regulation generated widespread dissatisfaction with government regulation. The result was a movement toward deregulation in the late 1970s and 1980s. Deregulation is the elimination or phasing out of government restrictions on economic activity. Initially, the major thrust of deregulation was in the transportation and telecommunications industries.

Deregulation
The elimination or phasing out of government restrictions on economic activity.

The Airline Deregulation Act of 1978 removed regulated airfares and restrictions against competition in air travel markets. The Staggers Rail Act of 1980 deregulated the railroads, the Motor Carrier Act of 1980 deregulated trucking, and the Bus Regulatory Reform Act of 1982 deregulated bus transportation. The Civil Aeronautics Board (CAB), established in 1938 to regulate airline fares and air routes, was abolished in 1984. The You're the Economist at the end of the chapter examines the effects on the airline industry.

In telecommunications, the most important case was the deregulation and dismantling of AT&T. As explained above, technological innovations made competition in telecommunications possible, and, as a result of an antitrust lawsuit, AT&T was broken up and forced to compete with MCI, Sprint, and other companies for long-distance service. In 1996, Congress passed a telecommunications bill that made additional changes in U.S. telecommunications. This bill deregulated cable television rates, while allowing local and long-distance telephone companies and cable companies to compete. This bill also required television manufacturers to equip new sets with a computer chip to block shows parents do not wish their children to watch.

For nearly 100 years electricity was a regulated industry in the United States. Privately held utility companies obtained the right to operate a monopoly in exchange for government regulations that set rates and capped profits. In 1992, Congress started the deregulation movement for power companies when it approved the Energy Policy Act, which opened competition at the wholesale level. By 2001, 24 states and the District of Columbia had approved deregulation plans, but the California power shortage created a deregulation backlash (see You're the Economist on California electricity deregulation).

The principal functions of the federal regulatory agencies discussed are summarized in Exhibit 3.

Three Cases for Government Regulation

Government regulation involves political, social, and economic factors, and the general justification for regulation is to protect the public. In this section, we examine three basic situations in which regulation is often imposed: (1) natural monopoly, (2) externalities, and (3) imperfect information. In each of these cases, the argument in favor of regulation is *market failure*. Recall from Chapter 4 that market failure is a situation in which the market operating on its own fails to lead to an efficient allocation of resources.

Natural Monopoly

The objective of antitrust policy is to create a level playing field for competing firms. Depending on the case, antitrust policy can result in breaking up a monopoly, preventing formation of a monopoly, and/or punishing anticompetitive business practices of a monopoly. But, what happens when it is inefficient for more than one company to operate in a particular market? Stated another way, creation of a level playing field for competitors may not be in the best interest of economic efficiency. This situation exists in a *natural monopoly*. As explained earlier in Exhibit 1 in Chapter 9 on monopoly, a natural monopoly is an industry in which long-run average cost is minimized when only one firm serves the market. Recall that the services of such public utilities as local telephone, gas, electric, cable TV, and water companies are natural monopolies subject to government regulation. To avoid abuse of this type of monopoly, the prices or rates these public utilities can charge are determined by a federal, state, or local regulatory commission or board.

EXHIBIT 3	Federal Regulatory Agencies

Agency	Year Created	Function
Interstate Commerce Commission (ICC)	1887*	Regulated interstate ground transportation, including the railroad, trucking, bus, and water carrier industries.
Food and Drug Administration (FDA)	1931	Protects the health of the nation against impure and unsafe foods, drugs, and cosmetics. Develops policy regarding labeling of all drugs.
Securities and Exchange Commission (SEC)	1934	Provides for complete financial disclosure and protects investors in stock and other securities against fraud.
Federal Communications Commission (FCC)	1934	Regulates television, radio, telephone, and telegraph services; satellite transmissions; and cable TV.
Civil Aeronautics Board (CAB)	1938†	Regulated airline fares and routes.
Occupational Safety and Health Administration (OSHA)	1970	Enforces rules in cases involving safety and health violations in the workplace.
Environmental Protection Agency (EPA)	1970	Regulates pollution in the areas of air, water, waste, noise, radiation, and toxic substances.
Consumer Product Safety Commission (CPSC)	1972	Protects the public against unreasonable risks of injury from consumer products.

*Abolished in 1995.
†Abolished in 1984.

Exhibit 4 illustrates the demand curve, long-run marginal cost curve ($LRMC$), and long-run average cost curve ($LRAC$) for a natural monopoly in the cable TV market—say, a company called Vision Cable. Because of *economies of scale,* the $LRAC$ curve is negatively sloped. Following the *marginal-average rule* explained in Chapter 7, the $LRMC$ curve is below the falling $LRAC$ curve. Given this condition, the firm's demand curve intersects the $LRAC$ curve at a quantity of 80,000 subscribers and a cost of $90 per month equal to the price (point B). Suppose this output is divided equally between Vision Cable and another cable company. As discussed earlier in Exhibit 1 of Chapter 9, the result of competition between cable TV companies is that the cost per subscriber is much higher—and even higher if output is divided among more than two cable companies.

To take advantage of the lower cost, the policy prescription is to create a cable TV market served by only one producer—Vision Cable. The policy problem now is how to keep this unregulated natural monopoly from enjoying a substantial monopoly profit. Instead of providing services for 80,000 customers, Vision Cable will service only 40,000 customers by following the $MR = MC$ rule to maximize profits. The price that corresponds to this output is $150 per month at point A. Because the profit-maximizing price exceeds the $LRAC$ curve, monopoly pricing creates too high a price and too small an output. Stated differently, the result is an inefficient cable TV market, in which there is an underallocation of resources to produce cable TV service.

For the cable television market to be efficient, regulators must set a price ceiling at $60 per month, which is equal to long-run marginal cost at point C on the demand curve. This pricing strategy follows the competitive principle of marginal cost pricing. Marginal cost pricing is a system of pricing in which the price charged

Marginal cost pricing

A system of pricing in which the price charged equals the marginal cost of the last unit produced.

EXHIBIT 4 — A Regulated Monopoly

If an unregulated monopolist serves the cable TV market, it will set $MR = LRMC$, charge a price of $150 per month, and provide service to only 40,000 customers (point A). To improve the efficiency of the market by taking advantage of the lower costs of a natural monopoly, government regulators could set the price at $60, which equals long-run marginal cost (point C). This policy is efficient, but losses require public subsidies. The typical solution is to set a "fair-return" price of $90, which allows the monopolist to earn zero economic profit and serve 80,000 customers at point B. This condition does not fully correct the underallocation of resources caused by an unregulated natural monopoly.

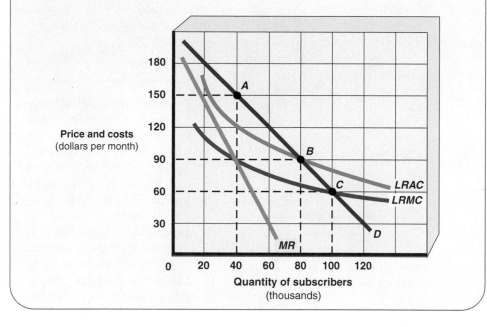

Price and costs
(dollars per month)

Quantity of subscribers
(thousands)

equals the marginal cost of the last unit produced. At a price of $60, Vision Cable suffers a loss because although the price covers long-run marginal cost, the price is not high enough to cover long-run average cost. This means the firm can survive in the long run only if the government subsidizes the loss.

What to do? Is there an option that does not require taxpayers' money? Yes! In practice, regulatory commissions have relaxed the objective of efficiency and have focused on establishing a "fair-return" price to be charged by the monopolist. In Exhibit 4, the commission would establish the fair-return price at $90 per month at point B, where the demand curve intersects the $LRAC$ curve. Because the price ceiling equals long-run average cost, Vision Cable earns zero economic profit and serves 80,000 customers in the long run. However, remember from the chapter on production costs that in economics cost includes a normal profit, which is just enough to keep the firm in the cable industry.

> **Conclusion** *Government regulators can achieve efficiency for a natural monopoly by setting a price ceiling equal to the intersection of the demand and the marginal cost curves, but this policy results in losses. An alternative is to set a price ceiling, called the fair-return price, that yields a normal profit, but is somewhat inefficient.*

In order to keep electricity cheap for its state, the California legislature in 1996 set a retail ceiling price of 10 cents per kilowatt-hour. Moreover, no new power-generating plants were built during the 1990s. The plan was to require utilities to sell their power plants and import electricity as needed from the "spot market" through high-speed transmission lines from other states. In the deregulated wholesale electricity market, a spot market is one in which the price of electricity is determined by supply and demand conditions each hour.

The stage was set for the forces of supply and demand to "turn out the lights." First, demand soared during a heat wave in the summer of 2000 as consumers turned on their air conditioners. Second, there was a leftward shift in supply. High natural gas prices increased the cost of producing electricity in all states. Also, low snowpacks and a drought in the Pacific Northwest reduced the capacity of hydroelectric dams in this region.

Facing shortages from both increased demand and decreased supply, California utilities had no choice but to buy electricity on the spot market as prices soared tenfold over their normal levels. Since customer rates were capped, the price paid by consumers did not cover what the utilities were paying for electricity. The utilities quickly found themselves facing bankruptcy, and this threat caused additional spot rate increases. Duke Power Company of North Carolina, for example, stated that 8 percent of its spot price was a premium to cover the risk of selling to California utilities that might not pay their bills. A subsequent investigation by the Federal Energy Regulatory Commission (FERC) reported evidence that power companies, such as Enron, developed strategies to drive up prices.

Faced with this crisis, Governor Gray Davis, who was governor of California at the time, called for more price caps. He convinced the FERC to cap wholesale prices in the West during hours of highest demand, combined with a daily regime of rolling blackouts, and calls for conservation. In April 2001, Davis abandoned the 1996 price ceiling, thus sharply increasing the retail electricity price.

ANALYZE THE ISSUE

Draw a graph illustrating California's electricity crisis. Put the label "Price of electricity (cents per kilowatt-hour)" on the vertical axis and "Quantity of electricity (megawatts per hour)" on the horizontal axis. As explained in Chapter 4, draw the changes in demand and supply for electricity in California described above. [Hint: Begin the graph in equilibrium below the price ceiling.]

CHECKPOINT
Why Doesn't The Water Company Compete?
The local water company is considered to be a natural monopoly, and the government prohibits other firms from competing with it. If a natural monopoly can produce water at a lower price than other firms, then why would the government protect the water company from competitors?

Externalities

The case of pollution was treated in detail in Exhibit 8(a) in Chapter 4. To refresh your memory, recall that the individual firm in a competitive market has no incentive to eliminate pollution voluntarily. Pollution is an *external cost* imposed on *third parties* who neither produce nor consume a good. Pollution causes polluting firms to overproduce, while causing firms that pay the cost of cleaning up the pollution to underproduce. Therefore, expenditures on pollution control would place firms at a competitive disadvantage with respect to firms that do not pay the cost of controlling pollution. If society wants less pollution, this type of market failure justifies government regulation from, say, the EPA. The exact nature of the regulation, however, may take a variety of forms, ranging from direct controls requiring specific pollution-control equipment to taxation.

Without repeating the explanation given in Exhibit 8(b) in Chapter 4, note that the *external benefits* of a good, such as a vaccination, can lead to underproduction of the good. Again, regulation is necessary if society is to respond to externalities. In this case, the government solution can take various forms, including requiring consumption or providing special subsidies.

Imperfect Information

In some cases, consumers lack important information about a product, and they cannot make rational decisions. Without complete and reliable information, consumers may be unaware of the dangers of unsafe drugs, hazardous chemicals, and defective products. The source of imperfect information about products may be company errors. Much worse, companies may be able to boost sales by withholding valuable information about a problem with their products.

Let's consider a hypothetical case in which an unsafe Tucker Motors (TM) truck is sold. Suppose the safety defect is a gas tank that is located too close to the side of the truck. As a result, another vehicle can crash into the side of the TM truck and hit the gas tank. Such an accident can cause a deadly explosion. Assume further that TM is aware of this safety problem, but the cost of recalling and fixing the trucks exceeds the estimated cost of lawsuits caused by the defective gas tanks. The market incentive is therefore for TM to withhold knowledge of this defect from uninformed consumers.

Exhibit 5 illustrates this case. With consumers unaware of the defect, the interaction of the supply and demand curves for TM trucks yields an equilibrium at E_1, with 100,000 trucks being sold per year at a price of $30,000 per truck. Next, suppose the Consumer Product Safety Commission (CPSC) exposes the problem, and the media report stories about crash victims who have been severely burned or even killed by the flames from the exploding gas tanks in TM trucks. Once the consuming public is aware of the defect, consumers' preferences for TM trucks change, and the demand curve decreases from D_1 to D_2. The result is a new equilibrium at E_2, with 75,000 TM trucks being sold per year at a price of $20,000 per truck. In other words, this case is an application of market supply and demand analysis as presented in Chapter 4.

> **Conclusion** *Deficient information on unsafe products can cause consumers to overconsume a product.*

© Fogstock LLC/Index Open.

A much-publicized case of deregulation is the airline industry. Under regulation by the Civil Aeronautics Board (CAB), airfare competition and the incentive to control costs were reduced or eliminated. The CAB set both fares and routes for carriers. Unable to compete with price, the carriers could compete only with costly nonprice competition, such as advertising. Once the CAB authorized a carrier to provide service between two cities, the frequency of service remained unregulated. When carriers purchased fleets of planes and provided too many flights for their protected routes, profits were squeezed because the percentage of seats filled with passengers (load factor) fell, and the average cost rose. Carriers would then attempt to boost profits by lobbying the CAB for higher fares. In addition to eliminating price competition between established carriers, the CAB restricted entrants into the industry. From 1938 until 1977, the CAB never awarded a major route to any new airline.

Successful deregulation of an industry would be expected to provide the following three results:

- The average price of the service falls.
- The volume and variety of services rise.
- New firms enter the industry, and other firms fail and exit the industry.

The Airline Deregulation Act of 1978 provided these results by changing the structure and business behavior of the airline industry. Although the Federal Aviation Administration (FAA) would still regulate the safety of air service, the CAB was eliminated under this act in 1984, and price competition produced the expected results of lower fares and greater quantity of service. The average passenger price per mile for a flight declined from 1978 to less than half that rate in 2008 on an inflation-adjusted basis, saving consumers billions of dollars in lower fares.[1] Over this same period, the fall in fares contributed to more than a tripling of passenger miles flown per year, from 227 billion to 797 billion.[2]

The airline deregulatory movement is not without criticism. One concern is that lots of airlines went "belly up," and these exits from the industry increased the percentage of all domestic air travel controlled by the industry's largest carriers. Moreover, under the pressure of competition, carriers searched for ways to cut costs, and they created the hub-and-spoke delivery system. This system allows carriers to gather passengers from the "spoke" routes by using smaller, less efficient planes and fly them from the hub in fully occupied, bigger planes at lower cost. Many carriers have gained near monopoly power in "hub" airports. These dominant hub carriers can control access to terminal gates, takeoff time slots, and baggage service, and they can charge smaller lines high rates for using these airport rights.

Today, deregulation continues to exert downward pressure on fares, and old-guard carriers scramble to compete with low-cost carriers such as Southwest and Jet Blue. Low-fare tickets, cyberfares, and frequent flyer miles are popular. Quality of service is higher measured by fewer consumer complaints today than in the regulation era.[3] Should the airlines remain deregulated or return to a government-enforced cartel? Critics point to airlines that are in financial trouble. Defenders of deregulation argue that growth of market concentration and its abuses can be controlled by enforcing antitrust laws and allowing global competition.

ANALYZE THE ISSUE

Prior to deregulation, critics argued that airline safety would suffer. Instead, although the Federal Aviation Administration's budget was cut following deregulation, the accident rate involving fatalities has fallen. Give a rationale for why the critics' prediction did not come to pass.

1. Annual Passenger Yields: U.S. Airlines, http://www.airlines.org/economics/finance/papricesyield.htm.
2. *Statistical Abstract of the United States, 2008, http://www.census.gov/compendia, Table 1038.*
3. Ibid. Table 1048.

EXHIBIT 5 — The Impact of Imperfect Information on the Market for TM Trucks

An initial equilibrium is established at point E_1, with 100,000 TM trucks purchased each year for $30,000 per truck. This equilibrium is reached without consumers having knowledge of a safety defect. Once consumers are informed of the safety defect, the demand curve shifts leftward from D_1 to D_2. At the new equilibrium point of E_2, 75,000 TM trucks are purchased each year for $20,000 per truck. Thus, imperfect information has resulted in a waste of the resources used to produce 25,000 TM trucks.

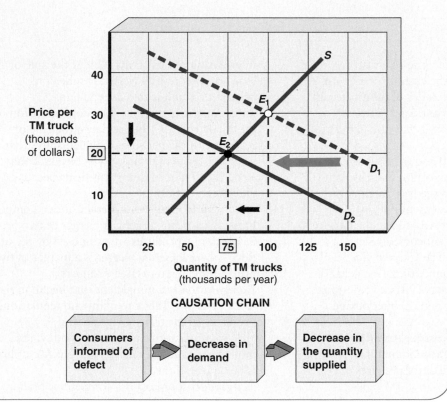

CAUSATION CHAIN

Consumers informed of defect → Decrease in demand → Decrease in the quantity supplied

In the TM truck example, resources were used to produce 25,000 trucks that consumers would not purchase when given complete information. These resources were misallocated because they could have been used to produce other goods and services. The solution is for government to prevent companies from making false or deceptive claims by gathering and disseminating accurate information to consumers. This is the rationale for the safety testing of cars, EPA mileage ratings on cars, and warning labels on cigarettes. In extreme cases, a product may be deemed too unsafe, and it is outlawed from sale. Others disagree with this view and argue that the government should only provide information. Once consumers have sufficient information, they should be free to choose.

KEY CONCEPTS

Trust
Predatory pricing
Sherman Act of 1890
Clayton Act of 1914
Federal Trade Commission
    Act of 1914

Robinson-Patman Act of 1936
Celler-Kefauver Act of 1950
Rule of reason
Per se rule
Horizontal merger
Vertical merger

Conglomerate merger
Deregulation
Marginal cost pricing

SUMMARY

- A *trust* is a cartel that places the assets of competing companies in the custody of a board of trustees. During the last decades of the nineteenth century, trusts engaged in anticompetitive strategies, such as *predatory pricing,* to eliminate competition and raise prices.

- The *Sherman Act of 1890* and the *Clayton Act of 1914* are the two most important antitrust laws. The Sherman Act marked the first attempt of the U.S. government to outlaw monopolizing behavior. Because this act was vague, the Clayton Act was passed to define anticompetitive behavior more precisely. The Clayton Act prohibited (1) price discrimination, (2) exclusive dealing, (3) tying contracts, (4) stock acquisition of competing companies, and (5) interlocking directorates.

- The *Federal Trade Commission Act of 1914* established the Federal Trade Commission (FTC) to investigate unfair competitive practices of firms.

- The *Robinson-Patman Act of 1936* strengthened the Clayton Act by prohibiting certain forms of price discrimination. This law is called the "Chain Store Act" because it was aimed at large retail chain stores that were obtaining volume discounts.

- The *Celler-Kefauver Act of 1950* strengthened the Clayton Act by declaring illegal the acquisition of the assets of one firm by another firm if the effect is to lessen competition.

- The *rule of reason* and the *per se rule* are the two main doctrines the courts have used in interpreting antitrust law. Under the rule of reason, monopolists were not subject to prosecution unless they acted in an anticompetitive manner. The court decision in the Alcoa case of 1945 replaced the rule of reason with the per se rule, which states that the mere existence of monopoly is illegal. Today, the trend is in favor of dominant firms because of global competition.

- A *horizontal merger* is a merger of two competing firms. A *vertical merger* is a merger of two firms in which one produces an input used by the other firm. A *conglomerate merger* is a merger of two firms producing unrelated products.

- *Deregulation* is a movement that began in the late 1970s and 1980s to eliminate regulations primarily in the transportation and telecommunications industries. Today, the movement to further deregulate electric utilities is being questioned.

- *Marginal cost pricing* is a competitive pricing strategy for a regulated natural monopoly. Using this approach, regulators set the monopolist's price equal to its marginal cost. Another method is for regulators to establish a fair-return price equal to long-run average cost, and the monopolist earns zero economic profit. Regulation of a natural monopoly is justified on the basis of market failure. Two other cases based on market failure include externalities and imperfect information.

Marginal cost pricing

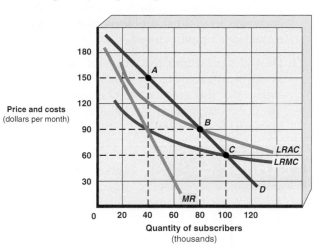

SUMMARY OF CONCLUSION STATEMENTS

- Government regulators can achieve efficiency for a natural monopoly by setting a price ceiling equal to the intersection of the demand and the marginal cost curves, but this policy results in losses. An alternative is to set a price ceiling, called the fair-return price, which yields a normal profit, but is somewhat inefficient.

- Deficient information on unsafe products can cause consumers to overconsume a product.

STUDY QUESTIONS AND PROBLEMS

1. Describe the major provisions of the Sherman Act and the Clayton Act. Who is responsible for enforcing these laws?

2. Two business practices outlawed by the Clayton Act are tying contracts and interlocking directorates. Explain the condition required for these two practices to be a violation of this antitrust law.

3. Distinguish between the Robinson-Patman Act of 1936 and the Celler-Kefauver Act of 1950.

4. Using cases presented in the text, explain the issue in the courts' interpretation of "monopoly versus monopolizing."

5. A controversy in many antitrust court cases involves the definition of the relevant market for a firm's product. How would you argue in the Alcoa case that the government's claim of the firm's high market share was in error?

6. In the MIT case, which students are harmed by the Ivy League schools' coordination of scholarship policy? Professional baseball is exempt from antitrust laws. Should colleges and universities also be exempt from antitrust laws?

7. Based on the antitrust laws, how would you expect the federal government to react to the following situations?
   a. A college bookstore deliberately reduces prices until its only rival is driven out of business. The bookstore then raises its prices.
   b. Real estate firms meet in an open meeting and agree to charge 6 percent commission on sales.
   c. Microsoft merges with Apple by a stock acquisition.
   d. A small tax preparation company merges with a regional grocery store chain.

8. Based on the cases discussed in the chapter, is the following statement correct? "The antitrust laws in reality deal less with monopolies than with oligopolies."

9. Assume a regulatory agency is given authority over prices and entry conditions for a given industry. Also assume the agency decides to allow new entry, as the CAB actually did before deregulation, only when it is proven to be "necessary." Would this condition be expected to favor (a) existing regulated firms, (b) new entrants, or (c) consumers? Explain.

10. Exhibit 6 represents a natural monopolist.
    a. If the monopolist is not regulated, what price will it charge, and what quantity will it produce?
    b. If the monopolist is required to use marginal cost pricing, what price will it charge, and what quantity will it produce? Why will the monopolist stay in business?
    c. Assume regulators set a fair-return price at P_b. Why would the monopolist stay in business?

11. Assume a natural monopolist is required to use marginal cost pricing and a government subsidy covers the loss. What problems might be associated with a public subsidy?

12. Do you agree that "cost does not really matter" as a principle for safety regulation, or do you believe that the cost of a safety device must be justified on the basis of the value of human life protected from a hazard?

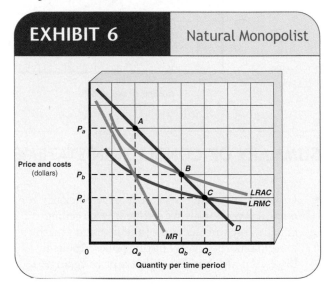

EXHIBIT 6   Natural Monopolist

For Online Exercises, go to the text Web site at www.cengage.com/economics/tucker.

CHECKPOINT ANSWERS

Does Price-Fixing Improve Your Education?

Accepting the schools' argument that they improve quality by price-fixing makes no more sense than allowing General Motors, Ford, Chrysler, and Japanese automakers to fix prices in order to improve quality. However, there is often a thin line between price-fixing and price leadership. Price leadership is not illegal as long as the price followers are not coerced. If you said price leadership is defendable and price-fixing is not, **YOU ARE CORRECT.**

Why Doesn't The Water Company Compete?

Suppose new firms are allowed to compete with the water company, which is a natural monopolist. The concern is that the rivals will be outcompeted. New water companies must build plants, dig up the streets, and lay new water pipes and duplicate other resources in the same neighborhood. Because the competitors cannot produce water at a lower cost, they will leave the industry, and the resources used to compete with the natural monopolist will be wasted. If you said the government is not protecting the natural monopolist from competition so much as it is protecting against inefficient competitors wasting resources, **YOU ARE CORRECT.**

PRACTICE QUIZ

For an explanation of the correct answers, please visit the tutorial at www.cengage. com/ economics/tucker.

1. Which of the following is illegal under the Sherman Act?
   a. Attempts to monopolize
   b. Price-fixing
   c. Formation of cartels
   d. All of the above are illegal.

2. Officers of five large building-materials companies meet and agree that none of them will submit bids on government contracts lower than an agreed-upon level. This is an example of
   a. price-fixing.
   b. vertical restriction.
   c. a tying contract.
   d. an interlocking directorate.

3. A fabric shop cannot sell Singer sewing machines if it also sells other brands of sewing machines. This is an example of
   a. resale price maintenance.
   b. territorial restrictions.
   c. a tying agreement.
   d. exclusive dealing.

4. Under the Clayton Act, horizontal mergers by stock acquisition were
   a. not considered.
   b. illegal if they could be shown to lessen competition.
   c. illegal under any circumstances.
   d. legal if they could be shown not to lessen competition.

5. Under the Clayton Act, which of the following was illegal even if it was *not* shown to lessen competition substantially?
   a. Price discrimination
   b. Tying contracts
   c. Horizontal mergers by stock acquisition
   d. Interlocking directorates

6. The importance of the Federal Trade Commission Act of 1914 is that it
   a. set up an independent antitrust agency with the power to investigate complaints.
   b. strengthened the law against mergers.

   c. strengthened the law against price discrimination.
   d. did none of the above.

7. Which of the following is concerned primarily with price discrimination?
   a. Sherman Act
   b. Clayton Act
   c. Robinson-Patman Act
   d. Celler-Kefauver Act

8. Which of the following is concerned primarily with mergers?
   a. Sherman Act
   b. Clayton Act
   c. Robinson-Patman Act
   d. Celler-Kefauver Act

9. The Utah Pie case was brought under which of the following laws?
   a. Sherman Act
   b. Federal Trade Commission Act
   c. Robinson-Patman Act
   d. Celler-Kefauver Act

10. Although U.S. Steel controlled nearly 75 percent of the domestic iron and steel industry, in 1920 the Supreme Court ruled that the firm was *not* in violation of the Sherman Act because there was no evidence of abusive behavior. What antitrust doctrine was the Court applying in this case?
    a. The rule of reason
    b. The per se rule
    c. The marginal cost pricing rule
    d. The natural monopoly rule

11. In which antitrust case did the courts first apply the per se rule to determine whether a firm was in violation of the Sherman Act?
    a. Standard Oil case
    b. Alcoa case
    c. IBM case
    d. MIT case

PRACTICE QUIZ CONTINUED

12. The Interstate Commerce Commission (ICC) was established in
    a. 1887.
    b. 1890.
    c. 1929.
    d. 1933.

13. Today, the Civil Aeronautics Board (CAB) regulates
    a. airline ticket prices.
    b. airline routes.
    c. airline safety.
    d. all of the above.
    e. none of the above; the CAB was abolished in 1984.

14. Which of the following provides the basis for regulation?
    a. Natural monopoly
    b. Externalities
    c. Imperfect information
    d. All of the above

15. Consider a regulated natural monopoly. If the regulatory commission wants to establish a fair-return price, then it should set a price ceiling where the demand curve crosses the monopoly's long-run
    a. marginal revenue curve.
    b. average revenue curve.
    c. marginal cost curve.
    d. average cost curve.

Environmental Economics

T he United States is the envy of many of the world's citizens for its quality of life. Americans can choose from an almost unlimited number of goods and services. When it comes to transportation, for example, the typical family may own two or three cars. This same family may own touring bikes, mountain bikes, and hybrids that incorporate features of each. Some U.S. citizens own boats, and others own jet skis. Those in colder climates may get around on snow skis, snowshoes, or snowmobiles. Some families even own their own planes. The choice of what to buy in the United States is a private decision. I will choose a snowmobile over snowshoes if I want to travel fast and am willing to spend the money. I will choose a jet ski over a kayak if I find high-speed travel more exciting than paddling along quietly. While my choice is private, my decision has consequences for others.

My jet ski may create waves that threaten to tip your kayak. The noise I make may spoil your desire for peace and quiet. It may also scare wildlife. And the fuel I use to power the jet ski not only adds to fuel consumption, but can contribute to water pollution. Engine exhaust may even make a small contribution to carbon emissions, which may contribute to climate change. Many fear that global warming is causing melting of the polar ice caps, resulting in rising ocean levels and massive flooding of coastal areas throughout the world, as well as climate shifts that could render today's farms tomorrow's deserts.

Up to this point, the competitive market has been shown to be the best engine to generate what consumers want at the lowest possible price. Yet the unbridled use of many of these goods, from jet skis and snowmobiles to Coke cans and cigarettes, may not be the best choice for society or the planet. Competitive markets work well when producers and consumers consider all costs in their decisions. But for some goods and services, decision-makers

351

fail to include the cost to others of their decision, such as revving the jet ski or snowmobile to the detriment of others, or throwing the Coke can or cigarette butt out the car window. Although these are local problems, other problems are global in scale, such as carbon emissions from gasoline-burning engines that many believe cause global warming. This chapter will begin by showing why competitive markets may fail to sufficiently protect the environment. First, we will see that competitive markets result in market failure by producing "too much pollution." Then we will see how we might correct the market failure. Finally, we will consider the pros and cons of government intervention to improve our environment.

In this chapter, you will learn to solve these economic puzzles:

- Why do competitive markets produce too many lawn mowers and charge too low a price for lawn mowers?

- How can government legislation, taxes, and permits help society achieve its environmental goals?

- Can government intervention actually reduce environmental quality?

Competitive Markets and Environmental Efficiency

While society values goods and services produced in markets, it also values air, water, and other environmental amenities. Air and water are shared resources that generally are not priced in the marketplace. The result is that markets often treat these resources as if they were free, resulting in their overuse. Competitive markets, which are the ideal in efficiently allocating many goods and services, fail to achieve preferred levels of output when they treat valuable resources such as air and water as if they were free.

The competitive market has been shown in earlier chapters to achieve *economic efficiency*. This efficiency exists when the price to consumers, reflecting marginal benefit, equals marginal cost. Consumers, such as jet ski buyers, consider purchase price, styling, and performance features, such as speed, when comparing models. Producers choose what type of jet ski to make based on profit maximization. Assuming perfect competition, profit maximization occurs where price equals marginal cost.

> **Private benefits and costs**
>
> Benefits and costs to the decisionmaker, ignoring benefits and costs to third parties. Third parties are people outside the market transaction who are affected by the product.

Buyers and sellers consider only their personal or private benefits and costs. Private benefits and costs are benefits and costs to the decisionmaker, ignoring benefits and costs to third parties. Third parties are people outside the market transaction who are affected by the product. As explained in Chapter 4, benefits and costs to third parties are known by a variety of names, including third-party effects, spillovers, and most commonly *external benefits and costs* or *externalities*. Recall that externalities are benefits or costs that are not considered by market buyers and sellers. Noise pollution is an externality that affects third parties not powering jet skis.

Other externalities that degrade the environment include sulfur emissions from coal-burning electric power plants and the emission of chlorofluorocarbons (CFCs) associated with aerosol sprays and air conditioners. Sulfur emissions are widely thought to contribute to acid rain, resulting in tree deaths and fish kills. CFCs may be linked to a hole in the atmosphere's ozone layer, which increases the chance of skin cancer from the sun's ultraviolet rays. Automobile emissions contribute to air pollution, which reduces visibility and impairs health.

Everyday externalities include the secondhand effects of cigarette smoke on the health of nonsmokers, as well as cigarette butts tossed out of car windows, farmers' use of pesticides that wash into soil and water with detrimental health effects, and even noise from your next-door neighbor who is having a loud party while you are trying to study for an economics exam. Externalities can be positive as well as negative. You benefit from your classmate's decision to get a flu vaccine.

When externalities are present, competitive markets are not likely to achieve economic efficiency. In competitive markets, price, which reflects marginal private benefit, equals marginal private cost. Efficiency for society requires consideration of both private and social benefits and costs. Social benefits are the sum of benefits to everyone in society, including both private benefits and external benefits. Social costs are the sum of costs to everyone in society, including both private costs and external costs. The condition for economic efficiency occurs when each unit of a good that is produced creates at least as much benefit to society as it does social cost. As a society, we do not want to produce any units of a good that creates more in additional social cost than it creates in extra social benefit. In other words, we do not want our scarce resources used up on items that will not enhance our collective well-being. A succinct way of stating this condition for maximizing social welfare is to produce units of any good up to the point where

> **Social benefits and costs**
> The sum of benefits to everyone in society, including both private benefits and external benefits. Social costs are the sum of costs to everyone in society, including both private costs and external costs.

Marginal social benefit = marginal social cost

Environmental regulations force market participants to include externalities in their decision making. For example, U.S. regulations prohibit the use of CFCs in air conditioners, aerosol cans, and other products. Although regulations like the ban on CFCs reduce emissions, they are not necessarily the most efficient approach to achieving less pollution.

Alternatively, instead of mandating the technology to achieve the goal, the government can specify the goal, but leave the method to achieve the goal up to the firm. Suppose businesses wish to expand in areas with high levels of pollution. As an alternative to reducing their own emissions, they can pay another party to reduce its emissions to meet the regulation. For example, a steel company wishing to expand can buy up old cars and retire them as a way of reducing emissions. It may be cheaper for the company to pay someone else to reduce emissions than to achieve an in-house reduction. We discuss this approach in more detail later in the chapter in the section on emissions trading.

Private and Social Costs

When a producer of jet skis or any other product chooses a production method, the producer is motivated by profit maximization. To maximize profit, the firm must choose the most efficient, least costly production method. Production costs include the costs of capital, labor, natural resources (such as land or energy), and entrepreneurship. External costs to others, such as pollution, are not included in production costs because the firm considers only its private costs. Social costs include private costs and external costs.

Competition and External Costs

Suppose considerable amounts of carbon emissions are produced by gasoline pow-ered lawn mowers. To reduce pollution, the manufacturer must redesign the engine. Also, suppose there is a lawn mower manufacturer, GreenAcres, that considers social costs. It will choose a different production method for lower emissions lawn mowers. This production method for lower emissions lawn mowers must have a higher cost than the method used by other, more polluting lawn mowers produced by other firms. If this were not the case, other companies would already be using this method.

In a perfectly competitive market, consumers perceive all products as identical. While there may be exceptions, the typical consumer will pay no more for an envi-ronmentally friendly GreenAcres mower than for other lawn mowers. In the short run, GreenAcres will earn less than other firms because its costs are higher. In the long run, GreenAcres will lose money and eventually go out of business. Only the lowest-cost firms will survive in the long run. Since price exactly equals minimum private average (and marginal) cost in the long run, average cost for the environ-mentally conscious company will lie above price, resulting in losses and eventual exit from the industry.

| EXHIBIT 1 | A Comparison of Costs for Typical and "Green" Firms |

A "green" firm has higher costs in both the short run and the long run. The typical firm considers only private costs, as shown by *MPC* (marginal private cost) in Part (a) and *APC* (average private cost) in Part (b). The "green" firm includes both private and external costs, as shown by *MSC* (marginal social cost) in Part (a) and *ASC* (average social cost) in Part (b). These curves reflect social costs. In the short run, price in a competitive industry equals marginal pri-vate cost. The "green" firm produces a smaller quantity than the competitive firm. In the long run, price equals mini-mum long-run average private cost in a competitive industry. Minimum cost for the "green" firm is above price, so the "green" firm loses money and eventually leaves the industry.

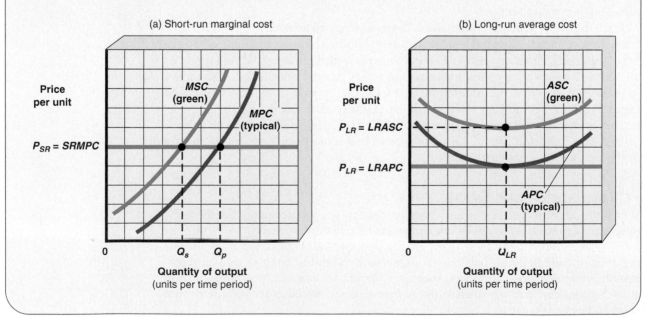

Exhibit 1(a) compares the typical and the "green" lawn mower companies in the short run. Exhibit 1(b) compares the two companies in the long run. The typical company chooses the lowest-cost method of production considering *private cost* only. Its marginal private cost and average private cost are shown as *MPC* and *APC*, respectively. The "green" company chooses the production method that has the lowest marginal and average *social cost*, shown as *MSC* and *ASC*, respectively. In the short run, *MSC* lies above *MPC*, so that the "green" company produces less. In the long run, *ASC* lies above *APC*, so the "green" company loses money and eventually exits the industry.

Competitive Market Inefficiency When Externalities Exist

In competition, only firms that choose the lowest-cost method of production will survive. Firms that choose higher-cost methods will lose money and eventually exit the industry. There is no room for GreenAcres or any firm that does not minimize cost.

Rewarding firms that ignore externalities while punishing firms that recognize externalities is not socially efficient. Efficiency requires that price reflect marginal social benefit and equal marginal social cost. Competition results in a price that reflects marginal private benefit and equals marginal private cost. Efficiency requires that all relevant opportunity costs be included in marginal social cost, while competition forces firms to consider only private costs if they are to survive. If they are allowed to, competitive firms will ignore harmful by-products of their products, such as pollution, climate change, and congestion.

Exhibit 2 shows lawn mower market equilibrium in a competitive market of traditional firms compared to a market of environmentally sensitive "green" firms. Competitive industry supply, S_P, sums the *marginal private costs* of "typical" individual firms that ignore externalities, while "green" industry supply, S_S, sums the *marginal social costs* of GreenAcres and other firms that recognize external costs in their engine design.

When externalities are present, competition leads to a lower price and a larger quantity than the socially efficient point (also see Exhibit 8(a) in Chapter 4). By ignoring external costs, competitive firms produce "too much," and the market equilibrium price is "too low," compared to a socially efficient industry. Competition leads to too many lawn mowers bought and sold because neither the buyers nor the sellers take into account the external cost of lawn mower engines that release emissions when used for mowing. When there are external costs, the efficient point is at the intersection of the demand curve and the social supply curve, S_S.

From society's point of view, the efficient outcome is an equilibrium quantity of Q_s lawn mowers sold at price P_s. Associated with this outcome is a smaller quantity of pollution than the quantity at the competitive equilibrium. The quantity of pollution associated with quantity Q_s of lawn mowers is the efficient quantity of pollution.

If left to the competitive market, profit-maximizing producers would have no reason to reduce emissions. Emissions reductions, if they occurred at all, would be only an unintended by-product of technological change. For example, if manufacturers substitute a smaller engine so as to reduce lawn mower fuel use, the smaller engine would emit fewer pollutants. The emissions reduction is a by-product of the market reward for a more fuel-efficient mower, which consumers want and are willing to pay for. For emissions reduction to be worthwhile in its own right in a competitive market, it is necessary that consumers be willing to pay for a lower emissions mower.

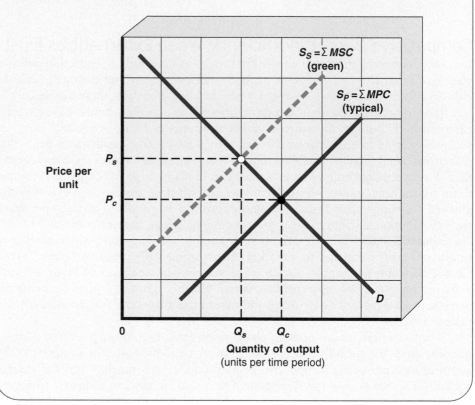

EXHIBIT 2   A Comparison of Equilibriums for Typical Competitive and "Green" Industries

A typical competitive industry operates at price P_c, below the socially efficient price P_s, which would be charged by "green" firms, including all social costs. The competitive industry produces too large a quantity Q_c compared to the socially efficient quantity Q_s and charges too low a price P_c compared to the socially efficient "green" industry price P_s.

Why won't consumers offer more for a cleaner mower, just as they might for a more fuel-efficient one? First, consider choosing between two mowers that are identical except that one mower uses one gallon of gas per acre, while the other uses two gallons per acre. You will be willing to pay more for the first mower because you will get to keep the full monetary benefit of reduced fuel purchases.

Now suppose you must choose between two identical mowers except that the "green" mower emits only half as much pollution as the other one. The typical consumer will not be willing to pay more for the "green" mower because individually he or she will get only a negligible benefit. Benefits will extend to everyone, in the form of cleaner air and reduced global warming. Furthermore, if others buy "green" mowers, you will get the benefits whether or not you purchase a low-emission machine. You are better off being a *free rider*. Recall from the definition of a public good in Chapter 4 that a free rider is someone who enjoys benefits without paying the cost. You will get the same benefit of cleaner air whether or not you buy the clean mower. So you will choose to be a free rider and pay nothing for cleaner

Free rider

An individual who enjoys benefits without paying the costs.

air, rather than paying extra to get a low-emission machine and still breathing the same cleaner air.

The end result is that no one buys a low-emission mower. Each individual chooses to free-ride, hoping to benefit from others who choose the "green" model. Once again, competitive markets are unlikely to be efficient.

> **Conclusion** *Unregulated competitive markets will oversupply and under-price products that pollute.*

Efficient Quantity of Pollution

The efficient production level for society is where marginal social benefit equals marginal social cost. The efficient amount of pollution is the amount generated at the socially efficient output level. It is of utmost importance to recognize that the efficient quantity of pollution is not zero. Zero pollution would require zero lawn mowers. Unless society is willing to abandon the American ideal of a neatly trimmed, emerald green lawn, there will continue to be lawn mowers. Nor is it likely that many Americans will return to manual push mowers that do not require fuel, but are slower and take more effort to use than gasoline-engine mowers.

Other alternatives to consider are reduced-emission or emission-free lawn mowers, such as electric mowers. For a parallel situation, consider alternatives to conventional gasoline-engine automobiles. Alternatives include solar and electric vehicles, as well as other transport modes, such as bus, rail, and bicycle. Solar cars, powered by photovoltaic cells, and hydrogen-powered cars are among the virtually emission-free alternatives. But a fundamental concept in economics is that there are tradeoffs. Currently, the cost of solar and hydrogen cars is too high given society's unwillingness to pay for reduced emissions. Performance may suffer as well; solar cars, for example, are slower and less able to climb mountainous terrain than gasoline-powered cars.

Achieving Environmental Efficiency

Competitive markets fail to produce the socially efficient quantity when there are externalities. Externalities are a cause of market failure. As explained in Chapter 4, market failure occurs when the private market fails to produce society's preferred outcome.

When there is market failure, we must consider alternatives to the market to achieve efficiency. Government has a potential role when market failure occurs. Just as government can apply antitrust laws when an industry is not competitive, government can apply environmental laws when an industry ignores external costs. Not only are cars required to have catalytic converters, but many states also require annual inspections to make sure the converters are working properly (and also to check that consumers have not removed the converters in order to improve gas mileage!).

In the environmental arena, as in other areas of government intervention, there is always the possibility of government failure. Government failure occurs when the government fails to correct market failure. Government officials may fail to achieve an efficient outcome either by doing too little about pollution or by doing too much.

Market failure
A situation in which market equilibrium results in too few or too many resources used in the production of a good or service.

Government failure
Government intervention or lack of intervention that fails to correct market failure.

Government officials motivated to keep their jobs may be influenced by large campaign contributors as well as by voter desires. A Michigan legislator is likely to be sympathetic to the concerns of the auto industry and will also be aware of the autoworker layoffs and unemployment that accompany reduced car production. The official may be less motivated by externalities that are borne by third parties who do not vote in Michigan. On the other hand, a New York legislator may support an overly strict emissions standard for automobiles. New York voters benefit from cleaner air and are less concerned about auto-industry job losses.

Much of the effort of environmental economists has gone toward improving the odds that government will help, rather than hinder, attempts to reach environmental goals. Economists generally favor incentive-based regulations over command-and-control regulations. Incentive-based (IB) regulations set an environmental goal, but are flexible as to how buyers and sellers achieve the goal. Incentive-based regulations can make it profitable for firms to reduce emissions. Command-and-control (CAC) regulations set an environmental goal and also dictate how the goal will be achieved. Firms unable to meet the goal are penalized, and those that exceed it are not rewarded.

The advantage of IB over CAC regulations is comparable to the advantages of a market system over those of a command system. Market systems are more efficient because they allow gains from comparative advantage. Businesses can pursue activities with low opportunity costs. Similarly, allowing firms to choose how to achieve environmental goals encourages firms that can improve at low cost to reduce emissions more than firms less able to achieve lower emissions.

More efficiency gains are obtainable from IB regulations than from CAC regulations in both the short run and long run. In the short run, allowing firms to choose how they will reduce emissions is more efficient than prescribing a single approach because firms incur different opportunity costs to lower emissions. In the long run, firms have an incentive to further reduce emissions by improving their technology. It is possible, though unlikely, that CAC regulations will be as efficient as IB regulations in the short run, just as it is possible, though unlikely, that a command system will happen to choose the lowest cost method of production. In the long run, however, command systems do not encourage innovative technology. There is no reward for improving, only a penalty for not meeting the standard. Let's consider how CAC and IB regulations reduce auto emissions.

Command-and-Control Regulations

In the 1970s, the U.S. government mandated the use of catalytic converters to reduce auto pollutants. The converter results in reduced hydrocarbon emissions associated with the burning of gasoline. While the catalytic converter undoubtedly reduces pollution, it suffers from several inefficiencies.

First, the requirement that cars have catalytic converters is uniform throughout the country. The marginal car in a high-pollution region, such as Los Angeles, has a much higher external cost than the same car driven across the prairies of Kansas. Efficiency calls for stricter regulations in automobile-intensive regions, such as Los Angeles. Second, there may be other technologies that can achieve the same reduced emissions at a lower cost. Finally, automakers have little incentive to invest in better future technology because the regulations require the firm to meet, but not beat, the standard.

A more subtle inefficiency is that CAC regulations may act as a barrier to entry to other firms, both domestic and international. The U.S. auto industry

---

Incentive-based regulations

Government regulations that set an environmental goal, but are flexible as to how buyers and sellers achieve the goal.

Command-and-control regulations

Government regulations that set an environmental goal and dictate how the goal will be achieved.

initially resisted environmental controls, knowing that controls would drive up costs. Foreign manufacturers, such as the Japanese automakers, already met the proposed U.S. standards, but achieved their goal with a different technology. Catalytic converters put the Japanese at a temporary cost disadvantage. Japanese cars were required to have catalytic converters even though they already met the air quality standard.

Another example of CAC regulations is the use of Corporate Average Fuel Economy (CAFE) standards. These oft-discussed standards require each automaker to achieve a minimum number of miles per gallon (mpg) for its fleet. For example, Ford's cars might be required to achieve at least 27 mpg. When this standard was imposed, Ford and other manufacturers invented minivans and sport utility vehicles (SUVs), which were classified as trucks and therefore not subject to the standard. Until the recent upswing in gas prices, consumers shifted to minivans and SUVs despite their lower fuel efficiency. In the end, Ford met the higher fuel standard, while the average mpg of vehicles actually on the road decreased!

Incentive-Based Regulations

Effluent Taxes   The simplest type of incentive-based (IB) regulation is an effluent tax. An effluent tax is a tax on the pollutant. If car manufacturers face a tax that depends on emissions, they can no longer ignore externalities. They must consider the tax based on emissions in addition to private resource costs. Exhibit 3 shows how an effluent tax can achieve efficiency.

A less direct way of reducing pollutants is a gasoline tax. By increasing the price of gasoline to car owners, the tax results in a smaller quantity demanded of gasoline and, in turn, lower emissions. Over time, consumers faced with high gas prices seek more fuel-efficient cars, lowering emissions even more.

Taxes can achieve efficiency directly or indirectly and can be placed on buyers or sellers. Although the tax approach may appear simple in theory, some important practical difficulties limit the use of pollution taxes. First, how do we measure external cost? There is no market that buys and sells air pollution or climate change. So the tax is at best an approximation of external cost. Second, studies that have attempted to measure external cost find it to be quite large, requiring a substantial tax. It is widely thought that the price of a gallon of gasoline would have to increase by $1 to approximate the external costs of auto emissions. Such a $1 tax, added to the approximately 40 cents in gasoline taxes that are already imposed to pay for roads, would be unpopular with voters and as a consequence are unattractive to politicians.

Those who favor the effluent tax approach propose that its revenues could be used for a variety of purposes, one of which could be a reduction in income taxes. If so, this approach is referred to as a *double dividend*. Lower pollution is one dividend, and lower taxes on income is another dividend because lower income taxes encourage work effort. But there is no guarantee that the funds from the effluent tax will be used to reduce incomes taxes.

Emissions Trading   What if there were a market in which air pollution or climate change could be traded? As a result of the 1990 amendments to the Clean Air Act, there are markets for emissions trading. Emissions trading allows firms to buy and sell the right to pollute. The most active market so far is for sulfur emissions. Sulfur dioxide causes increased rain acidity. Acid rain can cause damage to lakes, trees, and even cars.

Effluent tax
A tax on the pollutant.

Emissions trading
Firms buying and selling the right to pollute.

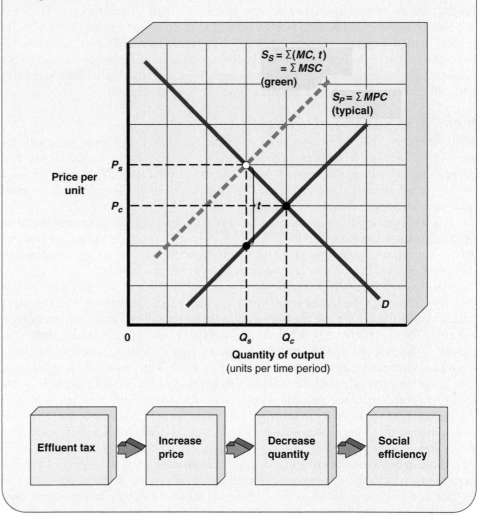

EXHIBIT 3   Using an Effluent Tax to Achieve Environmental Efficiency

An effluent tax can achieve efficiency. The tax, t, equals marginal external cost, which is the difference between marginal social cost (MSC) and marginal private cost (MPC) at the socially efficient quantity (Q_s). The firm's production costs now include both its private costs and the effluent tax, so it makes production decisions as if it considered marginal social cost.

$S_S = \Sigma(MC, t)$
$= \Sigma MSC$
(green)

$S_P = \Sigma MPC$
(typical)

Price per unit

P_s

P_c

t

D

0   Q_s Q_c

Quantity of output
(units per time period)

Effluent tax ⇨ Increase price ⇨ Decrease quantity ⇨ Social efficiency

There are markets for air pollution rights. A firm that wishes to build new factories that would add to pollution in an already polluted area may have to find *offsets* before it can relocate. An offset is a reduction in an existing pollution source that offsets a new pollution source. For example, U.S. Generating Company, an independent power producer, offered in 1992 to buy up automobile "clunkers" in return for permission to expand a coal-fired generating facility that would use the Deleware River and pollute the air. Under this program, the company offered to pay $500 to owners of cars that are at least 16 years old. The factory scraps the old

Offset

Reduction in an existing pollution source to counteract pollution from a new source.

clunkers, thereby offsetting its new source of pollution. The clunker approach makes use of the fact that a small percentage of cars are responsible for a disproportionate share of pollution.

To set up trading for lawn mower or car emissions, the government could require manufacturers to buy permits for each unit of emissions. In the short run, firms would include the cost of permits along with private costs as a component of price. The price would increase most for the dirtiest machines. In the long run, firms would have an incentive to build cleaner products. Firms with the cleanest products would need the fewest permits and might even profit by selling permits to companies that cannot improve as quickly. Whereas GreenAcres lawn mowers would go out of business in an unfettered competitive lawn mower industry, the company would now be in a position to succeed.

Alternatively, emissions trading for cars could be attached to CAFE standards. Auto manufacturers would have to possess permits based on gasoline use. This system would allow manufacturers with more fuel-efficient fleets to sell permits to manufacturers relying on larger less fuel-efficient cars.

A simple example can demonstrate the cost savings of an IB approach, such as emissions trading, compared to a CAC approach. Suppose two coal-fired electric plants each emit 100 tons of sulfur into the air. Plant A can reduce sulfur at a constant cost of $100/ton, while plant B can do so at a cost of $200/ton. The Environmental Protection Agency (EPA) announces that it wishes to cut sulfur emissions in half. Under CAC regulations, each plant will reduce its emissions to 50 tons, a reduction of 100 tons. The cost to plant A is $100/ton × (50 tons) = $5,000. The cost to plant B is $200/ton × (50 tons) = $10,000. The total cost to society of achieving a 100-unit reduction in sulfur emissions is $15,000.

Now suppose the EPA announces that it will give away 100 emissions permits, 50 to plant A and 50 to plant B. Each plant now is allowed to emit 50 units of sulfur. If the two plants do nothing more, each will have to reduce emissions from 100 to 50 tons, and each will do so at the same cost as with CAC regulations. However, there is a lower cost solution. Plant A is willing to sell its 50 permits at any price above $100/ton because it can reduce its emissions in-house for $100/ton. Plant B is willing to buy emissions permits at any price below $200/ton, the marginal cost of reducing its own emissions. Both plants can gain by plant A selling an additional 50 permits to plant B at a price between $100 and $200.

Suppose they agree to a price of $150/ton. Plant A now finds it profitable to eliminate all its emissions. Its marginal cost of reducing emissions is $100/ton. By reducing its emissions to zero, Plant A no longer needs any permits. It can sell its 50 permits for $150/ton, making a profit of $50 per ton by reducing its emissions to zero (at a cost of $100/ton) and selling its permits to Plant B (at a gain of $150/ton). In turn, plant B finds it cheaper to buy permits for $150/ton than to reduce emissions, at a cost of $200/ton.

In sum, the net cost to reduce emissions by 100 tons for Plant A is $100/ton × (100 tons) − $150/ton × (50 tons) = $2,500. The cost to plant B, now that it no longer reduces emissions, is $150/ton × (50 tons) = $7,500. The cost to society of achieving a 100-unit reduction in emissions is $10,000, which is $5,000 less than under the original CAC method.

The real world helps us see problems that textbook theory does not always reveal. Emissions trading has the theoretical potential to achieve environmental goals at the lowest cost, but, so far, real-world trading has fallen short of efficiency. There are a number of obstacles to efficient trading, some minor and some major.

Taking the factory and clunker example, one minor problem is a new-source bias. A new-source bias occurs when regulations provide an incentive to keep assets past the efficient point. A firm faced with the need to find offsets if it builds a new factory may stick with an older and dirtier factory rather than paying for offsets. If there were no offset program, it might have been economical to retire the old factory in favor of a less-polluting new factory. But if the new factory cannot meet the air quality standard without offsets, the lowest-cost solution becomes extending the life of the old plant. Electric utilities are also finding it worthwhile to continue to operate old coal-fired plants that are exempt from stringent regulations known as New Source Performance Standards that can only be met by newer technology. There also may be a type of free-rider problem. Car owners about to junk their 15-year-old clunkers for $25 may keep them another year if a firm might be willing to pay $500 for them. These minor problems are just growing pains of emissions trading, and future emissions markets will find ways to reduce these undesirable outcomes.

Other growing pains include small numbers of buyers or sellers, imperfect information about the value of a permit, and concerns about permit value in the future. Firms will trade actively only if trading is a better alternative than other alternatives. Some firms may shut down or perhaps relocate in other countries where permits are not needed. Also, emissions may be higher in regions where electric utilities buy permits rather than reduce emissions. The Tennessee Valley Authority has been a buyer of permits. Not only does Tennessee's air qualify suffer, but North Carolina believes its air quality is also compromised as pollution drifts east.

Nevertheless, emissions trading is here to stay. The government may initiate emissions trading by distributing permits according to production or pollution over a designated period, or it may sell permits through an auction to the highest bidders. Buyers may be electric utilities, or they may be environmentalists. Environmentalists can achieve pollution reduction by outbidding utilities for permits and then refusing to sell them to utilities, thereby forcing the utilities to reduce pollution.

The Chicago Board of Trade, or "Smog" Exchange, allows trading in pollution permits much like trading on the New York Stock Exchange. Companies are required to own a permit for each unit of emissions. Clean companies need fewer permits and offer to sell their extra permits on the exchange. Dirty companies need additional permits and are buyers on the exchange. They will only buy if the permit price is less than what it would cost them to reduce pollution by one more unit. Sellers of permits will charge at least what it costs them to reduce pollution by one more unit.

Exhibit 4 shows the permit price per ton of sulfur dioxide allowances since trading began in 1994. Over the years, the permit price has fluctuated widely from as low as $60 to a high of almost $1,600 after a sharp reduction in permits with the passage by the EPA of the Clean Air Interstate Act on March 10, 2005. Recently, the EPA has introduced a market for the trading of nitrogen oxides (NO_x), which contributes to smog.

There is concern that the benefits of emissions trading will be diminished by lack of trading and lingering opposition to the idea of creating a market for pollution rights, especially when permits are given away rather than auctioned. There is even a revival of interest in command-and-control regulation. If the government happens to pick the right approach and rewards cleaner technology, some economists favor CAC over the imperfect emissions trading to date. For example, there are supporters of California's approach to reducing auto emissions. California

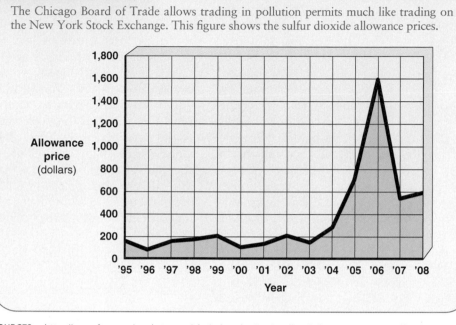

| EXHIBIT 4 | Monthly Average Price of Sulfur Dioxide Allowances under the Acid Rain Program |

The Chicago Board of Trade allows trading in pollution permits much like trading on the New York Stock Exchange. This figure shows the sulfur dioxide allowance prices.

SOURCES: http://www.ferc.gov/market-oversight/othr-mkts/emiss-allow/othr-emns-no-so-pr.pdf and http://www.epa.gov/airmarkets/progress/arp06.html.

considered a requirement that 10 percent of the cars sold within California must be emissions free. They anticipated that the mandate would be met with electric vehicles (EVs). California is now considering a requirement that a similar percentage of cars be hybrids, rather than EVs.

Critics of the California approach point out that EVs are not emissions free if they require electricity from a power plant. Certainly, power plants also pollute, although there may be an advantage to transferring pollution away from the most densely populated areas. EVs powered by photovoltaic cells (PVCs) that use solar energy are closer to being emissions free, but there is still pollution in the PVC production process. Perhaps the greatest drawback to EVs is their poor performance to date. They suffer from poor acceleration, limited range, and limited ability to climb hills. Critics maintain that inferior products continue to be the legacy of CAC approaches. In response to rising gas prices, Toyota and other car manufacturers responded with gas-electric hybrid vehicles. Critics suggest that the market has a superior ability to innovate, such as a hybrid vehicle with low emissions, as compared to CAC requiring zero emissions that could not be met by a gas-electric hybrid. However, even hybrid electricity use is not pollution free. Battery production is likely to lead to pollution. If the hybrid is recharged by plugging it in, there is still pollution at the electricity plant where the power is generated.

Conclusion *Economists generally believe that incentive-based regulations are more efficient than command-and-control regulations.*

YOU'RE THE ECONOMIST   Does Emissions Trading Work?

Applicable Concepts: emissions trading and command-and-control regulation

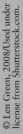

The New York State Legislature in 1894 created the Adirondack Forest Preserve as the first wild land preserve to gain constitutional protection in the United States. Today the Adirondack Park and Forest Preserve is the largest park in the nation outside of Alaska. When the Adirondacks began serving the public, each of its many lakes, rivers, and streams offered an abundant supply of fish and plants.

Now imagine your surprise if you were to approach the water and discover a sign saying "Toxic Water." The threat is real, and it is from the influx of acid rain due to weather patterns blowing in pollution from Southern and Midwestern factories. Attempts have been made to combat the ill effects to the lakes, but the acid rain keeps coming.

Acid rain occurs when coal-fired power plants emit sulfur and nitrogen into the atmosphere because the burning of fossil fuels reacts with moisture in the atmosphere to create nitric and sulfuric acid. The acid then falls to earth in the form of acid rain, snow, or fog.

A major provision in the 1990 Clean Air Act advocated by economists set up a marketplace in which companies can trade the right to pollute in the form of credits, as a commodity. The most active market has been for sulfur dioxide emissions that increase rain acidity. However, electric power plants and automobiles also release nitrogen, which has not been targeted by emissions trading.

A General Accounting Office study in 2000 found that sulfur levels had decreased substantially in 92 percent of the 48 of 52 Adirondack lakes examined, and nitrogen levels were dramatically higher in these tested lakes. The issue for New Yorkers is that a New York State law forced their utilities to cut emissions in the 1980s below federal law requirements. As a result, the good news was a windfall of pollution credits under the 1990 Clean Air Act to sell to companies outside New York that failed to meet the federal pollution standards. But the bad news is that this sale gives companies in other states the right to allow their pollution to blow through the air into New York.

ANALYZE THE ISSUE

1. What has been the primary benefit of emissions trading?
2. Why do investigators believe nitrogen levels have risen?
3. How could emissions trading be expanded to further reduce sulfur emissions and at the same time reduce nitrogen levels?

Source: Based on Raymond Hernandez, "Albany Battles Acid Rain Fed by Other States," May 2, 2000, http://www.nytimes.com.

Still, much of the public seems more comfortable with controls and rules than with prices and trading. There are a number of possible explanations for the public's view. First, people have difficulty accepting that any pollution is efficient. Nobody wants to think about a higher risk of cancer due to a leak from a nuclear power plant.

Another possible reason for the public's view is a mistrust of experts. People were told by experts that nuclear power would be safe, that hazardous waste disposal sites would not leak, and that people living near oil tanks would not have higher risks of cancer. When outcomes differ from what experts promise, the public favors safety over efficiency. No one wants to take a chance on illness or death if the experts are wrong again. And yet would you give up your car or favor a law that set the speed limit at 20 miles per hour? These laws might increase safety, but they would certainly be inefficient.

Government and Environmental Efficiency

Market failure is likely for products with external costs. To achieve efficiency, buyers and sellers must consider external costs. Government has the power to establish laws, taxes, or permit systems so that market participants pay for external costs.

Although government policy can potentially improve efficiency, there is no guarantee. The countries that emerged from the Soviet Union, where government played a far more dominant role than in the United States, have environmental problems that dwarf those in the United States. In these countries, air and water quality borders on ecocide, with high rates of illness due to environmental degradation. The Chernobyl disaster, in which a nuclear plant malfunctioned and released radioactivity, has caused thousands of premature deaths. In China, another nation where the government plays a major role in the economy, the Beijing weather report frequently calls for "smoky" skies.

In the United States, large numbers of U.S. Department of Defense sites are among the biggest environmental challenges. Hazardous wastes from the production of weapons are now leaking in burial sites, including Oak Ridge, Tennessee, and Richland, Washington. The U.S. Forest Service frequently permits lumber companies to harvest trees from national forests at subsidized prices. Government environmental officials have even gone to prison for illegally meeting with industry representatives to weaken environmental regulations. And government has tended to ignore the cost to firms of complying with hundreds of thousands of pages of environmental legislation, a set of regulations more voluminous than the U.S. Tax Code. For all these reasons, as well as the widespread dissatisfaction with government in general, there is concern about the effectiveness of government policy in achieving environmental goals. Government officials may pursue self-interest, which could favor polluting industries over societal interests as a whole, especially if industry executives are major campaign contributors.

The Coase Theorem   Ronald Coase, an economist at the University of Chicago and the winner of the 1991 Nobel Prize in economics, was among the first to caution against the assumption that government intervention in the environmental arena would improve upon private-sector environmental performance. In his famous 1960 paper, "The Problem of Social Cost," he even questioned the fundamental assumption of market failure. According to the Coase Theorem, the private sector could achieve social efficiency with minimal government intervention. The role of the government should be limited to the legal establishment of property rights, with environmental disputes resolved in court. The Coase Theorem is the proposition that private market negotiations can achieve social efficiency regardless of the initial definition of property rights.

As an example of how the Coase Theorem works, consider a train that throws off sparks and occasionally burns a farmer's crops. Exhibit 5 shows railroad profits increasing and farm profits decreasing as more trains run.

Each train has an external cost. Emitted sparks can cause fires, which reduce the farmer's crops. If the railroad ignores external cost, it appears that the railroad

Coase Theorem

The proposition that private market negotiations can achieve social efficiency regardless of the initial definition of property rights.

With the great success of emissions trading in sulfur dioxide, and the emergence of trading in nitrous oxides, we may well turn to emissions trading to reduce carbon emissions in the United States. In fact, Europe has already instituted such an exchange. In 2005, the European Union instituted a carbon-permit system for electric utilities and other major emitters such as steel companies. However, smaller emitters such as smaller industries and non-point sources such as automobiles are not covered.

In some ways, carbon would seem ideally positioned for emissions trading. To the extent that it contributes to global warming, the effect is the same regardless of where that emission takes place. Whether carbon is emitted in France, Spain, or for that matter the United States or China, its effect on the global atmosphere is the same. In this way, carbon is a better candidate for trading than sulfur, which has a greater impact in the vicinity of its release.

But there is increasing questioning of whether or not carbon trading is preferable to a tax on carbon. One contributing argument is the European experience to date, which has been disappointing. By mid-2006, the price of contracts had collapsed to 8 euros. The primary factor was that numerous national governments had issued enough permits that covered producers did not find it necessary to buy permits. In fact, carbon emissions increased in many countries during the first year of the carbon trading regime.

Since that time, there have been reforms in the trading system, and prices have risen. Nevertheless, the possibility that an emissions trading system might not reduce carbon emissions has given impetus to those who argue for a carbon tax.

For those who prefer the tax approach, perhaps the most widespread reason is that the tax will raise revenue. The revenue could provide a double dividend, if it is used to reduce taxes that discourage

would choose to run five trains so as to maximize profit, leaving the farmer with no crops. It also appears that to protect the farmer, there should be a law requiring the railroad to find a spark-free technology.

Suppose the courts establish a law that farmers have the right to spark-free trains. How could the railroad meet this tougher environmental standard? The railroad could change to a new, higher-cost technology. The cost must be higher, or the railroad would have chosen this environmentally friendly technology in the first place. If the cost is too high, the railroad might go out of business or relocate its tracks away from farms. Alternatively, it may be less expensive to offer the farmer money for any burned crops.

If the trains continue to throw off sparks, the first train will reduce the farmer's profits by $5 and will add $20 to the railroad's profits. The two parties will be able to negotiate a deal, with the farmer receiving a payment of between $5 and $20 from the railroad. What about a second train? This train will add another $20 to railroad profits, but will reduce farm profits by $10. Again, the farmer will permit the railroad to run a second train as long as the railroad pays the farmer at least $10. If a third train runs, marginal social benefit will equal marginal social cost.

productive activities, such as the income tax. Of course, the revenues could go toward research and development into carbon-reducing technologies or reduction of the national debt. (Or, tax opponents would point out, it could simply be wasted on pork barrel projects.) While permits could raise revenue if they were auctioned off, rather than given away, the auction would negate one of the main reasons for favoring permits—that industry is willing to support the permit approach because they do not have to pay for the permits.

Other reasons to favor the tax approach include its ability to be more comprehensive, covering all carbon emissions, rather than being limited primarily to large-point sources. It could also be fashioned to include other greenhouse gases, such as methane; farmers, for example, would pay a tax based on the number of cows they owned, and perhaps other animals that emit methane.[1] Some prefer the carbon tax on equity grounds. Particularly if coupled with a reduction in income taxes, the tax could offer relief to lower-income households. In contrast, the main beneficiaries of giving away permits are stockholders, which may represent wealthier citizens.[2]

While taxes are gaining momentum as compared to cap-and-trade, the arguments may turn out to be academic. At least since Ronald Reagan, politicians have shown the power of cutting taxes at the ballot booth. Despite the arguments in favor of the tax approach, trading is likely to face less opposition from industries and consumers. In the end, it may be necessary to learn from Europe's mistakes, and adopt a permit system, even if it is second best.

ANALYZE THE ISSUE

1. What are the advantages and disadvantages of carbon trading, as compared to sulfur dioxide trading?
2. What are the advantages and disadvantages of a tax system, as compared to carbon trading?
3. If a carbon tax is preferable to a trading system on economic grounds, why might we adopt a trading system anyway?

Source: From Fred Pearce, "European Trading in Carbon-Emission Permits Begins." Reprinted by permission of 'New Scientist Magazine'.

1. Jonathan A. Lesser, "Control of Greenhouse Gases Difficult with Cap-and-Trade or Tax-and-Spend," *Natural Gas and Electricity*, December 2007, Wiley Periodicals Inc., http://www3.interscience.wiley.com/cgi-bin/jhome/105559587.
2. Ian W. H. Parry, "Should We Abandon Cap and Trade in Favor of a CO_2 Tax?" *Resources*, Summer 2007, 6–10, *Resources for the Future*, http://www.rff.org/Documents/Rff-Resources-166_ShouldWeAbandoneCapAndTrade.pdf.

Society will benefit from more train service, but will lose from fewer crops. The third train will be marginally worthwhile, but additional trains will not run. The fourth train will add $20 to railroad profits, but will reduce farm profit by $30. Thus, the railroad will lose money if it runs the fourth train. By clearly establishing the farmer's right to spark-free trains, the number of trains will be decreased from five to three trains.

Notice that the farmer will be better off if he or she allows sparks as long as the railroad compensates the farmer for damage than if the government requires a spark-free technology. The farmer earns $105 when there are no sparks. With sparks, the farmer will earn at least $105, receiving between $5 and $20 for permitting the first train, at least $10 (and possibly as much as $20) for permitting the second train, and another $20 for the third train. With three trains, the farmer will still earn $70 from crops, in addition to a minimum of $35 for allowing trains, for a total of at least $105.

This outcome is similar to the government solutions examined earlier. Efficiency leads to the efficient amount of pollution, which is typically not zero. No sparks may mean no trains. But Coase asks, Why assume that society is best served

	EXHIBIT 5			Choosing the Efficient Amounts of Spark-Emitting Trains and Farm Crops		

Number of Trains	Total Railroad Profit	Marginal Railroad Profit	Number of Crops	Total Farm Profit	Marginal Farm Profit
0	$ 0		10.5	$105	
		$20			$ −5
1	20		10	100	
		20			−10
2	40		9	90	
		20			−20
3	60		7	70	
		20			−30
4	80		4	40	
		20			−40
5	100		0	0	

by assuming the railroad is the polluter and the farmer the victim? In the 1800s, sparking engines may have been the best available technology, and an occasional fire may have been a natural consequence.

So consider the outcome if property rights to produce sparks are given to the railroads so that trains are allowed to throw off sparks. If the farmer does nothing, the railroad will run five trains, and the farmer will end up with no crops and no profit. The farmer will increase profit by $40 if only four trains run. Since the fifth train will add only $20 to railroad profit, the farmer can afford to pay as much as $40 (or as little as $20) to stop the fifth train. Similarly, the farmer will gain $30 by stopping the fourth train, more than enough to pay the railroad for forgoing $20 in profit. Once again, negotiations will stop at three trains, the efficient number.

This example demonstrates the Coase Theorem: As long as the courts clearly establish property rights, markets may achieve social efficiency *regardless of the initial assignment of property rights*. Coase's great contribution was to focus attention on property rights, a focus that foreshadowed the emissions-trading approach that allows firms to negotiate by buying and selling the right to pollute. But Coase argues for an even more limited role for government. In his view, the government should establish courts and then let markets negotiate.

Some Limitations on the Coase Theorem　　Coase was instrumental in raising concern about government solutions. It might then seem a simple step to accept his claim that private markets would efficiently resolve environmental problems. In actuality, only a small number of environmental problems readily qualify for Coase Theorem solutions.

First, there are no transactions costs in the Coase Theorem. Transactions costs are the costs of negotiating and enforcing a contract. Turning to the courts is a costly process, in terms of both time and money. And dealing with the source of the externality has its own costs. Have you ever tried to negotiate with a noisy neighbor

Transactions costs

The costs of negotiating and enforcing a contract.

at 2 a.m.? However, there are also transactions costs associated with government solutions. So Coasean negotiations may be preferable to government intervention even when there are substantial private transactions costs.

Second, there are no differences in willingness to pay (WTP) and willingness to accept (WTA) in the Coase Theorem. Many studies have found that people's willingness to pay to acquire a property right, such as an improvement in air quality, is less than the compensation they require to give up a property right, such as accepting lower air quality. If the farmer has the right to spark-free air, he or she may require $50 to allow sparks. Alternatively, if the farmer has to buy that right, he or she may only be willing to pay $20. In other words, people may not view giving up an environmental right you already own as equivalent to buying a right you do not currently own.

Third, Coase assumes there are only two parties in the negotiation. Externalities are typically third-party problems, and there may be many third parties. Do all the farmers get together to negotiate with the railroad, and do all the neighbors get together to reduce noise from the party? With many participants, there is once again a free-rider problem. If noise levels decrease, I get the benefit whether or not I contribute to the negotiations. So why contribute? Stated as a concept, if some individuals benefit while others pay, the free-rider problem is that few will be willing to pay for improvement of the environment or other public goods. As a result, these goods are underproduced.

> **Free-rider problem**
> The problem that if some individuals benefit, while others pay, few will be willing to pay for improvement of the environment or other public goods. As a result, these goods are underproduced.

> **Conclusion** *Neither government nor the markets can be asserted to be the best solution to environmental problems. On balance, though, the effort to work toward improved government solutions seems worthwhile, given the outcome for the environment of purely self-interested markets.*

CHECKPOINT

Is It Efficient to Buy Odor-Reducing Technology If You Live Next to a Hog Farm?

You live next door to a hog farm. It is estimated that the smell from the hog farm reduces the value of your home by $7,000. For $5,000, you can purchase technology that reduces the hog smell by half, so your house value would decrease by only $3,500. Assuming the hog farm has the property right to locate next door and that it is not required to reduce the hog smell, what will you do? Will you do nothing or buy the new technology?

KEY CONCEPTS

Private benefits and costs
Social benefits and costs
Free rider
Market failure
Government failure

Incentive-based regulations
Command-and-control
    regulations
Effluent tax
Emissions trading

Offset
New-source bias
Coase Theorem
Transactions costs
Free-rider problem

SUMMARY

- *Externalities* are benefits or costs that fall on third parties who are neither buyers nor sellers. Pollution is a negative externality or an external cost that is a by-product of many industrial production processes.

- *Market failure* is present when the market produces a socially inefficient outcome. For example, when there are externalities. All firms, including competitive firms, consider private costs, but disregard external costs in making decisions.

- *Government failure* occurs when public-sector actions or lack of actions move us away from desired outcomes, such as efficiency. Government officials seeking campaign contributions and votes may choose environmental measures that favor wealthy contributors over society's best interests.

- *Command-and-control regulations* occur when the government dictates the approach to achieving an environmental goal. Command-and-control regulations are generally inefficient on three grounds: They do not distinguish between high- and low-pollution areas, they do not allow firms to choose lower-cost technologies that could

achieve the environmental standard, and they do not encourage investment in improved technology to lower future emissions.

- *Incentive-based regulations* build on markets to achieve environmental efficiency. **Effluent taxes** are taxes that reflect external costs. **Emissions trading** allows firms to buy and sell the "right to pollute."

- The *Coase Theorem* maintains that markets can be efficient in the presence of externalities with minimal government intervention. Even in the presence of externalities, markets may produce efficient outcomes so long as property rights are clearly established.

- *Transactions costs, income effects,* and *free-rider problems* are obstacles to achieving environmental efficiency through markets. Transactions costs are the costs of negotiating an agreement, income effects are present when limited income prevents one party from being able to afford the efficient solution, and free-rider problems are present when participants are better off hiding than revealing their willingness to pay for an environmental improvement.

SUMMARY OF CONCLUSION STATEMENTS

- Unregulated competitive markets will oversupply and underprice products that pollute.
- Economists generally believe that incentive-based regulations are more efficient than command-and-control regulations.
- Neither government nor the markets can be asserted to be the best solution to environmental

problems. On balance, though, the effort to work toward improved government solutions seems worthwhile, given the outcome for the environment of purely self-interested markets.

STUDY QUESTIONS AND PROBLEMS

1. Compare price and quantity in a competitive industry to those of a "green" industry for a product that generates pollution.

2. Suppose a car sells for $20,000 in a market with no pollution restrictions. Will the car sell for more than $20,000, less than $20,000, or $20,000 when there are pollution restrictions? Explain.

3. You are considering whether to buy one house for $100,000 or another identical house located near high-voltage electric power lines for $90,000. Assume that it has been established that living near high-voltage lines increases the risk of cancer due to electromagnetic fields (EMFs). If you choose the $90,000 house, is the radiation from EMFs an externality? Explain.

4. Restaurants have observed that large parties (eight or more) leave a lower average tip than smaller parties. Identify the effect, which also makes it more difficult to reach global environmental agreements, responsible for this phenomenon.

5. Suppose your instructor gives eight homework assignments during the semester. She indicates that anyone who does not turn in all eight assignments will automatically fail the course. Is this an example of a command-and-control or an incentive-based regulation? Explain any inefficiencies of your instructor's approach.

6. Environmentalists in Tennessee brought suit against the Champion Paper Company of North Carolina for polluting the Pigeon River, which flows from North Carolina into eastern Tennessee. Tennessee claimed that the coffee-colored water smelled bad and would not support fishing or swimming. Environmentalists requested that the river be restored to its pristine state, whereby water quality is restored to the level before the coming of industry. The Environmental Protection Agency heard the suit and applied an efficiency standard. Is pristine water an efficiency standard? Explain.

7. Draw a graph to demonstrate your answer to question 6.

8. California once proposed legislation that would have required 10 percent of its car fleet to be nearly emissions free by the year 2005. This mandate spurred electric vehicle research. Such vehicles could be powered by photovoltaic cells or by batteries that are recharged using an electrical outlet. Would you agree that it is correct to conclude that electric vehicles that use electrical outlets are emissions-free? What about electric vehicles powered by photovoltaic cells?

9. Explain why consumers would not be willing to pay the full costs of a less-polluting car in the absence of government regulations.

10. Evaluate the following statement: "When products pollute, government solutions are more efficient than market solutions."

11. Provide an example of a market where you think the Coase Theorem applies. Explain why you think the market satisfies assumptions regarding transactions costs, income effects, and free riders.

12. In a study of ranching laws in the 1800s, an economic researcher found that as these laws restricted the ability of cattle to roam freely, agricultural output increased. Does this researcher's finding support the Coase Theorem? Explain.

13. If we are to take action against global warming, we must reduce carbon emissions. Explain how to reduce carbon emissions by using
    a.   command-and-control regulation.
    b.   an effluent tax.
    c.   emissions trading.

14. A global agreement known as the Montreal Protocol led to the phase-out of chlorofluorocarbons (CFCs), chemical compounds found in aerosol cans and refrigerants. CFCs may have contributed to the growing hole in the ozone layer. With a diminished ozone layer, there is an increased chance of skin cancer. Explain the effect of this agreement on the price of deodorants and air-conditioning. Also, is a ban on CFCs an efficient approach to the ozone hole problem?

For Online Exercises, go to the text Web site at www.cengage.com/economics/tucker.

CHECKPOINT ANSWER

Is It Efficient to Buy Odor-Reducing Technology If You Live Next to a Hog Farm?

It is not efficient to purchase the new odor-reducing technology. It would cost $5,000, but would increase your house value by only $3,500. It is not efficient to cut the odor by half if the market will not compensate you sufficiently for reduced hog odors. If your only options are to do nothing or to buy the new technology, and you said do nothing, **YOU ARE CORRECT.** (A third option is to pay the hog farm to locate elsewhere. You would be willing to pay up to $7,000 to avoid the $7,000 lost due to the smell of the nearby farm.)

PRACTICE QUIZ

For an explanation of the correct answers, please visit the tutorial at www.cengage.com/economics/tucker.

1. Suppose the city of New Orleans discovered chemical compounds in its drinking water that may cause cancer. Since New Orleans's drinking water comes from the Mississippi River, the source of these chemicals is the waste discharges of industrial plants upstream from New Orleans. This is an example of
   a. an external cost imposed on the citizens of New Orleans by the industrial plants upstream.
   b. a market failure where the market price of the output of these industrial plants does not fully reflect the social cost of producing these goods.
   c. an externality where the marginal social costs of producing these industrial goods differ from the marginal private costs.
   d. all of the above.

2. A government policy that charges steel firms a fee per ton of steel produced (an "effluent charge") where the fee is determined by the amount of pollutants discharged into the air or water will lead to
   a. a decrease in the market equilibrium quantity of steel produced.
   b. a decrease in the market equilibrium price of steel.
   c. an increase in the market equilibrium price of steel.
   d. the results in (a) and (b).
   e. the results in (a) and (c).

3. Social costs are
   a. the full resource costs of an economic activity.
   b. usually less than private costs.
   c. the costs of an economic activity borne by the producer.
   d. all of the above.

4. As a general rule, if pollution costs are external, firms will produce
   a. too much of a polluting good.
   b. too little of a polluting good.
   c. an optimal amount of a polluting good.
   d. an amount that cannot be determined without additional information.

5. Many economists would argue that
   a. the optimal amount of pollution is greater than zero.
   b. all pollution should be eliminated.
   c. the market mechanism can handle pollution without any government intervention.
   d. central planning is the most efficient way to eliminate pollution.

6. Which of the following used marketable pollution permits as an incentive for reducing pollution?
   a. The Clean Air Act of 1970
   b. The Comprehensive Environmental Response, Compensation, and Liability Act of 1980
   c. The Clean Air Act amendments of 1990
   d. The Water Quality and Improvement Act of 1970

7. The disposable diaper industry is perfectly competitive. Which of the following is *true*?
   a. Since the industry is perfectly competitive, price and quantity are at the socially efficient levels.
   b. Competitive price is higher and competitive quantity lower than the socially efficient point.
   c. Competitive price is higher and competitive quantity higher than the socially efficient point.
   d. Competitive price is lower and competitive quantity higher than the socially efficient point.

8. An example of the command-and-control approach to environmental policy is
   a. placing a tax on high-sulfur coal to reduce its use and the corresponding sulfur emissions (which contribute to acid rain).
   b. requiring electric utilities to install scrubbers to reduce sulfur dioxide emissions (which contribute to acid rain).
   c. allowing coal producers to buy and sell permits to allow sulfur emissions.
   d. allowing individuals to sue coal producers if sulfur emissions exceed a government-set standard.

9. The profit-maximizing firm in Exhibit 6 creates water and air pollution as a consequence of producing its output of beef cattle. If pollution costs are borne by third parties, the firm will maximize economic profit by choosing to
   a. voluntarily incur costs to reduce its pollution.
   b. produce at output rate Q_3.

   c. produce at output rate Q_2.
   d. produce at output rate Q_4.

10. To maximize social welfare, the firm in Exhibit 6 should produce at output rate
    a. Q_1.
    b. Q_2.
    c. Q_3.
    d. Q_4.

11. As shown in Exhibit 7, if Orville has the property right to fly over Wilbur's house, but Wilbur is allowed to negotiate with Orville on the number of flights, what will be the number of flights?
    a. 2
    b. 3
    c. 4
    d. 5

12. As shown in Exhibit 7, if Wilbur has the property right to have no planes flying over his house, but Orville is allowed to negotiate with Wilbur, what will be the number of fights?
    a. 2
    b. 3
    c. 4
    d. 5

13. As shown in Exhibit 7, at the socially efficient number of flights, what will be the market value of Orville's house?
    a. $100,000
    b. $95,000
    c. $90,000
    d. $85,000
    e. $80,000

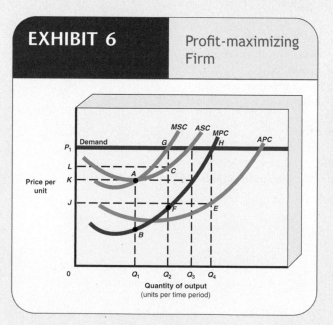

EXHIBIT 6 — Profit-maximizing Firm

EXHIBIT 7 — Impact of Flights on House Value

Number of Flights	Total Profits	Marginal Profits	Value of Wilbur's House
1	$10,000	$10,000	$100,000
2	18,000	8,000	95,000
3	24,000	6,000	90,000
4	28,000	4,000	85,000
5	30,000	2,000	80,000

MICROECONOMIC POLICY ISSUES

This road map feature helps you tie material in the part together as you travel the Economic Way of Thinking Highway. The following are review questions listed by chapter from the previous part. The key concept in each question is given for emphasis, and each question or set of questions concludes with an interactive game to reinforce the concepts. Click on the Tucker Web site, select the chapter, and play the visual causation chain game designed to make learning fun. Enjoy the cheers when correct and suffer the jeers if you miss.

For an explanation of the correct answers, please visit the tutorial at www.cengage.com/economics/tucker.

Chapter 13. Antitrust and Regulation

1. **Key Concept: Imperfect Information**
   Overconsumption of a product can be caused by
   a. excessive resources devoted to producing a product.
   b. consumers paying too low a price for a product.
   c. lack of knowledge about a product.
   d. All of the above are true.
   e. None of the above are true.

2. **Key Concept: Imperfect Information**
   Which of the following may be the result of a higher equilibrium price for a product?
   a. Advertising.
   b. Expectations.
   c. Imperfect information.
   d. All of the above are true.
   e. None of the above are true.

3. **Key Concept: Imperfect Information**
   Deficient information on unsafe products can cause
   a. overconsumption of a product.
   b. waste of resources used to produce a product.
   c. consumers to pay a higher price for a product.
   d. All of the above are true.
   e. None of the above are true.

Causation Chain Game
The Impact of Imperfect Information on the Market—Exhibit 6

Chapter 14. Environmental Economics

4. **Key Concept: Effluent Tax**
    Incentive-based regulations
    a. set an environmental goal, but are flexible on how to achieve the goal.
    b. obtain more efficiency gains than is obtainable from CAC regulations.
    c. include effluent taxes.
    d. All of the above are true.
    e. None of the above are true.

5. **Key Concept: Effluent Tax**
    In order to increase society's total welfare (social efficiency), a production process that produces a negative externality should be
    a. taxed.
    b. provided by the government.
    c. ignored.
    d. subsidized.

6. **Key Concept: Effluent Tax**
    A government policy that charges coal producers a fee per ton of coal produced (an "effluent charge") where the fee is determined by the amount of pollutants discharged into the air or water, will lead to a (an)
    a. decrease in the market equilibrium quantity of coal produced.
    b. decrease in the market equilibrium price of coal.
    c. increase in the market equilibrium price of coal.
    d. (a) and (c).

7. **Key Concept: Effluent Tax**
    In order to achieve efficiency, the size of an effluent tax should be based on
    a. the external cost created by the pollutant.
    b. people's willingness to pay for a cleaner environment.
    c. the expense of installing new "green" equipment.
    d. the number of free riders in the industry.

 Causation Chain Game
Environmental Efficiency and Effluent Taxes

Macroeconomic Fundamentals

The three chapters in this part explain key measures of how well the macroeconomy is performing. Knowledge of this material is vital to the discussion of macro theory and policy in the next part. The first chapter in this part explains GDP computation. The next chapter begins by teaching how to measure business cycles and concludes with an examination of unemployment. The final chapter in this part explores the measurement and consequences of inflation.

Gross Domestic Product

© David Muir/Digital Vision/Getty Images.

Measuring the performance of the economy is an important part of life. Suppose one candidate for president of the United States proclaims that the economy's performance is the best in a generation, and the opposing presidential candidate argues that the economy is performing poorly. Which statistics would you seek to tell how well the economy is doing? The answer requires understanding some of the nuts and bolts of *national income accounting.* National income accounting is the system used to measure the aggregate income and expenditures for a nation. Despite certain limitations, the national income accounting system provides a valuable indicator of an economy's performance. For example, you can visit the Internet and check the annual *Economic Report of the President* to compare the size or growth of the U.S. economy between years.

Prior to the Great Depression, there were no national accounting procedures for estimating the data required to assess the economy's performance. To provide accounting methodologies for macro data, the late economist Simon Kuznets published a small report in 1934 titled *National Income, 1929–32.* For his pioneering work, Kuznets, the "father of GDP," earned the 1971 Nobel Prize in economics. Today, thanks in large part to Kuznets, most countries use common national accounting methods. National income accounting serves a nation similar to the manner in which accounting serves a business or household. In each case, accounting methodology is vital for identifying economic problems and formulating plans for achieving goals.

Gross Domestic Product

The most widely reported measure throughout the world of a nation's economic performance is gross domestic product (GDP), which is the market value of all final goods and services produced in a nation during a period of time, usually a year. GDP therefore excludes production abroad by U.S. businesses. For example, GDP excludes General Motors' earnings on its foreign operations. On the other hand, GDP includes Toyota's profits from its car plants in the United States. Why is GDP important? One advantage of GDP is that it avoids the "apples and oranges" measurement problem. If an economy produces 10 apples one year and 10 oranges the next, can we say that the value of output has changed in any way? To answer this question, we must attach price tags in order to evaluate the relative monetary value of apples and oranges to society. This is the reason GDP measures value using dollars, rather than listing the number of cars, heart transplants, legal cases, toothbrushes, and tanks produced. Instead, the market-determined dollar value establishes the monetary importance of production. In GDP calculations, "money talks." That is, GDP relies on markets to establish the relative value of goods and services.

GDP is compiled by The Bureau of Economic Analysis (BEA), which is an agency of the Commerce Department. GDP requires that we give the following two points special attention: (1) GDP counts only new domestic production, and (2) it counts only final goods.

> **Gross domestic product (GDP)**
> The market value of all final goods and services produced in a nation during a period of time, usually a year.

GDP Counts Only New Domestic Production

National income accountants calculating GDP carefully exclude transactions in two major areas: secondhand transactions and nonproductive financial transactions.

Secondhand Transactions   *Current* GDP does not include the sale of a used car or the sale of a home constructed some years ago. Such transactions are merely exchanges of previously produced goods and not *current* production of new goods that add to the existing stock of cars and homes. However, the sales commission on a used car or a home produced in another GDP period counts in current GDP because the salesperson performed a service during the present period of time.

Nonproductive Financial Transactions   GDP does not count purely private or public financial transactions, such as giving private gifts, buying and selling stocks and bonds, and making transfer payments. A transfer payment is a government payment to individuals not in exchange for goods or services currently produced. Welfare, Social Security, veterans' benefits, and unemployment benefits are transfer payments. These transactions are considered nonproductive because they do not represent production of any new or *current* output. Similarly, stock market transactions represent only the exchange of certificates of ownership (stocks) or indebtedness (bonds) and not actual new production.

> **Transfer payment**
> A government payment to individuals not in exchange for goods or services currently produced.

GDP Counts Only Final Goods

The popular press usually defines GDP as simply "the value of all goods and services produced." This is technically incorrect because GDP counts only final goods, which are finished goods and services produced for the ultimate user. Including all goods and services produced would inflate GDP by *double counting* (counting many items more than once). In order to count only final goods and avoid overstating GDP, national income accountants must take care not to include intermediate goods. Intermediate goods are goods and services used as inputs for the production of final goods. Stated differently, intermediate goods are not produced for consumption by the ultimate user.

> **Final goods**
> Finished goods and services produced for the ultimate user.

> **Intermediate goods**
> Goods and services used as inputs for the production of final goods.

Suppose a wholesale distributor sells glass to an automaker. This transaction is not included in GDP. The glass is an intermediate good used in the production of cars. When a customer buys a new car from the car dealer, the value of the glass is included in the car's selling price, which is the value of a final good counted in GDP. Let's consider another example. A wholesale distributor sells glass to a hardware store. GDP does not include this transaction because the hardware store is not the final user. When a customer buys the glass from the hardware store to repair a broken window, the final purchase price of the glass is added to GDP as a consumer expenditure.

Measuring GDP

GDP is like an enormous puzzle with many pieces to fit together, including markets for products, markets for resources, consumers spending and earning money, and businesses spending and earning money. How can one fit all these puzzle pieces together? One way to understand how all these concepts fit together is to use a simple macroeconomic model called the circular flow model. The circular flow model shows the flow of products from businesses to households and the flow of resources from households to businesses. In exchange for these resources, money payments flow between businesses and households. Exhibit 1 shows the circular flow in a hypothetical economy with no government, no financial markets, and no foreign trade. In this ultra-simple pure market economy, only the households and the businesses make decisions.

> **Circular flow model**
> A diagram showing the flow of products from businesses to households and the flow of resources from households to businesses. In exchange for these resources, money payments flow between businesses and households.

The Circular Flow Model

The upper half of the diagram in Exhibit 1 represents *product markets,* in which households exchange money for goods and services produced by firms. The *supply* arrow in the top loop represents all finished products and the value of services produced, sold, and delivered to consumers. The *demand* arrow in the top loop shows why the businesses make this effort to satisfy the consuming households. When

EXHIBIT 1   The Basic Circular Flow Model

In this simple economy, households spend all their income in the upper loop and demand consumer goods and services from businesses. Businesses seek profits by supplying goods and services to households through the product markets. Prices and quantities in individual markets are determined by the market supply and demand model. In the factor markets in the lower loop, resources (land, labor, and capital) are owned by households and supplied to businesses that demand these factors in return for money payments. The forces of supply and demand determine the returns to the factors—for example, wages and the quantity of labor supplied. Overall, goods and services flow clockwise, and the corresponding payments flow counterclockwise.

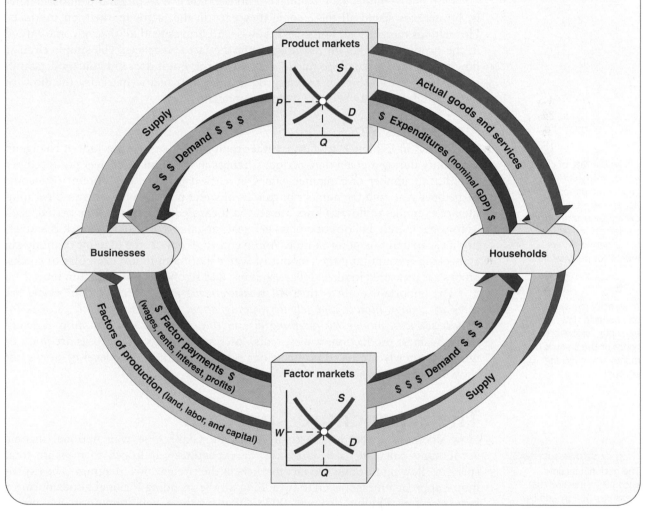

consumers decide to buy products, they are actually voting with their dollars. This flow of consumption expenditures from households is sales revenues to businesses and expenses from the viewpoint of households. Notice that the box labeled *product markets* contains a supply and demand graph. This means the forces of supply and demand in individual markets determine the price and quantity of each product exchanged without government interference.

The bottom half of the circular flow diagram consists of the *factor markets*, in which firms *demand* the natural resources, labor, capital, and entrepreneurship needed to produce the goods and services sold in the product markets. Our hypothetical economy is capitalistic, and the model assumes for simplicity that households own the factors of production. Businesses therefore must purchase all their resources from the households. The *supply* arrow in the bottom loop represents this flow of resources from households to firms, and the *demand* arrow is the flow of money payments for these resources. These payments are also income earned by households in the form of wages, rents, interest, and profits. As in the product markets, market supply and demand determine the price and quantity of factor payments.

Our simple model also assumes all households live from hand to mouth. That is, households spend all the income they earn in the factor markets on products. Households therefore do not save. Likewise, all firms spend all their income earned in the product markets on resources from the factor markets. The simple circular flow model therefore fails to mirror the real world. But it does aid your understanding of the relationships between product markets, factor markets, the flow of money, and the theory behind GDP measurement.

Flow versus Stock

The arrows in Exhibit 1 are flows, rather than stocks. A flow is a rate of change in a quantity during a given time period. Changes in the amount of steel produced per month, the number of computer games purchased per day, the amount of income earned per year, and the number of gallons of water pouring into a bathtub per minute are examples of flows. Flows are always measured in units per time period, such as tons per month, billions of dollars per year, or gallons per hour. A stock is a quantity measured at one point in time. An inventory of goods, the amount of money in a checking account, and the amount of water in a bathtub are examples of stocks. Stocks are measured in tons, dollars, gallons, and so on at a given point in time.

The important point is this: *All measurements in the circular flow model are rates of change (flows) and tell us nothing about the total amounts (stocks) of goods, services, money, or anything else in the economy.* Consumption expenditures, business production, wages, rents, interest payments, and profits are *flows* of money for newly produced products or resources that affect the level of *stocks* not shown in the model.

The Expenditure Approach

How does the government actually calculate GDP? One way national income accountants calculate GDP is to use the expenditure approach to measure total spending flowing through product markets in the circular flow diagram. The expenditure approach measures GDP by adding all the spending for final goods during a period of time. Exhibit 2 shows 2007 GDP using the expenditure approach, which breaks down expenditures into four components. The data in this exhibit show that all production in the U.S. economy is ultimately purchased by spending from households, businesses, government, or foreigners. Let's discuss each of these expenditure categories.

Personal Consumption Expenditures (*C*)

The largest component of GDP in 2007 was $9,734 billion for the category national income accountants call *personal consumption expenditures*, represented by the letter *C*. Personal consumption expenditures comprise total spending by households

---

Flow

A flow is a rate of change in a quantity during a given time period, such as dollars per year. For example, income and consumption are flows that occur per week, per month, or per year.

Stock

A quantity measured at one point in time. For example, an inventory of goods or the amount of money in a checking account.

Expenditure approach

The national income accounting method that measures GDP by adding all the spending for final goods during a period of time.

EXHIBIT 2	Gross Domestic Product Using the Expenditure Approach, 2007		
National Income Account		Amount (billions of dollars)	Percentage of GDP
Personal consumption expenditures (*C*)		$9,734	70%
Durable goods	$1,078		
Nondurable goods	2,833		
Services	5,823		
Gross private domestic investment (*I*)		2,125	15
Fixed investment	2,122		
Change in business inventories	3		
Government consumption expenditures and gross investment (*G*)		2,690	20
Federal	976		
State and local	1,714		
Net exports of goods and services (*X*−*M*)		−708	−5
Exports (*X*)	1,643		
Imports (*M*)	2,351		
Gross domestic product (**GDP**)		$13,841	100%

SOURCE: Bureau of Economic Analysis, *National Economic Accounts*, http://www.bea.gov/national/nipaweb/SelectTable.asp?Selected=Y, Table 1.1.5.

for durable goods, nondurable goods, and services. Durable goods include items such as automobiles, appliances, and furniture because they last longer than three years. Food, clothing, soap, and gasoline are examples of nondurables, because they are considered used up or consumed in less than three years. Services, which is the largest category, include recreation, legal advice, medical treatment, education, and any transaction not in the form of a tangible object.

Gross Private Domestic Investment (*I*)

In 2007, $2,125 billion was spent for what is officially called *gross private domestic investment* (*I*). This national income account includes "gross" (all) "private" (not government) "domestic" (not foreign) spending by businesses for investment in assets that are expected to earn profits in the future. Gross private domestic investment is the sum of two components: (1) *fixed investment* expenditures for newly produced capital goods, such as commercial and residential structures, machinery, equipment, and tools; and (2) change in *business inventories*, which is the net change in spending for unsold finished goods. Note that gross private domestic investment is simply the national income accounting category for "investment," defined in Chapter 2. The only difference is that investment in Exhibit 5 in Chapter 2 was in physical capital, such as manufacturing plants, oil wells, or fast-food restaurants, rather than the dollar value of capital used here.

Now we will take a closer look at gross private domestic investment. Note that national income accountants include the rental value of newly constructed residential housing in the $2,122 billion spent for fixed investment. A new factory, warehouse, or robot is surely a form of investment, but why include residential housing as business investment rather than consumption by households? The debatable answer is that a new home is considered investment because it provides services in the future that the owner can rent for financial return. For this reason, all newly produced housing is considered investment whether the owner rents or occupies the property.

Finally, the $3 billion change in business inventories means this amount of net dollar value of unsold finished goods and raw materials was added to the stock of inventories during 2007. A decline in inventories would reduce GDP because households consumed more output than firms produced during this year. When businesses have more on their shelves this year than last, more new production has taken place than has been consumed during this year.

Government Consumption Expenditures and Gross Investment (G)

This official category simply called *government spending* includes the value of goods and services government purchases at all levels measured by their costs. For example, spending for police and state university professors enters the GDP accounts at the prices the government pays for them. In addition, the government spends for investment additions to its stock of capital, such as tanks, schools, highways, bridges, and government buildings. In 2007, federal, state, and local government spending (G) totaled $2,690 billion. As the figures in Exhibit 2 reveal, government spending of state and local governments far exceeded those of the federal government. It is important to understand that the government spending category of GDP excludes *transfer payments* because, as explained at the beginning of the chapter, they do not represent newly produced goods and services. Instead, transfer payments are paid to those entitled to Social Security benefits, veterans' benefits, welfare, unemployment compensation, and benefits from other programs.

Net Exports (X–M)

The last GDP expenditure account is *net exports,* expressed in the formula (X–M). *Exports* (X) are expenditures by foreigners for U.S. domestically produced goods. *Imports* (M) are the dollar amount of our purchases of Japanese automobiles, French wine, toys from China, and other goods produced abroad. Because we are using expenditures for U.S. output to measure GDP, one might ask why imports are subtracted from exports. The answer is the result of how the government actually collects data from which GDP is computed. Spending for imports is not subtracted when spending data for consumption, investment, and government spending are reported. These three components of GDP therefore overstate the value of expenditures for U.S.-produced products.

Consider the data collected to compute consumption (C). In reality, personal consumption expenditures reported to the U.S. Department of Commerce include expenditures for both domestically produced and imported goods and services. For example, automobile dealers report to the government that consumers purchased a given dollar amount of new cars during 2007, but they are not required to separate their figures between sales of U.S. cars and sales of foreign cars. Because GDP measures only domestic economic activity, foreign sales must be removed. Subtracting imports in the net exports category removes all sales of foreign goods, including new foreign cars, from consumption (C) and likewise from investment (I) and government spending (G).

The overstatement of 2007 GDP expenditures is corrected by subtracting $2,351 billion in imports from $1,643 billion in exports to obtain net exports of

−$708 billion. The negative sign indicates that the United States is spending more dollars to purchase foreign products than it is receiving from the rest of the world for U.S. goods. The effect of a negative net exports figure is to reduce U.S. GDP when it is subtracted from the consumption, investment, and government components. Prior to the early 1980s, the United States was a consistent net exporter, selling more goods and services to the rest of the world than we purchased from abroad. Since 1983, the United States has been a net importer. International trade is discussed in more detail in the last section of the text.

A Formula for GDP

Using the expenditure approach, GDP is expressed mathematically in billions of dollars as

$$GDP = C + I + G + (X - M)$$

For 2007 (see Exhibit 2),

$$\$13{,}841 = \$9{,}734 + \$2{,}125 + \$2{,}690 + (\$1{,}643 - \$2{,}351)$$

This simple equation plays a central role in macroeconomics. It is the basis for analyzing macro problems and formulating macro policy. When economists study the macro economy, they can apply this equation to predict the behavior of the major sectors of the economy: consumption (C) is spending by households, investment (I) is spending by firms, government spending (G), and net exports ($X - M$) is net spending by foreigners.

The Income Approach

The second, somewhat more complex approach to measuring GDP is the income approach. The income approach measures GDP by adding all the incomes earned by households in exchange for the factors of production during a period of time. Both the expenditure approach and the income approach yield identical GDP calculations. As shown in the basic circular flow model, each dollar of expenditure paid by households to businesses in the product markets means a dollar of income flows to households through the factor markets as a payment for the land, labor, and capital required to produce the product. Using the income approach, GDP is expressed as follows:

> **Income approach**
> The national income accounting method that measures GDP by adding all incomes, including compensation of employees, rents, net interest, and profits.

$$GDP = \text{compensation of employees} + \text{rents} + \text{profits}$$
$$+ \text{ net interest} + \text{indirect taxes} + \text{depreciation}$$

In practice, it is necessary to add depreciation (capital consumption allowance) to factor payments so that national income equals GDP. Exhibit 3 presents actual 2007 GDP calculated following the income approach, and then each component is discussed in turn.

Compensation of Employees

Employees' compensation is the largest of the national income accounts. About 57 percent of GDP in 2007 ($7,874 billion) was income earned from wages, salaries, and certain supplements paid by firms and government to suppliers of labor. Since

EXHIBIT 3	Gross Domestic Product Using the Income Approach, 2007	

National Income Account	Amount (billions of dollars)	Percentage of GDP
Compensation of employees	$7,874	57%
Rental income	65	1
Profits	2,638	19
Proprietors' income	1,043	
Corporate profits	1,595	
Net interest	603	4
Indirect business taxes	1,041	7
Depreciation	1,620	12
Gross domestic product (GDP)	$13,841	100%

SOURCE: Bureau of Economic Analysis, *National Income Accounts*, http://www.bea.doc/bea.gov/national/nipaweb/SelectTable.asp?Selected=Y, Table 1.7.5.

labor services play such an important role in production, it is not surprising that employee compensation represents the largest share of the GDP income pie. The supplements consist of employer taxes for Social Security and unemployment insurance. Also included are fringe benefits from a variety of private health insurance and pension plans.

Rental Income
The smallest source of income is from rent and royalties received by property owners who permit others to use their assets during a time period. For example, this category includes house and apartment rents received by landlords. In 2007, $65 billion was earned in rental income.

Profits
Proprietors' Income   All forms of income earned by unincorporated businesses totaled $1,043 billion in 2007. Self-employed proprietorships and partnerships simultaneously own their businesses and pay themselves for labor services to their firms.

Corporate Profits   This income category includes all income earned by the stockholders of corporations regardless of whether stockholders receive it. The $1,595 billion of corporate profits in 2007 was the sum of three sources: (1) dividends, (2) undistributed corporate profits (retained earnings for expanding plant and equipment), and (3) corporate income taxes. Thus, corporate profits using the income approach are "before taxes."

Net Interest
Households both receive and pay interest. Persons who make loans to businesses earn interest income. Suppose you purchase a bond issued by General Motors.

When General Motors pays interest on its bonds, the interest payments are included in the national income accounts. Households also received interest from savings accounts and certificates of deposits (CDs). On the other hand, households borrow money and pay interest on, for example, credit cards, installment loans, and mortgage loans. The net interest of $603 billion in 2007 is the difference between interest income earned and interest payments.

Indirect Business Taxes

As reported in Exhibit 3, $1,041 billion was collected by government in the form of indirect business taxes. Why do national income accountants include business taxes in the income approach to GDP computation? Indirect business taxes are levied as a percentage of the prices of goods sold and therefore become part of the revenue received by firms. These taxes include sales taxes, federal excise taxes, license fees, business property taxes, and customs duties. Indirect taxes are not income payments to suppliers of resources. Instead, firms collect indirect taxes and send these funds to the government. Suppose you purchased a new automobile for $20,000, including a $1,000 federal excise tax and state sales tax. These taxes are included in the price, but are income for the government, which represents the public interest of households.

> **Indirect business taxes**
> Taxes levied as a percentage of the prices of goods sold and therefore collected as part of the firm's revenue. Firms treat such taxes as production costs. Examples include general sales taxes, excise taxes, and customs duties.

Depreciation

To reconcile the above income accounts with GDP requires adding the category labeled *consumption of fixed capital.* Consumption of fixed capital is an estimate of the depreciation of capital. This somewhat imposing term is simply an allowance for the portion of capital worn out producing GDP. Over time, capital goods, such as buildings, machines, and equipment, wear out and become less valuable. Depreciation (capital consumption allowance) is therefore a portion of GDP that is not available for income payments. Because it is impossible to measure depreciation accurately, an estimate is entered. In 2007, $1,620 billion was the estimated amount of GDP attributable to depreciation during the year.

Exhibit 4 presents the conceptual frameworks of the expenditure and income approaches to computing GDP.

CHECKPOINT

How Much Does Mario Add to GDP?

Mario works part-time at Pizza Hut and earns an annual wage plus tips of $15,000. He sold 4,000 pizzas at $15 per pizza during the year. He was unemployed part of the year, so he received unemployment compensation of $3,000. During the past year, Mario bought a used car for $5,000. Using the expenditure approach, how much has Mario contributed to GDP?

GDP in Other Countries

Exhibit 5 compares GDP for selected countries in 2007. The United States had the world's highest GDP. U.S. GDP, for example, was about three times Japan's GDP and over four times China's GDP.

GLOBAL ECONOMICS

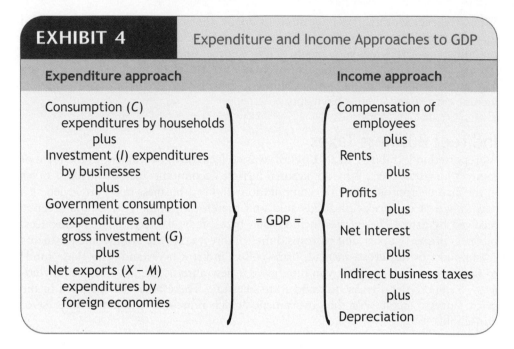

EXHIBIT 4 — Expenditure and Income Approaches to GDP

Expenditure approach		Income approach
Consumption (*C*) expenditures by households plus Investment (*I*) expenditures by businesses plus Government consumption expenditures and gross investment (*G*) plus Net exports (*X – M*) expenditures by foreign economies	= GDP =	Compensation of employees plus Rents plus Profits plus Net Interest plus Indirect business taxes plus Depreciation

GDP Shortcomings

For various reasons, GDP omits certain measures of overall economic well-being. Because GDP is the basis of government economic policies, there is concern that GDP may be giving us a false impression of the nation's material well-being. GDP is a less-than-perfect measure of the nation's economic pulse because it excludes the following factors.

Nonmarket Transactions

Because GDP counts only market transactions, it excludes certain unpaid activities, such as homemaker production, child rearing, and do-it-yourself home repairs and services. For example, if you take your dirty clothes to the laundry, GDP increases by the amount of the cleaning bill paid. But GDP ignores the value of laundering these same clothes if you wash them yourself at home.

There are two reasons for excluding nonmarket activities from GDP. First, it would be extremely imprecise to attempt to collect data and assign a dollar value to services people provide for themselves or others without compensation. Second, it is difficult to decide which nonmarket activities to exclude and which ones to include. Perhaps repairing your own roof, painting your own house, and repairing your own car should be included. Now consider the value of washing your car. GDP does include the price of cleaning your car if you purchase it at a car wash, so it could be argued that GDP should include the value of you washing your car at home.

The issue of unpaid, do-it-yourself activities affects comparisons of the GDPs of different nations. One reason some less-developed nations have lower GDPs than major industrialized nations is that a greater proportion of people in less-developed nations farm, clean, make repairs, and perform other tasks for their families rather than hiring someone else to do the work.

Distribution, Kind, and Quality of Products

GDP is blind to whether a small fraction of the population consumes most of a country's GDP or consumption is evenly divided. GDP also wears a blindfold with

EXHIBIT 5   An International Comparison of GDPs, 2007

This exhibit shows GDPs in 2007 for selected countries. The United States had the world's highest GDP. U.S. GDP, for example, was about three times the size of Japan's, and is over four times the GDP of China.

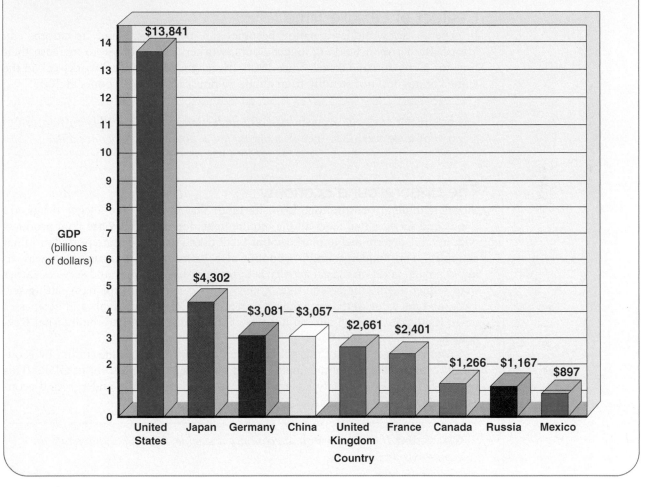

SOURCE: International Monetary Fund, *World Economic Outlook Database*, http://www.imf.org/external/pubs/ft/weo/2007/01/data/weoselgr.aspx.

respect to the quality and kinds of goods and services that make up a nation's GDP. Consider the fictional economies of Zuba and Econa. Zuba has a GDP of $2,000 billion, and Econa has a GDP of $1,000 billion. At first glance, Zuba appears to possess superior economic well-being. However, Zuba's GDP consists of only military goods, and Econa's products include computers, cell phones, tractors, wheat, milk, houses, and other consumer items. Moreover, assume the majority of the people of Zuba could care less about the output of military goods and would be happier if the country produced more consumer goods. Now consider for example the difference in quality between a digital phone purchased today and a cell phone with only few capabilities purchased years ago. Such qualitative improvements are not reflected in GDP.

> **Conclusion** *GDP is a quantitative, rather than a qualitative, measure of the output of goods and services.*

Neglect of Leisure Time

In general, the wealthier a nation becomes the more leisure time its citizens can afford. Rather than working longer hours, workers often choose to increase their time for recreation and travel. Since 1900, the length of the typical workweek in the United States declined steadily from about 50 hours to about 34 hours in 2007.[1]

> **Conclusion** *It can be argued that GDP understates national well-being because no allowance is made for people working fewer hours than they once did.*

The Underground Economy

Illegal gambling, prostitution, loan-sharking, illegal guns, and illegal drugs are goods and services that meet all the requirements for GDP. They are final products with a value determined in markets, but GDP does not include unreported criminal activities. The "underground" economy also includes tax evasion. One way to avoid paying taxes on a legal activity is to trade or barter goods and services rather than selling them. One person fixes a neighbor's car in return for baby-sitting services, and the value of the exchange is unreported. Other individuals and businesses make legal sales for cash and do not report the income earned to the Internal Revenue Service.

Estimates of the size of this subterranean economy vary. Some studies by economists estimate the size of the underground sector is about 9 percent of GDP.[2] This range of estimates is slightly less than the estimated size of the underground economy in most European countries.

> **Conclusion** *If the underground economy is sizable, GDP will understate an economy's performance.*

Economic Bads

More production means a larger GDP, regardless of the level of pollution created in the process. Recall from Chapter 4 the discussion of *negative externalities,* such as pollution caused by steel mills, chemical plants, and cigarettes. Air, water, and noise pollution are *economic bads* that impose costs on society not reflected in private market prices and quantities bought and sold. When a polluting company sells its product, this transaction increases GDP. However, critics of GDP argue that it fails to account for the diminished quality of life from the "bads" not reported in GDP. Stated another way, if production results in pollution and environmental damage, GDP overstates the nation's well-being.

---

1. *Economic Report of the President, 2008,* http://www.gpoaccess.gov/eop/, Table B-47.
2. Jim McTague, "Going Underground: America's Shadow Economy," *Frontpagemag.com,* Jan. 6, 2005, http://www.frontpagemag.com/Default.aspx.

© Vicki France, 2008/used under license from Shutterstock.com.

Suppose a factory in your community has been dumping hazardous wastes into the local water supply and people develop cancer and other illnesses from drinking polluted water. The Environmental Protection Agency (EPA) discovers this pollution and, under the federal "Superfund" law, orders a cleanup and imposes a fine for the damages. The company defends itself against the EPA by hiring lawyers and experts to take the case to court. After years of trial, the company loses the case and has to pay for the cleanup and damages.

In terms of GDP, an amazing "good" result occurs: The primary measure of national economic output, GDP, increases. GDP counts the millions of dollars spent to clean up the water supply. GDP even includes the health care expenses of anyone who develops cancer or other illnesses caused by drinking polluted water. GDP also includes the money spent by the company on lawyers and experts to defend itself against the EPA.

And GDP includes the money spent by the EPA to regulate the polluting company.

Now consider what happens when trees are cut down and oil and minerals are used to produce houses, cars, and other goods. The value of the wood, oil, and minerals is an intermediate good implicitly computed in GDP because the value of the final goods is explicitly computed in GDP. Using scarce resources to produce goods and services therefore raises GDP and is considered a "good" result. On the other hand, don't we lose the value of trees, oil, and minerals in the production process, so isn't this a "bad" result?

The Bureau of Economic Analysis (BEA) is an agency of the U.S. Department of Commerce. The BEA is the nation's economic accountant, and it publishes the *Survey of Current Business,* which is the source of GDP data cited throughout this text. Critics have called for a new measure designed to estimate the kinds of damage described above. These new accounts would adjust for changes in air and water quality and depletion of oil and minerals. These accounts would also adjust for changes in the stock of renewable natural resources, such as forests and fish stocks. In addition, accounts should be created to

measure global warming and destruction of the ozone layer.

As explained in this chapter, a dollar estimate of capital depreciation is subtracted from GDP to compute national income (NI). The argument here is that a dollar estimate of the damage to the environment should also be subtracted. To ignore measuring such environmental problems, critics argue, threatens future generations. In short, conventional GDP perpetuates a false dichotomy between economic growth and environmental protection.

Critics of this approach argue that assigning a dollar value to environmental damage and resource depletion requires a methodology that is extremely subjective and complex. Nevertheless, national income accountants have not ignored these criticisms, and the National Academy of Sciences has reviewed BEA proposals for ways to account for interactions between the environment and the economy.

ANALYZE THE ISSUE

Suppose a nuclear power plant disaster occurs. How could GDP be a "false beacon" in this case?

EXHIBIT 6	National Income Calculated from Gross Domestic Product, 2007

	Amount (billions of dollars)
Gross domestic product (GDP)	$13,841
Depreciation	−1,620
National income (NI)	$12,221

SOURCE: Bureau of Economic Analysis, *National Economic Accounts*, http://www.bea.gov/national/nipaweb/Select/Table?Table=Y.asp, Table 1.7.5.

Other National Income Accounts

In addition to GDP, the media often report several other national income accounts because they are necessary for studying the macro economy. We now take a brief look at each.

National Income (NI)

It can be argued that depreciation should be subtracted from GDP. Recall that GDP is not entirely a measure of newly produced output because it includes an estimated value of capital goods required to replace those worn out in the production process. The measurement designed to correct this deficiency is national income (NI), which is the gross domestic product minus depreciation of the capital worn out in producing output. Stated as a formula:

$$\text{NI} = \text{GDP} - \text{depreciation (consumption of fixed capital)}$$

In 2007, $1,620 billion was the estimated amount of GDP attributable to depreciation during the year. Exhibit 6 shows the actual calculation of NI from GDP in 2007. NI measures how much income is *earned* by households who own and supply resources. It includes the total flow of payments to the owners of the factors of production, including wages, rents, interest, and profits. Another way to compute national income is to add compensation of employees, rents, profits, net interest, and indirect business taxes using the income approach demonstrated in Exhibit 3. Exhibit 7 illustrates the transition from GDP to NI and two other measures of the macro economy.[3]

Personal Income (PI)

National income measures the total amount of money *earned*, but determining the amount of income actually *received* by households (not businesses) requires a measurement of personal income (PI). Personal income is the total income received by households that is available for consumption, saving, and payment of personal taxes. Suppose we want to measure the total amount of money individuals receive

---

National income (NI)

The total income earned by resource owners, including wages, rents, interest, and profits. NI is calculated as gross domestic product minus depreciation of the capital worn out in producing output.

Personal income (PI)

The total income received by households that is available for consumption, saving, and payment of personal taxes.

---

3. As a result of a revision in national income accounting, the only difference between net domestic product (NDP) and national income (NI) is a statistical discrepancy. Since NI is more widely reported in the media, and to simplify, NDP is not calculated here.

EXHIBIT 7	Four Measures of the Macro Economy

The four bars show major measurements of the U.S. macro economy in 2007 in billions of dollars. Beginning with gross domestic product, depreciation is subtracted to obtain national income. Next, personal income equals national income minus corporate profits and contributions for Social Security insurance (FICA payments) plus transfer payments and other income. Subtracting personal taxes from personal income yields disposable personal income.

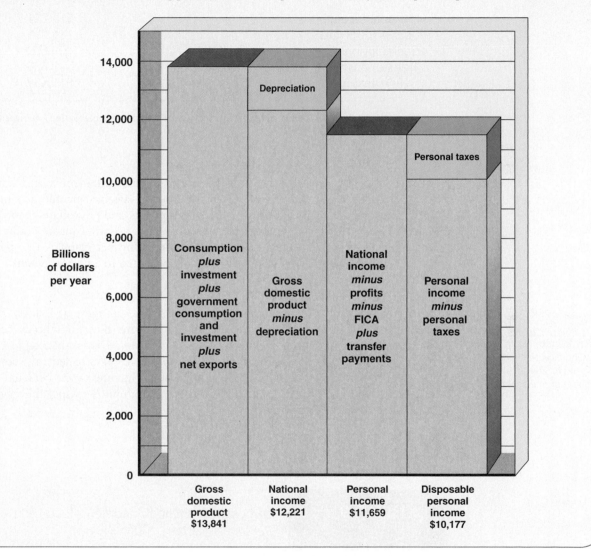

that they can use to consume products, save, and pay taxes. National income is not the appropriate measure for two reasons. First, NI excludes transfer payments, which constitute unearned income that can be spent, saved, or used to pay taxes. Second, NI includes corporate profits, but stockholders do not receive all these profits. A portion of corporate profits is paid in corporate taxes. Also, retained earnings are not distributed to stockholders, but are channeled back into business operations.

EXHIBIT 8	Personal Income Calculated from National Income, 2007
	Amount (billions of dollars)
National income (NI)	$12,221
Corporate profits	−1,595
Contributions for Social Security (FICA)	−603
Transfer payments and other income	1,636
Personal income (PI)	$11,659

SOURCE: Bureau of Economic Analysis, *National Economic Accounts*, http://www.bea.gov/national/nipaweb/SelectTable?Selected=Y.asp, Table 1.7.5.

Exhibit 7 illustrates the relationship between personal income and national income, and Exhibit 8 gives the figures for 2007. National income accountants adjust national income by subtracting corporate profits and payroll taxes for Social Security (FICA deductions). Next, *transfer payments* and other income individuals receive from net interest and dividends are added. The net result is the personal income received by households, which in 2007 amounted to $11,659 billion.

Disposable Personal Income (DI)

Disposable personal income (DI)

The amount of income that households actually have to spend or save after payment of personal taxes.

One final measure of national income is shown at the far right of Exhibit 7. Disposable personal income (DI) is the amount of income that households actually have to spend or save after payment of personal taxes. Disposable, or *after-tax*, income is equal to personal income minus personal taxes paid to federal, state, and local governments. Personal taxes consist of personal income taxes, personal property taxes, and inheritance taxes. As tabulated in Exhibit 9, disposable personal income in 2007 was $10,177 billion.

EXHIBIT 9	Disposable Personal Income Calculated from Personal Income, 2007
	Amount (billions of dollars)
Personal income (PI)	$11,659
Personal taxes	−1,482
Disposable personal income (DI)	$10,177

SOURCE: Bureau of Economic Analysis, *National Economic Accounts*, http://www.bea.gov/national/nipaweb/SelectTable?Selected=Y.asp, Table 2.1.

Changing Nominal GDP to Real GDP

So far, GDP has been expressed as nominal GDP. Nominal GDP is the value of all final goods based on the prices existing during the time period of production. Nominal GDP is also referred to as *current-dollar* or *money GDP*. Nominal GDP grows in three ways: First, output rises, and prices remain unchanged. Second, prices rise and output is constant. Third, in the typical case, both output and prices rise. The problem, then, is how to adjust GDP so it reflects only changes in output and not changes in prices. This adjusted GDP allows meaningful comparisons over time when prices are changing.

Nominal GDP

The value of all final goods based on the prices existing during the time period of production.

Changing prices can have a huge impact on how we compare dollar figures. Suppose a newspaper headline reports that a film entitled *The History of Economic Thought* is the most popular movie of all time. You ask, How could this be? What about *Gone with the Wind*? Reading the article reveals that this claim is based on the nominal measure of gross box-office receipts. This gives a recent movie with higher ticket prices an advantage over a movie released in 1939 when the average ticket price was only 25 cents. A better measure of popularity would be to compare "real" box office receipts by multiplying actual attendance figures for each movie by a base-year movie price.

Measuring the difference between changes in output and changes in the price level involves making an important distinction between nominal GDP and real GDP. Real GDP is the value of all final goods produced during a given time period based on the prices existing in a selected base year. The U.S. Department of Commerce currently uses 2000 as the base year.

Real GDP

The value of all final goods produced during a given time period based on the prices existing in a selected base year.

The GDP Chain Price Index

The most broadly based measure used to take the changes-in-the-price-level "air" out of the nominal GDP "balloon" and compute real GDP is officially called the GDP chain price index. The GDP chain price index is a measure that compares changes in the prices of all final goods produced during a given time period relative to the prices of those goods in a base year. The GDP chain price index is a broad "deflator" index calculated by a complex chain-weighted geometric series (you are spared the details). It is highly inclusive because it measures not only price changes of consumer goods, but also price changes of business investment, government spending, exports, and imports. Do not confuse the GDP chain price index with the *consumer price index* (CPI), which is widely reported in the news media. The CPI is a different index, measuring only consumer prices, which we will discuss in the chapter on inflation.

GDP chain price index

A measure that compares changes in the prices of all final goods during a given year to the prices of those goods in a base year.

Now it's time to see how it works. We begin with the following conversion equation:

$$\text{Real GDP} = \frac{\text{nominal GDP}}{\text{GDP chain price index}} \times 100$$

Using 2000 as the base year, suppose you are given the 2007 nominal GDP of $13,841 billion and the 2007 GDP chain price index of 119.66. To calculate 2007 real GDP, use the above formula as follows:

$$\$11,566 \text{ billion} = \frac{\$13,841 \text{ billion}}{119.66} \times 100$$

Exhibit 10 shows actual U.S. nominal GDP, real GDP, and the GDP chain price index computations for selected years. Column 1 reports nominal GDP, column 2

EXHIBIT 10   Nominal GDP, Real GDP, and the GDP Chain Price Index for Selected Years

Real GDP reflects output valued at 2000 base-year prices, but nominal GDP is annual output valued at prices prevailing during the current year. The intersection of real and nominal GDP occurs in 2000 because in the base year both nominal GDP and real GDP measure the same output at 2000 prices. Note that the nominal GDP curve has risen more sharply than the real GDP curve as a result of inflation included in the nominal figures.

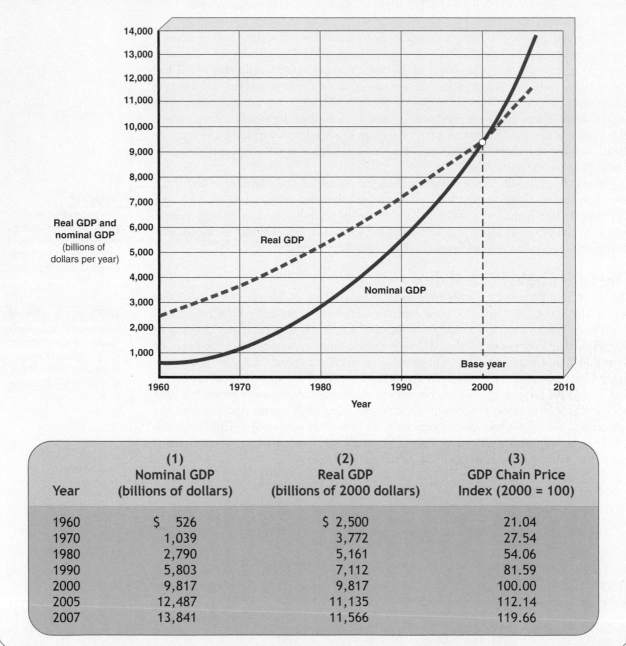

Year	(1) Nominal GDP (billions of dollars)	(2) Real GDP (billions of 2000 dollars)	(3) GDP Chain Price Index (2000 = 100)
1960	$ 526	$ 2,500	21.04
1970	1,039	3,772	27.54
1980	2,790	5,161	54.06
1990	5,803	7,112	81.59
2000	9,817	9,817	100.00
2005	12,487	11,135	112.14
2007	13,841	11,566	119.66

SOURCES: Bureau of Economic Analysis, *National Economic Accounts*, http://www.bea.gov/national/nipaweb/SelectTable?Selected=Y.asp, Tables 1.1.5, 1.1.6, and *Economic Report of the President*, http://www.gpoaccess.gov/eop/, Table B-3.

gives real GDP figures for these years, and column 3 lists corresponding GDP chain price indexes. Notice that the GDP chain price index exceeds 100 in years beyond 2000. This means that prices, on average, have risen since 2000, causing the real purchasing power of the dollar to fall. In years before 2000, the GDP chain price index is less than 100, which means the real purchasing power of the dollar was higher relative to the 2000 base year. At the base year of 2000, nominal and real GDP are identical, and the GDP price index equals 100.

The graph in Exhibit 10 traces real GDP and nominal GDP for the economy since 1960. Note that nominal GDP usually grows faster than real GDP because inflation is included in the nominal figures. For example, if we calculate the economy's growth rate in nominal GDP between 1990 and 2000, we find it was 6.9 percent. If instead we calculate real GDP growth between the same years, we find the growth rate was 3.8 percent. You must therefore pay attention to which GDP is being used in an analysis.

CHECKPOINT

Is the Economy Up or Down?

One person reports, "GDP rose this year by 8.5 percent." Another says, "GDP fell by 0.5 percent." Can both reports be right?

Drawing by Lorenz; © 1972 The New Yorker Magazine, Inc.

"And so, extrapolating from the best figures available, we see that current trends, unless dramatically reversed, will inevitably lead to a situation in which the sky will fall."

KEY CONCEPTS

Gross domestic product (GDP)   Stock   Disposable personal income (DI)
Transfer payment   Expenditure approach   Nominal GDP
Final goods   Income approach   Real GDP
Intermediate goods   Indirect business taxes   GDP chain price index
Circular flow model   National income (NI)
Flow   Personal income (PI)

SUMMARY

- *Gross domestic product (GDP)* is the most widely used measure of a nation's economic performance. GDP is the market value of all *final goods* produced in the United States during a period of time, regardless of who owns the factors of production. Secondhand and financial transactions are not counted in GDP. To avoid double counting, GDP also does not include *intermediate goods.* GDP is calculated by either the expenditure approach or the income approach.

- The *circular flow model* is a diagram representing the flow of products and resources between businesses and households in exchange for money payments. *Flows* must be distinguished from *stocks.* Flows are measured in units per time period—for example, dollars per year. Stocks are quantities that exist at a given point in time measured in dollars.

Circular flow model

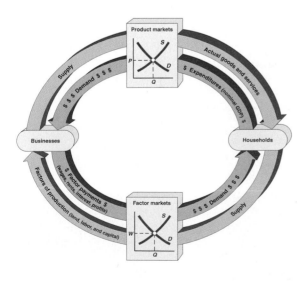

- The *expenditure approach* sums the four major spending components of GDP: consumption, investment, government spending, and net exports. Algebraically, GDP $= C + I + G + (X - M)$, where X equals foreign spending for domestic exports and M equals domestic spending for foreign products.

- The *income approach* sums the major income components of GDP, consisting of compensation of employees, rents, profits, net interest, *indirect business taxes,* and depreciation. Indirect business taxes are levied as a percentage of product prices and include sales taxes, excise taxes, and customs duties.

- *National income (NI)* is total income *earned* by households who own and supply resources. It is calculated as GDP minus depreciation.

- *Personal income (PI)* is the total income *received* by households and is calculated as NI minus corporate taxes and Social Security taxes plus transfer payments and other income.

- *Disposable personal income (DI)* is personal income minus personal taxes. DI is the amount of income a household has available to consume or save.

Measures of the macro economy

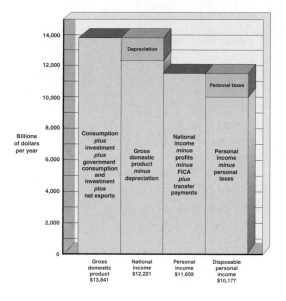

- *Nominal GDP* measures all final goods and services produced in a given time period, valued at the prices existing during the time period of production.
- *Real GDP* measures all final goods and services produced in a given time period, valued at the prices existing in a base year.
- The *GDP chain price index* is a broad price index used to convert nominal GDP to real GDP. The GDP chain price index measures changes in the prices of consumer goods, business investment, government spending, exports, and imports. Real GDP is computed by dividing nominal GDP for year X by year X's GDP chain price index and then multiplying the result by 100.

SUMMARY OF CONCLUSION STATEMENTS

- GDP is a quantitative, rather than a qualitative, measure of the output of goods and services.
- It can be argued that GDP understates national well-being because no allowance is made for people working fewer hours than they once did.
- If the underground economy is sizable, GDP will understate an economy's performance.

STUDY QUESTIONS AND PROBLEMS

1. Which of the following are final goods or services, and which are intermediate goods or services?
   a. A haircut purchased from a barber
   b. A new automobile
   c. An oil filter purchased in a new automobile
   d. Crude oil

2. Using the basic circular flow model, explain why the value of businesses' output of goods and services equals the income of households.

3. A small economy produced the following final goods and services during a given month: 3 million pounds of food, 50,000 shirts, 20 houses, 50,000 hours of medical services, 1 automobile plant, and 2 tanks. Calculate the value of this output at the following market prices:
   - $1 per pound of food
   - $20 per shirt
   - $50,000 per house
   - $20 per hour of medical services
   - $1 million per automobile plant
   - $500,000 per tank

4. An economy produces final goods and services with a market value of $5,000 billion in a given year, but only $4,500 billion worth of goods and services is sold to domestic or foreign buyers. Is this nation's GDP $5,000 billion or $4,500 billion? Explain your answer.

5. Explain why a new forklift sold for use in a warehouse is a final good even though it is fixed investment (capital) used to produce other goods. Is there a double-counting problem if this sale is added to GDP?

6. Explain why the government spending (G) component of GDP falls short of actual government expenditures.

7. Explain how net exports affect the U.S. economy. Describe both positive and negative impacts on GDP. Why do national income accountants use net exports to compute GDP, rather than simply adding exports to the other expenditure components of GDP?

8. Suppose the data in Exhibit 11 are for a given year from the annual *Economic Report of the President*. Calculate GDP, using the expenditure and the income approaches.

9. Using the data in Exhibit 11, compute national income (NI) by making the required subtraction from GDP. Explain why NI might be a better measure of economic performance than GDP.

10. Again using the data from Exhibit 11, derive personal income (PI) from national income (NI). Then make the required adjustments to PI to obtain disposable personal income (DI).

11. Suppose U.S. nominal GDP increases from one year to the next year. Can you conclude that these figures present a misleading measure of economic growth? What alternative method would provide a more accurate measure of the rate of growth?

12. Which of the following are counted in this year's GDP? Explain your answer in each case.
    a. Flashy Car Company sold a used car.
    b. Juanita Jones cooked meals for her family.
    c. IBM paid interest on its bonds.
    d. José Suarez purchased 100 shares of IBM stock.
    e. Bob Smith received a welfare payment.

EXHIBIT 11	National Income Data
	Amount (billions of dollars)
Corporate profits	$ 305
Depreciation	479
Gross private domestic investment	716
Personal taxes	565
Personal saving	120
Government spending	924
Imports	547
Net interest	337
Compensation of employees	2,648
Rental income	19
Exports	427
Personal consumption expenditures	2,966
Indirect business taxes	370
Contributions for Social Security (FICA)	394
Transfer payments and other income	967
Proprietors' income	328

f. Carriage Realty earned a brokerage commission for selling a previously owned house.
g. The government makes interest payments to persons holding government bonds.
h. Air and water pollution increase.
i. Gambling is legalized in all states.
j. A retired worker receives a Social Security payment.

13. Explain why comparing the GDPs of various nations might not tell you which nations are better off.

For Online Exercises, go to the text Web site at www.cengage.com/economics/tucker.

CHECKPOINT ANSWERS

How Much Does Mario Add to GDP?

Measuring GDP by the expenditure approach, Mario's output production is worth $60,000 because consumers purchased 4,000 pizzas at $15 each. Transfer payments and purchases of goods produced in other years are excluded from GDP. The $3,000 in unemployment compensation received and the $1,000 spent for a used car are therefore not counted in GDP. Mario's income of $15,000 is also not counted using the expenditure approach. If you said, using the expenditure approach to measure GDP,

Mario contributed $60,000 to GDP, **YOU ARE CORRECT.**

Is the Economy Up or Down?

Between 1973 and 1974, for example, nominal GDP rose from $1,382 to $1,500 billion—an 8.5 percent increase. During the same period, real GDP fell from $4,342 to $4,319 billion—a 0.5 percent decrease. If you said both reports can be correct because of the difference between nominal and real GDP, **YOU ARE CORRECT.**

PRACTICE QUIZ

For an explanation of the correct answers, please visit the tutorial at www.cengage. com/ economics/tucker.

1. The dollar value of all final goods and services produced within the borders of a nation is a
   a. GNP deflator.
   b. gross national product.
   c. net domestic product.
   d. gross domestic product.

2. Based on the circular flow model, money flows from businesses to households in
   a. factor markets.
   b. product markets.
   c. neither factor nor product markets.
   d. both factor and product markets.

3. The circular flow model does not include which of the following?
   a. The quantity of shoes in inventory on January 1
   b. The total wages paid per month
   c. The percentage of profits paid out as dividends each year
   d. The total profits earned per year in the U.S. economy

4. The expenditure approach measures GDP by adding all the expenditures for final goods made by
   a. households.
   b. businesses.
   c. government.
   d. foreigners.
   e. all of the above.

5. GDP is a less-than-perfect measure of the nation's economic pulse because it
   a. excludes nonmarket transactions.
   b. does not measure the quality of goods and services.
   c. does not report illegal transactions.
   d. all of the above.

6. Subtracting an allowance for depreciation of fixed capital from gross domestic product yields
   a. real GDP.
   b. nominal GDP.
   c. personal income.
   d. national income.

PRACTICE QUIZ CONTINUED

7. Adding all incomes earned by households from the sale of resources yields
   a. intermediate goods.
   b. indirect business taxes.
   c. national income.
   d. personal income.

8. Personal income equals disposable income plus
   a. personal savings.
   b. transfer payments.
   c. dividend payments.
   d. personal taxes.

9. Disposable personal income
   a. is the income people spend for personal items, such as homes and cars.
   b. includes transfer payments.
   c. excludes transfer payments.
   d. includes personal taxes.

10. Which of the following statements is *true*?
    a. National income is total income *earned* by households whereas personal income is total income *received* by households.
    b. Disposable personal income equals personal income minus personal taxes.
    c. The expenditure approach and the income approach yield the same GDP figure.
    d. All of the above are true.

11. Gross domestic product data that reflect actual prices as they exist in a given year are expressed in terms of
    a. fixed dollars.
    b. current dollars.
    c. constant dollars.
    d. real dollars.

12. The GDP chain price index is
    a. widely reported in the news.
    b. broadly based.
    c. adjusted for government spending.
    d. a measure of changes in consumer prices.

13. Which of the following statements is *true*?
    a. The inclusion of intermediate goods and services in GDP calculations would underestimate our nation's production level.
    b. The expenditure approach sums the compensation of employees, rents, profits, net interest, and nonincome expenses for depreciation and indirect business taxes.
    c. Real GDP has been adjusted for changes in the general level of prices due to inflation or deflation.
    d. Real GDP equals nominal GDP multiplied by the GDP deflator.

14. Which of the following is a shortcoming of GDP?
    a. GDP measures nonmarket transactions.
    b. GDP includes an estimate of illegal transactions.
    c. GDP includes an estimate of the value of household services.
    d. None of the above are true.

15. Which of the following items is included in the calculation of GDP?
    a. Purchase of 100 shares of General Motors stock
    b. Purchase of a used car
    c. The value of a homemaker's services
    d. Sale of Gulf War military surplus
    e. None of the above would be included

A Four-Sector Circular Flow Model

Sound the trumpets! This exhibit is going to put all the puzzle pieces together. Exhibit 1 presents a more complex circular flow model by adding three sectors: financial markets, government, and foreign markets. In addition to the spending of households for the output of firms shown in the simplified model in Exhibit 1, these additions add three *leakages* from the amount of income paid to households. First, part of households' income is saved. Second, part of it is taxed. Third, part of the income is spent on imports. On the other hand, this model includes three sources of spending *injections* for firms' output other than from households. First, firms purchase new plants, equipment, and inventories (investment) from other firms. Second, government spending are for goods and services from firms. Third, foreigners purchase exports from the firms.

EXHIBIT A.1   The Circular Flow Model of an Open Economy

This exhibit presents a circular flow model for an economy, such as the United States, that engages in international trade. The theoretical model includes links between the product and factor markets in the domestic economy and the financial markets, government, and foreign economies. To simplify the model, only dollar payments are shown for the foreign sector.

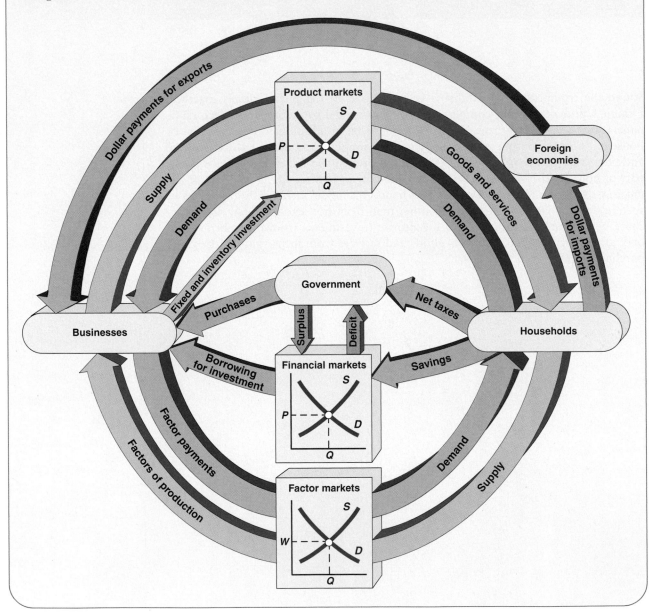

Business Cycles and Unemployment

T he headline in the morning newspaper reads, "The Economy Busts." Later in the day, a radio announcer begins the news by saying, "The unemployment rate rose for the fourth consecutive month." On television, the evening news broadcasts an interview with several economists who predict that the slump will last for another three months. Next, a presidential candidate appears on the screen and says, "It's time for change," and the media are abuzz with speculation on the political implications. The growth rate of the economy and the unemployment rate are headline-catching news. Indeed, these measures of macroeconomic instability are important because they affect your future. When real GDP rises and the economy "booms," jobs are more plentiful. A fall in real GDP means a "bust" because the economy forces some firms into bankruptcy and workers lose their jobs. Not being able to find a job when you want one is a painful experience not easily forgotten.

This chapter looks behind the macro economy at a story that touches each of us. It begins by discussing the business cycle. How are the expansions and contractions of business cycles measured? And what causes the business-cycle roller coaster? Finally, you will learn what the types of unemployment are, what "full employment" is, and what the monetary, nonmonetary, and demographic costs of unemployment are.

In this chapter, you will learn to solve these economic puzzles:

- What is the difference between a recession and a depression?

- Is a worker who has given up searching for work counted as unemployed?

- Can an economy produce more output than its potential?

The Business-Cycle Roller Coaster

A central concern of macroeconomics is the upswings and downswings in the level of real output called the business cycle. The business cycle consists of alternating periods of economic growth and contraction. Business cycles are inherent in market economies. A key measure of cycles is the rise and fall in real GDP, which mirrors changes in employment and other key measures of the macro economy. Recall from the previous chapter that changes in real GDP measure changes in the value of national output, while ignoring changes in the price level.

The Four Phases of the Business Cycle

Exhibit 1(a) illustrates a theoretical business cycle. Although business cycles vary in duration and intensity, each cycle is divided into four phases: peak, recession, trough, and recovery. The business cycle looks like a roller coaster. It begins at a peak, drops to a bottom, climbs steeply, and then reaches another peak. Once the trough is reached, the upswing starts again. Although forecasters cannot precisely predict the phases of a cycle, the economy is always operating along one of these phases. Over time, there has been a long-term upward trend with shorter-term cyclical fluctuations around the long-run trend.

Two *peaks* are illustrated in Exhibit 1(a). At each of these peaks, the economy is close to or at full employment. That is, as explained in Chapter 2, the economy is operating near its production possibilities curve, and real GDP is at its highest level relative to recent years. A macro setback called a *recession* or *contraction* follows each peak. A recession is a downturn in the business cycle during which real GDP declines, business profits fall, the percentage of the workforce without jobs rises, and production capacity is underutilized. A general rule is that a recession consists of at least two consecutive quarters (six months) in which there is a decline in real GDP. Stated differently, during a recession, the economy is functioning inside and farther away from its production possibilities curve.

What is the difference between a *recession* and a *depression*? According to the old saying: "A recession is when your neighbor loses his or her job, and a depression is when you also lose your job!" This one-liner is close to the true distinction between these two concepts. The answer is: Because no subsequent recession has approached the prolonged severity of the Great Depression from 1929 to 1933, the term *depression* is primarily a historical reference to this extremely deep and long recession. The Great Depression is discussed at the end of this chapter, the chapter on aggregate demand and supply, and the chapter on monetary policy.

The *trough* is where the level of real GDP "bottoms out." At the trough, unemployment and idle productive capacity are at their highest levels relative to recent years. The length of time between the peak and the trough is the duration of the recession. Since the end of World War II, recessions in the United States have averaged 10 months. As shown in Exhibit 2, the last recession lasted eight months from March 2001 to November 2001. The percentage decline in real GDP was 0.5 percent, and the national unemployment rate hit a high of 5.6 percent. Compared to the averages for previous recessions, the 2001 recession was mild.

The trough is both bad news and good news. It is simultaneously the bottom of the "valley" of the downturn and the foot of the "hill" of improving economic conditions called a *recovery* or *expansion*. A recovery is an upturn in the business

Business cycle

Alternating periods of economic growth and contraction, which can be measured by changes in real GDP.

Peak

The phase of the business cycle in which real GDP reaches its maximum after rising during a recovery.

Recession

A downturn in the business cycle during which real GDP declines, and the unemployment rate rises. Also called a *contraction*.

Trough

The phase of the business cycle in which real GDP reaches its minimum after falling during a recession.

Recovery

An upturn in the business cycle during which real GDP rises. Also called an *expansion*.

EXHIBIT 1 Hypothetical and Actual Business Cycles

Part (a) illustrates a hypothetical business cycle consisting of four phases: peak, recession, trough, and recovery. These fluctuations of real GDP can be measured by a growth trend line, which shows that over time real GDP has trended upward. In reality, the fluctuations are not so clearly defined as those in this graph.

Part (b) illustrates actual ups and downs of the business cycle. After a recession during 1990–1991, a strong upswing continued until another recession in 2001. The expansion lasted 10 years and was the longest in U.S. history.

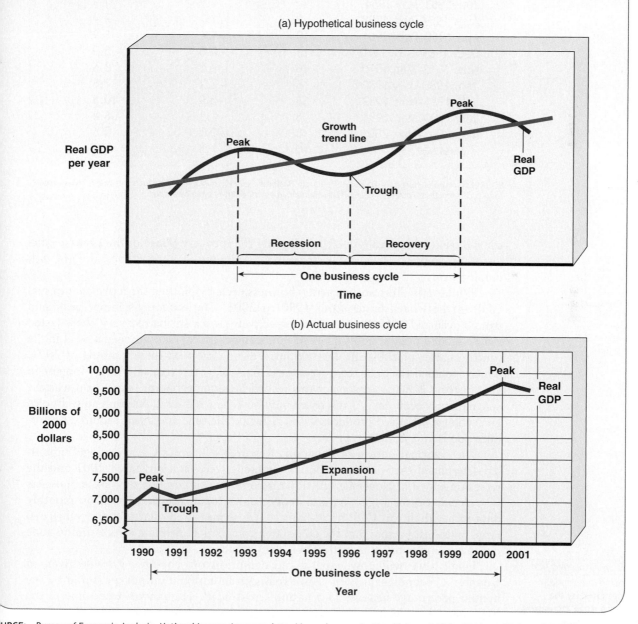

(a) Hypothetical business cycle

(b) Actual business cycle

URCE: Bureau of Economic Analysis, *National Income Accounts*, http://www.bea.gov/national/nipaweb/SelectTable.asp?Selected=Y, Table 1.1.6.

EXHIBIT 2	Severity of Post-World War II Recessions		
Recession Dates	Duration (months)	Percentage Decline in Real GDP	Peak Unemployment Rate
Nov. 1948–Oct. 1949	11	−1.7%	7.9%
July 1953–May 1954	10	−2.7	5.9
Aug. 1957–Apr. 1958	8	−1.2	7.4
Apr. 1960–Feb. 1961	10	−1.6	6.9
Dec. 1969–Nov. 1970	11	−0.6	5.9
Nov. 1973–Mar. 1975	16	−3.1	8.6
Jan. 1980–July 1980	6	−2.2	7.8
July 1981–Nov. 1982	16	−2.9	10.8
July 1990–Mar. 1991	8	−1.3	6.8
Mar. 2001–Nov. 2001	8	−0.5	5.6
Average	**10**	**−1.8**	**7.4**

SOURCE: National Bureau of Economic Research, *Business Cycle Expansion and Contractions,* http://www.nber .org/cycles/cyclesmain.html. Real GDP and unemployment rate data added by author.

cycle during which real GDP rises. During the recovery phase of the cycle, profits generally improve, real GDP increases, and employment moves toward full employment.

Exhibit 1(b) illustrates an actual business cycle by plotting the movement of real GDP in the United States from 1990 to 2001. The economy's initial peak and trough occurred in 1990 and 1991, respectively, and a strong recovery phase lasted until a second peak in 2000. The cycle indicates that real GDP reached a peak in the fourth quarter of 2000 and then declined during the next three quarters of 2001, which included the 9/11 terrorist attack. This 10-year expansion is the longest in U.S. history. A major reason for this record-breaking economic expansion was the so-called new economy. As discussed previously in Chapter 2, widespread technological change increased productivity by reducing the time and effort required to produce goods and services.

The National Bureau of Economic Research's Business Cycle Dating Committee determined that the U.S. economy entered a recession in March 2001 and the recession ended in November 2001. This committee is composed of six economists who decide on the beginning and ending dates for a recession based on monthly data rather than real GDP because real GDP is measured quarterly and subject to large revisions. Factors that the committee considers in defining a recession include decline in employment, industrial production, income, and sales.

Finally, we will now expand the definition of economic growth given in Chapter 2. Economic growth is an expansion in national output measured by the annual percentage increase in a nation's real GDP. The growth trend line in the hypothetical model in Exhibit 1(a) illustrates that over time our real GDP tends to rise. This general, long-term upward trend in real GDP persists in spite of the peaks, recessions, troughs, and recoveries. As shown by the dashed line in Exhibit 3, since 1929 real GDP in the United States has grown at an average annual rate of

Economic growth

An expansion in national output measured by the annual percentage increase in a nation's real GDP.

EXHIBIT 3   A Historical Record of Business Cycles in the United States, 1929–2007

Real GDP has increased at an average annual growth rate of 3.5 percent since 1929. Above-average annual growth rates have alternated with below-average annual growth rates. During a recession year, such as 1991, the annual growth rate was negative and therefore below the zero growth line. The economy entered the recovery phase in 1992 and reached a peak in 2000. In the recession year of 2001, the growth rate was less than 1 percent, and in 2007, the growth rate was 2.0 percent.

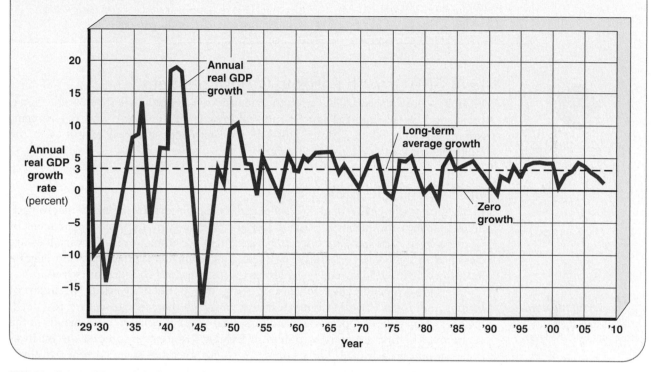

SOURCE: Bureau of Economic Analysis, *National Economic Accounts*, http://www.bea.gov/national/nipaweb/SelectTable.asp?Selected=Y, Table 1.1.6.

3.5 percent. This annual change may seem small, but about 3 percent annual growth will lead to a doubling of real GDP in only 24 years. One of our challenging policy goals is to maintain or increase that growth rate.

> **Conclusion** *We value economic growth as one of our nation's economic goals because it increases our standard of living—it creates a bigger "economic pie."*

Closer examination of Exhibit 3 reveals that the growth path of the U.S. economy over time is not a smooth, rising trend, but instead a series of year-to-year variations in real GDP growth. In 1991, for example, the economy was in recession and slipped below the zero growth line (negative growth), and in the recession year of 2001, the growth rate was less than 1 percent. In 2007, the growth rate was 2.0 percent, which was below the long-term 3.5 percent growth rate. As this text is written in 2008, the economy has continued to experience weak growth and there are fears of a recession.

CHECKPOINT

Where Are We on the Business-Cycle Roller Coaster?

Suppose the economy has been in a recession and everyone is asking when the economy will recover. To find an answer to the state of the economy's health, a television reporter interviews Terrence Carter, a local car dealer. Carter says, "I do not see any recovery. The third quarter of this year we sold more cars than the second quarter, but sales in these two quarters were far below the first quarter." Is Mr. Carter correct? Are his observations consistent with the peak, recession, trough, or recovery phase of the business cycle?

GLOBAL ECONOMICS

Real GDP Growth Rates in Other Countries

Exhibit 4 presents real GDP growth rates for selected countries in 2007. China, India, and Russia had the largest rates of growth at 10.0, 8.4, and 6.4 percent, respectively. The United States and other western industrialized countries in the exhibit had growth rates below 3 percent.

Business-Cycle Indicators

In addition to changes in real GDP, the media often report several other macro variables that measure business activity and are published by the U.S. Department of Commerce in *Business Conditions Digest*. These economic *indicator* variables are classified in three categories: leading indicators, coincident indicators, and lagging indicators. Exhibit 5 lists the variables corresponding to each indicator series.

The government's chief forecasting gauge for business cycles is the index of leading indicators. Leading indicators are variables that change before real GDP changes. This index captures the headlines when there is concern over swings in the economy. The first set of 10 variables in Exhibit 5 is used to forecast the business cycle months in advance. For example, a slump ahead is signaled when declines exceed advances in the components of the leading indicators data series. But beware! The leading indicators may rise for two consecutive months and then fall for the next three consecutive months. Economists are therefore cautious and wait for the leading indicators to move in a new direction for several months before forecasting a change in the cycle.

Is a recession near? The Conference Board's Consumer Confidence Index is often reported in the news as a key measure of the economy's health. It is based on a survey of 5,000 households who are asked their expectations of how well the economy will perform over the next six months. Prolonged consumer pessimism can result in less consumer spending and contribute to slowing economic growth. Stated differently, persistent consumer pessimism can result in lower personal consumption expenditures (*C*) and business investment (*I*) because businesses reduce investment when consumers' purchases of their products fall. The 9/11 terrorist attack on the United States in 2001 contributed to further erosion in consumer confidence and to the recession.

The second data series of variables listed in Exhibit 5 are four coincident indicators. Coincident indicators are variables that change at the same time that real GDP changes. For example, as real GDP rises, economists expect employment, personal income, industrial production, and sales to rise.

The third group of variables listed in Exhibit 5 are lagging indicators. Lagging indicators are seven variables that change after real GDP changes. For example, the duration of unemployment is a lagging indicator. As real GDP increases, the average

Leading indicators
Variables that change before real GDP changes.

Coincident indicators
Variables that change at the same time that real GDP changes.

Lagging indicators
Variables that change after real GDP changes.

EXHIBIT 4 | Global Comparison of Real GDP Growth Rates, 2007

The exhibit shows that China, India, and Russia had the largest rates of growth at 10.0, 8.4, and 6.4 percent, respectively. In contrast, the United States and other western industrialized countries had growth rates below 3 percent for the year. The United States had a growth rate of 2.0 percent.

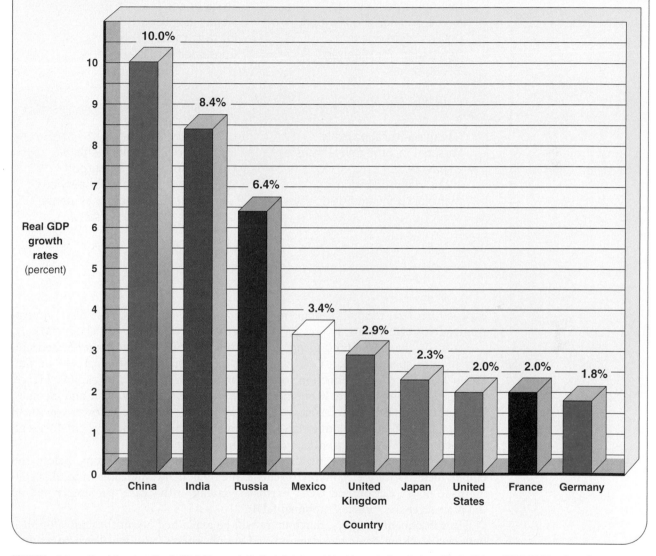

SOURCE: International Monetary Fund, *World Economic Outlook Database*, http://www.imf.org/external/pubs/ft/weo/2007/01/data/weselga.aspx.

time workers remain unemployed does not fall until some months after the beginning of the recovery.

Total Spending and the Business Cycle

The uneven historical pattern of economic growth for the U.S. economy gives rise to the following question: What causes business cycles? The theory generally accepted by economists today is that changes in total or aggregate expenditures are the cause of variations in real GDP. Recall from the previous chapter that aggregate

EXHIBIT 5	Business-Cycle Indicators

Leading Indicators

Average workweek	New building permits
Unemployment claims	Stock prices
New consumer goods orders	Money supply
Delayed deliveries	Interest rates
New orders for plant and equipment	Consumer expectations

Coincident Indicators	**Lagging Indicators**
Nonagricultural payrolls	Unemployment rate
Personal income minus transfer payments	Duration of unemployment
Industrial production	Labor cost per unit of output
Manufacturing and trade sales	Consumer price index for services
	Commercial and industrial loans
	Consumer credit to personal income ratio
	Prime rate

expenditures refer to total spending for *final goods* by households, businesses, government, and foreign buyers. Expressed as a formula: $GDP = C - I - G - (X - M)$.

Why do changes in total spending cause the level of GDP to change? Stated simply, if total spending increases, businesses find it profitable to increase output. When firms increase production, they use more land, labor, and capital. Hence, increased spending leads to economic growth in output, employment, and incomes. When total spending falls, businesses find it profitable to produce a lower volume of goods and avoid accumulating unsold inventory. In this case, output, employment, and incomes fall. These cutbacks, in turn, can lead to a recession.

The situation just described assumes the economy is operating below full employment. Once the economy reaches full employment, increases in total spending have no impact on real GDP. Further spending in this case will simply pull up the price level and "inflate" nominal GDP.

In subsequent chapters, much more will be explained about the causes of business cycles. Using aggregate demand and supply curves, you will learn to analyze why changes occur in national output, unemployment, and the price level.

Unemployment

Since the abyss of the Great Depression, a major economic goal of the United States has been to achieve a high level of employment. The Employment Act of 1946 declared it the responsibility of the federal government to use all practical means consistent with free competitive enterprise to create conditions under which all able individuals who are willing to work and seeking work will be afforded useful employment opportunities. Later, Congress amended this act with the Full

Employment and Balanced Growth Act of 1978, which established specific goals for unemployment and the level of prices.

Each month the Bureau of Labor Statistics (BLS) of the U.S. Department of Labor, in conjunction with the Bureau of the Census, conducts a survey of a random sample of about 60,000 households in the United States. Each member of the household who is 16 years of age or older is asked whether he or she is employed or unemployed. If a person works at least 1 hour per week for pay or at least 15 hours per week as an unpaid worker in a family business, he or she is counted as employed. If the person is not employed, the question then is whether he or she has looked for work in the last month. If so, the person is said to be unemployed. Based on its survey data, the BLS publishes the unemployment rate and other employment-related statistics monthly.

The unemployment rate is the percentage of people in the civilian labor force who are without jobs and are actively seeking jobs. But who is actually counted as an unemployed worker, and which people belong to the labor force? Certainly, all people without jobs are not classified as unemployed. Babies, full-time students, and retired persons are not counted as unemployed. Likewise, individuals who are ill or severely disabled are not included as unemployed. And there are other groups not counted.

Turn to Exhibit 6. The *civilian labor force* is the number of people 16 years of age and over who are either employed or unemployed, excluding members of the armed forces and other groups listed in the "persons not in labor force" category. Based on survey data, the BLS computes the *civilian unemployment rate*, using the following formula:

$$\text{Unemployment rate} = \frac{\text{unemployed}}{\text{civilian labor force}} \times 100$$

In 2007, the unemployment rate was

$$4.6\% = \frac{7.1 \text{ million persons}}{153.1 \text{ million persons}} \times 100$$

Exhibit 7 charts a historical record of the U.S. unemployment rate since 1929. Note that the highest unemployment rate reached was 25 percent in 1933 during the Great Depression. At the other extreme, the lowest unemployment rate we have attained was 1.2 percent in 1944. As this text is written in 2008, the unemployment rate surged to over 6 percent as a barely growing economy lost jobs amid fears of a recession.

Unemployment in Other Countries

Exhibit 8 shows unemployment rates for selected countries in 2007. France and other major industrialized countries had unemployment rates higher than the United States. The unemployment rate of France was about twice as high as the U.S. rate.

Unemployment Rate Criticisms

The unemployment rate is criticized for both understating and overstating the "true" unemployment rate. An example of *overstating* the unemployment rate occurs when respondents to the BLS survey falsely report they are seeking employment. The motivation may be that their eligibility for unemployment compensation or welfare benefits depends on actively pursuing a job. Or possibly an individual is "employed" in illegal activities.

Unemployment rate

The percentage of people in the civilian labor force who are without jobs and are actively seeking jobs.

Civilian labor force

The number of people 16 years of age and older who are employed or who are actively seeking a job, excluding armed forces, homemakers, discouraged workers, and other persons not in the labor force.

GLOBAL ECONOMICS

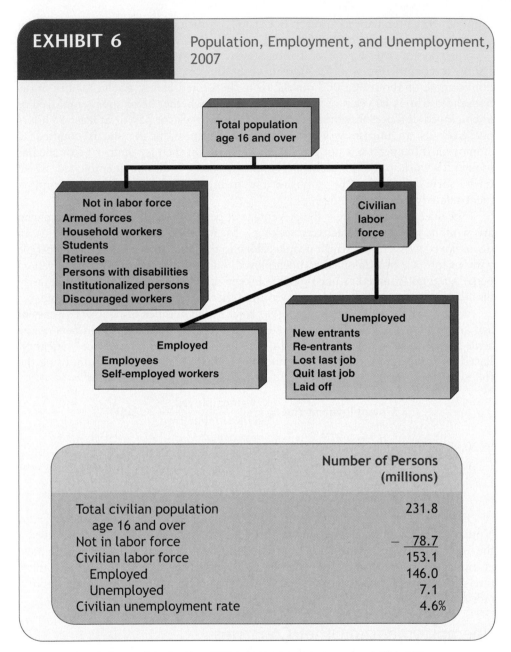

EXHIBIT 6   Population, Employment, and Unemployment, 2007

	Number of Persons (millions)
Total civilian population age 16 and over	231.8
Not in labor force	– 78.7
Civilian labor force	153.1
Employed	146.0
Unemployed	7.1
Civilian unemployment rate	4.6%

SOURCE: *Economic Report of the President*, 2008, http://www.gpoaccess.gov/eop/, Table B-35.

Discouraged worker

A person who wants to work, but who has given up searching for work because he or she believes there will be no job offers.

The other side of the coin is that the official definition of unemployment *understates* the unemployment rate by not counting so-called discouraged workers. A discouraged worker is a person who wants to work, but has given up searching for work because he or she believes there will be no job offers. After repeated rejections, discouraged workers often turn to their families, friends, and public welfare for support. The BLS counts a discouraged worker as anyone who has looked for work within the last 12 months, but is no longer actively looking. The BLS simply includes discouraged workers in the "not in labor force" category listed in Exhibit 6. Because

EXHIBIT 7	The U.S. Unemployment Rate, 1929-2007

This exhibit shows fluctuations in the civilian unemployment rate since 1929. The unemployment rate reached a high point of 25 percent in 1933 during the Great Depression. The lowest unemployment rate of 1.2 percent was achieved during World War II in 1944. In 2007, the unemployment rate was 4.6 percent. In 2008, the rate grew sharply to over 6 percent.

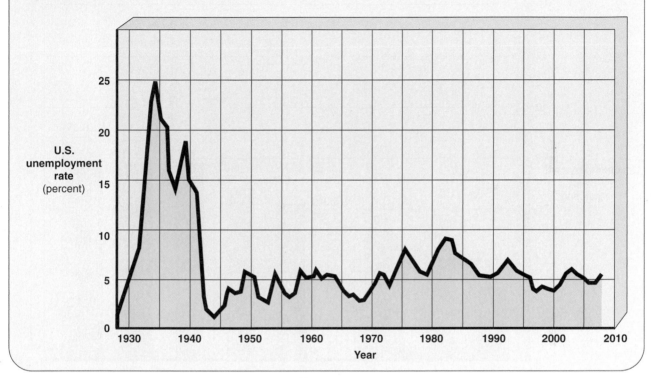

SOURCE: *Economic Report of the President*, 2008, http://www.gpoaccess.gov/eop/, Table B-35.

the number of discouraged workers rises during a recession, the underestimation of the official unemployment rate increases during a downturn.

Another example of *understating* the unemployment rate occurs because the official BLS data include all part-time workers as fully employed. These workers are actually partially employed, and many would work full time if they could find full-time employment.

Finally, the unemployment statistics do not measure *underemployment*. If jobs are scarce and a college graduate takes a job not requiring his or her level of skills, a human resource is underutilized. Or suppose an employer cuts an employee's hours of work from 40 to 20 per week. Such losses of work potential are greater during a recession, but are not reflected in the unemployment rate.

Types of Unemployment

The unemployment rate is determined by three different types of unemployment: *frictional*, *structural*, and *cyclical*. Understanding these conceptual categories of unemployment aids in understanding and formulating policies to ease the burden

| EXHIBIT 8 | Unemployment Rates for Selected Nations, 2007 |

In 2007, most of the major industrialized nations shown had a higher unemployment rate than the United States. The unemployment rate of France was about twice as high as the U.S. rate.

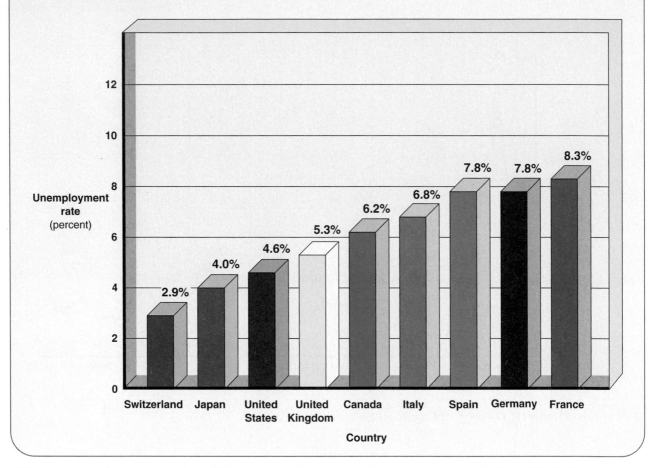

SOURCE: International Monetary Fund, *The World Economic Outlook Database*, http://www.imf.org/external/pubs/ft/weo/2007/01/data/weoselgr .aspx, Table 4.

of unemployment. In fact, each type of unemployment requires a different policy prescription to reduce it.

Frictional Unemployment

For some unemployed workers, the absence of a job is only temporary. At any given time, some people with marketable skills are fired, and others voluntarily quit jobs to accept or look for new ones. And there are always young people who leave school and search for their first job. Workers in some industries such as construction experience short periods of unemployment between projects, and temporary layoffs are common. Other workers are "seasonally unemployed." For example, ski resort workers will be employed in the winter, but not in the summer, and certain crops are harvested "in season." Because jobs requiring the skills of these unemployed workers are available, the unemployed workers and the job vacancies are matched and such workers are therefore considered "between jobs." This type of unemployment is called frictional unemployment, and it is not of great concern. Frictional unemployment is unemployment caused by the normal search time required by workers with marketable skills who are changing jobs, initially entering the labor force, or reentering the labor force. The cause of frictional unemployment is either the transition time to a new job or the lack of information required to match a job applicant immediately with a job vacancy. For this reason, frictional unemployment is sometimes called *transitional unemployment* or *search unemployment*.

The fact that job market information is imperfect and operates with "friction" causes frictional unemployment in the economy. Because it takes time to search for the information required to match employer and employees, some workers will always be frictionally unemployed. Frictional unemployment is therefore a normal condition in an economic system permitting freedom of job choice. Improved methods of distributing job information through job listings on the Internet help unemployed workers find jobs more quickly and reduce frictional unemployment.

Structural Unemployment

Unlike frictional unemployment, structural unemployment is not a short-term situation. Instead, it is long-term, or possibly permanent, unemployment resulting from the nonexistence of jobs for unemployed workers. Structural unemployment is unemployment caused by a mismatch of the skills of workers who are out of work and the skills required for existing job opportunities. Note that changing jobs and lack of job information are *not* problems for structurally unemployed workers. Unlike frictionally unemployed workers who have marketable skills, structurally unemployed workers require additional education or retraining. Changes in the structure of the economy create the following three cases of structural unemployment.

First, workers may face joblessness because they lack the education or the job-related skills to perform available jobs. This type of structural unemployment particularly affects teenagers and minority groups, but other groups of workers can be affected as well. For example, environmental concerns, such as protecting the spotted owl by restricting trees from being cut, cost some loggers their jobs. Reducing such structural unemployment requires retraining loggers for new jobs as, say, forest rangers. Another example involves the "peace dividend" from the reduction in defense spending after a war. This situation creates structural unemployment for discharged military personnel who require retraining after a war for, say, teaching, nursing, or police jobs.

Second, the consuming public may decide to increase the demand for Porsches and decrease the demand for Chevrolet Corvettes. This shift in demand would cause U.S. autoworkers who lose their jobs in Bowling Green, Kentucky, to become structurally unemployed. To regain employment, these unemployed autoworkers must retrain and find job openings in other industries, for example, manufacturing IBM computer printers in North Carolina.

Third, implementation of the latest technology may also increase the pool of structural unemployment in a particular industry and region. For example, the U.S. textile industry, located primarily in the South, can fight less expensive foreign textile imports by installing modern machinery. This new capital may replace textile workers. But suppose these unemployed textile workers do not wish to move to a new location where new types of jobs are available. The costs of moving, fear of the unknown, and family ties are understandable reasons for reluctance to move, and, instead, the workers become structurally unemployed.

There are many causes of structural unemployment, including poor schools, new products, new technology, foreign competition, geographic differences, restricted entry into jobs, and shifts in government priorities. Because of the numerous sources

Frictional unemployment

Unemployment caused by the normal search time required by workers with marketable skills who are changing jobs, initially entering the labor force, reentering the labor force, or seasonally unemployed.

Structural unemployment

Unemployment caused by a mismatch of the skills of workers out of work and the skills required for existing job opportunities.

of mismatching between skills and jobs, economists consider a certain level of structural unemployment inevitable. Public and private programs that train employees to fill existing job openings decrease structural unemployment. Conversely, one of the concerns about the minimum wage is that it may contribute to structural unemployment. In Exhibit 6 of Chapter 4, we demonstrated that a minimum wage set by legislation above the equilibrium wage causes unemployment. One approach intended to offset such undesirable effects of the minimum wage is a subminimum wage paid during a training period to give employers an incentive to hire unskilled workers.

Cyclical Unemployment

Cyclical unemployment

Unemployment caused by the lack of jobs during a recession.

Cyclical unemployment is directly attributable to the lack of jobs caused by the business cycle. Cyclical unemployment is unemployment caused by the lack of jobs during a recession. When real GDP falls, companies close, jobs disappear, and workers scramble for fewer available jobs. Similar to the game of musical chairs, there are not enough chairs (jobs) for the number of players (workers) in the game.

The Great Depression is a dramatic example of cyclical unemployment. There was a sudden decline in consumption, investment, government spending, and net exports. As a result of this striking fall in real GDP, the unemployment rate rose to about 25 percent (see Exhibit 7). Now notice what happened to the unemployment rate when real GDP rose sharply during World War II. To smooth out these swings in unemployment, a focus of macroeconomic policy is to moderate cyclical unemployment.

CHECKPOINT
What Kind of Unemployment Did the Invention of the Wheel Cause?

But Egor, what about the effect on labor?

Did the invention of the wheel cause frictional, structural, or cyclical unemployment?

The following is a classic article from the late 1980s that illustrates the types of unemployment and describes a recurring labor market situation:

People looking for job security have rarely chosen the music industry. But these days, musicians say, competition from machines has removed what little stability there was. Modern machines can effectively duplicate string sections, drummers, and even horn sections, so with the exception of concerts, the jobs available to live musicians are growing fewer by the day...

It is not the first time that technology has thrown a wrench into musical careers. When talking pictures helped usher in the death of vaudeville, and again, when recorded music replaced live music in radio station studios, the market for musicians took a beating from which it never fully recovered... The musicians' plight is not getting universal sympathy. Some industry insiders say that the current job problems are an inevitable price of progress, and that musicians should update their skills to deal with the new instruments...

But others insist that more than musicians' livelihood is at stake. Mr. Glasel, [Musicians' Union] Local 802's president, warns that unbridled computerization of music could eventually threaten the quality of music. Jobs for trumpet players, for instance, have dropped precipitously since the synthesizer managed a fair approximation of the trumpet. And without trumpet players, he asked, "where is the next generation going to get its Dizzy Gillespie?"[1]

The threat to musicians' jobs continues: The Toyota Motor Corp. unveiled its instrument-playing humanoid robots at the 2005 World Exposition. The robots played drums and horn instruments, such as trumpets and tubas.

And in 2008, a humanoid robot walked on the stage, said, "Hello, everyone," lifted the baton, and conducted the Detroit Symphony Orchestra. Its timing was judged to be impeccable, but the robot conductor lacked any spur-of-the-moment emotions.

Now there is a Robot Hall of Fame at Carnegie Mellon University. The robots fall into two categories—robots from science and robots from science fiction. A panel of experts, each serving a two-year term, chooses robots in each category to be inducted into the Hall of Fame. Envelope please! The first winners were: The Unimate, the first industrial robot; the Sojourner robot from NASA's Mars Pathfinder mission; R2D2, the "droid" from the Stars Wars films; and HAL-9000, the rogue computer from the film 2001: A Space Odyssey.

ANALYZE THE ISSUE

1. Are the musicians experiencing frictional, structural, or cyclical unemployment? Explain.
2. What solution would you propose for the trumpet players mentioned above?

James S. Newton, "A Death Knell Sounds for Musical Jobs," *The New York Times*, March 1, 1987, sec. 3, p. 9.

The Goal of Full Employment

In this section, we take a closer look at the meaning of full employment, also called the *natural rate of unemployment*. Because both frictional and structural unemployment are present in good and bad times, *full employment* does not mean "zero percent unemployment." Full employment is the situation in which an economy

Full employment
The situation in which an economy operates at an unemployment rate equal to the sum of the frictional and structural unemployment rates, also called the *natural rate of unemployment*.

operates at an unemployment rate equal to the sum of the frictional and structural unemployment rates. Full employment therefore is the rate of unemployment that exists without cyclical unemployment.

Unfortunately, economists cannot state with certainty what percentages of the labor force are frictionally and structurally unemployed at any particular point in time. In practice, therefore, full employment is difficult to define. Moreover, the full-employment rate of unemployment, or natural rate of unemployment, changes over time. In the 1960s, 4 percent unemployment was generally considered to represent full employment. In the 1980s, the accepted rate was 6 percent, and, currently, the consensus among economists is that the natural rate is close to 5 percent.

Several reasons are given for why full employment is not fixed. One reason is that between the early 1960s and the early 1980s, the participation of women and teenagers in the labor force increased. This change in the labor force composition increased the full-employment rate of unemployment because both women and young workers (under age 25) typically experience higher unemployment rates than men. Another frequently cited and controversial reason for the rise in the full-employment rate of unemployment is that larger unemployment compensation payments, food stamps, welfare, and Social Security benefits from the government make unemployment less painful. In the 1990s, the natural rate of unemployment declined somewhat because the entry of females and teenagers into the labor force slowed. Also, the baby boom generation has aged, and middle-aged workers have lower unemployment rates.

The GDP Gap

GDP gap

The difference between actual real GDP and potential or full-employment real GDP.

When people in an economy are unemployed, society forfeits the production of goods and services. To determine the dollar value of how much society loses if the economy fails to reach the natural rate of unemployment, economists estimate the GDP gap. The GDP gap is the difference between full-employment real GDP and actual real GDP. The level of GDP that could be produced at full employment is also called *potential real GDP*. Because the GDP gap is estimated on the basis of the difference between GDP at the full-employment rate of unemployment and GDP at the actual unemployment rate, the GDP gap measures the cost of cyclical unemployment. Expressed as a formula:

$$\text{GDP gap} = \text{actual real GDP} - \text{potential real GDP}$$

Exhibit 9 shows the size of the GDP gap (in 2000 prices) from 1990 to 2007, based on potential real GDP and actual real GDP for each of these years. When the two lines in the figure cross, the economy is performing at its peak. During the 1990–1991 recession, the economy operated below its potential (negative GDP gap), and society lost billions of dollars in potential real GDP. After the 1990–1991 recession, the economy operated below its potential until a brief period before the 2001 recession when the economy operated above its potential (positive gap). Since this recession, the U.S. economy has experienced negative GDP gaps.

> **Conclusion** *The gap between actual and potential real GDP measures the monetary losses of real goods and services to the nation from operating at less than full employment.*

amazon.com

Billing Address:
Benjamin Lee Grant
543 Massachusetts Avenue
Unit 2
Boston, MA 02118-1474
United States

Shipping Address:
Benjamin Lee Grant
63 Pinckney Street
Boston, MA 02114
United States

Your order of March 7, 2009 (Order ID:103 - 3349005 - 5623408)

Returns Are Easy!
Visit http://www.amazon.com/returns to return any item - including gifts - in unopened or original
condition within 30 days for a full refund (other restrictions apply)

SDT5px7x6R

Qty.	Item	Item Price	Total
	IN THIS SHIPMENT		
1	Economics for Today (** P22 63G3 **) (02268196 02268196) 0224591395 Hardcover	$163.16	$163.16

	Subtotal	$163.16
	Order Total	$163.16
	Paid via Mastercard	$163.16
	Balance Due	$0.00

This shipment completes your order

5102 (1 of 1)

amazon.com

EXHIBIT 9	Actual and Potential GDP, 1990–2007

The GDP gap is the difference between actual real GDP and potential real GDP. Because potential real GDP is based on full employment, a positive GDP gap measures the cost of cyclical unemployment in terms of real GDP. A positive GDP gap measures a boom in the economy when workers are employed overtime. In 2000, for example, the U.S. economy experienced a positive GDP gap. Since the recession in 2001, the U.S. economy has operated below its potential (negative GDP gaps).

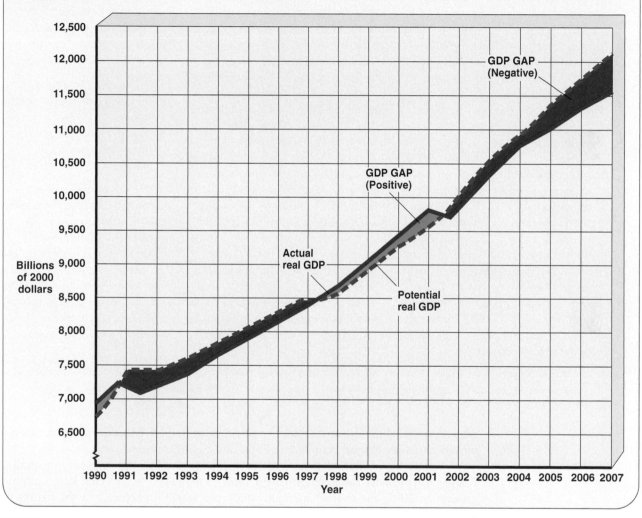

SOURCE: Economagic, www.economagic.com/.

Nonmonetary and Demographic Consequences of Unemployment

The burden of unemployment is more than the loss of potential output measured by the GDP gap. Unemployment also has nonmonetary costs. Some people endure unemployment pretty well because they have substantial savings to draw on, but others sink into despair. Without work, many people lose their feeling of worth. A person's self-image suffers when he or she cannot support a family and be a valuable member of society. Research has associated high unemployment with suicides,

YOU'RE THE ECONOMIST Brother Can You Spare a Dime?

Applicable Concept: human costs of unemployment

The unemployment rate does not measure the full impact of unemployment on individuals. Prolonged unemployment not only means lost wages, but it also impairs health and social relationships. The United States fought its most monstrous battle against unemployment during the Great Depression of the 1930s. Return to Exhibit 7 and note that the unemployment rate stayed at 20 percent or more from 1932 through 1935. In 1933, it reached almost 25 percent of the civilian labor force; that is, about one out of every four people who wanted to work could not. This meant 16 million Americans were out of work when our country's population was less than half its present size.[1] For comparison, at the low point of the 1990–1991 recession, about 10 million Americans were officially unemployed.

But these statistics tell only part of the horror story. Millions of workers were "discouraged workers" who had simply given up looking for work because there was no work available, and these people were not counted. People were standing in line for soup kitchens, selling apples on the street, and living in cardboard shacks. "Brother can you spare a dime?" was a common greeting. Some people jumped out of windows, and others roamed the country trying valiantly to survive. John Steinbeck's great novel *The Grapes of Wrath* described millions of midwesterners who drove in caravans to California after being wiped out by drought in what became known as the Dust Bowl.

A 1992 study estimated the frightening impact of sustained unemployment that is not reflected in official unemployment data.

Mary Merva, a University of Utah economist, co-authored a study of unemployment in 30 selected big cities from 1976 to 1990. The research found that a 1 percentage point increase in the national unemployment rate resulted in

- 6.7 percent more murders,
- 3.1 percent more deaths from stroke,
- 5.6 percent more death from heart disease, and
- 3.9 percent increase in suicides.[2]

Although these estimates are subject to statistical qualifications, they underscore the notion that prolonged unemployment poses a real danger to many individuals. As people change their behavior in the face of layoffs, cutbacks, or sudden drop in net worth, more and more Americans find themselves clinically depressed.

---

1. U.S. Bureau of the Census, *Historical Statistics of the United States, Colonial Times to 1957* (Washington, D.C.), Series D46–47, p. 73.
2. Robert Davis, "Recession's Cost: Lives," *USA Today*, Oct. 16, 1992, p. 1A.

---

crime, mental illness, heart attacks, and other maladies. Moreover, severe unemployment causes despair, family breakups, and political unrest.

Various labor market groups share the impact of unemployment unequally. Exhibit 10 presents the unemployment rates experienced by selected demographic groups. In 2007, the overall unemployment rate was 4.6 percent, but the figures in the exhibit reveal the unequal burden by race, age, and educational attainment. First, it is interesting to note that the unemployment rate for males and females was almost equal. Second, the unemployment rate for African-Americans was twice that for whites and higher than the rate for Hispanics. Third, teenagers experienced a high unemployment rate because they are new entrants to the workforce who have little employment experience, high quit rates, and little job mobility. Again, race is a strong factor, and the unemployment rate for African-American male or female teenagers was more than twice that for white male or female teenagers. Among the explanations are discrimination; the concentration of African-Americans in the inner city, where job opportunities for less skilled (blue-collar) workers are inadequate; and the minimum wage law.

EXHIBIT 10	Civilian Unemployment Rates by Selected Demographic Groups, 2007	
Demographic Group		**Unemployment Rate (percent)**
Overall		4.6%
Gender		
Male		4.7
Female		4.5
Race		
White		4.1
Hispanic		5.6
African-American		8.3
Teenagers (16–19 years old)		
All		15.7
White males		15.7
African-American males		33.8
White females		12.1
African-American females		25.3
Education (25 years and over)		
Less than high school diploma		7.1
High school graduates		4.4
Bachelor's degree and higher		2.0

SOURCES: *Economic Report of the President*, 2008, http://www.gpoacccess.gov/eop/, Table B-42 and Table B-43, and U.S Bureau of Labor Statistics, *Current Population Survey*, http://stats.bls.gov/cps/cpsatabs.htm, Table A-4.

Finally, comparison of the unemployment rates in 2007 by educational attainment reveals the importance of education as an insurance policy against unemployment. Firms are much less likely to lay off a higher-skilled worker with a college education, in whom they have a greater investment in terms of training and salaries, than a worker with only a high school diploma.

KEY CONCEPTS

Business cycle	Leading indicators	Frictional unemployment
Peak	Coincident indicators	Structural unemployment
Recession	Lagging indicators	Cyclical unemployment
Trough	Unemployment rate	Full employment
Recovery	Civilian labor force	GDP gap
Economic growth	Discouraged worker	

SUMMARY

- **Business cycles** are recurrent rises and falls in real GDP over a period of years. Business cycles vary greatly in duration and intensity. A cycle consists of four phases: peak, recession, trough, and recovery. The generally accepted theory today is that changes in the forces of demand and supply cause business cycles. A **recession** is officially defined as at least two consecutive quarters of real GDP decline. A **trough** is the turning point in national output between recession and recovery. During a **recovery,** there is an upturn in the business cycle, during which real GDP rises. A **peak** occurs when real GDP reaches its maximum level during a recovery.

Hypothetical Business Cycle

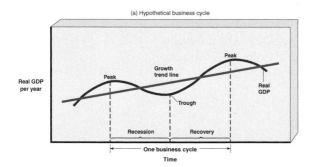

- **Economic growth** is measured by the annual percentage change in real GDP in a nation. The long-term average annual growth rate in the United States is 3.5 percent.
- **Leading, coincident,** and **lagging indicators** are economic variables that change before, at the same time as, and after changes in real GDP, respectively.
- The **unemployment rate** is the ratio of the number of unemployed to the number in the civilian labor force multiplied by 100. The nation's **civilian labor force** consists of people who are employed plus those who are out of work, but seeking employment.

- **Discouraged workers** are a reason critics say the unemployment rate is *understated*. Discouraged workers are persons who want to work, but have given up searching for work. Another criticism of the unemployment rate is that it *overstates* unemployment because respondents can falsely report they are seeking a job.

- **Frictional, structural,** and **cyclical unemployment** are different types of unemployment. **Frictional unemployment,** including seasonal unemployment, results when workers are seeking new jobs that exist. The problem is that imperfect information prevents matching the applicants with the available jobs. **Structural unemployment** is unemployment caused by factors in the economy, including lack of skills, changes in product demand, and technological change. **Cyclical unemployment** is unemployment resulting from insufficient aggregate demand.

- **Full employment** occurs when the unemployment rate is equal to the total of the frictional and structural unemployment rates. Currently, the full-employment rate of unemployment (natural rate of unemployment) in the United States is considered to be close to 5 percent. At this rate of unemployment, the economy is producing at its maximum potential.

- The **GDP gap** is the difference between full employment, or potential real GDP and actual real GDP. Therefore, the GDP gap measures the loss of output due to cyclical unemployment.

SUMMARY OF CONCLUSION STATEMENTS

- We value economic growth as one of our nation's economic goals because it increases our standard of living—it creates a bigger "economic pie."

- The gap between actual and potential real GDP measures the monetary losses of real goods and services to the nation from operating at less than full employment.

STUDY QUESTIONS AND PROBLEMS

1. What is the basic cause of the business cycle?

2. Following are real GDP figures for 10 quarters:

Quarter	Real GDP (billions of dollars)
1	$ 400
2	500
3	300
4	200
5	300
6	500
7	800
8	900
9	1,000
10	500

Plot these data points, and identify the four phases of the business cycle. Give a theory that may explain the cause of the observed business cycle. What are some of the consequences of a prolonged decline in real GDP? Is the decline in real GDP from $1,000 billion to $500 billion a recession?

3. In a given year, there are 10 million unemployed workers and 120 million employed workers in an economy. Excluding members of the armed forces and persons in institutions, and assuming these figures include only civilian workers, calculate the civilian unemployment rate.

4. Describe the relevant criteria that government statisticians use to determine whether a person is "unemployed."

5. How has the official unemployment rate been criticized for overestimating and underestimating unemployment?

6. Why is frictional unemployment inevitable in an economy characterized by imperfect job information?

7. How does structural unemployment differ from cyclical unemployment?

8. Is it reasonable to expect the unemployment rate to fall to zero for an economy? What is the relationship of frictional, structural, and cyclical unemployment to the full-employment rate of unemployment, or natural rate of unemployment?

9. In the 1960s, economists used 4 percent as their approximation for the natural rate of unemployment. Currently, full employment is on the order of 5 percent unemployment. What is the major factor accounting for this rise?

10. Speculate on why teenage unemployment rates exceed those for the overall labor force.

11. Explain the GDP gap.

For Online Exercises, go to the text Web site at www.cengage.com/economics/tucker.

following categories: food, housing, apparel, transportation, medical care, entertainment, and other expenditures. Exhibit 1 presents a more detailed breakdown of these categories and shows the relative importance of each as a percentage of total expenditures. The survey reveals, for example, that 33 cents out of each consumer dollar are spent for housing and 18 cents for transportation. The composition of the market basket generally remains unchanged from one period to the next, so the CPI is called a *fixed-weight price index*. If 33 percent of consumer spending was on housing during 1982–1984, the assumption is that 33 percent of spending is still spent on housing in, say, 2007. Over time, particular items in the CPI change. For example, personal computers, digital cameras, and cell phones have been added. The base period is changed periodically.

How the CPI Is Computed

Exhibit 2 illustrates the basic idea behind the CPI and shows how this price index measures inflation. Suppose, in 1982, a typical family in the United States lived a very meager existence and purchased a market basket of only hamburgers, gasoline, and jeans. Column 1 shows the quantity purchased for each of these items, and column 2 lists the corresponding average selling price. Multiplying the price times the quantity gives the market basket cost in column 3 of each consumer product purchased in 1982. The total cost paid by our typical family for the market basket, based on 1982 prices and quantities purchased, is $245.

Fourteen years later it is 1996, and we wish to know the impact of rising prices on consumer purchases. To calculate the CPI, we determine the cost of the *same* market basket, valued at 1996 *current-year prices,* and compare this to the cost at

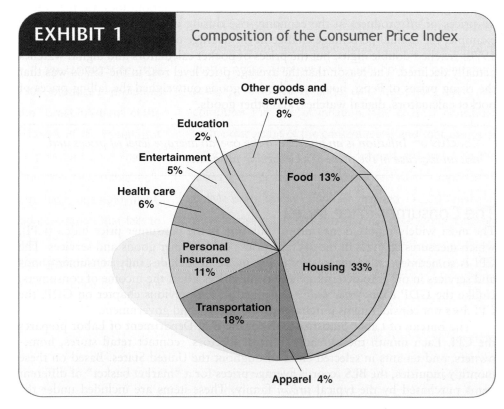

| EXHIBIT 1 | Composition of the Consumer Price Index |

SOURCE: Bureau of Labor Statistics, *Composition of Consumer Unit,* http:www.bls.gov/cex/#tables, Table 49.

EXHIBIT 2 — Consumer Price Index for a Simple Economy

Products in Consumers' Market Basket	(1) 1982 Quantity Purchased	(2) 1982 Price	(3) Market Basket Cost in 1982 [(1) × (2)]	(4) 1996 Price	(5) Market Basket Cost in 1996 [(1) × (4)]
Hamburgers	50	$ 0.80	$ 40	$ 1.00	$ 50
Gallons of gasoline	250	0.70	175	0.90	225
Jeans	2	15.00	30	30.00	60
			Total 1982 cost = $245		Total 1996 cost = $335

$$1996 \text{ CPI} = \frac{1996 \text{ market basket cost}}{1982 \text{ market basket cost}} \times 100$$

$$1996 \text{ CPI} = \frac{\$335}{\$245} \times 100 = 136.7$$

1982 *base-year prices*. A base year is a year chosen as a reference point for comparison with some earlier or later year. Expressed as a general formula:

$$\text{CPI} = \frac{\text{cost of market basket of products at current-year (1996) prices}}{\text{cost of same market basket of product at base-year (1982) prices}} \times 100$$

As shown in Exhibit 2, the 1996 cost for our market basket example is calculated by multiplying the 1996 price for each item in column 4 times the 1982 quantity purchased in column 1. Column 5 lists the result for each item in the market basket, and the total market basket cost in 1996 is $335. The CPI value of 136.7 is computed in Exhibit 2 as the ratio of the current 1996 cost of the market basket ($335) to the cost of the same market basket in the 1982 base year ($245) multiplied by 100.

The value of the CPI in the base year is always 100 because the numerator and the denominator of the CPI formula are the same in the base year. Currently, the CPI uses 1982–1984 spending patterns as its base year. Once the BLS selects the base year and uses the market basket technique to generate the CPI numbers, the annual *inflation rate* is computed as the percentage change in the official CPI from one year to the next. Mathematically,

$$\text{Annual rate of inflation} = \frac{\text{CPI in given year} - \text{CPI in previous year}}{\text{CPI in previous year}} \times 100$$

Exhibit 3 lists actual CPI data as reported in the *Economic Report of the President*. You can use the above formula and calculate the inflation rate for any given year using the base year of (1982–84 = 100). In 2006, for example, the CPI was 201.6, while in 2007, it was 207.3. The rate of inflation for 2007 is computed as follows:

$$2.8\% = \frac{207.3 - 201.6}{201.6} \times 100$$

Base year

A year chosen as a reference point for comparison with some earlier or later year.

EXHIBIT 3	Consumer Price Indexes and Inflation Rates, Selected Years	
Year	**CPI**	**Inflation Rate**
1931	15.2	—
1932	13.7	−9.9%
1979	72.6	—
1980	82.4	13.5
2000	172.2	—
2001	177.1	2.8
2002	179.9	1.6
2006	201.6	—
2007	207.3	2.8

SOURCE: *Economic Report of the President,* 2008, http://www.gpo.access.gov/eop/, Table B-60 and B-6A.

The negative inflation rate of 9.9 percent for 1932 was deflation, and the 13.5 percent inflation rate for 1980 illustrates a relatively high rate in recent U.S. history. The fall in the inflation rate from 2.8 percent to 1.6 percent between 2001 and 2002 was disinflation. Disinflation is a reduction in the rate of inflation. Disinflation does not mean that prices are falling; rather, it means that the rate of increases in prices is falling.

Disinflation
A reduction in the rate of inflation.

CHECKPOINT

The College Education Price Index
Suppose your *market basket* for a college education consisted of only the four items listed in the following table:

Item	2007	2008
Tuition and fees[1]	$2,500	$2,600
Room and board[2]	6,000	6,200
Books[3]	1,000	1,200
Soft drinks[4]	150	200

[1] Tuition for two semesters.
[2] Payment for nine months.
[3] Twenty books of 800 pages with full color.
[4] Three hundred 12-ounce Coca-Colas.

Using 2007 as your base year, what is the percentage change in the college education price index in 2008?

History of U.S. Inflation Rates

Exhibit 4 shows how prices have changed in the United States since 1929, as measured by annual changes in the CPI. During the early years of the Great Depression, the nation experienced *deflation,* and the CPI declined at almost a double-digit rate. In contrast, the CPI reached a double-digit inflation rate during and immediately following World War II. After 1950, the inflation rate generally remained below

EXHIBIT 4   The U.S. Inflation Rate, 1929–2007

During the Great Depression, the economy experienced deflation as prices plunged. During and immediately after World War II, the annual rate of inflation reached the double-digit level. After 1950, the inflation rate was generally below 3 percent until the inflationary pressures from the Vietnam War in the late 1960s. During the 1950–1968 period, the average inflation rate was only 2 percent. In contrast, the inflation rate climbed sharply to an average of 7.6 percent between 1969 and 1982. Since 1992, inflation moderated and averaged 2.7 percent annually. In 2007, the inflation rate was 2.8 percent.

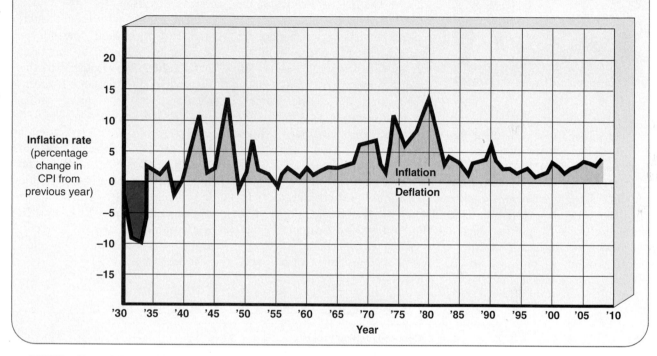

SOURCE: *Economic Report of the President, 2008,* http://www.gpoaccess.gov/eop/, Table B-64.

3 percent until the inflationary pressures from the Vietnam War in the late 1960s. In fact, the average inflation rate between 1950 and 1968 was only 2 percent. Then the inflation rate climbed to more than 10 percent in 1974, 1979, 1980, and 1981, reaching a high of 13.5 percent in 1980. During the 1973–1982 period, the average annual inflation rate was 8.8 percent. Following the 1990–1991 recession, the annual inflation rate moderated, and it averaged 2.7 percent between 1992 and 2003. Note that between 2001 and 2002 the rate of inflation declined, meaning that disinflation occurred. In 2007, the inflation rate was 2.8 percent. In 2008, as this text is written, there is concern that the inflation rate will be higher.

Consumer Price Index Criticisms

Just as there is criticism of the unemployment rate, the CPI is not a perfect measure of inflation, and it has been the subject of much public debate. There are reasons for this criticism:

1. Changes in the CPI are based on a typical market basket of products that does not match the actual market basket purchased by many consumers. Suppose you spend your nominal annual income entirely on lemonade, hot dogs, and

YOU'RE THE ECONOMIST   How Much More Does It Cost to Laugh?   *Applicable Concept: Consumer price index*

Are we paying bigger bucks for smaller yuks? Or is it a lower fee for more glee? Is there a bone to pick with the price of rubber chickens? Is the price of Groucho glasses raising eyebrows, the cost of *Mad* magazine driving you mad, and, well, you get the idea.

Malcolm Kushner, an attorney-turned-humor consultant based in Santa Cruz, California, developed an index based on a compilation of leading humor indicators to measure price changes in things that make us laugh. Kushner created the cost-of-laughing index to track how trends in laughter affect the bottom line. He is a humor consultant who advises corporate leaders on making humor work for business professionals. For example, humor can make executives better public speakers, and laughter reduces stress and can even cure illnesses. Kushner believes humor is America's greatest asset, and his consulting business gets a lot of publicity from publication of the index. To combat rising humor costs, Kushner has established a Web site at http://www.kushnergroup.com. It organizes links to databases of funny quotes, anecdotes, one-liners, and other material for business speakers and writers.

The exhibit with the Groucho face traces annual percentage changes in the cost of laughing that Kushner has reported to the media. On an annual basis, the inflation rate for laughing did a belly flop from 4.4 percent in 1995 to 3 percent in 1996, where it remained almost flat as a pancake through 2005. Then, in 2006, the humor index took a slippery slide on a banana peel to a disinflation rate of only 1/10 of 1 percent. In 2007, the index rose 4.7 percent, which was the largest increase since 1990.

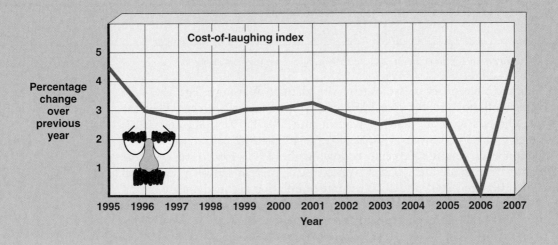

Closer examination of the cost-of-laughing index over the years gives both smiley and sad faces. The good news in 2007 is that the price of Groucho glasses and some other items did not rise, but the bad news is that the price of a dancing chick telegram rose. The major reason for more expensive humor is the price of writing a half-hour television situation comedy. Just like the CPI, Kushner's index has been criticized. Note that the fee for writing a TV sitcom dominates the index. Kushner responds to this issue by saying, "Well, I wanted the index to be truly national. The fact that this price dominates the index reflects that TV comedy shows dominate our national culture. If you can laugh for free at a sitcom, you don't need to buy a rubber chicken or go to a comedy club."

ANALYZE THE ISSUE

No question here. This one is just for fun.

Cost-of-Laughing Index

Item	2004	2005	2006	2007
Rubber chicken[1]	$ 51.00	$ 51.00	$ 51.00	$ 51.00
Groucho glasses[1]	15.00	15.00	15.00	15.00
Whoopee cushion[1]	5.40	5.40	5.40	5.40
Mad magazine[2]	2.99	3.50	3.99	3.99
Singing telegrams[3]				
Pink gorilla	105.00	125.00	125.00	150.00
Dancing chicken	105.00	125.00	125.00	150.00
Fee for writing a TV sitcom[4]	14,061.00	14,377.00	14,377.00	15,032.00
Comedy clubs[5]				
Atlanta: The Punch Line	22.00	22.00	22.00	22.50
Chicago: Second City	19.00	19.50	24.00	24.00
Houston: Laff Stop	21.49	25.00	24.65	35.00
Denver: Comedy Works	22.00	23.65	35.00	25.00
Indianapolis: Crackers Comedy	11.00	11.00	15.00	7.00
Los Angeles: Laugh Factory	15.00	17.00	17.00	20.00
New York: Comic Strip	17.00	19.00	20.00	20.00
Pittsburgh: The Funny Bone	15.00	15.00	15.00	15.00
San Francisco: Punch Line	15.00	15.00	20.00	20.00
Seattle: Comedy Underground	12.00	15.00	15.00	15.00
Total cost of humor basket	$14,514.88	$14,889.05	$14,910.04	$15,613.89
Annual inflation rate	2.6%	2.6%	0.1%	4.7%

[1] One dozen wholesale from Franco-American Novelty Company, Long Island City, New York.
[2] April issue.
[3] Available from Bellygrams, Manhattan, New York.
[4] Minimum fee under Writers Guild of America basic agreement.
[5] Admission on Saturday night.

Source: Data provided by Malcolm Kushner.

Inflation and Wealth

Wealth

The value of the stock of assets owned at some point in time.

Income is one measure of economic well-being, and wealth is another. Income is a flow of money earned by selling factors of production. Wealth is the value of the stock of assets owned at some point in time. Wealth includes real estate, stocks, bonds, bank accounts, life insurance policies, cash, and automobiles. A person can have a high income and little wealth, or great wealth and little income.

Inflation can benefit holders of wealth because the value of assets tends to increase as prices rise. Consider a home purchased in 2000 for $200,000. By 2007, this home might sell for $300,000. This 50 percent increase is largely a result of inflation. Also, people who own forms of wealth that increase in value faster than the inflation rate, such as real estate, are winners. (Use Exhibit 3 to calculate that the inflation rate between 2000 and 2007 was 20 percent.)

On the other hand, the impact of inflation on wealth penalizes people without it. Consider younger couples wishing to purchase a home. As prices rise, it becomes more difficult for them to buy a home or acquire other assets.

CHECKPOINT

What Is the Real Price of Gasoline?

In 1981, consumers were shocked when the average price for gasoline reached $1.35 per gallon because only a few years previously gasoline was selling for one half this price. If the CPI in 1981 was 90.9 and the CPI in 2007 was 207.3, what is the average inflation adjusted price in 2007 dollars?

"I've called the family together to announce that, because of inflation, I'm going to have to let two of you go."

• •

Drawing by Joseph Farris; © 1974, *The New Yorker Magazine*, Inc.

Inflation and the Real Interest Rate

Borrowers and savers may be winners or losers, depending on the rate of inflation. Understanding how this might happen requires making a distinction between the nominal interest rate and the real interest rate. The nominal interest rate is the actual rate of interest earned over a period of time. The nominal interest rate, for example, is the interest rate specified on a loan or savings account. If you borrow $10,000 from a bank at a 10 percent annual interest rate for five years, this is more accurately called a 10 percent annual nominal interest rate. Similarly, a $10,000 certificate of deposit that yields 10 percent annual interest is said to have a 10 percent annual nominal interest rate.

The real interest rate is the nominal interest rate minus the inflation rate. The occurrence of inflation means that the real rate of interest will be less than the nominal rate. Suppose the inflation rate during the year is 5 percent. This means that a 10 percent annual nominal interest rate paid on a $10,000 loan amounts to a 5 percent *real interest rate,* and a certificate of deposit that yields 10 percent annual nominal interest also earns 5 percent *real interest.*

To understand how inflation can make those who borrow winners, suppose you receive a one-year loan from your parents to start a business. Earning a profit is not your parents' motive, and they know you will repay the loan. Their only concern is that you replace the decline in purchasing power of the money they loaned you. Both you and your parents anticipate the inflation rate will be 5 percent during the year, so the loan is made and you agree to repay the principal plus the 5 percent to offset inflation. In short, both parties assume payment of a zero real interest rate (the 5 percent nominal interest rate minus the 5 percent rate of inflation). Now consider what happens if the inflation rate is actually 10 percent during the year of the loan. The clear unintentional winner is you, the debtor, because your creditor parents are paid the principal plus 5 percent interest, but their purchasing power still falls by 5 percent because the actual inflation rate is 10 percent. Stated differently, instead of zero, the real interest rate paid on the loan was −5 percent (the 5 percent nominal interest rate minus the 10 percent rate of inflation). In real terms, your parents paid you to borrow from them.

During the late 1970s, the rate of inflation rose frequently. This forced mortgage lenders to protect themselves against declining real interest rates on their loans by offering adjustable-rate mortgages (ARMs) in addition to conventional fixed-rate mortgages. As this text is written in 2008, a *subprime loan crisis* resulted from homeowners who were unable to make payments as the interest rate rose on their ARMs. This subject is discussed in more depth in the chapter on monetary policy.

A nest egg in the form of a savings account set aside for a rainy day is also affected by inflation. For example, if the interest rate on a one-year $10,000 certificate of deposit is 5 percent and the inflation rate is zero (5 percent real interest rate), the certificate holder will earn a 5 percent return on his or her savings. If the inflation rate exceeds the nominal rate of interest, the real interest rate is negative, and the saver is hurt because the interest earned does not keep pace with the inflation rate. This is the reason: Suppose, after one year, the saver withdraws the original $10,000 plus the $500 interest earned and the inflation rate during the year has been 10 percent. The real value of $10,500 adjusted for loss of purchasing power is only $9,500 [$10,000 + ($10,000 × −0.05)].

Finally, it is important to note that the nominal interest rate is never negative, but the real interest rate can be either positive or negative.

Nominal interest rate
The actual rate of interest without adjustment for the inflation rate.

Real interest rate
The nominal rate of interest minus the inflation rate.

Adjustable-rate Mortgage (ARM)
A home loan that adjusts the nominal interest rate to changing rates of inflation.

> **Conclusion** *When the real rate of interest is negative, lenders and savers lose because interest earned does not keep up with the inflation rate.*

Demand-Pull and Cost-Push Inflation

Economists distinguish between two basic types of inflation, depending on whether it originates from the buyers' or the sellers' side of the market. The analysis presented in this section returns to the cause-and-effect relationship between total spending and the business cycle discussed in the previous chapter.

Demand-Pull Inflation

Demand-pull inflation

A rise in the general price level resulting from an excess of total spending (demand).

Perhaps the most familiar type of inflation is demand-pull inflation, which is a rise in the general price level resulting from an excess of total spending (demand). Demand-pull inflation is often expressed as "too much money chasing too few goods." When sellers are unable to supply all the goods and services buyers demand, sellers respond by raising prices. In short, the general price level in the economy is "pulled up" by the pressure from buyers' total expenditures.

Demand-pull inflation occurs at or close to full employment, when the economy is operating at or near full capacity. Recall that at full employment all but the frictionally and structurally unemployed are working and earning income. Therefore, total, or aggregate demand, for goods and services is high. Businesses find it profitable to expand their plants and production to meet the buyers' demand, but cannot in the short run. As a result, national output remains fixed, and prices rise as buyers try to outbid one another for the available supply of goods and services. If total spending subsides, so will the pressure on the available supply of products, and prices will not rise as rapidly or may even fall.

A word of caution: Consumers may not be the only villain in the demand-pull story. Recall that total aggregate spending includes consumer spending (C), business investment (I), government spending (G), and net exports $(X - M)$. Even foreigners may contribute to inflation by bidding up the price of U.S. exports.

Cost-Push Inflation

Cost-push inflation

An increase in the general price level resulting from an increase in the cost of production.

An excess of total spending is not the only possible explanation for rising prices. For example, suppose the Organization of Petroleum Exporting Countries (OPEC) sharply increases the price of oil. This action means a significant increase in the cost of producing goods and services. The result could be cost-push inflation. Cost-push inflation is a rise in the general price level resulting from an increase in the cost of production.

The source of cost-push inflation is not always such a dramatic event as an OPEC price hike. Any sharp increase in costs to businesses can be a potential source of cost-push inflation. This means that upward pressure on prices can be caused by cost increases for labor, raw materials, construction, equipment, borrowing, and so on. Businesses can also contribute to cost-push inflation by raising prices to increase profits.

The influence of *expectations* on both demand-pull and cost-push inflation is an important consideration. Suppose buyers see prices rise and believe they should purchase that new house or car today before these items cost much more tomorrow. At or near full employment, this demand-pull results in a rise in prices. On the suppliers' side, firms might expect their production costs to rise in the future, so they raise prices in anticipation of the higher costs. The result is cost-push inflation.

Here you should take note of coming attractions. The chapter on aggregate demand and supply develops a modern macro model that you can use to analyze with more precision the factors that determine national output, employment, and the price level. In particular, the last section of this chapter applies the aggregate demand and supply model to the concepts of demand-pull and cost-push inflation. Also, the chapter on monetary policy will discuss the theory that inflation is the result of increases in the money supply in excess of increases in the production of goods and services.

Inflation in Other Countries

Exhibit 5 reveals that inflation rates vary widely among nations. In 2007, Zimbabwe, Iran, and other countries experienced very high rates of inflation. In contrast, the United States had a modest inflation rate of 2.8 percent, while Germany had only a 2.0 percent rate.

Inflation on a Rampage

Some people must carry a large stack of money to pay for a chocolate bar because of the disastrous consequences of hyperinflation. Hyperinflation is an extremely rapid rise in the general price level. There is no consensus on when a particular rate of inflation becomes "hyper." However, most economists would agree that an

GLOBAL ECONOMICS

Hyperinflation
An extremely rapid rise in the general price level.

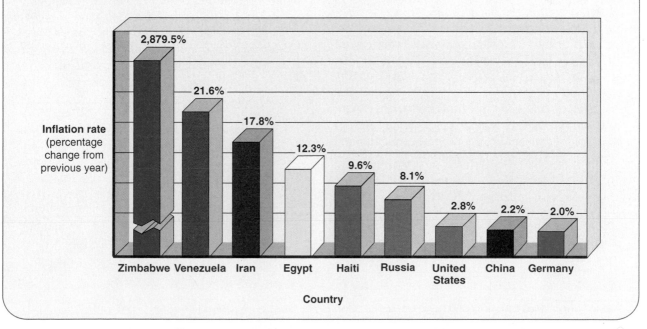

| EXHIBIT 5 | Average Annual Inflation Rates in Selected Countries, 2007 |

As shown by the bars, inflation was a serious problem in 2007 for Zimbabwe, Iran, and other countries. The United States experienced an inflation rate of 2.8 percent, while Germany had only a 2.0 percent rate.

Inflation rate (percentage change from previous year)

Zimbabwe 2,879.5%
Venezuela 21.6%
Iran 17.8%
Egypt 12.3%
Haiti 9.6%
Russia 8.1%
United States 2.8%
China 2.2%
Germany 2.0%

Country

SOURCE: International Monetary Fund, *World Economic Outlook Database*, http://www.imf.org/external/pubs/ft/weo/2007/01/data/weoselgr.aspx.

The following are two historical examples of hyperinflation:

A *Wall Street Journal* article described hyperinflation in La Paz, Bolivia:

> A courier stumbles into Banco Boliviano Americano, struggling under the weight of a huge bag of money he is carrying on his back. He announces that the sack contains 32 million pesos, and a teller slaps on a notation to that effect. The courier pitches the bag into a corner. "We don't bother counting the money anymore," explains Max Lowes Stah, a loan officer standing nearby. "We take the client's word for what's in the bag." Pointing to the courier's load, he says, "That's a small deposit." At that moment the 32 million pesos—enough bills to stuff a mail sack—were worth only $500. Today, less than two weeks later, they are worth at least $180 less. Life's like that with quadruple–digit inflation....
>
> Prices go up by the day, the hour or the customer. If the pace continues all year it would mean an annual rate of 116,000 percent. The 1,000-peso bill, the most commonly used, costs more to print than it purchases. To purchase an average-size television set with 1,000-peso bills, customers have to haul money weighing more than 68 pounds into the showroom. Inflation makes use of credit cards impossible here, and merchants generally can't take checks, either. Restaurant owners often covered their menus with cellophane and changed prices several times daily using a dry-erase marker.[1]

A *San Franciso Chronicle* article reported on hyperinflation in Zimbabwe:

> What is happening is no laughing matter. For untold numbers of Zimbabweans, bread, margarine, meat and even the morning cup of tea have become unimaginable luxuries. The city suffers rolling electrical blackouts because the state cannot afford parts or technicians to fix broken down power turbines. Mounds of uncollected garbage pile up on the streets of slums. Public-school fees and other ever-rising government surcharges have begun to exceed the monthly incomes of many urban families lucky enough to work. Those with spare cash put it not in banks, but in gilt-edged investments like bags of cornmeal and sugar, guaranteed not to lose their value.[2]

A *Newsweek* article made the following thoughtful observation:

> Hyperinflation is the worst economic malady that can befall a nation, wiping out the value of money, savings, assets, and thus work. It is worse even than a deep recession. Hyperinflation robs you of what you have now (savings), whereas a recession robs you of what you might have had (higher standards of living if the economy had grown). That's why it so often toppled governments and produced revolution. Recall that it was not the Great Depression that brought the Nazis to power in Germany but rather hyperinflation, which destroyed the middle class of that country by making its savings worthless.[3]

ANALYZE THE ISSUE

1. Can you relate inflation psychosis to these excerpts? Give an example of a debtor lender relationship that is jeopardized by hyper-inflation.

2. Explain why the workers in Bolivia were striking even though wages rose at an annual rate of 1,500 percent. Do you see any connection between hyperinflation and the political system?

---

1. Sonia L. Nazario, "When Inflation Rate Is 116,000 Percent, Prices Change by the Hour," *The Wall Street Journal*, Feb. 7, 1985, p. 1.
2. Michale Wines, "Zimbabwe: Inflation Capitol," *San Francisco Chronicle*, May 2, 2006, p. A-2.
3. Fareed Zakaria, "Is This the End of Inflation? Turkey's Currency Crisis May Be the Last Battle in the Global War Against Hyperinflation," *Newsweek*, Mar. 19, 2001, p. 38.

inflation rate of about 100 percent per year or more is hyperinflation. Runaway inflation is conducive to rapid and violent social and political change stemming from four causes.

First, individuals and businesses develop an *inflation psychosis,* causing them to buy quickly today in order to avoid paying even more tomorrow. Everyone feels pressure to spend their earnings before their purchasing power deteriorates. No matter whether you are paid once, twice, or any number of times per day, you will be eager to spend it immediately.

Second, huge unanticipated inflation jeopardizes debtor-lender contracts, such as credit cards, home mortgages, life insurance policies, pensions, bonds, and other forms of savings. For example, if nominal interest rates rise unexpectedly in response to higher inflation, borrowers find it more difficult to make their monthly payments.

Third, hyperinflation sets a wage-price spiral in motion. A wage-price spiral occurs in a series of steps when increases in nominal wage rates are passed on in higher prices, which, in turn, result in even higher nominal wage rates and prices. A wage-price spiral continues when management believes it can boost prices faster than the rise in labor costs. As the cost of living moves higher, however, labor must again demand even higher wage increases. Each round yields higher and higher prices as wages and prices chase each other in an upward spiral.

Wage-price spiral
A situation that occurs when increases in nominal wage rates are passed on in higher prices, which, in turn, result in even higher nominal wage rates and prices.

Fourth, because the future rate of inflation is difficult or impossible to anticipate, people turn to more speculative investments that might yield higher financial returns. To hedge against the high losses of purchasing power from hyperinflation, funds flow into gold, silver, stamps, jewels, art, antiques, and other currencies, rather than into new factories, machinery, and technological research, which expand an economy's production possibilities curve.

History reveals numerous hyperinflation examples. One of the most famous occurred during the 1920s in the German Weimar Republic. Faced with huge World War I reparations payments, the Weimar government simply printed money to pay its bills. By late 1923, the annual inflation rate in Germany had reached 35,000 percent per month. Prices rose frequently, sometimes increasing in minutes, and German currency became so worthless that it was used as kindling for stoves. No one was willing to make new loans, and credit markets collapsed. Wealth was redistributed because those who were heavily in debt easily paid their debts, and people's savings were wiped out.

Finally, hyperinflation is invariably the result of a government's ill-advised decision to increase a country's money supply. Moreover, hyperinflation is not a historical relic, as illustrated in the Global Economics article.

KEY CONCEPTS

Inflation	Nominal income	Adjustable-rate Mortgage (ARM)
Deflation	Real income	Demand-pull inflation
Consumer price index (CPI)	Wealth	Cost-push inflation
Base year	Nominal interest rate	Hyperinflation
Disinflation	Real interest rate	Wage-price spiral

SUMMARY

- *Inflation* is an increase in the general (average) price level of goods and services in the economy.
- *Deflation* is a decrease in the general level of prices. During the early years of the Great Depression, there was deflation, and the CPI declined at about a double-digit rate.
- The *consumer price index (CPI)* is the most widely known price-level index. It measures the cost of purchasing a market basket of goods and services by a typical household during a time period relative to the cost of the same bundle during a base year. The annual rate of inflation is computed using the following formula:

  Annual rate of inflation =
  $$\frac{\text{CPI in given year} - \text{CPI in previous year}}{\text{CPI in previous year}} \times 100$$

- *Disinflation* is a reduction in the inflation rate. This does not mean that prices were falling, only that the inflation rate fell.
- The *inflation rate* determined by the CPI is criticized because (1) it is not representative, (2) it has difficulty adjusting for quality changes, and (3) it ignores the relationship between price changes and the importance of items in the market basket.
- *Nominal income* is income measured in actual money amounts. Measuring your purchasing power requires converting nominal income into *real income,* which is nominal income adjusted for inflation.

- The *real interest rate* is the *nominal interest rate* adjusted for inflation. If real interest rates are negative, lenders incur losses.
- *Demand-pull inflation* is caused by pressure on prices originating from the buyers' side of the market. In contrast, *cost-push inflation* is caused by pressure on prices originating from the sellers' side of the market.
- *Hyperinflation* can seriously disrupt an economy by causing inflation psychosis, credit market collapses, a wage-price spiral, and speculation. A *wage-price spiral* occurs when increases in nominal wages cause higher prices, which, in turn, cause higher wages and prices.

SUMMARY OF CONCLUSION STATEMENTS

- Inflation is an increase in the overall average level of prices and not an increase in the price of any specific product.
- People whose nominal incomes rise faster than the rate of inflation gain purchasing power, while people whose nominal incomes do not keep pace with inflation lose purchasing power.
- When the real rate of interest is negative, lenders and savers lose because interest earned does not keep up with the inflation rate.

STUDY QUESTIONS AND PROBLEMS

1. Consider this statement: "When the price of a good or service rises, the inflation rate rises." Do you agree or disagree? Explain.

2. Suppose, in the base year, a typical market basket purchased by an urban family cost $250. In Year 1, the same market basket cost $950. What is the consumer price index (CPI) for Year 1? If the same market basket cost $1,000 in Year 2, what is the CPI for Year 2? What was the Year 2 rate of inflation?

3. What are three criticisms of the CPI?

4. Suppose you earned $100,000 in a given year. Calculate your real income, assuming the CPI is 200 for this year.

5. Explain how a person's purchasing power can decline in a given year even though he or she received a salary increase.

6. Who loses from inflation? Who wins from inflation?

7. Suppose you borrow $100 from a bank at 5 percent interest for one year and the inflation rate that year is 10 percent. Was this loan advantageous to you or to the bank?

8. Suppose the annual nominal rate of interest on a bank certificate of deposit is 12 percent. What would be the effect of an inflation rate of 13 percent?

9. When the economy approaches full employment, why does demand-pull inflation become a problem?

10. How does demand-pull inflation differ from cost-push inflation?

11. Explain this statement: "If everyone expects inflation to occur, it will."

For Online Exercises, go to the text Web site at www.cengage.com/economics/tucker.

CHECKPOINT ANSWERS

The College Education Price Index

$$\text{2007 college education price index} = \frac{\text{market basket cost at 2007 prices}}{\text{market basket cost at base-year (2007) prices}} \times 100 = \frac{\$9,650}{\$9,650} = 100$$

$$\text{2008 college education price index} = \frac{\text{market basket cost at 2008 prices}}{\text{market basket cost at base-year (2007) prices}} \times 100 = \frac{\$10,200}{\$9,650} = 105.7$$

$$\text{Percentage change in price level of college education} = \frac{105.7 - 100}{100} \times 100 = 5.7\%$$

If you said the price of a college education increased 5.7 percent in 2008, **YOU ARE CORRECT.**

What is the Real Price of Gasoline?

$$\text{Average gasoline price in 2007 dollars} = \$1.35 \times \frac{207.3}{90.9} = \$3.08$$

If you said the price of $1.35 per gallon for gasoline in 1981 was $3.08 per gallon in 2007 after adjusting for inflation over these years, **YOU ARE CORRECT.**
To update this calculation, click on the CPI Inflation Calculator at http://data.bls.gov/cgi-bin/cpicals.pl.

PRACTICE QUIZ

For an explanation of the correct answers, please visit the tutorial at www.cengage.com/economics/tucker.

1. Inflation is
   a. an increase in the general price level.
   b. not a concern during war.
   c. a result of high unemployment.
   d. an increase in the relative price level.

2. If the consumer price index in year X was 300 and the CPI in year Y was 315, the rate of inflation was
   a. 5 percent.
   b. 15 percent.
   c. 25 percent.
   d. 315 percent.

3. Consider an economy with only two goods: bread and wine. In the base year, the typical family bought four loaves of bread at $2 per loaf and two bottles of wine for $9 per bottle. In a given year, bread cost $3 per loaf, and wine cost $10 per bottle. The CPI for the given year is
   a. 100.
   b. 123.
   c. 126.
   d. 130.

4. As shown in Exhibit 6, the rate of inflation for Year 2 is
   a. 5 percent.
   b. 10 percent.
   c. 20 percent.
   d. 25 percent.

5. As shown in Exhibit 6, the rate of inflation for Year 5 is
   a. 4.2 percent.
   b. 5 percent.

EXHIBIT 6	Consumer Price Index

Year	Consumer Price Index
1	100
2	110
3	115
4	120
5	125

   c. 20 percent.
   d. 25 percent.

6. Deflation is a (an)
   a. increase in most prices.
   b. decrease in the general price level.
   c. situation that has never occurred in U.S. history.
   d. decrease in the inflation rate.

7. Which of the following would overstate the consumer price index?
   a. Substitution bias
   b. Improving quality of products
   c. Neither (a) nor (b)
   d. Both (a) and (b)

8. Suppose a typical automobile tire cost $50 in the base year and had a useful life of 40,000 miles. Ten years later, the typical automobile tire cost $75 and had a useful life of 75,000 miles. If no adjustment is made for mileage, the CPI would
   a. underestimate inflation between the two years.
   b. overestimate inflation between the two years.
   c. accurately measure inflation between the two years.
   d. not measure inflation in this case.

9. When the inflation rate rises, the purchasing power of nominal income
   a. remains unchanged.
   b. decreases.
   c. increases.
   d. changes by the inflation rate minus one.

10. Last year the Harrison family earned $50,000. This year their income is $52,000. In an economy with an inflation rate of 5 percent, which of the following is correct?
   a. The Harrisons' nominal income and real income have both risen.
   b. The Harrisons' nominal income and real income have both fallen.
   c. The Harrisons' nominal income has fallen, and their real income has risen.
   d. The Harrisons' nominal income has risen, and their real income has fallen.

11. If the nominal rate of interest is less than the inflation rate,
   a. lenders win.
   b. savers win.

c. the real interest rate is negative.
   d. the economy is at full employment.

12. Demand-pull inflation is caused by
   a. monopoly power.
   b. energy cost increases.
   c. tax increases.
   d. full employment.

13. Cost-push inflation is due to
   a. excess total spending.
   b. too much money chasing too few goods.
   c. resource cost increases.
   d. the economy operating at full employment.

14. Suppose you place $10,000 in a retirement fund that earns a nominal interest rate of 8 percent. If you expect inflation to be 5 percent or lower, then you are expecting to earn a real interest rate of at least
   a. 1.6 percent.
   b. 3 percent.
   c. 4 percent.
   d. 5 percent.

15. Which of the following statements is *true*?
   a. Demand-pull inflation is caused by excess total spending.
   b. Cost-push inflation is caused by an increase in resource costs.
   c. If nominal interest rates remain the same and the inflation rate falls, real interest rates increase.
   d. If real interest rates are negative, lenders incur losses.
   e. All of the above are true.

Road Map

PART 5

MACROECONOMIC FUNDAMENTALS

This road map feature helps you tie material in the part together as you travel the Economic Way of Thinking Highway. The following are review questions listed by chapter from the previous part. The key concept in each question is given for emphasis.

For an explanation of the correct answers, please visit the tutorial at www.cengage.com/economics/tucker.

Chapter 15. Gross Domestic Product

1. **Key Concept: Gross Domestic Product**
   Which of the following items is included in the calculation of GDP?
   a. Purchase of 100 shares of General Motors stock.
   b. Purchase of a used car.
   c. The value of a homemaker's services.
   d. Sale of Gulf War military surplus.
   e. None of the above would be included.

2. **Key Concept: Expenditure Approach**
   Using the expenditure approach, GDP equals
   a. $C + I + G + (X - M)$.
   b. $C + I + G + (X + M)$.
   c. $C + I - G + (X - M)$.
   d. $C + I + G - (X - M)$.

3. **Key Concept: GDP Shortcomings**
   If the underground economy is sizable, then GDP will
   a. understate the economy's performance.
   b. overstate the economy's performance.
   c. fluctuate unpredictably.
   d. accurately reflect this subterranean activity.

4. **Key Concept: Real GDP**
   The equation for determining real GDP for year X is

   a. $\dfrac{\text{nominal GDP for year } X}{\text{average nominal GDP}}$.

   b. $\dfrac{\text{nominal GDP for year } X}{\text{GDP for year } X} - 100$.

   c. $\dfrac{\text{nominal GDP for year } X}{\text{GDP chain-price index for year } X} \times 100$.

   d. $\dfrac{\text{nominal GDP for year } X}{\text{average family income}} \times 100$.

Chapter 16. Business Cycles and Unemployment

5. **Key Concept: Business Cycle**
   A business cycle is the
   a. period of time in which expansion and contraction of economic activity are equal.

   b.   period of time in which there are three phases: peak, depression, and
        recovery.
   c.   recurring growth and decline in real GDP.
   d.   period of time in which a business is established and ceases
        operations.

6. **Key Concept: Business Cycle**
    A business cycle is the period of time in which
    a.   a business is established and ceases operations.
    b.   there are four phases: peak, recession, trough, and recovery.
    c.   the price level varies with real GDP.
    d.   expansion and contraction of economic activity are equal.
    e.   none of the above are true.

7. **Key Concept: Unemployment**
    John Steinbeck's *Cannery Row* describes a character who takes his own life
    because of poor job prospects. If he was an unemployed person who gave up
    looking for work, he would be considered
    a.   chronically unemployed.
    b.   a discouraged worker.
    c.   a member of the labor force.
    d.   Frictionally unemployed.

8. **Key Concept: Unemployment**
    Consider a broom factory that permanently closes because of foreign competi-
    tion. If the broom factory's workers cannot find new jobs because their skills are
    no longer marketable, then they are classified as
    a.   seasonally unemployed.
    b.   frictionally unemployed.
    c.   structurally unemployed.
    d.   cyclically unemployed.

Chapter 17. Inflation

9. **Key Concept: Inflation**
    Inflation is measured by an increase in
    a.   homes, autos, and basic resources.
    b.   prices of all products in the economy.
    c.   the consumer price index (CPI).
    d.   none of the above.

10. **Key Concept: Consumer Price Index Bias**
    Suppose the price of gasoline rose and consumers cut back on their use of gaso-
    line relative to other consumer goods. This situation contributed to which bias in
    the consumer price index?
    a.   Substitution bias.
    b.   Transportation bias.
    c.   Quality bias.
    d.   Indexing bias.

11. **Key Concept: Real Income**

Real income in Year X is equal to

a. $\dfrac{\text{Year } X \text{ nominal income}}{\text{Year X real GDP}} \times 100$

b. $\dfrac{\text{Year } X \text{ nominal income}}{\text{Year } X \text{ real output}} \times 100$

c. $\dfrac{\text{Year } X \text{ nominal income}}{\text{CPI}/100}$

d. Year X nominal income × CPI.

12. **Key Concept: Cost-push Inflation**

Cost-push inflation is due to

a. labor cost increases.

b. energy cost increases.

c. raw material cost increases.

d. all of the above.

Macroeconomic Theory and Policy

This part begins with two chapters that present a theoretical model originating in a book published in 1936 by British economist John Maynard Keynes. The purpose of the Keynesian model is to understand the causes and cures of the Great Depression. The next chapter explains another theoretical macro model based on aggregate demand and aggregate supply. The following chapter discusses the federal government's taxing and spending policies, and the next chapter explains actual data measures of government spending and taxation patterns. The part concludes with a chapter on hotly debated topics: federal deficits, surpluses, and the national debt.

18

The Keynesian Model

I n U.S. history, the 1920s are known as the "Roaring 20s." It was a time of optimism and prosperity. Between 1920 and 1929, real GDP rose by 42 percent. Stock prices soared year after year and made many investors rich. As business boomed, companies invested in new factories, and the U.S. economy was a job-creating machine. People bought fine clothes, had parties, and danced the popular Charleston. Then the business cycle took an abrupt downturn on October 29, 1929, Black Thursday. The most severe recession in recent U.S. history had begun. During the Great Depression, stock prices fell. Wages fell. Real output fell. Banks failed. Businesses closed their doors, and the unemployment rate soared to 25 percent. Unemployed workers would fight over a job, sell apples on the corner to survive, and walk the streets in bewilderment.

The misery of the Great Depression created a revolution in economic thought. Prior to the Great Depression, economists recognized that over the years business downturns would interrupt the nation's prosperity, but they believed these episodes were temporary. They argued that in a short time the price system would automatically restore an economy to full employment without government intervention.

Why didn't the economy self-correct to its 1929 level of real output? What went wrong? The stage was set for a new idea offered by British economist John Maynard Keynes (pronounced "canes"). Keynes argued that the economy was not self-correcting and therefore could indeed remain below full employment indefinitely because of inadequate aggregate spending. Keynes's work not only explained the crash, but also offered cures requiring the government to play an active role in the economy.

Whether or not economists agree with Keynes's ideas, this famous economist still influences macroeconomics today. This chapter begins with a discussion of classical economic theory before Keynes. Then you will learn what determines the level of consumption and investment expenditures. Finally, these components form a simple Keynesian model.

In this chapter, you will learn to solve these economic puzzles:

- Why did economists believe the Great Depression was impossible?

- What are the components of the Keynesian Cross?

- Why did Keynes believe that "animal spirits" and government policy were important to maintain full employment?

Introducing Classical Theory and The Keynesian Revolution

Prior to the Great Depression of the 1930s, a group of economists known as the classical economists dominated economic thinking.[1] The founder of the classical school of economics was Adam Smith (discussed in the chapter on economies in transition). Macroeconomics had not developed as a separate economic theory, and classical economics was therefore based primarily on microeconomic market equilibrium theory. The classical school of economics was mainstream economics from the 1770s to the Great Depression era. The classical economists believed in the *laissez-faire* "leave it alone" theory that our economy was self-regulating and would correct itself without government interference. The classical economists believed, as you studied in Chapter 4, that the forces of supply and demand naturally achieve full employment in the economy because flexible prices (including wages and interest rates) in competitive markets bring all markets to equilibrium. After a temporary adjustment period, markets always clear because firms sell all goods and services offered for sale. In short, recessions would naturally cure themselves because the capitalistic price system would automatically restore full employment. The classical model is explained in more detail in the chapter on aggregate demand and supply.

> **Conclusion** *The classical economists believed that a continuing depression is impossible because markets eliminate persistent shortages or surpluses.*

The simple idea known as Say's Law, developed in the early 1800s by Jean Baptiste Say, convinced classical economists that a prolonged depression was impossible. Say's Law is the theory that supply creates its own demand. Say's Law was the cornerstone of classical economics. Simply put, this theory states that long-term underspending is impossible because the production of goods and services (supply) generates an equal amount of total spending (demand) for these goods and services. Recall the circular flow model explained in the chapter on GDP. Suppose a firm produces $1 worth of bread in the product market. This supply decision creates $1 of income to the household sector through the factor markets. In other

John Maynard Keynes
British economist (1883–1946) whose influential work offered an explanation of the Great Depression and suggested, as a cure, that the government should play an active role in the economy.

Classical economists
A group of economists whose theory dominated economic thinking from the 1770s to the Great Depression. They believed recessions would naturally cure themselves because the price system would automatically restore full employment.

Say's Law
The theory that supply creates its own demand.

---

1. The classical economists included Adam Smith, J. B. Say, David Ricardo, John Stuart Mill, Thomas Malthus, Alfred Marshall, and others.

words, Say's Law is a theory that a glut of unsold products causing workers to lose their jobs is a temporary problem because there is just the right amount of income in the economy to purchase all products without layoffs.

> **Conclusion** *In the classical view, unemployment is the result of a short-lived adjustment period in which wages and prices decline or people voluntarily choose not to work. Thus, there is a natural tendency for the economy to restore full employment over time.*

In 1936, seven years after the beginning of the Great Depression and three years before the beginning of World War II, John Maynard Keynes published *The General Theory of Employment, Interest, and Money*.[2] Keynes, a Cambridge University economist, wrote in a time of great uncertainty and instability. His book established macroeconomics as a separate field of economics and challenged the baffled classical economists by turning Say's Law upside down. Keynesian theory argues that "demand creates its own supply." Keynes explained that *aggregate expenditures* (*demand*) can be forever inadequate for an economy to achieve full employment. Aggregate expenditures are the sum of consumption (*C*), investment (*I*), government spending (*G*), and net exports (*X − M*). Aggregate expenditures are also known as *aggregate spending* and *aggregate demand*. Recall from the chapter on GDP that you learned that *C*, *I*, *G*, and (*X − M*) are national accounting categories used to calculate GDP following the expenditures approach. The remainder of this chapter is devoted to Keynes's theory for the determination of consumption and investment expenditures. The government and net exports expenditure components are developed in the next chapter.

The Consumption Function

What determines your family's spending for food, clothing, automobiles, education, and other consumer goods and services? According to Keynes, the most important factor is disposable income (personal income to spend after taxes; see Exhibit 9 in Chapter 15 on GDP). Keynes argued it is a fundamental psychological law that if take-home pay increases, consumers increase their spending and saving. Keynes's focus on the relationship between consumption and disposable income is represented by the consumption function. The consumption function shows the amount households spend for goods and services at different levels of disposable income. Recall from Exhibit 2 in Chapter 15 on GDP that consumption is the largest single component of aggregate expenditures.

Exhibit 1 provides data on real disposable income (Y_d) in column 1, consumption (*C*) in column 2, and saving (*S*) in column 3 for a hypothetical economy. Since households spend each dollar of real disposable income either for consumption or for saving, the formula for saving is

$$S = Y_d - C$$

From the above equation, it follows that

$$Y_d = C + S$$

Consumption function

The graph or table that shows the amount households spend for goods and services at different levels of disposable income.

---

2. John Maynard Keynes, *The General Theory of Employment, Interest, and Money* (New York: Harcourt, Brace, and World, 1936).

EXHIBIT 1	Consumption Function ($Y_d = C + S$)	
(1) Real Disposable Income (Y_d)	(2) Consumption (C)	(3) Saving (S)
$0	$1.00	−$1.00
1.00	1.75	−0.75
2.00	2.50	−0.50
3.00	3.25	−0.25
4.00	4.00	0
5.00	4.75	0.25
6.00	5.50	0.50
7.00	6.25	0.75
8.00	7.00	1.00

Note: All amounts are in trillions of dollars per year.

Exhibit 2 charts the consumption function using the real disposable income and consumption data given in columns 1 and 2 in Exhibit 1. At low levels of disposable income, households spend more on consumer goods and services than they earn during the year. If annual real disposable income is any level below $4 trillion, households dissave. Dissaving is the amount by which personal consumption expenditures exceed disposable income. Negative saving, or dissaving, is financed by drawing down previously accumulated financial assets, such as savings accounts, stocks, and bonds, or by borrowing. At a real disposable income of $2 trillion per year, for example, families spend $2.5 trillion and thereby dissave $0.5 trillion.

Note that if disposable income is zero, consumption expenditures will be $1 trillion of autonomous consumption. Autonomous consumption is consumption that is independent of the level of disposable income. It is the amount of consumption expenditures that occur even when disposable income is zero. In the event disposable income is zero, households will dissave to satisfy basic consumption needs.

Exhibit 2 represents dissaving as the vertical distance below the consumption function to the *45-degree line*. The 45-degree line is a geometric construct that makes it easier to identify the *break-even*, or *no-saving income*, which equates aggregate real disposable income measured on the horizontal axis and consumption on the vertical axis. In our example, $C = Y_d$ at $4 trillion, where households spend every dollar earned and saving is therefore zero.

The consumption function has a positive slope because consumption spending increases with real disposable income. At higher levels beyond the break-even income, households earn more income than they wish to spend, and a portion of income is saved. Saving is the part of disposable income households do not spend for consumer goods and services. Savings can be in various forms, such as funds in a passbook savings account, a certificate of deposit, stocks, or bonds. In Exhibit 2, positive saving is the vertical distance above the consumption function to the 45-degree line. For example, at a disposable income of $8 trillion, households save $1 trillion.

Dissaving
The amount by which personal consumption expenditures exceed disposable income.

Autonomous consumption
Consumption that is independent of the level of disposable income.

Saving
The part of disposable income households do not spend for consumer goods and services.

EXHIBIT 2   The Consumption Function

This exhibit shows the consumption function for a hypothetical economy. The break-even income is $4 trillion real disposable income, where households spend each dollar of real disposable income, $C = Y_d$, and savings are zero. Below $4 trillion, households spend more than their real disposable income by borrowing or withdrawing from past savings. Above the break-even income, households spend less than their real disposable income, and saving occurs. The marginal propensity to consume (MPC) is 0.75 because the slope of the consumption schedule shows that for each dollar increase in income (ΔY_d), consumption increases (ΔC) by 75 cents, and the remaining 25 cents is saved.

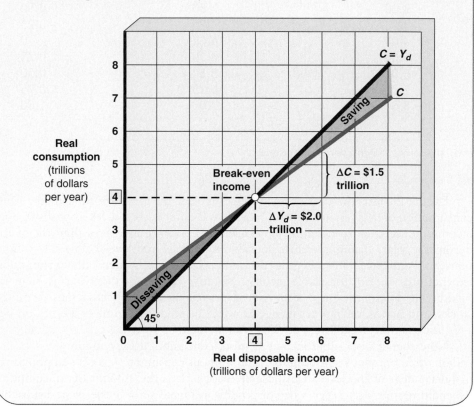

Conclusion *The 45-degree line is a geometric construct. It indicates all points where aggregate real income (measured on the horizontal axis) and consumption (measured on the vertical axis) are equal. Consequently, the 45-degree line makes it easier to identify the break-even, or no-saving, income level.*

Marginal propensity to consume (MPC)

The change in consumption resulting from a given change in real disposable income.

Marginal Propensities to Consume and Save

Keynes argued that as income grows, so does consumption, but by less than income. This crucial concept is called the marginal propensity to consume (MPC). The marginal propensity to consume is the "change in" or "extra" consumption resulting from a given change in real disposable income. Stated differently, the MPC is the ratio of the change in consumption (ΔC) to the change in real disposable income (ΔY_d). The Greek letter Δ (delta) means "a change in." Mathematically,

$$MPC = \frac{\text{change in consumption}}{\text{change in real disposable income}} = \frac{\Delta C}{\Delta Y_d}$$

Exhibit 3 reproduces and expands the data from Exhibit 1. As shown in column 4 of Exhibit 3, the MPC is 0.75. This means for every dollar increase (decrease) in disposable income (ΔY_d), consumption (ΔC) increases (decreases) 75 cents. In each model developed throughout this text, we assume the MPC is constant for all income levels. In our numerical example, real disposable income rises by $1 trillion between each level of income listed in column 1 of Exhibit 3, and consumption rises by $0.75 trillion. Mathematically,

$$MPC = \frac{\Delta C}{\Delta Y_d} = \frac{\$.75 \text{ trillion}}{\$1 \text{ trillion}} = 0.75$$

What do households do with an extra dollar of real disposable income if they do not spend it? There is only one other choice—they save it. The marginal propensity to save (MPS) is the change in saving resulting from a given change in real disposable income. That is, the MPS is the ratio of the change in saving (ΔS) to the change in real disposable income (ΔY_d). Mathematically,

$$MPS = \frac{\text{change in saving}}{\text{change in real disposable income}} = \frac{\Delta S}{\Delta Y_d}$$

Marginal propensity to save (MPS)

The change in saving resulting from a given change in real disposable income.

EXHIBIT 3	Consumption, Saving, *MPC*, and *MPS* Data			
(1) Real Disposable Income (Y_d)	(2) Consumption (C)	(3) Saving (S)	(4) Marginal Propensity to Consume (MPC) [$\Delta C/\Delta Y_d$ or $\Delta 2/\Delta 1$]	(5) Marginal Propensity to Save (MPS) [$\Delta S/\Delta Y_d$ or $\Delta 3/\Delta 1$]
$0	$1.00	−$1.00	–	–
1	1.75	−0.75	0.75	0.25
2	2.50	−0.50	0.75	0.25
3	3.25	−0.25	0.75	0.25
4	4.00	0	0.75	0.25
5	4.75	0.25	0.75	0.25
6	5.50	0.50	0.75	0.25
7	6.25	0.75	0.75	0.25
8	7.00	1.00	0.75	0.25

Note: All amounts are in trillions of dollars per year.

The *MPS* given in column 5 of Exhibit 3 is 0.25. Each dollar increase (decrease) in disposable income (Y_d) yields a rise (fall) of 25 cents in the amount of savings (ΔS). Mathematically,

$$MPS = \frac{\Delta S}{\Delta Y_d} = \frac{\$0.25 \text{ trillion}}{\$1 \text{ trillion}} = 0.25$$

As derived previously, $Y_d = C + S$, so it follows that $\Delta C + \Delta S = \Delta Y_d$. Dividing both sides of this equation by ΔY_d yields

$$\frac{\Delta C}{\Delta Y_d} + \frac{\Delta S}{\Delta Y_d} = \frac{\Delta Y_d}{\Delta Y_d}$$

or

$$MPC + MPS = 1$$

In our example, $0.75 + 0.25 = 1$, which means any change in real disposable income is divided between changes in consumption and changes in saving. Hence, if you know the *MPC*, you can calculate the *MPS* and vice versa. In addition to the consumption function, Exhibit 2 shows a graphic representation of the *MPC*. The *MPC* (slope) of the consumption function, C, between $4 trillion and $6 trillion is measured by dividing $\Delta C = \$1.5$ trillion (the rise) by $\Delta Y_d = \$2.0$ trillion (the run). Since the *MPC* is constant, the ratio $\Delta C/\Delta Y_d$ between any two levels of real disposable income is 0.75. As a formula:

$$\text{Slope of consumption function} = \frac{\text{rise}}{\text{run}} = \frac{\Delta C}{\Delta Y_d} = \frac{\$1.5 \text{ trillion}}{\$2.0 \text{ trillion}} = 0.75$$

The points along the consumption function, C, in Exhibit 2 can be expressed by the following equation:

$$C = a + bY_d$$

where *a* is autonomous consumption and *b* is the *MPC*, which falls between 0 and 1. Keynes used this basic equation to derive consumption (C), and it is called the Keynesian consumption function.

Using this equation,

$$C = \$1 \text{ trillion} + 0.75Y_d$$

For example, at $Y_d = \$4$ trillion,

$$C = \$1 \text{ trillion} + 0.75(\$4 \text{ trillion})$$
$$C = \$4 \text{ trillion}$$

Note that only at $4 trillion real disposable income does consumption equal this amount, as represented by the intersection of the C line and the 45-degree line. To demonstrate the relationship between the *MPC* and various levels of consumption, Exhibit 4 shows two consumption functions with the same autonomous

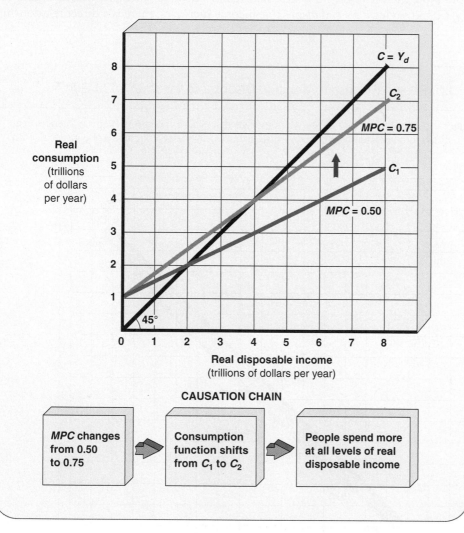

EXHIBIT 4   Consumption Functions for Two Marginal Propensities to Consume

The *MPC* is the slope of the consumption function. Here two consumption functions are shown for *MPCs* of 0.50 and 0.75. The autonomous consumption of $1 trillion is the same for both consumption functions. The higher the *MPC*, the steeper the consumption function.

CAUSATION CHAIN

| *MPC* changes from 0.50 to 0.75 | ⇒ | Consumption function shifts from C_1 to C_2 | ⇒ | People spend more at all levels of real disposable income |

consumption of $1 trillion, but each has a different slope. C_1 has an *MPC* of 0.50, and C_2 has a larger *MPC* of 0.75. Thus, the higher the marginal propensity to consume, the steeper the consumption function.

For example, suppose there is an income-tax cut. As a result, real disposable income (Y_d) increases and, in turn, induces an upward movement along the consumption function. An income-tax hike, on the other hand, reduces real disposable income and causes a downward movement along the consumption function.

> **Conclusion** *There is a direct relationship between changes in real disposable income and changes in consumption.*

A Historical Consumption Function

Exhibit 5 provides evidence that supports Keynes's theoretical consumption function. Note the use of the 45-degree line again. The dots represent historical data for Y_d, C, and savings. As real disposable income increases, there is a direct relationship

---

EXHIBIT 5   U.S. Personal Consumption and Disposable Income, 1930–2007

Keynes argued that a fundamental psychological law exists whereby real disposable income strongly influences real consumption. Actual data on real personal consumption expenditures and real disposable income are consistent with Keynes's theory.

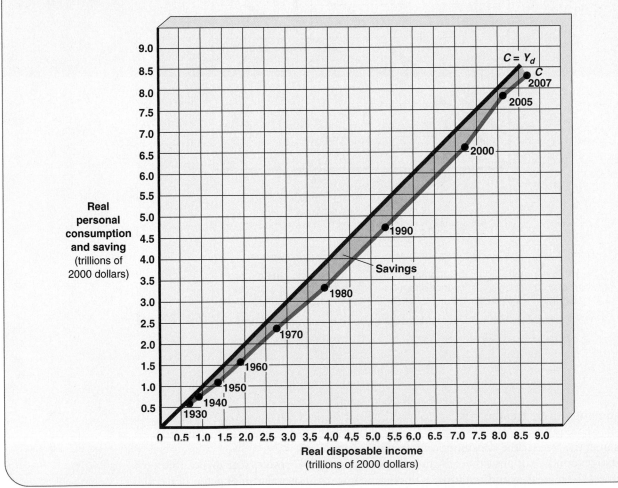

SOURCE: Bureau of Economic Research, *National Economic Accounts*, http://www.bea.gov/national/nipaweb/SelectTable.asp?Selected=Y, Tables 1.1.6 and 2.1.

with real consumption spending by households. The difference between the 45-degree line and the C line is saving.

> ## CHECKPOINT
> **What's Your *MPC*?**
> As your income increases over time, your marginal propensity to consume (*MPC*) can remain constant, or it can change. Would you expect your *MPC* to increase, decrease, or remain constant as your income increases throughout your career?

Reasons the Consumption Function Shifts

Just as nonprice factors in the market supply and demand model, such as consumer tastes and income, shift the demand curve, changes in certain *nonincome* factors cause the consumption function to shift.

> **Conclusion** *A change in real disposable income is the sole cause of a movement along the consumption function. A shift or relocation in the consumption schedule occurs when a factor other than real disposable income changes.*

Exhibit 6 illustrates this difference in terminology. The sole cause of the change in consumption spending from $3 trillion (point *A*) to $4 trillion (point *B*) along the stable consumption schedule, C_1, is a $2 trillion change in the level of real disposable income. A change in a nonincome determinant, on the other hand, can cause the consumption schedule to shift upward from $C_1 = a_1 + bY_d$ to $C_2 = a_2 + bY_d$. As a result, households spend an extra $1 trillion $(a_2 - a_1)$ at each point along C_2. This means that the level of autonomous consumption has increased by $1 trillion from $1.5 trillion to $2.5 trillion because of some influence other than current Y_d. Nonincome variables that can shift the consumption schedule include expectations, wealth, the price level, the interest rate, and the stock of durable goods.

Expectations

Consumer expectations are optimistic or pessimistic views of the future which can change consumption spending in the present. Expectations may involve the future inflation rate, the likelihood of becoming unemployed, the likelihood of receiving higher income, or the future shortage of products resulting from a war or other circumstances. Suppose households believe prices will be much higher next year and buy now, rather than paying more in the future. The effect of such expectations would be to trigger current spending and shift the consumption schedule upward. The anticipation of a recession and fears about losing jobs would make families more tightfisted in their current spending. This means an autonomous decrease in consumption, and the consumption function shifts downward.

Wealth

Holding all other factors constant, the more wealth households accumulate, the more they spend at any current level of disposable income, causing the consumption function to shift upward. Wealth owned by households includes both *real* assets,

EXHIBIT 6

Movement along and Shifts in the Consumption Function

The movement from real consumption spending of $3 trillion (point A) to $4 trillion (point B) along the stable consumption schedule, C_1, is a change in real consumption caused by a $2 trillion change in the level of real disposable income (Y_d). A change in a nonincome determinant causes the consumption function to shift. For example, some nonincome factors may increase autonomous consumption by $1 trillion from a_1 to a_2. As a result, the entire consumption function shifts upward from C_1 to C_2. Nonincome factors include changes in expectations, wealth, the price level, the interest rate, and the stock of durable goods.

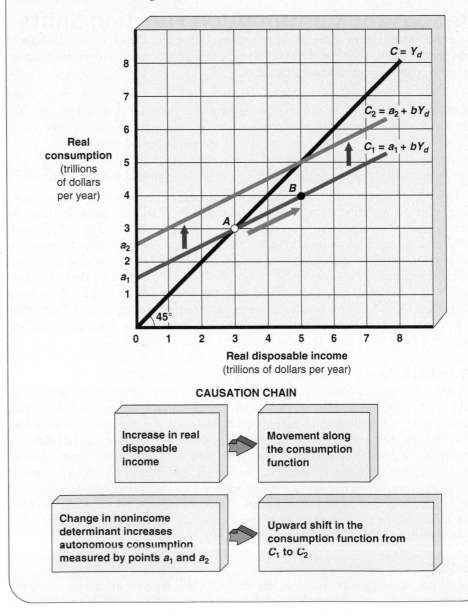

such as homes automobiles, and land, and *financial* assets, including cash, savings accounts, stocks, bonds, insurance policies, and pensions. Changes in prices of stocks, real estate, and other assets affect the value of wealth and, in turn, can shift the nation's consumption function. A so-called *wealth effect* occurred in the late 1990s dot.com era when stock values rose and households increased their spending. And during the financial turmoil in 2008, the fall in stock prices and housing prices was a significant factor in depressing consumption.

The Price Level

Any change in the general price level shifts the consumption schedule by reducing or enlarging the *purchasing power* of financial assets (wealth) with fixed nominal value. Suppose you own a $100,000 government bond or certificate of deposit. If the price level increases by, say, 10 percent, this same financial asset will buy approximately 10 percent less. Once the real value of financial wealth falls, families are poorer and spend less at any level of current disposable income. As a result, the consumption function shifts downward. The next chapter discusses this phenomenon in more detail.

The Interest Rate

The consumption schedule includes the option of borrowing to finance spending. A lower rate of interest on loans encourages consumers to borrow more, and a higher interest rate discourages consumer indebtedness. If interest rates fall, households may use more credit to finance consumer purchases. The result is a shift upward in the consumption schedule.

Stock of Durable Goods

When World War II ended, Americans had pent-up demand for many durable goods. During the war, automobiles, washing machines, refrigerators, and other goods were not produced. After the war ended, consumption exploded because people rushed out to make purchases and satisfy their long wish lists. This massive buying spree caused an upward shift in the consumption function.

Investment Expenditures

According to Keynes, changes in the private-sector components of aggregate expenditures (personal consumption and investment spending) are the major cause of the business cycle. And the more volatile of these two components is investment spending. Personal consumption may be more stable than investment spending because changes in nonincome determinants of personal consumption tend to offset each other. Or maybe people are simply reluctant to change their personal consumption habits. Whatever the reason for the stability of personal consumption, Exhibit 7 demonstrates this point. Over the years, the annual growth rate of real investment has indeed fluctuated much more than real personal consumption. Recall from Exhibit 2 in Chapter 15 on GDP that investment expenditures (gross private domestic investment) consist of spending on newly produced nonresidential structures, such as factories, equipment, changes in inventories, and residential structures.

The Investment Demand Curve

The classical economists believed that the interest rate alone determines the level of investment spending. Keynes disputed this idea. Instead, Keynes argued that

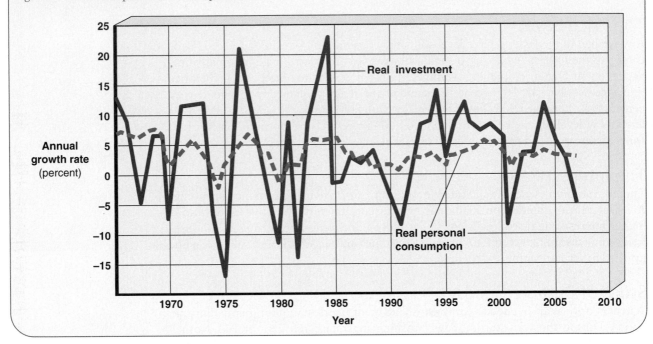

EXHIBIT 7

A Comparison of the Volatility of Real Investment and Real Consumption, 1965 to 2007

Real investment spending is highly volatile compared to real personal consumption. The data since 1965 confirm that the annual growth rate of real investment (gross private domestic investment) fluctuates much more than the annual growth rate of real personal consumption.

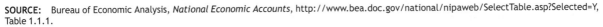

SOURCE: Bureau of Economic Analysis, *National Economic Accounts*, http://www.bea.doc.gov/national/nipaweb/SelectTable.asp?Selected=Y, Table 1.1.1.

expectations of future profits are the primary factor in determining investment, and the interest rate is the financing cost of any investment proposal.

Using a micro example to illustrate the investment decision-making process, suppose a consulting firm plans to purchase a new computer program for $1,000 that will be obsolete in a year. It anticipates that the new software will increase the firm's revenue by $1,100. Thus, assuming no taxes and other expenses exist, the expected rate of return or profit is 10 percent.

Now consider the impact of the cost of borrowing funds to finance the software investment. If the interest rate is less than 10 percent, the business will earn a profit, so it will make the investment expenditure to buy the computer program. On the other hand, a rate of interest higher than 10 percent means the software investment will be a loss, so this project will not be undertaken.

Understanding a single firm's investment decision from a micro perspective allows us to develop the investment demand curve from the macro vantage point. The investment demand curve shows the amount businesses spend for investment goods at different possible rates of interest. Exhibit 8 expresses the interest rate as annual percentages on the vertical axis. As shown in Part (a), changes in the interest rate generate movements along the firm's investment demand curve. If the interest rate falls from, say, 12 percent at point *A* to 8 percent at point *B*, an additional

Investment demand curve

The curve that shows the amount businesses spend for investment goods at different possible rates of interest.

EXHIBIT 8 — Movement along and a Shift in a Firm's Investment Demand

Part (a) shows that investment spending by a hypothetical business firm depends on the interest rate. Ceteris paribus, lowering the interest rate from 12 percent at point *A* to 8 percent at point *B* increases the quantity of real investment purchases from $5 million to $10 million during the year.

Keynes argued that investment spending is unstable because a change in volatile factors, such as expectations, technological change, capacity utilization, and business taxes, can shift the location of the investment demand curve. As shown in Part (b), the initial investment demand curve, I_1, has shifted rightward to I_2, and at an interest rate of 8 percent, $5 million in additional investment spending occurs between points *B* and *C*.

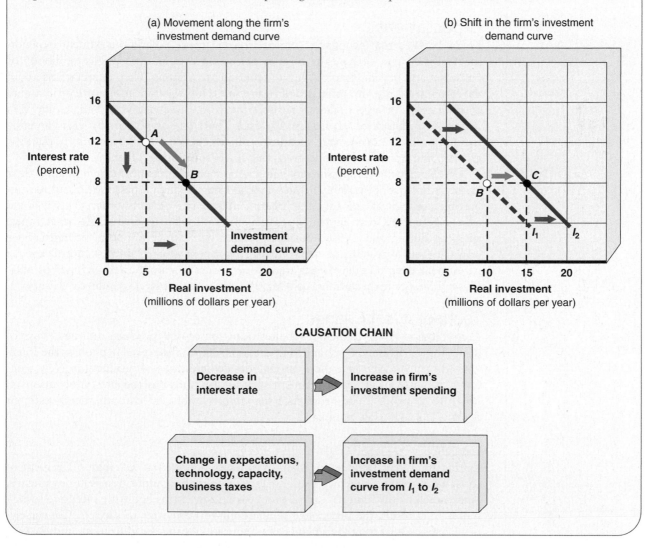

CAUSATION CHAIN

Decrease in interest rate	**Increase in firm's investment spending**
Change in expectations, technology, capacity, business taxes	**Increase in firm's investment demand curve from I_1 to I_2**

$5 million of real investment spending occurs because *marginal* planned projects become profitable. Stated another way, as a result of this fall in the rate of interest, the firm's real investment increases from $5 million to $10 million.

The relationship among the expected rate of profit, the interest rate, and investment follows this investment rule: *Businesses will undertake all planned investment projects for which the expected rate of profit equals or exceeds the interest rate.*

Why Investment Demand is Unstable

Why did Keynes view investment spending as so susceptible to ups and downs? The reason is there are several volatile determinants that cause the investment demand curve to be quite unstable. In short, any factor that changes the expected rate of profit shifts the investment demand curve and thereby changes the investment component of real GDP. As shown in Exhibit 8(b), the initial investment demand curve, I_1, has shifted rightward to I_2, and at an interest rate of 8 percent, $5 million of additional investment spending occurs between points B and C. The next sections discuss major factors that can shift the investment demand curve.

Expectations

Keynes argued that swings in "animal spirits" cause volatile investment expenditures. Translated, this means businesspersons are quite susceptible to moods of optimism and pessimism about future economic conditions. Their expectations about the future translate into estimates of future sales, future costs, and future profitability of investment projects. These forecasts involve a clouded crystal ball, requiring a degree of intuition or normative analysis. There are always many ever-changing factors, such as government spending and tax policies, world events, population growth, and stock market conditions, that make forecasting difficult.

When a wave of pessimism becomes pervasive, businesspeople reduce their expectations for profitability at each rate of interest. Such a pessimistic attitude can become contagious and shift the investment demand curve leftward. This was the case during the Great Depression, when the outlook was dismal. At other times, such as during the 1990s, businesspersons become very optimistic and revise upward their expected rate of profit for investment at each interest rate. If so, the investment demand curve shifts rightward. Thus, Keynes viewed changes in business confidence (expectations) as a major cause of investment spending volatility.

Technological Change

Technological progress includes the introduction of new products and new ways of doing things. Robots, personal computers, fax machines, cellular phones, the Internet, and similar new inventions provide less costly ways of production. New technologies create a flurry of investment spending as firms buy the latest innovations in order to improve their production capabilities, thereby causing the investment demand curve to shift rightward.

Capacity Utilization

During the Great Depression, many businesses operated at less than 50 percent of capacity. Capacity is defined as the maximum possible output of a firm or industry. Since much of the nation's capital stock stood idle, firms had little incentive to buy more. As a result, the investment demand curve shifted far to the left. Conversely, firms may be operating their plants at a high rate of capacity utilization, and the outlook for sales growth is optimistic. In this case, there is pressure on firms to invest in new investment projects, and the investment demand curve shifts to the right.

Business Taxes

As explained earlier, changes in income taxes on individuals affect disposable income and the level of consumption. Similarly, taxes on business firms can shift the investment demand curve. Business decisions, in reality, depend on the expected *after-tax* rate of profit. An increase in business taxes therefore would lower profitability and shift the investment demand curve to the left. On the other hand, the U.S. government may wish to encourage investment by allowing, say, a *tax credit* for new investment. A 10 percent *investment tax credit* means that if ExxonMobil decides to invest $10 million in a new plant, the corporation's tax bill to the IRS will be cut by $1 million. The effect of this tax policy is that the government increases the profitability of new investment projects by 10 percent and the investment demand curve shifts to the right.

Investment as an Autonomous Expenditure

Assuming none of the above factors changes in the short run, Keynes argued that investment spending is an autonomous expenditure. An autonomous expenditure is spending that does not vary with the current level of disposable income. Stated simply, autonomous expenditures in the Keynesian model remain a fixed amount, regardless of the level of disposable income. Exhibit 9 shows how the rate of interest determines the aggregate level of autonomous investment for all firms in an economy, regardless of or external to the level of real disposable income. In Part (a), at an interest rate of 8 percent, *all* businesses spend $1 trillion for capital goods and

> **Autonomous expenditure**
> Spending that does not vary with the current level of disposable income.

EXHIBIT 9 | The Aggregate Investment Demand and Autonomous Investment Demand Curves

In Part (a), the level of real investment for all firms in an economy is determined by the investment rule that all investment projects for which the expected rate of profit equals or exceeds the interest rate will be undertaken. If the interest rate is 8 percent, real autonomous investment will be $1 trillion, shown as point A on the investment demand curve, I.

In Part (b), autonomous real investment expenditures are shown to be independent of the level of real disposable income per year. This means firms will spend $1 trillion regardless of the level of real disposable income per year.

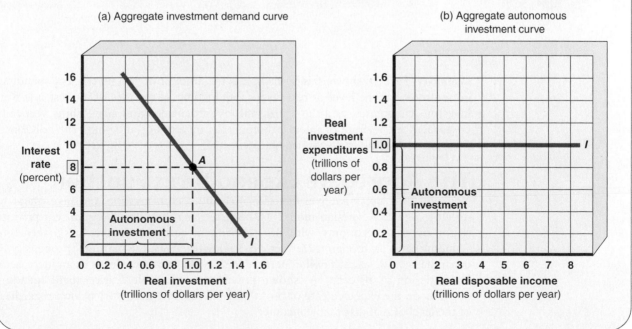

YOU'RE THE ECONOMIST Does a Stock Market Crash Cause
Recession? *Applicable Concept: aggregate expenditures function*

DOUG KANTER/AFP/Getty Images

The stock market soared during the "Roaring 20s." Lavish spending was in style as people enjoyed their new wealth. Then, on October 29, 1929, Black Thursday, the stock market crashed. During the Great Depression, banks failed, businesses closed their doors, real GDP plummeted, and unemployment soared. Over the years, much debate has occurred over whether the 1929 stock market crash was merely a symptom or a major cause of the downturn. Evidence

exists that the 1929 stock market crash only reflected an economic decline already in progress. For example, months before Black Thursday, national production had already fallen.

The argument over the impact of a stock market crash on the economy was renewed in 2001. The National Association for Business Economics (NABE) was holding its annual meeting in the World Trade Center when disaster struck the building on September 11, 2001. "The chandeliers shook, we heard a concussive sound, and as we were herding out, we could see that one tower was burning," said Carl Tannenbaum, the chief economist of LaSalle Bank in Chicago, who was attending the meeting.[1] Just the day before a panel of NABE economists predicted slow growth for the economy, but no

recession. That forecast became obsolete the moment the first plane hit. Analysts predicted a recession, and one reason was that they expected the stock market would dive as profit expectations fell. Indeed, as a result of the September terrorist attacks, the stock market suffered its worst one-week loss since the Great Depression. In the immediate aftermath, equities losses were estimated to be an extraordinary $1.2 trillion in value.[2]

Prior to the September attacks, the Dow Jones Industrial Average had reached a high of about 11,500 in May, but it had already fallen almost 2,000 points to a low of 9,431 on September 10, 2001. During this period of time, the economy was plagued by the implosion of the dot.com companies and sharp declines in high-tech

inventory. Part (b) shows this $1 trillion is the amount of real investment spending, no matter what the level of real disposable income. If the rate of interest is lower, investment increases, and the horizontal investment demand curve shifts vertically upward. A higher rate of interest discourages investment and shifts the horizontal investment demand curve vertically downward.

The Aggregate Expenditures Function
You will now use what you have learned about consumption and investment to develop a basic Keynesian model. To keep the analysis simple, visualize a private-sector domestic economy with no government sector (no taxes or government spending) and no foreign trade (net exports). Moreover, the marginal propensity to consume is 0.50, so each dollar increase in disposable income leads to an increase in consumption of 50 cents. As shown previously in Exhibit 9, investment spending depends on the expected rate of profit and interest rate and is $1 trillion regardless of the level of real disposable income.

468

stocks. After the attacks, the stock market closed for the remainder of the week and reopened the following Monday, September 17, 2001, with the famous statue of the Wall Street Bull decorated with American flags and the National Guard patrolling the streets. The result of trading was a huge selloff and another loss of 1,371 points during the week. Throughout the remainder of the year, the Dow Jones Industrial Average gradually rose toward its pre-September 11 levels, closing at 10,022 on December 31, 2001. Real GDP contracted at a 1.4 percent annual rate in the third quarter of 2001, and then it rose in the final three months of 2001 by 1.6 percent, which was a surprisingly strong performance under the circumstances. The six-member panel at the National Bureau of Economic Research (NBER), which is considered the nation's arbiter of U.S. business cycles, declared in November 2001 that a recession had begun in March and ended eight months later in November of that year.

Stock market plunges are widely reported headline news. One result of these plunges is that many Americans feel poorer because of the threat to their life's savings. In only a few hours, spectacular paper losses reduce the wealth that people are counting on to pay for homes, automobiles, college tuition, or retirement. Although not all U.S. households own stock, everyone fears a steep downhill ride on the Wall Street roller coaster. If a stock market crash leads to a recession, it would cause layoffs and cuts in profit-sharing and pension funds. Businesses fear that many families will postpone buying major consumer items in case they need their cash to tide them over the difficult economic times ahead. Reluctance of consumers to spend lowers aggregate demand, and, in turn, prices and profits fall. Falling sales and anxiety about a recession may lead many business executives to postpone modernization plans. Rather than buying new factories and equipment, businesses continue with used plants and machinery, which means lower private investment spending, employment, output, and income for the overall economy.

In early October 2008, stocks fell to their lowest since the 2001 terrorist attacks. The loss followed an initial failure of the House of Representative to pass a $700 billion financial-market bailout plan discussed in more detail in the You're the Economist in the chapter on monetary policy.

ANALYZE THE ISSUE

Immediately following the attack on the United States on September 11, 2001, the stock market plunged and many observers predicted a recession. Using the consumption and investment functions, explain their predictions.

---

1. "Worldwide, Hope for Recovery Dims," *Business Week*, Sept. 24, 2001, p. 42
2. "Economy under Siege," *Fortune*, October 15, 2001, p. 86

A little drum roll please! Now we are ready to finish this chapter by tying concepts together and pointing the spotlight on an important model necessary to understand Keynes's cure for the Great Depression. The table in Exhibit 10 gives various levels of real disposable income in column 1 and corresponding levels of consumption and investment in columns 2 and 3, respectively. The relationship between real disposable income and the sum of $C + I$ listed in column 4 is called the aggregate expenditures function (*AE*). The aggregate expenditures function is the total spending in an economy at a given level of real disposable income. The *AE* function is derived graphically in Exhibit 10 by summing the consumption function (*C*) and the investment demand curve (*I*) on the vertical axis at each level of disposable income on the horizontal axis. Note that the *C* and the $C + I$ functions are parallel. The slope of the consumption function is determined by the *MPC*, as explained earlier in Exhibit 2. Then the autonomous investment of $1 trillion is added at each level of real disposable income. As a result, the consumption function, *C*, shifts vertically by $1 trillion to become the *AE* function.

> **Aggregate expenditures function (*AE*)**
> The function that represents total spending in an economy at a given level of real disposable income.

EXHIBIT 10   Aggregate Expenditures Function Data

The aggregate expenditures function (*AE*) for a hypothetical economy begins with the consumption function (*C*). Then we add the investment demand curve (*I*) to obtain the *AE* function (*C* + *I*). Note that the *C* and *C* + *I* lines are parallel. Because *I* is assumed to be an autonomous expenditure of $1 trillion, the slope of the *C* + *I* function equals the slope (*MPC*) of the consumption function (*C*). At $6 trillion of real disposable income per year, aggregate income equals consumption plus investment, and the economy is in equilibrium.

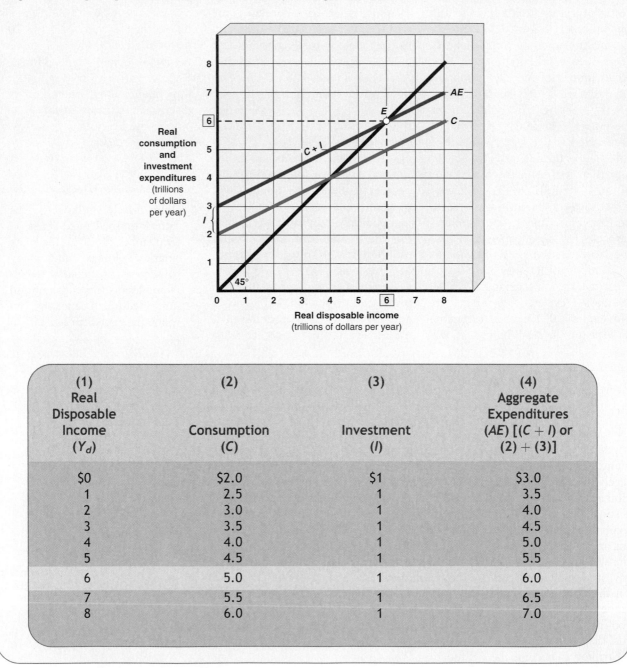

(1) Real Disposable Income (Y_d)	(2) Consumption (*C*)	(3) Investment (*I*)	(4) Aggregate Expenditures (*AE*) [(*C* + *I*) or (2) + (3)]
$0	$2.0	$1	$3.0
1	2.5	1	3.5
2	3.0	1	4.0
3	3.5	1	4.5
4	4.0	1	5.0
5	4.5	1	5.5
6	5.0	1	6.0
7	5.5	1	6.5
8	6.0	1	7.0

Note: All amounts are in trillions of dollars per year.

The aggregate expenditures function is sometimes called the *Keynesian Cross*. Note in Exhibit 10 that the *AE* line begins above the 45-degree line and then *crosses* it at $6 trillion of real disposable income. The *AE* line represents only private-sector spending in our hypothetical economy. For example, if real disposable income is $1 trillion per year, then consumers spend $2.5 trillion per year, businesses spend $1 trillion for investment, and *AE* = $3.5 trillion. This means the *AE* line is above the 45-degree line and a condition of dissaving exists. As a result, aggregate spending exceeds aggregate income by $2.5 trillion. Instead, if real disposable income is $8 trillion per year and investment remains fixed at $1 trillion, the *AE* line is below the 45-degree line. This means aggregate spending is $1 trillion less than real disposable income. At $6 trillion of real disposable income per year, the economy is in macro equilibrium because aggregate income equals aggregate spending by households and firms. Looking ahead to the next chapter, the discussion will expand the Keynesian Cross model by adding additional aggregate spending components and explaining macro equilibrium. Also, the aggregate expenditures model in this chapter has been developed with disposable income on the horizontal axis as originally developed by Keynes. In the next chapter, the broader measure of real GDP will be used instead.

KEY CONCEPTS

John Maynard Keynes
Classical economists
Say's Law
Consumption function

Dissaving
Autonomous consumption
Saving
Marginal propensity to consume (*MPC*)

Marginal propensity to save (*MPS*)
Investment demand curve
Autonomous expenditure
Aggregate expenditures function (*AE*)

SUMMARY

- *Say's Law* is the classical theory that "supply creates its own demand," and therefore the Great Depression was impossible. Say's Law is the theory that the value of production generates an equal amount of income and, in turn, total spending. The classical economists rejected the argument that underconsumption is possible because they believed flexible prices, wages, and interest rates would soon establish a balance between supply and demand.

- *John Maynard Keynes* rejected the classical theory that the economy self-corrects in the long run to full employment. The key in Keynesian theory is aggregate demand, rather than the classical economists' focus on aggregate supply. Unless aggregate spending is adequate, the economy can experience prolonged and severe unemployment.

- The *consumption function* (**C**) is determined by changes in the level of disposable income. *Autonomous consumption* is consumption that occurs even if disposable income equals zero. Changes in such nonincome determinants as expectations, wealth, the price level, interest rates, and the stock of durable goods can cause shifts in the consumption function.

- The *marginal propensity to consume* (**MPC**) is the change in consumption associated with a given change in disposable income. The *MPC* tells how much of an additional dollar of disposable income households will spend for consumption.

Consumption Function

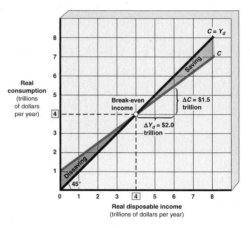

- The *marginal propensity to save* (**MPS**) is the change in saving associated with a given change in disposable income. The *MPS* measures how much of an additional dollar of disposable income households will save.

- The *investment demand curve* (**I**) shows the amount businesses spend for investment goods at different possible rates of interest. The determinants of this schedule are the expected rate of profit and rate of interest. Shifts in the investment demand curve result from changes in expectations, technology, capacity utilization, and business taxes.

Causation Chains

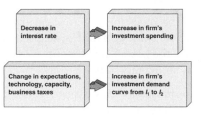

- An *autonomous expenditure* is spending that does not vary with the current level of disposable income. The Keynesian model applies this simplifying assumption to investment. As a result, the investment demand curve is a fixed amount determined by the rate of profit and the interest rate.
- The *aggregate expenditures function* (*AE*) shows the total spending in an economy at a given level of disposable income. Assuming investment spending is autonomous, the slope of the *AE* function is determined by the *MPC*.

Aggregate Expenditures Function

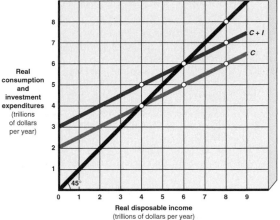

SUMMARY OF CONCLUSION STATEMENTS

- The classical economists believed that a continuing depression is impossible because markets eliminate persistent shortages or surpluses.
- In the classical view, unemployment is the result of a short-lived adjustment period in which wages and prices decline or people voluntarily choose not to work. Thus, there is a natural tendency for the economy to restore full employment over time.
- The 45-degree line is a geometric construct. It indicates all points where aggregate real income (measured on the horizontal axis) and consumption (measured on the vertical axis) are equal. Consequently, the 45-degree line makes it easier

to identify the break-even or no-saving income level.
- There is a direct relationship between changes in real disposable income and changes in consumption.
- A change in real disposable income is the sole cause of a movement along the consumption function. A shift or relocation in the consumption schedule occurs when a factor other than real disposable income changes.
- Businesses will undertake all planned investment projects for which the expected rate of profits equals or exceeds the interest rate.

STUDY QUESTIONS AND PROBLEMS

1. Explain how the classical economists concluded that Say's Law is valid and long-term unemployment impossible.

2. Use the consumption function data below to answer the following questions:

Keynesian Consumption Function
(billions of dollars per year)

Real Disposable Income	Consumption	Saving	MPC	MPS
$100	$150	$__	__	__
200	200	__	__	__
300	250	__	__	__
400	300	__	__	__
500	350	__	__	__

a. Calculate the saving schedule.
b. Determine the marginal propensities to consume (*MPC*) and save (*MPS*).
c. Determine the break-even income.
d. What is the relationship between the *MPC* and the *MPS*?

3. Explain why the MPC and the MPS must always add up to one.

4. How do households "dissave"?

5. Explain how each of the following affects the consumption function:
   a. The expectation is that a prolonged recession will occur in the next year.
   b. Stock prices rise sharply.
   c. The price level rises by 10 percent.
   d. The interest rate on consumer loans rises sharply.
   e. Income taxes increase.

6. Your college is considering investing $6 million to add 10,000 seats to its football stadium. The athletic department forecasts it can sell all these extra seats each game for a ticket price of $20 per seat, and the team plays six home games per year. If the school can borrow at an interest rate of 14 percent, should the school undertake this project? What would happen if the school expected a losing season and could sell tickets for only half of the 10,000 seats?

7. Why is the investment demand curve less stable than the consumption and saving schedules? What are the basic determinants that can shift the investment demand curve?

8. Suppose most business executives expect a slowdown in the economy. How might this situation affect the economy?

9. The levels of real disposable income and aggregate expenditures for a two-sector economy (consumption and investment) are given in the following table:

Real Disposable Income (trillions of dollars per year)	Aggregate Expenditures (trillions of dollars per year)
$0	$3.00
1	3.25
2	3.50
3	3.75
4	4.00
5	4.25
6	4.50
7	4.75
8	5.00

a. Construct a graph of the aggregate expenditures function (*AE*).
b. Determine the autonomous consumption, *MPC*, and *MPS* for this hypothetical economy.
c. What is the equilibrium level of real disposable income?
d. What will happen to the equilibrium level of real disposable income if autonomous investment increases?

For Online Exercises, go to the text Web site at www.cengage.com/economics/tucker.

CHECKPOINT ANSWER ✓

What's Your *MPC*?

Early in your career when your income is relatively low, you are likely to spend your entire income, and perhaps even dissave, just to afford necessities. During this stage of your life, your *MPC* will be close to 1. As your income increases and you have purchased the necessities, additional income can go to luxuries. If you become wealthier, you have a higher marginal propensity to save and consequently a lower marginal propensity to consume. If you said your *MPC* will probably decrease as your income increases, **YOU ARE CORRECT.**

PRACTICE QUIZ

For an explanation of the correct answers, please visit the tutorial at www.cengage.com/economics/tucker.

1. The French classical economist Jean-Baptiste Say transformed the equality of production and spending into a law that can be expressed as follows:
   a. The invisible hand creates its own supply.
   b. Wages always fall to the subsistence level.
   c. Supply creates its own demand.
   d. Aggregate output does not always equal consumption.

2. Autonomous consumption is
   a. positively related to the level of consumption.
   b. negatively related to the level of consumption.
   c. positively related to the level of disposable income.
   d. independent of the level of disposable income.

3. The consumption function represents the relationship between consumer expenditures and
   a. interest rates.
   b. saving.
   c. the price level.
   d. disposable income.

4. John Maynard Keynes's proposition that a dollar increase in disposable income will increase consumption, but by less than the increase in disposable income, implies a marginal propensity to consume that is
   a. greater than or equal to one.
   b. equal to one.
   c. less than one, but greater than zero.
   d. negative.

5. Above the break-even disposable income for the consumption function, which of the following occurs?
   a. Dissaving
   b. Saving
   c. Neither (a) nor (b)
   d. Both (a) and (b)

6. Which of the following changes produces an upward shift in the consumption function?
   a. An increase in consumer wealth
   b. A decrease in consumer wealth
   c. A decrease in autonomous consumption
   d. Both (b) and (c)

7. An upward shift in the consumption schedule, other things being equal, could be caused by households
   a. becoming optimistic about the state of the economy.
   b. becoming pessimistic about the state of the economy.
   c. expecting future income and wealth to decline.
   d. doing none of the above.

8. The investment demand curve represents the relationship between business spending for investment goods and
   a. GDP.
   b. interest rates.
   c. disposable income.
   d. saving.

PRACTICE QUIZ CONTINUED

EXHIBIT 11   Aggregate Expenditures Function

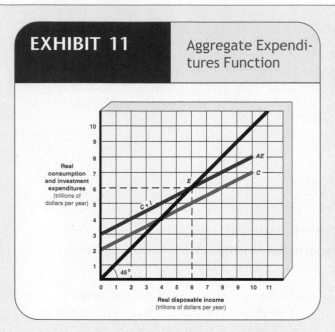

EXHIBIT 12   Aggregate Expenditures Function

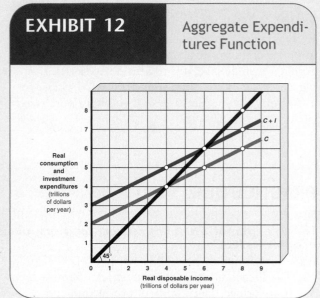

9. Which of the following changes produces a leftward shift in the investment demand curve?
   a. A wave of optimism about future profitability
   b. Technological change
   c. High plant capacity utilization
   d. An increase in business taxes

10. The aggregate expenditures function (*AE*) represents which of the following?
    a. The consumption function only
    b. Autonomous consumption only
    c. The investment demand curve only
    d. All three of the above combined
    e. A combination of (a) and (c)

11. In Exhibit 11, what is the households' marginal propensity to consume (*MPC*)?
    a. 0.50
    b. 0.67
    c. 0.75
    d. 0.80

12. In Exhibit 11, aggregate disposable income will equal consumption plus investment (aggregate expenditures), and the economy will be in equilibrium when real disposable income is
    a. $2.33 trillion.
    b. $3 trillion.

   c. $6 trillion.
   d. $10 trillion.

13. As shown in Exhibit 12, autonomous consumption is
    a. 0.
    b. $1 trillion.
    c. $2 trillion.
    d. $3 trillion.
    e. $6 trillion.

14. As shown in Exhibit 12, saving occurs
    a. at 0.
    b. between 0 and $4 trillion.
    c. where disposable income is greater than $4 trillion.
    d. at $2 trillion.

15. As shown in Exhibit 12, the marginal propensity to save (*MPS*) is
    a. 0.33.
    b. 0.50.
    c. 0.67.
    d. 0.75.

The Keynesian Model in Action

I n 1935, George Bernard Shaw received a letter from John Maynard Keynes, which stated, "I believe myself to be writing a book [*The General Theory*] on economic theory which will largely revolutionize—not, I suppose, at once but in the course of the next ten years—the way the world thinks about economic problems." Indeed, Keynes's macroeconomic theory offered powerful ideas whose time had come during the Great Depression. Building on the foundation of the previous chapter, this chapter describes how Keynes conceived the economy as driven by aggregate demand that can be separated and analyzed under the individual components of consumption (C), investment (I), government spending (G), and net exports ($X - M$).

You must keep in mind that during the Great Depression era, plants had idle capacity and unemployment was massive. Under these conditions, inflation was not the problem. The Keynesian model therefore generally ignores price level changes and focuses instead on how full-employment output can be achieved by changes in aggregate expenditures.

Like adding icing to a cake, this chapter begins by adding government spending and global trade to the aggregate expenditures line in the Keynesian model developed in the previous chapter. Next, you will learn how the economy gravitates to an equilibrium where aggregate expenditures equal aggregate output. And you will look at the link between the equilibrium output and the level of employment in an economy. The analysis will make clear why Keynes argued that there is no self-correction mechanism that eventually moves the nation to the full-employment equilibrium output.

Finally, you will understand one of Keynes's most powerful ideas—the spending multiplier. At the very heart of Keynesian theory is the concept that an initial increase in aggregate spending of $1 in an economy can increase equilibrium output by more than $1. Thus, Keynesian economics offers a cure for an economy in deep recession: government policies that expand aggregate demand, raise national output, create jobs, and restore full employment.

In this chapter, you will learn to solve these economic puzzles:

- Why did Keynes reject the classical theory that "supply creates its own demand"?

- Why did Keynes argue that the government should adopt active policies, rather than allowing the price system to prevail?

- Can the Keynesian model explain an ice cream war?

Adding Government and Global Trade to the Keynesian Model

In this chapter, we continue our study of the simple economy begun in the previous chapter (Exhibit 10). Consumption and investment are not the only forms of spending. As shown earlier in the chapter on GDP (Exhibit 2), consumption and investment represent 85 percent of total spending, while government spending and net exports account for the remaining 15 percent of GDP.

Government Spending

Government spending is the second largest component of aggregate expenditures in the United States. Like investment, government spending can be considered an autonomous expenditure. The reasoning is that government spending is primarily the result of political decisions made independent of the level of national output.

Exhibit 1(a) shows hypothetical government spending as a horizontal line labeled G at $1 trillion. If government officials increase government spending, the G line shifts upward to G_1, and reduced government spending shifts the G line downward to G_2. The amount of the shift is equal to the amount of change in government spending.

Here we must pause to take special note of the change from real disposable income to real GDP on the horizontal axis of the graph. Does it make a difference? No, it makes little difference. In the previous chapter, real disposable income was used, following the theory Keynes himself developed. However, it is important to connect aggregate output and income measures. Recall from Exhibit 7 in the chapter on GDP the adjustments required to convert GDP into disposable income (Y_d). As it turns out, real disposable income is a sizable portion of real GDP. Over the last decade, real disposable income, on average, has consistently been about 70 percent of real GDP. If we are willing to assume that real disposable income remains at the same high proportion of real GDP each year, then we can substitute real GDP for real disposable income in the Keynesian model. Changes in real GDP therefore reflect changes in both real national output and real disposable income.

Net Exports

Like investment and government spending exports and imports can be treated as autonomous expenditures unaffected by a nation's domestic level of real GDP.

GLOBAL ECONOMICS

EXHIBIT 1   Autonomous Government Spending and Net Exports Curves

In Part (a), government spending (G) is assumed to be determined by the political decision-making process. The autonomous government spending line, G, is therefore a horizontal line indicating that government spending is independent of the level of real GDP. An increase in government spending shifts G upward to G_1. A decrease shifts G downward to G_2.

Part (b) also shows that net exports are assumed to be independent of the level of GDP. Horizontal line $(X - M)_1$ is negative because imports exceed exports. If exports equal imports, then the net export line shifts upward to $(X - M)$. If exports exceed imports, the net exports line is represented by a positive net exports line, $(X - M)_2$.

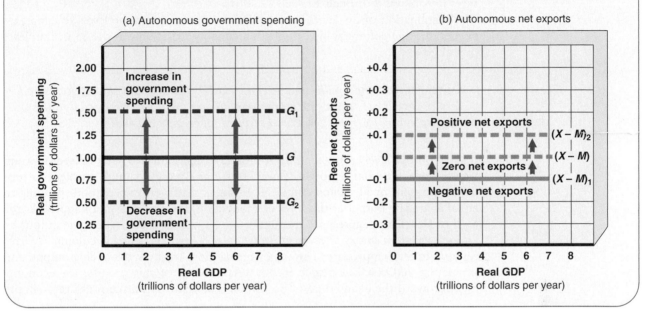

(a) Autonomous government spending

(b) Autonomous net exports

Economic conditions in the countries that buy U.S. products affect the level of our exports. On the other hand, the level of imports purchased by U.S. citizens is influenced by economic conditions in the United States. As shown in Exhibit 1(b), net exports, $(X - M)$, can be positive, zero, or negative. The level of net exports, or the $(X - M)$ line, is horizontal because net exports are assumed to be independent of the level of real GDP. Since for many years the value of imports we have purchased from foreigners has exceeded the value of exports we have been selling them, the model assumes net exports are negative at line $(X - M)_1$. If exports and imports are equal, the net exports line shifts upward to zero at line $(X - M)$. If exports exceed imports, the positive $(X - M)$ line shifts farther upward to line $(X - M)_2$.

The Aggregate Expenditures-Output Model

Keynes countered classical theory by developing an alternative theory that explained how a depressed economy can be stuck forever in a below-full-employment equilibrium without adequate aggregate expenditures. In this section, a simple Keynesian model is developed to explain what Keynes meant by his famous saying, "In the long run, we are all dead."

Tabular Analysis of Keynesian Equilibrium

Exhibit 2 presents data to illustrate the relationship between employment, aggregate output and income, and aggregate expenditures for our hypothetical economy. Real GDP (Y) is listed in column 1, consumption (C) is listed in column 2, and investment (I) in column 3 is an autonomous expenditure of $1 trillion from Exhibit 9(b) in the previous chapter. Government spending (G) in column 4 is also an autonomous expenditure of $1 trillion from Exhibit 1(a), and net exports ($X - M$) in column 5 are taken from Exhibit 1(b). The aggregate expenditures function (AE) in column 6 is the sum of the $C + I + G + (X - M)$ components of aggregate expenditures in columns 2 through 5.

Examination of the levels of real GDP in column 1 and the levels of aggregate expenditures in column 6 indicate that an equality exists only at the $5 trillion level of real GDP.

> **Conclusion** *At the equilibrium level of real GDP, the total value of goods and services produced (aggregate output and income, Y) is precisely equal to the total spending for these goods and services (aggregate expenditures, AE).*

All output levels other than $5 trillion are unsustainable macro disequilibrium levels. Consider what happens if businesses employ only enough workers to produce an output of $1 trillion real GDP. Business managers expect total spending to equal aggregate output at this level of production, but this does not happen. At the level of $1 trillion, aggregate expenditures of $3 trillion exceed aggregate output by an *unplanned inventory investment depletion* of $2 trillion, listed in column 7. Firms respond to this happy state of affairs by hiring more workers, expanding output, and generating additional aggregate income. As a result of this process, the economy moves toward the equilibrium of $5 trillion real GDP. Thus, the pressure of empty

EXHIBIT 2 — Equilibrium and Disequilibrium Levels of Employment, Output, and Income

(1) Aggregate Output and Income (real GDP) (Y)	(2) Consumption (C)	(3) Investment (I)	(4) Government (G)	(5) Net Exports (X − M)	(6) Aggregate Expenditures (AE)	(7) Unplanned Inventory Investment Depletion (−) or Accumulation (+)	(8) Direction of Real GDP and Employment
$ 0	$0.6	$1	$1	$−0.1	$2.5	$−2.5	Increase
1.0	1.1	1	1	−0.1	3.0	−2.0	Increase
2.0	1.6	1	1	−0.1	3.5	−1.5	Increase
3.0	2.1	1	1	−0.1	4.0	−1.0	Increase
4.0	2.6	1	1	−0.1	4.5	−0.5	Increase
5.0	3.1	1	1	−0.1	5.0	0	Equilibrium
6.0	3.6	1	1	−0.1	5.5	+0.5	Decrease
7.0	4.1	1	1	−0.1	6.0	+1.0	Decrease
8.0	4.6	1	1	−0.1	6.5	+1.5	Decrease

NOTE: All amounts are in trillions of dollars per year.

shelves and warehouses drives our hypothetical economy to create jobs and reduce the unemployment rate (not explicitly shown in the model).

The reverse is true for all levels of real GDP above the $5 trillion equilibrium level. Now suppose firms hire more workers and aggregate output is $7 trillion real GDP. At the real GDP disequilibrium level of $7 trillion, *unplanned inventory investment accumulation* occurs because aggregate expenditures of $6 trillion are insufficient to purchase $7 trillion of output. The result is that unwanted inventories worth $1 trillion remain unsold on the shelves and in the warehouses of business firms. Producers react to this undesirable condition by cutting the rate of output and employment. In this case, real GDP declines toward the equilibrium level of $5 trillion, jobs are lost, and unemployment rises.

> **Conclusion** *Aggregate expenditures in Keynesian economics pull aggregate output either higher or lower toward equilibrium in the economy as opposed to the classical view that aggregate output generates an equal amount of aggregate spending.*

Graphical Analysis of Keynesian Equilibrium

The tabular analysis of Keynesian theory can be presented graphically. Using the data from Exhibit 2, Exhibit 3 presents a graph measuring real aggregate expenditures on the y-axis and real GDP on the x-axis. Exhibit 3 illustrates the aggregate expenditures-output model. The aggregate expenditures-output model determines the equilibrium level of real GDP by the intersection of the aggregate expenditures and aggregate output (and income) curves. The 45-degree line now takes on a special significance. Each point along this line is equidistant from the horizontal and vertical axes. Therefore, each point reflects a *possible* equilibrium between real GDP aggregate output (Y) and aggregate expenditures (AE). Note that the AE line indicates aggregate expenditures along a line less steep than the 45-degree line. This is because the slope of the AE line is determined by the marginal propensity to consume (MPC), which is less than 1. Aggregate expenditures equal aggregate output at the $5 trillion real GDP level, and any other level of output is unstable. If businesses produce at some output level that is higher than equilibrium GDP, such as $7 trillion real GDP, the vertical distance between the 45-degree equilibrium line and the AE line measures an undesired inventory accumulation of $1 trillion. This leads businesses to reduce employment, and production drops downward until the economy reaches equilibrium at $5 trillion. You may have already recognized that the difference of $1 trillion between the equilibrium output (actual GDP) at point E and the full-employment output (potential GDP) is a positive *GDP gap*, discussed in the chapter on business cycles and unemployment (see Exhibit 9).

Now consider the case in which businesses hire only enough workers to produce aggregate output where the AE line is above the 45-degree equilibrium line. Since aggregate expenditures exceed aggregate output, businesses sell more than they currently produce, which depletes their inventories. Business managers react to this excess aggregate demand condition by hiring more workers and expanding production, causing movement upward along the AE function toward the equilibrium level of $5 trillion real GDP.

Now it's time to pause, take a deep breath, and appreciate what you have been studying so diligently. It's a powerful idea! Exhibit 3 illustrates the basic explanation

Aggregate expenditures-output model

The model that determines the equilibrium level of real GDP by the intersection of the aggregate expenditures and aggregate output (and income) curves.

EXHIBIT 3   The Keynesian Aggregate Expenditures-Output Model

Aggregate expenditures (AE) equal aggregate output (Y) at the equilibrium level of $5 trillion real GDP. Below the equilibrium level of real GDP, an undesired inventory depletion causes businesses to expand production, which pushes the economy toward equilibrium output. Above the equilibrium level of real GDP, an unintended inventory accumulation causes businesses to reduce production, which pushes the economy toward equilibrium output. In Keynesian theory, the full-employment output of $6 trillion real GDP can be reached only by shifting the AE curve upward until the full-capacity output of $6 trillion real GDP is reached.

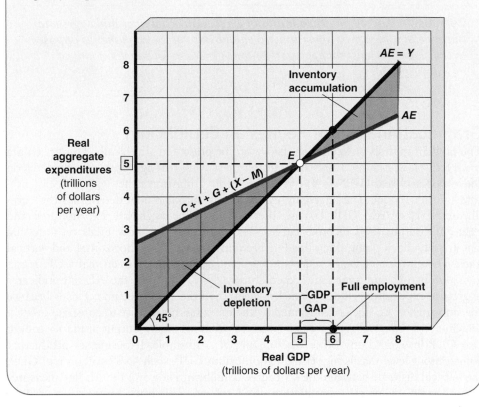

offered by Keynes for the Great Depression: *Contrary to classical theory, once an equilibrium is established between aggregate expenditures and aggregate output, there is no tendency for the economy to change, even when equilibrium is well below full employment.* The solution Keynes offered Western economies facing the Great Depression is to shift the AE line upward until the full-employment equilibrium is reached. Otherwise, prolonged unemployment persists indefinitely, and the economy never self-corrects. We now turn to the key idea behind changes in aggregate spending to stabilize the macro economy.

The Spending Multiplier Effect

Changes in aggregate expenditures in the Keynesian model make things happen. The crux of Keynesian macroeconomic policy depends on a change in aggregate

EXHIBIT 4   The Spending Multiplier Effect of a Change in Government Spending

This graph is an enlargement of the spending multiplier process beginning at the point where the economy is in equilibrium at $5 trillion. Then an initial increase of $500 billion in government spending shifts the aggregate expenditures line up vertically from AE_1 to AE_2. After all spending-output-spending rounds are complete, a new equilibrium is restored at point E_1 with a full-employment output of $6 trillion. Thus, the $500 billion initial increase in government spending has caused a $1 trillion increase in real GDP, and the value of the multiplier is 2.

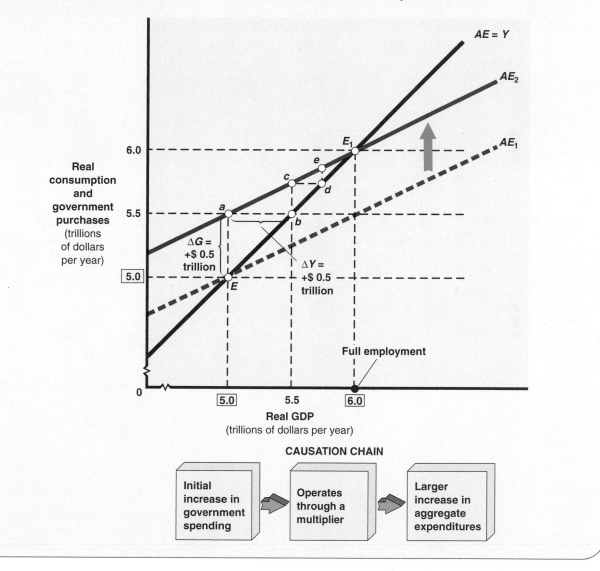

expenditures, which is multiplied or amplified by rounds of spending and respending throughout the economy. Exhibit 4 is an enlarged version of Exhibit 3. Our analysis begins at the initial equilibrium of $5 trillion real GDP (point E), which is below the full-employment output level of $6 trillion real GDP. Now let's assume the government decides to increase government spending by $0.5 trillion. An increase in autonomous government spending of $0.5 trillion per year shifts the aggregate expenditures curve *vertically* upward by this amount from point E on AE_1 to point a on AE_2. This means, at the initial output of $5 trillion real GDP, aggregate demand expands by $0.5 trillion to $5.5 trillion. The initial expansion of spending causes inventories (not shown in the graph) to decline by $0.5 trillion because aggregate spending of $5.5 trillion exceeds aggregate output of $5.0 trillion real GDP. Firms respond by stepping up output by $0.5 trillion real GDP per year to replace inventories. The exhibit shows this by the move from point a to point b. Now the marginal propensity to consume enters the picture. Assuming the MPC is 0.50, the expansion of output from $5 trillion to $5.5 trillion puts an extra $500 billion of income into the pockets of workers. Given the MPC of 0.50, these workers increase spending on goods and services by $250 billion (movement from point b to point c). This expansion of consumer spending again causes inventories to decline and output, in turn, to expand by $250 billion, represented by the distance between point c and point d. This again puts extra income into workers' pockets, of which $125 billion (the distance between points d and e) is spent ($MPC \times \Delta Y = 0.50 \times \$250$ billion = $125 billion).

This process of spending-output-spending continues through an infinite number of rounds until output reaches the new equilibrium level of $6 trillion per year at point E_1. Thus, an initial expansion of government spending of $0.5 trillion expands equilibrium output by $1 trillion, which is twice the magnitude of the increase in government spending. Hence, the spending multiplier is 2. The spending multiplier is the ratio of the change in real GDP to the initial change in any component of aggregate expenditures, including consumption, investment, government spending and net exports. The formula to compute the amount of change in government spending or other aggregate expenditures required to shift equilibrium aggregate output measured by real GDP is

$$\text{Spending multiplier} = \frac{\text{change in equilibrium rseal GDP}}{\textit{initial} \text{ change in aggregate expenditures}}$$

In the example presented in Exhibit 4, the spending multiplier is computed as

$$\text{Spending multiplier} = \frac{\Delta Y}{\Delta G} = \frac{\$1,000 \text{ billion}}{\$500 \text{ billion}} = 2$$

Spending Multiplier Arithmetic

The graphical presentation of the spending multiplier process should make the basic mechanics clear to you, but we need to be more specific and derive a formula. Therefore, let's pause to tackle the task of explaining in more detail the spending multiplier of 2 used in the above example. Exhibit 5 illustrates numerically the cumulative increase in aggregate expenditures resulting from a $500 billion increase in government spending. In the initial round, the government spends this amount for bridges, national defense, and so forth. Households receive this amount of income. In the second round, these households spend $250 billion (0.50 × $500 billion) on houses, cars, groceries, and other products. In the third round, the incomes of realtors, autoworkers, grocers, and others are boosted by $250 billion, and they spend $125 billion (0.50 × $250 billion). These rounds of spending create income

Spending multiplier (SM)

The ratio of the change in real GDP to an initial change in any component of aggregate expenditures, including consumption, investment, government spending, and net exports. As a formula, the spending multiplier equals $1/(1 - MPC)$ or $1/MPS$.

EXHIBIT 5	Spending Multiplier Effect	
Round	Component of Total Spending	New Consumption Spending
1	Government spending	$500
2	Consumption	250
3	Consumption	125
4	Consumption	63
.	.	.
.	.	.
.	.	.
All other rounds	Consumption	62
Total spending		$1,000

NOTE: All amounts are rounded to the nearest billion dollars per year.

for respending in a downward spiral throughout the economy in smaller and smaller amounts until the total level of aggregate expenditures rises by an extra $1,000 billion.

Conclusion *Any initial change in spending by the government, households, or firms creates a chain reaction of further spending, which causes a greater cumulative change in aggregate expenditures.*

You might recognize from algebra that the spending multiplier effect is a process based on an infinite geometric series. The formula for the sum of such a series of numbers is the initial number times $1/(1 - r)$, where r is the ratio that relates the numbers. Using this formula, the sum (total spending) is calculated as $500 billion $(\Delta G) \times [1/(1 - 0.50)] = \$1,000$ billion. By simply defining r in the infinite series formula as MPC, the spending multiplier for aggregate demand is expressed as

$$\text{Spending multiplier} = \frac{1}{1 - MPC}$$

Applying this formula to our example:

$$\text{Spending multiplier} = \frac{1}{1 - 0.50} = \frac{1}{0.50} = 2$$

Recall from the previous chapter that $MPC + MPS = 1$, and therefore $MPS = 1 - MPC$. Hence, the above multiplier formula can be rewritten as

$$\text{Spending multiplier} = \frac{1}{MPS}$$

EXHIBIT 6	Relationship between *MPC*, *MPS*, and the Spending Multiplier	
(1) Marginal Propensity to Consume (*MPC*)	**(2)** Marginal Propensity to Save (*MPS*)	**(3)** Spending Multiplier
0.90	0.10	10
0.80	0.20	5
0.75	0.25	4
0.67	0.33	3
0.50	0.50	2
0.33	0.67	1.5

Applying the multiplier formula to our example:

$$\text{Spending multiplier} = \frac{1}{MPS} = \frac{1}{1 - 0.50} = 2$$

Since *MPS* and *MPC* are related, the size of the multiplier depends on the size of the *MPC*. What will the result be if people spend 80 percent or 33 percent of each dollar of income instead of 50 percent? If the *MPC* increases (decreases), consumers spend a larger (smaller) share of each additional dollar of output/income in each round, and the size of the multiplier increases (decreases). Exhibit 6 lists the multiplier for different values of *MPC* and *MPS*. Economists use real-world macroeconomic data to estimate a more complex multiplier than the simple multiplier formula developed in this chapter. Their estimates of the long run real-world *MPC* range from 0.80 to 0.90. An *MPC* of 0.50 is used in the above examples for simplicity.

Recessionary and Inflationary Gaps

The multiplier is important in the Keynesian model because it means that the initial change in aggregate expenditures results in an amplified change in the equilibrium level of real GDP. Such inherent instability can mean bad or good news for an economy. The bad news occurs, for example, when the multiplier amplifies small declines in total spending from, say, consumer and business manager pessimism into downturns in national output, income, and employment. The good news is that, in theory, macroeconomic policy can manage, or manipulate, the economy's performance by a relatively small initial change in aggregate expenditures.

Recessionary Gap

Using Government Spending to Close a Recessionary Gap   Consider the aggregate expenditures function AE_1 in Exhibit 7. Beginning at point E_1, this hypothetical

---

EXHIBIT 7	A Recessionary Gap

The hypothetical economy begins in equilibrium at point E_1, with an equilibrium output of $4 trillion real GDP. With aggregate expenditures of AE_1, real GDP will not automatically increase to the $6 trillion full-employment output. The $1 trillion deficiency in total spending required to achieve full employment is the recessionary gap measured by the vertical distance between points a and E_2. Given a multiplier of 2, an initial increase in autonomous expenditures equal to the recessionary gap works through the spending multiplier and causes the economy to move from E_1 to E_2 and achieve full employment.

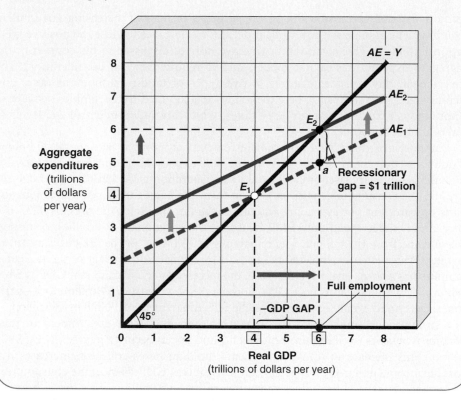

economy's initial equilibrium level is $4 trillion real GDP. The MPC is 0.50, and the spending multiplier is therefore 2. The full-employment output is $6 trillion real GDP, which means the economy faces a negative GDP gap of $2 trillion. Along the vertical line at the full-employment output level, look at the segment between point a on the initial AE_1 line and point E_2 on the AE_2 line, which is labeled a recessionary gap. A recessionary gap is the amount by which aggregate expenditures fall short of the amount required to achieve full-employment equilibrium. In our example, the recessionary gap is $1 trillion. What is the importance of the recessionary gap? The recessionary gap is the initial increase in autonomous spending required to trigger the multiplier, shift the aggregate expenditures function upward from AE_1 to AE_2, and eliminate the positive GDP gap. Stated as an expression,

Initial increase in autonomous expenditures × spending multiplier = increase in equilibrium output

Recessionary gap
The amount by which the aggregate expenditures curve must be increased to achieve full-employment equilibrium.

Using the data in our example,

$$\text{\$1 trillion} \times 2 = \text{\$2 trillion}$$

We now turn to the important question of how to inject an additional \$1 trillion spending into the economy, cause AE_1 to shift upward to AE_2, and thereby increase the equilibrium output from \$4 trillion to \$6 trillion real GDP. Under Keynesian theory, when market forces do not automatically do the job, then the central government should take aggressive action and adopt policies that boost autonomous spending [C, I, G, or $(X - M)$] by an amount equal to the recessionary gap.

Using a Tax Cut to Close a Recessionary Gap   Instead of increasing government spending, let's assume the government decides to cut taxes to close the positive GDP gap in Exhibit 7. This is an option we have not yet discussed in the context of the aggregate expenditures-output model, and it requires special consideration. The government may consider changes in two types of taxes: autonomous taxes and income taxes. For simplicity, here the analysis is confined to the simpler concept of autonomous taxes, such as property taxes, which are independent of the levels of real output and income.

Suppose in Exhibit 7 the government reduces autonomous taxes by \$800 billion. Would this tax cut be enough to restore full employment? Since real disposable income rises at every level of GDP, so does consumption at all levels of real GDP. As a result, the consumption function and, in turn, the aggregate expenditures function shifts upward, but not by the full amount of the tax cut. Since the *MPC* is 0.50, this means households spend only \$400 billion of the additional \$800 billion of disposable income from the tax cut. The remaining \$400 billion of the tax cut is added to savings. Hence, after multiplying the tax cut by the *MPC*, the result of the tax cut is computed as above. That is, in this case, the increase in equilibrium real GDP is \$400 billion × 2 = \$800 billion. Since GDP would increase only from \$4 trillion to \$4.8 trillion, the economy would operate below the full-employment real GDP of \$6 trillion.

An approach similar to a cut in taxes would be for the government to raise *transfer payments* (welfare, unemployment, and Social Security payments) by \$800 billion. This increase in transfer payments, holding taxes constant, increases disposable income dollar-for-dollar at each level of real GDP. Hence, the consumption and aggregate expenditures lines shift upward by \$400 billion. This initial boost in total spending is computed by multiplying the *MPC* of 0.50 times the increase of \$800 billion in transfer payments. The increase in transfer payments has the same effect as an identical cut in taxes, and the equilibrium real GDP increases by \$800 billion. Hence, a transfer payment is simply a cut in net taxes.

Another simpler method of calculating the impact of a change in taxes is to use a tax multiplier. The tax multiplier is the change in aggregate expenditures (total spending) resulting from an initial change in taxes. Expressed as a formula:

$$\text{Tax multiplier} = 1 - \text{spending multiplier}$$

After you calculate the tax multiplier, multiply your answer by the amount of the tax increase or decrease in order to determine the change in aggregate expenditures. Expressed as a formula:

$$\text{Change in taxes } (\Delta T) \times \text{tax multiplier} = \text{change in aggregate expenditures}$$

Tax multiplier

The change in aggregate expenditures (total spending) resulting from an initial change in taxes. As a formula, the tax multiplier equals 1 − spending multiplier.

YOU'RE THE ECONOMIST   The Great Ice Cream War

Applicable Concept: aggregate expenditures-output model

The following *Wall Street Journal* article provides a rare insight into the politics of global trade, and the Analyze the Issue connects trade policy to the macro model developed in this chapter:

While many people relish American-made ice cream with deliberately foreign-sounding names, few people realize that the U.S. government declared war on ice cream imports by restricting them to less than one-tenth of one percent of U.S. consumption. With quotas so low and transportation costs high, few countries bothered to ship any

ice cream at all to the United States. For example, in 1988 the United States exported hundreds of thousands of gallons of ice cream to Canada, yet Canadian ice cream was banned from the United States. Only 576 gallons was imported from New Zealand and 12 gallons from Denmark. This was not enough ice cream to stock a large grocery store on a summer Saturday.

The U.S. ice cream quotas dated back to December 31, 1970, when President Nixon decreed that future ice cream imports could not exceed 431,330 gallons a year. Why? That year, according to Deputy Secretary of Agriculture Ann Veneman, testifying before the ITC [U.S. International Trade Commission], the U.S. was hit with a "flood of imports." This so-called "flood" amounted to barely 1 percent of U.S. ice cream consumption.

How did Mr. Nixon decide to limit imports to exactly 431,330 gallons a year? Section 22 of the Agriculture Adjustment Act allowed the U.S. government to protect domestic

price-support programs by restricting imports to 50 percent of the annual average imports for a representative period. Ice cream imports did not begin until 1969, so the U.S. government chose 1969 and the two previous years with no ice cream imports in order to calculate a low annual average import quota for this product.

Finally, the article concluded that the U.S. government probably spent more than $1,000 in administrative expenses for each gallon of ice cream imported into the United States. The article's author concluded, "Global trade disputes are rapidly degenerating into a full employment program for government bureaucrats."

ANALYZE THE ISSUE

Assume the U.S. economy is in an inflationary gap condition. Use the Keynesian aggregate expenditures-output model to explain why increasing U.S. exports and restricting imports is or is not a desirable policy.

Returning to the example shown in Exhibit 7, suppose we wish to calculate the tax cut required to increase real GDP by $2 trillion from $4 trillion to $6 trillion and achieve full employment. Using the tax multiplier formula:

$$\text{Tax multiplier} = 1 - 2 = -1$$
$$\Delta T \times (-1) = \$2 \text{ trillion}$$
$$\Delta T = \$2 \text{ trillion}$$

Therefore, in this hypothetical economy, a $2 trillion tax cut will increase GDP by the $2 trillion required to achieve full employment.

CHECKPOINT

Full-Employment Output, Where are You?

Suppose the U.S. economy is in equilibrium at $3 trillion real GDP ($3,000 billion) with a recessionary gap. Given an *MPC* of 0.50, the government estimates that a tax cut of $200 billion is just enough to restore full employment. What is the full-employment real GDP target?

EXHIBIT 8 — An Inflationary Gap

The hypothetical economy begins in equilibrium at point E_1 with an equilibrium output of $6 trillion real GDP. Given an initial aggregate expenditures function of AE_1, real GDP will not self-correct to the full-employment output of $4 trillion. The $1 trillion excess of total spending over the amount required at full employment is the inflationary gap measured by the vertical distance between points a and E_2. Given a multiplier of 2, an initial decrease in autonomous expenditures of $1 trillion causes the economy to move from point E_1 to E_2, achieve full employment, and cool the upward pressure on prices.

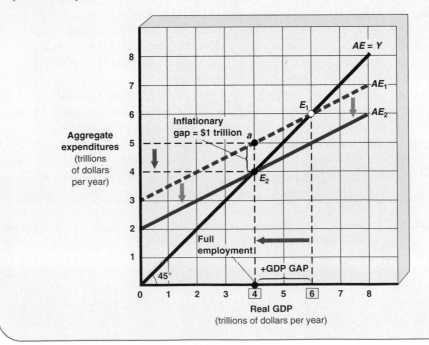

Inflationary Gap

Under other circumstances, an inflationary gap may burden an economy. An inflationary gap is the amount by which aggregate expenditures exceed the amount required to achieve full-employment equilibrium. In Exhibit 8, the inflationary gap of $1 trillion is the vertical distance between point a on the initial AE_1 line and point E_2 on the AE_2 line. Since the economy can produce only $4 trillion in real output, this excess aggregate demand puts upward pressure on prices as buyers compete for this limited real output. If aggregate spending declines from AE_1 to AE_2, the economy moves from an equilibrium of $6 trillion at point E_1 to the full-employment equilibrium of $4 trillion at point E_2, and the inflationary pressure cools.

Again, the Keynesian prescription is for the central government to take aggressive action and adopt policies that reduce autonomous spending [C, I, G, or ($X - M$)] by an amount equal to the inflationary gap. Note from the analysis in the previous section that the government could cut government spending or use a tax hike or a cut in transfer payments to reduce consumption. Stated as an expression,

Initial decrease in autonomous expenditures $\times$ spending multiplier
= decrease in equilibrium output

In our example, the *MPC* is 0.50, so the multiplier is 2. The actual real GDP of $6 trillion is greater than the potential real GDP of $4 trillion, so the negative real GDP gap is −$2 trillion. Hence,

−$1 trillion $\times$ 2 = −$2 trillion

> **Inflationary gap**
> The amount by which the aggregate expenditures curve must be decreased to achieve full-employment equilibrium.

CHECKPOINT

How Much Spending Must Uncle Sam Cut?

Suppose the U.S. economy is troubled by inflation. The economy is in equilibrium at a real GDP of $3.5 trillion ($3,500 billion), the *MPC* is 0.90, and the full-employment output is $3 trillion ($3,000 billion). If the government decides to eliminate the inflationary gap by cutting government spending, what will be the size of the cut?

KEY CONCEPTS

Aggregate expenditures-
   output model

Spending multiplier (SM)
Recessionary gap

Tax multiplier
Inflationary gap

SUMMARY

- The **Keynesian theory** argues that the economy is
inherently unstable and may require government
intervention to control aggregate expenditures
and restore full employment. If we assume that
real disposable income remains the same high
proportion of real GDP, then we can substitute
real GDP for real disposable income in the
Keynesian model. **Government spending** and **net
exports** can be treated as autonomous expenditures in the Keynesian model. **Net exports** are the
only component of aggregate expenditures that
changes from a positive to a negative value as real
GDP rises. Both exports and imports are determined by foreign or domestic income, tastes,
trade restrictions, and exchange rates.

Government Spending

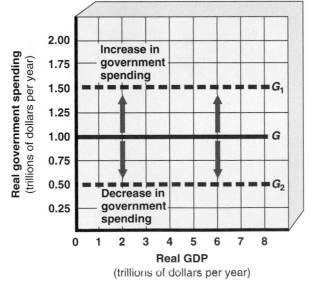

Autonomous government spending

Net Exports

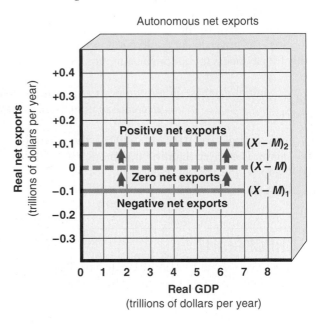

Autonomous net exports

- The **Keynesian aggregate expenditures-output
model** determines the equilibrium level of real
GDP by the intersection of the aggregate expenditures and the aggregate output and income
curves. Each equilibrium level in the economy is
associated with a level of employment and corresponding unemployment rate. Aggregate expenditures and real GDP are equal, graphically, where
the $AE = C + I + G + (X - M)$ line intersects the
45-degree line. At any output greater or less than
the equilibrium real GDP, unintended inventory
investment pressures businesses to alter aggregate
output and income until equilibrium at full-
employment real GDP is restored.

Keynesian Aggregate Expenditures-Output Model

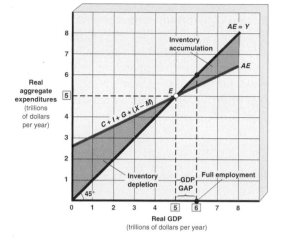

- The ***spending multiplier*** is the ratio of the change in equilibrium output to the initial change in any of the components of aggregate expenditures. Algebraically, the multiplier is the reciprocal of the marginal propensity to save. The multiplier effect causes the equilibrium level of real GDP to change by several times the initial change in spending.
- A ***recessionary gap*** is the amount by which aggregate expenditures fall short of the amount necessary for the economy to operate at full-employment real GDP. To eliminate a negative GDP gap, the Keynesian solution is to increase autonomous spending by an amount equal to the recessionary gap and operate through the multiplier to increase equilibrium output and income.

Recessionary Gap

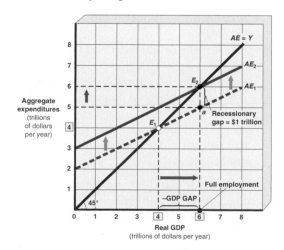

- The ***tax multiplier*** is the multiplier by which an initial change in taxes changes aggregate demand (total spending) after an infinite number of spending cycles. Expressed as a formula, the tax multiplier = 1 − spending multiplier.
- An ***inflationary gap*** is the amount by which aggregate expenditures exceed the amount necessary to establish full-employment equilibrium and indicates upward pressure on prices. To eliminate a positive GDP gap, the Keynesian solution is to decrease autonomous spending by an amount equal to the inflationary gap and operate through the multiplier to decrease equilibrium output and income.

Inflationary Gap

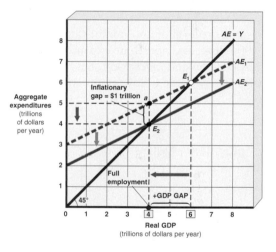

SUMMARY OF CONCLUSION STATEMENTS

- At the equilibrium level of real GDP, the total value of goods and services produced (aggregate output and income, Y) is precisely equal to the total spending for these goods and services (aggregate expenditures, AE).
- Aggregate expenditures in Keynesian economics pull aggregate output either higher or lower

toward equilibrium in the economy, as opposed to the classical view that aggregate output generates an equal amount of aggregate spending.

- Any initial change in spending by the government, households, or firms creates a chain reaction of further spending, which causes a greater cumulative change in aggregate expenditures.

STUDY QUESTIONS AND PROBLEMS

1. Assume the level of autonomous investment is $100 billion and aggregate expenditures equal consumption and investment. Based on the table below, answer the following questions.

Employment, Output, Consumption, and Unplanned Inventory

Possible Levels of Employment (millions of workers)	Real GDP (output) Equals Disposable Income (billions of dollars)	Consumption (billions of dollars)	Unplanned Inventory (billions of dollars)
40	$325	$300	$____
45	375	325	____
50	425	350	____
55	475	375	____
60	525	400	____
65	575	425	____
70	625	450	____

  a. Fill in the unplanned inventory column.
  b. Determine the MPC and MPS.
  c. If this economy employs a labor force of 40 million, what will happen to this level of employment? Explain and identify the equilibrium level of output.

2. Using the data given in Question 1, what is the impact of adding net exports? Let imports equal $75 billion, and assume exports equal $50 billion. What is the equilibrium level of employment and output?

3. Explain the determination of equilibrium real GDP by drawing an abstract graph of the aggregate expenditures-output model. Label the aggregate expenditures line AE and the aggregate output line AO. Explain why the interaction of AE and AO determines the Keynesian equilibrium level of real GDP.

4. Use the aggregate expenditures-output model to demonstrate the multiplier effect.

5. How are changes in the MPC, changes in the MPS, and the size of the multiplier related? Answer the following questions:
  a. What is the multiplier if the MPC is 0? 0.33? 0.90?
  b. Suppose the equilibrium real GDP is $100 billion and the MPC is 4/5. How much will the equilibrium output change if businesses increase their level of investment by $10 billion?
  c. Using the data given in Questions (b), what will be the change in equilibrium real GDP if the MPC equals 2/3?

6. Assume the MPC is 0.90 and autonomous investment increases by $500 billion. What will be the impact on real GDP?

7. Suppose autonomous investment increases by $100 billion and the *MPC* is 0.75.

   a. Use the following table to compute four rounds of the spending multiplier effect:

Round	Components of Total Spending	New Consumption Spending (billions of dollars)
1	Investment	$ _____
2	Consumption	_____
3	Consumption	_____
4	Consumption	_____
	Total spending	_____

   b. Use the spending multiplier formula to compute the final cumulative impact on aggregate spending.

8. First, use the data given in Question 1, and assume the level of autonomous investment is $50 billion. If the full-employment level of output is $525 billion, what is the equilibrium level of output and employment? Does a recessionary gap or an inflationary gap exist? Second, assume the level of autonomous investment is $150 billion. What is the equilibrium level of output and employment? Does a recessionary gap or an inflationary gap exist? Explain the consequences of an inflationary gap using the aggregate expenditures-output model.

9. Assume an economy is in recession with a *MPC* of 0.75 and there is a GDP gap of $100 billion. How much must government spending increase to eliminate the gap? Instead of increasing government spending by the amount you calculate, what would be the effect of the government cutting taxes by this amount?

10. Suppose the government wishes to eliminate an inflationary gap of $100 billion and the *MPC* is 0.50. How much must the government cut its spending? Instead of decreasing government spending by the amount you calculate, what would be the effect of the government increasing taxes by this amount?

For Online Exercises, go the text Web site at www.cengage.com/economics/tucker.

CHECKPOINT ANSWERS

Full-Employment Output, Where Are You

A tax cut of $200 billion boosts consumer income by this amount. Since the *MPC* is 0.50, consumers will spend $100 billion of the tax cut and save the remaining $100 billion. To compute the impact of the rise in consumption (ΔC) on real GDP (ΔY), use this formula:

$$\Delta C \times \text{multiplier} = \Delta Y$$

Where

$$\text{Multiplier} = \frac{1}{MPS} = \frac{1}{1 - MPS} = \frac{1}{1 - 0.50} = 2$$

Thus, $100 billion × 2 = $200 billion. The increase in real GDP from the tax cut equals $200 billion, which is added to the initial equilibrium real GDP of $3 trillion to achieve full-employment output. If you said the full-employment real GDP is $3.2 trillion, **YOU ARE CORRECT.**

How Much Spending Must Uncle Sam Cut?

The inflationary GDP gap is $500 billion real GDP. To calculate the size of the government spending cut (ΔG) required to decrease real GDP (ΔY) by $500 billion, use this formula:

$$\Delta G \times \text{multiplier} = \Delta Y$$

Where

$$\text{Multiplier} = \frac{1}{MPS} = \frac{1}{1 - MPC} = \frac{1}{1 - 0.90} = 10$$

Thus,

$$\Delta G = \frac{-\Delta Y}{\text{multiplier}} = \frac{-\$500 \text{ billion}}{10} = -\$50 \text{ billion}$$

If you said the size of the cut in government spending is $50 billion, **YOU ARE CORRECT.**

PRACTICE QUIZ

For an explanation of the correct answers, please visit the tutorial at www.cengage.com/economics/tucker.

1. The net exports line can be
   a. positive.
   b. negative.
   c. zero.
   d. any of the above.

2. There will be unplanned inventory investment accumulation when
   a. aggregate output (real GDP) equals aggregate expenditures.
   b. aggregate output (real GDP) exceeds aggregate expenditures.
   c. aggregate expenditures exceed aggregate output (real GDP).
   d. firms increase output.

3. John Maynard Keynes proposed that the multiplier effect can correct an economic depression. Based on this theory, an increase in equilibrium output would be created by an initial
   a. increase in investment.
   b. increase in government spending.
   c. decrease in government spending.
   d. both (a) and (b).
   e. both (a) and (c).

4. The spending multiplier is defined as
   a. 1/(1 − marginal propensity to consume).
   b. 1/(marginal propensity to consume).
   c. 1/(1 − marginal propensity to save).
   d. 1/(marginal propensity to consume + marginal propensity to save).

5. If the value of the marginal propensity to consume (*MPC*) is 0.50, the value of the spending multiplier is
   a. 0.50.
   b. 1.
   c. 2.
   d. 5.

6. If the marginal propensity to consume (*MPC*) is 0.80, the value of the spending multiplier is
   a. 2.
   b. 5.
   c. 8.
   d. 10.

7. If the marginal propensity to consume (*MPC*) is 0.75, a $50 billion decrease in government spending would cause equilibrium output to
   a. increase by $50 billion.
   b. decrease by $50 billion.
   c. increase by $200 billion.
   d. decrease by $200 billion.

8. If the marginal propensity to consume (*MPC*) is 0.90, a $100 billion increase in planned investment expenditure, other things being equal, will cause an increase in equilibrium output of
   a. $90 billion.
   b. $100 billion.
   c. $900 billion.
   d. $1,000 billion.

9. Keynes's criticism of the classical theory was that the Great Depression would not correct itself. The multiplier effect would restore an economy to full employment if
   a. government would follow a "least government is the best government" policy.
   b. government taxes were increased.
   c. government spending were increased.
   d. government spending were decreased.

10. The equilibrium level of real GDP is $1,000 billion, the full-employment level of real GDP is $1,250 billion, and the marginal propensity to consume (*MPC*) is 0.60. The full-employment target can be reached if government spending is
    a. increased by $60 billion.
    b. increased by $100 billion.
    c. increased by $250 billion.
    d. held constant.

11. In Exhibit 9, the spending multiplier for this economy is equal to
    a. 1⁷/₃.
    b. 2¹/₂.
    c. 3.
    d. 5.

EXHIBIT 9

The Keynesian Aggregate Expenditures-Output Model When the *MPC* is 3/5

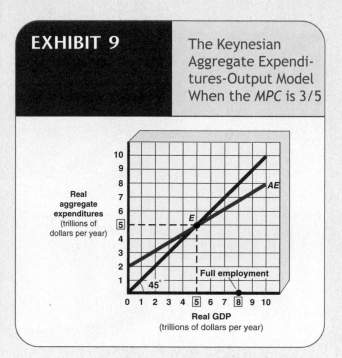

Real aggregate expenditures
(trillions of dollars per year)

Real GDP
(trillions of dollars per year)

12. To close the recessionary gap and achieve full-employment real GDP as shown in Exhibit 9, the government should increase spending by
   a. $1 trillion.
   b. $1.2 trillion.

   c. $2.0 trillion.
   d. $2.5 trillion.

13. To close the recessionary gap and achieve full-employment real GDP shown in Exhibit 9, the government should cut taxes by
   a. $0.60 trillion.
   b. $1 trillion.
   c. $2 trillion.
   d. $3 trillion.

14. Using the aggregate expenditure-output model, assume the aggregate expenditures (*AE*) line is above the 45-degree line at full-employment GDP. This vertical distance is called a (an)
   a. inflationary gap.
   b. recessionary gap.
   c. negative GDP gap.
   d. marginal propensity to consume gap.

15. Use the aggregate expenditures-output model and assume an economy is in equilibrium at $5 trillion, which is $250 billion below full-employment GDP. If the marginal propensity to consume (*MPC*) is 0.60, full-employment GDP can be reached if government spending
   a. decreases by $60 billion.
   b. decreases by $100 billion.
   c. decreases by $250 billion.
   d. is held constant.

Aggregate Demand and Supply

C lassical economic theory held that the economy would bounce back to full employment as long as prices and wages were flexible. As the unemployment rate soared and remained high during the Great Depression, British economist John Maynard Keynes formulated a new theory with new policy implications. Instead of taking a wait-and-see policy until markets self-correct the economy, Keynes argued that policymakers must take action to influence aggregate spending through changes in government spending. The prescription for the Great Depression was simple: Increase government spending and jobs will be created. Although Keynes was not concerned with the problem of inflation, his theory has implications for fighting demand-pull inflation. In this case, the government must cut spending or increase taxes to reduce aggregate demand.

In this chapter, you will use aggregate demand and supply analysis to study the business cycle. The chapter opens with a presentation of the aggregate demand curve and then the aggregate supply curve. Once these concepts are developed, the analysis shows why modern macroeconomics teaches that shifts in aggregate supply or aggregate demand can influence the price level, the equilibrium level of real GDP, and employment. You will probably return to this chapter often because it provides the basic tools with which to organize your thinking about the macro economy.

In this chapter, you will learn to solve these economic puzzles:

- Why does the aggregate supply curve have three different segments?

- Would the greenhouse effect cause inflation, unemployment, or both?

- Was John Maynard Keynes's prescription for the Great Depression right?

The Aggregate Demand Curve

Here we view the collective demand for *all* goods and services, rather than the *market* demand for a particular good or service. Exhibit 1 shows the aggregate demand curve (*AD*), which slopes downward and to the right for a given year. The aggregate demand curve shows the level of real GDP purchased by households, businesses, government, and foreigners (net exports) at different possible price levels during a time period, ceteris paribus. Stated differently, the aggregate demand curve shows us the total dollar amount of goods and services that will be demanded in the economy at various price levels. As for the demand curve for an individual market, the lower the economywide price level, the greater the aggregate quantity demanded for real goods and services, ceteris paribus.

The downward slope of the aggregate demand curve shows that at a given level of aggregate income, people buy more goods and services at a lower average price level. While the horizontal axis in the market supply and demand model measures *physical* units, such as bushels of wheat, the horizontal axis in the aggregate

> **Aggregate demand curve (*AD*)**
>
> The curve that shows the level of real GDP purchased by households, businesses, government, and foreigners (net exports) at different possible price levels during a time period, ceteris paribus.

EXHIBIT 1	The Aggregate Demand Curve

The aggregate demand curve (*AD*) shows the relationship between the price level and the level of real GDP, other things being equal. The lower the price level, the larger the GDP demanded by households, businesses, government, and foreigners. If the price level is 150 at point *A*, a real GDP of $4 trillion is demanded. If the price level is 100 at point *B*, the real GDP demanded increases to $6 trillion.

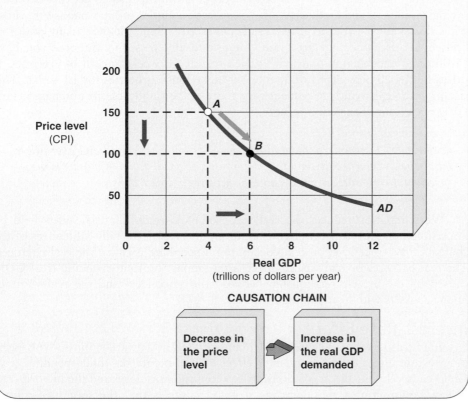

CAUSATION CHAIN

Decrease in the price level → Increase in the real GDP demanded

demand and supply model measures the value of *final* goods and services included in real GDP. Note that the horizontal axis represents the quantity of aggregate production demanded, measured in base-year dollars. The vertical axis is an *index* of the overall price level, such as the chain price index or the CPI, rather than the price per bushel of wheat. As shown in Exhibit 1, if the price level measured by the CPI is 150 at point *A,* a real GDP of $4 trillion is demanded in, say, a given year. If the price level is 100 at point *B,* a real GDP of $6 trillion is demanded.

Although the aggregate demand curve looks like a market demand curve, these concepts are different. As we move along a market demand curve, the price of related goods is assumed to be constant. But when we deal with changes in the general or average price level in an economy, this assumption is meaningless because we are using a market basket measure for *all* goods and services.

> **Conclusion** *The aggregate demand curve and the demand curve are not the same concept.*

Reasons for the Aggregate Demand Curve's Shape

The reasons for the downward slope of an aggregate demand curve include the *real balances effect,* the *interest-rate effect,* and the *net exports effect.*

Real Balances Effect

Recall from the discussion in the chapter on inflation that cash, checking deposits, savings accounts, and certificates of deposit are examples of financial assets whose real value changes with the price level. If prices are falling, the purchasing power of households rises and they are more willing and able to spend. Suppose you have $1,000 in a checking account with which to buy 10 weeks' worth of groceries. If prices fall by 20 percent, $1,000 will now buy enough groceries for 12 weeks. This rise in your real wealth may make you more willing and able to purchase a new DVD player out of current income.

> **Conclusion** *Consumers spend more on goods and services when lower prices make their dollars more valuable. Therefore, the real value of money is measured by the quantity of goods and services each dollar buys.*

Real balances
The impact on total spending (real GDP) caused by the inverse relationship between the price level and the real value of financial assets with fixed nominal value.

When inflation reduces the real value of fixed-value financial assets held by households, the result is lower consumption, and real GDP falls. The effect of the change in the price level on real consumption spending is called the real balances. The real balances or real wealth effect is the impact on total spending (real GDP) caused by the inverse relationship between the price level and the real value of financial assets with fixed nominal value.

Interest-rate effect
The impact on total spending (real GDP) caused by the direct relationship between the price level and the interest rate.

Interest-Rate Effect

A second reason why the aggregate demand curve is downward sloping involves the interest-rate effect. The interest-rate effect is the impact on total spending (real GDP) caused by the direct relationship between the price level and the interest rate. A key assumption of the aggregate demand curve is that the supply of money

EXHIBIT 2	Why the Aggregate Demand Curve Is Downward Sloping
Effect	**Causation Chain**
Real balances effect	Price level decreases → Purchasing power rises → Wealth rises → Consumers buy more goods → Real GDP demanded increases
Interest-rate effect	Price level decreases → Purchasing power rises → Demand for fixed supply of credit falls → Interest rates fall → Businesses and households borrow and buy more goods → Real GDP demanded increases
Net exports effect	Price level decreases → U.S. goods become less expensive than foreign goods → Americans and foreigners buy more U.S. goods → Exports rise and imports fall → Real GDP demanded increases

available for borrowing remains fixed. A high price level means people must take more dollars from their wallets and checking accounts in order to purchase goods and services. At a higher price level, the demand for borrowed money to buy products also increases and results in a higher cost of borrowing—that is, higher interest rates. Rising interest rates discourage households from borrowing to purchase homes, cars, and other consumer products. Similarly, at higher interest rates, businesses cut investment projects because the higher cost of borrowing diminishes the profitability of these investments. Thus, assuming fixed credit, an increase in the price level translates through higher interest rates into a lower real GDP.

Net Exports Effect

Whether American–made goods have lower prices than foreign goods is another important factor in determining the aggregate demand curve. A higher domestic price level tends to make U.S. goods more expensive than foreign goods, and imports rise because consumers substitute imported goods for domestic goods. An increase in the price of U.S. goods in foreign markets also causes U.S. exports to decline. Consequently, a rise in the domestic price level of an economy tends to increase imports, decrease exports, and thereby reduce the net exports component of real GDP. This condition is the net exports effect. The net exports effect is the impact on total spending (real GDP) caused by the inverse relationship between the price level and the net exports of an economy.

Exhibit 2 summarizes the three effects that explain why the aggregate demand curve in Exhibit 1 is downward sloping.

Nonprice-Level Determinants of Aggregate Demand

As was the case with individual demand curves, we must distinguish between *changes in real GDP demanded*, caused by changes in the price level, and *changes*

GLOBAL ECONOMICS

Net exports effect
The impact on total spending (real GDP) caused by the inverse relationship between the price level and the net exports of an economy.

in aggregate demand, caused by changes in one or more of the *nonprice-level determinants.* Once the ceteris paribus assumption is relaxed, changes in variables other than the price level cause a change in the location of the aggregate demand curve. Nonprice-level determinants include the consumption (C), investment (I), government purchases (G), and net exports ($X-M$) components of aggregate expenditures explained in the chapter on GDP.

> **Conclusion** *Any change in the individual components of aggregate expenditures shifts the aggregate demand curve.*

Exhibit 3 illustrates the link between an increase in expenditures and an increase in aggregate demand. Begin at point *A* on aggregate demand curve AD_1, with a price level of 100 and a real GDP of $6 trillion. Assume the price level remains constant at 100 and the aggregate demand curve increases from AD_1

EXHIBIT 3	A Shift in the Aggregate Demand Curve

At the price level of 100, the real GDP level is $6 trillion at point *A* on AD_1. An increase in one of the nonprice-level determinants of consumption (C), investment (I), government spending (G), or net exports ($X-M$) causes the level of real GDP to rise to $8 trillion at point *B* on AD_2. Because this effect occurs at any price level, an increase in aggregate expenditures shifts the *AD* curve rightward. Conversely, a decrease in aggregate expenditures shifts the *AD* curve leftward.

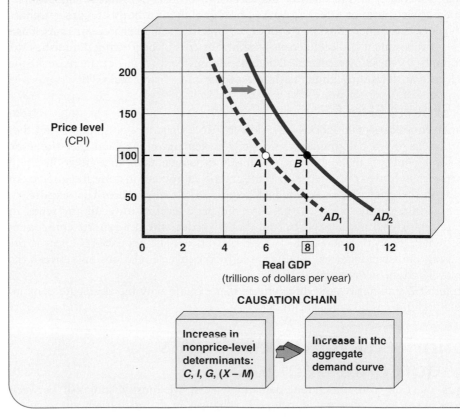

to AD_2. Consequently, the level of real GDP rises from $6 trillion (point A) to $8 trillion (point B) at the price level of 100. The cause might be that consumers have become more optimistic about the future and their consumption expenditures (C) have risen. Or possibly an increase in business optimism has increased profit expectations, and the level of investment (I) has risen because businesses are spending more for plants and equipment. The same increase in aggregate demand could also have been caused by a boost in government spending (G) or a rise in net exports ($X-M$). A swing to pessimistic expectations by consumers or firms will cause the aggregate demand curve to shift leftward. A leftward shift in the aggregate demand curve may also be caused by a decrease in government spending or net exports.

The Aggregate Supply Curve

Just as we must distinguish between the *aggregate* demand and *market* demand curves, the theory for a *market* supply curve does not apply directly to the *aggregate* supply curve. Keeping this condition in mind, we can define the aggregate supply curve (AS) as the curve that shows the level of real GDP produced at different possible price levels during a time period, ceteris paribus. Stated simply, the aggregate supply curve shows us the total dollar amount of goods and services produced in an economy at various price levels. Given this general definition, we must pause to discuss two opposing views—the Keynesian horizontal aggregate supply curve and the classical vertical aggregate supply curve.

> **Aggregate supply curve (AS)**
> The curve that shows the level of real GDP produced at different possible price levels during a time period, ceteris paribus.

Keynesian View of Aggregate Supply

In 1936, John Maynard Keynes published *The General Theory of Employment, Interest, and Money*. In this book, Keynes argued that price and wage inflexibility means that unemployment can be a prolonged affair. Unless an economy trapped in a depression or severe recession is rescued by an increase in aggregate demand, full employment will not be achieved. This Keynesian prediction calls for government to intervene and actively manage aggregate demand to avoid a depression or recession.

Why did Keynes assume that product prices and wages were fixed? During a deep recession or depression, there are many idle resources in the economy. Consequently, producers are willing to sell additional output at current prices because there are no shortages to put upward pressure on prices. Moreover, the supply of unemployed workers willing to work for the prevailing wage rate diminishes the power of workers to increase their wages, and union contracts prevent businesses from lowering wage rates. In fact, the CPI for the last month of each recession since 1948 was at or above the CPI for the first month of the recession. Given the Keynesian assumption of fixed or rigid product prices and wages, changes in the aggregate demand curve cause changes in real GDP along a horizontal aggregate supply curve. In short, Keynesian theory argues that only shifts in aggregate demand can revitalize a depressed economy.

Exhibit 4 portrays the core of Keynesian theory. We begin at equilibrium E_1, with a fixed price level of 100. Given aggregate demand schedule AD_1, the equilibrium level of real GDP is $6 trillion. Now government spending (G) increases, causing aggregate demand to rise from AD_1 to AD_2 and equilibrium to shift from E_1 to E_2 along the horizontal aggregate supply curve, (AS). At E_2, the economy moves to $8 trillion, which is closer to the full-employment GDP of $10 trillion.

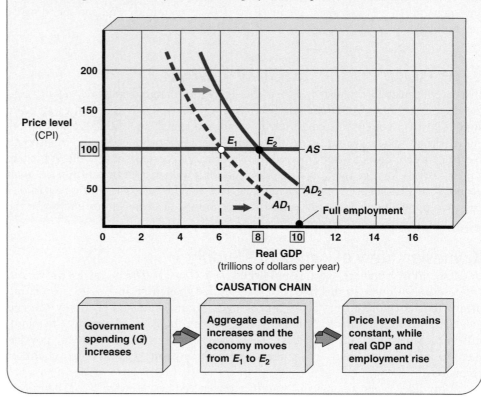

EXHIBIT 4 The Keynesian Horizontal Aggregate Supply Curve

The increase in aggregate demand from AD_1 to AD_2 causes a new equilibrium at E_2. Given the Keynesian assumption of a fixed price level, changes in aggregate demand cause changes in real GDP along the horizontal portion of the aggregate supply curve, *AS*. Keynesian theory argues that only shifts in aggregate demand possess the ability to restore a depressed economy to the full-employment output of $10 trillion.

CAUSATION CHAIN

| Government spending (*G*) increases | Aggregate demand increases and the economy moves from E_1 to E_2 | Price level remains constant, while real GDP and employment rise |

Conclusion *When the aggregate supply curve is horizontal and an economy is below full employment, the only effects of an increase in aggregate demand are increases in real GDP and employment, while the price level does not change. Stated simply, the Keynesian view is that "demand creates its own supply."*

Classical View of Aggregate Supply

Prior to the Great Depression, a group of economists known as the *classical economists* dominated economic thinking. The founder of the classical school of economics was Adam Smith. Exhibit 5 uses the aggregate demand and supply model to illustrate the classical view that the aggregate supply curve, *AS*, is a vertical line at the full employment output of $10 trillion. The vertical shape of the classical aggregate supply curve is based on two assumptions. First, the economy normally operates at its

EXHIBIT 5 | The Classical Vertical Aggregate Supply Curve

Classical theory teaches that prices and wages quickly adjust to keep the economy operating at its full-employment output of $10 trillion. A decline in aggregate demand from AD_1 to AD_2 will temporarily cause a surplus of $2 trillion, the distance from E' to E_1. Businesses respond by cutting the price level from 150 to 100. As a result, consumers increase their purchases because of the real balances or wealth effect, and wages adjust downward. Thus, classical economists predict the economy is self-correcting and will restore full employment at point E_2. E_1 and E_2 therefore represent points along a classical vertical aggregate supply curve, AS.

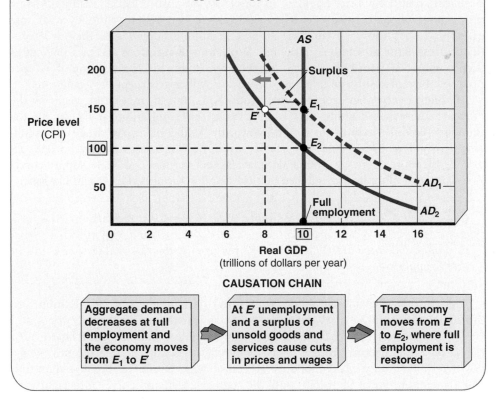

CAUSATION CHAIN

| Aggregate demand decreases at full employment and the economy moves from E_1 to E' | ⇨ | At E' unemployment and a surplus of unsold goods and services cause cuts in prices and wages | ⇨ | The economy moves from E' to E_2, where full employment is restored |

full-employment output level. Second, the price level of products and production costs change by the same percentage, that is, proportionally, in order to maintain a full-employment level of output. This classical theory of flexible prices and wages is at odds with the Keynesian concept of sticky (inflexible) prices and wages.

Exhibit 5 illustrates why classical economists believe a market economy automatically self-corrects to full employment. Following the classical scenario, the economy is initially in equilibrium at E_1, the price level is 150, real output is at its full-employment level of $10 trillion, and the aggregate demand curve AD_1 traces total spending. Now suppose private spending falls because households and businesses are pessimistic about economic conditions. This condition causes AD_1 to shift leftward to AD_2. At a price level of 150, the immediate effect is that aggregate output exceeds aggregate spending by $2 trillion ($E_1$ to E'), and unexpected inventory accumulation occurs. To eliminate unsold inventories resulting from the decrease in aggregate demand, business firms temporarily cut back on production and reduce the price level from 150 to 100.

At E', the decline in aggregate output in response to the surplus also affects prices in the factor markets. As a result of the economy moving from point E_1 to E', there is a decrease in the demand for labor, natural resources, and other inputs used to produce products. This surplus condition in the factor markets means that some workers who are willing to work are laid off and compete with those who still have jobs by reducing their wage demands. Owners of natural resources and capital likewise cut their prices.

How can the classical economists believe that prices and wages are completely flexible? The answer is contained in the *real balances effect*, explained earlier. When businesses reduce the price level from 150 to 100, the cost of living falls by the same proportion. Once the price level falls by 33 percent, a nominal or money wage rate of, say, $21 per hour will purchase 33 percent more groceries after the fall in product prices than it would before the fall. Workers will therefore accept a pay cut of 33 percent, or $7 per hour. Any worker who refuses the lower wage rate of $14 per hour will be replaced by an unemployed worker willing to accept the going rate.

Exhibit 5 shows an economywide proportional fall in prices and wages by the movement downward along AD_2 from E' to a new equilibrium at E_2. At E_2, the economy has self-corrected through downwardly flexible prices and wages to its full-employment level of $10 trillion worth of real GDP at the lower price level of 100. E_1 and E_2 therefore represent points along a classical vertical aggregate supply curve, AS. (The classical model is explained in more detail in the appendix to this chapter.)

> **Conclusion** *When the aggregate supply curve is vertical at the full-employment GDP, the only effect over time of a change in aggregate demand is a change in the price level. Stated simply, the classical view is that "supply creates its own demand."*[1]

Although Keynes himself did not use the *AD-AS* model, we can use Exhibit 5 to distinguish between Keynes's view and the classical theory of flexible prices and wages. Keynes believed that once the demand curve has shifted from AD_1 to AD_2, the surplus (the distance from E' to E_1) will persist because he rejected price-wage downward flexibility. The economy therefore will remain at the less-than-full-employment output of $8 trillion until the aggregate demand curve shifts rightward and returns to its initial position at AD_1.

Three Ranges of the Aggregate Supply Curve

Having studied the polar theories of the classical economists and Keynes, we will now discuss an eclectic or general view of how the shape of the aggregate supply curve varies as real GDP expands or contracts. The aggregate supply curve, *AS*, in Exhibit 6 has three quite distinct ranges or segments, labeled (1) *Keynesian range*, (2) *intermediate range*, and (3) *classical range*.

The Keynesian range is the horizontal segment of the aggregate supply curve, which represents an economy in a severe recession. In Exhibit 6, below real GDP Y_K, the price level remains constant as the level of real GDP rises. Between Y_K and

---

Keynesian range

The horizontal segment of the aggregate supply curve, which represents an economy in a severe recession.

---

1. This quotation is known as Say's Law, named after the French classical economist Jean Baptiste Say (1767–1832).

EXHIBIT 6   The Three Ranges of the Aggregate Supply Curve

The aggregate supply curve shows the relationship between the price level and the level of real GDP supplied. It consists of three distinct ranges: (1) a Keynesian range between 0 and Y_K wherein the price level is constant for an economy in severe recession; (2) an intermediate range between Y_K and Y_F, where both the price level and the level of real GDP vary as an economy approaches full employment; and (3) a classical range, where the price level can vary, while the level of real GDP remains constant at the full-employment level of output, Y_F.

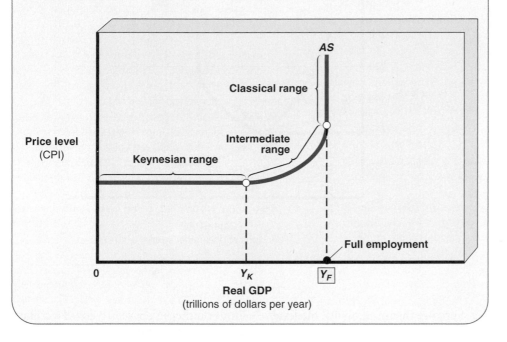

the full-employment output of Y_F, the price level rises as the real GDP level rises. The intermediate range is the rising segment of the aggregate supply curve, which represents an economy approaching full-employment output. Finally, at Y_F, the level of real GDP remains constant, and only the price level rises. The classical range is the vertical segment of the aggregate supply curve, which represents an economy at full-employment output. We will now examine the rationale for each of these three quite distinct ranges.

Aggregate Demand and Aggregate Supply Macroeconomic Equilibrium

In Exhibit 7, the *macroeconomic equilibrium* level of real GDP corresponding to the point of equality, *E,* is $6 trillion, and the equilibrium price level is 100. This is the unique combination of price level and output level that equates how much people want to buy with the amount businesses want to produce and sell. Because the entire real GDP value of final products is bought and sold at the price level of 100, there is no upward or downward pressure for the macroeconomic equilibrium to change. Note that the economy shown in Exhibit 7 is operating on the edge of the Keynesian range, with a GDP gap of $4 trillion.

Intermediate range
The rising segment of the aggregate supply curve, which represents an economy as it approaches full-employment output.

Classical range
The vertical segment of the aggregate supply curve, which represents an economy at full-employment output.

EXHIBIT 7

The Aggregate Demand and Aggregate Supply Model

Macroeconomic equilibrium occurs where the aggregate demand curve, *AD*, and the aggregate supply curve, *AS*, intersect. In this case, equilibrium, *E*, is located at the far end of the Keynesian range, where the price level is 100 and the equilibrium output is $6 trillion. In macroeconomic equilibrium, businesses neither overestimate nor underestimate the real GDP demanded at the prevailing price level.

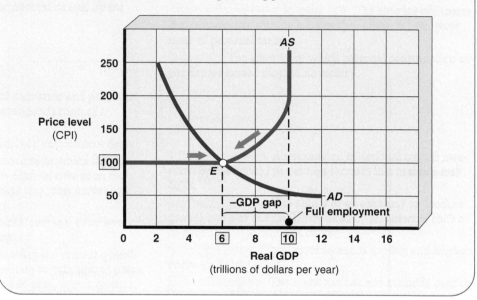

Suppose that in Exhibit 7 the level of output on the *AS* curve is below $6 trillion and the *AD* curve remains fixed. At a price level of 100, the real GDP demanded exceeds the real GDP supplied. Under such circumstances, businesses cannot fill orders quickly enough, and inventories are drawn down unexpectedly. Business managers react by hiring more workers and producing more output. Because the economy is operating in the Keynesian range, the price level remains constant at 100. The opposite scenario occurs if the level of real GDP supplied on the *AS* curve exceeds the real GDP in the intermediate range between $6 trillion and $10 trillion. In this output segment, the price level is between 100 and 200, and businesses face sales that are less than expected. In this case, unintended inventories of unsold goods pile up on the shelves, and management will lay off workers, cut back on production, and reduce prices.

This adjustment process continues until the equilibrium price level and output level are reached at point *E* and there is no upward or downward pressure for the price level to change. Here the production decisions of sellers in the economy equal the total spending decisions of buyers during the given period of time.

Conclusion *At macroeconomic equilibrium, sellers neither overestimate nor underestimate the real GDP demanded at the prevailing price level.*

Changes in the *AD-AS* Macroeconomic Equilibrium

One explanation of the business cycle is that the aggregate demand curve moves along a stationary aggregate supply curve. The next step in our analysis therefore is to *shift* the aggregate demand curve along the three ranges of the aggregate supply curve and observe the impact on real GDP and the price level. As the macroeconomic equilibrium changes, the economy experiences more or fewer problems with inflation and unemployment.

Keynesian Range

Keynes's macroeconomic theory offered a powerful solution to the Great Depression. Keynes perceived the economy as driven by aggregate demand, and Exhibit 8(a) demonstrates this theory with hypothetical data. The range of real GDP below $6 trillion is consistent with Keynesian price and wage inflexibility. Assume the economy is in equilibrium at E_1, with a price level of 100 and a real GDP of $4 trillion. In this case, the economy is in recession far below the full-employment GDP of $10 trillion. The Keynesian prescription for a recession is to increase aggregate demand until the economy achieves full employment. Because the aggregate supply curve is horizontal in the Keynesian range, "demand creates its own supply." Suppose demand shifts rightward from AD_1 to AD_2 and a new equilibrium is established at E_2. Even at the higher real GDP level of $6 trillion, the price level remains at 100. Stated differently, aggregate output can expand throughout this range without raising prices. This is because, in the Keynesian range, substantial idle production capacity (including property and unemployed workers competing for available jobs) can be put to work at existing prices.

> **Conclusion** *As aggregate demand increases in the Keynesian range, the price level remains constant as real GDP expands.*

Intermediate Range

The intermediate range in Exhibit 8(b) is between $6 trillion and $10 trillion worth of real GDP. As output increases in the range of the aggregate supply curve near the full-employment level of output, the considerable slack in the economy disappears. Assume an economy is initially in equilibrium at E_3 and aggregate demand increases from AD_3 to AD_4. As a result, the level of real GDP rises from $6 trillion to $8 trillion, and the price level rises from 100 to 125. In this output range, several factors contribute to inflation. First, *bottlenecks* (obstacles to output flow) develop when some firms have no unused capacity and other firms operate below full capacity. Suppose the steel industry is operating at full capacity and cannot fill all its orders for steel. An inadequate supply of one resource, such as steel, can hold up auto production even though the auto industry is operating well below capacity. Consequently, the bottleneck causes firms to raise the price of steel and, in turn, autos. Second, a shortage of certain labor skills while firms are earning higher profits causes businesses to expect that labor will exert its power to obtain sizable wage increases, so businesses raise prices. Wage demands are more difficult to reject when the economy is prospering because businesses fear workers will change jobs or strike. Besides, businesses believe higher prices can be passed on to consumers quite

EXHIBIT 8   Effects of Increases in Aggregate Demand

The effect of a rightward shift in the aggregate demand curve on the price and output levels depends on the range of the aggregate supply curve in which the shift occurs. In Part (a), an increase in aggregate demand causing the equilibrium to change from E_1 to E_2 in the Keynesian range will increase real GDP from $4 trillion to $6 trillion, but the price level will remain unchanged at 100.

In Part (b), an increase in aggregate demand causing the equilibrium to change from E_3 to E_4 in the intermediate range will increase real GDP from $6 trillion to $8 trillion, and the price level will rise from 100 to 125.

In Part (c), an increase in aggregate demand causing the equilibrium to change from E_5 to E_6 in the classical range will increase the price level from 150 to 200, but real GDP will not increase beyond the full-employment level of $10 trillion.

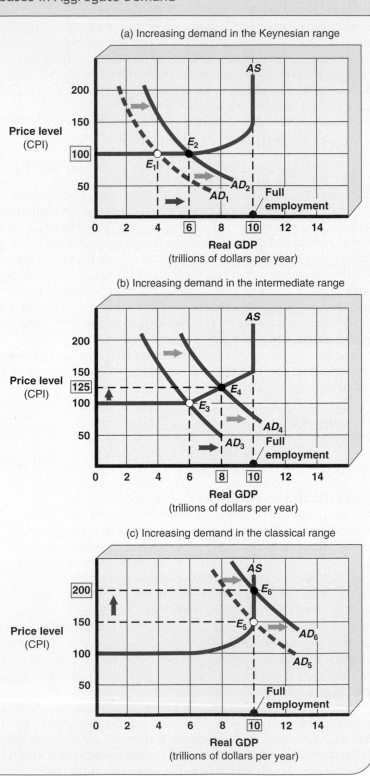

easily because consumers expect higher prices as output expands to near full capacity. Third, as the economy approaches full employment, firms must use less productive workers and less efficient machinery. This inefficiency creates higher production costs, which are passed on to consumers in the form of higher prices.

> **Conclusion** *In the intermediate range, increases in aggregate demand increase both the price level and the real GDP.*

Classical Range

While inflation resulting from an outward shift in aggregate demand was no problem in the Keynesian range and only a minor problem in the intermediate range, it becomes a serious problem in the classical or vertical range.

> **Conclusion** *Once the economy reaches full-employment output in the classical range, additional increases in aggregate demand merely cause inflation, rather than more real GDP.*

Assume the economy shown in Exhibit 8(c) is in equilibrium at E_5, which intersects AS at the full-capacity output. Now suppose aggregate demand shifts rightward from AD_5 to AD_6. Because the aggregate supply curve AS is vertical at $10 trillion, this increase in the aggregate demand curve boosts the price level from 150 to 200, but it fails to expand real GDP. The explanation is that once the economy operates at capacity, businesses raise their prices in order to ration fully employed resources to those willing to pay the highest prices.

In summary, the *AD-AS* model presented in this chapter is a combination of the conflicting assumptions of the Keynesian and the classical theories separated by an intermediate range, which fits neither extreme precisely. Be forewarned that in later chapters you will encounter a continuing great controversy over the shape of the aggregate supply curve. Modern-day classical economists believe the entire aggregate supply curve is steep or vertical. In contrast, Keynesian economists contend that the aggregate supply curve is much flatter or horizontal.

Nonprice-Level Determinants of Aggregate Supply

Our discussion so far has explained changes in real GDP supplied resulting from changes in the aggregate demand curve, given a stationary aggregate supply curve. Now we consider the situation when the aggregate demand curve is stationary and the aggregate supply curve shifts as a result of changes in one or more of the *nonprice-level determinants*. The nonprice-level factors affecting aggregate supply include resource prices (domestic and imported), technological change, taxes, subsidies, and regulations. Note that each of these factors affects production costs. At a given price level, the profit businesses make at any level of real GDP depends on production costs. If costs change, firms respond by changing their output. Lower production costs shift the aggregate supply curve rightward, indicating greater real GDP is supplied at any price level. Conversely, higher production costs shift the aggregate supply curve leftward, meaning less real GDP is supplied at any price level.

Exhibit 9 represents a supply-side explanation of the business cycle, in contrast to the demand-side case presented in Exhibit 8. (Note that for simplicity the aggregate supply curve can be drawn using only the intermediate segment.) The economy begins in equilibrium at point E_1, with real GDP at $7 trillion and the price level at 175. Then suppose labor unions become less powerful and their weaker bargaining position causes the wage rate to fall. With lower labor costs per unit of output, businesses seek to increase profits by expanding production at any price level. Hence, the aggregate supply curve shifts rightward from AS_1 to AS_2, and equilibrium changes from E_1 to E_2. As a result, real GDP increases $1 trillion, and the price level decreases from 175 to 150. Changes in other nonprice-level factors also cause an increase in aggregate supply. Lower oil prices, greater entrepreneurship, lower taxes, and reduced government regulation are other examples of conditions that lower production costs and therefore cause a rightward shift of the aggregate supply curve.

EXHIBIT 9 — A Rightward Shift in the Aggregate Supply Curve

Holding the aggregate demand curve constant, the impact on the price level and real GDP depends on whether the aggregate supply curve shifts to the right or the left. A rightward shift of the aggregate supply curve from AS_1 to AS_2 will increase real GDP from $7 trillion to $8 trillion and reduce the price level from 175 to 150.

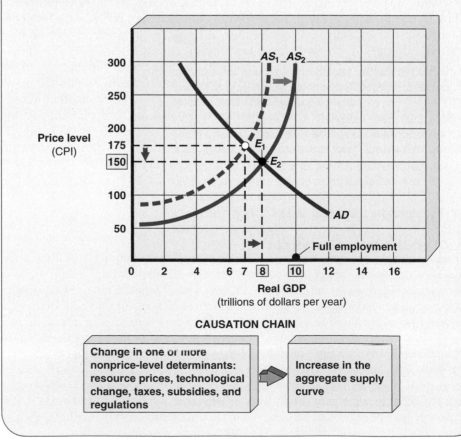

CAUSATION CHAIN

Change in one or more nonprice-level determinants: resource prices, technological change, taxes, subsidies, and regulations ⟹ Increase in the aggregate supply curve

EXHIBIT 10	Summary of the Nonprice-Level Determinants of Aggregate Demand and Aggregate Supply

Nonprice-Level Determinants of Aggregate Demand (Total Spending)	Nonprice-Level Determinants of Aggregate Supply
1. Consumption (*C*)	1. Resource prices (domestic and imported)
2. Investment (*I*)	2. Taxes
3. Government spending (*G*)	3. Technological change
4. Net exports (*X*−*M*)	4. Subsidies
	5. Regulation

What kinds of events might raise production costs and shift the aggregate supply curve leftward? Perhaps there is war in the Persian Gulf or the Organization of Petroleum Exporting Countries (OPEC) disrupts supplies of oil, and higher energy prices spread throughout the economy. Under such a "supply shock," businesses decrease their output at any price level in response to higher production costs per unit. Similarly, larger-than-expected wage increases, higher taxes to protect the environment (see Exhibit 8(a) in Chapter 4), or greater government regulation would increase production costs and therefore shift the aggregate supply curve leftward. A leftward shift in the aggregate supply curve is discussed further in the next section.

Exhibit 10 summarizes the nonprice-level determinants of aggregate demand and supply for further study and review. In the chapter on monetary policy, you will learn how changes in the supply of money in the economy can also shift the aggregate demand curve and influence macroeconomic performance.

Cost-Push and Demand-Pull Inflation Revisited

We now apply the aggregate demand and aggregate supply model to the two types of inflation introduced in the chapter on inflation. This section begins with a historical example of *cost-push inflation* caused by a decrease in the aggregate supply curve. Next, another historical example illustrates *demand-pull inflation*, caused by an increase in the aggregate demand curve.

During the late 1970s and early 1980s, the U.S. economy experienced stagflation. Stagflation is the condition that occurs when an economy experiences the twin maladies of high unemployment and rapid inflation simultaneously. How could this happen? The dramatic increase in the price of imported oil in 1973–1974 was a villain explained by a *cost-push inflation* scenario. Cost-push inflation, defined in terms of our macro model, is a rise in the price level resulting from a decrease in the aggregate supply curve while the aggregate demand curve remains fixed. As a result of cost-push inflation, real output and employment decrease.

Exhibit 11(a) uses actual data to show how a leftward shift in the supply curve can cause stagflation. In this exhibit, aggregate demand curve *AD* and aggregate supply curve AS_{73} represent the U.S. economy in 1973. Equilibrium was at point E_1,

Stagflation

The condition that occurs when an economy experiences the twin maladies of high unemployment and rapid inflation simultaneously.

EXHIBIT 11   Cost-Push and Demand-Pull Inflation

Parts (a) and (b) illustrate the distinction between cost-push inflation and demand-pull inflation. Cost-push inflationis inflation that results from a decrease in the aggregate supply curve. In Part (a), higher oil prices in 1973 caused the aggregate supply curve to shift leftward from AS_{73} to AS_{74}. As a result, real GDP fell from $4,341 billion to $4,319 billion, and the price level (CPI) rose from 44.4 to 49.3. This combination of higher price level and lower real output is called stagflation.

As shown in Part (b), demand-pull inflation is inflation that results from an increase in aggregate demand beyond the Keynesian range of output. Government spending increased to fight the Vietnam War without a tax increase, causing the aggregate demand curve to shift rightward from AD_{65} to AD_{66}. Consequently, real GDP rose from $3,191 billion to $3,399 billion, and the price level (CPI) rose from 31.5 to 32.4.

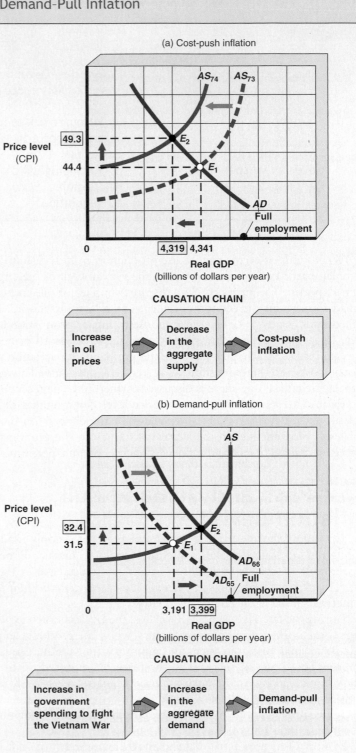

(a) Cost-push inflation

CAUSATION CHAIN

Increase in oil prices → Decrease in the aggregate supply → Cost-push inflation

(b) Demand-pull inflation

CAUSATION CHAIN

Increase in government spending to fight the Vietnam War → Increase in the aggregate demand → Demand-pull inflation

with the price level (CPI) at 44.4 and real GDP at $4,341 billion. Then, in 1974, the impact of a major supply shock shifted the aggregate supply curve leftward from AS_{73} to AS_{74}. The explanation for this shock was the oil embargo instituted by OPEC in retaliation for U.S. support of Israel in its war with the Arabs. Assuming a stable aggregate demand curve between 1973 and 1974, the punch from the energy shock resulted in a new equilibrium at point E_2, with the 1974 CPI at 49.3. The inflation rate for 1973 was 6.2 percent and for 1974 was 11 percent $[(49.3 - 44.4)/44.4] \times$ 100. Real GDP fell from $4,341 billion in 1973 to $4,319 billion in 1974, and the unemployment rate (not shown directly in the exhibit) climbed from 4.9 percent to 5.6 percent between these two years.[2]

In contrast, an outward shift in the aggregate demand curve can result in *demand-pull inflation*. Demand-pull inflation, in terms of our macro model, is a rise in the price level resulting from an increase in the aggregate demand curve while the aggregate supply curve remains fixed. Again, we can use aggregate demand and supply analysis and actual data to explain demand-pull inflation. In 1965, when the unemployment rate of 4.5 percent was close to the 4 percent natural rate of unemployment, real government spending increased sharply to fight the Vietnam War without a tax increase (an income tax surcharge was enacted in 1968). The inflation rate jumped sharply from 1.6 percent in 1965 to 2.9 percent in 1966.

Exhibit 11(b) illustrates what happened to the economy between 1965 and 1966. Suppose the economy was operating in 1965 at E_1, which is in the intermediate output range. The impact of the increase in military spending shifted the aggregate demand curve from AD_{65} to AD_{66}, and the economy moved upward along the aggregate supply curve until it reached E_2. Holding the aggregate supply curve constant, the *AD-AS* model predicts that increasing aggregate demand at near full employment causes demand-pull inflation. As shown in Exhibit 11(b), real GDP increased from $3,191 billion in 1963 to $3,399 billion in 1966, and the CPI rose from 31.5 to 32.4. Thus, the inflation rate for 1966 was 2.9 percent $[(32.4 - 31.5)/ 31.5] \times 100$. Corresponding to the rise in real output, the unemployment rate of 4.5 percent in 1965 fell to 3.8 percent in 1966.[3]

In summary, the aggregate supply and aggregate demand curves shift in different directions for various reasons in a given time period. These shifts in the aggregate supply and aggregate demand curves cause upswings and downswings in real GDP—the business cycle. A leftward shift in the aggregate demand curve, for example, can cause a recession. Whereas, a rightward shift of the aggregate demand curve can cause real GDP and employment to rise, and the economy recovers. A leftward shift in the aggregate supply curve can cause a downswing, and a rightward shift might cause an upswing.

> **Conclusion** *The business cycle is a result of shifts in the aggregate demand and aggregate supply curves.*

Cost-push inflation
An increase in the general price level resulting from an increase in the cost of production that causes the aggregate supply curve to shift leftward.

Demand-pull inflation
A rise in the general price level resulting from an excess of total spending (demand) caused by a rightward shift in the aggregate demand curve.

---

2. *Economic Report of the President*, 2008, http://www.gpoaccess.gov/eop/, Tables B-2, B-42, B-62, and B-64.
3. Ibid.

YOU'RE THE ECONOMIST   Was John Maynard Keynes Right?

Applicable Concepts: aggregate demand and aggregate supply analysis

In *The General Theory of Employment, Interest, and Money,* Keynes wrote:

> The ideas of economists and political philosophers, both when they are right and when they are wrong, are more powerful than is commonly understood. Indeed the world is ruled by little else. Practical men, who believe themselves to be quite exempt from any intellectual influences, are usually the slaves of some defunct economist. Madmen in authority, who hear voices in the air, are distilling their frenzy from some academic scribbler of a few years back.... There are not many who are influenced by new theories after they are twenty-five or thirty years of age, so that the ideas which civil servants and politicians and even agitators apply to current events are not likely to be the newest.[1]

Keynes (1883–1946) is regarded as the father of modern macroeconomics. He was the son of an eminent English economist, John Neville Keynes, who was a lecturer in economics and logic at Cambridge University. Keynes was educated at Eton and Cambridge in mathematics and probability theory, but ultimately he selected the field of economics and accepted a lectureship in economics at Cambridge.

Keynes was a many-faceted man who was an honored and supremely successful member of the British academic, financial, and political upper class. He amassed a $2 million personal fortune by speculating in stocks, international currencies, and commodities. (Use CPI index numbers to compute the equivalent amount in today's dollars.) In addition to making a huge fortune for himself, Keynes served as a trustee of King's College and increased its endowment over tenfold.

Keynes was a prolific scholar who is best remembered for *The General Theory,* published in 1936. This work made a convincing attack on the classical theory that capitalism would self-correct from a severe recession. Keynes based his model on the belief that increasing aggregate demand achieve full employment, while and wages remain inflexible. over, his bold policy prescripti for the government to raise its ing and/or reduce taxes in o increase the economy's ag demand curve and put the unem back to work.

Price Level, Real GDP, and ployment Rate, 1933–1941

Year	CPI	Real GDP (billions of 2000 dollars)	Une me (pe
1933	13.0	$ 635	
1939	13.9	951	
1940	14.0	1,034	
1941	14.7	1,211	

Sources: Bureau of Labor Statistics, ftp://ftp.bls. special.requests/cpi/cpiai.txt, Bureau of Econom sis, *National Economic Accounts,* http://www national/nipaweb/Table.asp?Selected=Y, Tab and *Economic Report of the President,* 2006, www.gpoaccess.gov/eop/index.html, Table B-

ANALYZE THE ISS

Was Keynes correct? Based following data, use the agg demand and aggregate s model to explain Keynes's that increases in aggregate de propel an economy towar employment.

1. J. M. Keynes, *The General Theory of Employment, Interest, and Money* (London: Macmillan, 1936), p. 383.

EXHIBIT 12 — A Rightward Shift in the Aggregate Demand and Supply Curves

From late 1995 through 2000, the aggregate demand curve increased from AD_{95} to AD_{00}. Significant increases in productivity from technology advances shifted the aggregate supply curve from AS_{95} to AS_{00}. As a result, the U.S economy experienced strong real GDP growth to full employment with mild inflation (the CPI increased from 152 to 172).

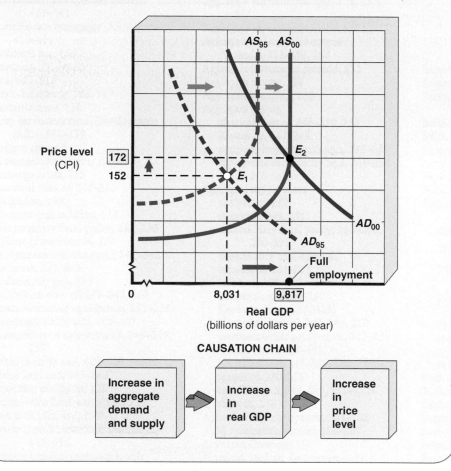

CAUSATION CHAIN

Increase in aggregate demand and supply ⟹ Increase in real GDP ⟹ Increase in price level

---

Increase in Both Aggregate Demand and Aggregate Supply Curves

Let the trumpets blow! Aggregate demand and supply curves will now edify you by explaining the U.S. economy from the mid-1990s through 2000. Begin in Exhibit 12 at E_1 with real GDP at $8,031 billion and the CPI at 152. As shown in the AD/AS model for 1995, the economy operated below full employment (5.6 percent unemployment rate, not explicitly shown). Over the next five years, the U.S. economy moved to E_2 in 2000 and experienced strong growth in real GDP (from $8,031 billion to $9,817 billion) and mild inflation (the CPI increased from 152 to 172, which is 13.1 percent, or 2.6 percent per year).

The movement from E_1 (below full employment) to E_2 (full employment) was caused by an increase in AD_{95} to AD_{00} and an increase in AS_{95} to AS_{00}. The rightward shift in the AS curve was the result of technological advances, such as the Internet and electronic commerce, which produced larger-than-usual increases in productivity at each possible price level. And, as shown earlier in Exhibit 9 of Chapter 16 on business cycles and unemployment, the economy has returned to operating below its full-employment potential real GDP since the recession of 2001.

CHECKPOINT

Would the Greenhouse Effect Cause Inflation, Unemployment, or Both?
You are the chair of the President's Council of Economic Advisers. There has been an extremely hot and dry summer due to a climatic change known as the greenhouse effect. As a result, crop production has fallen drastically. The president calls you to the White House to discuss the impact on the economy. Would you explain to the president that a sharp drop in U.S. crop production would cause inflation, unemployment, or both?

KEY CONCEPTS

Aggregate demand curve (*AD*)
Real balances effect
Interest-rate effect
Net exports effect

Aggregate supply curve (*AS*)
Keynesian range
Intermediate range
Classical range

Stagflation
Cost-push inflation
Demand-pull inflation

SUMMARY

- The **aggregate demand curve** shows the level of real GDP purchased in the economy at different price levels during a period of time.
- **Reasons why the aggregate demand curve is downward sloping** include the following three effects: (1) The **real balances effect** is the impact on real GDP caused by the inverse relationship between the purchasing power of fixed-value financial assets and inflation, which causes a shift in the consumption schedule. (2) The **interest-rate effect** assumes a fixed money supply; therefore, inflation increases the demand for money. As the demand for money increases, the interest rate rises, causing consumption and investment spending to fall. (3) The **net exports effect** is the impact on real GDP caused by the inverse relationship between net exports and inflation. An increase in the U.S. price level tends to reduce U.S. exports and increase imports, and vice versa.

Shift in the Aggregate Demand Curve

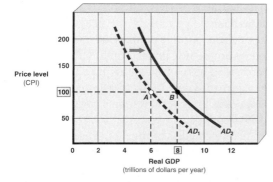

Real GDP
(trillions of dollars per year)

- The **aggregate supply curve** shows the level of real GDP that an economy will produce at different possible price levels. The shape of the aggregate supply curve depends on the flexibility of prices and wages as real GDP expands and contracts.

The aggregate supply curve has three ranges: (1) The **Keynesian range** of the curve is horizontal because neither the price level nor production costs will increase or decrease when there is substantial unemployment in the economy. (2) In the **intermediate range,** both prices and costs rise as real GDP rises toward full employment. Prices and production costs rise because of bottlenecks, the stronger bargaining power of labor, and the utilization of less-productive workers and capital. (3) The **classical range** is the vertical segment of the aggregate supply curve. It coincides with the full-employment output. Because output is at its maximum, increases in aggregate demand will only cause a rise in the price level.

Aggregate Supply Curve

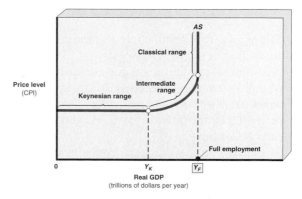

Real GDP
(trillions of dollars per year)

- **Aggregate demand and aggregate supply analysis** determines the equilibrium price level and the equilibrium real GDP by the intersection of the aggregate demand and aggregate supply curves. In macroeconomic equilibrium, businesses neither overestimate nor underestimate the real GDP demanded at the prevailing price level.

- *Stagflation* exists when an economy experiences inflation and unemployment simultaneously. Holding aggregate demand constant, a decrease in aggregate supply results in the unhealthy condition of a rise in the price level and a fall in real GDP and employment.
- *Cost-push inflation* is inflation that results from a decrease in the aggregate supply curve while the aggregate demand curve remains fixed. Cost-push inflation is undesirable because it is accompanied by declines in both real GDP and employment.

Cost-Push Inflation

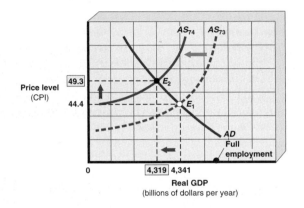

- *Demand-pull inflation* is inflation that results from an increase in the aggregate demand curve in both the classical and the intermediate ranges of the aggregate supply curve, while the aggregate supply curve is fixed.

Demand-Pull Inflation

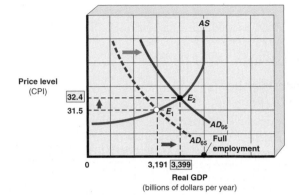

SUMMARY OF CONCLUSION STATEMENTS

- The aggregate demand curve and the demand curve are not the same concepts.
- Consumers spend more on goods and services when lower prices make their dollars more valuable. Therefore, the real value of money is measured by the quantity of goods and services each dollar buys.
- Any change in the individual components of aggregate expenditures shifts the aggregate demand curve.
- When the aggregate supply curve is horizontal and an economy is below full employment, the only effects of an increase in aggregate demand are increases in real GDP and employment, while the price level does not change. Stated simply, the Keynesian view is that "demand creates its own supply."
- When the aggregate supply curve is vertical at the full-employment GDP, the only effect over

time of a change in aggregate demand is a change in the price level. Stated simply, the classical view is that "supply creates its own demand."
- At macroeconomic equilibrium, sellers neither overestimate nor underestimate the real GDP demanded at the prevailing price level.
- As aggregate demand increases in the Keynesian range, the price level remains constant as real GDP expands.
- In the intermediate range, increases in aggregate demand increase both the price level and the real GDP.
- Once the economy reaches full-employment output in the classical range, additional increases in aggregate demand merely cause inflation, rather than more real GDP.
- The business cycle is a result of shifts in the aggregate demand and aggregate supply curves.

STUDY QUESTIONS AND PROBLEMS

1. Explain why the aggregate demand curve is downward sloping. How does your explanation differ from the reasons behind the downward-sloping demand curve for an individual product?

2. Explain the theory of the classical economists that flexible prices and wages ensure that the economy operates at full employment.

3. In which direction would each of the following changes in conditions cause the aggregate demand curve to shift? Explain your answers.
   a. Consumers expect an economic downturn.
   b. A new U.S. president is elected, and the profit expectations of business executives rise.
   c. The federal government increases spending for highways, bridges, and other infrastructure.
   d. The United States increases exports of wheat and other crops to Russia, Ukraine, and other former Soviet republics.

4. Identify the three ranges of the aggregate supply curve. Explain the impact of an increase in aggregate demand curve in each segment.

5. Consider this statement: "Equilibrium GDP is the same as full employment." Do you agree or disagree? Explain.

6. Assume the aggregate demand and aggregate supply curves intersect at a price level of 100. Explain the effect of a shift in the price level to 120 and to 50.

7. In which direction would each of the following changes in conditions cause the aggregate supply curve to shift? Explain your answers.
   a. The price of gasoline increases because of a catastrophic oil spill.
   b. Labor unions and all other workers agree to a cut in wages to stimulate the economy.
   c. Power companies switch to solar power, and the price of electricity falls.
   d. The federal government increases the excise tax on gasoline in order to finance a deficit.

8. Assume an economy operates in the intermediate range of its aggregate supply curve. State the direction of shift for the aggregate demand or aggregate supply curve for each of the following changes in conditions. What is the effect on the price level? On real GDP? On employment?
   a. The price of crude oil rises significantly.
   b. Spending on national defense doubles.
   c. The costs of imported goods increase.
   d. An improvement in technology raises labor productivity.

9. What shifts in aggregate supply or aggregate demand would cause each of the following conditions for an economy?
   a. The price level rises, and real GDP rises.
   b. The price level falls, and real GDP rises.
   c. The price level falls, and real GDP falls.
   d. The price level rises, and real GDP falls.
   e. The price level falls, and real GDP remains the same.
   f. The price level remains the same, and real GDP rises.

10. Explain cost-push inflation verbally and graphically, using aggregate demand and aggregate supply analysis. Assess the impact on the price level, real GDP, and employment.

11. Explain demand-pull inflation graphically using aggregate demand and supply analysis. Assess the impact on the price level, real GDP, and employment.

For Online Exercises, go to the text Web site at www.cengage.com/economics/tucker.

CHECKPOINT ANSWER ✓

Would the Greenhouse Effect Cause Inflation, Unemployment, or Both?

A drop in food production reduces aggregate supply. The decrease in aggregate supply causes the economy to contract, while prices rise. In addition to the OPEC oil embargo between 1972 and 1974, worldwide weather conditions destroyed crops and contributed to the supply shock that caused stagflation in the U. S. economy. If you said that a severe greenhouse effect would cause both higher unemployment and inflation, **YOU ARE CORRECT.**

PRACTICE QUIZ

For an explanation of the correct answers, please visit the tutorial at www.cengage.com/ economics/tucker.

1. The aggregate demand curve is defined as the
   a. net national product.
   b. sum of wages, rent, interest, and profits.
   c. real GDP purchased at different possible price levels.
   d. total dollar value of household expectations.

2. When the supply of credit is fixed, an increase in the price level stimulates the demand for credit, which, in turn, reduces consumption and investment spending. This effect is called the
   a. real balances effect.
   b. interest-rate effect.
   c. net exports effect.
   d. substitution effect.

3. The real balances effect occurs because a higher price level reduces the real value of people's
   a. financial assets.
   b. wages.
   c. unpaid debt.
   d. physical investments.

4. The net exports effect is the inverse relationship between net exports and the _____ of an economy.
   a. real GDP
   b. GDP deflator
   c. price level
   d. consumption spending

5. Which of the following will shift the aggregate demand curve to the left?
   a. An increase in exports
   b. An increase in investment
   c. An increase in government spending
   d. A decrease in government spending

6. Which of the following will *not* shift the aggregate demand curve to the left?
   a. Consumers become more optimistic about the future.
   b. Government spending decreases.
   c. Business optimism decreases.
   d. Consumers become pessimistic about the future.

7. The popular theory prior to the Great Depression that the economy will automatically adjust to achieve full employment is
   a. supply-side economics.
   b. Keynesian economics.
   c. classical economics.
   d. mercantilism.

8. Classical economists believed that the
   a. price system was stable.
   b. goal of full employment was impossible.
   c. price system automatically adjusts the economy to full employment in the long run.
   d. government should attempt to restore full employment.

9. Which of the following is *not* a range on the eclectic or general view of the aggregate supply curve?
   a. Classical range
   b. Keynesian range
   c. Intermediate range
   d. Monetary range

10. Macroeconomic equilibrium occurs when
   a. aggregate supply exceeds aggregate demand.
   b. the economy is at full employment.
   c. aggregate demand equals aggregate supply.
   d. aggregate demand equals the average price level.

11. Along the classical or vertical range of the aggregate supply curve, a decrease in the aggregate demand curve will decrease
   a. both the price level and real GDP.
   b. only real GDP.
   c. only the price level.
   d. neither real GDP nor the price level.

12. Other factors held constant, a decrease in resource prices will shift the aggregate
   a. demand curve leftward.
   b. demand curve rightward.
   c. supply curve leftward.
   d. supply curve rightward.

13. Assuming a fixed aggregate demand curve, a leftward shift in the aggregate supply curve causes a (an)
   a. increase in the price level and a decrease in real GDP.
   b. increase in the price level and an increase in real GDP.
   c. decrease in the price level and a decrease in real GDP.
   d. decrease in the price level and an increase in real GDP.

14. An increase in the price level caused by a rightward shift of the aggregate demand curve is called
   a. cost-push inflation.
   b. supply shock inflation.
   c. demand shock inflation.
   d. demand-pull inflation.

15. Suppose workers become pessimistic about their future employment, which causes them to save more and spend less. If the economy is on the intermediate range of the aggregate supply curve, then
   a. both real GDP and the price level will fall.
   b. real GDP will fall and the price level will rise.
   c. real GDP will rise and the price level will fall.
   d. both real GDP and the price level will rise.

20

The Self-Correcting Aggregate Demand and Supply Model

It can be argued that the economy is self-regulating. This means that over time the economy will move itself to full-employment equilibrium. Stated differently, this classical theory is based on the assumption that the economy might ebb and flow around it, but full employment is the normal condition for the economy regardless of gyrations in the price level. To understand this adjustment process, the *AD-AS* model presented in the chapter must be extended into a more complex model called the self-correcting *AD-AS* model. First, a distinction will be made between the short-run and long-run aggregate supply curves. Indeed, one of the most controversial areas of macroeconomics is the shape of the aggregate supply curve and the reasons for that shape. Second, we will explain long-run equilibrium using the self-correcting *AD-AS* model. Third, this appendix concludes by using the self-correcting *AD-AS* model to explain short-run and long-run adjustments to changes in aggregate demand.

Why the Short-Run Aggregate Supply Curve is Upward Sloping

Short-run aggregate supply curve (SRAS)

The curve that shows the level of real GDP produced at different possible price levels during a time period in which nominal incomes do not change in response to changes in the price level.

Exhibit A-1(a) shows the short-run aggregate supply curve (*SRAS*), which does not have either the perfectly flat Keynesian segment or the perfectly vertical classical segment developed in Exhibit 6 of this chapter. The short-run supply curve shows the level of real GDP produced at different possible price levels during a time period in which nominal wages and salaries (incomes) do not change in response to changes in the price level. Recall from the chapter on inflation that

$$\text{Real income} = \frac{\text{nominal income}}{\text{CPI (as decimal)}}$$

As explained by this formula, a rise in the price level measured by the CPI decreases real income, and a fall in the price level increases real income. Given the definition of the short-run aggregate supply curve, there are two reasons why one can assume nominal wages and salaries remain fixed in spite of changes in the price level:

1. **Incomplete knowledge.** In a short period of time, workers may be unaware that a change in the price level has changed their real incomes. Consequently, they do not adjust their wage and salary demands according to changes in their real incomes.
2. **Fixed-wage contracts.** Unionized employees, for example, have nominal or money wages stated in their contracts. Also, many professionals receive set salaries for a year. In these cases, nominal incomes remain constant, or "sticky," for a given time period regardless of changes in the price level.

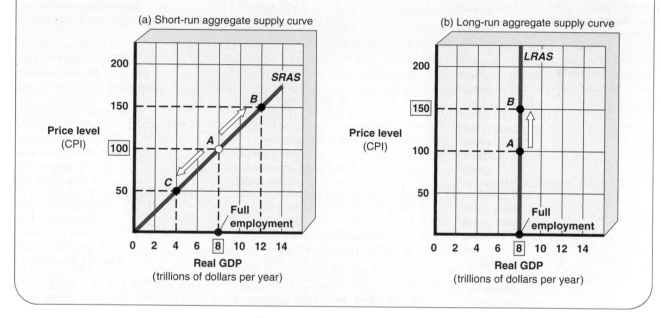

EXHIBIT A-1 — Aggregate Supply Curves

The short-run aggregate supply curve (*SRAS*) in Part (a) is based on the assumption that nominal wages and salaries are fixed based on an expected price level of 100 and full-employment real GDP of $8 trillion. An increase in the price level from 100 to 150 increases profits, real GDP, and employment, moving the economy from point *A* to point *B*. A decrease in the price level from 100 to 50 decreases profits, real GDP, and employment, moving the economy from point *A* to point *C*.

The long-run aggregate supply curve (*LRAS*) in Part (b) is vertical at full-employment real GDP. For example, if the price level rises from 100 at point *A* to 150 at point *B*, workers now have enough time to renegotiate higher nominal incomes by a percentage equal to the percentage increase in the price level. This flexible adjustment means that real incomes and profits remain unchanged, and the economy continues to operate at full-employment real GDP.

Given the assumption that changes in the prices of goods and services measured by the CPI do not in a short period of time cause changes in nominal wages, let's examine Exhibit A-1(a) and explain the *SRAS* curve's upward-sloping shape. Begin at point *A* with a CPI of 100 and observe that the economy is operating at the full-employment real GDP of $8 trillion. Also assume that labor contracts are based on this expected price level. Now suppose the price level unexpectedly increases from 100 to 150 at point *B*. At higher prices for products, firms' revenues increase, and with nominal wages and salaries fixed, profits rise. In response, firms increase output from $8 trillion to $12 trillion, and the economy operates beyond its full-employment output. This occurs because firms increase work hours and train and hire homemakers, retirees, and unemployed workers who were not profitable at or below full-employment real GDP.

Now return to point *A* and assume the CPI falls to 50 at point *C*. In this case, the prices firms receive for their products drop while nominal wages and salaries remain fixed. As a result, firms' revenues and profits fall, and they reduce output from $8 trillion to $4 trillion real GDP. Correspondingly, employment (not shown explicitly in the model) falls below full employment.

> **Conclusion** *The upward-sloping shape of the short-run aggregate supply curve (SRAS) is the result of fixed nominal wages and salaries as the price level changes.*

Why the Long-Run Aggregate Supply Curve is Vertical

Long-run aggregate supply curve (LRAS)

The curve that shows the level of real GDP produced at different possible price levels during a time period in which nominal incomes change by the same percentage as the price level changes.

The long-run aggregate supply curve (*LRAS*) is presented in Exhibit A-1(b). The long-run aggregate supply curve shows the level of real GDP produced at different possible price levels during a time period in which nominal incomes change by the same percentage as the price level changes. Like the classical vertical segment of the aggregate supply curve developed in Exhibit 6 of the chapter, the long-run aggregate supply curve is vertical at full-employment real GDP.

To understand why the long-run aggregate supply curve is vertical requires the assumption that sufficient time has elapsed for labor contracts to expire, so that nominal wages and salaries can be renegotiated. Stated another way, over a long-enough time, workers will calculate changes in their real incomes and obtain increases in their nominal incomes to adjust proportionately to changes in purchasing power. Suppose the CPI is 100 (or in decimal 1.0) at point *A* in Exhibit A-1(b) and the average nominal wage is $10 per hour. This means the average real wage is also $10 ($10 nominal wage divided by 1.0). But if the CPI rises to 150 at point *B*, the $10 average real wage falls to $6.67 ($10/1.5). In the long run, workers will demand and receive a new nominal wage of $15, returning their real wage to $10 ($15/1.5). Thus, both the CPI (rise from 100 to 150) and the nominal wage (rise from $10 to $15) changed by the same rate of 50 percent, and the economy moved from point *A* to point *B*, upward along the long-run aggregate supply curve. Note that because both the prices of products measured by the CPI and the nominal wage rise by the same percentage, profit margins remain unchanged in real terms, and firms have no incentive to produce either more or less than the full-employment real GDP of $8 trillion. And because this same adjustment process occurs between any two price levels along *LRAS*, the curve is vertical, and potential real GDP is independent of the price level. Regardless of rises or falls in the CPI, potential real GDP remains the same.

> **Conclusion** *The vertical shape of the long-run aggregate supply curve (LRAS) is the result of nominal wages and salaries eventually changing by the same percentage as the price level changes.*

Equilibrium in the Self-Correcting *AD-AS* Model

Exhibit A-2 combines aggregate demand with the short-run and long-run aggregate supply curves from the previous exhibit to form the self-correcting *AD-AS* model. Equilibrium in the model occurs at point *E*, where the economy's aggregate demand curve (*AD*) intersects the vertical long-run aggregate supply curve (*LRAS*) and the short-run aggregate supply curve (*SRAS*). In long-run equilibrium, the economy's price level is 100, and full-employment real GDP is $8 trillion.

EXHIBIT A-2 | Self-Correcting *AD-AS* Model

The short-run aggregate supply curve (*SRAS*) is based on an expected price level of 100. Point *E* shows that this equilibrium price level occurs at the intersection of the aggregate demand curve *AD*, *SRAS*, and the long-run aggregate supply curve (*LRAS*).

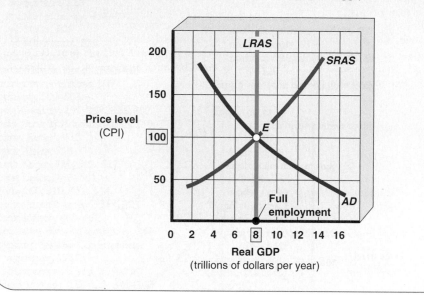

The Impact of an Increase in Aggregate Demand

Now you're ready for some actions and reactions using the model. Suppose that, beginning at point E_1 in Exhibit A-3, a change in a nonprice determinant (summarized in Exhibit 10 at the end of this chapter) causes an increase in aggregate demand from AD_1 to AD_2. For example, the shift could be the result of an increase in consumption spending (*C*), government spending (*G*), or business investment (*I*), or greater demand for U.S. exports. Regardless of the cause, the short-run effect is for the economy to move upward along $SRAS_{100}$ to the intersection with AD_2 at the temporary or short-run equilibrium point E_2 with a price level of 150. Recall that nominal incomes are fixed in the short run. Faced with higher demand, firms raise prices for products and, because the price of labor remains unchanged, firms earn higher profits and increase employment by hiring workers who were not profitable at full employment. As a result, for a short period of time, real GDP increases above the full-employment real GDP of $8 trillion to $12 trillion. However, the economy cannot produce in excess of full employment forever. What forces are at work to bring real GDP back to full-employment real GDP?

Assume time passes and labor contracts expire. The next step in the transition process at E_2 is that workers begin demanding nominal income increases that will eventually bring their real incomes back to the same real incomes established initially at E_1. Since firms are anxious to maintain their output levels, and they are competing for workers, firms meet the wage increase demands of labor. These increases

EXHIBIT A-3   Adjustments to an Increase in Aggregate Demand

Beginning at long-run equilibrium E_1, the aggregate demand curve increases from AD_1 to AD_2. Since nominal incomes are fixed in the short run, firms raise product prices, earn higher profits, and expand output to short-run equilibrium point E_2. After enough time passes, workers increase their nominal incomes to restore their purchasing power, and the short-run supply curve shifts leftward along AD_2 to a transitional point such as E_3. As the economy moves from E_2 to E_4, profits fall, and firms cut output and employment. Eventually, long-run equilibrium is reached at E_4 with full employment restored by the self-correction process.

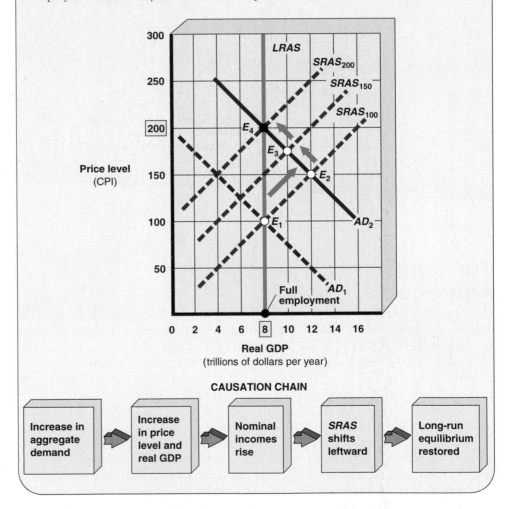

CAUSATION CHAIN

| Increase in aggregate demand | ⟹ | Increase in price level and real GDP | ⟹ | Nominal incomes rise | ⟹ | *SRAS* shifts leftward | ⟹ | Long-run equilibrium restored |

in nominal incomes shift the short-run aggregate supply curve leftward, which causes an upward movement along AD_2. One of the succession of possible intermediate adjustment short-run supply curves along AD_2 is $SRAS_{150}$. This short-run intermediate adjustment is based upon an expected price level of 150 determined by the intersection of $SRAS_{150}$ and $LRAS$. Although the short-run aggregate supply curve $SRAS_{150}$ intersects AD_2 at E_3, the adjustment to the increase in aggregate demand is not yet complete. Workers negotiated increases in nominal incomes based upon an expected price level of 150, but the leftward shift of the short-run aggregate supply curve raised the price level to about 175 at E_3. Workers must therefore negotiate another round of higher nominal incomes to restore purchasing power. This process continues until long-run equilibrium is restored at E_4, where the adjustment process ends.

The long-run forecast for the price level at full employment is now 200 at point E_4. $SRAS_{100}$ has shifted leftward to $SRAS_{200}$, which intersects $LRAS$ at point E_4. As a result of the shift in the short-run aggregate supply curve from E_2 to E_4 and the corresponding increase in nominal incomes, firms' profits are cut, and they react by raising product prices, reducing employment, and reducing output. At E_4, the economy has self-adjusted to both short-run and long-run equilibrium at a price level of 200 and full-employment real GDP of $8 trillion. If there are no further shifts in aggregate demand, the economy will remain at E_4 indefinitely. Note that nominal income is higher at point E_4 than it was originally at point E_1, but real wages and salaries remain unchanged, as explained in Exhibit A-1(b).

> **Conclusion** *An increase in aggregate demand in the long run causes the short-run aggregate supply curve to shift leftward because nominal incomes rise and the economy self corrects to a higher price level at full-employment real GDP.*

The Impact of a Decrease in Aggregate Demand

Point E_1 in Exhibit A-4 begins where the sequence of events described in the previous section ends. Now let's see what happens when the aggregate demand curve decreases from AD_1 to AD_2. The reason might be that a wave of pessimism from a stock market crash causes consumers to cut back on their spending and firms postpone buying new factories and equipment. As a result, firms find their sales and profits have declined, and they react by cutting product prices, output, and employment. Workers' nominal incomes remain fixed in the short run with contracts negotiated based on an expected price level of 200. The result of this situation is that the economy moves downward along $SRAS_{200}$ from point E_1 to short-run equilibrium point E_2. Here the price level falls from 200 to 150, and real GDP has fallen from $8 trillion to $4 trillion.

At E_2, the economy is in a serious recession, and after, say, a year, workers will accept lower nominal wages and salaries when their contracts are renewed in order to keep their jobs in a time of poor profits and competition from unemployed workers. This willingness to accept lower nominal incomes is made easier by the realization that lower prices for goods means it costs less to maintain the workers' standard of living. As workers make a series of downward adjustments in nominal incomes, the short-run aggregate supply curve moves downward along AD_2 toward E_4. $SRAS_{150}$ illustrates one possible intermediate position corresponding to the long-run expected price level of 150 determined by the intersection of $SRAS_{150}$ and $LRAS$. However, like E_2, E_3 is not the point of long-run equilibrium. Workers negotiated decreases in nominal increases based upon an expected price level of 150, but the rightward shift of the short-run aggregate supply curve has lowered the price

EXHIBIT A-4   Adjustments to a Decrease in Aggregate Demand

Assume the economy is initially at long-run equilibrium point E_1 and aggregate demand decreases from AD_1 to AD_2. Nominal incomes in the short run are fixed based on an expected price level of 200. In response to the fall in aggregate demand, firms' profits decline, and they cut output and employment. As a result, the economy moves downward along $SRAS_{200}$ to temporary equilibrium at E_2. When workers lower their nominal incomes because of competition from unemployed workers, the short-run aggregate supply curve shifts downward to an intermediate point, such as E_3. As workers decrease their nominal incomes based on the new long-run expected price level of 150 at point E_3, profits rise, and firms increase output and employment. In the long run, the short-run aggregate supply curve continues to automatically adjust downward along AD_2 until it again returns to long-run equilibrium at E_4.

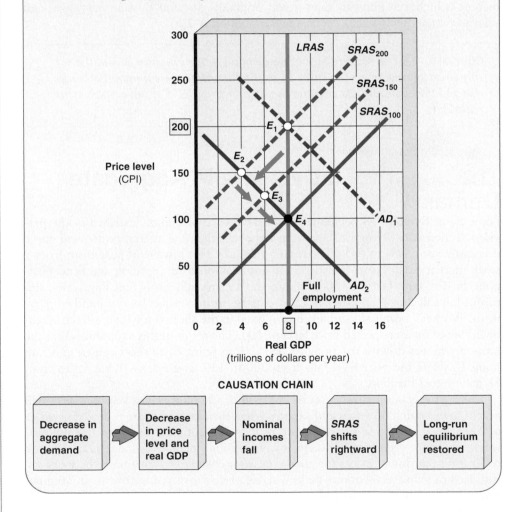

CAUSATION CHAIN

| Decrease in aggregate demand | ⇨ | Decrease in price level and real GDP | ⇨ | Nominal incomes fall | ⇨ | SRAS shifts rightward | ⇨ | Long-run equilibrium restored |

level to about 125 at E_3. Under pressure from unemployed workers who will work for still lower real wages and salaries, workers will continue this process of adjusting their nominal incomes lower until $SRAS_{150}$ shifts rightward to point E_4.

Eventually, the long-run expected full-employment price level returns to 100 at point E_4 where the economy has self-corrected to long-run full-employment equilibrium. The result of this adjustment downward along AD_2 between E_2 and E_4 is that lower nominal incomes raise profits and firms respond by lowering prices of products, increasing employment, and increasing output so that real GDP increases from $4 trillion to $8 trillion. Unless aggregate demand changes, the economy will be stable at E_4 indefinitely. Finally, observe that average nominal income has decreased by the same percentage between points E_1 and E_4 as the percentage decline in the price level. Therefore, real incomes are unaffected as explained in Exhibit A-1(b).

> **Conclusion** *A decrease in aggregate demand in the long run causes the short-run aggregate supply curve to shift rightward because nominal incomes fall and the economy self corrects to a lower price level at full-employment real GDP.*

Changes in Potential Real GDP

Like the aggregate demand and short-run aggregate supply curves, the long-run aggregate supply curve also changes. As explained in Chapter 2, changes in resources and technology shift the production possibilities curve outward. We now extend this concept of economic growth to the long-run aggregate supply curve as follows:

1. **Changes in resources.** For example, the quantity of land can be increased by reclaiming land from the sea or revitalizing soil. Over time, potential real GDP increases if the full-employment number of workers increases, holding capital and technology constant. Such growth in the labor force can result from population growth. Greater quantities of plants, production lines, computers, and other forms of capital also produce increases in potential real GDP. Capital includes *human capital,* which is the accumulation of education, training, experience, and health of workers.
2. **An advance in technology.** Technological change enables firms to produce more goods from any given amount of inputs. Even with fixed quantities of labor and capital, the latest computer-age machinery increases potential GDP.

> **Conclusion** *A rightward shift of the long-run aggregate supply curve represents economic growth in potential full-employment real GDP.*

Over time, the U.S. economy typically adds resources and improves technology, and growth occurs in full-employment output. Exhibit A-5 uses basic aggregate demand and supply analysis to explain a hypothetical trend in the price level measured by the CPI between the years the 2005, 2010, and 2015. The trend line connects the macro equilibrium points for each year. The following section uses real-world data to illustrate changes in the long-run aggregate supply curve over time.

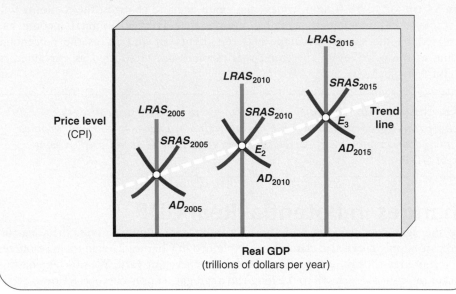

EXHIBIT A-5 | Trend of Macro Equilibrium Price Level over Time

Each hypothetical long-run equilibrium point shows the CPI and real GDP for a given year determined by the intersection of the aggregate demand curve, short-run aggregate supply curve, and the long-run aggregate supply curve. Over time, these curves shift, and both the price level and real GDP increase.

Increase in the Aggregate Demand and Long-Run Aggregate Supply Curves

The self-correcting *AD-AS* model shown in Exhibit A-5 revisits Exhibit 12 in this chapter, which illustrated economic growth that occurred between 1995 and 2000 in the U.S. economy. Exhibit A-6, however, uses short-run and long-run aggregate supply curves to expand the analysis. (For simplicity, the real GDP amounts have been rounded.) In 1995, the economy operated at point E_1, with the CPI at 152 and a real GDP of $8.0 trillion. Since $LRAS_{95}$ at E_1 was estimated to be $8.3 trillion real GDP, the economy was operating below its full-employment potential with an unemployment rate of 5.6 percent (not explicitly shown in the model). Over the next five years, the U.S. economy moved to full employment at point E_3 in 2000 and experienced growth in real GDP from $8.0 trillion to $9.8 trillion. The CPI increased from 152 to 172 (mild inflation), and the unemployment rate fell to 4.0 percent.

During this time period, extraordinary technological change and capital accumulation, particularly in high-tech industries, caused economic growth in potential real GDP, represented by the rightward shift in the vertical long-run supply curve from $LRAS_{95}$ to $LRAS_{00}$. The movement from E_1 below full-employment real GDP was caused by an increase in AD_{95} to AD_{00}, and a movement upward along short-run aggregate supply curve $SRAS_{95}$ to point E_2. Over time the nominal or money wage rate increased, and $SRAS_{95}$ shifted leftward to $SRAS_{00}$. At point E_3, the price level was 175 and equal to potential real GDP of $9.8 trillion.

EXHIBIT A-6	A Rightward Shift in the Aggregate Demand and Long-Run Aggregate Supply Curves

In 1995, the U.S. economy was operating at $8.0 trillion below full-employment real GDP of $8.3 trillion at $LRAS_{95}$. Between 1995 and 2000, the aggregate demand curve increased from AD_{95} to AD_{00} and the U.S economy moved upward along the short-run aggregate supply curve $SRAS_{95}$ from point E_1 to point E_2. Nominal or money incomes of workers increased, and $SRAS_{95}$ shifted leftward to $SRAS_{00}$, establishing long-run full-employment equilibrium at E_3 on long-run aggregate supply curve $LRAS_{00}$. Technological changes and capital accumulation over these years caused the rightward shift from $LRAS_{95}$ to $LRAS_{00}$, and potential real GDP grew from $8.3 trillion to $9.8 trillion.

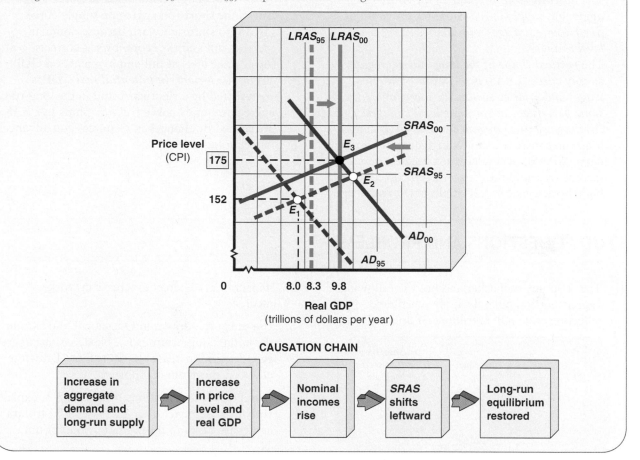

KEY CONCEPTS

Short-run aggregate supply curve (*SRAS*) Long-run aggregate supply curve (*LRAS*)

SUMMARY

- The *upward-sloping shape of the short-run aggregate supply curve (SRAS) is the result of fixed nominal wages and salaries as the price level changes.*
- The *vertical shape of the long-run aggregate supply curve (LRAS) is the result of nominal wages and salaries eventually changing by the same percentage as the price level changes.*
- An *increase in aggregate demand (AD)* in the long run causes the short-run aggregate supply curve (*SRAS*) to shift leftward because nominal incomes rise and the economy self corrects to a higher price level at full-employment real GDP.

- A *decrease in aggregate demand in the long run* causes the short-run aggregate supply curve (*SRAS*) to shift rightward because nominal incomes fall and the economy self corrects to a lower price level at full-employment real GDP.
- *Economic growth in potential real GDP* is represented by a rightward shift in the long-run aggregate supply curve (*LRAS*). Shifts in *LRAS* are caused by changes in resources and advances in technology.

STUDY QUESTIONS AND PROBLEMS

1. The economy of Tuckerland has the following aggregate demand and supply schedules, reflecting real GDP in trillions of dollars:

Price Level (CPI)	Aggregate Demand	Short-run Aggregate Supply
250	$4	$16
200	8	12
150	12	8
100	16	4

   a. Graph the aggregate demand curve and the short-run aggregate supply curve.
   b. What are short-run equilibrium real GDP and the price level?
   c. If Tuckerland's potential real GDP is $12 trillion, plot the long-run aggregate supply curve (*LRAS*) in the graph.

2. Using the graph from Question 1 and assuming long-run equilibrium at $12 trillion, explain the

impact of a 10 percent increase in workers' income.

3. Use the graph drawn in Question 1 and assume the initial equilibrium is E_1. Next, assume aggregate demand increases by $4 trillion. Draw the effect on short-run equilibrium.

4. Based on the assumptions of Question 3, explain verbally the impact of an increase of $4 trillion in aggregate demand on short-run equilibrium.

5. The economy shown in Exhibit A-7 is initially in equilibrium at point E_1, and the aggregate demand curve decreases from AD_1 to AD_2. Explain the long-run adjustment process.

6. In the first quarter of 2001, real GDP was $9.88 trillion, and the price level measured by the GDP chain price index was 101. Real GDP was approximately equal to potential GDP. In the third quarter, aggregate demand decreased to $9.83 trillion, and the price level rose to 103. Draw a graph of this recession.

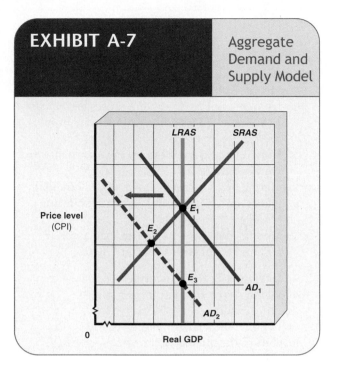

EXHIBIT A-7

Aggregate Demand and Supply Model

For Online Exercises, go to the text Web site at www.cengage.com/economics/tucker.

PRACTICE QUIZ

For an explanation of the correct answers, please visit the tutorial at www.cengage.com/economics/tucker.

1. An assumption for the short-run aggregate supply curve is that it is a period of time in which
   a. knowledge is complete.
   b. wages are fixed.
   c. wages are constant for under one year.
   d. prices firms charge for products are fixed.

2. The long-run aggregate supply curve is based on the assumption that
   a. both the price level and nominal incomes are fixed.
   b. prices are flexible after one year.
   c. both the price level and nominal incomes change by the same percentage.
   d. potential GDP is undetermined.

3. Graphically, long-run macro equilibrium occurs at the
   a. midpoint of the aggregate demand curve.

   b. intersection of the aggregate demand and long-run aggregate supply curves regardless of the short-run aggregate supply curve.
   c. midpoint of the long-run aggregate supply curve.
   d. intersection of the aggregate demand, short-run aggregate supply, and long-run aggregate supply curves.

4. An increase in nominal incomes of workers results in the
   a. aggregate demand curve shifting to the left.
   b. long-run aggregate supply curve shifting to the right.
   c. short-run aggregate supply curve shifting to the left.
   d. short-run aggregate supply curve shifting to the right.

PRACTICE QUIZ CONTINUED

5. An increase in aggregate demand in the long run will result in _____ in full-employment real GDP and _____ in the price level.
   a. no change; an increase
   b. an increase; no change
   c. a decrease; no change
   d. no change; a decrease

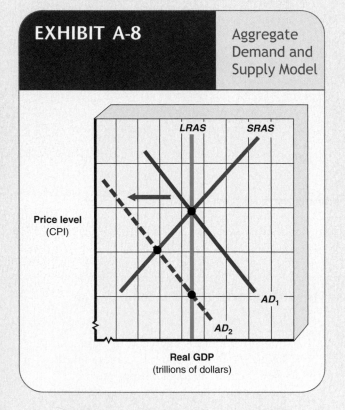

EXHIBIT A-8   Aggregate Demand and Supply Model

LRAS   SRAS

Price level (CPI)

AD_1

AD_2

Real GDP (trillions of dollars)

6. In Exhibit A-8, the intersection of AD_1 with *SRAS* indicates
   a. short-run equilibrium.
   b. long-run equilibrium.
   c. that the economy is not operating at full employment.
   d. that prices and wages are inflexible.

7. In Exhibit A-8, the intersection of AD_2 with *SRAS* indicates
   a. short-run equilibrium.
   b. long-run equilibrium.
   c. that the economy is operating at full employment.
   d. that prices and wages are inflexible.

8. In Exhibit A-8, the self-correcting *AD-AS* model argument is that competition
   a. from unemployed workers causes an increase in nominal wages and a rightward shift in *SRAS*.
   b. from unemployed workers causes a rightward shift in *LRAS*.
   c. among firms for workers increases nominal wages, and this causes a leftward shift in *SRAS*.
   d. among consumers causes an increase in the CPI and a rightward shift in *SRAS*.

9. In Exhibit A-8, the self-correcting *AD-AS* model theory is that in the long run the economy will
   a. remain where *SRAS* intersects AD_1.
   b. shift to the intersection of AD_2 and *SRAS*.
   c. shift to the intersection of AD_2 and *LRAS*.
   d. shift to the intersection of AD_2 and a new leftward-shifted *SRAS*.

10. In Exhibit A-8, the self-correcting *AD-AS* model predicts that the long-run result of the decrease from AD_1 to AD_2 will be a (an)
    a. higher price level and higher unemployment rate.
    b. lower price level and higher unemployment rate.
    c. unchanged price level and full employment.
    d. lower price level and full employment.

11. Which of the following is *most* likely to cause a leftward shift in the long-run aggregate supply curve?
    a. An increase in labor
    b. An increase in capital
    c. An advance in technology
    d. Destruction of resources

12. As shown in Exhibit A-9, and assuming the aggregate demand curve shifts from AD_1 and AD_2, the full-employment level of real GDP is
    a. $12 billion.
    b. $8 billion.
    c. $150 billion.
    d. unable to be determined.

13. Given the shift of the aggregate demand curve from AD_1 to AD_2 in Exhibit A-9, the real GDP and price level (CPI) in long-run equilibrium will be
    a. $8 billion and 150.
    b. $12 billion and 200.
    c. $8 billion and 250.
    d. $8 billion and 200.

14. Beginning from long-run equilibrium at point E_1 in Exhibit A-9, the aggregate demand curve shifts to AD_2. The real GDP and price level (CPI) in short-run equilibrium will be
    a. $12 billion and 200.
    b. $8 billion and 250.
    c. $8 billion and 150.
    d. $12 billion and 250.

15. Beginning from short-run equilibrium at point E_2 in Exhibit A-9, the economy's movement to a new position of long-run equilibrium would *best* be described as
    a. a movement along the AD_2 curve with a shift in the $SRAS_1$ curve.
    b. a movement along the $SRAS_2$ curve with a shift in the AD_2 curve.
    c. a shift in the $LRAS$ curve to an intersection at E_1.
    d. no shift of any kind.

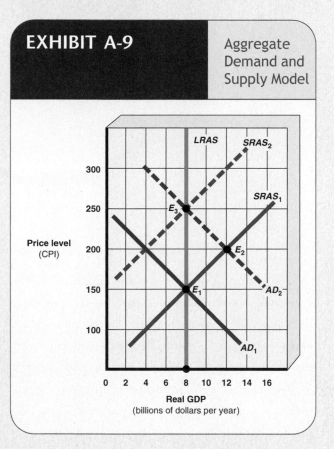

EXHIBIT A-9   Aggregate Demand and Supply Model

CHAPTER

21

Fiscal Policy

In the early 1980s, under President Ronald Reagan, the federal government reduced personal income tax rates. The goal was to expand aggregate demand and boost national output and employment in order to end the recession of 1980–1981. In the 1990s, a key part of President Bill Clinton's economic program was to stimulate economic growth by boosting government spending on long-term investment. This investment program included highways, bridges, fiber-optic communications networks, and education. In 2001, the United States experienced a recession, and President George W. Bush proposed and signed into law a tax cut in order to stimulate the economy. And in 2003, another tax cut bill was passed to create jobs and stimulate economic growth. From May to July 2008, Americans received about $170 billion in a tax-rebate stimulus package intended to trigger a spending spree that would enable the economy to avoid a recession.

Fiscal policy is one of the major issues that touches everyone's life. Fiscal policy is the use of government spending and taxes to influence the nation's output, employment, and price level. Federal government spending policies affect Social Security benefits, price supports for dairy farmers, and employment in the defense industry. Tax policies can change the amount of your paycheck and therefore influence whether you purchase a car or attend college.

Using fiscal policy to influence the performance of the economy has been an important idea since the Keynesian revolution of the 1930s. This chapter removes the political veil and looks at fiscal policy from the viewpoint of two opposing economic theories. First, you will study Keynesian demand-side fiscal policies that "fine-tune" aggregate demand so that the economy grows and achieves full employment with a higher price level. Second, you will study supply-side fiscal policy, which gained prominence during the Reagan administration. Supply-siders view aggregate supply as far more important than aggregate demand. Their fiscal policy prescription is to increase aggregate supply so that the economy grows and achieves full employment with a lower price level.

In this chapter, you will learn to solve these economic puzzles:

- Does an increase in government spending or a tax cut of equal amount provide the greater stimulus to economic growth?

- Can Congress fight a recession without taking any action?

- How could one argue that the federal government can increase tax revenues by cutting taxes?

Discretionary Fiscal Policy

Here we begin where the previous chapter left off—that is, discussing the use of discretionary fiscal policy, as Keynes advocated, to influence the economy's performance. Discretionary fiscal policy is the deliberate use of changes in government spending or taxes to alter aggregate demand and stabilize the economy. Exhibit 1 lists three basic types of discretionary fiscal policies and the corresponding ways in which the government can pursue each of these options. The first column of the table shows that the government can choose to increase aggregate demand by following an *expansionary* fiscal policy. The second column lists *contractionary* fiscal policy options the government can use to restrain aggregate demand.

Increasing Government Spending to Combat a Recession

Suppose the U.S. economy represented in Exhibit 2 has fallen into recession at equilibrium point E_1, where aggregate demand curve AD_1 intersects the aggregate supply curve, *AS*, in the near-full-employment range. (Note that for simplicity the aggregate demand and aggregate supply curves are drawn here as straight lines.) The price level measured by the CPI is 150, and a real GDP gap of $100 billion exists below the full-employment output of $6.1 trillion real GDP. As explained in the previous chapter (Exhibit 5), one approach the president and Congress can follow is provided by classical theory. The classical economists' prescription is to wait because the economy will self correct to full employment in the long run by adjusting downward along AD_1. But election time is approaching, so there is political pressure to do something about the recession now. Besides, recall Keynes's famous statement, "In the long run, we are all dead." Hence, policymakers follow Keynesian economics and decide to shift the aggregate demand curve rightward from AD_1 to AD_2 and thereby cure the recession.

How can the federal government do this? In theory, any increase in consumption (*C*), investment (*I*), or net exports (*X* − *M*) can spur aggregate demand. But these spending boosts are not directly under the government's control as is government spending (*G*). After all, there is always a long wish list of spending proposals for federal highways, health care, education, environmental programs, and so forth.

Fiscal policy
The use of government spending and taxes to influence the nation's spending, employment, and price level.

Discretionary fiscal policy
The deliberate use of changes in government spending or taxes to alter aggregate demand and stabilize the economy.

EXHIBIT 1	Discretionary Fiscal Policies
Expansionary Fiscal Policy	**Contractionary Fiscal Policy**
Increase government spending	Decrease government spending
Decrease taxes	Increase taxes
Increase government spending and taxes equally	Decrease government spending and taxes equally

Rather than crossing their fingers and waiting for things to happen in the long run, suppose that members of Congress gladly increase government spending to boost employment now.

But just how much new government spending is required? Note that the economy is operating $100 billion below its full-employment output, but the horizontal distance between AD_1 and AD_2 is $200 billion. This gap between AD_1 and AD_2 is indicated by the dotted line between points E_1 and X. This means that the aggregate demand curve must be shifted to the right by $200 billion. But it is not necessary to increase government spending by this amount. The following formula can be used to compute the amount of additional government spending required to shift the aggregate demand curve rightward and establish a new full-employment real GDP equilibrium:

Initial change in government spending (ΔG) × spending multiplier = change in aggregate demand (total spending)

Spending multiplier (SM)

The ratio of the change in real GDP to an initial change in any component of aggregate expenditures, including consumption, investment, government spending, and net exports. As a formula, spending multiplier equals $1/(1 - MPC)$ or $1/MPS$.

The spending multiplier (SM) in the formula amplifies the amount of new government spending. The spending multiplier is the change in aggregate demand (total spending) resulting from an initial change in any component of aggregate demand, including consumption, investment, government spending, and net exports. Assume the MPC is 0.75, and therefore the value for the spending multiplier in our example is 4. The next section explains the algebra behind the spending multiplier so our example can be solved:

$$\Delta G \times 4 = \$200 \text{ billion}$$
$$\Delta G = \$50 \text{ billion}$$

Note that the Greek letter Δ (delta) means "a change in." Thus, it takes $50 billion worth of new government spending to shift the aggregate demand curve to the right by $200 billion. As described in the previous chapter (Exhibit 6), bottlenecks occur throughout the upward-sloping range of the AS curve. This means prices rise as production increases in response to greater aggregate demand. Returning to Exhibit 2, you can see that $50 billion worth of new government spending shifts aggregate demand from AD_1 to AD_2. As a result, firms increase output upward along the aggregate supply curve, AS, and total spending moves upward

EXHIBIT 2 · Using Government Spending to Combat a Recession

The economy in this exhibit is in recession at equilibrium point E_1 on the intermediate range of the aggregate supply curve, AS. The price level is 150, with an output level of $6 trillion real GDP. To reach the full-employment output of $6.1 trillion in real GDP, the aggregate demand curve must be shifted to the right by $200 billion real GDP, measured by the horizontal distance between point E_1 on curve AD_1 and point X on curve AD_2. The necessary increase in aggregate demand from AD_1 to AD_2 can be accomplished by increased government spending. Given a spending multiplier of 4, a $50 billion increase in government spending brings about the required $200 billion rightward shift in the aggregate demand curve, and equilibrium in the economy changes from E_1 to E_2. Note that the equilibrium real GDP changes by $100 billion and not by the full amount by which the aggregate demand curve shifts horizontally.

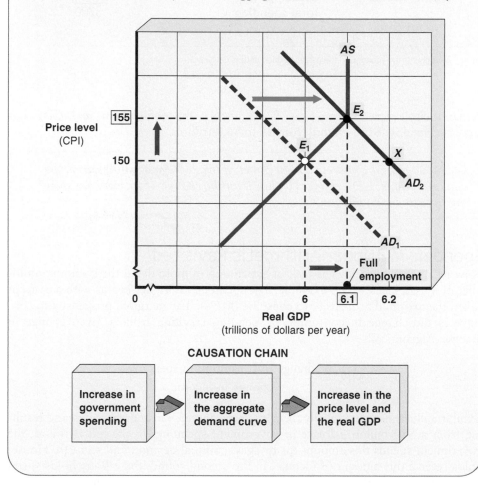

along aggregate demand curve AD_2. This adjustment mechanism moves the economy to a new equilibrium at E_2, with full employment, a higher price level of 155, and a real GDP of $6.1 trillion per year. At point E_2 the economy experiences *demand-pull inflation*. And here is the important point: Although the aggregate

EXHIBIT 3		The Spending Multiplier Effect
Round	Component of Total Spending	New Consumption Spending
1	Government spending	$ 50
2	Consumption	38
3	Consumption	29
4	Consumption	22
.	.	.
.	.	.
.	.	.
All other rounds	Consumption	61
	Total spending	$200

Note: All amounts are rounded to the nearest billion dollars per year.

demand curve has increased by $200 billion, the equilibrium real GDP has increased by only $100 billion, from $6 to $6.1 trillion.

> **Conclusion** *In the intermediate segment of the aggregate supply curve, the equilibrium real GDP changes by less than the change in government spending times the spending multiplier.*

Spending Multiplier Arithmetic Revisited[1]

Now let's pause to tackle the task of explaining in more detail the spending multiplier of 4 used in the above example. The spending multiplier begins with a concept called the marginal propensity to consume (*MPC*). The marginal propensity to consume is the change in consumption spending resulting from a given change in income. Algebraically,

Marginal propensity to consume (*MPC*)

The change in consumption spending resulting from a given change in income.

$$MPC = \frac{\text{change in consumption spending}}{\text{change in income}}$$

Exhibit 3 illustrates numerically the cumulative increase in aggregate demand resulting from a $50 billion increase in government spending. In the initial round, the government spends this amount for bridges, national defense, and so forth. Households receive this amount of income. In the second round, these households spend $38 billion (0.75 × $50 billion) on houses, cars, groceries, and other products. In the third round, the incomes of realtors, autoworkers, grocers, and others are boosted by $38 billion, and they spend $29 billion (0.75 × $38 billion). Each round

---

1. This section duplicates material presented earlier in the chapters titled "The Keynesian Model" and "The Keynesian Model in Action." The reason for repeating this material is that an instructor may choose to skip the Keynesian model presented in these two chapters.

of spending creates income for consumption re-spending in a downward spiral throughout the economy in smaller and smaller amounts until the total level of aggregate demand rises by an extra $200 billion.

> **Conclusion** *Any initial change in spending by the government, households, or firms creates a chain reaction of further spending, which causes a greater cumulative change in aggregate demand.*

You might recognize from algebra that the spending multiplier effect is a process based on an *infinite geometric series.* The formula for the sum of such a series of numbers is the initial number times $1/(1 - r)$, where r is the ratio that relates the numbers. Using this formula, the sum (total spending) is calculated as $50 billion $(\Delta G) \times [1/(1 - 0.75)] = 200 billion. By simply defining r in the infinite series formula as *MPC*, the spending multiplier for aggregate demand is expressed as

$$\text{Spending multiplier} = \frac{1}{1 - MPC}$$

Aplying this formula to our example:

$$\text{Spending multiplier} = \frac{1}{1 - 0.75} = \frac{1}{0.25} = 4$$

If households spend a portion of each extra dollar of income, then the remaining portion of each dollar is saved. The marginal propensity to save (*MPS*) is the change in saving resulting from a given change in income. Therefore:

$$MPC + MPS = 1$$

rewritten as

$$MPS = 1 - MPC$$

Hence, the above spending multiplier formula can be rewritten as

$$\text{Spending multiplier} = \frac{1}{MPS}$$

Since *MPS* and *MPC* are related, the size of the multiplier depends on the size of the *MPC*. What will the result be if people spend 80 percent or 33 percent of each dollar of income instead of 50 percent? If the *MPC* increases (decreases), consumers spend a larger (smaller) share of each additional dollar of output/income in each round, and the size of the multiplier increases (decreases). Exhibit 4 lists the multiplier for different values of *MPC* and *MPS*. Economists use real-world macroeconomic data to estimate a more complex multiplier than the simple multiplier formula developed in this chapter. Their estimates of the long run real-world *MPC* range from 0.80 to 0.90. An *MPC* of 0.50 is used in the above examples for simplicity.

Marginal propensity to save (*MPS*)

The change in saving resulting from a given change in income.

EXHIBIT 4	Relationship between *MPC*, *MPS*, and the Spending Multiplier		
(1) **Marginal Propensity to Consume** **(*MPC*)**	**(2)** **Marginal Propensity to Save** **(*MPS*)**	**(3)** **Spending Multiplier**
0.90	0.10	10
0.80	0.20	5
0.75	0.25	4
0.67	0.33	3
0.50	0.50	2
0.33	0.67	1.5

CHECKPOINT

What Is the *MPC* for Uncle Sam's Stimulus Package?

Assume there is concern that the economy is heading into a recession, and a stimulus package of $170 billion is passed by the federal government. The administration predicts that this measure will provide a $850 billion boost to GDP this year because consumers will spend their extra cash on plasma televisions and other items. For this amount of stimulus, what is the established value of *MPC* used in this forecast?

Cutting Taxes to Combat a Recession

Another expansionary fiscal policy intended to increase aggregate demand and restore full employment calls for the government to cut taxes. Let's return to point E_1 in Exhibit 2. As before, the problem is to shift the aggregate demand curve to the right by $200 billion. But this time, instead of a $50 billion increase in government spending, assume Congress votes for a $50 billion tax cut. How does this cut in taxes affect aggregate demand? First, *disposable personal income* (take-home pay) increases by $50 billion—the amount of the tax reduction. Second, once again assuming the *MPC* is 0.75, the increase in disposable personal income induces new consumption spending of $38 billion (0.75 × $50 billion). Thus, a cut in taxes triggers a multiplier process similar to, but smaller than, the spending multiplier.

Exhibit 5 demonstrates that a tax reduction adds less to aggregate demand than does an equal increase in government spending. Column 1 reproduces the effect of increasing government spending by $50 billion, and column 2 gives for comparison the effect of lowering taxes by $50 billion. Note that the only difference between increasing government spending and cutting taxes by the same amount is the impact in the initial round. The reason is that a tax cut injects zero new spending into the economy because the government has purchased no new goods and services.

EXHIBIT 5   Comparison of the Spending and Tax Multipliers

Round	Component of Total Spending	Increase in aggregate demand from	
		(1) $50 billion Increase in Government Spending ($+\Delta G$)	(2) $50 billion Cut in Taxes ($-\Delta T$)
1	Government spending	$ 50	$ 0
2	Consumption	38	38
3	Consumption	29	29
4	Consumption	22	22
·	·	·	·
·	·	·	·
·	·	·	·
All other rounds	Consumption	<u>61</u>	<u>61</u>
	Total spending	$200	$150

Note: All amounts are rounded to the nearest billion dollars per year.

The effect of a tax reduction in round 2 is that people spend a portion of the $50 billion boost in after-tax income from the tax cut introduced in round 1. Subsequent rounds in the tax multiplier chain generate a cumulative increase in consumption expenditures that totals $150 billion. Comparing the total changes in aggregate demand in columns 1 and 2 of Exhibit 4 leads to the following:

> **Conclusion** *A tax cut has a smaller multiplier effect on aggregate demand than an equal increase in government spending.*

The tax multiplier can be computed by using a formula and the information from column 2 of Exhibit 5. The tax multiplier is the change in aggregate demand (total spending) resulting from an initial change in taxes. Mathematically, the tax multiplier is given by this formula:

$$\text{Tax multiplier} = 1 - \text{spending multiplier}$$

Tax multiplier
The change in aggregate demand (total spending) resulting from an initial change in taxes. As a formula, tax multiplier equals 1 − spending multiplier.

Returning to Exhibit 2, the tax multiplier formula can be used to see how large a tax cut is needed to shift the aggregate demand curve rightward by $200 billion and restore full employment. Applying the formula given above and a spending multiplier of 4 yields a tax multiplier of −3. Note that the sign of the tax multiplier is always negative. Thus, a $66.6 billion tax cut is needed to shift the aggregate demand curve rightward by $200 billion and restore full-employment equilibrium at point E_2. Mathematically,

$$\text{Change in taxes } (\Delta T) \times \text{tax multiplier} = \text{change in aggregate demand}$$
$$\Delta T \times -3 = \$200 \text{ billon}$$
$$\Delta T = -\$66.6 \text{ billon}$$

A word of warning concerning the above analysis: In reality, the assumption that the *MPC* remains unchanged in response to a tax cut may be invalid. In 1964, Congress enacted President Kennedy's tax-cut proposal. The tax multiplier worked, and consumer spending lifted the economy out of a recession. On the other hand, in 1975, President Gerald Ford persuaded Congress to reduce income taxes to help increase aggregate demand during a recession. This time, however, the size of the tax multiplier fell because consumers reduced their *MPC*. This occurred because people saved much of the tax cut, rather than spending it. As a result, the anticipated boost to aggregate demand did not materialize.

Early in 2001, the United States experienced a recession that ended the longest economic expansion in U.S. history. In response, President Bush and Congress agreed to send out about $40 billion in tax rebates and phase in new lower marginal rates in coming years. In 2003, the personal income tax rate reductions scheduled for later years by the 2001 tax cut law were accelerated. Again, the key to the amount of real GDP growth depends on the size of the *MPC*, and in turn the tax multiplier. What proportion of the tax cut is spent for consumption? The answer means the difference between a deeper or milder recession, as well as the speed of recovery.

Using Fiscal Policy to Combat Inflation

So far, Keynesian expansionary fiscal policy, born of the Great Depression, has been presented as the cure for an economic downturn. Contractionary fiscal policy, on the other hand, can serve in the fight against inflation. Exhibit 6 shows an economy operating at point E_1 on the classical range of the aggregate supply curve, *AS*. Hence, this economy is producing the full-employment output of $6.1 trillion real GDP, and the price level is 160. In this situation, any increase in aggregate demand only causes inflation, while real GDP remains unchanged.

Suppose Congress and the president decide to use fiscal policy to reduce the CPI from 160 to 155 because they fear the wrath of voters suffering from the consequences of inflation. Although a fall in consumption, investment, or net exports might do the job, Congress and the president may be unwilling to wait, and they prefer taking direct action by cutting government spending. Given a marginal propensity to consume of 0.75, the spending multiplier is 4. As shown by the horizontal distance between point E_1 on AD_1 and point E' on AD_2 in Exhibit 6, aggregate demand must be decreased by $100 billion in order to shift the aggregate demand curve from AD_1 to AD_2 and establish equilibrium at E_2, with a price level of 155. Mathematically,

$$\Delta G \times 4 - -\$100 \text{ billion}$$
$$\Delta G = -\$25 \text{ billion}$$

Using the above formula, a $25 billion cut in real government spending would cause a $100 billion decrease in the aggregate demand curve from AD_1 to AD_2. The result is a temporary excess aggregate supply of $100 billion, measured by the distance

EXHIBIT 6   Using Fiscal Policy to Combat Inflation

The economy in this exhibit is in equilibrium at point E_1 on the classical range of the aggregate supply curve, AS. The price level is 160, and the economy is operating at the full-employment output of $6.1 trillion real GDP. To reduce the price level to 155, the aggregate demand curve must be shifted to the left by $100 billion, measured by the horizontal distance between point E_1 on curve AD_1 and point E' on curve AD_2. One way this can be done is by decreasing government spending. With MPC equal to 0.75, and therefore a spending multiplier of 4, a $25 billion decrease in government spending results in the needed $100 billion leftward shift in the aggregate demand curve. As a result, the economy reaches equilibrium at point E_2, and the price level falls from 160 to 155, while real output remains unchanged at full capacity.

An identical decrease in the aggregate demand curve can be obtained by a hike in taxes. A $33.3 billion tax increase works through a multiplier of 3 and provides the needed $100 billion decrease in the aggregate demand curve from AD_1 to AD_2.

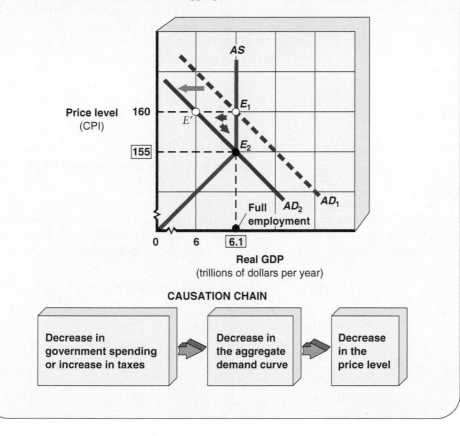

from E' to E_1. As explained in Exhibit 5 of the previous chapter, the economy follows classical theory and moves downward along AD_2 to a new equilibrium at E_2. Consequently, inflation cools with no change in the full-employment real GDP.

Another approach to the inflation problem would be for Congress and the president to raise taxes. Although tax increases are often considered political suicide, let's suppose Congress calculates just the correct amount of a tax hike required to reduce aggregate demand by $100 billion. Assuming a spending multiplier of 4, the tax multiplier is −3. Therefore, a $33.3 billion tax hike provides the necessary $100 billion leftward shift in the aggregate demand curve from AD_1 to AD_2. As a result, the desired equilibrium change from E_1 to E_2 is achieved, and the price level drops from 160 to 155 at the full-employment output of $6.1 trillion. Mathematically,

$$\Delta T \times -3 = -\$100 \text{ billion}$$
$$\Delta T = \$33.3 \text{ billion}$$

The Balanced Budget Multiplier

The analysis of Keynesian discretionary fiscal policy presented in the previous section supposes the federal government selects a change in *either* government spending or taxes as a remedy for recession or inflation. However, a controversial fiscal policy requires the government to match, or "balance," any new spending with new taxes. Understanding the impact on the economy of this fiscal policy requires derivation of the balanced budget multiplier. The balanced budget multiplier is an equal change in government spending and taxes, which changes aggregate demand by the amount of the change in government spending. Expressed as a formula,

Balanced budget multiplier

An equal change in government spending and taxes, which changes aggregate demand by the amount of the change in government spending.

Cumulative change in aggregate demand (ΔAD)
= government spending multiplier effect
+ tax multiplier effect

rewritten as

Cumulative change in aggregate demand (ΔAD)
= (initial change in government spending × spending multiplier)
+ (initial change in taxes × tax multiplier)

To see how the balanced budget multiplier works, suppose Congress enacts a $1 billion increase in government spending for highways and it finances these purchases with a $1 billion increase in gasoline taxes. Mathematically,

$$\Delta AD = \left(\$1 \text{ billion} \times \frac{1}{1 - MPC} \right) + \left(\$1 \text{ billion} \times 1 - \frac{1}{1 - MPC} \right)$$
$$= \left(\$1 \text{ billion} \times \frac{1}{1 - 0.75} \right) + \left(\$1 \text{ billion} \times 1 - \frac{1}{1 - 0.75} \right)$$
$$= (\$1 \text{ billion} \times 4) + (\$1 \text{ billion} \times -3)$$
$$= \$4 \text{ billion} - \$3 \text{ billion}$$
$$= \$1 \text{ billion}$$

Hence, the balanced budget multiplier is always equal to 1, and the cumulative change in aggregate demand is $1 billion—*the amount of the initial change in government spending.*

Conclusion *Regardless of the MPC, the net effect on the economy of an equal initial increase (decrease) in government spending and taxes is an increase (decrease) in aggregate demand equal to the initial increase (decrease) in government spending.*

CHECKPOINT

Walking the Balanced Budget Tightrope

Suppose the president proposes a $16 billion economic stimulus package intended to create jobs. A major criticism of this new spending proposal is that it is not matched by tax increases. Assume the U.S. economy is below full employment and Congress has passed a law requiring that any increase in spending be matched or balanced by an equal increase in taxes. The *MPC* is 0.75, and aggregate demand must be increased by $20 billion to reach full employment. Will the economy reach full employment if Congress increases spending by $16 billion and increases taxes by the same amount?

Automatic Stabilizers

Unlike discretionary fiscal policy, automatic stabilizers are policy tools built into the federal budget that help fight unemployment and inflation, while spending and tax laws remain unchanged. Automatic stabilizers are federal expenditures and tax revenues that automatically change levels in order to stabilize an economic expansion or contraction. Automatic stabilizers are sometimes referred to as *nondiscretionary fiscal policy*. Exhibit 7 illustrates the influence of automatic stabilizers on the economy. The downward-sloping line, *G*, represents federal government expenditures, including such *transfer payments* as unemployment compensation, Medicaid, and welfare. This line falls as real GDP rises. When the economy expands, unemployment falls, and government spending for unemployment compensation, welfare, and other transfer payments decreases. During a downturn, people lose their jobs, and government spending automatically increases because unemployed individuals become eligible for unemployment compensation and other transfer payments.

The direct relationship between tax revenues and real GDP is shown by the upward-sloping line, *T*. During an expansion, jobs are created, unemployment falls, and workers earn more income and therefore pay more taxes. Thus, income tax collections automatically vary directly with the growth in real GDP.

We begin the analysis of automatic stabilizers with a balanced federal budget. Federal spending, *G*, is equal to tax collections, *T*, and the economy is in equilibrium at $6 trillion real GDP. Now assume consumer optimism soars and a spending spree increases the consumption component (*C*) of total spending. As a result, the economy moves to a new equilibrium at $8 trillion real GDP. The rise in real GDP creates more jobs and higher tax collections. Consequently, taxes rise to $1,000 billion on line *T*, and the vertical distance between lines *T* and *G* represents a federal budget surplus of $500 billion. A budget surplus occurs when government revenues exceed government expenditures in a given time period.

Now begin again with the economy at $6 trillion in Exhibit 7, and let's change the scenario. Assume that business managers lower their profit expectations. Their revised outlook causes business executives to become pessimistic, so they cut investment spending (*I*), causing aggregate demand to decline. The corresponding decline in real GDP from $6 trillion to $4 trillion causes tax revenues to fall from $750 billion to $500 billion on line *T*. The combined effect of the rise in government spending and the fall in taxes creates a budget deficit. A budget deficit occurs when government expenditures exceed government revenues in a given time period.

Automatic stabilizers
Federal expenditures and tax revenues that automatically change levels in order to stabilize an economic expansion or contraction; sometimes referred to as *nondiscretionary fiscal policy*.

Budget surplus
A budget in which government revenues exceed government expenditures in a given time period.

Budget deficit
A budget in which government expenditures exceed government revenues in a given time period.

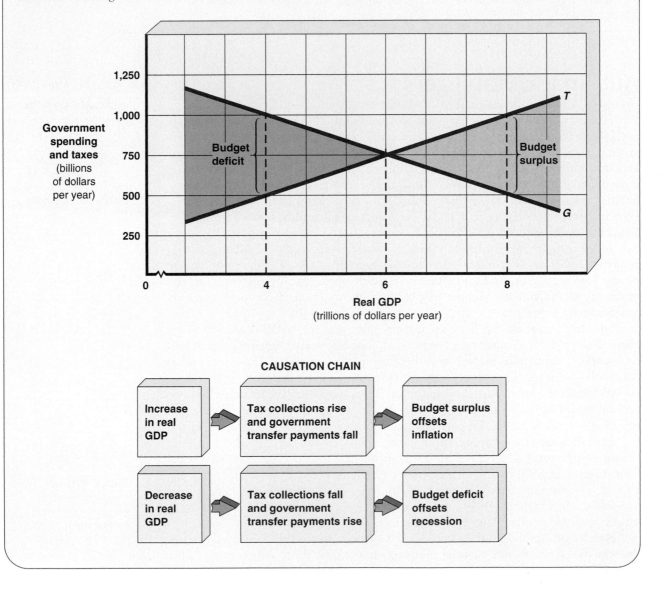

EXHIBIT 7   Automatic Stabilizers

Federal government spending varies inversely with real GDP and is represented by the downward-sloping line, G. Taxes, in contrast, vary directly with real GDP and are represented by the upward-sloping line, T. This means government spending for welfare and other transfer payments declines and tax collections rise as real GDP rises. Thus, if real GDP falls below $6 trillion, the budget deficit rises automatically. The size of the budget deficit is shown by the vertical distance between lines G and T. This budget deficit assists in offsetting a recession because it stimulates aggregate demand. Conversely, when real GDP rises above $6 trillion, a federal budget surplus increases automatically and assists in offsetting inflation.

CAUSATION CHAIN

Increase in real GDP → Tax collections rise and government transfer payments fall → Budget surplus offsets inflation

Decrease in real GDP → Tax collections fall and government transfer payments rise → Budget deficit offsets recession

The vertical distance between lines G and T at $4 trillion real GDP illustrates a federal budget deficit of $500 billion.

The key feature of automatic stabilization is that it "leans against the prevailing wind." In short, changes in federal spending and taxes moderate changes in aggregate demand. When the economy expands, the fall in government spending for transfer payments and the rise in the level of taxes result in a budget surplus. As the budget surplus grows, people send more money to Washington, which applies braking power against further increases in real GDP. When the economy contracts, the rise in government spending for transfer payments and the fall in the level of taxes yield a budget deficit. As the budget deficit grows, people receive more money from Washington to spend, which slows further decreases in real GDP.

> **Conclusion** *Automatic stabilizers assist in offsetting a recession when real GDP falls and in offsetting inflation when real GDP expands.*

Supply-Side Fiscal Policy

The focus so far has been on fiscal policy that affects the macro economy solely through the impact of government spending and taxation on aggregate demand. Supply-side economists, whose intellectual roots are in classical economics, argue that *stagflation* in the 1970s was the result of the federal government's failure to follow the theories of supply-side fiscal policy. Supply-side fiscal policy emphasizes government policies that increase aggregate supply in order to achieve long-run growth in real output, full employment, and a lower price level. Supply-side policies became an active economic idea with the election of Ronald Reagan as president in 1980. As discussed in the previous chapter, the U.S. economy in the 1970s experienced high rates of both inflation and unemployment. Stagflation aroused concern about the ability of the U.S. economy to generate long-term advances in the standard of living. This set the stage for a new macroeconomic policy.

Suppose the economy is initially at E_1 in Exhibit 8(a), with a CPI of 150 and an output of \$4 trillion real GDP. The economy is experiencing high unemployment, so the goal is to achieve full employment by increasing real GDP to \$6 trillion. As described earlier in this chapter, the federal government might follow Keynesian expansionary fiscal policy and shift the aggregate demand curve rightward from AD_1 to AD_2. Higher government spending or lower taxes operate through the multiplier effect and cause this increase in aggregate demand. The good news from such a demand-side fiscal policy prescription is that the economy moves toward full employment, but the bad news is that the price level rises. In this case, *demand-pull inflation* would cause the price level to rise from 150 to 200.

Exhibit 8(b) represents the supply-siders' alternative to Keynesian fiscal policy. Again, suppose the economy is initially in equilibrium at E_1. Supply-side economists argue that the federal government should adopt policies that shift the aggregate supply curve rightward from AS_1 to AS_2. An increase in aggregate supply would move the economy to E_2 and achieve the full-employment level of real GDP. Under supply-side theory, there is an additional bonus to full employment. Instead of rising as in Exhibit 8(a), the price level in Exhibit 8(b) falls from 150 to 100. Comparing the two graphs in Exhibit 8, you can see that the supply-siders have a better theoretical case than proponents of demand-side fiscal policy when both inflation and unemployment are concerns.

Note the causation chain under each graph in Exhibit 8. The demand-side fiscal policy options are from column 1 of Exhibit 1 in this chapter, and the supply-side policy alternatives are similar to Exhibit 9 in the previous chapter. For supply-side economics to be effective, the government must implement policies that increase the

Supply-side fiscal policy

A fiscal policy that emphasizes government policies that increase aggregate supply in order to achieve long-run growth in real output, full employment, and a lower price level.

EXHIBIT 8   Keynesian Demand-Side versus Supply-Side Effects

In Part (a), assume an economy begins in equilibrium at point E_1, with a price level of 150 and a real GDP of $4 trillion. To boost real output and employment, Keynesian economists prescribe that the federal government raise government spending or cut taxes. By following such demand-side policies, the policymakers work through the multiplier effect and shift the aggregate demand curve from AD_1 to AD_2. As a result, the equilibrium changes to E_2, where real GDP rises to $6 trillion, but the price level also rises to 200. Hence, full employment has been achieved at the expense of higher inflation.

The initial situation for the economy at point E_1 in Part (b) is identical to that shown in Part (a). However, supply-siders offer a different fiscal policy prescription than the Keynesians. Using some combination of cuts in resource prices, technological advances, tax cuts, subsidies, and regulation reduction, supply-side fiscal policy shifts the aggregate supply curve from AS_1 to AS_2. As a result, the equilibrium in the economy changes to E_2, and real GDP increases to $6 trillion, just as in Part (a). The advantage of the supply-side stimulus over the demand-side stimulus is that the price level falls to 100, rather than rising to 200.

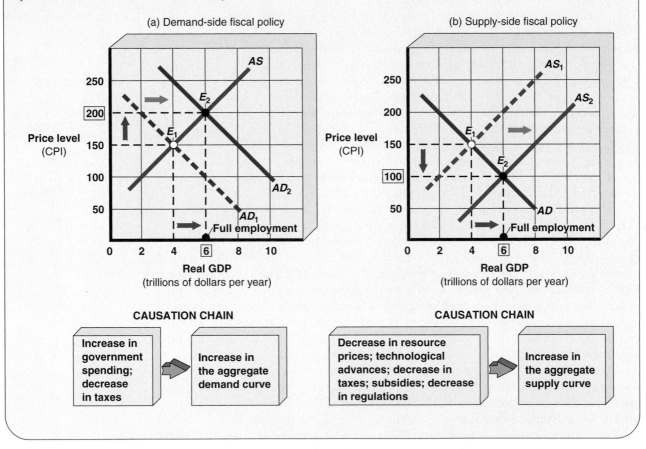

total output that firms produce at each possible price level. An increase in aggregate supply can be accomplished by some combination of cuts in resource prices, technological advances, subsidies, and reductions in government taxes and government regulations.

Although a laundry list of supply-side policies was advocated during the Reagan administration, the most familiar policy action taken was the tax cuts implemented in 1981. By reducing tax rates on wages and profits, the Reagan administration

EXHIBIT 9 — How Supply-Side Fiscal Policies Affect Labor Markets

Begin with equilibrium in the labor market at point E_1. Here the intersection of the labor supply and demand curves determines a wage rate of W_1 and L_1 hours of labor per year. By lowering tax rates, supply-side fiscal policies increase net after-tax earnings. This extra incentive causes workers to provide additional hours of labor per year. As a result, the labor supply curve increases and establishes a new equilibrium at point E_2. The new wage rate paid by employers falls to W_2, and they use more labor hours per year, L_2.

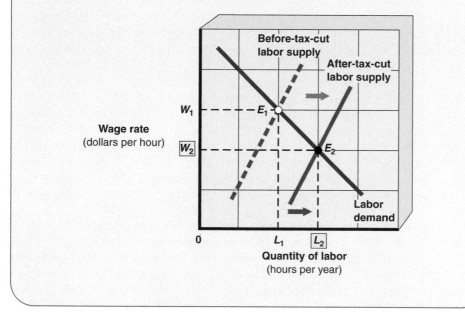

Wage rate (dollars per hour)

Before-tax-cut labor supply

After-tax-cut labor supply

Labor demand

Quantity of labor (hours per year)

sought to increase the aggregate supply of goods and services at any price level. However, tax cuts are a Keynesian policy intended to increase aggregate demand, so supply-siders must have a different view of the impact of tax cuts on the economy. To explain these different views of tax cuts, let's begin by stating that both Keynesians and supply-siders agree that tax cuts increase disposable personal income. In Keynesian economics, this boost in disposable personal income works through the *tax multiplier* to increase aggregate demand, as shown earlier in Exhibit 5. Supply-side economists argue instead that changes in disposable income affect the incentive to supply work, save, and invest.

Consider how a supply-side tax cut influences the labor market. Suppose supply and demand in the labor market are initially in equilibrium at point E_1 in Exhibit 9. Before a cut in personal income tax rates, the equilibrium hourly wage rate is W_1, and workers supply L_1 hours of labor per year at this wage rate. When the tax rates are cut, supply-side theory predicts the labor supply curve will shift rightward and establish a new equilibrium at E_2. The rationale is that an increase in the after-tax wage rate gives workers the incentive to work more hours per year. Those in the labor force will want to work longer hours and take fewer vacations. And because Uncle Sam takes a smaller bite out of workers' paychecks, many of those not already in the labor force will now supply their labor. As a result of the increase in the labor

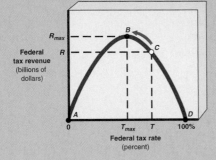

Federal tax revenue (billions of dollars)

R_{max}

R

Federal tax rate (percent)

T_{max} T 100%

Supply-side economics became popular during the presidential campaign of 1980. This fiscal policy prescription gained prominence after supply-side economist Arthur Laffer, using a paper napkin, explained what has come to be known as the Laffer curve to a journalist at a restaurant in Washington, D.C. The Laffer curve is a graph depicting the relationship between tax rates and total tax revenues. As shown in the figure, the hypothetical Laffer curve can be drawn with the federal tax rate on the horizontal axis and tax revenue on the vertical axis. The idea behind this curve is that the federal tax rate affects the incentive for people to work, save, invest, and produce, which in turn influences tax revenue. As the tax rate climbs, Laffer and other supply-siders argue that the erosion of incentives shrinks national income and total tax collections.

Here is how the Laffer curve works. Suppose the federal government sets the federal income tax rate at zero (point A). At a zero income tax rate, people have the maximum incentive to produce, and optimum national income would be earned, but there is zero tax revenue for Uncle Sam. Now assume the federal government sets the income tax rate at the opposite extreme of 100 percent (point D). At a 100 percent confiscating income tax rate, people have no reason to work, produce, and earn income. People seek ways to reduce their tax liabilities by engaging in unreported or underground transactions or by not working at all. As a result, no tax revenue is collected by the Internal Revenue Service. Because the government confiscates all reported income, the incentive to work and produce is much less at a 100 percent tax rate than at a zero percent tax rate.

Because the federal government does not want to collect zero tax revenue, Congress sets the federal income tax rate between zero and 100 percent. Assuming that the income tax rate is related to tax revenue as depicted in the figure, maximum tax revenue, R_{max}, is collected at a tax rate of T_{max} (point B). Laffer argued that the federal income tax rate of T (point C) in 1981 exceeded T_{max} and the result would be tax revenue of R, which is below R_{max}. In Laffer's view, reducing the federal income tax rate leads to an increase in tax revenue because people would increase their work effort, saving, and investment and would reduce their attempts to avoid paying taxes. Thus, Laffer argued that a cut in federal income tax rates would unleash economic activity and boost tax revenues needed to reduce the federal budget deficit. President Reagan's belief in the Laffer curve was a major reason why he thought that the federal government could cut personal income tax rates and still balance the federal budget.

The Laffer curve remains a controversial part of supply-side economics. There is still considerable uncertainty about the shape of the Laffer curve and at what point—B, C, or otherwise—along the curve the U.S. economy is operating. Thus, the existence and the usefulness of the Laffer curve are a matter of dispute.

ANALYZE THE ISSUE

Compare the common perception of how a tax rate cut affects tax revenues with economist Laffer's theory.

Laffer curve

A graph depicting the relationship between tax rates and total tax revenues.

supply curve, the price of labor falls to W_2 per hour, and the equilibrium number of labor hours increases to L_2.

Supply-side tax cuts of the early 1980s also provided tax breaks that subsidized business investment. Tax credits were available for new equipment and plants and for research and development to encourage technological advances. The idea here

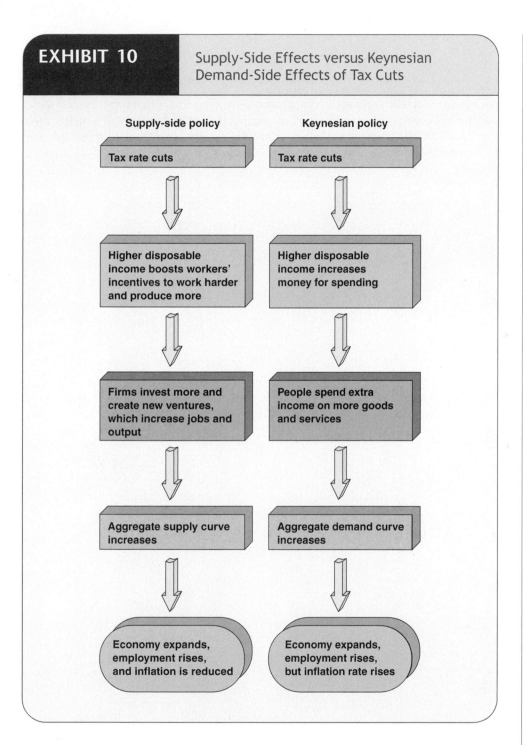

EXHIBIT 10   Supply-Side Effects versus Keynesian Demand-Side Effects of Tax Cuts

Supply-side policy

Tax rate cuts

Higher disposable income boosts workers' incentives to work harder and produce more

Firms invest more and create new ventures, which increase jobs and output

Aggregate supply curve increases

Economy expands, employment rises, and inflation is reduced

Keynesian policy

Tax rate cuts

Higher disposable income increases money for spending

People spend extra income on more goods and services

Aggregate demand curve increases

Economy expands, employment rises, but inflation rate rises

was to increase the nation's productive capacity by increasing the quantity and quality of capital. Consequently, the aggregate supply curve would shift rightward because businesses have an extra after-tax profit incentive to invest and produce more at each price level.

The idea of using tax cuts to shift the aggregate supply curve outward is controversial. Despite its logic, the Keynesians argue that the magnitude of any rightward shift in aggregate supply is likely to be small and occur only in the long run. They point out that it takes many years before tax cuts for business generate any change in actual plants and equipment or technological advances. Moreover, individuals can accept tax cuts with a "thank you, Uncle Sam" and not work longer or harder. Meanwhile, unless a reduction in government spending offsets the tax cuts, the effect will be a Keynesian increase in the aggregate demand curve and a higher price level. Exhibit 10 summarizes the important distinction between the supply-side and Keynesian theories on tax cut policy.

KEY CONCEPTS

Fiscal policy
Discretionary fiscal policy
Spending multiplier (*SM*)
Marginal propensity to consume (*MPC*)

Marginal propensity to save (*MPS*)
Tax multiplier
Balanced budget multiplier
Automatic stabilizers

Budget surplus
Budget deficit
Supply-side fiscal policy
Laffer curve

SUMMARY

- *Fiscal policy* is the use of government spending and taxes to stabilize the economy.
- *Discretionary fiscal policy* follows the Keynesian argument that the federal government should manipulate aggregate demand in order to influence the output, employment, and price levels in the economy. Discretionary fiscal policy requires new legislation to change either government spending or taxes in order to stabilize the economy.

Discretionary Fiscal Policies

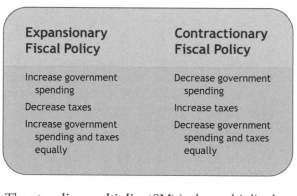

Expansionary Fiscal Policy	Contractionary Fiscal Policy
Increase government spending	Decrease government spending
Decrease taxes	Increase taxes
Increase government spending and taxes equally	Decrease government spending and taxes equally

- The *spending multiplier* (*SM*) is the multiplier by which an initial change in one component of aggregate demand, for example, government spending, alters aggregate demand (total spending) after an infinite number of spending cycles. Expressed as a formula, the spending multiplier = $1/(1 - MPC)$.
- *Expansionary fiscal policy* is a deliberate increase in government spending, a deliberate decrease in taxes, or some combination of these two options.

- *Contractionary fiscal policy* is a deliberate decrease in government spending, a deliberate increase in taxes, or some combination of these two options. Using either expansionary or contractionary fiscal policy, the government can shift the aggregate demand curve in order to combat recession, cool inflation, or achieve other macroeconomic goals.
- The *marginal propensity to consume* (*MPC*) is the change in consumption spending divided by the change in income.
- The *marginal propensity to save* (*MPS*) is the change in savings divided by the change in income.
- The *tax multiplier* is the change in aggregate demand (total spending) that result from an initial change in taxes after an infinite number of spending cycles. Expressed as a formula, the tax multiplier = 1 − spending multiplier.
- *Combating recession and inflation* can be accomplished by changing government spending or taxes. The total change in aggregate demand from a change in government spending is equal to the change in government spending times the spending multiplier. The total change in aggregate demand from a change in taxes is equal to the change in taxes times the tax multiplier.

Combating Recession

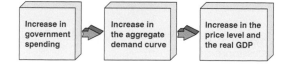

Combating Inflation

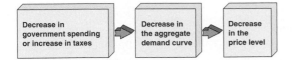

- The *balanced budget multiplier* is not neutral. A dollar of government spending increases real GDP more than a dollar cut in taxes. Thus, even though the government does not spend more than it collects in taxes, it is still stimulating the economy.
- A *budget surplus* occurs when government revenues exceed government expenditures. A *budget deficit* occurs when government expenditures exceed government revenues.
- *Automatic stabilizers* are changes in taxes and government spending that occur automatically in response to changes in the level of real GDP. The business cycle therefore creates braking power: A *budget surplus* slows an expanding economy; a *budget deficit* reverses a downturn in the economy.

Automatic Stabilizers

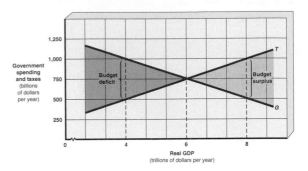

- According to *supply-side fiscal policy,* lower taxes encourage work, saving, and investment, which shift the aggregate supply curve rightward. As a result, output and employment increase without inflation.
- The *Laffer curve* represents the relationship between the income tax rate and the amount of income tax revenue collected by the government.

SUMMARY OF CONCLUSION STATEMENTS

- In the intermediate segment of the aggregate supply curve, the equilibrium real GDP changes by less than the change in government spending times the spending multiplier.
- Any initial change in spending by the government, households, or firms creates a chain reaction of further spending, which causes a greater cumulative change in aggregate demand.
- A tax cut has a smaller multiplier effect on aggregate demand than an equal increase in government spending.

- Regardless of the *MPC*, the net effect on the economy of an equal initial increase (decrease) in government spending and taxes is an increase (decrease) in aggregate demand equal to the initial increase (decrease) in government spending.
- Automatic stabilizers assist in offsetting a recession when real GDP falls and in offsetting inflation when real GDP expands.

STUDY QUESTIONS AND PROBLEMS

1. Explain how discretionary fiscal policy fights recession and inflation.

2. How does each of the following affect the aggregate demand curve?
   a.   Government spending increases.
   b.   The amount of taxes collected decreases.

3. In each of the following cases, explain whether the fiscal policy is expansionary, contractionary, or neutral.
   a.   The government decreases government spending.
   b.   The government increases taxes.
   c.   The government increases spending and taxes by an equal amount.

4. Why does a reduction in taxes have a smaller multiplier effect than an increase in government spending of an equal amount?

5. Suppose you are an economic adviser to the president and the economy needs a real GDP increase of $500 billion to reach full-employment equilibrium. If the marginal propensity to consume (MPC) is 0.75 and you are a Keynesian, by how much do you believe Congress must increase government spending to restore the economy to full employment?

6. Consider an economy that is operating at the full-employment level of real GDP. Assuming the MPC is 0.90, predict the effect on the economy of a $50 billion increase in government spending balanced by a $50 billion increase in taxes.

7. Why is a $100 billion increase in government spending for goods and services more expansionary than a $100 billion decrease in taxes?

8. What is the difference between discretionary fiscal policy and automatic stabilizers? How are federal budget surpluses and deficits affected by the business cycle?

9. Assume you are a supply-side economist who is an adviser to the president. If the economy is in recession, what would your fiscal policy prescription be?

10. Suppose Congress enacts a tax reform law and the average federal tax rate drops from 30 percent to 20 percent. Researchers investigate the impact of the tax cut and find that the income subject to the tax increases from $600 billion to $800 billion. The theoretical explanation is that workers have increased their work effort in response to the incentive of lower taxes. Is this a movement along the downward-sloping or the upward-sloping portion of the Laffer curve?

11. Indicate how each of the following would change either the aggregate demand curve or the aggregate supply curve.
    a. Expansionary fiscal policy
    b. Contractionary fiscal policy
    c. Supply-side economics
    d. Demand-pull inflation
    e. Cost-push inflation

For Online Exercises, go to the text Web site at www.cengage.com/economics/tucker.

CHECKPOINT ANSWERS ✓

What Is the *MPC* for Uncle Sam's Stimulus Package?

To calculate the value of the *MPC* required to increase real GDP (ΔY) by $850 billion from an increase in government spending (ΔG) of $170 billion, use this formula:

$$\Delta G \times \text{multiplier} = \Delta Y$$

where

$$\$170 \text{ billion} \times \text{multiplier} = \$850 \text{ billion}$$

Thus,

$$\text{Multiplier} = \frac{\$850 \text{ billion}}{\$170 \text{ billion}} = 5$$

Using Exhibit 6, if you said find that the *MPC* is 0.80, **YOU ARE CORRECT.**

Walking the Balanced Budget Tightrope

A $16 billion increase in government spending increases aggregate demand by $64 billion [government spending increase × spending multiplier, where the spending multiplier = 1/ (1 − MPC) = 1/0.25 = 4]. On the other hand, a $16 billion increase in taxes reduces aggregate demand by $48 billion (tax cut × tax multiplier, where the tax multiplier = 1 − spending multiplier = 1 − 4 = −3). Thus, the net effect of the spending multiplier and the tax multiplier is an increase in aggregate demand of $16 billion. If you said Congress has missed its goal of a $20 billion boost in aggregate demand by $4 billion and has not restored full employment, **YOU ARE CORRECT.**

PRACTICE QUIZ

For an explanation of the correct answers, please visit the tutorial at www.cengage. com/ economics/tucker.

1. Contractionary fiscal policy is deliberate government action to influence aggregate demand and the level of real GDP through
   a. expanding and contracting the money supply.
   b. encouraging business to expand or contract investment.
   c. regulating net exports.
   d. decreasing government spending or increasing taxes.

2. The spending multiplier is defined as
   a. 1/(1 − marginal propensity to consume).
   b. 1/(marginal propensity to consume).
   c. 1/(1 − marginal propensity to save).
   d. 1/(marginal propensity to consume + marginal propensity to save).

3. If the marginal propensity to consume (*MPC*) is 0.60, the value of the spending multiplier is
   a. 0.4.
   b. 0.6.
   c. 1.5.
   d. 2.5.

4. Assume the economy is in recession and real GDP is below full employment. The marginal propensity to consume (*MPC*) is 0.80, and the government increases spending by $500 billion. As a result, aggregate demand will rise by
   a. zero.
   b. $2,500 billion.
   c. more than $2,500 billion.
   d. less than $2,500 billion.

5. Mathematically, the value of the tax multiplier in terms of the marginal propensity to consume (*MPC*) is given by the formula
   a. *MPC* − 1.
   b. (*MPC* − 1)/*MPC*.
   c. 1/*MPC*.
   d. 1 − [1/(1 − *MPC*)].

6. Assume the marginal propensity to consume (*MPC*) is 0.75 and the government increases taxes by $250 billion. The aggregate demand curve will shift to the
   a. left by $1,000 billion.
   b. right by $1,000 billion.
   c. left by $750 billion.
   d. right by $750 billion.

7. If no fiscal policy changes are made, suppose the current aggregate demand curve will increase horizontally by $1,000 billion and cause inflation. If the marginal propensity to consume (*MPC*) is 0.80, federal policymakers could follow Keynesian economics and restrain inflation by decreasing
   a. government spending by $200 billion.
   b. taxes by $100 billion.
   c. taxes by $1,000 billion.
   d. government spending by $1,000 billion.

8. If no fiscal policy changes are implemented, suppose the future aggregate demand curve will exceed the current aggregate demand curve by $500 billion at any level of prices. Assuming the marginal propensity to consume (*MPC*) is 0.80, this increase in aggregate demand could be prevented by
   a. increasing government spending by $500 billion.
   b. increasing government spending by $140 billion.
   c. decreasing taxes by $40 billion.
   d. increasing taxes by $125 billion.

9. Suppose inflation is a threat because the current aggregate demand curve will increase by $600 billion at any price level. If the marginal propensity to consume (*MPC*) is 0.75, federal policymakers could follow Keynesian economics and restrain inflation by
   a. decreasing taxes by $600 billion.
   b. decreasing transfer payments by $200 billion.
   c. increasing taxes by $200 billion.
   d. increasing government spending by $150 billion.

10. If no fiscal policy changes are implemented, suppose the future aggregate demand curve will shift and exceed the current aggregate demand curve by $900 billion at any level of prices. Assuming the marginal propensity to consume (*MPC*) is 0.90, this increase in aggregate demand could be prevented by
    a. increasing government spending by $500 billion.
    b. increasing government spending by $140 billion.
    c. decreasing taxes by $40 billion.
    d. increasing taxes by $100 billion.

11. Which of the following is *not* an automatic stabilizer?
    a. Defense spending
    b. Unemployment compensation benefits
    c. Personal income taxes
    d. Welfare payments

12. Supply-side economics is most closely associated with
    a. Karl Marx.
    b. John Maynard Keynes.
    c. Milton Friedman.
    d. Ronald Reagan.

13. Which of the following statements is *true*?
    a. A reduction in tax rates along the downward-sloping portion of the Laffer curve would increase tax revenues.

b. According to supply-side fiscal policy, lower tax rates would shift the aggregate demand curve to the right, expanding the economy and creating some inflation.
c. The presence of automatic stabilizers tends to destabilize the economy.
d. To combat inflation, Keynesians recommend lower taxes and greater government spending.

14. The sum of the marginal propensity to consume (*MPC*) and the marginal propensity to save (*MPS*) always equals
    a. 1.
    b. 0.
    c. the interest rate.
    d. the marginal propensity to invest (*MPI*).

15. The marginal propensity to save is
    a. the change in saving induced by a change in consumption.
    b. (change in S) / (change in Y).
    c. $1 - MPC / MPC$.
    d. (change in $Y - bY$) / (change in Y).
    e. $1 - MPC$.

The Public Sector

I n the early 1980s, President Ronald Reagan adopted the Laffer curve theory that the federal government could cut tax rates and increase tax revenues. Critics said the result would be lower tax revenues. During the 2000 campaign for the Republican presidential nomination, Steve Forbes continued his attempt to win support for a flat tax, and George W. Bush advocated cutting individual marginal tax rates. However, President Bill Clinton said cutting taxes was not a good idea because ensuring the integrity of Social Security should come first. In 2001 and 2003, President George W. Bush signed laws that provided for phased-in cuts in the marginal tax rates, and he proposed increased spending for the war in Iraq and homeland defense. In 2004, Bush signed tax cut legislation for business and farmers. Critics argued that changing the tax structure while increasing spending would worsen the long-term federal budget outlook. And in 2008 John McCain and Barack Obama, as the presidential candidates, debated the issue of extending the Bush tax cuts beyond 2010.

These events illustrate the persistent real-world controversy surrounding fiscal policy. The previous chapter presented the theory behind fiscal policy. In this chapter, you will examine the practice of fiscal policy. Here the facts of taxation and government expenditures are clearly presented and placed in perspective. You can check, for example, the trend in federal taxes during the Reagan, Clinton, and both Bush administrations and compare the tax burden in the United States to that in other countries. And you will discover why the government uses different types of taxes and tax rates.

The final section of the chapter challenges the economic role of the public sector. Here you will learn a theory called *public choice,* which examines public sector decisions of politicians, government bureaucrats, voters, and special-interest groups.

Government Size and Growth

How big is the public sector in the United States? If we look at Exhibit 1, we see total government expenditures or outlays—including those of federal, state, and local governments—as a percentage of GDP for the 1929–2007 period. When we refer to *government expenditures*, we refer to more than the *government consumption expenditures and investment* (G) account used by national income accountants to calculate GDP (see Exhibit 3 in the chapter on GDP). Government expenditures, or outlays, equal government purchases plus *transfer payments*. Recall from the chapter on GDP that the government national income account (G) includes federal government spending for defense, highways, and education. Transfer payments, not in (G), include payments to persons entitled to welfare, Social Security, and unemployment benefits.

> **Government expenditures**
> Federal, state, and local government outlays for goods and services, including transfer payments.

As shown in Exhibit 1, total government expenditures skyrocketed as a percentage of GDP during World War II and then took a sharp plunge, but not to previous peacetime levels. Since 1950, total government expenditures have grown from about one-quarter of GDP to about one-third. In 2007, total government outlays were about 34 percent of GDP. The other side of the coin is that today the private sector's share of national output is approximately 66 percent of GDP. Note that in the 1990s, federal outlays decreased as a percentage of GDP, but this trend reversed after the recession and terrorist attacks in 2001.

Government Expenditures Patterns

Exhibit 2 shows program categories for federal government expenditures for the years 1970 and 2007. The largest category by far in the federal budget for 2007 was a category called *income security*. "Security" means these payments provide income to the elderly or disadvantaged, including Social Security, Medicare, unemployment compensation, public assistance (welfare), federal retirement, and disability benefits. These entitlements are transfer payments in the form of either direct cash payments or in-kind transfers that redistribute income among persons. In 2007, 44 percent of income security expenditures were spent for Social Security and 28 percent for Medicare.

The second largest category of federal government expenditures in 2007 was national defense. Note that the percentage of the federal budget spent for defense

EXHIBIT 1   The Growth of Government Expenditures as a Percentage of GDP in the United States, 1929–2007

The graph shows the growth of the federal, state, and local governments as measured by government expenditures for goods and services as a percentage of GDP since 1929. There was a dramatic rise in expenditures during World War II and a dramatic fall after the war, but not to previous peacetime levels. Taking account of all government outlays, including transfer payments, the government sector has grown from about one-quarter of GDP in 1950 to about one-third of GDP. After 2001, total government expenditures increased to about 34 percent of GDP.

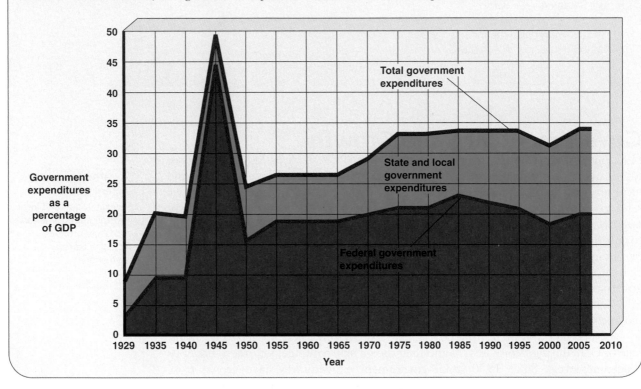

SOURCES: *Economic Report of the President*, 2008, http://www.gpo.access.gov/eop/, Table B-79; and Bureau of Economic Analysis, *National Income Accounts*, http://www.bea.gov/national/web/SelectTable.asp?Selected=Y, Tables 1.1.5 and 3.3.

declined from 40 percent in 1970 to 20 percent in 2007, while income security ("safety net") expenditures grew from 22 percent in 1970 to 49 percent in 2007. Hence, with a boost from an end to the Cold War, the dominant trend in federal government spending between 1970 and 2007 was an increase in the redistribution-of-income role of the federal government and a decrease in the portion of the budget spent for defense.

Federal expenditures for education and health were in third place in 2007, and net interest on the federal debt was in fourth place. Net interest paid is the interest on federal government borrowings minus the interest earned on federal government loans, and in 2007 this category of the budget was 9 percent. Thus, the federal government spent about the same proportion of the budget on financing its debt as on international affairs, veterans' benefits, agriculture, and transportation combined.

Finally, you need to be aware that the size and the growth of government are measured several ways. We could study *absolute* government spending rather than

EXHIBIT 2 — Federal Government Expenditures, 1970 and 2007

Between 1970 and 2007, income security became the largest category of federal expenditures. During the same period, national defense declined from the largest spending category to the second largest. Therefore, income security and national defense combined account for almost 70 percent of federal outlay in 2007.

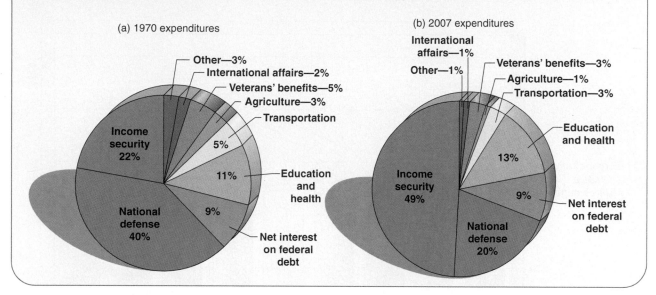

(a) 1970 expenditures

Other—3%
International affairs—2%
Veterans' benefits—5%
Agriculture—3%
Transportation
Income security 22%
5%
11% — Education and health
National defense 40%
9%
Net interest on federal debt

(b) 2007 expenditures

International affairs—1%
Other—1%
Veterans' benefits—3%
Agriculture—1%
Transportation—3%
Education and health
Income security 49%
13%
9%
National defense 20%
Net interest on federal debt

SOURCES: *Economic Report of the President*, 1975, Table C-65, p. 325; and *Economic Report of the President*, 2008, http://www.gpoaccess.gov/eop/, Table B-81.

percentages or compare the growth of spending after adjusting for inflation. Still another technique is to measure the proportion of the population that the public sector employs. Using any of these measurements confirms the conclusion reached from Exhibit 1:

> **Conclusion** *The government's share of total economic activity has generally increased since World War II ended in 1945. Most of the growth in combined government expenditures as a percentage of GDP reflects rapidly growing federal government transfer programs.*

Government Expenditures in Other Countries

In 2007, U.S. government spending for all levels as a percentage of GDP was lower than other advanced industrial countries. As shown in Exhibit 3, the governments of Sweden, France, Germany, and other countries spent a higher percentage of their GDPs than the federal, state, and local governments of the United States.

GLOBAL ECONOMICS

Financing Government Budgets

Where does the federal government obtain the funds to finance its outlays? Exhibit 4 tells the story. We find that the largest revenue source in 2007 was *individual income taxes* (45 percent), followed by *social insurance taxes* (34 percent), which

EXHIBIT 3	Government Expenditures in Other Countries, 2007

In 2007, the U.S. government was less of a spender than other advanced industrial countries. As shown in this exhibit, the governments of Sweden, France, Germany, and other countries spent a higher percentage of their GDPs than the federal, state, and local governments of the United States.

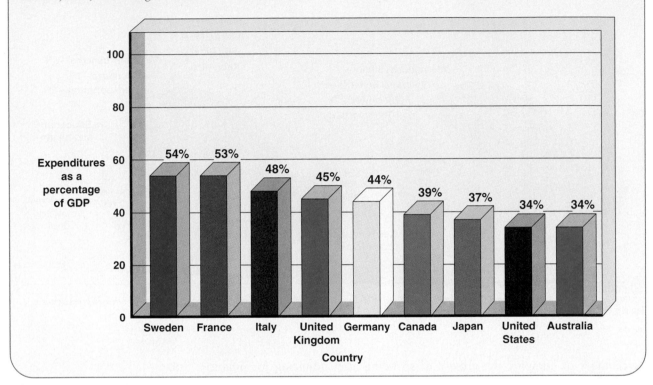

SOURCES: *OECD Economic Outlook* N. 82, December 2007, Annex Table 25, page 245.

include payroll taxes paid by employers and employees for Social Security, workers' compensation, and unemployment insurance. The third best revenue-getter was *corporate income taxes* (14 percent). An *excise tax* is a sales tax on the purchase of a particular good or service. Excise taxes contributed 3 percent of total tax receipts. The "Other" category includes receipts from such taxes as customs duties, estate taxes, and gift taxes.

GLOBAL ECONOMICS

The Tax Burden in Other Countries

Before turning our attention in the next section to the criteria for selecting which tax to impose, we must ask how burdensome overall taxation in the United States is. It may surprise you to learn that by international standards U.S. citizens are among the most lightly taxed people in the industrialized world. Exhibit 5 reveals that in 2007, the tax collector was clearly much more heavy-handed in most other advanced industrial countries based on the fraction of GDP paid in taxes. The Swedish, French, Italians, Germans, Canadians, Spanish, and British, for example, pay far higher taxes as a percentage of GDP than Americans. It should be noted that countries that tax

EXHIBIT 4 | Federal Government Receipts, 2007

In 2007, the largest source of revenue for the federal government was individual income taxes, and the second largest source was social insurance taxes.

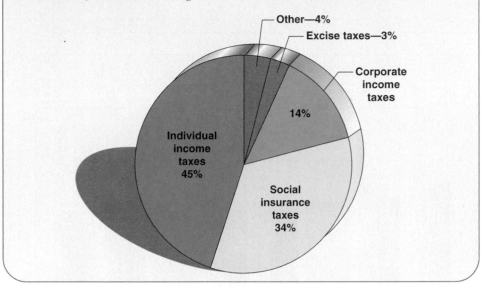

Other—4%

Excise taxes—3%

Corporate income taxes

14%

Individual income taxes 45%

Social insurance taxes 34%

SOURCES: *Economic Report of the President*, 2008, http://www.gpoaccess.gov/eop/, Table B-81.

more heavily also are expected to provide more public services—especially medical care—compared to the United States.

Another way to study the burden of taxation in the United States is to observe how it has changed over time. Exhibit 6 charts the growth of taxes as a percentage of GDP in the United States since 1929. Total government taxes, including federal, state, and local taxes, climbed from about 11 percent of GDP in 1929 to their highest level of 34 percent in 2000, and then fell to 32 percent in 2007. The exhibit also shows that in 2000, federal taxes as a percentage of GDP rose to a post-World War II high of 21 percent before falling to about 19 percent in 2007. Although federal taxes still take a larger share of GDP, there has been an upward trend in state and local government taxes as a percent of GDP. In 1950, the fraction was 7 percent, and in 2007 the fraction had grown to over 13 percent.

The Art of Taxation

Jean Baptiste Colbert, finance minister to King Louis XIV of France, once said, "The art of taxation consists of so plucking the goose as to obtain the largest amount of feathers while promoting the smallest amount of hissing." Each year with great zeal, members of Congress and other policymakers debate various ways of raising revenue without causing too much "hissing." As you will learn, the task is difficult because each kind of tax has a different characteristic. Government must decide which tax is "appropriate" based on two basic philosophies of fairness—benefits received and ability to pay.

EXHIBIT 5   The Tax Burden in Selected Countries, 2007

Americans were more lightly taxed in 2007 than the citizens of other advanced industrial countries. For example, the Swedes, French, Italians, Germans, Canadians, Spanish, and British pay higher taxes as a percentage of GDP.

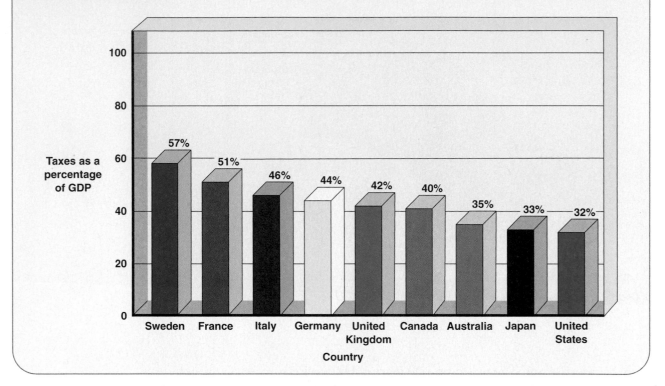

SOURCE: *OECD Economic Outlook* N. 82, December 2007, Annex Table 26, page 2.

The Benefits-Received Principle

What standard or guideline can we use to be sure everyone pays his or her "fair" share of taxes? One possibility is the benefits-received principle of taxation, which is the concept that those who benefit from government expenditures should pay the taxes that finance their benefits. The gasoline tax is an example of a tax that follows the *benefits-received principle*. The number of gallons of gasoline bought is a measure of the amount of highway services used, and the more gallons purchased, the greater the tax paid. Applying benefit-cost analysis, voters will approve additional highways only if the benefits they receive exceed the costs in gasoline taxes they must pay for highway construction and repairs.

Although the benefits-received principle of taxation is applicable to a private good like gasoline, the nature of *public goods* often makes it impossible to apply this principle. Recall from Chapter 4 that national defense is a public good, which users collectively consume. So how can we separate those who benefit from national defense and make them pay? We cannot, and there are other goods and services for which the benefits-received principle is inconsistent with societal goals. It would be foolish, for example, to ask families receiving food stamps to pay all the taxes required to finance their welfare benefits.

> **Benefits-received principle**
>
> The concept that those who benefit from government expenditures should pay the taxes that finance their benefits.

EXHIBIT 6 — The Growth of Taxes as a Percentage of GDP in the United States, 1929–2007

The graph shows the growth in federal, state, and local government taxes as a percentage of GDP since 1929. Total government taxes climbed from about 11 percent of GDP in 1929 to their highest level of 34 percent in 2000 before falling to 32 percent in 2007. In 2000, federal taxes as a percentage of GDP reached a post-World War II high of 21 percent before falling to 19 percent in 2007. State and local taxes have generally increased as a percentage of GDP since the 1950s.

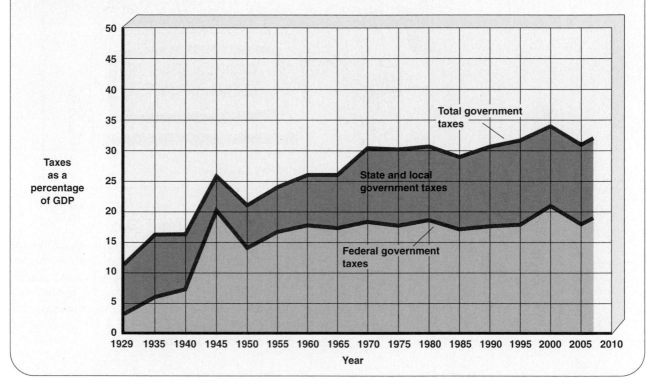

SOURCES: *Economic Report of the President*, 2008, http://www.bea.doc.gov/national/nipaweb/SelectTable.asp?Selected=Y, Table B-79; and *Bureau of Economic Analysis, National Income Accounts*, http://www.bea.doc.gov/national/nipaweb/SelectTable.asp?Selected=Y, Tables 1.1.5 and 3.3.

The Ability-to-Pay Principle

A second popular principle of fairness in taxation sharply contrasts with the benefits-received principle. The ability-to-pay principle of taxation is the concept that those who have higher incomes can afford to pay a greater proportion of their income in taxes, regardless of benefits received. Under this tax philosophy, the rich may send their children to private schools or use private hospitals, but they should bear a heavier tax burden because they are better able to pay. How could there possibly be a problem with such an approach? An individual who earns $200,000 per year should pay X more taxes than an individual who earns only $10,000 per year. The difficulty lies in determining exactly how much more the higher-income individual should pay in taxes to ensure he or she is paying a "fair" amount. Unfortunately, no scientific method can measure precisely what one's "ability" to pay taxes means in dollars or percentage of income. Nevertheless, in the U.S. economy, the ability-to-pay principle dominates the benefits-received principle.

> **Ability-to-pay principle**
>
> The concept that those who have higher incomes can afford to pay a greater proportion of their income in taxes, regardless of benefits received.

Where is the money I gave you last year?

Progressive, Regressive, and Proportional Taxes

As we have seen, governments raise revenues from various taxes, such as income taxes, sales taxes, excise taxes, and property taxes. For purposes of analysis, economists classify each of these taxes into three types of taxation—*progressive, regressive,* and *proportional.* The focus of these three classifications is the relationship between changes in the tax rates and increases or decreases in income. Income is the tax base because people pay taxes out of income, even though a tax is levied on property, such as land, buildings, automobiles, or furniture.

Progressive Taxes   Following the ability-to-pay principle, individual and corporate income taxes are progressive taxes. A progressive tax charges a higher percentage of income as income rises. For example, if a person earning $10,000 a year pays $1,500 in taxes, the *average* tax rate is 15 percent. If another person earns $100,000 a year and pays $28,000 in taxes, the average tax rate is 28 percent. This tax rate progressivity is the principle behind the federal and state income tax systems. Exhibit 8 illustrates the progressive nature of the federal income tax for a single person filing a 2005 tax return.

    Column 1 of Exhibit 7 lists the *taxable income* tax brackets. Taxable income is gross income minus the personal exemption and the standard deduction. The personal exemption and the standard deduction are adjusted each year so inflation does not push taxpayers into higher tax brackets. Column 2 shows the tax bill that a taxpayer at the upper income of each of the five lowest taxable income brackets must pay, and the figures in column 3 are the corresponding average tax rates. The average tax rate is the tax divided by the income:

$$\text{Average tax rate} = \frac{\text{total tax due}}{\text{total taxable income}}$$

Progressive tax

A tax that charges a higher percentage of income as income rises.

Average tax rate

The tax divided by the income.

| EXHIBIT 7 | Federal Individual Income Tax Rate Schedule for a Single Taxpayer, 2007 | | | | | |

(1) Taxable Income		(2) Tax*	(3) Average Tax Rate [(2)/(1)]	(4) Change in Taxable Income	(5) Change in Tax	(6) Marginal Tax Rate [(5)/(4)]
Over	But Not Over					
$ 0	$ 7,825	$ 782	10%	$ 7,825	$ 782	10%
7,825	31,850	4,386	14	24,025	3,604	15
31,850	77,100	15,699	20	45,250	11,313	25
77,100	160,850	39,149	24	83,750	23,450	28
160,850	349,700	101,470	29	188,850	62,321	33
349,700	...	...	...	...	...	35

* Tax calculated at the top of the taxable income brackets.
SOURCE: Internal Revenue Service, Publication 17, *Your Federal Income Tax*, 2007, http://www.irs.gov/publications/index.html, Tax Rate Schedules, p. 264.

Thus, at a taxable income of $31,850, the average tax rate is 14 percent ($4,386 divided by $31,850), and at $77,100, it is 20 percent ($15,699 divided by $77,100). A taxable income of over $349,700 is included to represent the upper-income bracket. As these figures indicate, our federal individual income tax is a progressive tax because the average tax rate rises as income increases.

Another key tax rate measure is the marginal tax rate, which is the fraction of additional income paid in taxes. The marginal tax rate formula is expressed as

> **Marginal tax rate**
> The fraction of additional income paid in taxes.

$$\text{Marginal tax rate} = \frac{\text{change in taxes due}}{\text{change in taxable income}}$$

Column 6 in Exhibit 7 computes the marginal tax rate for each federal tax bracket in the table. You can comprehend the marginal tax rate by observing in column 1 that when taxable income rises from $7,825 to $31,850 in the second lowest tax bracket, the tax rises from $782 to $4,386 in column 2. Column 4 reports this change in taxable income, and column 5 shows the change in the tax. The marginal tax rate in column 6 is therefore 15 percent ($3,604 divided by $24,025). Apply the same analysis when taxable income increases by $45,250 from $31,850 to $77,100 in the next bracket. An additional $11,313 is added to the $4,386 tax bill, so the marginal tax rate on this extra income is 25 percent ($11,313 divided by $45,250). Similar computations provide the marginal tax rates for the remaining taxable income brackets. The marginal tax rate is important because it determines how much a taxpayer's tax bill changes as his or her income rises or falls within each tax bracket.

Regressive Taxes   A tax can also be a regressive tax. A regressive tax charges a lower percentage of income as income rises. Suppose Mutt, who is earning $10,000 a year, pays a tax of $5,000, and Jeff, who earns $100,000 a year, pays $10,000 in taxes. Although Jeff pays twice the absolute amount, this would be regressive taxation

> **Regressive tax**
> A tax that charges a lower percentage of income as income rises.

because richer Jeff pays an average tax rate of 10 percent and poorer Mutt suffers a 50 percent tax bite. Such a tax runs afoul of the ability-to-pay principle of taxation.

We will now demonstrate that sales and excise taxes are regressive taxes. Assume that there is a 5 percent sales tax on all purchases and that the Jones family earned $80,000 during the last year, while the Jefferson family earned $20,000. A sales tax is regressive because the richer Jones family will spend a smaller portion of their income to buy food, clothing, and other consumption items. The Joneses, with an $80,000 income, can afford to spend $40,000 on groceries and clothes and save the rest, while the Jeffersons, with a $20,000 income, spend their entire income to feed and clothe their family. Because each family pays a 5 percent sales tax, the lower-income Jeffersons pay sales taxes of $1,000 (0.05 × $20,000), or 1/20 of their income. The higher-income Joneses, on the other hand, pay sales taxes of $2,000 (0.05 × $40,000), or only 1/40 of their income. Although the richer Jones family pays twice the amount of sales tax to the tax collector, the sales tax is regressive because their average tax rate is lower than the Jefferson family's tax rate.

In practice, an example of a regressive tax is the Social Security payroll tax, FICA. The payroll tax works like this: A fixed percentage of 12.4 percent is levied on each worker's earnings. The tax is divided equally between employers and employees. This means that an employee with a gross monthly wage of, say, $1,000 will have $62 (6.2 percent of $1,000) deducted from his or her check by the employer. In turn, the employer adds $62 and sends $124 to the government.

Payroll taxes are regressive for two reasons. First, only wages and salaries are subject to this tax, while other sources of income, such as interest and dividends, are not. Because wealthy individuals typically receive a larger portion of their income from sources other than wages and salaries than do lower-income individuals, the wealthy pay a smaller fraction of their total income in payroll taxes. Second, earnings above a certain level are exempt from the Social Security tax. Thus, the *marginal tax rate* above a given threshold level is zero. In 2007, this level was $102,000 for wage and salary income subject to Social Security tax. Hence, any additional dollars earned above this figure add no additional taxes, and the average tax rate falls. On the other hand, there is no wage base limit for the Medicare tax. It is noteworthy that one idea for reforming Social Security is to adjust or remove the limit on income subject to Social Security tax.

Finally, property taxes are also considered regressive for two reasons. First, property owners add this tax to the rent paid by tenants who generally are lower income persons. Second, property taxes are a higher percentage of income for poor families than rich families because the poor spend a much greater proportion of their incomes for housing.

Proportional Taxes There continues to be considerable interest in simplifying the federal progressive income tax by substituting a proportional tax, also called a *flat tax*. A proportional tax charges the same percentage of income, regardless of the size of income. For example, one way to reform the federal progressive tax rate system would be to eliminate all deductions, exemptions, and loopholes and simply apply the same tax rate, say, 17 percent of income to everyone. Such a reform is illustrated in Exhibit 8. This would avoid the "hissing" from taxpayers who would no longer require legions of accountants and lawyers to file their tax returns. Actually, most flat-tax proposals are not truly proportional because they exempt income below some level and are therefore somewhat progressive. Also, it is debatable that a 17 percent flat tax would raise enough revenue.

> **Proportional tax**
>
> A tax that charges the same percentage of income, regardless of the size of income. Also called a *flat tax rate* or simply a *flat tax*.

EXHIBIT 8   The Progressive Income Tax versus a Flat Tax

The taxable income tax brackets for 2007 are drawn from Exhibit 7. In contrast to the "stair step" tax rates, a flat tax would charge a single rate of, say, 17 percent. This reform proposal is controversial and is discussed in the You're the Economist, "Is It Time to Trash the 1040s?"

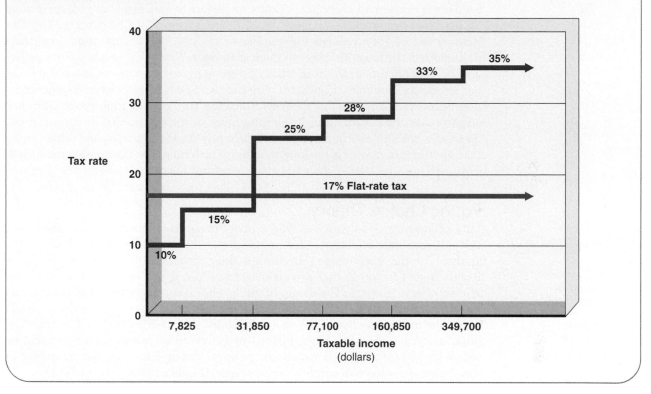

Let's look at whether the flat tax satisfies the benefits-received principle and the ability-to-pay principle. First, the flat tax does not necessarily relate to the benefits received from any particular government goods or services. Second, consider a 17 percent tax that collects $17,000 from Ms. "Rich," who is earning $100,000 a year, and $1,700 from Mr. "Poor," who is earning $10,000 a year. Both taxpayers pay the same proportional 17 percent of their incomes, but the $1,700 tax is thought to represent a much greater sacrifice to Mr. Poor than does the $17,000 tax paid by Ms. Rich. After paying her taxes, Ms. Rich can still live comfortably, but Mr. Poor complains that he desperately needed the $1,700 to buy groceries for his family. To be fair, one can argue that the $17,000 paid by Ms. Rich is not enough based on the ability-to-pay principle.

Reforming the Tax System

The Supreme Court declared the personal income tax unconstitutional in 1895. This changed in 1913 when the states ratified the Sixteenth Amendment to the Constitution, granting Congress the power to levy taxes on income. The federal income tax was an inconsequential source of revenue until World War II, but since then it has remained a major source. Currently, 41 states have income taxes, and personal income taxes may become an increasingly important source of state and local revenues in years to come.

Over the years, Congress has enacted various reforms of the federal tax system. The Tax Reform Act of 1986, for example, marked the first time Congress has completely rewritten the Federal Tax Code since 1954. This law removed millions of households from the tax rolls by roughly doubling the personal exemption allowed for each taxpayer and his or her dependents. Before the tax law changed, there were 15 marginal tax brackets for individuals, ranging from 11 to 50 percent. The Tax Reform Act of 1986 reduced the number of tax brackets to only four. Most taxpayers are in the lower brackets so the loss in tax revenue that resulted from lowering the individual tax rates was offset by raising taxes on corporations and closing numerous tax loopholes. Consistent with the two key taxation objectives, the intention of this major revision of the federal income tax law was to improve efficiency and to make the system fairer by shifting more of the tax burden to corporations. As shown in Exhibits 7 and 8, there are currently six tax brackets, and critics argue that another tax reform act is long overdue. The You're the Economist titled "Is It Time to Trash the 1040s" discusses ideas to reform the current federal tax system.

Public Choice Theory

James Buchanan, who won the 1986 Nobel Prize in economics, is the founder of a body of economic literature called public choice theory. Public choice theory is the analysis of the government's decision-making process for allocating resources. Recall from Chapter 4 that private-market failure is the reason for government intervention in markets. The theory of public choice considers how well the government performs when it replaces or regulates a private market. Rather than operating as the market mechanism to allocate resources, the government is a nonmarket, political decision-making force. Instead of behaving as private-interest buyers or sellers in the marketplace, actors in the political system have complex incentives in their roles as elected officials, bureaucrats, special-interest lobbyists, and voters.

Buchanan and other public choice theorists raise the fundamental issue of how well a democratic society can make efficient economic decisions. The basic principle of public choice theory is that politicians follow their own self-interest and seek to maximize their reelection chances, rather than promoting the best interests of society. Thus, a major contribution of Buchanan has been to link self-interest motivation to government officials, just as Adam Smith earlier identified the pursuit of self-interest as the motivation for consumers and producers. In short, individuals within any government agency or institution will act analogously to their private-sector counterparts; they will give first priority to improving their own earnings, working conditions, and status, rather than to being altruistic.

Given this introduction to the subject, let's consider a few public choice theories that explain why the public sector, like the private sector, may also "fail."

Majority-Rule Problem

To evaluate choices, economists often use a technique called benefit-cost analysis. Benefit-cost analysis is the comparison of the additional rewards and costs of an economic alternative. If a firm is considering producing a new product, its benefit ("carrots") will be the extra revenue earned from selling the product. The firm's cost ("sticks") is the opportunity cost of using resources to make the product. How many units of the product should the firm manufacture?

Public choice theory
The analysis of the government's decision-making process for allocating resources.

Benefit-cost analysis
The comparison of the additional rewards and costs of an economic alternative.

Applicable Concepts: flat tax and national sales tax

Two controversial fundamental tax reform ideas are often hot news topics. One proposal is the flat tax discussed earlier in this chapter, and the other is a national sales tax. The flat tax is favored by former presidential candidate and publisher Steve Forbes. It would grant a personal exemption of about $36,000 for a typical family and then tax income above this amount at 17 percent with no deductions. As stated by recent presidential candidate John McCain, the argument for a flat tax is that it would allow people to file their tax returns on a postcard and reduce the number of tax cheats. McCain proposes that the flat tax would be optional to the current tax system.

The flat-tax plan described above creates serious political problems by eliminating taxes on income from dividends, interest, capital gains, and inheritances. Also, eliminating deductions and credits would face strong opposition from the public. For example, eliminating the mortgage interest deduction and exemptions for health care and charity would be a difficult political battle. And there is the fairness question. People at the lower end of the current system of six progressive rates could face a tax increase while upper-income people would get the biggest tax break. The counterargument is that under the current tax system many millionaires pay nothing because they shelter their income. Under a flat-tax scheme, they would lose deductions and credits.

A national retail sales tax is another tax reform proposal. In 2008, Mike Huckabee, Republican candidate for president, made this idea central to his campaign. A consumption tax could eliminate all federal income taxes entirely (personal, corporate, and Social Security) and tax only consumer purchases at a given percentage— say, 30 percent. Like the flat tax, loopholes would be eliminated, and tax collection would become so simple that the federal government could save billions of dollars by cutting or eliminating the IRS. Taxpayers would save because they no longer need to hire accountants and lawyers to prepare their complicated 1040 tax returns. Also, the tax base would broaden because, while not everyone earns income, almost everyone makes purchases.

Critics of a national sales tax argue that retail businesses would have the added burden of being tax collectors for the federal government, and the IRS would still be required to ensure that taxes are collected on billions of sales transactions. Moreover, huge price increases from the national sales tax would lead to "black market" transactions. The counterargument is that this problem would be no worse than current income tax evasion, and a sales tax indirectly taxes participants in illegal markets when they spend their income in legal markets. Also, a sales tax is regressive because the poor spend a greater share of their income on food, housing, and other necessities. To offset this problem, sales tax advocates propose subsidy checks paid up to some level of income. Critics also point out that retired people who pay little or no federal income tax will not welcome paying a national sales tax.

ANALYZE THE ISSUE

Assume the federal government replaces the federal income tax with a national sales tax on all consumption expenditures. Analyze the impact of this tax change on taxation efficiency and equity. Note that the federal government already collects a nationwide consumption tax through excise taxes on gasoline, liquor, and tobacco.

> **Conclusion** *Rationally, a profit-maximizing firm follows the marginal rule and produces additional units so long as the marginal benefit exceeds the marginal cost.*

The basic rule of benefit-cost analysis is that undertaking a program whose cost exceeds its benefit is an inefficient waste of resources. In the competitive market system, undertaking projects that yield benefits greater than costs is a sure bet. In the long run, any firm that does not follow the benefit-cost rule will either go out of business or switch to producing products that yield benefits equal to or greater than their costs. Majority-rule voting, however, can result in the approval of projects whose costs outweigh their benefits. Exhibit 9 illustrates how an inefficient economic decision can result from the ballot box.

As shown in Exhibit 9, suppose Bob, Juan, and Theresa are the only voters in a mini-society that is considering whether to add two publicly financed park projects, *A* and *B*. The total cost to taxpayers of either park project is $300, and the marginal cost of park *A* or park *B* to each taxpayer is an additional tax of $100 (columns 2 and 5). Next, assume each taxpayer determines his or her additional dollar value derived from the benefits of park projects *A* and *B* (columns 3 and 6). Assuming each person applies marginal analysis, each will follow the *marginal rule* and vote for a project only if his or her benefit exceeds the cost of the $100 tax. Consider park project *A*. This project is worth $0 to Bob, $101 to Juan, and $101 to Theresa, and this means two Yes votes and one No vote: the majority votes for park *A* (column 4). This decision would not happen in the business world. The Disney company, for example, would rationally reject such a project because the total of all consumers' marginal benefits is only $202, which is less than its $300 marginal cost.

The important point here is that majority-rule voting can make the correct benefit-cost marginal analysis, but it can also lead to a rejection of projects with marginal total benefits that exceed marginal costs. Suppose park project *B* costs $300 as well, and Bob's benefits are $90, Juan's $90, and Theresa's $301 (column 6). The total of all marginal benefits from constructing park *B* is $481, and this project would be undertaken in a private-sector market. But because only Theresa's benefits exceed the marginal $100 tax, park project *B* in the political arena receives only one Yes vote against two No votes and fails.

Why is there a distinction between political majority voting and benefit-cost analysis? The reason is that dollars can measure the intensity of voter preferences

EXHIBIT 9	Majority-Rule Benefit-Cost Analysis of Two Park Projects					
	Park Project A			**Park Project B**		
(1)	(2)	(3)	(4)	(5)	(6)	(7)
Voter	Marginal Cost (taxes)	Marginal Benefit	Vote	Marginal Cost (taxes)	Marginal Benefit	Vote
Bob	$100	$ 0	No	$100	$ 90	No
Juan	100	101	Yes	100	90	No
Theresa	100	101	Yes	100	301	Yes
Total	$300	$202	Passes	$ 300	$ 481	Fails

and "one-person, one-vote" does not. A count of ballots can determine whether a proposal passes or fails, but this count may not be proportional to the dollar strength of benefits among the individual voters.

Special-Interest Group Effect

In addition to benefit-cost errors from majority voting, special-interest groups can create government support for programs with costs outweighing their benefits. The *special-interest effect* occurs when the government approves programs that benefit only a small group within society, but society as a whole pays the costs. The influence of special-interest groups is indeed a constant problem for effective government because the benefits of government programs to certain small groups are great and the costs are relatively insignificant to each taxpayer. For example, let's assume the benefits of support prices for dairy farmers are $100 million. Because of the size of these benefits to dairy farmers, this special-interest group can well afford to hire professional lobbyists and donate a million dollars or so to the reelection campaigns of politicians voting for dairy price supports.

In addition to the incentive of financial support from special interests, politicians can also engage in *logrolling*. Logrolling is the political practice of trading votes of support for legislated programs. Politician *A* says to politician *B*, "You vote for my dairy price support bill, and I will vote for your tobacco price support bill."

But who pays for these large benefits to special-interest groups? Taxpayers do, of course, but the extra tax burden per taxpayer is very low. Although Congress may enact a $200 million program to favor, say, a few defense contractors, this expenditure costs 100 million taxpayers only $2 per taxpayer. Because in a free society it is relatively easy to organize special-interest constituencies and lobby politicians to spread the cost, it is little wonder that spending programs are popular. Moreover, the small cost of each pet program per taxpayer means there is little reward for a single voter to learn the details of the many special-interest legislation proposals.

Rational Voter Ignorance

Politicians, appointed officials, and bureaucrats constitute the supply side of the political marketplace. The demand side of the political market consists of special-interest groups and voters who are subject to what economists call rational ignorance. Rational ignorance is a voter's decision that the benefit of becoming informed about an issue is not worth the cost. A frequent charge in elections is that the candidates are not talking about the issues. One explanation is that the candidates realize that a sizable portion of the voters will make a calculated decision not to judge the candidates based on in-depth knowledge of their positions on a wide range of issues. Instead of going to the trouble of reading position papers and doing research, many voters choose their candidates based simply on party affiliation or on how the candidate appears on television. This approach is rational if the perceived extra effort required to be better informed exceeds the marginal benefit of knowing more about the candidate.

Rational ignorance
The voter's choice to remain uninformed because the marginal cost of obtaining information is higher than the marginal benefit from knowing it.

The principle of rational ignorance also explains why eligible voters fail to vote on election day. A popular explanation is that low voter participation results from apathy among potential voters, but the decision can be an exercise in practical benefit-cost analysis. Nonvoters presumably perceive that the opportunity cost of going to the polls outweighs the benefit gained from any of the candidates or issues on the ballot. Moreover, nonvoters perceive that one extra vote is unlikely to change the outcome.

Public choice theorists argue that one reason benefits are difficult to measure is that the voter confronts an *indivisible* public service. In a grocery store, the consumer can decide to spend so much on apples, oranges, and other *divisible* items, but voting involves candidates who take stands on many issues. The point is that voting does not allow the voter to pick and choose among the candidate's good and bad positions. Most voters, in short, must "buy" a confusing mixture of "wants" and "unwants" that are difficult to interpret as a benefit.

Bureaucratic Inefficiency

The bureaucracy is the body of nonelected officials and administrators who operate government agencies. As government grows, one of the concerns is that the bureaucracy may become more powerful than the executive, legislative, and judicial branches. Public choice theory also considers how bureaucratic behavior affects economic decision making. One principle is that the government bureaucracy tends to be inefficient because of the absence of the profit motive.

What happens when a government agency performs poorly? First, there is no competition from other producers to take away market share. There are no shareholders demanding reform when profits are falling because taxpayers are a poor substitute for stockholder pressure. Second, the typical government response each year is to request a larger budget. Without profits as a measure of performance, the tendency is to use the size of an agency's budget and staff as an indicator of success. In brief, the basic incentive structure of government agencies encourages inefficient management because, unlike the market system, there is a lack of incentive to be cost-conscious or creative. Instead, the hallmark of the bureaucrat is to be extremely cautious and make all decisions "by the book." Such behavior may maximize prestige and security, but it usually fails to minimize costs.

Shortsightedness Effect

Finally, it can be argued that democracy has a bias toward programs offering clear benefits and hidden costs. The reason is that political officeholders must run for reelection after a relatively short period of two to six years. Given this reality, politicians tend to favor proposals providing immediate benefits, with future generations paying most of the costs. Conversely, they reject programs that have easily identifiable short-run high costs, but offer benefits only after a decade. Hence, the essence of the hidden costs bias, or *shortsightedness effect,* is that both voters and politicians suffer from a short time horizon. Such a myopic view of either future costs or future benefits can cause an irrational acceptance of a program, even though long-run costs exceed short-run benefits, or an irrational rejection of a program with long-run benefits that outweigh short-run costs.

CHECKPOINT

What Does Public Choice Say about a Budget Deficit?

In 2002, the situation switched from a few years in which the federal government spent less than it collected in taxes to spending more than tax revenues (discussed in the next chapter). James Buchanan predicted over 30 years ago that growing government deficits would be inevitable. He maintained that government officials would increase spending for their constituents in order to gain votes. Furthermore, politicians would shy away from tax increases for fear of alienating voters. The net effect would be deficits. Was Buchanan's prediction based on the rational ignorance effect, government inefficiency, or the shortsightedness effect?

KEY CONCEPTS

Government expenditures
Benefits-received principle
Ability-to-pay principle
Progressive tax

Average tax rate
Marginal tax rate
Regressive tax
Proportional or flat tax

Public choice theory
Benefit-cost analysis
Rational ignorance

SUMMARY

- *Government expenditures,* including transfer payments, have grown from about one-quarter of GDP in 1950 to about one-third of GDP today. After the recession and 9/11 terrorist attacks of 2001, federal outlays as a percentage of GDP have increased.

Government Expenditures

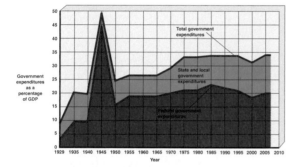

- *Federal tax revenues* are collected primarily from individual income taxes and social insurance taxes.

Federal Tax Revenues

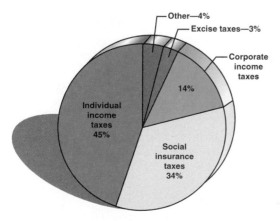

- The *taxation burden,* measured by taxes as a percentage of GDP, is lighter in the United States than in many other advanced industrial countries.

Taxation Burden

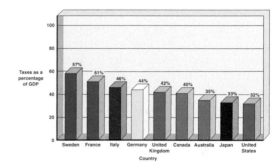

- *Total tax revenues* amounted to about 11 percent of GDP in 1929, and reached the highest level of close to 34 percent in 2000 before falling to about 32 percent in 2007. Federal taxes take a larger share of GDP than state and local governments.

Total Tax Revenues

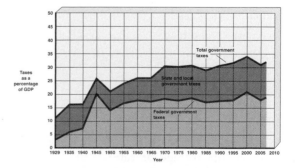

- The *benefits-received principle* and the *ability-to-pay principle* are two basic philosophies of taxation fairness. The gasoline tax is a classic example of the benefits-received principle because users of the highways pay the gasoline tax. Progressive income taxes follow the ability-to-pay principle because there is a direct relationship between the average tax rate and income size. Sales, excise, property, and flat-rate taxes violate this principle because each results in a greater burden on the poor than on the rich.
- *Public choice theory* reveals the government's decision-making process. For example, government failure can occur for any of the following reasons: (1) majority voting may not follow benefit-cost analysis; (2) special-interest groups can obtain large benefits and spread their costs over many taxpayers; (3) rational voter ignorance means a sizable portion of the voters will decide not to make informed judgments; (4) bureaucratic behavior may not lead to cost-effective decisions; and (5) politicians suffer from a short time horizon, leading to a bias toward hiding the costs of programs.

SUMMARY OF CONCLUSION STATEMENTS

- The government's share of total economic activity has generally increased since World War II ended in 1945. Most of the growth in combined government expenditures as a percentage of GDP reflects rapidly growing federal government transfer programs.

- Rationally, a profit-maximizing firm follows the marginal rule and produces additional units so long as the marginal benefit exceeds the marginal cost.

STUDY QUESTIONS AND PROBLEMS

1. Explain why federal, state, and local expenditures account for more than 30 percent of GDP, but total government spending (*G* in GDP) is only about 20 percent of GDP.

2. Identify the major differences between federal government outlays and spending by state and local governments.

3. What are the primary tax revenue sources at the federal, state, and local levels of government?

4. Which of the following taxes satisfy the benefits-received principle, and which satisfy the ability-to-pay principle?
   a. Gasoline tax
   b. Federal income tax
   c. Tax on Social Security benefits

5. What is the difference between the marginal tax rate and the average tax rate?

6. Explain why a 5 percent sales tax on gasoline is regressive.

7. Ms. Jones has a taxable income of $30,000, and she must pay $3,000 in taxes. Mr. Smith has a taxable income of $60,000. How much tax must Mr. Smith pay for the tax system to be
   a. progressive?
   b. regressive?
   c. proportional?

8. Explain why each of the following taxes is progressive or regressive:
   a. A $1 per pack federal excise tax on cigarettes
   b. The federal individual income tax
   c. The federal payroll tax

9. Complete the following table, which describes the sales tax paid by individuals at various income levels. Indicate whether the tax is progressive, proportional, or regressive.

Income	Total Spending	Sales Tax Paid	Sales Tax Paid as a Percentage of Income
$ 1,000	$ 1,000	$ 100	_____ %
5,000	3,500	350	_____
10,000	6,000	600	_____
100,000	40,000	4,000	_____

Income	Tax Paid	Average Tax Rate	Marginal Tax Rate
$ 0	$ 0	0%	0%
100	10	_____	_____
200	30	_____	_____
300	60	_____	_____
400	100	_____	_____
500	150	_____	_____

10. Calculate the average and the marginal tax rates in the following table, and indicate whether the tax is progressive, proportional, or regressive. What observation can you make concerning the relationship between marginal and average tax rates?

11. Compare "dollar voting" in private markets with "majority voting" in the political decision-making system.

For Online Exercises, go the text Web site at www.cengage.com/economics/tucker.

CHECKPOINT ANSWER

What Does Public Choice Say about a Budget Deficit?

The government uses the deficit to finance clear short-term benefits with little attention to long-term consequences. If you said public choice predicts that government officials will emphasize near-term benefits to gain votes (the shortsightedness effect), **YOU ARE CORRECT.**

PRACTICE QUIZ

For an explanation of the correct answers, please visit the tutorial at www.cengage.com/economics/tucker.

1. Since 1975, total government expenditures as a percentage of GDP in the United States have
   a. fallen by half.
   b. remained fairly constant at about one-third.
   c. grown from one-fourth to one-half.
   d. grown from one-quarter to one-third.

2. Which of the following accounted for the second largest percentage of total federal government expenditures in 2007?
   a. Income security
   b. National defense
   c. Interest on the national debt
   d. Education and health

3. Which of the following contributed the largest percentage of total federal government expenditures in 2007 (excluding federal grants)?
   a. Interest on the national debt
   b. Education and health
   c. National defense
   d. Income security

4. Which of the following countries devotes about the same percentage of its GDP to taxes as the United States?
   a. Sweden
   b. Italy
   c. United Kingdom
   d. Japan

PRACTICE QUIZ CONTINUED

5. "The poor should not pay income taxes." This statement reflects which of the following principles of taxation?
   a. Fairness of contribution
   b. Benefits-received
   c. Inexpensive-to-collect
   d. Ability-to-pay

6. Some cities finance their airports with a departure tax: every person leaving the city by plane is charged a small fixed dollar amount that is used to help pay for building and running the airport. The departure tax follows the
   a. benefits-received principle.
   b. ability-to-pay principle.
   c. flat-rate principle.
   d. public-choice principle.

7. Which of the following statements is *true*?
   a. The most important source of tax revenue for the federal government is individual income taxes.
   b. The most important source of tax revenue for state and local governments is sales taxes.
   c. The second most important source of revenue for state and local governments is local property taxes.
   d. The taxation burden, measured by taxes as a percentage of GDP, is lighter in the United States than in most other advanced industrial countries.
   e. All of the above are true.

8. Which of the following statements is *true*?
   a. A sales tax on food is a regressive tax.
   b. The largest source of federal government tax revenue is individual income taxes.
   c. The largest source of state and local government tax revenue is sales taxes.
   d. All of the above are true.

9. A tax that is structured so that people with higher incomes pay a larger percentage of their incomes for the tax than do people with smaller incomes is called a (an)
   a. income tax.
   b. regressive tax.

   c. property tax.
   d. progressive tax.

10. Generally, most economists feel that a _____ type of income tax is a fairer way to raise government revenue than a sales tax.
    a. regressive
    b. proportional
    c. flat-rate
    d. progressive

11. The federal personal income tax is an example of a (an)
    a. excise tax.
    b. proportional tax.
    c. progressive tax.
    d. regressive tax.

12. A 5 percent sales tax on food is an example of a
    a. flat tax.
    b. progressive tax.
    c. proportional tax.
    d. regressive tax.

13. Margaret pays a local income tax of 2 percent, regardless of the size of her income. This tax is
    a. proportional.
    b. regressive.
    c. progressive.
    d. a mix of (a) and (b).

14. Which of the following statements relating to public choice is *true*?
    a. A low voter turnout may result when voters perceive that the marginal cost of voting exceeds its marginal benefit.
    b. If the marginal cost of voting exceeds its marginal benefit, the vote is unimportant.
    c. Special-interest groups always cause the will of a majority to be imposed on a minority.
    d. All of the above are true.

15. According to the shortsightedness effect, politicians tend to favor projects with
    a. short-run benefits and short-run costs.
    b. short-run benefits and long-run costs.
    c. long-run benefits and short-run costs.
    d. long-run benefits and long-run costs.

Federal Deficits, Surpluses, and the National Debt

© David Muir/Digital Vision/Getty Images.

The U.S. government has been in the red almost continuously since the Revolutionary War forced the Continental Congress to borrow money. The only exception was a brief interlude more than a century and a half ago when our government was debt-free. In December 1834, President Andrew Jackson proudly reported to Congress what he considered to be a major accomplishment of his administration. By New Year's Day of 1835, the federal government would succeed in paying off the national debt. It was Jackson's second term as president. Since the close of the War of 1812, the country had experienced tremendous growth, and revenues flowed into the U.S. Treasury from import tariffs and the sale of public land. By early 1836, the nation had been out of debt for two years, and there was a budget surplus of $37 million. The dilemma in those days was how to use the surplus. In 1836, Congress simply decided to divide all but $5 million of the surplus among the states. Then the financial panic of 1837 caused the government to plunge into debt again, where it remains today and for the foreseeable future.

Unlike Andrew Jackson, Abraham Lincoln in his 1864 Annual Message to Congress expressed no concern for paying off the national debt. Lincoln stated:

> The great advantage of citizens being creditors as well as debtors, with relation to the public debt, is obvious. Men can readily perceive that they cannot be much oppressed by a debt which they owe to themselves.

In 2008, federal government borrowing to cover its budget deficits had accumulated a national debt over $9 trillion. To the average citizen, this is an incomprehensible amount of money for even the government to owe. Perhaps the best way to picture this sea of red ink is that your individual share is about $40,000.

In this chapter, you will learn to solve these economic puzzles:

- Can Uncle Sam go bankrupt?

- How does the national debt of the United States compare to the debt of other countries?

- Are we passing the debt burden to our children?

- Who owns the national debt?

The Federal Budget Balancing Act

What will happen next? Like a high-wire performer swinging one way and then another while the crowd below gazes transfixed, the public in the late 1990s and early 2000s watched the federal budget sway back and forth between deficits and surpluses. As you learned in the preceding chapter on fiscal policy, a federal budget deficit occurs whenever the government spends more than it collects in taxes. The accumulation of these budget deficits over the years is the origin of the national debt. When the federal government has a surplus in its budget, some or all of the surplus can be used to retire the national debt, and it decreases. Here you will take a closer look at the actual budgetary process that creates and finances our national debt.

The Federal Budgetary Process

In theory, Keynesian discretionary fiscal policy requires that legislation be enacted to change government spending or taxes in order to shift the aggregate demand curve represented in the *AD-AS* model. In practice, the federal budgetary process, which determines the level of spending and taxation, is not so orderly. The annual "battle of the budget" on Capitol Hill involves political decisions on how much the government plans to spend and where the money will come from to finance these outlays. Wrangling takes place between all sorts of camps: the president versus Congress, Republicans versus Democrats, national security versus economic equality, price stability versus full employment, health care versus tax cuts, and so on. Given the complexities of world events, special-interest groups, volatile public opinion, and political ambitions that complicate the budget process, it is no wonder actual fiscal policy often ignores textbook macroeconomics.

The following brief look at the federal budgetary process shows how Congress and the president make federal spending and tax decisions each year:

Stage 1: Formation of the Budget Between February and December, federal agencies develop and submit their budget requests for the upcoming fiscal year to the Office of Management and Budget (OMB). (The government's fiscal year begins on October 1 and ends on September 30, so the budgetary process begins in the preceding calendar year.) The Pentagon argues for more defense spending, the Department of Transportation for more highway funds, and so on. The OMB reviews each agency's request. After receiving advice from the president, officials from cabinet departments, the Council of Economic Advisors (CEA), and the Treasury, the OMB compiles all the proposals into a budget recommendation. Applying the administration's goals, the OMB sends the proposed budget to the president by December.

Stage 2: Presidential Budget Submission   In January, nine months before the new fiscal year begins on October 1, the president submits the proposed budget to Congress. The official title is *The Budget of the United States.* This unveiling of the administration's budget is always big news. Does the president recommend that less money be spent for defense and more for education? Is there an increase in the Social Security payroll tax or the income tax? And how large is the national debt? Is there a budget deficit or a budget surplus?

Stage 3: Budget Resolution   After the president submits the budget in January, Congress takes the lead in the budgetary process. The president's budget now becomes the starting point for congressional consideration. The Congressional Budget Office (CBO) employs a professional staff who advise Congress on the budget much the way the OMB advises the president. The CBO analyzes the budget by February and reports its evaluation at budget committee hearings in both the House of Representatives and the Senate. After debate, in May Congress approves an overall budget outline called the *budget resolution,* which sets target levels for spending, tax revenues, and the budget deficit or surplus.

Stage 4: Budget Passed   Throughout the summer, and supposedly ending by October 1, Congress and the president debate while congressional committees and subcommittees prepare specific spending and tax law bills. The budget resolution is supposed to guide the spending and revenue decisions of these committees. After Congress passes, and the president signs, the spending and revenue bills, the federal government has its actual budget for spending and tax collection.

As summarized in Exhibit 1, the budgetary process seems orderly enough, but in practice it does not work so smoothly. The process can, and often does, go astray. One problem is that Congress does not necessarily follow its own rules. The budget bills are not always passed on time, and when that happens, the fiscal year starts without a budget. Then federal agencies must operate on the basis of *continuing resolutions,* which means each agency operates as it did the previous year until spending bills are approved. In some years, Congress even fails to pass a continuing resolution, and the federal government must shut down and workers stay home until Congress approves the necessary funds.

Financing the National Debt

When the federal government must borrow money to finance a budget deficit, which occurs when it spends more than is collected in taxes, the deficit adds to the accumulated national debt. Exhibit 2 reveals that since 1960 the federal government has most often operated with a budget deficit. Exhibit 2(a) shows the growth of federal expenditures (spending for final goods and services plus transfer payments) and tax revenues, and Exhibit 2(b) traces the corresponding budget deficits or surpluses. A surplus occurs when the government collects more in tax than it spends. Note that between 1960 and 1997 a deficit occurred each year except 1969. Beginning in the early 1980s, the magnitude of the deficits increased sharply. In 1992, after the

EXHIBIT 1   Major Steps in the Federal Budgetary Process

The first step in the federal budgetary process is the OMB's formation of the budget based on requests from all federal agencies. The second step is the president's transmittal of the administration's budget to Congress. In the third step, Congress passes a budget resolution that sets targets for spending, taxes, and the deficit or surplus. In the final step, Congress passes the budget consisting of specific spending and tax bills. When the president signs the spending and revenue bills, the federal government has its actual budget.

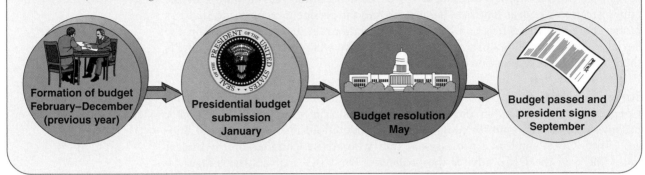

Formation of budget
February–December
(previous year)

Presidential budget
submission
January

Budget resolution
May

Budget passed and
president signs
September

1990–1991 recession, this trend reversed, and budget deficits declined sharply until a budget surplus occurred in 1998, and then surpluses continued to grow sharply through 2000. Then during the recession in 2001, the surplus declined. In 2002, deficits returned and are projected for future years. Note that after reaching a maximum in 2004, the deficits declined.

When the government overspends, the U.S. Treasury must borrow to finance the difference between expenditures and revenues. The U.S. Treasury borrows by selling Treasury bills (T-bills), notes, and bonds promising to make specified interest payments and to repay the loaned funds on a given date. These government securities are IOUs of the federal government. They are considered a safe haven for idle funds and are purchased by Federal Reserve banks, government agencies, private banks, corporations, individual U.S. citizens, and foreigners. If you own a U.S. government savings bond, for example, you have loaned your funds to the federal government. The stock of these federal government IOUs accumulated over the years is called the *gross public debt*, *federal debt*, or national debt. The national debt is the total amount owed by the federal government to owners of government securities.

National debt

The total amount owed by the federal government to owners of government securities.

Note that the national debt does not include state and local governments' debt. Also, as mentioned above, the national debt does include U.S. Treasury securities purchased by various federal agencies, such as the Social Security trust fund. Currently, the Social Security trust fund collects more in taxes than it pays out in retirement benefits, and it lends the extra money to the federal government for spending. In fact, federal budget deficits would be significantly higher, or budget surpluses would be significantly lower, without federal government borrowing from this trust fund. If we subtract the portion of the national debt held by all government agencies (what the federal government owes to itself), we can compute the net public debt. Beware! Confusion sometimes occurs when the media use the term *public debt* without specifying whether the reference is to "gross" or "net" public debt.

Net public debt

National debt minus all government interagency borrowing.

Before proceeding, let's pause and explain the Social Security trust fund in a little more detail. A misconception is that the Social Security Administration (SSA) collects the annual Social Security surpluses and stacks the cash with reserve cash

EXHIBIT 2	U.S. Federal Budget Expenditures, Revenues, and Budget Surpluses or Deficits, 1960–2007

Part (a) shows that until 1992 federal expenditures (including transfer payments) grew faster than federal tax revenues, causing deficits to increase rapidly. After 1992, this trend reversed, and the result was first declining budget deficits and then growing budget surpluses until 2000. After the recession of 2001, the trend was large deficits.

Part (b) shows that prior to 1998 the U.S. government was in surplus only in 1969. For much of the 1960s, the federal government was close to a balanced budget. During the early 1980s, however, federal budget deficits grew sharply. After 1992, the budget deficits declined, and from 1998 to 2000, there were sharply rising budget surpluses. In 2001, the budget surplus declined, and deficits returned in 2002. After reaching a maximum in 2004, deficits declined.

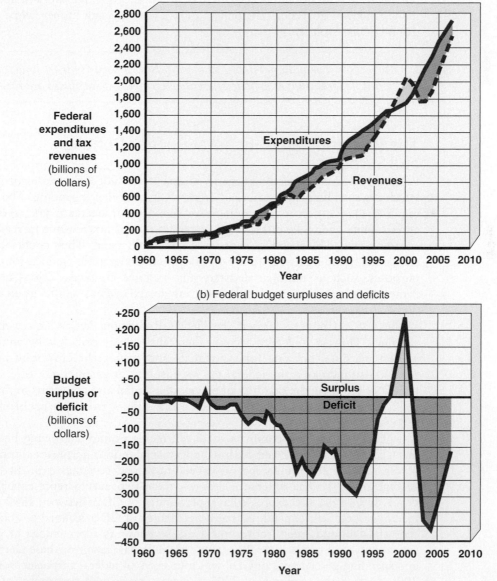

SOURCE: *Economic Report of the President*, 2008, http://www.gpoaccess./eop/, Table B-78.

from previous surpluses in a vault or special checking account. If the trust fund were to be in deficit as the baby boomers retire and the ratio of workers paying into the system to people drawing benefits shrinks, then the SSA will open the vault and/ or write a check to draw on trust fund reserves to pay its obligations.

Here is what really happens to Social Security tax dollars. When excess Social Security taxes are collected by the SSA, these surplus funds must, by law, be immediately withdrawn and given to the Treasury which, in turn, issues "nonmarketable" interest-bearing Treasury bonds to the SSA. The Treasury then spends this money on welfare, roads, tax cuts, defense, or whatever the federal government decides. On the other hand, if the trust fund cannot pay for retirees' needs, then the SSA will ask the Treasury to redeem its bonds for cash to pay benefits. In this situation, where will the Treasury get the money to repay the SSA? It will either print it, borrow it, levy additional taxes, or cut benefits. In short, the full faith and credit of the U.S. federal government promises to pay itself enough money when needed to pay for Social Security.

> **Conclusion** *The national debt includes the Social Security trust fund, and as a result, federal budget deficits are reduced or budget surpluses are raised.*

The Rise and Fall of Federal Budget Deficits and Surpluses

Restraint on federal spending began with the 1990 Budget Enforcement Act (BEA), which set spending caps on broad areas of discretionary spending. The BEA also required that any proposal to increase spending or decrease tax revenues over agreed limits had to be offset by an equal amount of tax revenue increases or new spending cuts. The spending caps were not totally rigid. They could be raised to reflect any spending that both the president and Congress designated for emergency purposes, such as national disasters and military conflicts. Critics argued that "emergency" spending is a loophole because exactly what qualifies as an emergency was not defined.

In 1993, Congress passed the Deficit Reduction Act, which increased tax revenues. This act took into account the ability-to-pay principle by increasing the highest marginal tax rate for individuals and raising the corporate income tax rate. It also increased the federal tax on gasoline. A gasoline tax offers the extra benefit of reducing the quantity of energy demanded and conforms to the benefits-received principle. However, a gasoline tax suffers from the problem of being regressive.

The spending caps combined with tax increases and a growing high-employment economy transformed federal budget deficits into surpluses during the late 1990s. Exhibit 3(a) shows federal expenditures and revenues expressed as a percentage of GDP. The difference between these two curves represents the federal deficit or surplus, also expressed as a percentage of GDP. Between 1992 and 2001, federal government expenditures as a percentage of GDP declined to about 18 percent of GDP, and federal government tax revenues as a percentage of GDP crept steadily upward to just over 20 percent of GDP. The result of these changes in tax and spending percentages of GDP was four years of federal surpluses from 1998 to 2001. During the recession of 2001, however, taxes as a percentage of GDP fell, and the federal budget returned to red ink in 2002. The reasons were primarily the recession's negative impact on tax collections, the tax cuts enacted in 2001 and

EXHIBIT 3

Federal Expenditures, Revenues, and Deficits as a Percentage of GDP, 1985–2007

Part (a) shows that after the 1990–1991 recession, federal government expenditures as a percentage of GDP declined until 2000, while federal government tax revenues rose steadily. The results were federal surpluses between 1998 and 2001. After 2000, federal government expenditures as a percentage of GDP rose and taxes as a percentage of GDP fell. In 2005, tax revenues as a percentage of GDP grew by about 1 percent. After 2004, tax revenues as a percentage of GDP grew and the deficit decreased.

Part (b) focuses on the federal deficit as a percentage of GDP. Between 1985 and 1994, the federal deficit as a percentage of GDP ranged from about 3 percent to 5 percent. After reaching a budget surplus peak of 2.4 percent in 2000, the federal budget deficit again grew to about 4 percent in 2004. In 2007, the federal deficit as a percentage of GDP fell to about 1 percent.

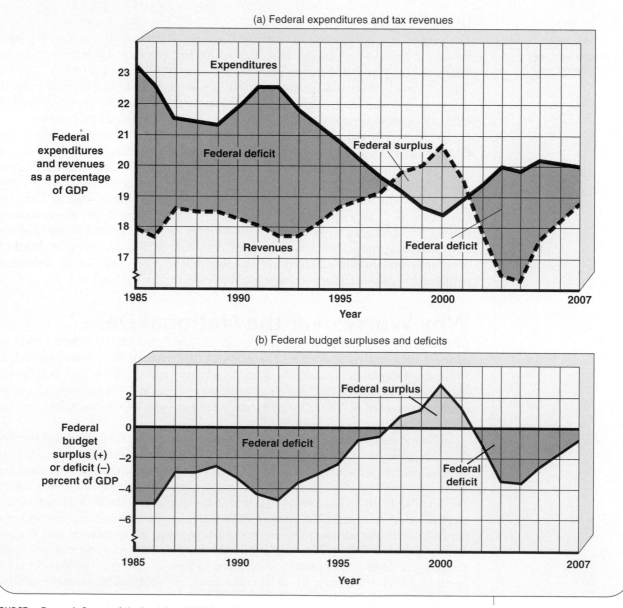

SOURCE: *Economic Report of the President*, 2008, http://www.gpoaccess/eop/, Table B-79.

2003, and spending on the war on terrorism. Also, the "pay-as-you-go" budget rules expired in 2002. Between 2004 and 2007, tax revenues as a percentage of GDP grew, while expenditures as a percentage of GDP remained constant. As a result, the federal deficit decreased.

Exhibit 3(b) provides an alternate graph of the federal budget deficit or surplus as a percentage of GDP. During President Reagan's first term in the early 1980s, the combined effect of recession, a military spending buildup, and a cut in income taxes caused a rise in the deficit to 5 percent of GDP. During the 1990–1991 recession, the deficit as a percentage of GDP again reached close to 5 percent. In the late 1990s, the federal government began running budget surpluses for a few years until 2002. Since 2002, federal budget deficits increased to almost 4 percent of GDP in 2004. In 2007, the federal deficit as a percentage of GDP fell to about 1 percent.

Debt Ceiling

Debt ceiling

A legislated legal limit on the national debt.

The debt ceiling is a method for curbing the national debt. A debt ceiling is a legislated legal limit on the national debt. This means that the federal government cannot legally allow its budget deficit to raise the national debt beyond the ceiling. It works like the credit limit on your charge card. When you reach the limit, you cannot charge any more and you must pay cash. When the federal government hits the debt limit, it cannot borrow any more to supplement its cash from taxes and other sources.

What usually happens when the budget pushes against the debt ceiling is that the ceiling is raised to accommodate the budget deficit. Raising the debt ceiling often provokes a fiery political debate over government spending. Failure to raise the debt ceiling means no money for the government to pay its bills, meet its payroll, or pay interest due on the present debt. In 1990, Congress rejected President George H. W. Bush's spending plan, and the government shut down throughout the three-day Columbus Day weekend. Most workers were off for the holiday, and few government agencies were affected. In 1995 and 1996, however, a deadlock between President Bill Clinton and the Republican Congress over a short-term spending bill caused the government to shut down for several weeks.

Why Worry over the National Debt?

As shown in Exhibit 4(a), the result of the accumulation of federal deficits is that the national debt has risen sharply. The national debt crossed $1 trillion in 1982. In 1986, the national debt broke the $2 trillion mark, and the $3 trillion barrier was breached in late 1990. The $4 trillion mark was passed in 1992, and the $5 trillion mark was crossed in 1996. In 2006, we were over the $8 trillion milestone, and over the $9 trillion milestone in 2008.

What are some major causes of the rising national debt? Observe in Exhibit 4(a) the increase in the debt during World War II. In wartime, the government must increase military expenditures sharply and escalate the national debt. Recession also causes the national debt to rise dramatically. Cyclical downturns like the 1930s, 1974–1975, 1981–1982, 1990–1991, and 2001 also cause the debt to rise rapidly because a decline in real GDP automatically increases the budget deficit due to lower tax collections and greater spending for unemployment compensation and welfare. As a result of the $700 billion bailout plan designed in 2008 to boost troubled credit markets, the federal government is expected to finance this plan with government borrowing that will cause a rise in federal deficits, the debt ceiling, the national debt, and net interest on the debt.

EXHIBIT 4 | The National Debt, 1930–2007

In Part (a), we see that the federal debt has skyrocketed since 1980. A concern is that sooner or later the U.S. government will be bankrupt. The counterargument is shown in Part (b). The national debt as a percentage of GDP has declined since the end of World War II, when it reached a peak of about 120 percent. Between 1980 and 1996, the federal debt as a percentage of GDP increased, but in recent years, the ratio has fallen back to its level of the late 1950s. It was about 65 percent in 2007.

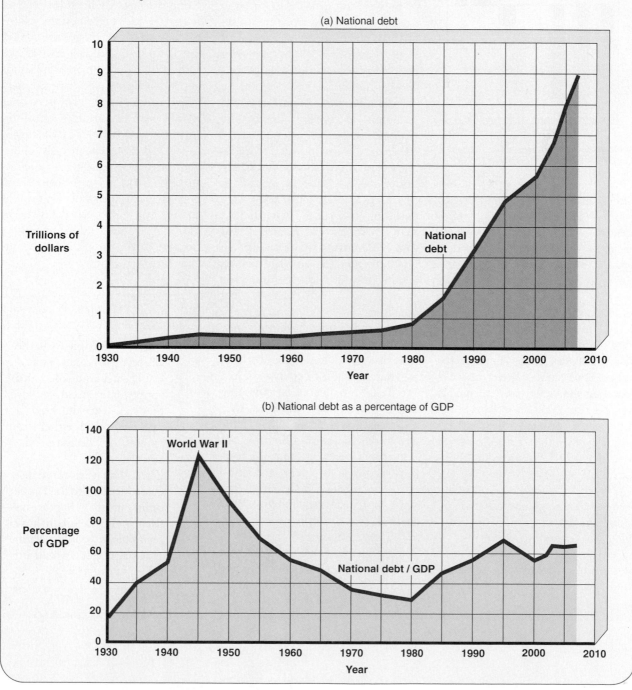

SOURCE: *Economic Report of the President*, 2008, http://www.gpoaccess./eop/, Tables B-78, and B-79.

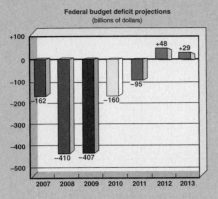

Federal budget deficit projections
(billions of dollars)

SOURCE: Office of Management and Budget, http://www.white-house.gov/budget/fy2007/tables.html, Table 5-1.

After 1969, it took 29 contentious years to eliminate federal budget deficits, and then surpluses occurred only between 1998 and 2001. These federal budget surpluses aroused as much controversy as deficits did in previous years. In short, the hotly contested debate involved whether the surplus should be saved, spent, or devoted to tax cuts. The case for tax cuts and smaller government is based on the view that a surplus is the result of excess tax collections. Proponents pointed out that in 2000, federal tax revenues as a percentage of GDP were the highest in a century. Moreover, tax cuts would spur the economy and prevent future Congresses from spending the surplus. The argument for spending a surplus is based on "unmet needs." Instead of tax cuts, the surplus could be used to finance spending for defense, public infrastructure, research and development, and social programs such as education or prescription drugs. Also, a large proportion of American households pay no income taxes. Tax cuts therefore do not benefit people who are not prosperous enough to pay taxes.

An alternative to tax cuts and spending is paying down the national debt. Former Federal Reserve Chairman Alan Greenspan supported this approach. He said Congress faced the quandary of trying to establish fiscal policy based on long-range forecasts that may prove inaccurate. He stated that if Congress cuts taxes, it also has to be prepared to cut spending significantly in the event that the forecasts on which the cuts were based are proved wrong. On the other hand, using the budget surplus to fund "irrevocable spending programs" would be "the worst of all outcomes." Testifying before the Senate Budget Committee in 2001, Greenspan suggested that the proposed tax cut bill include provisions that would limit the tax cuts if specified targets for the budget surpluses or debt reduction were not met. These provisions were not included in the 2001 tax bill.

The outcome of the "Great Budget Surplus Debate" was that President George W. Bush signed a $1.35 trillion bill in 2001 cutting taxes over 10 years. It was the largest and most widespread tax cut since the 1980s, during Ronald Reagan's presidency. The federal budget projections changed dramatically between 2001 and 2002. In August 2001, the Office of Management and Budget (OMB) projected continuously growing budget surpluses that would peak at about $400 billion in 2007. As shown in the graph, the OMB has dramatically changed its projections to deficits through 2011. The projected deficits have led critics of the tax cut to call for a rollback of the tax cuts. As actual deficit figures become available, check the accuracy of OMB estimates.

ANALYZE THE ISSUE

1. Refer to Exhibit 6 of the chapter on fiscal policy. Using demand-side and supply-side fiscal policy theories, explain how a tax cut could either increase or decrease the price level.

2. Using the Laffer curve discussed in You're the Economist in the chapter on fiscal policy, explain how proponents could claim that the tax cut would increase tax revenues.

Politicians and nonpoliticians alike often speak of the gloom and doom of the national debt. Should we lose sleep over it? To find out, we'll consider three controversial questions:

1. Can Uncle Sam Go Bankrupt?

Reasons to Worry   If households and firms persistently operate in the red, as the federal government does, they will sooner or later go bankrupt. How long can the national debt continue to rise before the U.S. government is broke?

Reasons Not to Worry   Whether private or public debt is the issue, debt must be judged relative to the debtor's ability to repay the principal and interest on the debt. Exhibit 4(b) shows that the national debt as a percentage of GDP is lower today than at the end of World War II. In 1945, the public debt was about 120 percent of GDP, but by 1980 the ratio of debt to GDP had fallen to 33 percent. This means the debt grew considerably slower than GDP between 1945 and 1980. Between 1980 and 1995, however, the trend reversed, and the debt grew faster than GDP, rising from 33 percent to 67 percent of GDP. Still, the United States was not bankrupt in 1945, and it is much farther from going bankrupt today. Moreover, the ratio in 2007 was 65 percent, which was the level in the mid-1950s.

There is an even more important point: Uncle Sam never has to pay off the national debt. At the maturity date on a government security, the U.S. Treasury has the constitutional authority to collect taxes levied by Congress, print money, or refinance its obligations. Suppose the government decides not to raise taxes or cause inflation by simply printing money, so it refinances the debt. When a $1 million government bond comes due, as described earlier in this chapter, the U.S. Treasury can simply "roll over" the debt. This financial trade expression means a borrower (here the federal government) pays off its $1 million bond that reaches maturity by issuing a new $1 million bond. In short, the federal government refinances its debt by replacing old bonds with new bonds. This means the federal government never has to pay off the national debt. These debts can be rolled over forever, provided bond buyers have faith in Uncle Sam.

Global Perspective on the National Debt   Exhibit 5 a provides global perspective on the national debt. This figure shows the ratio of national debt to GDP for several industrialized nations. Canada, the United Kingdom, Sweden, and Australia have a lower debt in relation to GDP than the United States. Japan, on the other hand, has a national debt-to-GDP ratio over twice as large as the U.S. ratio.

GLOBAL ECONOMICS

CHECKPOINT

What's Behind the National Debt?
Suppose the federal government has balanced budgets each year and the entire national debt comes due. How could the federal government pay off the national debt without refinancing, raising taxes, or printing money?

2. Are We Passing the Debt Burden to Our Children?

Reasons to Worry   The fear is that interest payments to finance the national debt will swallow an enormous helping of the federal government's budget pie. This means future generations will pay more of their tax dollars to the government's

EXHIBIT 5   A Global Comparison of National Debt Ratios, 2007

This exhibit shows the ratios of national debt to GDP in 2007 for selected industrialized countries. Japan, Italy, France, and Germany have higher debt-to-GDP ratios than the United States.

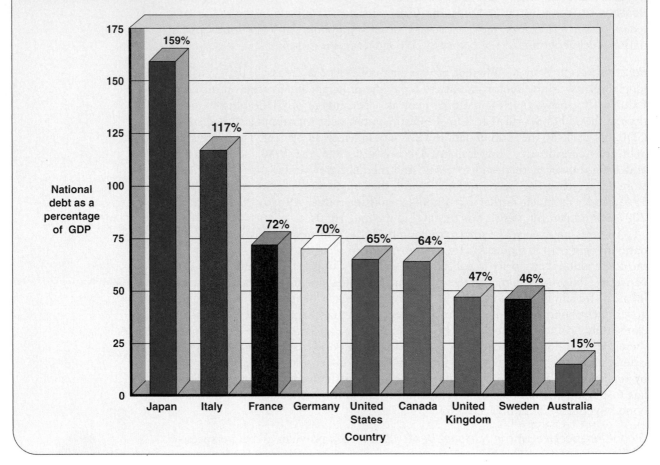

SOURCE: *OECD Economic Outlook.* N 82, December 2007, Annex Table 32, page 254.

creditors and have less to spend for highways, health care, defense, and other public-sector programs. Exhibit 6 shows net interest payments as a percentage of GDP. The net interest payment was only about 1.5 percent of GDP right after World War II, but it increased dramatically after the mid-1970s to more than 3 percent in the mid-1980s. In 2007, the interest payment burden declined to 1.6 percent of GDP.

Reasons Not to Worry   The burden of the national debt on present and future generations depends on who owns the accumulated national debt. Stated more precisely, the burden of the debt depends on whether it is held internally or externally. The bulk of the public debt is internal national debt. Internal national debt is the portion of the national debt owed to a nation's own citizens. Internal debt financing is viewed as "we owe it to ourselves." One U.S. citizen buys a government security and lends Uncle Sam the money to pay the interest and principal on a maturing government security held by another U.S. citizen. Although this redistribution of

Internal national debt

The portion of the national debt owed to a nation's own citizens.

EXHIBIT 6   Federal Net Interest as a Percentage of GDP, 1940–2007

Some fear that interest payments on the national debt will swallow an enormous portion of the federal budget. The exhibit shows that the net interest payment as a proportion of GDP was only about 1.5 percent right after World War II. In the 1980s and early 1990s, however, the interest rate burden increased dramatically. Since 1995, it declined to 1.6 percent of GDP in 2007.

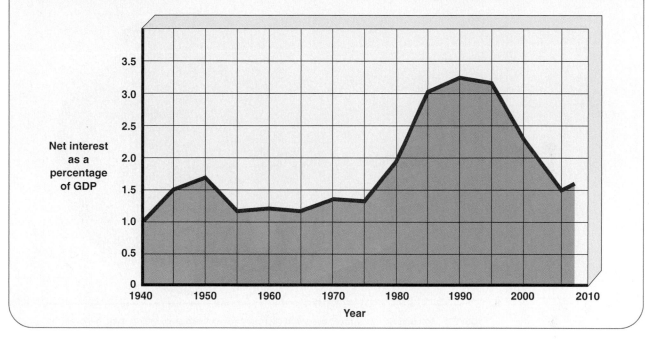

SOURCE: *Economic Report of the President*, 2008, http://www.gpoaccess/eop/, Tables B-1 and B-80.

income and wealth does indeed favor bondholders, who are typically upper-income individuals, transferring dollars between U.S. citizens does not alter the overall purchasing power in the U.S. economy.

Those on the "not to worry" side of this issue also concede that an external national debt is a concern. External national debt is the portion of the national debt owed to foreign citizens. Financing the external national debt means interest and principal payments are transfers of money from U.S. citizens to other nations. If foreign governments, banks, corporations, and individual investors hold part of the national debt, the "we owe it to ourselves" argument is weakened. Exhibit 7 shows who owns the securities the U.S. Treasury has issued. In 2007, foreigners owned 25 percent of the total national debt. Fifty-two percent was held by the federal, state, and local governments, primarily by federal agencies such as the U.S. Treasury, the Social Security Administration, and Federal Reserve banks. The Federal Reserve is an independent government agency, as explained in the next chapter. The private sector, consisting of individuals, banks, corporations, and insurance companies, held 23 percent of the national debt. The debt held by the private sector and government entities constitutes the internal national debt.

Although 75 percent of the national debt was internal, the 25 percent of total U.S. debt that is external debt is not necessarily undesirable. Foreign investment in the United States supplements domestic saving. Borrowing from abroad can prevent

External national debt

The portion of the national debt owed to foreign citizens.

| EXHIBIT 7 | Ownership of the National Debt, 2007 |

In 2007, about 52 percent of the national debt was held by the public sector, including federal, state, and local governments and Federal Reserve banks. The private sector, including individuals, banks, corporations, and insurance companies, held 23 percent, and foreigners owned the remaining 25 percent.

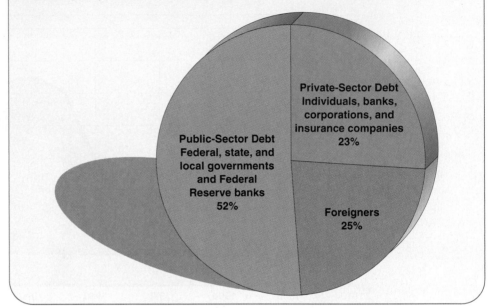

Private-Sector Debt
Individuals, banks,
corporations, and
insurance companies
23%

Public-Sector Debt
Federal, state, and
local governments
and Federal
Reserve banks
52%

Foreigners
25%

SOURCE: *Economic Report of the President,* 2008, http://www.gpoaccess.gov/eop/, Table B-89.

the higher interest rates that would exist if the U.S. Treasury relied only on domestic savers to purchase federal government securities. A lower interest rate increases U.S. investment and consumer spending, causing the aggregate demand curve to shift rightward.

If we do not need to worry about shifting the burden to future generations, can the current generation escape the debt burden? The answer is *No.* During World War II, for example, the United States operated at full employment along its *production possibilities curve.* As illustrated earlier in Exhibit 2 of Chapter 2, the people at that time in history were forced to trade off consumer goods production for military goods production. Because massive amounts of resources were diverted to fight World War II, people at that time were forced to give up private consumption of houses, cars, refrigerators, and so on. After the war was over, resources were again devoted to producing more consumer goods and fewer military goods. The same analysis can be used today. At full employment, the burden of the national debt on the current generation is the opportunity cost of private-sector goods forgone because land, labor, and capital are used to produce public-sector goods.

In other words, the burden of the national debt is incurred when production takes place; it is not postponed until the debt is paid by future generations. When the debt comes due in the future, the government can simply refinance the debt and redistribute money from one group of citizens to another. This redistribution of income does not cause a reallocation of resources away from consumer goods and services in favor of government programs.

3. Does Government Borrowing Crowd Out Private-Sector Spending?

Reasons to Worry   Critics of Keynesian fiscal policy believe that government spending financed by borrowing designed to boost aggregate demand has little, if any, effect on growth of real GDP. The reason is that the crowding-out effect dampens the stimulus to aggregate demand from increased federal government spending. The crowding-out effect is a reduction in private-sector spending as a result of higher interest rates caused by U.S. Treasury borrowing (selling securities) to finance government spending. For example, suppose the federal government spends and borrows, rather than collecting taxes, to finance new health care programs. In this case, the size of the national debt rises, and interest rates are pushed up in loan markets. Interest rates rise because the federal government competes with private borrowers for available savings, and less credit is available to consumers and business borrowers. The result of this crowding-out effect is lower consumption $(-\Delta C)$ and business investment $(-\Delta I)$, which offset the boost in aggregate demand $(+\Delta AD)$ from increased government spending $(+\Delta G)$ operating through the spending multiplier.

The crowding-out effect contradicts the theory, explained in the previous Reasons Not to Worry section, that future generations do not bear some of today's debt burden. Recall from Chapter 2 that current investment spending increases living standards in the future by shifting the production possibilities curve outward (Exhibit 5 in Chapter 2). If federal borrowing crowds out private investment in plants and equipment, future generations will have a smaller possible productive capacity.

The *AD-AS* model will help you understand the crowding-out concept. Exhibit 8 reproduces the situation in which government spending is used to combat a recession, depicted earlier in Exhibit 2 of the chapter on fiscal policy. Begin at E_1, with an equilibrium GDP of $4 trillion, and assume the government increases its spending and uses the spending multiplier to shift the aggregate demand curve rightward from AD_1 to AD_2. Following Keynesian theory, there is zero crowding out, and the economy achieves full employment at equilibrium point E_2, corresponding to real GDP of $8 trillion. Critics of Keynesian theory, however, argue that crowding out occurs. The result of expansionary fiscal policy is not E_2, but some equilibrium point along the *AS* line between E_1 and E_2. For example, a fall in private expenditures might partially offset the government spending stimulus. With incomplete crowding out, the aggregate demand curve increases only to AD'_2 because of the decline in consumption and investment. The economy therefore moves to E'_2 at a real GDP of $6 trillion and does not achieve full employment at E_2. Or crowding out can completely offset the multiplier effect of increased government spending. The fall in private expenditures by consumers and businesses can result in no change in aggregate demand curve AD_1. In this case, the economy remains at E_1, with unemployment unaffected by expansionary policy. Meanwhile, the deficit required to finance extra government spending increases the national debt.

Reasons Not to Worry   The crowding-out effect is controversial. Keynesian economists counter critics by saying that any crowding-out effect is small or nonexistent. Instead, at below full-employment real GDP, their counterargument is the crowding-in effect. For example, government capital spending for highways, dams, universities, and infrastructure financed by borrowing might offset any decline in private investment. Another Keynesian argument is that consumers and businesspersons may believe that federal spending is "just what the doctor ordered"

Crowding-out effect

A reduction in private-sector spending as a result of federal budget deficits financed by U.S. Treasury borrowing. When federal government borrowing increases interest rates, the result is lower consumption by households and lower investment spending by businesses.

Crowding-in effect

An increase in private-sector spending as a result of federal budget deficits financed by U.S. Treasury borrowing. At less than full employment, consumers hold more Treasury securities, and this additional wealth causes them to spend more. Businesses investment spending increases because of optimistic profit expectations.

EXHIBIT 8   Zero, Partial, and Complete Crowding Out

Beginning at equilibrium E_1, the federal government borrows to finance a deficit created by expansionary fiscal policy. Keynesian theory predicts zero crowding out, which means that an increase in government spending operates through the spending multiplier to shift aggregate demand from AD_1 to AD_2. If crowding out is zero, consumption and investment spending are unaffected by the increase in government spending financed by borrowing. Partial crowding out occurs when a decrease in private spending partially offsets the multiplier effect from an increase in deficit-financed government spending. Partial crowding out results in a shift only from AD_1 to AD_2' and an equilibrium at E_2', rather than E_2. If crowding out is complete, a decrease in private spending completely offsets the increase in government spending financed by debt. In this case, the aggregate demand curve remains at AD_1, and the economy remains at E_1.

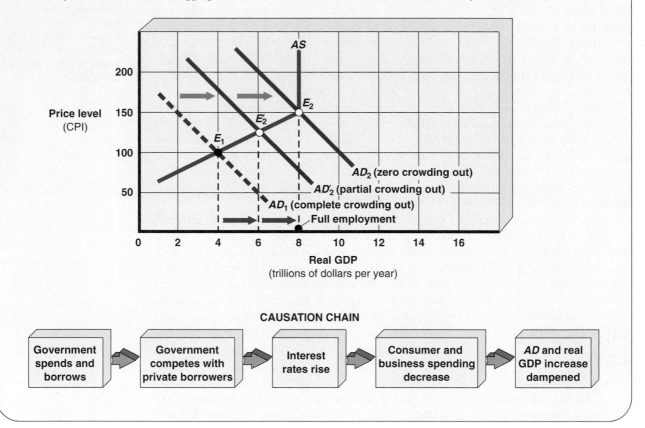

CAUSATION CHAIN

| Government spends and borrows | ⇒ | Government competes with private borrowers | ⇒ | Interest rates rise | ⇒ | Consumer and business spending decrease | ⇒ | *AD* and real GDP increase dampened |

for an ailing economy. Federal borrowing incurred to finance the new spending would boost consumption and therefore increase aggregate demand. The reason is because holders of Treasury bills, notes, and bonds feel richer. As a result of their greater wealth, consumers spend more now and plan to spend more in the future. Such a blush of optimism may also raise the profit expectations of business managers, and they may increase investment spending. The effect of increased private-sector spending could nullify some or all of the crowding-out effect, which would otherwise offset the boost in aggregate demand from increased government spending. Hence, as explained in the graphical analysis in Exhibit 8, the spending multiplier shifts the aggregate demand curve from AD_1 to AD_2, with zero crowding out.

Finally, both sides of the debate agree that complete crowding out occurs in one situation. Suppose the economy is operating at full employment (point E_2). This is comparable to being on the economy's production possibilities curve. If the

Applicable Concept: national debt and federal deficit

Perhaps the national debt and federal budget deficits are really not so large and threatening. For example, it can be argued that we should use real rather than nominal values to report in the national debt—similar to using real GDP to report economic growth. Suppose the national debt rises from $10 trillion to $10.3 trillion and the price level increases by 3 percent in a given year. The nominal value of the national debt therefore has risen by $300 billion because the government must issue $300 billion in newly issued government securities due to higher prices, and real growth in the national debt is therefore zero.

Critics also warn that federal accounting rules are an economic policy disaster. Private businesses, as well as state and local governments, use two budgets. One is the *operating budget,* which includes salaries, interest payments, and other current expenses. The second type of budget, called a *capital budget,* includes spending for investment items, such as machines, buildings, and roads. Expenditures on the capital budget yield benefits over time and may be paid for by long-term borrowing. The federal government does not use a capital budget. Capital budgeting allows spreading the cost of long-lasting assets over future years. For example, the federal budget makes no distinction between the rental cost of a federal office building and the cost of constructing a new federal office building to replace rented office space. However, payments on borrowing for a new building provide the benefit of a long-lasting asset that offsets rent payments. If a capital budgeting system were used, the public would see that most federal borrowing really finances assets yielding long-term benefits. In short, proponents of a capital budget believe the public's focus should be on the operating budget, which gives a truer measure of the federal deficit. Opponents of changing the accounting rules argue that controversial expenditures would be placed in the capital budget in order to manipulate the size of the deficit or surplus in the operating budget for political reasons.

Finally, some economists argue for other numerical adjustments that show the federal deficit or surplus is really not as it seems. They say it is not the federal deficit or surplus that really matters, but the combined deficits or surpluses of federal, state, and local governments. When state and local governments run budget surpluses, these surpluses are a source of savings in financial markets that adds to federal surpluses or offsets federal borrowing to finance its deficit.

ANALYZE THE ISSUE

1. Do households make a distinction between spending for current expenses and spending for capital expenses? Compare borrowing $5,000 to take a vacation in Hawaii to borrowing $125,000 to buy a condominium and move out of your rented apartment.

2. Critics of "new accounting" for federal borrowing argue that it does not matter what the government spends the money for. What matters is the total amount that the government spends minus taxes collected. Explain this viewpoint.

government shifts the aggregate demand curve rightward by increasing spending or cutting taxes, the result will be higher prices and a replacement of private-sector output with public-sector output.

Conclusion *Crowding out is complete if the economy is at full employment, but debatable at less than full employment.*

KEY CONCEPTS

National debt
Net public debt
Debt ceiling

Internal national debt
External national debt

Crowding-out effect
Crowding-in effect

SUMMARY

- The *national debt* is the dollar amount that the federal government owes holders of government securities. It is the cumulative sum of past deficits. The U.S. Treasury issues government securities to finance the deficits. The debt has increased sharply since 1980.

National Debt

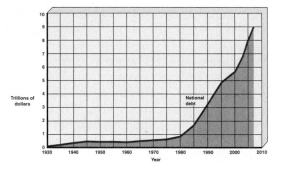

- The *net public debt* is the national debt minus all government interagency borrowing (the debt that the federal government owes to itself).
- A *debt ceiling* is a method used to restrict the growth of the national debt.
- *Internal national debt* is the percentage of the national debt a nation owes to its own citizens. In 2007, about 75 percent of the national debt was internally held by individuals, banks, corporations, insurance companies, and government entities. The "we owe it to ourselves" argument over the debt is that U.S. citizens own the bulk of the U.S. national debt. *External national debt* is a burden because it is the portion of the national debt a nation owes to foreigners. The interest paid on external debt transfers purchasing power to other nations. In 2007, approximately 25 percent of the national debt was external.

Internal and External National Debt

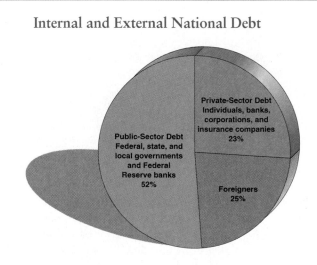

- The *burden of the debt debate* involves controversial questions:

  1. *Can Uncle Sam Go Bankrupt?* The U.S. government will not go bankrupt because it never has to pay off its debt. When government securities mature, the U.S. Treasury can refinance, or roll over, the debt by issuing new securities.

  2. *Are We Passing the Debt Burden to Our Children?* One side of this argument is that the burden of the debt falls only on the current generation when the tradeoff between public-sector goods and private-sector goods along the production possibilities curve occurs. In short, when resources are used to make missiles today, citizens are forced to give up, say, airplane production in the current period and not later. The counterargument is that there is a sizable external national debt that transfers purchasing power to foreigners.

  3. *Does Government Borrowing Crowd Out Private-Sector Spending?* The *crowding-out effect* is a burden of the national debt that occurs when the government borrows to

finance its deficit, causing the interest rate to rise. As the interest rate rises, consumption and business investment fall. If *crowding out* occurs, reduced private spending completely or partially offsets the multiplier effect of increased government spending.

Opponents believe in the ***crowding-in effect.*** In this view, government capital spending for highways, dams, universities, and infrastructure offsets any decline in business investment from crowding out.

Zero, Partial, and Complete Crowding Out

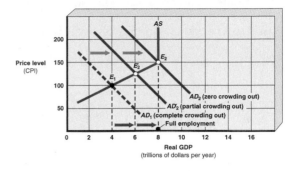

SUMMARY OF CONCLUSION STATEMENTS

- The national debt includes the Social Security trust fund, and, as a result, federal budget deficits are reduced or budget surpluses are raised.

- Crowding out is complete if the economy is at full employment, but it is debatable at less than full employment.

STUDY QUESTIONS AND PROBLEMS

1. Explain the relationship between budget deficits and the national debt.

2. Discuss various ways of measuring the size of the national debt.

3. Explain this statement: "The national debt is like taking money out of your left pocket and putting it into your right pocket."

4. Explain this statement: "The most unlikely problem of the national debt is that the government will go bankrupt."

5. Suppose the percentage of the federal debt owned by foreigners increases sharply. Would this trend concern you? Why or why not?

6. Explain the theory that crowding out can weaken or nullify the effect of expansionary fiscal policy financed by federal government borrowing.

7. Suppose the federal government has no national debt and spends $100 billion, while raising only $50 billion in taxes.
   a. What amount of government bonds will the U.S. Treasury issue to finance the deficit?

   b. Next year, assume tax revenues remain at $50 billion. If the government pays a 10 percent rate of interest, add the debt-servicing interest payment to the government's $100 billion expenditure for goods and services the second year.

   c. For the second year, compute the deficit, the amount of new debt issued, and the new national debt.

8. Suppose the media report that the federal deficit this year is $200 billion. The national debt was $5,000 billion last year, and it is $5,200 billion this year. The price level this year is 3 percent higher than it was last year. What is the real deficit?

9. During the presidential campaign of 1932 in the depth of the Great Depression, candidates Herbert Hoover and Franklin D. Roosevelt both advocated reducing the budget deficit, using tax hikes and/or expenditure reductions. Evaluate this fiscal policy.

10. Consider this statement: "Our grandchildren may not suffer the entire burden of a federal deficit." Do you agree or disagree? Explain.

11. Suppose you are the economic policy advisor to the president and are asked what should be done to eliminate a federal deficit. What would you recommend?

For Online Exercises, go the text Web site at www.cengage.com/economics/tucker.

CHECKPOINT ANSWER ✓

What's Behind the National Debt?
Every item owned by the federal government, including the White House, office buildings, tanks, and computers, is an asset standing behind the national debt. If you said the assets of the federal government could be sold to pay off the national debt, **YOU ARE CORRECT.**

PRACTICE QUIZ

For an explanation of the correct answers, please visit the tutorial at www.cengage.com/economics/tucker.

1. During the late 1990s, federal government budget deficits
   a. were completely removed.
   b. dropped significantly from a high of $300 billion.
   c. remained fairly stable at about $150 billion per year.
   d. exceeded $200 billion in each year.

2. The federal government finances a budget by
   a. taxing businesses and households.
   b. selling Treasury securities.
   c. printing more money.
   d. reducing its purchases of goods and services.

3. In 2007, the national debt was approximately
   a. $90 billion.
   b. $900 billion.
   c. $9 trillion.
   d. $8 trillion.

4. The national debt in 2007
   a. was about four times larger than in 1980.
   b. was twice as large in 1980.
   c. was approximately the same size in 1980.
   d. was none of the above.

5. Which of the following countries had the smallest national debt as a percentage of GDP in 2007?
   a. Italy
   b. Canada
   c. Australia
   d. Japan
   e. France

6. Which of the following is *false*?
   a. The national debt decreased steadily after World War II until 1980 and then increased sharply each year.
   b. The national debt increases whenever the federal government has a budget surplus.
   c. The national debt is currently about the same size as it was during World War II.
   d. All of the above are false.

7. In 2007, approximately what percentage of the U.S. national debt was owed to foreigners?
   a. 2.5 percent
   b. 25 percent
   c. 30 percent
   d. 60 percent

8. Which of the following own a portion of the national debt?
   a. Federal, state, and local governments
   b. Private U.S. citizens
   c. Banks
   d. Foreigners
   e. All of the above

9. The portion of the U.S. national debt held by foreigners
   a. represents a burden because it transfers purchasing power from U.S. taxpayers to other countries.
   b. is an accounting entry that represents no real burden.
   c. decreased as a proportion of the total debt during the 2000s.
   d. has been constant for many decades.

10. Which of the following statements about crowding out is *true*?
    a. It is caused by a budget surplus.
    b. It is not caused by a budget deficit.
    c. It cannot completely offset the multiplier effect of deficit government spending.
    d. It affects interest rates and, in turn, consumption and investment spending.

11. Which of the following statements about crowding out is *true*?
    a. It can completely offset the multiplier.
    b. It is caused by a budget deficit.
    c. It is not caused by a budget surplus.
    d. All of the above are true.

12. "Crowding in" refers to federal government deficits
    a. used for public infrastructure, which will offset any decline in business investment.
    b. which reduce private business and consumption spending.
    c. which reduce future rates of economic growth.
    d. all of the above.

13. When measured as a percentage of GDP, the U.S. national debt reached its highest levels as a result of
    a. World War II.
    b. The Vietnam War.
    c. The Reagan defense buildup and tax cuts.
    d. The Bush economic recovery program.

14. The national debt is unlikely to cause national bankruptcy because the
    a. national debt can be refinanced by issuing new bonds.
    b. interest on the public debt equals GDP.
    c. national debt cannot be shifted to future generations for repayment.
    d. federal government cannot repudiate the outstanding national debt.

15. Supply-side economists argue that less government spending
    a. will contract the productive side of the economy.
    b. will result in more crowding out.
    c. causes higher rates of unemployment and inflation.
    d. would cause interest rates to increase dramatically.
    e. would make more investment capital available at lower rates of interest to the private sector.

Road Map

PART 6

MACROECONOMIC THEORY AND POLICY ISSUES

This road map feature helps you tie material in the part together as you travel the Economic Way of Thinking Highway. The following are review questions listed by chapter from the previous part. The key concept in each question is given for emphasis, and each question or set of questions concludes with an interactive game to reinforce the concepts. Click on the Tucker Web site, select the chapter, and play the visual causation chain game designed to make learning fun. Enjoy the cheers when correct and suffer the jeers if you miss.

For an explanation of the correct answers, please visit the tutorial at www.cengage.com/economics/tucker.

Chapter 18. The Keynesian Model

1. **Key Concept: Consumption Function**
   The consumption function will shift for all of the following reasons except
   a. a change in a household's real assets.
   b. a change in interest rates.
   c. expectations of price changes.
   d. changes in a households' disposable incomes.
   e. changes in taxation policy.

   Causation Chain Game
   Movement Along and Shifts in the Consumption Function—Exhibit 6

2. **Key Concept: Investment Demand Curve**
   Which of the following will increase investment spending?
   a. More optimistic business expectations.
   b. An increase in interest rates.
   c. An increase in business taxes.
   d. A decrease in capacity utilization.
   e. All of the above.

   Causation Chain Game
   Movement Along and Shifts in a Firm's Investment Demand—Exhibit 8

3. **Key Concept: Spending Multiplier**
   The ratio of the change in GDP to an initial change in aggregate expenditures (*AE*) is the
   a. spending multiplier.
   b. permanent income rate.
   c. marginal expenditure rate.
   d. marginal propensity to consume.

   Causation Chain Game
   The Multiplier Effect and Government Spending—Exhibit 4

Chapter 20. Aggregate Demand and Supply

4. **Key Concept: Aggregate Demand Curve**

   Which of the following is *not* a reason for the downward slope of an aggregate demand curve?
   a. Real balance or wealth effect.
   b. Real interest rate effect.
   c. Net exports effect.
   d. All of the above are reasons.

   Causation Chain Game
   The Aggregate Demand Curve—Exhibit 1

5. **Key Concept: Aggregate Demand Curve**

   Which of the following could *not* be expected to shift the aggregate demand curve?
   a. Net exports fall.
   b. Consumption spending decreases.
   c. An increase in government spending.
   d. A change in real GDP.

   Causation Chain Game
   A Shift in the Aggregate Demand Curve—Exhibit 3

6. **Key Concept: Aggregate Supply Curve**

   The horizontal segment of the aggregate supply curve
   a. shows that real GDP can increase only by affecting the economy's price level.
   b. shows that real GDP can increase without affecting the economy's price level.
   c. depicts a positive relationship between real GDP and the price level.
   d. depicts a negative relationship between real GDP and the price level.
   e. marks the full-employment level of real GDP.

   Causation Chain Game
   The Keynesian Horizontal Aggregate Supply Curve—Exhibit 4

7. **Key Concept: Aggregate Supply Curve**

   According to classical theory, if the aggregate demand curve decreased and the economy experienced unemployment, then
   a. the economy would remain in this condition indefinitely.
   b. the government must increase spending to restore full employment.
   c. prices and wages would fall quickly to restore full employment.
   d. the supply of money would increase until the economy returned to full employment.

   Causation Chain Game
   The Classical Vertical Aggregate Supply Curve—Exhibit 5

8. **Key Concept: Aggregate Supply Curve**

   If a new method for obtaining oil from dry oil fields is found, then we will see
   a. the *AS* curve shift to the left.
   b. a movement to the left along the *AD* curve.
   c. the *AD* curve shift to the left.
   d. the *AD* curve shift to the right.
   e. the *AS* curve shift to the right.

    Causation Chain Game
   A Rightward Shift in the Aggregate Supply Curve—Exhibit 9

9. **Key Concept: Cost-push Inflation**

   Cost-push inflation occurs when the
   a. aggregate demand curve shifts leftward while the aggregate supply curve is fixed.
   b. aggregate supply curve shifts leftward while the aggregate demand curve is fixed.
   c. aggregate demand curve shifts rightward while the aggregate supply curve is fixed.
   d. aggregate supply curve shifts rightward.

    Causation Chain Game
   Cost-Push and Demand-Pull Inflation— Exhibit 11

10. **Key Concept: Demand-Pull Inflation**

    Demand-pull inflation is caused by
    a. an increase in aggregate demand.
    b. a decrease in aggregate demand.
    c. an increase in aggregate supply.
    d. a decrease in aggregate supply.

     Causation Chain Game
    Cost-Push and Demand-Pull Inflation— Exhibit 11

Chapter 21. Fiscal Policy

11. **Key Concept: Fiscal Policy**

    Which of the following would be an appropriate discretionary fiscal policy to use when the economy is in a recession?
    a. Increased government spending.
    b. Higher taxes.
    c. A balanced-budget reduction in both spending and taxes.
    d. An expansion in the money supply.

     Causation Chain Game
    Using Government Spending to Combat a Recession—Exhibit 2

12. **Key Concept: Fiscal Policy**

If no fiscal policy changes are implemented to fight inflation, suppose the aggregate demand curve will exceed the current aggregate demand curve by $900 billion at any level of prices. Assuming the marginal propensity to consume is 0.90, this increase in aggregate demand could be prevented by

a.   increasing government spending by $500 billion.
b.   increasing government spending by $140 billion.
c.   decreasing taxes by $40 billion.
d.   increasing taxes by $100 billion.

Causation Chain Game
Using Fiscal Policy to Combat Inflation—Exhibit 6

13. **Key Concept: Automatic Stabilizers**

Automatic stabilizers "lean against the prevailing wind" of the business cycle because

a.   wages are controlled by the minimum-wage law.
b.   federal expenditures and tax revenues change as the level of real GDP changes.
c.   the spending and tax multipliers are constant.
d.   they include the power of special interests.

Causation Chain Game
Automatic Stabilizers—Exhibit 5

14. **Key Concept: Supply-Side Economics**

An advocate of supply-side fiscal policy would advocate which of the following?

a.   Subsidies to produce technological advances.
b.   Reduction in regulation.
c.   Reduction in resource prices.
d.   Reduction in taxes.
e.   All of the above.

Causation Chain Game
Keynesian Demand-Side Versus Supply-Side Effects—Exhibit 8

Chapter 23. Federal Deficits, Surpluses, and the National Debt

15. **Key Concept: Federal Budget Process**

If Congress fails to pass a budget before the fiscal year starts, then federal agencies may continue to operate only if Congress has passed a

a.   balanced budget amendment.
b.   deficit reduction plan.
c.   conference resolution.
d.   continuing resolution.

Causation Chain Game
Major Steps in the Federal Budgetary Process—Exhibit 1

Money, Banking, and Monetary Policy

S tudents often find the material in these chapters the most interesting in their principles course because the topic is *money*. The first chapter begins the discussion of money with basic definitions and a description of the Federal Reserve System. Of special interest is a feature on the history of money in the colonies. The next chapter explains how the banking system and the Federal Reserve influence the supply of money. The following chapter compares different macroeconomic theories and concludes with a discussion of monetary policy in the Great Depression and the financial crisis of 2008. The final chapter in this part explores additional macro theories based on expectations.

Money and the Federal Reserve System

© David Muir/Digital Vision/Getty Images.

A s the lyrics of the old song go, "Money makes the world go around, the world go around, the world go around." Recall the circular flow model presented in the chapter on GDP. Households exchange *money* for goods and services in the product markets, and firms exchange *money* for resources in the factor markets. In short, money affects the way an economy works. In the chapter on aggregate demand and supply and the chapter on fiscal policy presented earlier in the text, the *AD-AS* model was developed without explicitly discussing money. In this chapter, and throughout this part, money takes center stage.

Exactly what is money? The answer may surprise you. Imagine yourself on the small South Pacific island of Yap. You are surrounded by exotic fowl, crystal-clear lagoons, delicious fruits, and sunny skies. Now suppose while leisurely strolling along the beach one evening, you

suddenly discover a beautiful bamboo hut for sale. As you will discover in this chapter, to pay for your dream hut, you must roll a 5-foot-diameter stone to the area of the island designated as the "bank."

We begin our discussion of money with the three functions money serves. Next, we identify the components of three different definitions of the money supply used in the United States. The remainder of the chapter describes the organization and services of the Federal Reserve System, our nation's central bank. Also, we discuss the Monetary Control Act of 1980 and its relationship to the savings and loan crisis of the 1980s and early 1990s. Beginning in this chapter and in the next three chapters, you will learn how the Federal Reserve System controls the stock of money in the economy. Then, using the *AD-AS* model, you will learn how variations in the stock of money in the economy affect total spending, unemployment, and prices.

What Makes Money *Money*?

Can exchange occur in an economy without money? It certainly can, using a trading system called barter. Barter is the direct exchange of one good or service for another good or service, rather than for money. The problem with barter is that it requires a *coincidence of wants*. Imagine for a moment that dollars and coins are worthless. Farmer Brown needs shoes, so he takes his bushels of wheat to the shoe store and offers to barter wheat for shoes. Unfortunately, the store owner refuses to barter because she wants to trade shoes for pencils, toothpaste, and coffee. Undaunted, Farmer Brown spends more time and effort to find Mr. Jones, who has pencils, toothpaste, and coffee he will trade for bushels of wheat. Although Farmer Brown's luck has improved, he and Mr. Jones must agree on the terms of exchange. Exactly how many pounds of coffee, for example, is a bushel of wheat worth? Assuming this exchange is worked out, Farmer Brown must spend more time returning to the shoe store and negotiating the terms of an exchange of pencils, coffee, and toothpaste for shoes.

> **Conclusion** *The use of money simplifies and therefore increases market transactions. Money also prevents wasting time that can be devoted to production, thereby promoting economic growth by increasing a nation's production possibilities.*

The Three Functions of Money

Suppose citizens of the planet of Starcom want to replace their barter system and must decide what to use for money. Assuming this planet is fortunate enough to have economists, they would explain that anything, regardless of its value, can serve as money if it conforms to the following definition. Money is anything that serves as a medium of exchange, unit of account, and store of value. Money is not limited to dimes, quarters, and dollar bills. Notice that "anything" meeting the three tests is a candidate to serve as money. This explains why precious metals, beaver skins, wampum (shells strung in belts), and cigarettes have all served as money. Let's discuss each of the three functions money serves.

Money as a Medium of Exchange   In a simple society, barter is a way for participants to exchange goods and services in order to satisfy wants. Barter, however, requires wasting time in the process of exchange that people could use for productive work. If the goal is to increase the volume of transactions and live in a modern

Barter
The direct exchange of one good or service for another good or service, rather than for money.

Money
Anything that serves as a medium of exchange, unit of account, and store of value.

Medium of exchange

The primary function of money to be widely accepted in exchange for goods and services.

economy, the most important function of money is to serve as a medium of exchange. Medium of exchange is the primary function of money to be widely accepted in exchange for goods and services. Money removes the problem of coincidence of wants because everyone is willing to accept money in payment, rather than goods and services. You give up two $20 bills in exchange for a ticket to see a rock concert. Because money serves as generalized purchasing power, all in society know that no one will refuse to trade their products for money. In short, money increases trade by providing a much more convenient method of exchange than a cumbersome barter system.

A fascinating question is whether people will find digital cash a more convenient means of payment. Each year more people avoid using checks, paper currency, or coins by transferring funds electronically from their accounts via various Internet-based and other systems. In fact, it is possible that widespread adoption of privately issued digital cash will ultimately replace government-issued currency. Vending and copy machines on many college campuses already accept plastic stored-value cards. Someday vending machines everywhere are likely to have smart card readers that accept electronic money.

Money as a Unit of Account   How does a wheat farmer know whether a bushel of wheat is worth one, two, or more pairs of shoes? How does a family compare its income to expenses or a business know whether it is making a profit? Government must be able to measure tax revenues collected and program expenditures made. And GDP is the *money* value of final goods and services used to compare the national output of the United States to, say, Japan's output. In each of these examples, money serves as a unit of account. Without money, we face the difficult task of, say, pricing pizzas in terms of other goods. Unit of account is the function of money to provide a common measurement of the relative value of goods and services. Without dollars, there is no common denominator. We must therefore decide if one pizza equals a box of pencils, 20 oranges equals one quart of milk, and so forth. Now let's compare the value of two items using money. If the price of one pizza is $10 and the price of a movie ticket is $5, then the value of one pizza equals two movie tickets. In the United States, the monetary unit is the dollar; in Japan, it is the yen; Mexico has its peso; and so on.

Unit of account

The function of money to provide a common measurement of the relative value of goods and services.

Money as a Store of Value   Can you save shrimp for months and then exchange them for some product? You could, but not without the extra expense of freezing the shrimp. Money, on the other hand, serves as a store of value in exchange for some item in the future. Store of value is the ability of money to hold value over time. You can bury money in your backyard or store it under your mattress for months or years and not worry about it spoiling. Stated differently, money allows us to synchronize our income more precisely with expenditures. However, recall from the chapter on inflation that hyperinflation can destroy money's store-of-value function and, in turn, its medium-of-exchange function.

Store of value

The ability of money to hold value over time.

> **Conclusion** *Money is a useful mechanism for transforming income in the present into future purchases.*

The key property of money is that it is completely *liquid*. This means that money is immediately available to spend in exchange for goods and services without any additional expense. Money is more liquid than real assets (real estate or gold) or paper assets (stocks or bonds). These assets also serve as stores of value, but liquidating (selling) them often involves expenses, such as brokerage fees, and time delays.

> **Conclusion** *Money is the most liquid form of wealth because it can be spent directly in the marketplace.*

Are Credit Cards Money?

Credit cards, such as Visa, MasterCard, and American Express, are often called "plastic money," but are these cards really money? Let's test credit cards for the three functions of money. First, because credit cards are widely accepted, they serve as a means of payment in an exchange for goods or services.

Second, the credit card statement, and not the card itself, serves as a unit of account. One of the advantages of credit cards is that you receive a statement listing the exact price in dollars paid for each item you charged. Your credit card statement clearly records the dollar amount you spent for gasoline, a dinner, or a trip.

But credit cards clearly fail to meet the store-of-value criterion and are therefore *not* money. The word *credit* means receiving money today to buy products in return for a promise to pay in the future. A credit card represents only a prearranged short-term loan up to a certain limit. If the credit card company goes out of business or for any reason decides not to honor your card, it is worthless. Hence, credit cards do not store value and are *not* money. If credit cards were money, you would be indifferent between receiving $1,000 in cash and an equal dollar increase in your credit limit.

> **CHECKPOINT**
> **Are Debit Cards Money?**
> Debit cards are used to pay for purchases, and the money is automatically deducted from the user's bank account. Are debit cards money?

Other Desirable Properties of Money

Once something has passed the three basic requirements to serve as money, there are additional hurdles to clear. First, an important consideration is *scarcity*. Money must be scarce, but not too scarce. Sand, for example, could theoretically serve as money, but sand is a poor choice because people can easily gather a bucketful to pay their bills. A Picasso painting would also be undesirable as money. Because there are so few for circulation, people would have to resort to barter.

Counterfeiting threatens the scarcity of money. Advances in computer graphics, scanners, and color copiers were allowing counterfeiters to win their ongoing battle with the U.S. Secret Service. In reponse, new bills were issued with a polymer security thread running through them. The larger off-center portraits on the bills allow for a watermark next to the portrait that is visible from both sides against a light.

> **Conclusion** *The supply of money must be great enough to meet ordinary transaction needs, but not be so plentiful that it becomes worthless.*

Applicable Concept: functions of money

On the tiny South Pacific island of Yap, life is easy, but the currency is hard as a rock. For nearly 2,000 years the Yapese have used large stone wheels to pay for major purchases, such as land, canoes, and permission to marry. The people of Yap have been using stone money ever since a Yapese warrior named Anagumang used canoes to bring the huge stones over the sea in ancient times from limestone caverns on neighboring Palau. Inspired by the moon, he fashioned the stones into large circles, and the rest is history. The stones' value remained high because of the difficulty and hazards involved in obtaining them over the rough seas.

Yap is a U.S. trust territory, and the dollar is used in grocery stores and gas stations, but reliance on stone money continues. Buying property with stones is "much easier than buying it with U.S. dollars," says John Chodad, who purchased a building lot with a 30-inch stone wheel. "We don't know the value of the U.S. dollar."[1] However, stone wheels don't make good pocket money, so Yapese use other forms of currency, such as beer for small transactions. Besides stone wheels and beer, the Yapese sometimes spend gaw, consisting of necklaces of stone beads strung together around a whale's tooth.

They also buy things with yar, a currency made from large seashells, but these are small change.

Stone disks may change ownership during marriage, transfer of land title, or other exchanges. Yapese lean the stone wheels against their houses or prop up rows of them in village "banks." Most of the stones are smaller in diameter, but some are as much as 12 feet in diameter. Each has a hole in the center so it can be slipped onto the trunk of a fallen betel–nut tree and carried. It takes 20 men to lift some wheels. Rather than risk a broken stone—or their backs—Yapese leave the larger stones where they are and make a mental accounting that the ownership has been transferred. There are some decided advantages to using massive stones for money. They are in short supply, difficult to steal, pose formidable obstacles to counterfeiting, and serve as a tourist attraction.

ANALYZE THE ISSUE

1. Explain how Yap's large stones pass the three tests in the definition of money.
2. Briefly discuss Yap's large stones in terms of other desirable properties of money.

---

1. Art Pine, "Fixed Assets, Or: Why a Loan in Yap Is Hard to Roll Over," *The Wall Street Journal*, Mar. 29, 1984, p. 1.

Second, money should be *portable* and *divisible*. That is, people should be able to reach into their pockets and make change to buy items at various prices. Statues of George Washington might be attractive money, but they would be difficult to carry and make change. Finally, money must be *uniform*. An ounce of gold is an ounce of gold. The quality differences of beaver skins and seashells, on the other hand, complicate using these items for money. Each exchange would involve the extra trouble of buyers and sellers arguing over which skins or shells are better or worse.

What Stands Behind our Money?

Historically, early forms of money played two roles. If, for example, a ruler declared beans as money, you could spend them or sell them in the marketplace. Precious metals, tobacco, cows, and other tangible goods are examples of commodity money. Commodity money is anything that serves as money while having market value in other uses. This means that money itself has intrinsic worth (the market value of

Commodity money

Anything that serves as money while having market value in other uses.

the material). For example, money can be pure gold or silver, both of which are valuable for nonmoney uses, such as making jewelry and serving other industrial purposes.

Today, United States's paper money and coins are no longer backed by gold or silver. Our paper money was exchangeable for gold or silver until 1934. As a result of the Great Depression, people rapidly tried to get rid of their paper money. The U.S. Treasury's stock of gold dropped so low that Congress passed a law in 1934 that prevented anyone from exchanging gold for $5 and larger bills. Later, in 1963, Congress removed the right to exchange $1 bills for silver. And in the mid-1960s, zinc, copper, and nickel replaced silver in coins.

The important consideration for money is acceptability. The acceptability of a dollar is due in no small degree to the fact that Uncle Sam decrees it to be fiat money. Fiat money is money accepted by law, and not because of its redeemability or intrinsic value. A dollar bill contains only about three cents worth of paper, printing inks, and other materials. A quarter contains maybe 10 cents worth of nickel and copper. Pull out a dollar bill and look at it closely. In the upper left corner on the front side is small print that proclaims, "THIS NOTE IS LEGAL TENDER FOR ALL DEBTS, PUBLIC AND PRIVATE." This means that your paper money is fiat money. Also notice that nowhere on the note is there any promise to redeem it for gold, silver, or anything else.

> **Conclusion** *An item's ability to serve as money does not depend on its own market value or the backing of precious metal.*

Fiat money
Money accepted by law and not because of its redeemability or intrinsic value.

Money Supply Definitions

Now that you understand the basic definition of money, we turn to exactly what constitutes the money supply of the U.S. economy. There is disagreement over the answer to this question because some economists define the money supply more narrowly than others. The following sections examine the methods used to measure the money supply, officially called M1 and M2.

M1: The Most Narrowly Defined Money Supply

M1 is the narrowest definition of the money supply. This money definition measures purchasing power immediately available to the public without borrowing or having to give notice. Specifically, M1 measures the currency and checkable deposits held by the public at a given time, such as a given day, month, or year. M1 does not include the money held by the government, Federal Reserve banks, or depository institutions. Expressed as a formula:

$$\text{M1} = \text{currency} + \text{checkable deposits}$$

Exhibit 1 shows the components of M1 and M2 money supply definitions based on daily averages during December 2007.

M1
The narrowest definition of the money supply. It includes currency, traveler's checks, and checkable deposits.

Currency Currency includes coins and paper money, officially called Federal Reserve notes, that the public holds for immediate spending. The purpose of currency is to enable us to make small purchases. Currency represents 56 percent of M1.

Currency
Money, including coins and paper money.

EXHIBIT 1	Definitions of the Money Supply, 2007

Each of the two pie charts represents the money supply in December 2007. M1, the most narrowly defined money supply, is equal to currency (coins and paper money) in circulation plus checkable deposits in financial institutions. M2 is a more broadly defined money supply, equal to M1 plus savings deposits and small time deposits of less than $100,000.

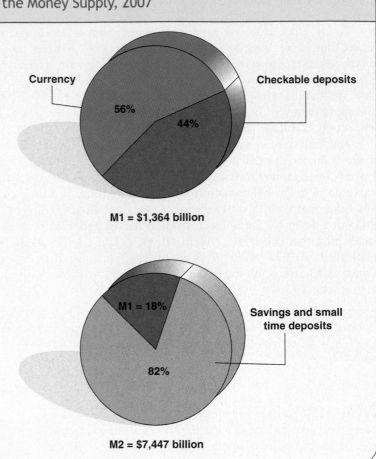

SOURCE: *Economic Report of the President*, 2008, http://www.gpoaccess.gov/eop/, Tables B-69 and B-70.

Checkable Deposits Most "big ticket" purchases are paid for with checks or credit cards (which are not money), rather than currency. Checks eliminate trips to the bank, and they are safer than cash. If lost or stolen, checks and credit cards can be replaced at little cost—money cannot. Exhibit 1 shows that a major share of M1 consists of checkable deposits. Checkable deposits are the total of checking account balances in financial institutions that are convertible to currency "on demand" by writing a check without advance notice. A checking account balance is a bookkeeping entry, often called a *demand deposit* because it can be converted into cash "on demand." Before the 1980s, only commercial banks could legally provide demand deposits. However, the law changed with the passage of the Depository Institutions Deregulation and Monetary Control Act of 1980. (This act will be discussed later in the chapter.) Today, checking accounts are available from many different financial institutions, such as savings and loan associations, credit unions, and mutual savings banks. For example, many people hold deposits in negotiable order of withdrawal (NOW) accounts or automatic transfer of savings (ATS) accounts, which serve as interest-bearing checking accounts. NOW and ATS accounts permit depositors to spend their deposits without a trip to the bank to withdraw funds. In December 2007, 44 percent of M1 was in traveler's checks and checkable deposits.

> **Checkable deposits**
>
> The total of checking account balances in financial institutions convertible to currency "on demand" when a check is written without advance notice.

M2: Adding Near Monies to M1

M2 is a broader measure of the money supply because it equals M1 plus *near money*. M1 is considered by many economists to be too narrow because it does not include near money accounts that can be used to purchase goods and services. These include passbook savings accounts, money market mutual funds, and time deposits of less than $100,000. Near monies are interest-bearing deposits easily converted into spendable funds. Written as a formula:

$$M2 = M1 + near\ monies$$

rewritten as

$$M2 = M1 + savings\ deposits + small\ time\ deposits\ of\ less\ than\ \$100,000$$

Savings Deposits   As shown in Exhibit 1, M1 was about one-fifth of M2 in December 2007, with savings deposits and small time deposits constituting the remainder of M2. Savings deposits are interest-bearing accounts that can be easily withdrawn. These deposits include passbook savings accounts, money market mutual funds, and other types of interest-bearing deposits with commercial banks, mutual savings banks, savings and loan associations, and credit unions.

Small Time Deposits   There is a distinction between a *checkable deposit* and a *time deposit*. A time deposit is an interest-bearing account in a financial institution that requires a withdrawal notice or must remain on deposit for a specified period unless an early withdrawal penalty is paid. Certificates of deposit (CDs) are deposits for a specified time, with a penalty charged for early withdrawal. Where is the line drawn between a small and a large time deposit? The answer is that time deposits of less than $100,000 are "small" and therefore are included in M2.

> **Conclusion** *M1 is more liquid than M2.*

To simplify the discussion throughout the remainder of this text, we will be referring to M1 when we discuss the money supply. However, one can argue that M2, or another measurement of the money supply, may be the best definition. Actually, the boundary lines for any definition of money are somewhat arbitrary.

The Federal Reserve System

Who controls the money supply in the United States? The answer is the Federal Reserve System, popularly called the "Fed." The Fed is the central banker for the nation and provides banking services to commercial banks, other financial institutions, and the federal government. The Fed regulates, supervises, and is responsible for policies concerning money. Congress and the president consult with the Fed to control the size of the money supply and thereby influence the economy's performance.

Other major nations have central banks, such as the Bank of England, the Bank of Japan, and the European Central Bank. The movement in the United States to establish a central banking system gained strength early in the twentieth century as a series of bank failures resulted in the Panic of 1907. In that year, stock prices fell, many businesses and banks failed, and millions of depositors lost their savings. The

---

M2

The definition of the money supply that equals M1 plus near monies, such as savings deposits and small time deposits of less than $100,000.

Federal Reserve System

The 12 central banks that service banks and other financial institutions within each of the Federal Reserve districts; popularly called the Fed.

HISTORY OF MONEY IN THE COLONIES

The early colonists left behind their well-developed money system in Europe. North American Indians accepted wampum as money. These are beads of polished shells strung in belts. Soon, a group of settlers learned to counterfeit wampum, and it lost its value. This meant that the main method of trading with the Indians was to barter. Later, trade developed with the West Indies, and Spanish coins called "pieces of eight" were circulated widely. Colonists often cut these coins into pieces to make change. Half of a coin became known as "four bits." A quarter part of the coin was referred to as "two bits." The first English colony to mint its own coins was Massachusetts in 1652. A striking pine tree was engraved on these coins called shillings. Other coins such as a six-pence and three-pence were also produced at a mint in Boston. Several

other colonies followed by authorizing their own coin issues.

The first national coin of the United States was issued in 1787 when Congress approved a one-cent copper coin. One side was decorated with a chain of 13 links encircling the words, "We Are One." The other side had a

prescription for preventing financial panic was for the government to establish more centralized control over banks. This desire for more safety in banking led to the creation of the Federal Reserve System by the Federal Reserve Act of 1913 during the administration of President Woodrow Wilson. No longer would the supply of money in the economy be determined by individual banks.

The Fed's Organizational Chart

The *Federal Reserve System* is an independent agency of the federal government. Congress is responsible for overseeing the Fed, but does not interfere with its day-to-day decisions. The chairman of the Fed reports to Congress twice each year and often coordinates its actions with the U.S. Treasury and the president. Although the Fed enjoys independent status, its independence can be revoked. If the Fed were to pursue policies contrary to the interests of the nation, Congress could abolish the Fed.

The Federal Reserve System consists of 12 central banks that service banks and other financial institutions within each of the Federal Reserve districts. Each Federal Reserve bank serves as a central banker for the private banks in its region. The United States is the only nation in the world to have 12 separate regional banks instead of a single central bank. In fact, the Fed's structure is the result of a compromise between the traditionalists, who favored a single central bank, and the populists, who distrusted concentration of financial power in the hands of a few. In addition, there are 25 Federal Reserve branch banks located throughout the country. The map in Exhibit 2 shows the 12 Federal Reserve districts.

sundial, the noonday sun, and the Latin word "*fugo*," meaning "time flies." Later, this coin became known as the Franklin cent, although there is no evidence that Benjamin Franklin played any role in its design.

In 1792, Congress established a mint in Philadelphia. It manufactured copper cents and half-cents about the size of today's quarters and nickels. In 1794, silver half-dimes and half-dollars increased the variety of available coins. The next year gold eagles ($10) and half-eagles ($5) appeared. The motto *E Pluribus Unum* ("out of many, one") was first used on the half-eagle in 1795. The next year America's first quarters and dimes were issued.

The first paper money in the Americas was printed in 1690. Massachusetts soldiers returned to the colony from fighting the French in Quebec, where they had unsuccessfully laid siege to the city. The colony had no precious metal to pay the soldiers. Hundreds of soldiers threatened mutiny, and the colony decided it must issue bills of credit, which were simply pieces of paper promising to pay the soldiers. Other colonies followed this example and printed their own paper money. Soon paper money was being widely circulated.

In 1775, the need to finance the American Revolution forced the Continental Congress to issue paper money called "continentals," but so much was issued that it rapidly lost its value. George Washington complained, "A wagon load of money will scarcely purchase a wagon load of provisions." This statement is today shortened to the phrase "not worth a continental."

The organizational chart of the Federal Reserve System, given in Exhibit 3, shows that the Board of Governors, located in Washington, D.C., administers the system. The Board of Governors is made up of seven members, appointed by the president and confirmed by the U.S. Senate, who serve for one nonrenewable 14-year term. Their responsibility is to supervise and control the money supply and the banking system of the United States. Fourteen-year terms for Fed governors create autonomy and insulate the Fed from short-term politics. These terms are staggered so one term expires every two years. This staggering of terms prevents a president from stacking the board with members favoring the incumbent party's political interests. A president usually makes two appointments in a one-term presidency and four appointments in a two-term presidency. The president designates one member of the Board of Governors to serve as chairman for a four-year term. The chair is the principal spokesperson for the Fed and has considerable power over policy decisions. In fact, it is often argued that the Fed's chairman is the most powerful individual in the United States next to the president. The current chairman is Ben Bernanke, who was appointed by President George W. Bush.

The Federal Reserve System receives no funding from Congress. This creates financial autonomy for the Fed by removing the fear of congressional review of its budget. Then where does the Fed get funds to operate? Recall from Exhibit 7 of the previous chapter that the Fed holds government securities issued by the U.S. Treasury. The Fed earns interest income from the government securities it holds and the loans it makes to depository institutions. Because the Fed returns any profits to the

Board of Governors of the Federal Reserve System
The seven members appointed by the president and confirmed by the U.S. Senate who serve for one nonrenewable 14-year term. Their responsibility is to supervise and control the money supply and the banking system of the United States.

Ben Bernanke
Chairman of the Board of Governors of the Federal Reserve System

EXHIBIT 2 The Twelve Federal Reserve Districts

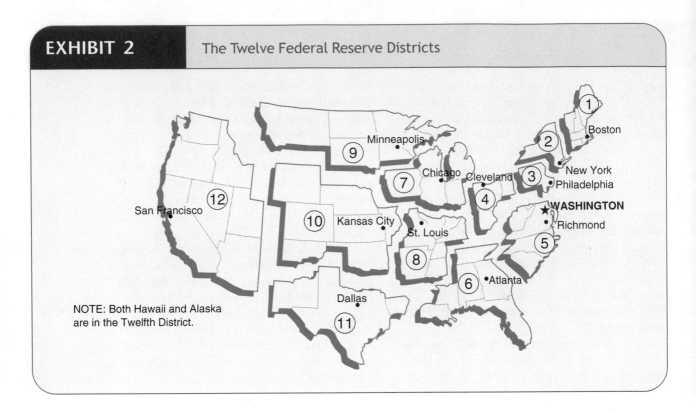

NOTE: Both Hawaii and Alaska are in the Twelfth District.

Treasury, it is motivated to adopt policies to promote the economy's well-being, rather than earning a profit. Moreover, the Board of Governors does not take orders from the president or any other politician. Thus, the Board of Governors is the independent, self-supporting authority of the Federal Reserve System.

On the left side of the organizational chart in Exhibit 3 is the very important Federal Open Market Committee (FOMC). The FOMC directs the buying and selling of U.S. government securities, which are major instruments for controlling the money supply. The FOMC consists of the seven members of the Board of Governors, the president of the New York Federal Reserve Bank, and the presidents of four other Federal Reserve district banks. The FOMC meets to discuss trends in inflation, unemployment, growth rates, and other macro data. FOMC members express their opinions on implementing various monetary policies and then issue policy statements known as *FOMC directives*. A directive, for example, might set the operation of the Fed to stimulate or restrain M1 in order to influence employment. The next two chapters explain the tools of monetary policy in more detail.

As shown on the right side of the chart, the *Federal Advisory Council* consists of 12 prominent commercial bankers. Each of the 12 Federal Reserve district banks selects one member each year. The council meets periodically to advise the Board of Governors.

Finally, at the bottom of the organizational chart is the remainder of the Federal Reserve System, consisting of only about 3,000 member banks of the approximately 8,000 commercial banks in the United States. Although these 3,000 Fed member banks represent only about one-third of U.S. banks, they have about 70 percent of all U.S. bank deposits. A sure sign of Fed membership is the word *National* in a bank's name. The U.S. comptroller of the currency charters national banks, and they

Federal Open Market Committee (FOMC)

The Federal Reserve's committee that directs the buying and selling of U.S. government securities, which are major instruments for controlling the money supply. The FOMC consists of the seven members of the Federal Reserve's Board of Governors, the president of the New York Federal Reserve Bank, and the presidents of four other Federal Reserve district banks.

EXHIBIT 3	The Organization of the Federal Reserve System

The Federal Open Market Committee (FOMC) and the Federal Advisory Council assist the Federal Reserve System's Board of Governors. The 12 regional Federal Reserve district banks and their 25 branches implement broad policies affecting the money supply.

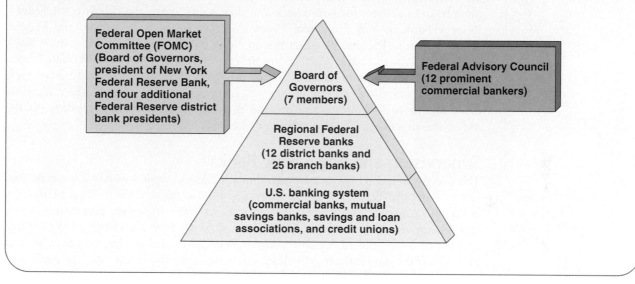

---

are required to be Fed members. Banks that do not have "National" in their title can also be Fed members. States can also charter banks, and these state banks have the option of joining the Federal Reserve. Less than 20 percent of state banks choose to join the Fed.

Nonmember depository institutions, including many commercial banks, savings and loan associations (S&Ls), savings banks, and credit unions, are not official members of the Fed team. They are, however, influenced by and depend on the Fed for a variety of services, which we will now discuss.

What a Federal Reserve Bank Does

The typical bank customer never enters the doors of a Federal Reserve district bank or one of its branch banks. The reason is that the Fed does not offer the public checking accounts, savings accounts, or any of the services provided by commercial banks. Instead, the Federal Reserve serves as a "banker's bank." Following are brief descriptions of some of the principal functions of the Federal Reserve.

Controlling the Money Supply

The primary role of the Fed is to control the nation's money supply. The mechanics of Fed control over the money supply are explained in the next two chapters. To most people, this is a wondrously mysterious process. So that you do not suffer in complete suspense, here is a sneak preview: The Fed has three policy tools, or levers, it can use to change the stock of money in the banking system. The potential macro outcome of changes in the money supply is to affect total spending and therefore real GDP, employment, and the price level.

Clearing Checks

Because most people and businesses use checks to pay for goods and services, check clearing is an important function. Suppose you live in Virginia and have a checking account with a bank in that state. While on vacation in California, you purchase tickets to Disneyland with a check for $200. Disneyland accepts your check and then deposits it in its business checking account in a California bank. This bank must collect payment for your check and does so by giving the check to the Federal Reserve bank in San Francisco. From there, your check is sent to the Federal Reserve bank in Richmond. At each stop along its journey, the check earns a black stamp mark on the back. Finally, the process ends when $200 is subtracted from your personal checking account. Banks in which checks are deposited have their Fed accounts credited, and banks on which checks are written have their accounts debited. The Fed clearinghouse process is much speedier than depending on the movement of a check between commercial banks.

Supervising and Regulating Banks

Federal Deposit Insurance Corporation (FDIC)

A government agency established in 1933 to insure commercial bank deposits up to a specified limit.

The Fed examines banks' books, sets limits for loans, approves bank mergers, and works with the Federal Deposit Insurance Corporation (FDIC). The FDIC is a government agency established by Congress in 1933 to insure commercial bank deposits up to a specified limit. Congress created the FDIC in response to the huge number of bank failures during the Great Depression and set the insurance limit at $25,000. If the government provides a safety net, people are less likely to panic and withdraw their funds from banks during a period of economic uncertainty. When deposits are insured and a bank fails, the government stands ready to pay depositors or transfer their deposits to a solvent bank. Banks that are members of the Fed are members of the FDIC. State agencies supervise state-chartered banks that are not members of either the Federal Reserve System or the FDIC. To shore up confidence in the U.S. banking system in the wake of bank failures in 2008, the $700 billion U.S. financial industry rescue law raised the FDIC coverage of bank deposits to $250, 000 per customer from $100, 000 through 2009.

Maintaining and Circulating Currency

Note that the Fed does *not* print currency—it *maintains* and *circulates* money. All Federal Reserve notes are printed at the Bureau of Engraving and Printing's facilities in Washington, D.C., and Fort Worth, Texas. The Treasury mints and issues all coins. Coins are made at U.S. mints located in Philadelphia and Denver. The bureau and the mints ship new notes and coins to the Federal Reserve banks for circulation. Much of this money is printed or minted simply to replace worn-out bills and coins. Another use of new currency is to meet public demand. Suppose it is the holiday season and banks need more paper money and coins to meet their customers' shopping needs. The Federal Reserve must be ready to ship extra money from its large vaults by armored truck.

Protecting Consumers

Since 1968, the Federal Reserve has played a role in protecting consumers by enforcing statutes enacted by Congress. Perhaps the most important is the *Equal Credit Opportunity Act,* which prohibits discrimination based on race, color, gender, marital status, religion, or national origin in the extension of credit. It also gives married women the right to establish credit histories in their own names. The Federal Reserve receives and tries to resolve consumer complaints against banks.

Maintaining Federal Government Checking Accounts and Gold

The Fed is also Uncle Sam's bank. The U.S. Treasury has the Fed handle its checking account. From this account, the federal government pays for such expenses as federal employees' salaries, Social Security, tax refunds, veterans' benefits, defense, and highways.

Finally, it is interesting to note that the New York Federal Reserve District Bank holds one of the oldest forms of money—*gold*. This gold belongs mainly to foreign governments and is one of the largest accumulations of this precious metal in the world. Viewing a Federal Reserve bank's vault is not something that most tourists typically have on their list of things to do, but I strongly recommend this tour.

The gold vault at the New York Federal Reserve Bank is nearly half the length of a football field and filled with steel and concrete walls several yards thick. Most cells contain the gold of only one nation, and only a few bank employees know the identities of the owners. When trade occurs between two countries, payment between the parties can be made by transferring gold bars from one compartment to another. Note that the Fed and the monetary system of the Yapese have a similarity. Recall from the Global Economics box that in Yap large stone wheels are not moved; rather they just change ownership.

The U.S. Banking Revolution

Prior to the 1980s, the U.S. banking system was simpler. It consisted of many commercial banks authorized by law to offer checking accounts. Then there were the other financial institutions, the so-called thrifts, which included S&Ls, mutual savings banks, and credit unions. The thrifts by law were permitted to accept only savings deposits with no checking privileges. The commercial banks, on the other hand, could not pay interest on checkable deposits. Moreover, a "maximum interest rate allowed by law" limited competition among commercial banks and other financial institutions. As will be explained momentarily, this relatively tranquil U.S. banking structure changed dramatically, and the stage was set for a fascinating banking "horror story."

The Monetary Control Act of 1980

A significant law affecting the U.S. banking system is the Depository Institutions Deregulation and Monetary Control Act of 1980, commonly called the Monetary Control Act. This law gave the Federal Reserve System greater control over nonmember banks and made all financial institutions more competitive. The act's four major provisions are the following:

> **Monetary Control Act**
> A law, formally titled the Depository Institutions Deregulation and Monetary Control Act of 1980, that gave the Federal Reserve System greater control over nonmember banks and made all financial institutions more competitive.

1. *The authority of the Fed over nonmember depository institutions was increased.* Before the Monetary Control Act, less than half the banks in the United States were members of the Fed and subject to its direct control. Under the act's provisions, the Federal Reserve sets uniform reserve requirements for *all* commercial banks, including state and national banks, S&Ls, and credit unions with checking accounts.

© Elena Elisseeva, 2008/Used under license from Shutterstock.com.

The case of Lincoln Savings and Loan is a classic example of what went wrong during one of the worst financial crises in U.S. history. In 1984, the Securities and Exchange Commission charged Charles Keating, Jr., with fraud in an Ohio loan scam, but regulators later allowed him to buy Lincoln Savings and Loan in California. Keating hired a staff to carry out his wishes and paid them and his relatives millions. Keating was also generous with politicians in Washington, D.C. Allegedly, five U.S. senators received $1.5 million in campaign contributions from Keating to influence regulators.

Where did Keating's money come from? It came from Lincoln Savings depositors and, ultimately, from taxpayers because the federal government insures deposits of failed S&Ls. When Keating took over Lincoln, it was a healthy S&L with assets of $1.1 billion. But because of deregulation mandated by the Monetary Control Act and other legislation and the lack of enforcement of regulations under the new laws, many S&Ls plunged into high-risk, but potentially highly profitable, ventures. Keating therefore took Lincoln out of sound home mortgage loans and into speculation in Arizona hotels costing $500,000 per room to build, raw land for golf courses, shopping centers, junk bonds, and currency futures.

In 1987, after it was already too late, California regulators became alarmed at the way Lincoln operated and asked the FBI and the FSLIC to take over Lincoln. Keating responded by contacting his friends in Washington, and the regulatory process moved at a snail's pace. Years passed before the government finally closed Lincoln and informed the public that their deposits were not safe in this S&L. During the time regulators were deciding what action to take, it is estimated that Lincoln cost taxpayers another $1 billion. Ultimately, the collapse of Lincoln cost U.S. taxpayers about $3 billion, making it the most expensive S&L failure of all.

Keating and other S&L entrepreneurs say they did nothing wrong. After all, Congress and federal regulators encouraged, or did not discourage, S&Ls to compete by borrowing funds at high interest rates and making risky, but potentially highly profitable, investments. If oil prices and land values fall unexpectedly and loans fail, this is simply the way a market economy works and not the fault of risk-prone wheeler-dealers like Keating.

In 1993, a federal judge sentenced Keating to 12 1/2 years in prison for swindling small investors. The sentence ran concurrently with a 10-year state prison sentence. The judge also ordered Keating to pay $122.4 million in restitution to the government for losses caused by sham property sales. However, the government has been unable to locate any significant assets. Keating served four years and nine months.

ANALYZE THE ISSUE

Critics of federal banking policy argue that deposit insurance is a key reason for banking failures. The banks enjoy a "heads I win, tails the government loses" proposition. Several possible reforms of deposit insurance have been suggested. For example, the limit on insured deposits can be raised, reduced, or eliminated. Do you think a change in deposit insurance would prevent bank failures?

2. *All depository institutions are able to borrow loan reserves from Federal Reserve banks.* This practice, called *discounting,* will be explained in the next chapter. Banks also have access to check clearing and other services of the Fed.

3. *The act allows commercial banks, thrifts, money market mutual funds, stock brokerage firms, and retailers to offer a wide variety of banking services.* For example, commercial banks and other financial institutions can pay unrestricted interest rates on checking accounts. Also, S&Ls and other financial institutions can offer checking accounts. Federal credit unions are authorized to make residential real estate loans, and other major corporations can offer traditional banking services.

4. *The act eliminated all interest rate ceilings. Before this act, S&Ls were allowed to pay depositors a slightly higher interest rate on passbook savings deposits than those paid by commercial banks.* The Monetary Control Act removed this advantage of S&Ls over other financial institutions competing for depositors.

Finally, the movement toward deregulation, which blurred the distinctions between financial institutions, continued in 1999 when the *Financial Services Modernization Act* was signed into law. This sweeping measure lifted Depression-era barriers and allows banks, securities firms, and insurance companies to merge and sell each other's products.

The Savings and Loan Crisis

Besides the current subprime loan housing crisis discussed in the chapter on monetary policy, the savings and loan crisis of the 1980s and early 1990s is one of the worst U.S. financial crisis since the Great Depression. After the Monetary Control Act removed interest rate ceilings on deposits, competition for customers forced S&Ls to pay higher interest rates on short-term deposits. Unlike the banks, however, S&Ls were earning their income from long-term mortgages at fixed interest rates below the rate required to keep or attract new deposits. The resulting losses enticed the S&Ls to forsake home mortgage loans, which they knew best, and seek high-interest, but riskier, commercial and consumer loans. Unfortunately, these risky higher-interest loans resulted in defaults and more losses. If conditions were not bad enough, lower oil prices depressed the oil-based state economies in Texas, Louisiana, and Oklahoma.

The Federal Savings and Loan Insurance Corporation (FSLIC) was the agency that insured deposits in S&Ls, similar to how the FDIC insures bank deposits. The magnitude of the losses exceeded the insurance fund's ability to pay depositors, and Congress placed the FSLIC's deposit-insurance fund under the FDIC's control. To close or sell ailing S&Ls and protect depositors, Congress enacted the Thrift Bailout Bill in 1989. One provision of this act created the Resolution Trust Corporation (RTC) to carry out a massive federal bailout of failed institutions. The RTC bought the assets and deposits of failed S&Ls and sold them to offset the cost borne by taxpayers. The RTC closed in 1995, and the ultimate cost to taxpayers totaled $125 billion!

KEY CONCEPTS

Barter
Money
Medium of exchange
Unit of account
Store of value
Commodity money
Fiat money

M1, M2
Currency
Checkable deposits
Federal Reserve System
Board of Governors of the
  Federal Reserve System

Federal Open Market Committee
  (FOMC)
Federal Deposit Insurance
  Corporation (FDIC)
Monetary Control Act

SUMMARY

- *Money* can be anything that meets these three tests. Money must serve as (1) a medium of exchange, (2) a unit of account, and (3) a store of value. Money facilitates more efficient exchange than barter. Other desirable properties of money include scarcity, portability, divisibility, and uniformity.
- *Medium of exchange* is the most important function of money. This means that money is widely accepted in payment for goods and services.
- *Unit of account* is another important function of money. Money is used to measure relative values by serving as a common yardstick for valuing goods and services.
- *Store of value* is the ability of money to hold its value over time. Money is said to be highly *liquid,* which means it is readily usable in exchange.
- *Credit cards* are not money. Credit cards represent a short-term loan and therefore fail as a store of value.
- *Commodity money* is money that has a marketable value, such as gold and silver. Today, the United States uses *fiat money,* which must be accepted by law, but is not convertible into gold, silver, or any commodity.
- *M1* is the narrowest definition of the money supply, which equals currency plus checkable deposits. *M2* is a broader definition of the money supply, which equals M1 plus *near monies,* such as savings deposits and small time deposits.

Definitions of Money Supply (M1 and M2)

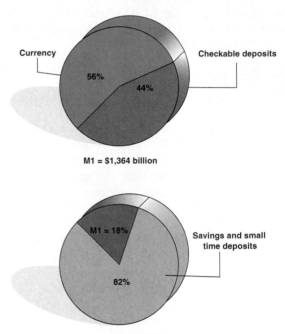

M1 = $1,364 billion

M2 = $7,447 billion

- The *Federal Reserve System,* our central bank, was established in 1913. The Fed consists of 12 Federal Reserve district banks with 25 branches. The *Board of Governors* is the Fed's governing body. The *Federal Open Market Committee* (FOMC) directs the buying and selling of U.S. government securities, which is a key method of controlling the money supply.

- *Basic Federal Reserve bank functions* are (1) controlling the money supply, (2) clearing checks, (3) supervising and regulating banking, (4) maintaining and circulating currency, (5) protecting consumers, and (6) maintaining the federal government's checking accounts and gold.

- The *Monetary Control Act of 1980* revolutionized U.S. banking by expanding the authority of the Federal Reserve System to all financial institutions. In addition, this law increased competition by blurring the distinctions between commercial banks, thrift institutions, and even nonfinancial institutions.

SUMMARY OF CONCLUSION STATEMENTS

- The use of money simplifies and therefore increases market transactions. Money also prevents wasting time that can be devoted to production, thereby promoting economic growth by increasing a nation's production possibilities.
- Money is a useful mechanism for transforming income in the present into future purchases.
- Money is the most liquid form of wealth because it can be spent directly in the marketplace.

- The supply of money must be great enough to meet ordinary transaction needs, but not be so plentiful that it becomes worthless.
- An item's ability to serve as money does not depend on its own market value or the backing of precious metal.
- M1 is more liquid than M2.

STUDY QUESTIONS AND PROBLEMS

1. Discuss this statement: "A man with a million dollars who is lost in the desert learns the meaning of money."

2. Could each of the following items potentially serve as money? Consider each as (1) a medium of exchange, (2) a unit of account, and (3) a store of value.
   a.   Visa credit card
   b.   Federal Reserve note
   c.   Dog
   d.   Beer mug

3. Consider each of the items in question 2 in terms of scarcity, portability, divisibility, and uniformity.

4. What backs the U.S. dollar? Include the distinction between commodity money and fiat money in your answer.

5. What are the components of the most narrowly defined money supply in the United States?

6. Distinguish between M1 and M2. What are near monies?

7. What is the major purpose of the Federal Reserve System? What is the major responsibility of the Board of Governors and the Federal Open Market Committee?

8. Should the Fed be independent or a government agency subordinate to Congress and the president?

9. Which banks must be insured by the FDIC? Which banks can choose not to be insured by the FDIC?

10. Briefly discuss the importance of the Depository Institutions Deregulation and Monetary Control Act of 1980.

For Online Exercises, go to the text Web site at www.cengage.com/economics/tucker.

CHECKPOINT ANSWER

Are Debit Cards Money?

Debit cards serve as a means of payment, and debit card statements serve as a unit of account. Finally, unlike credit cards, debit cards serve as a store of value because they are a means of accessing checkable deposits and not an extension of credit. If you said debit cards are money because they serve all three functions required for money, **YOU ARE CORRECT.**

PRACTICE QUIZ

For an explanation of the correct answers, please visit the tutorial at www.cengage.com/economics/tucker.

1. Which of the following is a problem with barter?
   a. Individuals will not exchange goods.
   b. Individuals' wants must coincide in order for there to be exchange.
   c. Goods can be exchanged, but services cannot.
   d. None of the above is a problem.

2. Which of the following is *not* a characteristic of money?
   a. It provides a way to measure the relative value of goods and services.
   b. It is always backed by something of high intrinsic value, such as gold or silver.
   c. It is generally acceptable as a medium of exchange.
   d. It allows for saving and borrowing.

3. Which of the following is *not* a store of value?
   a. Dollar
   b. Money market mutual fund share
   c. Checking account balance
   d. Credit card

4. The easier it is to convert an asset directly into goods and services without loss, the
   a. less secure it is.
   b. more secure it is.
   c. more liquid it is.
   d. less liquid it is.

5. M1 refers to
   a. the most narrowly defined money supply.
   b. currency held by the public plus checking account balances and traveler's checks.
   c. the smallest dollar amount of the money supply definitions.
   d. all of the above.

6. The M1 definition of the money supply consists of
   a. coins and currency in circulation.
   b. coins and currency in circulation, checkable deposits, and traveler's checks.
   c. Federal Reserve notes, gold certificates, and checkable deposits.
   d. Federal Reserve notes and bank loans.

7. Which of the following items is *not* included when computing M1?
   a. Coins in circulation
   b. Currency in circulation
   c. Savings accounts
   d. Checking account entries

8. Which of the following is part of the M2 definition of the money supply, but not part of M1?
   a. Checkable Deposits
   b. Currency held in banks
   c. Currency in circulation
   d. Money market mutual fund shares

9. Which of the following is *not* part of M1?
   a. Checking accounts
   b. Coins
   c. Credit cards
   d. Paper currency

10. Which definition of the money supply includes credit cards, or "plastic money"?
    a. M1
    b. M2
    c. All of the above
    d. None of the above

11. Which of these institutions has the responsibility to control the money supply?
    a. Commercial banks
    b. Congress
    c. U.S. Treasury Department
    d. Federal Reserve System

12. Which of the following is *not* one of the functions of the Federal Reserve?
    a. Clearing checks
    b. Printing currency
    c. Supervising and regulating banks
    d. Controlling the money supply

13. Which of the following is in charge of the buying and selling of government securities by the Fed?
    a. The president
    b. Federal Open Market Committee (FOMC)

c. Congress
d. None of the above

14. The major protection against sudden mass attempts to withdraw cash from banks is the
    a. Federal Reserve.
    b. Consumer Protection Act.
    c. deposit insurance provided by the FDIC.
    d. gold and silver backing the dollar.

15. Which of the following is *not* part of the Federal Reserve System?
    a. Council of Economic Advisors
    b. Board of Governors
    c. Federal Open Market Committee
    d. 12 Federal Reserve District Banks
    e. Federal Advisory Council

Money Creation

I t has been said that the most important person in Washington, D.C., is the chair of the Federal Reserve because he or she can influence the money supply and therefore the performance of the economy. This chapter builds on your knowledge of money and the Federal Reserve System gained in the previous chapter. You will discover that the Federal Reserve (the Fed) and the banks work together to determine the money supply. The chapter begins with a brief history of the evolution of banking. Then we examine the mechanics of how banks create money in a simplified system. This remarkable process depends on the ability of banks to amplify checkable deposits by generating a spiral of new loans and, in turn, deposits for new spending in the economy. Finally, the Fed's toolkit swings open, and we discuss the three tools used by the Fed to change the money supply.

A common misconception is that banks (including savings and loans and other depository institutions)

accept deposits and make loans, and that's about the end of the story. But there is another very important chapter to tell. Banking transactions expand or contract the money supply. Without minting coins or using the printing presses to make paper money, your local bank and other banks can create money; that is, banks can increase the money supply (M1).

The reason people do not understand money creation is that they think the federal government controls the money supply by turning the printing presses on and off. As explained in the previous chapter, this notion is only partly true because money consists primarily of bookkeeping entries, rather than pieces of paper and coins. Consequently, writing checks, using an automatic teller machine, and getting a loan affect the size of the checkable deposits component of the money supply.

In this chapter, you will learn to solve these economic puzzles:

- Exactly how is money created in the economy? That is, how does the money supply increase?

- What are the major tools the Federal Reserve uses to control the supply of money?

- Why is there nothing "federal" about the federal funds rate?

Money Creation Begins

In the Middle Ages, gold was the money of choice in most European nations. One of the problems with gold is that it is a heavy commodity, which makes it difficult to use in transactions or to hide from thieves. The medieval solution was to keep it safely deposited with the people who worked with gold, called *goldsmiths*. This demand for their services inspired goldsmith entrepreneurs to become the founders of modern-day banking.

The goldsmiths sat on their benches with ledgers close by and recorded the amounts of gold placed in their vaults. In fact, the word *bank* is derived from the Italian word for bench, which is *banco*. After assessing the purity of the gold, a goldsmith issued a receipt to the customer for the amount of gold deposited. In return, the goldsmith collected a service charge, just as you pay today for services at your bank. Anyone who possessed the receipt and presented it to the goldsmith could make a withdrawal for the amount of gold written on the receipt.

With these gold receipts in circulation, people began paying their debts with these pieces of paper, rather than actually exchanging gold. Thus, goldsmith receipts became paper money. At first, the goldsmiths were very conservative and issued receipts exactly equal to the amount of gold stored in their vaults. However, some shrewd goldsmiths observed that net withdrawals in any period were only a *fraction* of all the gold "on reserve." This observation produced a powerful idea. Goldsmiths discovered that they could make loans for more gold than they actually held in their vaults. As a result, goldsmiths made extra profit from interest on loans, and borrowers had more money for spending in their hands.

How a Single Bank Creates Money

The medieval goldsmiths were the first to practice fractional reserve banking. Modern fractional reserve banking is a system in which banks keep only a percentage of their deposits on reserve as vault cash and deposits at the Fed. In a 100 percent reserve banking system, banks would be unable to create money by making loans. However, as you will learn momentarily, holding less than 100 percent on reserve allows banks to make loans and, in turn, to create money in the economy.

> **Fractional reserve banking**
> A system in which banks keep only a percentage of their deposits on reserve as vault cash and deposits at the Fed.

631

Banker Bookkeeping

We begin our exploration of how the fractional reserve banking system operates in the United States by looking at the balance sheet of a single bank, Typical Bank. A balance sheet is a statement of the assets and liabilities of a bank at a given point in time. Balance sheets are called *T-accounts*. The hypothetical T-account of Typical Bank in Balance Sheet 1 lists only major categories and omits details to keep things simple.

On the right side of the balance sheet are the bank's *liabilities*. Liabilities are the amounts the bank owes to others. In our example, the only liabilities are *checkable deposits,* or demand deposits. Note that checkable deposits are assets on the customers' personal balance sheets, but they are debt obligations of Typical Bank. If a depositor writes a check against his or her checking account, the bank must pay this amount. Therefore, checkable deposits are liabilities to the bank.

On the left side of the balance sheet, we see Typical Bank's *assets*. Assets are amounts the bank owns. In our example, these assets consist of required reserves, *excess reserves,* and *loans.* Required reserves are the minimum balance that the Fed requires a bank to hold in vault cash or on deposit with the Fed. Note that the Fed is a Scrooge and pays no interest on reserves held with the Fed. And because reserves earn no return, Typical Bank will maximize profits by trying to keep only the minimum amount possible in required reserves.

The required reserve ratio determines the minimum required reserves. The required reserve ratio is the percentage of deposits that the Fed requires a bank to hold in vault cash or on deposit with the Fed. Here we assume that the Fed's required reserve ratio is 10 percent. Thus, the bank must have required reserves of $5 million (10 percent of $50 million). This leaves Typical Bank with $45 million in loans that provide profit to the bank.

Exhibit 1 shows that the actual required reserve ratio depends on the level of a bank's checkable deposits. Note that the Fed requires a lower percentage for a smaller bank. In the real world, Typical Bank's required reserve ratio would be 3 percent if its checkable deposits were between $7.8 million and $48.3 million.

Typical Bank has zero excess reserves so far in our analysis. Excess reserves are potential loan balances held in vault cash or on deposit with the Fed in excess of required reserves. We will see shortly that excess reserves play a starring role in

---

Required reserves

The minimum balance that the Fed requires a bank to hold in vault cash or on deposit with the Fed.

Required reserve ratio

The percentage of deposits that the Fed requires a bank to hold in vault cash or on deposit with the Fed.

Excess reserves

Potential loan balances held in vault cash or on deposit with the Fed in excess of required reserves.

Typical Bank

Balance Sheet 1			
Assets		**Liabilities**	
Required reserves	$ 5 million	Checkable deposits	$50 million
Excess reserves	0		
Loans	45 million		
Total	$50 million	Total	$50 million

Note: The Fed requires the bank to keep 10 percent of its checkable deposits in reserves. Holding $5 million in required reserves, the bank has zero excess reserves and $45 million in loans to earn profit.

EXHIBIT 1	Required Reserve Ratio of the Federal Reserve
Type of Deposit	**Required Reserve Ratio**
Checkable deposits	
$7.8–$48.3 million	3%
Over $48.3 million	10

SOURCE: Federal Reserve Bank of Minneapolis, *Reserve Requirements*, http://woodrow.mpls.frb. fed.us/info/policy/res-req.cfm.

the banking system's ability to change the money supply. The relationship between reserves accounts can be expressed as follows:

$$\text{Total reserves} = \text{required reserves} + \text{excess reserves}$$

or

$$\text{Excess reserves} = \text{total reserves} - \text{required reserves}$$

The final entry on the asset side of Typical Bank's balance sheet is loans, which are interest-earning assets of the bank. Loans are bank assets because they represent outstanding credit payable to the bank. In a fractional reserve banking system, the bank uses balances not held in reserves to earn income. In our example, loan officers have written loans totaling $45 million. Finally, note that Typical Bank's assets equal its liabilities. As you will see momentarily, any change on one side of the T-account must be accompanied by an equal amount of change on the other side of the balance sheet.

Step One: Accepting a New Deposit

You are now prepared to see how a bank creates money. Assume the required reserve ratio is 10 percent and one of Best National Bank's depositors, Brad Rich, takes $100,000 in cash from under his mattress and deposits it in his checking account. Balance Sheet 2 records this change by increasing the bank's checkable deposits on the liability side by $100,000. Brad's deposit is a liability of the bank because Brad could change his mind and withdraw his money. On the asset side, Brad's deposit increases assets because the bank has an extra $90,000 to lend after setting aside the proper amount of required reserves. Balance Sheet 2 shows that total reserves are divided between required reserves of $10,000 (10 percent of the deposit) and excess reserves of $90,000 (90 percent of the deposit). Thus, the bank's assets and liabilities remain equal when Brad makes his deposit.

Before proceeding, we must pause to make an important point. Depositing coins or paper currency in a bank has no initial effect on the money supply (M1). Recall from the previous chapter that M1 includes currency in circulation. Therefore, the transfer of $100,000 in cash from the mattress to the bank creates no money because M1 already counts this amount. Moreover, the money supply would *not* have increased had Brad Rich's initial $100,000 deposit been a check

Best National Bank

Balance Sheet 2				
Assets		**Liabilities**		**Change in M1**
Required reserves	+$ 10,000	Brad Rich account	+$100,000	0
Excess reserves	+ 90,000			
Total	$100,000	Total	$100,000	

Step 1: Brad Rich deposits $100,000 in cash, which increases checkable deposits. The Fed requires the bank to keep 10 percent of its new deposit in required reserves, so this account is credited with $10,000. The remaining 90 percent is excess reserves of $90,000. There is no effect on the money supply.

written on another bank. In this case, an increase in the assets and liabilities of Best National Bank by $100,000 would simply decrease the assets and liabilities of the other bank by $100,000. Recall that M1 also includes checkable deposits.

> **Conclusion** *Transferring currency to a bank and moving deposits from one bank to another do not affect the money supply (M1).*

Step Two: Making a Loan

So far, M1 has not changed, as shown in Balance Sheet 2, because Brad has simply taken $100,000 in currency and transferred it to a checkable deposit. Stated differently, the public holds the same $100,000 for spending, and only the form has changed from cash to a checkable deposit. In step two, the actual money creation process occurs. The profit motive provides the incentive for bank officials not to let $90,000 from a new deposit sit languishing in excess reserves. Instead, Best National Bank is eager to make loans and earn a profit by charging interest. Suppose, coincidentally, that Connie Jones walks in with a big smile, asking for a $90,000 loan to purchase equipment for her health spa. Connie has a fine credit record, so the bank accepts Connie's note (IOU) agreeing to repay the loan. As shown in Balance Sheet 3, three entries on the assets side have changed. First, the loan to Connie Jones boosts the loans account to $90,000. Second, the bank must increase required reserves by $9,000 because of the $90,000 increase in checkable deposits on the liabilities side. (Recall that required reserves are 10 percent of checkable deposits.) Third, transferring $9,000 from excess reserves to required reserves reduces the bank's excess reserves from $90,000 to $81,000. Total reserves remain at $100,000 in both Balance Sheet 2 and Balance Sheet 3.

The corresponding entry on the liabilities side of the balance sheet is the bread and butter of money creation. Checkable deposits have increased by $90,000 to $190,000. The reason is that the bank issued a check in Connie's name drawn on a checking account in the bank. Thus, Best National Bank has performed money magic with this transaction. Look what happened to the $100,000 deposited by Brad Rich. It has generated a new $90,000 *loan*, which promptly added this amount to checkable deposits and therefore increased the money supply by $90,000.

Best National Bank

Balance Sheet 3				
Assets		**Liabilities**		**Change in M1**
Required reserves	$ 19,000	Brad Rich account	$100,000	
Excess reserves	81,000	Connie Jones account	+90,000	+$90,000
Loans	+90,000			
Total	$190,000	Total	$190,000	

Step 2: The bank loans Connie Jones $90,000 by crediting her checking account with this amount. A corresponding $90,000 balance is added to the loan account. The result is an increase in the money supply of $90,000.

> **Conclusion** *When a bank makes a loan, it creates deposits, and the money supply increases by the amount of the loan because the money supply includes checkable deposits.*

Before proceeding further, you need to pause and take a breath. After resting, take particular notice of the impact of these transactions on the money supply. In step one, Brad's initial deposit did not change M1. But in step two, M1 increased by $90,000 when Best National Bank created money out of thin air by making the loan to Connie Jones. Now Connie has more money in her checking account than she did before, and no one else has less. Connie can now use this money to buy goods and services.

Step Three: Clearing the Loan Check

Now Connie Jones can use her new money to purchase equipment for her spa. Suppose Connie buys equipment for her business from Better Health Spa and writes a check for $90,000 drawn on Best National Bank. The owner of Better Health Spa then deposits the check in the firm's account at Yazoo National Bank. Yazoo National will send the check to its Federal Reserve district bank for collection. Recall that each bank maintains reserves at the Fed. The Fed clears the check by debiting the reserve account of Best National Bank and crediting the reserve account of Yazoo National Bank. The Fed then returns the check to Best National Bank, and this bank reduces Connie Jones's checking account by $90,000. As shown in Balance Sheet 4, Connie Jones's checking account falls to zero, and Best National Bank's liabilities are reduced by $90,000. On the asset side of the balance sheet, required reserves decrease by $9,000, and excess reserves return to zero. Now that all the dust has settled, Best National Bank has required reserves of $10,000 and an IOU for $90,000. Note that this check-clearing process in step three has no effect on M1. The $90,000 increase in M1 created by Best National Bank's loan to Connie remains on deposit at Yazoo National Bank in Better Health Spa's checking account.

Finally, if Brad Rich withdraws $100,000 in cash from Best National Bank, the process described above operates in reverse. The result is a $90,000 decline (destruction) in the money supply.

Best National Bank

Balance Sheet 4

Assets		Liabilities		Change in M1
Required reserves	$ 10,000	Brad Rich account	$100,000	0
Excess reserves	0	Connie Jones account	0	
Loans	90,000			
Total	$100,000	Total	$100,000	

Step 3: Connie Jones pays Better Health Spa with a $90,000 check drawn on Best National Bank. Better Health Spa deposits the check in Yazoo National Bank, which collects from Best National Bank. The result is a debit to Connie's account and her bank's reserves accounts.

Multiplier Expansion of Money by the Banking System

The process of money creation (loans) does not stop at the doors of Best National Bank. Just like the spending multiplier from the chapter on fiscal policy, there is a money multiplier process. Let's continue our story by following the effect on Yazoo National after Better Health Spa deposits $90,000 from Connie Jones. As shown in Balance Sheet 5, Yazoo National's checkable deposits increase by $90,000. Given a required reserve ratio of 10 percent, Yazoo National Bank must keep $9,000 in required reserves, and the remaining $81,000 goes into excess reserves.

Yazoo National's loan officer now has $81,000 in additional excess reserves to lend and thus create additional checkable deposits, excess reserves, and eventually loans in other banks. Exhibit 2 presents the expansion of the money supply created when Brad Rich makes his initial $100,000 deposit and then banks make loans that are deposited in other banks.

In Exhibit 2, we see that, lo and behold, an initial deposit of $100,000 in Best National Bank can eventually create a $900,000 increase in the money supply (M1). This is because Brad Rich's initial $100,000 deposit eventually creates total excess reserves of $900,000, which are available for new loans and, in turn, new deposits in

Yazoo National Bank

Balance Sheet 5

Assets		Liabilities	
Required reserves	+$ 9,000	Better Health Spa account	+$90,000
Excess reserves	+81,000		
Total	$90,000	Total	$90,000

Note: Given a required reserve ratio of 10 percent, Better Health Spa's deposit of $90,000 from Connie Jones creates $81,000 in additional excess reserves that the bank can lend, and thus create additional checkable deposits.

EXHIBIT 2		Expansion of the Money Supply		
Round	Bank	Increase in Checkable Deposits	Increase in Required Reserves	Increase in Excess Reserves
1	Best National Bank	$ 100,000	$ 10,000	$ 90,000
2	Yazoo National Bank	90,000	9,000	81,000
3	Bank A	81,000	8,100	72,900
4	Bank B	72,900	7,290	65,610
5	Bank C	65,610	6,561	59,049
6	Bank D	59,049	5,905	53,144
7	Bank E	53,144	5,314	47,830
.	.	.	.	.
.	.	.	.	.
.	.	.	.	.
Total all other banks		478,297	47,830	430,467
Total increase		$1,000,000	$100,000	$900,000

Note: A $100,000 cash deposit in Best National Bank creates $900,000 in new deposits in other banks. Each round creates excess reserves, which are loaned to a customer who deposits the loan check in another bank in the next round.

different banks. As this process continues, each bank accepts smaller and smaller increases in checkable deposits because 10 percent of each deposit is held as required reserves. As shown in Exhibit 2, the banking system as a whole can create new checkable deposits of $900,000, equal to the total of newly created excess reserves in individual banks. Note that the initial $100,000 was from cash already counted in M1, and so it is not counted in the expansion of the money supply.

The Money Multiplier

Fortunately, we do not need to calculate all the individual bank transactions listed in Exhibit 2 in order to derive the change in the money supply initiated by a deposit or withdrawal. Instead, we can use the money multiplier, or *deposit multiplier*. The money multiplier gives the *maximum* change in the money supply (checkable deposits) due to an initial change in the excess reserves held by banks.[1] The money multiplier is equal to 1 divided by the required reserve ratio. Expressed as a formula:

$$\text{Money multiplier} = \frac{1}{\text{required reserve ratio}} = \frac{1}{1/10} = 10$$

The actual change in the money supply is computed by the following formula:

$$\text{Actual money supply change} = \text{initial change in excess reserves } (ER) \\ \times \text{ money multiplier } (MM)$$

> **Money multiplier**
> The maximum change in the money supply (checkable deposits) due to an initial change in the excess reserves banks hold. The money multiplier is equal to 1 divided by the required reserve ratio.

---

1. The money multiplier (MM) is the sum of the infinite geometric progression $1 + (1 - r) + (1 - r)^2 + (1 - r)^3 + \ldots + (1 - r)^\infty$ where r equals the required reserve ratio.

Symbolically, using the data in Exhibit 2,

$$\Delta M1 = \Delta ER \times MM$$
$$\$900{,}000 = \$90{,}000 \times 10$$

The Real-World Money Multiplier

In reality, for several reasons, the size of the money multiplier can be considerably smaller than our handy little formula indicates. First, Connie Jones, or any customer along the money creation process, can decide to put a portion of the loan in her pocket, rather than writing a check to Better Health Spa for the full amount of the loan. Money outside the banking system in someone's wallet or purse or underneath the mattress is a cash leakage, which reduces the value of the money multiplier.

Second, the size of the money multiplier falls when banks do not use all their excess reserves to make loans. Perhaps some banks anticipate large deposit account withdrawals and prepare for them by holding excess reserves. Or some banks can hold excess reserves because they lack enough "worthy" loan applications. When banks decide for whatever reason to retain excess reserves, the money multiplier will be smaller.

How Monetary Policy Creates Money

The previous chapter explained that the principal function of the Fed is to control the money supply, using three policy tools, or levers. The Fed's use of these tools to influence the economy is more precisely called monetary policy. Monetary policy is the Federal Reserve's use of open market operations, changes in the discount rate, and changes in the required reserve ratio to change the money supply (M1). Using these three tools, or levers, of monetary policy, the Fed can limit or expand deposit creation by the banks and thereby change the money supply.

Monetary policy

The Federal Reserve's use of open market operations, changes in the discount rate, and changes in the required reserve ratio to change the money supply (M1).

Open Market Operations

You have seen how decisions of the public—including those of Brad Rich, Connie Jones, and Better Health Spa—worked through the banking system and increased M1. In this section, you will build on this foundation by learning how the Fed can expand or contract the money supply. We begin with the aggregated Balance Sheet 6 of the 12 Federal Reserve banks of the Federal Reserve System. Total assets of the Fed on June 18, 2008, were $903 billion. The majority of these assets ($479 billion) were held in U.S. government securities in the form of Treasury bills, Treasury notes, and Treasury bonds, and loans to banks were $304 billion. This contrasts with commercial banks, which hold most of their assets in loans. Finally, the other assets of the Fed include coins, cash items in the process of collection, bank property, and foreign currencies.

The major liability of the Fed was $787 billion worth of Federal Reserve notes—paper currency. This is in contrast to the major liability of commercial banks, which is checkable deposits. As explained in the previous chapter, the Fed issues, but does not actually print, Federal Reserve notes. Instead, the Fed decides how much to issue and then calls the Bureau of Engraving and Printing to order new batches of $10, $20, $50, and $100 bills, which the Fed sends to the banks in armored trucks.

Another important liability of the Fed is the deposits of banks and the U.S. Treasury. The Fed therefore serves as a bank for these banks and the Treasury.

Federal Reserve System

Balance Sheet 6
June 18, 2008 (billions of dollars)

Assets		Liabilities	
U.S. government securities	$479	Federal Reserve notes	$787
Loans to banks	304	Deposits	29
Other assets	120	Other liabilities and net worth	87
Total assets	$903	Total liabilities and net worth	$903

SOURCE: Federal Reserve Board, *Factors Affecting Reserve Balances*, http://www.federalreserve.gov/releases/h41/Current/.

Note that these bank deposits include the required reserve deposits discussed at the beginning of the chapter. On June 18, 2008, total liabilities and net worth equaled total assets of $903 billion. Again, some details of the balance sheet are intentionally omitted.

Recall the Federal Open Market Committee (FOMC) introduced in the previous chapter. The FOMC, as its name implies, determines the money supply through open market operations. Open market operations are the buying and selling of government securities by the Federal Reserve System. The New York Federal Reserve Bank's trading desk executes these orders. Suppose the FOMC decides to increase the money supply and instructs the New York Fed trading desk to *buy* $100,000 worth of 90-day U.S. Treasury bills (called T-bills).[2]

The Fed contacts securities dealers in the private sector for competitive bids. Suppose the Fed accepts the lowest bid, buys $100,000 worth of T-bills, and pays the dealer with a check drawn against itself. As shown in Balance Sheet 7, the Fed's assets increase by $100,000 worth of U.S. government IOUs. Once the securities dealer deposits the Fed's check in the firm's account at Best National Bank, the bank will send the $100,000 check back to the Fed. When the Fed receives the check, it will increase Best National's reserves account at the Fed by this amount. The Fed therefore increases its liabilities by $100,000, and M1 increases immediately by $100,000 because the security dealer's checking account increases at Best National Bank. Like a magician waving a magic wand, the Fed has created new money: The initial $100,000 checkable deposit and excess reserves for loans. Given a 10 percent reserve requirement, Best National Bank's required reserves increase by $10,000, and its excess reserves increase by $90,000. Therefore, the money supply will potentially increase by $1 million (the $100,000 initial increase in M1 when the Fed buys the security multiplied by the money multiplier of 10). Note that unlike the example shown previously in Exhibit 2 involving an initial $100,000 cash deposit already counted in M1, here the initial deposit

Open market operations
The buying and selling of government securities by the Federal Reserve System.

---

2. The U.S. Treasury issues T-bills in minimum denominations of $10,000. These marketable obligations of the federal government mature in three months, six months, or one year and are used to finance the budget deficit, as explained in the chapter on this topic. The Treasury sells three-month bills at weekly auctions and six-month and one-year bills less often.

Federal Reserve Bank

Balance Sheet 7		
Assets	Liabilities	Initial change in M1
U.S. government securities +$100,000	Reserves of Best National Bank +$100,000	+$100,000

Note: To increase the money supply, the Fed conducted open market operations by purchasing $100,000 in government securities. The Fed pays a securities dealer with a Fed check, which the dealer deposits in its bank. The initial change in the money supply is an increase of $100,000.

was created by the Fed and therefore not already counted in M1. Expressed as a formula:

Actual money supply change = initial checkable deposit (*CD*) + (initial change in excess reserves × money multiplier)

$$\Delta M1 = \Delta CD + \Delta ER \times MM$$
$$\$1,000,000 = \$100,000 + (\$90,000 \times 10)$$

The process goes into reverse if the FOMC directs the New York Fed trading desk to *sell* U.S. government securities for the Fed's portfolio. As shown in Balance Sheet 8, the goal of the Fed is to decrease the money supply by selling, say, $100,000 in Treasury bonds from the asset side of its balance sheet. In this case, the Fed accepts the best offer from a securities dealer. Again, assume the securities dealer's $100,000 check payable to the Fed is written on the firm's account with Best National Bank. When the Fed accepts the check, it reduces the reserves recorded on the liabilities side of Balance Sheet 8, and Best National Bank reduces the checkable deposits account of the securities dealer. By subtracting $100,000 from Best National Bank's reserves, the Fed decreases M1 initially by $100,000. Again, the Fed has waved its magic wand and extinguished money in the banking system. Given a 10 percent reserve requirement, the money supply can potentially fall by $1 million (the $100,000 initial decrease in M1 when the Fed sells the security multiplied by the money multiplier of 10).

Federal Reserve Bank

Balance Sheet 8		
Assets	Liabilities	Initial change in M1
U.S. government securities −$100,000	Reserves of Best National Bank −$100,000	−$100,000

Note: To decrease the money supply, the Fed conducted open market operations by selling $100,000 in government securities. The Fed accepts a securities dealer's check drawn on the dealer's bank. The initial change in the money supply is a decrease of $100,000.

Another way to study open market operations is to look at a typical day at the trading desk, located at the Federal Reserve Bank of New York. The manager of the trading desk starts the day by studying estimates of excess reserves in the banking system. If excess reserves are low, few banks have funds to lend. High excess reserves mean many banks can make loans. After collecting this information and other data, the manager looks at the directive from the FOMC and formulates the day's "game plan." Then the manager makes conference calls to several members of the FOMC for approval. With their blessing, the manager has traders in the trading room call dealers who trade in government securities for price quotations. The open market operation has two alternative objectives: purchase or sell government securities.

> **Conclusion** *A purchase of government securities by the Fed injects reserves into the banking system and increases the money supply. A sale of government securities by the Fed reduces reserves in the banking system and decreases the money supply.*

Exhibit 3 illustrates the Federal Reserve's open market operations.

CHECKPOINT

Who Has More Dollar Creation Power?
You find a $1,000 bill hidden beneath the floorboards in your house and decide to deposit it in your checking account. On the same day, the Fed decides to buy $1,000 in government securities from your bank. Assuming a 10 percent reserve requirement, which of these actions creates more money in the economy?

The Discount Rate

So far, money creation in the banking system depends on excess reserves acquired from new checkable deposits. Actually, the Fed itself provides another option for banks to obtain reserves through its *discount window*. This is a department within each of the Federal Reserve district banks and not an actual window. Suppose Best National Bank has no excess reserves and Brad Rich does not walk in with a deposit. Also assume the Fed does not purchase government securities and pay a dealer with a check deposited in Best National Bank. Now enter Connie Jones, who asks for a loan. In this situation, the bank has no money to lend, but it can borrow reserves from the Fed for a short period and pay the discount rate. The discount rate is the interest rate the Fed charges on loans of reserves to banks. All banks and other depository institutions have the privilege of occasionally borrowing at the Fed to cover reserve deficiencies. Changes in the discount rate often signal the Fed's monetary policy direction and therefore can affect the public's expectations about the economy. A lower discount rate encourages banks to borrow reserves and make loans.

Discount rate
The interest rate the Fed charges on loans of reserves to banks.

> **Conclusion** *A higher discount rate discourages banks from borrowing reserves and making loans. If the Fed wants to expand the money supply, it reduces the discount rate. If the objective is to contract the money supply, the Fed raises the discount rate.*

EXHIBIT 3   Open Market Operations

When the Fed buys government securities from dealers, it increases the reserves of the banks. Banks can use these reserves to make loans, which operate through the money multiplier to expand the money supply. When the Fed sells government securities to dealers, it decreases the reserves of the banks. Thus, the banks' capacity to lend diminishes, and as a consequence, the money supply decreases.

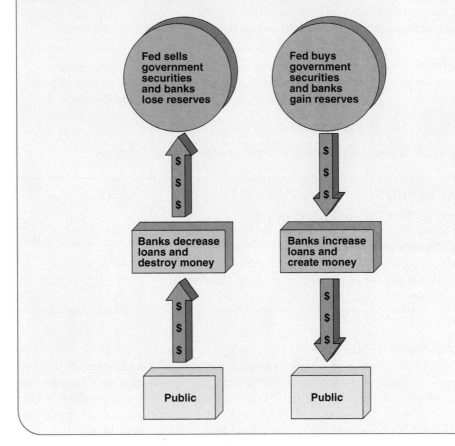

Federal funds market

A private market in which banks lend reserves to each other for less than 24 hours.

Federal funds rate

The interest rate banks charge for overnight loans of reserves to other banks.

Banks wanting to expand their reserves in order to seek profitable loan opportunities can also turn to the federal funds market. The federal funds market is a private market in which banks lend reserves to each other for less than 24 hours. The word *federal* does not mean it is a government market. It simply means this is an economywide or national market. In this market, a bank short of reserves can borrow some reserves from another bank. Using the interbank loan market, Best National Bank can borrow excess reserves from Yazoo National and pay the federal funds rate. The federal funds rate is the interest rate banks charge for overnight loans of reserves to other banks. Reserves borrowed in the federal funds market have no effect on the money supply because such borrowing simply moves reserves from one bank to another. Note that most banks borrow money to meet their reserve requirements primarily through the federal funds market and not the discount window. Also, the federal funds rate is a primary barometer of Fed policy reported in the media. The following You're the Economist provides further explanation of the federal funds rate.

The Required Reserve Ratio

Under the Monetary Control Act of 1980, discussed in the preceding chapter, the Fed can set reserve requirements by law for all banks and savings and loan associations. By changing the required reserve ratio, the Fed can change banks' excess reserves and therefore banks' lending ability. This is potentially an extremely powerful policy lever. Recall that the money multiplier equals 1 divided by the required reserve ratio. Suppose the Fed is concerned about inflation, so it wants to restrain the money supply and thereby dampen aggregate demand in the economy. If the Fed increases the required reserve ratio, the effect is to reduce excess reserves and generate a smaller change in the money supply because the money supply multiplier is smaller. For example, a required reserve ratio of 10 percent yields a money multiplier of 10 (1/0.10). If the Fed increases the ratio to 20 percent, the money multiplier falls to 5 (1/0.20).

> **Conclusion** *There is an inverse relationship between the size of the required reserve ratio and the money multiplier.*

Raising the required reserve ratio can sharply reduce the lending power of banks. Consider an initial increase in excess reserves of $10 billion in the banking system when the required reserve ratio is 10 percent. The potential value of loans (deposits) is $100 billion ($10 billion of excess reserves × 10). Now assume the Fed raises the required reserve ratio to 20 percent. The potential value of loans (deposits) falls to $50 billion ($10 billion of excess reserves × 5).

> **Conclusion** *If the Fed wishes to increase the money supply, it decreases the required reserve ratio. If the objective is to decrease the money supply, the Fed increases the required reserve ratio. In reality, changing the required reserve ratio is considered a heavy-handed approach that is an infrequently used tool of monetary policy.*

Exhibit 4 presents a summary of the impact of monetary policy tools.

The Fed used all three of its monetary policy tools to increase the money supply and battle the 1990–1991 recession. In the fall of 1990, the Fed recognized the economy was slipping into a recession, so it purchased federal government securities to inject new reserves into the banking system. The discount rate was lowered eight times between the end of 1990 and early 1992. In early 1992, the reserve requirement on demand deposits was also lowered from 12 percent to 10 percent.

Shortly after the terrorist attacks of September 11, 2001, the Fed lowered the discount rate and increased its loans to banks. The Fed also increased its open market purchases of government securities and arranged to provide dollars to foreign central banks to meet their needs in this crisis. In 2002, the Fed responded to the recession by using open market purchases of securities to increase the money supply, and it decreased the discount rate numerous times. These responses by the Fed eased the negative effects of the terrorist attacks and the recession on the U.S. and world economies.

In 2008, the Fed dramatically expanded its scope in response to the loss in confidence among lenders and panic sweeping financial markets that resulted in the flow of credit falling sharply. Using Depression-era emergency powers, the Fed took the radical step of becoming a "lender of last resort" source of short-term loans for major companies other than banks. The source of the money for these loans was

YOU'RE THE ECONOMIST   How Does the FOMC Really Work?

Applicable Concept: monetary policy

© Josef Bosak, 2008/Used under license from Shutterstock.com.

The Federal Open Market Committee (FOMC), which is the Fed's most powerful monetary policy-making group, meets eight times a year at the Federal Reserve in Washington, D.C. Often it seems that the whole world is watching for the results. Before the meeting, board members are given three books prepared by the Fed staff. The "Green Book" forecasts aggregate demand and various prices based on a variety of equations and the assumptions that monetary policy does or does not

change. The "Blue Book" might discuss as many as three monetary policy options, the rationale for each option, and the impact of each option on the economy. There is also a "Beige Book," published eight times per year, that gathers anecdotal information on current economic conditions obtained from interviews with key businesspersons, economists, bankers, and other sources.

The meeting begins at precisely 9:00 a.m. with a discussion of foreign currency operations and domestic open market operations illustrated with colorful graphics. Next, the staff presents their analysis of recent developments and forecasts for the economy laid out in the Green Book. Then each board member around the impressive 27-foot oval mahogany table expresses their views about

the analyses, except for the chair, who may choose not to participate in this round. Now, it's coffee time and everyone relaxes beneath a 23-foot ceiling with a 1,000-pound chandelier.

After the coffee break, the staff discusses each policy option from the Blue Book without recommending a particular option. Generally, three options are presented. Option A is always a decline in interest rates, Option B is always no change in interest rates, and Option C is always an increase. After the staff presentation, board members politely discuss the policy options, but with an important difference. In this policy round, the chair goes first. He leads the discussion and advocates a policy decision. After other board members express their views, the chair summarizes the

---

Term auction facility (TAF)

A monetary policy tool created in 2007 during the financial crisis to encourage banks to borrow reserves and thereby extend new loans. Under this program, banks in sound financial condition are allowed to make interest rate bids for short-term collateralized Federal Reserve loans.

provided by the Treasury Department. Also, the Fed introduced a monetary policy tool called the term auction facility (TAF) as a new way of encouraging banks to borrow reserves and thereby extend new loans. This auction allows banks to make interest rate bids for Fed loans. Under this program, the Fed auctions short-term collateralized loans to depository institutions that are in sound financial condition and are expected to remain so over the term of TAF loans. Depending on its success, the Fed may use the TAF as a permanent policy tool. The housing crisis is discussed in the You're the Economist in the next chapter.

Monetary Policy Shortcomings

Monetary policy, like fiscal policy, has its limitations. The Fed's control over the money supply is imperfect for the following reasons.

Money Multiplier Inaccuracy

If the Fed is to manage the money supply, it must know the size of the money multiplier so that it can forecast the increase in the money supply resulting from a change

consensus and reads a draft of the Directive to be voted upon. The Directive gives instructions to the Fed's staff on how to conduct open market operations until the next FOMC meeting. For example, the New York Fed's trading desk may be instructed to increase the money supply in the range of 1 to 5 percent and lower interest rates by buying 90-day U.S. Treasury bills. After discussion, board members vote on the Directive, with the chair voting first and the decision going to the majority. The chair is always expected to be on the winning side.

The Directive is sent to the New York Fed's trading desk, and soon about four dozen bond dealers receive the Fed's call. If there is a change in policy, it will be announced at 2:15 that afternoon. To maintain confidentiality, minutes of the meeting will become available the Thursday following the next meeting. A full transcript of the meeting will not be available for five years.

The Fed now communicates its changes in monetary policy by announcing changes in its targets for the federal funds rate. Recall that the Fed does not set this interest rate, but it can influence the rate through open market operations. If the Fed buys bonds, the supply of excess reserves in the banking system increases, and the rate falls. If the Fed sells bonds, the supply of excess reserves in the banking system decreases, and the rate increases. As a result, interest rates in general are influenced. In 2001, the Fed was fighting against a recession. To accomplish this goal, the Fed cut the federal funds rate 11 times, the most since the last recession in 1990–1991. The next chapter explains in more detail the link between changes in the interest rate and changes in other key macro measures. In 2002 and 2003, the Fed again cut the federal funds rate target to support economic recovery. Between 2004 and 2006, the Fed became concerned about inflation

and increased the federal funds rate 17 times. When measuring inflation, the Fed pays closest attention to the *core* CPI—the CPI excluding food and fuel—because it is less volatile than the total CPI inflation rate. In 2007, the Fed changed its focus again because it became concerned that a housing slump and credit crunch would slow the economy, and it cut this key rate for the first time in four years. In 2008, the Fed continued cutting the federal funds rate until it reached it's lowest level since 2004. The housing crisis is discussed in the next chapter.

ANALYZE THE ISSUE

What happened at the last FOMC meeting? Would you like to send the Fed your comments on monetary policy? Visit http://www.federalreserve.gov/fomc/default.htm.

in excess reserves. The value of the money multiplier, however, can be uncertain and subject to decisions independent of the Fed. As explained earlier in the chapter, the public's decision to hold cash and the willingness of banks to make loans affect the total expansion from an initial change in excess reserves. These decisions vary with conditions of prosperity and recession. When the business cycle is in an upturn, banks are very willing to use their excess reserves for making loans, and the money supply expands. During a downturn, bankers are less willing to use their excess reserves for making loans, and the money supply tends to contract.

Nonbanks

Nonbanks provide financial services, but do not offer checkable deposits included in M1. Nonbanks are not directly under the Fed's jurisdiction. Insurance companies, pension funds, brokerage houses, finance companies, and other corporations hold large amounts of funds and make loans with the potential to offset changes in the money supply. For example, customers turned down for a loan at their bank can turn to Household Finance Corporation, or another finance company, for cash.

	EXHIBIT 4	The Effect of Monetary Policy Tools on the Money Supply	

Type of Monetary Policy	Monetary Policy Action	Mechanism	Change in the Money Supply
Expansionary	Open market operations purchase	Reserves increase	Increases
Contractionary	Open market operations sale	Reserves decrease	Decreases
Expansionary	Discount rate decreases	Borrowing reserves becomes cheaper	Increases
Contractionary	Discount rate increases	Borrowing reserves becomes costlier	Decreases
Expansionary	Require reserve ratio decreases	Money multiplier increases	Increases
Contractionary	Required reserve ratio increases	Money multiplier decreases	Decreases

Which Money Definition Should the Fed Control?

As discussed in the previous chapter, there are different definitions of the money supply. What if the Fed masterfully controls M1, but the public transfers more of its deposits to M2? For example, banks can pay higher interest and attract more customers to invest in certificates of deposits. Consequently, the Fed might respond by focusing on M2 instead of M1. In fact, in recent years, the Fed has focused more on M2 than M1 because M2 more closely correlates with changes in GDP.

Lags in Monetary Policy versus Fiscal Policy

Fiscal policy does not happen instantaneously, and neither does monetary policy. Like fiscal policy, monetary policy is subject to time lags. First, an *inside lag* exists between the time a policy change is needed and the time the Fed identifies the problem and decides which policy tool to use. The inside lag is fairly short because financial data are available daily, data on inflation and unemployment monthly, and data on real GDP within three months. Once the Fed has the data, it can quickly decide which policy changes are needed and make appropriate adjustments. The inside lag for monetary policy is shorter than for fiscal policy because fiscal policy is the result of a long political budget process.

Second, there is an *outside lag* between the time a policy decision is made and the time the policy change has its effect on the economy. This lag refers to the length of time it takes the money multiplier or spending multiplier to have its full effect on aggregate demand and, in turn, employment, the price level, and real GDP.

Now it's time to answer an important question: Who is the hare and who is the tortoise in the race to the finish line of stabilizing the economy? In the popular version of this story, the hare is much faster, but goofs off along the way and eventually loses to the tortoise at the finish line. In our economics story, however, the Fed is the hare and wins easily over fiscal policy (the tortoise). Although computer model estimates differ widely, the total lag (inside plus outside lags) for monetary policy can be 3 to 12 months. In contrast, the total lag for fiscal policy is not less than a year, and a total lag of three years is quite possible.

KEY CONCEPTS

Fractional reserve banking
Required reserves
Required reserve ratio
Excess reserves

Money multiplier
Monetary policy
Open market operations
Discount rate

Federal funds market
Federal funds rate
Term auction facility (TAF)

SUMMARY

- *Fractional reserve banking,* the basis of banking today, originated with the goldsmiths in the Middle Ages. Because depository institutions (banks) are not required to keep all their deposits in vault cash or with the Federal Reserve, banks create money by making loans.

- *Required reserves* are the minimum balance that the Fed requires a bank to hold in vault cash or on deposit with the Fed. The percentage of deposits that must be held as required reserves is called the *required reserve ratio.*

- *Excess reserves* exist when a bank has more reserves than required. Excess reserves allow a bank to create money by exchanging loans for deposits. The money supply is reduced when excess reserves are reduced and loans are repaid.

- The *money multiplier* is used to calculate the maximum change (positive or negative) in checkable deposits (money supply) due to a change in excess reserves. As a formula:

$$\text{Money multiplier} = \frac{1}{\text{required reserve ratio}}$$

The actual change is computed as

Money multiplier
× initial change in excess reserves =
money supply change

- *Monetary policy* is action taken by the Fed to change the money supply. The Fed uses three basic tools: (1) *open market operations,* (2) *changes in the discount rate,* and (3) *changes in the required reserve ratio.*

- *Open market operations* are the buying and selling of government securities by the Fed through its trading desk at the New York Federal Reserve Bank. *Buying government securities* creates extra bank reserves and loans, thereby *expanding* the money supply. *Selling government securities*

reduces bank reserves and loans, thereby *contracting* the money supply.

Open Market Operations

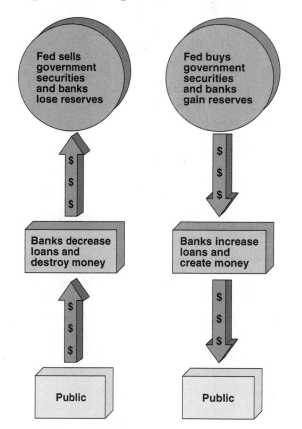

- *Changes in the discount rate* occur when the Fed changes the rate of interest it charges on loans of reserves to banks. Lowering the discount rate makes it easier for banks to borrow reserves from the Fed and expands the money supply. Raising the discount rate discourages banks from borrowing reserves from the Fed and contracts the money supply.

- *Changes in the required reserve ratio* and the size of the money multiplier are *inversely* related. Thus, if the Fed decreases the required reserve ratio, the money multiplier and money supply increase. If the Fed increases the required reserve ratio, the money multiplier and money supply decrease.

- *Monetary policy limitations* include the following: (1) The money multiplier can vary. (2) Nonbanks, such as insurance companies and finance companies, can offer loans and other financial services not directly under the Fed's control. (3) The Fed might control M1, but the public can shift funds to M2, M3, or another money supply definition. (4) Time lags occur.

SUMMARY OF CONCLUSION STATEMENTS

- Transferring currency to a bank and moving deposits from one bank to another do not affect the money supply (M1).
- When a bank makes a loan, it creates deposits, and the money supply increases by the amount of the loan because the money supply includes checkable deposits.
- A purchase of government securities by the Fed injects reserves into the banking system and increases the money supply. A sale of government securities by the Fed reduces reserves in the banking system and decreases the money supply.
- A higher discount rate discourages banks from borrowing reserves and making loans. If the Fed wants to expand the money supply, it reduces the discount rate. If the objective is to contract the money supply, the Fed raises the discount rate.

- There is an inverse relationship between the size of the required reserve ratio and the money multiplier.
- If the Fed wishes to increase the money supply, it decreases the required reserve ratio. If the objective is to decrease the money supply, the Fed increases the required reserve ratio. In reality, changing the required reserve ratio is considered a heavy-handed approach, so it is an infrequently used tool of monetary policy.

STUDY QUESTIONS AND PROBLEMS

1. Relate Shakespeare's admonition "Neither a borrower nor a lender be" to the goldsmiths' evolutionary use of fractional reserve banking.

2. If you deposit a $20 bill into a checking account and your bank has a 10 percent reserve requirement, by how much will the bank's excess reserves rise?

3. Consider this statement: "Banks do not create money because this is the Fed's responsibility." Do you agree or disagree? Explain.

4. In what form does a bank hold its required reserves? Assume the Fed has a 20 percent required reserve ratio. What amount of checkable deposits can be supported by $10 million in required reserves?

5. Suppose you deposit your paycheck drawn on another bank. Explain the impact on the money supply.

6. Suppose you remove $1,000 from under your mattress and deposit it in First National Bank. Using a balance sheet, show the impact of your deposit on the bank's assets and liabilities. If the required reserve ratio is 10 percent, what is the maximum amount the bank can loan from this deposit?

7. Suppose it is the holiday season and you withdraw $1,000 from your account at First National Bank to purchase presents. Using a balance sheet, show the impact on this bank's assets and liabilities. If the required reserve ratio is 20 percent, what is the impact on the bank's loans?

8. Suppose the Federal Reserve's trading desk buys $500,000 in T-bills from a securities dealer who then deposits the Fed's check in Best National Bank. Use a balance sheet to show the impact on the bank's loans. Consider the money multiplier and assume the required reserve ratio is 10 percent.

What is the maximum increase in the money supply that can result from this open market transaction?

9. Assume the required reserve ratio is 10 percent and a bank's excess reserves are $50 million. Explain why checkable deposits resulting from new loans based on excess reserves are not likely to generate the maximum of $500 million.

10. Briefly describe the effect on the money supply of the following monetary policies:

a. The Fed purchases $20 million worth of U.S. Treasury bonds.
b. The Fed increases the discount rate.
c. The Fed decreases the discount rate.
d. The Fed sells $40 million worth of U.S. T-bills.
e. The Fed decreases the required reserve ratio.

11. What are some problems faced by the Fed in controlling the money supply?

For Online Exercises, go the text Web site at www.cengage.com/economics/tucker.

CHECKPOINT ANSWER ✓

Who Has More Dollar Creation Power?

Your action adds $1,000 to your bank's liabilities. Also, assets in the form of required reserves increase by $100 (0.10 × $1,000). This means excess reserves increase by $900, allowing the bank to make this amount of new loans. When the Fed buys $1,000 in government securities, the bank again receives $1,000 in reserves. But the Fed's transaction does not change the bank's liabilities; therefore, the full $1,000 can go into loans. Comparing the effect on the total money supply, the money multiplier effect shows a $9,000 addition to the money supply from your action and a $10,000 addition from the Fed's action. If you said the Fed's action creates more money, **YOU ARE CORRECT.**

PRACTICE QUIZ

For an explanation of the correct answers, please visit the tutorial at www.cengage.com/economics/tucker.

1. If a bank has total deposits of $100,000 with $10,000 set aside to meet reserve requirements of the Fed, its required reserve ratio is
   a. $10,000.
   b. 10 percent.
   c. 0.1 percent.
   d. 1 percent.

2. Assume a simplified banking system in which all banks are subject to a uniform required reserve ratio of 30 percent and checkable deposits are the only form of money. A bank that receives a new deposit of $10,000 is able to extend new loans up to a maximum of
   a. $3,000.
   b. $7,000.

   c. $10,000.
   d. $30,000.

3. The Best National Bank operates with a 10 percent required reserve ratio. One day a depositor withdraws $400 from his or her checking account at the bank. As a result, the bank's excess reserves
   a. fall by $400.
   b. fall by $360.
   c. rise by $40.
   d. rise by $400.

4. If an increase of $100 in excess reserves in a simplified banking system can lead to a total expansion in bank deposits of $400, the required reserve ratio must be
   a. 40 percent.

PRACTICE QUIZ CONTINUED

b. 400 percent.
c. 25 percent.
d. 4 percent.
e. 2.5 percent.

5. In a simplified banking system in which all banks are subject to a 25 percent required reserve ratio, a $1,000 open market sale by the Fed would cause the money supply to
a. increase by $1,000.
b. decrease by $1,000.
c. decrease by $4,000.
d. increase by $4,000.

6. In a simplified banking system in which all banks are subject to a 20 percent required reserve ratio, a $1,000 open market purchase by the Fed would cause the money supply to
a. increase by $100.
b. decrease by $200.
c. decrease by $5,000.
d. increase by $5,000.

7. The cost to a member bank of borrowing from the Federal Reserve is measured by the
a. reserve requirement.
b. price of securities in the open market.
c. discount rate.
d. yield on government bonds.

8. The required reserve ratio in Exhibit 5 is
a. 10 percent.
b. 15 percent.
c. 20 percent.
d. 25 percent.

9. If the bank in Exhibit 5 received $100,000 in new deposits, its addition to required reserves would be
a. $10,000.
b. $20,000.
c. $30,000.
d. $40,000.

10. Suppose Brad Jones deposits $1,000 in the bank shown in Exhibit 5. The result would be
a. a $200 increase in excess reserves.
b. a $200 increase in required reserves.
c. a $1,200 increase in required reserves.
d. zero change in required reserves.

11. If all banks in the system were identical to Best National Bank in Exhibit 5, the money multiplier would be
a. 5.
b. 10.
c. 15.
d. 20.

EXHIBIT 5 — Balance Sheet of Best National Bank

Assets		Liabilities	
Required reserves	$_____	Checkable deposits	$100,000
Excess reserves			
Loans	80,000		
Total	$100,000	Total	$100,000

EXHIBIT 6 — Balance Sheet of Tucker National Bank

Assets		Liabilities	
Required reserves	$_____	Checkable deposits	$100,000
Excess reserves	5,000		
Loans	70,000		
Total	$100,000	Total	$100,000

12. Assume all banks in the system are identical to Best National Bank in Exhibit 5. A $1,000 open market sale by the Fed would
    a. expand the money supply by $1,000.
    b. expand the money supply by $15,000.
    c. contract the money supply by $1,000.
    d. contract the money supply by $5,000.

13. The required reserve ratio in Exhibit 6 is
    a. 10 percent.
    b. 15 percent.
    c. 20 percent.
    d. 25 percent.

14. In Exhibit 6, the bank could
    a. extend new loans by $5,000.
    b. extend new loans by $20,000.
    c. call in $5,000 existing loans.
    d. call in $20,000 existing loans.

15. If all banks in the system shown in Exhibit 6 were identical to Tucker National Bank, the money multiplier for the system would be
    a. 4.
    b. 5.
    c. 10.
    d. 25.

26

Monetary Policy

© David Muir/Digital Vision/Getty Images.

V ladimir Lenin, the first communist leader of the Soviet Union, once said the best way to destroy a nation is to destroy its money. Adolf Hitler had the same idea. During World War II, he planned to counterfeit British currency and drop it from planes flying over England. Both cases illustrate that the amount of money in circulation matters. A sudden increase in the quantity of money can render a nation's money valueless. As a consequence, people must resort to barter and waste time making direct exchanges of goods and services, rather than being productive.

The previous two chapters provided the prerequisites for understanding the market for money. You have learned two definitions for the money supply, how the banking system creates money, and how the Fed can control the money supply. Here you will begin by studying the demand for and the supply of money and how they interact to determine the rate of interest.

Then we add to this story by linking changes in the money supply to the aggregate demand and aggregate supply model. Using this tool of analysis, you will understand how changes in the demand for money affect interest rates and, in turn, real GDP, employment, and prices.

The first half of this chapter explores how Keynesian economists view the relationship between monetary policy and the economy. The second half of the chapter presents the opposing view of the monetarists. This debate is a clash between two radically different perspectives over the channels through which monetary policy influences the economy. This ideologically charged confrontation is important to the United States' future and is still far from resolved. The chapter concludes with two You're the Economists that allow you to analyze the Keynesian and monetarist views applied to the current housing crisis and the Great Depression.

In this chapter, you will learn
to solve these economic puzzles:

- Why do people wish to hold money balances?

- What is a monetary policy transmission mechanism?

- Why would a Nobel Laureate economist suggest replacing the Federal Reserve with an intelligent horse?

The Keynesian View of the Role of Money

The Demand for Money

Why do people hold (demand) currency and checkable deposits (M1), rather than putting their money to work in stocks, bonds, real estate, or other nonmoney forms of wealth? Because money yields no direct return, people (including businesses) who hold cash or checking account balances incur an *opportunity cost* of forgone interest or profits on the amount of money held. So what are the benefits of holding money? Why would people hold money and thereby forgo earning interest payments? John Maynard Keynes, in his 1936 book *The General Theory of Employment, Interest, and Money,* gave three important motives for doing so: transactions demand, precautionary demand, and speculative demand.

Transactions Demand for Money The first motive to hold money is the transactions demand. The transactions demand for money is the stock of money people hold to pay everyday predictable expenses. The desire to have "walking around money" to make quick and easy purchases is the principal reason for holding money. Students, for example, have a good idea of how much money they will spend on rent, groceries, utilities, gasoline, and other routine purchases. A business can also predict its payroll, utility bill, supply bills, and other routine expenses. Without enough cash, the public must suffer forgone interest and possibly withdrawal penalties as a result of converting their stocks, bonds, or certificates of deposit into currency or checkable deposits in order to make transactions.

> **Transactions demand for money**
> The stock of money people hold to pay everyday predictable expenses.

Precautionary Demand for Money In addition to holding money for ordinary expected purchases, people have a second motive to hold money, called the precautionary demand. The precautionary demand for money is the stock of money people hold to pay unpredictable expenses. This is the "mattress money" people hold to guard against those proverbial rainy days. For example, your car might break down, or your income may drop unexpectedly. Similarly, a business might experience unexpected repair expenses or lower-than-anticipated cash receipts from sales. Because of unforeseen events that could prevent people from paying their bills on time, people hold precautionary balances. This affords the peace of mind that unexpected payments can be made without having to cash in interest-bearing financial assets or to borrow.

> **Precautionary demand for money**
> The stock of money people hold to pay unpredictable expenses.

Speculative demand for money

The stock of money people hold to take advantage of expected future changes in the price of bonds, stocks, or other nonmoney financial assets.

Speculative Demand for Money   The third motive for holding money is the speculative demand. The speculative demand for money is the stock of money people hold to take advantage of expected future changes in the price of bonds, stocks, or other nonmoney financial assets. In addition to the transactions and precautionary motives, individuals and businesses demand "betting money" to speculate, or guess, whether the prices of alternative assets will rise or fall. This desire to take advantage of profit-making opportunities when the prices of nonmoney assets fall is the driving force behind the speculative demand. When the interest rate is high, people buy, say, IBM 30-year bonds because the opportunity cost of holding money is the high forgone interest earned on these nonmoney assets. When the interest rate is low, people hold more money because there is less opportunity cost in forgone interest earned on investing in bonds. Suppose the interest rate on IBM 30-year bonds is low. If so, people decide to hold more of their money in the bank and *speculate* that soon the interest rate will climb higher.

> **Conclusion** *As the interest rate falls, the opportunity cost of holding money falls, and people increase their speculative balances.*

Demand for money curve

A curve representing the quantity of money that people hold at different possible interest rates, ceteris paribus.

The Demand for Money Curve   The three motives for holding money combine to create a demand for money curve, which represents the quantity of money people hold at different possible interest rates, ceteris paribus. As shown in Exhibit 1, people increase their money balances when interest rates fall. The reason is that many people move their money out of, for example, money market mutual funds and into checkable deposits (M1).

> **Conclusion** *There is an inverse relationship between the quantity of money demanded and the interest rate.*

What determines the shape of the demand for money curve? Let's start with the transactions and the precautionary demands for money. These money balances are computed as a given proportion of real GDP. Suppose real GDP is $5,000 billion and people wish to hold, say, 10 percent for transactions and precautionary purposes. This means the first $500 billion read along the horizontal axis in Exhibit 1 are held to make purchases and handle unforeseen events.

Now consider the impact of changes in the interest rate on the speculative demand for money. As the interest rate falls, people add larger speculative balances to their transactions and precautionary balances. For example, when the rate is 8 percent per year, the total quantity of money demanded at point *A* is $1,000 billion, of which $500 billion are speculative balances. If the interest rate is 4 percent, the total quantity of money demanded increases to $1,500 billion at point *B*, of which $1,000 billion are speculative balances. Therefore, the demand for money curve, labeled *MD*, looks much like any other demand curve.

> **Conclusion** *The speculative demand for money at possible interest rates gives the demand for money curve its downward slope.*

EXHIBIT 1 — The Demand for Money Curve

Assume the level of real GDP is $5,000 billion. Also assume households and businesses demand to hold 10 percent of real GDP ($500 billion) for transactions and precautionary balances. The speculative demand for money varies inversely with the interest rate. At an interest rate of 8 percent, the quantity of money demanded (M1) is $1,000 billion (point *A*), calculated as the sum of transactions and precautionary demand ($500 billion) and speculative demand ($500 billion). At a lower interest rate, a greater total quantity of money is demanded because the opportunity cost of holding money is lower.

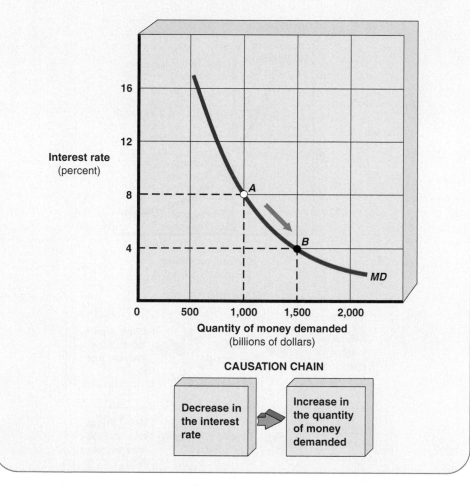

Interest rate
(percent)

Quantity of money demanded
(billions of dollars)

CAUSATION CHAIN

Decrease in the interest rate ➡ Increase in the quantity of money demanded

The Equilibrium Interest Rate

We are now ready to form the money market and determine the equilibrium interest rate by putting the demand for money and the supply of money together. In Exhibit 2, the money demand curve (*MD*) is identical to that in Exhibit 1. The supply of money curve (*MS*) is a vertical line because the $1,000 billion quantity of money supplied does not respond to changes in the interest rate. The reason is that our model assumes the Fed has used its tools to set the money supply at this quantity of money regardless of the interest rate.

EXHIBIT 2   The Equilibrium Interest Rate

The money market consists of the demand for and the supply of money. The market demand curve represents the quantity of money people are willing to hold at various interest rates. The money supply curve is a vertical line at $1,000 billion, based on the assumption that this is the quantity of money supplied by the Fed. The equilibrium interest rate is 8 percent and occurs at the intersection of the money demand and the money supply curves (point *E*). At any other interest rate, for example, 12 percent or 4 percent, the quantity of money people desire to hold does not equal the quantity available.

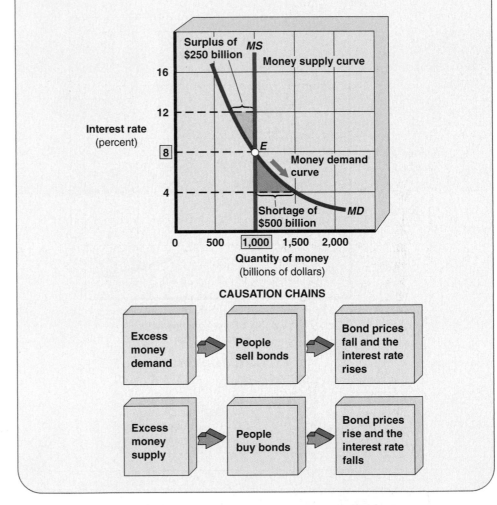

At point *E,* the equilibrium interest rate is 8 percent, determined by the intersection of the demand for money curve and the vertical supply of money curve. People wish to hold exactly the amount of money in circulation, and, therefore, there is neither upward nor downward pressure on the interest rate.

Excess Quantity of Money Demanded   Suppose the interest rate in Exhibit 2 is 4 percent instead of 8 percent. Such a low opportunity cost of money means that people desire to hold a greater quantity of money than the quantity supplied.

To eliminate this shortage of $500 billion, individuals and businesses adjust their asset portfolios. They seek more money by selling their bonds or other nonmoney assets. When many sell or try to sell their bonds, there is an increase in the supply of bonds for sale. Consequently, the price of bonds falls, and the interest rate rises. This rise in the interest rate ceases at the equilibrium interest rate of 8 percent because people are content with their portfolio of money and bonds at point *E*.

Here we need to pause and look at an example to understand what is happening. Suppose Apple pays 4 percent on its $1,000 30-year bonds. This means Apple pays a bondholder $40 in interest each year and promises to repay the original $1,000 price (face amount) at the end of 30 years. However, a holder of these bonds can sell them before maturity at a market-determined price. If bondholders desire to hold more money than is supplied, they will sell more of these bonds. Then the increase in the supply of bonds causes the price of bonds to fall to, say, $500. As a result, the interest rate rises to 8 percent ($40/$500).

Excess Quantity of Money Supplied   The story reverses for any rate of interest above 8 percent. Let's say the interest rate is 12 percent. In this case, people are holding more money than they wish. Stated differently, they wish to hold less money than is currently in circulation. In this case, the quantity of money demanded is $250 billion less than the quantity supplied. To correct this imbalance, people will move out of cash and checkable deposits by buying bonds. This increase in the demand for bonds will drive up the price of bonds and lower the interest rate. As the interest rate falls, the quantity of money demanded increases as people become more willing to hold money. Finally, the money market reaches equilibrium at point *E*, and people are content with their mix of money and bonds.

> **Conclusion** *There is an inverse relationship between bond prices and the interest rate that enables the money market to achieve equilibrium.*

How Monetary Policy Affects the Interest Rate

Assuming a stationary demand for money, the equilibrium rate of interest changes in response to changes in monetary policy. As we learned in Exhibit 4 of the previous chapter, the Federal Reserve can alter the money supply through open market operations, changes in the required reserve ratio, or changes in the discount rate. In this section, you will see that the Fed's power to change the money supply can also alter the equilibrium rate of interest.

Increasing the Money Supply   Exhibit 3(a) shows how increasing the money supply will cause the equilibrium rate of interest to fall. Our analysis begins at point E_1, with the money supply at $1,000 billion, which is equal to the quantity of money demanded, and with the equilibrium interest rate at 12 percent. Now suppose the Fed increases the money supply to $1,500 billion by buying government securities in the open market. The impact of the Fed's expansionary monetary policy is to create a $500 billion surplus of money at the prevailing 12 percent interest rate.

How will people react to this excess money in their pockets or checking accounts? Money becomes a "hot potato," and people buy bonds. The rush to purchase bonds drives the price of bonds higher and the interest rate lower. As the

| EXHIBIT 3 | The Effect of Changes in the Money Supply |

In Part (a), the Federal Reserve increases the money supply from $1,000 billion ($MS_1$) to $1,500 billion ($MS_2$). At the initial interest rate of 12 percent (point E_1), there is an excess of $500 billion beyond the amount people wish to hold. They react by buying bonds, and the interest rate falls until it reaches a new lower equilibrium interest rate at 8 percent (point E_2).

The reverse happens in Part (b). The Fed decreases the money supply from $1,500 billion ($MS_1$) to $1,000 billion ($MS_2$). Beginning at 8 percent (point E_1), people wish to hold $500 billion more than is available. This shortage disappears when people sell their bonds. As the price of bonds falls, the interest rate rises to the new higher equilibrium interest rate of 12 percent at point E_2.

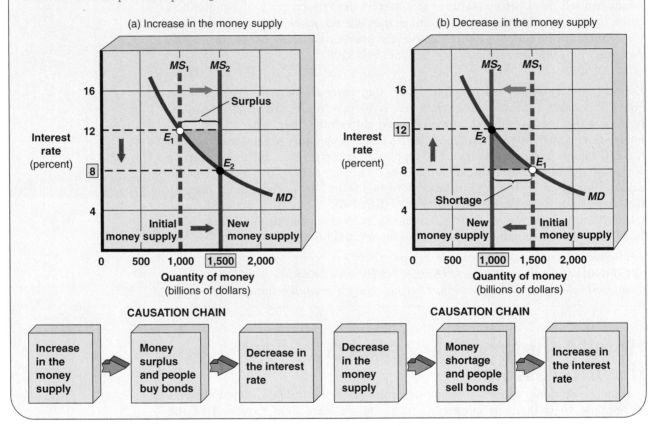

interest rate falls, people are *willing* to hold larger money balances. Or, stated differently, the quantity of money demanded increases until the new equilibrium at E_2 is reached. At the lower interest rate of 8 percent, the opportunity cost of holding money is also lower, and the imbalance between the money demand and money supply curves disappears.

Decreasing the Money Supply Exhibit 3(b) illustrates how the Fed can put upward pressure on the interest rate with contractionary monetary policy. Beginning at point E_1, the money market is in equilibrium at an interest rate of 8 percent. This time the Fed shrinks the money supply by selling government securities through its trading desk, raising the required reserve ratio, or raising the discount rate. As a result, the money supply decreases from $1,500 billion to $1,000 billion.

At the initial equilibrium interest rate of 8 percent, this decrease in the money supply causes a shortage of $500 billion.

Individuals and businesses wish to hold more money than is available. How can the public put more money in their pockets and checking accounts? They can sell their bonds for cash. This selling pressure lowers bond prices, causing the rate of interest to rise. At point E_2, the upward pressure on the interest rate stops. Once the equilibrium interest rate reaches 12 percent, people willingly hold the $1,000 billion money supply.

CHECKPOINT

What Does the Money Supply Curve Look Like When the Fed Targets the Federal Funds Rate?

Suppose the Fed has a policy of adjusting the money supply to achieve interest rate targets. For example, the Fed might set a 6 percent target federal funds rate. If an increase in the demand for money boosts the rate above 6 percent, the Fed adjusts the money supply until the 6 percent rate is restored. Under such a monetary policy, is the supply of money curve vertical, horizontal, or upward sloping with respect to the federal funds rate?

How Monetary Policy Affects Prices, Output, and Employment

The next step in our journey is to understand how monetary policy alters the macro economy. Here you should pause and study Exhibit 4. This exhibit illustrates the causation chain linking monetary policy and economic performance.

> **Conclusion** *In the Keynesian model, changes in the supply of money affect interest rates. In turn, interest rates affect investment spending, aggregate demand, and, finally, real GDP, employment, and prices.*

The Impact of Monetary Policy Using the AD-AS Model How do changes in the rate of interest affect aggregate demand? Begin with Exhibit 5(a), which is identical to Exhibit 3(a) and represents the money market. As explained earlier, we assume

---

EXHIBIT 4   The Keynesian Monetary Policy Transmission Mechanism

Keynesians focus on how changes in the money supply affect interest rates and investment spending. In turn, aggregate demand shifts and affects prices, real GDP, and employment.

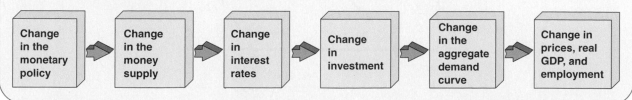

Change in the monetary policy ⇨ Change in the money supply ⇨ Change in interest rates ⇨ Change in investment ⇨ Change in the aggregate demand curve ⇨ Change in prices, real GDP, and employment

EXHIBIT 5   The Effect of Expansionary Monetary Policy on Aggregate Demand

In Part (a), the money supply is initially MS_1, and the equilibrium rate of interest is 12 percent. The equilibrium point in the money market changes from E_1 to E_2 when the Fed increases the money supply to MS_2. This causes the quantity of money people wish to hold to increase from $1,000 billion to $1,500 billion, and a new lower equilibrium interest rate is established at 8 percent.

The fall in the rate of interest shown in Part (b) causes a movement downward along the investment demand curve from point A to point B. Thus, the quantity of investment spending per year increases from $800 billion to $850 billion.

In Part (c), the investment component of the aggregate demand curve increases, causing this curve to shift outward from AD_1 to AD_2. As a result, the aggregate demand and supply equilibrium in the product market changes from E_1 to E_2, and the real GDP gap is eliminated. The price level also changes from 150 to 155.

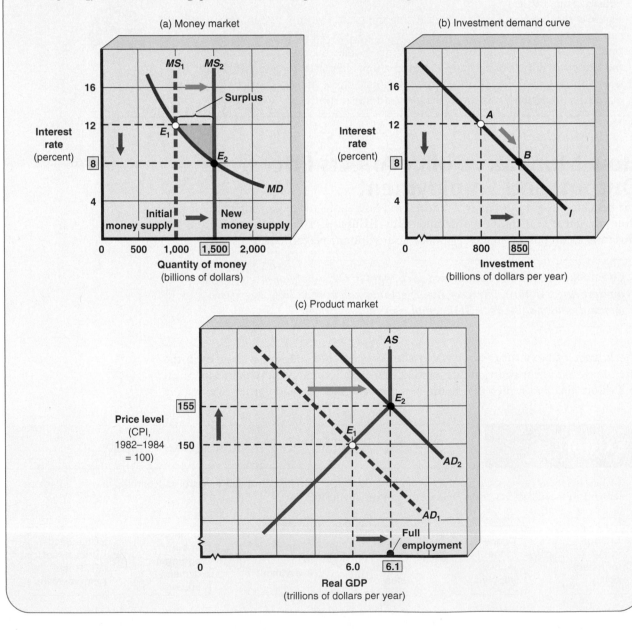

that the Fed increases the money supply from $1,000 billion ($MS_1$) to $1,500 billion ($MS_2$) and the equilibrium interest rate falls from 12 percent to 8 percent. In Part (b), we can see that the falling rate of interest causes an increase in the quantity of investment spending from $800 billion to $850 billion per year. Stated another way, there is a movement downward along the *investment demand curve (I)*, which you recall from the chapter on GDP is a component of total spending or aggregate demand. The investment demand curve shows the amount businesses spend for investment goods at different possible interest rates.

The classical economists believed that the interest rate alone determines the level of investment spending. Keynes disputed this idea. Instead, Keynes argued that the expectation of future profits is the primary factor determining investment and the interest rate is the financing cost of any investment proposal. Using a micro example to illustrate the investment decision-making process, suppose a consulting firm plans to purchase a new computer program for $1,000 that will be obsolete in a year. The firm anticipates the new software will increase its revenue by $1,100. Thus, assuming no taxes and other expenses, the expected rate of return or profit is 10 percent.

Now consider the impact of the cost of borrowing funds to finance the software investment. If the interest rate is less than 10 percent, the business will earn a profit, and it will make the investment expenditure to obtain the computer program. On the other hand, a rate of interest higher than 10 percent means the software investment will be a loss, so this purchase will not be made. The expected rate of the profit-interest rate-investment relationship follows this rule: *Businesses will undertake all investment projects for which the expected rate of profit equals or exceeds the interest rate.*

In Exhibit 5(c), we use the fiscal policy aggregate demand and aggregate supply analysis developed earlier. Begin at point E_1, with a real GDP per year of $6 trillion and a price level of 150. Now consider the link to the change in the money supply.

The increase in investment resulting from the fall in the interest rate works through the *spending multiplier* and shifts the aggregate demand curve rightward from AD_1 to AD_2. At the new equilibrium point, E_2, the level of real GDP rises from $6 trillion to $6.1 trillion, and full employment is achieved. In addition, the price level rises from 150 to 155. Exhibit 5(a) also demonstrates the effect of a contractionary monetary policy. In this case, the money supply shifts inward from MS_2 to MS_1, causing the equilibrium rate of interest to rise from 8 percent to 12 percent. The Fed's "tight" money policy causes the level of investment spending to fall from $850 billion to $800 billion, which, in turn, decreases the equilibrium level of real GDP per year from $6.1 trillion to $6 trillion. As a result, the unemployment rate rises, and the inflation rate falls because the price level falls from 155 to 150.

The Monetarist View of the Role of Money

The Monetarist Transmission Mechanism

Monetarists believe Keynesians suffer from the delusion that monetary policy operates only indirectly, causing changes in the interest rate before affecting aggregate demand and then prices, real GDP, and employment. The opposing school of economic thought, called monetarism, challenges this view. Monetarism is the theory that changes in the money supply directly determine changes in prices, real

Monetarism

The theory that changes in the money supply directly determine changes in prices, real GDP, and employment.

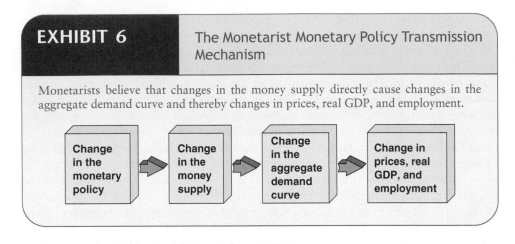

EXHIBIT 6   The Monetarist Monetary Policy Transmission Mechanism

Monetarists believe that changes in the money supply directly cause changes in the aggregate demand curve and thereby changes in prices, real GDP, and employment.

Change in the monetary policy ➡ Change in the money supply ➡ Change in the aggregate demand curve ➡ Change in prices, real GDP, and employment

GDP, and employment. Exhibit 6 illustrates the monetarist transmission mechanism. Comparison of this figure with Exhibit 4 shows that the monetarist model omits the Keynesian interest rate-investment linkage.

The Equation of Exchange   Monetarists put the spotlight on the money supply. They argue that to predict the condition of the economy, you simply look at the money supply. If it expands too much, higher rates of inflation will be the forecast. If it contracts too much, unemployment lines will lengthen. Monetarism has its intellectual roots in classical economics, introduced in the chapter on aggregate demand and supply. Monetarists proudly wear *laissez faire* on their sleeves and believe the price system is the macro economy's best friend. To understand monetarism, we begin with the equation of exchange developed by the classical economists in the nineteenth century. The equation of exchange is an accounting identity that states the money supply times the velocity of money equals total spending. Expressed as a formula, the equation of exchange is written as

$$MV = PQ$$

Let's begin with the left side of the equation ($M \times V$). M is the money supply (more precisely M1) in circulation, and V represents the velocity of money. The velocity of money is the average number of times per year a dollar of the money supply is spent on final goods and services. Assume you have one crisp $20 bill and this is the only money in an ultrasimple economy. Suppose you spend this money on a pizza and soda at Zeno's Pizza Hut. Once Mr. Zeno puts your money in his pocket, he decides to buy an economics book and learn how the views of Keynesians and monetarists differ. And so, Mr. Zeno buys the book at the Wise Professor Book Store for exactly $20. At this point, both Mr. Zeno and Ms. Wise have sold $20 worth of goods. Thus, a single $20 bill has financed $40 worth of total spending. And as long as this $20 bill passes from hand to hand during, say, one year, the value of sales will increase. For example, assume the $20 travels from hand to hand five times. This means the velocity of money is 5, and the equation of exchange is expressed as

$$\$20 \times 5 = 100$$

The equation of exchange is an *identity*—true by definition—that expresses the fact that the value of what people spend is equal to, or exchanged for, what they buy. What people buy is nominal GDP, or ($P \times Q$). Recall that nominal, or money, GDP

Equation of exchange

An accounting identity that states the money supply times the velocity of money equals total spending.

Velocity of money

The average number of times per year a dollar of the money supply is spent on final goods and services.

is equal to the average selling price during the year (*P*) multiplied by the quantity of actual output of final goods and services (*Q*). In our simple economy, total spending equals $100. Note that the identity between *MV* and *PQ* does not say what happens to either *P* or *Q* if *MV* increases. Although we know by how much the total value of output (*PQ*) increases, we do not know whether the price level (*P*) or the quantity of output (*Q*) or both increase.

Consider a more realistic example. Suppose that nominal GDP last year was $5 trillion and M1 was $1 trillion. How many times did each dollar of the money supply have to be spent to generate this level of total spending in the economy? Using the equation of exchange,

$$M \times V = P \times Q$$
$$\$1 \text{ trillion} \times V = \$5 \text{ trillion}$$
$$MV = PQ$$

Thus, each dollar was spent an average of five times per year.

The Quantity Theory of Money   The equation of exchange is converted from an *identity* to a *theory* by making certain assumptions. The classical economists became the forerunners of modern-day monetarists by arguing that the velocity of money (*V*) and real output (*Q*) are fairly constant. The classical economists viewed *V* as constant because people's habits of holding a certain quantity of money, and therefore the number of times a dollar is spent, are slow to change. Recall from the chapter on aggregate demand and supply that classical economists believed in price and wage flexibility. Hence, they believed the economy would automatically adjust to long-run full-employment output (*Q*).

Because *V* and *Q* are constant by assumption, we have one of the oldest theories of inflation, called the quantity theory of money. The quantity theory of money states that changes in the money supply are directly related to changes in the price level. Monetary policy based on the quantity theory of money therefore directly affects the price level. To illustrate, we will modify the equation of exchange by putting a bar (–) over *V* and over *Q* to indicate they are fixed or constant in value:

> **Quantity theory of money**
> The theory that changes in the money supply are directly related to changes in the price level.

$$M \times \bar{V} = P \times \bar{Q}$$

What if the money supply doubles? The price level also doubles. Or, if the Fed cuts the money supply in half, then the price level is also cut in half. Meanwhile, real output of goods and services, *Q*, remains unchanged.

> **Conclusion** *According to the quantity theory of money, any change in the money supply must lead to a proportional change in the price level.*

In short, monetarists say the cause of inflation is "too much money chasing too few goods." The quantity theory of money denies any role for nonmonetary factors, such as supply shocks from a hike in oil prices, which cause cost-push inflation [see Exhibit 11(a) in the chapter on aggregate demand and supply]. Moreover, this theory ignores the impact of fiscal policy changes in taxation and spending on the price level.

What do the data reveal about the link between changes in the money supply and changes in the rate of inflation? Although the relationship does not exist for all years, the evidence supports the general conclusion that sustained levels of higher growth in the money supply correspond to increases in the inflation rate. For example, when the money supply growth rate was low and averaged 1.5 percent between 1953 and 1962, the inflation rate averaged 1.3 percent. During 1973–1982, the money supply grew at a higher average rate of 6.7 percent, and the average inflation rate rose to 8.8 percent. More recently, between 1993 and 2002, the money supply increased at a lower average rate of 1.8 percent, and the average inflation rate dropped to 2.5 percent. Globally, a similar direct correlation exists between changes in the money supply and inflation. For example, Argentina's money supply grew at an average rate of 369 percent during 1980–1990 and the average annual inflation rate was 395 percent over this 10-year period.

Modern Monetarism   Today's monetarists have changed the assumptions of the classical quantity theory of money. The evidence indicates that velocity is not constant and the economy does not always operate at full employment. Although M and P are correlated, they do not change proportionally. *Monetarists argue that although velocity is not unchanging, it is nevertheless predictable.* Suppose the predicted velocity of money is 5 and the money supply increases by $100 billion this year. Monetarists would predict that nominal GDP will increase by about $500 billion ($\Delta M \times \hat{V}$). [The circumflex ($\wedge$) indicates velocity is predicted.] If the economy is far below full employment, most of the rise in total spending will be in real output. If the economy is near full employment, much of the increase will be in rising prices.

Monetarists refute the Keynesian view that the rate of interest is so important. Instead, the monetarist view is often expressed in the famous single-minded statement that "money does matter." Instead of working through the rate of interest to affect investment and, in turn, the economy, changes in the money supply directly determine economic performance.

> **Conclusion** *To avoid inflation and unemployment, the monetarists' prescription is to be sure that the money supply is at the proper level.*

Fixed Money Target   Monetarism gained credibility in the late 1950s and 1960s, led by Professor Milton Friedman at the University of Chicago. The monetarists have an answer for how we make sure the economy grows at the right rate: Instead of risking policy errors, forget about the rate of interest and follow a steady, predictable monetary policy. Recall from the chapter on money creation that there are limitations on the Fed's ability to control the money supply because of the independent actions of households, firms, banks, and the U.S. Treasury. Monetarists would stop the Fed from tinkering with the money supply, missing the target, and making the economy worse, rather than better. Instead, they say the money supply should expand at the same rate as the potential growth rate in real GDP. That is, it should increase somewhere between 3 percent and 5 percent per year. The Fed should therefore pick a rate and stick to it, even if unexpected changes in velocity cause short periods of inflation or unemployment. This is called following a *monetary rule.* Monetarists argue that their "straitjacket" approach would reduce the intensity and duration of unemployment and inflation by eliminating the monetarists' public enemy number one—the

Fed's discretion to change the money supply. A Keynesian once summarized the fixed money supply approach as "Don't do something, just stand there."

> **Conclusion** *Monetarists advocate that the Federal Reserve increase the money supply by a constant percentage each year.*

How Stable Is Velocity?   How stable, or predictable, is the velocity of money? This is a critical question in the Keynesian-monetarist debate. Keynesians do not accept the monetarists' argument that over long periods of time velocity is stable and predictable. Hence, a change in the money supply can lead to a much larger or smaller change in GDP than the monetarists would predict. As shown in Exhibit 7,

EXHIBIT 7   The Velocity of Money, 1945–2007

The velocity of money (*V*) equals GDP divided by the supply of money (M1). Keynesians argue that velocity is not stable. During the 1980s, early 1990s, and years after 2001 velocity became quite unpredictable. Monetarists believe velocity is stable over the long term and point to the periods of 1946–1981 and 1993–2000. During these years, velocity rose at a predictable annual rate.

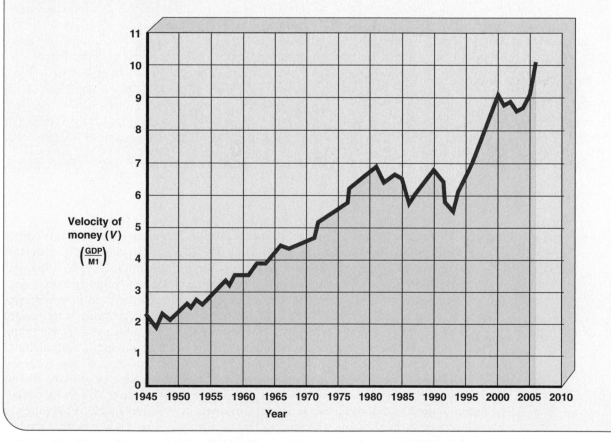

SOURCE: *Economic Report of the President*, 1980 and 2008, http://www.gpoaccess.gov/eop/, Tables B-52, B-1, and B-69.

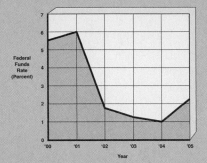

SOURCE: FRB Federal Open Market Committee, http://www.federalreserve.gove/fomc/fundsrate.htm.

The story of the worst collapse of the housing market and most serious financial crisis since the Great Depression is filled with villains and no action hero to sweep down from the sky and save the day. It is a story with plenty of blame to go around: homeowners who bought a Trojan horse, rampant speculation, predatory lenders, slick Wall Street operators, greedy CEOs, lax regulators, and debatable Fed pol-

icy. Perhaps a phrase by Alan Greenspan, former Fed chairman, best described the bust of the housing market bubble when he said, "How do we know when irrational exuberance has unduly escalated asset values?"

The stage was set for the housing crisis by the Fed's response to the recession of 2001. The annual change in the money supply jumped from –3.1 percent in 2000 to 8.7 percent in 2001.[1] And, as shown in the above exhibit, the Fed decreased interest rates sharply after 2001 and kept them historically low in order to boost aggregate demand and prevent another recession. Then in 2004, Greenspan addressed the Credit Union Association and said, "American consumers might benefit if lenders provided greater mortgage product alternatives to the traditional fixed rate mortgage." And as if following the Fed chairman's advice, *adjustable rate mort-*

gages (ARMs) became the loan of choice for *subprime borrowers* who have poor or less than ideal credit scores. Mailboxes were stuffed with offers to borrow 100 percent or more of a home's value with zero down. Payments and "Teaser" interest rates were held artificially low for the first few years of the loan and then they would jump sharply upward. Forget worrying about not affording the home, your income would not be checked following a "no document" lending practice. Thus, using risky ARMs, banks lent billions of dollars to home buyers who could not pay the bank when the payments and interest rates rose.

Faced with accumulating portfolios of risky debt, banks and mortgage companies sold these risky mortgages to New York investment firms such as Bear Stearns (acquired by J. P. Morgan Chase with financial backing from

---

1. *Economic Report of the President 2008*, http://www.gpoaccess.gov/eop/, Table B-69.

Keynesians are quick to point out the turbulent variations in velocity. Velocity gyrated up and down during the 1980s, early 1990s, and years after 2001. Monetarists counter by pointing to the evidence that during the periods of 1946–1981 and 1993–2000 velocity generally rose at a quite predictable or steady annual rate.

Keynesians focus on short-run variations in V that accompany any long-run velocity growth rate. They therefore argue that following a monetary rule is folly. Suppose the money supply increases at a constant rate, but velocity is greater than expected. This means that total spending will be greater than predicted, causing inflation. Lower-than-predicted velocity results in unemployment because the economy expands too little. The Keynesians believe that the Federal Reserve must be free to change the money supply to offset unexpected changes in velocity. Monetarists counter that the Fed *cannot* predict short-run variations in V, so its "quick-fix" changes in the money supply will often be wrong. This is why monetarists advocate that the Fed follow a monetary rule. Keynesians are willing to accept occasional policy errors and

the Fed) and Merrill Lynch who pooled them with other securities. These packages, often called collateralized debt obligations or CDOs, were sold to customers around the world—all with the blessing of ratings agencies such as Standard & Poor's. With each of these transactions, large fees were collected, and in short, consummation of the deal was the criterion and not validity of the assessment of risk.

Expansion of the housing market bubble was based on an assumption by all the players that real estate prices would always go up. However, beginning in the summer of 2005, subprime foreclosures rose and home prices dropped as people's payments rose under their ARMs. Also, once the value of homes fell below the loan value, people could not refinance loans to get lower payments. When people walked away from their mortgages, Wall Street and foreign investors were stuck with bad loans in their CDOs to write off, CEOs were fired, and many real estate executives were indicted

for mortgage fraud. As a result, lenders greatly tightened their lending standards to avoid further risky loans, and home financing became difficult to obtain.

In 2008, the Fed announced that it would allow Wall Street investment firms to receive emergency loans and exchange risky investments for Treasury securities. Also, the Housing and Economic Recovery Act of 2008 was passed that allows some borrowers to refinance their mortgages with new fixed-rate loans backed by a federal guarantee, and it provides grants for state and local governments in the hardest-hit communities to buy foreclosed property. It also includes a tax credit for first-time home buyers who buy housing that is unoccupied. And the Treasury Department was given authority to take over Fannie Mae and Freddie Mac, the troubled government-created firms that fund the vast majority of mortgage loans in the United States.

In addition, a massive $700 billion bailout plan was enacted in 2008 that gave the Treasury the

authority to buy and resale bad mortgage debt from financial institutions. Also, the federal government decided to take partial ownership in private U.S. banks until they regain stability and increase lending. Participating banks must curtail executive bonuses and other perks. Moreover, lenders in Congress have promised the biggest changes in regulation of financial companies since the 1930s. Meanwhile, the final price tag to the taxpayers for this financial crisis is unknowable.

ANALYZE THE ISSUE

In support of the Fed's monetary policy prior to the deflation of the home prices bubble, one can argue that the reality is that increasing the money supply and low-interest rates were required to sustain expansion. Based on the Monetarist school of thought, criticize the Fed's policy.

reject this idea in favor of maintaining Fed flexibility to change the money supply in order to affect interest rates, aggregate demand, and the economy.

CHECKPOINT

A Horse of Which Color?

A famous economist once proposed replacing the Fed with an intelligent horse. Each New Year's Day, the horse would stand in front of Fed headquarters to answer monetary policy questions. Reporters would ask, "What is going to happen to the money supply this year?" The horse would tap its hoof four times, and the next day headlines would read "Fed to Once Again Increase the Money Supply 4 Percent." Is this famous economist a Keynesian or a monetarist?

A Comparison of Macroeconomic Views

By now, your head is probably spinning with dueling schools of economic thought. The debate among the classicals, Keynesians, and monetarists can be quite confusing. This chapter has presented differences in monetary policy between these schools. To refresh your memory and complete the discussion, this section presents a brief review of key differences in fiscal policy introduced in earlier chapters. Exhibit 8 gives a thumbnail summary of the key differences between the three camps. Note the similarity between the classical and the monetarist schools.

Classical Economics

As discussed in the chapter on aggregate demand and supply, the dominant school of economic thought before the Great Depression was classical economics. The

EXHIBIT 8	Comparison of Macroeconomic Theories		
Issue	**Classical**	**Keynesian**	**Monetarist**
	Adam Smith	John Maynard Keynes	Milton Friedman
Stability of economy	Stable in long run at full employment	Inherently unstable at less than full employment	Stable in long run at full employment
Price-wage flexibility	Yes	No	Yes
Velocity of money	Stable	Unstable	Predictable
Cause of inflation	Excess money supply	Excess aggregate demand	Excess money supply
Causes of unemployment	Short-run price and wage adjustment	Inadequate aggregate demand	Short-run price and wage adjustment
Effect of monetary policy	Changes aggregate demand and prices	Changes interest rate, which changes investment and real GDP	Changes aggregate demand and prices
Effect of fiscal policy	Not necessary	Spending multiplier changes aggregate demand	No effect because of crowding-out effect

Monetarists and Keynesians still debate the causes of the Great Depression. Monetarists Milton Friedman and Anna Schwartz, in their book *A Monetary History of the United States,* argued that the Great Depression was caused by the decline in the money supply, as shown in Exhibit 9(a). The accompanying Parts (b), (c), and (d) present changes in the price level, real GDP, and unemployment rate.

During the 1920s, the money supply expanded steadily, and prices were generally stable. In response to the great stock market crash of 1929, bank failures, falling real GDP, and rising unemployment, the Fed changed its monetary policy. Through the Great Depression years from 1929 to 1933, M1 declined by 27 percent. Assuming velocity is relatively constant, how will a sharp reduction in the quantity of money in circulation affect the economy? Monetarists predict a reduction in prices, output, and employment. As Exhibit 9(b) shows, the price level declined by 24 percent between 1929 and 1933. In addition to deflation, Exhibit 9(c) shows that real GDP was 27 percent lower in 1933 than

in 1929. Unemployment rose from 3.2 percent in 1929 to 24.9 percent in 1933.

Friedman and Schwartz argued that the ineptness of the Fed's monetary policy during the Great Depression caused the trough in the business cycle to be more severe and sustained. For proof, let's look at the period after 1933. The money supply grew and was followed closely by an increase in prices, real GDP, and employment.

The Great Depression was indeed not the Fed's finest hour. In the initial phase of the contraction, foreign banks were fearful and withdrew large amounts of their gold from U.S. banks. To stop the outflow of gold to other countries, the Fed raised the discount rate in 1931. As a result, banks borrowed less of their required reserves from the Fed's discount window, and the money supply fell. Later, the discount rate fell, but only after the economy was deeper into the Great Depression.

What should the Fed have done? Friedman and Schwartz argued that the Fed should not have waited until 1931 to use open market operations to increase the

money supply. Thus, they concluded that the Fed was to blame for not pursuing an expansionary policy, which would have reduced the severity and duration of the contraction.

Finally, although the emphasis here is monetary policy, note that both monetary and fiscal policies worsened the situation. President Herbert Hoover attempted to balance the budget, rather than using expansionary fiscal policy.

ANALYZE THE ISSUE

1. Explain why monetarists believe the Fed should have expanded the money supply during the Great Depression.
2. The Keynesians challenge the Friedman-Schwartz monetarists' monetary policy cure for the Great Depression. Use the *AD-AS* model to explain the Keynesian view. (Hint: Your answer must include the investment demand curve.)

Source: From Friedman, Milton; *Monetary History of the United States, 1867–1960.* © 1963 NBER, 1991 renewed. Reprinted by permission of Princeton University Press.

basic theory of the classical economists, introduced by Adam Smith in *The Wealth of Nations,* was that a market-directed economy will automatically correct itself to full employment. Consequently, there is no need for fiscal policy designed to restore full employment.

Recall that a key assumption of classical theory is that, given time to adjust, prices and wages will decrease to ensure the economy operates at full employment.

EXHIBIT 9   The Great Depression Economic Data, 1929–1934

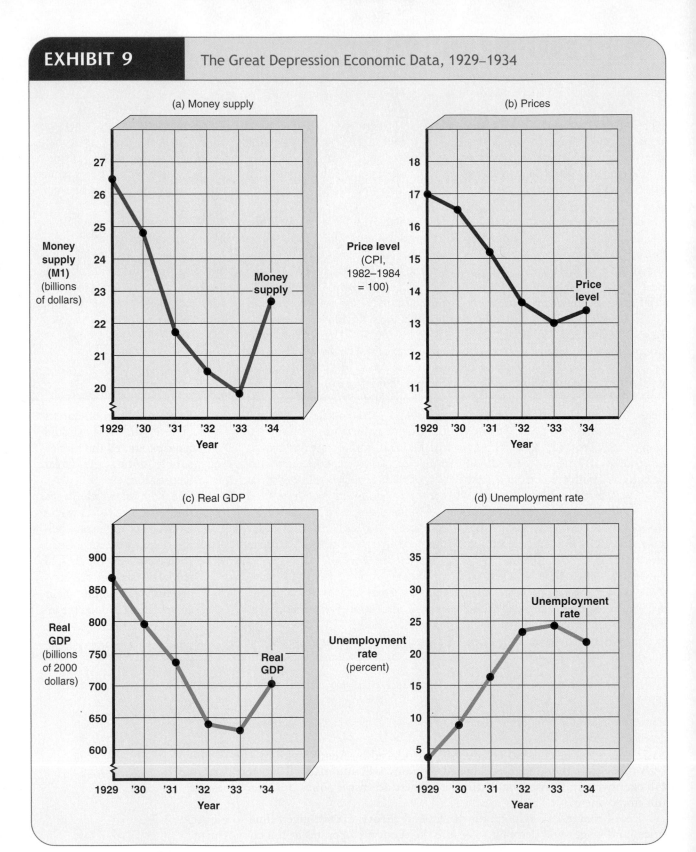

A decrease in the aggregate demand curve causes a temporary surplus, which, in turn, causes businesses to cut prices, and, in turn, causes more goods to be purchased because of the real balances effect. As a result, wages adjust downward, and employment rises. Classical economists therefore view the economy as operating in the long run along a vertical aggregate supply curve originating at the full-employment real GDP.

Keynesian Economics

The Great Depression challenged the classical prescription to wait until markets adjust and full employment is automatically restored. As the unemployment rate rose to 24.9 percent in 1933, people asked how long it would take for the market mechanism to adjust. John Maynard Keynes responded with his famous saying, "In the long run we are all dead." Keynes, in his book *The General Theory*, attacked classical theory and in the process revolutionized macroeconomic thought.

As explained in the chapter on fiscal policy, using fiscal policy to affect aggregate demand is a cornerstone of Keynesian economics. While Keynesians believe monetary policy is often not very powerful, especially during a downturn, they regard fiscal policy as their "top banana." However, Keynesians recognize that one of the potential problems of fiscal policy is the *crowding-out effect*. As shown earlier in Exhibit 8 of the chapter on federal deficits and the national debt, financing a federal deficit by borrowing competes with private borrowers for funds. Given a fixed money supply, the extra demand from the federal government to finance its deficit causes the interest rate to rise. As a result, businesses cut back on investment spending and offset the expected increase in aggregate demand. The Keynesian view, however, is that the investment demand curve is not very sensitive to changes in the interest rate, and therefore only a relatively small amount of investment spending will be crowded out. Thus, the decline in investment only slightly counteracts or offsets an increase in aggregate demand created by a deficit.

> **Conclusion** *Keynesians view the shape of the investment demand curve as rather steep or vertical, so the crowding-out effect is insignificant.*

Monetarism

Monetarists are iconoclasts because they attack the belief in the ability of either the Fed or the federal government to stabilize the economy. They argue that fiscal policy is an essentially useless tool that has little or no impact on output or employment because of a total crowding-out effect. Suppose the money supply remains fixed and the federal government borrows to finance its deficit. The intended goal is to increase aggregate demand and restore full employment. According to the monetarists, financing the deficit will drive up the interest rate and crowd out a substantial, not a small, amount of investment spending. The reason is that the monetarists view the investment demand curve as sensitive to changes in the interest rate; therefore, greater amounts of investment spending will be crowded out. As a result, the net effect is no increase in aggregate demand and no reduction in unemployment.

> **Conclusion** *Monetarists view the shape of the investment demand curve as less steep or relatively flat, so the crowding-out effect is significant.*

Although the monetarists do not trust the Federal Reserve to use discretionary monetary policy, they are quick to point out that only money is important. Changes in the money supply, the basic lever of monetary policy, have a powerful impact. Instead of ineffectual government deficit spending to cure unemployment, an increase in the money supply would definitely stimulate the economy based on the quantity theory of money. In short, changes in the money supply directly result in changes in real GDP.

KEY CONCEPTS

Transactions demand for
  money
Precautionary demand for money
Speculative demand for money

Demand for money curve
Monetarism
Equation of exchange
Velocity of money

Quantity theory of money
Adjustable-rate mortgages
  (ARM)
Subprime borrowers

SUMMARY

- The *demand for money* in the Keynesian view
  consists of three reasons why people hold money:
  (1) *Transactions demand* is money held to pay
  for everyday predictable expenses. (2) *Precautionary demand* is money held to pay unpredictable expenses. (3) *Speculative demand* is money
  held to take advantage of price changes in nonmoney assets.

- The *demand for money curve* shows the quantity
  of money people wish to hold at various rates of
  interest. As the interest rate rises, the quantity of
  money demanded is less than when the interest
  rate is lower.

Demand for Money Curve

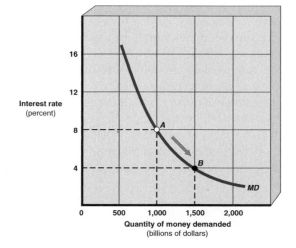

- The *equilibrium interest rate* is determined in
  the money market by the intersection of the
  demand for money and the supply of money
  curves. The money supply (M1), which is determined by the Fed, is represented by a vertical
  line.

The Equilibrium Interest Rate

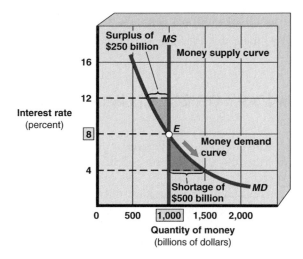

- An *excess quantity of money demanded* causes
  households and businesses to increase their
  money balances by selling bonds. This causes
  the price of bonds to fall, thus driving up the
  interest rate.

- An *excess quantity of money supplied* causes
  households and businesses to reduce their money
  balances by purchasing bonds. The effect is to
  cause the price of bonds to rise, and, thereby, the
  rate of interest falls.

- The *Keynesian view of the monetary policy
  transmission mechanism* operates as follows:
  First, the Fed uses its policy tools to change the
  money supply. Second, changes in the money
  supply change the equilibrium interest rate,
  which affects investment spending. Finally, a
  change in investment changes aggregate demand
  and determines the level of prices, real GDP, and
  employment.

- *Monetarism* is the simpler view that changes in monetary policy directly change aggregate demand, and thereby prices, real GDP, and employment. Thus, monetarists focus on the money supply, rather than on the rate of interest.
- The *equation of exchange* is an accounting identity that is the foundation of monetarism. The equation ($MV = PQ$) states that the money supply multiplied by the *velocity of money* is equal to the price level multiplied by real output. The velocity of money is the number of times each dollar is spent during a year. Keynesians view velocity as volatile, but monetarists disagree.
- The *quantity theory of money* is a monetarist argument that the velocity of money (V) and the output (Q) variables in the equation of exchange are relatively constant. Given this assumption, changes in the money supply yield proportionate changes in the price level. The monetarist solution to inept Fed tinkering with the money supply that causes inflation or recession is to have the Fed simply pick a rate of growth in the money supply that is consistent with real GDP growth and stick to it.
- *Keynesians' and monetarists' views on fiscal policy* are also different. Keynesians believe the investment demand curve is relatively vertical, and monetarists view it as relatively flat. Monetarists assert that the *crowding-out effect* is large and, therefore, fiscal policy is ineffective. Keynesians argue that the crowding-out effect is small and that fiscal policy is effective.

SUMMARY OF CONCLUSION STATEMENTS

- As the interest rate falls, the opportunity cost of holding money falls, and people increase their speculative balances.
- There is an inverse relationship between the quantity of money demanded and the interest rate.
- The speculative demand for money at possible interest rates gives the demand for money curve its downward slope.
- There is an inverse relationship between bond prices and the interest rate that enables the money market to achieve equilibrium.
- In the Keynesian model, changes in the supply of money affect interest rates. In turn, interest rates affect investment spending, aggregate demand, and, finally, real GDP, employment, and prices.

- According to the quantity theory of money, any change in the money supply must lead to a proportional change in the price level.
- To avoid inflation and unemployment, the monetarists' prescription is to be sure that the money supply is at the proper level.
- Monetarists advocate that the Federal Reserve increase the money supply by a constant percentage each year.
- Keynesians view the shape of the investment demand curve as rather steep or vertical, so the crowding-out effect is insignificant.
- Monetarists view the shape of the investment demand curve as less steep or relatively flat, so the crowding-out effect is significant.

STUDY QUESTIONS AND PROBLEMS

1. How much money do you keep in cash or checkable deposits on a typical day? Under the following conditions, would you increase or decrease your demand for money? Also identify whether the condition affects your transactions demand, precautionary demand, or speculative demand.
   a. Your salary doubles.
   b. The rate of interest on bonds and other assets falls.
   c. An automatic teller machine (ATM) is installed next door, and you have a card.
   d. Bond prices are expected to rise.
   e. You are paid each week instead of monthly.

2. What are the basic motives for the transactions demand, precautionary demand, and speculative demand? Explain how these three demands are combined in a graph to show the total demand for money.

3. Suppose a bond pays annual interest of $80. Compute the interest rate per year that a bondholder can earn if the bond has a face value of $800, $1,000, and $2,000. State the conclusion drawn from your calculations.

EXHIBIT 10 — Money Market

Interest Rate (percent)	Demand for Money (billions of dollars)	Supply of Money (billions of dollars)
8%	$100	$200
6	200	200
4	300	200
2	400	200

4. Using the demand and supply schedule for money shown in Exhibit 10, do the following:
   a. Graph the demand for and the supply of money curves.
   b. Determine the equilibrium interest rate.
   c. Suppose the Fed increases the money supply by $100 billion. Show the effect in your graph, and describe the money market adjustment process to a new equilibrium interest rate. What is the new equilibrium rate of interest?

5. Assume you are the chair of the Federal Reserve Board of Governors and the condition of the economy is as shown in Exhibit 5. Assume you are a Keynesian, and start at point E_1 in the money market and the product market. State the likely direction of change in the price level, real GDP, and employment caused by each of the following monetary policies:
   a. The Fed makes an open market sale of government bonds.
   b. The Fed reduces the required reserve ratio.
   c. The Fed increases the discount rate.

6. "A monetarist investigator might say that the sewer flow of 6,000 gallons an hour consisted of an average of 200 gallons in the sewer at any one time with a complete turnover of the water 30 times every hour."[1] Interpret this statement using the equation of exchange.

7. What is the quantity theory of money, and what does each term in the equation represent?

8. Exhibit 6 shows the monetarist monetary policy transmission mechanism. Assume the economy is in a recession. At each arrow, identify a reason why the transmission process could fail.

9. Explain the difference between the Keynesian and the monetarist views on how an increase in the money supply causes inflation.

10. Based on the quantity theory of money, what would be the impact of increasing the money supply by 25 percent?

11. Suppose the investment demand curve is a vertical line. Would the Keynesian or the monetarist view of the impact of monetary policy on investment spending be correct?

12. Why is the shape of the aggregate supply curve important to the Keynesian-monetarist controversy? (Hint: Review Exhibit 6 in the chapter on aggregate demand and supply.)

For Online Exercises, go the text Web site at www.cengage.com/economics/tucker.

---

1. Werner Sichel and Peter Eckstein, *Basic Economic Concepts* (Chicago, Rand McNally, 1974), p. 344.

CHECKPOINT ANSWERS ✓

What Does the Money Supply Curve Look Like When the Fed Targets the Federal Funds Rate?

In Exhibit 11, consider the effect of a shift in the money demand curve from MD_1 to MD_2 when the Fed follows a federal funds rate target of 6 percent. The initial effects are an excess demand for money and upward pressure on the rate. Because the Fed sets the rate target at 6 percent, it will increase the money supply along the money supply curve, MS, and establish a new equilibrium at E_2. At the new equilibrium, the money supply has increased from \$800 billion to \$850 billion, and the rate is unchanged at 6 percent. Therefore, the money supply curve is traced by an infinite number of possible equilibrium points along the MS curve. If you said the money supply curve is horizontal when the Fed sets a federal funds rate target, **YOU ARE CORRECT.**

A Horse of Which Color?

The famous economist is Milton Friedman, who favors a monetary rule for the Fed. The horse is a sarcastic way of rejecting Keynesian activist policies that destabilize the economy. Friedman even argues that the Board of Governors of the Federal Reserve

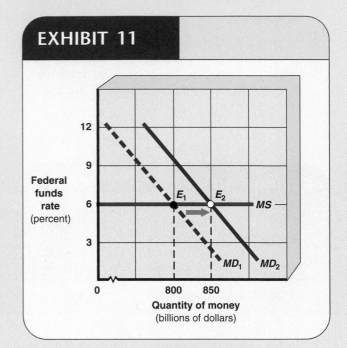

EXHIBIT 11

System should announce the growth rate for the money supply each year and must resign if the target is missed. If you said the economist is a monetarist, **YOU ARE CORRECT.**

PRACTICE QUIZ

For an explanation of the correct answers, please visit the tutorial at www.cengage.com/ economics/tucker.

1. Keynes gave which of the following as a motive for people holding money?
   a. Transactions demand
   b. Speculative demand
   c. Precautionary demand
   d. All of the above

2. A decrease in the interest rate, other things being equal, causes a (an)
   a. upward movement along the demand curve for money.
   b. downward movement along the demand curve for money.
   c. rightward shift of the demand curve for money.
   d. leftward shift of the demand curve for money.

3. Assume the demand for money curve is stationary and the Fed increases the money supply. The result is that people
   a. increase the supply of bonds, thus driving up the interest rate.
   b. increase the supply of bonds, thus driving down the interest rate.
   c. increase the demand for bonds, thus driving up the interest rate.
   d. increase the demand for bonds, thus driving down the interest rate.

4. Assume the demand for money curve is fixed and the Fed decreases the money supply. The result is a temporary
   a. excess quantity of money demanded.
   b. excess quantity of money supplied.
   c. increase in the price of bonds.
   d. increase in the demand for bonds.

5. Assume the demand for money curve is fixed and the Fed increases the money supply. The result is that the price of bonds
   a. rises.
   b. remains unchanged.
   c. falls.
   d. None of the above occurs.

6. Using the aggregate supply and demand model, assume the economy is in equilibrium on the intermediate portion of the aggregate supply curve. A decrease in the money supply will decrease the price level and
   a. lower both the interest rate and real GDP.
   b. raise both the interest rate and real GDP.
   c. lower the interest rate and raise real GDP.
   d. raise the interest rate and lower real GDP.

7. Based on the equation of exchange, the money supply in the economy is calculated as
   a. $M = V/PQ$.
   b. $M = V(PQ)$.
   c. $MV = PQ$.
   d. $M = PQ - V$.

8. The V in the equation of exchange represents the
   a. variation in the GDP.
   b. variation in the CPI.
   c. variation in real GDP.
   d. average number of times per year a dollar is spent on final goods and services.

9. Which of the following is *not* an issue in the Keynesian-monetarist debate?
   a. The importance of monetary versus fiscal policy
   b. The importance of a change in the money supply
   c. The importance of the crowding-out effect
   d. All of the above

10. Keynesians reject the influence of monetary policy on the economy. One argument supporting this Keynesian view is that the
    a. money demand curve is horizontal at any interest rate.
    b. aggregate demand curve is nearly flat.
    c. investment demand curve is nearly vertical.
    d. money demand curve is vertical.

11. Starting from an equilibrium at E_1 in Exhibit 12, a rightward shift of the money supply curve from MS_1 to MS_2 would cause an excess
    a. demand for money, leading people to sell bonds.
    b. supply of money, leading people to buy bonds.

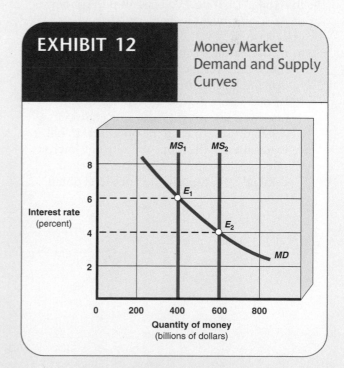

EXHIBIT 12   Money Market Demand and Supply Curves

PRACTICE QUIZ CONTINUED

c. supply of money, leading people to sell bonds.
d. demand for money, leading people to buy bonds.

12. Beginning from an equilibrium at E_2 in Exhibit 12, a decrease in the money supply from $600 billion to $400 billion causes people to
a. sell bonds and drive the price of bonds down.
b. buy bonds and drive the price of bonds up.
c. buy bonds and drive the price of bonds down.
d. sell bonds and drive the price of bonds up.

13. In Exhibit 13, a move from M_1 to M_2
a. increases the money supply, causing the interest rate to rise from i_2 to i_1.
b. increases the money supply, causing the interest rate to fall from i_1 to i_2.
c. decreases the money supply, causing the interest rate to rise from i_2 to i_1.
d. decreases the money supply, causing the interest rate to fall from i_1 to i_2.
e. has no effect on the money supply or the interest rate.

14. In Exhibit 13, if the Fed believes the economy is at AD_3, how might it engineer a decline in the price level?
a. By decreasing the money supply, the interest rate falls, investment rises, and aggregate demand falls, causing the price level to fall.
b. By decreasing the money supply, the interest rate rises, investment rises, and aggregate demand rises, causing the price level to fall.
c. By decreasing the money supply, the interest rate rises, investment falls, and aggregate demand falls, causing the price level to fall.

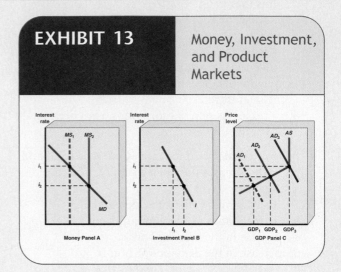

EXHIBIT 13   Money, Investment, and Product Markets

Money Panel A

Investment Panel B

GDP Panel C

d. By increasing the money supply, the interest rate rises, investment rises, and aggregate demand falls, causing the price level to fall.
e. By increasing the money supply, the interest rate rises, investment falls, and aggregate demand rises, causing the price level to fall.

15. The monetarist transmission mechanism through which monetary policy affects the price level, real GDP, and employment depends on the
a. indirect impact of changes on the interest rate.
b. indirect impact of changes on profit expectations.
c. direct impact of changes in fiscal policy on aggregate demand.
d. direct impact of changes in the money supply on aggregate demand.

Policy Disputes Using the Self-Correcting Aggregate Demand and Supply Model

In the appendix to the chapter on aggregate demand and supply, the classical self-correcting aggregate demand and supply model was explained without disagreement. Expansionary and contractionary fiscal policy was discussed in the chapter on fiscal policy, and this chapter explained monetary policy. In this appendix, we combine these topics and examine contrasting fiscal and monetary policies using the self-correcting model.

The Classical versus Keynesian Views of Expansionary Policy

The Keynesian activist approach rejects classical nonintervention policy to stabilize the economy using discretionary fiscal policy or activist monetary policy. Exhibit A-1 illustrates opposing theories for restoring an economy in recession to full employment. In both Parts (a) and (b), the economy starts with a real GDP of $8 trillion and a price level of 150 at macro equilibrium E_1. Since full-employment real GDP is $12 trillion, the recessionary gap equals $4 trillion. In Part (a), the economy closes the gap through the self-correction process. The key classical assumption is that nominal wages are flexible and fall as a result of competition among unemployed workers for jobs. Over time, the result is that the short-term aggregate supply curve ($SRAS_1$) shifts rightward to $SRAS_2$ and the economy automatically adjusts to long-run macro full-employment equilibrium at E_2 with a price level of 100.

Part (b) illustrates the opposing Keynesian theory. This view argues that nominal wages are fixed in the short run. In contrast to the self-correction model, Keynesians advocate using discretionary fiscal policy in which the federal government manages the aggregate demand curve (AD) by increasing government spending or cutting taxes. Both of these policy options work through the multiplier process and increase AD_1 to AD_2. The result is that the economy achieves full employment at macro equilibrium point E_2 where the price level is 200.

Activist monetary policy can also stabilize the economy. The Federal Reserve can increase the money supply, which lowers the interest rate, and in response, business investment spending increases. As a result, AD_1 shifts to AD_2 in Part (b) of Exhibit A-1, and full employment is restored at E_2.

Note that both approaches in Parts (a) and (b) restore full-employment real GDP; however, the impact on the price level is quite different. If classical theory is correct, the price level falls from 150 to 100. In contrast, if Keynesian theory is correct, the price level rises from 150 to 200, resulting in a higher inflation rate.

EXHIBIT A-1   Opposing Anti-Recession Theories

Part (a) illustrates classical theory, which advocates noninterventionist fiscal and monetary policy. The classical assumption is that nominal wages are flexible. At point E_1, unemployed workers compete for jobs, and the wage rate falls causing the short-run aggregate supply curve to shift from $SRAS_1$ to $SRAS_2$. Full employment is therefore automatically restored at point E_2.

In Part (b), Keynesian policy advocates interventionist fiscal and monetary policy. Discretionary fiscal policy increases government spending or cuts taxes to increase the aggregate demand curve from AD_1 to AD_2. Discretionary monetary policy would increase the money supply to increase AD_1 to AD_2.

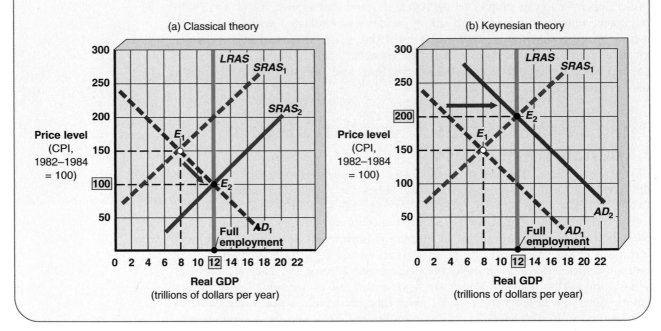

Conclusion *The classical approach to a recession is to let market forces shift the short-run aggregate supply curve rightward and restore the economy to full employment. The opposing Keynesian approach to cure a recession is to use discretionary fiscal and monetary policy to increase aggregate demand and achieve full-employment real GDP.*

Classical versus Keynesian Views of Contractionary Policy

Exhibit A-2 shows alternative theories for closing an inflationary gap. The classical nonintervention policy relies on competition between firms in response to a shortage of labor. In Parts (a) and (b), the economy is at macro equilibrium at point E_1 where the price level is 150 and real GDP is \$16 trillion. There is an inflationary gap of \$4 trillion greater than the potential real GDP of \$12 trillion. In Part (a), classical theory assumes flexible wages, so nominal wages rise, causing the $SRAS_1$ to shift upward to $SRAS_2$, and the economy reaches full-employment real GDP at point E_2 with a price level of 200.

EXHIBIT A-2 | Opposing Anti-Inflation Theories

In Part (a), the classical assumption is that at point E_1 firms face a labor shortage and their competition for available workers drives up the nominal wage rate. Under a noninterventionist policy, the short-run aggregate supply curve shifts leftward from $SRAS_1$ to $SRAS_2$, and the economy is automatically restored to full employment at E_2.

Part (b) shows the effect of Keynesian contractionary policy. Discretionary fiscal policy decreases government spending or increases taxes to shift the aggregate demand curve leftward from AD_1 to AD_2. Discretionary monetary policy would decrease the money supply to decrease AD_1 to AD_2.

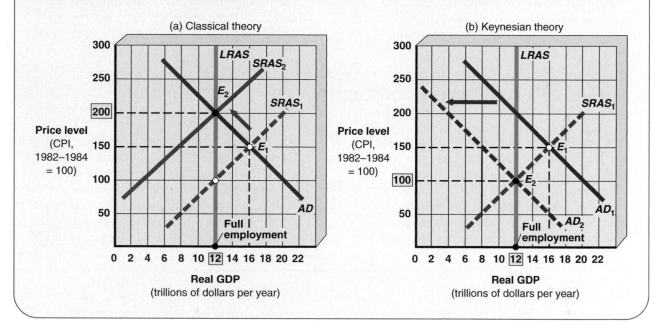

In Part (b), Keynesian contractionary policy aims at decreasing AD_1 to AD_2 using cuts in government spending or tax hikes. Working through the multiplier process, the inflationary gap is eliminated, and the economy moves from point E_1 to E_2 where the price level falls from 150 to 100 and full-employment real GDP of \$12 trillion is achieved.

Monetary policy can also be used to shift the aggregate demand curve leftward. In this case, the Federal Reserve could follow a contractionary policy and decrease the money supply, resulting in a higher interest rate, and firms respond by decreasing their investment spending. Consequently, AD_1 decreases to AD_2, and full-employment real GDP is reached at E_2.

As shown in the previous exhibit, opposing theories have different impacts on the price level. In Part (a) of Exhibit A-2, the classical approach leads to an increase in the price level from 150 to 200. In contrast, the Keynesian approach yields a decrease in the price level from 150 to 100.

> **Conclusion** *The classical approach to an inflationary gap is to let market forces shift the short-run aggregate supply curve leftward and restore the economy to full employment. The opposing Keynesian approach to cure inflation uses discretionary fiscal and monetary policy to decrease aggregate demand and achieve full-employment real GDP.*

SUMMARY

- The *Keynesian prescription for a recession* rejects the classical assumption that wages are flexible and will fall, causing the short-run aggregate supply curve to shift downward and restore full-employment GDP. Instead, Keynesians support expansionary fiscal and monetary policy to increase aggregate demand and return the economy to the natural rate of unemployment.

- The *Keynesian cure for inflation* also rejects the classical assumption that wages are flexible and will rise, causing the short-run aggregate supply curve to shift upward and restore full-employment GDP. In contrast, Keynesian theory advocates contractionary fiscal and monetary policy to decrease aggregate demand and achieve full-employment macro equilibrium.

SUMMARY OF CONCLUSION STATEMENTS

- The classical approach to a recession is to let market forces shift the short-run aggregate supply curve rightward and restore the economy to full employment. The opposing Keynesian approach to cure a recession is to use discretionary fiscal and monetary policy to increase aggregate demand and achieve full-employment real GDP.

- The classical approach to an inflationary gap is to let market forces shift the short-run aggregate supply curve leftward and restore the economy to full employment. The opposing Keynesian approach to cure inflation uses discretionary fiscal and monetary policy to decrease aggregate demand and achieve full-employment real GDP.

PRACTICE QUIZ

For an explanation of the correct answers, please visit the tutorial at www.cengage.com/economics/tucker.

1. Assume the economy is experiencing a recessionary gap. Classical economists would support which of the following policies?
   a. Contractionary
   b. Expansionary
   c. Noninterventionist
   d. Fixed wage

2. Assume the economy is in short-run equilibrium at a real GDP below its potential real GDP. According to classical self-correction theory, which of the following policies should be followed?
   a. The Federal Reserve should increase the money supply.
   b. The federal government should increase spending.
   c. The federal government should cut taxes.
   d. None of the above.

3. Assuming the economy is in a recession, classical economists predict that
   a. wages will remain fixed.
   b. monetary policy will sell government securities.
   c. higher wages will shift the short-run aggregate supply curve leftward.
   d. lower wages will shift the short-run aggregate supply curve rightward.

4. Assume the economy is operating at a real GDP below full-employment real GDP. Keynesian economists would prescribe which of the following policies?
   a. Noninterventionist
   b. Fixed rule
   c. Contractionary
   d. Expansionary

5. Assume the economy is in short-run equilibrium at a real GDP above its potential real GDP. According to Keynesian theory, which of the following policies should be followed?
    a. The Federal Reserve should use open market operations and buy U.S. government securities.
    b. The Federal Reserve should follow a fixed rule.
    c. The federal government should cut taxes.
    d. Fiscal policy and monetary policy should be contractionary.

6. Assume the economy is experiencing an inflationary gap. Keynesian economists would believe that
    a. wages will remain inflexible.
    b. the federal government should decrease spending to shift the aggregate demand curve leftward.
    c. the Federal Reserve should lower the interest rate.
    d. the federal government should increase spending to shift the aggregate demand curve rightward.

The Phillips Curve and Expectations Theory

© David Muir/Digital Vision/Getty Images.

This chapter explores the Phillips curve, expectations theory, and incomes policies (wage and price controls). The Phillips curve traces the relationship between two of the greatest problems of economies everywhere—inflation and unemployment. One of the most fascinating puzzles in economics is whether a stable tradeoff exists between these two economic evils. If true, policymakers face a dilemma described by the old saying "Inside each solution there is another problem looking to work its way out." If policymakers reduce the unemployment rate, the inflation rate worsens. Or, if they reduce the inflation rate, the unemployment rate rises. In the 1960s, most economists and policymakers thought the way to achieve a particular inflation-unemployment point on the Phillips curve menu was to use Keynesian demand-management policies.

Just as the reality of the Great Depression refuted classical theory, the Great Stagflations of the 1970s and early 1980s challenged the Phillips curve and Keynesian policies. To explain how varying rates of inflation can occur at the same rate of unemployment, we explore two competing ways of thinking called *adaptive expectations* and *rational expectations*. Both of these theories are attacks on the Keynesians who urge the government to interfere with the market economy in order to achieve full employment.

The chapter begins with a discussion of the Phillips curve and why both expectations camps believe there is no permanent inflation-unemployment tradeoff. In the last part of this chapter, you will see what happens when policymakers fight inflation using policies to control wages and prices (incomes), rather than monetary and fiscal policies.

The Phillips Curve

In a celebrated article published in 1958, Australian economist A. W. Phillips of the London School of Economics plotted data on unemployment rates and the rate of change in wage rates between 1861 and 1957 in the United Kingdom.[1] Phillips showed there was a remarkably stable inverse relationship between changes in money wages and the unemployment rate. Economists have since extended this concept to the following definition of the Phillips curve. The Phillips curve is a curve showing an inverse relationship between the inflation rate and the unemployment rate. The reason it is acceptable to use the inflation rate, rather than the change in wages, is that wages are the main component of prices. At low rates of unemployment, labor has the market power to push up wages and, in turn, prices. When many workers are pounding the pavement eager for jobs, labor lacks bargaining power to ask for raises. As a result, the upward pressure on prices eases.

> **Phillips curve**
> A curve showing an inverse relationship between the inflation rate and the unemployment rate.

The Phillips Curve in Theory

Exhibit 1 shows the relationship between the *AD-AS* model developed earlier and the Phillips curve. In Part (a), we assume that the aggregate supply curve, *AS*, is stationary. Thus, points *A-D* represent possible equilibrium points depending on the location of the aggregate demand curve. As the aggregate demand curve increases from AD_1 to AD_4, real GDP rises from $6.0 trillion to $6.6 trillion, more workers are employed, and the price level (CPI) rises from 100 to 112. The astute reader will recognize from the chapter on aggregate demand and supply that we are discussing *demand-pull inflation.*

The inverse relationship between the price level and unemployment in Part (a) determines the shape of the Phillips curve in Part (b). Points *A-D* in both figures correspond. If the economy operates at point *A*, the annual rate of inflation is zero, and the unemployment rate is 8 percent. If the economy is at point *B*, the annual

---

1. A. W. Phillips, "The Relation between Unemployment and the Rate of Change in Money Wage Rates in the United Kingdom, 1861–1957," *Economica* 25 (November 1958): 283–299.

EXHIBIT 1   The Theoretical Relationship between Changes in Aggregate Demand and the Phillips Curve

In Part (a), the aggregate demand curve shifts upward, while the aggregate supply curve remains stationary. The result is a series of equilibrium points *A-D*. As aggregate demand rises along the *AS* curve, the price level (CPI), real GDP, and employment increase. Points *A-D* in Parts (a) and (b) correspond. An increase in aggregate demand from AD_1 to AD_4 causes the unemployment rate to fall, but the inflation rate rises. Thus, the increase in aggregate demand results in a movement upward along the Phillips curve.

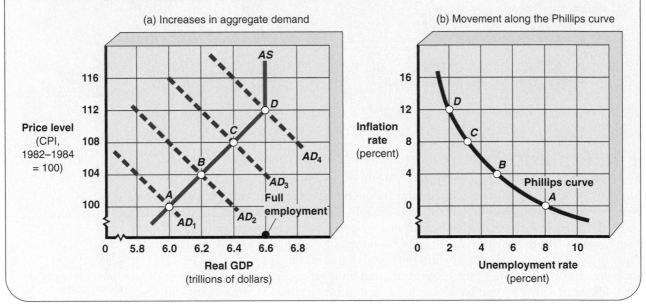

(a) Increases in aggregate demand

(b) Movement along the Phillips curve

rate of inflation is 4 percent, and the unemployment rate is 5 percent. Similarly, points *C* and *D* correspond in both graphs. Note that below point *A* the price level is below 100 and the economy experiences deflation.

> **Conclusion** *Changes in aggregate demand cause a movement along a stationary Phillips curve.*

The Phillips Curve in Practice

So far so good. If the world works this way, policymakers must choose from a menu of inflation rate and unemployment rate combinations along the Phillips curve. Do we want *X* percent less unemployment with an opportunity cost of *Y* percent more inflation? Early studies verified the Phillips curve for the U.S. economy in the 1960s. As shown in Exhibit 2, the data fit the Phillips curve very well. Based on this evidence, most economists, including Nobel Laureates Paul Samuelson and Robert Solow of MIT, believed the Phillips curve was stable. Policymakers might choose low inflation and high unemployment, as in 1961. Or they may prefer higher inflation and lower unemployment, as, for example, in 1969. And the most popular way in the 1960s to reach a particular point on the Phillips curve was to "fine tune" the economy using Keynesian demand-management policies.

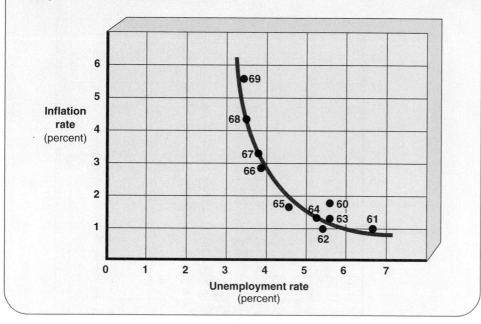

EXHIBIT 2   The Phillips Curve for the United States in the 1960s

The figure plots the inflation rate and unemployment rate combinations for the period 1960–1969. A freehand curve drawn through the points conforms very well to the Phillips curve.

SOURCE: *Economic Report of the President*, 2008, http://www.gpoaccess.gov/eop/, Tables B-35 and B-64.

Then, just as policymakers and economists became comfortable with the Phillips curve, the dream turned into a nightmare. As shown in Exhibit 3, the points for 1970–2007 show the Phillips curve in chaos. The pattern disappeared, and many points moved far above and to the right of the 1960s data. At higher unemployment rates, the corresponding inflation rate was much higher than the Phillips curve predicted. For example, look at the years 1975, 1979, 1980, and 1981. These data reflect bouts with stagflation, which occurred in the 1970s and early 1980s. Recall from Exhibit 11(a) in the chapter on aggregate demand and supply that *cost-push inflation* is the result of a leftward shift of the aggregate supply curve. In the Great Stagflations of 1973–1974 and 1979–1980, the influence of such "supply shocks" as soaring oil prices pushed up production costs and shifted the economy's aggregate supply curve inward. Thus, the Phillips curve theory was in shambles as the nation simultaneously experienced both high inflation and high unemployment. Policymakers therefore turned their focus from the Phillips curve, based on tradeoffs, to a "misery index," which added the inflation and unemployment rates.

The Long-Run Phillips Curve
The simple idea of a stable tradeoff between unemployment and inflation was an overnight sensation in the 1960s. By the early 1970s, the Phillips curve was becoming a "has-been." Since Keynesian demand-management policies generate the curve,

EXHIBIT 3   Inflation and Unemployment Rates for the United States, 1970–2007

After the 1960s, the Phillips curve became unstable. Clearly, many points have been established upward and to the right. The inflation rate therefore can be much higher at any unemployment rate than the Phillips curve of the 1960s predicted.

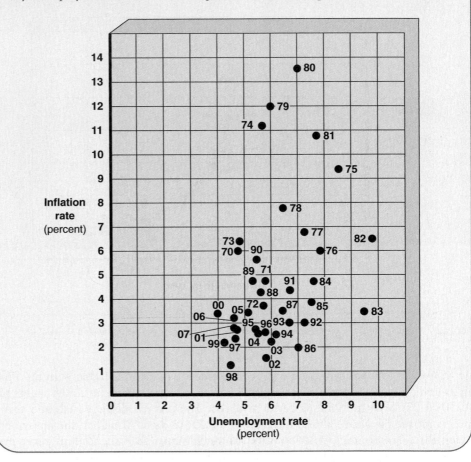

SOURCE: *Economic Report of the President*, 2008, http://www.gpoaccess.gov/eop/, Tables B-35 and B-64.

it will come as no surprise that monetarists such as Milton Friedman and Edmund S. Phelps always believed the Phillips curve was just a transitory, short-run relationship. In the mid-1960s, they suggested that the unemployment rate and the rate of inflation are unrelated in the long run. As shown in Exhibit 4, the challengers argued that after a few years the Phillips curve is a vertical line. As explained below, this monetarist view is also debatable.

Natural Rate Hypothesis

If the Phillips curve is vertical in the long run, there are profound implications for macroeconomic policy. Expansionary monetary and fiscal policies can at best produce a short-lived lowering of unemployment. This is the so-called natural rate hypothesis. The natural rate hypothesis argues that the economy will self-correct to

Natural rate hypothesis

The hypothesis that argues the economy will self-correct to the natural rate of unemployment. The long-run Phillips curve is therefore a vertical line at the natural rate of unemployment.

EXHIBIT 4   The Short-Run and Long-Run Phillips Curves

Beginning at point *A*, the economy is operating at the 6 percent natural rate of unemployment. The actual and anticipated inflation rates are 3 percent. An increase in aggregate demand temporarily causes the inflation rate to rise to 6 percent. Under adaptive expectations theory, real wages fall, profits rise, and more workers are employed. The unemployment rate falls to 4 percent, and the economy moves along the short-run Phillips curve PC_1 to point *B*. Over time, workers demand and get nominal wage rate hikes, and profits fall. Workers lose their jobs, and the unemployment rate returns to 6 percent at point *C* on the short-run Phillips curve PC_2. This process will repeat each time expansionary policy attempts to reduce unemployment below the natural rate. The long-run Phillips curve is therefore a vertical line at the natural rate of unemployment. This suggests that Keynesian expansionary policies create only inflation over time.

Under rational expectations theory, workers do not rely only on recent experience. They adjust their nominal wages quickly in proportion to changes in prices. Expansionary policy will move the economy directly upward along the long-run Phillips curve.

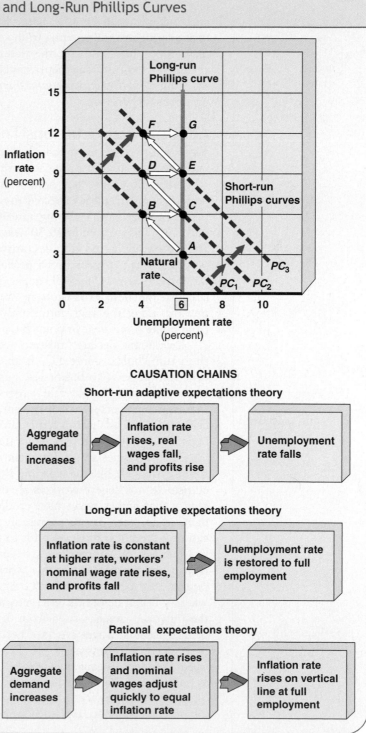

CAUSATION CHAINS

Short-run adaptive expectations theory

| Aggregate demand increases | ⇒ | Inflation rate rises, real wages fall, and profits rise | ⇒ | Unemployment rate falls |

Long-run adaptive expectations theory

| Inflation rate is constant at higher rate, workers' nominal wage rate rises, and profits fall | ⇒ | Unemployment rate is restored to full employment |

Rational expectations theory

| Aggregate demand increases | ⇒ | Inflation rate rises and nominal wages adjust quickly to equal inflation rate | ⇒ | Inflation rate rises on vertical line at full employment |

the natural rate of unemployment. The long-run Phillips curve is therefore a vertical line at the natural rate of unemployment. Recall from the chapter on business cycles and unemployment that the natural rate of unemployment, or the full-employment unemployment rate, is equal to the sum of the frictional and structural unemployment rates. In Exhibit 4, the natural rate of unemployment is 6 percent. Two versions of expectations theory explain the natural rate model. We begin our analysis using *adaptive expectations theory* and then turn to the more recent *rational expectations theory*.

Adaptive Expectations Theory

To explain the reasoning behind the natural rate hypothesis, let us begin in Exhibit 4 with the economy operating at point *A*, with a 3 percent inflation rate and a 6 percent unemployment rate. Assume the inflation rate has been 3 percent in recent years and this trend is expected to continue. Based on this recent 3 percent rise in the CPI, collective bargaining agreements call for hourly nominal or money wages of $10.00 this year and $10.30 next year. Now suppose an election is approaching and the president and Congress strive to make voters happy by reducing the unemployment rate to 4 percent. Or perhaps policymakers incorrectly believe 4 percent is the natural rate of unemployment. Regardless of the reason for setting this goal, suppose the new expansionary fiscal policy shifts the aggregate demand curve upward along the aggregate supply curve and the economy moves unexpectedly from point *A* this year to point *B* the next year.

Keynesians declare "mission accomplished" when the economy moves up the short-run Phillips curve PC_1 from point *A* to point *B*. This unexpected change brings good news to businesses. Based on an expected inflation rate of 3 percent, employers agreed to pay real wages of $10.00 at point *B*. However, if the inflation rate rises unexpectedly to 6 percent, real wages fall to $9.72 as prices rise.[2] With cheaper labor costs in real terms, profits increase, more workers are hired, real GDP expands, and the unemployment rate drops to 4 percent.

So far, Keynesians and monetarists agree that policymakers and businesses are running the race like the hare and the workers are acting like the tortoise. But monetarists do not believe workers are caught flat-footed as time passes. Workers soon realize that higher prices have eroded their purchasing power. Consequently, they demand an extra 3 percent raise in the nominal wage rate so that their real wages can be restored to the level prior to the unexpected rise in the inflation rate from 3 to 6 percent. When workers get their raise to offset the higher cost-of-living, business profits decline, and some workers are laid off until the unemployment rate returns to 6 percent at point *C*. At point *C*, the unemployment rate is right back where it began before the government unsystematically changed its fiscal policy, but the inflation rate has risen from 3 to 6 percent. Keynesians, on the other hand, believe nominal wages are fixed because workers do not demand and get an extra 3 percent rise in nominal wages. In the Keynesian view, demand stimulus reduced unemployment in exchange for the higher inflation rate, and the economy remains at point *B* and does not automatically move in time to point *C*.

Our story describes a *wage-price spiral*, defined in the chapter on inflation, and we need a theory to explain how people form their inflationary expectations. The

---

2. Assume the price level at point *A* is 100 and the price level rises to 106 at point *B*. The real wage is computed as the nominal wage multiplied by the initial price level divided by the new price level. Thus, the real wage rate at point *B* is equal to $10.30 × (100/106) = $9.72. If the price level had risen to 103, as expected, the real wage at point *B* would equal $10.30 × (100/103) = $10.00.

reason the economy moved from point *A* to point *B* is based on adaptive expectations theory. Adaptive expectations theory is the concept that people believe the best indicator of the future is recent information. As a result, people persistently underestimate inflation when it is accelerating and overestimate it while it is slowing down. Adaptive expectations theory assumes ignorance of future events, including changes in fiscal and monetary policies. People learn from recent experience and gradually adjust their anticipated inflation rate to the actual inflation rate. This means that at point *C* workers expect a higher rate of inflation at any unemployment rate because last year the actual rate of inflation was 6 percent. Unions therefore expect a 6 percent rate of inflation and are no longer satisfied with a contract with less than a 6 percent increase in the nominal wage rate, since anything less would mean a cut in real wages. Thus, workers *adapt* their expectations to 6 percent instead of 3 percent, and the short-run Phillips curve shifts outward from PC_1 to PC_2 in Exhibit 4. In other words, the economy moves from point *A* to point *C* on the vertical long-run Phillips curve. If policymakers follow a contractionary policy, adaptive expectations operate in reverse, and the inflation rate declines (see You're the Economist: The Political Business Cycle).

Suppose policymakers figure expansionary policy worked last time, so why not try it again? So they take another stab at creating jobs by stimulating aggregate demand. This time the economy will ride up the new short-run Phillips curve PC_2 from point *C* to point *D*, and the whole process will repeat. When the actual inflation rate rises from 6 to 9 percent, nominal wage increases will be a step slow in catching up with price hikes. In time, workers will demand and get a nominal wage hike, which restores their real wage rate, and the economy will reach point *E*. Faced with the new short-run Phillips curve PC_3, the government will cause an inflation rate of 12 percent at point *F* if it persists in trying to achieve 4 percent unemployment. Eventually, nominal wages will rise (reducing profits), some workers will lose their jobs, and the economy will move from point *F* to point *G*.

> **Conclusion** *According to adaptive expectations theory, expansionary monetary and fiscal policies to reduce the unemployment rate are useless in the long run. After a short-run reduction in unemployment, the economy will self-correct to the natural rate of unemployment, but at a higher inflation rate. Thus, there is no long-run tradeoff between inflation and unemployment.*

The Long-Run Phillips Curve and the Labor Market

We can now give one explanation for the tendency of the inflation-unemployment points shown earlier in Exhibit 3 to shift upward to the right in the 1970s and early 1980s. Demand stimulus policies in the 1960s caught people by surprise, and there was a movement upward along a short-run Phillips curve. As inflation worsened during the 1970s and the early 1980s, adaptive expectations caused the short-run Phillips curves to shift outward. As the inflation rate dropped sharply during the late 1980s, people's inflationary expectations adapted in the downward direction, and the short-run Phillips curve shifted inward. Moreover, as discussed in the chapter on business cycles and unemployment, economists estimated that the *natural rate of unemployment* increased from the 1960s to the 1980s. Recall that the natural rate of unemployment is the full-employment unemployment rate at which the economy operates at capacity (potential GDP). This means the vertical long-run

Adaptive expectations theory
The concept that people believe the best indicator of the future is recent information. As a result, people persistently underestimate inflation when it is accelerating and overestimate it while it is slowing down.

YOU'RE THE ECONOMIST   The Political Business Cycle

Applicable Concept: adaptive expectations

The basic ideal of Keynesian economics is that the government uses monetary and fiscal policies to stabilize the economy. On the other hand, the government may be diabolical and deliberately cause business cycles. The political business cycle is therefore Keynesianism in reverse. A political business cycle is a business cycle caused by policymakers to improve politicians' reelection chances.

A basic assumption of the political business cycle model is that democratic government causes business cycles. This theory views politics as by nature a short-run game. The rational self-interest goal of politicians is to maximize votes today and worry about tomorrow when tomorrow comes. This means a politician who faces an election must act now and not later. Voters are also short-sighted and want good news now, rather than promises of long-term solutions. If people want jobs, for example, the politicians who seek reelection will use expansionary policies to create jobs. The political process will therefore gladly force a lower unemployment rate now in exchange for a higher inflation rate in the future. The politician who commits the sin of truth and tells the voters a "quick fix" is harmful will probably taste defeat.

Given the realities of politics, politicians may find it easier to let the Fed stimulate the economy. Expansionary fiscal policy requires Congress to approve tax cuts or spending increases. Since members of Congress belong to opposing parties, each side has an incentive to prevent the other party from taking credit for legislation. Even if a bill eventually passes, it may be too late for the election. Fiscal policy takes considerable time to implement and actually affect the economy and, in turn, the voters.

If the Fed is independent, why would the Fed be willing to create political business cycles? Recall that the president appoints the Fed chair and members of the Board of Governors. Thus, the Fed is a semiseparate branch of government and often wishes to avoid conflict with Congress or the president. If the Fed is willing to stimulate aggregate demand before an election, incumbent politicians will benefit at the expense of their opponents. Once the election is over, the Fed will slow down the economy to reduce the inflation rate. Then the concern becomes recession until the next election looms and the Fed stimulates the economy again. Meanwhile, politicians can blame the Fed for driving up prices or starting the downturn.

Exhibit 5 reveals that the money supply has generally been on the rise before presidential elections. In 1964, 1968, 1972, 1976, 1980 (slight), 1988, and 1992, the money supply rose before the presidential election and then fell after the presidential election. The 1984, 1996, 2000, and 2004 elections were exceptions.

ANALYZE THE ISSUE

Based on adaptive expectations theory, assume an expansionary monetary policy has moved the economy to point C in Exhibit 4. Now suppose the election is over and inflation concerns policymakers, so the Fed applies the brakes to monetary policy. Use this diagram to explain the short-run and long-run effects of a contractionary monetary policy.

Political business cycle

A business cycle caused by policymakers to improve politicians' reelection chances.

Phillips curve intersecting each short-run Phillips curve shifted to the right. The explanation, in part, is because women and teenagers became a larger percentage of the labor force, and these groups of workers often experience higher rates of unemployment. It is also argued that the following measures might reduce the natural rate of unemployment: revising unemployment compensation, changing the minimum wage law, providing better education and training, improving information on available jobs, removing discrimination, and reducing the monopoly power of unions and businesses.

EXHIBIT 5	Money Supply Growth and Presidential Elections, 1960–2004

Since 1960, the money supply has often increased prior to presidential elections. The 1984, 1996, 2000, and 2004 elections were exceptions.

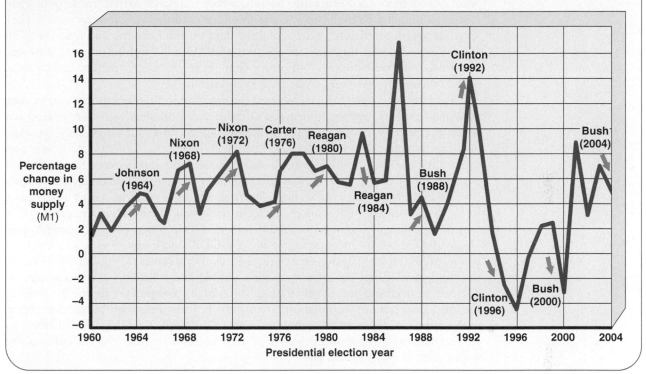

SOURCE: *Economic Report of the President*, 2008, http://www.gpoaccess.gov/eop/, Table B-69.

The Theory of Rational Expectations

Whether expectations are formed "adaptively" or "rationally" is a hotly contested debate among economists. In the mid-1970s, Robert Lucas of the University of Chicago (1995 Nobel Laureate) is generally credited with introducing the theory of rational expectations, which is the competing view that adaptive expectations theory is too simplistic. Rational expectations theory is the belief that people use all available information to predict the future, including future monetary and fiscal policies. Systematic and predictable macroeconomic policies can therefore be negated when businesses and workers anticipate the effects of these policies on the economy. According to the rational expectations hypothesis, people do not simply think inflation will be about the same next year as last year. Although everyone's crystal ball is clouded, people are intelligent and informed on how the economy works. They not only consider past price changes, but also how changes in the federal deficit or money supply will affect inflation next year. Suppose businesses and workers predict that a surge in the money supply or a tax cut will raise the actual inflation rate to, say, 6 percent. They will immediately raise their expectations of the inflation rate to 6 percent even though the most recent rate of inflation was 3 percent. In short, rational expectationists believe that both nominal wages and prices are flexible.

Rational expectations theory

The belief that people use all available information to predict the future, including future monetary and fiscal policies. Systematic and predictable macroeconomic policies can therefore be negated when businesses and workers anticipate the effects of these policies on the economy.

Let's reconsider the case in which the government is trying to reduce the unemployment rate. Begin at point *A* in Exhibit 4, and suppose policymakers strive to reduce unemployment, using new expansionary policies to stimulate demand. Under rational expectations theory, workers are not caught napping. Workers will not simply wait until the actual inflation rate exceeds the expected inflation rate at point *B* and then ask for a raise. Although they may lack formal training in forecasting, workers are quite sophisticated in understanding the macro economy. They watch news on television, check economic data on the Internet, and read the *Wall Street Journal, Time,* the local newspapers, and AFL-CIO publications for information on government policies and future changes in prices. When new information becomes available, workers revise their expectations.

Since workers wisely use all relevant information to predict future changes, they anticipate that the aggregate demand curve is going to shift rightward, causing a rise in the price level and a fall in real wages. They know that unless they get wage hikes to match the price increases, they will be losers. Consequently, workers rationally raise their nominal wage demands so that no gap between the actual and expected rates of inflation occurs. In fact, many collective bargaining agreements contain escalator clauses, providing automatic nominal wage increases as the price level rises. Assuming that workers correctly anticipate the inflation rate, real wages remain unchanged because nominal wages and prices rise proportionately. This means the temporary increase in profits, real GDP, and employment does *not* happen as predicted by adaptive expectationists. In short, rational expectationists refute the short-run Phillips curves drawn in Exhibit 4. There would be, for example, no decrease in unemployment from 6 percent (point *A*) to 4 percent (point *B*). Instead, the only movement in the inflation rate is directly from 3 percent (point *A*) to 6 percent (point *C*). This means higher anticipated inflation is added without delay to current nominal wages and prices, which generates a vertical Phillips curve along such points as *A, C, E,* and *G*.

> **Conclusion** *According to rational expectations theory, systematic and predictable expansionary monetary and fiscal policies used to reduce unemployment are not only useless, but also harmful because the only result is higher inflation.*

On the brighter side, rational expectations theory argues that a credible "stay the course" contractionary fiscal and monetary policy can quickly cool inflation without increasing unemployment. Suppose the economy is at the natural rate of unemployment and the Fed decreases the money supply to lower the rate of inflation. Workers analyze available information on the future impact of the Fed's action from AFL-CIO economists and other sources. They are convinced that policymakers are committed to decreasing aggregate demand until the price level recedes. Armed with this analysis, workers are not surprised, and they reduce their nominal wages as prices fall. In this case, there is no short-run Phillips curve. Contrary to adaptive expectations, inflation can be cured without recession, since workers are not caught off-guard.

Keynesians reject rational expectations theory because they argue that prices and wages are "sticky" downward (see Exhibit 4 of the chapter on aggregate demand and supply). On the other hand, the classical economists believed that the economy automatically adjusts after short-run delays to full employment in the long run. But in the rational expectations model, not so! There is no short run. Nevertheless, because the theory of rational expectations is similar to the self-correction model of the classical economists, rational expectationists are called *new classical* economists.

> **Conclusion** *According to rational expectations theory, if people are not surprised by monetary and fiscal policy changes, the economy's self-correction mechanism will restore the natural rate of unemployment. Preannounced, stable policies to achieve low and constant money supply growth and a balanced federal budget are therefore the best way to lower the inflation rate.*

CHECKPOINT

Does Rational Expectations Theory Work in the Classroom?
An economics professor is considering improving class attendance and preparation by giving pop quizzes. Two approaches are being considered: (1) If rational expectations theory operates in the classroom, should the professor give pop quizzes on days when homework is due or (2) keep it a secret and give pop quizzes randomly?

Applying the *AD-AS* Model to the Great Expectations Debate

The distinction between adaptive expectations and rational expectations can be analyzed using the aggregate demand-aggregate supply model presented in Exhibit 6. Assume the economy is currently in equilibrium at point E_1, with a full-employment output of $6 trillion. Now suppose the Fed pursues an expansionary monetary policy designed to create jobs and further reduce unemployment. Hence, the aggregate demand curve shifts rightward from AD_1 to AD_2 along the short-run aggregate supply curve $SRAS_1$. Based on adaptive expectations theory, a monetarist urges the Fed to leave the economy alone. The monetarist's prediction is that the economy will move from equilibrium at E_1 to E_2, causing real GDP to rise from the potential GDP of $6 trillion to the GDP of $6.5 trillion. Recall from Exhibit 9 of the chapter on business cycles and unemployment that this condition in the economy is a negative GDP gap of $0.5 trillion. In addition, the price level (CPI) increases from 100 to 105. Eventually, at equilibrium E_2, with unemployment below the natural rate, workers are no longer "caught off-guard" and demand higher nominal wages to offset the rise in prices. As a result, production costs rise, causing the short-run aggregate supply curve to shift leftward from $SRAS_1$ to $SRAS_2$; and, therefore, a new equilibrium is established at E_3. This response drives up the unemployment rate to the natural rate as real output returns to the initial level of $6 trillion. However, Fed activism has not had a neutral effect on the price level because it has risen from the initial level of 100 to 110. The monetarist's prediction is therefore higher inflation and no impact on employment and real GDP in the long run.

A rational expectationist sees events differently. Most people are not "fooled." They are able to rationally predict the consequences of expansionary monetary policies. People anticipate that the economy will move from point E_1 to point E_3,

EXHIBIT 6 — Adaptive Expectations versus Rational Expectations

Suppose policymakers use expansionary policies to increase the aggregate demand curve from AD_1 to AD_2. Adaptive expectations theory argues that labor adjusts nominal wages sluggishly. As a result, the path of the economy is E_1 to E_2 to E_3 with a temporary increase in real GDP to $6.5 trillion and lower unemployment at point E_2. The theory of rational expectations is the competing view that the expansionary policy used to increase the aggregate demand curve from AD_1 to AD_2 is anticipated. Workers anticipate that the price level (CPI) will rise to 110, so they increase their nominal wages without a period of adjustment. As a result, the aggregate supply curve shifts from $SRAS_1$ to $SRAS_2$, causing the economy to move directly from equilibrium point E_1 to point E_3. The result of Keynesian expansionary policies under both theories is that inflation becomes worse and there is no effect on real GDP or employment.

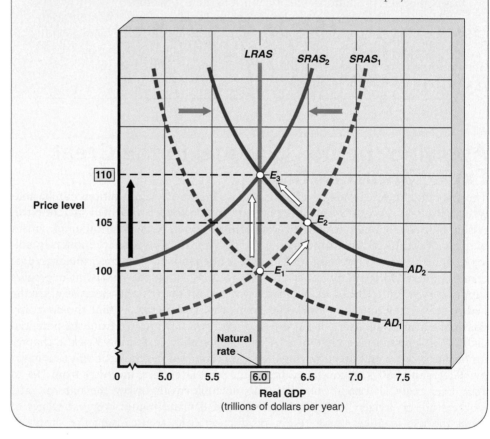

the price level will rise from 100 to 110, and real GDP will not change. Consequently, businesses and workers do not stumble around in the dark, unable to see what the actual inflation rate is going to be. They know, or *anticipate*, that the inflation rate is going to rise 10 percent, and they react immediately by raising prices and wages 10 percent. Since prices and wages increase quickly and proportionately, rational expectations theory predicts a direct path of change in the economy's equilibrium from E_1 to E_3. Stated differently, if firms and workers formulate expectations rationally, any impact of stimulative monetary policy is nullified. Under rational expectations theory, only *unanticipated* or *surprise* policies can influence output and employment.

If workers foresee inflation and prevent erosion of their real wages by demanding and receiving nominal wage raises in advance, aggregate supply is the vertical curve, *LRAS*. When real wages remain unchanged, there is no incentive for businesses to alter production as prices rise. If rational expectations theory is correct, the economy does not enjoy the short-lived pleasure of lower unemployment at point E_2, as predicted by adaptive expectations theory.

Incomes Policy

Suppose we accept the power of unions and businesses to raise wages and prices as inevitable. Let's also assume Milton Friedman is correct that discretionary monetary and fiscal policies are useless or counterproductive. Then what approach is left to fight inflation? There is another way, used in the past, which is a collection of regulatory policies called incomes policies. Incomes policies are federal government policies designed to affect the real incomes of workers by controlling nominal wages and prices. Such policies include presidential jawboning, wage-price guidelines, and wage-price controls.

Presidential Jawboning

The mildest form of incomes policies is jawboning. Jawboning is oratory intended to pressure unions and businesses to reduce wage and price increases. The government attempts to prevent or roll back wage and price hikes by appealing to labor and business leaders. The most spectacular success with this technique occurred in 1962. President John F. Kennedy called major U.S. steel manufacturers and convinced them to rescind their price increases. But President Kennedy jawboned with a club in hand. He threatened to sell government stockpiles of steel at lower prices. The president also informed the firms that those failing to cooperate would lose government contracts to firms that would lower prices. President Lyndon Johnson followed Kennedy's example and jawboned even more. Then there was the "Blow the Whistle" program under President Richard Nixon. An official agency was established to monitor unwarranted price increases and publicly announce violators of the national interest.

Most economists argue that firms raise prices when changes in demand or cost make it profitable to do so. Jawboning may do a little good for a while, but over time it is a blunt weapon against inflation.

Wage and Price Guidelines

A more formal policy to cool down the inflation rate is to establish wage and price guidelines. Wage and price guidelines are voluntary standards set by the government for "permissible" wage and price increases. The Truman and Eisenhower administrations made unsystematic attempts to discourage business and labor from raising prices and wages. But the first systematic wage and price guideline program was initiated during the Kennedy administration, and this approach was also used during the Johnson and Carter administrations. For example, the Carter administration asked labor unions to limit their wage increases to 7 percent. Violators were identified in hopes that adverse publicity would force the unions to comply.

Incomes policies
Federal government policies designed to affect the real incomes of workers by controlling nominal wages and prices. Such policies include presidential jawboning, wage-price guidelines, and wage-price controls.

Jawboning
Oratory intended to pressure unions and businesses to reduce wage and price increases.

Wage and price guidelines
Voluntary standards set by the government for "permissible" wage and price increases.

Without any enforcement mechanism, the dominant view among economists is that guidelines accomplish little against self-interest.

Wage and Price Controls

When guidelines have the force of law, the economy moves to a mandatory system of wage and price controls. Wage and price controls are legal restrictions on wage and price increases. Violations can result in fines and imprisonment. Once people believe wages and prices are under control by law, the good news is that they expect lower prices. The bad news is that controls are government interference with market supply and demand.

As discussed in Chapter 4, a ceiling price established below the equilibrium price will cause shortages in markets (see Exhibit 5 in Chapter 4). This usually means rationing of such scarce items as gasoline. When price is not allowed to serve as the rationing device, consumers must incur higher opportunity costs by waiting in long lines for gasoline. This happened in 1979, when the government imposed a price ceiling on gasoline. Another rationing device is government ration coupons that give the right to buy a good. Ration coupons were used for many goods during World War II. Shortages also lead to *black markets,* which are illegal markets for goods at unregulated prices. To enforce the system requires a government bureaucracy at taxpayers' expense.

Long lines for products, ration coupons, and black markets are not popular. This explains why wage and price controls appear primarily during war and rarely in peacetime. The United States has imposed wage and price controls during World War II, the Korean War, and, most recently during the Nixon administration. President Nixon hoped to combat high inflationary expectations built up during the Vietnam War. The inflation rate from 1969 to 1971 averaged 5.2 percent, an alarming rate in those days. The plan was to control inflation and then fight unemployment, which averaged 4.8 percent over the same period. The first phase of the attack was a 90-day freeze on wages and prices in August 1971. A 15-member Pay Board and a 7-member Price Commission administered the controls. For three months businesses could not raise prices, wages were frozen, and landlords could not charge higher rents. The intent was to give inflationary expectations a shock treatment. Then the freeze lifted, and wage and price controls were established to limit increases between 1971 and 1974. The bottom line is that in 1971 the inflation rate was 4.4 percent. In 1973, the inflation rate climbed to 6.2 percent. When the experiment with controls ended in 1974, the inflation rate rose to 11 percent. During the same period, the unemployment rate remained between 5 and 6 percent. Obviously, controls did not slay the inflation dragon, although some economists have argued that controls made the dragon less fierce.

In 1968, the Council of Economic Advisors eloquently stated the opinion of most economists on wage and price controls:

> *While such controls may be necessary under conditions of an all-out war, it would be folly to consider them as a solution to inflationary pressures that accompany high employment under any other circumstance.... Although such controls may be unfortunately popular when they are in effect, the appeal quickly disappears once people live under them.*[3]

---

3. *Annual Report of the Council of Economic Advisors* (Washington, D.C.: Government Printing Office, 1968), p. 119.

YOU'RE THE ECONOMIST

Ford's Whip Inflation Now (WIN) Button

Applicable Concept: incomes policies

The most interesting historical artifact of the fight against inflation is gathering dust in the White House attic. In October 1974, President Gerald Ford proposed the "WIN" button to a joint session of Congress. The idea was that Americans would wear their "Whip Inflation Now" buttons, and this would break the wage-price spiral. The WIN button represented an appeal to patriotism that would discourage businesses and labor from raising prices and wages.

The logical question is, What circumstances drove the president of the United States to use a button against inflation? We will begin the story in 1971, when the Nixon administration approved wage and price controls to cool inflationary expectations. Beginning in 1972, bad crops caused food prices to soar, and the OPEC oil embargo boosted the price of crude oil. These supply shocks boosted the inflation rate from 3.2 percent in 1972 to 6.2 percent in 1973. Clearly, the wage and price control program was falling apart before controls ended in 1974.

Following the demand-management prescription against inflation, the Fed raised the discount rate in late 1973. Federal Reserve Chair Arthur Burns stated that the Fed must follow a contractionary monetary policy for years to come. Despite the Fed's restrictive policy, the inflation rate rose to an annual rate of about 14 percent in early 1974. By late 1974, the unemployment rate had risen to 6 percent, but policymakers remained committed to anti-inflation policies. The Fed raised the discount rate again in the fall of 1974, and President Ford called an economic summit meeting. The outcome of the summit was a resolve to stick to the battle plan and beat inflation before turning to the worsening unemployment problem. Aiming for public support, President Ford unveiled the WIN button, accompanied by a tax surcharge and federal spending ceiling proposals. While the fight against inflation preoccupied policymakers, the unemployment rate rose from 5.6 percent in 1974 to 8.5 percent in 1975. The percentage change in real GDP between 1974 and 1975 was –0.6 percent, and recession suddenly replaced inflation as the number one enemy. In response, Congress approved a $22.8 billion tax cut bill in 1975, and the Fed increased the money supply. In 1974, the inflation rate was 11.0 percent, and in 1975, the inflation rate was still at the high rate of 9.1 percent.

What caused this puzzling twist in stabilization policy to deal with stagflation? Many economists explain this turn of events by the absence of a conceptual framework to understand the effects of supply shocks on the aggregate supply curve. Instead, policymakers tried to shift the aggregate demand curve back and forth while asking people to wear a WIN button.

ANALYZE THE ISSUE

Assume the economy is in equilibrium at full employment and the public anticipates restrictive monetary and fiscal policies, including WIN buttons, which decrease aggregate demand in order to combat inflation. Use the *AD-AS* model depicted in Exhibit 6 to explain the new classical predictions of the impact on the price level, real GDP, and the unemployment rate.

The majority view is that controls destroy the efficient allocation of resources provided by the price system and intrude on economic freedom. Defenders of controls believe this is a small price to pay.

EXHIBIT 7   How Different Macroeconomic Models Cure Inflation

School of thought
Monetarism

Milton Friedman

Inflation prescription
Monetarists see the cause of inflation as "too much money chasing too few goods," based on the quantity of money theory ($MV = PQ$). To cure inflation, they would cut the money supply and force the Fed to stick to a fixed money supply growth rate. In the short run, the unemployment rate will rise, but in the long run, it self-corrects to the natural rate.

School of thought
Keynesianism

John Maynard Keynes

Inflation prescription
Keynesians believe in using contractionary fiscal and monetary policies to cool an overheated economy. To decrease aggregate demand, they advocate that the government use tax hikes and/or spending cuts. The Fed should reduce the money supply and cause the rate of interest to rise. The opportunity cost of reducing inflation is greater unemployment. Keynesians also believe that incomes policies are effective.

School of thought
Supply-side economics

Arthur Laffer

Inflation prescription
Supply-siders view the cause of inflation as "not enough goods." Their approach is to increase aggregate supply by cuts in marginal tax rates, government regulations, and import barriers. The effect provides incentives to work, invest, and expand production capacity. Thus, both the inflation rate and the unemployment rate fall.

School of thought
New classical school

Robert Lucas

Inflation prescription
The theory of rational expectations asserts that the public must be convinced that policymakers will stick to restrictive and persistent fiscal and monetary policies. If policymakers have credibility, the inflation rate will be anticipated and quickly fall without a rise in unemployment.

CHECKPOINT

Can Wage and Price Controls Cure Stagflation?

Suppose war in the Persian Gulf destroyed much of the world's oil reserves. As a result, the U.S. economy is experiencing a bout of stagflation. You are a member of Congress, and a bill is introduced to fight the problems of high inflation and high unemployment by imposing wage and price controls. Using the *AD-AS* model, will you vote in favor of controls to cure stagflation by freezing the price level? [Hint: Look at Exhibit 5 of Chapter 4 and Exhibit 11(a) in the chapter on aggregate demand and supply.]

How Different Macroeconomic Theories Attack Inflation

If incomes policies do not cure an overheated economy during peacetime, policy-makers must decide which macroeconomic school "hat" to wear. Exhibit 7 gives a brief description of how four basic macroeconomic models deal with inflation. Recall the monetarist view presented in the previous chapter and supply-side economics explained in the chapter on fiscal policy.

KEY CONCEPTS

Phillips curve
Natural rate hypothesis
Adaptive expectations theory

Political business cycle
Rational expectations theory
Incomes policies

Jawboning
Wage and price guidelines
Wage and price controls

SUMMARY

- The *Phillips curve* shows a stable inverse relationship between the inflation rate and the unemployment rate. If policymakers reduce inflation, unemployment increases, and vice versa. During the 1960s, the curve closely fit the inflation and unemployment rates in the United States. Since 1970, the Phillips curve has not conformed to the stable inflation-unemployment tradeoff pattern of the 1960s.

The Phillips Curve for the United States in the 1960s

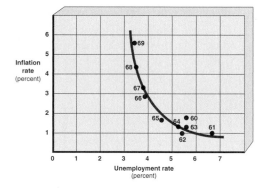

- The *natural rate hypothesis* argues that the economy self-corrects to the natural rate of unemployment. Over time, changes in the rate of inflation are fully anticipated, and prices and wages rise or fall proportionately. As a result, the long-run Phillips curve is a vertical line at the natural rate of unemployment. Thus, Keynesian demand-management policies ultimately cause only higher or lower inflation, and the natural rate of unemployment remains unchanged.

- *Adaptive expectations theory* is the proposition that people base their economic forecasts on recent past information, rather than future information. Once the government causes the inflation rate to rise or fall, people adapt their inflationary expectations to the current inflation rate. The result is a short-run Phillips curve that intersects the vertical long-run Phillips curve. Over time, the economy self-corrects to the natural rate of unemployment.

- The *political business cycle* is a business cycle created by the incentive for politicians to manipulate the economy to get reelected. Using expansionary policies, officeholders can stimulate the economy before an election. Unemployment falls, and the price level rises. After the election, the strategy is to contract the economy to fight inflation and unemployment rises.

- *Rational expectations theory* argues that it is naive to believe that people change their inflationary expectations based only on the current inflation rate. Rational expectationists belong to the new classical school. Assuming the impact of government policy is predictable, people immediately anticipate higher or lower inflation. Workers quickly change their nominal wages as businesses change prices. Consequently, inflation worsens or improves, and unemployment remains unchanged at the natural rate. Thus, there is no short-run Phillips curve, and the vertical long-run Phillips curve is identical to adaptive expectations theory.

- *Incomes policies* are a variety of federal government programs aimed at directly controlling wages and prices. Incomes policies include jawboning, wage-price guidelines, and wage-price controls. Over time, incomes policies tend to be ineffective.

- *Wage and price controls* are legal restrictions on wages and prices. Most economists do not favor wage and price controls in peacetime. Such controls are expensive to administer, destroy efficiency, and intrude on economic freedom.

SUMMARY OF CONCLUSION STATEMENTS

- Changes in aggregate demand cause a movement along a stationary Phillips curve.
- According to adaptive expectations theory, expansionary monetary and fiscal policies to reduce the unemployment rate are useless in the long run. After a short-run reduction in unemployment, the economy will self-correct to the natural rate of unemployment, but at a higher inflation rate. Thus, there is no long-run tradeoff between inflation and unemployment.
- According to rational expectations theory, systematic and predictable expansionary monetary and fiscal policies used to reduce unemployment are not only useless, but also harmful because the only result is higher inflation.
- According to rational expectations theory, if people are not surprised by monetary and fiscal policy changes, the economy's self-correction mechanism will restore the natural rate of unemployment. Preannounced, stable policies to achieve low and constant money supply growth and a balanced federal budget are therefore the best way to lower the inflation rate.

STUDY QUESTIONS AND PROBLEMS

1. What is a Phillips curve? Assuming the economy's aggregate supply curve is stable, how would an increase in aggregate demand affect the unemployment rate and the inflation rate?

2. What were the inflation rate and the unemployment rate last year? Do these rates lie on a Phillips curve?

3. What happened in the 1970s and early 1980s to cast doubt on the Phillips curve?

4. Suppose you flipped an honest coin 10 times and heads came up 8 times. You are about to toss the coin another 10 times. Using adaptive expectations, how many heads do you expect? Based on rational expectations, how many heads do you expect?

5. According to adaptive expectations, what happens to the inflation rate and the unemployment rate in the following situations?
   a. Initially, the economy is operating at the natural rate of 6 percent unemployment. The anticipated rate of inflation is 6 percent, and the actual rate is also 6 percent.
   b. In the next period, there is an unexpected rise in the inflation rate to 10 percent.
   c. In the next period, there is an unexpected rise in the inflation rate to 12 percent.

6. Explain what happens under adaptive expectations theory when monetary and fiscal policymakers use expansionary policy to achieve an unemployment rate below the natural rate.

7. Keynesians believe monetary and fiscal policymakers should stabilize the business cycle. Compare the political business cycle to Keynesian policy objectives.

8. Use Exhibit 8 to answer the questions below.
   a. Which points represent the natural unemployment rate?
   b. Which points represent an unemployment rate below the natural unemployment rate?
   c. Which points represent an unemployment rate above the natural unemployment rate?

EXHIBIT 8 — Long-Run and Short-Run Phillips Curves

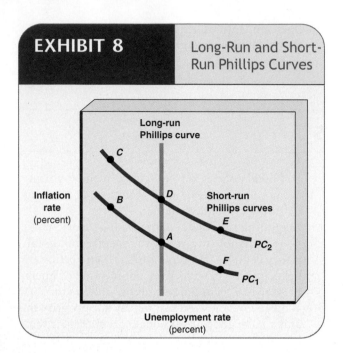

d. Explain points *A* and *D* on the graph.
e. Explain points *B* and *C* on the graph.
f. Explain points *E* and *F* on the graph.
g. Why is curve PC_2 to the right of curve PC_1?

9. Based on rational expectations theory, what happens to the inflation rate and the unemployment rate in the following situations?
    a. Initially, the economy is operating at the natural unemployment rate of 4 percent, and the inflation rate is also 4 percent. People correctly anticipate that an increase in the money supply will increase the inflation rate to 6 percent next year.
    b. In the next period, people correctly forecast that a tax cut will cause the inflation rate to rise to 8 percent.
    c. In the next period, they anticipate that the Fed's hike in the discount rate will cause the inflation rate to fall to 4 percent.

For Online Exercises, go to the text Web site at www.cengage.com/economics/tucker.

CHECKPOINT ANSWERS

Does Rational Expectations Theory Work in the Classroom?

Under rational expectations, if the students know what is going to happen, they will use this information to negate the policy. If pop quizzes are given on the same day homework is due, the rational students will be certain to attend class on those days and take cuts on other days. If quizzes are random, quiz dates are unknown, so there is always a chance that missing a class may mean missing a quiz. If you said the professor will keep pop quizzes a secret and give them randomly, **YOU ARE CORRECT.**

Can Wage and Price Controls Cure Stagflation?

Assume the economy begins in equilibrium at E_1 in Exhibit 9 and an oil shock causes the economy to move to a new equilibrium at E_2. Without wage and price controls, the price level increases from 150 to 200, and real GDP decreases from \$4 trillion to

EXHIBIT 9 — Aggregate Demand and Aggregate Supply Curves

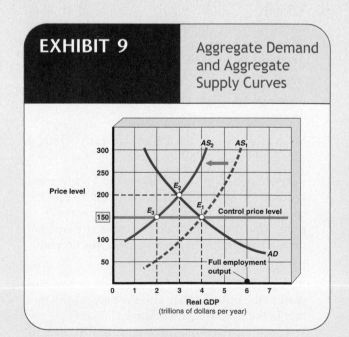

$3 trillion. Now assume laws keep the price level frozen at 150. This means firms cannot raise prices to meet higher costs, so under controls they are forced to lay off more workers and cut production even further. The economy's equilibrium moves from E_2 to E_3, and real GDP is $2 trillion, rather than $3 trillion, causing unemployment to climb even higher.

Using wage and price controls to fight inflation would cause an even more severe decrease in real GDP; therefore, unemployment is greater than would otherwise be the case. If you voted *no* on the wage and price controls bill because they cause greater shortages and a deeper recession, **YOU ARE CORRECT.**

PRACTICE QUIZ

For an explanation of the correct answers, please visit the tutorial at www.cengage.com/economics/tucker.

1. The Phillips curve depicts the relationship between the
   a. unemployment rate and the change in GDP.
   b. inflation rate and the interest rate.
   c. level of investment spending and the interest rate.
   d. inflation rate and the unemployment rate.

2. A difficulty in using the Phillips curve as a policy menu is
   a. that the natural rate of unemployment does not exist.
   b. that the curve does not remain in one position.
   c. deciding between monetary and fiscal policies.
   d. that Democrats choose one point on the curve and Republicans choose another point.

3. Since the 1970s, the
   a. Phillips curve has not been stable.
   b. inflation rate and the unemployment rate have been about equal.
   c. Phillips curve has proven to be a reliable model to guide public policy.
   d. relationship between the inflation rate and the unemployment rate moved in a counterclockwise direction.

4. According to the natural rate hypothesis,
   a. the Phillips curve is quite flat, so a large reduction in employment can be achieved without inflation.
   b. workers adapt their wage demands to inflation only after a considerable time lag.

   c. the Phillips curve is vertical in the long run at full employment.
   d. workers cannot anticipate the inflationary effects of expansionary public policies.

5. Adaptive expectations theory
   a. argues that the best indicator of the future is recent information.
   b. underestimates inflation when it is accelerating.
   c. overestimates inflation when it is slowing down.
   d. does none of the above.
   e. does all of the above.

6. The conclusion of adaptive expectations theory is that expansionary monetary and fiscal policies intended to reduce the unemployment rate are
   a. effective in the long run.
   b. effective in the short run.
   c. unnecessary and cause inflation in the long run.
   d. necessary and reduce inflation in the long run.

7. Most macroeconomic policy changes, say the rational expectations theorists, are
   a. unpredictable.
   b. predictable.
   c. slow to take place.
   d. irrational.

8. Rational expectations theorists advise the federal government to
   a. change policy often.
   b. pursue stable policies.

PRACTICE QUIZ CONTINUED

c. do the opposite of what the public expects.
d. ignore future economic predictions.

9. Suppose the government shown in Exhibit 10 uses contractionary monetary policy to reduce inflation from 9 to 6 percent. If people have *adaptive* expectations, then
   a. the economy will remain stuck at point E_1.
   b. the natural rate will permanently increase to 8 percent.
   c. unemployment will rise to 8 percent in the short run.
   d. Unemployment will remain at 6 percent as the inflation rate falls.

10. Suppose the government shown in Exhibit 10 uses contractionary monetary policy to reduce inflation from 9 to 6 percent. If people have *rational* expectations, then
    a. the economy will remain stuck at point E_1.
    b. the natural rate will permanently increase to 8 percent.
    c. unemployment will rise to 8 percent in the short run.
    d. unemployment will remain at 6 percent as the inflation rate falls.

11. Voluntary wage-price restraints are known as
    a. wage-price controls.
    b. price rollbacks.
    c. wage-price guidelines.
    d. anti-inflation commitments.

12. Which of the following government policies is an incomes policy?
    a. A reduction in welfare expenditures
    b. The publication of a list of guidelines suggesting maximum wage and price increases
    c. An increase in the money supply
    d. All of the above

13. As shown in Exhibit 11, if people behave according to adaptive expectations theory, an increase in the aggregate demand curve from AD_1 to AD_2 will cause the price level to move
    a. directly from 100 to 110 and then remain at 110.
    b. directly from 100 to 105 and then remain at 105.

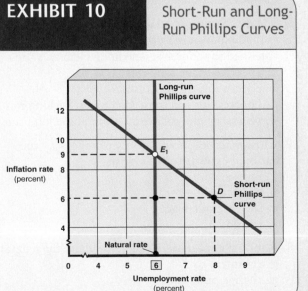

EXHIBIT 10   Short-Run and Long-Run Phillips Curves

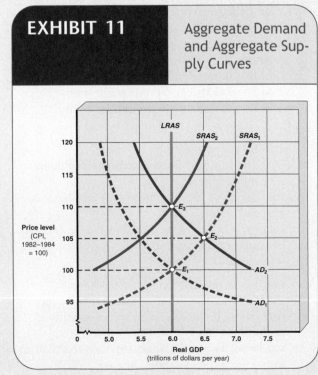

EXHIBIT 11   Aggregate Demand and Aggregate Supply Curves

c. from 100 to 105 initially and then eventually move back to 100.

d. from 100 to 105 initially and then eventually move to 110.

14. As shown in Exhibit 11, if people behave according to rational expectations theory, an increase in the aggregate demand curve from AD_1 to AD_2 will cause the economy to move

a. directly from E_1 to E_3 and then remain at E_3.

b. directly from E_1 to E_2 and then remain at E_2.

c. from E_1 to E_2 initially and then eventually move back to E_1.

d. from E_1 to E_2 initially and then eventually move to E_3.

15. As shown in Exhibit 11, if people behave according to rational expectations theory, an increase in the aggregate demand curve from AD_1 to AD_2 will cause

a. labor to adjust nominal wages sluggishly.

b. the aggregate supply curve to remain at $SRAS_1$.

c. the price level to eventually rise from 100 to 110.

d. none of the above.

Road Map

This road map feature helps you tie material in the part together as you travel the Economic Way of Thinking Highway. The following are review questions listed by chapter from the previous part. The key concept in each question is given for emphasis, and each question or set of questions concludes with an interactive game to reinforce the concepts. Click on the Tucker Web site, select the chapter, and play the visual causation chain game designed to make learning fun. Enjoy the cheers when correct and suffer the jeers if you miss.

For an explanation of the correct answers, please visit the tutorial at www.cengage.com/economics/tucker.

Chapter 24. Money and the Federal Reserve System

1. **Key Concept: Money Supply Definitions**
    Suppose you transfer $1,000 from your checking account to your savings account. How does this action affect the M1 and M2 money supplies?
    a.   M1 and M2 are both unchanged.
    b.   M1 falls by $1,000, and M2 rises by $1,000.
    c.   M1 is unchanged, and M2 rises by $1,000.
    d.   M1 falls by $1,000, and M2 is unchanged.

2. **Key Concept: Federal Reserve System**
    Which of the following groups oversees and administers the Federal Reserve System?
    a.   The House of Representatives.
    b.   The President's Council of Economic Advisors.
    c.   The U.S. Treasury Department.
    d.   None of the above; the Fed is an independent agency.

3. **Key Concept: Monetary Control Act**
    The Monetary Control Act of 1980
    a.   allowed savings and loan associations to offer checking accounts.
    b.   allowed more institutions to offer checking account services.
    c.   created greater competition among various financial institutions.
    d.   all of the above.
    e.   none of the above.

Chapter 25. Money Creation

4. **Key Concept: Open Market Operations**
    When the Fed sells government securities, it
    a.   lowers the cost of borrowing from the Fed, encouraging banks to make loans to the general public.
    b.   raises the cost of borrowing from the Fed, discouraging banks from making loans to the general public.

c.   increases the amount of excess reserves that banks hold, encouraging them
     to make loans to the general public.
d.   increases the amount of excess reserves that banks hold, discouraging them
     from making loans to the general public.
e.   decreases the amount of excess reserves that banks hold, discouraging them
     from making loans to the general public.

5. **Key Concept: Open Market Operations**
   When the Fed buys government securities, it
   a.   lowers the cost of borrowing from the Fed, encouraging banks to make loans
        to the general public.
   b.   raises the cost of borrowing from the Fed, discouraging banks from making
        loans to the general public.
   c.   increases the amount of excess reserves that banks hold, encouraging them
        to make loans to the general public.
   d.   increases the amount of excess reserves that banks hold, discouraging them
        from making loans to the general public.
   e.   decreases the amount of excess reserves that banks hold, discouraging them
        from making loans to the general public.

Chapter 26. Monetary Policy

6. **Key Concept: Money Demand Curve**
   In a two-asset economy with money and T-bills, the quantity of money that
   people will want to hold, other things being equal, can be expected to
   a.   decrease as real GDP increases.
   b.   increase as the interest rate decreases.
   c.   increase as the interest rate increases.
   d.   all of the above.

   Causation Chain Game
   Demand for Money Curve—Exhibit 1

7. **Key Concept: Equilibrium Interest Rate**
   Assume the Fed decreases the money supply, and the demand for money curve is
   fixed. In response, people will
   a.   sell bonds, thus driving up the interest rate.
   b.   buy bonds, thus driving down the interest rate.
   c.   buy bonds, thus driving up the interest rate.
   d.   sell bonds, thus driving down the interest rate.

8. **Key Concept: Equilibrium Interest Rate**
   Assume a fixed demand for money curve, and the Fed increases the money supply. In response, people will
   a.   sell bonds, thus driving up the interest rate.
   b.   sell bonds, thus driving down the interest rate.
   c.   buy bonds, thus driving up the interest rate.
   d.   buy bonds, thus driving down the interest rate.

   Causation Chain Game
   The Equilibrium Interest Rate—Exhibit 2

9. **Key Concept: Change in Money Supply**

   Assume the demand for money curve is stationary, and the Fed increases the money supply. The result is that people
   a. increase the supply of bonds, thus driving up the interest rate.
   b. increase the supply of bonds, thus driving down the interest rate.
   c. increase the demand for bonds, thus driving up the interest rate.
   d. increase the demand for bonds, thus driving down the interest rate.

10. **Key Concept: Change in Money Supply**

    Assume a fixed demand for money curve, and the Fed decreases the money supply. In response, people will
    a. sell bonds, thus driving up the interest rate.
    b. sell bonds, thus driving down the interest rate.
    c. buy bonds, thus driving up the interest rate.
    d. buy bonds, thus driving down the interest rate.

Causation Chain Game
The Effect of Changes in the Money Supply—Exhibit 3

11. **Key Concept: Keynesian Transmission Mechanism**

    The Keynesian cause-and-effect sequence predicts that a decrease in the money supply will cause interest rates to
    a. fall, boosting investment and shifting the AD curve rightward, leading to an increase in real GDP.
    b. fall, boosting investment and shifting the AD curve rightward, leading to a decrease in real GDP.
    c. rise, cutting investment and shifting the AD curve rightward, leading to an increase in real GDP.
    d. rise, boosting investment and shifting the AD curve rightward, leading to an increase in real GDP.
    e. rise, cutting investment and shifting the AD curve leftward, leading to a decrease in real GDP.

Causation Chain Game
The Keynesian Monetary Policy Transmission Mechanism—Exhibit 4

12. **Key Concept: Monetarists Transmission Mechanism**

    Most monetarists favor
    a. frequent changes in the growth rate of the money supply to avoid inflation.
    b. placing the Federal Reserve under the Treasury.
    c. a steady, gradual shrinkage of the money supply.
    d. a constant increase in the money supply year after year equal to the potential annual growth rate in real GDP.

Causation Chain Game
The Monetarist Policy Transmission Mechanism—Exhibit 6

Chapter 27. The Phillips Curve and Expectations Theory

13. Key Concept: Adaptive Expectations

According to adaptive expectations theory, expansionary monetary and fiscal policies to reduce the unemployment rate are
a. useless in the long run.
b. useless in the short run.
c. ineffective on the price level.
d. None of the above.

14. Key Concept: Rational Expectations

The belief that the government can do absolutely nothing in either the short run or the long run to reduce the unemployment rate, because people will anticipate the government's actions, is held by the
a. rational expectations school.
b. neo-Keynesian school.
c. classical school.
d. supply-side school.
e. Keynesian school.

Causation Chain Game
The Short-Run and Long-Run Phillips Curve—Exhibit 4

The International Economy

T he final part of this text is devoted to global topics. The first
chapter explains the importance of free trade and the
mechanics of trade bookkeeping and exchange rates. Here you will
find a feature on the birth of the euro. The second chapter takes
a historical look at the theoretical debate over capitalism and the
transition of Cuba, Russia, and China toward this system. The final
chapter provides comparisons of advanced and developing countries. The chapter concludes with the fascinating economic success
story of Hong Kong.

International Trade and Finance

Just imagine your life without world trade. For openers, you could not eat bananas from Honduras or chocolate from Nigerian cocoa beans. Nor could you sip French wine, Colombian coffee, or Indian tea. Also forget about driving a Japanese motorcycle or automobile. In addition, you could not buy Italian shoes and most DVDs, televisions, fax machines, and personal computers because they are foreign made. Taking your vacation in London would also be ruled out if there were no world trade. And the list goes on and on, so the point is clear. World trade is important because it gives consumers more power by expanding their choices. Today, the speed of transportation and communication means producers must compete on a global basis for the favor of consumers.

Trade is often highly controversial. Regardless of whether it is a World Trade Organization (WTO) meeting or a G-8 summit meeting, trade talks face protesters in the streets complaining that globalization has triggered a crisis in the world economy, such as global warming, poverty, soaring oil prices, or food shortages. And in the United States, outsourcing jobs to lower paid workers overseas continues to be a hotly debated issue.

The first part of this chapter explains the theoretical reason why countries should specialize in producing certain goods and then trade them for imports. Also, you will study arguments for and against the United States protecting itself from "unfair" trade practices by other countries. In the second part of the chapter, you will learn how nations pay each other for world trade. Here you will explore international bookkeeping and discover how supply and demand forces determine that, for example, 1 dollar is worth 100 yen.

In this chapter, you will learn to solve these economic puzzles:

- How does Babe Ruth's decision not to remain a pitcher illustrate an important principle in global trade?

- Is there a valid argument for trade protectionism?

- Should the United States return to the gold standard?

Why Nations Need Trade

Exhibit 1 reveals which regions are our major trading partners (exports plus imports). Leading the list of nations are Canada, our largest trading partner, followed by China, Mexico, and Japan. Leading U.S. exports are chemicals, machinery, airplanes, and computers. Major imports include cars, trucks, petroleum, electronics, and clothing. Why does a nation even bother to trade with the rest of the world? Does it seem strange for the United States to import goods it could produce for itself? Indeed, why doesn't the United States become self-sufficient by growing all its own food, including bananas, sugar, and coffee, making all its own cars, and prohibiting sales of all foreign goods? This section explains why specialization and trade are a nation's keys to a higher standard of living.

The Production Possibilities Curve Revisited

Consider a world with only two countries—the United States and Japan. To keep the illustration simple, also assume *both* countries produce only two goods—grain and steel. Accordingly, we can construct in Exhibit 2 a *production possibilities curve* for each country. We will also set aside the *law of increasing opportunity costs*, explained in Chapter 2, and assume workers are equally suited to producing grain or steel. This assumption transforms the bowed-out shape of the production possibilities curve into a straight line.

Comparing Parts (a) and (b) of Exhibit 2 shows that the United States can produce more grain than Japan. If the United States devotes all its resources to this purpose, 100 tons of grain are produced per day, represented by point A in Exhibit 2(a). The maximum grain production of Japan, on the other hand, is only 40 tons per day because Japan has less labor, land, and other factors of production than the United States. This capability is represented by point D in Exhibit 2(b).

Now consider the capacities of the two countries for producing steel. If all their respective resources are devoted to this output, the United States produces 50 tons per day (point C), and Japan produces only 40 tons per day (point F). Again, the greater potential maximum steel output of the United States reflects its greater resources. Both countries are also capable of producing other combinations of grain and steel along their respective production possibilities curves, such as point B for the United States and point E for Japan.

EXHIBIT 1	U.S. Trading Partners, 2007

In 2007, Canada, China, Mexico, and Japan accounted for 43 percent of U.S. trade (exports plus imports).

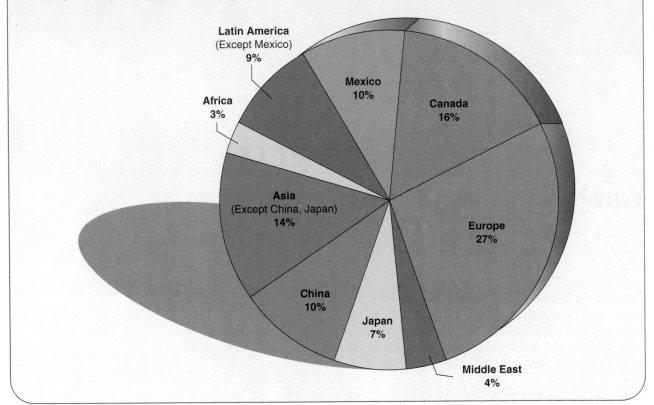

SOURCE: Bureau of Economic Analysis, *U.S. International Transactions by Area*, http://www.bea/gov/international/index.htm, Table 12.

Specialization without Trade

Assuming no world trade, the production possibilities curve for each country also defines its *consumption possibilities*. Stated another way, we assume that both countries are *self-sufficient* because without imports they must consume only the combination chosen along their production possibilities curve. Under the assumption of self-sufficiency, suppose the United States prefers to produce and consume 60 tons of grain and 20 tons of steel per day (point *B*). Also assume Japan chooses to produce and consume 30 tons of grain and 10 tons of steel (point *E*). Exhibit 3 lists data corresponding to points *B* and *E* and shows that the total world output is 90 tons of grain and 30 tons of steel.

Now suppose the United States specializes by producing and consuming at point *A*, rather than point *B*. Suppose also that Japan specializes by producing and consuming at point *F*, rather than point *E*. As shown in Exhibit 3, specialization in each country increases total world output per day by 10 tons of grain and 10 tons of steel. Because this extra world output has the potential for making both countries better off, why wouldn't the United States and Japan specialize and produce at points *A* and *F*, respectively? The reason is that although production at these points

EXHIBIT 2   The Benefits of Trade

As shown in Part (a), assume the United States chooses point B on its production possibilities curve, $PPC_{U.S.}$. Without trade, the United States produces and consumes 60 tons of grain and 20 tons of steel. In Part (b), assume Japan also operates along its production possibilities curve, PPC_{Japan}, at point E. Without trade, Japan produces and consumes 30 tons of grain and 10 tons of steel.

Now assume the United States specializes in producing grain at point A and imports 20 tons of Japanese steel in exchange for 30 tons of grain. Through specialization and trade, the United States moves to consumption possibility point B, outside its production possibilities curve. Japan also moves to a higher standard of living at consumption possibility point E′, outside its production possibilities curve.

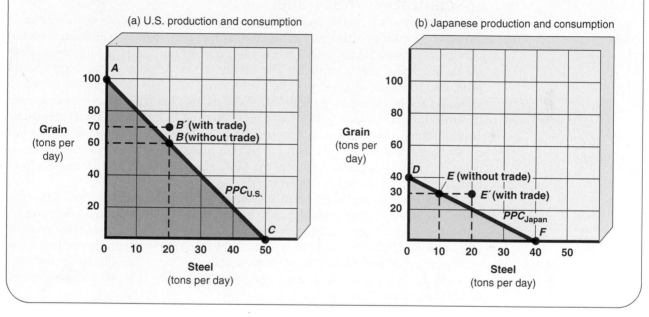

(a) U.S. production and consumption

(b) Japanese production and consumption

EXHIBIT 3   Effect of Specialization on World Output

	Grain Production (tons per day)	Steel Production (tons per day)
Before specialization		
United States (at point B)	60	20
Japan (at point E)	30	10
Total world output	90	30
After specialization		
United States (at point A)	100	0
Japan (at point F)	0	40
Total world output	100	40

is clearly possible, neither country wants to consume these combinations of output. The United States prefers to consume less grain and more steel at point *B* compared to point *A*. Japan, on the other hand, prefers to consume more grain and less steel at point *E,* rather than point *F*.

> **Conclusion** *When countries specialize, total world output increases, and, therefore, the potential for greater total world consumption also increases.*

Specialization with Trade

Now let's return to Exhibit 2 and demonstrate how world trade benefits countries. Suppose the United States agrees to specialize in grain production at point *A* and to import 20 tons of Japanese steel in exchange for 30 tons of its grain output. Does the United States gain from trade? The answer is Yes. At point *A*, the United States produces 100 tons of grain per day. Subtracting the 30 tons of grain traded to Japan leaves the United States with 70 tons of its own grain production to consume. In return for grain, Japan unloads 20 tons of steel on U.S. shores. Hence, specialization and trade allow the United States to move from point *A* to point *B′*, which is a consumption possibility *outside* its production possibilities curve in Exhibit 2(a). At point *B′*, the United States consumes the same amount of steel and 10 more tons of grain compared to point *B* (without trade).

Japan also has an incentive to specialize by moving its production mix from point *E* to point *F*. With trade, Japan's consumption will be at point *E′*. At point *E′*, Japan has as much grain to consume as it had at point *E*, plus 10 more tons of steel. After trading 20 of the 40 tons of steel produced at point *F* for grain, Japan can still consume 20 tons of steel from its production, rather than only 10 tons of steel at point *E*. Thus, point *E′* is a consumption possibility that lies *outside* Japan's production possibilities curve.

> **Conclusion** *Global trade allows a country to consume a combination of goods that exceeds its production possibilities curve.*

Comparative and Absolute Advantage

Why did the United States decide to produce and export grain instead of steel? Why did Japan choose to produce steel, rather than grain? Here you study the economic principle that determines specialization and trade.

Comparative Advantage

Engaging in world trade permits countries to escape the prison of their own production possibilities curves by producing bread, cars, or whatever goods they make best. The decision of the United States to specialize in and export grain and the decision of Japan to specialize in and export steel are based on comparative advantage. Comparative advantage is the ability of a country to produce a good at a lower opportunity cost than another country. Continuing our earlier example, we can calculate opportunity costs for the two countries and use comparative advantage to determine which country should specialize in grain and which in steel. For the

Comparative advantage
The ability of a country to produce a good at a lower opportunity cost than another country.

United States, the opportunity cost of producing 50 tons of steel is 100 tons of grain not produced, so 1 ton of steel costs 2 tons of grain. For Japan, the opportunity cost of producing 40 tons of steel is 40 tons of grain, so 1 ton of steel costs 1 ton of grain. Japan's steel is therefore cheaper in terms of grain forgone. This means Japan has a comparative advantage in steel production because it must give up less grain to produce steel than the United States. Stated differently, the opportunity cost of steel production is lower in Japan than in the United States.

The other side of the coin is to measure the cost of grain in terms of steel. For the United States, 1 ton of grain costs 1/2 ton of steel. For Japan, 1 ton of grain costs 1 ton of steel. The United States has a comparative advantage in grain because its opportunity cost in terms of steel forgone is lower. Thus, the United States should specialize in grain because it is more efficient in grain production. Japan, on the other hand, is relatively more efficient at producing steel and should specialize in this product.

> **Conclusion** *Comparative advantage refers to the relative opportunity costs between different countries of producing the same goods. World output and consumption are maximized when each country specializes in producing and trading goods for which it has a comparative advantage.*

Absolute Advantage

So far, a country's production and global trade decisions depend on comparing what a country gives up to produce more of a good. It is important to note that comparative advantage is based on opportunity costs, regardless of the absolute costs of resources used in production. We have not considered how much labor, land, or capital either the United States or Japan uses to produce a ton of grain or steel. For example, Japan might have an absolute advantage in producing *both* grain and steel. Absolute advantage is the ability of a country to produce a good using fewer resources than another country. In our example, Japan might use fewer resources per ton to produce grain and steel than the United States. Maybe the Japanese work harder or are more skilled. In short, the Japanese may be more productive producers, but their absolute advantage does not matter in specialization and world trade decisions. If the United States has a comparative advantage in grain, it should specialize in grain even if Japan can produce both grain and steel with fewer resources.

> **Absolute advantage**
> The ability of a country to produce a good using fewer resources than another country.

Perhaps another example will clarify the difference between absolute advantage and comparative advantage. When Babe Ruth played for the New York Yankees, he was the best hitter and the best pitcher, not only on the team, but in all of major league baseball. In fact, before Ruth was traded to the Yankees and switched to the outfield, he was the best left-handed pitcher in the American League for a few seasons with the Boston Red Sox. His final record was 99–46. In other words, he had an *absolute advantage* in both hitting and throwing the baseball. Stated differently, Babe Ruth could produce the same home runs as any other teammate with fewer times at bat. The problem was that if he pitched, he would bat fewer times because pitchers need rest after pitching. The coaches decided that the Babe had a *comparative advantage* in hitting. A few pitchers on the team could pitch almost as well as the Babe, but no one could touch his hitting. In terms of opportunity costs, the Yankees would lose fewer games if the Babe specialized in hitting.

CHECKPOINT

Do Nations with an Advantage Always Trade?
Comparing labor productivity, suppose the United States has an absolute advantage over Costa Rica in the production of calculators and towels. In the United States, a worker can produce 4 calculators or 400 towels in 10 hours. In Costa Rica, a worker can produce 1 calculator or 100 towels in the same time. Under these conditions, are specialization and trade advantageous?

Free Trade Versus Protectionism

In theory, global trade should be based on comparative advantage and free trade. Free trade is the flow of goods between countries without restrictions or special taxes. In practice, despite the advice of economists, every nation protects its own domestic producers to some degree from foreign competition. Behind these barriers to trade are special interest groups whose jobs and incomes are threatened, so they clamor to the government for protectionism. Protectionism is the government's use of embargoes, tariffs, quotas, and other restrictions to protect domestic producers from foreign competition.

Free trade
The flow of goods between countries without restrictions or special taxes.

Protectionism
The government's use of embargoes, tariffs, quotas, and other restrictions to protect domestic producers from foreign competition.

Embargo

Embargo
A law that bars trade with another country.

Embargoes are the strongest limit on trade. An embargo is a law that bars trade with another country. For example, the United States and other nations in the world imposed an arms embargo on Iraq in response to its invasion of Kuwait in 1990. The United States also maintains embargoes against Cuba, Iran, and North Korea.

Tariff

Tariff
A tax on an import.

Tariffs are the most popular and visible measures used to discourage trade. A tariff is a tax on an import. Tariffs are also called customs duties. Suppose the United States imposes a tariff of 2.9 percent on autos. If a foreign car costs $40,000, the amount of the tariff equals $1,160 ($40,000 × 0.029), and the U.S. price, including the tariff, is $41,160. The current U.S. tariff code specifies tariffs on nearly 70 percent of U.S. imports. A tariff can be based on weight, volume, or number of units, or it can be *ad valorem* (figured as a percentage of the price). The average U.S. tariff is less than 5 percent, but individual tariffs vary widely. Tariffs are imposed to reduce imports by raising import prices and to generate revenues for the U.S. Treasury. Exhibit 4 shows the trend of the average tariff rate since 1930.

During the worldwide depression of the 1930s, when one nation raised its tariffs to protect its industries, other nations retaliated by raising their tariffs. Under the Smoot-Hawley tariffs of the 1930s, the average tariff in the United States reached a peak of 20 percent. Durable imports, which were one-third of imports, were subject to an unbelievable tariff rate of 60 percent. In 1947, most of the world's industrialized nations mutually agreed to end the tariff wars by signing the *General Agreement on Tariffs and Trade (GATT)*. Since then, GATT nations have met periodically to negotiate lower tariff rates. GATT agreements have significantly reduced tariffs over the years among member nations. In the 1994 *Uruguay round,* member nations signed a GATT agreement that decreased tariffs and reduced other

EXHIBIT 4	The United States Average Tariff Rate, 1930–2007

Under the Smoot-Hawley Act of 1930, the average tariff rate peaked at 20 percent. Since the GATT in 1947 and other trade agreements, tariffs have declined to less than 5 percent.

SOURCES: *Economic Report of the President 1989,* http://www.gpoaccess.gov/eop/, p. 151; United States International Trade Commission, *The Economic Effect of Significant U.S. Import Restraints,* June 2002, p. 146, http://www.USITC.gov/; and *Trade Profiles,* http://stat.wto.org/CountryProfiles/US_e.htm.

trade barriers. The most divisive element of this agreement was the creation in 1995 of the Geneva-based World Trade Organization (WTO) to enforce rulings in global trade disputes. The WTO has 150 members and a standing appellate body to render final decisions regarding disputes between WTO members. Critics fear that the WTO might be far more likely to rule in favor of other countries in their trade disputes with the United States. Some people argue that the WTO is unaccountable, and these critics reject free trade and globalization.

To illustrate an interesting case, the United States imposed tariffs in 2002 on steel imports to protect jobs in the struggling U.S. steel industry against foreign competition. The WTO ruled these tariffs were illegal, and countries in Europe and Asia prepared a list of retaliatory tariffs. These levies targeted products such as citrus fruit grown in Florida and apparel produced in southern states crucial to President Bush's reelection. Meanwhile, U.S. automakers and other steel-consuming industries complained because the tariffs increased their costs. Facing these threats, the United States removed the tariffs on steel imports in 2003. It is interesting to compare this case to the You're the Economist titled World Trade Slips on Banana Peel.

World Trade Organization (WTO)

An international organization of member countries that oversees international trade agreements and rules on trade disputes.

Quota

Quota

A limit on the quantity of a good that may be imported in a given time period.

Another way to limit foreign competition is to impose a quota. A quota is a limit on the quantity of a good that may be imported in a given time period. For example, the United States may allow 10 million tons of sugar to be imported over a one-year period. Once this quantity is reached, no more sugar can be imported for the year. About 12 percent of U.S. imports are subject to import quotas. Examples include import quotas on sugar, dairy products, textiles, steel, and even ice cream. Quotas can limit imports from all foreign suppliers or from specific countries. In 2005, for example, global quotas were lifted from Chinese imports. The United States and other European countries demanded quotas to protect their countries from Chinese textiles. Critics argue that, like all barriers to trade, quotas invite nations to retaliate with their own measures to restrict trade, and consumers are harmed by higher prices because of the lack of competition from lower-priced imports. In addition to embargoes, tariffs, and quotas, some nations use subtler measures to discourage trade, such as setting up an overwhelming number of bureaucratic steps that must be taken in order to import a product.

Arguments for Protection

Free trade provides consumers with lower prices and larger quantities of goods from which to choose. Thus, removing import barriers might save each family a few hundred dollars a year. The problem, however, is that imports could cost some workers their jobs and thousands of dollars per year from lost income. Thus, it is no wonder that, in spite of the greater total benefits from free trade to consumers, trade barriers exist. The reason is primarily because workers and owners from import-competing firms have more at stake than consumers, so they go to Washington and lobby for protection. The following are some of the most popular arguments for protection. These arguments have strong political or emotional appeal, but weak support from economists.

Infant Industry Argument

As the name suggests, the *infant industry argument* is that a new domestic industry needs protection because it is not yet ready to compete with established foreign competitors. An infant industry is in a formative stage and must bear high start-up costs to train an entire workforce, develop new technology, establish marketing channels, and reach economies of scale. With time to grow and protection, an infant industry can reduce costs and "catch up" with established foreign firms.

Economists ask where one draws the arbitrary line between an "infant" and a "grown-up" industry. It is also difficult to make a convincing case for protecting an infant industry in a developed country, such as the United States, where industries are well established. The infant industry argument, however, may have some validity for less-developed countries. Yet, even for these countries, there is a danger. Once protection is granted, the new industry will not experience the competitive pressures necessary to encourage reasonably quick growth and participation in world trade. Also, once an industry is given protection, it is difficult to take it away.

National Security Argument

Another common argument is that defense-related industries must be protected with embargoes, tariffs, and quotas to ensure national security. By protecting critical defense industries, a nation will not be dependent on foreign countries for the essential defense-related goods it needs to defend itself in wartime. The *national defense argument* has been used to protect a long list of industries, including petro-chemicals, munitions, steel, and rubber.

This argument gained validity during the War of 1812. Great Britain, the main trading partner of the United States, became an enemy that blockaded our coast. Today, this argument makes less sense for the United States. The government stock-piles missiles, sophisticated electronics, petroleum, and most goods needed in wartime.

Employment Argument

The *employment argument* suggests that restricting imports increases domestic jobs in protected industries. According to this protectionist argument, the sale of an imported good comes at the expense of its domestically produced counterpart. Lower domestic output therefore leads to higher domestic unemployment than would otherwise be the case.

It is true that protectionism can increase output and save jobs in some indus-tries at home. Ignored, however, are the higher prices paid by consumers because protectionism reduces competition between domestic goods and imported goods. In addition, there are employment reduction effects to consider. For example, suppose a strict quota is imposed on steel imported into our nation. Reduced foreign compe-tition allows U.S. steelmakers to charge higher prices for their steel. As a result, prices rise and sales fall for cars and other products using steel, causing production and employment to fall in these industries. Thus, the import quota on steel may save jobs in the steel industry but at the expense of more jobs lost in the steel-consuming industries. Also, by selling U.S. imports, foreigners earn dollars that they can use to buy U.S. exports. Import quotas cause foreigners to have fewer dollars to spend on U.S. exports, resulting in a decrease in employment in U.S. export indus-tries. In short, protectionism may cause a net reduction in the nation's total employment.

Cheap Foreign Labor Argument

Another often heard popular claim is the *cheap labor argument*. It goes something like this: "How can we compete with such unfair competition? Labor costs $10 an hour in the United States, and firms in many developing countries pay only $1 an hour. Without protection against outsourcing our jobs, U.S. wages will be driven down, and our standard of living will fall."

A major flaw in this argument is that it neglects the reason for the difference in the wage rates between countries. A U.S. worker has more education, training, capi-tal, and access to advanced technology. Therefore, if U.S. workers produce more output per hour than workers in another country, U.S. workers will earn higher wages without a competitive disadvantage. Suppose textile workers in the United States are paid $10 per hour. If a U.S. worker takes 1 hour to produce a rug, the labor cost per rug is $10. Now suppose a worker in India earns $1 per hour, but requires 20 hours to produce a rug on a handloom. In this case, the labor cost per rug is $20. Although the wage rate is 10 times higher in the United States, U.S. pro-ductivity is 20 times higher because a U.S. worker can produce 20 rugs in 20 hours, while the worker in India produces only 1 rug in the same amount of time.

Sometimes U.S. companies move their operations to foreign countries where labor is cheaper. Such moves are not always successful because the savings from paying foreign workers a lower wage rate are offset by lower productivity. Other disadvantages of foreign operations include greater transportation costs to U.S. markets and political instability.

Growing bananas for European markets was a multi-billion-dollar bright spot for Latin America's struggling economies. In fact, about half of this region's banana exports traditionally were sold to Europe. Then, in 1993, the European Union (EU) adopted a package of quotas and tariffs aimed at cutting Europe's banana imports from Latin America. The purpose of these restrictions was to give trade preference to 66 banana-growing former colonies of European nations in Africa, the Caribbean, and the Pacific. Ignored was the fact that growers in Latin America grow higher-quality bananas at half the cost of EU-favored growers because of their low labor costs and flat tropical land near port cities.[1]

In 1999, the World Trade Organization (WTO) ruled that the EU was discriminating in favor of European companies importing the fruit and the WTO imposed $191.4 million per year in punitive tariffs on European goods. This was the first time in the four years the WTO had been in existence that such retaliation had been approved, and only the second time going back to its predecessor, the General Agreement on Tariffs and Trade. When the EU failed to comply with the WTO findings, the United States enforced its WTO rights by imposing increased duties on EU imports, including goods ranging from cashmere sweaters and Italian handbags to sheep's milk cheese, British biscuits, and German coffeemakers. The effect of the U.S. sanctions was to double the wholesale prices of these items. Denmark and the Netherlands were exempt from the U.S. tariffs because they were the only nations that voted against the EU banana rules.

Critics charged that the United States was pushing the case for political reasons. American companies, including Chiquita Brands International and Dole Food Company, grow most of their bananas in Latin America. With America's trade deficit running at a record level, U.S. trade experts also argued that the United States had little choice but to act against

Free Trade Agreements

The trend in recent years has been for nations to negotiate a reduction in trade barriers. In 1993, Congress approved the *North American Free Trade Agreement (NAFTA)*, which linked the United States to its first- and third-largest trading partners, Canada and Mexico. Under NAFTA, which became effective January 1, 1994, tariffs were phased out, and other impediments to trade and investment were eliminated among the three nations. For example, elimination of trade restrictions allows the United States to supply Mexico with more U.S. goods and to boost U.S. jobs. On the other hand, NAFTA was expected to raise Mexico's wages and standard of living by increasing Mexican exports to the United States. Note that NAFTA made no changes in restrictions on labor movement and workers must enter the United States under a limited immigration quota or illegally. The success of NAFTA remains controversial. At the conclusion of this chapter, we will use data to examine its impact.

The United States and other countries are considering other free trade agreements. In Europe, 27 nations have joined the *European Union (EU)*, which is dedicated to removing all trade barriers within Europe and thereby creating a single

the EU for failing to abide by the WTO's ruling. Moreover, with increasing voices in the United States questioning the wisdom of global trade and globalization, it was important that the WTO prove that it could arbitrate these disputes.

In 2001, it appeared that the banana dispute might be resolved. The EU agreed to increase market access for U.S. banana distributors, and the United States lifted its retaliatory duties on EU products. The agreement also provided that the United States could reimpose the duties if the EU did not complete its phased-in reductions in restrictions on banana imports.[2]

And the banana story just kept "slipping along."

European Union anti-fraud officials say that illegal banana trafficking is proving more lucrative than that in cocaine. A recently exposed scheme saw Italian banana importers use false licences to pay greatly reduced customs duties on non-quota fruit. The fraud netted smugglers hundreds of millions of euros over a two-year period. Italian public prosecutor, Fabio Scavone, says more is being made from simple customs fraud than from serious crimes such as narcotics trafficking.[3]

And in 2004, Latin American growers again complained that the EU was discriminating against their bananas in favor of producers from African and Caribbean countries. Under the 2001 WTO ruling, the EU was compelled to replace its complex quota and tariff system on bananas with a tariff-only regime. So the EU placed a 176 euro tariff per ton on Latin American suppliers to get into the EU market, while bananas from African and Caribbean countries can export up to 775,000 tons duty-free. A memorandum issued by the Swedish government attacked the "considerable overprice" European consumers pay for banana protection.[4] The banana war continued in 2008 when a WTO dispute panel ruled for the third time that the EU tariff/quota banana regime was unfair.

ANALYZE THE ISSUE

Make an argument in favor of the European import restrictions. Make an argument against this plan.

---

1. James Brooke, "Forbidden Fruit in Europe: Latin Bananas Face Hurdles," *The New York Times,* April 5, 1993, p. A1.
2. "U.S. Lifts Sanctions in Banana War," *The Food Institute Report,* July 9, 2001, p. 9.
3. "Banana Scam Beats Cocaine," *Australian Business Intelligence,* July 24, 2002.
4. "Bananas: Commission Proposes New Import Tariff at Euro 230 aTon," *European Report,* Oct. 30, 2004, p. 506.

European economy almost as large as the U.S. economy. See the Birth of the Euro box insert in this chapter.

The *Asian-Pacific Economic Cooperation (APEC)* was formed in 1989 and today has 21 member nations, including China, Hong Kong, Russia, Japan, and Mexico. This organization is based on a nonbinding agreement to reduce trade barriers between member nations.

In 2003, trade ministers from 34 nations met in Miami to create a plan for the world's largest free-trade area that would tear down trade barriers from Alaska to Argentina. The *Free Trade Area of the Americas (FTAA)* would span the Western Hemisphere except Cuba. In 2005, the *Central American Free Trade Agreement (CAFTA)* extended the free-trade zone to six Central American countries that signed, including Costa Rica, Guatemala, El Salvador, Honduras, Nicaragua, and the Dominican Republic. The success or failure of CAFTA will have an impact on future negotiation for FTAA.

Critics are concerned that regional free trade accords will make global agreements increasingly difficult to achieve. Some fear that trading blocs may erect new barriers, creating "Fortress North America," "Fortress Europe," and similar impediments to the worldwide reduction of trade barriers.

BIRTH OF THE EURO

In 1958, several European nations formed a Common Market to eliminate trade restrictions among member countries. The Common Market called for gradual removal of tariffs and import quotas on goods traded among member nations. Later, the name was changed to the *European Economic Community (EEC)*, and it is now called the *European Union (EU)*. This organization established a common system of tariffs for imports from nonmember nations and created common policies for economic matters of joint concern, such as agriculture and transportation. The EU now comprises the 27 nations listed in the table.

In 1999, 11 European countries, joined later by Greece, followed the United States as an example and united in the *European Economic and Monetary Union (EMU)*. In the United States, 50 states are linked with a common currency, and the Federal Reserve serves as the central bank by conducting monetary policy for the nation. Among the states, trade, labor, and investment enjoy

© Mikael Damkier, 2008/Used under license from Shutterstock.com.

freedom of movement. In 2002, the EMU members replaced their national currencies with a single currency, the euro. The objective was to remove exchange rate fluctuations that impede cross-border transactions. This is why the U.S. Congress created a national currency in 1863 to replace state and private bank currencies.

The EU faces many unanswered questions. Unlike the states of the United States, the EU's member nations do not share a common language or government. This makes maintaining common macro policies difficult.

The Balance of Payments

When trade occurs between the United States and other nations, many types of financial transactions are recorded in a summary called the balance of payments. The balance of payments is a bookkeeping record of all the international transactions between a country and other countries during a given period of time. This summary is the best way to understand interactions between economies because it records the value of a nation's spending inflows and outflows made by individuals, firms, and governments. Exhibit 5 presents a simplified U.S. balance of payments for 2007.

Note the pluses and minuses in the table. A transaction that is a payment to the United States is entered as a positive amount. A payment by the United States to another country is entered with a minus sign. As our discussion unfolds, you will learn that the balance of payments provides much useful information.

Current Account

The first section of the balance of payments is the *current account*, which includes, as the name implies, trade in currently produced goods and services. The most widely reported and largest part of the current account is the balance of trade, also

Balance of payments

A bookkeeping record of all the international transactions between a country and other countries during a given period of time.

Balance of trade

The value of a nation's goods imports subtracted from its goods exports.

France, for example, might seek to control inflation, while Germany has reducing unemployment as its highest priority. Coordinating monetary policy among EU nations is also difficult. Although the EU has established the *European Central Bank* headquartered in Frankfurt, Germany with sole authority over the supply of euros, the central banks of member nations still function. But these national central banks operate similar to the district banks of the Federal Reserve System in the United States. Only time will tell whether EU nations will perform better with a single currency than with separate national currencies. It is possible that the euro could become a strong alternative to the U.S. dollar as a key currency for the global financial systems. Currently, the United Kingdom, Denmark, and Sweden still use their own currencies.

European Union (EU) Members			
Austria	Finland	Latvia	Romania
Belgium	France	Lithuania	Slovakia
Bulgaria	Germany	Luxembourg	Slovenia
Cyprus	Greece	Malta	Spain
Czech Republic	Hungary	Netherlands	Sweden
Denmark	Ireland	Poland	United Kingdom
Estonia	Italy	Portugal	

called the trade balance. The balance of trade is the value of a nation's goods imports subtracted from its goods exports. As shown in Exhibit 5, the United States had a *balance of trade deficit* of −$819 billion in 2007. A trade deficit occurs when the value of a country's imports of goods (not services) exceeds the value of its exports of goods. When a nation has a trade deficit, it is called an *unfavorable balance of trade* because more is spent for imports than is earned from exports. Recall that net exports can have a positive (favorable) or negative (unfavorable) effect on $GDP = C + I + G + (X - M)$.

Exhibit 6 charts the annual balance of trade for the United States from 1975 through 2007. Observe that the United States experienced a *balance of trade surplus* in 1975. A trade surplus arises when the value of a country's merchandise exports is greater than the value of its merchandise imports. This is called a *favorable balance of trade* because the United States earned more from exports than it spent for imports. Since 1975, however, sizable trade deficits have occurred. These trade deficits have attracted much attention because in part they reflect the popularity of foreign goods and the lack of competitiveness of goods "Made in U.S.A." In 2001, the U.S. trade deficit narrowed slightly due to the recession. Because of this weakness in the economy, spending for imports fell slightly relative to exports and the gap was reduced.

EXHIBIT 5	U.S. Balance of Payments, 2007 (billions of dollars)
Type of Transaction	
Current account	
1. Goods exports	$ +1,149
2. Goods imports	−1,968
Trade balance (lines 1–2)	−819
3. Service exports	+497
4. Service imports	−378
5. Investment income (net)	+82
6. Unilateral transfers (net)	−113
Current account balance (lines 1-6)	−731
Capital account	
7. U.S. capital inflow	+2,058
8. U.S. capital outflow	−1,290
Capital account balance (lines 7-8)	+768
9. Statistical discrepancy	−37
Net balance (lines 1–9)	0

SOURCE: Bureau of Economic Analysis, *U.S. International Transactions*, http://www.bea.gov/international/index.htm, Table 1.

By the end of 2007, the U.S. trade deficit reached over $800 billion due in part to the rising price of oil imports. Between 2001 and 2007, the price per barrel doubled, and the U.S. trade deficit with OPEC countries grew from $40 billion to $126 billion. Also, our trade deficit with China tripled over the same time period from $83 billion to $257 billion. China is discussed in more detail in the next chapter.

Lines 3–6 of the current account in Exhibit 5 list ways other than goods to move dollars back and forth between the United States and other countries. For example, a Japanese tourist who pays a hotel bill in Hawaii buys an export of services, which is a plus or credit to our current account (line 3). Similarly, an American visitor to foreign lands buys an import of services, which is a minus or debit to our services and therefore a minus to our current account (line 4). Income flowing back from U.S. investments abroad, such as plants, real estate, and securities, is a payment for use of the services of U.S. capital. Foreign countries also receive income flowing from the services of their capital owned in the United States. In 2007, line 5 of the table reports a net flow of $82 billion to the United States.

Finally, we consider line 6, unilateral transfers. This category includes gifts made by our government, charitable organizations, or private individuals to other governments or private parties elsewhere in the world. For example, this item includes U.S. foreign aid to other nations. Similar unilateral transfers into the United States must be subtracted to determine the *net* unilateral transfers. Net unilateral transfers for the United States were –$113 billion in 2007.

Adding lines 1–6 gives the current account balance deficit of –$731 billion in 2007. This deficit means that foreigners sent us more goods and services than we sent to them. Because the current account balance includes *both* goods and services, it is a broader measure than the trade balance. Since 1982, the trend in the current account balance has followed the swing into the red shown by the trade balance in Exhibit 6.

Capital Account

The second section of the balance of payments is the *capital account,* which records payment flows for financial capital, such as real estate, corporate stocks, bonds,

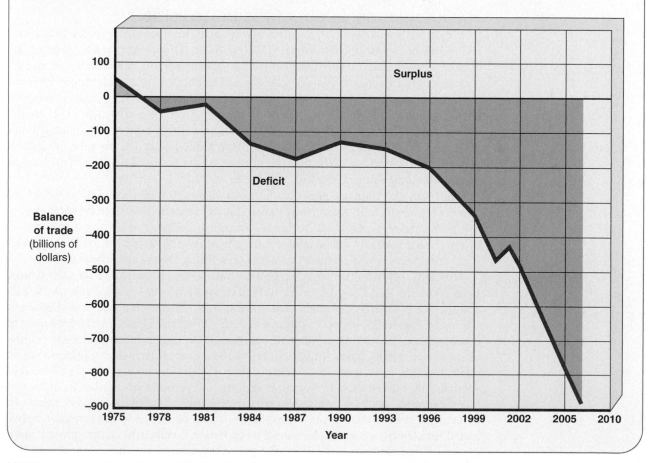

EXHIBIT 6   U.S. Balance of Trade, 1975–2007

Since 1975, the United States has experienced trade deficits, in which the value of goods imports has exceeded the value of exports. These goods trade deficits attract much attention because in part they reflect the popularity of foreign goods in the United States. During the recession in 2001, the U.S. trade deficit narrowed as spending for imports fell relative to exports. After the U.S. economy recovered, the deficit continued to grow to over $800 billion in 2007.

SOURCE: Bureau of Economic Analysis, *U.S. International Transactions,* http://www.bea.gov/international/index, Table 1.

government securities, and other debt instruments. For example, when Japanese investors buy U.S. Treasury bills, Rockefeller Center, or farmland in Hawaii, there is an inflow of dollars into the United States. As Exhibit 5 shows, foreigners made payments of $2,058 billion to our capital account (line 7). This exceeded the −$1,290 billion outflow (line 8) from the United States to purchase foreign-owned financial capital.

An important feature of the capital account is that the United States finances any deficit in its current account through this account. The capital account balance in 2007 was $768 billion. This surplus indicates that there was more foreign investment in U.S. assets than U.S. investment in foreign assets during this year.

> **Conclusion** *A current account deficit is financed by a capital account surplus.*

The current account deficit should equal the capital account surplus, but line 9 in the exhibit reveals that the balance of payments is not perfect. The capital account balance does not exactly offset the current account balance. Hence, a credit amount is simply recorded as a statistical discrepancy; therefore, the balance of payments always balances, or equals zero.

The International Debt of the United States

If each nation's balance of payments is always zero, why is there so much talk about a U.S. balance of payments problem? The problem is with the *composition* of the balance of payments. Suppose the United States runs a $500 billion deficit in its current account. This means that the current account deficit must be financed by a net annual capital inflow in the capital account of $500 billion. That is, foreign lenders, such as banks and businesses, must purchase U.S. assets and grant loans to the United States that on balance equal $500 billion. For example, a Japanese bank could buy U.S. Treasury bonds. Recall from Exhibit 7 in the chapter on federal deficits and the national debt that the portion of the national debt owed to lenders outside the United States is called *external debt.*

In 1984, the United States became a net debtor for the first time in about 70 years. This means that investments in the United States accumulated by foreigners—stocks, bonds, real estate, and so forth—exceeded the stock of foreign assets owned by the United States. In fact, during the decade of the 1980s, the United States moved from being the world's largest creditor nation to being the largest debtor nation.

Exhibit 7 shows that the United States has its largest trade deficits with China, Japan, Mexico, and Canada, respectively. The concern over continuing trade deficits and the rising international debt that accompanies them is that the United States is artificially enjoying a higher standard of living. When the United States continues to purchase more goods and services abroad than it exports, it might find itself "enjoying now and paying later." Suppose the Japanese and other foreigners decide not to make new U.S. investments and loans. In this case, the United States will be forced to eliminate its trade deficit by bringing exports and imports into balance. In fact, if other countries not only refuse to provide new capital inflows, but also decide to liquidate their investments, the United States would be forced to run a trade surplus. Stated differently, we would be forced to tighten our belts and accept a lower standard of living. How a change in foreign willingness to purchase U.S. assets also affects the international value of the dollar is the topic to which we now turn.

| EXHIBIT 7 | U.S. Balance of Trade with Selected Countries, 2007 |

The United States has its greatest trade deficits with China, Japan, Mexico, and Canada.

U.S. trade deficit (billions of dollars)

- China: −257
- Japan: −85
- Mexico: −78
- Canada: −71
- Germany: −45
- Venezuela: −30
- Italy: −21
- France: −14
- United Kingdom: −8

Country

SOURCE: Bureau of Economic Analysis, *U.S. International Transactions by Area*, http://www.bea.gov/international/indes.htm, Table 12.

CHECKPOINT

Should Everyone Keep a Balance of Payments?
Nations keep balances of payments and calculate accounts such as their merchandise trade deficit or surplus. If nations need these accounts, the 50 states should also maintain balances of payments to manage their economies. Or should they? What about cities?

Exchange Rates

Each transaction recorded in the balance of payments requires an exchange of one country's currency for that of another. Suppose you buy a Japanese car made in Japan, say, a Mazda. Mazda wants to be paid in yen and not dollars, so dollars must be traded for yen. On the other hand, suppose Pink Panther Airline Company in France purchases an airplane from Boeing in the United States. Pink Panther has euros to pay the bill, but Boeing wants dollars. Consequently, euros must be exchanged for dollars.

The critical question for Mazda, Pink Panther, Boeing, and everyone involved in world trade is, "What is the exchange rate?" The exchange rate is the number of units of one nation's currency that equals one unit of another nation's currency. For example, assume 1.81 dollars can be exchanged for 1 British pound. This means the exchange rate is 1.81 dollars = 1 pound. Alternatively, the exchange rate can be expressed as a reciprocal. Dividing 1 British pound by 1.81 dollars gives 0.552 pounds per dollar. Now suppose you are visiting England and want to buy a T-shirt with a price tag of 10 pounds. Knowing the exchange rate tells you the T-shirt costs $18.10 (10 pounds × $1.81/pound).

> **Conclusion** *An exchange rate can be expressed as a reciprocal.*

Exchange rate

The number of units of one nation's currency that equals one unit of another nation's currency.

Supply and Demand for Foreign Exchange

The exchange rate for dollars, or any nation's currency, is determined by global forces of supply and demand. For example, consider the exchange rate of yen to dollars, shown in Exhibit 8. Like the price and the quantity of any good traded in markets, the quantity of dollars exchanged is measured on the horizontal axis, and the price per unit is measured on the vertical axis. In this case, the price per unit is the value of the U.S. dollar expressed as the number of yen per dollar.

The demand for dollars in the world currency market comes from Japanese individuals, corporations, and governments that want to buy U.S. exports. Because the Japanese buyers must pay for U.S. exports with dollars, they *demand* to exchange their yen for dollars. As expected, the demand curve for dollars or any foreign currency is downward sloping. A decline in the number of yen per dollar means that one yen buys a larger portion of a dollar. This means U.S. goods and investment opportunities are less expensive to Japanese buyers because they must pay fewer yen for each dollar. Thus, as the yen price of dollars decreases, the quantity of dollars demanded by the Japanese to purchase Fords, stocks, land, and other U.S. products and investments increases. For example, suppose a CD recording of the hottest rock group has a $20 price tag. If the exchange rate is 200 yen to the dollar, a Japanese importer would pay 4,000 yen. If the price of dollars to Japanese buyers falls to 100 yen each, the same $20 CD will cost Japanese importers only 2,000 yen. This lower price causes Japanese buyers to increase their orders, which, in turn, increases the quantity of dollars demanded.

The supply curve of dollars is upward sloping. This curve shows the amount of dollars offered for exchange at various yen prices per dollar in the world currency exchange market. Similar to the demand for dollars, the supply of dollars in this market flows from individuals, corporations, and governments in the United States that want to buy Mazdas, stocks, land, and other products and investments from Japan. Because U.S. citizens must pay for the Japanese goods and services in yen,

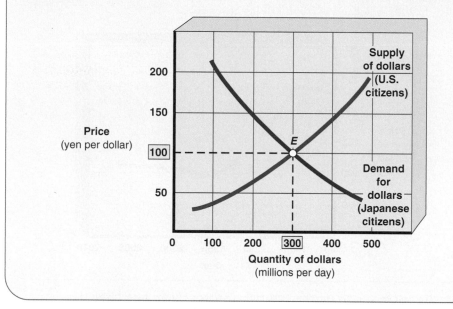

EXHIBIT 8   The Supply of and Demand for Dollars

The number of Japanese yen per dollar in the foreign exchange market is determined by the demand for dollars by Japanese citizens and the supply of dollars by U.S. citizens. The equilibrium exchange rate is 100 yen per dollar, and the equilibrium quantity is $300 million per day.

they must exchange dollars for yen. An example will illustrate why the supply curve of dollars slopes upward. Suppose a Nikon camera sells for 100,000 yen in Tokyo and the exchange rate is 100 yen per dollar or 0.01 dollar per yen ($1/100 yen). This means the camera costs an American tourist $1,000. Now assume the exchange rate rises to 250 yen per dollar or 0.004 dollar per yen ($1/250 yen). The camera will now cost the American buyer only $400. Because the prices of the Nikon camera and other Japanese products fall when the number of yen per dollar rises, Americans respond by purchasing more Japanese imports, which, in turn, increases the quantity of dollars supplied.

The foreign exchange market in Exhibit 8 is in equilibrium at an exchange rate of 100 yen for $1. As you learned in Chapter 3, if the exchange rate is above equilibrium, there will be a surplus of dollars in the world currency market. Citizens of the United States are supplying more dollars than the Japanese demand, and the exchange rate falls. On the other hand, below equilibrium, there will be a shortage of dollars in the world currency market. In this case, the Japanese are demanding more dollars than Americans supply, and the exchange rate rises.

Shifts in Supply and Demand for Foreign Exchange

For most of the years between World War II and 1971, currency exchange rates were *fixed*. Exchange rates were based primarily on gold. For example, the German mark was fixed at about 25 cents. The dollar was worth 1/35 of an ounce of gold, and 4 German marks were worth 1/35 of an ounce of gold. Therefore, 1 dollar

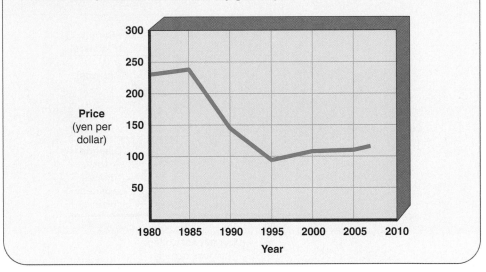

EXHIBIT 9 — Changes in the Yen-per-Dollar Exchange Rate, 1980–2007

Today, most economies are on a system of flexible exchange rates. As the demand and supply curves for currencies change, exchange rates change. In 1980, 1 dollar was worth about 230 Japanese yen. By 1995, the exchange rate had dropped to 94 yen per dollar. In 2007, a dollar was worth 118 Japanese yen.

SOURCE: *Economic Report of the President*, 2008, http://www.gpoaccess.gov/eop/, Table B-110.

equaled 4 marks, or 25 cents equaled 1 mark. In 1971, Western nations agreed to stop fixing their exchange rates and to allow their currencies to *float* according to the forces of supply and demand. Exhibit 9 illustrates that these rates can fluctuate widely. For example, in 1980, 1 dollar was worth about 230 Japanese yen. After gyrating up and down over the years, the exchange rate hit a postwar low of 94 yen per dollar in 1995. In 2007, the exchange rate was about 118 yen per dollar.

Recall from Chapter 3 that the equilibrium price for products changes in response to shifts in the supply and demand curves. The same supply and demand analysis applies to equilibrium exchange rates for foreign currency. There are four important sources of shifts in the supply and demand curves for foreign exchange. Let's consider each in turn.

Tastes and Preferences   Exhibit 10(a) illustrates one important factor that causes the demand for foreign currencies to shift. Suppose the Japanese lose their "taste" for tobacco, U.S. government bonds, and other U.S. products and investment opportunities. This decline in the popularity of U.S. products in Japan decreases the demand for dollars at each possible exchange rate, and the demand curve shifts leftward from D_1 to D_2. This change causes the equilibrium exchange rate to fall from 150 yen to the dollar at E_1 to 100 yen to the dollar at E_2. Because the number of yen to the dollar declines, the dollar is said to *depreciate* or become *weaker*. Depreciation of currency is a fall in the price of one currency relative to another.

What happens to the exchange rate if the "Buy American" idea changes our tastes and the demand for Japanese imports decreases? In this case, U.S. citizens

Depreciation of currency

A fall in the price of one currency relative to another.

EXHIBIT 10   Changes in the Supply and Demand Curves for Dollars

In Part (a), U.S. exports become less popular in Japan. This change in tastes for U.S. products and investments decreases the demand for dollars, and the demand curve shifts leftward from D_1 to D_2. As a result, the equilibrium exchange rate falls from 150 yen to the dollar at E_1 to 100 yen to the dollar at E_2.

Part (b) assumes U.S. citizens are influenced by the "Buy American" idea. In this case, our demand for Japanese imports decreases, and U.S. citizens supply fewer dollars to the foreign currency market. The result is that the supply curve shifts leftward from S_1 to S_2, and the equilibrium exchange rate rises from 100 yen per dollar at E_1 to 150 yen per dollar at E_2.

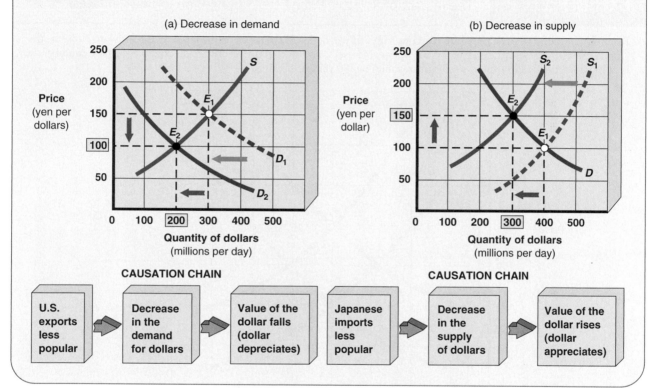

supply fewer dollars at any possible exchange rate, and the supply curve in Exhibit 10(b) shifts leftward from S_1 to S_2. As a result, the equilibrium exchange rate rises from 100 yen to the dollar at E_1 to 150 yen to the dollar at E_2. Because the number of yen per dollar rises, the dollar is said to *appreciate* or become *stronger*. Appreciation of currency is a rise in the price of one currency relative to another.

Relative Incomes   Assume income in the United States rises, while income in Japan remains unchanged. As a result, U.S. citizens buy more domestic products and more Japanese imports. The results are a rightward shift in the supply curve for dollars and a decrease in the equilibrium exchange rate. Paradoxically, growth of U.S. income leads to the dollar depreciating, or becoming weaker, against the Japanese yen.

> **Appreciation of currency**
> A rise in the price of one currency relative to another.

Conclusion *An expansion in relative U.S. income causes a depreciation of the dollar.*

Relative Price Levels   Now we consider a more complex case, in which a change in a factor causes a change in both the supply and the demand curves for dollars. Assume the foreign exchange rate begins in equilibrium at 100 yen per dollar, as shown at point E_1 in Exhibit 11. Now assume the price level increases in Japan, but remains constant in the United States. The Japanese therefore want to buy more

---

EXHIBIT 11   The Impact of Relative Price Level Changes on Exchange Rates

Begin at E_1, with the exchange rate equal to 100 yen per dollar. Assume prices in Japan rise relative to those in the United States. As a result, the demand for dollars increases, and the supply of dollars decreases. The new equilibrium is at E_2 when the dollar appreciates (rises in value) to 200 yen per dollar.

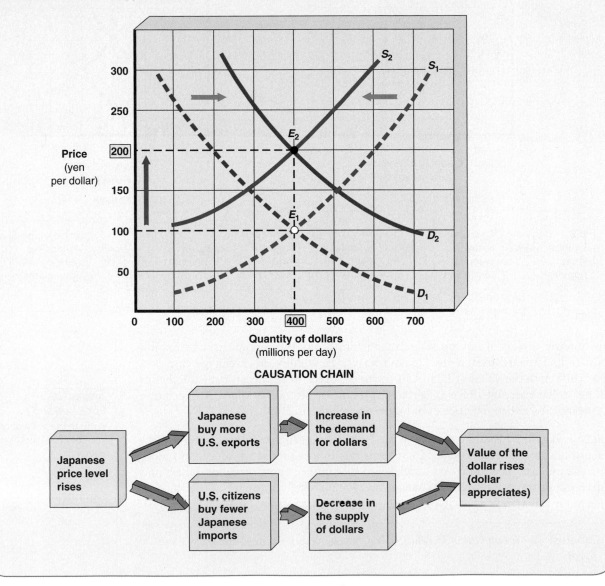

U.S. exports because they have become cheaper relative to Japanese products. This willingness of the Japanese to buy U.S. goods and services shifts the demand curve for dollars rightward from D_1 to D_2. In addition, U.S. products are cheaper for U.S. citizens compared to Japanese imports. As a result, the willingness to import from Japan is reduced at each exchange rate, which means the supply curve of dollars decreases from S_1 to S_2. The result of the shifts in both the demand and the supply curves for dollars is to establish a new equilibrium at point E_2, and the exchange rate reaches 200 yen per dollar.

> **Conclusion** *A rise in a trading partner's relative price level causes the dollar to appreciate.*

Relative Real Interest Rates   Changes in relative real (inflation-adjusted) interest rates can have an important effect on the exchange rate. Suppose real interest rates in the United States rise, while those in Japan remain constant. To take advantage of more attractive yields, Japanese investors buy an increased amount of bonds and other interest-bearing securities issued by private and government borrowers in the United States. This change increases the demand for dollars, which increases the equilibrium exchange rate of yen to the dollar, causing the dollar to appreciate (or the yen to depreciate).

There can also be an effect on the supply of dollars. When real interest rates rise in the United States, our citizens purchase fewer Japanese securities. Hence, they offer fewer dollars at each possible exchange rate, and the supply curve for dollars shifts leftward. As a result, the equilibrium exchange rate increases, and the dollar appreciates from changes in both the demand for and the supply of dollars.

The Impact of Exchange Rate Fluctuations

Now it is time to stop for a minute, take a breath, and draw some important conclusions. As you have just learned, exchange rates between most major currencies are flexible. Instead of being pegged to gold or another fixed standard, their value is determined by the laws of supply and demand. Consequently, shifts in supply and demand create a weaker or a stronger dollar. But it should be noted that exchange rates do not fluctuate with total freedom. Governments often buy and sell currencies to prevent wide swings in exchange rates. In summary, the strength or weakness of any nation's currency has a profound impact on its economy.

A weak dollar is a "mixed blessing." Ironically, a weak dollar makes U.S. producers happy because they can sell their less expensive exports to foreign buyers. As export sales rise, jobs are created in the United States. On the other hand, a weak dollar makes foreign producers and domestic consumers unhappy because the prices of Japanese cars, French wine, and Italian shoes are higher. As U.S. imports fall, jobs are lost in foreign countries.

> **Conclusion** *When the dollar is weak or depreciates, U.S. goods and services cost foreign consumers less, so they buy more U.S. exports. At the same time, a weak dollar means foreign goods and services cost U.S. consumers more, so they buy fewer imports.*

Gold is always a fascinating story: *The Wonderful Wizard of Oz* was first published in 1900 and this children's tale has been interpreted as an allegory for political and economic events of the 1890s. For example, the Yellow Brick Road represents the gold standard, Oz in the title is an abbreviation for ounce, Dorothy is the naïve public, Emerald City symbolizes Washington, D.C., the Tin Woodman represents the industrial worker, the Scarecrow is the farmer, and the Cyclone is a metaphor for a political revolution. In the end, Dorothy discovers magical powers in her *silver* shoes (changed to ruby in the 1939 film) to find her way home and not the fallacy of the Yellow Brick Road. Although the author of the story, L. Frank Baum, never stated it was his intention, it can be argued that the issue of the story concerns the election of 1896. Democratic presidential nominee William Jennings Bryan (the Cowardly Lion) supported fixing the value of the dollar to both gold and silver (bimetallism), but Republican William McKinley (the Wicked Witch) advocated using only the gold standard. Since McKinley won, the United States remained on the Yellow Brick Road.[1]

The United States adopted the gold standard in 1873 and until the 1930s, most industrial countries were on the gold standard. The gold standard served as an international monetary system in which currencies were defined in terms of gold. Under the gold standard, a nation with a balance of payments deficit was required to ship gold to other nations to finance the deficit. Hence, a large excess of imports over exports meant a corresponding outflow of gold from a nation. As a result, that nation's money supply decreased, which, in turn, reduced the aggregate demand for goods and services. Lower domestic demand led to falling prices, lower production, and fewer jobs. In contrast, a nation with a balance of payments surplus would experience an inflow of gold and the opposite effects. In this case, the nation's money supply increased, and its aggregate demand for goods and services rose. Higher aggregate spending, in turn, boosted employment and the price level. In short, the gold standard meant that governments could not control their money supplies and thereby conduct monetary policy.

The gold standard worked fairly well as a fixed exchange rate system so long as nations did not face sudden or severe swings in flows from their stocks of gold. The Great Depression marked the beginning of the end of the gold standard. Nations faced with trade deficits and high unemployment began going off the gold standard, rather than contracting their money supplies by following the gold standard.

In 1933, President Franklin D. Roosevelt took the United States off the gold standard and ordered all 1933 gold double eagle coins already manufactured

A strong dollar is also a "mixed blessing." A strong dollar makes our major trading partners happy because the prices of Japanese cars, French wine, and Italian shoes are lower. A strong dollar, contrary to the implication of the term, makes U.S. producers unhappy because their exports are more expensive and related jobs decline. Conversely, a strong dollar makes foreign producers happy because the prices of their goods and services are lower, causing U.S. imports to rise.

> **Conclusion** *When the dollar is strong or appreciates, U.S. goods and services cost foreign consumers more, so they buy fewer U.S. exports. At the same time, a strong dollar means foreign goods and services cost U.S. consumers less, so they buy more foreign imports.*

to be melted down and not circulated. Through a long twisted story worthy of a Sherlock Holmes mystery novel involving the Smithsonian Institution, the former king of Egypt, the Treasury Department, the Justice Department, the U.S. Mint, and a long list of intriguing supporting characters, one 1933 double eagle surfaced and was sold for $7.59 million in 2002. This was double the previous record for a coin.

Once the Allies felt certain they would win World War II, the finance ministers of Western nations met in 1944 at Bretton Woods, New Hampshire, to establish a new international monetary system. The new system was based on fixed exchange rates and an international central bank called the *International Monetary Fund* (*IMF*). The IMF makes loans to countries faced with short-term balance of payments problems. Under this system, nations were expected to maintain fixed exchange rates within a narrow range. In the 1960s and early 1970s, the Bretton Woods system became strained as conditions changed. In the 1960s, inflation rates in the United States rose relative to those in other countries, causing U.S. exports to become more expensive and U.S. imports to become less expensive. This situation increased the supply of dollars abroad and caused an increasing surplus of dollars, thus putting downward pressure on the exchange rate. Monetary authorities in the United States worried that central banks would demand gold for their dollars, the U.S. gold stock would diminish sharply, and the declining money supply would adversely affect the economy.

Something had to give, and it did. In August 1971, President Richard Nixon announced that the United States would no longer honor its obligation to sell gold at $35 an ounce. By 1973, the gold standard was dead, and most of our trading partners were letting the forces of supply and demand determine exchange rates.

Today, some people advocate returning to the gold standard. These gold buffs do not trust the government to control the money supply without the discipline of a gold standard. They argue that if governments have the freedom to print money, political pressures will sooner or later cause them to increase the money supply too much and let inflation rage.

One argument against the gold standard is that no one can control the supply of gold. Big gold discoveries can cause inflation and have done so in the past. On the other hand, slow growth in the stock of mined gold can lead to slow economic growth and a loss of jobs. Governments therefore are unlikely to return to the gold standard because it would mean turning monetary policy over to uncontrollable swings in the stock of gold.

ANALYZE THE ISSUE

Return to Exhibit 8, and assume the equilibrium exchange rate is 150 yen per dollar and the equilibrium quantity is $300 million. Redraw this figure, and place a horizontal line through the equilibrium exchange rate to represent a fixed exchange rate. Now use this figure to explain why a country would abandon the gold standard.

---

1. Bradley A. Hansen, "The Fable of the Allegory," *Journal of Economic Education*, Summer 2002, pp. 254–264.

Finally, as promised earlier in this chapter, we return to the discussion of NAFTA in order to illustrate the impact of this free trade agreement and the effect of a strong dollar. Recall that in January 1994, NAFTA began a gradual phaseout of tariffs and other trade barriers. Exhibit 12 provides trade data for the United States and Mexico for the years surrounding NAFTA. As the exhibit shows, both exports and imports of goods increased sharply after NAFTA. On the other hand, a small U.S. trade surplus of $2 billion with Mexico in 1993 turned into a huge trade deficit of $78 billion in 2007.

Before blaming this trade deficit entirely on NAFTA, you must note that the exchange rate rose from 3.12 to 10.93 pesos per dollar. Since 1995, the peso was devalued and the stronger dollar has put the price of U.S. goods out of reach for many Mexican consumers. This is one reason U.S. exports to Mexico have been

EXHIBIT 12	U.S. Trade Balances with Mexico, 1993–2007			
Year	U.S. Exports to Mexico (billions of dollars)	U.S. Imports from Mexico (billions of dollars)	Exchange Rate (pesos per dollar)	U.S. Trade Surplus (+) or Deficit (−) (billions of dollars)
1993	$ 42	$ 40	3.12	$ +2
1995	46	63	6.45	−17
1997	71	87	7.92	−16
1999	87	111	9.55	−24
2001	101	132	9.34	−31
2003	97	139	10.79	−42
2005	120	171	10.89	−51
2007	136	214	10.93	−78

SOURCES: Bureau of Economic Analysis, *U.S. International Transactions by Area,* http://gov/international/index.htm, Table 12, and *Economic Report of the President 2008*, http://www.gpoaccess.gov/eop/, Table 110.

lower than they would have been otherwise. At the same time, Mexican goods became less expensive for U.S. consumers, so U.S. imports from Mexico have risen.

KEY CONCEPTS

Comparative advantage
Absolute advantage
Free trade
Protectionism
Embargo

Tariff
World Trade Organization (WTO)
Quota
Balance of payments
Balance of trade

Exchange rate
Depreciation of currency
Appreciation of currency

SUMMARY

- *Comparative advantage* is a principle that allows nations to gain from trade. Comparative advantage means that each nation *specializes* in a product for which its opportunity cost is lower in terms of the production of another product, and then nations trade. When nations follow this principle, they gain. The reason is that world output increases, and each nation ends up with a higher standard of living by consuming more goods and services than would be possible without specialization and trade.

Comparative Advantage

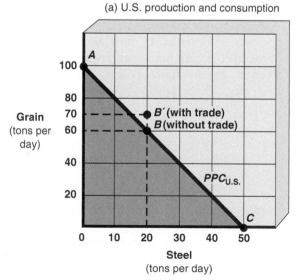

(a) U.S. production and consumption

(b) Japanese production and consumption

- *Free trade* benefits a nation as a whole, but individuals may lose jobs and incomes because of competition from foreign goods and services.
- *Protectionism* is a government's use of embargoes, tariffs, quotas, and other methods to impose barriers intended to both reduce imports and protect particular domestic industries. *Embargoes* prohibit the import or export of particular goods. *Tariffs* discourage imports by making them more expensive. *Quotas* limit the quantity of imports or exports of certain goods. These trade barriers often result primarily from domestic groups that exert political pressure on government in order to gain from these barriers.
- The *balance of payments* is a summary bookkeeping record of all the international transactions a country makes during a year. It is divided into different accounts, including the *current*

account, the *capital account,* and the *statistical discrepancy.* The current account summarizes all transactions in currently produced goods and services. The overall balance of payments is always zero after an adjustment for the statistical discrepancy.

- The **balance of trade** measures only goods (not services) that a nation exports and imports. A balance of trade can be in deficit or in surplus. The balance of trade is the most widely reported and largest part of the current account. Since 1975, the United States has experienced balance of trade deficits.

Balance of Trade

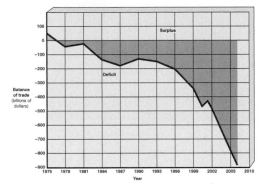

- An **exchange rate** is the price of one nation's currency in terms of another nation's currency. Foreigners who wish to purchase U.S. goods, services, and financial assets demand dollars. The supply of dollars reflects the desire of U.S. citizens to purchase foreign goods, services, and financial

assets. The intersection of the supply and demand curves for dollars determines the number of units of a foreign currency per dollar.

Exchange Rate

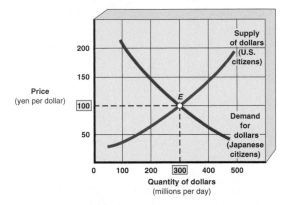

- ***Shifts in supply and demand for foreign exchange*** result from changes in such factors as tastes, relative price levels, relative real interest rates, and relative income levels.
- ***Depreciation of currency*** occurs when one currency becomes worth fewer units of another currency. If a currency depreciates, it becomes weaker. Depreciation of a nation's currency increases its exports and decreases its imports.
- ***Appreciation of currency*** occurs when one currency becomes worth more units of another currency. If a currency appreciates, it becomes stronger. Appreciation of a nation's currency decreases its exports and increases its imports.

SUMMARY OF CONCLUSION STATEMENTS

- When countries specialize, total world output increases, and, therefore, the potential for greater total world consumption also increases.
- Global trade allows a country to consume a combination of goods that exceeds its production possibilities curve.
- Comparative advantage refers to the relative opportunity costs between countries of producing the same goods. World output and consumption are maximized when each country specializes in

producing and trading goods for which it has a comparative advantage.
- A current account deficit is financed by a capital account surplus.
- An exchange rate can be expressed as a reciprocal.
- An expansion in relative U.S. income causes a depreciation of the dollar.
- A rise in a trading partner's relative price level causes the dollar to appreciate.

- When the dollar is weak or depreciates, U.S. goods and services cost foreign consumers less, so they buy more U.S. exports. At the same time, a weak dollar means foreign goods and services cost U.S. consumers more, so they buy fewer imports.

- When the dollar is strong or appreciates, U.S. goods and services cost foreign consumers more, so they buy fewer U.S. exports. At the same time, a strong dollar means foreign goods and services cost U.S. consumers less, so they buy more foreign imports.

STUDY QUESTIONS AND PROBLEMS

1. The countries of Alpha and Beta produce diamonds and pearls. The production possibilities schedule below describes their potential output in tons per year:

Points on Production Possibilities Curve	Alpha		Beta	
	Diamonds	Pearls	Diamonds	Pearls
A	150	0	90	0
B	100	25	60	60
C	50	50	30	120
D	0	75	0	180

Using the data in the table, answer the following questions:

a. What is the opportunity cost of diamonds for each country?

b. What is the opportunity cost of pearls for each country?

c. In which good does Alpha have a comparative advantage?

d. In which good does Beta have a comparative advantage?

e. Suppose Alpha is producing and consuming at point B on its production possibilities curve and Beta is producing and consuming at point C on its production possibilities curve. Use a table such as Exhibit 3 to explain why both nations would benefit if they specialize.

f. Draw a graph, and use it to explain how Alpha and Beta benefit if they specialize and Alpha agrees to trade 50 tons of diamonds to Beta and Alpha receives 50 tons of pearls in exchange.

2. Bill can paint either two walls or one window frame in one hour. In the same time, Frank can paint either three walls or two window frames. To minimize the time spent painting, who should specialize in painting walls, and who should specialize in painting window frames?

3. Consider this statement: "The principles of specialization and trade according to comparative advantage among nations also apply to states in the United States." Do you agree or disagree? Explain.

4. Would the U.S. government gain any advantage from using tariffs or quotas to restrict imports?

5. Suppose the United States passed a law stating that we would not purchase imports from any country that imposed any trade restrictions on our exports. Who would benefit and who would lose from such retaliation?

6. Now consider question 5 in terms of the law's impact on domestic producers that export goods. Does this policy adversely affect domestic producers that export goods?

7. Consider this statement: "Unrestricted foreign trade costs domestic jobs." Do you agree or disagree? Explain.

8. Do you support a constitutional amendment to prohibit the federal government from imposing any trade barriers, such as tariffs and quotas, except in case of war or national emergency? Why or why not?

9. Discuss this statement: "Because each nation's balance of payments equals zero, it follows that there is actually no significance to a balance of payments deficit or surplus."

10. For each of the following situations, indicate the direction of the shift in the supply curve or the demand curve for dollars, the factor causing the change, and the resulting movement of the equilibrium exchange rate for the dollar in terms of foreign currency:
    a. American-made cars become more popular overseas.
    b. The United States experiences a recession, while other nations enjoy economic growth.
    c. Inflation rates accelerate in the United States, while inflation rates remain constant in other nations.
    d. Real interest rates in the United States rise, while real interest rates abroad remain constant.
    e. The Japanese put quotas and high tariffs on all imports from the United States.
    f. Tourism from the United States increases sharply because of a fare war among airlines.

11. The following table summarizes the supply and the demand for euros:

	U.S. Dollars per Euro				
	$0.05	$0.10	$0.15	$0.20	$0.25
Quantity demanded (per day)	500	400	300	200	100
Quantity supplied (per day)	100	200	300	400	500

Using the above table:
a. Graph the supply and demand curves for euros.
b. Determine the equilibrium exchange rate.
c. Determine what the effect of a fixed exchange rate at $0.10 per euro would be.

For Online Exercises, go to the text Web site at www.cengage.com/economics/tucker.

CHECKPOINT ANSWERS

Do Nations with an Advantage Always Trade?

In the United States, the opportunity cost of producing 1 calculator is 100 towels. In Costa Rica, the opportunity cost of producing 1 calculator is 100 towels. If you said because the opportunity cost is the same for each nation, specialization and trade would not boost total output, and therefore Costa Rica would not trade these products, **YOU ARE CORRECT.**

Should Everyone Keep a Balance of Payments?

The principal purpose of the balance of payments is to keep track of payments of national currencies. Because states and cities within the same nation use the same national currency, payments for goods and services traded between these parties do not represent a loss (outflow) or gain (inflow). If you said only nations need to use the balance of payments to account for flows of foreign currency across national boundaries, **YOU ARE CORRECT.**

PRACTICE QUIZ

For visual explanation of the correct answers, please visit the tutorial at www.cengage.com/ economics/tucker.

1. With trade, the production possibilities for two nations lie
   a. outside their consumption possibilities.
   b. inside their consumption possibilities.
   c. at a point equal to the world production possibilities curve.
   d. none of the above.

2. Free trade theory suggests that when trade takes place
   a. both nations will be worse off.
   b. one nation must gain at the other nation's expense.
   c. both nations will be better off.
   d. one nation will gain and the other nation will be neither better nor worse off.

3. Which of the following is *true* when two countries specialize according to their comparative advantage?
   a. It is possible to increase their total output of all goods.
   b. It is possible to increase their total output of some goods only if both countries are industrialized.
   c. One country is likely to gain from trade, while the other loses.
   d. None of the above is true.

4. According to the theory of comparative advantage, a country should produce and
   a. import goods in which it has an absolute advantage.
   b. export goods in which it has an absolute advantage.
   c. import goods in which it has a comparative advantage.
   d. export goods in which it has a comparative advantage.

5. In Exhibit 13, which country has the comparative advantage in the production of potatoes?
   a. The United States because it requires fewer resources to produce potatoes
   b. The United States because it has the lower opportunity cost of potatoes
   c. Ireland because it requires fewer resources to produce potatoes

EXHIBIT 13	Potatoes and Wheat Output (tons per hour)	
Country	**Potatoes**	**Wheat**
United States	1	3
Ireland	1	2

   d. Ireland because it has the lower opportunity cost of potatoes

6. In Exhibit 13, the opportunity cost of wheat is
   a. 1/3 ton of potatoes in the United States and 1/2 ton of potatoes in Ireland.
   b. 2 tons of potatoes in the United States and 1 1/2 tons of potatoes in Ireland.
   c. 8 tons of potatoes in the United States and 4 tons of potatoes in Ireland.
   d. 1/2 ton of potatoes in the United States and 2/3 ton of potatoes in Ireland.

7. In Exhibit 13, the opportunity cost of potatoes is
   a. 1/2 ton of wheat in the United States and 2/3 ton of wheat in Ireland.
   b. 2 tons of wheat in the United States and 1 1/2 tons of wheat in Ireland.
   c. 16 tons of wheat in the United States and 6 tons of wheat in Ireland.
   d. 3 tons of wheat in the United States and 2 tons of wheat in Ireland.

8. If the countries in Exhibit 13 follow the principle of comparative advantage, the United States should
   a. buy all of its potatoes from Ireland.
   b. buy all of its wheat from Ireland.
   c. buy all of its potatoes and wheat from Ireland.
   d. produce both potatoes and wheat and not trade with Ireland.

9. A tariff increases
   a. the quantity of imports.
   b. the ability of foreign goods to compete with domestic goods.

PRACTICE QUIZ CONTINUED

c. the prices of imports to domestic buyers.
d. all of the above.

10. The infant industry argument for protectionism is based on which of the following views?
    a. Foreign buyers will absorb all of the output of domestic producers in a new industry.
    b. The growth of an industry that is new to a nation will be too rapid unless trade restrictions are imposed.
    c. Firms in a newly developing domestic industry will have difficulty growing if they face strong competition from established foreign firms.
    d. It is based on none of the above.

11. The figure that results when goods imports are subtracted from goods exports is
    a. the capital account balance.
    b. the balance of trade.
    c. the current account balance.
    d. always less than zero.

12. Which of the following international accounts records payments for exports and imports of goods, military transactions, foreign travel, investment income, and foreign gifts?
    a. The capital account
    b. The merchandise account
    c. The current account
    d. The official reserve account

13. Which of the following international accounts records the purchase and sale of financial assets and real estate between the United States and other nations?
    a. The balance of trade account
    b. The current account
    c. The capital account
    d. The balance of payments account

14. If a Japanese radio priced at 2,000 yen can be purchased for $10, the exchange rate is
    a. 200 yen per dollar.
    b. 20 yen per dollar.
    c. 20 dollars per yen.
    d. none of the above.

15. The United States
    a. was on a fixed exchange rate system prior to late 1971, but now is on a flexible exchange rate system.
    b. has been on a fixed exchange rate system since 1945.
    c. has been on a flexible exchange rate system since 1945.
    d. was on a flexible exchange rate system prior to late 1983, but now is on a fixed exchange rate system.

16. Suppose the exchange rate changes so that fewer Japanese yen are required to buy a dollar. We would conclude that
    a. the Japanese yen has depreciated in value.
    b. U.S. citizens will buy fewer Japanese imports.
    c. Japanese will demand fewer U.S. exports.
    d. none of the above will occur.

17. Which of the following would cause a decrease in the demand for euros by those holding U.S. dollars?
    a. Inflation in France, but not in the United States
    b. Inflation in the United States, but not in France
    c. An increase in the real rate of interest on investments in France above the real rate of interest on investments in the United States
    d. None of the above

18. An increase in the equilibrium price of a nation's money could be caused by a (an)
    a. decrease in the supply of the money.
    b. decrease in the demand for the money.
    c. increase in the supply of the money.
    d. increase in the quantity of money demanded.

19. If the dollar appreciates (becomes stronger), this causes
    a. the relative price of U.S. goods to increase for foreigners.
    b. the relative price of foreign goods to decrease for Americans.
    c. U.S. exports to fall and U.S. imports to rise.
    d. a balance of trade deficit for the United States.
    e. all of the above to occur.

20. Which of the following would cause the U.S. dollar to depreciate against the Japanese yen?
    a. Greater popularity of U.S. exports in Japan
    b. A higher price level in Japan
    c. Higher real interest rates in the United States
    d. Higher incomes in the United States

Economies in Transition

The inherent vice of capitalism is the unequal sharing of blessings. The inherent virtue of communism is the equal sharing of miseries.

Winston Churchill

The rapid emergence of the market system in Russia, China, and other countries continues to fascinate us. Newspapers and periodicals report the astonishing news that leaders of countries that used to be devoted followers of Marxist ideology now say they believe that capitalism, private property, and profit are ideas superior to the communist system. The failure of communism and the transformation toward a market system is personified by the success of McDonald's in Russia and Wal-Mart in China. Today, Russia and other countries continue to experience economic problems during their restructuring, but the commitment to free-market reforms remains. What caused this astonishing turn of events?

To understand how the pieces of the global economic puzzle fit together, this chapter begins with a discussion of the three basic types of economies. Then you will examine the pros and cons of the "isms"— capitalism, socialism, and communism. Here you will explore the worldwide clash between the ideas of Adam Smith and Karl Marx and study their current influence on economic systems. Finally, you will examine economic reforms in Cuba, Russia, and China.

In this chapter, you will learn to solve these economic puzzles:

- Why did drivers in the former Soviet Union remove the windshield wipers and side mirrors whenever they parked their cars?

- What did Adam Smith mean when he said that an "invisible hand" promotes the public interest?

- If the Soviet Union was foolish to run its economy on five-year plans, why do universities, businesses, and governments in a capitalistic economy plan?

Basic Types of Economic Systems

An economic system consists of the organizations and methods used to determine what goods and services are produced, how they are produced, and for whom they are produced. As explained earlier in Chapter 2, scarcity forces each economic system to decide what combination of goods to produce, how to produce such goods, and who gets the output once produced. The decision-making process involves interaction among many aspects of a nation's culture, such as its laws, form of government, ethics, religions, and customs. Economist Robert L. Heilbroner established a simple way to look at the basic methods society can employ. Each economic system can be classified into one of three basic types: (1) *traditional*, (2) *command*, and (3) *market*.

The Traditional Economy

Why does England have a king or queen? Tradition is the answer. Historically, the traditional economy has been a common system for making economic decisions. The traditional economy is a system that answers the *What, How,* and *For Whom* questions the way they have always been answered. People in this type of society learn that copying the previous generation allows them to feel accepted. Anyone who changes ways of doing things asks for trouble from others. This is because people in such a society believe that what was good yesterday, and years ago, must still be a good idea today.

Although most traditional economies have switched to keep pace with modern economic trends, traditional systems are used today, for example, by the Ainu of Japan, the native people of Brazil's rain forest, the pygmies of Central Africa, and the Amish of Pennsylvania. In these societies, the way past generations decided what crops are planted, how they are harvested, and to whom they are distributed remains unchanged over time. People perform their jobs in the manner established by their ancestors. The Amish are well known for rejecting tractors and using horse-drawn plows. Interestingly, the Amish reject Social Security because their society voluntarily redistributes wealth to members who are needy.

The Traditional Economy's Strengths and Weaknesses

The benefit of the traditional approach is that it minimizes friction among members because relatively little is disputed. Consequently, people in this system may cooperate more freely with one another. In today's industrial world, the Amish and other traditional economies appear very satisfied with their relatively uncomplicated systems. However, critics argue that the traditional system restricts individual initiative and therefore does not lead to the production of advanced goods, new technology, and economic growth.

The Command Economy

In a command economy, a dictator or group of central planners makes economic decisions for society. In this system, the *What, How,* and *For Whom* questions are answered by planners with central authority. The former Soviet Union and China in the past and Cuba, North Korea, and Burma today are examples of nations with command economies using national economic plans implemented through powerful government committees. Politically selected committees decide on everything, including the number, color, size, quality, and price of autos, brooms, sweaters, and tanks. The state owns the factors of production and dictates answers to the three basic economic questions. The authorities might decide to produce modern weapons instead of schools, or they might decide to devote resources to building huge monuments like the pyramids, built by the rulers of ancient Egypt to honor their dead kings and queens.

In the old Soviet economy, for example, the three basic economic questions were answered by a central planning agency called the *Gosplan*. Following the policies of the political authority (the Politburo), the Gosplan set production quotas and prices for farms, factories, mines, housing construction, medical care, and other producing units. What should the cows be fed? If it is hay, how much land can be used to grow it? How much milk should the cows give? How many people will be dairy farmers? What wages should a dairy farmer earn? Should milk be given to everyone, to a few, or to any persons chosen by the leaders? If there was a shortage of goods in the shops, then goods would be rationed through queuing. The Gosplan tried to make all these decisions. Today, in Russia and the other former Soviet republics, the Gosplan is a distant memory of the discarded Soviet command system.

We can represent the command economy by the pyramid shown in Exhibit 1. At the top of the pyramid is a supremely powerful group of central planners, such as the old Soviet Gosplan. That agency established production targets and prices for goods and services. Then the Gosplan transmitted this information to a second layer of specialized state planning agencies. One of these specialized government

---

EXHIBIT 1   The Command Economy Pyramid

The principal feature of a command economy is the central planning board at the top, which transmits economic decisions down to the various producing and consuming units below. This process begins with an overall plan from a supreme planning board, such as the old Soviet Gosplan. The Gosplan established production targets and was the ultimate authority over a layer of specialized planning agencies, which authorized capital expansion, raw material purchases, prices, wages, and all other production decisions for individual producing units. Finally, the factories, farms, mines, and other producers distributed the specified output to consumers according to the approved master plan.

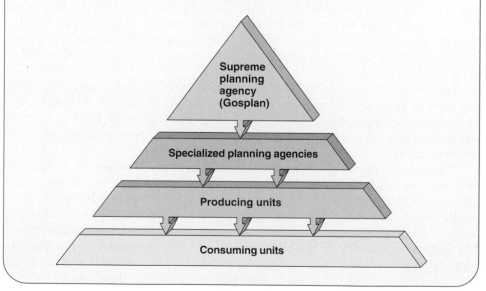

bureaucracies purchased raw materials, another agency established fashion trends, another set prices, and another government bureaucracy made decisions based on employment and wages.

Production objectives were transmitted from the upper authority layers to the individual producing units, represented by the third layer of the pyramid in Exhibit 1. These producers supplied goods and services to the consumers, as commanded by the central authorities. The bottom portion of the pyramid illustrates the distribution, according to the master plan, of output to consuming units of individuals and households.

The Command Economy's Strengths and Weaknesses

Believe it or not, the command system can be defended. Proponents argue that economic change occurs much faster than in a traditional economy. This is one reason those dissatisfied with a traditional society might advocate establishment of a command system. The central authorities can ignore custom and order new ways of doing things. Another reason for adopting a command economy is the controversial belief that the government will provide economic security and equity. It is alleged that central authorities ensure that everyone is provided food, clothing, shelter, and medical care regardless of their ability to contribute to society.

The absolute power of central authorities to make right decisions is also the power to be absolutely wrong. Often the planners do not set production goals accurately, and either shortages or surpluses of goods and services are the result. For example, at one point the planners miscalculated and produced too few windshield wipers and side mirrors for Soviet cars. Faced with shortages of these parts, Soviet drivers removed windshield wipers and side mirrors whenever they parked their cars to prevent theft. On the other hand, the Gosplan allocated some collective farms far more fertilizer than they could use. To receive the same amount of fertilizer again the next year, farmers simply burned the excess fertilizer. As a result of such decision-making errors, people waited in long lines or stole goods. How does any decision-making group really know how many windshield wipers to produce each year and how much workers making them should earn?

Because profit is not the motive of producers in a command economy, quality and variety of goods also suffer. If the Gosplan ordered a state enterprise to produce 400,000 side mirrors for cars, for example, producers had little incentive to make the extra effort required to create a quality product in a variety of styles. The easiest way to meet the goal was to produce a low-quality product in one style regardless of consumer demand.

Exhibit 2 illustrates how the pricing policy of central planners causes shortages. The demand curve for side mirrors conforms to the law of demand. At lower prices in rubles, the quantity demanded increases. The supply curve is fixed at 400,000 side mirrors because it is set by the central planners and is therefore unresponsive to price variations.

Suppose one of the principal goals of the command economy is to keep the price low. To reach this goal, the central planners set the price of side mirrors at 20 rubles, which is below the equilibrium price of 40 rubles. At 20 rubles, more people can afford a side mirror than at the equilibrium price set by an uncontrolled marketplace. The consequence of this lower price set by the planners is a shortage. The quantity demanded at 20 rubles is 800,000 side mirrors, and the quantity supplied is only 400,000 mirrors. Thus, the model explains why side mirrors disappeared from stores long before many who were willing to buy them could do so.

EXHIBIT 2 | Central Planners Fixing Prices

The central planners' goal is to keep prices low, so they set the price of a side mirror for a car at 20 rubles, which is below the market-determined equilibrium price of 40 rubles. At the set price, however, the quantity demanded is 800,000 side mirrors per year. Also set by the planners, the quantity supplied is 400,000 per year. Thus, the shortage at the government-established price is 400,000 side mirrors per year. As a result, long lines form to buy side mirrors, and black markets appear.

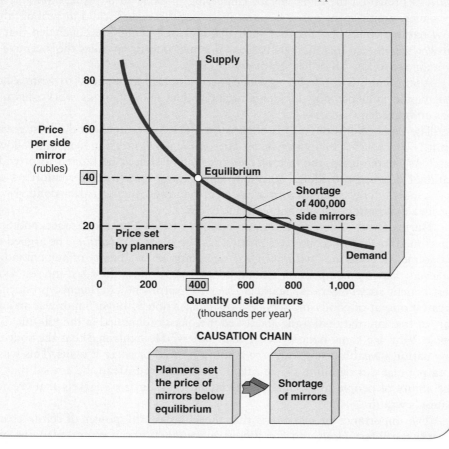

The same graphical analysis applies to centrally planned rental prices for apartments. The central planners in the former Soviet Union set rents below the equilibrium rental prices for apartments. As the model predicts, low rents resulted in a shortage of housing. Meanwhile, the planners promised that improvements in housing would come in time.

> **Conclusion** *When central planners set prices below equilibrium for goods and services, they create shortages, which mean long lines, empty shelves, and black markets.*[1]

---

1. Recall from Exhibit 5 of Chapter 4 that a black market is an illegal market that emerges when a price ceiling is imposed in a free market.

The Market Economy and the Ideas of Adam Smith

Market economy

An economic system that answers the *What, How,* and *For Whom* questions using prices determined by the interaction of the forces of supply and demand.

Adam Smith (1723–1790) The father of modern economics who wrote *The Wealth of Nations,* published in 1776.

Invisible hand

A phrase that expresses the belief that the best interests of a society are served when individual consumers and producers compete to achieve their own private interests.

In a market economy, neither customs nor a single person or group of central planners answers the three basic economic questions facing society. The market economy is an economic system that answers the *What, How,* and *For Whom* questions using prices determined by the interaction of the forces of supply and demand. One of the first people to explain the power of a market economy was the Scottish economist Adam Smith. In the same year that the American colonies declared their political independence, Smith's *An Inquiry into the Nature and Causes of the Wealth of Nations* presented the blueprint for employing markets to improve economic performance. Smith spent over 10 years observing the real world and writing about how nations could best improve their material well-being. He concluded that the answer was to use free markets because this mechanism provides the incentive for everyone to follow his or her *self-interest.*

Adam Smith is the *father of modern economics.* He intended to write a book that would influence popular opinion, and unlike many famous works, his book was an immediate success.

The basic philosophy of his book is "the best government is the least government." This belief is known as *laissez faire,* a French expression meaning "allow to act." As Smith stated, the role of the government should be limited to providing national defense, providing education, maintaining infrastructure, enforcing contracts, and little else. Smith also advocated free trade among nations and rejected the idea that nations should impose trade barriers.

During Smith's lifetime, European nations such as England, France, and Spain intervened to control economic activities. In *The Wealth of Nations,* he argued that economic freedoms are "natural rights" necessary for the dignity of humankind. He believed that free competition among people who follow their self-interest would best benefit society because markets free of government interference produce the greatest output of goods and services possible. As noted above, Smith was an advocate of free international trade and asked the question implied in the full title of his book: Why are some nations richer than others? He explained that the source of any nation's wealth is not really the amount of gold or silver it owns. This was an idea popular during Smith's time called *mercantilism.* Instead, he argued that it is the ability of people to produce products and trade in free markets that creates a nation's wealth.

The importance of markets is that they harness the power of self-interest to answer the *What, How,* and *For Whom* questions. Without central planning, markets coordinate the actions of millions of consumers and producers. Smith said that the market economy seemed to be controlled by an invisible hand. The invisible hand is a phrase that expresses the belief that the best interests of a society are served when individual consumers and producers compete to achieve their own private interests. Guided by an invisible hand, producers must compete with one another to win consumers' money. The *profit motive* in a competitive marketplace provides profits as a reward for efficient producers, while losses punish inefficient producers. Smith saw profit as the necessary driving force in an individualistic market system. The profit motive leads the butcher, the baker, and other producers to answer the *What, How,* and *For Whom* questions at the lowest prices. Consumers also compete with one another to purchase the best goods at the lowest price. Competition automatically regulates the economy and provides more goods and services than a system in which government attempts to accomplish the same task in the *public interest*. In Smith's own words:

> *Every individual necessarily labours to render the annual revenue of the society as great as he can. He generally, indeed, neither intends to promote the public interest, nor knows how much he is promoting it. By ... directing that industry in such a manner as its produce may be of the greatest value, he intends only his own gain, and he is in this, as in many other cases, led by an invisible hand to promote an end which was no part of his intention. Nor is it always the worse for the society that it was no part of it. By pursuing his own interest he frequently promotes that of the society more effectually than when he really intends to promote it.*[2]

The Market Economy's Strengths and Weaknesses

In a market system, if consumers want Beanie Babies, they can buy them because sellers seek to profit from the sale of Beanie Babies. No single person or central planning board makes a formal decision to shift resources and tell firms how to produce what many might view as a frivolous product. Because no central body or set of customs interferes, the market system provides a wide variety of goods and services that buyers and sellers exchange at the lowest prices.

> **Conclusion** *A market economy answers the What to produce and How to produce questions very effectively.*

Those who attack the market economy point out the market failure problems of lack of competition, externalities, public goods, and income inequality, discussed in Chapter 4. For example, critics contend that competition among buyers and sellers results in people who are very wealthy and people who are very poor. In a market economy, output is divided in favor of people who earn higher incomes and own property. Some people will dine on caviar in a fine restaurant, while others will wander the street and beg for food and shelter. Supporters of the market system argue that this inequality of income must exist to give people incentives or rewards for the value of their contributions to others.

The Mixed Economy

In the real world, no nation is a pure traditional, command, or market economy. Even primitive tribes employ a few markets in their system. For example, members of a tribe may exchange shells for animal skins. In China, the government allows many private shops and farms to operate in free markets. Although the United States is best described as a market economy, it is also a blend of the other two systems. As mentioned earlier, the Amish operate a well-known traditional economy in our nation. The draft during wartime is an example of a command economy in which the government obtains involuntary labor. In addition, taxes "commanded" from taxpayers fund government programs, such as national defense and Social Security. If the economic systems of most nations do not perfectly fit one of the

2. Adam Smith, *An Inquiry into the Nature and Causes of the Wealth of Nations* (1776; reprint, New York: Random House, 1937), p. 423.

GLOBAL ECONOMICS
Another Planet

Choosing an Economic System on

Applicable Concept: basic types of economic systems

Suppose we discover life on a new planet and the chief of their society learns of the successful economy of the United States and summons an economic advisor to learn the secret. Sitting at the head of a huge oval table, the chief addresses the advisor seated at the other end saying, "Our economic system depends on tradition and command. It works, but not nearly so well as the U.S. economy. Our men and women lead a highly tradition-bound way of life. Men farm and hunt like their forefathers. Women work only in the home and care for children following the role approved by their elders. There is no confusion over how things are done, and there is no chaos over what work, or what output will be produced. People are simply assigned jobs by their leaders and told how much to produce. Likewise, people are told to work on community projects for our planet's benefit. If anyone refuses to follow instructions, they are shunned or banished. Tell me, how could there possibly be a better way to organize our economy?" The advisor confidently responds, "Yes, there is definitely a better way. Replace tradition and command systems with the 'invisible hand' of the market system. This idea was explained long ago by a scholar named Adam Smith, the father of modern economics."

The chief is puzzled. "I have never heard of Adam Smith or the market economy. In a nutshell, explain to me how it differs from our system."

"Very well," says the advisor. "In a market economy, each person is allowed to decide for himself or herself what to do based on price signals."

The chief is horrified and takes umbrage. "But what happens when they do not choose correctly? Let's talk about something specific, like computer production. Unless we designate people to make computers, how do we know the right number will select this job? What if women want to work in this industry? Who decides how much these workers should be paid and how many computers should be produced to satisfy the demand for them?"

"You may rest assured," says the advisor. "Using prices determined in markets free from intervention will answer all your questions better than if leaders try to control everything."

The chief interrupts triumphantly. "Do you really expect me to believe that without instructions from the leaders, too few or too many products will not be bought and sold?"

"Ah, exactly!" the advisor quickly answers. "The market will automatically do all these wonderful things. People will be more motivated by their own rational self-interest than by tradition or central authority. In short, the system runs itself."

"The economy runs without my leaders' directions!" says the chief. "That's absurd, and you have wasted my time. I thought you had a meaningful proposal. Good day!"

ANALYZE THE ISSUE

1. Describe how a traditional or a command system would make employment and production decisions compared to a market system.

2. Why might the leader find a market system inconceivable? Is it possible for economic activities not based on self-interest to take place in a market economy?

Source: Adapted from Robert L. Heilbroner, *The Making of Economic Society*, 9/e, © 1993. Electronically reproduced by permission of Pearson Education, Inc., Upper Saddle River, NJ.

Mixed economy

An economic system that answers the *What, How,* and *For Whom* questions through a mixture of traditional, command, and market systems.

basic definitions, what term best describes their economies? A more appropriate description is that most countries employ a blend of the basic types of economic systems, broadly called a mixed economy. A mixed economy is a system that answers the *What, How,* and *For Whom* questions through a mixture of traditional, command, and market systems.

The traditional, command, and market economies can exist in a wide variety of political situations. For instance, the United States and Japan are politically "free" societies in which the market system flourishes. But China uses the market system to a limited degree in spite of its lack of political freedom. Moreover, some of the Western democracies engage in central economic planning. French officials representing government, business, and labor meet annually to discuss economic goals for industry for the next five-year period, but compliance is voluntary. In Japan, a government agency called the *Ministry of Economy, Trade and Industry (METI)* engages in long-term planning. One of the goals of the METI is to encourage exports so that Japan can earn the foreign currencies it needs to pay for oil and other resources.

The "ISMS"

What type of economic system will a society choose to answer the *What, How,* and *For Whom* questions? We could call most economies "mixed," but this would be too imprecise. In the real world, economic systems are labeled with various forms of the popular "isms"—capitalism, socialism, and communism—which are based on the basic types of systems.

Capitalism

The popular term for the market economy discussed previously is capitalism. *Capitalism is an economic system characterized by private ownership of resources and markets.* *Capitalism* is also called the *free enterprise system.* Regardless of its political system, a capitalist economic system must possess two characteristics: (1) private ownership of resources and (2) decentralized decision making using markets.

Private Ownership   Ownership of resources determines to a great degree who makes the *What, How,* and *For Whom* decisions. In a capitalist system, resources are primarily *privately* owned and controlled by individuals and firms, rather than having property rights be *publicly* held by government on behalf of society. In the United States, most capital resources are privately owned, but the term *capitalism* is somewhat confusing because it stresses private ownership of factories, raw materials, farms, and other forms of *capital* even though public ownership of land exists as well.

Decentralized Decision Making   This characteristic of capitalism allows buyers and sellers to exchange goods in markets without government involvement. A capitalist system operates on the principle of consumer sovereignty. Consumer sovereignty is the freedom of consumers to cast their dollar votes to buy, or not to buy, at prices determined in competitive markets. As a result, consumer spending determines what goods and services firms produce. In a capitalist system, most allocative decisions are coordinated by consumers and producers interacting through markets and making their own decisions guided by Adam Smith's invisible hand. Friedrick von Hayek, an Austrian economist who was a 1974 recipient of the Nobel Prize and author of *The Road to Serfdom,* argued that political and economic freedoms are inseparable.

In the real world, many U.S. markets are not perfectly open or free markets with the consumer as sovereign. For example, consumers cannot buy illegal drugs or body organs. In Chapter 4, you learned that the U.S. government sets minimum prices (support prices) for wheat, milk, cheese, and other products. These markets are free only if the market price is above the support price. Similarly, the minimum-wage law

Capitalism

An economic system characterized by private ownership of resources and markets.

Consumer sovereignty

The freedom of consumers to cast their dollar votes to buy, or not to buy, at prices determined in competitive markets.

forces employers to pay a wage above some dollar amount per hour regardless of market conditions.

> **Conclusion** *No nation in the world precisely fits the two criteria for capitalism; however, the United States comes close.*

Capitalism's Strengths and Weaknesses

One of the major strengths of capitalism is its capacity to achieve *economic efficiency* because competition and the profit motive force production at the lowest cost. Another strength of pure capitalism is *economic freedom* because economic power is widely dispersed. Individual consumers, producers, and workers are free to make decisions based on their own self-interest. Economist Milton Friedman makes a related point: Private ownership limits the power of government to deny goods, services, or jobs to their adversaries.

Critics of capitalism cite several shortcomings. First, capitalism tends toward an unequal distribution of income. This inequality of income among citizens results for several reasons. Private ownership of capital and the other factors of production can cause these factors to become concentrated in the hands of a few individuals or firms. Also, people do not have equal labor skills, and the marketplace rewards those with greater skills. These inequalities may be perpetuated because the rich can provide better education, legal aid, political platforms, and wealth to their heirs. Second, pure capitalism is criticized for its failure to protect the environment. The pursuit of profit and self-interest can take precedence over damage or pollution to the air, rivers, lakes, and streams. Recall the graphical model used in Chapter 4 to illustrate the socially unacceptable impact of producers who pollute the environment.

Socialism

Socialism

An economic system characterized by government ownership of resources and centralized decision making.

The idea of socialism has existed for thousands of years. Its basis is the command system. Socialism is an economic system characterized by government ownership of resources and centralized decision making. Socialism is also called *command socialism*. Under a socialist economy, a command system owns and controls in the *public interest* the major industries, such as steel, electricity, and agriculture. However, some free markets can exist in farming, retail trade, and certain service areas. Just as no pure capitalist system exists in the real world, none of the socialist countries in the world today practices pure socialism. In fact, there are as many variants of socialism as there are countries called socialist.

Before discussing socialism further, you must realize that socialism is an economic system, and politics should not be confused with economics. Great Britain, France, and Italy have representative democracies, but many of their major industries are or have been nationalized. In the United States, the federal government owns and operates the Tennessee Valley Authority (TVA), the National Aeronautics and Space Administration (NASA), and the U.S. Postal Service, while at the same time allowing private utilities and mail service firms to operate.

The Ideas of Karl Marx

Despite the transition to capitalism in Russia and Eastern Europe, socialism still prevails in China, Cuba, and many less-developed countries. The theory for socialism and *communism* can be traced to Karl Marx. Marx was a nineteenth-century German philosopher, revolutionary, and economist. Unlike other economists of the time who followed Adam Smith, Marx rejected the concept of a society operating through private interest and profit.

Karl Marx was born in Germany, the son of a lawyer. He was an outstanding student at Berlin University. In 1841, after receiving a doctorate in philosophy, he turned to journalism. In 1843, Marx married the daughter of a wealthy family and moved to Paris, but his political activities forced him to leave Paris for England. From the age of 31, he lived and wrote his books in London. In London, Marx lived an impoverished life while he and his lifelong friend Friedrich Engels wrote the *Communist Manifesto,* published in 1848. A massive work followed, titled *Das Kapital,* which was published in three volumes in 1867, 1884, and 1885.

These two works made Karl Marx the most influential economist in the history of socialism. In fact, he devoted his entire life to a revolt against capitalism. As Marx read *The Wealth of Nations,* he saw profits as unjust payments to owners of firms—the capitalists. Marx predicted that the market system would destroy itself because wealthy owners would go too far and exploit workers because unrelenting greed for profits would lead the owners to pay starvation wages. Moreover, the owners would force laborers to work in unsafe conditions, and many would not have a job at all.

Marx believed that private ownership and exploitation would produce a nation driven by a class struggle between a few "haves" and many "have-nots." As he stated in the *Communist Manifesto,* "The history of all existing society is the history of class struggle. Freeman and slave, patrician and plebeian, lord and serf, guildmaster and journeyman, in a word, oppressor and oppressed."[3] In Marx's vision, capitalists were the modern-day oppressors, and the workers were the oppressed proletariat. Someday, Marx predicted, the workers would rise up in a spontaneous bloody revolution against a system benefiting only the owners of capital. Marx believed communism to be the ideal system, which would evolve in stages from capitalism through socialism. Communism is a stateless, classless economic system in which all the factors of production are owned by the workers and people share in production according to their needs. This is the highest form of socialism toward which the revolution should strive.

Under communism, no private property exists to encourage self-interest. There is no struggle between classes of people, and everyone cooperates. In fact, there is no reason to commit crime, and police, lawyers, and courts are unnecessary. Strangely, Marx surpassed Adam Smith in advocating a system with little central government. Marx believed that those who work hard, or are more skilled, will be public spirited. Any "haves" will give voluntarily to "have-nots" until everyone has exactly the same material well-being. In Marx's own words, people would be motivated by the principle "from each according to his ability, to each according to his need." World peace would evolve as nation after nation accepted cooperation and rejected profits and competition. Under the idealized society of communism, there would be no state. No central authority would be necessary to pursue the interests of the people.

Today, we call the economic systems that existed in the former Soviet Union and Eastern Europe, and still exist in China, Cuba, and other countries *communist*. However, the definition for *socialism* given in this chapter more accurately describes their real-world economic systems. Actually, no nation has achieved the ideal communist society described by Marx, nor has capitalism self-destructed as he predicted. The 1917 communist revolution in Russia did not fit Marx's theory. At that time, Russia was an underdeveloped country, rather than an industrial country filled with greedy capitalists who exploited workers.

Karl Marx (1818–1883) His criticism of capitalism advanced communism. He wrote *Communist Manifesto* and *Das Kapital.*

The Print Collector/Alamy

Communism

A stateless, classless economic system in which all the factors of production are owned by the workers, and people share in production according to their needs. In Marx's view, this is the highest form of socialism toward which the revolution should strive.

3.   Karl Marx and Friedrich Engels, *The Communist Manifesto* (New York: International Press, 1848), p. 31.

Characteristics of Socialism

Regardless of a society's political system, a socialist economy has two basic characteristics: (1) public ownership and (2) centralized decision making.

Public Ownership   Under socialism, the government owns most of the factors of production, including factories, farms, mines, and natural resources. Agriculture in the old Soviet Union illustrates how even this real-world socialist country deviated from total public ownership. In the Soviet Union, there were three rather distinct forms of agriculture: state farms, collective farms, and private plots. In both the state-farm and the collective-farm sectors, central planning authorities determined prices and outputs. In contrast, the government allowed those holding small private plots on peasant farms to operate primarily in free markets that determined price and output levels. Reforms now allow farmers to buy land, tractors, trucks, and other resources from the state. If these reforms continue, they will dramatically end the collectivization of agriculture begun under Josef Stalin.

Centralized Decision Making   Instead of the pursuit of *private interest,* the motivation of pure socialism is the *public interest* of the whole society. For instance, a factory manager cannot decide to raise or lower prices to obtain maximum profits for the factory. Regardless of inventory levels or the opportunity to raise prices, the planners will not permit this action. Instead of exploiting the ups and downs of the market, the goal of the socialist system is to make centralized decisions that protect workers and consumers from decentralized market decisions. Critics argue that the main objective of this centralization is to perpetuate the personal dictatorships of leaders such as Stalin in the old Soviet Union and Fidel Castro in Cuba.

Before the open market reforms, Soviet planners altered earnings to attract workers into certain occupations and achieve planned goals. For example, if space projects needed more engineers, then the state raised the earnings of engineers until the target number of people entered the engineering profession.

As shown earlier in Exhibit 2, central planners in the Soviet Union also manipulated consumer prices. If consumers desired more cars than were available, the authorities increased the price of cars. If people wished to purchase less of an item than was available, planners lowered prices. The problem was that this decision process took time. And while the market awaited its orders from the Soviet planners, excess inventories of some items accumulated, and consumers stood in line for cheap products that never seemed to be available. There was an old Soviet saying, "If you see a line, get in it. Whatever it is, it's scarce, and you will not see it tomorrow."

The Soviet factory system did not adhere completely to the command system. The government rewarded successful managers with bonuses that could be substantial. Better apartments, nice vacations, and medals were incentives for outstanding performance. Under economic reforms, plant managers now make decisions based on profitability instead of centralized controls.

CHECKPOINT

To Plan or Not to Plan—That Is the Question

You make plans. You planned to go to college. You plan which career to follow. You plan to get married, and so on. Businesses plan. They plan to hire employees, expand their plants, increase profits, and so forth. Because individuals and businesses plan in a market economy, there is really no difference between our system and a command economy. Or is there?

Socialism's Strengths and Weaknesses

Proponents of the socialism model argue that this system is superior in achieving an equitable distribution of income. This is because government ownership of capital and other resources prevents a few individuals or groups from acquiring a disproportionate share of the nation's wealth. Also, supporters argue that rapid economic growth is achieved when planners have the power to direct more resources to producing capital goods and fewer resources to producing consumer goods (see Exhibit 5 of Chapter 2).

National goals may seem to be easily formulated and pursued under state directives, but there are problems. For example, proponents of such an economy can claim there is no unemployment because the government assigns all workers a job and allocates resources to complete their production goals. However, economic inefficiency results because the government often uses many workers to perform work requiring only one or two workers. Critics also point out that the absence of the profit motive discourages entrepreneurship and innovation and thus suppresses economic growth.

Socialism is particularly vulnerable to the charge that it ignores the goal of economic freedom and instead creates a privileged class of government bureaucrats who assume the role of "capitalists." Central planners are the key translators of information about consumer preferences and production capabilities flowing to millions of economic units. This complex and cumbersome process is subject to errors and unresponsiveness to the wants of the majority of the population. Critics also question whether the distribution of income under socialism is more equitable than under capitalism. In the socialist system, "perks" for government officials, nepotism, and the illegal use of markets create disparities in income.

Comparing Economic Systems

In reality, all nations operate economic systems that blend capitalism and socialism. Exhibit 3 presents a continuum that attempts to place countries between the two extremes of pure socialism on the left and pure capitalism on the right. Economies

---

EXHIBIT 3   A Classification of Economic Systems

No nation has an economic system that is pure socialism or pure capitalism. All nations mix government ownership and reliance on markets. North Korea and Cuba are closest to pure socialism, while Hong Kong comes closest to pure capitalism. Other real-world economies are placed between these two extremes on the basis of their use of government ownership versus markets.

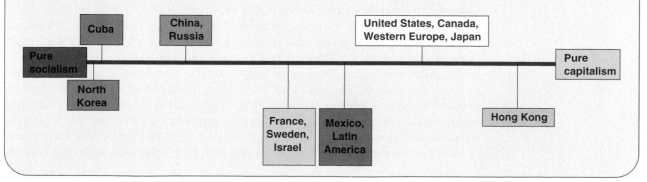

characterized by a high degree of both private ownership and market allocation are closest to pure capitalism. Hong Kong (now part of China), Japan, the United States, and Canada fall at the capitalism end of the line. Conversely, economies characterized by much government ownership of resources and central planning are closest to pure socialism. North Korea and Cuba fall close to the pure socialism end of the spectrum, with China and Russia further away from pure socialism.

Economies in Transition

By the early 1990s, the centrally planned economies in the old Soviet Union and Eastern Europe had collapsed. After more than 70 years in the Soviet Union and over 40 years in Eastern Europe and China, the failed communist economies made a startling switch to embrace capitalism. Faced with severe shortages of food, housing, cars, and other consumer goods, communism could no longer claim better living standards for its citizens. The following is a brief discussion of reforms aimed at introducing market power into the economic systems of Cuba, Russia, and China.

Cuba

Cuba often experiences daily power blackouts, fuel shortages, housing shortages, and other economic hardships. But regardless of its economics woes, Cuba remains wedded to the communist system. Nevertheless, the collapse of Soviet bloc aid coupled with the effects of the U.S. trade embargo have forced Fidel Castro and the country's new leader, Raul Castro, die-hard Marxists, to reluctantly adopt limited free market reforms. To earn foreign exchange, the dollar has been legalized, and the Cuban government has poured capital into tourism by building several new state-owned hotels and restoring historic sections of Havana. Interestingly, Cuba operates special medical tourist hospitals that treat foreigners and diplomats, while excluding Cubans. Cuba has also set up quasi-state enterprises that accept only hard currency. Because few Cubans have dollars or other hard currency, many are earning it by turning to illegal schemes, such as driving gypsy cabs, engaging in prostitution, or selling Cuba's famous cigars and coffee on the black market. Other Cubans have abandoned state jobs and opened small businesses under these new rules. However, these small-scale businesses cannot employ anyone beyond the family of the owner. Also, spare rooms in houses can be rented, and artisans can sell their work to tourists. In addition, state farm enterprises have been broken into worker-owned units, and the government allows farmers to sell produce leftover after they have met the state's quota. As a result of this free market, some farmers have become venture capitalists, and more food, and a greater variety of food, are becoming available. In 2008, a series of changes opened access to cell phones, computers, and DVD players. Cubans are now also allowed to patronize tourist hotels. However, such luxuries are prohibitive for most Cubans.

Despite the private enterprise reforms, Cuba remains essentially a communist system. Workers receive free education, housing, health care, low state salaries in pesos, and rations of staples, such as a monthly allowance of rice, beans, and milk. Profits from hotels and shops go directly into the central bank and help finance Castro's government. The state also discourages private enterprises by taxing them heavily on expected earnings, rather than on actual sales. In addition, there are highly restrictive regulations. For example, restaurants in Havana are limited to 12 seats and cannot expand regardless of demand. And Cuba has halted new licenses for some types of self-employment, including jewelers, mousetrap makers, and magicians or clowns. Currently, Hugo Chavez, president of Venezuela, is using his country's tremendous oil reserves to throw Cuba an economic lifeline and counter the U.S. embargo against Cuba.

Russia

In 1991, communist rule ended in Russia. To function efficiently, markets must offer incentives, so workers, the public, and even foreign investors were permitted to buy state property. This meant individuals could own the factors of production and earn profits. Such market incentives were a dagger thrust into the heart of a system previously devoted to rejecting capitalism.

A key reform for Russia was to allow supply and demand to set higher prices for basic consumer goods. As shown earlier in Exhibit 2, without central planners, when prices rise to their equilibrium level, the quantity supplied increases and the quantity demanded decreases. At the beginning of 1992, the Russian government removed direct government price controls on most market goods. As the model predicts, average prices rose, leaping 1,735 percent in 1992, and a greater variety of goods started appearing on the shelves. Although workers had to pay more for basic consumer goods, they could at least find goods to buy.

Since 1992, Russia has established an independent central bank and implemented anti-inflationary monetary policies. As a result, the inflation rate fell to 15 percent in 1997. By 2007, the inflation rate had fallen to 8 percent and Russians have become accustomed to high growth rates in real GDP in excess of 6 percent. Cities throughout Russa now have restaurants, megamalls, decent hotels, and streets choked with foreign cars. Russian entrepreneurial spirit and acceptance of it in society is in an embryonic stage, and corruption, including the legal system, is a frequent way of life. Today, Russia's economy is heavily dependent on oil and natural gas exports. Russia holds the world's largest natural gas reserves, and the eighth largest oil reserves. Although Russia is far from a successful market economy, the nation is struggling to achieve an amazing economic transition. Russian privatization plans are being implemented and steps are continuing to create a dynamic economy embracing capitalism. And *Forbes* magazine reports that there are now several billionaires who reside in Russia.

The People's Republic of China

Unlike Russia, China has sought economic reform under the direction of its Communist Party. Fundamental economic reforms began in China after the death of Mao Tse-Tung in 1976. Much of this reform was due to the leadership of Deng Xiaoping. Mao was devoted to the egalitarian ideal of communist ideology. Under his rule, thoughts of self-interest were counterrevolutionary, and photographs of Marx, Lenin, and Mao hung on every street corner and in every office and factory. Deng shifted priorities by increasing production of consumer goods and steering China toward becoming a global economic power. And the results have been dramatic. International trade expanded from less than 1 percent of U.S. trade in 1975 to 10 percent in 2007. China joined the WTO in 2001 and agreed to open some markets closed to foreigners. China's real GDP growth rate averaged 9.8 percent between 2001 and 2007, making it the world's fastest growing economy.

To make China an industrial power in the twenty-first century, Chinese planners introduced a two-tier system for industry and agriculture in 1978. Each farm and state enterprise was given a contract to produce a quota. Any amount produced

Applicable Concept: comparative economic systems

Gavin Heller/Jupiter images

For more than 2,000 years, China had a "self reliance" policy that caused its economy to lag far behind advanced economies. In 1978, China adopted new economic reforms that are continuing to transform one of the poorest economies in the world into one of the fastest growing. Under this reform system, households operate in a mixed world of state controls and free markets. A two-track pricing system still exists for some key goods and services, such as coal, petroleum, steel, transportation, and agriculture. The rural economy is central to China's economic reforms. In the past, farmers worked collectively in people's communes. The government told the farmers what to produce and how much to produce. They could sell their products only to the state at a price fixed by the government, rather than in markets. A so-called household contract responsibility system was created as a reform to assign land owned by the state to farmers. The farmers must pay an annual share of their profits to the government, and the state does not cover losses. Farmers, however, have the authority to decide what to produce and the price at which to sell in open markets. As a result, both farmers and consumers are noticeably better off because everyone can find and afford more food.

As farming productivity rose sharply, fewer farmers were needed to work on the land, and this surplus labor moved into emerging township and village nonstate enterprises. These enterprises were mostly in light industry and owned collectively by townships or villages. As a result, the composition of rural output has changed. When the reforms began in the late 1970s, farming accounted for 70 percent of the total rural output and industry for 20 percent. Currently, the over the quota could be sold in an open market. The Chinese government also encouraged the formation of nonstate enterprises owned jointly by managers and their workforces and special economic zones open to foreign investment. In other words, a blend of capitalism and socialism would provide the incentives needed to increase output. As Deng Xiaoping explained, "It doesn't matter whether the cat is black or white as long as it catches mice." These reforms worked, leading to huge increases in farm and industrial output in the 1980s. In fact, some peasant farmers became the wealthiest people in China. After Deng's death in the mid-1990s, leadership of China passed to leaders who continued the policy of free market reforms. Today, forests of glossy skyscrapers, expressways, upscale apartments, and enormous shopping malls in Beijing, Shanghai, and other cities attest to the market-oriented reforms begun years ago. And life in China's fast lane now includes the opportunity of dining at Kentucky Fried Chicken and McDonalds restaurants located in cities throughout the country. Also, despite government censorship, China has the largest number of Internet users in the world. (See *Global Economics: China's Quest for Free Market Reform.*)

Today, China is a huge nation transforming itself swiftly into a powerful player in the global economy. U.S. exporters are overjoyed at the prospect of selling products to over a billion Chinese consumers. For example, swarms of bicyclists

structure of the economy has changed dramatically. In 2006, agriculture accounted for only 13 percent of GDP and industry's share had risen to 48 percent.[1]

A 1993 article in the *Boston Globe* provides an interesting observation on China's economic transformation:

> Stuffing the genie back into the bottle might prove difficult. The flood of money has created a bubble, particularly in stocks and property, making some people in China very rich, very fast. The China Daily, China's official English-language newspaper, recently heralded the existence of 1 million millionaires.... These millionaires, many of whom just five years ago were still wearing Mao outfits and following the party's socialist-dictates, now sport stylish Western-style suits with the label ostentatiously left on the cuff.[2]

A 2001 *Time* article described China's controversial womb police, who have spent two decades attempting to control the nation's population by fining citizens with more than one child. They have succeeded remarkably well. Today, the average Chinese woman has two children, compared with six 30 years ago. "For all the bad press, China has achieved the impossible," says Sven Burmester, the U.N. Population Fund representative in Beijing.

"The country has solved its population problem." In fact, China's population will actually start declining in 2042, according to U.N. projections.[3]

At the sixteenth Communist Party Congress in 2003, President Hu Jintao and Communist Party leaders announced "another turning point and a new starting point in China's reform process." A key debate concerned reforms that would move China closer to capitalism, including the first-ever guarantee of private property under communist rule.[4] In 2006, *USA Today* reported that China has 15 billionaires, and Rupert Hoogewerft, CEO of *Human Report*, says China's recent surge in mega-wealth is "comparable to the U.S. at the end of the 19th century, when you had the Rockefellers and Carnegies."[5]

ANALYZE THE ISSUE

1. Why would China abandon the goal of income equality and shift from a centrally planned system to a more market-oriented economy?

2. Which groups in China are likely to resist the reforms?

1. The World Bank, *Key Development Data & Statistics*, http://www.worldbank.org/.
2. Maggie Farley, "China's Economic Boom Energizing Inflation," *Boston Globe*, Aug. 13, 1993, p. 1A.
3. "China's Lifestyle Choice: Changes to the Famous One-Child Policy Miss the Point," *Time*, Aug. 6, 2001, p. 32.
4. Joe McDonald, "China Debates Private Property," *Sun News*, Oct. 12, 2003, p. 14A.
5. Calum MacLeod, "Worth on 'Forges' List Jumps for Communist Country's Rich," *USA Today*, Nov. 2, 2006, p. 1A.

once synonymous with urban China are being pushed off the road by consumers who now can afford cars and trucks. Rolls-Royce and Bentley, the ultra-luxury cars, have expanded into China, and it is estimated that by 2030 China will have more cars on the road than the United States Also, more Chinese are traveling by air. Consequently, the Chinese are buying more Boeing airplanes and American-made cars. The other side of the coin is the threat of what goods the industrious Chinese workers, with increasing training and foreign investment, might produce and sell abroad. For example, China manufactures most of the world's copiers, microwave ovens, DVD players, and shoes. A ballooning United States trade deficit with China is often cited as evidence that China is not playing fair, and the political rhetoric has intensified on both sides of the issue. Other countries fear that China will eliminate their export business with the United States. Moreover, there is concern that lowering trade barriers under free trade agreements will increase Chinese imports into domestic markets and eliminate jobs. In 2007, one Chinese-made product after another was removed from U.S. shelves, for example, lethal pet food, toxic toothpaste, and other contaminated products. This prompted calls for more stringent safety regulations for imports.

Currently, China's leaders are dealing with an economy that is experiencing overheating. Factories suffer electricity shortages, while ports and railways cannot handle all the cargo flowing in and out of the country. China is consuming huge quantities of crude oil, copper, steel, and aluminum. Moreover, there is discontent over labor issues, pollution, and income inequality. While some dig through trash bins, there are now wealthy private business owners. Despite the unease, China remains a market of great profit and promise as it continues its transition from a communist command economy to capitalism. In 2008, China announced the largest stimulus package in its history to counter the impact of the global economic downturn. And the debate continues over whether China, a socialist economy, is a strategic trading partner or an emerging rival that will dominate the world economy.

KEY CONCEPTS

Economic system
Traditional economy
Command economy
Market economy

Invisible hand
Mixed economy
Capitalism
Consumer sovereignty

Socialism
Communism

SUMMARY

- An *economic system* is the set of established procedures by which a society answers the *What, How,* and *For Whom to produce* questions.
- *Three basic types of economic systems* are the traditional, command, and market systems. The *traditional system* makes decisions according to custom, and the *command system,* shown in the figure below, answers the three economic questions through some powerful central authority. In contrast, the *market system* uses the impersonal mechanism of the interaction of buyers and sellers in markets to answer the *What, How,* and *For Whom* questions.

Command Economy

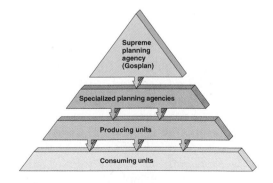

- *Capitalism* is an economic system in which the factors of production are privately owned and economic choices are made by consumers and firms in markets. As prescribed by Adam Smith, government plays an extremely limited role, and self-interest is the driving force, held in check, or regulated, by competition.
- *Consumer sovereignty* is the freedom of consumers to determine the types and quantities of products that are produced in an economy by choosing to buy or not to buy.
- *Socialism* is an economic system in which the government owns the factors of production.

The central authorities make the myriad of society's economic decisions according to a national plan. The collective good, or public interest, is the intended guiding force behind the central planners' decisions.
- *Communism* is an economic system envisioned by Karl Marx to be an ideal society in which the workers own all the factors of production. Marx believed that workers who work hard will be public spirited and voluntarily redistribute income to those who are less productive. Such a communist nation described by Marx does not exist.

SUMMARY OF CONCLUSION STATEMENTS

- When central planners set prices below equilibrium for goods and services, they create shortages, which mean long lines, empty shelves, and black markets.
- A market economy answers the *What* to produce and *How* to produce questions very effectively.

- No nation in the world precisely fits the two criteria for capitalism; however, the United States comes close.

STUDY QUESTIONS AND PROBLEMS

1. Give an example of how a nation's culture affects its economic system.

2. Explain the advantages and the disadvantages of any two of the three basic types of economic systems.

3. Suppose a national program of free housing for the elderly is paid for by a sizable increase in income taxes. Explain a tradeoff that might occur between economic security and efficiency.

4. "The schools are not in the business of pleasing parents and students, and they cannot be allowed to set their own agendas. Their agendas are set by politicians, administrators, and various constituencies that hold the keys to political power. The public system is built to see to it that the schools do what their government wants them to do—that they conform to the higher-order values their governors seek to impose."[4] Relate this statement to Exhibit 1.

5. Suppose you are a farmer. Explain why you would be motivated to work in traditional, command, and market economies.

6. Karl Marx believed the market system was doomed. Why do you think he was right or wrong?

---
4. John Chubb and Terry More, *Politics, Markets, and the Nation's Public Schools* (Washington, D.C.: Brookings Institution, 1990), p. 38.

7. If all real-world economies are mixed economies, why is the U.S. economy described as capitalist, while the Cuban economy is described as communist?

8. Suppose you are a factory manager. Describe how you might reach production goals under a system of pure capitalism and under a system of pure socialism.

For online Exercises, go the text Web site at www.cengage.com/economics/tucker.

CHECKPOINT ANSWER ✓

To Plan or Not to Plan—That Is the Question

When an individual or a business plans in a market economy, other individuals are free to make and follow their own plans. Suppose Hewlett-Packard decides to produce X number of laser printers and sell them at a certain price. The decision does not prohibit IBM from producing Y number of laser printers and selling them for less than Hewlett Packard's printers.

If either firm makes a mistake, only that firm suffers, and other industries are for the most part unaffected. Under a command system, a central economic plan would be made for all laser printer manufacturers. If the central planners order the wrong quantity or quality, there could be major harm to other industries and society. If you said there is a major difference between individual planning and central planning for all society, **YOU ARE CORRECT.**

PRACTICE QUIZ

For visual explanation of the correct answers, please visit the tutorial at www.cengage.com/economics/tucker.

1. The economic system in which all of the basic decisions are made through a centralized authority, such as a government agency, is termed a
   a. market economy.
   b. capitalistic economy.
   c. command economy.
   d. traditional economy.

2. Command economies typically suffer from
   a. unemployment, but not underemployment.
   b. neither unemployment nor underemployment.
   c. both unemployment and underemployment.
   d. underemployment, but not unemployment.

3. Adam Smith stated that the role of government in society should be to
   a. provide defense.
   b. enforce contracts.
   c. do absolutely nothing.
   d. do both (a) and (b).

4. When making economic decisions, Adam Smith urged society to
   a. follow the principle of self interest.
   b. follow the principle of public interest.
   c. transfer wealth according to need.
   d. provide equal income for all citizens.

5. The doctrine of *laissez faire*
   a. advocates an economic system with extensive government intervention and little individual decision making.
   b. was advocated by Adam Smith in his book *The Wealth of Nations*.
   c. was advocated by Karl Marx in his book *Das Kapital*.
   d. is described by none of the above.

6. In Adam Smith's competitive market economy, the question of what goods to produce is determined by the
   a. "invisible hand" of the price system.
   b. "invisible hand" of government.
   c. "visible hand" of public interest.
   d. "visible hand" of laws and regulations.

7. Adam Smith wrote that the
   a. economic problems of eighteenth-century England were caused by free markets.
   b. government should control the economy with an "invisible hand."
   c. pursuit of private self interest promotes the public interest in a market economy.
   d. public or collective interest is not promoted by people pursuing their self interest.

8. Adam Smith, in his book *The Wealth of Nations*, advocated
   a. socialism.
   b. an economy guided by an "invisible hand."
   c. government control of the "invisible hand."
   d. the adoption of mercantilism.

9. The economic system in which private individuals own the factors of production is
   a. a planned economy.
   b. capitalism.
   c. collectivism.
   d. socialism.

10. Which of the following is *not* a basic characteristic of capitalism?
    a. Economic decisions occur in markets.
    b. Factors of production are privately owned.
    c. Income is distributed on the basis of need.
    d. Businesses make their own product and price decisions.

11. According to Karl Marx, under capitalism,
    a. profits would be shared fairly.
    b. incomes would be distributed equally.
    c. workers would be exploited and revolt against owners of capital.
    d. workers would actually own the factors of production.

12. Karl Marx predicted which of the following?
    a. The market system would self-destruct.
    b. The "haves" would revolt against the "have-nots."
    c. The wealthy were entitled to profits as their reward for risk taking.
    d. None of the above.

13. How many nations in the world today operate totally according to Karl Marx's theory of communism?
    a. None
    b. Several
    c. Only the United States
    d. Many

14. In Marx's ideal communist society, the state
    a. actively promotes income equality.
    b. follows the doctrine of *laissez faire*.
    c. owns resources and conducts planning.
    d. does not exist.

15. Karl Marx was a (an)
    a. nineteenth-century German philosopher.
    b. eighteenth-century Russian economist.
    c. fourteenth-century Polish banker.
    d. nineteenth-century Russian journalist.

Growth and the Less-Developed Countries

H ow would your life be different if you lived in Rwanda or Haiti instead of the United States? It is unlikely that anyone in your family would have a telephone or a car. You surely would not own a personal computer or a compact disc player. You would not have new clothes and be enrolled in a college or university studying economics. You would not be going out to restaurants or movies. You would be fortunate to have shoes and one full meal each day. You would receive little or no medical care and live in unsanitary surroundings. Hunger, disease, and squalor would engulf you. In fact, the World Bank estimates that over 20 percent of people in developing countries survive on less than $1 per day.

It is exceedingly difficult for Americans to grasp that one-fifth of the world's population lives at such a meager subsistence level. This brings us to this chapter's important task of unraveling the secrets of economic growth and development. Why do some countries prosper while others decline?

At different times in history, Egypt, China, Italy, and Greece were highly developed by the standards of their time. On the other hand, at one time the United States was a struggling, relatively poor country on the path to becoming a rich country. Its growth came in three stages: First, was the agricultural stage. Then came the manufacturing stage when industries such as railroads, steel, and automobiles were driving forces toward economic growth. And, finally, there has been a shift toward service industries. This is the U.S. success story, but it is not the only road countries can follow to lift themselves from the misery of poverty.

In this chapter, you will learn
to solve these economic puzzles:

- Is there a difference between economic growth and economic development?

- Why are some countries rich and others poor?

- Is trade a better "engine of growth" than foreign aid and loans?

Comparing Developed and Less-Developed Countries

Income disparity exists not only among families within the United States but also among nations. In this section, the great inequality of income between the families of nations will be used to classify nations as rich or poor.

Classifying Countries by GDP per Capita

There are about 225 countries in the world. Exhibit 1 shows a ranking of selected countries from high to low GDP per capita. GDP per capita is the value of final goods produced (GDP) divided by the total population. Although any system of defining rich versus poor countries is arbitrary, GDP per capita or average GDP is a fundamental measure of a country's economic well-being. At the top of the income ladder are 27 developed countries called the industrially advanced countries (IACs). Industrially advanced countries are high-income nations that have market economies based on large stocks of technologically advanced capital and well-educated labor. The United States, Canada, Australia, New Zealand, Japan, and most of the countries of Western Europe are IACs. Excluded from the IACs are countries with high incomes whose economies are based on oil under the sand, and not on widespread industrial development. The United Arab Emirates is an example of such a country.

Countries of the world other than IACs are classified as underdeveloped or less-developed countries (LDCs). Less-developed countries are nations without large stocks of technologically advanced capital and well-educated labor. Their economies are based on agriculture, as in most countries of Africa, Asia, and Latin America. Over three-fourths of the world's population, consisting of about 150 countries, live in LDCs and share widespread poverty.

A closer examination of Exhibit 1 reveals that the differences in living standards between the IACs and LDCs are enormous. For example, the GDP per capita in the United States was $45,490 greater than the average income in Ethiopia. Stated differently, the 2007 average income in the United States was about 224 times larger than the average income in Ethiopia ($45,490/$203). What a difference! Imagine trying to live on only $203 for a year in the United States. You probably would not survive.

Exhibit 2 compares GDP per capita for IACs to LDCs by regions of the world for 2007. The average citizen in the IACs enjoyed an income of $40,226, which was

GDP per capita
The value of final goods produced (GDP) divided by the total population.

Industrially advanced countries (IACs)
High-income nations that have market economies based on large stocks of technologically advanced capital and well-educated labor. The United States, Canada, Australia, New Zealand, Japan, and most of the countries of Western Europe are IACs.

Less-developed countries (LDCs)
Nations without large stocks of technologically advanced capital and well-educated labor. LDCs are economies based on agriculture, such as most countries of Africa, Asia, and Latin America.

EXHIBIT 1	Annual GDP per Capita for Selected Countries, 2007		
Country	**GDP per capita**	**Country**	**GDP per capita**
Industrially Advanced Countries (IACs)			
Luxembourg	$93,301	France	37,899
Norway	74,848	Germany	37,746
Switzerland	53,352	Australia	39,320
Ireland	58,168	Italy	34,120
Denmark	55,603	Spain	30,289
United States	45,490	Singapore	32,506
Sweden	46,400	New Zealand	27,285
Netherlands	43,386	Hong Kong	28,982
Austria	42,126	Greece	30,603
Japan	33,668	Israel	21,220
Finland	42,878	Portugal	20,029
United Kingdom	43,735	South Korea	19,485
Belgium	39,798	Taiwan	15,759
Canada	38,382		
Less-Developed Countries (LDCs)			
Mexico	8,530	China	2,310
Chile	9,026	Egypt	1,755
Russia	8,209	Indonesia	1,812
South Africa	5,680	Bolivia	1,212
Turkey	5,882	Georgia	2,123
Panama	5,571	Pakistan	893
Brazil	6,220	India	871
Romania	7,311	Vietnam	798
Iran	3,184	Haiti	590
Thailand	3,304	Bangladesh	486
Jordan	2,778	Mozambique	382
Ukraine	2,649	Rwanda	287
Morocco	2,028	Ethiopia	203

SOURCE: International Monetary Fund, *World Economic Outlook Database*, http://www.imf.org/external/pubs/ft/weo/2007/01/data/weoselgr.aspx.

EXHIBIT 2	Average GDP per Capita for IACs and LDCs by Region, 2007

This exhibit shows average GDP per capita by regions of the world for 2007. The differences between the rich, industrially advanced countries (IACs) and the poor less-developed countries (LDCs) in the various regions of the world are enormous. For example, the average citizen in the IACs had an income 52 times that of the average citizen in the LDCs of South Asia.

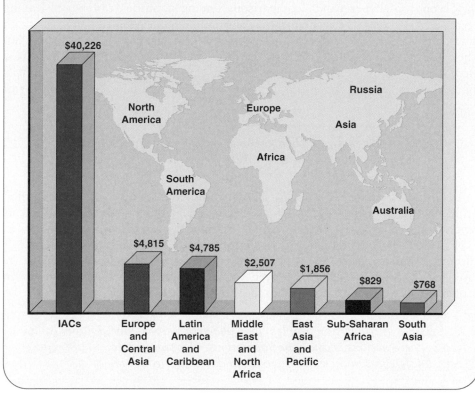

SOURCE: World Bank Group, *Key Development Data & Statistics*, http://www.worldbank.org.

52 times that of the average citizen in South Asia ($40,266/$768). The exhibit also reveals that the greatest concentrations of world poverty are located in the rural areas of South Asia and Sub-Saharan Africa. The East Asia and Pacific region has many countries characterized by bleak and pervasive poverty, but there are notable exceptions, nicknamed the "Four Tigers" of East Asia—Hong Kong, Singapore, South Korea, and Taiwan. These Pacific Rim countries are newly industrialized economies, which we discuss at the end of this chapter.

Problems with GDP per Capita Comparisons

Several problems are associated with using GDP per capita to compare rich versus poor countries. First, there is a measurement problem because countries tabulate GDP with differing degrees of accuracy. LDCs in general do not use sophisticated methods of gathering and processing GDP and population data. For example, in countries whose economies are based largely on agriculture, a family is more likely to produce goods and services outside the price system. In LDCs, families often grow their own food, make their own clothes, and build their own homes. Estimating the value of this output at market prices is difficult.

> **Conclusion** *LDCs' GDP per capita is subject to greater measurement errors than data for IACs.*

Second, GDP per capita comparisons among countries can be misleading because they ignore the relative income distribution. Some countries have very high per capita incomes, yet most of the income goes to just a few wealthy families. The United Arab Emirates' GDP per capita is higher than that of several IACs. However, the United Arab Emirates earns its income from oil exports, and its income is actually distributed disproportionately to a relatively small number of wealthy families.

> **Conclusion** *GDP per capita comparisons among nations can be misleading because GDP per capita does not measure income distribution.*

Third, GDP per capita comparisons between nations are subject to conversion problems. Making these data comparisons requires converting one nation's currency, say, Japan's yen, into a common currency, the U.S. dollar. Because, as explained in the chapter on international trade and finance, the value of a country's currency can rise or fall for many reasons, the true value of a nation's output can be distorted. For example, during a given year, one government might maintain an artificially high exchange rate and another government might not.

> **Conclusion** *A conversion problem may widen or narrow the GDP per capita gap between nations because the fluctuations in exchange rates do not reflect actual differences in the value of goods and services produced.*

Quality-of-Life Measures of Development

GDP per capita measures market transactions, but this measure does not give a complete picture of differences in living standards among nations. Exhibit 3 presents other selected socioeconomic indicators of the quality of life. These are variables such as life expectancy at birth, infant mortality rate, illiteracy rate, per capita energy consumption and economic freedom ranking. Take a close look at the statistics in Exhibit 3. These data reflect the dimensions of poverty in many of the LDCs. For example, a person born in Japan has a life expectancy that is much longer than a person born in Mozambique, and the infant mortality rate is dramatically higher in Mozambique. Per capita energy consumption measures the use of nonhuman energy to perform work. In IACs, most work is done by machines, and in LDCs, virtually all work is done by people. For example, the average American uses 7,893 kilograms of (oil-equivalent) energy per year, while the average person in Bangladesh uses only 159 kilograms. Finally, it is interesting to note that GDP per capita and other quality-of-life indicators are related to the ranking in economic freedom.

EXHIBIT 3	Quality-of-Life Indicators for Selected Countries, 2007					
Country	(1) GDP Per Capita	(2) Life Expectancy at Birth (years)	(3) Infant Mortality Rate[1]	(4) Illiteracy Rate[2]	(5) Per Capita Energy Consumption[3]	(6) Economic Freedom Rank[4]
United States	$45,490	77	7%	1%	7,893	5
Japan	33,668	82	4	1	4,152	22
China	2,310	72	24	8	1,316	86
Egypt	1,755	71	35	29	841	76
India	871	64	76	39	491	69
Bangladesh	486	64	69	57	159	101
Mozambique	382	42	138	52	497	91

[1]Per 1,000 live births.
[2]Percentage age 15 and over who cannot read and write.
[3]Kilograms of oil equivalent.
[4]The Fraser Institute.

SOURCES: The CIA World Factbook, http://www.cia.gov/library/publications/the-factbook/geos.mz; World Bank Group, *Key Development Data & Statistics,* http://www.worldbank.org/; and The Fraser Institute, http://www.freetheworld.com.

How good an indicator of the quality of life is GDP per capita? Exhibit 3 reflects the principle that lower GDP per capita is highly correlated with measures of the quality of life.

> **Conclusion** *In general, GDP per capita is highly correlated with alternative measures of quality of life.*

Economic Growth and Development around the World

Economic growth and development are major goals of IACs and LDCs. People all over the world strive for a higher quality of life for their generation and future generations. However, growth is closer to a life-or-death situation for many LDCs, such as Bangladesh and Mozambique.

Economic growth and economic development are somewhat different, but related, concepts. As shown in Exhibit 4, recall from Chapter 2 that economic growth is the ability of an economy to produce greater levels of output, represented by an outward shift of its production possibilities curve (*PPC*). Thus, economic growth is defined on a *quantitative* basis using the percentage change in GDP per capita. When a nation's GDP rises more rapidly than its population, GDP per capita rises, and the nation experiences economic growth. Conversely, if GDP expands less than the population of a nation, GDP per capita falls, and the nation experiences negative economic growth.

EXHIBIT 4   Economic Growth

The economy begins with the capacity to produce combinations along production possibilities curve PPC_1. Growth in the resource base or technological advance shifts the production possibilities curve outward from PPC_1 to PPC_2. Points along PPC_2 represent new production possibilities that were previously impossible. The distance that the curve shifts represents an increase in the nation's productive capacity.

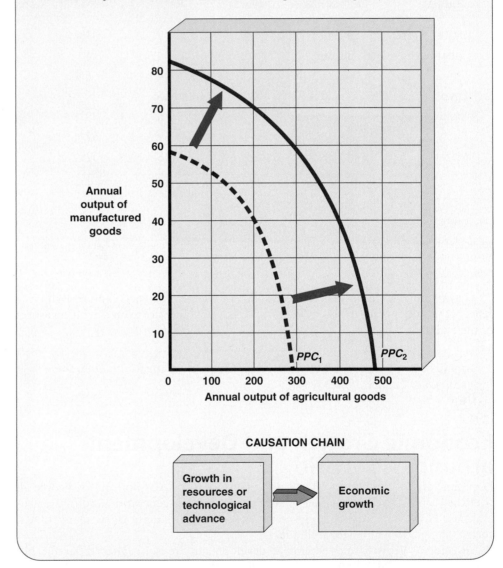

CAUSATION CHAIN

Growth in resources or technological advance → Economic growth

Economic development is a broader concept that is more *qualitative* in nature. Economic development encompasses improvement in the quality of life, including economic growth in the production of goods and services. In short, continuous economic growth is necessary for economic development, but economic growth is not the only consideration. For example, as explained earlier, GDP per capita does not measure the distribution of income or the political environment that provides the legal, monetary, education, and transportation structures necessary for economic growth.

Economic growth and development involve a complex process that is determined by several interrelated factors. Like the performance of an NBA basketball team, success depends on the joint effort of team players, and one or two weak players can greatly reduce overall performance. However, there is no precise formula for winning. If your team has a player like former NBA great Michael Jordan, it can win even with a few weak players. The remainder of this section examines the key factors, or players, that operate together to produce a nation's economic well-being.

Endowment of Natural Resources

Most of the LDCs have comparatively limited bases of natural resources, including mineral deposits and arable land resources. In these countries, most of the available land is used for agricultural production, and clearing tropical forests to obtain more land can cause soil erosion. Also, tropical climates prevail in Central and South America, Africa, the Indian subcontinent, and Southeast Asia. The hot, humid climate in these regions is conducive to weed and insect infestations that plague agriculture.

Although a narrow base of resources does pose a barrier to economic growth and development, no single conclusion can be drawn. For example, how have Hong Kong, Japan, and Israel achieved high standards of living in spite of limited natural resource bases? Each has practically no minerals, little fertile land, and no domestic sources of energy. Nonetheless, these economies have become prosperous. In contrast, Argentina, Venezuela, and Brazil have abundant fertile land and minerals. Yet these and other countries have been growing slowly or not at all. Venezuela, for example, is one of the most oil-rich countries in the world. Ghana, Kenya, and Bolivia are also resource-rich countries that are poor, with little or no economic growth.

> **Conclusion** *Natural resource endowment can promote economic growth, but a country can develop without a large natural resource base.*

Investment in Human Resources

A low level of human capital can also present a barrier to economic growth and development. Recall that human capital is the education, training, experience, and health that improve the knowledge and skills of workers to produce goods and services. In most of the LDCs, investment in human capital is much less than in the IACs. Look back at column 4 in Exhibit 3. Consider how the illiteracy rate rises for the poorer countries. A country with a higher illiteracy rate has less ability to educate its labor force and create a basic foundation for economic growth. In fact, often the skills of workers in the poor countries are suited primarily to agriculture, rather than being appropriate for a wide range of industries and economic growth. Further complicating matters is a "brain drain" problem because the best educated and trained workers of poor countries pursue their education in wealthier countries. Column 2 of Exhibit 3 also gives a measure of health among countries with varying levels of GDP per capita. As the GDP per capita falls, the life expectancy at birth falls. Thus, richer countries have the advantage of a better-educated and healthier workforce.

> **Conclusion** *Investment in human capital generally results in increases in GDP per capita.*

Thus far, the discussion has been about the quality of labor. We must also talk about the quantity of labor because productivity is related to both the quality and the quantity of labor. Overpopulation is a problem for LDCs. In a nutshell, here is why: Other factors held constant, population (labor force) growth can increase a country's GDP. Yet rapid population growth can convert an expanding GDP into a GDP per capita that is stagnant, slow growing, or negative. Stated another way, there is no gain if an increase in output is more than matched by an increase in the number of mouths that must be fed. Suppose the GDP of an LDC grows at, say, 3 percent per year. If there is no growth in population, GDP per capita also grows at 3 percent per year. But what if the population also grows at 3 percent per year? The result is that GDP per capita remains unchanged. If the population growth is instead only 1 percent per year, GDP per capita rises 2 percent per year. Obstacles to population control are great and include strong religious and sociocultural arguments against birth control programs.

> **Conclusion** *Rapid population growth combined with low human capital investment explains why many countries are LDCs.*

CHECKPOINT

Does Rapid Growth Mean a Country Is Catching Up?

Suppose country Alpha has a production possibilities curve closer to the origin than the curve for country Beta. Now assume Alpha experiences a 3 percent growth rate in GDP for 10 years and Beta experiences a 6 percent growth rate in GDP for 10 years. At the end of five years, which of the following is the best prediction for the standard of living? (1) Alpha's residents are better off. (2) Beta's residents are better off. (3) Which country's residents are better off cannot be determined.

Accumulation of Capital

It did not take long for Robinson Crusoe on a deserted island to invest in a net in order to catch more fish than he could catch with his hands. Similarly, farmers working with modern tractors can cultivate more acres than farmers working with horse-drawn plows. Recall from Chapter 1 that capital in economics means factories, tractors, trucks, roads, computers, irrigation systems, electricity-generating facilities, and other human-made goods used to produce goods and services.

LDCs suffer from a critical shortage of capital. A family in Somalia owns little in the way of tools except a wooden plow. To make matters worse, roads are terrible, there are few plants generating electricity, and telephone lines are scarce.

As shown in Exhibit 5, recall from Chapter 2 that a high-investment country can shift its production possibilities curve outward, but investment in capital goods is not a "free lunch." When more resources are used to produce more factories and machines, there is an opportunity cost of fewer resources available for the production of current consumer goods. This means that LDCs are often caught in a vicious circle of poverty. A vicious circle of poverty is the trap in which countries are poor and cannot afford to save. And low savings translate into low investment. Low investment results in low productivity, which, in turn, keeps incomes low. Any savings that do exist among higher-income persons in poor LDCs are often invested in IACs. This phenomenon is often called "capital flight." These wealthy individuals are afraid to save in their own countries because they fear that their governments may be overthrown and their savings could be lost.

The United States and other nations have attempted to provide LDCs with foreign aid so that they might grow. These countries desperately need more factories and infrastructure. Infrastructure is capital goods usually provided by the government, including highways, bridges, waste and water systems, and airports. Unfortunately, the amount of capital given to the LDCs is relatively small, and, as explained above, workers in the LDCs lack the skills necessary to use the most modern forms

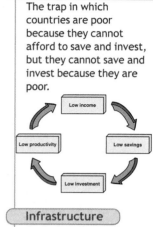

Vicious circle of poverty
The trap in which countries are poor because they cannot afford to save and invest, but they cannot save and invest because they are poor.

Infrastructure
Capital goods usually provided by the government, including highways, bridges, waste and water systems, and airports.

EXHIBIT 5   Alpha's and Beta's Present and Future Production Possibilities Curves

In Part (a), each year Alpha produces only enough capital (K_a) to replace existing capital that is worn out. Without greater capital and assuming other resources remain fixed, Alpha is unable to shift its production possibilities curve outward. In Part (b), each year Beta produces K_b capital, which is more than the amount required to replenish its depreciated capital. In 2010, this expanded capital provides Beta with the extra production capacity to shift its production possibilities curve to the right. If Beta chooses point B on its curve, it has the production capacity to increase the amount of consumer goods from C_b to C_c without producing fewer capital goods.

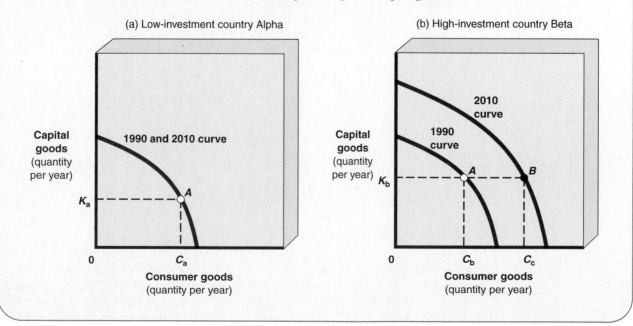

of capital. More specifically, LDCs face a major obstacle to capital accumulation because of the lack of entrepreneurs to assume the risks of capital formation.

> **Conclusion** *There is a significant positive relationship between investment and economic growth and development.*

Technological Progress

As explained earlier in Chapter 2, holding natural resources, labor, and capital constant, advancing the body of knowledge applied to production shifts the production possibilities curve of a country. In fact, technological advances have been at the heart of economic growth and development in recent history. During the last 250 years, brainpower has discovered new power-driven machines, advanced communication devices, new energy sources, and countless ways to produce more output with the same resources. How have innovative products improved your productivity? Consider, to name just a few products, the impact of CD-ROMs, fax machines, DVDs, personal computers, word-processing software, cell phone photography, and the Internet. In contrast, in many poor countries, waterwheels still bring water to the surface, cloth is woven on handlooms, and oxcarts are the major means of transportation. Consequently, large inputs of human effort are used relative to capital resources.

The United States and other IACs have provided the world with an abundant accumulation of technological knowledge that might be adopted by those LDCs without the resources to undertake the required cost of research and development. However, the results of this transfer process have been mixed. For example, countries such as China, Hong Kong, Singapore, Taiwan, South Korea, and Japan have surely achieved rapid growth in part from the benefit of technological borrowing. Currently, Russia and other Eastern European nations are attempting to apply existing technological knowledge to boost their rates of growth.

The other side of the coin is that much available technology is not suited to LDCs. The old saying "You need to learn to walk before you can run" often applies to the LDCs. For example, small farms of most LDCs are not suited for much of the agricultural technology developed for IACs' large farms. And how many factories in the LDCs are ready to use the most modern robotics in the production process? Stated differently, LDCs need appropriate technology, rather than necessarily the latest technology.

> **Conclusion** *Many LDCs continue to experience low growth rates even though IACs have developed advanced technologies that the world can utilize.*

Political Environment

The discussion above leads to the generalization that in order for LDCs to achieve economic growth and development, they must wisely use natural resources, invest in human and physical capital, and adopt advanced technology. This list of policies is not complete. LDC governments must also create a political environment favorable to economic growth. All too often a large part of the problem in poor countries is that resources are wasted as a result of war and political instability. Political leaders must not be corrupt and/or incompetent. Instead of following policies that favor a small elite ruling class, LDC governments must adopt appropriate domestic and international economic policies, discussed under the following three headings of law and order, infrastructure, and international trade.

Law and Order   A basic governmental function is to establish domestic law and order. This function includes many areas, such as a stable legal system, stable money and prices, competitive markets, and private ownership of property. In particular, expropriation of private property rights among LDCs is a barrier to growth. Well-defined private property rights have fostered economic growth in the IACs because this institutional policy has encouraged an entrepreneurial class. Private ownership provides individuals with the incentive to save money and invest in businesses. A stable political environment that ensures private ownership of profits also provides an incentive for individuals in other countries to invest in developing poor countries.

Infrastructure   Assuming an LDC government maintains law and order and the price system is used to allocate goods and services, it is vital that wise decisions be made concerning infrastructure. Indeed, inadequate infrastructure is one of the greatest problems of LDCs. Without such public goods as roads, schools, bridges, and public health and sanitation services, poor countries are unable to generate the substantial external benefits that are an important ingredient in economic growth and development. From the viewpoint of individual firms, government must provide infrastructure because these public goods projects are too costly for a firm to undertake.

International Trade   In general, LDCs can benefit from an expanding volume of trade. This is the theory behind the North American Free Trade Agreement (NAFTA), the General Agreement on Tariffs and Trade (GATT), and the World Trade Organization (WTO) discussed in the chapter on international trade and finance. As explained earlier in this chapter, policies such as tariffs and quotas restrain international trade and thereby inhibit economic growth and development. These trade policies are antigrowth because they restrict the ability of people in one country to trade with people in other countries. Similarly, a country that fixes the exchange rate of its own currency above the market-determined exchange rate makes that country's exports less attractive to foreigners. This means, in turn, that domestic citizens sell less of their goods to foreigners and earn less foreign currency with which to buy imports.

> **Conclusion** *Exchange rate controls artificially set by government above the market exchange rates reduce the volume of both exports and imports (international trade).*

Exhibit 6 summarizes the key factors explained above that determine the economic growth and development of countries. Analysis of this exhibit reveals that economic growth and development are the result of a multidimensional process. This means that it is difficult for countries to break the poverty barrier because they must follow various avenues and improve many factors in order to increase their economic well-being. But it is important to remember that lack of one or more key

EXHIBIT 6	Key Categories that Determine Economic Growth and Development

There are five basic categories that interact to determine the economic growth and development of countries: natural resources, human resources, capital, technological progress, and the political environment. The exhibit also indicates important factors that influence investment in human resources, capital, technological advances, and the political environment. LDCs are faced with a formidable task. Because economic growth and development are multidimensional, LDCs must improve many factors in order to achieve economic progress.

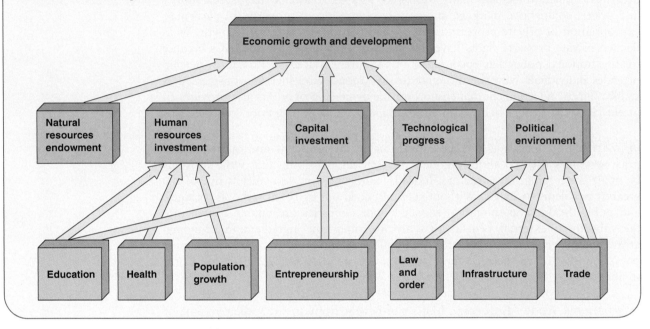

factors, such as natural resources, does not necessarily keep an LDC in the trap of underdevelopment.

> **Conclusion** *There is no single strategy for economic growth and development.*

The Helping Hand of Advanced Countries

How can poor countries escape the vicious circle of poverty? Low GDP per capita leads to low savings and investment, which lead, in turn, to low growth. Although there is no easy way for poor countries to become richer, the United States and other advanced countries can be an instrument of growth. The necessary funds can come from the LDCs' own domestic savings, or it can come from external sources that include foreign private investment, foreign aid, and foreign loans.

Exhibit 7 illustrates how external funds can shift a country's production possibilities curve outward. Here you should look back and review Exhibit 5. Suppose country Alpha is trapped in poverty and produces only enough capital (K_a) to replace the existing capital being worn out. Alpha's consumption level is at C_a, corresponding to point A on production possibilities curve PPC_1. Because C_a is at the subsistence level, Alpha cannot save and invest by substituting capital for current

| EXHIBIT 7 | The Effect of External Financing on an LDC's Production Possibilities Curve |

The poor country of Alpha is initially operating at point A on production possibilities curve PPC_1, with only enough capital (K_a) to replace depreciation. If C_a is the consumption level of subsistence, Alpha's economy cannot grow by reducing consumption. An inflow of external funds from abroad permits the LDC to increase its capital from K_a to K_b and its production possibilities curve shifts outward to PPC_2. At PPC_2, Alpha is able to increase its production of consumer goods from C_a to C_b.

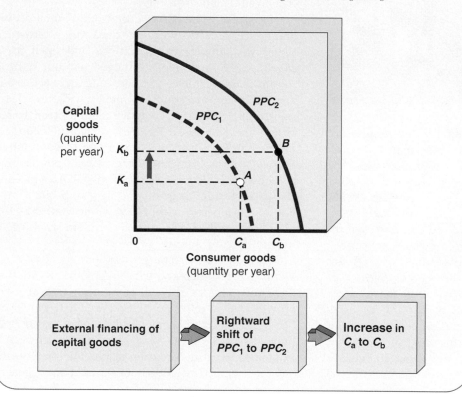

consumption and move upward along PPC_1. This inability to increase capital means Alpha cannot use internal sources of funds to increase its production possibilities curve in the future. There is a way out of the trap using external sources. Now assume Alpha receives an inflow of funds from abroad and buys capital goods that increase its rate of investment from K_a to K_b. At K_b, the rate of capital formation exceeds the value of capital depreciated, and Alpha's production possibilities curve shifts rightward to PPC_2. Economic growth made possible by external investment means Alpha can improve its standard of living by increasing its consumption level from C_a at point A on PPC_1 to C_b at point B on PPC_2.

Foreign Private Investment

Many countries' development benefits from private-sector foreign investment from private investors. For example, Microsoft might finance construction of a plant in the Philippines to manufacture software, or Bank of America may make loans to the

Sanjay Pindiyath/morguefile

As the map shows, the Pacific Rim economies are located along an arc extending from Japan and South Korea in the north to New Zealand in the south. The Four Tigers of East Asia are Hong Kong, Singapore, South Korea, and Taiwan. These "miracle economies" have often experienced higher economic growth rates, lower inflation rates, and lower unemployment rates than many long-established advanced countries.

Hong Kong is a great success story. When Adam Smith published his famous book, *The Wealth of Nations,* in 1776, Hong Kong was little more than a small barren rock island void of natural resources except fish. Today, Hong Kong is a bustling model of free enterprise in spite of the fact that seven million inhabitants are crowded into only about 400 square miles—one of the highest population densities in the world.

What is the reason for Hong Kong's success? Following the doctrine of Adam Smith, this economy is a paragon of *laissez faire.* Hong Kong has among the lowest individual and corporate income tax rates in the world and almost no legal restrictions on business. It has no capital gains tax, no interest tax, no sales tax, and no withholding tax. Hong Kong has become the largest banking center in the Pacific region after Tokyo. International trade is also largely unrestricted, and Hong Kong depends to a large extent on trade through its magnificent harbor for its economic success. Tariffs on imported goods are low, and Hong Kong is known as a safe-haven warehouse and trading center, with little or no interference from the government.

Hong Kong has proved that industrious people and entrepreneurs working hard on a crowded island with minimum regulations and open trade can improve their living standard without natural resources. Nevertheless, Hong Kong faces economic and political uncertainty. Under a 99-year lease signed in 1898, the United Kingdom transferred Hong Kong to the People's Republic of China in 1997. Will China allow Hong Kong to continue to follow Adam Smith's *laissez-faire* philosophy, resulting in high growth rates, or will Hong Kong change direction? It is anyone's guess. So far China has not tampered with Hong Kong's laissez-faire economy, and its economic freedom ranking is higher than any country in the world.[1]

After a 10 percent growth rate in 2000, the falloff in global demand triggered by the recession in the United States slowed Hong Kong's real GDP growth rate to only 0.6 percent in 2001. However, between 2004 and 2007 Hong Kong's growth rate jumped to 7.1 percent and this East Asian tiger is leaping forward and roaring again. The map on the next page compares 2008 data for the Four Tigers of East Asia.

ANALYZE THE ISSUE

One of the keys to Hong Kong's success is its free trade policy. Why is this so important for a developing country? What would be the effect of Hong Kong attempting to protect its domestic industries by raising tariffs and following other protectionist trade policies?

---

1. Frazer Institute, http://www.freetheworld.com/.

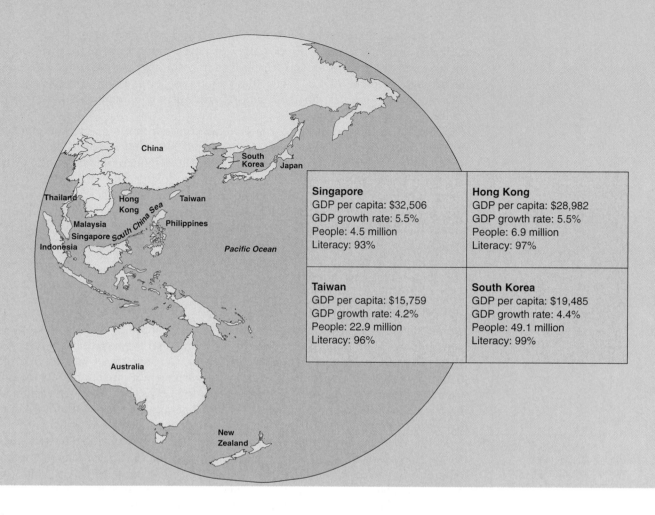

Singapore
GDP per capita: $32,506
GDP growth rate: 5.5%
People: 4.5 million
Literacy: 93%

Hong Kong
GDP per capita: $28,982
GDP growth rate: 5.5%
People: 6.9 million
Literacy: 97%

Taiwan
GDP per capita: $15,759
GDP growth rate: 4.2%
People: 22.9 million
Literacy: 96%

South Korea
GDP per capita: $19,485
GDP growth rate: 4.4%
People: 49.1 million
Literacy: 99%

government of Haiti. These large multinational corporations and commercial banks supply scarce capital to the LDCs. A multinational corporation is a firm with headquarters in one country and one or more branch plants in other countries. Multinational firms often seek new investment opportunities in LDCs because these poor countries offer abundant supplies of low-wage labor and raw materials. But the political environment in the LDCs must be conducive to investment. Multinational corporations often become the largest employers, largest taxpayers, and largest exporters in the LDCs.

Foreign Aid

About 1 percent of the U.S. federal budget is spent on foreign aid. Foreign aid is the transfer of money or resources from one government to another with no repayment required. These transfers may be made as outright grants, technical assistance, or food supplies. Foreign aid flows from country to country through governments and voluntary agencies, such as the Red Cross, CARE, and Church World Relief. The United States distributes most of its official development assistance through the Agency for International Development (AID), established in 1961. The AID is the agency of the U.S. State Department that is in charge of U.S. aid to foreign countries.

Foreign aid
The transfer of money or resources from one government to another for which no repayment is required.

Agency for International Development (AID)
The agency of the U.S. State Department that is in charge of U.S. aid to foreign countries.

One reason that countries like the United States provide foreign aid to LDCs is the belief that it is a moral responsibility of richer countries to share their wealth with poorer countries. A second reason is that it is in the best economic interest of the IACs to help the LDCs. When these countries become more prosperous, the IACs have more markets for their exports, and thereby all countries benefit from trade.

The LDCs often complain that foreign aid comes with too many economic and political strings attached. Loans are often offered on a "take it or leave it" basis, tied to policies other than basic trade policies, such as human rights, politics, or the military. Consequently, many LDCs argue for "trade, not aid." If the IACs would simply buy more goods from the LDCs, the LDCs could use their gains in export earnings to purchase more capital and other resources needed for growth. Many people in the United States feel that most foreign aid is a waste of money because it is misused by the recipient countries. This belief has caused Congress to grow increasingly reluctant to send taxpayers' money abroad except in the clearest cases of need or for reasons of national security.

Foreign Loans

A third source of external funds that can be used to finance LDCs' domestic investment is loans from abroad. Governments, international organizations, and private banks all make loans to LDCs. Like foreign private investment and foreign aid, loans give LDCs the opportunity to shift their production possibilities curves outward. There are various types of loan sources for LDCs. Bilateral loans are made directly from one country to another. The principal agent for official U.S. bilateral loans is the U.S. Agency for International Development, introduced earlier.

World Bank

The lending agency that makes long-term low-interest loans and provides technical assistance to less-developed countries.

One prominent multilateral lending agency is the World Bank. The 184-member World Bank is the lending agency affiliated with the United Nations that makes long-term low-interest loans and provides technical assistance to LDCs. Loans are made only after a planning period lasting a year or more. The World Bank was established in 1944 by major nations meeting in Bretton Woods, New Hampshire. Its first charge was to assist with reconstruction after World War II. Today, the World Bank is located in Washington, D.C., and its main purpose is to channel funds from rich countries to poor countries. Voting shares are in proportion to the money provided by the members. The World Bank makes "last resort" loans to LDCs that are limited to financing basic infrastructure projects, such as schools, health centers, dams, irrigation systems, and transportation facilities, for which private financing is not available. In addition, the World Bank helps LDCs get loans from private lenders by insuring the loans. Thus, the poor countries are able to complete projects and use the economic returns to pay off the lender with interest.

International Monetary Fund (IMF)

The lending agency that makes short-term conditional low-interest loans to developing countries.

The World Bank is not the only multilateral lending agency making loans to LDCs. The World Bank's partner institution is the International Monetary Fund (IMF). The International Monetary Fund is the lending agency that makes short-term conditional low-interest loans to developing countries. The IMF was also established at Bretton Woods in 1944. Its purpose is to help countries overcome short-run financial difficulties. Typically, the IMF makes conditional loans that require the debtor countries to implement fiscal and monetary policies that will alleviate balance-of-payments deficit problems and promote noninflationary economic growth. The 184-member IMF is not a charitable institution. It operates like a credit union with funding quotas that earn interest on the loans. The United States is the IMF's largest shareholder and thus has effective veto power over IMF decisions.

In recent years, the IMF has performed a major role in providing short-term loans to developing countries and to economies making the transition to capitalism. In the late 1990s, the IMF provided multibillion-dollar bailouts to Russia, several Asian countries, Brazil, and other countries experiencing economic turmoil. Critics argue that as long as governments believe the IMF will bail them out, they will fail to correct their own problems. IMF supporters counter that if the IMF does not intervene, troubled economies will default on outstanding loans and cause a world-wide ripple effect. Critics respond that a flood of low-cost short-term loans from the IMF encourages bad government policies and excessive risk taking by banks. Consequently, a bailout in a crisis generates new financial crises and reduces world economic growth.

Finally, private banks also engage in lending to LDCs. Until the 1970s, LDCs borrowed primarily from the World Bank and foreign governments. In the 1970s, private banks began to lend to both governments and private firms in LDCs. During the 1980s, the news was full of stories that some U.S. banks had made so many risky loans to LDCs that default on these loans would lead to the failure of one major U.S. bank after another. As the story goes, "If you can't repay the bank for your car loan, you're in trouble. If a government can't repay the bank a billion dollars, the bank's in trouble."

In the late 1980s, the debt crisis was avoided by (1) writing off some of the loans, (2) lowering the interest rate of remaining loans, and (3) lending LDCs more money to pay interest on their debt. The U.S. government, other Western governments, and the IMF were active in these solutions. Was this a case of "throwing good money after bad" because many loans would never be repaid? The answer is No. Easing the debt burden salvaged some payments and was in the best interest of both rich and poor countries because a fresh start encouraged trade. Nevertheless, the huge outstanding debts of some LDCs make another debt crisis a lingering possibility. In 2005, the wealthiest countries (G-8) reached a groundbreaking agreement to eliminate the debt of some of the world's most impoverished countries.

CHECKPOINT

Is the Minimum Wage an Antipoverty Solution for Poor Countries?
Imagine you are an economic advisor to the president of a poor LDC. The president is seeking policies to promote economic growth and a higher standard of living for citizens of this country. You are asked whether adopting a minimum wage equal to the average of the IACs' average hourly wages would achieve these goals. Recall the discussion of the minimum wage from Chapter 4 and evaluate this policy.

KEY CONCEPTS

GDP per capita
Industrially advanced
  countries (IACs)
Less-developed countries
  (LDCs)

Vicious circle of poverty
Infrastructure
Foreign aid
Agency for International
  Development (AID)

World Bank
International Monetary
  Fund (IMF)

SUMMARY

- *GDP per capita* provides a general index of a country's standard of living. Countries with low GDP per capita and slow growth in GDP per capita are less able to satisfy basic needs for food, shelter, clothing, education, and health.
- *Industrially advanced countries* (*IACs*) are countries with high GDP per capita and output is produced by technologically advanced capital. Countries that have high incomes without widespread industrial development, such as the oil-rich Arab countries, are not included in the IAC list.
- *Less-developed countries* (*LDCs*) are countries with low production per person. In these countries, output is produced without large amounts of technologically advanced capital and well-educated labor. The LDCs account for about three-fourths of the world's population.
- The *Four Tigers of the Pacific Rim* are Hong Kong, Singapore, South Korea, and Taiwan. These newly industrialized countries have achieved high growth rates and standards of living.
- *GDP per capita comparisons* are subject to four problems: (1) the accuracy of LDC data is questionable, (2) GDP per capita ignores income distribution, (3) fluctuations in exchange rates affect GDP per capita gaps between countries, and (4) there is no adjustment for cost-of-living differences between countries.

- *Economic growth* and *economic development* are related, but somewhat different concepts. Economic growth is measured quantitatively by GDP per capita, while economic development is a broader concept. In addition to GDP per capita, economic development includes quality-of-life measures, such as life expectancy at birth, adult literacy rate, and per capita energy consumption. Economic growth and development are the result of a complex process that is determined by five major factors: (1) natural resources, (2) human resources, (3) capital, (4) technological progress, and (5) the political environment. There is no single correct strategy for economic development, and a lack of strength in one or more of the five areas does not prevent growth.
- The *vicious circle of poverty* is a trap in which an LDC is too poor to save and therefore it cannot invest and shift its production possibilities curve outward. As a result, the LDC remains poor. One way for a poor country to gain savings, invest, and grow is to use funds from external sources such as foreign private investment, foreign aid, and foreign loans. Borrowing by many LDCs led to the debt crisis of the 1980s, which was resolved by writing off and restructuring the loans.

SUMMARY OF CONCLUSION STATEMENTS

- LDCs' GDP per capita is subject to greater measurement errors than data for IACs.
- GDP per capita comparisons among nations can be misleading because GDP per capita does not measure income distribution.
- A conversion problem may widen or narrow the GDP per capita gap between nations because the fluctuations in exchange rates do not reflect actual differences in the value of goods and services produced.
- Differences in purchasing power that affect living standards can alter the interpretation of international comparisons of GDP per capita.
- In general, GDP per capita is highly correlated with alternative measures of quality of life.

- Natural resource endowment can promote economic growth, but a country can develop without a large natural resource base.
- Investment in human capital generally results in increases in GDP per capita.
- Rapid population growth combined with low human capital investment explains why many countries are LDCs.
- Nations that grow slowly or experience declines in GDP per capita will fail to catch up with the IACs' standard of living.
- There is a significant positive relationship between investment and economic growth and development.

- Many LDCs continue to experience low growth rates even though IACs have developed advanced technologies that the world can utilize.
- Exchange rate controls artificially set by government above the market exchange rates reduce the volume of both exports and imports (international trade).
- There is no single strategy for economic growth and development.

STUDY QUESTIONS AND PROBLEMS

1. What is the difference between industrially advanced countries (IACs) and less-developed countries (LDCs)? List five IACs and five LDCs.

2. Explain why GDP per capita comparisons among nations are not a perfect measure of differences in economic well-being.

3. Assume you are given the following data for country Alpha and country Beta:

Country	GDP Per Capita
Alpha	$25,000
Beta	15,000

   a. Based on the GDP per capita data given above, in which country would you prefer to live?
   b. Now assume you are given the following additional quality-of-life data. In which country would you prefer to reside?

Country	Life Expectancy at Birth (years)	Daily per Capita Calorie Supply	Per Capita Energy Consumption*
Alpha	65	2,500	3,000
Beta	70	3,000	4,000

   *Kilograms of oil equivalent.

4. What is the difference between economic development and economic growth? Give examples of how each of these concepts can be measured.

5. Do you agree with the argument that the rich nations are getting richer and the poor nations are getting poorer? Is this an oversimplification? Explain.

6. Explain why it is so difficult for poor LDCs to generate investment in capital in order to increase productivity and growth and therefore improve their standard of living.

7. Why is the quest for economic growth and development complicated?

8. Indicate whether each of the following is associated with a high or low level of economic growth and development:

	High	Low
a. Overpopulation	___	___
b. Highly skilled labor	___	___
c. High savings rate	___	___
d. Political stability	___	___
e. Low capital accumulation	___	___
f. Advanced technology	___	___
g. Highly developed infrastructure	___	___
h. High proportion of agriculture	___	___
i. High degree of income inequality	___	___

9. Without external financing from foreign private investment, foreign aid, and foreign loans, poor countries are caught in the vicious circle of poverty. Explain. How does external financing help poor countries achieve economic growth and development?

10. What are some of the problems for LDCs of accepting foreign aid?

11. Why would an LDC argue for "trade, not aid"?

12. Explain the differences among the Agency for International Development (AID), the World Bank, and the International Monetary Fund (IMF).

For Online Exercises, go to the text Web site at www.cengage.com/economics/tucker.

CHECKPOINT ANSWERS ✓

Does Rapid Growth Mean a Country Is Catching Up?

GDP growth alone does not measure the standard of living. You must also consider population. Even though Beta experienced a greater GDP growth rate, its GDP per capita might be less than Alpha's because its population growth rate is greater. Of course, the reverse is also possible, but without population data, we cannot say. If you said which country's people are better off cannot be determined because the GDP must be divided by the population to measure the average standard of living, **YOU ARE CORRECT.**

Is the Minimum Wage an Antipoverty Solution for Poor Countries?

An important source of foreign investment for LDCs is multinational corporations that locate plants and other facilities in these countries. LDCs compete with each other for the economic growth and development benefits that these multinational corporations can provide. For an LDC to win the competition, it must offer political stability, adequate infrastructure, a favorable business climate, and a cheap labor force. If you said you would not support the president's proposal to raise the minimum wage because it would place the LDC at a competitive disadvantage in the labor market, thereby reducing foreign private investment and growth, **YOU ARE CORRECT.**

PRACTICE QUIZ

For an explanation of the correct answers, please visit the tutorial at www.cengage.com/economics/tucker.

1. An LDC is defined as a country
   a. without large stocks of advanced capital.
   b. without well-educated labor.
   c. with low GDP per capita.
   d. that is described by all of the above.

2. According to the definition given in the text, which of the following is *not* an LDC?
   a. India
   b. Egypt
   c. China
   d. Ireland

3. Which of the following is *true* when making GDP per capita comparisons among nations?
   a. The GDP per capita is subject to greater measurement errors for LDCs compared to IACs.

   b. The GDP per capita does not measure income distribution.
   c. The GDP per capita is subject to fluctuations from changes in exchange rates.
   d. All of the above are true.

4. LDCs are characterized by
   a. high life expectancy.
   b. high adult literacy.
   c. high infant mortality.
   d. all of the above.
   e. none of the above.

5. According to the classification in the text, which of the following is *not* an IAC?
   a. United Arab Emirates
   b. Israel
   c. Hong Kong
   d. Greece

6. When the government fixes the exchange rate above market exchange rates,
   a. international trade falls.
   b. the infrastructure improves.
   c. real GDP per capita rises.
   d. the vicious circle of poverty is broken.

7. Which of the following statements is *true*?
   a. An LDC is a country with a low GDP per capita, low levels of capital, and uneducated workers.
   b. The vicious circle of poverty exists because GDP must rise before people can save and invest.
   c. LDCs are characterized by rapid population growth and low levels of investment in human capital.
   d. All of the above are true.

8. An outward shift of the production possibilities curve represents
   a. economic growth.
   b. a decline in economic development.
   c. a decrease in human capital.
   d. a decrease in resources.

9. Which of the following problems do LDCs face?
   a. Low per capita income and high GDP growth rate
   b. Low population growth and low per capita income
   c. Rapid population growth and low human capital
   d. Low per capita income and high saving rate

10. Which of the following *best* defines the vicious circle of poverty?
    a. The GDP per capita must rise before people can save and invest.
    b. People cannot save while capital accumulates.
    c. Increased GDP per capita relates to lower population growth.
    d. Poverty, saving, and investment are related like a circle.

11. Which of the following is infrastructure?
    a. International Harvester tractor plant
    b. Waste and water system provided by government
    c. US Airways airplane
    d. Service of postal workers

12. Economic growth and development in LDCs are low because many of them lack
    a. capital investment.
    b. technological progress.
    c. a favorable political environment.
    d. all of the above.
    e. none of the above.

13. Which of the following makes short-term conditional low-interest loans to developing countries?
    a. Agency for International Development (AID)
    b. World Bank
    c. International Monetary Fund (IMF)
    d. New International Economic Order (NIEO)

14. Which of the following groups makes long-term low-interest loans to less-developed countries (LDCs)?
    a. Agency for International Development (AID)
    b. New International Economic Order (NIEO)
    c. International Monetary Fund (IMF)
    d. World Bank

15. In order for Ethiopia to increase its future economic growth, it must choose a point that is
    a. below its production possibilities curve.
    b. further along on its production possibilities curve toward the capital goods axis.
    c. further along on its production possibilities curve toward the consumption goods axis.
    d. further along on its production possibilities curve away from the population axis.
    e. above its production possibilities curve.

THE INTERNATIONAL ECONOMY

This road map feature helps you tie material in the part together as you travel the Economic Way of Thinking Highway. The following are review questions listed by chapter from the previous part. The key concept in each question is given for emphasis, and each question or set of questions concludes with an interactive game to reinforce the concepts. Click on the Tucker Web site, select the chapter, and play the visual causation chain game designed to make learning fun. Enjoy the cheers when correct and suffer the jeers if you miss.

For an explanation of the correct answers, please visit the tutorial at www.cengage.com/economics/tucker.

Chapter 28. International Trade and Finance

1. **Key Concept: Exchange Rate Changes**
   Which of the following would cause the U.S. demand curve for Japanese yen to shift to the right?
   a. An increase in the U.S. inflation rate compared to the rate in Japan.
   b. A higher real rate of interest on investments in Japan than on investments in the United States.
   c. The popularity of Japanese products increases in the United States.
   d. All of the above.

2. **Key Concept: Exchange Rate Changes**
   Which of the following would cause the supply of dollars curve in the United States to shift to the right?
   a. Japanese imports become less popular.
   b. The value of the dollar falls.
   c. The supply of dollars decreases.
   d. Japanese imports became more popular.

   Causation Chain Game
   Changes in Supply and Demand Curves for Dollars—Exhibit 10

3. **Key Concept: Impact of Relative Price Level Changes**
   An increase in inflation in the United States relative to the rate in France would make
   a. U.S. goods relatively less expensive in the United States and in France.
   b. French goods relatively less expensive in the United States and U.S. goods relatively more expensive in France.
   c. French goods relatively more expensive in the United States and in France.
   d. French goods relatively more expensive in the United States and U.S. goods relatively less expensive in France.

4. **Key Concept: Impact of Relative Price Level Changes**
   If the Japanese price level falls relative to the price level in the United States, then
   a. Japanese buy less U.S. exports.
   b. the demand for dollars decreases.

c.   the supply of dollars increases.

d.   the value of the dollar falls.

e.   all of the above are true.

Causation Chain Game

The Impact of Relative Price Level Changes on Exchange Rates—Exhibit 11

5.   **Key Concept: Command Economy**

Which of the following statements is *true* about a command economy?

a.   Shortages occur because of complexities in the planning process.

b.   Planners determine what, how many, and for whom goods and services are to be produced.

c.   Planners often allocate goods and services through a rationing system.

d.   The quality of produced goods and services tends to be inferior.

e.   All of the above are true.

6.   **Key Concept: Command Economy**

Which of the following statements *best* describes the role played by prices in a command economy such as the former Soviet Union?

a.   Prices were used to allocate resources.

b.   Prices played the same role as in a market economy.

c.   Prices were used to ration final goods and services but not to allocate resources.

d.   None of the above statements is descriptive.

Causation Chain Game

Central Planners Fixing Prices—Exhibit 2

Chapter 30. Growth and the Less-Developed Countries

7.   **Key Concept: Economic Growth**

An outward shift of an economy's production possibilities curve is caused by an

a.   increase in capital.

b.   increase in labor.

c.   advance in technology.

d.   all of the above are true.

8.   **Key Concept: Economic Growth**

Which of the following is *correct*?

a.   Economic development is more quantitative than economic growth.

b.   A country cannot achieve economic growth with a limited base of natural resources.

c.   Infrastructure is capital provided by the private sector.

d.   All of the above are true.

e.   All of the above are false.

Causation Chain Game

Economic Growth—Exhibit 4

9. **Key Concept: Achieving Economic Growth**
   Which of the following can be a barrier to an LDC's economic growth and development?
   a.   Low population growth.
   b.   A low level of human capital.
   c.   Faster capital accumulation.
   d.   More infrastructure.

10. **Key Concept: Economic Growth and Development**
    To grow and prosper, less-developed countries must *not*
    a.   invest in human capital.
    b.   build a strong infrastructure.
    c.   shift resources out of the production of consumer goods and into the production of capital goods.
    d.   shift resources out of the production of capital goods and into the production of consumer goods.
    e.   improve the quality of the water supply.

Causation Chain Game
The Effect of External Financing on an LDC's Production Possibilities Curve—Exhibit 7

Answers to Odd-Numbered Study Questions and Problems*

Chapter 1 Introducing the Economic Way of Thinking

1. A poor nation with many people who lack food, clothing, and shelter certainly experiences wants beyond the availability of goods and services to satisfy these unfulfilled wants. On the other hand, no wealthy nation has all the resources necessary to produce everything everyone in the nation wishes to have. Even if you had $1 million and were completely satisfied with your share of goods and services, other desires would be unfulfilled. There is never enough time to accomplish all the things that you can imagine would be worthwhile.

3. a. capital

5. a. microeconomic issue
   b. macroeconomic issue
   c. microeconomic issue
   d. macroeconomic issue

7. The real world is full of complexities that make it difficult to understand and predict the relationships between variables. For example, the relationship between changes in the price of gasoline and changes in consumption of gasoline requires abstraction from the reality that such variables as the fuel economy of cars and weather conditions often change at the same time as the price of gasoline.

9. The two events are associated, and the first event (cut in military spending) is the cause of the second event (higher unemployment in the defense industry). The point is that association does not necessarily mean causation, but it might.

11. d. statement of normative economics

Appendix to Chapter 1 Applying Graphs to Economics

1. a. The probability of living is *inversely* related to age. This model could be affected by improvements in diet, better health care, reductions in hazards to health in the workplace, or changes in the speed limit.

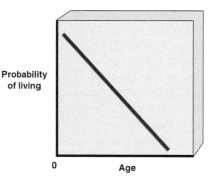

   b. Annual income and years of formal education are *directly* related. This relationship might be influenced by changes in such human characteristics as intelligence, motivation, ability, and family background. An example of an institutional change that could affect this relationship over a number of years is the draft.

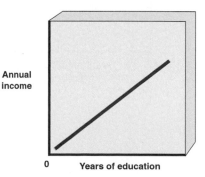

---

*Note: Answers to even-numbered questions and problems are in the Instructor's Manual.

c. Inches of snow and sales of bathing suits are *inversely* related. The weather forecast and the price of travel to sunny vacation spots can affect this relationship.

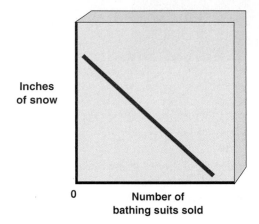

d. Most alumni and students will argue that the number of football games won is *directly* related to the athletic budget. They reason that winning football games is great advertising and results in increased attendance, contributions, and enrollment that, in turn, increase the athletic budget. Success in football can also be related to other factors, such as school size, age and type of institution, number and income of alumni, and quality of the faculty and administrators.

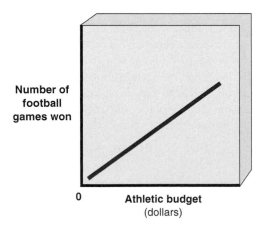

Chapter 2 Production Possibilities, Opportunity Cost, and Economic Growth

1. Because the wants of individuals and society exceed the goods and services available to satisfy these desires, choices must be made. The consumption possibilities of an individual with a fixed income are limited, and as a result, additional consumption of one item necessarily precludes an expenditure on another next-best choice. The forgone alternative is called the opportunity cost, and this concept also applies to societal decisions. If society allocates resources to the production of guns, then those same resources cannot be used at the same time to make butter.

3. Regardless of the price of a lunch, economic resources—land, labor, and capital—are used to produce the lunch. These scarce resources are no longer available to produce other goods and services.

5. Using marginal analysis, students weigh the benefits of attending college against the costs. There is an incentive to attend college when the benefits (improved job opportunities, income, intellectual improvement, social life, and so on) outweigh the opportunity costs.

7.

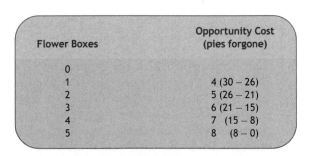

Flower Boxes	Opportunity Cost (pies forgone)
0	
1	4 (30 − 26)
2	5 (26 − 21)
3	6 (21 − 15)
4	7 (15 − 8)
5	8 (8 − 0)

9. Movements along the curve are efficient points and conform to the well-known "free lunch" statement. However, inefficient points are exceptions because it is possible to produce more of one output without producing less of another output.

11.

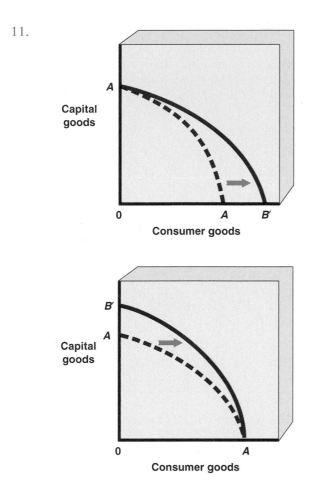

Chapter 3 Market Demand and Supply

1. If people buy a good or service because they associate higher quality with higher price, this is a violation of the ceteris paribus assumption. An increase in the quantity demanded results only from a decrease in price. Quality and other nonprice determinants of demand, such as tastes and preferences and the price of related goods, are held constant in the model.

3. a. Demand for cars decreases; oil and cars are *complements*.
   b. Demand for insulation increases; oil and home insulation are *substitutes*.
   c. Demand for coal increases; oil and coal are *substitutes*.
   d. Demand for tires decreases; oil and tires are *complements*.

5. One reason that the demand curve for word processing software shifted to the right might be that people desire new, higher-quality output features. The supply curve can shift to the right when new technology makes it possible to offer more software for sale at different prices.

7. a. Demand shifts to the right.
   b. Supply shifts to the left.
   c. Supply shifts to the right.
   d. Demand shifts to the right.
   e. Demand shifts to the right.
   f. Supply of corn shifts to the left.

9. a. The supply of CD players shifts rightward.
   b. The demand for CD players is unaffected.
   c. The equilibrium price falls, and the equilibrium quantity increases.
   d. The demand for CDs increases because of the fall in the price of CD players (a complementary good).

11. The number of seats (quantity supplied) remains constant, but the demand curve shifts because tastes and preferences change according to the importance of each game. Although demand changes, the price is a fixed amount, and to manage a shortage, colleges and universities use amount of contributions, number of years as a contributor, or some other rationing device.

Appendix to Chapter 3 Consumer Surplus, Producer Surplus, and Market Efficiency

1. $80

3.

Price	$30	$15
Consumer surplus	$80	$105
Producer surplus	$25	$5
Total surplus	$105	$110

The lower price results in higher total surplus because in this case the rise in consumer surplus exceeds fall in producer surplus.

Chapter 4 Markers in Action

1.

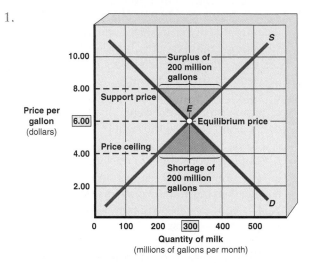

a. The equilibrium price is $6.00 per gallon, and the equilibrium quantity is 300 million gallons per month. The price system will restore the market's $6.00 per gallon price because either a surplus will drive prices down or a shortage will drive prices up.

b. The support price results in a persistent surplus of 200 million gallons of milk per month, which the government purchases with taxpayers' money. Consequently, taxpayers who do not drink milk are still paying for milk. The purpose of the support price is to bolster the incomes of dairy farmers.

c. The ceiling price will result in a persistent shortage of 200 million gallons of milk per month, but 200 million gallons are purchased by consumers at the low price of $4.00 per gallon. The shortage places a burden on the government to ration milk in order to be fair and to prevent black markets. The government's goal is to keep the price of milk below the equilibrium price of $6.00 per gallon, which would be set by a free market.

3. The labor market can be divided into two separate markets, one for skilled union workers and one for unskilled workers. If the minimum wage is above the equilibrium wage rate and is raised, the effect will be to increase the demand for, and the wage of, skilled union workers because the two groups are substitutes.

5. The equilibrium price rises.

7. The government can reduce emissions by (a) regulations that require smoke-abatement equipment or (b) imposing pollution taxes that shift supply leftward.

9. Pure public goods are not produced in sufficient quantities by private markets because there is no feasible method to exclude free riders.

Chapter 5 Price Elasticity of Demand and Supply

1. Demand is elastic because the percentage change in quantity is greater than the percentage change in price.

3. If the price of used cars is raised 1 percent, the quantity demanded will fall 3 percent. If the price is raised 10 percent, the quantity demanded will fall 30 percent.

5.
$$E_d = \frac{\%\Delta Q}{\%\Delta P} = \frac{\dfrac{4,500 - 5,000}{5,000 + 4,500}}{\dfrac{3,500 - 3,000}{3,000 + 3,500}} = \frac{\dfrac{1}{19}}{\dfrac{1}{13}} = 0.68$$

The price elasticity of demand for the university is inelastic.

7. Demand for popcorn is perfectly inelastic, and total revenue will increase.

9. a. Sunkist oranges
   b. Cars
   c. Foreign travel in the long run

11. Furniture sales fall by 30 percent and physician services by only 3 percent. Thus, the demand for physician services is much less responsive to a reduction in income than the demand for furniture.

13. The negative number tells you car tires are complements. If the price of cars rises by 10 percent, the quantity demanded of car tires falls by 20 percent.

15. As the demand for a product becomes more inelastic, the greater the amount of a tax on this product that sellers can pass on to consumers by raising the product's price.

Chapter 6 Consumer Choice Theory

1. Utility is a subjective concept, and, therefore, this statement may or may not be true.

3. Marginal utility is 10 utils. When you attend the fourth party, total utility will increase, but marginal utility will be less than 10 utils.

5. In consumer equilibrium, the marginal utility ratio is 3/4, which is equal to the price ratio.

7. As people consume more of any product, eventually the satisfaction per unit decreases. Since the marginal utility from additional units falls, people will not buy a greater quantity unless the price falls.

9. The initial consumer equilibrium is as follows:

$$\frac{MU \text{ of steak meal}}{\text{Price of steak meal}} = \frac{MU \text{ of hamburger meal}}{\text{Price of hamburger meal}}$$

$$\frac{12 \text{ utils}}{\$10} = \frac{6 \text{ utils}}{\$10}$$

The marginal utility per dollar for each good equals 1.2. If the price of a hamburger meal falls to $2, this equality no longer holds. Now the marginal utility per dollar for a hamburger meal becomes higher at 3 (6 utils/$2). James can now increase his total utility by purchasing more hamburger meals per month. Given the law of diminishing returns, the marginal utility of hamburger meals falls until consumer equilibrium is restored.

Appendix to Chapter 6 Indifference Curve Analysis

1. $MRS = 3$ (3 slices of pizza per Coke), but the ratio of prices is 1/2 ($1.00 per Coke/$2.00 per slice of pizza). Since $MRS >$ slope (the ratio of prices), the consumer is not maximizing total utility. Therefore, the consumer should consume less pizza and more Coke in order to maximize total utility by moving downward along the consumer's indifference curve until consumer equilibrium is achieved where $MRS =$ price ratio $= 1/2$.

3. a and b

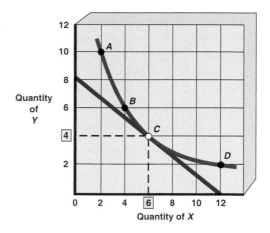

c. Consumer equilibrium occurs at point C with 6 units of X and 4 units of Y purchased.

d. $MRS = P_x/P_y = \dfrac{\$1}{\$1.50} = \dfrac{2}{3}$

e. Hold the price of Y constant at $1.50 and decrease the price of X from $1.00 to $0.50. The new budget line will shift northeastward from the Y axis intercept point of 8 units. Now draw a new indifference curve and determine the new equilibrium point. Finally, draw a graph with various prices of X on the vertical axis and the quantity of X on the horizontal axis. Connecting the two consumer equilibrium points will allow you to draw a downward-sloping demand curve.

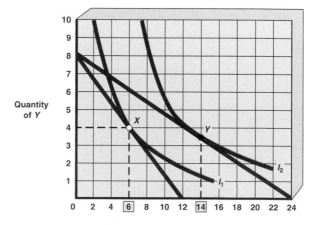

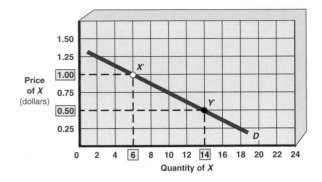

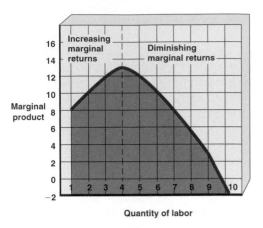

Chapter 7 Production Costs

1. a. explicit cost
   b. explicit cost
   c. implicit cost
   d. implicit cost
   e. explicit cost
   f. implicit cost

3. a.

Labor	Marginal Product
1	8
2	10
3	12
4	13
5	12
6	10
7	8
8	6
9	3
10	−2

b.

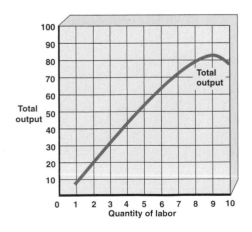

5. None. The position of a firm's short-run average total cost curve is not related to the demand curve.

7. The ATC and AVC curves converge as output expands because $ATC = AVC + AFC$. As output increases, AFC declines, so most of ATC is therefore AVC.

9. The average total cost-marginal cost rule states that when the marginal cost is below the average total cost, the addition to total cost is below the average total cost, and the average total cost falls. When the marginal cost is greater than the average total cost, the average total cost rises. In this case, the average total cost is at a minimum because it is equal to the marginal cost.

11. The marginal product for any number of workers is the slope of the total output curve. The marginal product is the derivative of the total output curve dTO/dQ, where TO is the total output and Q is the number of workers.

Chapter 8 Perfect Competition

1. A perfectly competitive firm will not advertise. Because all firms in the industry sell the same product, there is no reason for customers to be influenced by ads into buying one firm's product rather than another firm's product.

3.

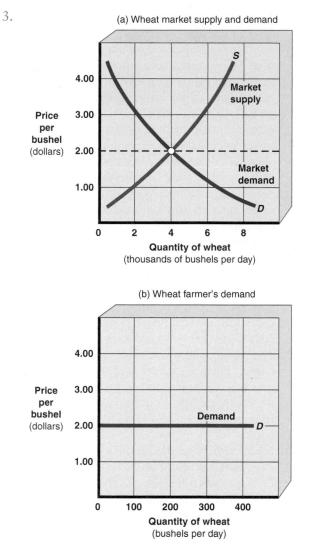

(a) Wheat market supply and demand

Price per bushel (dollars)

Quantity of wheat (thousands of bushels per day)

(b) Wheat farmer's demand

Price per bushel (dollars)

Quantity of wheat (bushels per day)

A single wheat farmer is a price taker facing a perfectly elastic demand curve because in perfect competition one seller has no control over its price. The reason is that each wheat farmer is one among many, sells a homogeneous product, and must compete with any new farmer entering the wheat market.

5. At a price of $150, the firm produces 4 units and earns an economic profit of $70 ($TR - TC = $600 - 530). The firm breaks even at an output of 2 units.

7. This statement is incorrect. A firm can earn maximum profit (or minimum loss) when marginal revenue equals marginal cost. The confusion is between the "marginal" and the "total" concepts.

Marginal cost is the change in total cost from one additional unit of output, and marginal revenue is the change in total revenue from one additional unit of output.

9. The statement is incorrect. The perfectly competitive firm must consider both its marginal revenue and its marginal cost. Instead of trying to sell all the quantity of output possible, the firm will sell the quantity where $MR = MC$ because beyond this level of output the firm earns less profit.

11. Advise the residential contractor to shut down because the market price exceeds the average variable cost and the firm cannot cover its operating costs.

Chapter 9 Monopoly

1. Each market is served by a single firm providing a unique product. There are no close substitutes for local telephone service, professional football in San Francisco, and first-class mail service. A government franchise imposes a legal barrier to potential competitors in the telephone and first-class mail services. An NFL franchise grants monopoly power to its members in most geographic areas.

3. The reason may be that the hospital has monopoly power because it is the only hospital in the area and patients have no choice. On the other hand, there may be many drugstores competing to sell drugs, and this keeps prices lower than those charged by the hospital.

5. In a natural monopoly, a single seller can produce electricity at a lower cost because the $LRAC$ curve declines. One firm can therefore sell electricity at a cheaper price and drive its competitor out of business over time. Another possibility would be for two competing firms to merge and earn greater profit by lowering cost further.

7. In this special case, sales maximization and profit maximization are the same. The monopolist should charge $2.50 per unit, produce 5 units of output, and earn $12.50 in profit. When the marginal cost curve is not equal to zero, the monopolist's $MR = MC$ output is less than 5 units, the price is higher than $2.50 per unit, and profit is below $12.50.

9. a. increase output
   b. decrease output

11. a. not price discrimination
    b. price discrimination
    c. not price discrimination if justified by a transportation cost difference
    d. price discrimination
13. Answers vary with students.

Chapter 10 Monopolistic Competition and Oligopoly

1. The monopolistically competitive firm's demand curve is less elastic (steeper) than a perfectly competitive firm's demand curve, but more elastic (flatter) than a monopolist's demand curve.
3. a. P_1
   b. Q_1
   c. Q_3
   d. greater than the marginal cost ($B > A$)
5.

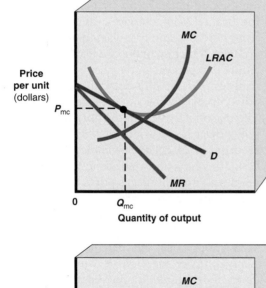

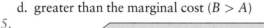

Because $P_{mc} > MC$, the monopolistically competitive firm fails to achieve allocative efficiency.

The monopolistically competitive firm is also inefficient because it charges a higher price and produces less output than under perfect competition. The perfectly competitive firm sets P_{pc} equal to MC and produces a level of output corresponding to the minimum point on the $LRAC$ curve.

7. Answers might include automobiles, airline travel, personal computers, and cigarettes. An oligopoly differs from monopolistic competition by having few sellers, rather than many sellers; either a homogeneous or a differentiated product, rather than all differentiated products; and difficult entry rather than easy entry.
9. Any maverick jeans firm that raises or lowers its price will earn less profits. Therefore, firms in the jeans industry face a kinked demand curve, and prices remain rigid. Although firms do not engage in price competition, they can engage in nonprice competition. Each firm can use advertising and style to market its brand-name product.
11. The pricing behavior follows the price leadership model. The price leader is Hewlett-Packard, which is the largest and most dominant firm in the computer printer industry. After a price war, IBM followed each of Hewlett-Packard's price hikes.
13. If both firms spend no money advertising, they each earn a profit of $8 billion in cell A. If either firm does not advertise and the other firm does in cell B or cell C, then the advertising firm attracts more customers and earns $10 billion compared to a −$2 billion loss for the rival without ads. This outcome forces both firms to advertise and reduce mutual profits at cell D. As a result of both firms spending large budgets on advertising, their mutual profits are reduced to $5 billion. If the government bans all cigarette advertising, the result is that both firms will move to the mutually high profit cell A.

Chapter 11 Labor Markets

1. This statement is incorrect. Workers supply their labor to employers. Demand refers to the quantity of labor employers hire at various wage rates based on the marginal revenue product of labor.
3. The MRP of the second worker is this person's contribution to total revenue, which is $50 ($150 − $100). Because $MRP = P \times MP$ and

$MP = MRP/P$, the second worker's marginal product (MP) is no 10 ($50/$5).

5. The firm in a perfectly competitive labor market is a price taker. Because a single firm buys the labor of a relatively small portion of workers in an industry, it can hire additional workers and not drive up the wage rate. For the industry, however, all firms must offer higher wages to attract workers from other industries.

7. Students investing in education are increasing their human capital. A student with greater human capital increases his or her marginal product. At a given product price, the MRP is higher, and firms find it profitable to hire the better-educated worker and pay higher wages.

9. At a wage rate of $90 per day, Zippy Paper Company hires 3 workers because each worker's MRP exceeds or equals the wage rate. Setting the wage rate at $100 per day causes Zippy Paper Company to cut employment from 3 to 2 workers because the third worker's MRP is $10 below the union-caused wage rate of $100 per day.

11. As shown in the exhibit below, for a monopsony, the optimum quantity of labor is 3 quarterbacks, determined at point A, where the MFC curve intersects the MRP curve. However, the team can attract and hire 3 quarterbacks for an annual salary of $300,000 each at point B on the supply of labor curve, rather than paying a quarterback's contribution to the team's revenues (MRP), which is $500,000 per year at point A. In a competitive labor market, the Jacksonville Jaguars hire 4 quarterbacks and pay each $400,000 per year.

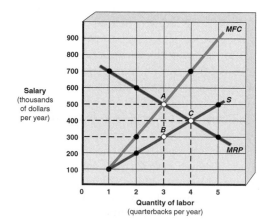

Chapter 12 Income Distribution, Poverty, and Discrimination

1. a.

Percentage of Families	Alpha		Beta	
	Percentage Share	Cumulative Share	Percentage Share	Cumulative Share
Lowest fifth	17.7%	17.7%	9.0%	9.0%
Second-lowest fifth	19.9	37.6	14.2	23.2
Middle fifth	20.4	58.0	17.5	40.7
Second-highest fifth	20.7	78.7	21.9	62.6
Highest fifth	21.3	100.0	37.4	100.0

b.

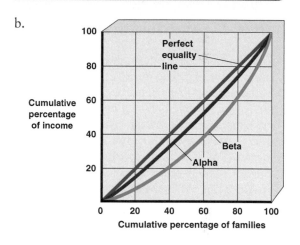

c. Because the Lorenz curve for Alpha is closest to the perfect equality line, Alpha's distribution of income is more equal compared to Beta.

3. Absolute poverty is defined as a dollar figure that represents some level of income per year required to purchase some minimum amount of goods and services essential to meeting a person's or a family's basic needs. Relative poverty is defined as a level of income required to place a person or family in, say, the lowest 20 percent among all persons or families receiving incomes. The poverty line is based on the absolute definition.

5. In-kind transfers are payments in the form of goods and services rather than cash. Examples include such government programs as food stamps, Medicaid, and housing. Noncash income is not counted in a family's income to determine whether the family's income is below the poverty line.

7. The percentage of families in the United States classified as poor was about 12 percent. Poor families are more likely to live in the South. The age, race,

and education of the head of the family are also important characteristics of poor families.

9. The three major criticisms are that welfare: (1) reduces the work incentive, (2) is inefficient because the programs cost too much to administer, and (3) treats poor persons with the same needs unequally because the states pay different benefits.

11. This is an opinion question. To agree, you assume that markets are perfectly competitive and discrimination is therefore unprofitable. To disagree, you can argue that in reality labor markets will never be perfectly competitive and the government must therefore address the institutional causes of poverty.

Chapter 13 Antitrust and Regulation

1. The Sherman Act outlaws price-fixing or anticompetitive practices designed to eliminate rivals. The Clayton Act clarifies the Sherman Act by outlawing specific business practices, including price discrimination, exclusive dealing, tying contracts, stock acquisition, and interlocking directorates. The U.S. Department of Justice and Federal Trade Commission (FTC) are responsible for enforcing these laws. Private firms can also bring suit against other firms under these laws.

3. Both the Robinson-Patman Act and the Celler-Kefauver Act were amendments to close loopholes in the Clayton Act. The Robinson-Patman Act expanded the list of illegal price discrimination practices to include quantity discounting, free advertising, and promotional allowances offered that "substantially lessen competition or tend to create a monopoly." The Celler-Kefauver Act closed the loophole in the Clayton Act whereby competing firms could merge by asset acquisition (not outlawed in the Clayton Act), rather than by acquiring stock (outlawed in the Clayton Act).

5. In fact, Alcoa argued that metals such as copper and steel are substitutes for aluminum. Therefore, the relevant industry to compute market share was the metals industry and not the aluminum industry. If the court had chosen the U.S. metals industry as the relevant industry, Alcoa would not have a monopoly.

7. a. The federal government will charge the bookstore with predatory pricing in order to monopolize its college market for books, which is a violation of the Sherman Act.

b. The federal government will charge the real estate firms with collusion to fix prices, which is a violation of the Sherman Act.

c. The federal government will charge a violation of the Clayton Act because the combined market share of this horizontal merger would substantially lessen competition in the personal computer market.

d. The federal government will not charge a violation because this is a conglomerate merger between firms in unrelated industries.

9. The "necessary" condition would be expected to favor existing regulated firms by eliminating or greatly restricting competition and raising prices. The existing regulated firms are better organized politically than either new competitors or consumers. While consumers favor competition and lower prices, regulators would be expected to interpret "necessary" to mean that the service provided by existing firms is sufficient without new firms.

11. Although a public subsidy achieves efficiency, marginal-cost pricing is usually unpopular with voters, who must provide the monopolist with public funds. Moreover, a public subsidy gives the monopolist a disincentive to minimize costs.

Chapter 14 Environmental Economics

1. A competitive industry selling a pollution-generating product will charge a lower price and sell a larger quantity than would be the case for a "green" industry. The competitive industry has lower costs because it fails to include external costs. Lower costs allow a lower price. A lower price leads to a larger quantity demanded and sold.

3. If you choose the $90,000 house, the EMF radiation is *not* an externality. An externality is a third-party effect, whereby buyers and sellers of a product ignore the spillover effects of their transaction. In this case, the market reflects the risk of cancer, with the seller accepting a lower price and the buyer saving $10,000 to reflect the cancer risk.

Houses have many characteristics that influence their price, including number of rooms, location, nearby schools, and environmental amenities. If you are willing to buy a house near a nuclear plant, or near EMFs, you, the buyer, bear the consequences, not a third party.

5. An instructor who automatically flunks students who do not turn in all homework assignments is exhibiting command-and-control regulation. She is dictating the production process for achieving knowledge. The inefficiencies are that students may turn in poorly done assignments or may copy assignments and that some students may understand the material without doing the homework or may have an alternative production method, such as the use of computer software, to achieve knowledge. The instructor's method is particularly inefficient if her assignments are busywork and do not really help the students to achieve knowledge.

7.

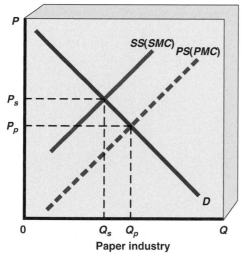

Paper industry

At Q_p, pollution from paper production leads to coffee-colored rivers. At socially efficient Q_s, there is less pollution, and rivers are less polluted. The rivers are unlikely to be pristine, which requires no production at all.

9. Consumers will share in the benefits of cleaner air if any individual buys a less polluting car. Since they enjoy the same benefit whether they pay extra or their neighbor pays extra for a cleaner car, they will let the neighbor buy the cleaner car. Of course, since their neighbor uses the same reasoning, no one ends up paying extra to buy a cleaner car.

11. Convincing examples should be sent to the author of the text. It is very difficult to find markets where the transaction costs of reaching an agreement are near zero. It is also difficult to find two-party situations, since most pollution spills over to many individuals. With many individuals involved, the free-rider problem arises, as a given individual wants to benefit from pollution agreements, but let others bear the cost. There can often be income effects, as fighting pollution may take a large amount of one's income. Candidates for markets where the Coase Theorem might apply include convincing your neighbor to leash her dog (you might help finance invisible fencing), enforcing laws concerning the fencing of cattle (see question 12 for further discussion), and settling disputes when one builder interferes with the views of existing homes.

13. a. Command-and-control regulation would dictate the use of an alternative technology with lower carbon emissions.

   b. An effluent tax would place a tax on carbon emissions so that firms could no longer ignore these costs. In turn, prices of carbon-emitting products would increase, and quantities would decrease.

   c. Permits would be issued giving the right to emit carbon. The number of permits would equal the socially efficient emissions level. Firms would be allowed to buy or sell these permits. Firms with higher marginal costs of emissions abatement would buy permits, while firms that could reduce emissions at a lower cost would profit from selling permits.

Chapter 15 Gross Domestic Product

1. a. final service
   b. final good
   c. intermediate good
   d. intermediate good

3.
3 million pounds of food × $1 per pound	= $3 million
50,000 shirts × $20 per shirt	= 1 million
20 houses × $50,000 per house	= 1 million
50,000 hours of medical services × $20 per hour	= 1 million
1 automobile plant × $1 million per plant	= 1 million
2 tanks × $500,000 per tank	= 1 million
Total value of output	= $8 million

5. Capital is not excluded from being a final good. A final good is a finished good purchased by an ultimate user and not for resale. The ultimate user is the warehouse, so the sale would be included in GDP and there would be no double-counting problem.

7. Using the expenditure approach, net exports are exports minus imports. If the expenditures by foreigners for U.S. products exceed the expenditures by U.S. citizens for foreign products, net exports will be a positive contribution to GDP. If foreigners spend less for U.S. products than U.S. citizens spend for foreign products, GDP is reduced. Net exports are used by national income accountants because actual consumption, investment, and government spending figures reported to the U.S. Department of Commerce do not exclude the amount of expenditures for imports.

9. $NI = GDP -$ depreciation
$\$4,007 = \$4,486 - \$479$

The depreciation charge is not a measure of newly produced output. It is an estimate, subject to error, of the value of capital worn out in the production of final goods and services. Errors in the capital consumption allowance overstate or understate GDP.

11. When the price level is rising, nominal GDP overstates the rate of change between years. Dividing nominal GDP by the GDP chain price index results in real GDP by removing the distortion from inflation. Comparison of real GDP changes between years reflects only changes in the market value of all final products and not changes in the price level.

13. GDP does not tell the mix of output in two nations, say, between military and consumer goods. GDP also does not reveal whether GDP is more equally distributed in one nation compared to another.

Chapter 16 Business Cycles and Unemployment

1. The generally accepted theory of business cycles is that they are the result of changes in the level of total spending, or aggregate demand. Total spending includes spending for final goods by households, businesses, government, and foreign buyers. Expressed as a formula, $GDP = -C + I + G + (X-M)$.

3. **Civilian unemployment rate**

$$= \frac{\textbf{unemployed}}{\textbf{civilian labor force}} \times 100$$

where the civilian labor force = unemployed + employed. Therefore,

$$7.7\% = \frac{\textbf{10 million persons}}{\textbf{130 million persons}} \times 100$$

5. The official unemployment rate is overstated when respondents to the BLS falsely report that they are seeking employment. The unemployment rate is understated when *discouraged workers* who want to work have given up searching for a job.

7. Structural unemployment occurs when those seeking jobs do not possess the skills necessary to fill the available jobs. Cyclical unemployment is caused by deficient total spending.

9. The increasing participation of women and teenagers in the labor force has increased the rate of unemployment. Women take more time out of the labor force than do men for childbearing and child rearing.

11. The GDP gap is the difference between potential real GDP and actual real GDP. Because potential real GDP is estimated on the basis of the full-employment rate of unemployment, the GDP gap measures the cost of *cyclical* unemployment in terms of real GDP.

Chapter 17 Inflation

1. This statement is incorrect. The price of a single good or service can rise while the average price of all goods and services falls. In short, the inflation rate rises when the average price of consumer goods and services rises.

3. First, the CPI is based on a typical market basket purchased by the urban family. Any group not buying the same market basket, such as retired persons, is not experiencing the price changes measured by changes in the CPI. Second, the CPI fails to adjust for quality changes. Third, the CPI ignores the law of demand and the substitution effect as prices of products change.

5. If the percentage increase in the CPI exceeds the salary increase, a person's purchasing power declines in a given year.

7. The loan is advantageous to you because the real interest rate is −5 percent (5 percent nominal interest rate minus 10 percent inflation). In one year, you must repay $105. If prices rise by 10 percent during the year, the real value of the $105 will be only $95. Therefore, you have borrowed $100 worth of purchasing power and are repaying $95 worth of purchasing power.

9. At full employment, the economy operates at full capacity and produces the maximum output of goods and services. As buyers try to outbid one another for the fixed supply of goods and services, prices rise rapidly.

11. If buyers think prices will be higher tomorrow, they may buy products today and cause demand-pull inflation. If businesses believe prices for inputs will be higher in the future, many will raise prices today and cause cost-push inflation.

Chapter 18 The Keynesian Model

1. Classical economists argued that underconsumption and unemployment could not exist in the long run because of price-wage flexibility. Unsold merchandise would force firms to compete and lower product prices, and unemployed workers would accept a lower wage rate.

3. Consumers have only two options for any extra disposable income they receive. The *MPC* and *MPS* must add up to one because the portion of extra income that is not spent must be saved.

5. a. The consumption schedule downshifts, and the saving schedule downshifts.
   b. The consumption schedule upshifts, and the saving schedule downshifts.
   c. The consumption schedule downshifts, and the saving schedule upshifts.
   d. The consumption schedule downshifts, and the saving schedule downshifts.
   e. Both the consumption and the saving schedules downshift.

7. Changes in the nonincome determinants of the consumption and saving schedules tend to offset each other, and people are reluctant to change their consumption and saving habits. On the other hand, Keynes considered the volatility of businesses' decisions to invest as a major cause of the business cycle. The potentially unstable determinants of investment spending include expectations, technological change, the stock of capital goods, and business taxes.

9. a.

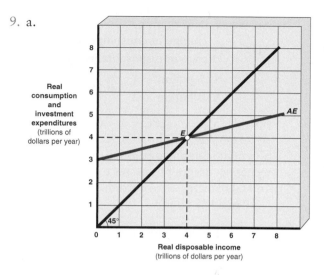

b. The autonomous consumption is $3 trillion, and the $MPC = 0.25$. Note that each $1 trillion increase in real disposable income results in a $0.25 trillion increase in aggregate expenditures. Since $MPS = (1 − MPC)$, $MPS = (1 − 0.25) = 0.75$.

c. The equilibrium level of real disposable income equals $4 trillion where the *AE* line intersects the 45° line.

d. An increase in autonomous investment adds new spending by businesses at each level of aggregate spending. The *AE* line would therefore shift upward, and the equilibrium level of real disposable income increases.

Chapter 19 The Keynesian Model in Action

1.

Possible Levels of Employment (millions)	Real GDP (output) Equals Disposable Income (billions of dollars)	Consumption (billions of dollars)	Unplanned Inventory (billions of dollars)
40	325	300	−75
45	375	325	−50
50	425	350	−25
55	475	375	0
60	525	400	25
65	575	425	50
70	625	450	75

a. Answers are given in the above table.

b.
$$MPC = \frac{\text{change in consumption}}{\text{change in disposable income}}$$

$$= \frac{\$25 \text{ billion}}{\$50 \text{ billion}} = \frac{1}{2} = 0.50$$

since $MPS = 1 - MPC = 1 - 0.50 = 0.50$

c. At an employment level of 40 million workers, $75 million in unplanned inventory investment encourages businesses to expand output, and GDP increases toward the equilibrium real GDP of $475 billion.

3.

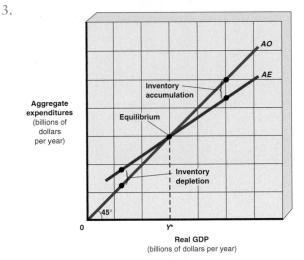

Aggregate expenditures (billions of dollars per year)

Real GDP (billions of dollars per year)

The aggregate expenditures (AE) line intersects the aggregate output (AO) line at the equilibrium level of real GDP, Y^*. Below Y^*, an unplanned inventory depletion causes businesses to expand output, which pushes the economy toward equilibrium output. Above Y^*, an unintended inventory accumulation pushes the economy toward Y^* by pressuring businesses to reduce production.

5.
$$\text{Multiplier} = \frac{1}{1 - MPC} = \frac{1}{MPS}$$

The greater the MPC, the smaller the MPS and the greater the size of the multiplier.

a. 1, 1.5, 10

b. $Y = M \times I = 5 \times \$10 \text{ billion} = \$50 \text{ billion}$

c. $Y = M \times I = 3 \times \$10 \text{ billion} = \$30 \text{ billion}$

7. a.

Round	Component of Total Spending	New Consumption Spending (billions of dollars)
1	Investment	$100
2	Consumption	75
3	Consumption	56
4	Consumption	42
	Total spending	$273

b. The spending multiplier is

$$\frac{1}{(1 - MPC)} = \frac{1}{(1 - 0.75)} = \frac{1}{0.25} = 4$$

Therefore, change in investment spending × spending multiplier = change in aggregate spending ($100 billion × 4 = $400 billion).

Note: This problem demonstrates how useful the spending multiplier formula is because it avoids working through individual steps in the multiplier process.

9. **Spending multiplier**

$$= \frac{\text{change in GDP}}{\text{change in government spending}} = \frac{\Delta Y}{\Delta G}$$

Since $MPC = 0.75$,

$$\textbf{Spending multiplier} = \frac{1}{(1 - MPC)} = \frac{1}{0.25} = 4$$

rewritten as

$$4 = \frac{\$100 \text{ billion}}{\Delta G}$$

Therefore,

$$\Delta G = \frac{\$100 \text{ billion}}{4} = \$25 \text{ billion}$$

Given that the MPC is 0.75, this means households spend only $18.75 billion of the additional $25 billion of disposable income from the tax cut. Therefore,

$\Delta C \times$ **spending multiplier** = **change in GDP**
$18.75 billion × 4 = $75 billion

Because GDP must increase by $100 billion, a tax cut of $25 billion would not be enough to restore full-employment GDP.

Chapter 20 Aggregate Demand and Supply

1. There are three reasons why the aggregate demand curve is downward sloping:
   a. The *real balances effect* means that a lower price level increases the purchasing power of money and other financial assets. The result is an increase in consumption, which increases the quantity of real GDP demanded.
   b. The *interest-rate effect* assumes a fixed money supply, and, therefore, a lower price level reduces the demand for borrowing and the interest rate. The lower rate of interest increases spending for consumption and investment.
   c. The *net exports effect* encourages foreign customers to buy more of an economy's domestic exports relative to its domestic purchases of imports when the price level falls. An increase in net exports increases aggregate expenditures.
   Rationales for the downward-sloping demand curve for an individual market are the income effect, the substitution effect, and the law of diminishing marginal utility, which are quite different from the three effects that determine the aggregate demand curve.

3. a. A leftward shift occurs because of a decrease in the consumption schedule.
   b. A rightward shift occurs because of an increase in autonomous investment spending.
   c. A rightward shift occurs because of an increase in government spending.
   d. A rightward shift occurs because of an increase in net exports.

5. This statement may not be correct. The equilibrium GDP is not necessarily the same as the full-employment GDP. Equilibrium GDP refers to the equality between the aggregate demand and the aggregate supply curves, which does not necessarily equal the full capacity of the economy to produce goods and services.

7. a. leftward because of an increase in resource prices
   b. rightward because of a decrease in resource prices

   c. rightward because technological change reduces the cost of production
   d. leftward because an increase in taxes means the price must cover the tax at each possible quantity supplied

9. a. Aggregate demand increases.
   b. Aggregate supply increases.
   c. Aggregate demand decreases.
   d. Aggregate supply decreases.
   e. Aggregate demand decreases along the classical range.
   f. Aggregate demand increases along the Keynesian range.

11. Assuming the aggregate supply curve remains constant, a rightward shift of the aggregate demand curve from AD_1 to AD_2 in the upward-sloping or the vertical range of the aggregate supply curve causes the price level to rise from P_1 to P_2. In addition to demand-pull inflation, the level of real GDP increases from Q_1 to Q_2 and provides the economy with new jobs. In the classical range, inflation is the only undesirable result, and real GDP remains unaffected at Q_2.

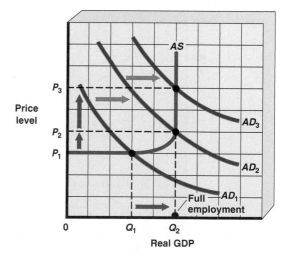

Appendix to Chapter 20
The Self-Correcting Aggregate Demand and Supply Model

1. a.–c.

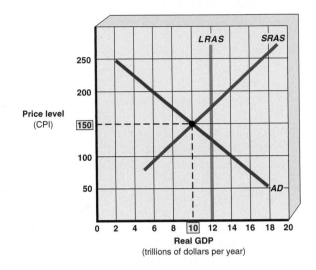

Price level (CPI)

Real GDP
(trillions of dollars per year)

3.

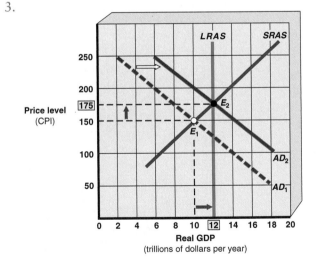

Price level (CPI)

Real GDP
(trillions of dollars per year)

5. Nominal incomes of workers in the short run are fixed. In response to the fall in aggregate demand, firms' profits decline, and they cut output and employment. As a result, the economy moves downward along $SRAS$ to temporary equilibrium at E_2. When workers lower their nominal incomes because of competition from unemployed workers, the short-run aggregate supply curve shifts rightward to E_3 and returns to long-run equilibrium. Profits rise and firms increase output and employment while the price level falls.

Chapter 21 Fiscal Policy

1. *Expansionary* fiscal policy refers to increasing government spending and/or decreasing taxes in order to increase aggregate demand and eliminate a GDP gap. *Contractionary* fiscal policy is designed to cool inflation by decreasing aggregate demand. This result is accomplished by decreasing government spending and/or increasing taxes.
3. a. contractionary fiscal policy
   b. contractionary fiscal policy
   c. expansionary fiscal policy
5. The spending multiplier is

$$\frac{1}{1 - MPC} = \frac{1}{0.25} = \frac{1}{1/4} = 4$$

The spending multiplier (SM) times the change in government spending (ΔG) equals the change in aggregate demand (ΔAD). Therefore,

$$\Delta G \times SM = AD$$
$$G \times 4 = \$500 \text{ billion}$$
$$G = \$125 \text{ billion}$$

The government must increase government spending by \$125 billion in order to eliminate the GDP gap.

7. The tax multiplier equals the spending multiplier minus one. Thus, the impact of the expansion in government spending exceeds the impact of an equal amount of tax cut.
9. As a supply-side economist, you would argue that the location of the aggregate supply curve is related to the tax rates. Ceteris paribus, if the tax rates are cut, there will be strong incentives for workers to supply more work, households to save more, and businesses to invest more in capital goods. Thus, cutting tax rates shifts the aggregate supply curve rightward, the level of real GDP rises, and the price level falls.
11. a. rightward shift in the aggregate demand curve
    b. leftward shift in the aggregate demand curve
    c. rightward shift in the aggregate supply curve
    d. rightward shift in the aggregate demand curve
    e. leftward shift in the aggregate supply curve

Chapter 22 The Public Sector

1. Transfer payments account for the difference between total government expenditures, or outlays, and total government spending. Transfers do not

"use up" resources; they reallocate purchasing power by collecting taxes from one group and paying benefits to other groups.

3. The primary sources are individual income taxes at the federal level, sales and excise taxes at the state level, and property taxes at the local level.

5. The marginal tax rate is the percentage of additional income paid in taxes. The average tax rate is the amount of taxes paid as a percentage of income.

7. a. more than $6,000
   b. less than $6,000
   c. $6,000

9. Sales tax paid as a percentage of income:
   10%
   7%
   6%
   4%
   Because the sales tax paid as a percentage of income falls as income rises, the tax is regressive.

11. A profit-maximizing firm follows the marginal rule that units will be produced so long as the marginal benefit exceeds or equals the marginal cost. Dollars can measure the intensity of benefits in relation to costs. A "one-person, one-vote" system does not necessarily measure benefits in proportion to the dollar value of benefits among individual voters. Thus, a majority of voters can approve projects for which costs exceed benefits and reject projects for which benefits exceed costs.

Chapter 23 Federal Deficits, Surpluses, and the National Debt

1. The national debt is the sum of past federal budget deficits. When budget deficits are large, the national debt increases at a rapid rate. When budget deficits are small, the national debt increases at a lower rate.

3. The statement makes the argument that most of the debt is internal national debt that one U.S. citizen owes to another U.S. citizen. Suppose the federal government finances a deficit by having the Treasury sell government bonds to one group of U.S. citizens, thereby increasing the national debt. When the bonds mature, the government can pay the interest and principal by issuing new government bonds (rolling over the debt) to another group of U.S. citizens. This argument ignores the income distribution problem that results because

interest payments go largely to those who are better off financially.

5. When the government makes interest payments on internally held debt, the money remains in the hands of U.S. citizens. External debt is very different. Repayment of interest and principal to foreigners withdraws purchasing power from U.S. citizens in favor of citizens abroad.

7. a. In year one, the federal deficit begins at $50 billion, and the U.S. Treasury issues $50 billion worth of bonds to finance the deficit.
   b. The next year the federal government must pay interest of $5 billion to service the debt ($50 billion bonds × 0.10 interest rate). Adding the interest payment to the $100 billion spent for goods and services yields a $105 billion expenditure in year two.
   c. For the second year, the deficit is $55 billion ($105 billion in expenditures − $50 billion in taxes), and the U.S. Treasury borrows this amount by issuing new bonds. The new national debt is $105 billion, consisting of the $50 billion in bonds issued in the first year and the $55 billion in bonds issued in the second year.

9. During a depression, tax hikes and/or expenditure cuts would only reduce aggregate demand and, in turn, real GDP, jobs, and income. Because the economy is operating in the Keynesian segment of the aggregate demand curve, this fiscal policy would have no impact on the price level.

11. This answer should be logical and supported by a thoughtful explanation.

Chapter 24 Money and the Federal Reserve System

1. Money is worthless in and of itself. The value of money is to serve as a medium of exchange, a unit of account, and a store of value.

3. a. The quantity of credit cards can be controlled. Credit cards are portable, divisible, and uniform in quality.
   b. The quantity of Federal Reserve notes is controlled by the U.S. government. These notes are portable, divisible, and uniform in quality.
   c. The quantity of dogs is difficult to control. Dogs are not very portable or divisible, and they are certainly not uniform.
   d. The quantity of beer mugs can be controlled. Beer mugs are not very portable or divisible, but they could be made fairly uniform.

5. The narrowest definition of money in the United States is M1. M1 = currency (coins plus paper bills) + checkable deposits.

7. The Fed's most important function is to regulate the U.S. money supply. The *Board of Governors* is composed of seven persons who have the responsibility to supervise and control the money supply and the U.S. banking system. The *Federal Open Market Committee (FOMC)* controls the money supply by directing the buying and selling of U.S. government securities.

9. Banks that belong to the Fed must join the FDIC. Banks chartered by the states may affiliate with the FDIC. There are relatively few nonmember, noninsured state banks.

Chapter 25 Money Creation

1. At first, the goldsmiths followed Shakespeare's advice and gave receipts only for gold on deposit in their vaults. They then realized that at any given time new deposits were coming in that could offset old deposits people were drawing down. The conclusion is that banking does not require a 100 percent required reserve ratio. Therefore, loans can be made, which stimulate the economy.

3. Banks can and do create money by granting loans to borrowers. These loans are deposited in customers' checking accounts, and, therefore, banks are participants in the money supply creation process.

5. There is no impact on the money supply. A check deposited in bank *A*, drawn on bank *B*, increases deposits, reserves, and lending at bank *A*. However, bank *B* experiences an equal reduction in deposits, reserves, and lending.

7.

First National Bank

Balance Sheet

Assets		Liabilities	
Reserves	−$1,000	Checkable deposits	−$1,000
Required	−$100		
Excess	−$900		
Total assets	−$1,000	Total liabilities	−$1,000

Negative excess reserves mean that loans must be reduced by $1,000.

9. Some customers may hold cash, rather than writing a check for the full amount of the loan. Some banks may hold excess reserves, rather than using these funds to make loans.

11. The decision of the public to hold cash and the willingness of banks to use excess reserves for loans affect the money multiplier. Variations in the money multiplier can cause unexpected changes in the money supply. Nonbanks can make loans and offer other financial services that are not under the direct control of the Federal Reserve. Finally, the public can decide to transfer funds from *M1* to *M2* or other definitions of the money supply.

Chapter 26 Monetary Policy

1. a. Transactions and precautionary balances increase.
   b. Speculative balances decrease.
   c. Transactions and precautionary balances decrease.
   d. Speculative balances increase.
   e. Transactions and precautionary balances decrease.

3.

Bond price	Interest rate
$ 800	10%
1,000	8
2,000	4

There is an inverse relationship between the price of a bond and the interest rate.

5. a. The price level declines slightly. Real GDP and employment fall substantially.
   b. The price level, real GDP, and employment rise.
   c. The price level declines slightly. Real GDP and employment fall substantially.

7. In the monetarist view, the velocity of money, *V*, and the output, *Q*, variables in the equation of exchange are constant. Therefore, the quantity theory of money is stated as

$$M \times V = P \times Q$$

Given this equation, changes in the money supply, *M1*, yield proportionate changes in the price level, *P*.

9. In the Keynesian view, an increase in the money supply decreases the interest rate and causes investment spending, which increases aggregate demand through the multiplier effect and causes demand-pull inflation. In the monetarist view, money supply growth gives people more money to spend. This direct increase in aggregate demand causes demand-pull inflation.

11. Under such conditions, the Keynesian view is correct. The Fed would have no influence on investment because changes in the interest rate failed to alter the quantity of investment goods demanded.

Chapter 27 The Phillips Curve and Expectations Theory

1. The Phillips curve is an inverse relationship between the inflation rate and the unemployment rate. The increase in aggregate demand would cause the inflation rate to increase and the unemployment rate to decrease.

3. In the 1970s and early 1980s, the economy experienced supply shocks from skyrocketing oil and food prices. The result was a leftward shift in the aggregate supply curve and stagflation.

5. a. The inflation rate is 6 percent, and the unemployment rate is 6 percent.
   b. The inflation rate rises to 10 percent, and the employment rate falls in the short run. In the long run, the unemployment rate returns to 6 percent.
   c. The inflation rate rises to 12 percent, and the unemployment rate falls in the short run. In the long run, the unemployment rate returns to 6 percent.

7. The economy is stimulated prior to an election, and there is a boom. After the election, the strategy is to contract the economy, causing recession until the next election approaches. Thus, political policies are counter to Keynesian policies because political policies cause the business cycle instead of stabilizing it.

9. a. Both prices and nominal wages will rise immediately, causing the inflation rate to rise from 4 percent to 6 percent. The unemployment rate remains unchanged at the 4 percent natural rate.
   b. Both prices and nominal wages will rise immediately, causing the inflation rate to rise from 6 percent to 8 percent. The unemployment rate remains unchanged at the 4 percent natural rate.
   c. Both prices and nominal wages will fall immediately, causing the inflation rate to fall from 8 percent to 4 percent. The unemployment rate remains unchanged at the 4 percent natural rate.

Chapter 28 International Trade and Finance

1. a. In Alpha, the opportunity cost of producing 1 ton of diamonds is 1/2 ton of pearls. In Beta, the opportunity cost of producing 1 ton of diamonds is 2 tons of pearls.
   b. In Alpha, the opportunity cost of producing 1 ton of pearls is 2 tons of diamonds. In Beta, the opportunity cost of producing 1 ton of pearls is 1/2 ton of diamonds.
   c. Because Alpha can produce diamonds at a lower opportunity cost than Beta can, Alpha has a comparative advantage in the production of diamonds.
   d. Because Beta can produce pearls at a lower opportunity cost than Alpha can, Beta has a comparative advantage in the production of pearls.
   e.

	Diamonds (tons per year)	Pearls (tons per year)
Before specialization		
Alpha (at point *B*)	~~100~~	~~25~~
Beta (at point *C*)	30	120
Total output	130	145
After specialization		
Alpha (at point *A*)	~~150~~	~~0~~
Beta (at point *D*)	0	180
Total output	150	180

As shown in the above table, specialization in each country increases total world output per year by 20 tons of diamonds and 35 tons of pearls.

f.

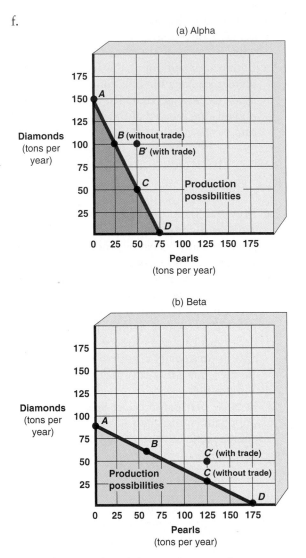

(a) Alpha

(b) Beta

Without trade, Alpha produces and consumes 100 tons of diamonds and 25 tons of pearls at point *B* on its production possibilities curve. Without trade, Beta produces and consumes 30 tons of diamonds and 120 tons of pearls (point *C*). Now assume Alpha specializes in producing diamonds at point *A* and imports 50 tons of pearls in exchange for 50 tons of diamonds. Through specialization and trade, Alpha moves its consumption possibility to point *B'*, outside its production possibilities curve.

3. The principle of specialization and trade according to comparative advantage applies to both nations and states in the United States. For example, Florida grows oranges, and Idaho grows

potatoes. Trade between these states, just like trade between nations, increases the consumption possibilities.

5. U.S. industries (and their workers) that compete with restricted imports would benefit. Consumers would lose from the reduced supply of imported goods from which to choose and from higher prices for domestic products, resulting from lack of competition from imports.

7. Although some domestic jobs may be lost, new ones are created by international trade. Stated differently, the economy as a whole gains when nations specialize and trade according to the law of comparative advantage, but imports will cost jobs in some specific industries.

9. Although each nation's balance of payments equals zero, its current and capital account balances usually do not equal zero. For example, a current account deficit means a nation purchased more in imports than it sold in exports. On the other hand, this nation's capital account must have a surplus to offset the current account deficit. This means that foreigners are buying more domestic capital (capital inflow) than domestic citizens are buying foreign capital (capital outflow). Thus, net ownership of domestic capital stock is in favor of foreigners.

11. a.

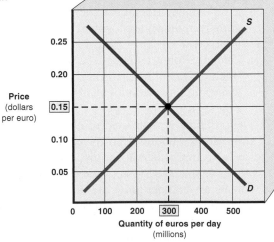

b. $0.15 per euro

c. An excess quantity of 200 million euros would be demanded.

Chapter 29 Economies in Transition

1. Americans prefer large cars and canned soup. Europeans predominantly buy small cars and dry soup. The role of women and minorities in the workplace is an excellent example of how culture relates to the labor factor of production.

3. Such a program would provide additional economic security for the elderly, but higher taxes could reduce the incentive to work, and economic efficiency might be reduced.

5. In a traditional agricultural system, a benefit would be that members of society would cooperate by helping to build barns, harvest, and so on. Under the command system, worrying about errors and crop failures would be minimized because the state makes the decisions and everyone in society has a basic income. In a market economy, a bumper crop would mean large profits and the capacity to improve one's standard of living.

7. Because most economies are mixed systems, this term is too broad to be very descriptive. The terms *capitalism* and *communism* are more definitive concerning the role of private ownership, market allocations, and decentralized decision making. Embracing a market-oriented system means a transfer of power from the command bureaucracy to consumers. Markets are incompatible with the principle that socialist citizens are supposed to be concerned with the collective interest.

Chapter 30 Growth and the Less-Developed Countries

1. The difference between IACs and LDCs is based on GDP per capita. This classification is somewhat arbitrary. A country with a high GDP per capita and narrow industrial development based on oil, such as the United Arab Emirates, is excluded from the IAC list. There are 27 economies listed in the text as IACs, including Switzerland, Japan, the United States, Singapore, and Hong Kong. The following countries are considered to be LDCs: Argentina, Mexico, South Africa, Jordan, and Bangladesh.

3. a. Based only on GDP per capita, you would conclude that Alpha is a better place to live because this country produces a greater output of goods and services per person.

   b. Based on the additional evidence, you would change your mind and prefer to live in Beta because the quality-of-life data indicate a higher standard of living in this country.

5. The average growth rate of GDP per capita for IACs exceeds the GDP per capita growth rate for LDCs. This evidence is consistent with the argument. The argument is oversimplified because there is considerable diversity among the LDCs. In a given year, a LDC may have a GDP per capita growth rate greater than many IACs.

7. Economic growth and development are complicated because there is no single prescription that a country can follow. The text presents a multidimensional model with five basic categories: natural resources, human resources, capital, technological progress, and political environment. Because an LDC is weak in one or more of the key factors, such as natural resources, does not necessarily mean that the LDC cannot achieve economic success.

9. Because they are poor countries with low GDP per capita, they lack domestic savings to invest in capital; and lacking investment, they remain poor. The rich in these poor countries often put their savings abroad because of the fear of political instability. An inflow of external funds from abroad permits the LDC to increase its capital without reducing its consumption and to shift its production possibilities curve outward.

11. Poor countries are too poor to save enough to finance domestic capital formation. International trade is a way LDCs can generate savings from abroad. Exports provide the LDCs with foreign exchange to pay for imports of capital stock that is necessary for economic growth and development.

APPENDIX

B Answers to Practice Quizzes

Chapter 1 Introducing the Economic Way of Thinking

1. c   2. d   3. c   4. c   5. a   6. a   7. a   8. a
9. a   10. c   11. a   12. b   13. c   14. d   15. d

Appendix to Chapter 1 Applying Graphs to Economics

1. d   2. d   3. a   4. d   5. d   6. c   7. c   8. c
9. d   10. d   11. d   12. b

Chapter 2 Production Possibilities, Opportunity Cost, and Economic Growth

1. c   2. a   3. c   4. c   5. b   6. c   7. c   8. e
9. a   10. c   11. b   12. d   13. e   14. c   15. a

Chapter 3 Market Demand and Supply

1. e   2. a   3. b   4. b   5. a   6. b   7. c   8. b
9. c   10. b   11. c   12. c   13. d   14. d   15. c
16. d   17. d   18. c   19. d   20. d

Appendix to Chapter 3 Consumer Surplus, Producer Surplus, and Market Efficiency

1. c   2. b   3. d   4. e   5. d   6. d   7. b   8. d
9. a   10. b

Chapter 4 Markets in Action

1. a   2. a   3. c   4. d   5. d   6. d   7. c.   8. b
9. a   10. b   11. c   12. a   13. c   14. d   15. d

Chapter 5 Price Elasticity of Demand and Supply

1. a   2. b   3. a   4. a   5. a   6. d   7. a   8. a
9. d   10. c   11. c   12. c   13. c   14. b   15. b

Chapter 6 Consumer Choice Theory

1. c   2. d   3. a   4. a   5. d   6. d   7. c   8. b
9. a   10. a   11. b   12. a   13. d   14. a   15. d

Appendix to Chapter 6 Indifference Curve Analysis

1. d   2. d   3. c   4. d   5. c   6. b   7. d   8. b
9. d   10. a   11. c   12. b   13. a

Chapter 7 Production Costs

1. d   2. b   3. c   4. c   5. d   6. d   7. c   8. d
9. d   10. c   11. c   12. b   13. c   14. b   15. d
16. c   17. d   18. e   19. c   20. d

Chapter 8 Perfect Competition

1. b   2. b   3. b   4. b   5. c   6. d   7. b   8. d
9. b   10. b   11. a   12. d   13. b   14. d   15. d
16. a   17. d   18. d   19. b   20. a

Chapter 9 Monopoly

1. d   2. d   3. d   4. d   5. b   6. d   7. b   8. d
9. b   10. d   11. e   12. b   13. b   14. d   15. e

Chapter 10 Monopolistic Competition and Oligopoly

1. b   2. b   3. d   4. d   5. d   6. d   7. a   8. a
9. b   10. d   11. d   12. a   13. c   14. b   15. a
16. a   17. d   18. a   19. a   20. d

Chapter 11 Labor Markets

1. d   2. a   3. c   4. a   5. c   6. b   7. d   8. b
9. c   10. c   11. b   12. c   13. c   14. a   15. b

Chapter 12 Income Distribution, Poverty, and Discrimination

1. a   2. c   3. c   4. a   5. b   6. d   7. d   8. a
9. d   10. c   11. a   12. d   13. d   14. d   15. c

Chapter 13 Antitrust and Regulation

1. d   2. a   3. d   4. b   5. d   6. a   7. c   8. d
9. c   10. a   11. b   12. a   13. e   14. d   15. d

Chapter 14 Environmental Economics

1. d   2. e   3. a   4. a   5. a   6. c   7. d   8. b
9. d   10. b   11. b   12. b   13. c

Chapter 15 Gross Domestic Product

1. d   2. a   3. a   4. e   5. d   6. d   7. c   8. d
9. b   10. d   11. b   12. b   13. c   14. d   15. e

Chapter 16 Business Cycles and Unemployment

1. c   2. d   3. d   4. d   5. d   6. d   7. c   8. b
9. a   10. d   11. d   12. d   13. c   14. e   15. e

Chapter 17 Inflation

1. a   2. a   3. b   4. b   5. a   6. b   7. d   8. b
9. b   10. d   11. c   12. d   13. c   14. b   15. e

Chapter 18 The Keynesian Model

1. c   2. d   3. d   4. c   5. b   6. a   7. a   8. b
9. d   10. d   11. a   12. c   13. c   14. c   15. b

Chapter 19 The Keynesian Model in Action

1. d   2. b   3. d   4. a   5. c   6. b   7. d   8. d
9. c   10. b   11. b   12. b   13. c   14. a   15. b

Chapter 20 Aggregate Demand and Supply

1. c   2. b   3. a   4. c   5. d   6. a   7. c   8. c
9. d   10. c   11. c   12. d   13. a   14. d   15. a

Appendix to Chapter 20 The Self-Correcting Aggregate Demand and Supply Model

1. b   2. c   3. d   4. c   5. a   6. b   7. a   8. a
9. c   10. d   11. d   12. b   13. c   14. a   15. a

Chapter 21 Fiscal Policy

1. d   2. a   3. d   4. b   5. d   6. c   7. a   8. d
9. c   10. d   11. a   12. d   13. a   14. a   15. e

Chapter 22 The Public Sector

1. a   2. b   3. d   4. d   5. d   6. a   7. e   8. d
9. d   10. d   11. c   12. d   13. a   14. a   15. b

Chapter 23 Federal Deficits, Surpluses, and the National Debt

1. a   2. b   3. c   4. d   5. c   6. d   7. b   8. e
9. a   10. d   11. d   12. a   13. a   14. a   15. e

Chapter 24 Money and the Federal Reserve System

1. b   2. b   3. d   4. c   5. d   6. b   7. c   8. d
9. c   10. d   11. d   12. b   13. b   14. c   15. a

Chapter 25 Money Creation

1. b   2. b   3. b   4. c   5. c   6. d   7. c   8. c
9. b   10. b   11. a   12. d   13. d   14. a   15. a

Chapter 26 Monetary Policy

1. d   2. b   3. d   4. a   5. a   6. d   7. c   8. d
9. d   10. c   11. b   12. a   13. b   14. c   15. d

Appendix to Chapter 26 Policy Disputes Using the Self-Correcting Aggregate Demand and Supply Model

1. c   2. d   3. d   4. d   5. d   6. b

Chapter 27 The Phillips Curve and Expectations Theory

1. d   2. b   3. a   4. c   5. e   6. c   7. b   8. c
9. c   10. d   11. c   12. b   13. d   14. a   15. d

Chapter 28 International Trade and Finance

1. b   2. c   3. a   4. d   5. d   6. a   7. d   8. a
9. c   10. c   11. b   12. c   13. c   14. a   15. a
16. b   17. a   18. a   19. e   20. d

Chapter 29 Economies in Transition

1. c   2. d   3. d   4. a   5. b   6. a   7. c   8. b
9. b   10. c   11. c   12. a   13. a   14. d   15. a

Chapter 30 Growth and the Less Developed Countries

1. d   2. d   3. d   4. c   5. a   6. a   7. d   8. a
9. c   10. a   11. b   12. d   13. c   14. d   15. b

Answers to Road Map Questions

Part 1

1. e 2. c 3. c 4. d 5. a 6. e 7. d 8. d
9. d 10. b

Part 2

1. b 2. c 3. a 4. a 5. d 6. d 7. d 8. c
9. c 10. b 11. c

Part 3

1. c 2. e 3. c 4. b 5. a 6. a 7. b 8. c
9. d 10. b 11. d

Part 4

1. c 2. d 3. d 4. d 5. a 6. d 7. a

Part 5

1. e 2. a 3. a 4. c 5. c 6. b 7. b 8. d
9. a 10. a 11. c 12. d

Part 6

1. d 2. a 3. a 4. d 5. d 6. b 7. c 8. e
9. b 10. a 11. a 12. d 13. b 14. e 15. d

Part 7

1. d 2. d 3. d 4. e 5. c 6. b 7. a 8. d
9. d 10. a 11. e 12. d 13. a 14. a

Part 8

1. d 2. d 3. b 4. e 5. e 6. c 7. d 8. e
9. b 10. d

GLOSSARY

A

Ability-to-pay principle The concept that those who have higher incomes can afford to pay a greater proportion of their income in taxes, regardless of benefits received.

Absolute advantage The ability of a country to produce a good using fewer resources than another country.

Adaptive expectations theory The concept that people believe the best indicator of the future is recent information. As a result, people persistently underestimate inflation when it is accelerating and overestimate it while it is slowing down.

Adjustable-rate mortgage (ARM) A home loan that adjusts the nominal interest rate to changing rates of inflation.

Agency for International Development (AID) The agency of the U.S. State Department that is in charge of U.S. aid to foreign countries.

Aggregate demand curve (AD) The curve that shows the level of real GDP purchased by households, businesses, government, and foreigners (net exports) at different possible price levels during a time period, ceteris paribus.

Aggregate expenditures function (AE) The function that represents total spending in an economy at a given level of real disposable income.

Aggregate expenditures-output model The model that determines the equilibrium level of real GDP by the intersection of the aggregate expenditures and aggregate output (and income) curves.

Aggregate supply curve (AS) The curve that shows the level of real GDP produced at different possible price levels during a time period, ceteris paribus.

Appreciation of currency A rise in the price of one currency relative to another.

Arbitrage The practice of earning a profit by buying a good at a low price and reselling the good at a higher price.

Automatic stabilizers Federal expenditures and tax revenues that automatically change levels in order to stabilize an economic expansion or contraction; sometimes referred to as *nondiscretionary fiscal policy*.

Autonomous consumption Consumption that is independent of the level of disposable income.

Autonomous expenditure Spending that does not vary with the current level of disposable income.

Average fixed cost (AFC) Total fixed cost divided by the quantity of output produced.

Average tax rate The tax divided by the income.

Average total cost (ATC) Total cost divided by the quantity of output produced.

Average variable cost (AVC) Total variable cost divided by the quantity of output produced.

B

Balance of payments A bookkeeping record of all the international transactions between a country and other countries during a given period of time.

Balance of trade The value of a nation's goods imports subtracted from its goods exports.

Balanced budget multiplier An equal change in government spending and taxes, which changes aggregate demand by the amount of the change in government spending.

Barter The direct exchange of one good or service for another good or service, rather than for money.

Base year A year chosen as a reference point for comparison with some earlier or later year.

Benefit-cost analysis The comparison of the additional rewards and costs of an economic alternative.

Benefits-received principle The concept that those who benefit from government expenditures should pay the taxes that finance their benefits.

Board of Governors of the Federal Reserve System The seven members appointed by the president and confirmed by the U.S. Senate who serve for one nonrenewable 14-year term. Their responsibility is to supervise and control the money supply and the banking system of the United States.

Budget deficit A budget in which government expenditures exceed government revenues in a given time period.

Budget line A line that shows the different combinations of two goods a consumer can purchase with a given amount of money and prices for the goods.

Budget surplus A budget in which government revenues exceed government expenditures in a given time period.

Business cycle Alternating periods of economic growth and contraction, which can be measured by changes in real GDP.

C

Capital The physical plants, machinery, and equipment used to produce other goods. Capital goods are human-made goods that do not directly satisfy human wants.

Capitalism An economic system characterized by private ownership of resources and markets.

Cartel A group of firms that formally agree to control the price and the output of a product.

Celler-Kefauver Act A 1950 amendment to the Clayton Act that prohibits one firm from merging with a competitor by purchasing its physical assets if the effect is to substantially lessen competition.

Ceteris paribus A Latin phrase that means while certain variables change, "all other things remain unchanged."

Change in demand An increase or a decrease in the quantity demanded at each possible price. An increase in demand is a rightward shift in the entire demand curve. A decrease in demand is a leftward shift in the entire demand curve.

Change in quantity demanded A movement between points along a stationary demand curve, ceteris paribus.

Change in quantity supplied A movement between points along a stationary supply curve, ceteris paribus.

Change in supply An increase or a decrease in the quantity supplied at each possible price. An increase in supply is a rightward shift in the entire supply curve. A decrease in supply is a leftward shift in the entire supply curve.

Checkable deposits The total of checking account balances in financial institutions convertible to currency "on demand" when a check is written without advance notice.

Circular flow model A diagram showing the flow of products from businesses to households and the flow of resources from households to businesses. In exchange for these resources, money payments flow between businesses and households.

Civilian labor force The number of people 16 years of age and older who are employed or who are actively seeking a job, excluding armed forces, homemakers, discouraged workers, and other persons not in the labor force.

Classical economists A group of economists whose theory dominated economic thinking from the 1770s to the Great Depression. They believed recessions would naturally cure themselves because the price system would automatically restore full employment.

Classical range The vertical segment of the aggregate supply curve, which represents an economy at full-employment output.

Clayton Act A 1914 amendment that strengthens the Sherman Act by making it illegal for firms to engage in certain anticompetitive business practices.

Coase Theorem The proposition that private market negotiations can achieve social efficiency regardless of the initial definition of property rights.

Coincident indicators Variables that change at the same time that real GDP changes.

Collective bargaining The process of negotiating labor contracts between the union and management concerning wages and working conditions.

Command economy A system that answers the *What, How,* and *For Whom* questions by central authority.

Command-and-control regulations Government regulations that set an environmental goal and dictate how the goal will be achieved.

Commodity money Anything that serves as money while having market value in other uses.

Communism A stateless, classless economic system in which all the factors of production are owned by the workers, and people share in production according to their needs. In Marx's view, this is the highest form of socialism toward which the revolution should strive.

Comparable worth The principle that employees who work for the same employer must be paid the same wage when their jobs, even if different, require similar levels of education, training, experience, and responsibility. A nonmarket wage-setting process is used to evaluate and compensate jobs according to point scores assigned to different jobs.

Comparative advantage The ability of a country to produce a good at a lower opportunity cost than another country.

Complementary good A good that is jointly consumed with another good. As a result, there is an inverse relationship between a price change for one good and the demand for its "go together" good.

Conglomerate merger A merger between firms in unrelated markets.

Constant returns to scale A situation in which the long-run average cost curve does not change as the firm increases output.

Constant-cost industry An industry in which the expansion of industry output by the entry of new firms has no effect on the individual firm's average total cost curve.

Consumer equilibrium A condition in which total utility cannot increase by spending more of a given budget on one good and spending less on another good.

Consumer price index (CPI) An index that measures changes in the average prices of consumer goods and services.

Consumer sovereignty The freedom of consumers to cast their dollar votes to buy, or not to buy, at prices determined in competitive markets.

Consumer surplus The value of the difference between the price consumers are willing to pay for a product on the demand curve and the price actually paid for it.

Consumption function The graph or table that shows the amount households spend for goods and services at different levels of disposable income.

Cost-push inflation An increase in the general price level resulting from an increase in the cost of production that causes the aggregate supply curve to shift leftward.

Cross-elasticity of demand The ratio of the percentage change in the quantity demanded of a good or service to a given percentage change in the price of another good or service.

Crowding-in effect An increase in private-sector spending as a result of federal budget deficits financed by U.S. Treasury borrowing. At less than full employment, consumers hold more Treasury securities, and this additional wealth causes them to spend more. Businesses investment spending increases because of optimistic profit expectations.

Crowding-out effect A reduction in private-sector spending as a result of federal budget deficits financed by U.S. Treasury borrowing. When federal government borrowing increases interest rates, the result is lower consumption by households and lower investment spending by businesses.

Currency Money, including coins and paper money.

Cyclical unemployment Unemployment caused by the lack of jobs during a recession.

D

Deadweight loss The net loss of consumer and producer surplus for underproduction or over-production of a product.

Debt ceiling A legislated legal limit on the national debt.

Decreasing-cost industry An industry in which the expansion of industry output by the entry of new firms decreases the individual firm's average total cost curve (cost curve shifts downward).

Deflation A decrease in the general (average) price level of goods and services in the economy.

Demand A curve or schedule showing the various quantities of a product consumers are willing to purchase at possible prices during a specified period of time, ceteris paribus.

Demand curve for labor A curve showing the different quantities of labor employers are willing to hire at different wage rates in a given time period, ceteris paribus. It is equal to the marginal revenue product of labor.

Demand for money curve A curve representing the quantity of money that people hold at different possible interest rates, ceteris paribus.

Demand-pull inflation A rise in the general price level resulting from an excess of total spending (demand) caused by a rightward shift in the aggregate demand curve.

Depreciation of currency A fall in the price of one currency relative to another.

Deregulation The elimination or phasing out of government restrictions on economic activity.

Derived demand The demand for labor and other factors of production that depends on the consumer demand for the final goods and services the factors produce.

Direct relationship A positive association between two variables. When one variable increases, the other variable increases, and when one variable decreases, the other variable decreases.

Discount rate The interest rate the Fed charges on loans of reserves to banks.

Discouraged worker A person who wants to work, but who has given up searching for work because he or she believes there will be no job offers.

Discretionary fiscal policy The deliberate use of changes in government spending or taxes to alter aggregate demand and stabilize the economy.

Diseconomies of scale A situation in which the long-run average cost curve rises as the firm increases output.

Disinflation A reduction in the rate of inflation.

Disposable personal income (DI) The amount of income that households actually have to spend or save after payment of personal taxes.

Dissaving The amount by which personal consumption expenditures exceed disposable income.

E

Economic growth An expansion in national output measured by the annual percentage increase in a nation's real GDP.

Economic growth The ability of an economy to produce greater levels of output, represented by an outward shift of its production possibilities curve.

Economic profit Total revenue minus explicit and implicit costs.

Economic system The organizations and methods used to determine what goods and services are produced, how they are produced, and for whom they are produced.

Economics The study of how society chooses to allocate its scarce resources to the production of goods and services in order to satisfy unlimited wants.

Economies of scale A situation in which the long-run average cost curve declines as the firm increases output.

Effluent tax A tax on the pollutant.

Elastic demand A condition in which the percentage change in quantity demanded is greater than the percentage change in price.

Embargo A law that bars trade with another country.

Emissions trading Firms buying and selling the right to pollute.

Entrepreneurship The creative ability of individuals to seek profits by taking risks and combining resources to produce innovative products.

Equation of exchange An accounting identity that states the money supply times the velocity of money equals total spending.

Equilibrium A market condition that occurs at any price and quantity where the quantity demanded and the quantity supplied are equal.

Excess reserves Potential loan balances held in vault cash or on deposit with the Fed in excess of required reserves.

Exchange rate The number of units of one nation's currency that equals one unit of another nation's currency.

Expenditure approach The national income accounting method that measures GDP by adding all the spending for final goods during a period of time.

Explicit costs Payments to nonowners of a firm for their resources.

External national debt The portion of the national debt owed to foreign citizens.

Externality A cost or benefit imposed on people other than the consumers and producers of a good or service.

F

Federal Deposit Insurance Corporation (FDIC) A government agency established in 1933 to insure commercial bank deposits up to a specified limit.

Federal funds market A private market in which banks lend reserves to each other for less than 24 hours.

Federal funds rate The interest rate banks charge for overnight loans of reserves to other banks.

Federal Open Market Committee (FOMC) The Federal Reserve's committee that directs the buying and selling of U.S. government securities, which are major instruments for controlling the money supply. The FOMC consists of the seven members of the Federal Reserve's Board of Governors, the president of the New York Federal Reserve Bank, and the presidents of four other Federal Reserve district banks.

Federal Reserve System The 12 central banks that service banks and other financial institutions within each of the Federal Reserve districts; popularly called the Fed.

Federal Trade Commission Act The federal act that in 1914 established the Federal Trade Commission (FTC) to investigate unfair competitive practices of firms.

Fiat money Money accepted by law and not because of its redeemability or intrinsic value.

Final goods Finished goods and services produced for the ultimate user.

Fiscal policy The use of government spending and taxes to influence the nation's spending, employment, and price level.

Fixed input Any resource for which the quantity cannot change during the period of time under consideration.

Flow A flow is a rate of change in a quantity during a given time period, such as dollars per year. For example, income and consumption are flows that occur per week, per month, or per year.

Foreign aid The transfer of money or resources from one government to another for which no repayment is required.

Fractional reserve banking A system in which banks keep only a percentage of their deposits on reserve as vault cash and deposits at the Fed.

Free rider An individual who enjoys benefits without paying the costs.

Free-rider problem The problem that if some individuals benefit, while others pay, few will be willing to pay for improvement of the environment or other public goods. As a result, these goods are underproduced.

Free trade The flow of goods between countries without restrictions or special taxes.

Frictional unemployment Unemployment caused by the normal search time required by workers with marketable skills who are changing jobs, initially entering the labor force, reentering the labor force, or seasonally unemployed.

Full employment The situation in which an economy operates at an unemployment rate equal to the sum of the frictional and structural unemployment rates, also called the *natural rate of unemployment*.

G

Game Theory A model of the strategic moves and counter-moves of rivals.

GDP chain price index A measure that compares changes in the prices of all final goods during a given year to the prices of those goods in a base year.

GDP gap The difference between actual real GDP and potential or full-employment real GDP.

GDP per capita The value of final goods produced (GDP) divided by the total population.

Government expenditures Federal, state, and local government outlays for goods and services, including transfer payments.

Government failure Government intervention or lack of intervention that fails to correct market failure.

Gross domestic product (GDP) The market value of all final goods and services produced in a nation during a period of time, usually a year.

H

Horizontal merger A merger of firms that compete in the same market.

Human capital The accumulation of education, training, experience, and health that enables a worker to enter an occupation and be productive.

Hyperinflation An extremely rapid rise in the general price level.

I

Implicit costs The opportunity costs of using resources owned by the firm.

Incentive-based regulations Government regulations that set an environmental goal, but are flexible as to how buyers and sellers achieve the goal.

In-kind transfers Government payments in the form of goods and services, rather than cash, including such government programs as food stamps, Medicaid, and housing.

Income approach The national income accounting method that measures GDP by adding all incomes, including compensation of employees, rents, net interest, and profits.

Income effect The change in quantity demanded of a good or service caused by a change in real income (purchasing power).

Income elasticity of demand The ratio of the percentage change in the quantity demanded of a good or service to a given percentage change in income.

Incomes policies Federal government policies designed to affect the real incomes of workers by controlling nominal wages and prices. Such policies include presidential jawboning, wage-price guidelines, and wage-price controls.

Increasing-cost industry An industry in which the expansion of industry output by the entry of new firms increases the individual firm's average total cost curve (cost curve shifts upward).

Independent relationship A zero association between two variables. When one variable changes, the other variable remains unchanged.

Indifference curve A curve showing the different combinations of two products that yield the same satisfaction or total utility to a consumer.

Indifference map A selection of indifference curves with each curve representing a different level of satisfaction or total utility.

Indirect business taxes Taxes levied as a percentage of the prices of goods sold and therefore collected as part of the firm's revenue. Firms treat such taxes as production costs. Examples include general sales taxes, excise taxes, and customs duties.

Industrially advanced countries (IACs) High-income nations that have market economies based on large stocks of technologically advanced capital and well-educated labor.

The United States, Canada, Australia, New Zealand, Japan, and most of the countries of Western Europe are IACs.

Inelastic demand A condition in which the percentage change in quantity demanded is less than the percentage change in price.

Inferior good Any good for which there is an inverse relationship between changes in income and its demand curve.

Inflation An increase in the general (average) price level of goods and services in the economy.

Inflationary gap The amount by which the aggregate expenditures curve must be decreased to achieve full-employment equilibrium.

Infrastructure Capital goods usually provided by the government, including highways, bridges, waste and water systems, and airports.

Interest-rate effect The impact on total spending (real GDP) caused by the direct relationship between the price level and the interest rate.

Intermediate goods Goods and services used as inputs for the production of final goods.

Intermediate range The rising segment of the aggregate supply curve, which represents an economy as it approaches full-employment output.

Internal national debt The portion of the national debt owed to a nation's own citizens.

International Monetary Fund (IMF) The lending agency that makes short-term conditional low-interest loans to developing countries.

Inverse relationship A negative association between two variables. When one variable increases, the other decreases, and when one variable decreases, the other variable increases.

Investment demand curve The curve that shows the amount businesses spend for investment goods at different possible rates of interest.

Investment The accumulation of capital, such as factories, machines, and inventories, that is used to produce goods and services.

Invisible hand A phrase that expresses the belief that the best interests of a society are served when individual consumers and producers compete to achieve their own private interests.

J

Jawboning Oratory intended to pressure unions and businesses to reduce wage and price increases.

John Maynard Keynes British economist (1883–1946) whose influential work offered an explanation of the Great Depression and suggested, as a cure, that the government should play an active role in the economy.

K

Keynesian range The horizontal segment of the aggregate supply curve, which represents an economy in a severe recession.

Kinked demand curve A demand curve facing an oligopolist that assumes rivals will match a price decrease, but ignore a price increase.

L

Labor The mental and physical capacity of workers to produce goods and services.

Laffer curve A graph depicting the relationship between tax rates and total tax revenues.

Lagging indicators Variables that change after real GDP changes.

Land A shorthand expression for any natural resource provided by nature.

Law of demand The principle that there is an inverse relationship between the price of a good and the quantity buyers are willing to purchase in a defined time period, ceteris paribus.

Law of diminishing marginal utility The principle that the extra satisfaction of a good or service declines as people consume more in a given period.

Law of diminishing returns The principle that beyond some point the marginal product decreases as additional units of a variable factor are added to a fixed factor.

Law of increasing opportunity costs The principle that the opportunity cost increases as production of one output expands.

Law of supply The principle that there is a direct relationship between the price of a good and the quantity sellers are willing to offer for sale in a defined time period, ceteris paribus.

Leading indicators Variables that change before real GDP changes.

Less-developed countries (LDCs) Nations without large stocks of technologically advanced capital and well-educated labor. LDCs are economies based on agriculture, such as most countries of Africa, Asia, and Latin America.

Long run A period of time so long that all inputs are variable.

Long-run aggregate supply curve (LRAS) The curve that shows the level of real GDP produced at different possible price levels during a time period in which nominal incomes change by the same percentage as the price level changes.

Long-run average cost curve (LRAC) The curve that traces the lowest cost per unit at which a firm can produce any level of output when the firm can build any desired plant size.

Lorenz curve A graph of the actual cumulative distribution of income compared to a perfectly equal cumulative distribution of income.

M

M1 The narrowest definition of the money supply. It includes currency, traveler's checks, and checkable deposits.

M2 The definition of the money supply that equals M1 plus near monies, such as savings deposits and small time deposits of less than $100,000.

Macroeconomics The branch of economics that studies decision making for the economy as a whole.

Marginal analysis An examination of the effects of additions to or subtractions from a current situation.

Marginal cost (MC) The change in total cost when one additional unit of output is produced.

Marginal cost pricing A system of pricing in which the price charged equals the marginal cost of the last unit produced.

Marginal factor cost (MFC) The additional total cost resulting from a one-unit increase in the quantity of a factor.

Marginal product The change in total output produced by adding one unit of a variable input, with all other inputs used being held constant.

Marginal propensity to consume (MPC) The change in consumption resulting from a given change in real disposable income.

Marginal propensity to consume (MPC) The change in consumption spending resulting from a given change in income.

Marginal propensity to save (MPS) The change in saving resulting from a given change in income.

Marginal propensity to save (MPS) The change in saving resulting from a given change in real disposable income.

Marginal rate of substitution (MRS) The rate at which a consumer is willing to substitute one good for another without a change in total utility. The MRS equals the slope of the indifference curve at any point on the curve.

Marginal revenue (MR) The change in total revenue from the sale of one additional unit of output.

Marginal revenue product (MRP) The increase in a firm's total revenue resulting from hiring an additional unit of labor or other variable resource.

Marginal-average rule The rule that states when marginal cost is below average cost, average cost falls. When marginal cost is above average cost, average cost rises. When marginal cost equals average cost, average cost is at its minimum point.

Marginal tax rate The fraction of additional income paid in taxes.

Marginal utility The change in total utility from one additional unit of a good or service.

Market Any arrangement in which buyers and sellers interact to determine the price and quantity of goods and services exchanged.

Market economy An economic system that answers the *What, How,* and *For Whom* questions using prices determined by the interaction of the forces of supply and demand.

Market failure A situation in which market equilibrium results in too few or too many resources used in the production of a good or service. This inefficiency may justify government intervention.

Market failure A situation in which market equilibrium results in too few or too many resources used in the production of a good or service.

Market structure A classification system for the key traits of a market, including the number of firms, the similarity of the products they sell, and the ease of entry into and exit from the market.

Means test A requirement that a family's income not exceed a certain level to be eligible for public assistance.

Medium of exchange The primary function of money to be widely accepted in exchange for goods and services.

Microeconomics The branch of economics that studies decision making by a single individual, household, firm, industry, or level of government.

Mixed economy An economic system that answers the *What, How,* and *For Whom* questions through a mixture of traditional, command, and market systems.

Model A simplified description of reality used to understand and predict the relationship between variables.

Monetarism The theory that changes in the money supply directly determine changes in prices, real GDP, and employment.

Monetary Control Act A law, formally titled the Depository Institutions Deregulation and Monetary Control Act of 1980, that gave the Federal Reserve System greater control over nonmember banks and made all financial institutions more competitive.

Monetary policy The Federal Reserve's use of open market operations, changes in the discount rate, and changes in the required reserve ratio to change the money supply (M1).

Money multiplier The maximum change in the money supply (checkable deposits) due to an initial change in the excess reserves banks hold. The money multiplier is equal to 1 divided by the required reserve ratio.

Money Anything that serves as a medium of exchange, unit of account, and store of value.

Monopolistic competition A market structure characterized by (1) many small sellers, (2) a differentiated product, and (3) easy market entry and exit.

Monopoly A market structure characterized by (1) a single seller, (2) a unique product, and (3) impossible entry into the market.

Monopsony A labor market in which a single firm hires labor.

Mutual interdependence A condition in which an action by one firm may cause a reaction from other firms.

N

National debt The total amount owed by the federal government to owners of government securities.

National income (NI) The total income earned by resource owners, including wages, rents, interest, and profits. NI is calculated as gross domestic product minus depreciation of the capital worn out in producing output.

Natural monopoly An industry in which the long-run average cost of production declines throughout the entire market. As a result, a single firm can supply the entire market demand at a lower cost than two or more smaller firms.

Natural rate hypothesis The hypothesis that argues the economy will self-correct to the natural rate of unemployment. The long-run Phillips curve is therefore a vertical line at the natural rate of unemployment.

Negative income tax (NIT) A plan under which families below a certain break-even level of income would receive cash payments that decrease as their incomes increase.

Net exports effect The impact on total spending (real GDP) caused by the inverse relationship between the price level and the net exports of an economy.

Net public debt National debt minus all government interagency borrowing.

New-source bias Bias that occurs when regulations provide an incentive to keep assets past the efficient point.

Nominal GDP The value of all final goods based on the prices existing during the time period of production.

Nominal income The actual number of dollars received over a period of time.

Nominal interest rate The actual rate of interest without adjustment for the inflation rate.

Nonprice competition The situation in which a firm competes using advertising, packaging, product development, better quality, and better service, rather than lower prices.

Normal good Any good for which there is a direct relationship between changes in income and its demand curve.

Normal profit The minimum profit necessary to keep a firm in operation. A firm that earns normal profits earns total revenue equal to its total opportunity cost.

Normative economics An analysis based on value judgment.

O

Offset Reduction in an existing pollution source to counteract pollution from a new source.

Oligopoly A market structure characterized by (1) few sellers, (2) either a homogeneous or a differentiated product, and (3) difficult market entry.

Open market operations The buying and selling of government securities by the Federal Reserve System.

Opportunity cost The best alternative sacrificed for a chosen alternative.

P

Peak The phase of the business cycle in which real GDP reaches its maximum after rising during a recovery.

Per se rule The antitrust doctrine that the existence of monopoly alone is illegal, regardless of whether or not the monopoly engages in illegal business practices.

Perfect competition A market structure characterized by (1) a large number of small firms, (2) a homogeneous product, and (3) very easy entry into or exit from the market. Perfect competition is also referred to as *pure competition.*

Perfectly competitive firm's short-run supply curve The firm's marginal cost curve above the minimum point on its average variable cost curve.

Perfectly competitive industry's long-run supply curve The curve that shows the quantities supplied by the industry at different equilibrium prices after firms complete their entry and exit.

Perfectly competitive industry's short-run supply curve The supply curve derived from horizontal summation of the marginal cost curves of all firms in the industry above the minimum point of each firm's average variable cost curve.

Perfectly elastic demand A condition in which a small percentage change in price brings about an infinite percentage change in quantity demanded.

Perfectly elastic demand A condition in which the quantity demanded does not change as the price changes.

Perfectly inelastic demand A condition in which the quantity demanded does not change as the price changes.

Personal income (PI) The total income received by households that is available for consumption, saving, and payment of personal taxes.

Phillips curve A curve showing an inverse relationship between the inflation rate and the unemployment rate.

Political business cycle A business cycle caused by policymakers to improve politicians' reelection chances.

Positive economics An analysis limited to statements that are verifiable.

Poverty line The level of income below which a person or a family is considered to be poor.

Precautionary demand for money The stock of money people hold to pay unpredictable expenses.

Predatory pricing The practice of one or more firms temporarily reducing prices in order to eliminate competition and then raising prices.

Price ceiling A legally established maximum price a seller can charge.

Price discrimination The practice of a seller charging different prices for the same product that are not justified by cost differences.

Price elasticity of demand The ratio of the percentage change in the quantity demanded of a product to a percentage change in its price.

Price elasticity of supply The ratio of the percentage change in the quantity supplied of a product to the percentage change in its price.

Price floor A legally established minimum price a seller can be paid.

Price leadership A pricing strategy in which a dominant firm sets the price for an industry and the other firms follow.

Price maker A firm that faces a downward-sloping demand curve and therefore it can choose among price and output combinations along the demand curve.

Price system A mechanism that uses the forces of supply and demand to create an equilibrium through rising and falling prices.

Price taker A seller that has no control over the price of the product it sells.

Private benefits and costs Benefits and costs to the decisionmaker, ignoring benefits and costs to third parties. Third parties are people outside the market transaction who are affected by the product.

Producer surplus The value of the difference between the actual selling price of a product and the price producers are willing to sell it for on the supply curve.

Product differentiation The process of creating real or apparent differences between goods and services.

Production function The relationship between the maximum amounts of output that a firm can produce and various quantities of inputs.

Production possibilities curve A curve that shows the maximum combinations of two outputs an economy can produce in a given period of time with its available resources and technology.

Progressive tax A tax that charges a higher percentage of income as income rises.

Proportional tax A tax that charges the same percentage of income, regardless of the size of income. Also called a *flat-tax rate* or simply a *flat tax*.

Protectionism The government's use of embargoes, tariffs, quotas, and other restrictions to protect domestic producers from foreign competition.

Public choice theory The analysis of the government's decision-making process for allocating resources.

Public good A good or service with two properties: (1) users collectively consume benefits, and (2) there is no way to bar people who do not pay (free riders) from consuming the good or service.

Q

Quantity theory of money The theory that changes in the money supply are directly related to changes in the price level.

Quota A limit on the quantity of a good that may be imported in a given time period.

R

Rational expectations theory The belief that people use all available information to predict the future, including future monetary and fiscal policies. Systematic and predictable macroeconomic policies can therefore be negated when businesses and workers anticipate the effects of these policies on the economy.

Rational ignorance The voter's choice to remain uninformed because the marginal cost of obtaining information is higher than the marginal benefit from knowing it.

Real balances effect The impact on total spending (real GDP) caused by the inverse relationship between the price level and the real value of financial assets with fixed nominal value.

Real GDP The value of all final goods produced during a given time period based on the prices existing in a selected base year.

Real income The actual number of dollars received (nominal income) adjusted for changes in the CPI.

Real interest rate The nominal rate of interest minus the inflation rate.

Recession A downturn in the business cycle during which real GDP declines, and the unemployment rate rises. Also called a *contraction*.

Recessionary gap The amount by which the aggregate expenditures curve must be increased to achieve full-employment equilibrium.

Recovery An upturn in the business cycle during which real GDP rises. Also called an *expansion*.

Regressive tax A tax that charges a lower percentage of income as income rises.

Required reserve ratio The percentage of deposits that the Fed requires a bank to hold in vault cash or on deposit with the Fed.

Required reserves The minimum balance that the Fed requires a bank to hold in vault cash or on deposit with the Fed.

Resources The basic categories of inputs used to produce goods and services. Resources are also called *factors of production*. Economists divide resources into three categories: land, labor, and capital.

Robinson-Patman Act A 1936 amendment to the Clayton Act that strengthens the Clayton Act against price discrimination.

Rule of reason The antitrust doctrine that the existence of monopoly alone is not illegal unless the monopoly engages in illegal business practices.

S

Saving The part of disposable income households do not spend for consumer goods and services.

Say's Law The theory that supply creates its own demand.

Scarcity The condition in which human wants are forever greater than the available supply of time, goods, and resources.

Sherman Act The federal antitrust law enacted in 1890 that prohibits monopolization and conspiracies to restrain trade.

Short run A period of time so short that there is at least one fixed input.

Short-run aggregate supply curve (*SRAS*) The curve that shows the level of real GDP produced at different possible price levels during a time period in which nominal incomes do not change in response to changes in the price level.

Shortage A market condition existing at any price where the quantity supplied is less than the quantity demanded.

Slope The ratio of the change in the variable on the vertical axis (the rise or fall) to the change in the variable on the horizontal axis (the run).

Social benefits and costs The sum of benefits to everyone in society, including both private benefits and external benefits. Social costs are the sum of costs to everyone in society, including both private costs and external costs.

Socialism An economic system characterized by government ownership of resources and centralized decision making.

Speculative demand for money The stock of money people hold to take advantage of expected future changes in the price of bonds, stocks, or other nonmoney financial assets.

Spending multiplier (SM) The ratio of the change in real GDP to an initial change in any component of aggregate expenditures or aggregate demand, including consumption, investment, government spending, and net exports. As a formula, the spending multiplier equals $1/(1-MPC)$ or $1/MPS$.

Stagflation The condition that occurs when an economy experiences the twin maladies of high unemployment and rapid inflation simultaneously.

Stock A quantity measured at one point in time. For example, an inventory of goods or the amount of money in a checking account.

Store of value The ability of money to hold value over time.

Structural unemployment Unemployment caused by a mismatch of the skills of workers out of work and the skills required for existing job opportunities.

Subprime mortgage loan A home loan made to borrowers with an above-average risk of default.

Substitute good A good that competes with another good for consumer purchases. As a result, there is a direct relationship between a price change for one good and the demand for its "competitor" good.

Substitution effect The change in quantity demanded of a good or service caused by a change in its price relative to substitutes.

Supply A curve or schedule showing the various quantities of a product sellers are willing to produce and offer for sale at possible prices during a specified period of time, ceteris paribus.

Supply curve of labor A curve showing the different quantities of labor workers are willing to offer employers at different wage rates in a given time period, ceteris paribus.

Supply-side fiscal policy A fiscal policy that emphasizes government policies that increase aggregate supply in order to achieve long-run growth in real output, full employment, and a lower price level.

Surplus A market condition existing at any price where the quantity supplied is greater than the quantity demanded.

T

Tariff A tax on an import.

Tax incidence The share of a tax ultimately paid by consumers and sellers.

Tax multiplier The change in aggregate expenditures (total spending) resulting from an initial change in taxes. As a formula, tax multiplier equals $1-$spending multiplier.

Tax multiplier The change in aggregate demand (total spending) resulting from an initial change in taxes. As a formula, tax multiplier equals $1-$spending multiplier.

Technology The body of knowledge applied to how goods are produced.

Term auction facility (TAF) A monetary policy tool created in 2007 during the financial crisis to encourage banks to borrow reserves and thereby extend new loans. Under this program, banks in sound financial condition are allowed to make interest rate bids for short-term collateralized Federal Reserve loans.

Total cost (TC) The sum of total fixed cost and total variable cost at each level of output.

Total fixed cost (TFC) Costs that do not vary as output varies and that must be paid even if output is zero. These are payments that the firm must make in the short run, regardless of the level of output.

Total revenue The total number of dollars a firm earns from the sale of a good or service, which is equal to its price multiplied by the quantity demanded.

Total utility The amount of satisfaction received from all the units of a good or service consumed.

Total variable cost (TVC) Costs that are zero when output is zero and vary as output varies.

Traditional economy A system that answers the *What, How,* and *For Whom* questions the way they always have been answered.

Transactions costs The costs of negotiating and enforcing a contract.

Transactions demand for money The stock of money people hold to pay everyday predictable expenses.

Transfer payment A government payment to individuals not in exchange for goods or services currently produced.

Trough The phase of the business cycle in which real GDP reaches its minimum after falling during a recession.

Trust A combination or cartel consisting of firms that place their assets in the custody of a board of trustees.

U

Unemployment compensation The government insurance program that pays income for a short time period to unemployed workers.

Unemployment rate The percentage of people in the civilian labor force who are without jobs and are actively seeking jobs.

Unit of account The function of money to provide a common measurement of the relative value of goods and services.

Unitary elastic demand A condition in which the percentage change in quantity demanded is equal to the percentage change in price.

Utility The satisfaction, or pleasure, that people receive from consuming a good or service.

V

Variable input Any resource for which the quantity can change during the period of time under consideration.

Velocity of money The average number of times per year a dollar of the money supply is spent on final goods and services.

Vertical merger A vertical merger is a merger of a firm with its suppliers.

Vicious circle of poverty The trap in which countries are poor because they cannot afford to save and invest, but they cannot save and invest because they are poor.

W

Wage and price controls Legal restrictions on wage and price increases. Violations can result in fines and imprisonment.

Wage and price guidelines Voluntary standards set by the government for "permissible" wage and price increases.

Wage-price spiral A situation that occurs when increases in nominal wage rates are passed on in higher prices, which, in turn, result in even higher nominal wage rates and prices.

Wealth The value of the stock of assets owned at some point in time.

Wealth effect A decrease in consumption spending when the value of assets, such as stocks and homes, falls and an increase in consumption spending when the value of these assets rises.

World Bank The lending agency that makes long-term low-interest loans and provides technical assistance to less-developed countries.

World Trade Organization (WTO) An international organization of member countries that oversees international trade agreements and rules on trade disputes.